CALIFORNIA
CAMPING

FOGHORN ✂ OUTDOORS

CALIFORNIA CAMPING

The Complete Guide to More Than 1,500 Campgrounds

TWELFTH EDITION

Tom Stienstra

AVALON
TRAVEL
publishing

FOGHORN OUTDOORS: CALIFORNIA CAMPING
The Complete Guide to More Than 1,500 Campgrounds

TWELFTH EDITION
Tom Stienstra

GV
191.42
. C2
S85
2001

Published by
Avalon Travel Publishing, Inc.
5855 Beaudry St.
Emeryville, CA 94608, USA

ISBN: 1-56691-245-8
ISSN: 1531-8109

Editors: Karen Bleske, Marisa Solís
Copy Editor: Julie Leigh
Index: Sondra Nation
Illustrations: Bob Race
Graphics Coordinator: Erika Howsare
Production: Carey Wilson, David Hurst
Map Editor: Mike Ferguson
Cartography: Mike Morgenfeld

Front cover photo: Larry Prosor © 2001

Printing History
First edition—1987
12th edition—January 2001
5 4 3 2 1

Please send all comments, corrections, additions,
amendments, and critiques to:
**FOGHORN OUTDOORS:
CALIFORNIA CAMPING**
Twelfth Edition
**AVALON TRAVEL PUBLISHING, INC.
5855 BEAUDRY ST.
EMERYVILLE, CA 94608, USA**
email: info@travelmatters.com
www.foghorn.com

Printed in the U.S.A. by R.R. Donnelley
Distributed in the United States and Canada by Publishers Group West.

TABLE OF CONTENTS

NORTHERN CALIFORNIA

CENTRAL CALIFORNIA

MAPS

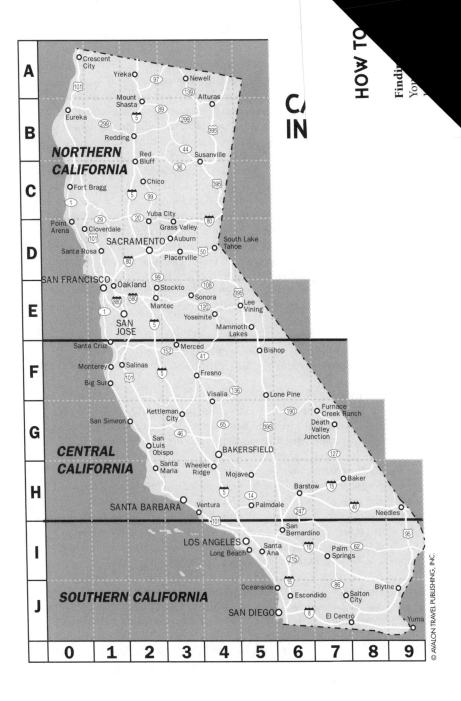

USE THIS BOOK

...ig a Campground

...a can search for your ideal campground in two ways:

1. If you know the name of the campground you'd like to visit or the nearest town or geographical feature (national or state forest, national or state park or recreation area, wildlife area, park, lake, river, mountain), look it up in the index beginning on page 904 to locate it and turn to the corresponding page.

2. If you'd like to camp in a particular part of the state and want to find out what camps are available there, turn to the California state map on the preceding page or in the back of this book. Find the zone where you'd like to camp (such as E1 for the San Francisco Bay Area or H3 for Santa Barbara), then turn to the corresponding chapter. Each chapter opens with a map that clearly numbers every campground in that area. Locate individual camping destinations on the map and then turn to those numbered sites in the chapter for detailed descriptions.

This book is conveniently divided into Northern, Central, and Southern California. These sections are further divided into individually mapped grids to allow for greater detail.

Northern California, pages 98–549 (maps AØ-E5)
Central California, pages 550–756 (maps F1-H9)
Southern California, pages 757–892 (maps I2-J9)

About the Maps

The maps in this book are designed to show the general location of each campground. Readers are advised to buy a detailed state map before heading out to any campground, particularly when venturing into remote areas.

What the Ratings Mean

Every camping spot in this book is designated with a scenic beauty rating of 1 through 10. Other factors that can influence a trip, such as noise or restroom cleanliness, can change from day-to-day and do not affect the ratings. That is why it is possible to have a great trip at a campground that is rated a 1 or a 2. In addition, like most people, I don't think high grades should be easy to come by, so we tend to be tough graders.

What the Symbols Mean

Listings in this book feature activity symbols that represent the recreational offerings at or within walking distance of the campground. Other symbols identify whether there are sites for RVs or tents, or any wheelchair-accessible facilities. Wheelchair accessibility has been indicated when it is mentioned by campground managers, and concerned persons should call the contact number to ensure that their specific needs will be met.

The 5 Percent Club

Approximately 100 of the camps in *California Camping* are marked with the "5 Percent Club" symbol: %. It has been documented that 95 percent of American vacationers use only 5 percent of the available recreation areas. Campgrounds that display % are for the other 5 percent of us—those who want to escape the crowds and camp in California's hard-to-reach, hidden sites.

About Pricing

California state parks are already among the most beautiful places on earth. But starting in 2001, they are also the best recreation deal in North America.

A state budget surplus has allowed the governor and legislature to fully fund the California State Parks Department for the first time in nearly 20 years. The biggest cuts are in camping fees, reduced to $12 at even the most popular family campsites with full facilities, $18 for camps with full hookups for RVs, and just $1 for many walk-in camps. Many current add-on charges will be eliminated, such as the $7.50 reservation fee, and fees for pets, premium sites, and boat launching.

This is the only book available that has these updated prices for each state park camp. In many cases, we worked directly with rangers as the prices were being set.

ACTIVITY SYMBOLS

🚶	hiking	🐕	pets permitted
🚲	biking	🛝	playground
🏊	swimming	♿	wheelchair access
🐟	fishing	5%	5 percent club
🚙	boating	🚐	RV sites
〰️	hot springs	⛺	tent sites

Our Commitment

We are committed to making *California Camping* the most accurate, thorough, and enjoyable camping guide to the state. With this twelfth edition, you can rest assured that every camping spot in this book has been carefully reviewed and accompanied by the most up-to-date information available. It is possible in few cases, primarily at a small number of private RV parks, that some campground fees will be raised after we have gone to press. If you have a specific need or concern, it's a good idea to call the campground ahead of time.

If you would like to comment on the book, whether it's to suggest a tent or RV spot we overlooked, or to let us know about any noteworthy experience—good or bad—that occurred while using *California Camping* as your guide, we would appreciate hearing from you. Please address correspondence to:

California Camping, 12th Edition
Avalon Travel Publishing
5855 Beaudry Street
Emeryville, CA 94608
U.S.A
email: info@travelmatters.com

ACKNOWLEDGMENTS

U.S. Forest Service

Michael Dombeck, chief, Washington D.C. Headquarters
Matt Mathes and Mary Hale, Pacific Region Headquarters
Terrie Trippel, Angeles National Forest, Los Angeles River Ranger District
Gwen Smith, Angeles National Forest, San Gabriel River Ranger District
Diane McCombs, Carol Richmond and Tom Kaucher, Angeles National Forest, Santa Clara/Mojave Rivers Ranger District
Karen Findlaysen and Jenni Bradley, Camino Office
Anne Carey, Cleveland National Forest, Descanso Ranger District
Russ Lajoie, Cleveland National Forest, Palomar Ranger District
Don Wolff, Cleveland National Forest, Trabuco Ranger District
Terry Holm and Tina Garcia, Eldorado National Forest, Amador Ranger District
Jean Clark, Karen Kessler and Leanna Albrecht, Eldorado National Forest, Eldorado Information Center
Jon Jue, Eldorado National Forest, Georgetown Ranger District
Kris Schroeder, Eldorado National Forest, Pacific Ranger District
Molly Brown, Humboldt-Toiyabe National Forest, Bridgeport and Carson Ranger Districts
Mike Johnson, Inyo National Forest, Mammoth Lakes Ranger District
Lynne Ingram, Inyo National Forest, Mono Basin Visitor Center
Liz Nelson and Jan Cutts, Inyo National Forest, Mt. Whitney Ranger Station
Jim Stout, Klamath National Forest, Goosenest Ranger District
Pat Garrahan, Klamath National Forest, Happy Camp Ranger District
Al Buchter, Klamath National Forest, Salmon River Ranger District
Jim Lipke, Klamath National Forest, Scott River Ranger District
Gay Eitel, Lake Tahoe Basin Management Unit
Janie Ackley, Lassen National Forest, Almanor Ranger Station
Mike Zunino and Bob Phillips, Lassen National Forest, Eagle Lake Ranger Station
Jim Barnhardt, Lassen National Forest, Hat Creek Ranger Station
Rudy Segobia, Manuel Madrigal and Katy Ross, Los Padres National Forest, Monterey Ranger District
Mike Foster, Los Padres National Forest, Mount Pinos Ranger District
Joseph Signorino, Los Padres National Forest, Ojai Ranger District
Carole Anderson, Los Padres National Forest, Santa Barbara Ranger District
Gina Thompson, Los Padres National Forest, Santa Lucia Ranger District
Brooks Smith, Mendocino National Forest, Covelo Ranger District
Fred Bell, Mendocino National Forest, Grindstone Ranger District
Lori Pacheco, Mendocino National Forest, Upper Lake Ranger District
Robert Haggard and Jami Nield, Modoc National Forest
Beverly Way, Modoc National Forest, Big Valley Ranger District
Mike Kegg, Modoc National Forest, Doublehead Ranger District
Pandora Valle, Plumas National Forest, Beckwourth Ranger District
Carol Durnell and Linda Braxton, Plumas National Forest, Feather River Ranger District
Judy Abrams, Plumas National Forest, Mt. Hough Ranger District

Tom Spencer, San Bernardino National Forest
Bob Wood, San Bernardino National Forest, Arrowhead Ranger District
Helen Cheek, San Bernardino National Forest, Lytle Creek Ranger District
Alfredo Zarate, Jr., San Bernardino National Forest, Mill Creek Ranger Station
Ron Lawson, San Bernardino National Forest, San Jacinto Ranger District
Dick Reynolds and Cheryl Baller, Sequoia National Forest, Cannell Meadows Ranger District
Dave Baskin, Sequoia National Forest, Greenhorn Ranger District
Irene Burlingame and Maxine Chittender, Sequoia National Forest, Hume Lake
    Ranger District
Janann Faure, Sequoia National Forest, Tule River and Hot Springs Ranger District
Jean Cooke, Marti Parachini and Cindy Beckstead, Shasta-Trinity National Forest, Big
    Bar Ranger District
Steve Ryberg and Pat Smith, Shasta-Trinity National Forest, Hayfork and Yolla Bolla
    Ranger Districts
Barbara Paolinetti, Shasta-Trinity National Forest, McCloud Ranger District
Don Lee, Shasta-Trinity National Forest, Mount Shasta Ranger District
Anna Draper and Cathy Southwick, Shasta-Trinity National Forest, Shasta Lake
    Ranger District
Marla Schardin and Fay Mok, Shasta-Trinity National Forest, Weaverville Ranger District
Debe Arndt and Retha Gomez, Sierra National Forest, Kings River and Pineridge
    Ranger Districts
Mike LeFevre, Sierra National Forest, Mariposa-Minerats Ranger District
John Theuerkauf, Six Rivers National Forest, Gasquet District
Mike Mitchell and Mark Burrows, Six Rivers National Forest, Lower Trinity Ranger District
Jean Hawthorne, Six Rivers National Forest, Mad River and Orleans Ranger Districts
Roy Morris, Stanislaus National Forest, Calaveras Ranger District
Dorothy Riddell, Stanislaus National Forest, Groveland Ranger District
Chuck James, Stanislaus National Forest, Mi-Wok Ranger District
Steve Bailey, Stanislaus National Forest, Summit Ranger District
Joe Chavez, Tahoe National Forest, Downieville Ranger District
Ed Moore, Tahoe National Forest, Foresthill Ranger District
Patti Mahaffey, Tahoe National Forest, Nevada City Ranger District
Diane Suarez and Mary Westmoreland, Tahoe National Forest, Truckee Ranger District

U.S. Army Corps of Engineers
Phil Turner, South Pacific Region
Joe Holmberg, Sacramento District
Greg Volkman, Cordoniz Recreation Area
Valerie Mavis, Lake Mendocino
Sue Layden, Lake Sonoma
Dan Benedetti, New Hogan
Alison Wilson, Pine Flat Field Office
Robert Moreno, Tule Recreation Area

Bureau of Land Management
Diana Milton, Alturas Field Office
Brian Logan, Arcata Field Office

John Bogacki, Bakersfield Field Office
Harold Johnson, Barstow Field Office
Joy Manga, Bishop Field Office
Stan Bales, Eagle Lake Field Office
Joya Szalwinski, El Centro Field Office
Anna Atkinson, Palm Springs Field Office
Bill Crothers, Redding Field Office
Scott Adams, Ukiah Field Office
Mary Lowans, Yuma Field Office

National Parks

Carol Spears, Channel Islands National Park
Laura Lusk, Death Valley National Park
Kris Landers, Devil's Postpile National Monument
Mary Risser, Joshua Tree National Park
Nancy Bailey, Lassen Volcanic National Park
Craig Dorman, Lava Beds National Monument
Ruby Newton, Mojave National Preserve
Carol McCall, Redwood National Park
Kris Fister, Sequoia & Kings Canyon National Parks
Trish Ford, Whiskeytown National Recreation Area
Sheri Ogden, Yosemite National Park

State Parks

Vic Maris, Superintendent of Park Operations
Roy Stearns, Deputy Director of Communications
Fred Jee, Anza-Borrego Desert State Park
James Burke, Tom Kline and Laura Itogawa, Cuyamaca Rancho State Park
Charles Kuntzman, Patrick's Point State Park
Steve Ortiz, Humboldt Lagoons State Park
Ron Munson, Russian River/Mendocino District
Kim Trefry, Folsom Lake State Recreation Area
Meadow Bell, Standish-Hickey State Recreation Area
Beverly Rivas, Humboldt Redwoods State Park
Dick Goss, Lake Earl & Talawa State Park
Alan Wilkinson, North Coast Redwoods District
Kim Preston, Northern Buttes District
Karen Broderick, Salt Point State Park
Ian Mion, Austin Creek State Recreation Area
Holly Palmer, Clear Lake State Park
Al Vosher, Bothe-Napa Valley State Park
Bob Birkland, Sugarloaf Ridge State Park
Rich Silver, Donner Memorial State Park
Katie Bernarding, Tomales Bay State Park
Cassandra Gill, Colusa-Sacramento River State Recreation Area
Craig Miller, Indian Grinding Rock State Historic Park

Bill Rathbone, D.L. Bliss State Park
Mike Hanes, Samuel P. Taylor State Park
Jim Mazzucotelli, China Camp State Park
Jill Dampier, Auburn State Recreation Area
Roger Nelson, Half Moon Bay State Beach
Becky Bradford, Butano State Park
Bill Mentzer, Mt. Tamalpais State Park
Dan Winkelman, Angel Island State Park
Andrea Kelly, Brannan Island State Recreation Area
Barry Breckling, Henry Coe State Park
David Totino, McConnell State Recreation Area
Cindy Smith, Calaveras Big Trees State Park
Mike Wintch, Mt. Diable State Park
Valerie Foster, Millerton Lake State Recreation Area
Adam Elsholz, Caswell Memorial State Park
Lucy Hernandez, San Luis Reservoir State Recreation Area
Cameron Morrison, New Brighton State Beach
Mary Negron, Sunset State Beach
Matt Mahan, Manresa Uplands State Beach
Becky Nobriga, Henry Cowell Redwoods State Park
Holly Praytor, Pfeiffer Big Sur State Park
Nedra Martinez, Fremont Peak State Park
Laura Wong, Seacliff State Beach
Chris Stokes, Turlock Lake State Recreation Area
John Tranmer, Morro Bay State Park
Nate Bitt, San Simeon State Park
Beth Roche and Tony Villareal, Pismo State Beach
Mary Peltier, Colonel Allensworth State Historic Park
Dennis Doberneck, Oceano Dunes State Vehicular Recreation Area
Tom Tanner, Mojave Desert Sector
Wes Chapin, Fred Soderlund and Rondy Robinson, Channel Coast District
Linda Tornello, Carpinteria State Beach
Timothy Wallace, Richardson Grove State Park
Maria Almanza, Four Rivers District
William Dall, Lake Perris State Recreation Area
Richard Campbell, Mount San Jacinto State Park
Matthew Maechler, McGrath State Beach
Brian Elliott, Bolsa Chica State Beach
Denise Estrada, Doheny State Beach
Bobby Matos, San Clemente State Beach
Susan Rodgers, Angeles District
Dylan Farmer, San Elijo State Beach
Kim Miller, Palomar Mountain State Park
Dana Burdex and Tamara Kinnison, Silverwood Lake State Recreation Area
Mickie Jensen, Picacho State Recreation Area
Edy Davis, San Onofre State Beach
Derek Jones, Orange Coast District

Beverly White, Salton Sea State Recreation Area
Bradley Massey, South Carlsbad State Beach
JoAnn Ebright, Ocotillo Wells State Vehicular Recreation Area
Bill Carter, Carnegie State Vehicular Recreation Area

State Forests

Chris Avina, Boggs Mountain Demonstration State Forest
Debbie Lotten, Jackson Demonstration State Forest
Scott McDonald, Latour Demonstration State Forest
Jose Medina, Mountain Home State Forest

Other

Sandy Hall, Pacific Gas & Electric Company, Land Projects
Lizeth Meza, San Diego County Parks
Kriste Reinhard, U.S. Department of Reclamation
John Reginato, Shasta Cascade Wonderland Association
Robert Stienstra, Jr., Fieldscout
Bob Simms, Fieldscout
Michael Furniss, Fieldscout
Jeffrey Patty, Fieldscout

CREDITS

Research editor . . . . Stephani Cruickshank
Research assistant . . . . A. Ashalyn

LEARNING TO CAMP

While working on this edition of the book, I received this note from a new California resident:

"My wife and I moved to California six weeks ago from Rhode Island, and one of the first things we noticed is there seems to be a lot of good places to go camping and hiking. The problem is that we like to hike, but we have never gone camping. So how do we learn how to camp? How can we find out if we like it without spending a fortune on equipment?"

—Keith Arsenault.

A lot of California residents can empathize with Keith Arsenault: New to the area, ready to play, but not quite ready to make a full buy-in on equipment.

Yet with the problems of driving in heavy traffic on freeways in the Bay Area, Sacramento, Los Angeles Basin and San Diego areas, many are figuring out that by camping overnight, the driving problem is solved, because you then wake up where you want to be for the day. It also allows the ultimate way to enjoy California's beautiful weather (nine months a year), as well as a chance to enjoy nature, wildlife, stargazing, or fishing or boating amid some of North America's most beautiful landscapes.

The number of people new to California is staggering, and many are curious about the region's stellar getaways. In the past 20 years, the population has climbed from 23 million to 34 million, and according to the most recent research information, about 2 million people who lived here 20 years ago no longer do. That equates to about 13 million new people in the state, with many arriving during the recent economic boom.

These new arrivals are often stunned to discover the amount of recreation available. California has 1,200 miles of coast, 20 million acres of national forest, 18 million acres of land managed by the Bureau of Land Management, 185 major streams, 375 lakes you can drive to, 483 significant lakes you can hike to, and a landscape that includes Yosemite Valley, the Redwood Empire, the high Sierra, Death Valley, coastal mountain ranges, the high desert and the Channel Islands.

So right off, many newcomers are sold on the outdoors. Yet they are often not sold quite enough to buy a ton of equipment for an outing (camping) they have never before tried.

But there is an answer to this, and it can work for anybody.

The best way to start is by choosing an area you want to explore, then renting a rustic cabin to use as a base camp. The only camping equipment you will need is a sleeping bag and a pillow, a cooler for drinks and food, and plates and utensils, along with personal items.

I finished a detailed survey of sites with cabin rentals, and there are roughly 500 places where cabins or cottages are available; hundreds are listed in this book.

For a first-time camp, this is the best way to go, for many reasons. But the three most important are these:

1. You guarantee yourself a good night of sleep, the most important factor in enjoying a camping trip.
2. You have a roof over your head, to protect you from any weather, like surprise thunderstorms in the Sierra and foggy dew on the coast.
3. You don't have to make a huge equipment buy-in just to get started.
   If the cabin trips work well, then you can take the next step.

You can buy or rent a little more equipment, such as a camp stove, lantern, Therm-a-Rest pad, foam sleeping cushion or a cot, and then rent a primitive cabin, camping cabin or yurt. If you don't want to make these purchases, camping equipment rentals are available at REI outdoor equipment stores, as well as at other outdoor shops.

The key again, is to make sure you get a good night's sleep. Many people do not spend enough pre-trip concern making sure they will be comfortable sleeping at camp. Newcomers often end up uncomfortable, waking up many times in a night. A camping joke is that you sleep eight hours all right, but that it comes in 20 installments. A suggestion is to practice getting comfortable "camping" at home before heading out.

If I go a week or so without a night in my sleeping bag, I start festering, and often put up an army cot and jump in my bag for the night. It helps takes the edge off until the next trip. After so many years, I now sleep better when camping than at any other time.

Eventually, you will be ready for tenting, and in turn, backpacking. Again, you can rent the equipment, then buy items as you get comfortable in the sport. Most people accumulate their gear over years, not in one fell swoop. The best first tent sites are at state parks, where rangers and camp hosts are available to answer questions.

In time, as you learn to love the primal experience of the great outdoors, the evolution of to walk-in sites, and eventually to the wilderness, where camping can be like a trip in a time machine to hundreds of years ago.

By then, you will no longer wonder whether or not to buy more equipment. You will suddenly discover that without any plan, that over the years you have bought just about everything imaginable.

TAKING A BREAK
ON THE PACIFIC COAST TRAIL

INTRODUCTION

If this book looks different from any previous edition of *California Camping,* well, that's because it is.

More than 5,000 updates and upgrades have been made in the campground listings of this edition, the biggest makeover in five years, and the third major makeover in the 15-year history of the book. To reflect that, we've added a new cover style, art work and photographs. Our mission is to make this the most accurate, easy-to-use and comprehensive outdoor guidebook ever created.

In many cases, directions have been rewritten and simplified, often detailed down to the nearest tenth of a mile. Part of the latter is so the book can be downloaded into a Palm Pilot and linked to a GPS for precision, the first guidebook in the United States designed with this accuracy in mind. In addition, every fee has been checked. Every phone number has been dialed. And 25 years of experiences from roaming around California, looking for hiking trails, hidden lakes and fishing spots, has been weaved into the camp descriptions. We have also added all new reservation numbers, website information, and the RV camps that accept credit cards and are wheelchair accessible, among many new improvements.

To do this, not only did the entire book go through my keyboard in the year 2000, but copies of the page galleys were reviewed by hundreds of field-scouts, including 200 rangers at Forest Service districts and state parks. Research editor Stephani Cruickshank faxed the galleys out to field stations, then personally reviewed each listing with rangers. A similar process was completed for every page.

We were blessed by the support of Michael Dombeck, chief of the U.S. Forest Service in Washington D.C., Matt Mathes out of regional Forest Service headquarters in Vallejo, and State Parks Superintendent of Park Operations, Vic Maris. The upgrades and details in this book would not have been possible without their support. I am also indebted to Stephani Cruickshank, who directed the fact-checking operation. Research Assistant A. Ashalyn worked over the privately-owned RV parks, as well some county, city and regional facilities. The new look, including art work and photography, was designed by editor Marisa Solís and her talented staff at Foghorn Outdoors and Avalon Travel Publishing.

Many of these upgrades have been inspired by letters from readers. Jean and Bill Pawek, for instance, who spend much of the year traveling in their RV, became fieldscouts and provided many suggestions. We are always looking for ways to improve the book, and your comments are welcome; write me at my website at www.TomStienstra.com, or at Avalon Travel Publishing, 5855 Beaudry Street, Emervyille, CA 94608.

When I first started this book years ago, the idea was simply to find all the campgrounds so I would never get stuck again looking for a spot. In the end, that is still its greatest value: You will always be able to find a spot for the night.

Never get stuck again! In the end, that's what keeps this book as my personal favorite.

—Tom Stienstra

CAMPING TIPS

Food and Cooking Gear

It was a warm, crystal clear day, the kind of day when if you had ever wanted to go skydiving, you would go skydiving. That was exactly the case for my old pal Foonsky, who had never before tried the sport. But a funny thing happened after he jumped out of the plane and pulled on the rip cord: His parachute didn't open.

In total free fall, Foonsky watched the earth below getting closer and closer. Not one to panic, he calmly pulled the rip cord on the emergency parachute. Again nothing happened. No parachute, no nothing.

The ground was getting ever closer, and as he tried to search for a soft place to land, Foonsky detected a small object shooting up toward him, growing larger as it approached. It looked like a camper.

Figuring this was his last chance, Foonsky shouted as they passed in midair, "Hey, do you know anything about parachutes?"

The other fellow just yelled back as he headed off into space, "Do you know anything about lighting camping stoves?"

Well, Foonsky got lucky and his parachute opened. As for the other guy, well, he's probably in orbit like a NASA weather satellite. If you've ever had a mishap while lighting a camping stove, you know exactly what I'm talking about.

When it comes to camping, all gear is not created equal. Nothing is more important than lighting your stove easily and having it reach full heat without feeling as if you're playing with a short fuse to a miniature bomb. If your stove does not work right, your trip can turn into a disaster, regardless of how well you have planned the other elements. In addition, a bad stove will add an underlying sense of foreboding to your day. You will constantly have the inner suspicion that your darn stove is going to foul up again.

Camping Stoves

If you are buying a camping stove, remember this one critical rule: Do not leave the store with a new stove unless you have been shown exactly how to use it.

Know what you are getting. Many stores that specialize in outdoor recreation equipment now provide experienced campers/employees who will demonstrate the use of every stove they sell and while they're at it, describe their respective strengths and weaknesses.

An innovation by Peak 1 is a two-burner backpacking stove that allows you to boil water and heat a pot of food simultaneously. While that has long been standard for car campers using Coleman's legendary camp stove, it was previously unheard of for wilderness campers in high-elevation areas. Another recent invention is the flameless stove (no kidding) that allows campers to cook in a tent safely for the first time.

A stove that has developed a cultlike following is the little Sierra, which burns small twigs and pinecones, then uses a tiny battery-driven fan to develop increased heat and cooking ability. It's an excellent alternative for long-distance backpacking trips, as it solves the problem of carrying a fuel bottle, especially on expeditions for which large quantities of fuel would otherwise be needed. Some tinkering with the flame (a very hot one) is required, and they are legal and functional only in the alpine zone where dry wood is available. Also note that in years with high fire danger, the U.S. Forest Service will enact rules prohibiting open flames, and fires are also often prohibited above an elevation of 10,000 feet.

I prefer a small, lightweight stove that uses white gas so I can closely gauge fuel consumption. My pal Foonsky uses one with a butane bottle because it lights so easily. We have contests to see who can boil a pot of water faster, and the difference is usually negligible. Thus, other factors are important when choosing a stove.

Of these, ease of cleaning the burner is the most important. If you camp often, especially with a smaller stove, the burner holes will eventually become clogged. Some stoves have a built-in cleaning needle; a quick twist of the knob and you're in business. Others require disassembly and a protracted session using special cleaning tools. If a stove is difficult to clean, you will tend to put off doing it, and your stove will sputter and pant while you feel humiliated watching the cold pot of water sitting there.

Before making a purchase, have the salesperson show you how to clean the burner head. Except in the case of large, multiburner family camping stoves, which rarely require cleaning, this test can do more to determine the long-term value of a stove than any other factor.

Fuels for Camping Stoves

White gas and butane have long been the most popular camp fuels, but a newly developed fuel could dramatically change that.

LPG (liquid petroleum gas) comes in cartridges for easy attachment to a stove or lantern. At room temperature, LPG is delivered in a combustible gaseous form. When you shake the cartridge, the contents sound liquid; that is because the gas liquefies under pressure, which is why it is so easy to use. Large amounts of fuel are compressed into small canisters.

While convenience has always been the calling card for LPG, recent innovations have allowed it to become a suitable choice for winter and high-altitude mountaineering expeditions, coming close to matching white gas performance specs. For several years now, MSR, Epi (Coleman), Coleman, Primus, Camping Gaz, Markill, and other makers have been mixing propane, butane, and isobutane to improve performance capabilities.

Two important hurdles that stood in the way of LPG's popularity were recently leaped. Coleman, working in cooperation with the U.S. Postal Service, has developed a program in which three-packs of 170-gram Coleman Max fuel cartridges can be shipped by mail to any address or post office in the 50 states and Puerto Rico. Also, each Coleman Max fuel cartridge is now made of aluminum and comes with a special device that allows the consumer to puncture the cartridge safely once the fuel is gone and then toss it into any aluminum recycling container.

The following details the benefits and drawbacks of other available fuels:

White gas: White gas is the most popular camp fuel because it is available at most outdoor recreation stores and many supermarkets and is inexpensive and effective. It burns hot, has virtually no smell, and evaporates quickly when spilled. If you are caught in wet, miserable weather and can't get a fire going, you can use white gas as an emergency fire starter; however, if you do so, use it sparingly and never on an open flame.

White gas is a popular fuel both for car campers, who use the large, two-burner stoves equipped with a fuel tank and a pump, and for hikers who carry a lightweight backpacking stove. On the latter, lighting can require priming with a gel called priming paste, which some people dislike. Another problem with white gas is that it can be extremely explosive.

As an example, I once almost burned my beard completely off in a mini-explosion while lighting one of the larger stoves designed for car camping. I was in the middle of cooking dinner when the flame suddenly shut down. Sure enough, the fuel tank was empty, and after refilling it, I pumped the tank 50 or 60 times to regain pressure. When I lit a match, the sucker ignited from three feet away. The resulting explosion was like a stick of

Stoves are available in many styles and burn a variety of fuels. These are three typical examples. Top: **White gas** *stoves are the most popular because they are inexpensive and easy to find; they do require priming and can be explosive. Middle:* Gas canister *stoves burn propane, butane, isobutane, and mixtures of the three. These are the easiest to use but have two disadvantages: 1) Because the fuel is bottled, determining how much fuel is left can be difficult. 2) The fuel is limited to above-freezing conditions. Bottom:* **Liquid fuel** *stoves burn Coleman Fuel, denatured alcohol, kerosene, and even gasoline; these fuels are economical and have a high heat output, but most must be primed.*

dynamite going off, and immediately the smell of burning beard was in the air. In a flash, my once thick, dark beard had been reduced to a mass of little yellow burned curlicues.

My error? After filling the tank, I forgot to shut the fuel cock off while pumping up the pressure in the tank. As a result, the stove burners were slowly producing the gas/air mixture as I pumped the tank, filling the air above the stove. Then strike a match from even a few feet away and ka-boom!

During high fire danger the U.S. Forest Service will enact rules prohibiting open flames. Fires are also often prohibited above an elevation of 10,000 feet.

Butane: The explosive problem can be solved by using stoves that burn bottled butane fuel. Butane requires no pouring, pumping, or priming, and butane stoves are the easiest to light. Just turn a knob and light—that's it. On the minus side, because it comes in bottles, you never know precisely how much fuel you have left. And when a bottle is empty, you have a potential piece of litter. (Never litter. Ever.)

The other problem with butane is that it just plain does not work well in cold weather or when there is little fuel left in the cartridge. Since you cannot predict mountain weather in spring or fall, you can wind up using more fuel than originally projected. That can be frustrating, particularly if your stove starts wheezing when there are still several days left to go. In addition, with most butane cartridges, if there is any chance of the temperature falling below freezing, you often have to sleep with the cartridge to keep it warm or forget about using it come morning.

Coleman Max Performance Fuel: This new fuel offers a unique approach to solving the consistent burn challenge facing all pressurized gas cartridges: operating at temperatures at or below 0 degrees Fahrenheit. Using a standard propane/butane blend for high-octane performance, Coleman gets around the drop-off in performance other cartridges experience by utilizing a version of fuel injection. A hose inside the cartridge pulls liquid fuel into the stove, where it vaporizes—a switch from the standard approach of pulling only a gaseous form of the fuel into a stove. By drawing liquid out of the cartridge, Coleman gets around the tendency of propane to burn off first and allows each cartridge to deliver a consistent mix of propane and butane to the stove's burners throughout the cartridge's life.

Butane/Propane: This blend offers higher octane performance than butane alone, solving the cold temperature doldrums somewhat. However, propane burns off before butane, so there will be a performance drop as the fuel level in the cartridge lowers.

Propane: Now available for single-burner stoves using larger, heavier cartridges to accommodate higher pressures, propane offers the very best performance of any of the pressurized gas canister fuels.

Primus Tri-Blend: This blend is made up of 20% propane, 70% butane, and 10% isobutane and is designed to burn with more consistent heat and efficiency than standard propane/butane mixes.

Denatured alcohol: Though this fuel burns cleanly and quietly and is virtually explosion proof, it generates much less heat than pressurized or liquid gas fuels. *Kerosene:* Never buy a stove that uses kerosene for fuel. Kerosene is smelly and messy, generates low heat, needs priming, and is virtually obsolete as a camp fuel in the United States. As a test I once tried using a kerosene stove. I could scarcely boil a pot of water. In addition, some kerosene leaked out when the stove was packed, ruining everything it touched. The smell of kerosene never did go away. Kerosene remains popular in Europe only because most campers there haven't yet heard much about white gas. When they do, they will demand it.

Building Fires

One summer expedition took me to the Canadian wilderness in British Columbia for a 75-mile canoe trip on the Bowron Lake Circuit, a chain of 13 lakes, six rivers, and seven portages. It is one of the truly great canoe trips in the world, a loop that ends just a few hundred feet from its starting point. But at the first camp at Kibbee Lake, my stove developed a fuel leak at the base of the burner, and the nuclear-like blast that followed just about turned Canada into a giant crater.

As a result, the final 70 miles of the trip had to be completed without a stove, cooking on open fires each night. The problem was compounded by the weather. It rained eight of the 10 days. Rain? In Canada, raindrops the size of silver dollars fall so hard they actually bounce on the lake surface. We had to stop paddling a few times in order to empty the rainwater out of the canoe. At the end of the day we'd make camp and then face the test: either make a fire or go to bed cold and hungry.

Keep It Wild Tip 1: Campfires

1. Fire use can scar the backcountry. If a fire ring is not available, use a lightweight stove for cooking.
2. Where fires are permitted, use existing fire rings away from large rocks or overhangs.
3. Don't char rocks by building new rings.
4. Gather sticks from the ground that are no larger than the diameter of your wrist.
5. Don't snap branches of live, dead, or downed trees, which can cause personal injury and also scar the natural setting.
6. Put the fire "dead out" and make sure it's cold before departing. Remove all trash from the fire ring and sprinkle dirt over the site.
7. Remember that some forest fires can be started by a campfire that appears to be out. Hot embers burning deep in the pit can cause tree roots to catch fire and burn underground. If you ever see smoke rising from the ground, seemingly from nowhere, dig down and put the fire out.

With an ax, at least we had a chance for success. As soaked as all the downed wood was, I was able to make my own fire-starting tinder from the chips of split logs; no matter how hard it rains, the inside of a log is always dry. In miserable weather, matches don't stay lit long enough to get the tinder started. Instead we used either a candle or the little waxlike fire-starter cubes that remain lit for several minutes. From those we could get the tinder going. Then we added small, slender strips of wood that had been axed from the interior of the logs. When the flame reached a foot high, we added the logs, their dry interior facing in. By the time the inside of the logs had caught fire, the outside would be drying from the heat. It wasn't long before a royal blaze was brightening the rainy night.

That's a worst-case scenario, and hopefully you will never face anything like it. Nevertheless, being able to build a good fire and cook on it can be one of the more satisfying elements of a camping trip. At times just looking into the flames can provide a special satisfaction at the end of a good day.

However, never expect to build a fire for every meal or in some cases even to build one at all. Many state and federal campgrounds have been picked clean of downed wood, or forest fire danger forces rangers to prohibit fires altogether during the fire season. In either case you must use your camp stove or go hungry.

But when you can build a fire and the resources for doing so are available, it will enhance the quality of your camping experience. Of the campgrounds listed in this book, those where you are permitted to build fires will usually have fire rings. In primitive areas where you can make your own fire, you should dig a ring eight inches deep, line the edges with rock, and clear all the needles and twigs in a five-foot radius. The next day, when the fire is dead, you can discard the rocks, fill over the black charcoal with dirt, and then scatter pine needles and twigs over it. Nobody will even know you camped there. That's the best way I know to keep a secret spot a real secret.

When you start to build a campfire, the first thing you will notice is that no matter how good your intentions, your fellow campers will not be able to resist moving the wood around. Watch. You'll be getting ready to add a key piece of wood at just the right spot, and your companion will stick his mitts in, confidently believing he has a better idea. He'll shift the fire around and undermine your best-thought-out plans.

So I enforce a rule on camping trips: One person makes the fire while everybody else stands clear or is involved with other camp tasks such as gathering wood, getting water, putting up tents, or planning dinner. Once the fire is going strong, then it's fair game; anyone adds logs at his or her discretion. But in the early, delicate stages of the campfire, it's best to leave the work to one person.

Before a match is ever struck, you should gather a complete pile of firewood. Then start small, with the tiniest twigs you can find, and slowly add larger twigs as you go, crisscrossing them like a miniature tepee. Eventually you will get to the big chunks that will produce high heat. The key is to get one piece of wood burning into another, which then burns into another, setting off what I call the chain of flame. Conversely, single pieces of wood set apart from each other will not burn.

On a dry summer evening at a campsite where plenty of wood is available, about the only way you can blow the deal is to get impatient and try to add the big pieces too quickly. Do that and you'll get smoke, not flames, and it won't be long before every one of your fellow campers is poking at your fire. It will drive you crazy, but they just won't be able to help it.

Cooking Gear

I like traveling light, and I've found that all I need for cooking is a pot, small frying pan, metal pot grabber, fork, knife, cup, and matches. If you want to keep the price of food low and also cook customized dinners each night, a small pressure cooker can be just the ticket. (See "Keeping the Price Down" on page 30.) I store all my gear in one small bag that fits into my pack. If I'm camping out of my four-wheel-drive rig, the little bag of cooking gear is easy to keep track of. Going simple, not complicated, is the key to keeping a camping trip on the right track.

You can get more elaborate by purchasing complete kits with plates, a coffeepot, large pots, and other cookware, but what really counts is having a single pot that makes you happy. It needs to be just the right size, not too big or small, and stable enough so it won't tip over, even if it is at a slight angle on a fire, full of water at a full boil. Mine is just six inches wide and four-and-a-half inches deep. It holds better than a quart of water and has served me well for several hundred camp dinners.

The rest of your cook kit is easy to complete. The frying pan should be small, light-gauge aluminum, and Teflon-coated, with a fold-in handle so it's no hassle to store. A pot grabber is a great addition. It's a little aluminum gadget that clamps to the edge of pots and allows you to lift them and pour water with total control without burning your fingers. For cleanup take a plastic scrubber and a small bottle filled with dish cleaner, and you're in business.

A sierra cup, a wide aluminum cup with a wire handle, is an ideal item to carry because you can eat out of it as well as use it for drinking. This means no plates to scrub after dinner, so cleanup is quick and easy. In addition, if you go for a hike, you can clip it to your belt with its handle.

If you want a more formal setup complete with plates, glasses, silverware, and the like, you can end up spending more time preparing and cleaning up from meals than you do enjoying the country you are exploring. In addition, the more equipment you bring, the more loose ends you will have to deal with, and loose ends can cause plenty of frustration. If you have a choice, go simple.

And remember what Thoreau said: "A man is rich in proportion to what he can do without."

Food and Cooking Tricks

On a trip to the Bob Marshall Wilderness in western Montana, I woke up one morning, yawned, and said, "What've we got for breakfast?"

The silence was ominous. "Well," finally came the response, "we don't have any food left."

"What!?"

"Well, I figured we'd catch trout for meals every other night."

On the return trip, we ended up eating wild berries, buds, and, yes, even roots (not too tasty). When we finally landed the next day at a suburban pizza parlor, we nearly ate the wooden tables.

Running out of food on a camping trip can do more to turn reasonable people into violent grumps than any other event. There's no excuse for it, not when a system for figuring meals can be outlined with precision and little effort. You should not go out and buy a bunch of food, throw it in your rig, and head off for yonder. That leaves too much to chance. And if you've ever been in the woods and real hungry, you'll know it's worth taking a little effort to make sure a day or two of starvation will not occur. Here's a three-step solution:

1. Draw up a general meal-by-meal plan and make sure your companions like what's on it.
2. Tell your companions to buy any specialty items (like a special brand of coffee) on their own and not to expect you to take care of everything.
3. Put all the food on your living room floor and literally plan out every day of your trip, meal by meal, putting the food in plastic bags as you go. That way you will know exact food quotas and will not go hungry.

Fish for your dinner? There's one guarantee as far as that goes: If you expect to catch fish for meals, you will most certainly get skunked. If you don't expect to catch fish for meals, you will probably catch so many they'll be coming out of your ears. I've seen it a hundred times.

Keeping the Price Down

"There must be some mistake," I said with a laugh. "Whoever paid $750 for camp food?"

But the amount was as clear as the digital numbers on the cash register: $753.27.

"How is this possible?" I asked the clerk.

"Just add it up," she responded, irritated.

Then I started figuring. The freeze-dried backpack dinners cost $6 apiece. A small pack of beef jerky went for $2, the beef sticks for 75 cents, granola bars for 50 cents. Multiply it all by four hungry men, including Foonsky, for 21 days. This food was to sustain us on a major expedition—four guys hiking 250 miles over three weeks from Mount Whitney to Yosemite Valley.

The dinners alone cost close to $500. Add in the usual goodies—jerky, granola bars, soup, dried fruit, oatmeal, Tang, candy, and coffee—and I felt as if an earthquake had struck when I saw the tab.

How to Make Beef Jerky in Your Own Kitchen

Start with a couple pieces of meat: lean top round, sirloin, or tri-tip. Cut it into 3/16-inch strips across the grain, trimming out the membrane, gristle, and fat. Marinate the strips for 24 hours in a glass dish. The fun begins in picking a marinade. Try two-thirds teriyaki sauce, one-third Worcestershire sauce. You can customize the recipe by adding pepper, ground mustard, bay leaf, red wine vinegar, garlic, and, for the brave, Tabasco sauce.

After a day or so, squeeze out each strip of meat with a rolling pin, lay them in rows on a cooling rack over a cookie sheet, and dry them in the oven at 125 degrees for 12 hours. Thicker pieces can take as long as 18 to 24 hours.

That's it. The hardest part is cleaning the cookie sheet when you're done. The easiest part is eating your own homemade jerky while sitting at a lookout on a mountain ridge. The do-it-yourself method for jerky may take a day or so, but it is cheaper and can taste better than any store-bought jerky.

A lot of campers have received similar shocks. In preparation for their trips, campers shop with enthusiasm. Then they pay the bill in horror.

Well, there are solutions, lots of them. You can eat gourmet style in the outback without having your wallet cleaned out. But it requires do-it-yourself cooking, more planning, and careful shopping. It also means transcending the push-button I-want-it-now attitude that so many people can't leave behind when they go to the mountains.

The secret is to bring along a small pressure cooker. A reader in San Francisco, Mike Bettinger, passed this tip on to me. Little pressure cookers weigh about two pounds, which may sound like a lot to backpackers and backcountry campers. But when three or four people are on a trip, it actually saves weight.

The key is that it allows campers to bring items that are difficult to cook at high altitudes, such as brown and white rice; red, black, pinto, and lima beans; and lentils. You pick one or more for a basic staple and then add a variety of freeze-dried ingredients to make a complete dish. Available are packets of meat, vegetables, onions, shallots, and garlic. Sun-dried tomatoes, for instance, reconstitute wonderfully in a pressure cooker. Add herbs, spices, and maybe a few rainbow trout and you will be eating better out of a backpack than most people do at home.

"In the morning, I have used the pressure cooker to turn dried apricots into apricot sauce to put on the pancakes we made with sourdough starter," Bettinger said. "The pressure cooker is also big enough for washing out cups and utensils. The days when backpacking meant eating terrible freeze-dried food are over. It doesn't take a gourmet cook to prepare these meals, only some thought beforehand."

Now when Foonsky, Mr. Furnai, Rambob, and I sit down to eat such a meal, we don't call it "eating." We call it "hodgepacking" or "time to pack your

Basic steps to cleaning a fish: *First, slit belly from anal vent to gills. Then sever lower junctions of gills. Next, pull out innards and gills. And last but not least, run thumbnail along cavity to clean out dark matter.*

hodge." After a particularly long day on the trail, you can do some serious hodgepacking.

If your trip is a shorter one, say for a weekend, you can bring more fresh food to add some sizzle to the hodge. You can design a hot soup/stew mix that is good enough to eat at home.

Start by bringing a pot of water to a full boil, then adding pasta, ramen noodles, or macaroni. While it simmers, cut in a potato, carrot, onion, and garlic clove, and cook for about 10 minutes. When the vegetables have softened, add in a soup mix or two, maybe some cheese, and you are just about in business. But you can still ruin it and turn your hodge into slodge. Make sure you read the directions on the soup mix to determine cooking time. It can vary widely. In addition, make sure you stir the whole thing up; otherwise you will get these hidden dry clumps of soup mix that taste like garlic sawdust.

How do I know? Well, it was up near Kearsage Pass in the Sierra Nevada, where, feeling half-starved, I dug into our nightly hodge. I will never forget that first bite—I damn near gagged to death. Foonsky laughed at me, until he took his first bite (a nice big one) and then turned green.

Another way to trim food costs is to make your own beef jerky, the trademark staple of campers for more than 200 years. A tiny packet of beef jerky costs $2, and for that 250-mile expedition, I spent $150 on jerky alone. Never again. Now we make our own and get big strips of jerky that taste better than anything you can buy.

If all this still doesn't sound like your idea of a gourmet but low-cost camping meal, well, you are forgetting the main course: rainbow trout. Remember: If you don't plan on catching them for dinner, you'll probably snag more than you can finish in one night's hodgepacking.

Some campers go to great difficulties to cook their trout, bringing along frying pans, butter, grills, tinfoil, and more, but all you need is some seasoned salt and a campfire.

Rinse the gutted trout, and while it's still wet, sprinkle on a good dose of seasoned salt, both inside and out. Clear any burning logs to the side of the campfire, then lay the trout right on the coals, turning it once so both sides are cooked. Sound ridiculous? Sound like you are throwing the fish away? Sound like the fish will burn up? Sound like you will have to eat the campfire ash? Wrong on all counts. The fish cooks perfectly, the ash doesn't stick, and after cooking trout this way, you may never fry trout again.

But if you can't convince your buddies, who may insist the trout should be fried, then make sure you have butter to fry them in, not oil. Also make sure you cook them all the way through, so the meat strips off the backbone in two nice, clean fillets. The fish should end up looking like one that Sylvester the Cat just drew out of his mouth—only the head, tail, and a perfect skeleton.

You can supplement your eats with sweets, nuts, freeze-dried fruits, and drink mixes. In any case, make sure you keep the dinner menu varied. If you and your buddies look into your dinner cups and groan, "Ugh, not this again," you will soon start dreaming of cheeseburgers and french fries instead of hiking, fishing, and finding beautiful campsites.

If you are car camping and have a big ice chest, you can bring virtually anything to eat and drink. If you are on the trail and don't mind paying the price, the newest freeze-dried dinners provide another option.

Some of the biggest advances in the outdoors industry have come in the freeze-dried dinners now available to campers. Some of them are almost good enough to serve in restaurants. Sweet-and-sour pork over rice, tostadas, Burgundy chicken—it sure beats the poopy goop we used to eat, like the old soupy chili-mac dinners that tasted bad and looked so unlike food that consumption was near impossible, even for my dog, Rebel. Foonsky usually managed to get it down, but just barely.

To provide an idea of how to plan a menu, consider what my companions and I ate while hiking 250 miles on California's John Muir Trail:

- Breakfast: instant soup, oatmeal (never get plain), one beef or jerky stick, coffee or hot chocolate.

- Lunch: one beef stick, two jerky sticks, one granola bar, dried fruit, half cup of pistachio nuts, Tang, one small bag of M&Ms.

- Dinner: instant soup, one freeze-dried dinner, one milk bar, rainbow trout.

What was that last item? Rainbow trout? Right! Unless you plan on it, you can catch them every night.

Clothing and Weather Protection

What started as an innocent pursuit of a perfect campground evolved into one heck of a predicament for Foonsky and me.

We had parked at the end of a logging road and then bushwhacked our way down a canyon to a pristine trout stream. On my first cast—a little flip into the plunge pool of a waterfall—I caught a 16-inch rainbow trout, a real beauty that jumped three times. Magic stuff.

Then just across the stream, we saw it: The Perfect Camping Spot. On a sandbar on the edge of the forest, there lay a flat spot, high and dry above the river. Nearby was plenty of downed wood collected by past winter storms that we could use for firewood. And, of course, this beautiful trout stream was bubbling along just 40 yards from the site.

But nothing is perfect, right? To reach it, we had to wade across the river, although it didn't appear to be too difficult. The cold water tingled a bit, and the river came up surprisingly high, just above the belt. But it would be worth it to camp at The Perfect Spot.

Once across the river, we put on some dry clothes, set up camp, explored the woods, and fished the stream, catching several nice trout for dinner. But late that afternoon, it started raining. What? Rain in the summertime? Nature makes its own rules. By the next morning, it was still raining, pouring like a Yosemite waterfall from a solid gray sky.

That's when we noticed The Perfect Spot wasn't so perfect. The rain had raised the river level too high for us to wade back across. We were marooned, wet, and hungry.

"Now we're in a heck of a predicament," said Foonsky, the water streaming off him.

Getting cold and wet on a camping trip with no way to warm up is not only unnecessary and uncomfortable, it can be a fast ticket to hypothermia, the number one killer of campers in the woods. By definition, hypothermia is a condition in which body temperature is lowered to the point that it causes illness. It is particularly dangerous because the afflicted are usually unaware it is setting in. The first sign is a sense of apathy, then a state of confusion, which can lead eventually to collapse (or what appears to be sleep), then death.

You must always have a way to get warm and dry in short order, regardless of any conditions you may face. If you have no way of getting dry, then you must take emergency steps to prevent hypothermia. Those steps are detailed in the first-aid section on page 64.

But you should never reach that point. For starters, always have spare sets of clothing tucked away so no matter how cold and wet you might get, you have something dry to put on. On hiking trips I always carry a second set of clothes, sealed to stay dry, in a plastic garbage bag. I keep a third set waiting back at the truck.

If you are car camping, your vehicle can cause an illusory sense of security. But with an extra set of dry clothes stashed safely away, there is no illusion. The security is real. And remember, no matter how hot the weather is when you start your trip, always be prepared for the worst. Foonsky and I learned the hard way.

So both of us were soaking wet on that sandbar, and with no other choice we tried holing up in the tent for the night. A sleeping bag with Quallofil or another polyester fiberfill can retain warmth even when wet, because the fill is hollow and retains its loft. So as miserable as it was, we made it through the night.

The rain stopped the next day and the river dropped a bit, but it was still rolling big and angry. Using a stick as a wading staff, Foonsky crossed about 80% of the stream before he was dumped, but he made a jump for it and managed to scramble to the riverbank. He waved for me to follow. "No problem," I thought.

It took me 20 minutes to reach nearly the same spot where Foonsky had been dumped. The heavy river current was above my belt and pushing hard. Then in the flash of an instant, my wading staff slipped on a rock. I teetered in the river current and was knocked over like a bowling pin. I became completely submerged. I went tumbling down the river, heading right toward the waterfall. While underwater I looked up at the surface, and I can remember how close it seemed yet how out of control I was. Right then this giant hand appeared, and I grabbed it. It was Foonsky. If it weren't for that hand, I would have sailed right over the waterfall.

My momentum drew Foonsky right into the river, and we scrambled in the current, but I suddenly sensed the river bottom under my knees. On all fours, the two of us clambered ashore. We were safe.

"Thanks ol' buddy," I said.

"Man, we're wet," he responded. "Let's get to the rig and get some dry clothes on."

The Art of Layering

The most important element in enjoying the outdoor experience in any condition is to stay dry and warm. There is no substitute. You must stay dry and you must stay warm.

Thus comes the theory behind layering, which suggests that as your body temperature fluctuates or the weather shifts, you simply peel off or add available layers as needed—and have a waterproof shell available in case of rain.

The introduction of a new era of outdoor clothing has made it possible for campers to turn choosing clothes into an art form. Like art, it comes much more expensive than throwing on a pair of blue jeans, a T-shirt, and some flannel, but for many it is worth the price.

In putting together your ideal layering system, there are some general considerations. What you need to do is create a system that effectively combines elements of breathability, wicking, rapid drying, insulation, durability, wind resistance, and water repellence while still being lightweight and offering the necessary freedom of movement, all with just a few garments.

The basic intent of a base layer is to manage moisture. Your base layer will be the first article of clothing you put on and the last to come off. Since your own skin will be churning out the perspiration, the goal of this second skin is to manage the moisture and move it away from you without trapping your body's heat. The only time that cotton should become a part of your base layer is if you wish to keep cool, not warm, such as in a hot desert climate where evaporative cooling becomes your friend, not your enemy.

That is why the best base layer available is from bicomponent knits, that is, blends of polyester and cotton, which work to provide wicking and insulating properties in one layer. The way it works is that the side facing your skin is water hating, while the side away from your skin is water loving; thus it pulls or "wicks" moisture through. You'll stay dry and happy, even with only one layer on, something not possible with old single-function weaves. The best include Thermax, Capilene, Driclime, Lifa, and Polartec 100.

Stretch fleece and microdenier pile also provide a good base layer, though they can be used as a second layer as well. Microdenier pile can be worn alone or layered under or over other pieces, and it has excellent wicking capability as well as more windproof potential.

The next layer should be a light cotton shirt or a long-sleeved cotton/wool shirt, or both, depending on the coolness of the day. For pants, many just wear blue jeans when camping, but blue jeans can be hot and tight, and once wet, they tend to stay that way. Putting on wet blue jeans on a cold morning is a torturous way to start the day. (I tell you this from experience, since I have suffered that fate a number of times.) A better choice is pants made from a cotton/canvas mix, which are available at outdoors stores. They are light, have a lot of give, and dry quickly. If the weather is quite warm, shorts that have some room to them can be the best choice.

Finally, you'll top the entire ensemble off with a thin windproof, water-resistant layer. You want this layer to breathe like crazy, yet not be so porous that rain runs through it like floodwaters through a leaking dike. Patagonia's Velocity shell is one of the best. Its outer fabric is DWR (durable water-repellent) treated, and the coating is by Gore. Patagonia calls it Pneumatic (Gore now calls it Activent, while Marmot, Moonstone, and North Face all offer their own versions). Though condensation will still build up inside, it manages to get rid of enough moisture.

It is critical to know the difference between "water-resistant" and "waterproof." This is covered later in the chapter under the "Rain Gear" section.

But hey, why does anybody need all this fancy stuff just to go camping? Fair question. Like the introduction of Gore-Tex years ago, all this fabric and fiber mumbo jumbo has its skeptics, including me. You don't have to opt for this aerobic-function fashion statement; it is unnecessary on many camping trips. But the fact is you must be ready for anything when you venture into the outdoors. And the truth is that the new era of outdoor clothing works, and it works better than anything that has come before.

Regardless of what you choose, weather should never be a nuisance or cause discomfort, regardless of what you experience. Instead it should provide a welcome change of pace.

About Hats

One final word of advice: Always pack along a warm hat for those times when you need to seal in warmth. You lose a large percentage of heat through your head. I almost always wear a wide-brimmed hat, something like the legendary outlaws wore 150 years ago. There's actually logic behind it: My hat is made out of kangaroo skin (waterproof), is rigged with a lariat (it can be cinched down when it's windy), and has a wide brim that keeps the tops of my ears from being sunburned (years ago they once were burned to a red crisp on a trip where I was wearing a baseball hat). But to be honest, I like how it looks, kind of like my pal Waylon Jennings.

Vests and Parkas

In cold weather you should take the layer system one step further with a warm vest and a parka jacket. Vests are especially useful because they provide warmth without the bulkiness of a parka. The warmest vests and parkas are either filled with down or Quallofil, or are made with a cotton/wool mix. Each has its respective merits and problems. Down fill provides the most warmth for the amount of weight, but becomes useless when wet, closely resembling a wet dishrag. Quallofil keeps much of its heat-retaining quality even when wet, but is expensive. Vests made of cotton/wool mixes are the most attractive and also are quite warm, but they can be as heavy as a ship's anchor when wet.

Sometimes the answer is combining the two. One of my best camping companions wears a good-looking cotton/wool vest and a parka filled with Quallofil. The vest never gets wet, so weight is not a factor.

Rain Gear

One of the most miserable nights I ever spent in my life was on a camping trip where I didn't bring my rain gear or a tent. Hey, it was early August, the temperature had been in the 90s for weeks, and if anybody had said it was going to rain, I would have told him to consult a brain doctor. But rain it did. And as I got wetter and wetter, I kept saying to myself, "Hey, it's summer, it's not supposed to rain." Then I remembered one of the ten commandments of camping: Forget your rain gear and you can guarantee it will rain.

To stay dry, you need some form of water-repellent shell. It can be as simple as a $5 poncho made out of plastic or as elaborate as a Gore-Tex rain

Waterproof: impervious to water. Though rain won't penetrate waterproof material, if you're at all mobile you'll soon find yourself wet from perspiration that can't evaporate.

Water-resistant: resistant but not impervious to water. You'll stay dry using water-resistant material only if it isn't pouring.

jacket-and-pants set that costs $300. What counts is not how much you spend, but how dry you stay.

The most important thing to realize is that waterproof and water-resistant are completely different things. In addition, there is no such thing as rain gear that is both waterproof and breathable. The more waterproof a jacket is, the less it breathes. Conversely, the more breathable a jacket is, the less waterproof it becomes.

If you wear water-resistant rain gear in a downpour, you'll get soaked. Water-resistant rain gear is appealing because it breathes and will keep you dry in the light stuff, such as mist, fog, even a little splash from a canoe paddle. But in rain? Forget it.

So what is the solution?

I've decided that the best approach is a set of fairly light but 100%-waterproof rain gear. I recently bought a hooded jacket and pants from Coleman, and my assessment is that it is the most cost-efficient rain gear I've ever had. All I can say is, hey, it works: I stay dry, it doesn't weigh much, and it didn't cost a fortune.

You can also stay dry with any of the waterproof plastics and even heavy-duty rubber-coated outfits made for commercial fishermen. But these are uncomfortable during anything but a heavy rain. Because they are heavy and don't breathe, you'll likely get soaked anyway (that is, from your own sweat), even if it isn't raining hard.

On backpacking trips, I still stash a super lightweight water-repellent slicker for day hikes, and a poncho, which I throw over my pack at night to keep it dry. But otherwise I never go anywhere—*anywhere*—without my rain gear.

Some do just fine with a cheap poncho, and note that ponchos can serve other uses in addition to a raincoat. Ponchos can be used as a ground tarp, as a rain cover for supplies or a backpack, or can be roped up to trees in a pinch to provide a quick storm ceiling if you don't have a tent. The problem with ponchos is that in a hard rain, you just don't stay dry. First your legs get wet, then they get soaked. Then your arms follow the same pattern. If you're wearing cotton, you'll find that once part of the garment gets wet, the water will spread until, alas, you are dripping wet, poncho and all. Before long you start to feel like a walking refrigerator.

One high-cost option is buying a Gore-Tex rain jacket and pants. Gore-Tex is actually not a fabric as is commonly believed, but a laminated film that coats a breathable fabric. The result is lightweight, water-repellent, breathable jackets and pants. They are perfect for campers, but they cost a fortune.

Some hiking buddies of mine have complained that the older Gore-Tex rain gear loses its water-repellent quality over time. However, manufacturers insist that this is the result of water seeping through seams, not leaks in the jacket. At each seam, tiny needles have pierced the fabric, and as tiny as the holes are, water will find a way through. An application of Seam Lock, especially at major seams around the shoulders of a jacket, can usually fix the problem.

If you don't want to spend the big bucks for Gore-Tex rain gear but want more rain protection than a poncho affords, a coated nylon jacket is the compromise that many choose. They are inexpensive, have the highest water-repellency of any rain gear, and are warm, providing a good outer shell for your layers of clothing. But they are not without fault. These jackets don't breathe at all, and if you zip them up tight, you can sweat a river.

My brother Rambob gave me a nylon jacket prior to a mountain climbing expedition. I wore that $20 special all the way to the top with no complaints; it's warm and 100% waterproof. The one problem with nylon is when temperatures drop below freezing. It gets so stiff that it feels as if you are wearing a straitjacket. But at $20, it seems like a treasure, especially compared to a $180 Gore-Tex jacket.

There's one more jacket-construction term to know: DWR, or durable water-repellent finish. All of the top-quality jackets these days are DWR treated. The DWR causes water to bead up on the shell. When the DWR wears off, even a once-waterproof jacket will feel like a wet dishrag.

Also note that ventilation is the key to coolness. The only ventilation on most shells is often the zipper. But waterproof jackets need additional openings. Look for mesh-backed pockets and underarm zippers, as well as cuffs, waists, and hems that can be adjusted to open wide. Storm flaps (the baffle over the zipper) that close with hook-and-loop material or snaps let you leave the zipper open for airflow into the jacket.

Other Gear—and a Few Tips

What are the three items most commonly forgotten on a camping trip? A hat, sunglasses, and lip balm.

A hat is crucial, especially when you are visiting high elevations. Without one you are constantly exposed to everything nature can give you. The sun will dehydrate you, sap your energy, sunburn your head, and in worst cases, cause sunstroke. Start with a comfortable hat. Then finish with sunglasses, lip balm, and sunscreen for additional protection. They will help protect you from extreme heat.

To guard against extreme cold, it's a good idea to keep a pair of thin ski gloves stashed away with your emergency clothes, along with a wool ski cap. The gloves should be thick enough to keep your fingers from stiffening up, but pliable enough to allow full movement so you don't have to take them off to complete simple tasks, like lighting a stove. An alternative to gloves is glovelets, which look like gloves with no fingers. In any case, just because the weather turns cold doesn't mean that your hands have to.

And if you fall into a river as Foonsky and I did—well, I hope you have a set of dry clothes waiting back at your rig. Oh, and a hand reaching out to you.

Hiking and Foot Care

We had set up a nice little camp in the woods, and my buddy, Foonsky, was strapping on his hiking boots, sitting against a big Douglas fir.

"New boots," he said with a grin. "But they seem pretty stiff."

We decided to hoof it down the trail for a few hours, exploring the mountain wildlands that are said to hide Bigfoot and other strange creatures. After just a short while on the trail, a sense of peace and calm seemed to settle in. The forest provides the chance to be purified with clean air and the smell of trees, freeing you from all troubles.

But it wasn't long before a look of trouble was on Foonsky's face. And no, it wasn't from seeing Bigfoot.

"Got a hot spot on a toe," he said.

Immediately we stopped. He pulled off his right boot, then his socks, and inspected the left side of his big toe. Sure enough, a blister had bubbled up, filled with fluid, but hadn't popped. From his medical kit, Foonsky cut a small piece of moleskin to fit over the blister and taped it to hold it in place. In a few minutes we were back on the trail.

A half hour later, there was still no sign of Bigfoot. But Foonsky stopped again and pulled off his other boot. "Another hot spot." On the little toe of his left foot was another small blister, over which he taped a Band-Aid to keep it from further chafing against the inside of his new boot.

In just a few days, ol' Foonsky, a strong, 6-foot-5, 200-plus-pound guy, was walking around like a sore-hoofed horse that had been loaded with a month's worth of supplies and ridden over sharp rocks. Well, it wasn't the distance that had done Foonsky in; it was those blisters. He had them on eight of his 10 toes and was going through Band-Aids, moleskin, and tape like a walking emergency ward. If he used any more tape, he would've looked like a mummy from an Egyptian tomb.

If you've ever been in a similar predicament, you know the frustration of wanting to have a good time, wanting to hike and explore the area where you have set up a secluded camp, only to be turned gimp-legged by several blisters. No one is immune—all are created equal before the blister god. You can be forced to bow to it unless you get your act together.

That means wearing the right style boots for what you have in mind and then protecting your feet with carefully selected socks. If you are still so unfortunate as to get a blister or two, it means knowing how to treat them fast so they don't turn your walk into a sore-footed endurance test.

What causes blisters? In almost all cases, it is the simple rubbing of a foot against the rugged interior of a boot. That can be worsened by several factors:

1. A very stiff boot or one in which your foot moves inside as you walk, instead of the boot flexing as if it were another layer of skin.

2. Thin, ragged, or dirty socks. This is the fastest route to blisters. Thin socks will allow your feet to move inside of your boots, ragged socks will allow your skin

to chafe directly against the boot's interior, and dirty socks will wrinkle and fold, also rubbing against your feet instead of cushioning them.

3. Soft feet. By themselves, soft feet will not cause blisters, but in combination with a stiff boot or thin socks, they can cause terrible problems. The best way to toughen up your feet is to go barefoot. In fact, some of the biggest, toughest-looking guys you'll ever see, from Hell's Angels to pro football players, have feet that are as soft as a baby's butt. Why? Because they never go barefoot and don't hike much.

Selecting the Right Boots

One summer I hiked 400 miles, including 250 miles in three weeks, along the crest of California's Sierra Nevada, and another 150 miles over several months in an earlier general training program. In that span I got just one blister, suffered on the fourth day of the 250-miler. I treated it immediately and suffered no more. One key is wearing the right boot, and for me, that means a boot that acts as a thick layer of skin that is flexible and pliable to my foot. I want my feet to fit snugly in them, with no interior movement.

There are three kinds of boots: mountaineering boots, hiking (or backpacking) boots, and canvas walking shoes. Select the right one for you or pay the consequences.

Mountaineering boots

The stiffest of the lot is the mountaineering boot. These boots are often identified by mid-range tops, laces that extend almost as far as the toe area, and ankle areas that are as stiff as a board. The lack of "give" is what endears them to mountaineers. Their stiffness is preferred when rock climbing, walking off-trail on craggy surfaces, or hiking down the edge of streambeds where walking across small rocks can cause you to turn your ankle. Because these boots don't give on rugged, craggy terrain, they reduce ankle injuries and provide better traction.

The drawback to stiff boots is that if you don't have the proper socks and your foot starts slipping around in the boot, you will get a set of blisters that would raise even Foonsky's eyebrows. But if you just want to go for a walk or a good tromp with a backpack, then hiking shoes or backpacking boots will serve you better.

Canvas walking shoes

Canvas walking shoes are the lightest of all boots, designed for day walks or short backpacking trips. Some of the newer models are like rugged tennis shoes, designed with a canvas top for lightness and a lug sole for traction. These are perfect for people who like to walk but rarely carry a backpack. Because they are flexible, they are easy to break in, and with fresh socks they rarely cause blister problems. Because they are light, general hiking fatigue is greatly reduced.

On the negative side, because canvas shoes have shallow lug soles, traction can be far from good on slippery surfaces. In addition, they provide less than ideal ankle support, which can be a problem in rocky areas, such as along a stream where you might want to go trout fishing. Turn your ankle and your trip can be ruined.

Backpacking boots

My preference is for a premium backpacking boot, the perfect medium between the stiff mountaineering boot and the soft canvas walking shoe. The deep lug bottom provides traction, the high ankle coverage provides support, yet the soft, waterproof leather body gives each foot a snug fit. Add it up and that means no blisters. On the negative side, they can be quite hot, weigh a ton, and if they get wet, take days to dry.

There are a zillion styles, brands, and price ranges to choose from. If you wander about comparing all their many features, you will get as confused as a kid in a toy store. Instead, go into the store with your mind clear about what you want, find it, and buy it. If you want the best, expect to spend $85-110 for canvas walking shoes, from $130-180 and sometimes more for hiking or mountaineering boots. I have spent as much as $250 for hiking boots that I have worn for close to 2,000 miles. Yet another time I spent $185, thinking I was getting stellar quality, but they turned out to be miserable blister makers, and even after a year of trying to get my money's worth, they never worked right on the trail and now occupy a dark place deep in my closet.

This is one area where you don't want to scrimp, so try not to yelp about the high cost. Instead, walk out of the store believing you deserve the best, and that's exactly what you just paid for. Another trick I have learned is to bring several pairs of different style hiking boots on adventures, then change them constantly according to the terrain. Use heavy boots for steep trails with loose footing, lightweight models for flat routes with a hard surface. This works wonders to avoid blisters and muscle soreness because you are constantly changing what I call "the point of attack."

If you plan on using the advice of a shoe salesperson, first look at what kind of boots he or she is wearing. If he or she isn't even wearing boots, then any advice the salesperson might tender may not be worth a plugged nickel.

Keep It Wild Tip 2: Travel Lightly

1. Visit the backcountry in small groups.
2. Below tree line, always stay on designated trails.
3. Don't cut across switchbacks.
4. When traveling cross-country where no trails are available, follow animal trails or spread out with your group so no new routes are created.
5. Read your map and orient yourself with landmarks, a compass, and an altimeter. Avoid marking trails with rock cairns, tree scars, or ribbons.

Most people I know who own quality boots, including salespeople, will wear them almost daily if their job allows, since boots are the best footwear available. However, even these well-meaning folks can offer sketchy advice. Every hiker I've ever met will tell you he wears the world's greatest boot.

Instead, enter the store with a precise use and style in mind. Rather than fish for suggestions, tell the salesperson exactly what you want, try two or three brands of the same style, and always try on both boots in a pair simultaneously so you know exactly how they'll feel. If possible, walk up and down stairs with them. Are they too stiff? Are your feet snug yet comfortable, or do they slip? Do they have that "right" kind of feel when you walk?

If you get the right answers to those questions, then you're on your way to blister-free, pleasure-filled days of walking.

Socks

The poor gent was scratching his feet as if ants were crawling over them. I looked closer. Huge yellow calluses covered the bottoms of his feet, and at the ball and heel, the calluses were about a quarter inch thick, cracking and sore.

"I don't understand it," he said. "I'm on my feet a lot, so I bought a real good pair of hiking boots. But look what they've done to my feet. My feet itch so much I'm going crazy."

People can spend so much energy selecting the right kind of boot that they virtually overlook wearing the right kind of socks. One goes with the other.

Your socks should be thick enough to cushion your feet as well as fit snugly. Without good socks you might try to get the bootlaces too tight—and that's like putting a tourniquet on your feet. You should have plenty of clean socks on hand, or plan on washing what you have on your trip. As socks are worn, they become compressed, dirty, and damp. Any one of those factors can cause problems.

My camping companions believe I go overboard when it comes to socks, that I bring too many and wear too many. But it works, so that's where the complaints stop. So how many do I wear? Well, it varies. On day hikes, I have found a sock called a SmartWool that makes my size 13s feel as if I'm walking on pillows. But on long expeditions, the 200-milers, I sometimes wear three socks on each foot, believe it or not. It may sound like overkill, but each has its purpose, and like I said, it works.

The interior sock is thin, lightweight, and made of polypropylene or silk synthetic materials designed to transport moisture away from your skin. With a poly interior sock, your foot stays dry when it sweats. Without a poly sock, your foot can get damp and mix with dirt, which can cause a hot spot to start on your foot. Eventually you get blisters, lots of them.

The second sock is for comfort and can be cotton, but a thin wool-based composite is ideal. Some made of the latter can wick moisture away from the skin, much like polypropylene does. If wool itches your feet, a thick cotton sock can be suitable, though cotton collects moisture and compacts more quickly than other socks. If you're on a short hike though, cotton will do just fine.

The exterior sock should be made of high-quality, thick wool—at least 80% wool. It will cushion your feet, provide that just right snug fit in your boot, and give you some additional warmth and insulation in cold weather. It is critical to keep the wool sock clean. If you wear a dirty wool sock over and over again, it will compact and lose its cushion and start wrinkling while you hike, then your feet will catch on fire from the blisters that start popping up. Of course, when wearing multiple socks, especially a wool composite, you will likely need to go up a boot size so they fit comfortably.

A Few More Tips

If you are like most folks—that is, the bottoms of your feet are rarely exposed and quite soft—you can take additional steps in their care. The best tip is keeping a fresh foot pad made of sponge rubber in your boot. Another cure for soft feet is to get out and walk or jog on a regular basis prior to your camping trip.

If you plan to use a foot pad and wear three socks, you will need to use these items when sizing boots. It is an unforgiving error to wear thin cotton socks when buying boots and later try to squeeze all this stuff, plus your feet, into them. There just won't be enough room.

The key to treating blisters is fast work at the first sign of a hot spot. But before you remove your socks, check to see if the sock has a wrinkle in it, a likely cause of the problem. If so, either change socks or pull them tight, removing the tiny folds, after taking care of the blister. Cut a piece of moleskin to cover the offending toe, securing the moleskin with white medical tape. If moleskin is not available, small Band-Aids can do the job, but these have to be replaced daily, and sometimes with even more frequency. At night, clean your feet and sleep without socks.

Two other items that can help your walking is an Ace bandage and a pair of gaiters.

For sprained ankles and twisted knees, an Ace bandage can be like an insurance policy to get you back on the trail and out of trouble. Over the years I have had serious ankle problems and have relied on a good wrap with a four-inch bandage to get me home. The newer bandages come with the clips permanently attached, so you don't have to worry about losing them.

Gaiters are leggings made of plastic, nylon, or Gore-Tex that fit from just below your knees, over your calves, and attach under your boots. They are of particular help when walking in damp areas or in places where rain is common. As your legs brush against ferns or low-lying plants, gaiters will deflect the moisture. Without them, your pants will be soaking wet in short order.

Should your boots become wet, a good tip is never to try to force dry them. Some well-meaning folks will try to dry them quickly at the edge of a campfire or actually put the boots in an oven. While this may dry the boots, it can also loosen the glue that holds them together, ultimately weakening them until one day they fall apart in a heap.

A better bet is to treat the leather so the boots become water repellent. Silicone-based liquids are the easiest to use and least greasy of the treatments available.

A final tip is to have another pair of lightweight shoes or moccasins that you can wear around camp and in the process give your feet the rest they deserve.

Sleeping Gear

One mountain night in the pines on an eve long ago, my dad, brother, and I had rolled out our sleeping bags and were bedded down for the night. After the pre-trip excitement, a long drive, an evening of trout fishing, and a barbecue, we were like three tired doggies who had played too much.

But as I looked up at the stars, I was suddenly wide awake. This kid was still wired. A half hour later? No change—wide awake.

And as little kids can do, I had to wake up ol' dad to tell him about it. "Hey, Dad, I can't sleep."

"This is what you do," he said. "Watch the sky for a shooting star and tell yourself that you cannot go to sleep until you see at least one. As you wait and watch, you will start getting tired, and it will be difficult to keep your eyes open. But tell yourself you must keep watching. Then you'll start to really feel tired. When you finally see a shooting star, you'll go to sleep so fast you won't know what hit you."

Well, I tried it that night and I don't even remember seeing a shooting star, I went to sleep so fast.

It's a good trick, and along with having a good sleeping bag, ground insulation, maybe a tent, or a few tricks for bedding down in a pickup truck or motor home, you can get a good night's sleep on every camping trip.

More than 20 years after that camping episode with my dad and brother, we made a trip to the planetarium at the Academy of Sciences in San Francisco to see a show on Halley's Comet. The lights dimmed, and the ceiling turned into a night sky, filled with stars and a setting moon. A scientist began explaining phenomena of the heavens.

After a few minutes, I began to feel drowsy. Just then, a shooting star zipped across the planetarium ceiling. I went into a deep sleep so fast it was like I was in a coma. I didn't wake up until the show was over, the lights were turned back on, and the people were leaving.

Feeling drowsy, I turned to see if ol' Dad had liked the show. Oh yeah? Not only had he gone to sleep too, but he apparently had no intention of waking up, no matter what. Just like a camping trip.

Sleeping Bags

Question: What could be worse than trying to sleep in a cold, wet sleeping bag on a rainy night without a tent in the mountains?

Answer: Trying to sleep in a cold, wet sleeping bag on a rainy night without a tent in the mountains when your sleeping bag is filled with down.

*Even with the warmest
sleeping bag in the world, if you just lay
it down on the ground and try to sleep, you will likely
get as cold as a winter cucumber. That is because the cold ground will
suck the warmth right out of your body. The solution? A sleeping pad.*

Water will turn a down-filled sleeping bag into a mushy heap. Many campers do not like a high-tech approach, but the state-of-the-art polyfiber sleeping bags can keep you warm even when wet. That factor, along with temperature rating and weight, is key when selecting a sleeping bag.

A sleeping bag is a shell filled with heat-retaining insulation. By itself it is not warm. Your body provides the heat, and the sleeping bag's ability to retain that heat is what makes it warm or cold.

The old-style canvas bags are heavy, bulky, cold, and when wet, useless. With other options available, their use is limited. Anybody who sleeps outdoors or backpacks should choose otherwise. Buy and use a sleeping bag filled with down or one of the quality poly-fills. Down is light, warm, and aesthetically pleasing to those who don't think camping and technology mix. If you choose a down bag, be sure to keep it double wrapped in plastic garbage bags on your trip in order to keep it dry. Once wet, you'll spend your nights howling at the moon.

The polyfiber-filled bags are not necessarily better than those filled with down, but they can be. Their one key advantage is that even when wet, some poly-fills can retain up to 85% of your body heat. This allows you to sleep and get valuable rest even in miserable conditions. And my camping experience is that no matter how lucky you may be, there comes a time when you will get caught in an unexpected, violent storm and everything you've got will get wet, including your sleeping bag. That's when a poly-fill bag becomes priceless. You either have one and can sleep, or you don't have one and suffer. It is that simple. Of the synthetic fills, Quallofil made by Dupont is the industry leader.

But just because a sleeping bag uses a high-tech poly-fill doesn't necessarily make it a better bag. There are other factors.

The most important are a bag's temperature rating and weight. The temperature rating of a sleeping bag refers to how cold it can get before you start actually feeling cold. Many campers make the mistake of thinking, "I only camp in the summer, so a bag rated at 30 or 40 degrees should be fine." Later they find out it isn't so fine, and all it takes is one cold night to convince them of that. When selecting the right temperature rating, visualize the coldest weather you might ever confront, and then get a bag rated for even colder weather.

For instance, if you are a summer camper, you may rarely experience a night in the low 30s or high 20s. A sleeping bag rated at 20 degrees would be appropriate, keeping you snug, warm, and asleep. For most campers, I advise bags rated at zero or 10 degrees.

If you buy a poly-filled sleeping bag, never leave it squished in your stuff sack between camping trips. Instead, keep it on a hanger in a closet or use it as a blanket. One thing that can reduce a poly-filled bag's heat-retaining qualities is if you lose the loft out of the tiny hollow fibers that make up the fill. You can avoid this with proper storage.

The weight of a sleeping bag can also be a key factor, especially for backpackers. When you have to carry your gear on your back, every ounce becomes important. Sleeping bags that weigh just three pounds are available, although they are expensive. But if you hike much, it's worth the price to keep your weight to a minimum. For an overnighter, you can get away with a four- or four-and-a-half-pound bag without much stress. However, bags weighing five pounds and up should be left back at the car.

I have two sleeping bags: a seven-pounder that feels like a giant sponge, and a little three-pounder. The heavy-duty model is for pickup truck camping in cold weather and doubles as a blanket at home. The lightweight bag is for hikes. Between the two, I'm set.

Insulation Pads

Even with the warmest sleeping bag in the world, if you just lay it down on the ground and try to sleep, you will likely get as cold as a winter cucumber. That is because the cold ground will suck the warmth right out of your body. The solution is to have a layer of insulation between you and the ground. For this you can use a thin Insulite pad, a lightweight Therm-a-Rest inflatable pad, a foam pad or mattress, air bed, or a cot. Here is a capsule summary of all three:

- **Insulite pads:** They are light, inexpensive, roll up quick for transport, and can double as a seat pad at your camp. The negative side is that in one night, they will compress, making you feel that you are sleeping on granite.

- **Therm-a-Rest pads:** These are a real luxury because they do everything an Insulite pad does, but also provide a cushion. The negative side is that they are expensive by comparison, and if they get a hole in them, they become worthless without a patch kit.

- **Air beds, foam mattresses, and cots:** These are excellent for car campers. The new line of air beds available are outstanding, especially the thicker ones, and inflate quickly with an electric motor inflator that plugs into a power plug or cigarette lighter in your vehicle. Foam mattresses are also excellent, in fact, the most comfortable of all, but their size precludes many from considering them. I've found that cots work great, too. I finally wore out an old wood one just before this book went to press; replaced it immediately with one of the new high-tech and light metal ones. For camping in the back of a pick-up truck with a camper shell, the cots with three-inch legs are best, of course.

A Few Tricks

When surveying a camp area, the most important consideration should be to select a good spot to sleep. Everything else is secondary. Ideally, you want a flat spot that is wind sheltered and on ground soft enough to drive stakes into. Yeah, and I want to win the lottery, too.

Sometimes that ground will have a slight slope to it. In that case, always sleep with your head on the uphill side. If you sleep parallel to the slope, every time you roll over, you'll find yourself rolling down the hill. If you sleep with your head on the downhill side, you'll get a headache that feels as if an ax is embedded in your brain.

When you've found a good spot, clear it of all branches, twigs, and rocks, of course. A good tip is to dig a slight indentation in the ground where your hip will fit. Since your body is not flat, but has curves and edges, it will not feel comfortable on flat ground. Some people even get severely bruised on the sides of their hips when sleeping on flat, hard ground. For that reason alone they learn to hate camping. What a shame, especially when the problem is solved easily with a Therm-a-Rest pad, foam insulation, air bed or a cot.

After the ground is prepared, throw a ground cloth over the spot, which will keep much of the morning dew off you. In some areas, particularly where fog is a problem, morning dew can be heavy and get the outside of your sleeping bag quite wet. In that case, you need overhead protection, such as a tent or some kind of roof, like a poncho or tarp with its ends tied to trees.

Tents and Weather Protection

All it takes is to get caught in the rain once without a tent and you will never go anywhere without one again. A tent provides protection from rain, wind, and mosquito attacks. In exchange, you can lose a starry night's view, though some tents now even provide moon roofs.

A tent can be as complex as a four-season, tubular-jointed dome with a rain fly or as simple as two ponchos snapped together and roped up to a tree. They can be as cheap as a $10 tube tent, which is nothing more than a hollow piece of plastic, or as expensive as a $500 five-person deluxe expedition dome model. They vary greatly in size, price, and put-up time. If you plan on getting a good one, plan on doing plenty of shopping and asking lots of questions. With a little bit of homework, you can get the right answers to these questions:

Will it keep me dry?

On many one-person and two-person tents, the rain fly does not extend far enough to keep water off the bottom sidewalls of the tent. In a driving rain, water can also drip from the rain fly and to the bottom sidewalls of the tent. Eventually the water can leak through to the inside, particularly through the seams where the tent has been sewn together.

You must be able to stake out your rain fly so it completely covers all of the tent. If you are tent shopping and this does not appear possible, then don't buy the tent. To prevent potential leaks, use a seam waterproofer such as Seam Lock, a gluelike substance, to close potential leak areas on tent seams. For large umbrella tents, keep a patch kit handy. Another way to keep water out of your tent is to store all wet garments outside the tent, under a poncho. Moisture from wet clothes stashed in the tent will condense on the interior tent walls. If you bring enough wet clothes into the tent, by the next morning you can feel as if you're camping in a duck blind.

How hard is it to put up?

If a tent is difficult to erect in full sunlight, you can just about forget it at night. Some tents can go up in just a few minutes, without requiring help from another camper. This might be the kind of tent you want.

The way to compare put-up time of tents when shopping is to count the number of connecting points from the tent poles to the tent and the number of stakes required. The fewer the better. Think simple. My tent has seven connecting points and, minus the rain fly, requires no stakes. It goes up in a few minutes. If you need a lot of stakes, it is a sure tip-off to a long put-up time. Try it at night or in the rain, and you'll be ready to cash your chips and go for broke.

Another factor is the tent poles themselves. Some small tents have poles that are broken into small sections that are connected by bungee cords. It takes only an instant to convert them to a complete pole.

*A-frame style **tents** have gone the way of the dinosaur. With the world going high-tech, tents of today vary greatly in complexity, size, price, and put-up time. And they wouldn't be fit for the new millennium without offering options such as moon roofs, rain flies, and tent wings. Be sure to buy the one that's right for your needs.*

Some outdoor shops have tents on display on their showroom floor. Before buying the tent, have the salesperson take the tent down and put it back up. If it takes him more than five minutes, or he says he doesn't have time, then keep looking.

Is it roomy enough?
Don't judge the size of a tent on floor space alone. Some tents small on floor space can give the illusion of roominess with a high ceiling. You can be quite comfortable in them and snug.

But remember that a one-person or two-person tent is just that. A two-person tent has room for two people plus gear. That's it. Don't buy a tent expecting it to hold more than it is intended to.

How much does it weigh?
If you're a hiker, this becomes the preeminent question. If it's much more than six or seven pounds, forget it. A 12-pound tent is bad enough, but get it wet and it's like carrying a piano on your back. On the other hand, weight is scarcely a factor if you camp only where you can take your car. My dad, for instance, used to have this giant canvas umbrella tent that folded down to a neat little pack that weighed about 500 pounds.

Family Tents
It is always worth spending the time and money to buy a tent you and your family will be happy with.

Though many good family tents are available for $125-175, particularly from Coleman, Cabela's, and Remington, here is a synopsis of two of the best tents available anywhere, without regard to cost, generally ranging from $350-600:

Sierra Designs Mondo 5CD
tel. (800) 736-8551

10.14 pounds

82 square feet / 20-square-foot covered entry / Inside peak height: five feet, five inches

If you've got a family that likes to head for distant camps, then this is your tent. It's light enough to pack along, yet big enough to accommodate a family of four. Using speed clips, this tent is by far the easiest and quickest to set up of any family tent I've used. A generous rain fly and covered entry area (new adjustment features allow various awning configurations) mean more than adequate protection from the elements, no matter how hard they are pelting down.

Kelty Domolite 6
tel. (800) 423-2320

16.4 pounds

81.5 square feet / Inside peak height: five feet, seven inches

Using three 18-foot-long fiberglass poles, the Domolite boasts a sleek, low profile that slips the wind very nicely. Each pole slides easily through continuous pole sleeves, thanks to rubber-tipped ends, making set-up a snap. Kelty has an optional covered entry area, since without it, the tent is barely adequate shelter should you have to weather a deluge in cramped quarters. Floor seams are taped for added waterproofness. A great package.

Bivouac Bags

If you like going solo and choose not to own a tent at all, a bivy bag, short for bivouac bag, can provide the weather protection you require. A bivy bag is a water-repellent shell in which your sleeping bag fits. It is light and tough, and for some is the perfect alternative to a heavy tent. My own bivy weighs 31 ounces and cost me $240, made by OR (Outdoor Research), and I just plain love the thing on expeditions. On the downside, however, it can be a bit difficult getting settled just right in it, and some say they feel claustrophobic at the close quarters. My biggest fear was the idea of riding out a storm. You can hear the rain hitting you, and sometimes even feel the pounding of the drops through the bivy bag. For some, it can be unsettling to try and sleep under such circumstances. On the other hand, I've always looked forward to it. In cold weather, it also helps to keep you warm.

Pickup Truck Campers

If you own a pickup truck with a camper shell, you can turn it into a self-contained campground with a little work. This can be an ideal way to go: it's fast, portable, and you are guaranteed a dry environment.

But that does not necessarily mean it is a warm environment. In fact, without insulation from the metal truck bed, it can be like trying to sleep on an iceberg. That is because the metal truck bed will get as cold as the air temperature, which is often much colder than the ground temperature. Without insulation, it can be much colder in your camper shell than it would be on the open ground.

When I camp in my rig, I use a large piece of foam for a mattress and insulation. The foam measures four inches thick, 48 inches wide, and 76 inches long. It makes for a bed as comfortable as anything one might ask for. In fact, during the winter, if I don't go camping for a few weeks because of writing obligations, I sometimes will throw the foam on the floor, lie down the old sleeping bag, light a fire, and camp right in my living room. It's in my blood, I tell you. Air beds and cots are also extremely comfortable and I've used both many times. Whatever you choose, just make sure you have a comfortable sleeping unit. Good sleep makes for great camping trips.

RVs

The problems RVers encounter come from two primary sources: lack of privacy and light intrusion.

The lack of privacy stems from the natural restrictions of where a land yacht can go. Without careful use of the guide portion of this book, motor home owners can find themselves in parking lot settings, jammed in with plenty of neighbors. Because RVs often have large picture windows, you lose your privacy, causing some late nights; then, come daybreak, light intrusion forces an early wake up. The result is you get shorted on your sleep.

The answer is to carry inserts to fit over the inside of your windows. This closes off the outside and retains your privacy. And if you don't want to wake up with the sun at daybreak, you don't have to. It will still be dark.

First Aid and Insect Protection

The mountain night could not have been more perfect, I thought as I lay in my sleeping bag.

The sky looked like a mass of jewels and the air tasted sweet and smelled of pines. A shooting star fireballed across the sky, and I remember thinking, "It just doesn't get any better."

Just then, as I was drifting into sleep, a mysterious buzz appeared from nowhere and deposited itself inside my left ear. Suddenly awake, I whacked my ear with the palm of my hand, hard enough to cause a minor concussion. The buzz disappeared. I pulled out my flashlight and shined it on my palm, and there, lit in the blackness of night, lay the squished intruder: a mosquito, dead amid a stain of blood.

Satisfied, I turned off the light, closed my eyes, and thought of the fishing trip planned for the next day. Then I heard them. It was a squadron of mosquitoes flying landing patterns around my head. I tried to grab them with an open hand, but they dodged the assault and flew off. Just 30 seconds later another landed in my left ear. I promptly dispatched the invader with a rip of the palm.

Now I was completely awake, so I got out of my sleeping bag to retrieve some mosquito repellent. But en route, several of the buggers swarmed and nailed me in the back and arms. After I applied the repellent and settled snugly again in my sleeping bag, the mosquitoes would buzz a few inches from my ear. After getting a whiff of the poison, they would fly off. It was like sleeping in a sawmill.

The next day, drowsy from little sleep, I set out to fish. I'd walked but 15 minutes when I brushed against a bush and felt this stinging sensation on the inside of my arm, just above the wrist. I looked down: A tick had his clamps in me. I ripped it out before he could embed his head into my skin.

After catching a few fish, I sat down against a tree to eat lunch and just watch the water go by. My dog, Rebel, sat down next to me and stared at the beef jerky I was munching as if it were a T-bone steak. I finished eating, gave him a small piece, patted him on the head, and said, "Good dog." Right then, I noticed an itch on my arm where a mosquito had drilled me. I unconsciously scratched it. Two days later, in that exact spot, some nasty red splotches started popping up. Poison oak. By petting my dog and then scratching my arm, I had transferred the oil residue of the poison oak leaves from Rebel's fur to my arm.

When I returned home, Foonsky asked me about the trip.

"Great," I said. "Mosquitoes, ticks, poison oak. Can hardly wait to go back."

"Sorry I missed out," he answered.

Mosquitoes, No-See-Ums, Gnats, and Horseflies

On a trip to Canada, Foonsky and I were fishing a small lake from the shore when suddenly a black horde of mosquitoes could be seen moving across the lake toward us. It was like when the French army looked across the Rhine and saw the Wehrmacht coming. There was a buzz in the air. We fought them off for a few minutes, then made a fast retreat to the truck and jumped in, content the buggers had been fooled. But somehow still unknown to us, the mosquitoes gained entry to the truck. In 10 minutes, we squished 15 of them as they attempted to plant their oil drills into our skin. Just outside the truck, the black horde waited for us to make a tactical error like rolling down a window. It finally took a miraculous hailstorm to foil the attack.

When it comes to mosquitoes, no-see-ums, gnats, and horseflies, there are times when there is nothing you can do. However, in most situations you can muster a defense to repel the attack.

The first key with mosquitoes is to wear clothing too heavy for them to drill through. Expose a minimum of skin, wear a hat, and tie a bandanna around your neck, preferably one that has been sprayed with repellent. If you try to get by with just a cotton T-shirt, you will be declared a federal mosquito sanctuary.

So first your skin must be well covered, exposing only your hands and face. Second, you should have your companion spray your clothes with repellent. Third, you should dab liquid repellent directly on your skin.

Mosquito Repellent: Taking vitamin B1 and eating garlic are reputed to act as natural insect repellents, but I've met a lot of mosquitoes that are not convinced. A better bet is to examine the label of the repellent in question for **N,N-diethyl-metatoluamide**, commonly known as DEET. That is the poison, and the percentage of it in the container must be listed and will indicate that brand's effectiveness. Inert ingredients are mainly fluids used to fill the bottles.

At night, the easiest way to get a good sleep without mosquitoes buzzing in your ear is to sleep in a bug-proof tent. If the nights are warm and you want to see the stars, new tent models are available that have a skylight covered with mosquito netting. If you don't like tents on summer evenings, mosquito netting rigged with an air space at your head can solve the problem. Otherwise prepare to get bitten, even with the use of mosquito repellent.

If your problems are with no-see-ums or biting horseflies, then you need a slightly different approach.

No-see-ums are tiny black insects that look like nothing more than a sliver of dirt on your skin. Then you notice something stinging, and when you rub the area, you scratch up a little no-see-um. The results are similar to mosquito bites, making your skin itch, splotch, and when you get them bad, swell. In addition to using the techniques described to repel mosquitoes, you should go one step further.

The problem is that no-see-ums are tricky little devils. Somehow they can actually get under your socks and around your ankles where they will bite to their hearts' content all night long while you sleep, itch, sleep, and itch some more. The best solution is to apply a liquid repellent to your ankles, then wear clean socks.

Horseflies are another story. They are rarely a problem, but when they get their dander up, they can cause trouble you'll never forget.

One such episode occurred when Foonsky and I were paddling a canoe along the shoreline of a large lake. This giant horsefly, about the size of a fingertip, started dive-bombing the canoe. After 20 minutes, it landed on Foonsky's thigh. He immediately slammed it with an open hand, then let out a blood-curdling "Yeeeee-ow!" that practically sent ripples across the lake. When Foonsky whacked it, the horsefly had somehow turned around and bit him on the hand, leaving a huge red welt.

In the next 10 minutes, that big fly strafed the canoe on more dive-bomb runs. I finally got my canoe paddle, swung it as if it were a baseball bat, and nailed that horsefly as if I'd hit a home run. It landed about 15 feet from the boat, still alive and buzzing in the water. While I was trying to figure what it would take to kill this bugger, a large rainbow trout surfaced and snatched it out of the water, finally avenging the assault.

If you have horsefly or yellow jacket problems, you'd best just leave the area. One, two, or a few can be dealt with. More than that and your fun camping trip will be about as fun as being roped to a tree and stung by an electric shock rod.

On most trips, you will spend time doing everything possible to keep from getting bitten by mosquitoes or no-see-ums. When that fails, you must know what to do next, and fast, if you are among those ill-fated campers who get big red lumps from a bite inflicted from even a microscopic mosquito.

A fluid called After Bite or a dab of ammonia should be applied immediately to the bite. To start the healing process, apply a first-aid gel (not a liquid), such as the one made by Campho-Phenique.

DEET Versus "Natural" Repellents

What is DEET? You're not likely to find the word DEET on any repellent label. That's because DEET stands for N,N diethyl-metatoluamide. If the label contains this scientific name, the repellent contains DEET. Despite fears of DEET-associated health risks and the increased attention given natural alternatives, DEET-based repellents are still acknowledged as by far the best option when serious insect protection is required.

What are the health risks associated with using DEET? A number of deaths and a number of medical problems have been attributed in the press to DEET in recent years—events that those in the DEET community vehemently deny as being specifically DEET related, pointing to reams of scientific documentation as evidence. It does seem logical to assume that if DEET can peel paint, melt nylon, destroy plastic, wreck wood finishes, and damage fishing line, then it must be hell on the skin—perhaps worse.

On one trip, I had a small bottle of mosquito repellent in the same pocket as a Swiss army knife. Guess what happened? The mosquito repellent leaked a bit and literally melted the insignia right off the knife. DEET will also melt synthetic clothes. That is why in bad mosquito country, I'll expose a minimum of skin, just hands and face (with full beard), and apply the repellent only to my cheeks and the back of my hands, perhaps wear a bandanna sprinkled with a few drops as well. That does the trick, with a minimum of exposure to the repellent.

Although nothing definitive has been published, there is a belief among a growing number in the scientific community that repeated applications of products containing low percentages of DEET can be potentially dangerous. It is theorized that this actually puts consumers at a greater risk for absorbing high levels of DEET into the body than if they had just used one application of a 30 to 50% DEET product with an efficacy of four to six hours. Also being studied is the possibility that low levels of DEET, which might not otherwise be of toxicological concern, may become hazardous if they are formulated with solvents or dilutents (considered inert ingredients) that may enhance the absorption rate.

Are natural alternatives a safer choice? To imply that essential oils are completely safe because they are a natural product is not altogether accurate. Essential oils, while derived from plants that grow naturally, are chemicals too. Some are potentially hazardous if ingested, and most are downright painful if they find their way into the eyes or onto mucus membranes. For example, pennyroyal is perhaps the most toxic of the essential oils used to repel insects and can be deadly if taken internally. Other oils used include citronella (perhaps the most common, it's extracted from an aromatic grass indigenous to Southern Asia), eucalyptus, cedarwood, and peppermint.

Three citronella-based products, Buzz Away (manufactured by Quantum), Avon's Skin-So-Soft, and Natrapel (manufactured by Tender), have received EPA registration and approval for sale as repellents for use in controlling mosquitoes, flies, gnats, and midges.

Keep It Wild Tip 4: Sanitation

If no refuse facility is available:

1. Deposit human waste in "cat holes" dug six to eight inches deep. Cover and disguise the cat hole when finished.

2. Deposit human waste at least 75 paces (200 feet) from any water source or camp.

3. Use toilet paper sparingly. When finished, carefully burn it in the cat hole, then bury it.

4. If no appropriate burial locations are available, such as in popular wilderness camps above tree line in granite settings, then all human refuse should be double-bagged and packed out.

5. At boat-in campsites, chemical toilets are required. Chemical toilets can also solve the problem of larger groups camping for long stays at one location where no facilities are available.

6. To wash dishes or your body, carry water away from the source and use small amounts of biodegradable soap. Scatter dishwater after all food particles have been removed.

7. Scour your campsites for even the tiniest piece of trash and any other evidence of your stay. Pack out all the trash you can, even if it's not yours. Finding cigarette butts, for instance, provides special irritation for most campers. Pick them up and discard them properly.

8. Never litter. Never. Or you become the enemy of all others.

How effective are natural repellents? While there are numerous studies cited by those on the DEET and citronella sides of the fence, the average effective repelling time of a citronella product appears to range from 1.5 to two hours. Tests conducted at Cambridge University, England, comparing Natrapel to DEET-based Skintastic (a low-percentage DEET product) found citronella to be just as effective in repelling mosquitoes. The key here is effectiveness and the amount of time until reapplication.

Citronella products work for up to two hours and then require reapplication (the same holds true for other natural formulations). Products using a low-percentage level of DEET also require reapplication every two hours to remain effective. So if you're going outside for only a short period in an environment where insect bites are more an irritant than a hazard, you would do just as well to go natural.

What other chemical alternatives are there? Another line of defense against insects is the chemical permethrin, used on clothing, not on skin. Permethrin-based products are designed to repel and kill arthropods or crawling insects, making them a preferred repellent for ticks. The currently available products will remain effective, repelling and killing mosquitoes, ticks, and chiggers, for two weeks and through two launderings.

Ticks

Ticks are nasty little vermin that will wait in ambush, jump on unsuspecting prey, and then crawl to a prime location before filling their bodies with their victim's blood.

I call them Dracula bugs, but by any name they can be a terrible camp pest. Ticks rest on grass and low plants and attach themselves to those who brush against the vegetation (dogs are particularly vulnerable). Typically they are no more than 18 inches above ground, and if you stay on the trails, you can usually avoid them.

There are two common species of ticks. The common coastal tick is larger, brownish in color, and prefers to crawl around prior to putting its clamps on you. The latter habit can be creepy, but when you feel it crawling, you can just pick it off and dispatch it. The coastal tick's preferred destination is usually the back of your neck, just where the hairline starts. The other species, the wood tick, is small and black, and when he puts his clamps in, it's immediately painful. When a wood tick gets into a dog for a few days, it can cause a large red welt. In either case, ticks should be removed as soon as possible.

If you have hiked in areas infested with ticks, it is advisable to shower as soon as possible, washing your clothes immediately. If you just leave your clothes in a heap, a tick can crawl out and invade your home. They like warmth, and one way or another, they can end up in your bed. Waking up in the middle of the night with a tick crawling across your chest can really give you the creeps.

Once a tick has its clampers on you, you must decide how long it has been there. If it has been a short time, the most painless and effective method for removal is to take a pair of sharp tweezers and grasp the little devil, making certain to isolate the mouth area, then pull him out. Reader Johvin Perry sent in the suggestion to coat the tick with Vaseline, which will cut off its oxygen supply, after which it may voluntarily give up the hunt.

If the tick has been in longer, you may wish to have a doctor extract it. Some people will burn a tick with a cigarette, or poison it with lighter fluid, but this is not advisable. No matter how you do it, you must take care to remove all of it, especially its clawlike mouth.

The wound, however small, should then be cleansed and dressed. This is done by applying liquid peroxide, which cleans and sterilizes, and then applying a dressing coated with a first-aid gel such as First-Aid Cream, Campho-Phenique, or Neosporin.

Lyme disease, which can be transmitted by the bite of the deer tick, is rare but common enough to warrant some attention. To prevent tick bites, some people tuck their pant legs into their hiking socks and spray tick repellent, called Permamone, on their pants.

The first symptom of Lyme disease is that the bite area will develop a bright red, splotchy rash. Other possible early symptoms include headache, nausea, fever, and/or a stiff neck. If this happens, or if you have any doubts, you should see your doctor immediately. If you do get Lyme disease, don't panic. Doctors say it is easily treated in the early stages with simple antibiotics. If you are nervous about getting Lyme disease, carry a small plastic bag with you when you hike. If a tick manages to get his clampers into you, put it in the plastic bag after you pull it out. Then give it to your doctor for analysis to see if the tick is a carrier of the disease.

During the course of my hiking and camping career, I have removed ticks from my skin hundreds of times without any problems. However, if you are worried about ticks, you can buy a tick removal kit from any outdoors store. These kits allow you to remove ticks in such a way that their toxins are guaranteed not to enter your bloodstream.

If you are particularly wary of ticks or perhaps even have nightmares of them, wear long pants that are tucked into the socks, as well as a long-sleeved shirt tucked securely into the pants and held with a belt. Clothing should be light in color, making it easier to see ticks, and tightly woven so ticks have trouble hanging on. On one hike with my mom, Eleanor, I brushed more than 100 ticks off my blue jeans in less than an hour, while she did not pick up a single one on her polyester pants.

Perform tick checks regularly, especially on the back of the neck. The combination of DEET insect repellents applied to the skin and permethrin repellents applied directly to clothing is considered to be the most effective line of defense against ticks.

Poison Oak

After a nice afternoon hike, about a five-miler, I was concerned about possible exposure to poison oak, so I immediately showered and put on clean clothes. Then I settled into a chair with my favorite foamy elixir to watch the end of a baseball game. The game went 18 innings; meanwhile, my dog, tired from the hike, went to sleep on my bare ankles.

A few days later I had a case of poison oak. My feet looked as though they had been on fire and put out with an ice pick. The lesson? Don't always trust your dog, give him a bath as well, and beware of extra-inning ball games.

You can get poison oak only from direct contact with the oil residue from the leaves. It can be passed in a variety of ways, as direct as skin-to-leaf contact or as indirect as leaf to dog, dog to sofa, sofa to skin. Once you have it, there is little you can do but itch yourself to death. Applying Caladryl lotion or its equivalent can help because it contains antihistamines, which attack and dry the itch.

Avoiding Poison Oak:
Remember the old Boy Scout saying: "Leaves of three, let them be."

A tip that may sound crazy but seems to work is advised by my pal Furniss. You should expose the afflicted area to the hottest water you can stand, then suddenly immerse it in cold water. The hot water opens the skin pores and gets the "itch" out, and the cold water then quickly seals the pores.

In any case, you're a lot better off if you don't get poison oak to begin with. Remember that poison oak can disguise itself. In the spring, it is green; then it gradually turns reddish in the summer. By fall, it becomes a bloody, ugly-looking red. In the winter, it loses its leaves altogether and appears to be nothing more than barren, brown sticks of a small plant. However, at any time and in any form, its contact with skin can quickly lead to infection.

Some people are more easily afflicted than others, but if you are one of the lucky few who aren't, don't cheer too loudly. While some people can be exposed to the oil residue of poison oak with little or no effect, the body's resistance can gradually be worn down with repeated exposure. At one time I could practically play in the stuff and the only symptom would be a few little bumps on the inside of my wrist. Now, over 15 years later, my resistance has broken down. If I merely rub against poison oak now, in a few days the exposed area can look as if it were used for a track meet.

So regardless of whether you consider yourself vulnerable or not, you should take heed to reduce your exposure. That can be done by staying on trails when you hike and making sure your dog does the same. Remember, the worst stands of poison oak are usually brush-infested areas just off the trail. Protect yourself also by dressing so your skin is completely covered, wearing long-sleeved shirts, long pants, and boots. If you suspect you've been exposed, immediately wash your clothes and then wash yourself with aloe vera, rinsing with a cool shower.

And don't forget to give your dog a bath as well.

Sunburn

The most common injury suffered on camping trips is sunburn, yet some people wear it as a badge of honor, believing that it somehow enhances their virility. Well, it doesn't. Neither do suntans. And too much sun can lead to serious burns or sunstroke.

It is easy enough to avoid. Use a high-level sunscreen on your skin, apply lip balm with sunscreen, and wear sunglasses and a hat. If any area gets burned, apply first-aid cream, which will soothe and provide moisture for your parched, burned skin.

The best advice is not to get even a suntan. Those who do are involved in a practice that can be eventually ruinous to their skin and possibly lead to cancer.

A Word about Giardia and Cryptosporidium

You have just hiked in to your backwoods spot, you're thirsty and a bit tired, but you smile as you consider the prospects. Everything seems perfect—there's not a stranger in sight, and you have nothing to do but relax with your pals.

You toss down your gear, grab your cup, dip it into the stream, and take a long drink of that ice-cold mountain water. It seems crystal pure and sweeter than anything you've ever tasted. It's not till later that you find out it can be just like drinking a cup of poison.

Whether you camp in the wilderness or not, if you hike, you're going to get thirsty. And if your canteen runs dry, you'll start eyeing any water source. Stop! Do not pass Go. Do not drink.

By drinking what appears to be pure mountain water without first treating it, you can ingest a microscopic protozoan called *Giardia lamblia*. The pain of the ensuing abdominal cramps can make you feel that your stomach and intestinal tract are in a knot, ready to explode. With that comes long-term diarrhea that is worse than even a bear could imagine.

Doctors call the disease *giardiasis*, or giardia for short, but it is difficult to diagnose. One friend of mine who contracted giardia was told he might have stomach cancer before the proper diagnosis was made.

Drinking directly from a stream or lake does not mean you will get giardia, but you are taking a giant chance. There is no reason to assume such a risk, potentially ruining your trip and enduring weeks of misery.

A lot of people are taking that risk. I made a personal survey of campers in the Yosemite National Park wilderness, and found that roughly only one in 20 was equipped with some kind of water-purification system. The result, according to the Public Health Service, is that an average of 4% of all backpackers and campers suffer giardiasis. According to the Parasitic Diseases Division of the Center for Infectious Diseases, the rates range from 1% to 20% across the country.

But if you get giardia, you are not going to care about the statistics. "When I got giardia, I just about wanted to die," said Henry McCarthy, a California camper. "For about 10 days, it was the most terrible thing I have ever experienced. And through the whole thing, I kept thinking, 'I shouldn't have drunk that water, but it seemed all right at the time.'"

That is the mistake most campers make. The stream might be running free, gurgling over boulders in the high country, tumbling into deep, oxygenated pools. It looks pure. Then in a few days, the problems suddenly start. Drinking untreated water from mountain streams is a lot like playing Russian roulette. Sooner or later the gun goes off.

Filters

There's really no excuse for going without a water filter: Handheld filters are getting more compact, lighter, easier to use, and often less expensive. Having to boil water or endure chemicals that leave a bad taste in the mouth has been all but eliminated.

With a filter, you just pump and drink. Filtering strains out microscopic contaminants, rendering the water clear and some-what pure. How pure? That depends on the size of the filter's pores—what manufacturers call pore-size efficiency. A filter with a pore-size efficiency of one micron or smaller will re-move protozoa like *Giardia lamblia,* and cryptosporidium, as well as parasitic eggs and larva, but it takes a pore-size effi-ciency of less than 0.4 microns to remove bacteria. All but one of the filters recommended here do that.

A good backcountry water filter weighs less than 20 ounces, is easy to grasp, simple to use, and a snap to clean and main-tain. At the very least, buy one that will remove protozoa and bacteria. (A number of cheap, pocket-size filters remove only *Giardia lamblia,* and cryptosporidium. That, in my book, is risking your health to save money.) Consider the flow rate, too: A liter per minute is good.

All filters will eventually clog—it's a sign that they've been doing their job. If you force water through a filter that's be-coming difficult to pump, you risk injecting a load of microbial nasties into your bottle. Some models can be backwashed, brushed, or, as with ceramic elements, scrubbed to extend their useful lives. And if the filter has a prefilter to screen out the big stuff, use it: It will give your filter a boost in mileage, which can then top out at about 100 gallons per disposable element. Any of the filters reviewed here will serve well on an outing into the wilds, providing you always play by the manufacturer's rules. They cost about $35-75, up to over $200, depending on the volume of water they are constructed to filter.

Water filters *are a wise investment since all wilderness water should be considered contam-inated. Make sure the filter can be easily cleaned or has a replaceable cartridge. The filter pores must be .04 microns or less to remove bacteria.*

- **First Need Deluxe:** The 15-ounce First Need Deluxe from General Ecology does something no other handheld fil-ter will do: It removes protozoa, bacteria, and viruses without using chemicals. Such effectiveness is the result of a fancy three-stage matrix system. Un-fortunately, if you drop the filter and unknowingly crack the cartridge, all the little nasties can get through. General Ecology's solution is to in-clude a bottle of blue dye that indicates breaks. The issue hasn't scared off too many folks, though: the First Need has been around since 1982. Additional cartridges cost $30. A final note: The filter pumps smoothly and puts out more than a liter per minute. A favorite of mine.

- **PentaPure Oasis:** The PentaPure Oasis Water Purification System from WTC/Ecomaster offers drinkable water with a twist: You squeeze and sip instead of pumping. Weighing 6.5 ounces, the system packages a three-stage filter inside a 21-ounce-capacity sport bottle with an angled and sealing drinking nozzle, ideal for mountain bikers. The filter removes and/or kills protozoa, bacteria, and viruses, so it's also suitable for world travel. It's certainly convenient: just fill the bottle with untreated water, screw on the cap, give it a firm squeeze (don't expect the easy flow of a normal sport bottle; there's more work being done), and sip. The Oasis only runs into trouble if the water source is shallow; you'll need a cup for scooping.

- **Basic Designs Ceramic:** The Basic Designs Ceramic Filter Pump weighs eight ounces and is as stripped-down a filter as you'll find. The pump is simple, easy to use, and quite reliable. The ceramic filter effectively removes protozoa and bacteria, making it ideal and cost effective for backpacking—but it won't protect against viruses. Also, the filter element is too bulbous to work directly from a shallow water source; like the PentaPure, you'll have to decontaminate a pot, cup, or bottle to transfer your unfiltered water. It's a great buy, though, for anyone worried only about *Giardia lamblia* and cryptosporidium.

- **SweetWater WalkAbout:** The WalkAbout is perfect for the day hiker or backpacker who obsesses on lightening the load. The filter weighs just 8.5 ounces, is easily cleaned in the field, and removes both protozoa and bacteria: a genuine bargain. There are some trade-offs, however, for its diminutiveness. Water delivery is a tad slow at just under a liter per minute, but redesigned filter cartridges ($12.50) are now good for up to 100 gallons.

- **MSR MiniWorks:** Like the WalkAbout, the bargain-priced MiniWorks has a bigger and more expensive water-filtering brother. But in this case the differences are harder to discern: The new 14.3-ounce MiniWorks looks similar to the $140 WaterWorks II, and like the WaterWorks is fully field-maintainable, while guarding against protozoa, bacteria, and chemicals. But the Mini is the best-executed, easiest-to-use ceramic filter on the market, and it attaches directly to a standard one-quart Nalgene water bottle. Too bad it takes 90 seconds to filter that quart.

- **PUR Explorer:** The Explorer offers protection from all the bad guys—viruses as well as protozoa and bacteria—by incorporating an iodine matrix into the filtration process. An optional carbon cartridge ($20) neutralizes the iodine's noxious taste. The Explorer is also considered a trusty veteran among water filters because of its smooth pumping action and nifty back-washing feature: With a quick twist, the device switches from filtering mode to self-cleaning mode. It may be on the heavy side (20 ounces) and somewhat pricey, but the Explorer works very well on iffy water anywhere.

- **Katadyn U.S.A. Mini Filter:** The Mini Filter is a much more compact version of Katadyn's venerable Pocket Filter. This one weighs just eight ounces, ideal for the minimalist backcountry traveler, and it effectively removes protozoa and bacteria. A palm-of-the-hand-size filter, however, makes it challenging to put any kind of power behind the pump's tiny handle, and the filtered water comes through at a paltry half-liter per minute. It also requires more cleaning than most filters—though the good news is that the element is made of long-lasting ceramic. Ironically, one option lets you buy the Mini Filter with a carbon element instead of the ceramic. The pumping is easier, the flow rate is better, and the price is way down ($99), but I'd only go that route if you'll be pumping from clear mountain streams.

- **MSR WaterWorks II Ceramic:** At 17.4 ounces the WaterWorks II isn't light, but for the same price as the Katadyn you get a better flow rate (90 seconds per liter), an easy pumping action, and—like the original Mini Filter—a long-lasting ceramic cartridge. This filter is a good match for the person who encounters a lot of dirty water—its three-stage filter weeds out protozoa, bacteria, and chemicals—and is mechanically inclined. The MSR can be completely disassembled afield for troubleshooting and cleaning. (If you're not so endowed, take the filter apart at home only, as the potential for confusion is somewhat high.) By the way, the company has corrected the clogging problem that plagued a previous version of the WaterWorks.

The big drawback with filters is that if you pump water from a mucky lake, the filter can clog in a few days. Therein lies the weakness. Once plugged up, it is useless, and you have to replace it or take your chances.

One trick to extend the filter life is to fill your cook pot with water, let the sediment settle, then pump from there. As an insurance policy, always have a spare filter canister on hand.

Boiling water

Except for water filtration, this is the only treatment that you can use with complete confidence. According to the federal Parasitic Diseases Division, it takes a few minutes at a rolling boil to be certain you've killed *Giardia lamblia*. At high elevations, boil for three to five minutes. A side benefit is that you'll also kill other dangerous bacteria that live undetected in natural waters.

But to be honest, boiling water is a thorn for most people on backcountry trips. For one thing, if you boil water on an open fire, what should taste like crystal-pure mountain water tastes instead like a mouthful of warm ashes. If you don't have a campfire, it wastes stove fuel. And if you are thirsty *now*, forget it. The water takes hours to cool.

The only time boiling always makes sense, however, is when you are preparing dinner. The ash taste will disappear in whatever freeze-dried dinner, soup, or hot drink you make.

Water-purification pills
Pills are the preference for most backcountry campers, and this can get them in trouble. At just $3-8 per bottle, which can figure up to just a few cents per canteen, they do come cheap. In addition, they kill most of the bacteria, regardless of whether you use iodine crystals or potable aqua iodine tablets.

The problem is they just don't always kill *Giardia lamblia,* and that is the one critter worth worrying about on your trip. That makes water-treatment pills unreliable and dangerous.

Another key element is the time factor. Depending on the water's temperature, organic content, and pH level, these pills can take a long time to do the job. A minimum wait of 20 minutes is advised. Most people don't like waiting that long, especially when they're hot and thirsty after a hike and thinking, "What the heck, the water looks fine."

And then there is the taste. On one trip, my water filter clogged and we had to use the iodine pills instead. It doesn't take long to get tired of the iodine-tinged taste of the water. Mountain water should be one of the greatest tasting beverages of the world, but the iodine kills that.

No treatment
This is your last resort and, using extreme care, can be executed with success. One of my best hiking buddies, Michael Furniss, is a nationally renowned hydrologist, and on wilderness trips he has showed me the difference between safe and dangerous water sources.

Long ago, people believed that just finding water running over a rock was a guarantee of its purity. Imagine that. What we've learned is that the safe water sources are almost always small springs in high, craggy mountain areas. The key is making sure no one has been upstream from where you drink.

Furniss mentioned that another potential problem in bypassing water treatment is that even in settings free of *Giardia lamblia,* you can still ingest other bacteria that cause stomach problems.

Hypothermia
No matter how well planned your trip might be, a sudden change in weather can turn it into a puzzle for which there are few answers. Bad weather or an accident can set in motion a dangerous chain of events.

Such a chain of episodes occurred for my brother Rambob and me on a fishing trip one fall day just below the snow line. The weather had suddenly turned very cold, and ice was forming along the shore of the lake. Suddenly, the canoe became terribly imbalanced, and just that quick it flipped. The little life vest seat cushions were useless, and using the canoe as a paddleboard, we tried to kick our way back to shore where my dad was going crazy at the thought of his two sons drowning before his eyes.

It took 17 minutes in that 38-degree water, but we finally made it to shore. When they pulled me out of the water, my legs were dead, not strong enough even to hold up my weight. In fact, I didn't feel so much cold as tired, and I just wanted to lie down and go to sleep.

I closed my eyes, and my brother-in-law, Lloyd Angal, slapped me in the face several times, then got me on my feet and pushed and pulled me about.

In the celebration over our making it to shore, only Lloyd had realized that hypothermia was setting in. Hypothermia is the condition in which the temperature of the body is lowered to the point that it causes poor reasoning, apathy, and collapse. It can look like the afflicted person is just tired and needs to sleep, but that sleep can be the first step toward a coma.

Ultimately my brother and I shared what little dry clothing remained. Then we began hiking around to get muscle movement, creating internal warmth. We ate whatever munchies were available because the body produces heat by digestion. But most important, we got our heads as dry as possible. More body heat is lost through wet hair than any other single factor.

A few hours later, we were in a pizza parlor replaying the incident, talking about how only a life vest can do the job of a life vest. We decided never again to rely on those little flotation seat cushions that disappear when the boat flips.

Almost by instinct we had done everything right to prevent hypothermia: Don't go to sleep, start a physical activity, induce shivering, put dry clothes on, dry your head, and eat something. That's how you fight hypothermia. In a dangerous situation, whether you fall in a lake or a stream or get caught unprepared in a storm, that's how you can stay alive.

After being in that ice-bordered lake for almost 20 minutes and then finally pulling ourselves to the shoreline, we discovered a strange thing. My canoe was flipped right-side up and almost all of its contents were lost: tackle box, flotation cushions, and cooler. But remaining were one paddle and one fishing rod, the trout rod my grandfather had given me for my 12th birthday.

Lloyd gave me a smile. "This means that you are meant to paddle and fish again," he said with a laugh.

Getting Unlost

You could not have been more lost. But there I was, a guy who is supposed to know about these things, transfixed by confusion, snow, and hoofprints from a big deer.

I discovered it is actually quite easy to get lost. If you don't get your bearings, getting found is the difficult part. This occurred on a wilderness trip where I'd hiked in to a remote lake and then set up a base camp for a deer hunt.

"There are some giant bucks up on that rim," confided Mr. Furnai, who lives near the area. "But it takes a mountain man to even get close to them."

That was a challenge I answered. After four-wheeling it to the trailhead, I tromped off with pack and rifle, gut-thumped it up 100 switchbacks over the rim, then followed a creek drainage up to a small but beautiful lake. The area was stark and nearly treeless, with bald granite broken only by large boulders. To keep from getting lost, I marked my route with piles of small rocks to act as directional signs for the return trip.

But at daybreak the next day, I stuck my head out of my tent and found eight inches of snow on the ground. I looked up into a gray sky filled by huge, cascading snowflakes. Visibility was about 50 yards, with fog on the mountain rim. "I better get out of here and get back to my truck," I said to myself. "If my truck gets buried at the trailhead, I'll never get out."

After packing quickly, I started down the mountain. But after 20 minutes, I began to get disoriented. You see, all the little piles of rocks I'd stacked to mark the way were now buried in snow, and I had only a smooth white blanket of snow to guide me. Everything looked the same, and it was snowing even harder now.

Five minutes later I started chewing on some jerky to keep warm, then suddenly stopped. Where was I? Where was the creek drainage? Isn't this where I was supposed to cross over a creek and start the switchbacks down the mountain?

Right then I looked down and saw the tracks of a huge deer, the kind Mr. Furnai had talked about. What a predicament: I was lost and snowed in and seeing big hoofprints in the snow. Part of me wanted to abandon all safety and go after that deer, but a little voice in the back of my head won out. "Treat this as an emergency," it said.

The first step in any predicament is to secure your present situation, that is, to make sure it does not get any worse. I unloaded my rifle (too easy to slip, fall, and have a misfire), took stock of my food (three days' worth), camp fuel (plenty), and clothes (rain gear keeping me dry). Then I wondered, "Where the hell am I?"

*To keep from getting lost (above tree line or in sparse vegetation), mark your route with **trail ducks,** small piles of rocks, which act as directional signs for the return trip.*

I took out my map, compass, and altimeter, then opened the map and laid it on the snow. It immediately began collecting snowflakes. I set the compass atop the map and oriented it to north. Because of the fog, there was no way to spot landmarks, such as prominent mountaintops, to verify my position. Then I checked the altimeter, which read 4,900 feet. Well, the elevation at my lake was 5,320 feet. That was critical information.

I scanned the elevation lines on the map and was able to trace the approximate area of my position, somewhere downstream from the lake, yet close to a 4,900-foot elevation. "Right here," I said, pointing to a spot on the map with a finger. "I should pick up the switchback trail down the mountain somewhere off to the left, maybe just 40 or 50 yards away."

Slowly and deliberately, I pushed through the light, powdered snow. In five

The **topographical map** is easier to read than you think. Lines close together mean steep gradients; lines farther apart mean gentle gradients; V-shaped sets of lines pointing to higher elevations mean gulleys or streambeds; V-shaped sets of lines pointing to lower elevations mean ridges.

minutes, I suddenly stopped. To the left, across a 10-foot depression in the snow, appeared a flat spot that veered off to the right. "That's it! That's the crossing."

In minutes, I was working down the switchbacks, on my way, no longer lost. I thought of the hoofprints I had seen, and now that I knew my position, I wanted to head back and spend the day hunting. Then I looked up at the sky, saw it filled with falling snowflakes, and envisioned my truck buried deep in snow. Alas, this time logic won out over dreams.

In a few hours, now trudging through more than a foot of snow, I was at my truck at a spot called Doe Flat, and next to it was a giant, all-terrain U.S. Forest Service vehicle and two rangers.

"Need any help?" I asked them.

They just laughed. "We're here to help you," one answered. "It's a good thing you filed a trip plan with our district office in Gasquet. We wouldn't have known you were out here."

"Winter has arrived," said the other. "If we don't get your truck out now, it will be stuck here until next spring. If we hadn't found you, you might have been here until the end of time."

They connected a chain from the rear axle of their giant rig to the front axle of my truck and started towing me out, back to civilization. On the way to pavement, I figured I had gotten some of the more important lessons of my life. Always file a trip plan and have plenty of food, fuel, and a camp stove you can rely on. Make sure your clothes, weather gear, sleeping bag, and tent will keep you dry and warm. Always carry a compass, altimeter, and map with elevation lines, and know how to use them, practicing in good weather to get the feel of it.

And if you get lost and see the hoofprints of a giant deer, well, there are times when it is best to pass them by.

Catching Fish, Avoiding Bears, and Having Fun

Feet tired and hot, stomachs hungry, we stopped our hike for lunch beside a beautiful little river pool that was catching the flows from a long but gentle waterfall. My brother Rambob passed me a piece of jerky. I took my boots off, then slowly dunked my feet into the cool, foaming water.

I was gazing at a towering peak across a canyon when suddenly, Wham! There was a quick jolt at the heel of my right foot. I pulled my foot out of the water to find that, incredibly, a trout had bitten it.

My brother looked at me as if I had antlers growing out of my head. "Wow!" he exclaimed. "That trout almost caught himself an outdoors writer!"

It's true that in remote areas trout sometimes bite on almost anything, even feet. On one high-country trip I caught limits of trout using nothing but a bare hook. The only problem is that the fish will often hit the splitshot sinker instead of the hook. Of course, fishing isn't usually that easy. But it gives you an idea of what is possible.

America's wildlands are home to a remarkable abundance of fish and wildlife. Deer browse with little fear of man, bears keep an eye out for your food, and little critters like squirrels and chipmunks are daily companions. Add in the fishing, and you've got yourself a camping trip.

Your camping adventures will evolve into premium outdoor experiences if you can work in a few good fishing trips, avoid bear problems, and occasionally add a little offbeat fun with some camp games.

Trout and Bass

He creeps up on the stream as quiet as an Indian scout, keeping his shadow off the water. With his little spinning rod he'll zip his lure within an inch or two of its desired mark, probing along rocks, the edges of riffles, pocket water, or wherever he can find a change in river habitat. Rambob is trout fishing, and he's a master at it.

In most cases he'll catch a trout on his first or second cast. After that it's time to move up the river, giving no spot much more than five minutes' due. Stick and move, stick and move, stalking the stream like a bobcat zeroing in on an unsuspecting rabbit. He might keep a few trout for dinner, but mostly he releases what he catches. Rambob doesn't necessarily fish for food. It's the feeling that comes with it.

You don't need a million dollars' worth of fancy gear to catch fish. What you need is the right outlook, and that can be learned. That goes regardless of whether you are fishing for trout or bass, the two

Why We Fish: Fishing can give you a sense of exhilaration, like taking a hot shower after being coated with dust. On your walk back to camp, the steps come easy. You suddenly understand what John Muir meant when he talked of developing a oneness with nature, because you have it. That's what fishing can provide.

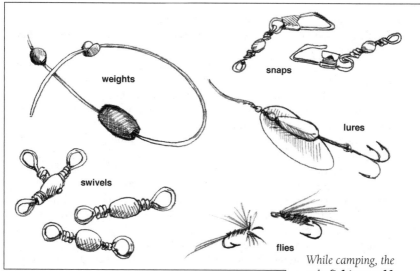

weights

snaps

lures

swivels

flies

*While camping, the only **fishing tackle** you should bring is the essentials: several varying weights, about 20 lures, and around 20 flies, splitshot, and snap swivels. These should all fit into a container just bigger than a deck of cards.*

most popular fisheries in the United States. Your fishing tackle selection should be as simple and clutter free as possible.

At home I've got every piece of fishing tackle you might imagine, more than 30 rods and many tackle boxes, racks and cabinets filled with all kinds of stuff. I've got one lure that looks like a chipmunk and another that resembles a miniature can of beer with hooks. If I hear of something new, I want to try it and usually do. It's a result of my lifelong fascination with the sport.

But if you just want to catch fish, there's an easier way to go. And when I go fishing, I take that path. I don't try to bring everything. It would be impossible. Instead I bring a relatively small amount of gear. At home I will scan my tackle boxes for equipment and lures, make my selections, and bring just the essentials. Rod, reel, and tackle will fit into a side pocket of my backpack or a small carrying bag.

So what kind of rod should be used on an outdoor trip? For most camper/anglers, I suggest the use of a light, multipiece spinning rod that will break down to a small size. The lowest-priced, quality six-piece rod on the market is the Daiwa 6.5-foot pack rod, No. 6752, which is made of a graphite/glass composite that gives it the quality of a much more expensive model. And it comes in a hard plastic carrying tube for protection. Other major rod manufacturers, such as Fenwick, offer similar premium rods. It's tough to miss with any of them.

The use of graphite/glass composites in fishing rods has made them lighter and more sensitive, yet stronger. The only downside to graphite as a rod material is that it can be brittle. If you rap your rod against something, it can crack or cause a weak spot. That weak spot can eventually snap under even light pressure, like setting a hook or casting. Of course, a bit of care will prevent that from ever occurring.

If you haven't bought a fishing reel in some time, you will be surprised at the quality and price of micro spinning reels on the market. The reels come tiny and strong, with rear-control drag systems. Sigma, Shimano, Cardinal, Abu, and others all make premium reels. They're worth it. With your purchase, you've just bought a reel that will last for years and years.

The one downside to spinning reels is that after long-term use, the bail spring will weaken. The result is that after casting and beginning to reel, the bail will sometimes not flip over and allow the reel to retrieve the line. Then you have to do it by hand. This can be incredibly frustrating, particularly when stream fishing, where instant line pickup is essential. The solution is to have a new bail spring installed every few years. This is a cheap, quick operation for a tackle expert.

You might own a giant tackle box filled with lures, but on your fishing trip you are better off to fit just the essentials into a small container. One of the best ways to do that is to use the Plano Micro-Magnum 3414, a tiny two-sided tackle box for trout anglers that fits into a shirt pocket. In mine, I can fit 20 lures in one side of the box and 20 flies, splitshot, and snap swivels in the other. For bass lures, which are bigger, you need a slightly larger box, but the same principle applies.

There are more fishing lures on the market than you can imagine, but a few special ones can do the job. I make sure these are in my box on every trip. For trout, I carry a small black Panther Martin spinner with yellow spots, a small gold Kastmaster, a yellow Roostertail, a gold Z-Ray with red spots, a Super Duper, and a Mepps Lightning spinner.

You can take it a step further using insider's wisdom. My old pal Ed "the Dunk" showed me his trick of taking a tiny Dardevle spoon, spray painting it flat black, and dabbing five tiny red dots on it. It's a real killer, particularly in tiny streams where the trout are spooky.

The best trout catcher I've ever used on rivers is a small metal lure called a Met-L Fly. On days when nothing else works, it can be like going to a shooting gallery. The problem is that the lure is nearly impossible to find. Rambob and I consider the few we have remaining so valuable that if the lure is snagged on a rock, a cold swim is deemed mandatory for its retrieval. These lures are as hard to find in tackle shops as trout can be to catch without one.

For bass, you can also fit all you need into a small plastic tackle box. I have fished with many bass pros, and all of them actually use just a few lures: a white spinner bait, a small jig called a Gits-It, a surface plug called a Zara Spook, and plastic worms. At times, as when the bass move into shoreline areas during the spring, shad minnow imitations like those made by Rebel or Rapala can be dynamite. My favorite is the one-inch, blue-silver Rapala. Every spring as the lakes begin to warm and the fish snap out of their winter doldrums, I like to float and paddle around in my small raft. I'll cast that little Rapala along the shoreline and catch and release hundreds of bass, bluegill, and sunfish. The fish are usually sitting close to the shoreline, awaiting my offering.

Fishing Tips

There's an old angler's joke about how you need to think like a fish. But if you're the one getting zilched, you may not think it's so funny.

The irony is that it is your mental approach, what you see and what you miss, that often determines your fishing luck. Some people will spend a lot of money on tackle, lures, and fishing clothes, and that done, just saunter up to a stream or lake, cast out, and wonder why they are not catching fish. The answer is their mental outlook. They are not attuning themselves to their surroundings.

You must live on nature's level, not your own. Try this and you will become aware of things you never believed even existed. Soon you will see things that will allow you to catch fish. You can get a head start by reading about fishing, but to get your degree in fishing, you must attend the University of Nature.

On every fishing trip, regardless what you fish for, try to follow three hard-and-fast rules:

1. Always approach the fishing spot so you will be undetected.
2. Present your lure, fly, or bait in a manner so it appears completely natural, as if no line was attached.
3. Stick and move, hitting one spot, working it the best you can, then move to the next.

Approach

No one can just walk up to a stream or lake, cast out, and start catching fish as if someone had waved a magic wand. Instead, give the fish credit for being smart. After all, they live there.

Your approach must be completely undetected by the fish. Fish can sense your presence through sight and sound, though this is misinterpreted by most people. By sight, this rarely means the fish actually see you; more likely they will see your shadow on the water or the movement of your arm or rod while casting. By sound, it doesn't mean they hear you talking, but that they will detect the vibrations of your footsteps along the shore, kicking a rock, or the unnatural plunking sound of a heavy cast hitting the water. Any of these elements can spook them off the bite. In order to fish undetected, you must walk softly, keep your shadow off the water, and keep your casting motion low. All of these keys become easier at sunrise or sunset, when shadows are on the water. At midday a high sun causes a high level of light penetration in the water, which can make the fish skittish to any foreign presence.

Like hunting, you must stalk the spots. When my brother Rambob sneaks up on a fishing spot, he is like a burglar sneaking through an unlocked window.

Presentation

Your lure, fly, or bait must appear in the water as if no line were attached, so it looks as natural as possible. My pal Mo Furniss has skin-dived in rivers to watch what the fish see when somebody is fishing.

"You wouldn't believe it," he said. "When the lure hits the water, every trout within 40 feet, like 15, 20 trout, will do a little zigzag. They all see the lure and are aware something is going on. Meanwhile, onshore the guy casting doesn't get a bite and thinks there aren't any fish in the river."

If your offering is aimed at fooling a fish into striking, it must appear as part of its natural habitat, like an insect just hatched or a small fish looking for a spot to hide. That's where you come in.

After you have sneaked up on a fishing spot, you should zip your cast upstream and start your retrieval as soon as it hits the water. If you let the lure sink to the bottom and then start the retrieval, you have no chance. A minnow, for instance, does not sink to the bottom, then start swimming. On rivers, the retrieval should be more of a drift, as if the "minnow" is in trouble and the current is sweeping it downstream.

When fishing on trout streams, always hike and cast upriver and retrieve as the offering drifts downstream in the current. This is effective because trout will sit almost motionless, pointed upstream, finning against the current. This way they can see anything coming their direction, and if a potential food morsel arrives, all they need to do is move over a few inches, open their mouths, and they've got an easy lunch. Thus you must cast upstream.

Conversely, if you cast downstream, your retrieval will bring the lure from behind the fish, where he cannot see it approaching. And I've never seen a trout that had eyes in its tail. In addition, when retrieving a downstream lure, the river current will tend to sweep your lure inshore to the rocks.

Finding Spots

A lot of anglers don't catch fish, and a lot of hikers never see any wildlife. The key is where they are looking.

The rule of the wild is that fish and wildlife will congregate wherever there is a distinct change in the habitat. This is where you should begin your search. To find deer, for instance, forget probing a thick forest, but look for where it breaks into a meadow or a clear-cut has splayed a stand of trees. That's where the deer will be.

In a river, it can be where a riffle pours into a small pool, a rapid that plunges into a deep hole and flattens, a big boulder in the middle of a long riffle, a shoreline point, a rock pile, a submerged tree. Look for the changes. Conversely, long, straight stretches of shoreline will not hold fish—the habitat is lousy.

On rivers, the most productive areas are often where short riffles tumble into small oxygenated pools. After sneaking up from the downstream side and staying low, you should zip your cast so the lure plops gently into the white water just above the pool. Start your retrieval instantly; the lure will drift

The rule of the wild is that wildlife will congregate wherever there is a distinct change in habitat. To find **where fish are hiding,** look where a riffle pours into a small pond, where a rapid plunges into a deep hole and flattens, and around submerged trees, rock piles, and boulders in the middle of a long riffle.

downstream and plunk into the pool. Bang! That's where the trout will hit. Take a few more casts and then head upstream to the next spot.

With a careful approach and lure presentation and by fishing in the right spots, you have the ticket to many exciting days on the water.

Of Bears and Food

The first time you come nose-to-nose with a bear can make your skin quiver.

Even the sight of mild-mannered black bears, the most common bear in America, can send shock waves through your body. They weigh 250-400 pounds and have large claws and teeth that are made to scare campers. When they bound, the muscles on their shoulders roll like ocean breakers.

Bears in camping areas are accustomed to sharing the mountains with hikers and campers. They have become specialists in the food-raiding business. As a result, you must be able to make a bear-proof food hang or be able to scare the fellow off. Many campgrounds provide bear- and raccoon-proof food lockers. You can also stash your food in your vehicle, but that limits the range of your trip.

If you are staying at one of the easy backpack sites listed in this book, there will be no food lockers available. Your car will not be there, either. The solution is to make a bear-proof food hang, suspending all of your food wrapped in a plastic garbage bag from a rope in midair, 10 feet from the trunk of a tree and 20 feet off the ground. (Counterbalancing two bags with a rope thrown over a tree limb is very effective, but finding an appropriate limb can be difficult.)

This is accomplished by tying a rock to a rope, then throwing it over a high but sturdy tree limb. Next, tie your food bag to the rope and hoist it in the air. When you are satisfied with the position of the food bag, tie off the end of the rope to another tree. In an area frequented by bears, a good food bag is a necessity—nothing else will do.

I've been there. On one trip my pal Foonsky and my brother Rambob left to fish, and I was stoking up an evening campfire when I felt the eyes of an intruder on my back. I turned around and saw a big bear heading straight for our camp. In the next half hour I scared the bear off twice, but then he got a whiff of something sweet in my brother's pack.

The bear rolled into camp like a truck, grabbed the pack, ripped it open, and plucked out the Tang and the Swiss Miss. The 350-pounder then sat astride a nearby log and lapped at the goodies like a thirsty dog drinking water.

Once a bear gets his mitts on your gear, he considers it his. I took two steps toward the pack, and that bear jumped off the log and galloped across the camp right at me. Scientists say a man can't outrun a bear, but they've never seen how fast I can go up a granite block with a bear on my tail.

Shortly thereafter, Foonsky returned to find me perched on top of the rock and demanded to know how I could let a bear get our Tang. It took all three of

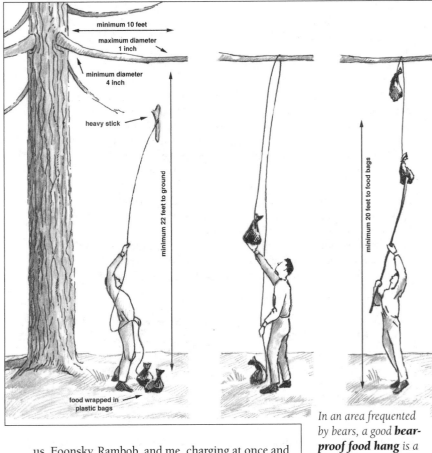

minimum 10 feet

maximum diameter 1 inch

minimum diameter 4 inch

heavy stick

minimum 22 feet to ground

minimum 20 feet to food bags

food wrapped in plastic bags

us, Foonsky, Rambob, and me, charging at once and shouting like madmen, to clear the bear out of camp and send him off over the ridge. We learned never to let food sit unattended.

*In an area frequented by bears, a good **bear-proof food hang** is a must. Food should be stored in a plastic bag 10 feet from the trunk of the tree and at least 20 feet from the ground.*

The Grizzly

When it comes to grizzlies, well, my friends, you need what we call an attitude adjustment. Or that big ol' bear may just decide to adjust your attitude for you, making your stay at the park a short one.

Grizzlies are nothing like black bears. They are bigger, stronger, have little fear, and take what they want. Some people believe there are many different species of this critter, like Alaskan brown, silvertip, cinnamon, and Kodiak, but the truth is they are all grizzlies. Any difference in appearance has to do with diet, habitat, and life habits, not speciation. By any name, they all come big.

The first thing you must do is determine if there are grizzlies in the area where you are camping. That can usually be done by asking local rangers. If you are heading into Yellowstone or Glacier National Park, or the Bob Marshall Wilderness of Montana, well, you don't have to ask. They're out there, and they're the biggest and potentially most dangerous critters you could run into.

One general way to figure the size of a bear is from his footprint. Take the width of the footprint in inches, add one to it, and you'll have an estimated length of the bear in feet. For instance, a nine-inch footprint equals a 10-foot bear. Any bear that big is a grizzly, my friends. In fact, most grizzly footprints average about nine to 10 inches across, and black bears (though they may be brown in color) tend to have footprints only four and a half to six inches across.

Most encounters with grizzlies occur when hikers fall into a silent march in the wilderness with the wind in their faces, and they walk around a corner and right into a big, unsuspecting grizzly. If you do this and see a big hump just behind its neck, well, don't think twice. It's a grizzly.

What should you do? Get up a tree, that's what. Grizzlies are so big that their claws cannot support their immense weight, and thus they cannot climb trees. And although their young can climb, they rarely want to get their mitts on you.

Grizzly bears are distinguished from **black bears** by a pronounced shoulder hump and a concave facial profile. Grizzlies are generally brown and average 10 to 11 feet in length, while black bears (which can also be brown) maintain lengths of five to seven feet.

Bear Territory

If you are hiking in a wilderness area that may have grizzlies, it becomes a necessity to wear bells on your pack. That way the bear will hear you coming and likely get out of your way. Keep talking, singing, or maybe even debating the country's foreign policy, but do not fall into a silent hiking vigil. And if a breeze is blowing in your face, you must make even more noise (a good excuse to rant and rave about the government's domestic affairs). Noise is important, because your smell will not be carried in the direction you are hiking. As a result the bear will not smell you coming.

If a bear can hear you and smell you, it will tend to get out of the way and let you pass without your knowing it was even close by. The exceptions are if you are carrying fish or lots of sweets in your pack or if you are wearing heavy, sweet deodorants or makeup. All of these are bear attractants.

If you do get grabbed, every instinct in your body will tell you to fight back. Don't believe it. Play dead. Go limp. Let the bear throw you around a little, because after awhile you become unexciting play material and the bear will get bored. My grandmother was grabbed by a grizzly in Glacier National Park and after a few tosses and hugs, was finally left alone to escape.

Some say it's a good idea to tuck your head under his chin, since that way the bear will be unable to bite your head. I'll take a pass on that one. If you are taking action, any action, it's a signal that you are a force to be reckoned with, and he'll likely respond with more aggression. And bears don't lose many wrestling matches.

What grizzlies really like to do, believe it or not, is to pile a lot of sticks and leaves on you. Just let them, and keep perfectly still. Don't fight them; don't run. And when you have a 100% chance (not 98 or 99) to dash up a nearby tree, that's when you let fly. Once safely in a tree, you can hurl down insults and let your aggression out.

In a wilderness camp there are special precautions you should take. Always hang your food at least 100 yards downwind of camp and get it high, 30 feet is reasonable. In addition, circle your camp with rope and hang the bells from your pack on it. Thus, if a bear walks into your camp, he'll run into the rope, the bells will ring, and everybody will have a chance to get up a tree before ol' griz figures out what's going on. Often the unexpected ringing of bells is enough to send him off in search of a quieter environment.

You see, more often than not, grizzlies tend to clear the way for campers and hikers. So be smart, don't act like bear bait, and always have a plan if you are confronted by one.

My pal Foonsky had such a plan during a wilderness expedition in Montana's northern Rockies. On our second day of hiking, we started seeing scratch marks on the trees 13 to 14 feet off the ground.

"Mr. Griz made those," Foonsky said. "With spring here, the grizzlies are coming out of hibernation and using the trees like a cat uses a scratch board to stretch the muscles."

The next day, I noticed Foonsky had a pair of track shoes tied to the back of his pack. I just laughed.

"You're not going to outrun a griz," I said. "In fact, there's hardly any animal out here in the wilderness that man can outrun."

Foonsky just smiled.

"I don't have to outrun a griz," he said. "I just have to outrun you!"

Fun and Games

"Now what are we supposed to do?" the young boy asked his dad.

"Yeah, Dad, think of something," said another son.

Well, Dad thought hard. This was one of the first camping trips he'd taken with his sons and one of the first lessons he received was that kids don't appreciate the philosophic release of mountain quiet. They want action and lots of it. With a glint in his eye, Dad searched around the camp and picked up 15 twigs, breaking them so each was four inches long. He laid them in three separate rows, three twigs in one row, five twigs in another, and seven in the other.

"OK, this game is called 3-5-7," said Dad. "You each take turns picking up sticks. You are allowed to remove all or as few as one twig from a row, but here's the catch: You can pick only from one row per turn. Whoever picks up the last stick left is the loser."

I remember this episode well because those two little boys were my brother Bobby, as in Rambobby, and me. And to this day, we still play 3-5-7 on campouts, with the winner getting to watch the loser clean the dishes. What I have learned in the span of time since that original episode is that it does not matter what your age is: campers need options for camp fun.

Some evenings, after a long hike or ride, you are likely to feel too worn-out to take on a serious romp downstream to fish, or a climb up to a ridge for a view. That is especially true if you have been in the outback for a week or more. At that point a lot of campers will spend their time resting and gazing at a map of the area, dreaming of the next day's adventure, or just take a seat against a rock, watching the colors of the sky and mountain panorama change minute by minute. But kids in the push-button video era, and a lot of adults too, want more. After all, "I'm on vacation; I want some fun."

There are several options, like the 3-5-7 twig game, and they should be just as much a part of your trip planning as arranging your gear.

For kids, plan on games, the more physically challenging the competition, the better. One of the best games is to throw a chunk of wood into a lake and challenge the kids to hit it by throwing rocks. It wreaks havoc on the fishing, but it can keep kids totally absorbed for some time. Target practice with a wrist-rocket slingshot is also all consuming for kids, firing rocks away at small targets like pinecones set on a log.

You can also set kids off on little missions near camp, such as looking for the footprints of wildlife, searching out good places to have a "snipe hunt," picking up twigs to get the evening fire started, or having them take the water purifier to a stream to pump some drinking water into a canteen. The latter is an easy, fun, yet important task that will allow kids to feel a sense of equality they often don't get at home.

For adults, the appeal should be more to the intellect. A good example is star and planet identification, and while you are staring into space, you're bound to spot a few asteroids or shooting stars. A star chart can make it easy to locate and identify many distinctive stars and constellations, such as Pleiades (the Seven Sisters), Orion, and others from the zodiac, depending on the time of year. With a little research, this can add a unique perspective to your trip. You could point to Polaris, one of the most easily identified of all stars, and note that navigators in the 1400s used it to find their way. Polaris, of course, is the North Star and is at the end of the handle of the Little Dipper. Pinpointing Polaris is quite easy. First find the Big Dipper and then locate the outside stars of the ladle of the Big Dipper. They are called the "pointer stars" because they point right at Polaris.

A tree identification book can teach you a few things about your surroundings. It is also a good idea for one member of the party to research the history of the area you have chosen and another to research the geology. With shared knowledge, you end up with a deeper love of wild places.

Another way to add some recreation into your trip is to bring a board game, a number of which have been miniaturized for campers. The most popular are chess, checkers, and cribbage. The latter comes with an equally miniature set of playing cards. And if you bring those little cards, that opens a vast set of other possibilities. With kids along, for instance, just take three queens out of the deck and you can play Old Maid.

But there are more serious card games, and they come with high stakes. Such occurred on one high country trip where Foonsky, Rambob, and I sat down for a late afternoon game of poker. In a game of seven-card stud, I caught a straight on the sixth card and felt like a dog licking on a T-bone. Already I had bet several Skittles and peanut M&Ms on this promising hand.

Then I examined the cards Foonsky had face up. He was showing three sevens, and acting as happy as a grizzly with a pork chop—or a full house. He matched my bet of two peanut M&Ms, then raised me three SweetTarts, one Starburst, and one sour apple Jolly Rancher. Rambob folded, but I matched Foonsky's bet and hoped for the best as the seventh and final card was dealt.

Just after Foonsky glanced at that last card, I saw him sneak a look at my grape stick and beef jerky stash.

"I raise you a grape stick," he said.

Rambob and I both gasped. It was the highest bet ever made, equivalent to a million dollars laid down in Las Vegas. Cannons were going off in my chest. I looked hard at my cards. They looked good, but were they good enough?

Even with a great hand like I had, a grape stick was too much to gamble, my last one with 10 days of trail ahead of us. I shook my head and folded my cards. Foonsky smiled at his victory.

But I still had my grape stick.

Old Tricks Don't Always Work

Most people are born honest, but after a few camping trips, they usually get over it.

I remember some advice I got from Rambob, normally an honest soul, on one camping trip. A giant mosquito had landed on my arm and he alerted me to some expert advice.

"Flex your arm muscles," he commanded, watching the mosquito fill with my blood. "He'll get stuck in your arm, then he'll explode."

For some reason, I believed him. We both proceeded to watch the mosquito drill countless holes in my arm.

Alas, the unknowing face sabotage from their most trusted companions on camping trips. It can arise at any time, usually in the form of advice from a friendly, honest-looking face, as if to say, "What? How can you doubt me?" After that mosquito episode, I was a little more skeptical of my dear old brother. Then the next day, when another mosquito was nailing me in the back of the neck, out came this gem:

"Hold your breath," he commanded. I instinctively obeyed. "That will freeze the mosquito," he said, "then you can squish him."

But in the time I wasted holding my breath, the little bugger was able to fly off without my having the satisfaction of squishing him. When he got home, he probably told his family, "What a dummy I got to drill today!"

Over the years, I have been duped numerous times with dubious advice:

On a grizzly bear attack: "If he grabs you, tuck your head under the grizzly's chin; then he won't be able to bite you in the head." This made sense to me until the first time I came face-to-face with a nine-foot grizzly 40 yards away. In seconds, I was at the top of a tree, which suddenly seemed to make the most sense.

On coping with animal bites: "If a bear bites you in the arm, don't try to jerk it away. That will just rip up your arm. Instead force your arm deeper into his mouth. He'll lose his grip and will have to open it to get a firmer hold, and right then you can get away." I was told this in the Boy Scouts, and when I was 14, I had a chance to try it out when a friend's dog bit me as I tried to pet it. What happened? When I shoved my arm deeper into his mouth, he bit me three more times.

On cooking breakfast: "The bacon will curl up every time in a camp frying pan. So make sure you have a bacon stretcher to keep it flat." As a 12-year-old Tenderfoot, I spent two hours looking for the bacon stretcher until I figured out the camp leader had forgotten it. It wasn't for several years until I learned that there is no such thing.

Keep It Wild Tip 5: Keep the Wilderness Wild

1. Let nature's sound prevail. Avoid loud voices and noises.
2. Leave radios and tape players at home. At drive-in camping sites, never open car doors with music playing.
3. Careful guidance is necessary when choosing any games to bring for children. Most toys, especially any kind of gun toys with which children simulate shooting at each other, shouldn't be allowed on a camping trip.
4. Control pets at all times or leave them with a sitter at home.
5. Treat natural heritage with respect. Leave plants, rocks, and historical artifacts where you find them.

On preventing sore muscles: "If you haven't hiked for a long time and you are facing a rough climb, you can keep from getting sore muscles in your legs, back, and shoulders by practicing the 'Dead Man's Walk.' Simply let your entire body go slack, and then take slow, wobbling steps. This will clear your muscles of lactic acid, which causes them to be so sore after a rough hike." Foonsky pulled this one on me. Rambob and I both bought it and tried it while we were hiking up Mount Whitney, which requires a 6,000-foot elevation gain in six miles. In one 45-minute period, about 30 other hikers passed us and looked at us as if we were suffering from some rare form of mental aberration.

Fish won't bite? No problem: "If the fish are not feeding or will not bite, persistent anglers can still catch dinner with little problem. Keep casting across the current, and eventually, as they hover in the stream, the line will feed across their open mouths. Keep reeling and you will hook the fish right in the side of the mouth. This technique is called 'lining.' Never worry if the fish will not bite, because you can always line 'em." Of course, heh, heh, heh, that explains why so many fish get hooked in the side of the mouth.

How to keep bears away: "To keep bears away, urinate around the borders of your campground. If there are a lot of bears in the area, it is advisable to go right on your sleeping bag." Yeah, surrrrrre.

What to do with trash: "Don't worry about packing out trash. Just bury it. It will regenerate into the earth and add valuable minerals." Bears, raccoons, skunks, and other critters will dig up your trash as soon as you depart, leaving one huge mess for the next camper. Always pack out everything.

Often the advice comes without warning. That was the case after a fishing trip with a female companion, when she outcaught me two to one, the third such trip in a row. I explained this to a shopkeeper, and he nodded, then explained why.

"The male fish are able to detect the female scent on the lure, and thus become aroused into striking."

Of course! That explains everything!

Getting Revenge

I was just a lad when Foonsky pulled the old snipe-hunt trick on me. It took nearly 30 years to get revenge.

You probably know about snipe hunting. That is where the victim is led out at night in the woods by a group, then is left holding a bag.

"Stay perfectly still and quiet," Foonsky explained. "You don't want to scare the snipe. The rest of us will go back to camp and let the woods settle down. Then when the snipe are least expecting it, we'll form a line and charge through the forest with sticks, beating bushes and trees, and we'll flush the snipe out right to you. Be ready with the bag. When we flush the snipe out, bag it. But until we start our charge, make sure you don't move or make a sound or you will spook the snipe and ruin everything."

I sat out there in the woods with my bag for hours, waiting for the charge. I waited, waited, and waited. Nothing happened. No charge, no snipe. It wasn't until well past midnight that I figured something was wrong. When I finally returned to camp, everybody was sleeping.

Well, I tell ya, don't get mad at your pals for the tricks they pull on you. Get revenge. Some 25 years later, on the last day of a camping trip, the time finally came.

"Let's break camp early," Foonsky suggested to Mr. Furnai and me. "Get up before dawn, eat breakfast, pack up, and be on the ridge to watch the sun come up. It will be a fantastic way to end the trip."

"Sounds great to me," I replied. But when Foonsky wasn't looking, I turned his alarm clock ahead three hours. So when the alarm sounded at the appointed 4:30 a.m. wake-up time, Mr. Furnai and I knew it was actually only 1:30 a.m.

Foonsky clambered out of his sleeping bag and whistled with a grin. "Time to break camp."

"You go ahead," I answered. "I'll skip breakfast so I can get a little more sleep. At the first sign of dawn, wake me up, and I'll break camp."

"Me, too," said Mr. Furnai.

Foonsky then proceeded to make some coffee, cook a breakfast, and eat it, sitting on a log in the black darkness of the forest, waiting for the sun to come up. An hour later, with still no sign of dawn, he checked his clock. It now read 5:30 a.m. "Any minute now we should start seeing some light," he said.

He made another cup of coffee, packed his gear, and sat there in the middle of the night, looking up at the stars, waiting for dawn. "Anytime now," he said. He ended up sitting there all night long.

Revenge is sweet. Prior to a fishing trip at a lake, I took Foonsky aside and explained that the third member of the party, Jimbobo, was hard of hearing and very sensitive about it. "Don't mention it to him," I advised. "Just talk real loud."

Meanwhile, I had already told Jimbobo the same thing. "Foonsky just can't hear very good."

We had fished less than 20 minutes when Foonsky got a nibble.

"GET A BITE?" shouted Jimbobo.

"YEAH!" yelled back Foonsky, smiling. "BUT I DIDN'T HOOK HIM!"

"MAYBE NEXT TIME!" shouted Jimbobo with a friendly grin.

Well, they spent the entire day yelling at each other from the distance of a few feet. They never did figure it out. Heh, heh, heh.

That is, I thought so, until we made a trip salmon fishing. I got a strike that almost knocked my fishing rod out of the boat. When I grabbed the rod, it felt as if Moby Dick were on the other end. "At least a 25-pounder," I said. "Maybe bigger."

The fish dove, ripped off line, and then bulldogged. "It's acting like a 40-pounder," I announced, "Huge, just huge. It's going deep. That's how the big ones fight."

Some 15 minutes later, I finally got the "salmon" to the surface. It turned out to be a coffee can that Foonsky had clipped on the line with a snap swivel. By maneuvering the boat, he made the coffee can fight like a big fish.

This all started with a little old snipe hunt years ago. You never know what your pals will try next. Don't get mad. Get revenge.

Camping Options

Boat-in Seclusion

Most campers would never think of trading in their car, pickup truck, or RV for a boat, but people who go by boat on a camping trip enjoy virtually guaranteed seclusion and top-quality outdoor experiences.

Camping with a boat is a do-it-yourself venture in living under primitive circumstances. Yet at the same time you can bring along any luxury item you wish, from giant coolers, stoves, and lanterns to portable gasoline generators. Weight is almost never an issue.

Many outstanding boat-in campgrounds in beautiful surroundings are available in California. The best are on the shores of lakes accessible by canoe or skiff, and at offshore islands reached by saltwater cruisers. Several boat-in camps are detailed in this book.

If you want to take the adventure a step further and create your own boat-in camp, perhaps near a special fishing spot, this is a go-for-it deal that provides the best way possible to establish your own secret campsite. But most people who set out freelance style forget three critical items for boat-in camping: a shovel, a sunshade, and an ax. Here is why these items can make a key difference in your trip:

Shovel: Many lakes and virtually all reservoirs have steep, sloping banks. At reservoirs subject to drawdowns, what was lake bottom in the spring can be a campsite in late summer. If you want a flat area for a tent site, the only answer is to dig one out yourself. A shovel gives you that option.

Sunshade: The flattest spots to camp along lakes often have a tendency to support only sparse tree growth. As a result, a natural shield from sun and rain is rarely available. What? Rain in the summer? Oh yeah, don't get me started. A light tarp, set up with poles and staked ropes, solves the problem.

Ax: Unless you bring your own firewood, which is necessary at some sparsely wooded reservoirs, there is no substitute for a good, sharp ax. With an ax, you can almost always find dry firewood, since the interior of an otherwise wet log will be dry. When the weather turns bad is precisely when you will most want a fire. You may need an ax to get one going.

In the search to create your own personal boat-in campsite, you will find that the flattest areas are usually the tips of peninsulas and points, while the protected back ends of coves are often steeply sloped. At reservoirs, the flattest areas are usually near the mouths of the feeder streams and the points are quite steep. On rivers, there are usually sandbars on the inside of tight bends that make for ideal campsites.

Almost all boat-in campsites developed by government agencies are free of charge, but you are on your own. Only in extremely rare cases is piped water available.

Any way you go, by canoe, skiff, or power cruiser, you end up with a one-in-a-million campsite you can call your own.

Desert Outings

It was a cold, snowy day in Missouri when 10-year-old Rusty Ballinger started dreaming about the vast deserts of the West.

"My dad was reading aloud from a Zane Grey book called Riders of the Purple Sage," Ballinger said. "He would get animated when he got to the passages about the desert. It wasn't long before I started to have the same feelings."

That was in 1947. Ballinger, now in his 60s, has spent a good part of his life exploring the West, camping along the way. "The deserts are the best part. There's something about the uniqueness of each little area you see," Ballinger said. "You're constantly surprised. Just the time of day and the way the sun casts a different color. It's like the lady you care about. One time she smiles, the next time she's pensive. The desert is like that. If you love nature, you can love the desert. After awhile, you can't help but love it."

A desert adventure is not just an antidote for a case of cabin fever in the winter. Whether you go by RV, pickup truck, car, or on foot, it provides its own special qualities.

If you go camping in the desert, your approach has to be as unique as the setting. For starters, don't plan on any campfires, but bring a camp stove instead. And unlike in the mountains, do not camp near a water hole. That's because an animal such as a badger, coyote, or desert bighorn might be desperate for water, and if you set up camp in the animal's way, you may be forcing a confrontation.

In some areas, there is a danger of flash floods. An intense rain can fall in one area, collect in a pool, then suddenly burst through a narrow canyon. If you are in its path, you could be injured or drowned. The lesson? Never camp in a gully.

"Some people might wonder, 'What good is this place?'" Ballinger said. "The answer is that it is good for looking at. It is one of the world's unique places."

Camp Ethics and Politics

The perfect place to set up a base camp turned out to be not so perfect. In fact, according to Doug Williams of California, it did not even exist.

Williams and his son, James, had driven deep into Angeles National Forest, prepared to set up camp and then explore the surrounding area on foot. But when they reached their destination, no campground existed.

"I wanted a primitive camp in a national forest where I could teach my son some basics," said the senior Williams. "But when we got there, there wasn't much left of the camp, and it had been closed. It was obvious that the area had been vandalized."

It turned out not to be an isolated incident. A lack of outdoor ethics practiced by a few people using the unsupervised campgrounds available on national forestland has caused the U.S. Forest Service to close a few of them and make extensive repairs to others.

"There have been sites closed, especially in Angeles and San Bernardino national forests in Southern California," said David Flohr, regional campground co-

---

Keep It Wild Tip 6: Respect Other Users

1. Horseback riders have priority over hikers. Step to the downhill side of the trail and talk softly when encountering horseback riders.
2. Hikers and horseback riders have priority over mountain bikers. When mountain bikers encounter other users even on wide trails, they should pass at an extremely slow speed. On very narrow trails they should dismount and get off to the side so hikers or horseback riders can pass without having their trip disrupted.
3. Mountain bikes aren't permitted on most single-track trails and are expressly prohibited in designated wilderness areas and all sections of the Pacific Crest Trail. Mountain bikers breaking these rules should be confronted and told to dismount and walk their bikes until they reach a legal area.
4. It's illegal for horseback riders to break off branches that may be in the path of wilderness trails.
5. Horseback riders on overnight trips are prohibited from camping in many areas and are usually required to keep stock animals in specific areas where they can do no damage to the landscape.

---

food cache
(hang downwind)

escape tree

minimum 100 feet

minimum 100 feet

minimum 200 feet

minimum 200 feet

6-8 inch "cat hole" for
depositing human waste

In setting up camp, always be mindful of potential ecological disturbances. Pitch tents and dispose of human waste at least 200 feet from the water's edge. In grizzly bear territory, increase the distance between your tent and your cooking area, food-hang, and the water's edge threefold. In other words, if you're in grizzly country, do all your cooking 200 yards (not feet) downwind of your sleeping area. If you can establish an escape tree nearby, all the better.

ordinator for the U.S. Forest Service. "It's an urban type of thing, affecting forests near urban areas, and not just Los Angeles. They get a lot of urban users and they bring with them a lot of the same ethics they have in the city. They get drinking and they're not afraid to do things. They vandalize and run. Of course, it is a public facility, so they think nobody is getting hurt."

But somebody is getting hurt, starting with the next person who wants to use the campground. And if the ranger district budget doesn't have enough money to pay for repairs, the campground is then closed for the next arrivals. Just ask Doug and James Williams.

In an era of considerable fiscal restraint for the U.S. Forest Service, vandalized campgrounds could face closure instead of repair in the next few years. Williams had just a taste of it, but Flohr, as camping coordinator, gets a steady diet.

"It starts with behavior," Flohr said. "General rowdiness, drinking, partying, and then vandalism. It goes all the way from the felt-tip pen things (graffiti) to total destruction, blowing up toilet buildings with dynamite. I have seen toilets destroyed totally with shotguns. They burn up tables, burn barriers. They'll burn up signs for firewood, even the shingles right off the roofs of the bathrooms. They'll shoot anything, garbage cans, signs. It can get a little hairy. A favorite is to remove the stool out of a toilet building. We've had people fall in the open hole."

The National Park Service had a similar problem some years back, especially with rampant littering. Park Director Bill Mott responded by creating an interpretive program that attempts to teach visitors the wise use of natural areas, and to have all park workers set examples by picking up litter and reminding others to do the same.

The U.S. Forest Service has responded with a similar program, making brochures available that detail the wise use of national forests. The four most popular brochures are titled: "Rules for Visitors to the National Forest," "Recreation in the National Forests," "Is the Water Safe?" and "Backcountry Safety Tips." These include details on campfires, drinking water from lakes or streams, hypothermia, safety, and outdoor ethics. They are available for free by writing to Public Affairs, U.S. Forest Service, 630 Sansome Street, San Francisco, CA 94111.

Flohr said even experienced campers sometimes cross over the ethics line unintentionally. The most common example, he said, is when campers toss garbage into the outhouse toilet, rather than packing it out in a plastic garbage bag.

"They throw it in the vault toilet bowls, which just fills them up," Flohr said. "That creates an extremely high cost to pump it. You know why? Because some poor guy has to pick that stuff out piece by piece. It can't be pumped."

At most backcountry sites, the U.S. Forest Service has implemented a program called "Pack it in, pack it out," even posting signs that remind all visitors to do so. But a lot of people don't do it, and others may even uproot the sign and burn it for firewood.

On a trip to a secluded lake near Carson Pass in the Sierra Nevada, I arrived at a small, little-known camp where the picnic table had been spray painted and garbage had been strewn about. A pristine place, the true temple of God, had been defiled.

Getting Along with Fellow Campers

The most important thing about a camping, fishing, or hunting trip is not where you go, how many fish you catch, or how many shots you fire. It often has little to do with how beautiful the view is, how easy the campfire lights, or how sunny the days are.

Oh yeah? Then what is the most important factor? The answer: The people you are with. It is that simple.

Who would you rather camp with? Your enemy at work or your dream mate in a good mood? Heh, heh.

Two Dogs: "There are two dogs inside of you," my dad once said, "a good one, and a bad one. The one you feed is the one that will grow. Always try to feed the good dog."

You get the idea. A camping trip is a fairly close-knit experience, and you can make lifetime friends or lifelong enemies in the process. That is why your choice of companions is so important. Your own behavior is equally consequential.

Yet most people spend more time putting together their camping gear than considering why they enjoy or hate the company of their chosen companions. Here are 10 rules of behavior for good camping mates:

1. **No whining:** Nothing is more irritating than being around a whiner. It goes right to the heart of adventure, since often the only difference between a hardship and an escapade is simply whether or not an individual has the spirit for it. The people who do can turn a rugged day in the outdoors into a cherished memory. Those who don't can ruin it with their incessant sniveling.

2. **Activities must be agreed upon:** Always have a meeting of the minds with your companions over the general game plan. Then everybody will possess an equal stake in the outcome of the trip. This is absolutely critical. Otherwise they will feel like merely an addendum to your trip, not an equal participant, and a whiner will be born (see No. 1).

3. **Nobody's in charge:** It is impossible to be genuine friends if one person is always telling another what to do, especially if the orders involve simple camp tasks. You need to share the space on the same emotional plane, and the only way to do that is to have a semblance of equality, regardless of differences in experience. Just try ordering your mate around at home for a few days. You'll quickly see the results, and they aren't pretty.

4. **Equal chances at the fun stuff:** It's fun to build the fire, fun to get the first cast at the best fishing spot, and fun to hoist the bagged food for a bear-proof food hang. It is not fun to clean the dishes, collect firewood, or cook every night. So obviously there must be an equal distribution of the fun stuff and the not-fun stuff, and everybody on the trip must get a shot at the good and the bad.

5. **No heroes:** No awards are bestowed for achievement in the outdoors, yet some guys treat mountain peaks, big fish, and big game as if they are prizes in a trophy competition. Actually, nobody cares how wonderful you are, which is always a surprise to trophy chasers. What people care about is the heart of the adventure, the gut-level stuff.

6. **Agree on a wake-up time:** It is a good idea to agree on a general wake-up time before closing your eyes for the night, and that goes regardless of whether you want to sleep in late or get up at dawn. Then you can proceed on course regardless of what time you crawl out of your sleeping bag in the morning, without the risk of whining (see No. 1).

7. **Think of the other guy:** Be self-aware instead of self-absorbed. A good test is to count the number of times you say, "What do you think?" A lot of potential problems can be solved quickly by actually listening to the answer.

8. **Solo responsibilities:** There are a number of essential camp duties on all trips, and while they should be shared equally, most should be completed

solo. That means that when it is time for you to cook, you don't have to worry about me changing the recipe on you. It means that when it is my turn to make the fire, you keep your mitts out of it.

9. **Don't let money get in the way:** Of course everybody should share equally in trip expenses, such as the cost of food, and it should be split up before you head out yonder. Don't let somebody pay extra, because that person will likely try to control the trip. Conversely, don't let somebody weasel out of paying a fair share.

10. **Accordance on the food plan:** Always have complete agreement on what you plan to eat each day. Don't figure that just because you like Steamboat's Sludge, everybody else will, too, especially youngsters. Always, always, always check for food allergies such as nuts, onions, or cheese, and make sure each person brings his or her own personal coffee brand. Some people drink only decaffeinated; others might gag on anything but Burma monkey beans.

Obviously, it is difficult to find companions who will agree on all of these elements. This is why many campers say that the best camping buddy they'll ever have is their mate, someone who knows all about them and likes them anyway.

Outdoors with Kids

How do you get a boy or girl excited about the outdoors? How do you compete with the television and remote control? How do you prove to a kid that success comes from persistence, spirit, and logic, which the outdoors teaches, and not from pushing buttons?

The answer is in the **Ten Camping Commandments for Kids**. These are lessons that will get youngsters excited about the outdoors, and will make sure adults help the process along, not kill it. I've put this list together with the help of my own kids, Jeremy and Kris, and their mother, Stephani. Some of the commandments are obvious, some are not, but all are important:

1. Take children to places where there is a guarantee of action. A good example is camping in a park where large numbers of wildlife can be viewed, such as squirrels, chipmunks, deer, and even bears. Other good choices are fishing at a small pond loaded with bluegill, or hunting in a spot where a kid can shoot a .22 at pinecones all day. Boys and girls want action, not solitude.

2. Enthusiasm is contagious. If you aren't excited about an adventure, you can't expect a child to be. Show a genuine zest for life in the outdoors, and point out everything as if it is the first time you have ever seen it.

3. Always, always, always be seated when talking to someone small. This allows the adult and child to be on the same level. That is why fishing in a small boat is perfect for adults and kids. Nothing is worse for youngsters than having a big person look down at them and give them orders. What fun is that?

4. Always show how to do something, whether it is gathering sticks for a campfire, cleaning a trout, or tying a knot. Never tell—always show. A

button usually clicks to "off" when a kid is lectured. But kids can learn behavior patterns and outdoor skills by watching adults, even when the adults are not aware they are being watched.

5. Let kids be kids. Let the adventure happen, rather than trying to force it within some preconceived plan. If they get sidetracked watching pollywogs, chasing butterflies, or sneaking up on chipmunks, let them be. A youngster can have more fun turning over rocks and looking at different kinds of bugs than sitting in one spot, waiting for a fish to bite.

6. Expect short attention spans. Instead of getting frustrated about it, use it to your advantage. How? By bringing along a bag of candy and snacks. Where there is a lull in the camp activity, out comes the bag. Don't let them know what goodies await, so each one becomes a surprise.

7. Make absolutely certain the child's sleeping bag is clean, dry, and warm. Nothing is worse than discomfort when trying to sleep, but a refreshing sleep makes for a positive attitude the next day. In addition, kids can become quite scared of animals at night. A parent should not wait for any signs of this, but always play the part of the outdoor guardian, the one who will take care of everything.

8. Kids quickly relate to outdoor ethics. They will enjoy eating everything they kill, building a safe campfire, and picking up all their litter, and they will develop a sense of pride that goes with it. A good idea is to bring extra plastic garbage bags to pick up any trash you come across. Kids long remember when they do something right that somebody else has done wrong.

9. If you want youngsters hooked on the outdoors for life, take a close-up photograph of them holding up fish they have caught, blowing on the campfire, or completing other camp tasks. Young children can forget how much fun they had, but they never forget if they have a picture of it.

10. The least important word you can ever say to a kid is "I." Keep track of how often you are saying "Thank you" and "What do you think?" If you don't say them very often, you'll lose out. Finally, the most important words of all are: "I am proud of you."

Predicting Weather

Foonsky climbed out of his sleeping bag, glanced at the nearby meadow, and scowled hard.

"It doesn't look good," he said. "Doesn't look good at all."

I looked at my adventure companion of 20 years, noting his discontent. Then I looked at the meadow and immediately understood why: "When the grass is dry at morning light, look for rain before the night."

"How bad you figure?" I asked him.

"We'll know soon enough, I reckon," Foonsky answered. "Short notice, soon to pass. Long notice, long it will last."

When you are out in the wild, spending your days fishing and your nights camping, you learn to rely on yourself to predict the weather. It can make or break you. If a storm hits the unprepared, it can quash the trip and possibly endanger the participants. But if you are ready, a potential hardship can be an adventure.

You can't rely on TV weather forecasters, people who don't even know that when all the cows on a hill are facing north, it will rain that night for sure. God forbid if the cows are all sitting. But what do you expect from TV's talking heads?

Foonsky made a campfire, started boiling some water for coffee and soup, and we started to plan the day. In the process, I noticed the smoke of the campfire: It was sluggish, drifting and hovering.

"You notice the smoke?" I asked, chewing on a piece of homemade jerky.

"Not good," Foonsky said. "Not good." He knew that sluggish, hovering smoke indicates rain.

"You'd think we'd have been smart enough to know last night that this was coming," Foonsky said. "Did you take a look at the moon or the clouds?"

"I didn't look at either," I answered. "Too busy eating the trout we caught." You see, if the moon is clear and white, the weather will be good the next day. But if there is a ring around the moon, the number of stars you can count inside the ring equals the number of days until the next rain. As for clouds, the high, thin clouds called cirrus indicate a change in the weather.

We were quiet for a while, planning our strategy, but as we did so, some terrible things happened: A chipmunk scampered past with his tail high, a small flock of geese flew by very low, and a little sparrow perched on a tree limb quite close to the trunk.

"We're in for trouble," I told Foonsky.

"I know, I know," he answered. "I saw 'em, too. And come to think of it, no crickets were chirping last night either."

"Damn, that's right!"

These are all signs of an approaching storm. Foonsky pointed at the smoke of the campfire and shook his head as if he had just been condemned. Sure enough, now the smoke was blowing toward the north, a sign of a south wind. "When the wind is from the south, the rain is in its mouth."

"We'd best stay hunkered down until it passes," Foonsky said.

I nodded. "Let's gather as much firewood now as we can, get our gear covered up, then plan our meals."

"Then we'll get a poker game going."

As we accomplished these camp tasks, the sky clouded up, then darkened. Within an hour we had gathered enough firewood to make a large pile, enough wood to keep a fire going no matter how hard it rained. The day's meals had been separated out of the food bag so it wouldn't have to be retrieved during the storm. We buttoned two ponchos together, staked two of the corners with ropes to the ground, and tied the other two with ropes to different tree limbs to create a slanted roof/shelter.

As the first raindrop fell with that magic sound on our poncho roof, Foonsky was just starting to shuffle the cards.

"Cut for deal," he said.

Just as I did so, it started to rain a bit harder. I pulled out another piece of beef jerky and started chewing on it. It was just another day in paradise.

Weather lore can be valuable. Small signs provided by nature and wildlife can be translated to provide a variety of weather information. Here is the list I have compiled over the years:

When the grass is dry at morning light,
Look for rain before the night.

Short notice, soon to pass.
Long notice, long it will last.

When the wind is from the east,
'Tis fit for neither man nor beast.

When the wind is from the south,
The rain is in its mouth.

When the wind is from the west,
Then it is the very best.

Red sky at night, sailors' delight.
Red sky in the morning, sailors take warning.

When all the cows are pointed north,
Within a day rain will come forth.

Onion skins very thin, mild winter coming in.
Onion skins very tough, winter's going to be very rough.

When your boots make the squeak of snow,
Then very cold temperatures will surely show.

If a goose flies high, fair weather ahead.
If a goose flies low, foul weather will come instead.

A thick coat on a woolly caterpillar means a big, early snow is coming.

Chipmunks will run with their tails up before a rain.

Bees always stay near their hives before a rainstorm.

When the birds are perched on large limbs near tree trunks, an intense but short storm will arrive.

On the coast, if groups of seabirds are flying a mile inland, look for major winds.

If crickets are chirping very loud during the evening, the next day will be clear and warm.

If the smoke of a campfire at night rises in a thin spiral, good weather is assured for the next day.

If the smoke of a campfire at night is sluggish, drifting, and hovering, it will rain the next day.

If there is a ring around the moon, count the number of stars inside the ring, and that is how many days until the next rain.

If the moon is clear and white, the weather will be good the next day.

High, thin clouds, or cirrus, indicate a change in the weather.

Oval-shaped lenticular clouds indicate high winds.

Two levels of clouds moving in different directions indicate changing weather soon.

Huge, dark, billowing clouds, called cumulonimbus, suddenly forming on warm afternoons in the mountains mean that a short but intense thunderstorm with lightning can be expected.

When squirrels are busy gathering food for extended periods, it means good weather is ahead in the short term, but a hard winter is ahead in the long term.

And God forbid if all the cows are sitting down . . . .

Beating the Time Trap

If the great outdoors is so great, then why don't people enjoy it more? The answer is because of the time trap, and I will tell you exactly how to beat it.

For many, the biggest problem is finding the time to go, whether it is camping, hiking, fishing, boating, backpacking, biking, or even just for a good drive in the country. The solution? Well, believe it or not, the answer is to treat your fun just as you treat your work, and I'll tell you how.

Consider how you treat your job: Always on time? Go there every day you are scheduled? Do whatever it takes to get there and get it done? Right? No foolin' that's right. Now imagine if you took the same approach to the outdoors. Suddenly your life would be a heck of a lot better.

The secret is to schedule all of your outdoor activities. For instance, I go fishing every Thursday evening, hiking every Sunday morning, and on an overnight trip every new moon (when stargazing is best). No matter what, I'm going. Just like going to work, I've scheduled it. The same approach works with longer adventures. The only reason I was able to hike from Mount Whitney to Yosemite was because I scheduled three weeks to do it. It was so much fun that I then hiked Yosemite to Tahoe a few years later. You know how I found the time? Right: I scheduled it. It's a great way to beat the time trap. It works especially well when planning trips with your loved ones or best friends: Because once the dates are locked in, they can't get out of it. The reason I spend 125 to 150 days a year in the field is that I schedule them. In my top year, I had nearly 200 days where at least part of the day was enjoyed taking part in outdoor recreation.

If you get out your calendar and write in the exact dates you are going, then you'll go. If you don't, you won't. Suddenly, with only a minor change in your life plan, you can be living the life you were previously dreaming about.

See you out there.

—Tom Stienstra

CAMPING GEAR CHECKLIST

COOKING GEAR

- Camp fuel
- Camp stove
- Dish soap and scrubber
- Fire-starter cubes or candle
- Itemized food
- Knife, fork
- Matches stored in resealable (such as Ziploc) bags
- Plastic spade
- Pot, pan, cup
- Pot grabber
- Salt, pepper, spices

Optional Cooking Gear
- Ax or hatchet
- Can opener
- Clothespins
- Dustpan
- Grill
- Ice chest
- Spatula
- Tablecloth
- Tinfoil
- Whisk broom
- Wood or charcoal for barbecue

CAMPING CLOTHES

- Cotton/canvas pants
- Cotton shirt
- Hat
- Long-sleeved cotton/wool shirt
- Parka
- Polypropylene underwear
- Rain jacket, pants, or poncho

- Sunglasses
- Vest

Optional Clothing
- Gloves
- Seam Lock
- Shorts
- Ski cap
- Swimsuit

HIKING GEAR

- Backup lightweight shoes
- 80% wool socks
- Gaiters
- Innersole or foot cushion
- Moleskin and medical tape
- Polypropylene socks

- Quality hiking boots
- Strong bootlaces
- Thick cotton socks
- Water-repellent boot treatment

SLEEPING GEAR

- Sleeping bag
- Insulite or Therm-a-Rest pad
- Ground tarp
- Tent

Optional Sleeping Gear
- Air pillow
- Catalytic heater
- Foam pad for truck bed
- Mosquito netting
- RV Windshield light screen

FIRST AID

- Ace bandage
- Adhesive bandages
- After-Bite or ammonia
- Aspirin
- Athletic tape
- Biodegradable soap
- Caladryl or Tecnu
- Campho-Phenique gel
- First-aid cream
- Moleskin
- Mosquito repellent
- Neosporin
- Roller gauze
- Sterile gauze pads
- Sunscreen
- Thermometer
- Towelettes
- Tweezers

Optional First Aid

- Coins for emergency phone calls
- Extra set of matches
- Mirror for signaling
- Water purification system

FISHING/RECREATION GEAR

- Fishing reel with fish-line split-shot, snap swivels
- Fishing rod
- Knife
- Pliers

Optional Recreation Gear

- Backpacking cribbage board
- Deck of cards
- Knapsack for each person
- Stargazing chart
- Tree identification handbook

MISCELLANEOUS

- Camera and film
- Compass
- Feminine hygiene products
- Flashlight
- Handkerchief
- Lantern and fuel
- Lip balm
- Maps
- Nylon rope for food hang
- Plastic garbage bags
- Toilet paper
- Toothbrush and toothpaste
- Watch

Optional Miscellaneous

- Binoculars
- Notebook and pen
- Towel

NORTHERN CALIFORNIA
CHAPTER AO

OVERLOOKING ISLAND LAKE, SIX
RIVERS NATIONAL FOREST

MAP A0

One inch equals approximately 11 miles.

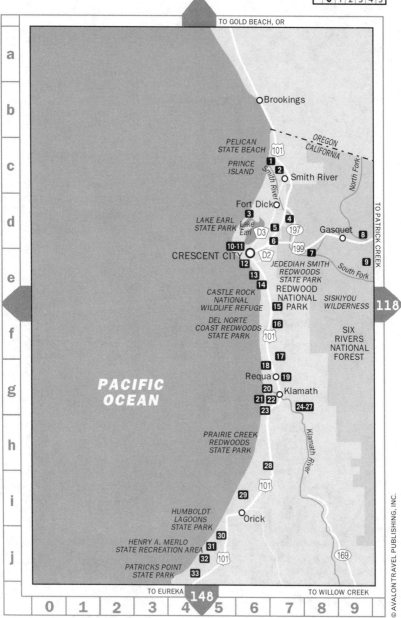

TO GOLD BEACH, OR

O Brookings

PELICAN
STATE BEACH
[101]

PRINCE
ISLAND

1
2

O Smith River

Smith River

OREGON
CALIFORNIA

North Fork

TO PATRICK CREEK

Fort Dick O

3

LAKE EARL
STATE PARK

Lake
Earl

D3

4

5

[197]

Gasquet
O

8

6

10-11

D2

[199]

7

9

CRESCENT CITY O

12

JEDEDIAH SMITH
REDWOODS
STATE PARK

South Fork

13

14

CASTLE ROCK
NATIONAL
WILDLIFE REFUGE

REDWOOD
NATIONAL
PARK

15

SISKIYOU
WILDERNESS

118

DEL NORTE
COAST REDWOODS
STATE PARK

16

[101]

SIX
RIVERS
NATIONAL
FOREST

17

18

19

Requa O

**PACIFIC
OCEAN**

20

Klamath

21 **22**

24-27

23

Klamath River

PRAIRIE CREEK
REDWOODS
STATE PARK

28

29

[101]

HUMBOLDT
LAGOONS
STATE PARK

Orick O

HENRY A. MERLO
STATE RECREATION AREA

30

31

[169]

32

[101]

PATRICKS POINT
STATE PARK

33

TO EUREKA **148**

TO WILLOW CREEK

© AVALON TRAVEL PUBLISHING, INC.

NORTHERN CALIFORNI

CHAPTER A0

1 Salmon Harbor Resort

     6

If location is everything, then this privately operated campground rates high for salmon fishermen in the fall. It is set near the mouth of the Smith River, where salmon enter and school in the deep river holes in October. The fish are big, occasionally even surpassing 40 pounds. Year-round this is a good layover for RV cruisers looking for a spot near the Oregon border. It is actually an RV parking area with hookups, set within a mobile home park. Salmon Harbor Resort overlooks the ocean, with good beachcombing and driftwood and agate hunting nearby.

Location: On the Smith River; map A0, grid c7.

Campsites, facilities: There are 98 sites for tents or RVs, 88 with full hookups and cable TV. Picnic tables and fire grills are provided. Drinking water, flush toilets, showers, telephones and modem hookups and a recreation room are available. A coin laundry, ice, gas, a restaurant, a bar, and a bait and tackle shop are available within three miles. Leashed pets are permitted.

s, fees: Reservations are accepted $5 per night. (800) 332-6139. Open round.

ctions: From Crescent City, drive north on U.S. 101 for 13 miles to the town of Smith River. Continue three miles north on U.S. 101 to the Salmon Harbor Road exit. Turn left on Salmon Harbor Road, drive two blocks, and look for Salmon Harbor Resort at the end of the road.

Contact: Salmon Harbor Resort, tel. (707) 487-3341; website: www.allcampgrounds.com/salmonharbor/.

❷ Ship Ashore Resort Best Western RV Park

 7

This is a famous spot for Smith River fishermen, where the tales get taller as the evening gets late. The park is set on five acres of land adjacent to the lower Smith River. The salmon and steelhead seem to come in one size here—giant—but they can be as elusive as Bigfoot. If you want to hear how big, just check into the Captain's Galley restaurant any fall or winter evening. In the summer, the resort has become quite popular with people cruising the coast on U.S. 101.

Location: On the Smith River; map A0, grid c7.

Campsites, facilities: There are 200 RV sites, most with full hookups, and a separate area for 10 to 15 tents. Picnic tables are provided. Flush toilets, showers, boat dock, boat ramp, and some patios are available. A coin laundry, LP gas, and groceries are also available. Leashed pets are permitted.

Reservations, fees: Reservations are accepted; $10 for two people for the first night, $15 per night thereafter. Major credit cards accepted. Open year-round.

Directions: From Crescent City, drive north on U.S. 101 for 16 miles, three miles past the town of Smith River, to the Ship Ashore sign at Chinook Street. At Chinook Street, turn left and drive a short distance (less than half a block) to the camp store at the campground entrance.

Contact: Ship Ashore Resort Best Western RV Park, tel. (707) 487-3141, ext. 6, or fax (707) 487-7070.

❸ Lake Earl/Talawa State Park

 9

This campground is one of the great discoveries available to people who love the outdoors. The walk-in sites are extremely secluded, quiet, and sheltered, set off little spur trails from the main access trail/road. With forested rolling hills, a benign climate, and a combination of marshes, sandy soil, and proximity to the ocean, the Smith River and Lake Earl are not only pretty and pleasant, but attract a wide variety of bird life. The access trail provides an outstanding bicycle trip. The campgrounds are not set near Lake Earl, but the lake is accessible with a short drive. Lakes Earl and Talawa are connected by a curving piece of water, with Talawa to the west and Earl to the east. Talawa borders coastal sand dunes and, after heavy rainfall, sometimes runs into the ocean. That is how sea-run cutthroat trout and flounder enter the brackish waters, caught rarely at the narrows between the lakes. Lakes Earl and Talawa offer 7.5 miles of ocean frontage, 15 miles of horseback riding trails, numerous hiking trails, opportunities for canoeing and kayaking, and the bonus of having the Smith River nearby to the north. Guided walks are conducted by a state park ranger in July and August and also by reservation.

Location: Near Crescent City; map A0, grid d6.

Campsites, facilities: There are six primitive sites and a ride-in horse camp with 16 individual corrals and food lockers. There is no drinking water, but picnic tables are provided. Firewood and pit toilets are available. Fire rings are provided for the walk-in sites and fire pits for the horse camp. Leashed pets are permitted.

Reservations, fees: No reservations; $7 per night for walk-in sites. In the horse camp, there is a $3 fee per night per horse and rider, and a group rate of $45 per night for 15 or more riders. Registration is required at either Del Norte Coast Redwoods State Park or Jedediah Smith Redwoods State Park.

Directions: In Crescent City, drive on U.S. 101 to the lighted intersection at Northcrest Drive. Turn left (northwest) and drive about five miles (Northcrest becomes Lake Earl Drive) to Lower Lake Road. Turn left and drive 2.5 miles. Turn left on Kellogg Road and drive one-half mile. A small metal gate, for which the combination is given at registration, and parking area large enough for a few cars is the access point on the right side of the road.

For the horse camp: In Crescent City, turn northwest on Northcrest Drive and drive five miles to Lower Lake Road. At Lower Lake Road, turn left and drive about seven miles to Pala Road. At Pala Road, turn left and drive to the parking area. The horse camp is about a mile southwest of the Pala Road parking lot.

For trail and walk-in beach access: In Crescent City, turn northwest on Northcrest Drive and continue 1.5 miles to Old Mill Road. Turn west (left) on Old Mill Road and drive three miles to Sand Hill Road. For the state park trailhead, turn left at Sand Hill Road and drive 0.25 mile to the trail entrance. For Fish and Game trail and walk-in beach access, continue on Old Mill Road to the locked gate at the road's end (about 100 yards past the Sand Hill Road turnoff). The trail begins at the parking lot.

For the Lake Earl boat launch: In Crescent City, turn northwest on Northcrest Drive and drive about 3.5 miles to Lake View Road. At Lake View Road, turn left and drive a mile to the road's end at Lake Earl.

For the drive-in beach access: From Crescent City, turn northwest on Northcrest Drive and drive north for about five miles to Lower Lake Road. At Lower Lake Road, turn left and drive 2.5 miles to Kellogg Road. At Kellogg Road, turn left and drive 1.5 miles to the beach parking lot at the end of the road.

For picnicking and bird-watching: In Crescent City, turn northwest on Northcrest Drive and drive north for about five miles to Lower Lake Road. At Lower Lake Road, turn left and drive about seven miles to Pala Road on the left. Note: Refer to trail notes and walk-in beach access.

Contact: Lake Earl State Park, tel. (707) 464-6101, ext. 5151.

4 Ramblin' Rose Resort

 8

Ramblin' Rose is an RV park set amid redwood trees, some of them giant. The big trees are the highlight of the area, of course, with Redwood National Park and Jedediah Smith Redwoods State Park just to the east on U.S. 199. Nearby attractions include the beach to the immediate west and the Smith River to the north.

Location: Near the Smith River; map A0, grid d7.

Campsites, facilities: There are 93 RV sites with full hookups and seven tent sites. Picnic tables are provided. Restrooms, drinking water, showers, and a recreation hall are available. A mini convenience store, ice, and a coin laundry are also available. Some facilities are wheelchair accessible. Leashed pets are permitted.

Reservations, fees: Reservations are accepted; $20 per night for RV sites and $15 per night for tent sites. For reservations, tel. (877) 387-4831. Open year-round.

Directions: From Crescent City, take U.S. 101 north for four miles to the junction of U.S. 199. Continue north on U.S. 101 for another four miles to the campground, 6701 U.S. 101 North in Crescent City.

Contact: Ramblin' Rose Resort, tel. (707) 487-4831; website: www.ramblinroserv.com.

5 Crescent City Redwoods KOA

      6

This KOA camp is on the edge of a recreation wonderland, a perfect jump-off spot for a vacation. The camp itself includes those little KOA Kamping Kabins, which are cute log cabins with electricity and heat; just make sure you bring your sleeping bag and pillows. In addition, there are two nine-hole golf courses nearby. The camp is only a 10-minute drive to Redwood National Park, Jedediah Smith Redwoods State Park, and the Smith River National Recreation Area. It is also only a 10-minute drive to the beach and Lake Earl Wildlife Area to the east, and to Crescent City Harbor to the south.

Location: 5 miles north of Crescent City; map A0, grid d7.

Campsites, facilities: There are 44 tent sites and 44 sites with full hookups for RVs up to 40 feet long. Cabins are also available. Picnic tables and fire grills are provided. A sanitary disposal station, flush toilets, showers, a coin laundry, and a playground are available. LP gas, groceries, ice, and wood are also available. Leashed pets are permitted.

Reservations, fees: Reservations are accepted; $21 per night ($38 to $45 for two-room cabins). Major credit cards accepted. For reservations, tel. (800) KOA-5754. Open year-round.

Directions: From Crescent City, take U.S. 101 north for five miles to the junction of U.S. 101 and U.S. 199. Continue north on U.S. 101 for one mile and look for the campground entrance on the right (east) side of the road.

Contact: Crescent City Redwoods KOA, tel. (707) 464-5744; website: www.koa.com.

6 Hiouchi Hamlet RV Resort

      7

The folks who run this outfit are among the nicest you'll ever find, and hey, the fried chicken at the Hamlet is always good for a quick hit. The park is out of the wind and fog you get on the coast and set instead in the heart of the forest country. It makes a good base camp for a steelhead trip in winter. An excellent side trip is to drive just east of Hiouchi on U.S. 199, turn right, and cross over two bridges, where you will reach a fork in the road. Turn left for a great scenic drive along the South Fork Smith River or turn right to get backdoor (and free) access to Jedediah Smith Redwoods State Park and three great trailheads for hiking in the redwoods. My favorite of the latter is the Boy Scout Tree Trail.

Location: Near the Smith River; map A0, grid d7.

Campsites, facilities: There are 120 sites for tents or RVs, most with full hookups. Flush toilets, showers, and a sanitary disposal station are available. A coin laundry, LP gas, groceries, and a golf course are available within three miles. Some facilities are wheelchair accessible. Pets are permitted.

Reservations, fees: Reservations are accepted; $15 to $22 per night. Furnished homes are also available for $48 per day or $242 per week. Open year-round.

Directions: From Crescent City, drive five miles north on U.S. 101 to U.S. 199. Turn east (right) on U.S. 199 and drive about five miles (just past the entrance to Jedediah Smith State Park) to the town of Hiouchi. In Hiouchi, turn left at the well-signed campground entrance.

Contact: Hiouchi Hamlet RV Resort, tel. (800) 722-9468 or (707) 458-3321, or fax (707) 458-4223.

7 Jedediah Smith Redwoods State Park

    10

This is a beautiful park set along the Smith River, where the campsites are sprinkled amid a grove of redwoods. During the summer reservations are usually a necessity. The park has hiking trails that lead right out of the campground; one is routed along the beautiful Smith

River, and another heads through forest, across U.S. 199, and hooks up with the Simpson-Reed Interpretive Trail. In the summer, interpretive programs are available. There is also a good put-in spot at the park for river access in a drift boat, canoe, or raft. The fishing is best for steelhead from mid-January through March. An excellent side trip is available on the opposite bank of the Smith River; for access, see the entry for Hiouchi Hamlet RV Resort.

Location: On the Smith River; map A0, grid e8.

Campsites, facilities: There are 107 sites for tents or RVs up to 36 feet long and trailers up to 31 feet long, and five hike-in/bike-in sites. Picnic tables, fire grills, and food lockers are provided. Drinking water, flush toilets, coin-operated showers, and a sanitary disposal station are available. Propane gas, groceries, and a coin laundry are available within one mile. Leashed pets are permitted only in the campground and on roads. Some facilities are wheelchair accessible.

Reservations, fees: Reserve at (800) 444-PARK (800-444-7275) or website: www.ReserveAmerica.com; $12 per night, and $1 per person per night for hike-in, bike-in sites. Open year-round.

Directions: From Crescent City, drive north on U.S. 101 for five miles to the junction with U.S. 199. Turn east at U.S. 199 and drive nine miles. Turn right at the well-signed entrance station.

Contact: Redwood National and State Parks, tel. (707) 464-6101, ext. 5112 or 5064.

8 Panther Flat

 8

This is an ideal alternative to the often crowded Jedediah Smith Redwoods State Park. The park provides easy road access since it is set right along U.S. 199, the two-laner that runs aside the Smith River. This is the largest and one of the feature campgrounds in the Smith River National Recreation Area, with excellent prospects for salmon and steelhead fish-

ing in the fall [...] standing hikir [...] mer. A great n [...] Trail, an easy v [...] River; the trail [...] Stoney Creek R [...] a short drive to [...] ness is a short c [...] roads detailed on Forest Service maps. The wild and scenic Smith River system provides swimming, sunbathing, kayaking for experts, and beautiful scenery.

Location: On the Smith River in Six Rivers National Forest; map A0, grid d9.

Campsites, facilities: There are 39 sites for tents, trailers up to 40 feet long, and RVs up to 35 feet long. Picnic tables and fire grills are provided. Drinking water, flush toilets, hot showers, and a camp host are available. Propane gas, groceries, and coin laundry are available nearby. Several campsites are wheelchair accessible. Leashed pets are permitted.

Reservations, fees: Reservations are recommended. Reservations tel. (877) 444-6777 ($8.65 reservation fee), or at website: www.reserveusa.com. $15 per night, $5 fee for extra vehicles. Open year-round.

Directions: From Crescent City, drive north on U.S. 101 for five miles to the junction with U.S. 199. At U.S. 199, turn east and drive 15 miles to Gasquet. From Gasquet, continue for 2.3 miles east on U.S. 199 and look for the entrance to the campground on the left side of the highway.

Contact: Smith River National Recreation Area, Six Rivers National Forest, P.O. Box 228, Gasquet, CA 95543; tel. (707) 457-3131 or fax 707 457-3794.

9 Big Flat

 7

This camp provides an ideal setting for those who know of it, which is why it gets quite a bit of use for a relatively remote camp. Set along Hurdygurdy Creek, near where

he South Fork of the Smith
es nearby access to the South
ll, an outstanding hiking route
you are walking for a few hours or
packing for days. In the summer, it is a
good layover for rafters or kayakers paddling
the South Fork of the Smith River. In winter,
though the campground is closed, there is fishing access here for steelhead, with a good stretch of water nearby.

Location: On Hurdygurdy Creek in Six Rivers National Forest; map A0, grid e9.

Campsites, facilities: There are 28 sites for tents or RVs up to 22 feet long. Picnic tables and fire grills are provided. Vault toilets are available. There is no drinking water and you must pack out your garbage. Leashed pets are permitted.

Reservations, fees: No reservations; $8 per night, $5 per night for each extra vehicle. Open May through mid-September.

Directions: From Crescent City, drive north on U.S. 101 for five miles to the junction with U.S. 199, turn east on U.S. 199, and drive five miles to Hiouchi. Continue just past Hiouchi, turn right at South Fork Road, and cross two bridges. At the Y, turn left on South Fork Road and drive about 14 miles to Big Flat Road/County Road 405. At Big Flat Road, turn left and drive one-quarter mile to the campground entrance road (Forest Road 15N59) on the left. Turn left and drive a short distance to the camp on the left.

Contact: Smith River National Recreation Area, Six Rivers National Forest, P.O. Box 228, Gasquet, CA 95543; tel. (707) 457-3131 or fax (707) 457-3794.

10 Bayside RV Park

   6

If you are towing a boat, you just found your own personal heaven: this RV park is directly adjacent to the boat docking area in Crescent City Harbor. There are several walks in the immediate area, including exploring the harbor and ocean frontage. For a quick change of scenery, it is only a 15-minute drive to Redwood National Park and Jedediah Smith Redwoods State Park along U.S. 199 to the north.

Location: In Crescent City; map A0, grid d5.

Campsites, facilities: There are 110 RV sites with full hookups. Picnic tables are provided. Flush toilets, showers, and a coin laundry are available. Leashed pets are permitted.

Reservations, fees: Reservations are accepted; $15 per night. Open year-round.

Directions: From U.S. 101 at the southern end of Crescent City, turn west at Citizen Dock Road and drive a very short distance to the campground.

Contact: Bayside RV Park, tel. (707) 464-9482.

11 Village Camper Inn

    8

Woods and water, that's what attracts visitors to California's north coast. Village Camper Inn provides nearby access to big woods and big water. This RV park is on 20 acres of wooded land, with the giant redwoods along U.S. 199 about a 10-minute drive away. In addition, you find some premium beachcombing for driftwood and agates a mile away on the spectacular rocky beaches just west of town.

Location: In Crescent City; map A0, grid d5.

Campsites, facilities: There are 135 RV sites, most with full hookups, and a separate area for tents. Picnic tables are provided. Drinking water, a sanitary disposal station, flush toilets, and showers are provided; a coin laundry and cable TV hookups are available. Leashed pets are permitted.

Reservations, fees: Reservations are accepted; $14 to $18 per night. Major credit cards accepted. Open year-round.

Directions: On U.S. 101, driving north in Crescent City: Drive north on U.S. 101 to the Parkway Avenue exit and drive one-half mile to the campground on the right.

On U.S. 101, driving south in Crescent City: Drive south on U.S. 101 to the Washington Boulevard exit. Turn left on Washington Boulevard and drive one block to Parkway Drive.

Turn left on Parkway and drive one block to the campground on the right.
Contact: Village Camper Inn, tel. (707) 464-3544.

12 Sunset Harbor RV Park

      4

People camp here with their RVs in order to be close to the action in Crescent City and the nearby harbor and beach frontage. For starters, drive a few minutes to the northwest side of town, where the sea is sprinkled with gigantic rocks and boulders, for dramatic ocean views and spectacular sunsets. For finishers, go down to the west side of town for great walks along the ocean parkway or south to the harbor and adjacent beach, which is long and expansive.

Location: In Crescent City; map A0, grid e6.
Campsites, facilities: There are 69 sites with full hookups for RVs up to 40 feet long. Picnic tables are provided. Flush toilets and showers are available. A coin laundry, grocery store, and a recreation room are available nearby. Restrooms and showers are wheelchair accessible. Leashed pets are permitted.

Reservations, fees: Reservations are accepted; $17 to $20 per night. Major credit cards accepted. Open year-round.

Directions: In Crescent City on U.S. 101, drive to King Street. At King Street, turn east and drive one block to the park entrance.

Contact: Sunset Harbor RV Park, tel. (707) 464-3423.

13 Harbor RV Anchorage

      7

The Crescent City Harbor, restaurants, and a beach walk are all within close walking distance. The beach walk, immediately to the south, is spectacular during low tides for beachcombing, especially for driftwood. Get the picture? This park is right on the ocean, complete with salt air. If you don't mind the largely asphalt surroundings, more of a parking lot than anythin...
classic setup r...
Location: In C...
Campsites, f...
full hookups...
tables are p...
sanitary di...
cable TV hookups...
are permitted.

Reservations, fees: Reservations are accepted; $16 per night. Open year-round.

Directions: From U.S. 101 at the southern end of Crescent City, turn west at Anchor Way and drive a short distance to Starfish Way. At Starfish Way, turn right and drive to the campground.

Contact: Harbor RV Anchorage, tel. (707) 464-1724.

14 Nickel Creek Walk-In

    8

This camp is set 100 yards from the beach on a bluff, right near the mouth of Nickel Creek. One of the least-known national park campgrounds in the whole state, Nickel Creek Walk-In provides a backpacking-type experience, yet requires only a short walk. In return for the effort, you get seclusion and beach frontage, with seashore walks and tide pool exploration available.

Location: In Redwood National Park; map A0, grid e6.

Campsites, facilities: There are five hike-in tent sites. There is no drinking water. Picnic tables and fire grills are provided. Composting toilets are available. You must pack out garbage. No pets are allowed.

Reservations, fees: No reservations, no fee. Open year-round.

Directions: From Crescent City, drive south on U.S. 101 for two miles to Enderts Beach Road, turn right on Enderts Beach Road, and drive about a mile to the trailhead at the end of the road. From the trailhead, hike in a half mile to the campground.

...d National and State Parks,
...reet, Crescent City, CA 95531;
...-6101, or fax (707) 464-1812.

el Norte Coast Redwoods State Park

      8

The campsites are set in a series of loops in the forest, so while there are a lot of camps, you still feel a sense of privacy here. In addition to redwoods, there are also good stands of alders, along with a rambling stream fed by several creeks. It makes for a very pretty setting, with a good loop hike available right out of the camp. One reason for the lush growth is what rangers call the "nurturing" coastal climate. Nurturing, in this case, means rain like you wouldn't believe in the winter and lots of fog in the summer. Interpretive programs are conducted here. Insider's note: Hike-in and bike-in campers beware. There is a 900-foot elevation change over the course of two miles between the U.S. 101 access road and the campground.

Location: Near Crescent City; map A0, grid f7.

Campsites, facilities: There are 38 tent sites and 107 sites for tents or RVs up to 31 feet long and trailers up to 27 feet long. Hike-in/bike-in sites are also available. Picnic tables, fire grills, and food lockers are provided. Drinking water, sanitary disposal station, flush toilets, and coin-operated showers are available. Some facilities are wheelchair accessible. Leashed pets are permitted only in the campground.

Reservations, fees: Reserve at (800) 444-PARK (800-444-7275) or website: www.ReserveAmerica.com; $12 per night; $1 per person per night for hike-in/bike-in sites. Open May through September.

Directions: From Crescent City, drive seven miles south on U.S. 101 to a signed access road for Del Norte Coast Redwoods State Park. Turn left at the park entrance.

Contact: Redwood National and State Park, tel. (707) 464-6101, ext. 5120 or 5064.

De Martin

 8

This camp is primarily used by overnighters who are hiking the Pacific Coastal Trail. It is set in a grassy prairie area on a bluff overlooking the ocean along the De Martin section of the trail, right aside Wilson Creek. Sound good? You can chase the waves, hike the Coastal Trail, or just hunker down and let the joy of a peaceful spot renew your spirit.

Location: In Redwood National Park; map A0, grid f7.

Campsites, facilities: There are 10 tent sites. Caches for food storage are provided. Composting toilets are available. There is no drinking water and you must pack out your garbage. No pets are allowed.

Reservations, fees: No reservations; no fee. Open year-round.

Directions: From Crescent City, drive south for approximately 18 miles on U.S. 101 to Wilson Creek Road. At Wilson Creek Road, turn left and drive a quarter mile to the trailhead at the end of the road. From the trailhead, hike in about 2.5 miles to the campground.

Contact: Redwood National and State Parks, 1111 Second Street, Crescent City, CA 95531; tel. (707) 464-6101 or fax (707) 464-1812.

Camp Marigold

     7

Camp Marigold is surrounded by Redwood National Park, towering redwoods, Pacific Ocean beaches, driftwood, agates, fossilized rocks, blackberries, Fern Canyon, Lagoon Creek Park, and the Trees of Mystery. It also has world-famous fishing nearby for chinook and silver salmon, steelhead, sturgeon, trout, red tail perch, and candlefish. The camp has 3.5 acres of landscaped gardens with hiking trails ... get the idea? Well, there's more: it is only two miles to the Klamath River, in case you can't find enough to do already.

Location: Near the Klamath River; map A0, grid f7.

Campsites, facilities: There are 40 sites for tents or RVs with full hookups. Picnic tables and barbecues are provided. Restrooms, hot showers, cable TV, and a coin laundry are available. Cabins (with fully equipped kitchenettes and bedding, for two to six people) and a group lodge (with kitchen, for up to 15 people) are also available. Small leashed pets are permitted.

Reservations, fees: Reservations are recommended; $10 to $15 per night; cabins rent for $47.52 to $77.76 per night; the lodge rents for $180 per night for the first 10 people, $5 for each additional person (maximum 15). Major credit cards are accepted. Open year-round.

Directions: From Eureka, drive 60 miles north on U.S. 101 to the campground at 16101 U.S. 101, four miles north of the Klamath River Bridge, on the right side of the road. The camp is a mile south of the Trees of Mystery.

Contact: Camp Marigold, tel. (800) 621-8513.

18 Mystic Forest RV Park

     6

Yes, Paul Bunyan exists. After all, how do you think the Mojave got turned into a desert? Babe, the giant blue ox, is still around too, as you will discover at the Trees of Mystery north of Klamath, where a dinosaur-size Paul Bunyan guards the parking lot. Less than a mile away is the Mystic Forest RV Park. Though Mystic Forest and the Trees of Mystery are not associated commercially, the link is obvious as soon as you arrive.

Location: Near the Klamath River; map A0, grid g6.

Campsites, facilities: There are 30 RV sites, many with full hookups (15 are drive-through), and a separate area for tents. Picnic tables and fire rings are provided. Drinking water, flush toilets, showers, playground, two jacuzzis, a coin laundry, and wood are available. Some facilities are wheelchair accessible. Leashed pets are permitted.

Reservations, fees: Reservations are ac-

cepted; $14 to $16 per night. Major credit cards accepted. Open year-round.

Directions: From Eureka, drive north on U.S. 101 to Klamath and continue north for four miles. Look for the entrance sign on the left side of the road. If you reach the Trees of Mystery, you have gone a mile too far north.

Contact: Mystic Forest RV Park, tel. (707) 482-4901 or fax (707) 482-0704; website: www.campgrounds.com/mysticforest.

19 Riverside RV Park

     7

This is one in a series of RV parks near the town of Klamath along the lower Klamath River. It provides an option for RV cruisers looking for a layover spot on a U.S. 101 tour or a base of operations for a Klamath River fishing trip. There's good salmon fishing starting in late summer, peaking at Labor Day, and continuing into fall on the Klamath River.

Location: On the Klamath River; map A0, grid g7.

Campsites, facilities: There are 93 RV sites with full hookups (30 drive-through). Flush toilets, showers, cable TV, restaurant, boutique shop, and a recreation room are available. Boat rentals and a dock are also available. Leashed pets are permitted.

Reservations, fees: Reservations are accepted; $5 to $17 per night. Open April through October.

Directions: From Eureka, drive north on U.S. 101 to Klamath. Continue north for two miles to the campground on the left.

Contact: Riverside RV Park, tel. (707) 482-2523.

20 Chinook RV Resort

     7

Chinook RV Resort is another of the more well-known parks on the lower Klamath. A boat ramp, fishing supplies, and all the advice you can ask for are available. The camping area consists of grassy RV sites that overlook the river.

Location: On the Klamath River; map A0, grid g6.

Campsites, facilities: There are 70 RV sites with full hookups. Picnic tables and fire grills are provided. Flush toilets, showers, cable television and modem hookups, a playground, coin laundry and recreation room, LP gas, groceries, RV supplies, boat ramp, boat rentals, and a tackle shop are available. Leashed pets are permitted.

Reservations, fees: Reservations are accepted; $18 per night, plus $1.50 per person per night for more than two people. Major credit cards accepted. Open year-round.

Directions: From Eureka, drive north on U.S. 101 to Klamath. After crossing the bridge at the Klamath River, continue north on U.S. 101 for a mile to the campground.

Contact: Chinook RV Resort, tel./fax (707) 482-3511; website: www.campgrounds.com/chinook.

Flint Ridge Walk-In

 7

This little-known camp is on a grassy bluff overlooking the ocean, along the Flint Ridge section of the Pacific Coastal Trail. From the parking area at the trailhead, it's only a five-minute walk to reach a meadow surrounded by a thicket of wild blackberries, alders, and redwoods, with the ocean looming huge to the west. The parking area, by the way, is an excellent perch to watch for the "puff-of-smoke" spouts from passing whales. A hike out of camp is routed into the forest, a two-mile climb to reach a hill filled solid with redwoods. The only problem is that there is no real destination; just in, then back.

Location: In Redwood National Park; map A0, grid g6.

Campsites, facilities: There are 10 hike-in tent sites. Composting toilets are available. There is no drinking water. You must pack out garbage. No pets are allowed.

Reservations, fees: No reservations; no fee. Open year-round.

Directions: From Eureka, drive north on U.S. 101 to the Klamath River. Just before reaching the bridge at the Klamath River, take the Coastal Drive exit and head west up the hill for four miles to a dirt parking area on the right side of the road. Park here. The campground trailhead is adjacent to the parking area on the east side of the road. Hike five minutes to the camp.

Contact: Redwood National and State Parks, 1111 Second Street, Crescent City, CA 95531; tel. (707) 464-6101 or fax (707) 464-1812.

Camper Corral

 6

This resort offers 3,000 feet of Klamath River frontage, grassy tent sites, berry picking, access to the ocean, and hiking trails nearby. And, of course, in the fall it has salmon, the main attraction on the lower Klamath.

Location: On the Klamath River; map A0, grid g6.

Campsites, facilities: There are 140 sites for tents or RVs, many with full hookups. Picnic tables and fire grills are provided. Drinking water, flush toilets, showers, a heated swimming pool, recreation hall, playground, sanitary disposal station, coin laundry, cable TV, ice, and a bait and tackle shop are available. Leashed pets are permitted.

Reservations, fees: Reservations are accepted; $14 to $20 per night, $2 per night for each additional vehicle, $2 per person per night for more than two people. Major credit cards accepted. Open April through October.

Directions: From Eureka, drive north on U.S. 101 to Klamath. Just after crossing the Klamath River Bridge, take the Terwer Valley Road exit. Drive a short distance west to the campground.

Contact: Camper Corral, tel. (707) 482-5741 or fax (707) 482-6625; website: www.campgrounds.com/campercorral.

23 Riverwoods Campground

      7

Riverwoods Campground provides direct access to the Klamath River, with pretty sites in a grove of alder trees. Although the camp is set beside the Klamath, it is actually very close to the ocean as well, so the river is often more like a big lagoon. From mid-August through September, salmon will enter the Klamath and hold here, becoming acclimated to changes in salinity and water temperature. In the spring, usually late March and April, lampreys will enter this area and provide unusual shoreline fishing prospects. Nearby hiking is available on the Coastal Trail, with a trailhead a five-minute drive to the west on Klamath Beach Road, taking you to a spectacular ocean bluff.

Location: On the Klamath River; map A0, grid g6.

Campsites, facilities: There are 74 RV sites, many with full hookups, and a separate area for tents. Picnic tables and fire grills are provided. Drinking water, flush toilets, showers, and a sanitary disposal station are available. Ice and wood are also available. Satellite TV is available with full-hookup sites. A few rental trailers are available. A convenience store and fishing tackle store are at the campground. Some facilities are wheelchair accessible. Leashed pets are permitted.

Reservations, fees: Reservations are accepted; $14 to $20 per night. Open year-round.

Directions: From the town of Klamath, drive a mile south on U.S. 101 to Klamath Beach Road. Turn right on Klamath Beach Road and drive two miles. Look for the campground entrance on the right side of the road.

Contact: Riverwoods Campground, tel. (707) 482-5591.

24 Crivelli's Trailer Park

      5

Crivelli's Trailer Park is adjacent to a motel, surrounded by trees, and only a quarter-mile away from the Klamath River. It's a good base camp for a salmon fishing trip during the fall run so when the salmon arrive en masse, it can be difficult to get a reservation. Some regulars show up every year, same time, same place, staying for a week or more and fishing daily for salmon in the lower river. A cafe and lounge are available

Location: Near the Klamath River; map A0, grid g7.

Campsites, facilities: There are 31 RV sites with full hookups, including some pull-through sites. Some facilities are wheelchair accessible. Flush toilets, showers, a coin laundry, restaurant, and a lounge are available. Leashed pets are permitted.

Reservations, fees: Reservations are accepted; $10 to $15 per night. Open year-round.

Directions: From Eureka, drive north on U.S. 101 to Klamath and the junction with Highway 169. Turn east (right) on Highway 169 and drive 2.5 miles to the trailer park entrance.

Contact: Crivelli's Trailer Park, tel. (707) 482-3713; website: www.wcinet.net/@crivellis.

25 Steelhead Lodge

     6

Many anglers use this park as headquarters when the salmon and steelhead get going in August. The park has grassy sites near the Klamath River.

Location: On the Klamath River; map A0, grid g7.

Campsites, facilities: There are 36 RV sites (10 drive-through) with full hookups. Picnic tables are provided. Drinking water, flush toilets, showers, and ice are available. A bar, restaurant, and motel are also available. Bar and restaurant are wheelchair accessible. Leashed pets are permitted.

Reservations, fees: Reservations are accepted; $15 per night. Major credit cards accepted. Open year-round.

Directions: From Eureka, drive north on U.S. 101 to Klamath and the junction with Highway

169. Turn east on Highway 169 and drive 3.2 miles to Terwer Riffle Road. Turn right (south) on Terwer Riffle Road and drive one block to Steelhead Lodge.

Contact: Steelhead Lodge, tel. (707) 482-8145. For a fishing report, phone (707) 482-7775.

26 Redwood Rest

      7

While there are quite a few privately operated parks on the lower Klamath River, Redwood Rest is the only park with redwood trees actually in the campground and a 20-foot-tall wooden Indian at the entrance. Reservations are advised during summer and are a necessity when salmon fishing picks up in mid-August.

Location: On the Klamath River; map A0, grid g7.

Campsites, facilities: There are 100 sites for tents or RVs (30 drive-through) with full or partial hookups. Picnic tables are provided. Drinking water, flush toilets, showers, and wood are available. Leashed pets are permitted.

Reservations, fees: Reservations are accepted; $12 to $14 per night, $2 for each additional person after the first two people. Open May through October.

Directions: From Eureka, drive north on U.S. 101 to Klamath and the junction with Highway 169. Turn east (right) on Highway 169 and drive three miles to the park.

Contact: Redwood Rest, tel. (707) 482-5033 or fax (707) 482-5033.

27 Terwer Park

     7

This RV park is situated near the Terwer Riffle, one of the better shore-fishing spots for steelhead and salmon on the lower Klamath River. You get grassy sites, river access, and some fair trails along the Klamath. When the salmon arrive in late August and September, Terwer Riffle can be loaded with fish, as well as boaters and shore anglers—a wild scene.

Location: On the Klamath River; map A0, grid g7.

Campsites, facilities: There are 98 RV sites with full hookups. Picnic tables are provided. Flush toilets, hot showers, a coin laundry, cable TV, and a dock with fee boat launching are available. Leashed pets are permitted.

Reservations, fees: Reservations are accepted; $16 per night. Open year-round.

Directions: From Eureka, drive north on U.S. 101 to Klamath and the junction with Highway 169. Turn east on Highway 169 and drive 3.5 miles to Terwer Riffle Road. Turn right on Terwer Riffle Road and drive seven blocks (about a half mile) to the park, 641 Terwer Riffle Road.

Contact: Terwer Park, tel. (707) 482-3855.

28 Elk Prairie

     9

Herds of Roosevelt elk wander free in this remarkable park. Great opportunities for photographs abound, often right beside the highway. Where there are meadows, there are elk; it's about that simple. An elky here, an elky there, making this one of the best places to see wildlife in California. Remember that these are wild animals, are huge, and can be unpredictable; in other words, enjoy them, but don't harass them or get too close. The park also has excellent hiking and some mountain biking, including a trailhead for a great bike ride at the campground. There are many additional trailheads and a beautiful tour of giant redwoods along the Drury Scenic Parkway. A museum and summer interpretive programs are available.

Location: In Prairie Creek Redwoods State Park; map A0, grid h6.

Campsites, facilities: There are 75 sites for tents, RVs up to 27 feet long, or trailers up to 24 feet long. Picnic tables, fire grills, and food lockers are provided. Drinking water, flush toilets, and coin-operated showers are available. Some facilities are wheelchair accessible. Leashed pets are permitted.

Reservations, fees: Call (800) 444-PARK

(800-444-7275) or website: www.ReserveAmerica.com; $12 per night. Open year-round.

Directions: From Eureka, drive 45 miles north on U.S. 101 to Orick. At Orick, continue north on U.S. 101 for five miles to the Newton B. Drury Scenic Parkway. Take the exit for the Newton B. Drury Scenic Parkway and drive north for a mile to the park. Turn left at the park entrance.

Contact: Prairie Creek Redwoods State Park, tel. (707) 464-6101, ext. 5301 or 5064.

29 Gold Bluff Beach

     8

The campsites here are set in a sandy, exposed area with man-made windbreaks with a huge, expansive beach on one side and a backdrop of 100 to 200-foot cliffs on the other side. You can walk for miles at this beach, often without seeing another soul, and there is a great trail routed north through forest, with many hidden little waterfalls. In addition, the Fern Canyon Trail, one of the best 30-minute hikes in California, is at the end of Davison Road. Hikers walk along a stream in a narrow canyon, its vertical walls covered with magnificent ferns. There are some herds of elk in the area, often right along the access road. These camps are rarely used in the winter because of the region's heavy rain and winds.

Location: In Prairie Creek Redwoods State Park; map A0, grid i6.

Campsites, facilities: There are 25 sites for tents or RVs up to 24 feet long (no trailers or vehicles wider than eight feet). Fire grills, food lockers, and tables are provided. Drinking water, flush toilets, and solar showers are available. Leashed pets are permitted.

Reservations, fees: No reservations; $12 per night. Open year-round, weather permitting.

Directions: From Eureka, drive north on U.S. 101 for 45 miles to Orick. At Orick, continue north on U.S. 101 for three miles to Davison Road. Turn left (west) on Davison Road and drive four miles to the campground on the left. Note: No vehicles more than 24 feet long or more than eight feet wide are permitted on Davison Road, which is narrow and very bumpy.

Contact: Prairie Creek Redwoods State Park, tel. (707) 464-6101, ext. 5301 or 5064.

30 Stone Lagoon Boat-In

     10

Virtually nobody knows about this ideal spot for canoeists. While Stone Lagoon is directly adjacent to U.S. 101, the camp is set in a cove that is out of sight of the highway. That makes it a secret spot for many. It is a great place to explore by canoe or kayak, especially paddling upstream to the lagoon's inlet creek. After setting up camp, it is possible to hike to a secluded sand spit and stretch of beachfront. You may see elk in this area on the rare occasion. The water is usually calm in the morning, but often gets choppy from afternoon winds. Translation: Get your paddling done early on Stone Lagoon. There is also good fishing for cutthroat trout here.

Location: In Humboldt Lagoons State Park; map A0, grid j5.

Campsites, facilities: There are six primitive tent sites accessible by boat only. There is no drinking water. Picnic tables, food lockers, and fire rings are provided. Pit toilets are available. Garbage must be packed out. No pets are allowed.

Reservations, fees: No reservations; $7 per night. Open year-round.

Directions: From Eureka, drive 41 miles north on U.S. 101 (15 miles north of Trinidad) to Stone Lagoon. At Stone Lagoon, turn left at the visitor information center. The boat-in campground is in a cove directly across the lagoon from the visitor center. The campsites are dispersed in an area covering about 300 yards in the landing area.

Contact: Humboldt Lagoons State Park, tel. (707) 488-2041 or fax (707) 488-5555.

31 Dry Lagoon Walk-In

    8

This is a walk-in camp; that is, you need to walk about 200 yards from the parking area to reach the campsites. This makes it a dream for members of the 5 Percent Club, because many tourists are unwilling to walk at all. It is beautiful here, set in the woods, with ocean views and beach access.

Location: In Humboldt Lagoons State Park; map A0, grid j5.

Campsites, facilities: There are six primitive tent sites. Picnic tables, fire rings, and food lockers are provided. Pits toilets are available. There is no drinking water. Garbage must be packed out. No pets are allowed.

Reservations, fees: No reservations, but all campers must register at the Patrick's Point State Park entrance station to obtain the combination to the gate lock; $7 per night. Open year-round.

Directions: From Eureka, drive north on U.S. 101 for 22 miles to Trinidad. At Trinidad, continue north on U.S. 101 for 13 miles to Dry Lagoon Road. Turn left and drive approximately one mile to the gate at the end of the road. Open gate combination (see previous note) and drive one-quarter mile to the trailhead. Park and walk 200 yards to the camp.

Contact: Humboldt Lagoons State Park, tel. (707) 488-2041.

32 Big Lagoon County Park

      7

This is a remarkable, huge lagoon that borders the Pacific Ocean. It provides good boating, excellent exploring, fair fishing, and good duck hunting in the winter. It's a good spot to paddle a canoe around on a calm day. A lot of out-of-towners cruise by, note the lagoon's proximity to the ocean, and figure it must be saltwater. Wrong! Not only is it fresh water, but it provides a long shot for anglers trying for rainbow trout. One reason not many RV drivers stop here is that most of them are drawn far-

ther north (another eight miles) to Freshwater Lagoon, where there is a wide shoulder along the highway that allows them to line up their rigs, like a convoy parking parade—an unbelievable sight.

Location: Overlooking the Pacific Ocean; map A0, grid j5.

Campsites, facilities: There are 26 sites for tents or RVs. Picnic tables and fire grills are provided. Drinking water and flush toilets are available. A boat ramp is also available. Pets are permitted.

Reservations, fees: No reservations; $12 per night, $1 pet fee. Open year-round.

Directions: From Eureka, drive 22 miles north on U.S. 101 to Trinidad. At Trinidad, continue north on U.S. 101 for eight miles to Big Lagoon Park Road. Turn left (west) at Big Lagoon Park Road and drive two miles to the park.

Contact: Humboldt County Parks, tel. (707) 445-7651.

33 Patricks Point State Park

     9

This pretty park is filled with Sitka spruce, dramatic coastal lookouts, and several beautiful beaches, including one with agates, one with tidepools, and another with an expansive stretch of beachfront leading to a lagoon. You can best see all of it on the Rim Trail, which has many little cut-off routes to the lookouts and down to the beaches. The campground is sheltered in the forest, and while it is often foggy and damp in the summer, it is always beautiful. A Native American village, constructed by the Yurok tribe, is also available. At the north end of the park, a short hike to see the bizarre "Octopus Trees" is a good side trip, with trees that are growing atop downed logs, with their root systems exposed like octopus tentacles. In addition, there are several miles of pristine beach to the north that extend to the lagoons. Interpretive programs are available. For camping, plan on making reservations.

Location: Near Trinidad; map A0, grid j4.

Campsites, facilities: There are 124 sites for tents or RVs up to 31 feet long. A cabin and yurt are also available. Fire grills, food lockers, and picnic tables are provided. Drinking water, flush toilets, and coin-operated showers are available. Some facilities are wheelchair accessible. Leashed pets are permitted at campsites, but not on trails or beaches.

Reservations, fees: Reserve at (800) 444-PARK (800-444-7275) or website: www.ReserveAmerica.com; $12 per night. The yurt is $20 per night, cabin $29 per night. Open year-round.

Directions: From Eureka, drive north on U.S. 101 for 22 miles to Trinidad. At Trinidad, continue north on U.S. 101 for 5.5 miles and to Patrick's Point Drive. Take that exit and at the stop sign, turn left and drive a one-half mile to the park entrance.

Contact: Patricks Point State Park, tel. (707) 677-3570 or tel. (707) 488-5555.

A SEA OF CONIFERS
IN THE SISKIYOU WILDERNESS

MAP A1

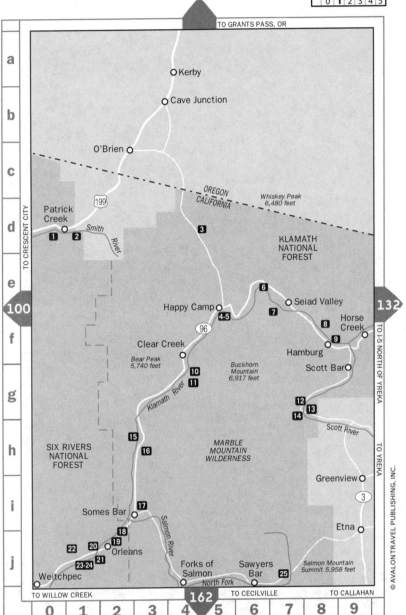

TO GRANTS PASS, OR

O Kerby

O Cave Junction

O'Brien O

199

OREGON
CALIFORNIA

Whiskey Peak
6,480 feet

Patrick
Creek

1 **2**

Smith River

3

KLAMATH
NATIONAL
FOREST

6

Happy Camp O

4-5

7

O Seiad Valley

8

Horse
Creek

96

Clear Creek

Bear Peak
5,740 feet

10

11

Klamath River

Buckhorn
Mountain
6,917 feet

Hamburg

9

Scott Bar O

12

13

14

Scott River

SIX RIVERS
NATIONAL
FOREST

15

16

MARBLE
MOUNTAIN
WILDERNESS

Greenview O

3

Somes Bar

17

Etna O

18

22

20

19

Orleans

23-24 **21**

Salmon River

Weitchpec

Forks of
Salmon

North Fork

Sawyers
Bar

25

Salmon Mountain
Summit 5,958 feet

TO WILLOW CREEK

162

TO CECILVILLE

TO CALLAHAN

TO CRESCENT CITY

100

132

TO I-5 NORTH OF YREKA

TO YREKA

© AVALON TRAVEL PUBLISHING, INC.

a b c d e f g h i j

0 1 2 3 4 5 6 7 8 9

CHAPTER A1

1 Grassy Flat

    4

This is one in a series of three easy-to-reach Forest Service camps set near U.S. 199 along the beautiful Smith River. It's a classic wild river, popular in the summer with kayakers, and the steelhead come huge in the winter for the crafty few. The camp itself is set directly across from a CalTrans waste area, and if you hit it when the crews are working, it can be noisy here. Most of the time, however, it is peaceful and quiet. In the winter when the camp is closed, fishermen will often park at the piped gate, and then walk past the camp to a good steelhead spot.

Location: On the Smith River in Six Rivers National Forest; map A1, grid d0.

Campsites, facilities: There are five tent sites and 14 sites for tents or RVs up to 30 feet long. Picnic tables and fire grills are provided.

Drinking water and vault toilets are available. Propane gas and groceries are available nearby. Some facilities are wheelchair accessible. Leashed pets are permitted.

Reservations, fees: Reserve at (877) 444-6777 ($8.65 reservation fee) or website: www.reserveusa.com; $10 per night, $5 for each extra vehicle. Open late May through mid-September.

Directions: From Crescent City, drive north on U.S. 101 for four miles to the junction with U.S. 199, turn east on U.S. 199 and drive 15 miles to Gasquet. From Gasquet, continue east on U.S. 199 for 4.4 miles and look for the campground entrance on the right side of the road.

Contact: Smith River National Recreation Area, Six Rivers National Forest, P.O. Box 228, Gasquet, CA 95543; tel. (707) 457-3131 or fax (707) 457-3794.

2 Patrick Creek

 8

This is one of the prettiest spots along U.S. 199, where Patrick Creek enters the upper Smith River. This section of the Smith looks something like a large trout stream, rolling green past a boulder-lined shore, complete with forest canopy. There are no trout of course, but rather salmon and steelhead in the fall and winter, and only their little smolts pooling up in the summer. A big plus for this camp is its nearby access to excellent hiking in the Siskiyou Wilderness, especially the great day hike to Buck Lake. It is essential to have a map of Six Rivers National Forest, both for driving directions to the trailhead and for the hiking route. You can buy maps at the information center for the Smith River National Recreation Area on the north side of U.S. 199 in Gasquet. An option at this camp is Patrick Creek Lodge, on the opposite side of the highway from the campground, which has a fine restaurant and bar.

Location: In Six Rivers National Forest; map A1, grid d1.

Campsites, facilities: There are 13 sites for tents and RVs up to 35 feet long. Picnic tables and fire grills are provided. Drinking water, flush toilets, and restrooms are available. Some facilities are wheelchair accessible. Leashed pets are permitted.

Reservations, fees: Reserve at (877) 444-6777 ($8.65 reservation fee) or website: www.reserveusa.com; $13 per night, $5 for each extra vehicle. Open late May through mid-September.

Directions: From Crescent City, drive north on U.S. 101 for three miles to the junction with U.S. 199, turn east on U.S. 199, and drive 15 miles to Gasquet. From Gasquet, continue east on U.S. 199 for 7.5 miles and look for the campground entrance on the right side of the road.

Contact: Smith River National Recreation Area, Six Rivers National Forest, P.O. Box 228, Gasquet, CA 95543; tel. (707) 457-3131 or fax (707) 457-3794.

3 West Branch

 6

This is a virtually unknown, no-charge camp, set in a canyon near Indian Creek, deep in Klamath National Forest. It is a 20-minute drive from the town of Happy Camp at 2,200 feet in elevation. The best side trip here is the winding four-mile drive on a bumpy dirt road to Kelly Lake, little known and little used. A remote Forest Service station is on the opposite side of Indian Creek Road from the campground.

Location: In Klamath National Forest; map A1, grid d4.

Campsites, facilities: There are 15 sites for tents or RVs up to 32 feet long. Picnic tables and fire grills are provided. Drinking water and vault toilets are available. There are sanitary disposal stations in Happy Camp at the Elk Creek Campground and the Happy Camp Open Dump. Pack out your garbage. Leashed pets are permitted.

Reservations, fees: No reservations; $4 per night. Two vehicles maximum per site. Open May through October.

Directions: From Happy Camp on Highway 96, turn north on Indian Creek Road (a paved road) and drive 14.5 miles to the camp on the right side of the road.

Contact: Klamath National Forest, Happy Camp Ranger District, tel. (530) 493-2243 or fax (530) 493-1796.

4 Elk Creek Campground

 8

Elk Creek Campground is a year-round RV park set where Elk Creek pours into the Klamath River. It is a beautiful facility, with sites right on the water in a pretty, wooded setting. The section of the Klamath River nearby is perfect for inflatable kayaking and rafting. Guided trips are available for families or experts, with a wide scope of white water available, rated all the way from the easy Class I stuff all the way to the Class V to hell-and-back rapids. In addition, the water is quite warm in the summer and flows are maintained throughout the year, making it ideal for water sports. The park also has 25 miniature show horses boarded on the property with surreys and buckboards. In addition, horseshoe tournaments are occasionally held.

Location: On the Klamath River; map A1, grid f5.

Campsites, facilities: There are 78 RV sites, many with full or partial hookups, and a separate area for tents. Picnic tables and fire grills are provided. Restrooms, hot showers, recreation room, beach, coin laundry, sanitary disposal station, ice, propane, and wood are available. Leashed pets are permitted. Private horse boarding is available,

Reservations, fees: Reservations are accepted; $7 per person for tent campers, $18 to $20 for RVs. Open year-round.

Directions: From Highway 96 in the town of Happy Camp, turn south on Elk Creek Road and drive one mile to the campground.

Contact: Elk Creek Campground, tel. (530) 493-2208.

5 Curly Jack

 7

This campground is set at 1,075 feet in elevation on the Klamath River, providing opportunities for fishing, light rafting, and kayaking. What's special about Curly Jack, though, is that the water is generally warm enough through the summer for swimming.

Location: On the Klamath River in Klamath National Forest; map A1, grid f5.

Campsites, facilities: There are 17 sites for tents or RVs up to 22 feet and two group sites. Fire grills are provided. Drinking water and vault toilets are available. Some facilities are wheelchair accessible. Leashed pets are permitted.

Reservations, fees: Reservations required for group camps only; $10 per night, $30 per night for a group campsite ($15 reservation fee required). A maximum of two vehicles is allowed per site. Open year-round, but services available only from May through September.

Directions: From the town of Happy Camp on Highway, turn south on Elk Creek Road and drive about one mile. Turn right on Curly Jack Road and drive one block to the campground entrance.

Contact: Klamath National Forest, Happy Camp Ranger District, tel. (530) 493-2243 or fax (530) 493-1796.

6 Fort Goff

 7

This small, primitive campground is set right along the Klamath River, an ideal location for both fishing and rafting. Many of the most productive shoreline fishing spots on the Klamath River are in this area, with fair trout fishing in summer, good steelhead fishing in the fall and early winter, and a wild card for salmon in late September. There are pullouts along Highway 96 for parking, with short trails/scrambles down to the river. This is also a good spot for rafting, especially in inflatable kayaks, and commercial rafting operations have trips available on this stretch of river. On the opposite side of Highway 96 (within walking distance to the west) is a trailhead for a hike that is routed along Little Fort Goff Creek, an uphill tromp for five miles to Big Camp and the Boundary National Recreation Trail. The creek also runs near the camp.

Location: In Klamath National Forest; map A1, grid e6.

Campsites, facilities: There are five tent sites. Picnic tables and fire grills are provided. Vault toilets are available. There is no drinking water and you must pack out your garbage. Supplies are available in Seiad Valley. Leashed pets are permitted.

Reservations, fees: No reservations; no fee.

Directions: From Yreka, drive north on Interstate 5 to the junction with Highway 96. At Highway 96, turn west and drive to Seiad Valley. At Seiad Valley, contin-

ue west on Highway 96 for five miles to the campground on the left side of the road.
Contact: Klamath National Forest, Happy Camp Ranger District, tel. (530) 493-2243 or fax (530) 493-1796.

�7 Grider Creek

 6

This obscure little camp is used primarily by hikers, since a trailhead for the Pacific Crest Trail is available, and by deer hunters in the fall. The camp is set at 1,700 feet along Grider Creek. From here, the Pacific Crest Trail is routed uphill along Grider Creek into the Marble Mountain Wilderness, about an 11-mile ripper to Huckleberry Mountain at 6,303 feet. There are no lakes along the route, only small streams and feeder creeks.
Location: In Klamath National Forest; map A1, grid f7.
Campsites, facilities: There are 10 sites for tents or RVs up to 16 feet long. Picnic tables and fire grills are provided. Vault toilets are available. No drinking water is provided. Garbage must be packed out. Leashed pets are permitted.
Reservations, fees: No reservations; no fee. Two vehicles maximum per site.
Directions: From Yreka, drive north on Interstate 5 to the junction with Highway 96. At Highway 96, turn west and drive to Walker Creek Road/Forest Road 46N64, one mile before Seiad Valley. Turn left to enter Walker Creek Road and stay to the right as it runs adjacent to the Klamath River to Grider Creek Road. At Grider Creek Road, turn left and drive south for three miles to the camp entrance.
Contact: Klamath National Forest, Happy Camp Ranger District, tel. (530) 493-2243 or fax (530) 493-1796.

⓼ O'Neil Creek

 7

This camp is set near O'Neil Creek, and though not far from the Klamath River, access to the river is not easy. To fish or raft, most people will use this as a base camp, then drive out for recreation during the day. That creates a predicament for RV owners, who lose their campsites every time they drive off. During the fall hunting season, this is a good base camp for hunters branching out into the surrounding national forest. There are also historic mining sites nearby.
Location: In Klamath National Forest; map A1, grid f8.
Campsites, facilities: There are 18 sites for tents or RVs up to 22 feet. Picnic tables and fire grills are provided. Vault toilets are available. No drinking water is available and garbage must be packed out. Supplies can be obtained in Seiad Valley. Leashed pets are permitted.
Reservations, fees: No reservations; $4 per night. A maximum of two vehicles is allowed per site.
Directions: From Yreka drive, north on Interstate 5 to the junction with Highway 96. Turn west on Highway 96 and drive past Hamburg, continuing west for three miles to the campground.
Contact: Klamath National Forest, Happy Camp Ranger District, tel. (530) 493-2243 or fax (530) 493-1796.

⓽ Sarah Totten

 7

This is one of the more popular Forest Service camps on the Klamath River, and it's no mystery why. In the summer, its placement is perfect for rafters, who camp here and use it as a put-in spot. In fall and winter, fishermen arrive for the steelhead run. It's in the "banana belt," or good weather area of the Klamath, in a pretty grove of oak trees. Fishing is often good here for salmon in early October and for steelhead from November through spring, providing there are fishable water flows.
Location: On the Klamath River in Klamath National Forest; map A1, grid f8.
Campsites, facilities: There are 12 tent sites, five sites for tents and RVs up to 22 feet long,

and a group site. Picnic tables and fire grills are provided. Drinking water and vault toilets are available. There's a small grocery store nearby. Leashed pets are permitted.

Reservations, fees: Reservations for the group site only; phone (877) 444-6777; $10 per night for family sites, $30 per night for the group site ($15 reservation fee required). Two vehicles maximum per site.

Directions: From Yreka, drive north on Interstate 5 to the junction with Highway 96. At Highway 96, turn west and drive to Horse Creek, continuing west for five miles to the campground on the right side of the road. If you reach the town of Hamburg, you have gone a half mile too far.

Contact: Klamath National Forest, Happy Camp Ranger District, tel. (530) 493-2243 or fax (530) 493-1796.

10 Sulphur Springs

 8

This hidden spot is set along Elk Creek on the border of the Marble Mountain Wilderness. The camp is at a trailhead that provides access to miles and miles of trails that follow streams into the backcountry of the wilderness area. It is a 12-mile backpack trip one way and largely uphill to Spirit Lake, one of the prettiest lakes in the entire wilderness. Sulphur Springs Camp is set at 3,100 feet. The nearby hot springs (which are actually lukewarm) provide a side attraction. There are also some swimming holes nearby in Elk Creek, but these aren't hot springs, so expect the water to be cold.

Location: On Elk Creek in Klamath National Forest; map A1, grid g4.

Campsites, facilities: There are several walk-in tent sites. Picnic tables and fire grills are provided. Vault toilets are available. No drinking water is available. Pack out your garbage. Leashed pets are permitted.

Reservations, fees: No reservations; no fee. Two vehicles maximum per site.

Directions: From Yreka, drive north on Inter-

state 5 to the junction with Highway 96. At Highway 96, turn west and drive to Happy Camp. In Happy Camp, turn south on Elk Creek Road and drive 14 miles to the campground.

Contact: Klamath National Forest, Happy Camp Ranger District, tel. (530) 493-2243 or fax (530) 493-1796.

11 Norcross

 7

Set at 2,400 feet in elevation, this camp serves as a staging area for various trails that provide access into the Marble Mountain Wilderness. There is also access to the popular Kelsey Trail and to swimming and fishing activities.

Location: Near Happy Camp in Klamath National Forest; map A1, grid g4.

Campsites, facilities: There are eight sites for tents or RVs. Picnic tables and fire pits are provided. Vault toilets are available. No drinking water is available. Pack out all garbage. Leashed pets are permitted.

Reservations, fees: No reservations, no fee. Open year-round. Two vehicles maximum per site.

Directions: From Yreka on Interstate 5, drive west on Highway 96 to the town of Happy Camp. In Happy Camp, turn south onto Elk Creek Road and drive 16 miles to the campground.

Contact: Klamath National Forest, Happy Camp Ranger District, tel. (530) 493-2243 or fax (530) 493-1796.

12 Indian Scotty

 7

This popular camp provides direct access to the adjacent Scott River. Because it is easy to reach (no gravel roads) and shaded, it gets a lot of use. The camp is set at 2,400 feet. The levels, forces, and temperatures on the Scott River fluctuate greatly from spring to fall. In the spring, it can be a raging cauldron, cold from snowmelt. Come summer it quiets, with some deep pools providing swimming holes. By fall, it can be reduced to a trickle. Keep your expectations flexible according to the season.

Location: On the Scott River in Klamath National Forest; map A1, grid g7.

Campsites, facilities: There are 28 sites and a group site for tents or RVs up to 22 feet long. Picnic tables and fire grills are provided. Drinking water and vault toilets are available. There is a playground in the group-use area. Leashed pets are permitted.

Reservations, fees: Reservations are accepted; $6 per night during summer and free during winter, $30 per night for the group site. Open year-round.

Directions: From Redding, drive north on Interstate 5 to Yreka. In Yreka, turn southwest on Highway 3 and travel 16.5 miles to Fort Jones. In Fort Jones, turn right on Scott River Road and drive 18 miles to a concrete bridge and the adjacent signed campground entrance.

Contact: Klamath National Forest, Scott River Ranger District, tel. (530) 468-5351 or fax (530) 468-1290.

13 Bridge Flat

 7

This camp is set at 2,000 feet along the Scott River. Though commercial rafting trips are only rarely available here, the river is accessible during the early spring for skilled rafters and kayakers, with a good put-in and take-out spot four miles downriver. For backpackers a trailhead for the Kelsey Trail is nearby, leading into the Marble Mountain Wilderness.

Location: In Klamath National Forest; map A1, grid g8.

Campsites, facilities: There are four sites for tents or RVs up to 22 feet long. Picnic tables and fire grills are provided. Vault toilets are available and wheelchair accessible. There is no drinking water. Garbage must be packed out. Leashed pets are permitted.

Reservations, fees: No reservations; no fee. Open year-round.

Directions: From Redding, drive north on Interstate 5 to Yreka. In Yreka, turn southwest on Highway 3 and drive 16.5 miles to Fort Jones. In Fort Jones, turn right on Scott River Road and drive 21 miles to the campground on the right side of the road.

Contact: Klamath National Forest, Scott River Ranger District, tel. (530) 468-5351 or fax (530) 468-1290.

14 Lovers Camp

 5

Lovers Camp isn't set up for lovers at all, but for horses and backpackers. This is a trailhead camp set at 4,300 feet at the edge of the Marble Mountain Wilderness, one of the best in the entire wilderness for packers with horses. The trail here is routed up along Canyon Creek to the beautiful Marble Valley at the foot of Black Marble Mountain. The most common destination is Sky High Lakes, a good one-day huff-and-puff away. Now there's a place for lovers.

Location: In Klamath National Forest; map A1, grid g7.

Campsites, facilities: There are five walk-in sites. Picnic tables and fire grills are provided. Vault toilets are available and wheelchair accessible. There are also facilities for stock unloading and a corral. There is no drinking water, but water is available for stock. Garbage must be packed out. Leashed pets are permitted.

Reservations, fees: No reservations; no fee. Open June through October.

Directions: From Redding, drive north on Interstate 5 to Yreka. In Yreka, turn southwest on Highway 3 and drive to Fort Jones. In Fort Jones, turn right and drive 18 miles on Scott River Road to Forest Road 43N45. Turn south on Forest Road 43N45 and drive nine miles to the campground at the end of the road.

Contact: Klamath National Forest, Scott River Ranger District, tel. (530) 468-5351 or fax (530) 468-1290.

15 Dillon Creek

 7

This is a prime base camp for rafting or a steelhead fishing trip. A put-in spot for rafting is adjacent to the camp, with an excellent river run available from here on down past Presido Bar to the takeout at Ti-Bar. If you choose to go on, make absolutely certain to pull out at Somes Bar, or risk death at Ishi Pishi Falls. The water is warm here in the summer, and there are also many excellent swimming holes in the area. In addition, this is a good stretch of water for steelhead fishing in September and October, best from Dillon Beach to Ti-Bar. The elevation is 800 feet.

Location: On the Klamath River in Klamath National Forest; map A1, grid h2.

Campsites, facilities: There are 10 tent sites and 11 RV sites. Picnic tables and fire grills are provided. Drinking water and vault toilets are available. There is a sanitary disposal station in Happy Camp 25 miles north of the campground and at Aikens Creek nine miles west of the town of Orleans. Leashed pets are permitted.

Reservations, fees: No reservations; $9 fee per night. Open year-round.

Directions: From Yreka on Interstate 5, turn west on Highway 96 and drive to the town of Happy Camp. Continue west from Happy Camp for 35 miles and look for the campground on the right side of the road. Coming from the west, from Somes Bar, drive 15 miles north on Highway 96.

Contact: Six Rivers National Forest, Orleans Ranger District, tel. (530) 627-3291 or fax (530) 627-3401.

16 Marble Mountain Ranch

 6

The lodge is set just across the road from the Klamath River, an ideal location as headquarters for a rafting trip in the summer or a steelhead fishing trip in the fall. Commercial rafting trips are available here, as this piece of river is beautiful and fresh with lots of wildlife and birds, yet not dangerous. However, be absolutely certain to take out at Somes Bar before reaching Ishi Pishi Falls, which cannot be run. If you like privacy and comfort, the cabin rentals available here are a nice bonus. There's also a full pack station for guided trail rides lasting from one hour to overnight. Guided mountain bike trips are also available. In addition, there is a sporting clays target range.

Location: Near the Klamath River; map A1, grid h3.

Campsites, facilities: There are 30 tent sites, 11 cabins, two houses, and 30 RV sites with full hookups. Picnic tables and fire grills are provided. Restrooms, drinking water, hot showers, coin laundry, ice, wood, recreation room, horseshoe pits, and volleyball and basketball courts are available. Leashed pets are permitted.

Reservations, fees: Reservations are accepted; $5 to $14 per night, $60 per night for cabins, $100 per night for houses. Major credit cards are accepted. Open year-round.

Directions: From the junction of U.S. 101 and Highway 299 near Arcata, turn east on Highway 299 and drive to Willow Creek. In Willow Creek, turn north (left) on Highway 96 and drive to Somes Bar. At Somes Bar, continue for 7.5 miles to Marble Mountain Ranch.

Contact: Marble Mountain Ranch, tel. (530) 469-3322 or (800) KLAMATH/552-6284, or fax (530) 469-3357; website: www.marblemountainranch.com.

17 Oak Bottom on the Salmon River

 7

This camp is just far enough off Highway 96 that it gets missed by zillions of out-of-towners every year. It is set across the road from the lower Salmon River, a pretty, clean, and cold stream that pours out of the surrounding wilderness high country. Swimming is very good in river holes, though the water is cold, especially when nearby Wooley Creek is full of snowmelt pouring out of the Marble Mountains to the north. In the fall, there is good shoreline fishing for steelhead, though the canyon bottom is shaded almost all day and gets very cold.

Location: In Klamath National Forest; map A1, grid i3.

Campsites, facilities: There are 26 sites for tents and small RVs and some group sites. Picnic tables and fire grills are provided. Drinking water and vault toilets are available. There is a sanitary disposal station at the Elk Creek Campground in Happy Camp and at Aikens Creek, 13 miles west of the town of Orleans. Supplies are available in Somes Bar. Leashed pets are permitted.

Reservations, fees: No reservations; $9 per night. Open April through November, weather permitting.

Directions: From the junction of U.S. 101 and Highway 299 near Arcata, turn east on Highway 299 and drive to Willow Creek. At Willow Creek, turn north on Highway 96 and drive to Somes Bar. At Somes Bar, turn right on Somes Bar-Etna Road and drive three miles to the campground on the left side of the road.

Contact: Klamath National Forest, Ukonom Ranger District, tel. (530) 627-3291 or fax (530) 627-3401.

18 Pearch Creek

 7

This is one of the premium Forest Service camps on the Klamath River because of its easy access from the highway and easy access to the river. The camp is set on Pearch Creek, about a quarter mile from the Klamath at a deep bend in the river. It is open year-round. Indeed, the fishing is often excellent for one- to five-pound steelhead from August through November. The elevation is 400 feet.

Location: On the Klamath River in Six Rivers National Forest; map A1, grid j2.

Campsites, facilities: There are nine sites for tents and two sites for tents or RVs up to 22

feet long. Picnic tables and fire grills are provided. Drinking water, vault toilets, and a camp host in summer are available. A grocery store, coin laundry, and propane gas are available within one mile. Leashed pets are permitted.

Reservations, fees: No reservations; $9 per night; $5 for each additional vehicle. Open year-round.

Directions: From Interstate 5 in Redding, turn west on Highway 299 and drive to Willow Creek. In Willow Creek, turn north on Highway 96, drive past Weitchpec, and continue to Orleans. In Orleans, continue for one mile and look for the campground entrance on the right side of the road.

Contact: Six Rivers National Forest, Orleans Ranger District, tel. (530) 627-3291 or fax (530) 627-3401.

19 The Pines Trailer Park

 6

This is an option for RV cruisers touring Highway 96, looking for a stopover in Orleans. The steelhead fishing is good in this area in the fall. The campground is in a wooded setting, across the highway from the Klamath River.

Location: On the Klamath River; map A1, grid j2.

Campsites, facilities: There are 25 sites for RVs up to 40 feet long, all with full hookups, and a separate area for tents. Picnic tables are provided. Restrooms, showers, cable TV hookups, a sanitary disposal station, and a coin laundry are available. Leashed pets are permitted.

Reservations, fees: Reservations are accepted; $13 per night. Open year-round.

Directions: From the junction of U.S. 101 and Highway 299 near Arcata, drive east on Highway 299 to Willow Creek. At Willow Creek, turn north (left) on Highway 96, drive past Weitchpec, and continue to Orleans. In Orleans, look for the park entrance on the left side of the road.

Contact: The Pines Trailer Park, tel. (530) 627-3425.

20 Klamath Riverside RV Park and Campground

 8

Klamath Riverside RV Park and Campground is an option for RV cruisers touring Highway 96 and looking for a place in Orleans to tie up the horse for the night. The camp has large grassy sites set amid pine trees, right on the river. There are spectacular views of Mount Orleans and the surrounding hills. There has been a continuing evolution of changes and improvements in the past 10 years here. One big plus is that the park offers guided trips during the season for fishing and rafting.

Location: On the Klamath River; map A1, grid j1.

Campsites, facilities: There are 45 RV sites with full hookups and a separate area for tents. Picnic tables and fire rings are provided. Restrooms, showers, a hot tub, group pavilion, a small store, and a coin laundry are available. Horseback riding, river rafting services, and seasonal drift boat fishing are available within nine miles. Leashed pets are permitted.

Reservations, fees: Reservations are accepted; phone (800) 627-9779; $12 to $19 per night. Group rates available. Open year-round.

Directions: From the junction of U.S. 101 and Highway 299 near Arcata, drive east on Highway 299 to Willow Creek, turn north (left) on Highway 96, and drive past Weitchpec to Orleans. This campground is at the west end of the town of Orleans on Highway 96.

Contact: Klamath Riverside RV Park and Campground, tel. (800) 627-9779 or (530) 627-3239, or fax (530) 627-3755; website: www.campgrounds.com/klamathriverside.

21 Sivshaneen

 7

This makes a good base camp for a Klamath River fishing trip from August to December. That is when the steelhead and the "half-pounders," actually juvenile steelhead in the 12- to 16-inch class, arrive in huge numbers in this stretch of river. In the summer, the river is warm, with a good put-in spot for rafters available nearby.

Location: On the Klamath River; map A1, grid j1.

Campsites, facilities: There are 25 RV sites, all with full hookups. Restrooms, showers, cable and modem hookups, a coin laundry, and sanitary disposal station are available. Leashed pets are permitted.

Reservations, fees: Reservations are accepted; $12 per night. Open Memorial Day through October.

Directions: From the junction of U.S. 101 and Highway 299 near Arcata, drive east on Highway 299 to Willow Creek. At Willow Creek, turn north (left) on Highway 96, drive past Weitchpec, and continue to Orleans. In Orleans, turn south (right) on Red Cap Road and drive 1.5 miles to the campground.

Contact: Sivshaneen, tel. (530) 627-3354.

22 Fish Lake

 8

This is a pretty little lake that provides good fishing for stocked rainbow trout from the season opener on Memorial Day weekend through July. The camp gets little pressure in other months. It's in the heart of Bigfoot country, with numerous Bigfoot sightings reported near Bluff Creek. No powerboats are permitted on the lake, but it's too small for that anyway, being better suited for a canoe, float tube, raft, or pram. The elevation is 1,800 feet. The presence here of Port Orford cedar root disease, spread by spores in the mud, forces closure in the months from October through April.

Location: In Six Rivers National Forest; map A1, grid j1.

Campsites, facilities: There are 10 sites for tents and 14 sites for tents or RVs up to 35 feet long. Picnic tables and fire grills are provided. Drinking water, vault toilets, and a camp host are available. Leashed pets are permitted.

Reservations, fees: No reservations; $9 per night. Open May through September, weather permitting.

Directions: From Interstate 5 in Redding, turn west on Highway 299 and drive to Willow Creek. At Willow Creek, turn north on Highway 96 and drive to Weitchpec, continuing seven miles north on Highway 96 to Fish Lake Road. Turn left on Fish Lake Road and drive five miles (stay to the right at the Y) to Fish Lake.
Contact: Six Rivers National Forest, Orleans Ranger District, tel. (530) 627-3291 or fax (530) 627-3401.

23 Aikens Creek West

      7

The Klamath River is warm and green here in summer, and this camp provides an ideal put-in spot for a day of easy rafting, especially for newcomers in inflatable kayaks. The camp is set at 340 feet in elevation along the Klamath. From here to Weitchpec is an easy paddle, with the takeout on the right side of the river just beyond Muddy Creek. The river is set in a beautiful canyon with lots of birds and enters the Hoopa Valley Indian Reservation. The steelhead fishing can be good in this area from August through mid-November, and best downstream at Johnson's Bar from a boat, boondogging Glo Bugs. Highway 96 is a scenic but slow cruise. Note: The camp may be closed periodically due to flooding. In winter and spring, check status before planning your trip.
Location: On the Klamath River in Six Rivers National Forest; map A1, grid j1.
Campsites, facilities: There are dispersed sites for tents or RVs. Picnic tables and fire grills are provided. Vault toilets are available. No drinking water is available. All garbage must be packed out. Leashed pets are permitted.
Reservations, fees: No reservations; $7 per night. Open year-round.
Directions: From the junction of U.S. 101 and Highway 299 near Arcata, turn east on Highway 299 and drive to Willow Creek. In Willow Creek, turn north on Highway 96 and drive to

Weitchpec, continuing on Highway 96 for five miles to the campground on the right side of the road.
Contact: Six Rivers National Forest, Orleans Ranger District, tel. (530) 627-3291 or fax (530) 627-3401.

24 E-Ne-Nuck

     7

The campground gets its name from a Karuk Indian chief who lived in the area in the late 1800s. It's a popular spot for anglers; Bluff Creek and the Klamath are within walking distance and Fish Lake is eight miles to the west. Bluff Creek is the legendary site where the Bigfoot film of the 1960s was shot. Whether the film is genuine or a phony, it still has put Bluff Creek on the map.
Location: In Six Rivers National Forest; map A1, grid j1.
Campsites, facilities: There are 11 campsites for tents or RVs up to 22 feet long. Picnic tables and cast iron fire box stoves are provided. Drinking water, vault toilets, and a camp host are available. Leashed pets are permitted.
Reservations, fees: No reservations; $9 per night, $5 per additional vehicle. Open July through November 5.
Directions: From the junction of U.S. 101 and Highway 299 near Arcata, turn east on Highway 299 and drive to Willow Creek. In Willow Creek, turn north on Highway 96 and drive to Weitchpec, continuing on Highway 96 for about five miles to the campground. E-Ne-Nuck is just beyond Aikens Creek West Campground.
Contact: Six Rivers National Forest, Orleans Ranger District, tel. (530) 627-3291 or fax (530) 627-3401.

25 Idlewild

     8

This is one of the prettiest drive-to camps in the region, set near the confluence of the Salmon River and its south fork, a beautiful, cold, clear stream and a major tributary to the

Klamath River. Most campers are using the camp for its nearby trailhead (two miles north on a dirt Forest Service road out of camp). The hike here is routed to the north, climbing alongside the Salmon River for miles into the Marble Mountain Wilderness (wilderness permits are required). It's a rugged 10-mile, all-day climb to Lake of the Island with several other lakes (highlighted by Hancock Lake) to the nearby west, accessible on weeklong trips.

Location: On the North Fork of the Salmon River in Klamath National Forest; map A1, grid j7.

Campsites, facilities: There are 23 sites, including two group sites, for tents or RVs up to 22 feet long. Picnic tables and fire grills are provided. Drinking water and vault toilets are available. Leashed pets are permitted.

Reservations, fees: No reservations; $6 per night. Open June through October.

Directions: From Redding, drive north on Interstate 5 to Yreka. In Yreka, turn southwest on Highway 3 and drive to Etna. In Etna, turn west on Etna-Somes Bar Road (Main Street in town) and drive about 16 miles to the campground on the right side of the road. Note: A shorter but more complete route on Gazelle-Callahan Road, north of Weed, is also available.

Contact: Klamath National Forest, Salmon River Ranger District, tel. (530) 468-5351 or fax (530) 468-1290.

TRAIL BUDDIES

MAP A2

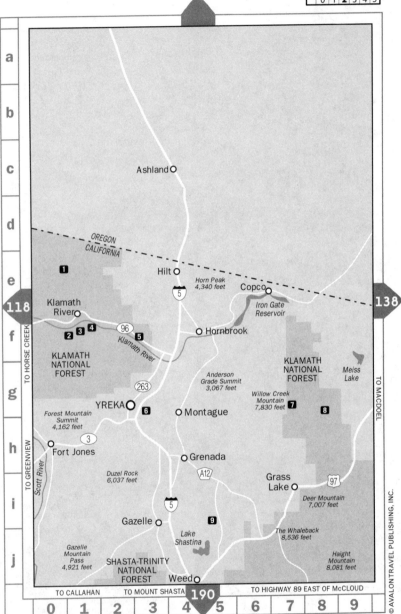

118

138

190

TO HORSE CREEK

TO GREENVIEW

TO MACDOEL

Ashland

OREGON
CALIFORNIA

1

Hilt

Horn Peak
4,340 feet

Copco

Iron Gate
Reservoir

Klamath
River

2 **3** **4**

96

5

Hornbrook

Klamath River

KLAMATH
NATIONAL
FOREST

KLAMATH
NATIONAL
FOREST

Meiss
Lake

263

Anderson
Grade Summit
3,067 feet

Willow Creek
Mountain
7,830 feet

7

8

YREKA

6

Montague

Forest Mountain
Summit
4,162 feet

Scott River

3

Fort Jones

Grenada

A12

Grass
Lake

97

Duzel Rock
6,037 feet

Deer Mountain
7,007 feet

5

Gazelle

9

The Whaleback
8,536 feet

Lake
Shastina

Gazelle
Mountain
Pass
4,921 feet

Haight
Mountain
8,081 feet

SHASTA-TRINITY
NATIONAL
FOREST

Weed

TO CALLAHAN   TO MOUNT SHASTA   TO HIGHWAY 89 EAST OF McCLOUD

© AVALONTRAVEL PUBLISHING, INC.

CHAPTER A2

1 Beaver Creek

 8

This camp is set along Beaver Creek, a feeder stream to the nearby Klamath River, with two small creeks entering Beaver Creek on the far side of the river near the campground. It is quiet and pretty. There are several historic mining sites in the area; you'll need a map of Klamath National Forest (available for $4 at the district office) in order to find them. In the fall, this campground is usually taken by deer hunters.

Location: In Klamath National Forest; map A2, grid e0.

Campsites, facilities: There are eight sites for tents or small RVs. Picnic tables and fire grills are provided. Drinking water and vault toilets are available. Garbage must be packed out. Leashed pets are permitted.

Reservations, fees: No reservations; no fee. Open year-round.

Directions: From Redding, drive north on Interstate 5 to Highway 96. Turn west on High-way 96 and drive approximately 15 miles (if you reach the town of Klamath River, you have gone a half mile too far) to Beaver Creek Road. Turn right on Beaver Creek Road/Forest Road 11 and drive four miles to the campground.

Contact: Klamath National Forest, Scott River Ranger District, tel. (530) 468-5351 or fax (530) 468-1290.

2 The Oaks RV Park

 7

Fishing? Rafting? Canoeing? Hiking? This camp provides a good headquarters for all of these adventures. This stretch of the Klamath is ideal for boating, with summer flows warm and often at perfect levels for rafting and canoeing. Fishing is best in the fall, when salmon, and later steelhead, migrate through the area.

Location: On the Klamath River; map A2, grid f1.

Campsites, facilities: There are 10 sites for tents and 12 sites for RVs. Picnic tables and fire grills are provided. Drinking water, restrooms, hot showers, snack bar, and coin laundry are available. A restaurant and lounge are available within walking distance. Groceries can be obtained within three miles in the town of Klamath River. A golf course is nearby. Leashed pets are permitted.

Reservations, fees: Reservations are accepted; $10 to $12 per night. Open year-round.

Directions: From Redding, drive north on Interstate 5 to Highway 96. Turn west on Highway 96 and drive approximately 20 miles to the town of Klamath River. Look for the park entrance across from the town post office.

Contact: The Oaks RV Park, tel. (530) 465-2323 or fax (530) 465-2312.

3 Quigley's General Store and Trailer Park

      7

This year-round, privately operated park is set along the Klamath River. Many of the parking sites have clear views of the river, as well as good mountain views. Quigley's General Store is well stocked for such a remote little shop, and you can usually get reliable fishing information here, too.

Location: On the Klamath River; map A2, grid f1.

Campsites, facilities: There are 20 RV sites with full hookups. Picnic tables are provided. Restrooms, hot showers, a store, and coin laundry are available. Some facilities are wheelchair accessible. Leashed pets are permitted.

Reservations, fees: Reservations are accepted; $15 per night. For more than two people, $1 per person per night. Major credit cards accepted. Open year-round.

Directions: From Redding, drive north on Interstate 5 to Highway 96. Turn west on Highway 96 and drive approximately 15 miles to the town of Klamath River. Look for the campground entrance on the left.

Contact: Quigley's General Store and Trailer Park, tel. (530) 465-2224 or fax (530) 465-2422.

4 Klamath River Trailer Park

       8

This privately operated RV park is in one of the prettiest areas of the Klamath River. There's a good piece of river here for summer rafting or fall steelhead fishing. For rafting, the river is sprinkled with Class II and III rapids, ideal for inflatable kayaks, and several commercial rafting companies operate in this area. Every site has a view of the river and the beautiful Siskiyou Mountains.

Location: On the Klamath River; map A2, grid f1.

Campsites, facilities: There are 17 RV sites with full hookups. Restrooms, hot showers, and a coin laundry are available. Some facilities are wheelchair accessible. Leashed pets are permitted.

Reservations, fees: Reservations are accepted; $10 per night. For more than two people, $1 extra per person per night. Open year-round.

Directions: From Redding, drive north on Interstate 5 to Highway 96. Turn west on Highway 96 and drive approximately 15 miles to the campground entrance on the left (if you reach the town of Klamath River, you have gone a mile too far).

Contact: Klamath River Trailer Park, tel. (530) 465-2324.

5 Tree of Heaven

    7

This outstanding riverside campground provides excellent access to the Klamath River for fishing, rafting, and hiking. The best deal is to put in your raft, canoe, or drift boat upstream at the ramp below Iron Gate Reservoir, then make the all-day run down to the takeout at Tree of Heaven. This section of river is an easy paddle and also provides excellent steelhead fishing in the winter. There is also a trail out of the camp that is routed along the river and probes through vegetation, ending at a fair fishing spot (a better spot is nearby at the mouth of the Shasta River). On the drive in from the highway, you can watch the landscape turn from high chaparral to forest.

Location: In Klamath National Forest; map A2, grid f3.

Campsites, facilities: There are 10 tent sites and 11 sites for moderate-sized RVs. Picnic tables and fire grills are provided. Drinking water and vault toilets are available. A spot for put-in and take-out for rafts and drift boats is available. Some facilities are wheelchair accessible. Leashed pets are permitted.

Reservations, fees: For reservations, phone tel. (530) 468-5351, $10 per night. Open year-round.

Directions: From Redding, drive north on Interstate 5 to Highway 96. Turn west on Highway 96 and drive seven miles to the campground entrance on the left side of the road.

Contact: Klamath National Forest, Scott River Ranger District, tel. (530) 468-5351 or fax (530) 468-1290.

6 Waiiaka Trailer Haven

    4

If it's late, you're tired, and you're hunting for a spot to hunker down for the night, this is your only bet in the immediate Yreka vicinity. A string of fast-food restaurants is available nearby on the west side of the highway. The campground is not exactly paradise, but the view of Mount Shasta to the south is beautiful. The best side trip is heading north on Interstate 5 to the Klamath River; an exit with river access is available at the Interstate 5 bridge.

Location: Near Yreka; map A2, grid g3.

Campsites, facilities: There are 60 RV sites with full hookups. Restrooms, showers, playground, and a recreation room are provided. A coin laundry and propane gas are available. Leashed pets are permitted.

Reservations, fees: Reservations are accepted; $22 per night. Major credit cards accepted. Open year-round.

Directions: From Redding, drive north on Interstate 5 to Yreka, take the Fort Jones exit, and drive one block east to Fairlane Road. At Fairlane Road, turn right (north) and drive to Sharps Road. At Sharps Road, bear left (east) and drive one block to the RV park entrance (just past the fairgrounds parking lot).

Contact: Waiiaka Trailer Heaven, tel. (530) 842-4500.

7 Martins Dairy

     8

This camp is set at 6,000 feet, where the deer get big and the country seems wide open. A large meadow is nearby, directly across the road from this remote camp, with fantastic wildflower displays in late spring. This is one of the prettiest camps around in the fall, with dramatic color from aspens and other hardwoods. It also makes a good base camp for hunters in the fall. Before heading into the surrounding backcountry, obtain a map of Klamath National Forest, available for $6 at the Goosenest Ranger Station on Highway 97, on your way in to camp.

Location: On the Little Shasta River in Klamath National Forest; map A2, grid g7.

Campsites, facilities: There are eight sites for tents or small RVs and a horse camp site. Picnic tables and fire grills are provided. Drinking water and wheelchair-accessible vault toilets are available. Leashed pets are permitted.

Reservations, fees: No reservations; $8 per night. Open Memorial Day weekend through mid-October, weather permitting.

Directions: From Redding, drive north on Interstate 5 to Weed. In Weed, turn north on U.S. 97 and drive to Grass Lake. Continue about seven miles to Forest Road 70/46N10 (if you reach Hebron Summit, you have driven about a mile too far). Turn left, drive about 10 miles to a Y, take the left fork, and drive three miles (including a very sharp right turn) to the campground on the right side of the road. A map of Klamath National Forest is advised.

Contact: Klamath National Forest, Goosenest Ranger District, tel. (530) 398-4391 or fax (530) 398-4599.

8 Juanita Lake

   7

Small and relatively unknown, this camp is set along the shore of Juanita Lake at 5,100 feet. It is stocked with rainbow trout, brown trout, bass, and catfish, but a problem with golden shiners has cut into the lake's fishing productivity. It's a small lake and forested, set near the Butte Valley Wildlife Area in the plateau country just five miles to the northeast. The latter provides an opportunity to see waterfowl and, in the winter, bald eagles. Campers will discover a network of Forest Service roads in the area, providing an opportunity for mountain biking. There is also a paved trail around the lake that is wheelchair accessible and spans approximately 1.25 miles.

Location: In Klamath National Forest; map A2, grid g8.

Campsites, facilities: There are 12 tent sites, 11 sites for RVs up to 32 feet, and a group site that can accommodate 50 people. Picnic tables and fire grills are provided. Drinking water and vault toilets are available. Boating is allowed, but no motorboats are permitted on the lake. Many facilities are wheelchair accessible. Leashed pets are permitted.

Reservations, fees: No reservations for family sites, $10 per night; group site is $30 per night, reservations required at tel. (530) 398-4391. Open May through October.

Directions: From Redding, drive north on Interstate 5 to Weed. In Weed, turn north on U.S. 97 and drive approximately 37 miles. Turn left on Ball Mountain Road and drive 2.5 miles, veer right at the fork, and continue to the campground entrance at the lake.

Contact: Klamath National Forest, Goosenest Ranger District, tel. (530) 398-4391 or fax (530) 398-4599.

9 Lake Shastina

 7

Lake Shastina is set at the northern foot of Mount Shasta. It offers spectacular views, good swimming on hot summer days, and fishing for catfish and bass in the spring and summer, an occasional opportunity for crappie, and good fishing for trout when the wind is down in late winter and spring. One reason the views of Mount Shasta are so good is that this is largely high sagebrush country with few trees. As such, it can get very dusty, windy, and in the winter, nasty cold. When the lake is full and the weather is good, there are few complaints. This is one of the few lakes in Northern California that has property with lakeside housing, consisting of several small developments. Alas, the water slide, once offering great fun for kids, is now off-limits to the public.

Location: Near Klamath National Forest and Weed; map A2, grid i5.

Campsites, facilities: There is a small primitive area designated for camping. There is no drinking water. A chemical toilet is available and a boat launch is available nearby. Garbage must be packed out. Supplies can be obtained five miles away in Weed. Leashed pets are permitted.

Reservations, fees: No reservations; no fee. Open May through September.

Directions: From Redding, drive north on Interstate 5 to Weed. In Weed, turn north on U.S. 97 and drive about five miles to Big Springs Road. Turn left (west) on Big Springs Road and drive about one mile to Jackson Ranch Road. Turn left (west) on Jackson Ranch Road and drive a half mile to Emerald Isle Road (watch for the signed turnoff). Turn right and drive two miles to the campground.

Contact: Siskiyou County Public Works, tel. (530) 842-8250.

GARY R. ZAHM

DUCKS RISING

MAP A3

TO BEND, OR

a

b

c

97

140

Klamath
Falls

d

140

Midland

e

LOWER
KLAMATH
NATIONAL
WILDLIFE
REFUGE

Worden

39

132

144

Dorris

Merrill

f

97

Mahogany
Mountain
6,255 feet

Lower
Klamath
Lake

161

OREGON

CALIFORNIA

Tulelake

g

TO WEED

Macdoel

Tule
Lake

1

TULE LAKE
NATIONAL
WILDLIFE
REFUGE

CLEAR LAKE
NATIONAL
WILDLIFE
REFUGE

Mount Hebron

Newell

h

2

Clear
Lake
Reservoir

LAVA BEDS
NATIONAL
MONUMENT

i

TO U.S. 97 EAST OF WEED

KLAMATH
NATIONAL
FOREST

MODOC
NATIONAL
FOREST

139

3

TO GOOSE LAKE

Tennant

j

4-7

Medicine
Lake

9 **8**

TO BARTLE

222

TO CANBY   TO HIGHWAY 199

0   1   2   3   4   5   6   7   8   9

© AVALON TRAVEL PUBLISHING, INC.

CHAPTER A3

1 Shady Lane Trailer Park

  3

There isn't much shade in Modoc County, but this private park manages to provide some. Good side trips include the Tule Lake Wildlife Refuge, one of the best places in America (during the winter) to see bald eagles and a good bet year-round for bird-watching. Nearby is Lava Beds National Monument, whose northern edge is an excellent place to see deer in late fall and early winter. There is also a network of lava tubes and ice caves, making for a great getaway adventure. The Tulelake unit of the Klamath National Wildlife Refuge is only four miles away, and the Lower Klamath Lake unit is eight miles away; both provide excellent waterfowl hunting in early fall.

Location: In Tulelake; map A3, grid g5.

Campsites, facilities: There are 60 RV sites with full hookups, some with cable hookups. Restrooms, showers, patios, and a coin laundry are available. Leashed pets are permitted.

Reservations, fees: Reservations are accepted; $15 per night. Open year-round.

Directions: From Redding, turn east on Highway 299 and drive to the junction with Highway 139 at Canby. At Highway 139 turn left (north) and drive 52 miles to Tulelake. At Tulelake take the south exit of East West Road, drive to Modoc Avenue, turn left, and drive to the trailer park.

Contact: Shady Lane Trailer Park, 795 Modoc Avenue, P.O. Box 297, Tulelake, CA 96134; tel. (530) 667-2617.

2 Shafter

      4

This is a little-used camp with trout fishing at nearby Butte Creek for small rainbows, primarily six- to eight-inchers. Little Orr Lake, about a 10-minute drive away on the southwest flank of Orr Mountain, provides fishing for bass and larger rainbow trout, 10- to 12-inchers, as well as a sprinkling of smaller brook trout. A boat ramp and restroom with vault toilets were opened in 2000. This camp is primitive and not well known, set in a juniper- and sage-filled landscape. A great side trip is to the nearby Orr Mountain Lookout, where there are spectacular views of Mount Shasta. A Forest Service touch that is like gold in the summer is that the road adjacent to the campground is paved, which keeps the dust down.

Location: In Klamath National Forest; map A3, grid h0.

Campsites, facilities: There are 14 sites for tents or small RVs. Picnic tables and fire grills are provided. Drinking water, a restroom, vault toilets, and boat ramp are available. Pack out all garbage. Leashed pets are permitted.

Reservations, fees: No reservations; $6 per night. Open year-round. Services available in summer only.

Directions: From Redding, drive north on Interstate 5 to Weed, turn north on Highway 97, and drive 40 miles to Ball Mountain Road. At Ball Mountain Road, turn right and drive 2.5 miles to a T with Old State Highway 97. Turn right and drive 4.25 miles (crossing railroad tracks) to the campground on the right side of the road.

Contact: Klamath National Forest, Goosenest Ranger District, tel. (530) 398-4391 or fax (530) 398-4599.

3 Indian Well

  9

This is a one-in-a-million spot with more than 400 lava tube caves, Schonchin Butte (a cinder cone with a hiking trail), Mammoth Crater, Native American pictographs, battlefields and campsites from the Modoc Indian War, and wildlife overlooks of Tule Lake. After winter's first snow, this is one of the best places in the west to photograph deer. Nearby is Klamath National Wildlife Refuge, the largest bald eagle wintering area in the lower 48. If you are new to the outdoors, an interpretive center is available to explain it all to you.

Location: In Lava Beds National Monument; map A3, grid i5.

Campsites, facilities: There are 42 sites for tents or RVs up to 30 feet long. Picnic tables, fire rings, and cooking grills are provided. From Memorial Day to Labor Day, water and flush toilets are available. Drinking water and flush toilets are always available in the B Loop and at the visitor center. Note that during the off-season in the A Loop, only pit toilets are available. Some facilities are wheelchair accessible. The town of Tulelake (30 miles north) is the nearest supply station. Leashed pets are permitted.

Reservations, fees: No reservations; $10 per night, $5 per vehicle park entrance fee. Open year-round.

Directions: From Redding, drive north on Interstate 5 to Central Weed. Take that exit, turn right and continue for one mile to U.S. 97. Drive north on U.S. 97 for 54 miles to Highway 161. Turn east on Highway 161 and drive 20 miles to Hill Road. Turn right (south) and drive 18 miles to the visitor center and the campground entrance on the left. Turn left and drive a quarter mile to the campground.

Contact: Lava Beds National Monument, tel. (530) 667-2282 or fax (530) 667-2737.

4 Medicine

 7

Lakeside campsites tucked away in conifers make this camp a winner. Medicine Lake was formed in the crater of an old volcano and is surrounded by lodgepole pine and fir trees. The lake is stocked with rainbow and brook trout in the summer, gets quite cold in the fall, and freezes over in winter. Many side trips are possible, including nearby Blanche Lake and Ice Caves (both signed and off the access road) and Lava Beds National Monument just 15 miles north. At 6,700 feet, temperatures can turn cold in summer and the season is short.

Location: On Medicine Lake in Modoc National Forest; map A3, grid j3.

Campsites, facilities: There are 22 sites for tents or RVs up to 30 feet long. Picnic tables and fire grills are provided. Drinking water and vault toilets are available. A boat ramp is available nearby. A small restaurant for breakfast and lunch and with a bar is available in Bartle, otherwise no supplies are available within an hour's drive. Leashed pets are permitted.

Reservations, fees: No reservations; $7 per vehicle per night. Open late May through early October, weather permitting.

Directions: From Redding, drive north on Interstate 5 past Dunsmuir to Highway 89. Go east on Highway 89 and drive 28 miles to Bartle. Just past Bartle, turn left on Forest Road 49 and drive 31 miles (it becomes Medicine Lake Road) to the lake. From Bartle, the route is signed.

Contact: Modoc National Forest, Doublehead Ranger District, tel. (530) 667-2246 or fax (530) 667-8609.

5 A. H. Hogue

 7

This camp was created in 1990 when the original Medicine Lake Campground was divided in half. For more information, see the entry for Medicine.

Location: On Medicine Lake in Modoc National Forest; map A3, grid j3.

Campsites, facilities: There are 24 sites for tents or RVs up to 30 feet long. Picnic tables and fire grills are provided. Drinking water and vault toilets are available. A boat ramp is available nearby. Leashed pets are permitted. A small restaurant for breakfast and lunch and with a bar is available in Bartle, otherwise no supplies are available within an hour's drive.

Reservations, fees: No reservations; $7 per vehicle per night. Open late May through early October, weather permitting.

Directions: From Redding, drive north on Interstate 5 past Dunsmuir to Highway 89. Turn east on Highway 89 and drive 28 miles to Bartle. Just past Bartle, turn left on Forest Road 49 and drive 31 miles (it becomes Medicine Lake Road) to the lake. From Bartle, the route is signed.

Contact: Modoc National Forest, Doublehead Ranger District, tel. (530) 667-2246 or fax (530) 667-8609.

6 Hemlock

 7

This is one in a series of campgrounds on Medicine Lake operated by the Forest Service. A special attraction at Hemlock is the natural sand beach. For more information, see the entry for Medicine Camp.

Location: On Medicine Lake in Modoc National Forest; map A3, grid j3.

Campsites, facilities: There are 19 sites for tents or RVs up to 22 feet long. Picnic taables and fire grills are provided. Drinking water and vault toilets are available. A boat ramp is available nearby. A small restaurant for breakfast and lunch and with a bar is available in Bartle, otherwise no supplies are available within an hour's drive.

Reservations, fees: No reservations; $7 per vehicle per night. Open late May through early October, weather permitting.

Directions: From Redding, drive north on Interstate 5 past Dunsmuir to Highway 89. Turn east on Highway 89 and drive 28 miles to Bartle. Just past Bartle, turn left on Forest Road 49 and drive 31 miles (it becomes Medicine Lake Road) to the lake. From Bartle, the route is signed.

Contact: Modoc National Forest, Doublehead Ranger District, tel. (530) 667-2246 of fax (530) 667-8609.

7 Headquarters

 7

This is one of four campgrounds set beside Medicine Lake. For more information, see the entry for Medicine.

Location: On Medicine Lake in Modoc National Forest; map A3, grid j3.

Campsites, facilities: There are nine sites for tents and RVs up to 16 feet long. Picnic tables and fire grills are provided. Drinking water and vault toilets are available. A boat ramp is available nearby. A small restaurant for breakfast and lunch and with a bar is available in Bartle, otherwise no supplies are available within an hour's drive.

Reservations, fees: No reservations; $7 per vehicle per night. Open late May through early October, weather permitting.

Directions: From Redding, drive north on Interstate 5 past Dunsmuir to Highway 89. Go east on Highway 89 and drive 28 miles to Bartle. Just past Bartle, turn left on Forest Road 49 and drive 31 miles (it becomes Medicine Lake Road) to the lake. From Bartle, the route is signed.

Contact: Modoc National Forest, Doublehead Ranger District, tel. (530) 667-2246 or fax (530) 667-8609.

8 Bullseye Lake

 7

This tiny lake gets overlooked every year, mainly because of its proximity to nearby Medicine Lake. Bullseye Lake is shallow, but because snow keeps it locked up until late May or early June, the water stays plenty cold for small trout through July. It is stocked with just 750 six- to eight-inch rainbow trout, not much to crow about—or to catch, for that matter. Nearby are some ice caves, created by ancient volcanic action, which are fun to poke around in and explore. The place is small, quiet, and pretty, but most of all, small. This camp is set at an elevation of 6,500 feet.

Location: Near Medicine Lake in Modoc National Forest; map A3, grid j3.

Campsites, facilities: There are a few primitive campsites. A vault toilet is available. No drinking water or other facilities are available. Garbage must be packed out. Supplies are available in McCloud. A small restaurant for breakfast and lunch and with a bar is available in Bartle, otherwise no supplies are available within an hour's drive. Leashed pets are permitted.

Reservations, fees: No reservations; no fee. Open late May through early October, weather permitting.

Directions: From Redding, drive north on Interstate 5 past Dunsmuir to Highway 89. Go east on Highway 89 and drive 28 miles to Bartle. Just past Bartle, turn left on Forest Road 49 and drive 30 miles (if you reach Medicine Lake, you have gone about two miles too far). Turn right at the Bullseye Lake access road and drive a short distance to the lake.

Contact: Modoc National Forest, Doublehead Ranger District, tel. (530) 667-2246 or fax (530) 667-8609.

9 Payne Springs

   8

This camp is set by a small spring in a very pretty riparian area. It's small, but it is special.

Location: Near Medicine Lake in Modoc National Forest; map A3, grid j3.

Campsites, facilities: There are six dispersed and primitive campsites for tents or RVs up to 20 feet long. A vault toilet is available. No drinking water is available. A small restaurant for breakfast and lunch and with a bar is available in Bartle, otherwise no supplies are available within an hour's drive. Supplies are available in McCloud. Leashed pets are permitted.

Reservations, fees: No reservation; no fee. Open late May through early October, weather permitting.

Directions: From Redding, on Interstate 5 drive past Dunsmuir to Highway 89. Turn east on Highway 89 and drive 28 miles. Just past Bartle, turn left on Forest Road 49 and drive 30 miles. A quarter mile past the Bullseye Lake access road, turn left onto the Payne Springs access road. (If you reach Medicine Lake, you have gone too far.)

Contact: Modoc National Forest, Doublehead Ranger District, tel. (530) 667-2246 or fax (530) 667-8609.

GARY R. ZAHM

SANDHILL CRANES
IN FLIGHT

MAP A4

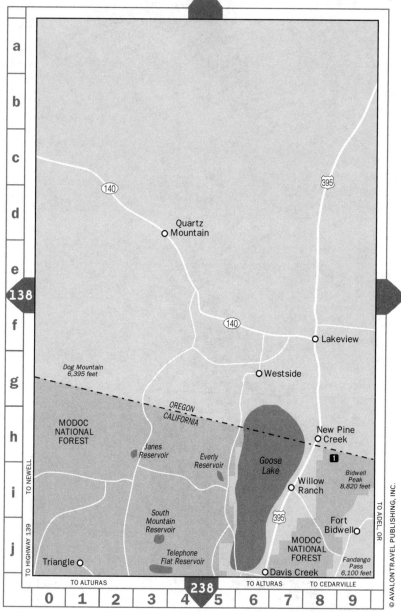

140

395

Quartz
Mountain

138

140

Lakeview

Dog Mountain
6,395 feet

Westside

OREGON
CALIFORNIA

MODOC
NATIONAL
FOREST

Janes
Reservoir

Everly
Reservoir

New Pine
Creek

Goose
Lake

Bidwell
Peak
8,820 feet

1

Willow
Ranch

TO NEWELL

TO ADEL, OR

South
Mountain
Reservoir

395

Fort
Bidwell

TO HIGHWAY 139

MODOC
NATIONAL
FOREST

Telephone
Flat Reservoir

Fandango
Pass
6,100 feet

Triangle

Davis Creek

TO ALTURAS

238

TO ALTURAS

TO CEDARVILLE

0 1 2 3 4 5 6 7 8 9

© AVALON TRAVEL PUBLISHING, INC.

CHAPTER A4

❶ Cave Lake

 8

A pair of lakes can be discovered out here in the middle of nowhere, with Cave Lake on one end and Lily Lake on the other. Together they make a nice set, very quiet, extremely remote, with good fishing for rainbow trout and brook trout. Of the two lakes, it is nearby Lily Lake that is prettier and provides the better fishing. Cave Lake is set at 6,600 feet. By camping here, you become a member of the 5 Percent Club; that is, the 5 percent of campers who know of secret, isolated little spots such as this one.

Location: In Modoc National Forest; map A4, grid h8.

Campsites, facilities: There are six sites for tents or RVs up to 15 feet long; trailers are not advised due to the steep access road. Picnic tables and fire grills are provided. Drinking water and vault toilets are available. Garbage must be packed out. A boat ramp is available for small boats, but all motors are prohibited on the lake, including electric. Supplies are available in New Pine Creek, Fort Bidwell, and Davis Creek. Leashed pets are permitted.

Reservations, fees: No reservations; no fee. Open July through September.

Directions: From Redding, turn east on Highway 299 and drive 146 miles to Alturas. In Alturas, turn north on U.S. 395 and drive 40 miles to Forest Road 2 (if you reach the town of New Pine Creek on the Oregon/California border, you have driven a mile too far). Turn right on Forest Road 2 (a steep dirt road—trailers are not recommended) and drive six miles to the campground entrance on the left side of the road, just beyond the Lily Lake picnic area.

Contact: Modoc National Forest, Warner Mountain Ranger; tel. (530) 279-6116 or fax (530) 279-8309.

CHAPTER BO

SHELTER IN
THE REDWOODS

MAP BO

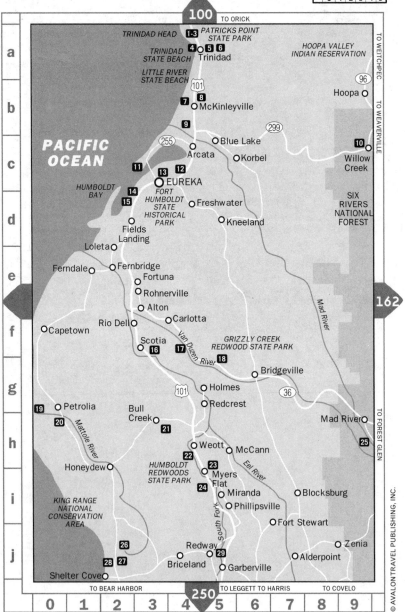

100 TO ORICK

TRINIDAD HEAD **1-3** PATRICKS POINT STATE PARK

HOOPA VALLEY INDIAN RESERVATION

TO WEITCHPEC

a

4 **5** **6**
TRINIDAD
STATE BEACH
Trinidad

LITTLE RIVER
STATE BEACH
101

96

Hoopa

b

7 **8**
McKinleyville

9

299

TO WEAVERVILLE

PACIFIC
OCEAN

255

Blue Lake

10

c

11

Arcata
Korbel

Willow
Creek

13 **12**
EUREKA

HUMBOLDT
BAY

14
15
FORT
HUMBOLDT
STATE
HISTORICAL
PARK
Freshwater

SIX
RIVERS
NATIONAL
FOREST

d

Kneeland

Fields
Landing

Loleta

e

Ferndale
Fernbridge
Fortuna

Rohnerville

Mad River

162

Rio Dell
Alton

Carlotta

f

Capetown

Scotia
16 **17**
Van Duzen River
18

GRIZZLY CREEK
REDWOOD STATE PARK

g

101
Holmes
Redcrest

36

Bridgeville

19
Petrolia

TO FOREST GLEN

20

Bull
Creek

21

Mad River

25

h

Mattole River

Weott
22
McCann

Eel River

Honeydew

HUMBOLDT
REDWOODS
STATE PARK

23
Myers
Flat
24

Miranda

Blocksburg

i

KING RANGE
NATIONAL
CONSERVATION
AREA

South Fork

Phillipsville

Fort Stewart

Zenia

26

Redway
29

j

28 **27**
Shelter Cove

Briceland

Garberville

Alderpoint

© AVALON TRAVEL PUBLISHING, INC.

TO BEAR HARBOR **250** TO LEGGETT TO HARRIS TO COVELO

| 0 | 1 | 2 | 3 | 4 | 5 | 6 | 7 | 8 | 9 |

CHAPTER B0

1 Sounds of the Sea

     6

The Trinidad area, about 20 miles north of Eureka, is one of the great places on this planet. Nearby Patricks Point State Park is one of the highlights, with a Sitka spruce forest, beautiful coastal lookouts, a great easy hike on the Rim Trail, and access to several secluded beaches. To the nearby south at Trinidad Head is a small harbor and dock, with deep-sea and salmon fishing trips available. A breezy beach is to the immediate north of the Seascape Restaurant. A bonus at this privately operated RV park is good berry picking.

Location: In Trinidad; map B0, grid a4.

Campsites, facilities: There are 52 RV sites with full hookups. Picnic tables and fire rings are provided. Restrooms, showers, a sanitary disposal station, a coin laundry, grocery store, gift shop, cable TV, and ice are available. Leashed pets are permitted.

Reservations, fees: Reservations are accepted; $21 per night. Major credit cards accepted. Open year-round.

Directions: From Eureka, drive north on U.S. 101 for 28 miles to Trinidad. In Trinidad, continue north on U.S. 101 for five miles to the Patricks Point exit. Take the Patricks Point exit, turn left, and drive a half mile to the campground.

Contact: Sounds of the Sea, tel. (707) 677-3271; website: www.northcoast.com/~gupie.

2 Sylvan Harbor RV Park and Cabins

    6

This is one of several privately operated parks in the Trinidad area, offering a choice of shaded or open sites near the ocean. For more information about recreation options nearby, see the entry for Sounds of the Sea.

Location: In Trinidad; map B0, grid a4.

Campsites, facilities: There are 73 RV sites with full hookups and three cabins for rent. Restrooms, showers, a sanitary disposal station, a coin laundry, and LP gas are available. Leashed pets are permitted.

Reservations, fees: No reservations except for cabins; $12 to $16 per night for RV sites, $2 per person for more than two people; call for cabin fees. Open year-round.

Directions: From Eureka, drive north on U.S. 101 for 28 miles to Trinidad. Take the Trinidad exit, turn left at the stop sign, and drive a short distance under the freeway to Patricks Point Drive. Turn right and drive one mile to the campground.

Contact: Sylvan Harbor RV Park and Cabins, tel. or fax (707) 677-9988.

3 View Crest Campground

       8

View Crest Campground is one of the premium spots in Trinidad, with pretty cottages available as well as campsites for RVs and tents. A bonus here is the remarkable flights of swallows, many of which have nests at the cottages. Recreation options include deep-sea and salmon fishing at Trinidad Harbor to the nearby south, and outstanding easy hiking at Patricks Point State Park to the nearby north.

Location: In Trinidad; map B0, grid a4.

Campsites, facilities: There are 25 RV sites with full hookups, including nine drive-through sites, and a separate area for tents. Seven cottages are available. Picnic tables and fire rings are provided. Restrooms, showers, playground, a sanitary disposal station, cable TV

hookups, RV storage, a coin laundry, and wood are available. Leashed pets are permitted.

Reservations, fees: Reservations are accepted; $16 to $20 per night, $1 per person per night for more than two people. Cottages rent from $70 to $160 per night. Major credit cards accepted. Open year-round.

Directions: From Eureka, drive north on U.S. 101 for 28 miles to Trinidad. At the Trinidad exit, turn left at the stop sign on Seawood Drive and drive a short distance under the freeway to Patricks Point Drive. Turn right on Patricks Point Drive and drive two miles to the campground on the right.

Contact: View Crest Campground, tel. (707) 677-3393 or fax (707) 677-9363; website: www.viewcrestlodge.com.

4 Midway RV Park

     6

This is one of several privately developed campgrounds in Trinidad. In the summer, salmon fishing can be excellent just off Trinidad Head. In the fall, rockfishing is the way to go, and in winter, crabbing is tops. Patricks Point State Park provides a nearby side trip option to the north.

Location: In Trinidad; map B0, grid a4.

Campsites, facilities: There are 65 RV sites with full hookups and four sites for tents. Picnic tables are provided. Restrooms, showers, cable TV, club room, a playground, and RV storage are available. Some facilities are wheelchair accessible. Leashed pets are permitted.

Reservations, fees: Reservations are recommended in the summer; $16 to $21 per night, $3 per person per night for more than two people. Major credit cards accepted. Open year-round.

Directions: From Eureka, drive north on U.S. 101 for 28 miles to Trinidad. Take the Trinidad exit, turn left at the stop sign, and drive a short distance under the freeway to Patricks Point Drive. Turn right on Patricks Point Drive and drive a half mile to the campground.

Contact: Midway RV Park, tel. or fax (707) 677-3934; website: www.midwayrv@humboldt1.com.

5 Hidden Creek

      5

To tell you the truth, there really isn't much hidden about this RV park, but you might be hardpressed to find year-round Parker Creek. Regardless, it is still in a pretty location in Trinidad, with the Trinidad pier, adjacent harbor, restaurants, and beach all within a drive of just a minute or two. Some of California's best deep-sea fishing for salmon, lingcod, and rockfish is available on boats out of Trinidad Harbor, and there are annual lingcod and halibut derbies. Crab and albacore tuna are also caught here, and there's beachcombing for agates and driftwood on the beach to the immediate north.

Location: In Trinidad; map B0, grid a5.

Campsites, facilities: There are 56 RV sites (six drive-through) with full or partial hookups, and three sites for tents. Several group sites are also available. Picnic tables are provided. Patios, restrooms, showers, LP gas, and a sanitary disposal station are available. Leashed pets are permitted.

Reservations, fees: Reservations are recommended in the summer; $14 to $21 per night, $2 per person per night for more than two people. Open year-round.

Directions: From Eureka, drive north on U.S. 101 for 28 miles to Trinidad. Take the Trinidad exit to the stop sign. Turn right at Westhaven Drive and drive a short distance to the RV park at 199 North Westhaven.

Contact: Hidden Creek, tel. (707) 677-3775 or fax (707) 677-3886.

6 Emerald Forest

      5

This campground is set on 12 acres of redwoods, often dark and wet, with the ocean at Trinidad Head only about a five-minute drive away. Nice spot with nice folks.

Location

Campsite
tents or R
full or part
ins with kitc
barbecues a
free cable TV
ground are av
coin laundry,
fireplace (seats ... gas are also
available. Leash..u pets are permitted, except
in the tent sites.

Reservations, fees: Reservations are recommended in the summer; $18 to $25 per night, $2 per person per night for more than two people, $1 pet fee (dogs must be under 35 pounds); cabins $69 to $155 per night. Major credit cards accepted. Open year-round.

Directions: From Eureka, drive north on U.S. 101 for 28 miles to Trinidad. Take the Trinidad exit, turn left at the stop sign, and drive a short distance under the freeway to Patricks Point Drive. Turn right on Patricks Point Drive and drive about 0.9 mile north to the campground on the right side of the road.

Contact: Emerald Forest, tel. (707) 677-3554 or fax (707) 677-0963; website: campgrounds.com/emeraldforest.

7 Clam Beach County Park

    7

Here awaits a beach that seems to stretch on forever, one of the great places to bring a lover, dog, children, or, hey, all three. While the campsites are a bit exposed, making winds out of the north a problem in the spring, the direct beach access largely makes up for it. The park gets its name from the good clamming that is available, but you must come equipped with a clam gun or special clam shovel, and then be out when minus low tides arrive at daybreak. Most people just enjoy playing tag with the waves, taking long romantic walks, or throwing sticks for the dog.

...cilities: There are 50 sites for ...Vs. Picnic tables and fire rings are ...ed. Drinking water and vault toilets are ...ailable. Propane gas, grocery store, and a coin laundry are available in McKinleyville. Leashed pets are permitted.

Reservations, fees: No reservations; $8 per night. Open year-round.

Directions: From Eureka, drive north on U.S. 101 to McKinleyville. Just past McKinleyville, turn west at the sign for Clam Beach and drive two blocks to the campground, which is adjacent to Little River State Beach.

Contact: Clam Beach County Park, tel. (707) 445-7652.

8 Widow White Creek RV Park

 5

This privately operated park provides extremely easy access from the highway. Nearby recreation options include the Mad River, where there is a nice picnic site near the hatchery, productive steelhead fishing in the winter, and good perch fishing in the surf where the Mad River enters the ocean. Ocean fishing for salmon is nearby in the summer. Get this—nearby are the "world's largest totem poles." They'll tell you all about it.

Location: In McKinleyville; map B0, grid b4.

Campsites, facilities: There are 40 RV sites with full hookups and a separate area for tents. Picnic tables are provided. Restrooms, showers, playground, a sanitary disposal station, and a coin laundry are available. Some facilities are wheelchair accessible. Leashed pets are permitted.

Reservations, fees: Reservations are accepted; $12.50 to $18 per night. Open year-round.

Directions: From Eureka, drive north on U.S. 101 and continue for 4.5 miles past the junction with Highway 299 to the Murray Road exit. Take the exit, turn right (east) on Murray Road, and drive one-half block to the campground.

Contact: Widow White Creek RV Park, tel. (707) 839-1137; website: www.campgrounds.com/widowwhite.

9 Mad River Rapids RV Park

 7

This camp is near the farmlands on the outskirts of town, in a pastoral, quiet setting. There is a great bike ride nearby on a trail routed along the Mad River, and it is also excellent for taking a dog for a walk. Nearby Arcata is a unique town, a bit of the old and a bit of the new, and the Arcata Marsh at the north end of Humboldt Bay provides a scenic and easy bicycle trip, as well as an excellent destination for hiking, sight-seeing, and bird-watching.

Location: In Arcata; map B0, grid b4.

Campsites, facilities: There are 92 RV sites (40 drive-through) with full hookups. Picnic tables are provided. Fire grills are provided at two sites. Patios, restrooms, showers, a sanitary disposal station, recreation room, tennis courts, fitness room, playground, basketball courts, horseshoe pits, swimming pool, spa, cable TV, VCR rentals, grocery store, and coin laundry are available. Some facilities are wheelchair accessible. Leashed pets are permitted.

Reservations, fees: Reservations are accepted; $26 to $29 per night. Major credit cards accepted. Open year-round.

Directions: From the junction of U.S. 101 and Highway 299 in Arcata, drive a quarter mile north on U.S. 101 to the Guintoli Lane exit. At the exit, turn left (west) on Janes Road and drive two blocks west to the campground.

Contact: Mad River Rapids RV Park, tel. (800) 822-7776 or (707) 822-7275 or fax (707) 822-7286; website: www.madriverrv.com.

10 Boise Creek

 7

This camp features a quarter-mile-long trail down to Boise Creek and nearby access to the Trinity River. If you have ever wanted to see Bigfoot, you can do it while camping here because there's a giant wooden Bigfoot on display in nearby Willow Creek. After your Bigfoot experience, your best bet during summer is to head north on nearby Highway 96 (turn north in Willow Creek) to the campground at Tish Tang, where there is excellent river access, swimming, and rafting in the late summer's warm flows. The Trinity River also provides good salmon and steelhead fishing during fall and winter, respectively, with the best nearby access upriver along Highway 299 at Burnt Ranch. Note that fishing is prohibited in nearby Willow Creek.

Location: In Six Rivers National Forest; map B0, grid c9.

Campsites, facilities: There are several sites for bicyclists and hikers and 17 sites for tents or RVs up to 35 feet long. Picnic tables and fire grills are provided. Drinking water, vault toilets, and a camp host are available. A grocery store, gas station, restaurant, and propane gas are available nearby. Leashed pets are permitted.

Reservations, fees: No reservations; $10 per night, $4 for an extra vehicle. Open year-round, with limited services in winter.

Directions: From the intersection of U.S. 101 and Highway 299 near Arcata, drive 38 miles east on Highway 299 and look for the campground entrance on the left side of the road. If you reach the town of Willow Creek, you have gone 1.5 miles too far.

Contact: Six Rivers National Forest, Lower Trinity Ranger District, tel. (530) 629-2118 or fax (530) 629-2102.

11 Samoa Boat Launch County Park

 7

The nearby vicinity of the boat ramp, with access to Humboldt Bay and the Pacific Ocean, makes this a star attraction for campers towing their fishing boats. At the park you get good beachcombing and clamming at low tides and a chance to see a huge variety of seabirds, highlighted by egrets and herons. There's a reason: directly across the bay is the Humboldt Bay National Wildlife Refuge. This park is set near the famed all-you-can-eat, logger-style Samoa Cookhouse.

Location: On Humboldt Bay; map B0, grid c3.

Campsites, facilities: There are 10 tent sites and 40 RV sites. Picnic tables and fire grills are provided. Drinking water and flush toilets are available. A boat ramp, grocery store, LP gas, and a coin laundry are available in Eureka (about five miles away). Leashed pets are permitted.

Reservations, fees: No reservations; $10 per night, $1 pet fee. Open year-round.

Directions: From U.S. 101 in Eureka, turn west on Highway 255 and drive two miles until it dead-ends at New Navy Base Road. At New Navy Base Road, turn left and drive five miles to the end of the Samoa Peninsula and the campground entrance.

Contact: Samoa Boat Launch County Park, tel. (707) 445-7652 or fax (707) 445-7409.

12 Eureka KOA

 2

This is a year-round KOA camp for U.S. 101 cruisers looking for a layover spot in Eureka. A bonus here is a few of those little KOA Kamping Kabins, the log-style jobs that win on cuteness alone. The closest significant recreation option is the Arcata Marsh on Humboldt Bay, a richly diverse spot with good trails for biking and hiking or just parking and looking at the water. Another option is excellent salmon fishing in June, July, and August, with party boats available just south of Eureka at King Salmon Charters.

Location: In Eureka; map B0, grid c4.

Campsites, facilities: There are eight bike-in/hike-in sites, 26 tent sites, and 140 RV sites (42 drive-through with full hookups and some partial hookups). Group sites and 10 camping cabins are available. Picnic tables and fire pits are provided. Drinking water, flush toilets, showers, playground, recreation room, heated swimming pool, two hot tubs, grocery store, coin laundry, sanitary disposal station, LP gas, ice, wood, fax machine, and computer kiosks are available. Some facilities are wheelchair accessible. Pets are permitted.

Reservations, fees: Reservations are accepted, tel. (800) 562-3136; $20 to $26 per night. Cabins are $35 per night for two people, $3 per day per person for more than two people. $3 per day for pets. Major credit cards accepted. Open year-round.

Directions: From Eureka, drive north on U.S. 101 for four miles to KOA Drive (well signed on east side of highway). Turn right on KOA Drive and drive to 4050 North U.S. 101.

Contact: Eureka KOA, tel. (707) 822-4243, fax (707) 822-0126; website: www.koa.com.

Ebb Tide Park

 2

This year-round RV park provides easy access off the highway and to stores and movie theaters—not exactly a primitive spot in pristine wilderness. It is what it is: a place to park the rig for the night.

Location: In Eureka; map B0, grid c3.

Campsites, facilities: There are 81 RV sites (58 drive-through) with full or partial hookups, and four tent sites. Picnic tables are provided. Restrooms, showers, patios, a sanitary disposal station, RV storage, and coin laundry are available. Leashed pets are permitted.

Reservations, fees: Reservations are accepted; $18 to $20 per night, $10 for tent sites. Open year-round.

Directions: In Eureka, drive north on U.S. 101, take the Mall 101 exit. Look for the park at the end of the road. Driving south on U.S. 101, take the V Street exit and drive to the first stoplight. Turn left and drive to Sixth Street. Turn left on Sixth Street and drive into Mall 101 and straight ahead to the park.

Contact: Ebb Tide Park, tel. (707) 445-2273.

E-Z Landing RV Park and Marina

 7

This is a good base camp for salmon trips in July and August when big schools of king and coho salmon often teem just west of the entrance of Humboldt Bay. A boat ramp with access to Humboldt Bay and party boat fishing trips are available out of E-Z Landing. It's not the prettiest camp in the world, with quite a bit of asphalt, but most people use this camp as a simple parking spot for sleeping and getting down to the business of the day: fishing. This spot is ideal for ocean fishing, clamming, beachcombing, and boating.

Location: On Humboldt Bay; map B0, grid c3.

Campsites, facilities: There are 55 RV sites (20 drive-through) with full hookups. Patios, flush toilets, showers, a sanitary disposal station, modem hookups, marine gas, ice, coin laundry, boat docks, boat launch, party boat rentals, bait, and tackle are available. Some facilities are wheelchair accessible. Leashed pets are permitted.

Reservations, fees: Reservations are accepted; $20 per night. Major credit cards accepted. Open year-round.

Directions: From Eureka, drive 3.5 miles south on U.S. 101. Turn west (right) on King Salmon Avenue (it becomes Buhne Drive) and drive for a half mile. Turn left (south) on Buhne Drive and go a half mile to 1875 Buhne Drive.

Contact: E-Z Landing RV Park and Marina, tel. (707) 442-1118 or fax (707) 442-1999.

15 Johnny's Marina and RV Park

     5

This is a good base camp for salmon fishing during the peak season in June, July, and August. Mooring for private boats is available, a nice plus for campers trailering boats. Other recreation activities include beachcombing, clamming, and perch fishing from shore. Charter fishing trips are available from King Salmon Charters, with one boat available. The owners have run this place for more than 50 years.

Location: On Humboldt Bay; map B0, grid d2.

Campsites, facilities: There are 53 RV sites (four drive-through) with full hookups. Patios, restrooms, showers, and a sanitary disposal station are provided. A coin laundry and boat dock are available. Pets must be controlled.

Reservations, fees: Reservations are accepted; $18 per night. Open year-round.

Directions: From Eureka, drive 3.5 miles south on U.S. 101. Turn west (right) on King Salmon Avenue (it becomes Buhne Drive). Continue about a half mile to 1821 Buhne Drive.

Contact: Johnny's Marina and RV Park, tel. (707) 442-2284 or fax (707) 443-4608.

16 Stafford RV Park

      6

This is a privately operated park for RVs that provides several side trip options: a tour of the giant sawmill in Scotia, a tour of giant redwoods on the Avenue of the Giants, access to the nearby Eel River, and best of all, the nearby Redwood National Park. One of the better park information centers in California is here, with maps and information about hikes, bike rides, and driving tours.

Location: Near Scotia; map B0, grid f3.

Campsites, facilities: There are 50 RV sites (14 drive-through) with full or partial hookups and 30 tent sites. Group sites are available. Picnic tables and fire grills are provided. Drinking water, flush toilets, showers, and a coin laundry are available. Some facilities are wheelchair accessible. Leashed pets are permitted.

Reservations, fees: Reservations are accepted; $10 to $20 per night, $2 pet fee. Major credit cards accepted. Open year-round, with reduced number of sites in the winter.

Directions: From Eureka, drive south on U.S. 101 to Scotia. At Scotia, continue south for three miles to Stafford Road. Turn right on Stafford Road and at the first stop sign, turn left under the overpass, and drive a short distance to North Road. At North Road, turn right and drive a quarter mile to 385 North Road.

Contact: Stafford RV Park, tel. (707) 764-3416.

17 Van Duzen County Park

    6

This campground is set at the headwaters of the Van Duzen River, one of the Eel River's major tributaries. The river is subject to tremendous fluctuations in flows and height, so low in the fall that it is often temporarily closed to fishing by the Department of Fish and Game, so high in the winter that only fools would stick their toes in. For a short period in late spring, it provides a benign run for rafting and canoeing, putting in at Grizzly Creek and taking out at Van Duzen. In October, you'll find an excellent salmon fishing spot where the Van Duzen enters the Eel.

Location: On the Van Duzen River; map B0, grid f4.

Campsites, facilities: There are 30 sites for tents or RVs. Picnic tables and fire grills are provided. Drinking water, flush toilets, and showers are available. A grocery store and coin laundry are available nearby. Pets are permitted.

Reservations, fees: No reservations; $12 per night, $1 pet fee. Open year-round.

Directions: From Eureka, drive south on U.S. 101 to the junction of Highway 36 at Alton. Turn east on Highway 36 and drive 12 miles to the campground.

Contact: Van Duzen County Park, tel. (707) 445-7652 or fax (707) 445-7409.

18 Grizzly Creek Redwoods State Park

 7

Most summer vacationers hit the campgrounds on the Redwood Highway, that is, U.S. 101. However, this camp is just far enough off the beaten path to provide some semblance of seclusion. It is set in redwoods, quite beautiful, with fair hiking and good access to the adjacent Van Duzen River. In the winter one of the better holes for steelhead fishing is accessible here.

Location: Near Bridgeville; map B0, grid g5.

Campsites, facilities: There are 18 tent sites and 12 sites for RVs up to 30 feet long or trailers up to 18 feet. Picnic tables and fire grills are provided. Drinking water, flush toilets, and showers are available. A grocery store is available within 3.5 miles. Some facilities are wheelchair accessible. Leashed pets are permitted.

Reservations, fees: Reserve at (800) 444-PARK (800-444-7275) or website: www.ReserveAmerica.com; $12 per night. Open year-round.

Directions: From Eureka, drive south on U.S. 101 to the junction of Highway 36 at Alton. Turn east on Highway 36 and drive about 17 miles to the campground on the right.

Contact: Grizzly Creek Redwoods State Park, tel. (707) 777-3683 or fax (707) 777-3159.

19 Mattole

 8

This is a little-known camp set at the mouth of the Mattole River, right where it pours into the Pacific Ocean. It is beautiful and isolated. An outstanding hike is available to the Punta Gorda Lighthouse. Hike from the campground to the ocean and head south. It's a level walk, and at low tide, there's a chance to observe tidepool life. Perch fishing is good

where the Mattole flows into the ocean, best during low tides. In the winter, the Mattole often provides excellent steelhead fishing. Check the Department of Fish and Game regulations for closed areas. Be sure to have a full tank on the way out—the nearest gas station is quite distant.

Location: On the Pacific Ocean; map B0, grid g0.

Campsites, facilities: There are 14 sites for tents or RVs up to 15 feet long. Picnic tables and fire rings are provided. Pit toilets are available. No drinking water is available. Leashed pets are permitted.

Reservations, fees: No reservations; $5 per night suggested donation. Open year-round.

Directions: From U.S. 101 north of Garberville, take the South Fork-Honeydew exit and drive west to Honeydew. At Honeydew, turn right on Mattole Road and drive toward Petrolia. At the second bridge over the Mattole River, one mile before Petrolia, turn west on Lighthouse Road and drive five miles to the campground at the end of the road.

Contact: Bureau of Land Management, Arcata Field Office, tel. (707) 825-2300 or fax (707) 825-2301.

20 A. W. Way County Park

 8

This secluded camp provides a home for visitors to the "Lost Coast," the beautiful coastal stretch of California far from any semblance of urban life. The highlight here is the Mattole River, a great steelhead stream when flows are suitable between January and mid-March. Nearby is excellent hiking in the King Range National Conservation Area. For the great hike out to the abandoned Punta Gorda Lighthouse, drive to the trailhead on the left side of Lighthouse Road (see previous listing). This area is typically bombarded with monsoon-level rains in winter.

Location: On the Mattole River; map B0, grid h0.

Campsites, facilities: There are 30 sites for

tents or RVs. Picnic tables and fire grills are provided. Drinking water, flush toilets, and showers are available. A grocery store, coin laundry, and propane gas are available nearby. Pets are permitted.

Reservations, fees: No reservations; $12 per night, $1 pet fee.

Directions: From Garberville, drive north on U.S. 101 to the South Fork-Honeydew exit. Turn west on South Fork-Honeydew Road and drive 31 miles (the road alternates between pavement, gravel, dirt, then pavement again) to the park entrance on the left side of the road. The park is 7.5 miles south of the town of Petrolia.

Contact: A.W. Way County Park, tel. (707) 445-7652 or fax (707) 445-7409.

Albee Creek

    8

Humboldt Redwoods State Park is known for some unusual giant trees in the Federation Grove and Big Tree Area. A series of excellent hikes, both short and long, is available here. The camp is set in a redwood grove, and the smell of these trees has a special magic. Nearby Albee Creek, a benign trickle most of the year, can flood in the winter after heavy rains.

Location: In Humboldt Redwoods State Park; map B0, grid h3.

Campsites, facilities: There are 39 sites for tents and 33 sites for RVs up to 31 feet long and trailers up to 21 feet long. Picnic tables, fire grills, and food lockers are provided. Drinking water, flush toilets, and showers are available. Leashed pets are permitted.

Reservations, fees: Reserve at (800) 444-PARK (800-444-7275) or website: www .ReserveAmerica.com; $12 per night. Open May through September.

Directions: From Eureka, drive south on U.S. 101 about 11 miles to the Honeydew exit (if you reach Weott, you have gone two miles too far). At Mattole Road, turn west and drive five miles to the campground on the right.

Contact: Humboldt Redwoods State Park, tel. (707) 946-2409 or tel. (707) 946-2326.

Burlington

     7

This camp is often at capacity during the tourist months. You get shady campsites with big redwood stumps that kids can play on. There's good hiking on trails routed through the redwoods, and in winter, steelhead fishing is often good on the nearby Eel River. The park has 100 miles of trails, but it is the little half-mile Founders Grove Nature Trail that has the quickest payoff and requires the least effort.

Location: In Humboldt Redwoods State Park; map B0, grid h4.

Campsites, facilities: There are 57 sites for tents or RVs up to 33 feet long or trailers up to 24 feet. Picnic tables, fire grills, and food lockers are provided. Drinking water, flush toilets, and showers are available. Some facilities are wheelchair accessible. Leashed pets are permitted.

Reservations, fees: Reserve at (800) 444-PARK (800-444-7275) or website: www .ReserveAmerica.com; $12 per night. Open year-round.

Directions: From Eureka, drive south on U.S. 101 for 45 miles to the Weott/Newton Road exit. Turn right on Newton Road and continue to the T junction where Newton Road meets the Avenue of the Giants. Turn left on the Avenue of the Giants and drive two miles to the campground entrance on the left.

Contact: Humboldt Redwoods State Park, tel. (707) 946-2409 or fax (707) 946-2326.

Hidden Springs

    7

This camp gets heavy use from May through September, but the campsites have been situated in a way that offers relative seclusion. Side trips include good hiking on trails routed through redwoods and a touring drive on Avenue of the Giants. The park has more than 100 miles of hiking trails, many of them amidst spectacular giant redwoods, including the Bull Creek Flats Trail and Founders Grove Nature Trail. Bears are occasionally spotted by mountain bikers on rides out to the park's outskirts. In winter, nearby High Rock on the Eel River is one of the better shoreline fishing spots for steelhead.

Location: In Humboldt Redwoods State Park; map B0, grid h5.

Campsites, facilities: There are 154 sites for tents or RVs up to 33 feet long or trailers up to 24 feet. Picnic tables, fire grills, and food lockers are provided. Drinking water, flush toilets, and showers are available. A grocery store and coin laundry are available within one mile in Myers Flat. Leashed pets are permitted.

Reservations, fees: Reserve at (800) 444-PARK (800-444-7275) or website: www.ReserveAmerica.com; $12 per night. Open May through September.

Directions: From Eureka, drive south 50 miles on U.S. 101 to the Myers Flat/Avenue of the Giants exit. Continue south and drive less than a mile to the campground entrance on the left.

Contact: Humboldt Redwoods State Park, tel. (707) 946-2409 or fax (707) 946-2326.

24 Giant Redwoods RV and Camp

 8

This privately operated park is set in a grove of redwoods and covers 23 acres, much of it fronting the Eel River. Trip options include the scenic drive on Avenue of the Giants.

Location: On the Eel River; map B0, grid i4.

Campsites, facilities: There are 26 tent sites and 57 RV sites (34 drive-through), many with full or partial hookups. Picnic tables and fire rings are provided. Restrooms, showers, modem hookups, a sanitary disposal station, a store, ice, coin laundry, playground, and a recreation room are available. Some facilities are wheelchair accessible. Pets are welcome with a dog "freedom area" available at the river bar.

Reservations, fees: Reservations are recommended in the summer; $19 to $27 per night, $2.50 per person per night for more than two people, $2 per night per dog. Major credit cards accepted. Open year-round.

Directions: From Eureka, drive south 50 miles on U.S. 101 to the Myers Flat/Avenue of the Giants exit. Turn right on Avenue of the Giants and make a quick left onto Myers Avenue. Drive a quarter mile on Myers Avenue to the campground entrance.

Contact: Giant Redwoods RV Camp, tel. (707) 943-3198 or fax (707) 943-3359; website: www.campgrounds.com/giantredwoods.

25 Mad River

 7

This Forest Service campground is set in a giant manzanita forest, often hot, always remote, in a relatively unknown section of Six Rivers National Forest at an elevation of 2,600 feet. The headwaters of the Mad River pour right past the campground, about two miles downstream from the Ruth Lake Dam. People making weekend trips to Ruth Lake sometimes end up at this little-used camp. Ruth Lake is a designated Watchable Wildlife Site, and is the only major recreation lake within decent driving range of Eureka, offering a small marina with boat rentals and a good boat ramp for access to trout fishing, bass fishing, and water-skiing.

Location: In Six Rivers National Forest; map B0, grid h9.

Campsites, facilities: There are 40 sites, a few of which are for RVs up to 22 feet long or trailers up to 30 feet long. Picnic tables and fire grills are provided. Drinking water is available from approximately mid-May to mid-October. Vault toilets are available. Leashed pets are permitted.

Reservations, fees: No reservations; $12 per night, $5 per extra vehicle. Open year-round.

Directions: From Eureka, drive south on U.S. 101 to Alton. Turn east on Highway 36 and drive about 50 miles to the town of Mad River. Turn southeast on Lower Mad River Road and drive four miles to the camp on the right side of the road.

Contact: Six Rivers National Forest, Mad River Ranger District, tel. (707) 574-6233 or fax (707) 574-6273.

26 Horse Mountain

 6

Few people know of this spot. The campground is set along the northwest flank of Horse Mountain. A primitive road (Saddle Mountain Road) leads west from the camp and then goes left at the Y, up to Horse Mountain (1,929 feet), which offers spectacular ocean and coastal views on clear days. If you turn right at the Y, the road leads to the trailhead for the King Crest Trail near Saddle Mountain (3,290 feet). This hike is an ambitious climb to King Peak (4,087 feet), rewarding hikers with a fantastic panorama, including Mount Lassen poking up above the Yolla Bolly Wilderness to the east.

Location: In the King Range; map B0, grid j2.

Campsites, facilities: There are nine sites for tents or RVs up to 20 feet long. Picnic tables and fire rings are provided. Pit toilets are available. No drinking water is available. Leashed pets are permitted.

Reservations, fees: No reservations; $5 per night. Open year-round.

Directions: From Eureka, drive 60 miles south on U.S. 101. Take the Redway/Shelter Cove exit onto Redwood Drive in the town of Redway. Look on the right for the King Range Conservation Area sign. Turn right on Briceland-Thorne Road (which will become Shelter Cove Road) and drive 17 miles to King Peak Road (Horse Mountain). Turn right and continue six miles to the campground on the right.

Contact: Bureau of Land Management, Arcata Field Office, tel. (707) 825-2300 or fax (707) 825-2301.

27 Shelter Cove RV Park & Campground

 9

This is a prime oceanside spot to set up a base camp for deep-sea fishing, whale-watching, tidepool gazing, beachcombing, and hiking. A relatively new six-lane boat ramp makes it perfect for campers who have trailered boats and don't mind the long drive. Reservations are strongly advised here. The park's backdrop is the King Range National Conservation Area, offering spectacular views. The deli is world famous for its fish-and-chips. The salmon fishing is quite good here in July and August, crabbing in December, clamming during winter's low tides, and hiking in the King Mountain Range during the summer. There is heavy rain in winter. On Saturday nights from Memorial Day through Labor Day, there are barbecues with live entertainment, weather permitting.

Location: Overlooking the Pacific Ocean; map B0, grid j2.

Campsites, facilities: There are 105 sites for tents or RVs (15 drive-through), many with full hookups. Picnic tables and fire rings are provided. Restrooms, showers, a sanitary disposal station, a coin laundry, grocery store, deli, LP gas, ice, RV supplies, and a boat ramp are available. Some facilities are wheelchair accessible. Leashed pets are permitted.

Reservations, fees: Reservations are recommended; $16 to $27 per night, $3 per person per night for more than two people. Major credit cards accepted. Open year-round.

Directions: From Eureka, drive 60 miles south on U.S. 101 to the Redway/Shelter Cove exit. Drive 2.5 miles north on Redwood Road to Briceland-Shelter Cove Road. Turn right (west) and drive 24 miles (following the truck/RV route signs) to Upper Pacific Drive. Turn south on Upper Pacific Drive and proceed a half mile to the park.

Contact: Shelter Cove, tel. (707) 986-7474.

28 Tolkan

 6

This remote camp is set at 1,840 feet, a short drive south of Horse Mountain. For nearby side trip options, see the entry for Horse Mountain.

Location: In the King Range; map B0, grid j2.

Campsites, facilities: There are nine sites for tents or RVs up to 20 feet long. Picnic tables and fire rings are provided. Drinking water and vault toilets are available. Some facilities are wheelchair accessible. Leashed pets are permitted.

Reservations, fees: No reservations; $8 per night. Open year-round.

Directions: From Eureka, drive 60 miles south on U.S. 101 to the Redway exit. Take the Redway/Shelter Cove exit onto Redwood Drive into the town of Redway. Look on the right for the King Range Conservation Area sign, turn right on Briceland-Thorne Road (which will become Shelter Cove Road), and drive 17 miles to Kings Peak (Horse Mountain) Road. Turn right on Kings Peak Road and continue 3.5 miles to the campground on the right.

Contact: Bureau of Land Management, Arcata Field Office, tel. (707) 825-2300 or fax (707) 825-2301.

29 Dean Creek Resort

 7

This year-round RV park is set on the South Fork of the Eel River. In the summer, it makes a good base camp for a redwood park adventure, with the adjacent Humboldt Redwoods State Park providing 100 miles of hiking trails, many routed through awesome stands of giant trees. In the winter heavy rains feed the South Fork Eel, inspiring steelhead upstream on their annual winter journey. Fishing is good in this area, best by shore at nearby High Rock. Bank access is good at several other spots, particularly upstream near Benbow and in Cooks Valley. An excellent side trip is to drive on Avenue of the Giants, a tour through giant redwood trees three miles from the park. The campground also offers volleyball, shuffleboard, badminton, and horseshoes. You get the idea.

Location: On the South Fork of the Eel River; map B0, grid j5.

Campsites, facilities: There are 64 RV sites with full or partial hookups and 12 drive-through sites; an 11-unit motel is also available. Picnic tables and fire grills are provided. Restrooms, showers, a recreation room, a coin laundry, store, RV supplies, wood, ice, giant spa, sauna, pool, sanitary disposal station, and a playground are available. Miniature golf is available on site. Some facilities are wheelchair accessible. Leashed pets are permitted.

Reservations, fees: Reservations are recommended in the summer; $14 to $29 per night, $3.50 per person per night for more than two people, $1.50 pet fee, $1.50 per vehicle per night for more than one vehicle. Major credit cards accepted. Open year-round.

Directions: From Eureka, drive 60 miles south on U.S. 101 to the Redway/Shelter Cove exit. Exit onto Redwood Drive and continue about one block to the campground entrance on the right.

Contact: Dean Creek Resort, tel. (707) 923-2555 or fax (707) 923-2547; website: www.campgrounds.com/deancreek.

CHAPTER B1

JEFFREY PATTY

ON SAWTOOTH RIDGE, NEAR
THOMPSON PEAK IN THE
TRINITY ALPS WILDERNESS

MAP B1

TO FORKS OF SALMON **118** TO SAWYERS BAR · TO YREKA

TO WEED

a ○Weitchpec
⑨96

KLAMATH
NATIONAL FOREST

Callahan○

SIX RIVERS
NATIONAL FOREST

❶

Salmon River South Fork

❺

❻

❹

b **❼**
❾

❷ ○Cecilville

❸

❽

TRINITY ALPS
WILDERNESS

11

12

c ○Salyer
10
○Denny

SHASTA-TRINITY
NATIONAL FOREST

24

TO CARRVILLE

⑭299
Trinity River

13

Trinity Center

25

d **14**
Burnt○
Ranch

17 ○Dedrick

26

Del
Loma

27-31

e **15-16**

18 Helena

38
39

33-37 **32**

Trinity
Lake

40

190

148 Big Bar **19** **20** **21** **22**
23

③3

Junction City

41

42

43

f **53**
○Hyampom

Trinity River

Weaverville○

44
45 **46** Lewiston
Lake

47

50

48-49 ○Lewiston

TO REDDING

g Hayfork○
③3

Douglas City○

52 **51**

French Gulch

②299 Buckhorn Summit
3,213 feet

Hayfork Summit
3,660 feet

h **54**
Peanut○

55

i Forest
Glen
56-57
③36
○Wildwood

○Ono

Ⓐ16

TO IGO

j Ruth
Lake
58

Platina○

59
○Ruth

○Beegum

60

③36

Mad River

61

SHASTA-TRINITY
NATIONAL FOREST

TO RED BLUFF

266

TO WILLOW CREEK · TO MAD RIVER

© AVALON TRAVEL PUBLISHING, INC.

0 1 2 3 4 5 6 7 8 9

CHAPTER B1

(CONTINUED ON NEXT PAGE)

1 Matthews Creek

 8

This camp is set in a dramatic river canyon, with the beautiful South Fork of the Salmon River nearby. Rafters call it the "Cal Salmon," and good put-in and take-out spots are found every few miles all the way to the confluence with the Klamath. In early summer the water is quite cold from snowmelt, but by midsummer it warms up significantly. The best fishing for steelhead on the Salmon is in December in the stretch of river downstream from Forks of Salmon (check regulations for closed areas). In winter the mountain rims shield the canyon floor from sunlight and it gets so cold you'll feel like a human glacier. The elevation is 1,700 feet.

Location: On the Salmon River in Klamath National Forest; map B1, grid a4.

Campsites, facilities: There are seven sites for tents or RVs up to 16 feet long and seven sites for tents only. Picnic tables and fire grills are provided. Drinking water and vault toilets are available during the summer season. The toilets are wheelchair accessible. Leashed or controlled pets are permitted.

Reservations, fees: No reservations; $8 per night, free during the off-season. Open year-round, weather permitting.

Directions: From the junction of U.S. 101 and Highway 299 near Arcata, head east on Highway 299 and drive to Willow Creek. In Willow Creek, turn north on Highway 96 and drive past Orleans to Somes Bar. At Somes Bar, turn east on Salmon River Road/Forest Road 2B01 and drive to the town of Forks of Salmon. Turn right on Cecilville Road/Forest Road 1002/ and drive about nine miles to the campground. Cecilville Road is very narrow.

Contact: Klamath National Forest, Salmon River Ranger District, tel. (530) 468-5351 or fax (530) 468-1290.

2 East Fork

    6

This is one of the more spectacular areas in the fall when the leaves turn different shades of gold. It's set at 2,400 feet along the Salmon River, just outside the town of Cecilville. Directly adjacent to the camp is Forest Road 37N02, which leads to a Forest Service station four miles away, and a trailhead for the Trinity Alps Wilderness three miles beyond that. Note to steelhead anglers: Check the Department of Fish and Game regulations for closed areas on the Salmon River.

Location: On the Salmon River in Klamath National Forest; map B1, grid b6.

Campsites, facilities: There are six tent sites and three sites for RVs up to 16 feet long. Picnic tables and fire grills are provided. Vault toilets are available. No drinking water is available. Leashed pets are permitted.

Reservations, fees: No reservations; no fee. Open year-round, weather permitting.

Directions: From Redding, drive north on Interstate 5 past Weed to the Edgewood exit. Take the Edgewood exit, turn left at the stop sign, and drive a short distance to another stop sign at Old Stage Road. Turn right at Old Stage Road, drive to Gazelle, turn left on Gazelle-Callahan Road, and drive to Callahan. In Callahan, turn southwest on Cecilville Road and drive about 30 miles to the campground on the right side of the road. If you reach the town of Cecilville, you have gone two miles too far.

Contact: Klamath National Forest, Salmon River Ranger District, tel. (530) 468-5351 or fax (530) 468-1290.

3 Shadow Creek

 7

This tiny spot, secluded and quiet, is along little Shadow Creek where it enters the East Fork Salmon River, adjacent to a deep bend in the road. An unusual side trip is to take the Forest Service road out of camp (turn north off Cecilville Road) and follow it as it winds back and forth, finally arriving at Grouse Point, 5,409 feet in elevation, for a view of the western slopes of the nearby Russian and Trinity Alps Wilderness Areas. There are three trailheads six miles to the east of the camp: Fish Creek, Long Gulch, and Trail Gulch. Note: The river adjacent to the campground is a spawning area and is closed to salmon and steelhead fishing, but you can take trout.

Location: In Klamath National Forest; map B1, grid b7.

Campsites, facilities: There are five tent sites and five sites for RVs up to 16 feet long. Picnic tables and fire grills are provided. Vault toilets are available. No drinking water is available. All garbage must be packed out. Leashed pets are permitted.

Reservations, fees: No reservations; no fee. Open year-round.

Directions: From Redding, drive north on Interstate 5 past Weed to the Edgewood exit. Take the Edgewood exit, turn left at the stop sign, and drive a short distance to another stop sign at Old Stage Road. Turn right at Old Stage Road, drive to Gazelle, turn left on Gazelle-Callahan Road, and drive to Callahan. In Callahan, turn southwest on Cecilville Road and drive about 25 miles to the campground on the left side of the road.

Contact: Klamath National Forest, Salmon River Ranger District, tel. (530) 468-5351 or fax (530) 468-1290.

4 Trail Creek

 7

This simple and quiet camp is set beside Trail Creek, a small tributary to the upper Salmon River, at an elevation of 4,700 feet. A trailhead is about a mile to the south, accessible via a Forest Service road, providing access to a two-mile trail routed along Fish Creek and leading to little Fish Lake. From Fish Lake the trail climbs steeply, switchbacking at times, for another two miles to larger Trail Gull Lake, a very pretty spot set below Deadman Peak (7,741 feet).

Location: In Klamath National Forest; map B1, grid a8.

Campsites, facilities: There are seven sites for tents or RVs up to 22 feet long and eight sites for tents only. Picnic tables and fire grills are provided. Drinking water and vault toilets are available. Leashed pets are permitted.

Reservations, fees: No reservations; $6 per night. Open May through October.

Directions: From Redding, drive north on Interstate 5 past Weed to the Edgewood exit. Take the Edgewood exit, turn left at the stop sign, and drive a short distance to another stop sign at Old Stage Road. Turn right at Old Stage Road and drive to Gazelle. In Gazelle, turn left on Gazelle-Callahan Road and continue to Callahan. In Callahan, turn southwest on Cecilville Road and drive 17 miles to the campground.

Contact: Klamath National Forest, Scott River Ranger District, tel. (530) 468-5351 or fax (530) 468-1290.

5 Hidden Horse

 7

Hidden Horse Camp provides an alternate horse camp to nearby Carter Meadows. The horse camps are in close proximity to the Pacific Crest National Scenic Trail, which passes through the area and serves as access to the Russian Wilderness to the north and the Trinity Alps Wilderness to the south. Trail Creek and East Fork are nearby.

Location: In Klamath National Forest; map B1, grid a7.

Campsites, facilities: There are six sites for tents or RVs. Picnic tables and fire grills are provided. Drinking water and vault toilets are available. A horse-mounting ramp and corral hitching posts are also available. There is no designated water for stock available. Some facilities are wheelchair accessible.

Reservations, fees: No reservations; $10 per night. Open late May to mid-October, weather permitting.

Directions: From Redding, drive north on Interstate 5 past Weed. Take the Edgewood exit, turn left at the stop sign, and drive a short distance. Turn right on Old Stage Road, drive to Gazelle, turn left on Gazelle-Callahan Road, and continue to Callahan. In Callahan turn southwest on Cecilville Road and drive 11 miles to Carter Meadows Horse Camp. Continue one-quarter mile to the campground on the left.

Contact: Klamath National Forest, Scott River Ranger District, tel. (530) 468-5351 or fax (530) 468-1290.

6 Carter Meadows Horse Camp

   7

Carter Meadows offers an extensive trail network for riding and hiking. The Pacific Crest National Scenic Trail passes through the area and serves as access to the Russian Wilderness to the north and the Trinity Alps Wilderness to the south. Stream fishing is another option here. Trail Creek and East Fork are nearby.

Location: In Klamath National Forest; map B1, grid a9.

Campsites, facilities: There is one group equestrian site for tents or RVs, with three large horse corrals. Group barbecues and picnic tables are provided. Drinking water and vault toilets are available. One toilet is wheel-chair accessible. Stock water troughs are also available.

Reservations, fees: Reservations required, phone (800) 444-6777 ($8.65 reservation fee) or website: www.reserveusa.com; $30 per night. Open mid-June to mid-October, weather permitting.

Directions: From Redding, drive north on Interstate 5 past Weed. Take the Edgewood exit, turn left at the stop sign, and drive a short distance. Turn right on Old Stage Road, drive to Gazelle, turn left on Gazelle-Callahan Road, and continue to Callahan. In Callahan turn southwest on Cecilville Road and drive 11 miles to the campground.

Contact: Klamath National Forest, Scott River Ranger District, tel. (530) 468-5351 or fax (530) 468-1290.

7 East Fork Willow Creek

     9

This is a beautiful spot along Willow Creek. Set at a 2,000-foot elevation, it's one of the prettiest campgrounds in the area. In August and September the river is often quite warm, ideal for swimming or tubing. In the winter it is one of the better camps for shoreline steelhead fishing. Way back in the 1950s and early 1960s this was one of the better-known campgrounds in the area, but the flood of 1964 wiped it out. Only recently have rehabilitation efforts restored it to life.

Location: On Willow Creek; map B1, grid b0.

Campsites, facilities: There are 13 sites for tents and RVs up to 35 feet long. Picnic tables and fire rings are provided. Vault toilets with wheelchair access are available. No drinking water is available. Leashed pets are permitted.

Reservations, fees: No reservations; $8 per night, $5 per night for additional vehicles, two vehicles maximum per site.

Directions: From the junction of U.S. 101 and Highway 299 near Arcata, turn east on Highway 299 and drive 32 miles (past Willow Creek) and look for the camp's entrance road (well signed) on the right (south) side of the road.

Contact: Six Rivers National Forest, Lower Trinity Ranger District, tel. (530) 629-2118 or fax (530) 629-2102. For a map, send $6 to U.S. Forest Service, Attn: Map Sales, P.O. Box 587, Camino, CA 95709; tel. (530) 647-5390, fax (530) 647-5389, or website: www.r5.fs.fed.us/visitorcenter. Major credit cards accepted. Ask for the Six Rivers National Forest.

8 Tish Tang

     8

This campground is adjacent to one of the best swimming holes in all of Northern California. By late July the adjacent Trinity River is warm and slow, perfect for tubing, falling in "by accident," and paddling a canoe. There is a large gravel beach, and some people will bring along their shorty lawn chairs and just take a seat on the edge of the river in a few inches of water. Though Tish Tang is a good put-in spot for rafting in the late spring and early summer, it is too easy for most rafters to even ruffle a feather during the summer. The elevation is 400 feet.

Location: In Six Rivers National Forest; map B1, grid c0.

Campsites, facilities: There are 21 sites for tents and 19 sites for tents or RVs up to 30 feet long and trailers up to 22 feet long. Picnic tables and fire grills are provided. Drinking water, vault toilets, and a camp host are available. Leashed pets are permitted.

Reservations, fees: No reservations; $10 per night, $5 for each additional vehicle, $15 per night for multiple-family sites. Open late May to late October.

Directions: From the junction of U.S. 101 and Highway 299 near Arcata, turn east on Highway 299 and drive to Willow Creek. In Willow Creek, turn north on Highway 96 and drive eight miles north to the campground entrance on the right side of the road.

Contact: Hoopa Valley Tribal Council, Forestry Department, tel. (530) 625-4284 or fax (530) 625-4230.

9 Mill Creek Lake Hike-In

   4

In 1999, a forest fire severely affected this area and caution should be used when hiking. Occasional falls of dead trees are inevitable. Because of the fire, few people are expected to visit the lake. In time, this will again become something of a secret camp. It now is surrounded largely by tree skeletons. Mill Creek Lake is a secret three-acre lake set at 5,000 feet on the edge of the Trinity Alps Wilderness. Reaching it requires a two-mile hike from the wilderness boundary, with the little lake set just north of North Trinity Mountain (6,362 feet). This is a rare chance to reach a wilderness lake with such a short walk, backpacking without having to pay the penalty of days of demanding hiking. The lake features excellent swimming, with warmer water than in higher and more remote wilderness lakes, and decent fishing for rainbow trout. It is stocked with fingerlings yearly by airplane.

Location: On the border of the Trinity Alps Wilderness; map B1, grid b1.

Campsites, facilities: There are three primitive tent sites at locations around the lake. Fire rings are provided. No drinking water is available. Pack out all garbage. Leashed pets are permitted.

Reservations, fees: No reservations; no fee. A free wilderness permit is required from the U.S. Forest Service. Open when weather permits access.

Directions: From the junction of U.S. 101 and Highway 299 near Arcata, turn east on Highway 299 and drive to Willow Creek. In Willow Creek turn north on Highway 96, drive into the Hoopa Valley, turn east on Big Hill Road, and drive 12 miles to the national forest boundary. Turn right on Forest Road 10N02 and drive about 3.5 miles, where you will reach another junction. Turn left at the signed junction to the Mill Creek Lake Trailhead and drive a short distance to the parking area. A one-hour walk is then required to reach the lake.

Contact: Six Rivers National Forest, Lower Trinity Ranger District, tel. (530) 629-2118 or fax (530) 629-2102. For a map, send $6 to U.S. Forest Service, Attn: Map Sales, P.O. Box 587, Camino, CA 95709; tel. (530) 647-5390, fax (530) 647-5389, or website: www.r5.fs.fed.us/visitorcenter. Major credit cards accepted. Ask for the Six Rivers National Forest.

Denny

       8

This is a secluded and quiet campground along the New River, a tributary to the Trinity River and a designated Wild and Scenic River. The stream here is OK for swimming, but too cold to even dip a toe in until late summer. If you drive north from the camp on Denny Road, you will find several trailheads for trips into the Trinity Alps Wilderness. The best of them is at the end of the road, where there is a good parking area, with a trail that is routed along the East Fork New River up toward Limestone Ridge. Note that the stretch of river near the camp is closed to fishing year-round. The campground is set at 1,400 feet.

Location: On the New River in Shasta-Trinity National Forest; map B1, grid c2.

Campsites, facilities: There are 16 tent sites and six sites for tents or RVs up to 25 feet long. Picnic tables and fire grills are provided. Vault toilets are available. No drinking water is available. All garbage must be packed out. Leashed pets are permitted. Supplies are available about one hour away in Salyers Bar.

Reservations, fees: No reservations; no fee. Open year-round.

Directions: From the junction of U.S. 101 and Highway 299 near Arcata, turn east on Highway 299 and drive to Willow Creek. In Willow Creek, continue east on Highway 299 and, after reaching Salyer, continue for four miles to Denny Road/County Road 402. Turn north on Denny Road and drive about 14 miles on a paved but very windy road to the campground.

Contact: Shasta-Trinity National Forest, Big Bar Ranger Station, tel. (530) 623-6106 or tel. (530) 623-6123.

Goldfield

  6

For hikers, this camp makes a perfect first stop after a long drive. You wake up, get your gear organized, then take the trailhead to the south. It is routed along Boulder Creek, and with a left turn at the junction (about four miles in), will take you to Boulder Lake (another two miles), set inside the edge of the Trinity Alps Wilderness. Former 49er coach George Seifert first told me about the beauty of this place, and how perfectly this campground is located for the hike. Campground elevation is 3,000 feet.

Location: In Shasta-Trinity National Forest; map B1, grid c8.

Campsites, facilities: There are six tent sites. Picnic tables and fire grills are provided. Vault toilets and hitching posts for horses are available. No drinking water is available. Pack out all garbage. Leashed pets are permitted.

Reservations, fees: No reservations; no fee. Open year-round.

Directions: From Redding, head east on Highway 299 and drive to Weaverville. Turn north on Highway 3 and drive just past the north end of Trinity Lake to Coffee Creek Road/Forest Road 104, adjacent to a Forest Service ranger station. Turn left on Coffee Creek Road and drive 6.5 miles to the campground on the left side of the road.

Contact: Shasta-Trinity National Forest, Weaverville Ranger Station, tel. (530) 623-2121 or fax (530) 623-6010.

Big Flat

   8

This is a great jump-off spot for a wilderness backpacking trip into the adjacent Trinity Alps. An 11-mile hike will take you into the beautiful Caribou Lakes Basin for lakeside campsites, excellent swimming, dramatic sunsets, and fair trout fishing. The trail is routed out of camp, crosses the stream, then rises up a series of switchbacks to the ridge. From here it gets easier, rounding a mountain and depositing you in the basin. Bypass Little Caribou, Lower Caribou, and Snowslide Lakes, and instead head all the way to Caribou, the biggest and best of the lot. Big Flat is set at 5,000 feet in elevation along Coffee Creek, and on the drive in, you'll see big piles of boulders along the stream, evidence of past gold mining activity.

Location: On Coffee Creek in Klamath National Forest; map B1, grid c9.

Campsites, facilities: There are nine sites for tents or RVs up to 16 feet long. Picnic tables and fire grills are provided. Vault toilets are available. No drinking water is available. Garbage must be packed out. Leashed pets are permitted.

Reservations, fees: No reservations; no fee. Open year-round, weather permitting.

Directions: From Redding, turn east on Highway 299 and drive to Weaverville. In Weaverville, turn north on Highway 3 and drive just past the north end of Trinity Lake to Coffee Creek Road/Forest Road 104, adjacent to a Forest Service ranger station. Turn left on Coffee Creek Road and drive 21 miles to the campground at the end of the road.

Contact: Klamath National Forest, Salmon River Ranger District, tel. (530) 468-5351 or fax (530) 468-1290.

13 Hobo Gulch

 7

Only the ambitious need apply. This is a trailhead camp set on the edge of the Trinity Alps Wilderness, and the reason only the ambitious show up is that it is a 20-mile uphill haul all the way to Grizzly Lake, set at the foot of the awesome Thompson Peak (8,663 feet), with no other lakes available en route. The camp is set at 2,900 feet along the North Fork of the Trinity River. The adjacent slopes of the wilderness are known for little creeks, woods, and a few pristine meadows, and are largely devoid of lakes.

Location: On the North Fork of the Trinity River in Shasta-Trinity National Forest; map B1, grid d5.

Campsites, facilities: There are 10 sites for tents or RVs. Picnic tables and fire grills are provided. Vault toilets are available. No drinking water is available. Garbage must be packed out. Supplies can be obtained in Junction City, about one hour away. Leashed pets are permitted.

Reservations, fees: No reservations; no fee. Open year-round, weather permitting.

Directions: From Redding, turn west on Highway 299, drive past Weaverville, and continue 13 miles to Helena. In Helena, turn right and drive four miles on County East Fork Road to Hobo Gulch Road. At Hobo Gulch Road, turn north and drive 16 miles to the end of the road at the campground.

Contact: Shasta-Trinity National Forest, Big Bar Ranger Station, tel. (530) 623-6106 or fax (530) 623-6123.

14 Burnt Ranch

 7

This campground is set on a bluff above the Trinity River and is one of its most compelling spots. Burnt Ranch Falls isn't much of a waterfall, but provides a fantastic spot to watch salmon and steelhead leap like hurdlers to make it past the falls and into a calm pool above. The peak migration periods are in mid-September for salmon and in early winter and early spring for steelhead. On their migratory route, the fish will hold below the falls, gaining strength for their upriver surge, making it a natural fishing spot. This section of river is very pretty, with deep, dramatic canyons nearby. The elevation is 1,000 feet.

Location: On the Trinity River in Shasta-Trinity National Forest; map B1, grid d1.

Campsites, facilities: There are 16 sites for tents or RVs up to 25 feet long. Picnic tables and fire grills are provided. Drinking water and vault toilets are available.

Garbage must be packed out. Supplies can be obtained in Hawkins Bar about one hour away. Leashed pets are permitted.

Reservations, fees: No reservations; $8 per night in season. Open year-round, weather permitting.

Directions: From Redding, take Highway 299 west and drive past Weaverville to Burnt Ranch. In Burnt Ranch, continue a half mile and look for the campground entrance on the right side of the road.

Contact: Shasta-Trinity National Forest, Big Bar Ranger Station, tel. (530) 623-6106 or fax (530) 623-6123.

15 Del Loma RV Park and Campground

     7

RV cruisers looking for a layover spot near the Trinity River will find just that at Del Loma. Shady sites and sandy beaches are available here along the Trinity. Rafting and tubing trips are popular in this area during the summer. Salmon fishing is best in the fall, steelhead fishing in the winter.

Location: On the Trinity River; map B1, grid e2.

Campsites, facilities: There are 41 RV sites with full or partial hookups. Picnic tables, fire grills, flush toilets, hot showers, and a sanitary disposal station are provided. A grocery store, RV supplies, firewood, coin laundry, recreation room, volleyball, and horseshoe pits are available. Leashed pets are permitted.

Reservations, fees: Reservations are accepted; phone (800) 839-0194; $18.75 per night. Open year-round.

Directions: From the junction of U.S. 101 and Highway 299 in Arcata, turn east on Highway 299 and drive to Burnt Ranch. From Burnt Ranch, continue 10 miles east on Highway 299 to the town of Del Loma and look for the campground entrance along the road.

Contact: Del Loma RV Park and Campground, tel. (530) 623-2834.

16 Hayden Flat

      7

This campground is split into two pieces, with most of the sites grouped in a large, shaded area across the road from the river and a few on the river side. A beach is available along the river; it is a good spot for swimming as well as a popular put-in and takeout for rafters. The elevation is 1,200 feet.

Location: On the Trinity River in Shasta-Trinity National Forest; map B1, grid e2.

Campsites, facilities: There are 35 sites for tents or RVs up to 25 feet long and five sites for RVs up to 35 feet in length. Picnic tables and fire grills are provided. Drinking water and vault toilets are available. Some facilities are wheelchair accessible. Leashed pets are permitted.

Reservations, fees: No reservations; $8 to $10 per night in season, free in winter. Open year-round.

Directions: From the junction of U.S. 101 and Highway 299 in Arcata, head east on Highway 299 and drive to Burnt Ranch. From Burnt Ranch, continue 10 miles east on Highway 299 and look for the campground entrance along the left side of the road. If you reach the town of Del Loma, you have gone a half mile too far.

Contact: Shasta-Trinity National Forest, Big Bar Ranger Station, tel. (530) 623-6106 or fax (530) 623-6123.

17 Ripstein

    8

This is one of the great trailhead camps for the neighboring Trinity Alps. It is set at 2,600 feet on the southern edge of the wilderness and is a popular spot for a late-night arrival followed by a backpacking trip the next morning. Waiting are the Canyon Creek Lakes via a six-mile uphill hike along Canyon Creek. The destination is extremely beautiful—two alpine lakes set in high granite mountains. The route passes Canyon Creek Falls, a set of two different waterfalls, about 3.5 miles out.

Location: On Canyon Creek in Shasta-Trinity National Forest; map B1, grid e5.

Campsites, facilities: There are 10 tent sites. Picnic tables and fire grills are provided. Vault toilets are available. No drinking water is available. Garbage must be packed out. Supplies can be obtained 45 minutes away in Junction City. Leashed pets are permitted.

Reservations, fees: No reservations; no fee. Open year-round.

Directions: From Redding, head west on Highway 299 and drive to Junction City. At Junction City, turn right on Canyon Creek Road and drive 15 miles to the campground on the left side of the road.

Contact: Shasta-Trinity National Forest, Big Bar Ranger Station, tel. (530) 623-6106 or fax (530) 623-6123.

18 Big Flat

 6

This level campground is set off Highway 299, just across the road from the Trinity River. The sites are close together, and it can be hot and dusty in midsummer. No problem. That is when you will be on the Trinity River, taking the lowest-priced rafting trip available anywhere in the West—as low as $25 to rent an inflatable kayak from Trinity River Rafting in nearby Big Bar, which includes shuttle service. It's fun, exciting, easy (newcomers are welcome), and cheap.

Location: On the Trinity River in Shasta-Trinity National Forest; map B1, grid e3.

Campsites, facilities: There are 10 sites for tents or RVs up to 25 feet long. Picnic tables and fire grills are provided. Drinking water and vault toilets are available. Leashed pets are permitted.

Reservations, fees: No reservations; $8 per night in season, free in winter.

Directions: From Redding, turn west on Highway 299, drive past Weaverville, Junction City, and Helena, and continue for about seven miles. Look for the campground entrance on the right side of the road. If you reach the town of Big Bar, you have gone three miles too far.

Contact: Shasta-Trinity National Forest, Big Bar Ranger Station, tel. (530) 623-6106 or fax (530) 623-6123.

19 Big Bar

 6

You name it, you got it—a quiet, small campground with easy access, good fishing nearby (in the fall), and piped water. In addition, there is a good put-in spot for inflatable kayaks and rafts. It is an ideal piece of water for newcomers, with Trinity River Rafting offering inflatable rentals for as low as $25, including shuttle service. The elevation is 1,200 feet. If the shoe fits. . . .

Location: Near the Trinity River in Shasta-Trinity National Forest; map B1, grid e3.

Campsites, facilities: There are three tent sites. Picnic tables and fire grills are provided. Vault toilets are available. No drinking water is available. Supplies are available one mile away. Leashed pets are permitted.

Reservations, fees: No reservations; no fee. Open year-round.

Directions: From Redding, turn west on Highway 299 and drive past Weaverville and continue for 25 miles to the ranger station one mile east of Big Bar and look for Corral Bottom Roads (across from the ranger station). Turn left and drive a quarter mile to the campground on the left.

Contact: Shasta-Trinity National Forest, Big Bar Ranger Station, tel. (530) 623-6106 or fax (530) 623-6123.

20 Skunk Point Group Camp

 7

This is an ideal site for groups on rafting trips. You get easy access to the nearby Trinity River with a streamside setting and privacy for the group. A beach on the river is nearby. In the spring, this section of river offers primarily Class II rapids (only more difficult during high water), but most of it is rated Class I. By late summer, the water is warm and benign, ideal for families. Guided rafting trips and inflatables are available for hire and rent in nearby Big Flat. The camp elevation is 1,200 feet.

Location: On the Trinity River in Shasta-Trinity National Forest; map B1, grid e3.

Campsites, facilities: There are two group sites that hold up to 30 people each. Picnic tables and fire grills are provided. Vault toilets are available. No drinking water is available. Some facilities are wheelchair accessible. Leashed pets are permitted.

Reservations, fees: Reservations required at tel. (530) 623-6106; $20 per night for 10 or fewer campers, $2 each additional camper to a maximum of 30 people. Open year-round.

Directions: From Redding, head west on Highway 299, driving past Weaverville, Junction City, and Helena, and continue for about seven miles. Look for the campground entrance on the left side of the road. If you reach the town of Big Bar, you have gone two miles too far.

Contact: Shasta-Trinity National Forest, Big Bar Ranger Station at tel. (530) 623-6106 or fax (530) 623-6123.

21 Pigeon Point

 7

In the good old days, huge flocks of bandtail pigeons flew the Trinity River Canyon, swooping and diving in dramatic shows. Nowadays you don't see too many pigeons, but this camp still keeps its namesake. It is better known for its access to the Trinity River, with a large beach for swimming. The elevation is 1,100 feet.

Location: On the Trinity River in Shasta-Trinity National Forest; map B1, grid e4.

Campsites, facilities: There are 10 sites for tents or RVs up to 25 feet long. Picnic tables and fire grills are provided. Vault toilets are available. No drinking water is available. Supplies can be obtained within 10 miles in Big Bar or Junction City. Some facilities are wheelchair accessible. Leashed pets are permitted.

Reservations, fees: No reservations; $6 per night. Open mid-May through October.

Directions: From Redding, head west on Highway 299 and drive to Weaverville. Continue west on Highway 299 to Helena and continue a half mile to the campground on the left (south) side of the road.

Contact: Shasta-Trinity National Forest, Big Bar Ranger Station, tel. (530) 623-6106 or fax (530) 623-6123.

22 Bigfoot Campground and RV Park

 8

This private RV park is set along the Trinity River. It is a popular layover for Highway 299 cruisers but provides the option for longer stays with rafting, gold panning, and in the fall and winter, fishing for salmon and steelhead, respectively. RV sites are exceptionally large, and a bonus is that a storage area is available.

Location: On the Trinity River; map B1, grid e5.

Campsites, facilities: There are 45 RV sites with full or partial hookups, a separate area for tent camping, and two cabins. From December 1 to May 1 only, self-contained vehicles are allowed. Flush toilets, hot showers (for a fee), a coin laundry, grocery store, sanitary disposal station, television, propane gas, swimming pool, and horseshoe pits are available. Television and modem hookups, fishing licenses, and a tackle shop are also available. Some facilities are wheelchair accessible. Leashed pets are permitted.

Reservations, fees: Reservations are recommended from July through October; $15 per night, $2 per night per person for more than two people; cabins are $75 per night. Major credit cards accepted. Open year-round.

Directions: From Redding, turn west on Highway 299 and drive to Junction City. Continue west on Highway 299 for three miles to the camp.

Contact: Bigfoot Campground and RV Park, tel. (800) 422-5219 or (530) 623-6088, fax (530) 623-3573.

23 Junction City

     7

Some of the Trinity River's best fall salmon fishing is in this area in September and early October, with steelhead following from mid-October into the winter. That makes it an ideal base camp for a fishing or camping trip.

Location: On the Trinity River in Shasta-Trinity National Forest; map B1, grid e5.

Campsites, facilities: There are 26 sites for tents and RVs up to 30 feet long. Picnic tables, fire grills, and bear-proof food lockers are provided. Drinking water, vault toilets, and camp hosts are available; note that from November through April, drinking water is available only from the pump house. Groceries and propane gas are available within two miles in Junction City. Leashed pets are permitted.

Reservations, fees: No reservations; $8 per night from May through October. Open year-round.

Directions: From Redding, turn west on Highway 299 and drive to Junction City. At Junction City, continue west on Highway 299 for 1.5 miles to the camp on the right.

Contact: Bureau of Land Management, Redding Field Office, tel. (530) 224-2100, or fax (530) 224-2172.

24 Wyntoon Resort

     8

This huge resort is an ideal family vacation destination. Set in a wooded area on the north shore of Trinity Lake, it provides opportunities for fishing, boating, swimming, and water-skiing, with access within walking distance. The lake sits at the base of the dramatic Trinity Alps, one of the most beautiful regions in the state.

Location: On Trinity Lake; map B1, grid d9.

Campsites, facilities: There are 78 tent sites, 136 full-hookup sites for trailers or RVs, 19 cottages and five trailers. Picnic tables and fire rings are provided. Drinking water, restrooms, showers, a coin laundry, a playground, pool, sanitary disposal station, gasoline, hardware store, grocery store, bicycle rentals, fish cleaning area, boat rentals, slips, and a boat launch are available. Some facilities are wheelchair accessible. Leashed pets are permitted.

Reservations, fees: Reservations are accepted, tel. (800) 715-3337; $21 to $25 per night, $2 per person for more than two people; $40 to $80 per night for trailers, $90 to $135 per night for cottages. Major credit cards accepted. Open year-round

Directions: From Redding, turn west on Highway 299 and drive to Weaverville at Highway 3. Turn north on Highway 3 and drive to Trinity Lake. At Trinity Center, continue a half mile north on Highway 3 to the resort.

Contact: Wyntoon Resort, tel. (530) 266-3337 or fax (530) 266-3820; website: wyntoonresort.com.

25 Preacher Meadow

    7

The winter of 2000 was one of the strangest on record here, where a localized wind storm knocked down 66 trees and put this campground temporarily out of commission. It reopened in summer of 2000. The anomaly of a tree blowdown makes a constant subject of discussion. But it isn't long and your attention will shift to the view of the Trinity Alps, excellent from the right vantage point. Otherwise, compared to all the other camps in the area so close to Trinity Lake, it has trouble matching up in the quality department. If the lakeside camps are full, this camp provides an overflow option.

Location: In Shasta-Trinity National Forest; map B1, grid d9.

Campsites, facilities: There are 45 sites for tents or RVs up to 32 feet long. Picnic tables and fire grills are provided. Drinking water, vault toilets, and a camp host are available. Supplies, a coin laundry, and a small airport are available nearby. Leashed pets are permitted.

Reservations, fees: No reservations; $8 per night. Open mid-May through October.

Directions: From Redding, turn west on Highway 299 and drive to Weaverville at Highway 3. Head north on Highway 3 and drive to Trinity Lake. Continue toward Trinity Center and look for the campground entrance on the left side of the road (if you reach Trinity Center you have gone two miles too far).

Contact: Shasta-Trinity National Forest, Weaverville Ranger Station, tel. (530) 623-2121 or fax (530) 623-6010.

26 Alpine View

    9

This is an attractive area, set on the shore of Trinity Lake at a creek inlet. The boat ramp nearby provides a bonus. It's a very pretty spot, with views to the west across the lake arm and to the Trinity Alps, featuring Granite Peak. The Forest Service also runs tours from the campground to historic Bowerman Barn, which was built in 1894. The elevation is 2,400 feet.

Location: On Trinity Lake in Shasta-Trinity National Forest; map B1, grid e9.

Campsites, facilities: There are 66 sites for tents or RVs up to 32 feet long. Picnic tables and fire grills are provided. Drinking water, flush toilets, and a camp host are available. Some facilities are wheelchair accessible. The Bowerman Boat Ramp is next to the camp. Leashed pets are permitted.

Reservations, fees: No reservations; $12 to $18 per night, $5 for an extra vehicle. Open mid-May through mid-September (rarely, it is closed temporarily when lake levels are extremely low).

Directions: From Redding, turn west on Highway 299 and drive to Weaverville. In Weaverville, turn north on Highway 3 and drive to Covington Mill (six miles south of Trinity Center). Turn right (south) on Guy Covington Road and drive three miles to the camp (one mile past Bowerman Boat Ramp) on the right side of the road.

Contact: Shasta-Trinity National Forest, Weaverville Ranger Station, tel. (530) 623-2121 or fax (530) 623-6010.

27 Stoney Creek Group Camp

      7

A series of camps sits on the northern shore of the Stuarts Fork arm of Trinity Lake. This is one of two designed for groups (the other is Bushy Tail), and it is clearly the better. It is set along the Stoney Creek arm, a cove with a feeder creek, with the camp large but relatively private. A swimming beach nearby is a bonus. The elevation is 2,400 feet.

Location: On Trinity Lake in Shasta-Trinity National Forest; map B1, grid e9.

Campsites, facilities: This group campground can hold up to 50 people. Sites are for tents only. Drinking water (spring, summer, and fall only; no drinking water in the winter), flush toilets, picnic tables, and fire grills are available. Leashed pets are permitted.

Reservations, fees: Reservations required at tel. (877) 444-6777 ($8.65 reservation fee) or website: www.reserveusa.com; $50 per night during season. Open year-round.

Directions: From Redding, turn west on Highway 299 and drive to Weaverville. In Weaverville, turn north on Highway 3 and drive 14.5 miles (about a half mile past the Stuarts Fork Bridge) to the campground.

Contact: Shasta-Trinity National Forest, Weaverville Ranger Station, tel. (530) 623-2121 or fax (530) 623-6010.

28 Bushy Tail Group Camp

      7

This is a huge group camp at Trinity Lake, the kind of place where you might want to have a political convention. Then you could tell some politician to go jump in a lake. (Haven't you always wanted to do that?) What the heck, it's pretty enough to want to jump in yourself, and with a boat launch nearby, you get a bonus. The elevation is 2,500 feet.

Location: On Trinity Lake in Shasta-Trinity National Forest; map B1, grid e9.

Campsites, facilities: This group campground can hold up to 200 people in 30 sites. Sites are for tents or RVs up to 20 feet long. Picnic tables and fire grills are provided. Drinking water and flush toilets are available. Supplies and a boat ramp are available nearby. Leashed pets are permitted.

Reservations, fees: Reservations required at tel. (877) 444-6777 ($8.65 reservation fee) or website: www.reserveusa.com; $60 group fee per night. Open May through September.

Directions: From Redding, head west on Highway 299 and drive to Weaverville. In Weaverville, turn north on Highway 3 and drive about 16 miles (approximately 3.5 miles past the Stuarts Fork Bridge) to the campground entrance road on the right. Turn right and drive a short distance to the camp on the left side of the road.

Contact: Shasta-Trinity National Forest, Weaverville Ranger Station, tel. (530) 623-2121 or fax (530) 623-6010.

29 Clark Springs

This used to be a day-use-only picnic area, but due to popular demand, the Forest Service has opened it for camping. That makes sense because people were bound to declare it a campground anyway, since it has a nearby boat ramp and a beach. The elevation is 2,400 feet.

Location: On Trinity Lake in Shasta-Trinity National Forest; map B1, grid e9.

Campsites, facilities: There are 21 tent sites. Picnic tables and fire grills are provided. Drinking water (spring, summer, and fall only) and flush toilets are available. A grocery store and boat ramp are available nearby. Leashed pets are permitted.

Reservations, fees: No reservations; $8 per night, free in winter. Open year-round, but no drinking water is available in the winter.

Directions: From Redding, head west on Highway 299 and drive to Weaverville. In Weaverville, turn north on Highway 3 and drive 16.5 miles (about four miles past the Stuarts Fork Bridge) to the campground entrance road on the right.

Contact: Shasta-Trinity National Forest, Weaverville Ranger Station, tel. (530) 623-2121 or fax (530) 623-6010.

30 Mariners Roost Boat-In Camp

A perfect boat camp? This comes close at Trinity since it's positioned perfectly for boaters, with spectacular views of the Trinity Alps to the west, and is an ideal spot for water-skiers. That is because it is on the western side of the lake's major peninsula, topped by Bowerman Ridge. Secluded and wooded, this area is set at 2,400 feet elevation.

Location: On Trinity Lake in Shasta-Trinity National Forest; map B1, grid e9.

Campsites, facilities: There are seven tent sites. Picnic tables and fire grills are provided. Vault toilets are available. No drinking water is available. Boat ramps are available at Clark Springs campground, near Alpine View campground, or farther north at Trinity Center. Leashed pets are permitted.

Reservations, fees: No reservations; no fee. Open year-round.

Directions: From Redding, head west on Highway 299 and drive to Weaverville. In Weaverville, turn north on Highway 3 and drive seven miles to the Stuarts Fork arm of Trinity Lake. You'll find boat launches at Stuarts Fork. After launching, drive your boat to the mouth of Stuarts Fork and look for the camp on the peninsula, just east and on the opposite shore of Ridgeville Island Boat-In Camp.

Contact: Shasta-Trinity National Forest, Weaverville Ranger Station, tel. (530) 623-2121 or fax (530) 623-6010.

3.1 Fawn Group Camp

 7

If you want Trinity Lake all to yourself, one way to do it is to get a group together and then reserve this camp near the shore of Trinity Lake. The elevation is 2,500 feet.

Location: On Trinity Lake in Shasta-Trinity National Forest; map B1, grid e9.

Campsites, facilities: This group campground can hold up to 300 people. Sites are for tents or RVs up to 37 feet long. Picnic tables and fire grills are provided. Drinking water and flush toilets are available. Leashed pets are permitted.

Reservations, fees: Reservations required at tel. (877) 444-6777 ($8.65 reservation fee) or website: www.reserveusa.com; $60 group fee per night. Open May through September.

Directions: From Redding, head west on Highway 299 and drive to Weaverville. In Weaverville, turn north on Highway 3 and drive 15 miles to the campground.

Contact: Shasta-Trinity National Forest, Weaverville Ranger Station, tel. (530) 623-2121 or fax (530) 623-6010.

3.2 Tannery Gulch

 8

This is one of the more popular Forest Service camps on the southwest shore of huge Trinity Lake. There's a nice beach near the campground, provided the infamous Bureau of Reclamation hasn't drawn the lake level down too far. It can be quite low in the fall. The elevation is 2,400 feet.

Location: On Trinity Lake in Shasta-Trinity National Forest; map B1, grid e8.

Campsites, facilities: There are 83 sites for tents or RVs up to 40 feet long and four multifamily sites. Picnic tables and fire grills are provided. Drinking water, flush and vault toilets, a boat ramp, and a camp host are available. A grocery store is available nearby. Leashed pets are permitted.

Reservations, fees: Reserve at tel. (877) 444-6777 ($8.65 reservation fee) or website: www.reserveusa.com; $12 to $18 per night, $5 for an extra vehicle. Open May through September.

Directions: From Redding, head west on Highway 299 and drive to Weaverville. In Weaverville, turn north on Highway 3 and drive 13.5 miles north to County Road 172. Turn right on County Road 172 and drive 1.5 miles to the campground on the left side of the road.

Contact: Shasta-Trinity National Forest, Weaverville Ranger Station at tel. (530) 623-2121 or fax (530) 623-6010.

3.3 Ridgeville Island Boat-In Camp

 9

This is one of the 100 featured campgrounds in my book *Easy Camping in Northern California*. Why? Well, how would you like to be on a deserted island for a week? You'll learn the answer from this tiny, little-known island with a great view of the Trinity Alps. It is one of several boat-in camps in the Trinity Lake region. The elevation is 2,500 feet. Note that the lake level at Trinity Lake is typically dropped significantly from September through October.

Location: On Trinity Lake in Shasta-Trinity National Forest; map B1, grid e8.

Campsites, facilities: There are three tent sites. Picnic tables and fire grills are provided. Vault toilets are available. No drinking water is available. Garbage must be packed out. Boat ramps can be found at Clark Springs campground, Bowerman Boat Ramp at Alpine View, or farther north at Trinity Center. Leashed pets are permitted.

Reservations, fees: No reservations; no fee. Open year-round.

Directions: From Redding, head west on Highway 299 and drive to Weaverville. In Weaverville, turn north on Highway 3 and drive seven miles to the Stuarts Fork arm of Trinity Lake. You'll find boat launches at Stuarts Fork. After launching, drive your boat to the mouth of Stuarts Fork; the campground is set on a small island here.

Contact: Shasta-Trinity National Forest, Weaverville Ranger Station, tel. (530) 623-2121 or fax (530) 623-6010.

34 Ridgeville Boat-In Camp

 9

This is one of the ways to get a camping spot to call your own—go by boat. The camp is exposed on a peninsula, providing beautiful views. Good prospects for water-skiing and trout or bass fishing make for a highlight film. The early part of the season is the prime time here for boaters, prior to the furnace heat of full summer, with both trout and bass on the bite. A great view of the Trinity Alps is a bonus. The only downer is the typical lake drawdown at the end of summer and beginning of fall, when this boat-in camp is left a long traipse from water's edge.

Location: On Trinity Lake in Shasta-Trinity National Forest; map B1, grid e8.

Campsites, facilities: There are 11 tent sites. Picnic tables and fire grills are provided. Vault toilets are available. No drinking water is available. Garbage must be packed out. Boat ramps can be found near Clark Springs, Alpine View, or farther north at Trinity Center. Leashed pets are permitted.

Reservations, fees: No reservations; no fee. Open year-round.

Directions: From Redding, head west on Highway 299 and drive to Weaverville. In Weaverville, turn north on Highway 3 and drive seven miles to the Stuarts Fork arm of Trinity Lake. You'll find boat launches at Stuarts Fork. After launching, drive your boat to the mouth of Stuarts Fork. The campground is set on the western shore at the end of a peninsula at the entrance to that part of the lake.

Contact: Shasta-Trinity National Forest, Weaverville Ranger Station, tel. (530) 623-2121 or fax (530) 623-6010.

35 Hayward Flat

 7

When giant Trinity Lake is full of water, Hayward Flat is one of the prettiest places you could ask for. The camp has become one of the most popular Forest Service campgrounds on Trinity Lake because it sits right along the shore and offers a "private" beach for Hayward Flat campers only. The elevation is 2,400 feet.

Location: On Trinity Lake in Shasta-Trinity National Forest; map B1, grid e8.

Campsites, facilities: There are 94 sites for tents or RVs up to 40 feet long and four multi-family sites. Picnic tables and fire grills are provided. Drinking water, flush toilets, and a camp host are available. Supplies and a boat ramp are available nearby. Leashed pets are permitted.

Reservations, fees: Reserve at tel. (877) 444-6777 ($8.65 reservation fee) or website: www.reserveusa.com; $12 to $18 per night, $5 for each additional vehicle. Open mid-May through mid-September.

Directions: From Redding, head west on Highway 299 and drive to Weaverville. In Weaverville, turn north on Highway 3 and drive about 20 miles, approximately three miles past the Mule Creek Ranger Station. Turn right at the signed access road for Hayward Flat and drive about three miles to the campground at the end of the road.

Contact: Shasta-Trinity National Forest, Weaverville Ranger Station, tel. (530) 623-2121 or fax (530) 623-6010.

36 Minersville

 7

The setting is near lakeside, quite beautiful when Trinity Lake is fullest in the spring and early summer. This is a good camp for boaters, with a boat ramp in the cove a short distance to the north. But note that the boat ramp is not always functional. When the lake level is 65 feet below full, the ramp is not useable. The elevation is 2,500 feet.

Location: On Trinity Lake in Shasta-Trinity National Forest; map B1, grid e8.

Campsites, facilities: There are 21 sites for tents or RVs up to 18 feet long. Picnic tables and fire grills are provided. Drinking water (spring, summer, and fall only), flush toilets, a camp host, and a low-water boat ramp are provided. Leashed pets are permitted.

Reservations, fees: No reservations; $10 to $17 per night, free in winter. Open year-round, but note that there is no piped water in the winter.

Directions: From Redding, head west on Highway 299 to Weaverville. Turn north on Highway 3 and drive about 18 miles (if you reach the Mule Creek Ranger Station, you have gone a half mile too far). Turn right at the signed campground access road and drive a half mile to the camp.

Contact: Shasta-Trinity National Forest, Weaverville Ranger Station, tel. (530) 623-2121 or fax (530) 623-6010.

37 Stoney Point

      7

This is a popular spot at Trinity Lake, easily discovered and easily reached. Set near the inlet of Stuarts Fork, it often fills up, but two other campgrounds close by provide overflow options. The elevation is 2,400 feet.

Location: On Trinity Lake in Shasta-Trinity National Forest; map B1, grid e8.

Campsites, facilities: There are 22 sites for tents only. Picnic tables and fire grills are provided. Drinking water and flush toilets are available. Leashed pets are permitted.

Reservations, fees: No reservations; $10 per night in season, free in winter. Open year-round, weather permitting.

Directions: From Redding, head west on Highway 299 and drive to Weaverville. In Weaverville, turn north on Highway 3 and drive 14

miles (about a quarter mile past the Stuarts Fork Bridge) to the campground.

Contact: Shasta-Trinity National Forest, Weaverville Ranger Station, tel. (530) 623-2121 or fax (530) 623-6010.

38 Bridge Camp

   8

This remote spot is an ideal jump-off point for backpackers. It's at the head of Stuarts Fork Trail, about two miles from the western shore of Trinity Lake. The trail leads into the Trinity Alps Wilderness, along Stuarts Fork, past Oak Flat and Morris Meadows, and up to Emerald Lake and the Sawtooth Ridge. It is a long and grueling climb, but fishing is excellent at Emerald Lake as well as at neighboring Sapphire Lake. There's a great view of the Alps from this camp. It is set at 2,700 feet and remains open year-round, but there's no piped water in the winter and it gets mighty cold up here.

Location: On Stuarts Fork in Shasta-Trinity National Forest; map B1, grid e7.

Campsites, facilities: There are 10 sites for tents or trailers up to 12 feet long. Picnic tables and fire grills are provided. Drinking water, vault toilets, a camp host, and horse corrals are available. Leashed pets are permitted.

Reservations, fees: No reservations; $8 per night, free in winter. Open year-round, weather permitting.

Directions: From Redding, head west on Highway 299 and drive to Weaverville. In Weaverville, turn north on Highway 3 and drive 17 miles to Trinity Alps Road (at Stuarts Fork of Trinity Lake). At Trinity Alps Road, turn left and drive about 2.5 miles to the campground on the right side of the road.

Contact: Shasta-Trinity National Forest, Weaverville Ranger Station, tel. (530) 623-2121 or fax (530) 623-6010.

39 Pinewood Cove Campground

 7

This is a privately operated camp with full boating facilities at Trinity Lake. If you don't have a boat but want to get on Trinity Lake, this can be a good starting point. A reservation is advised during the peak summer season. The elevation is 2,300 feet.

Location: On Trinity Lake; map B1, grid e7.

Campsites, facilities: There are 50 sites with full or partial hookups for RVs up to 40 feet long, and 28 tent sites. There are also six trailer rentals, six park-model cabins, and one A-frame cabin. Picnic tables and fire grills are provided. Restrooms, showers, a coin laundry, sanitary disposal station, RV supplies, free movies three nights a week, recreation room, pinball and video machines, grocery store, ice, fishing tackle, library, boat dock with 32 slips, beach, and boat rentals are available. Some facilities are wheelchair accessible. Leashed pets are permitted.

Reservations, fees: Reservations are recommended in the summer; $18 to $24 per night. Major credit cards accepted. Open mid-April through October.

Directions: From Redding, turn west on Highway 299 and drive to Weaverville. In Weaverville, turn north (right) on Highway 3 and drive 14 miles to the campground entrance on the right.

Contact: Pinewood Cove Campground, tel. (800) 988-5253 or (530) 286-2201, fax at (530) 286-2202; website: www.pinewoodcove.com.

40 Rush Creek

 4

This small, primitive camp provides overflow space during busy holiday weekends when the camps at Lewiston and Trinity Lakes are near capacity. It may not be much, but hey, at least if you know about Rush Creek you'll never get stuck for a spot. The camp borders Rush Creek and is secluded, but again, it's nearly five miles to the nearest access point to Trinity Lake.

Location: In Shasta-Trinity National Forest, north of Weaverville; map B1, grid e7.

Campsites, facilities: There are 10 sites for tents only. Picnic tables and fire pits are provided. Vault toilets are available. No drinking water is available.

Reservations, fees: No reservations; $5 per night. Open May to mid-September.

Directions: From Redding, go west on Highway 299 and drive to Weaverville. In Weaverville, turn north on Highway 3 and drive about eight miles to the signed turnoff on the left side of the road. Turn left and drive a quarter mile on the short spur road to the campground on the left side of the road. If you get to Forest Road 113, you've gone too far.

Contact: Shasta-Trinity National Forest, Weaverville Ranger Station at tel. (530) 623-2121 or fax (530) 623-6010.

41 East Weaver

    6

This camp is set along East Weaver Creek. Another mile to the west on East Weaver Road, the road dead-ends at a trailhead, a good side trip. From here, the hiking trail is routed four miles, a significant climb, to tiny East Weaver Lake, set to the southwest of Monument Peak (7,771 feet elevation). The elevation at East Weaver is 2,700 feet.

Location: On the east branch of Weaver Creek in Shasta-Trinity National Forest; map B1, grid f7.

Campsites, facilities: There are eight tent sites and seven sites for tents or RVs up to 16 feet long. Picnic tables and fire grills are provided. Drinking water (spring, summer, and fall only) and vault toilets are available. Supplies and a coin laundry are available in Weaverville. Leashed pets are permitted.

Reservations, fees: No reservations; $8 per night. Open year-round.

Directions: From Redding, go west on Highway 299 and drive to Weaverville. In Weaverville, turn north on Highway 3 and drive about two miles to East Weaver Road. Turn left on East Weaver Road and drive 3.5 miles to the campground.

Contact: Shasta-Trinity National Forest, Weaverville Ranger Station, tel. (530) 623-2121 or fax (530) 623-6010.

42 Captain's Point Boat-In Camp

       7

The Trinity River arm of Trinity Lake is a massive piece of water, stretching north from the giant Trinity Dam for nearly 20 miles. This camp is the only boat-in camp along this entire stretch of shore, and it is situated at a prominent spot, where a peninsula juts well out into the main lake body. This is a perfect boat-in site for water-skiers or fishermen. The fishing is often excellent for smallmouth bass in the cove adjacent to Captain's Point, using grubs. The elevation is 2,400 feet.

Location: On Trinity Lake in Shasta-Trinity National Forest; map B1, grid f8.

Campsites, facilities: There are three tent sites. Picnic tables and fire grills are provided. Vault toilets are available. No drinking water is available. Garbage must be packed out. Boat ramps can be found near Clark Springs and Alpine View, or farther north at Trinity Center. Leashed pets are permitted.

Reservations, fees: No reservations; no fee. Open year-round.

Directions: From Redding, head west on Highway 299 and drive to Weaverville. In Weaverville, turn north on Highway 3 and drive about seven miles to the signed turnoff on the right side of the road for the Trinity Alps Marina. Turn right and drive approximately 10 miles to the marina and boat ramp. Launch your boat and cruise north about four miles up the main Trinity River arm of the lake. Look for Captain's Point on the left side of the lake.

Contact: Shasta-Trinity National Forest, Weaverville Ranger Station, tel. (530) 623-2121 or fax (530) 623-6010.

43 Tunnel Rock

    7

This is a very small, primitive alternative to Ackerman, which is more developed and another mile up the road to the north. The proximity to the Pine Cove boat ramp and fish-cleaning station, less than two miles to the south, is a primary attraction. The elevation is 1,700 feet.

Location: On Lewiston Lake in Shasta-Trinity National Forest; map B1, grid f8.

Campsites, facilities: There are six tent sites. Picnic tables and fire grills are provided. Vault toilets are available. No drinking water is available. Leashed pets are permitted.

Reservations, fees: No reservations; $5 per night. Open year-round.

Directions: From Redding, go west on Highway 299, drive over Buckhorn Summit, and continue for five miles to County Road 105/Buckeye Creek Road. Turn right on County Road 105/Buckeye Creek Road, drive four miles to Lewiston, and then continue another seven miles north on County Road 105/Buckeye Creek Road to the campground.

Contact: Shasta-Trinity National Forest, Weaverville Ranger Station, tel. (530) 623-2121 or fax (530) 623-6010.

44 Ackerman

    7

Of the camps and parks at Lewiston Lake, Ackerman is closest to the lake's headwaters. This stretch of water below Trinity Dam is the best area for trout fishing on Lewiston Lake. Nearby Pine Cove boat ramp, two miles south of the camp, offers the only boat launch on Lewiston Lake with docks and a fish-cleaning station—a popular spot for anglers. When the Trinity powerhouse is running, trout fishing is excellent in this area. The elevation is 2,000 feet.

Location: On Lewiston Lake in Shasta-Trinity National Forest; map B1, grid f8.

Campsites, facilities: There are 66 sites for tents or RVs up to 40 feet long. Picnic tables and fire grills are provided. Drinking water (spring, summer, and fall only; no drinking water in the winter), flush toilets, a sanitary disposal station, and camp host are available. Leashed pets are permitted.

Reservations, fees: No reservations; $5 to $10 per night. Open year-round.

Directions: From Redding, head west on Highway 299, drive over Buckhorn Summit, and continue for five miles to County Road 105. Turn right on County Road 105 and drive four miles to Lewiston. Continue north on County Road 105 (Buckeye Creek Road) for eight miles to the campground.

Contact: Shasta-Trinity National Forest, Weaverville Ranger Station, tel. (530) 623-2121 or fax (530) 623-6010.

45 Lakeview Terrace Resort

 8

This might be your Golden Pond. It's a terraced RV park—with cabin rentals also available—that overlooks Lewiston Lake, one of the prettiest drive-to lakes in the region. Fishing for trout is excellent from Lakeview Terrace on upstream toward the dam. Lewiston Lake is perfect for fishing, with a 10 mph speed limit in effect (all the hot boats go to nearby Trinity Lake), along with excellent prospects for rainbow and brown trout. The topper is that Lewiston Lake is always full to the brim, just the opposite of the up-and-down nightmare of its neighboring big brother, Trinity.

Location: On Lewiston Lake; map B1, grid f8.

Campsites, facilities: There are 40 RV sites with full hookups, and cabins with one to five bedrooms. Restrooms, hot showers, laundry room, heated pool, propane gas, and boat rentals are available. Supplies are available within five miles. Leashed pets are permitted.

Reservations, fees: Reservations are recommended; $21 per night; cabins are $60 to $120 per night. Major credit cards accepted. Open year-round.

Directions: From Redding, drive west on Highway 299, drive over Buckhorn Summit, and continue for five miles to County Road 105/Trinity Dam Boulevard. Turn right on Trinity Dam Boulevard and drive 10 miles (five miles past Lewiston) to the resort on the left side of the road.

Contact: Lakeview Terrace Resort, tel. (530) 778-3803 or fax (530) 778-3960; website: www.campgrounds.com/lakeview.

46 Cooper Gulch

 8

Here is a nice spot along a beautiful lake, featuring a short trail to Baker Gulch, where a pretty creek enters Lewiston Lake. The trout fishing is good on the upper end of the lake (where the current starts) and upstream. The lake was recently designated as a wildlife viewing area, with large numbers of waterfowl and other birds often spotted near the tules off the shore of Lakeview Terrace. Bring all of your own supplies and plan on hunkering down here for a while.

Location: On Lewiston Lake in Shasta-Trinity National Forest; map B1, grid f8.

Campsites, facilities: There are five sites for tents or RVs up to 16 feet long. Picnic tables and fire grills are provided. Vault toilets are available. No drinking water is available. Some facilities are wheelchair accessible. Supplies and a coin laundry are available in Lewiston. Leashed pets are permitted.

Reservations, fees: No reservations; $10 per night. Open April through November.

Directions: From Redding, head west on Highway 299, drive over Buckhorn Summit, and continue for five miles to County Road 105/Buckeye Creek Road. Turn right on County Road 105/Buckeye Creek road, drive four miles to Lewiston, and then continue another four miles north on County Road 105/Buckeye Creek Road to the campground.

Contact: Shasta-Trinity National Forest, Weaverville Ranger Station, tel. (530) 623-2121 or fax (530) 623-6010.

47 Mary Smith

    10

This is one of the prettiest spots you'll ever see, set along the southwestern shore of Lewiston Lake. When you wake up and peek out of your sleeping bag, the natural beauty of this serene lake can take your breath away. Hand-launched boats, such as canoes, are ideal here. Trolling for trout is only fair in this end of the lake; most of the fish are below the Trinity Dam. Bird-watching is good, however. The elevation is 2,000 feet.

Location: On Lewiston Lake in Shasta-Trinity National Forest; map B1, grid f8.

Campsites, facilities: There are 18 sites for tents only, some requiring a very short walk. Picnic tables and fire grills are provided. Drinking water, flush and vault toilets, and a camp host are available. Supplies and a coin laundry are available in Lewiston. Leashed pets are permitted.

Reservations, fees: No reservations; $9 per night. Open May through October.

Directions: From Redding, head west on Highway 299, drive over Buckhorn Summit, and continue for five miles to County Road 105. Turn right on County Road 105/Buckeye Creek Road, drive four miles to Lewiston, and then continue 2.5 miles north on County Road 105/Buckeye Creek Road to the campground.

Contact: Shasta-Trinity National Forest, Weaverville Ranger Station, tel. (530) 623-2121 or fax (530) 623-6010.

48 Old Lewiston Bridge RV Resort

    7

Though much of the water from Trinity and Lewiston Lakes is diverted via tunnel to Whiskeytown Lake (en route to the valley and points south), enough escapes downstream to provide a viable fishery on the stretch of river near the town of Lewiston. This upstream portion below Lewiston Lake is prime in the early summer for trout, particularly the chance for a huge brown trout (special regulations in effect). In the winter, the stretch near Steelbridge is often good for steelhead. The campground is in a hilly area but has level sites, with nearby Lewiston Lake a major attraction. Damage from a major fire in the general area in summer of 1999, set as a "controlled burn," is still evident and will remain a topic of intense emotions for many years.

Location: On the Trinity River; map B1, grid f7.

Campsites, facilities: There are 52 RV sites with full hookups and a separate area for tents. Picnic tables are provided. Restrooms, hot showers, a coin laundry, a grocery store, and propane gas refills are available. A group picnic area is available by reservation. Supplies can be obtained within walking distance in Lewiston. Leashed pets are permitted.

Reservations, fees: Reservations are accepted; $21 per night for RVs, $12 per night per vehicle for tent campers. Major credit cards accepted. Open year-round.

Directions: From Redding, head west on Highway 299, drive over Buckhorn Summit, and continue for five miles to County Road 105. Turn right on County Road 105, drive four miles to Lewiston, and continue north to the junction of Rush Creek Road and Trinity Dam Road. Turn left (west) on Rush Creek Road and drive three-quarters of a mile to the resort.

Contact: Old Lewiston Bridge RV Resort, tel. (800) 922-1924, tel. or fax (530) 778-3894; website: www.campgrounds.com/oldlewistonbridge.

49 Trinity River Lodge RV Resort

     7

For many, this privately operated park has an ideal location. You get level, grassy sites with shade trees along the Trinity River, yet it is just a short drive north to Lewiston Lake or a bit farther to giant Trinity Lake. Lake or river, take your pick.

Location: On the Trinity River; map B1, grid f7.

Campsites, facilities: There are 60 sites with full hookups for RVs up to 40 feet long, and five tent sites. Restrooms, hot showers, a coin laundry, cable TV, recreation room, lending library, clubhouse, recreation field, propane gas, camp store, ice, wood, furnished trailer rentals, boat and trailer storage, and horseshoes are available. Some facilities are wheelchair accessible. There is lake fishing less than 10 minutes away. Leashed pets are permitted.

Reservations, fees: Reservations are recommended; $14 to $21 per night. Major credit cards accepted. Open year-round.

Directions: From Redding, go west on Highway 299, drive over Buckhorn Summit, and continue for five miles to County Road 105. Turn right on County Road 105 and drive four miles to Lewiston. Turn right at Trinity Dam Boulevard and drive six miles, crossing the Trinity River. Just after the bridge, turn left on Rush Creek Road and drive to the campground on the left.

Contact: Trinity River Lodge RV Resort, tel. (800) 761-2769 or (530) 778-3791; website: www.campgrounds.com/trinityriver.

50 Steelbridge

      7

Very few campers know of this spot, yet it was renovated in 2000 and it can be a prime spot for anglers and campers. It's one of the better stretches of water in the area for steelhead, with good shore fishing access. The prime time is from October through December. In the summer, the shade of conifers will keep you cool. Don't forget to bring your own water. The elevation is 1,700 feet.

Location: On the Trinity River; map B1, grid f7.

Campsites, facilities: There are 10 sites for tents or RVs up to 25 feet long. Picnic tables and fire grills are provided. Pit toilets and a summer camp host are available. No drinking water is available. Supplies are available within three miles in Douglas City. Leashed pets are permitted.

Reservations, fees: No reservations; $5 per night. Open year-round.

Directions: From Redding, head west on Highway 299, drive over Buckhorn Summit, and continue toward Douglas City to Steel Bridge Road (if you reach Douglas City, you have gone 2.3 miles too far). At Steel Bridge Road, turn right and drive about four miles to the campground at the end of the road.

Contact: Bureau of Land Management, Redding Field Office, tel. (530) 224-2100 or fax (530) 224-2172.

51 Indian Creek RV Park

  6

This privately operated RV park is set in the heart of Trinity River country across the road from the Trinity River. The elevation is 1,650 feet.

Location: On the Trinity River; map B1, grid g6.

Campsites, facilities: There are 12 RV sites with full hookups. Picnic tables are provided. Drinking water, showers, flush toilets, TV hookups, and a coin laundry are available. Supplies are available in Douglas City. Some facilities are wheelchair accessible. Leashed pets are permitted.

Reservations, fees: Reservations are accepted; $18 per night. Open year-round.

Directions: From Redding, drive west on Highway 299 for 36 miles to the Indian Creek Park sign on the left. Turn left at the sign, drive a short distance, and look for the park office on the left.

Contact: Indian Creek RV Park, tel. (530) 623-6332.

52 Douglas City & Steiner Flat

 7

If you want to camp along this stretch of the main Trinity River, these camps are your best bet (located along the river about two miles from each other). They are set off the main road, near the river, with good bank fishing access (the prime season is from mid-August through winter for salmon and steelhead). There's paved parking and two beaches at Douglas City Campground. Steiner Flat, a more primitive camp, provides better access for fishing. This can be a good base camp for an off-season fishing trip on the Trinity River or a lounging spot during the summer. The elevation is 1,700 feet.

Location: On the Trinity River; map B1, grid g6.

Campsites, facilities: There are 19 sites for tents or RVs up to 35 feet long at Douglas City with dispersed camping at Steiner Flat. At Douglas City, picnic tables and fire grills are provided. Restrooms, flush toilets, and sinks are available. Drinking water is available in summer only. At Steiner Flat, a pit toilet is available. No drinking water is available. Supplies are available within one mile in Douglas City. Leashed pets are permitted.

Reservations, fees: No reservations; $10 per night. Open year-round.

Directions: From Redding, go west on Highway 299 and continue over the bridge at the Trinity River near Douglas City to Steiner Flat Road. Turn left on Steiner Flat Road and drive a half mile to Douglas City campground on the left. To reach Steiner Flat, continue two more miles and look for the campground on the left.

Contact: Bureau of Land Management, Redding Field Office, tel. (530) 224-2100 or fax (530) 224-2172.

53 Big Slide

 7

This camp is literally out in the middle of nowhere. Free? Of course it's free. Otherwise, someone would actually have to show up now and then to collect. It's a tiny, secluded, little-visited spot set along the South Fork of the Trinity River. The elevation is 1,200 feet.

Location: On the South Fork of the Trinity River in Shasta-Trinity National Forest; map B1, grid f1.

Campsites, facilities: There are four tent sites and four sites for tents or RVs. Picnic tables and fire grills are provided. Vault toilets are available. No drinking water is available. Leashed pets are permitted.

Reservations, fees: No reservations; no fee. Open May through October.

Directions: From Redding, head west on Highway 299 and drive over the Buckhorn Summit to the junction with Highway 3 near Douglas City. Turn south on Highway 3 and drive to Hayfork. From Hayfork, turn right on County Road 301 and drive about 20 miles to the town of Hyampom. In Hyampom, turn right on Lower South Fork Road /County Road 311 and drive five miles on County Road 311 to the campground on the right.

Contact: Shasta-Trinity National Forest, Hayfork Ranger Station, tel. (530) 628-5227 or fax (530) 628-5212.

54 Philpot

 7

It's time to join the 5 Percent Club; that is, the 5 percent of the people who know the little-used, beautiful spots in California. This is one of those places, set on the North Fork of Salt Creek on national forest land. The elevation is 2,600 feet. Remember: 95 percent of the people use just 5 percent of the available open space. Why would anyone come here? To join the 5 Percent Club, that's why. Note: The road is too rough for many vehicles, and the sites too small for most RVs.

Location: On the North Fork of Salt Creek in Shasta-Trinity National Forest; map B1, grid h3.

Campsites, facilities: There are six sites for tents or small RVs. Picnic tables and fire grills are provided. Vault toilets are available. No drinking water is available. Leashed pets are permitted.

Reservations, fees: No reservations; no fee. Open May through October.

Directions: From Redding, turn west on Highway 299, drive over the Buckhorn Summit, and continue to the junction with Highway 3 near Douglas City. Turn south on Highway 3 and drive to Hayfork. From Hayfork, continue south on Highway 3 for about six miles to Plummer Lookout Road in Peanut. Turn right on Plummer Lookout Road and drive one mile to the campground on the left. Plummer Lookout Road is very rough and not recommended for RVs.

Contact: Shasta-Trinity National Forest, Hayfork Ranger Station, tel. (530) 628-5227 or fax (530) 628-5212.

55 Deerlick Springs

    8

It's a long, twisty drive to this remote and primitive camp set on the edge of the Chanchelulla Wilderness in the transition zone where the valley's oak grasslands give way to conifers. This quiet little spot is set along Browns Creek. A trailhead just north of camp provides a streamside walk. The elevation is 3,100 feet.

Location: On Browns Creek in Shasta-Trinity National Forest; map B1, grid h5.

Campsites, facilities: There are 13 sites for tents or RVs up to 20 feet long. Picnic tables and fire grills are provided. Vault toilets are available. No drinking water is available. Leashed pets are permitted.

Reservations, fees: No reservations; no fee. Open May through October.

Directions: From Red Bluff, turn west on Highway 36 (very twisty) and drive to the For-est Service ranger station in Platina. In Platina, turn north on Harrison Gulch Road and drive 10 miles to the campground on the left.

Contact: Shasta-Trinity National Forest, Yolla Bolla Ranger Station, tel. (530) 352-4211 or fax (530) 352-4312.

56 Hell Gate

    7

This is a pretty spot bordering the South Fork of the Trinity River that is visited by virtually no one. The prime feature is for hikers. The South Fork National Recreation Trail begins at the campground and follows the river for many miles. Additional trails branch off and up into the South Fork Mountains. This area is extremely hot in summer. The elevation is 2,300 feet.

Location: On the South Fork of the Trinity River in Shasta-Trinity National Forest; map B1, grid i0.

Campsites, facilities: There are 10 tent sites and seven sites for tents or RVs up to 15 feet long. Picnic tables and fire grills are provided. Drinking water and vault toilets are available. Some facilities are wheelchair accessible. Leashed pets are permitted. If Hell Gate is full, there are 10 additional campsites that will take tents and RVs up to 20 feet long, just a half mile beyond this campground at Scott's Flat Campground.

Reservations, fees: No reservations; $8 per night. Open May through October.

Directions: From Red Bluff, turn west on Highway 36 (very twisty) and drive past Platina to the junction with Highway 3. Continue west on Highway 36 for 10 miles to the campground entrance on the left side of the road. If you reach Forest Glen, you have gone a mile too far.

Contact: Shasta-Trinity National Forest, Hayfork Ranger Station, tel. (530) 628-5227 or fax (530) 628-5212.

57 Forest Glen

 7

If you get stuck for a spot in this region, this camp almost always has sites open, even during three-day weekends. It is on the edge of a forest near the South Fork of the Trinity River.

Location: On the South Fork of the Trinity River in Shasta-Trinity National Forest; map B1, grid i0.

Campsites, facilities: There are 15 sites for tents or RVs up to 15 feet long. Picnic tables and fire grills are provided. Vault toilets are available. No drinking water is available. Some facilities are wheelchair accessible. Leashed pets are permitted.

Reservations, fees: No reservations; $6 per night. Open May through October.

Directions: From Red Bluff, turn west on Highway 36 (very twisty) and drive past Platina to the junction with Highway 3. Continue west on Highway 36 for 11 miles to Forest Glen. The campground is at the west end of town on the right side of the road.

Contact: Shasta-Trinity National Forest, Hayfork Ranger Station, tel. (530) 628-5227 or fax (530) 628-5212.

58 Bailey Cove

 7

Ruth Lake is the only major lake within a reasonable driving distance of U.S. 101, although some people might argue with you over how reasonable this twisty drive is. Regardless, you end up at a camp along the east shore of Ruth Lake, where fishing for trout or bass and water-skiing are popular. What really wins out is that it is hot and sunny all summer, the exact opposite of the fogged-in Humboldt coast. The elevation is 2,600 feet.

Location: On Ruth Lake in Six Rivers National Forest; map B1, grid i0.

Campsites, facilities: There are 25 sites, a few of which are for RVs up to 22 feet long. Picnic tables and fire grills are provided. Drinking water and vault toilets are available.

A boat ramp and small marina are available nearby. Leashed pets are permitted.

Reservations, fees: No reservations; $12 per night, $5 for an extra vehicle. Open May through October.

Directions: From Eureka, drive south on U.S. 101 to Alton and the junction with Highway 36. Turn east on Highway 36 and drive about 50 miles to the town of Mad River. Turn right at the sign for Ruth Lake/Lower Mad River Road and drive 13 miles to the campground on the right side of the road.

Contact: Six Rivers National Forest, Mad River Ranger District, tel. (707) 574-6233 or fax (707) 574-6273.

59 Fir Cove

 7

This spot is situated along Ruth Lake adjacent to Bailey Cove. Groups can reserve a portion of the campground Mondays through Thursdays. The elevation is 2,600 feet.

Location: On Ruth Lake in Six Rivers National Forest; map B1, grid j0.

Campsites, facilities: There are 19 single or three group sites. Several sites can accommodate RVs up to 22 feet long. Picnic tables and fire grills are provided. Drinking water and vault toilets are available. Leashed pets are permitted.

Reservations, fees: The campground is available for single family camping on summer weekends only, from Friday after 2 p.m. to Monday at 2 p.m. No reservations for single sites; $12 per night, $5 per night for additional vehicles. Reserve group sites through the Mad River Ranger Station at tel. (707) 574-6233; $40 to $50 per night. Open May through October.

Directions: From Eureka, drive south on U.S. 101 to Alton and the junction with Highway 36. Turn east on Highway 36 and drive about 50 miles to the town of Mad River. Turn right at the sign for Ruth Lake/Lower Mad River Road and drive 12 miles to the campground on the right side of the road.

Contact: Six Rivers National Forest, Mad River Ranger District, tel. (707) 574-6233 or fax (707) 574-6273.

60 Basin Gulch

 5

This is one of three little-known campgrounds in the vicinity that rarely gets much use. A trail out of this camp climbs Noble Ridge, eventually rising to a good lookout at 3,933 feet, providing sweeping views of the north valley. Of course, you could also just drive there, taking a dirt road out of Platina. There are many backcountry Forest Service roads in the area so your best bet is to get a Shasta-Trinity National Forest map, which details the roads. The elevation is 2,600 feet.

Location: In Shasta-Trinity National Forest; map B1, grid j5.

Campsites, facilities: There are 13 sites for tents or RVs up to 20 feet. Picnic tables and fire grills are provided. Vault toilets are available. No drinking water is available. Leashed pets are permitted.

Reservations, fees: No reservations; $6 per night. Open May through October.

Directions: From Red Bluff, drive about 45 miles west on Highway 36 to the Yolla Bolly District Ranger Station. From the ranger station, turn south on Stuart Gap Road and drive two miles to the campground on the left.

Contact: Shasta-Trinity National Forest, Yolla Bola Ranger Station, tel. (530) 352-4211 or fax (530) 352-4312.

61 Beegum Gorge

 8

If you want to get the heck away from anything and everything, this spot should be your calling. The camp is set along little Beegum Creek. The road to this camp dead-ends another mile down the road (west), at a trailhead for a hike that is routed along the creek for nearly five miles to North Fork Beegum campground. Another route heads up nearby Little Red Mountain, but it involves a 2,000-foot climb, often across dry, hot terrain. The payoffs include incredible views of the Yolla Bolly-Middle Eel Wilderness and spectacular wildflower displays in the spring. The elevation at the camp is 2,200 feet.

Location: In Shasta-Trinity National Forest; map B1, grid j5.

Campsites, facilities: There are two sites for tents only. Picnic tables and fire grills are provided. Vault toilets are available. No drinking water is available. Garbage must be packed out. Leashed pets are permitted.

Reservations, fees: No reservations; no fee. Open May through October.

Directions: From Red Bluff, turn west on Highway 36 and drive to Platina. In Platina, turn south on Forest Road 29N06 and drive 6.5 miles to the campground.

Contact: Shasta-Trinity National Forest, Yolla Bolla Ranger Station, tel. (530) 352-4211 or fax (530) 352-4312.

CHAPTER B2

LOWER FALLS,
MCCLOUD RIVER

MAP B2

TO GAZELLE   132 TO WEED   TO HIGHWAY 97

KLAMATH NATIONAL FOREST

Mount Shasta 14,162 feet

SHASTA-TRINITY NATIONAL FOREST

Mount Eddy 9,038 feet

Mount Shasta

Scott Mountain Summit 5,401 feet

Lake Siskiyou

McCloud

Snowmans Hill Summit 4,470 feet

CASTLE CRAGS STATE PARK

Dunsmuir

Castella

SHASTA-TRINITY NATIONAL FOREST

Carrville

Grizzly Peak Lookout 6,253 feet

Sacramento River

McCloud River

SHASTA–TRINITY NATIONAL FOREST

Trinity Lake

La Moine

Iron Canyon Reservoir

Big Bend

Lakehead

Pit River

Wengler

O'Brien

Shasta Lake

Montgomery Creek

Hatchet Mountain Summit 4,368 feet

Round Mountain

Shasta Lake

Ingot

Whiskeytown

Shasta

Bella Vista

Oak Run

Whitmore

Whiskeytown Lake

REDDING

Enterprise

Igo

Palo Cedro

Millville

Viola

Anderson

Shingletown

Cottonwood

Manton

TO BEEGUM   TO RED BLUFF   284   TO DALES STATION   TO MINERAL

© AVALON TRAVEL PUBLISHING, INC.

CHAPTER B2

(CONTINUED ON NEXT PAGE)

1 Scott Mountain

   7

This camp is a jump-off point for hikers, with the Pacific Crest Trail passing right by here. If you hike southwest, it leads into the Scott Mountains and skirts the northern edge of the Trinity Alps Wilderness. Another option here is driving on Forest Road 40N08, which begins directly across from camp and Highway 3. On this road, it's only two miles to Big Carmen Lake, a small, largely unknown and pretty little spot. Campground elevation is 5,400 feet.

Location: In Shasta-Trinity National Forest; map B2, grid a0.

Campsites, facilities: There are seven tent sites. Picnic tables and fire grills are provided. Vault toilets are available. No drinking water is available. All garbage must be packed out. Leashed pets are permitted.

Reservations, fees: No reservations; no fee. Open year-round.

Directions: From Redding, drive north on Interstate 5 just past Weed and take the Edgewood turnoff. At the stop sign, turn left and drive a short distance to the stop sign at Old Stage Road. Turn right on Old Stage Road and drive six miles to Gazelle. In Gazelle, turn left at Gazelle-Callahan Road and drive to Callahan. In Callahan, turn south on Highway 3 and drive to Scott Mountain Summit and look for the campground on the right side of the road.

Contact: Shasta-Trinity National Forest, Weaverville Ranger Station, tel. (530) 623-2121 or fax (530) 623-6010.

2 Kangaroo Lake/Walk-In

 10

A remote paved road leads right to Kangaroo Lake, set at 6,050 feet, providing a genuine rarity: a beautiful and pristine mountain lake with a walk-in campground, good fishing for brook and rainbow trout, and an excellent trailhead for hikers. The walk to the campsites is very short, five minutes tops, with many sites within a minute's walk. Reaching the lake requires another five minutes, but a paved wheelchair-accessible trail is available. In addition, a switchbacked ramp for wheelchairs makes it one of the best wheelchair-accessible fishing areas in California. For hiking, a trail rises up steeply out of the campground and connects to the Pacific Crest Trail, from which you turn left to gain a dramatic lookout of Northern California peaks as well as the lake below.

Location: In Klamath National Forest; map B2, grid a1.

Campsites, facilities: There are 13 drive-in sites for RVs or trailers up to 25 feet and five walk-in sites for tents. Picnic tables and fire grills are provided. Drinking water and vault toilets are available. Some facilities are wheelchair-accessible, including a nearby fishing pier. Leashed pets are permitted.

Reservations, fees: No reservations; $10 per

night. Open June through October, weather permitting.

Directions: From Redding, drive north on Interstate 5 just past Weed and take the Edgewood turnoff. At the stop sign, turn left and drive a short distance to the stop sign at Old Stage Road. Turn right on Old Stage Road and drive six miles to Gazelle. In Gazelle, turn left at Gazelle-Callahan Road and drive over the summit. From the summit, continue about five miles to Rail Creek Road. Turn left at Rail Creek Road and drive approximately five miles to where the road dead-ends at Kangaroo Lake Walk-In.

Contact: Klamath National Forest, Scott River Ranger Station, tel. (530) 468-5351 or fax (530) 468-1290.

❸ KOA Mount Shasta

     7

Despite this KOA camp's relative proximity to the town of Mount Shasta, the extended driveway, wooded grounds, and view of Mount Shasta offer some feeling of seclusion. A bonus here is that those cute little KOA log cabins are available, providing additional privacy. There are many excellent side trips. The best is driving up Everitt Memorial Highway, which rises up the slopes of Mount Shasta to tree line at Bunny Flat, where you can take outstanding, short day hikes with great views to the south of the Sacramento River Canyon and Castle Crags. In the winter, you can play in the snow.

Location: In Mount Shasta City; map B2, grid a5.

Campsites, facilities: There are 41 RV sites with full hookups, four camping cabins, and 89 additional sites for tents or RVs (partial hookups). Picnic tables and fire grills are provided. Restrooms, showers, a playground, propane gas, a grocery store, horseshoe pit, shuffleboard, a swimming pool, and coin laundry are available. Some facilities are wheelchair accessible. Leashed pets are permitted.

Reservations, fees: Reservations at tel. (800) 562-3617; $18 to $25 per night. Cabins are $34 to $39 per night. Major credit cards accepted. Open year-round.

Directions: From Redding, drive north on Interstate 5 to the town of Mount Shasta. Continue past the first Mount Shasta exit and take the Central Mount Shasta exit. Turn right at the stop sign and drive to the stoplight at Mount Shasta Boulevard. Turn left and drive a half mile to East Hinckley Boulevard. Turn right on East Hinckley, drive a very short distance, then turn left at the entrance to the extended driveway for Mount Shasta KOA.

Contact: KOA Mount Shasta, tel. or fax, (530) 926-4029; website: www.koa.com.

❹ McBride Springs

   8

This camp is set on the slopes of the awesome Mount Shasta (14,162 feet), California's most majestic mountain. Stargazing is fantastic here, and during full moons, an eerie glow is cast on the adjoining high mountain slopes. A good side trip is to drive to the end of Everitt Memorial Highway, which tops out above 7,000 feet. You get great lookouts to the west and a jump-off point for a Shasta expedition or day hike to Panther Meadows.

Location: In Shasta-Trinity National Forest; map B2, grid a5.

Campsites, facilities: There are 10 sites for tents or small RVs. Picnic tables and fire grills are provided. Drinking water (from a single well with a hand pump at the north end of the campground) and vault toilets are available. Supplies and a coin laundry are available in the town of Mount Shasta. Leashed pets are permitted.

Reservations, fees: No reservations; $12 per night. Open Memorial Day weekend through October, weather permitting.

Directions: From Redding drive north on Interstate 5 to the town of Mount Shasta and take the Central Mount Shasta exit. Turn right and continue on Lake Street through town; once out of town, it turns to the left and becomes Everitt Memorial Highway. Continue on Everitt Memorial Highway for four miles to the campground entrance on the left side of the road.

Contact: Shasta-Trinity National Forest, Mount Shasta Ranger District, tel. (530) 926-4511 or fax (530) 926-5120.

5 Panther Meadows Walk-In

   9

This quiet site, on the slopes of Mount Shasta at 7,400 feet, features access to the pristine Panther Meadows, a high mountain meadow set just below tree line. It's a sacred place, regardless of your religious orientation. The hiking is excellent here, with a short hike out to Gray Butte (8,108 feet) for a perfect look to the south of Castle Crags, Mount Lassen, and the Sacramento River Canyon.

Location: In Shasta-Trinity National Forest; map B2, grid a6.

Campsites, facilities: There are 10 walk-in tent sites (trailers not recommended). Picnic tables and fire grills are provided. Vault toilets are available. No drinking water is available. Garbage must be packed out. Supplies are available in the town of Mount Shasta. Leashed pets are permitted.

Reservations, fees: No reservations; no fee. Open mid-June to mid-October, weather permitting.

Directions: From Redding, drive north on Interstate 5 to the town of Mount Shasta and take the Central Mount Shasta exit. Turn right and continue on Lake Street through town; once out of town, Lake Street turns to the left and becomes Everitt Memorial Highway. Continue on Everitt Memorial Highway for about 10 miles to the Bunny Flat parking area (where the road is gated). Park, walk past the gate, and continue for one mile to the campground entrance on the right side of the road. Note: When the gate is open, the walk takes only a few minutes.

Contact: Shasta-Trinity National Forest,

Mount Shasta Ranger District, tel. (530) 926-4511 or fax (530) 926-5120.

6 Horse Flat

    6

This camp is used by commercial pack operations as well as horse owners preparing for trips into the Trinity Alps. The camp even has a corral, though it was unused on our visit. A trail starts right out of camp and is routed deep into the Trinity Alps Wilderness. It starts at 3,200 feet in elevation, then climbs all the way along Eagle Creek to Eagle Peak, where it intersects with the Pacific Crest Trail, then drops over the ridge to little Telephone Lake, a nine-mile hike. Note: Horse owners should call for the condition of the corral prior to making the trip.

Location: On Eagle Creek in Shasta-Trinity National Forest; map B2, grid b0.

Campsites, facilities: There are five tent sites and 11 sites for tents or RVs up to 16 feet long. Picnic tables and fire grills are provided. Vault toilets are available. No drinking water is available. Horse corrals are available. Garbage must be packed out. Leashed pets are permitted.

Reservations, fees: No reservations; no fee. Open mid-May through October.

Directions: From Redding, drive west on Highway 299 to Weaverville and Highway 3. Turn north on Highway 3 and drive to Trinity Center at the north end of Trinity Lake. From Trinity Center, continue north on Highway 3 for 16.5 miles to Eagle Creek Campground (on the right) and Forest Road 38N27 on the left. Turn left on Forest Road 38N27 and drive two miles to the campground.

Contact: Shasta-Trinity National Forest, Weaverville Ranger Station, tel. (530) 623-2121 or fax (530) 623-6010.

7 Eagle Creek

    7

This campground is set where little Eagle Creek enters the north Trinity River. Some campers use it as a base camp for a fishing trip, with the rainbow trout often abundant but predictably small in this stretch of water. The campground is open year-round, but there is no drinking water in the winter. The elevation is 2,800 feet.

Location: In Shasta-Trinity National Forest; map B2, grid c0.

Campsites, facilities: There are five tent sites and 12 sites for tents or RVs up to 27 feet long. Picnic tables and fire grills are provided. Drinking water (spring, summer, and fall only), vault toilets, and a camp host are available. Leashed pets are permitted.

Reservations, fees: No reservations; $8 per night. Open year-round.

Directions: From Redding, drive west on Highway 299 to Weaverville and Highway 3. Turn north on Highway 3 and drive to Trinity Center at the north end of Trinity Lake. From Trinity Center, continue north on Highway 3 for 16.5 miles to the campground on the right side of the road.

Contact: Shasta-Trinity National Forest, Weaverville Ranger Station, tel. (530) 623-2121 or fax (530) 623-6010.

8 Trinity River

 7

This camp offers easy access off Highway 3, yet is fairly secluded and provides streamside access to the upper Trinity River. It's a good base camp for a fishing trip when the upper Trinity is loaded with small trout. The elevation is 2,500 feet.

Location: In Shasta-Trinity National Forest; map B2, grid c0.

Campsites, facilities: There are seven sites for tents or RVs up to 32 feet long. Picnic tables and fire grills are provided. Drinking water (spring, summer, and fall only), vault toilets, and a camp host are available. Leashed pets are permitted.

Reservations, fees: No reservations; $8 per night. Open year-round, but there's no drinking water in the winter.

Directions: From Redding, drive west on Highway 299 to Weaverville and Highway 3. Turn north on Highway 3 and drive to Trinity Center at the north end of Trinity Lake. From Trinity Center, continue north on Highway 3 for 9.5 miles to the campground on the left side of the road.

Contact: Shasta-Trinity National Forest, Weaverville Ranger Station, tel. (530) 623-2121 or fax (530) 623-6010.

9 Gumboot Lake

 8

This pretty spot provides a few small camps set beside a small yet beautiful high mountain lake, the kind of place many think you can only reach with long hikes. Not so with Gumboot. In addition, the fishing is good here, with rainbow trout in the 12-inch class. The lake is small, almost too small for even a canoe, and better suited to a pram, raft, or float tube. When the fishing gets good, it can get crowded, with both out-of-towners and locals making casts from the shoreline. An option is hiking 10 minutes through forest to Upper Gumboot Lake, which is more of a pond with small trout. Another excellent hike is available here, tromping off-trail beyond Upper Gumboot Lake and up the back slope of the lake to the Pacific Crest Trail, then turning left and scrambling to a great lookout of Mount Shasta in the distance and Gumboot in the foreground.

Location: In Shasta-Trinity National Forest; map B2, grid b3.

Campsites, facilities: There are four sites for tents or RVs up to 10 feet long, and across the creek there are four tent sites. Picnic tables are provided. Vault toilets are available. No drinking water is available. Garbage must be packed out. Leashed pets are permitted.

Reservations, fees: No reservations; no fee. Open May through October, weather permitting.

Directions: From the town of Mount Shasta on Interstate 5, take the Central Mount Shasta exit and drive to the stop sign. Turn west and continue a short distance to Old Stage Road. Turn left and drive a quarter mile to a Y at W. A. Barr Road. Bear right on W. A. Barr Road and drive past Box Canyon Dam and the Lake Siskiyou Campground entrance. Continue 10 miles to a fork, signed for Gumboot Lake. Bear left and drive one-half mile to the lake and campsites.

Contact: Shasta-Trinity National Forest, Mount Shasta Ranger District, tel. (530) 926-4511 or fax (530) 926-5120.

10 Toad Lake Walk-In

 9

If you want the remote beauty and splendor of an alpine lake on the Pacific Crest Trail, yet don't want to walk far to get there, this is the place. Little Toad Lake is no easy trick to get to, with a bone-jarring ride for the last half hour, followed by a 15-minute walk, but it's worth the effort. It's a beautiful little lake in the Mount Eddy Range, with lakeside sites, excellent swimming, fair fishing for small trout, and great hiking. The best of the latter is a 45-minute hike out of the Toad Lake Basin (follow the trail counterclockwise around the lake and up to the ridge) to Porcupine Lake, a pristine mountain lake.

Location: In Shasta-Trinity National Forest; map B2, grid b3.

Campsites, facilities: There are six walk-in tent sites. A vault toilet is provided, but not always functioning. No drinking water is available. All garbage must be packed out. Leashed pets are permitted.

Reservations, fees: No reservations; no fee. Access roads may be closed due to flooding; call ahead for status. Open May through October, weather permitting.

Directions: From the town of Mount Shasta on Interstate 5, take the Central Mount Shasta exit and drive to the stop sign. Turn west and drive a short distance to Old Stage Road. Turn left and drive a quarter mile to a Y at W. A. Barr Road. Bear right and drive past Box

Canyon Dam and the entrance to Lake Siskiyou, and continue up the mountain (the road becomes Forest Road 26). Just past a concrete bridge, turn right at the sign for Toad Lake, drive 0.2 mile, then turn left on a dirt Forest Service road and continue for 11 miles to the parking area. The road is extremely bumpy and twisty, and the final half mile to the trailhead is rocky and rough. High-clearance, four-wheel-drive vehicles are recommended. Walk in about one-half mile to the lake and campsites.

Contact: Shasta-Trinity National Forest, Mount Shasta Ranger District, tel. (530) 926-4511 or fax (530) 926-5120.

11 Castle Lake

 10

Castle Lake is a beautiful spot, a deep blue lake set in a granite bowl with a spectacular wall on the far side. The views of Mount Shasta are great, fishing is good (especially ice fishing in winter), canoeing or floating around on a raft is a lot of fun, and there is a terrific hike that loops around the left side of the lake, rising to the ridge overlooking the lake for dramatic views. The campground is not right beside the lake, to ensure the pristine clear waters remain untouched, but is rather just a short distance downstream along Castle Lake Creek. The elevation is 5,450 feet.

Location: In Shasta-Trinity National Forest; map B2, grid b4.

Campsites, facilities: There are six sites for tents or RVs up to 16 feet long. Picnic tables and fire grills are provided. Vault toilets are available. No drinking water is available. Leashed pets are permitted.

Reservations, fees: No reservations; no fee. Open May through October, weather permitting.

Directions: From the town of Mount Shasta on Interstate 5, take the Central Mount Shasta exit and drive to the stop sign. Turn west and drive a short distance to Old Stage Road. Turn left and drive a quarter mile to a Y at W. A.

Barr Road. Bear right on W. A. Barr Road and drive past Box Canyon Dam. Turn left at Castle Lake Road and drive seven miles to the campground access road on the left. Turn left and drive a short distance to the campground. Note: Castle Lake is another quarter mile up the road; there are no legal campsites along the lake's shoreline.

Contact: Shasta-Trinity National Forest, Mount Shasta Ranger District, tel. (530) 926-4511 or fax (530) 926-5120.

12 Lake Siskiyou Campground and Marina

    8

This true gem of a lake, virtually in the shadow of Mount Shasta, is almost always full and offers a variety of recreation options. The campground complexes are huge, yet they are tucked into the forest so visitors don't get their style cramped. The lake is within walking distance, but fishermen will want to drive since a good boat ramp is available. The 10-mph speed limit is strictly enforced. There is an excellent beach and swimming area, the latter protected by a buoy line.

Location: Near Mount Shasta; map B2, grid b5.

Campsites, facilities: There are 150 RV sites (25 with partial and 125 with full hookups) and 225 additional sites for tents, four of which are group areas. There are also 11 RV rentals and 24 lodging units available, including cabins. Picnic tables and fire grills are provided. Drinking water, flush toilets, showers, playground, propane, grocery store, gift shop, deli, coin laundry, and a sanitary disposal station are available. There are also marinas, boat rentals (canoes, kayaks, motorized boats), free boat launching, fishing dock, fish-cleaning station, beach, and a banquet room. A free movie plays every night in the summer. Some facilities are wheelchair accessible. Leashed pets are permitted.

Reservations, fees: Reservations are accepted; $16.50 to $22.50 per night, $4 per night each additional vehicle. RVs rent for $50 to $85 per night. Lodging units are $85 per night. A $1 day-use fee per person is charged at the entrance station. Major credit cards are accepted. Open April through October, weather permitting.

Directions: From the town of Mount Shasta on Interstate 5, take the Central Mount Shasta exit and drive to the stop sign. Turn west and drive a short distance to Old Stage Road. Turn left and drive one-quarter mile to a Y at W. A. Barr Road. Bear right on W. A. Barr Road and drive past Box Canyon Dam. Two miles farther, turn right at the entrance road for Lake Siskiyou Campground and Marina and drive a short distance to the entrance station.

Contact: Lake Siskiyou Campground and Marina, tel. (530) 926-2618 or (888) 926-2618; web-site: www.lakesis.com.

13 Friday's RV & McCloud Fly Fishing Ranch

     8

With two fishing ponds, a fishable stream running through the camp, and the nearby McCloud River's wild trout section a half-hour drive to the south, Friday's offers great fishing opportunities for every member of the family. The park covers 400 wooded and grassy acres with nearby access to the Pacific Crest Trail for hiking. Owner Bob Friday is quite a character, and figured out by planting giant rainbow trout in the ponds for catch-and-release fishing that flyfishers will stop to catch a monster and take a photograph, then tell people they caught the fish on the McCloud River, where they are smaller and elusive. Also available is a public golf course on Squaw Valley Road, plus the dinner and excursion train that runs out of McCloud on summer weekends. See Ah-Di-Na and McCloud Dance Country RV Park for other information and side trip options.

Location: Near McCloud; map B2, grid c6.

Campsites, facilities: There are 30 sites for RVs of any length with full hookups, and a large, grassy area for dispersed tent camping. Picnic tables and fire pits are provided. Drinking water, restrooms with hot showers and flush toilets, cableTV, laundry room, pay phone, propane gas, and a recreation room are available. There is a one-acre stocked fishpond for the youngsters, another three-acre pond with wild and stocked trout, and a scheduled fly-fishing school. No fishing license is required on the premises. Some facilities are wheelchair accessible. Leashed pets are permitted.

Reservations, fees: Reservations are advised; $14 to $21 per night for two people, $3 for each additional camper; weekly rates are $124. Open May through October, weather permitting.

Directions: From Redding, drive north on Interstate 5 and continue just past Dunsmuir to the junction with Highway 89. Bear right on Highway 89 and drive 11 miles to McCloud and Squaw Valley Road. Turn right at Squaw Valley Road and drive six miles to the park entrance on the right.

Contact: Friday's, tel. (530) 964-2878; website: www.fridaysflyshop.com.

14 McCloud Dance Country RV Park

     7

Dance Country RV Park is very popular with square dancers in the summer. The town of McCloud is the home of McCloud Dance Country Hall, a large dance hall dedicated to square and round dancing activities. The park is sprinkled with old-growth pine trees and bordered by Squaw Valley Creek, a pretty stream. The RV sites are grassy and manicured, many shaded. McCloud River's three waterfalls are accessible from the McCloud River Loop, five miles south of the park on Highway 89. Mount Shasta Ski Park also offers summer activities such as biking, mountain climbing, and chairlift rides to great views of the surrounding forests. The ski park access road is six miles west of McCloud off Highway 89 at Snowman's Hill Summit. The McCloud River Railroad runs an excursion and a dinner train on summer weekends out of McCloud; reservations are available in town. If you're lucky you might see "Old Engine No. 25," one of the few remaining steam engines in service. For more information, see Fowler's Camp.

Location: In McCloud; map B2, grid c6.

Campsites, facilities: There are 134 sites for RVs of any length, 98 with full hookups and 36 with partial hookups. A grassy area is available for tent camping. Picnic tables are provided. Drinking water, restrooms with hot showers, a central barbecue and campfire area, cableTV, modem hookups, laundry room, fish-cleaning station, and two pet walks are available. Some facilities are wheelchair accessible. Large groups are welcome. Leashed pets are permitted.

Reservations, fees: Reservations are recommended; $18.50 to $23 per night for two people, $1.50 for each additional child from 6 to 12 years old, and $3 for each additional camper 13 years of age or older. Tent sites $15. Open year-round.

Directions: From Redding, drive north on Interstate 5 and continue just past Dunsmuir to the junction with Highway 89. Turn east on Highway 89 and drive 11 miles to McCloud. Turn right on Squaw Valley Road and then turn immediately left into the park entrance.

Contact: Dance Country RV Park, P.O. Box 486, McCloud, CA 96057; tel. (530) 964-2252.

15 Fowler's Camp

      10

This campground is set beside the beautiful McCloud River, providing the chance for an easy hike to two waterfalls, including one of the most dramatic in Northern California. From the camp, the trail is routed upstream through forest, a near-level walk for only 15 minutes, then arrives at awesome Middle

Falls, a wide-sweeping and powerful cascade best viewed in April. By summer, the flows subside and warm to the point that some people will swim in the pool at the base of the falls. Another trail is routed from camp downstream to Lower Falls, an outstanding swimming hole in midsummer. Fishing the McCloud River here is fair, with trout stocks made from Lakim Dam on downstream to the camp. If this camp is full, Cattle Camp and Algoma offer overflow areas.

Location: On the McCloud River in Shasta-Trinity National Forest; map B2, grid c7.

Campsites, facilities: There are 39 sites for tents or RVs up to 30 feet long. Picnic tables and fire grills are provided. Drinking water and vault toilets are available. Some facilities are wheelchair accessible. Leashed pets are permitted.

Reservations, fees: No reservations; $12 per night.

Directions: From Redding, drive north on Interstate 5 and continue just past Dunsmuir to the junction with Highway 89. Turn east on Highway 89 and drive 12 miles to McCloud. From McCloud, drive five miles southeast on Highway 89 to the campground entrance road on the right. Turn right and drive a short distance to a Y, then turn left at the Y to the campground.

Contact: Shasta-Trinity National Forest, McCloud Ranger District, tel. (530) 964-2184 or fax (530) 964-2938.

16 Cattle Camp

 5

This campground is ideal for RV campers who want a rustic setting, or as an overflow area if the more attractive Fowler's Camp is filled. One of the best swimming holes in the McCloud River is near the camp, although the water is typically cold. There are several good side trips in the area, including fishing on the nearby McCloud River, visiting the three waterfalls near Fowler's Camp, and exploring the north slopes of Mount Shasta (a map of

Shasta-Trinity National Forest details the back roads).

Location: On the McCloud River in Shasta-Trinity National Forest; map B2, grid c8.

Campsites, facilities: There are 29 sites for tents or RVs. Picnic tables and fire grills are provided. Drinking water and vault toilets are available. Some facilities are wheelchair accessible, including toilets. Leashed pets are permitted.

Reservations, fees: No reservations; $10 per night.

Directions: From Redding, drive north on Interstate 5 and continue just past Dunsmuir to the junction with Highway 89. Turn east on Highway 89 and drive to McCloud. From McCloud, drive 11 miles east on Highway 89 to the campground entrance road on the right. Turn right and drive a half mile to the campground on the left side of the road.

Contact: Shasta-Trinity National Forest, McCloud Ranger District, tel. (530) 964-2184 or fax (530) 964-2938.

17 Algoma

 7

This little-known, undeveloped spot along the McCloud River is quite dusty in August. It is an alternative to Fowler's Camp and Cattle Camp. (See those entries for side trip options.) A dirt road out of Algoma Camp (turn right at the junction) follows along the headwaters of the McCloud River, past Cattle Camp to Upper Falls. There is a parking area for a short walk to view Middle Falls and on to Fowler's Camp and Lower Falls.

Location: On the McCloud River in Shasta-Trinity National Forest; map B2, grid c9.

Campsites, facilities: There are eight sites for tents or RVs. Picnic tables and fire grills are provided. A vault toilet is available intermittently. No drinking water is available. Leashed pets are permitted.

Reservations, fees: No reservations; no fee.

Directions: From Redding, drive north on Interstate 5 and continue just past Dunsmuir to the junction with Highway 89. Turn east on Highway 89 and drive to McCloud. From McCloud, drive 14 miles east on Highway 89 to the campground entrance road on the right. Turn right and drive one mile to the campground on the right side of the road.

Contact: Shasta-Trinity National Forest, McCloud Ranger District, tel. (530) 964-2184 or fax (530) 964-2938.

18 Railroad Park Resort RV Park

     7

This camp was designed in the spirit of the railroad, when steam trains ruled the rails. The property features old stage cars (available for overnight lodging) and a steam locomotive. Many good side trips are available in the area, including excellent hiking and sightseeing at Castle Crags State Park (where there is a series of awesome granite spires) and outstanding trout fishing on the upper Sacramento River.

Location: South of Dunsmuir; map B2, grid c4.

Campsites, facilities: There are 60 sites, many with full hookups, and a separate area for tents only. Restrooms, hot showers, satellite TV hookups, modem hookups, grocery store, ice, laundry room, restaurant, recreation room, playground, and horseshoes are available. Some facilities are wheelchair accessible. Leashed pets are permitted.

Reservations, fees: Deposit required with reservation; $16 to $24 fee per night, $2 per person per night for more than two people. Major credit cards accepted. Open April through October.

Directions: From Redding, drive north on Interstate 5 for 45 miles to Railroad Park Road. Turn west and drive a half mile to the campground.

Contact: Railroad Park Campground, tel. (530) 235-0420; website: www.rrpark.com

19 Castle Crags State Park

     9

Ancient granite spires tower 6,000 feet above the park, and beyond to the north is the giant Mount Shasta, making for a spectacular natural setting. The campsites are set in forest, shaded, very pretty, and sprinkled along a paved access road. At the end of the access road is a parking area for the two-minute walk to the Crags Lookout, a beautiful view. Nearby is the trailhead (at 2,500 feet elevation) for hikes up the Crags, featuring a six-mile round-trip that rises to Castle Dome at 4,966 feet, the leading spire on the crag's ridge. Trout fishing is good in the nearby Sacramento River, but requires driving, walking, and exploring to find the best spots. This is a popular state park, with reservations often required in summer, but with your choice of any campsite even in late spring.

Location: On the Sacramento River; map B2, grid c4.

Campsites, facilities: There are 64 sites for tents or RVs up to 27 feet. Picnic tables, food lockers, and fire grills are provided. Drinking water, wood, hot showers, and flush toilets are available. Leashed pets are permitted at campsites only.

Reservations, fees: Reserve at (800) 444-PARK (800-444-7275) or website: www.ReserveAmerica.com; $12 per night. Open year-round.

Directions: From Redding, drive north on Interstate 5 for 45 miles to the Castle Crags State Park exit. Turn west and drive to the well-signed park entrance on the right side of the road.

Contact: Castle Crags State Park, tel. (530) 235-2684.

20 Best in the West Resort

     3

This is a good layover spot for RV cruisers looking to take a break. The proximity to Castle Crags State Park, the Sacramento River, and Mount Shasta make the location a winner.

Location: Near Dunsmuir; map B2, grid c4.

Campsites, facilities: There are 16 RV sites, most with full hookups. Five cabins are also available. Picnic tables are provided. Restrooms, hot showers, cable TV, coin laundry, and playground are available. Leashed pets are permitted.

Reservations, fees: Reservations are accepted; $15 per night. Cabins $45 to $65 per night. Open year-round.

Directions: From Redding, drive north on Interstate 5 for about 40 miles to the Sims Road exit. Take the Sims Road exit and drive one block west on Sims Road to the campground on the left.

Contact: Best in the West Resort, tel. (530) 235-2603; website:eggerbestwest.com.

21 Sims Flat

 7

The upper Sacramento River is again becoming one of the best trout streams in the West that provides easy and direct access off an interstate highway. This camp is a good example. Sitting beside the upper Sacramento River, it provides access to some of the better spots for trout fishing, particularly from mid-May through July. The trout population has largely recovered since the devastating spill from a train derailment that occurred in 1991. There is a wheelchair-accessible interpretive trail. If you want to literally get away from it all, there is a trailhead about three miles east on Sims Flat Road which climbs along South Fork, including a terrible, steep, one-mile section near the top, eventually popping out at Tombstone Mountain.

Location: On the Sacramento River; map B2, grid c4.

Campsites, facilities: There are 19 sites for tents or RVs up to 16 feet. Picnic tables and fire grills are provided. Drinking water and flush and vault toilets are available. A grocery store is nearby. Some facilities are wheelchair accessible. Leashed pets are permitted.

Reservations, fees: No reservations; $12 per night. Open April through October.

Directions: From Redding, drive north on Interstate 5 for about 40 miles to the Sims Road exit. Take the Sims Road exit (on the east side of the highway) and drive south for a mile to the campground.

Contact: Shasta-Trinity National Forest, Mount Shasta Ranger District, tel. (530) 926-4511 or fax (530) 926-5120.

22 Ah-Di-Na

 9

This is the perfect base camp for trout fishing on the lower McCloud River, with campsites just a cast away from one of the prettiest streams in California. Downstream of the camp is a special two-mile stretch of river governed by the Nature Conservancy, where all fish must be released, no bait is permitted, single, barbless hooks are mandated, and only 10 rods are allowed on the river at any one time. Wildlife is abundant in the area, the Pacific Crest Trail passes adjacent to the camp, and an excellent nature trail is also available along the river in the McCloud Nature Conservancy.

Location: On the McCloud River in Shasta-Trinity National Forest; map B2, grid c6.

Campsites, facilities: There are 16 tent sites. Picnic tables and fire grills are provided. Drinking water and flush toilets are available. Leashed pets are permitted.

Reservations, fees: No reservations; $8 per night.

Directions: From Redding, drive north on Interstate 5 past Dunsmuir to the junction with Highway 89. Turn right and drive to McCloud. In McCloud, turn right on Squaw Valley Road and drive to Lake McCloud. Turn right at Lake McCloud and continue along the lake to a signed turnoff on the right side of the road (at a deep cove in the lake). Turn right (the road turns to dirt) and drive four miles to the campground entrance on the left side of the road. Turn left and drive a short distance to the campground.

Contact: Shasta-Trinity National Forest, McCloud Ranger District, tel. (530) 964-2184 or fax (530) 964-2938.

23 Jackass Springs

 6

If you're poking around for a more secluded campsite on this end of the lake, halt your search and pick the best spot you can find at this campground, since it's the only one in this area of Trinity Lake. The campground is one mile from Trinity Lake, but you can't see the lake from the camp. It is most popular in the fall as a base camp for deer hunters. The elevation is 2,500 feet.

Location: On Trinity Lake in Shasta-Trinity National Forest; map B2, grid d0.

Campsites, facilities: There are 21 sites for tents or RVs up to 32 feet long. Picnic tables and fire grills are provided. Vault toilets are available. No drinking water is available. Garbage must be packed out. Leashed pets are permitted.

Reservations, fees: No reservations; no fee. Open year-round, weather permitting.

Directions: From Redding head west on Highway 299 and drive to Weaverville and the junction with Highway 3. Turn north on Highway 3 and drive 29 miles to Trinity Center. Continue five miles past Trinity Center to County Road 106. Turn right on County Road 106 and drive 12 miles to the Jackass Springs/County Road 119 turnoff. Turn right on County Road 119 and drive five miles to the campground at the end of the road.

Contact: Shasta-Trinity National Forest, Weaverville Ranger Station, tel. (530) 623-2121 or fax (530) 623-6010.

24 Clear Creek

 6

This is a primitive, little-known camp that gets little use. It is set near Clear Creek at 3,500 feet elevation. In fall hunters will occasionally turn it into a deer camp, with the adjacent slopes of Blue Mountain and Damnation Peak in the Trinity Divide country providing fair numbers of large bucks, three points or better. Trinity Lake is only seven miles to the west, but it seems like it's in a different world.

Location: In Shasta-Trinity National Forest; map B2, grid e0.

Campsites, facilities: There are two tent sites and six sites for tents or RVs up to 22 feet long. Picnic tables and fire grills are provided. Vault toilets are available. No drinking water is available. Garbage must be packed out. Leashed pets are permitted.

Reservations, fees: No reservations; no fee. Open year-round.

Directions: From Redding, turn west on Highway 299 and drive 17 miles to Trinity Lake Road (just west of Whiskeytown Lake). Turn north on Trinity Lake Road and continue past the town of French Gulch for about 12 miles to the Trinity Mountain Ranger Station. Turn right on County Road 106/East Side Road (gravel) and drive north for about 11 miles to the campground access road (dirt) on right. Turn right on the access road and drive two miles to the campground.

Contact: Shasta-Trinity National Forest, Weaverville Ranger District, tel. (530) 623-2121 or fax (530) 623-6010.

25 Deadlun

 8

Deadlun is a pretty campground set in the forest, shaded and quiet, with a five-minute walk or one-minute drive to the Deadlun Creek arm of Iron Canyon Reservoir. Drive? If you have a canoe to launch or fishing equipment to carry, driving is the choice. Trout fishing is good here, both in April and May, then again in October and early November. One downer is that the shoreline is often very muddy here in March and early April. Because of an engineering error with the dam, the lake never fills completely, causing the lakeshore to be strewn with stumps and quite muddy after spring rains and snowmelt.

Location: On Iron Canyon Reservoir in Shasta-Trinity National Forest; map B2, grid d7.

Campsites, facilities: There are 30 sites for tents or RVs up to 24 feet long. Picnic tables and fire grills are provided. Vault toilets are available. No drinking water is available. A small boat ramp is available one mile from the camp. Leashed pets are permitted.

Reservations, fees: No reservations; no fee. Open year-round.

Directions: From Redding, drive east on Highway 299 for 37 miles to Big Bend Road. At Big Bend Road, turn left and drive 15.2 miles to the town of Big Bend. Continue for five miles to the lake, bearing right at the T intersection, and continue for two miles (past the boat launch turnoff) to the campground turnoff on the left side of the road. Turn left and drive one mile to the campground.

Contact: Shasta-Trinity National Forest, Shasta Lake Ranger District, tel. (530) 275-1587 or fax (530) 275-1512, or Shasta Lake Visitor Center, tel. (530) 275-1589.

26 Hawkins Landing

 7

The adjacent boat ramp makes Hawkins Landing the better of the two camps at Iron Canyon Reservoir for campers with trailered boats (though Deadlun is far more secluded). Iron Canyon provides good fishing for trout, has a resident bald eagle or two, and also has nearby hot springs in the town of Big Bend. One problem with this lake is the annual drawdown in late fall, which causes the shoreline to be extremely muddy in the spring. The lake usually rises high enough to make the boat ramp functional by mid-April. This camp is set at an elevation of 2,700 feet.

Location: On Iron Canyon Reservoir; map B2, grid e6.

Campsites, facilities: There are 10 sites for tents or RVs up to 30 feet long. Picnic tables and fire grills are provided. Drinking water,

vault toilets, and a small boat ramp are available. Supplies can be obtained in Big Bend. Leashed pets are permitted.

Reservations, fees: No reservations; $10 per night, $1 dog fee, $3 per night per extra vehicle, $7 per night for extra RV. Open Memorial Day weekend to Labor Day weekend, weather permitting.

Directions: From Redding, drive east on Highway 299 for 37 miles to Big Bend Road. At Big Bend Road turn left and drive 15.2 miles to the town of Big Bend. Continue for 2.1 miles to Forest Road 38N11. Turn left and drive 3.3 miles to the Iron Canyon Reservoir Spillway. Turn right and drive 1.1 miles to a dirt road. Turn left and drive 0.3 miles to the campground.

Contact: PG&E Building and Land Services, tel. (916) 386-5164.

27 Lakeshore Villa RV Park

 7

This is a large campground with level, shaded sites for RVs, set near the northern Sacramento River arm of giant Shasta Lake. Prime time is April through July, when lake levels are highest and bass and trout are on the bite.

Location: On Shasta Lake; map B2, grid e2.

Campsites, facilities: There are 86 sites with full or partial hookups for RVs and six sites for RVs or tents. Restrooms, hot showers, sanitary disposal station, cable TV, coin laundry, playground, recreation room, and a boat dock are available. Leashed pets are permitted.

Reservations, fees: A deposit is required with reservation; $18 per night. Major credit cards are accepted. Open year-round.

Directions: From Redding, drive north on Interstate 5 for 24 miles to the Lakeshore-Antlers Road exit in Lakehead. Take that exit, turn left at the stop sign, and drive under the freeway to Lakeshore Drive. Turn left on Lakeshore Drive and drive a half mile to the campground on the right.

Contact: Lakeshore Villa RV Park and Camp, tel. (800) 238-8688 or (530) 238-8688.

Lakeshore Inn & RV

 7

Shasta Lake is a boater's paradise, and an ideal spot for campers with boats, with a nearby boat ramp and private marina available. It is on the Sacramento River arm of Shasta Lake.

Location: On Shasta Lake; map B2, grid e2.

Campsites, facilities: There are 35 RV sites with partial and full hookups and 10 cabins. Picnic tables are provided. Restrooms, hot showers, swimming pool, playground, video arcade, coin laundry, bar (open weekends), restaurant, and a small grocery store are available. Family barbecues are held on Sundays in season, 5 p.m. to 9 p.m. Live music is scheduled most weekends. A marina and boat rentals are available nearby. Some facilities are wheelchair accessible. Leashed pets are permitted.

Reservations, fees: Reservations are recommended; $18 to $20 per night; cabins are $70 to $90 per night. A lakeside cabin is $150 per night. Major credit cards accepted. Open year-round.

Directions: From Redding, drive north on Interstate 5 for 24 miles to the Lakeshore-Antlers Road exit in Lakehead. Take that exit, turn left at the stop sign, and drive under the freeway to Lakeshore Drive. Turn left on Lakeshore Drive and drive one mile to the campground.

Contact: Lakeshore, tel. (888) 238-2003 (California only), (530) 238-2004 or fax (530) 238-2832; website: www.travel-west.com/lakeshore.

Shasta Lake RV Resort and Camp

 7

Shasta Lake RV Resort and Camp is one of a series on the upper end of Shasta Lake with easy access off Interstate 5 by car, then easy access by boat to premium trout or bass fishing as well as water-skiing.

Location: On Shasta Lake; map B2, grid e2.

Campsites, facilities: There are 21 tent sites and 53 RV sites with full hookups. Picnic tables, barbecues, and fire rings are provided. Restrooms, hot showers, grocery store, wood, coin laundry, playground, and a swimming pool are available. There is also a private dock with 36 boat slips. Pets are permitted.

Reservations, fees: A deposit is required with reservation; $14 to $21 per night. Major credit cards accepted. Open year-round.

Directions: From Redding, drive north on Interstate 5 for 24 miles to the Lakeshore-Antlers Road exit in Lakehead. Take that exit, turn left at the stop sign, and drive under the freeway to Lakeshore Drive. Turn left on Lakeshore Drive and drive 1.5 miles to the campground.

Contact: Shasta Lake RV Resort and Camp, tel. (800) 374-2782 or (530) 238-2370; website: www.shastalakerv.com.

Lakeshore East

 7

Lakeshore East is near the full-service community of Lakehead and is on the Sacramento arm of Shasta Lake. It's a nice spot, with a good boat ramp and marina nearby at Antlers or Sugarloaf.

Location: On Shasta Lake in Shasta-Trinity National Forest; map B2, grid e2.

Campsites, facilities: There are 26 sites for tents or RVs up to 30 feet long. Picnic tables and fire grills are provided. Drinking water, flush toilets, and a camp host are available. A boat ramp, grocery store, and coin laundry are available nearby. Some facilities are wheelchair accessible. Leashed pets are permitted.

Reservations, fees: Reserve at (877) 444-6777 ($8.65 reservation fee) or website: www.reserveusa.com; $15 per night for single sites, $25 for double sites. Open May through September.

Directions: From Redding, drive north on Interstate 5 for 24 miles to the Antlers exit at Lakehead. Take the Antlers exit, turn left at the stop sign, and drive under the freeway to Lakeshore Drive. Turn left on Lakeshore Drive and drive three miles. Look for the campground entrance on the left side of the road.

Contact: Shasta-Trinity National Forest, Shasta Lake Ranger District, tel. (530) 275-1587 or fax (530) 275-1512; or Shasta Lake Visitor Center, (530) 275-1589.

31 Antlers RV Park and Campground

 7

Antlers Park is set along the Sacramento River arm of Shasta Lake at 1,215 feet. The prime time to visit is from March through summer when the lake levels are highest. This is a full-service spot for campers, boaters, and anglers.

Location: On Shasta Lake; map B2, grid e3.

Campsites, facilities: There are 36 tent sites and 70 RV sites, many with full hookups, and a separate area for tents. Restrooms, hot showers, snack bar, seasonal grocery store, ice, laundry room, recreation room, playground, volleyball court, swimming pool, boat rental, houseboats, moorage, and a complete marina are available. Some facilities are wheelchair accessible. Pets are permitted.

Reservations, fees: A deposit is required with reservation; $11 to $27.50 per night. Major credit cards accepted. Open year-round.

Directions: From Redding, drive north on Interstate 5 for 24 miles to the Lakeshore-Antlers Road exit in Lakehead. Take that exit, turn left at the stop sign, and drive a short distance to Antlers Road. At Antlers Road, turn right and drive one mile south to the campground.

Contact: Antlers RV Resort and Campground, tel. (530) 238-2322.

32 Gregory Creek

 7

This is one of the more secluded Forest Service campgrounds on Shasta Lake, and it has

become extremely popular with the younger crowd. It is set just above lakeside, on the eastern shore of the northern Sacramento River arm of the lake. When the lake is fullest in the spring and early summer, this is a great spot.

Location: On Shasta Lake in Shasta-Trinity National Forest; map B2, grid e3.

Campsites, facilities: There are five tent sites and 13 sites for tents or RVs up to 24 feet long. Picnic tables and fire grills are provided. Drinking water and flush toilets are available. Leashed pets are permitted.

Reservations, fees: No reservations; $12 per night, $5 for each additional vehicle. Open May through September.

Directions: From Redding, drive north on Interstate 5 for 21 miles to the Salt Creek/Gilman Road exit. Take that exit and drive over the freeway to Gregory Creek Road. Turn right and drive 10 miles to the campground at the end of the road.

Contact: Shasta-Trinity National Forest, Shasta Lake Ranger District, tel. (530) 275-1587 or fax (530) 275-1512; or Shasta Lake Visitor Center, (530) 275-1589.

33 Antlers

 7

This spot is set on the primary Sacramento River inlet of giant Shasta Lake. Antlers is a well-known spot that attracts returning campers and boaters year after year. It is the farthest upstream marina/camp on the lake. Because of that, lake levels can fluctuate greatly from spring through fall, and the operators will move their docks to compensate. Easy access off Interstate 5 is a big plus for boaters.

Location: On Shasta Lake in Shasta-Trinity National Forest; map B2, grid e3.

Campsites, facilities: There are 41 single sites and 18 double sites for tents or RVs up to 30 feet long. Picnic tables and fire grills are provided. Drinking water, flush and vault toilets, and a camp host in summer are available. A boat ramp, grocery store, and coin laundry are available nearby. Leashed pets are permitted.

Reservations, fees: Reservations are accepted at tel. (877) 444-6777 ($8.65 reservation fee) or website: www.reserveusa.com; $15 per night for a single site, $25 for a double site, $5 for an extra vehicle. Open year-round.

Directions: From Redding, drive north on Interstate 5 for 24 miles to the Lakeshore-Antlers Road exit in Lakehead. Take that exit, turn right at the stop sign, and drive a short distance to Antlers Road. At Antlers Road, turn right and drive one mile south to the campground.

Contact: Shasta-Trinity National Forest, Shasta Lake Ranger District, tel. (530) 275-1587, or fax (530) 275-1512; or Shasta Lake Visitors Center, (530) 275-1589.

34 Moore Creek

 7

The McCloud arm of Shasta Lake is the most beautiful of the five arms at Shasta, with its emerald green waters and limestone canyon towering overhead to the east. That beautiful setting is taken advantage of at this camp, with a good view of the lake and limestone, along with good trout fishing on the adjacent section of water.

Location: On Shasta Lake in Shasta-Trinity National Forest; map B2, grid e4.

Campsites, facilities: There are 12 sites for tents or RVs up to 16 feet long. Picnic tables and fire grills are provided. Drinking water and vault toilets are available. Leashed pets are permitted.

Reservations, fees: Group reservations only, tel. (877) 444-6777 ($8.65 reservation fee) or website: www.reserveusa.com; for single sites, $12 per night, $5 for each additional vehicle, $90 for group site. Open May through September.

Directions: From Redding, drive north on Interstate 5 for about 20 miles to the Salt Creek/Gilman exit. Take that exit and turn right on Gilman Road/County Road 7H009 and drive northeast for 11 miles to the campground on the right side of the road.

Contact: Shasta-Trinity National Forest, Shasta Lake Ranger District, tel. (530) 275-1587 or fax (530) 275-1512; Shasta Lake Visitor Center, (530) 275-1589.

35 Dekkas Rock Group Camp

 8

The few people who know about this camp love this little spot. It is an ideal group camp, set on a flat above the McCloud arm of Shasta Lake, shaded primarily by bays and oaks, with a boat ramp two miles to the south at Hirz Bay. The views are pretty here, looking across the lake at the limestone ridge that borders the McCloud arm. In late summer and fall when the lake level drops, it can be a hike from the camp down to water's edge.

Location: On Shasta Lake in Shasta-Trinity National Forest; map B2, grid e4.

Campsites, facilities: There one group site including four parking spaces for RVs up to 16 feet long. A central meeting area with preparation tables, picnic tables, and large barbecue is provided. Drinking water and vault toilets are available. Leashed pets are permitted.

Reservations, fees: Reserve at (877) 444-6777 ($8.65 reservation fee) or website: www.reserveusa.com; $90 per night for the group site for up to 60 campers.

Directions: From Redding, drive north on Interstate 5 for about 20 miles to the Salt Creek/Gilman exit. Turn right on Gilman Road/County Road 7H009 and drive northeast for 11 miles to the campground on the right side of the road.

Contact: Shasta-Trinity National Forest, Shasta Lake Ranger District, tel. (530) 275-1587 or fax (530) 275-1512; Shasta Lake Visitor Center, (530) 275-1589.

36 Ellery Creek

 7

This camp is set at a pretty spot where Ellery Creek empties into the upper McCloud arm of Shasta Lake. Several sites are set on the pavement with an unobstructed view of the beautiful McCloud arm. This stretch of water is excellent for trout fishing in the summer, with bank-fishing access available two miles upstream at the McCloud Bridge. In the spring, there are tons of small spotted bass along the shore from the camp on upstream to the inlet of the McCloud River. Boat launching facilities are available five miles south at Hirz Bay.

Location: On Shasta Lake in Shasta-Trinity National Forest; map B2, grid e4.

Campsites, facilities: There are 19 sites for tents or RVs up to 30 feet long. Picnic tables and fire grills are provided. Drinking water, vault toilets, and a camp host are available. Toilet facilities are wheelchair accessible. Leashed pets are permitted.

Reservations, fees: Reserve at (877) 444-6777 ($8.65 reservation fee) or website: www.reserveusa.com; $12 per night, $5 for each additional vehicle. Open April through September.

Directions: From Redding, drive north on Interstate 5 for about 20 miles to the Salt Creek/Gilman exit. Turn right on Gilman Road/County Road 7H009 and drive northeast for 15 miles to the campground on the right side of the road.

Contact: Shasta-Trinity National Forest, Shasta Lake Ranger District, tel. (530) 275-1587 or fax (530) 275-1512; Shasta Lake Visitor Center, (530) 275-1589.

37 Pine Point

 7

Pine Point is a pretty little camp, set on a ridge above the McCloud arm of Shasta Lake amid oak trees and scattered ponderosa pines. The view is best in spring, when lake levels are generally highest. Boat launching facilities are available at Hirz Bay; boaters park their boats on shore below the camp while the rest of their party arrives at the camp by car. That provides a chance not only for camping, but also for boating, swimming, water-skiing, and fishing. Note: From July through September, this campground can be reserved as a group site only.

Location: On Shasta Lake in Shasta-Trinity National Forest; map B2, grid e4.

Campsites, facilities: There are 14 sites for tents or RVs up to 24 feet. Picnic tables and fire rings are provided. Drinking water and vault toilets are available. Leashed pets are permitted.

Reservations, fees: Reservations only for groups; tel. (877) 444-6777 ($8.65 reservation fee) or website: www.reserveusa.com, $90 per night. For single site use, no reservations; $12 per night, $5 for each additional vehicle. Open May through September.

Directions: From Redding, drive north on Interstate 5 for about 20 miles to the Salt Creek/Gilman exit. Turn right on Gilman Road/County Road 7H009 and drive northeast for 17 miles to the campground entrance road on the right.

Contact: Shasta-Trinity National Forest, Shasta Lake Ranger District, tel. (530) 275-1587 or fax (530) 275-1512; Shasta Lake Visitor Center, (530) 275-1589.

38 McCloud Bridge

 7

Even though reaching this camp requires a long drive, it remains popular. That is because the best shore-fishing access at the lake is available at nearby McCloud Bridge. It is common to see 15 or 20 people shore fishing here for trout on summer weekends. In the fall, big brown trout migrate through this section of lake en route to their upstream spawning grounds.

Location: On Shasta Lake in Shasta-Trinity National Forest; map B2, grid e4.

Campsites, facilities: There are 20 sites for tents or RVs up to 16 feet long. Picnic tables and fire grills are provided. Drinking water, flush toilets, vault toilets, and a group picnic area are available. Some facilities are wheelchair accessible, including the picnic area. Leashed pets are permitted.

Reservations, fees: Reserve at (877) 444-6777 ($8.65 reservation fee) or website: www.reserveusa.com; $15 per night for single sites, $25 for double sites, $5 for each additional vehicle. Open May through October.

Directions: From Redding, drive north on Interstate 5 for about 20 miles to the Salt Creek/Gilman exit. Turn right on Gilman Road/County Road 7H009 and drive northeast for 18.5 miles. Cross the McCloud Bridge and drive one mile to the campground entrance on the right.

Contact: Shasta-Trinity National Forest, Shasta Lake Ranger District, tel. (530) 275-1587 or fax (530) 275-1512; Shasta Lake Visitor Center, (530) 275-1589.

39 Salt Creek RV Park and Campground

       5

This camp is on a ridge across the highway from Shasta Lake. The sites are wooded, set about a half mile from Shasta Lake. There's boating, water-skiing, swimming, and fishing on the upper end of Shasta Lake. Some private, shaded RV sites are available.

Location: Near Shasta Lake; map B2, grid f3.

Campsites, facilities: There are 50 sites for tents or RVs, many with full hookups, and one cabin. Picnic tables and fire grills are provided. Restrooms, hot showers, sanitary disposal station, grocery store, wood, laundry room, playground, video game room, heated pool, horseshoes, and a volleyball court are available. Some facilities are wheelchair accessible. Leashed pets are permitted.

Reservations, fees: Reservations are accepted; $15.50 to $20.50 per night. Major credit cards accepted. Open year-round.

Directions: From Redding, drive north on Interstate 5 for about 20 miles to the Salt Creek/Gilman Road exit. Take that exit, turn left and drive over the freeway to Salt Creek Road. Turn right on Salt Creek Road and drive a quarter mile to Statton Road. Turn right and drive under the freeway to North Ramp Road. Turn left and drive a quarter mile to the park on the right side of the road (route is well signed; do not re-enter Interstate 5).

Contact: Salt Creek RV Park and Campground, tel. (800) 954-1824 or (530) 238-8500; website: www.saltcreekrv.com.

40 Nelson Point

      7

This is an easy-to-reach campground, only a few minutes from Interstate 5. It's set beside the Salt Creek inlet of Shasta Lake, deep in a cove. In low water years, or when the lake level is low in the fall and early winter, this camp can seem quite distant from water's edge.

Location: On Shasta Lake in Shasta-Trinity National Forest; map B2, grid f3.

Campsites, facilities: There are nine sites for tents or RVs up to 16 feet long. Vault toilets, picnic tables, and fire grills are provided. No drinking water is available. A grocery store and coin laundry are nearby in Lakehead. Leashed pets are permitted.

Reservations, fees: Reservations only for groups, July through September; tel. (877) 444-6777 ($8.65 reservation fee) or website: www.reserveusa.com, $65 per night. For single site use, limited reservations are available at same number; $8 per night, $5 for each additional vehicle. Open May through September.

Directions: From Redding, drive north on Interstate 5 for about 20 miles to the Salt Creek Road/Gilman Road exit. Take that exit, turn left and drive a quarter mile to Gregory Creek Road. Turn right and drive one mile to Conflict Point Road. Turn left and drive one mile to the campground on the left.

Contact: Shasta-Trinity National Forest, Shasta Lake Ranger District, tel. (530) 275-

1587 or fax (530) 275-1512; Shasta Lake Visitor center, (530) 275-1589.

41 Holiday Harbor

 7

This camp is one of the more popular year-round, all-service resorts on Shasta Lake. It is set on the lower McCloud arm of the lake, which is extremely beautiful with a limestone mountain ridge off to the east. It is an ideal jump-off for all water sports, especially house-boating and fishing. A good boat ramp, boat rentals, and store with all the goodies are bonuses. Another plus is the side trip to Shasta Caverns, a privately guided adventure (fee charged) into limestone caves.

Location: On Shasta Lake; map B2, grid f3.

Campsites, facilities: There 27 sites with full hookups for RVs up to 40 feet long. Picnic tables and barbecues are provided. Restrooms, hot showers, grocery store, coin laundry, boat moorage, playground, propane gas, and boat rentals are available. Some facilities are wheelchair accessible. Leashed pets are permitted.

Reservations, fees: Reservations are accepted; $24.50 per night for two people, $3 per night for each additional camper over three years old, $4.50 per night for each additional vehicle, and $8 per night for boat moorage. Major credit cards accepted. Open April through October.

Directions: From Redding, drive 18 miles north on Interstate 5 to the Shasta Caverns Road exit. Turn right at Shasta Caverns Road and drive about one mile to the campground entrance on the right.

Contact: Holiday Harbor, tel. (530) 238-2383, ext. 23, or tel. (800) 776-2628.

42 Trail In RV Campground

 7

This is a privately operated campground near the Salt Creek arm of giant Shasta Lake. Open, level sites are available. The lake is about a quarter mile away and offers fishing, boating, and swimming. Its proximity to Interstate 5 makes this a popular spot, fast and easy to reach, which is extremely attractive for drivers of RVs and trailers who want to avoid the many twisty roads surrounding Shasta Lake.

Location: Near Shasta Lake; map B2, grid f3.

Campsites, facilities: There are 39 sites, 10 pull-through, with full hookups. Picnic tables and fire grills are provided. Restrooms, hot showers, TVs, sanitary disposal station, swimming pool, grocery store, ice, wood, and coin laundry are available. Leashed pets are permitted.

Reservations, fees: A deposit is required with reservation; $19.25 per night, $2 per person per night for more than two people; $2 per night for pets. Major credit cards accepted. Open year-round.

Directions: From Redding, drive 22 miles north on Interstate 5. Take the Gilman Road/Salt Creek Road exit and drive a short distance west on Gilman Road to Gregory Creek Road. Turn north on Gregory Creek Road and drive one mile to the campground (route is well signed).

Contact: Trail In RV Campground, tel. (530) 238-8533.

43 Hirz Bay Group Camp

 7

This is the spot for your own private party—providing you get a reservation—set on a point at the entrance of Hirz Bay on the McCloud River arm of Shasta Lake. A boat ramp is only a half mile away on the camp access road, giving access to the McCloud River arm. This is an excellent spot to make a base camp for a fishing trip, with great trolling for trout in this stretch of the lake.

Location: On Shasta Lake in Shasta-Trinity National Forest; map B2, grid f4.

Campsites, facilities: There are two group sites for tents and RVs up to 24 feet long. Picnic tables and fire grills are provided. Drinking water, vault toilets, and a group picnic area are available. Leashed pets are permitted.

Reservations, fees: Reserve at (877) 444-6777 ($8.65 reservation fee) or website: www.re-serveusa.com; Camp One accommodates up to 120 people and is $90 per night; Camp Two accommodates up to 80 people and is $65 per night. Open year-round.

Directions: From Redding, drive north on Interstate 5 for about 20 miles to the Salt Creek/Gilman exit. Turn right on Gilman Road/County Road 7H009 and drive northeast for 10 miles to the campground/boat launch access road. Turn right and drive a half mile to the camp on the left side of the road. The group camp is past the family campground.

Contact: Shasta-Trinity National Forest, Shasta Lake Ranger District, tel. (530) 275-1587 or fax (530) 275-1512; Shasta Lake Visitor Center, (530) 275-1589.

44 Hirz Bay

    7

This is one of two camps in the immediate area (the other is Hirz Bay Group Camp) that provides nearby access to a boat ramp (a half mile down the road) and the McCloud River arm of Shasta Lake. The camp is set on a point at the entrance of Hirz Bay. This is an excellent spot to make a base camp for a fishing trip, with great trolling for trout in this stretch of the lake.

Location: On Shasta Lake in Shasta-Trinity National Forest; map B2, grid f4.

Campsites, facilities: There are 38 single sites and 10 double sites for tents or RVs up to 30 feet long. Picnic tables and fire grills are provided. Drinking water, flush and vault toilets are available. A boat ramp is nearby. Some facilities are wheelchair accessible. Leashed pets are permitted.

Reservations, fees: Reservations are accepted Reserve at (877) 444-6777 ($8.65 reservation fee) or website: www.reserveusa.com;

$15 per night for a single, $25 for a double, $5 for an extra vehicle. Reduced rates and services in the winter. Open year-round.

Directions: From Redding, drive north on Interstate 5 for about 20 miles to the Salt Creek/Gilman exit. Turn right on Gilman Road/County Road 7H009 and drive northeast for 10 miles to the campground/boat launch access road. Turn right and drive a half mile to the camp on the left side of the road.

Contact: Shasta-Trinity National Forest, Shasta Lake Ranger District, tel. (530) 275-1587 or fax (530) 275-1512; Shasta Lake Visitor Center, (530) 275-1589.

45 Gooseneck Cove Boat-In

     4

You want a camp all to yourself? There's a good chance of that here at Gooseneck Cove. One reason is because it is well hidden, set well back in a cove on the west side of the Sacramento River arm of giant Shasta Lake. The other reason is there was some fire damage here in 1999, and some burned oaks and manzanita will take years to outgrow. So there is a blackened hill in view. That will likely keep the few who know of this place away. So there you have it, a chance any day of the year to have a campground all to yourself. The fishing on the Sacramento River arm of Shasta Lake is very good, both trolling for trout all summer, especially at the headwaters in midsummer, and for bass in the spring on plastic worms. Water-skiing is also excellent here, with water temperatures in the high 70s for most of summer.

Location: On Shasta Lake in Shasta-Trinity National Forest; map B2, grid f2.

Campsites, facilities: There are eight boat-in sites for tents. Picnic tables and fire grills are provided. Vault toilets are available. No drinking water is available. Garbage must be packed out. Small stores with supplies are available at Antlers. Leashed pets are permitted.

Reservations, fees: No reservations, no fee. A $5 fee is charged for boat launching. Open year-round.

Directions: From Redding, drive north on Interstate 5 for 24 miles to the Lakeshore-Antlers Road exit in Lakehead. Take that exit, turn left at the stop sign, and drive a short distance to Antlers Road. At Antlers Road, turn right and drive one mile south to the campground and nearby boat launch. Launch your boat and cruise seven miles south to the boat-in campground.

Contact: Shasta-Trinity National Forest, Shasta Lake Ranger District, tel. (530) 275-1587 or fax (530) 275-1512; Shasta Lake Visitor Center, (530) 275-1589.

46 Greens Creek Boat-In

 10

This is one of my favorite spots on the planet on a warm spring day, maybe mid-April, but it is always special. This boat-in campsite provides an exceptional base camp and boat-in headquarters for a recreation paradise. The camp is set at the foot of dramatic limestone formations on the McCloud arm of Shasta Lake. On land, there is a steep but fantastic hike that leads to a dramatic lookout of the lake. By boat, this is one of the best fishing spots, trolling for 16- to 18-inch trout with Z-Rays, Kastmasters, and Cripplures; proper depth is critical, and experts using downriggers have a huge advantage. The campsites are in a region well wooded, little traveled, with good opportunities in the evening to see wildlife.

Location: On Shasta Lake in Shasta-Trinity National Forest; map B2, grid f4.

Campsites, facilities: There are nine boat-in sites for tents. Picnic tables and fire grills are provided. Vault toilets are available. No drinking water is available. Garbage must be packed out. Small stores with supplies are available at Holiday Harbor. Leashed pets are permitted.

Reservations, fees: No reservations, no fee. A $5 fee is charged for boat launching. Open year-round.

Directions: From Redding, drive north on In-

terstate 5 over the Pit River Bridge at Shasta Lake to O'Brien Road/Shasta Caverns Road exit. Turn east (right)on Shasta Caverns Road and drive one-quarter mile to a signed turnoff for Bailey Cove. Turn right and drive one mile to Bailey Cove Boat Ramp. Launch boat and cruise four miles northeast up the McCloud Arm. Land your boat and pick your campsite.

Contact: Shasta-Trinity National Forest, Shasta Lake Ranger District, tel. (530) 275-1587 or fax (530) 275-1512; Shasta Lake Visitor Center, (530) 275-1589.

47 Arbuckle Flat Boat-In

 8

How could anything be secluded on Northern California's most popular recreation lake? Well, here is your answer. Arbuckle Flat is a truly secluded boat-in campground well up the Pit River arm of the lake, set far back in a deep cove. You will feel a million miles away from all the fast traffic back at the main lake body. Specifically, it is five miles east of the Jones Valley Boat Ramp, set on the right (south) side of a deep cove. You pay a small price for this seclusion. After landing your boat, you must then carry your gear up a hill to the campsites. When the lake is low, this is like a march up Cardiac Hill. The landscape surrounding the campsites is peppered with oak. The fishing in the area is often good for bass, and where you find submerged trees, for crappie as well.

Location: On Shasta Lake in Shasta-Trinity National Forest; map B2, grid f4.

Campsites, facilities: There are 11 boat-in sites for tents. Picnic tables and fire grills are provided. Vault toilets are available. No drinking water is available. Garbage must be packed out. Small stores with supplies are available at Silverthorn Resort and Jones Valley Resort. Leashed pets are permitted.

Reservations, fees: No reservations, no fee. A $5 fee is charged for boat launching. Open year-round.

Directions: From Redding, drive north on Interstate 5 to the Oasis exit and drive east to Bear Mountain Road. Turn right and drive to Dry Creek Road. Turn left on Dry Creek Road and drive seven miles to a fork in the road. Bear right at the fork and drive to Jones Valley Boat Ramp (a left at the fork takes you to Silverthorn Resort). Launch your boat, head east (to the right) for five miles. The last major arm off to your right hides the campground at the back of the cove, in the oaks above the shore. Land and pick your campsite.

Contact: Shasta-Trinity National Forest, Shasta Lake Ranger District, tel. (530) 275-1587 or fax (530) 275-1512; Shasta Lake Visitor Center, (530) 275-1589.

48 Ski Island Boat-in

     8

Could there be any secrets left about Shasta Lake? You bet, with boat-in campsites providing the best of all worlds for people willing to rough it just a little. Ski Island is an outstanding place to set up camp, then boat, fish, ski or explore this giant lake. It is on the Pit River Arm of the lake about three miles upstream from the Pit River (I-5) bridge. The closest boat ramp to Ski Island is at Silverthorn Resort, which is in a cove on the Pit River arm of the lake. Here you will find this three-acre island with a boat-in campground and several little trails. It is well out of sight, and out of mind for most campers as well. One note: In wet weather, the reddish, iron-based soil on the island will turn the bottom of your boat rust colored with even a minimum of tracking in.

Location: On Shasta Lake in Shasta-Trinity National Forest; map B2, grid g3.

Campsites, facilities: There are 23 boat-in sites for tents. Picnic tables and fire grills are provided. Vault toilets are available. No drinking water is available. Garbage must be packed out. Small stores with supplies are available at Silverthorn Resort and Jones Valley Resort. Leashed pets are permitted.

Reservations, fees: No reservations, no fee. A $5 fee is charged for boat launching. Open year-round.

Directions: From Redding, drive north on Interstate 5 to the Oasis exit and drive east to Bear Mountain Road. Turn right and drive to Dry Creek Road. Turn left on Dry Creek Road and drive seven miles to a fork in the road. Bear right at the fork and drive to Jones Valley Boat Ramp (a left at the fork takes you to Silverthorn Resort). Launch your boat, head west (to the left) for four miles to Ski Island. Land and pick your campsite.

Contact: Shasta-Trinity National Forest, Shasta Lake Ranger District, tel. (530) 275-1587 or fax (530) 275-1512; Shasta Lake Visitor center, (530) 275-1589.

49 Madrone Camp

     7

Tired of people? Then you've come to the right place. This remote camp is set along Squaw Creek, a feeder stream of Shasta Lake to the southwest. It's way out there, far away from anybody. Even though Shasta Lake is relatively close, about 10 miles away, it is literally in another world. A network of four-wheel-drive roads provides a recreation option, detailed on a map of Shasta-Trinity National Forest.

Location: On Squaw Creek in Shasta-Trinity National Forest; map B2, grid f7.

Campsites, facilities: There are 13 sites for tents or RVs up to 16 feet long. Picnic tables and fire grills are provided. Vault toilets and a camp host in summer are available. No drinking water is available. Leashed pets are permitted.

Reservations, fees: No reservations; no fee. Open year-round, with limited winter facilities.

Directions: From Redding, drive 29 miles east on Highway 299 to the town of Montgomery Creek. Turn left on Fenders Ferry Road/Forest Road 27 and drive 22 miles to the camp (the road starts as gravel and then becomes dirt).

Contact: Shasta-Trinity National Forest, Shasta Lake Ranger District, tel. (530) 275-1587 or fax (530) 275-1512; Shasta Lake Visitor Center, (530) 275-1589.

50 Upper and Lower Jones Valley Camps

 7

Lower Jones is a small, pretty camp sheltered by oaks and bays along a deep cove in the remote Pit River arm of Shasta Lake. There is a trailhead at camp that provides access to the Clickapudi Trail, a great hiking and biking trail that traces the lake's shore, routed through pretty woodlands. Two nearby resorts, Jones Valley and Silverthorn, provide boat rentals and supplies.

Location: On Shasta Lake in Shasta-Trinity National Forest; map B2, grid g4.

Campsites, facilities: There are 21 sites for tents or RVs up to 16 feet long in two adjacent campgrounds. Picnic tables and fire grills are provided. Drinking water and vault toilets are available. Some facilities are wheelchair accessible. A boat ramp at Jones Valley is two miles from camp. Leashed pets are permitted.

Reservations, fees: Reserve at (877) 444-6777 ($8.65 reservation fee) or website: www.reserveusa.com; Upper Jones sites are $15 per night, Lower Jones sites are $15 for a single site and $25 for a double. Lower Jones is open year-round. Upper Jones is open May through September.

Directions: From Redding, turn east on Highway 299 and drive 7.5 miles just past the town of Bella Vista. At Dry Creek Road, turn left and drive nine miles to a Y in the road. Bear right at the Y (left will take you to Silverthorn Resort) and drive a short distance to the campground entrances, on the left side for Lower Jones and on the right side for Upper Jones.

Contact: Shasta-Trinity National Forest, Shasta Lake Ranger District, tel. (530) 275-1587 or fax (530) 275-1512; Shasta Lake Visitor Center, (530) 275-1589.

51 Jones Valley Inlet

 7

This is one of the few primitive camp areas on Shasta Lake, set on the distant Pit River arm of the lake. It is an ideal camp for hiking and biking, with the nearby Clickapudi Trail routed for miles along the lake's shore, in and out of coves, and then entering the surrounding foothills and oak/bay woodlands. The camp is pretty, if a bit exposed, with two nearby resorts, Jones Valley and Silverthorn, providing boat rentals and supplies.

Location: On Shasta Lake in Shasta-Trinity National Forest; map B2, grid g4.

Campsites, facilities: There is an area for dispersed, primitive camping for tents or RVs up to 30 feet long. Drinking water and vault toilets are available. A boat ramp at Jones Valley is two miles from camp. Groceries available nearby. Leashed pets are permitted.

Reservations, fees: No reservations; $6 per vehicle per night, $4 fee for each additional vehicle. Open March through mid-October.

Directions: From Redding, turn east on Highway 299 and drive 7.5 miles just past the town of Bella Vista. At Dry Creek Road turn left and drive nine miles to a Y in the road. Bear right at the Y (left will take you to Silverthorn Resort) and drive a short distance to the campground entrance on the left side of the road.

Contact: Shasta-Trinity National Forest, Shasta Lake Ranger District, tel. (530) 275-1587 or fax (530) 275-1512; Shasta Lake Visitor Center, (530) 275-1589.

52 Shasta

 6

This campground is between Shasta Dam and the Sacramento River, and adjacent to an off-highway-vehicle staging area. Get the idea? Right, this place is for ATVs and dirt bikes, loud and wild, and hey, it's a perfect spot for them. It's barren because of past mining activities in the area, but the view of the river and Shasta Dam are incredible. Nearby dam tours are unique and memorable.

Location: On the Sacramento River in Shasta-Trinity National Forest; map B2, grid g2.

Campsites, facilities: There are 22 sites for tents or RVs up to 24 feet long. Picnic tables and fire rings are provided. Drinking water and vault toilets are available. A boat ramp is nearby. Groceries and bait are available in Shasta Lake City. Leashed pets are permitted.

Reservations, fees: No reservations; $10 per night, $5 for each additional vehicle. Open year-round.

Directions: From Interstate 5 in Redding, drive north for three miles to the exit for the town of Shasta Lake City and Shasta Dam Boulevard. Take that exit and bear west on Shasta Dam Boulevard and drive three miles to Lake Boulevard. Turn right on Lake Boulevard and drive two miles. Cross Shasta Dam and continue four miles to the signed campground.

Contact: Shasta-Trinity National Forest, Shasta Lake Ranger District, tel. (530) 275-1587 or fax (530) 275-1512; Shasta Lake Visitor Center, (530) 275-1589.

53 Wonderland Mobile Home & RV Park

    5

This RV park is within a mobile home park south of Shasta Lake. The tour of Shasta Caverns is a recreation option, via a short drive to Holiday Harbor. Other options include the city of Redding's extensive visitor center, the Carter House Natural History Museum in Caldwell Park, public golf courses, and the Sacramento River trails, which are paved, making them accessible for wheelchairs and bikes.

Location: Near Shasta Lake; map B2, grid g3.

Campsites, facilities: There are 36 RV sites, many with full hookups. Restrooms, showers, coin laundry, cable TV, seasonally-heated swimming pool, and horseshoes are available. Some facilities are wheelchair accessible. Leashed pets are permitted.

Reservations, fees: Reservations are required with a deposit; $10 to $14.50 per night, $1.50 per person per night for more than two people. Major credit cards accepted. Open year-round.

Directions: From Redding, drive north on Interstate 5 for 11 miles to the Fawndale exit. Exit west onto Wonderland Boulevard and drive a quarter mile to 15203 Wonderland Boulevard.

Contact: Wonderland Mobile Home & RV Park, tel. (530) 275-1281.

54 Bear Mountain RV Resort

      3

This is a privately operated park set up primarily for RVs in the remote Jones Valley area along Shasta Lake.

Location: Near Shasta Lake; map B2, grid g3.

Campsites, facilities: There are 17 tent sites and 97 RV sites with full or partial hookups. Picnic tables and fire rings are provided. Drinking water, flush toilets, laundry room, store, sanitary disposal station, a pool, recreation hall, arcade, and horseshoe pit are available. Some facilities are wheelchair accessible. Within three miles, there is a boat launch ramp. Leashed pets are permitted.

Reservations, fees: Reservations are accepted; $12 to $20 per night, $2 per person per night for more than two people. Open year-round.

Directions: From Redding, drive north on Interstate 5 for three miles to the Oasis Road exit. Turn right on Oasis Road/Old Oregon Trail and drive 3.5 miles. Turn right on Bear Mountain Road and drive 3.5 miles to the campground.

Contact: Bear Mountain RV Resort, tel. (530) 275-4728, tel. (800) 952-0551, or fax (530) 275-8459; website: www.bearmtnrvresort.com.

55 Brandy Creek

      7

For campers with boats, this is the best place to stay at Whiskeytown Lake, with a boat ramp less than a quarter mile away. Whiskeytown is popular for sailing and windsurfing, getting a lot more wind than other lakes in the region. Fishing for kokanee salmon is good in the early morning prior to the wind coming up.

Location: On Whiskeytown Lake; map B2, grid h0.

Campsites, facilities: There are 46 RV sites for self-contained vehicles up to 30 feet long. Drinking water and a sanitary disposal station are available. Leashed pets are permitted.

Reservations, fees: No reservations; $14 per night during the summer season, $7 per night during off season. Open year-round.

Directions: From Redding, drive 10 miles west on Highway 299. Turn left at the visitor center (Kennedy Memorial Drive) and drive five miles to the campground entrance road on the right. Turn right and drive a short distance to the camp.

Contact: Whiskeytown National Recreation Area, tel. (530) 242-3400 or fax (530) 246-5154.

56 Oak Bottom

     7

The prettiest hiking trails at Whiskeytown Lake are at the far western end of the reservoir, and this camp provides excellent access to them. One hiking and biking trail skirts the north shoreline of the lake and is routed to the lake's inlet at the Judge Carr Powerhouse. The other, with the trailhead just a short drive to the west, is routed along Mill Creek, a pristine, clear-running stream with the trail jumping over the water many times. The campground sites seem a little close, but the location is next to a beach area. There are junior ranger programs for kids 6 to 12 years old, and evening seminars at the Oak Bottom Amphitheater are available three nights per week from mid-June through Labor Day. A self-guided nature trail is five miles away at the visitor center.

Location: On Whiskeytown Lake; map B2, grid h0.

Campsites, facilities: There are 101 walk-in tent sites with picnic tables and fire grills. There are 22 RV sites in the large parking area near the launch ramp and restrooms. Drinking water, flush toilets, coin-operated showers, groceries, ice, wood, sanitary disposal station, boat ramp, and boat rentals are available. Some facilities are wheelchair accessible. Leashed pets are permitted.

Reservations, fees: No reservations in the off-season; reservations are required in the summer. Reserve at (800) 365-CAMP (800-365-2267) or website: http://reservations.nps.gov/; $7 to $18 per night. Open year-round.

Directions: From Redding, drive 15 miles west on Highway 299 (past the visitor center) to the campground entrance road on the left. Turn left and drive a short distance to the campground.

Contact: Whiskeytown National Recreation Area, tel. (530) 242-3400 or fax (530) 246-5154.

57 Dry Creek Group Camp

      7

If you're in a group and take the time to reserve this spot, you'll be rewarded with some room and the quiet that goes along with it. This is the most remote drive-to camp at Whiskeytown Lake. A boat ramp is about two miles away (to the east) at Brandy Creek. You'll pass it on the way in. Note: Reservations are an absolute must, available five months in advance.

Location: On Whiskeytown Lake; map B2, grid h0.

Campsites, facilities: There are two group sites that can accommodate 50 people each. Picnic tables and fire grills are provided. Drinking water and pit toilets are available. Leashed pets are permitted.

Reservations, fees: Reserve at (800) 365-CAMP (800-365-2267) or website: http://reservations.nps.gov/; $75 per night. Open year-round, weather permitting.

Directions: From Redding, drive 10 miles west on Highway 299. Turn left at the visitor center (Kennedy Memorial Drive) and drive six miles to the campground on the right side of the road.

Contact: Whiskeytown National Recreation Area, tel. (530) 242-3400, ext. 221, or fax (530) 246-5154.

58 KOA of Redding

 2

If you're stuck with no place to go, this large park could be your savior, but expect very hot weather in the summer. Nearby recreation options include the waterslide park across the road, the Sacramento River which runs through town, Whiskeytown Lake to the west, and Shasta Lake to the north.

Location: In Redding; map B2, grid h2.

Campsites, facilities: There are 111 RV sites, 53 with full hookups, 22 with partial hookups, a separate area for tents, and one cabin. Picnic tables and fire grills are provided. Drinking water, flush toilets, showers, playground, swimming pool, laundry room, sanitary disposal station, cable hookups, a grocery store, and propane gas are available. Leashed pets are permitted.

Reservations, fees: Reservations are accepted; $19.50 to $24.50 per night, $2 per person per night for more than two people. The cabin is $35 per night. Major credit cards accepted. Open year-round.

Directions: In Redding, drive north on Interstate 5 to the Lake Boulevard/Burney-Alturas exit. Turn west (left) on Lake Boulevard and drive a quarter mile to North Boulder Drive. Turn right (north) on North Boulder Drive and drive one block to the campground.

Contact: KOA of Redding, tel. (530) 246-0101 or tel. (800) 562-0899; website: www.koa.com.

59 Twin View Terrace RV Park

 2

This is one of several RV parks open year-round in the Redding area. It is within a mobile home park.

Location: Near Redding; map B2, grid h2.

Campsites, facilities: There are 48 drive-through RV sites with full hookups for RVs up to 34 feet long. Restrooms, showers, a coin laundry, and swimming pool are available. Some facilities are wheelchair accessible. Leashed pets are permitted.

Reservations, fees: No reservations; $19 per night. Open year-round.

Directions: In Redding, take the Twin View exit off Interstate 5. Turn south (right) on Twin View and drive one mile on Twin View Boulevard to the RV park.

Contact: Twin View Terrace RV Park, tel. (530) 243-8114.

60 Marina RV Park

 6

The riverside setting is a highlight here, with the Sacramento River providing relief from the dog days of summer. An easy, paved walking and bike trail is available nearby at the Sacramento River Parkway, providing river views and sometimes a needed breeze on hot summer evenings. A miniature golf course is nearby.

Location: On the Sacramento River; map B2, grid h1.

Campsites, facilities: There are 42 RV sites with full or partial hookups. Restrooms, hot showers, a coin laundry, small store, swimming pool, whirlpool, boat ramp, and sanitary disposal station are on park grounds. Pets are permitted.

Reservations, fees: Reservations are accepted; $22 per night. Open year-round.

Directions: In Redding turn west on Highway 299 and drive to Park Marina Drive. At Park Marina Drive turn left (south) and drive one mile to the park.

Contact: Marina RV Park, tel. (530) 241-4396.

61 Sacramento River RV Park

      7

This makes a good headquarters for a fall fishing trip on the Sacramento River, where the salmon come big from August through October. In the summer trout fishing is very good from this area as well, but a boat is a must. No problem; there's a boat ramp at the park. In addition, you can hire fishing guides who launch from here daily. The park is open year-round, and if you want to stay close to home, a three-acre pond is available at the park. You also get great views of Mount Shasta and Mount Lassen.

Location: South of Redding; map B2, grid j2.

Campsites, facilities: There are 20 tent sites and 140 RV sites with full hookups. Restrooms, hot showers, grocery store, coin laundry, sanitary disposal station, cable TV, bait shop, propane gas, boat launch, two tennis courts, and a large swimming pool are available. Some facilities are wheelchair accessible. Leashed pets are permitted.

Reservations, fees: Reservations are accepted; $14 to $21 per night. Most discount coupons are honored for RVs. Major credit cards accepted. Open April through October, weather permitting.

Directions: From Redding, drive south on Interstate 5 for five miles to the Knighton Road exit. Turn west (right) and drive a short distance to Riverland Drive. Turn left on Riverland Drive and drive two miles to the end of the road.

Contact: Sacramento River RV Park, tel. (530) 365-6402 or fax (530) 365-2601.

62 Old Cow Meadows

    7

Nobody finds this campground without this book. You want quiet? You don't want to be bugged by anybody? You want piped water, too? Well, two out of three ain't bad. This tiny camp, virtually unknown, is set at 5,900 feet in a wooded area along Old Cow Creek. Recreation options include all-terrain vehicle use on existing roads and walking the dirt roads that crisscross the area.

Location: In Latour Demonstration State Forest; map B2, grid i9.

Campsites, facilities: There are three sites for tents or RVs. Picnic tables and fire grills are provided. Pit toilets are available. No drinking water is available. Leashed pets are permitted.

Reservations, fees: No reservations; no fee. Open June through October.

Directions: In Redding, turn east on Highway 44 and drive about 9.5 miles to Millville Road. Turn left on Millville Road and drive a half mile to the intersection of Millville Road and Whitmore Road. Turn right on Whitmore Road and drive 13 miles, through Whitmore, until Whitmore Road becomes Tamarac Road. Continue for one mile to a fork at Bateman Road. Take the right fork on Bateman Road, drive 3.5 miles (where the road turns to gravel), and then continue 12 miles to the entrance to the campground.

Contact: Latour Demonstration State Forest, tel. (530) 225-2505 or tel. (530) 225-2438, or fax (530) 225-2514.

63 South Cow Creek Meadows

     6

This camp is set in a pretty, wooded area next to a small meadow along South Cow Creek. It's mostly used in the fall for hunting, with off-highway-vehicle use on the surrounding roads in the summer. The camp is set at 5,600 feet. If you want to get away from it all without leaving your vehicle, this is one way to do it. The creek is a reliable water source providing you use a water filtration pump.

Location: In Latour Demonstration State Forest; map B2, grid i9.

Campsites, facilities: There are two sites for tents or RVs. Picnic tables and fire grills are provided. Pit toilets are available. No drinking water is available. Leashed pets are permitted.

Reservations, fees: No reservations; no fee. Open June through October.

Directions: In Redding, turn east on Highway 44 and drive about 9.5 miles to Millville Road. Turn left on Millville Road and drive one-half mile to the intersection of Millville Road and Whitmore Road. Turn right on Whitmore Road and drive 13 miles, through Whitmore, until Whitmore Road becomes Tamarac Road. Continue for one mile to the fork at Bateman Road. Take the right fork on Bateman Road, drive 3.5 miles (where the road turns to gravel), and then continue for 11 miles to South Cow Creek Road. Turn right (east) and drive one mile to the campground.

Contact: Latour Demonstration State Forest, tel. (530) 225-2505 or tel. (530) 225-2438, or fax (530) 225-2514.

64 Macumber Reservoir

 7

Here's a small lake, easy to reach from Redding, that is little known and rarely visited. Macumber Reservoir is set at 3,500 feet and is stocked with 6,000 rainbow trout each year, providing fair fishing. No gas motors are permitted here. That's fine—it guarantees quiet, calm water, ideal for car-top boats: prams, canoes, rafts, and small aluminum boats.

Location: On Macumber Reservoir; map B2, grid j9.

Campsites, facilities: There are seven sites for tents or RVs and five walk-in sites. Picnic tables and fire grills are provided. Drinking water and vault toilets are available. Leashed pets are permitted.

Reservations, fees: No reservations; $13 per night, $3 per night for extra vehicles, $7 per night for extra RV, $1 pet fee. Open mid-May to mid-September, weather permitting.

Directions: In Redding, turn east on Highway 44 and drive toward Viola to Lake Macumber Road (if you reach Viola, you have gone four

miles too far). At Lake Macumber Road, turn left and drive two miles to the reservoir and campground.

Contact: PG&E Building and Land Services, tel. (916) 386-5164.

65 Mt. Lassen KOA

 6

This popular KOA camp is 14 miles from the entrance of Lassen Volcanic National Park and has pretty, wooded sites. Location is always the critical factor on vacations, and this park is set up perfectly for launching trips to the nearby east. Hat Creek provides trout fishing along Highway 89, and just inside the Highway 44 entrance station at Lassen Park is Manzanita Lake, providing good fishing and hiking.

Location: Near Lassen Volcanic National Park; map B2, grid j7.

Campsites, facilities: There are 50 sites for tents or RVs; some are drive-through sites with full or partial hookups. Picnic tables and fire grills are provided. Flush toilets, hot showers, playground, heated pool, a sanitary disposal station, groceries, ice, wood, coin laundry, and propane gas are available. Leashed pets are permitted.

Reservations, fees: Phone (800) 562-3403. A deposit is required with reservation; $18 to $23 per night. Major credit cards accepted. Open year-round.

Directions: From Redding, turn east on Highway 44 and drive to Shingletown. In Shingletown, continue east for four miles and look for the KOA sign.

Contact: KOA Lassen/Shingletown, tel. (530) 474-3133; website: www.koa.com.

66 Mill Creek Park

 7

This year-round park is set up primarily for RVs, but has sites for tents. The elevation is 4,000 feet, and it's set amid conifers on the western slopes of Mount Lassen. The proximity to Lassen Volcanic National Park is a key attraction.

Location: Near Shingletown; map B2, grid j7.

Campsites, facilities: There are 34 sites for tents or RVs; some are drive-through sites with full or partial hookups. Four cabins are available. Picnic tables and fire grills are provided. Drinking water, flush toilets, sanitary disposal station, and a laundry room are available. A fishing pond and creek are also available nearby. Leashed pets are permitted.

Reservations, fees: A deposit is required with reservation; $11 for tent sites, $15.40 to $20 per night for RV sites; $38.50 to $55 for cabins. Major credit cards accepted. Open year-round.

Directions: From Redding, drive east on Highway 44 to Shingletown. In Shingletown, continue east on Highway 44 for two miles to the campground.

Contact: Mill Creek Park, tel. (530) 474-5384 or fax (530) 474-1236; website: www.millcreekrvpark.com.

MCARTHUR–BURNEY FALLS
STATE PARK

MAP B3

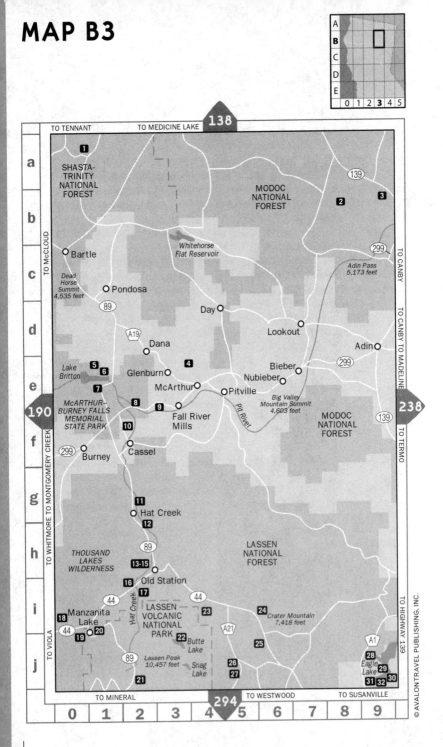

© AVALON TRAVEL PUBLISHING, INC.

CHAPTER B3

1 Harris Springs

 3

This camp is a hidden spot in remote Shasta-Trinity National Forest, nestled in the long, mountainous ridge that runs east from Mount Shasta to the Lava Beds National Monument. The camp is set at 4,800 feet, with a part-time fire station within a quarter mile on the opposite side of the access road. The area is best explored by four-wheel drive, venturing to a series of small buttes, mountaintops, and lookouts in the immediate area. A map of Shasta-Trinity National Forest is a must.

Location: In Shasta-Trinity National Forest; map B3, grid a0.

Campsites, facilities: There are 15 sites for tents or RVs up to 32 feet long. Picnic tables and fire grills provided. Drinking water (spring water, not piped) and vault toilets are available. Garbage must be packed out. Leashed pets are permitted.

Reservations, fees: No reservations; no fee.

Directions: From Redding, drive north on Interstate 5 past Dunsmuir to the junction with Highway 89. Turn east on Highway 89, drive to McCloud, and then continue on Highway 89 for 17 miles just past the town of Bartle. Turn left (north) on Medicine Lake Road and drive about five miles to the Y intersection. Turn left at the Y on Harris Springs Road/Forest

Road 15 and drive 12 miles. Turn right at a Forest Service road signed for the Harris Springs Ranger Station, drive a short distance, and look for the campground entrance on the right side of the road.

Contact: Shasta-Trinity National Forest, McCloud Ranger District, tel. (530) 964-2184 or fax (530) 964-2938.

② Cottonwood Flat

    6

The camp is wooded and shady, set at 4,700 feet in elevation in the rugged and remote Devil's Garden area of Modoc National Forest. The region is known for large mule deer, and Cottonwood Flat is well situated as a base camp for a hunting trip in the fall. Temperatures can get extremely cold early and late in the season.

Location: In Modoc National Forest; map B3, grid b8.

Campsites, facilities: There are 10 sites for tents or RVs up to 16 feet long. Picnic tables and fire grills are provided. Drinking water (spring water) and vault toilets are available. Garbage must be packed out. Supplies are available within five miles in Canby. Leashed pets are permitted.

Reservations, fees: No reservations; no fee. Open June through September.

Directions: From Redding, drive east on Highway 299 for about 100 miles to Adin. Continue on Highway 299 for about 20 miles to the Canby Bridge at the Pit River and the junction with Forest Road 84. Turn left on Forest Road 84 and drive about eight miles to Forest Road 42N95. Turn right and drive a half mile to the campground entrance on the left side of the road. Note: The access road is not recommended for RVs longer than 14 to 16 feet.

Contact: Modoc National Forest, Devil's Garden Ranger District, tel. (530) 233-5811 or fax (530) 233-5817.

③ Howard's Gulch

      6

This is the nearest campground to Duncan Reservoir, three miles to the north and stocked with trout each year by the Department of Fish and Game. The camp is set in the typically sparse woods of Modoc National Forest, but a beautiful grove of aspen is three miles to the west on Highway 139, on the left side of the road. By the way, Highway 139 isn't much of a highway at all, but it is paved and will get you there. The elevation is 4,700 feet.

Location: Near Duncan Reservoir in Modoc National Forest; map B3, grid b9.

Campsites, facilities: There are 11 sites for tents or RVs up to 22 feet long. Picnic tables and fire grills are provided. Drinking water and vault toilets are available. Some facilities are wheelchair accessible. Supplies are available within five miles in Canby. Leashed pets are permitted.

Reservations, fees: No reservations; $6 per night. Open May through October.

Directions: From Redding, drive east on Highway 299 for about 100 miles to Adin. Continue on Highway 299 for about 25 miles. Turn left (northwest) on Highway 139 and drive six miles to the campground on the left side of the road.

Contact: Modoc National Forest, Devil's Garden Ranger District, tel. (530) 233-5811 or fax (530) 233-8709.

④ Ahjumawi Lava Springs Boat-In

      9

This is a unique boat-in camp set on Big Lake and connecting Horr Pond. Access is by non-motorized boat only, ideal for canoes, and in addition, the lake is not well known outside of the region. Ahjumawi means "where the waters come together," named by the Pit River Native Americans who inhabit the area near the confluence of Big Lake, Tule River, Ja She Creek, Lava Creek and Fall River. Together the waters form one of the largest freshwater springs in the world. Springs flowing from the lava are prominent along the shoreline. This is a place of exceptional and primeval beauty. Much of the land is covered by recent (in geologic terms) lava flows, including vast areas of jagged black basalt, along with lava tubes and spattercone and conic depressions. There are brilliant aqua bays and for campers, peace and quiet. However, you may be joined by armies of mosquitoes. Bass fishing is often good, and know-hows tell stories of a few giant but elusive brown trout caught by accident on bass lures, and a sprinkling of rainbow trout. There are also nesting areas around the lake for bald eagles, ospreys and blue herons. A series of connecting trails are accessible from camp.

Location: At Big Lake; map B3, grid e3.

Campsites, facilities: There are nine boat-in sites. No motors are permitted on boats. Picnic tables and fire pits are provided. Vault toilets are available. No drinking water is available. Leashed pets are permitted.

Reservations, fees: No reservations; $7 per night. Open year-round, weather permitting.

Directions: From Redding, drive east on Highway 299 for 73 miles to McArthur and Main Street. Turn left on Main Street and drive 3.5 miles (becomes a dirt road) to the Rat Farm boat launch at Big Lake. Launch boat and paddle or row 1 to 2.5 miles to one of the nine boat-in campsites.

Contact: Ahjumawi Lava Springs State Park, tel. (530) 225-2065.

5 McArthur-Burney Falls State Park

     9

Burney Falls is a 129-foot waterfall, a beautiful cascade split at the top by a little grove of trees, with small trickles oozing and falling out of the adjacent moss-lined wall. Since it is fed primarily by a spring, it runs strong and glorious most of the year. The Headwaters Trail provides an outstanding hike, both to see the waterfall and Burney Creek, as well as for an easy adventure and fishing access to the stream. An excellent flyfishing section of the Pit River is available below the dam. There are other stellar recreation options at this state park. At the end of the campground access road is a boat ramp for Lake Britton, with rentals available for canoes and paddleboats. This is a beautiful lake, with awesome canyon walls on its upper end, and good smallmouth bass and crappie fishing. There is also a good swimming beach. The Pacific Crest Trail is routed right through the park and provides an additional opportunity for a day hike, best explored downstream from the dam. Reservations for sites are essential during the summer.

Location: In McArthur-Burney Falls Memorial State Park; map B3, grid e1.

Campsites, facilities: There are 128 sites for tents or RVs up to 35 feet long. Picnic tables and fire grills are provided. Drinking water, flush toilets, hot showers, and a sanitary disposal station are available. Some facilities are wheelchair accessible. A grocery store and boat rentals are available in the summer. Leashed pets are permitted, except on the trails and the beach.

Reservations, fees: Reserve at (800) 444-PARK (800-444-7275) or website: www.ReserveAmerica.com; $12 per night. Open year-round.

Directions: From Redding, drive east on Highway 299 to Burney and then continue for five miles to the junction with Highway 89. At Highway 89, drive north for six miles to the campground entrance on the left side of the road.

Contact: McArthur-Burney Falls State Park, tel. (530) 335-2777.

6 Dusty Campground

 8

This is one in a series of campgrounds near the north shore of Lake Britton. See the entry for Northshore for more information. The camp is set an elevation of 2,800 feet.

Location: On Lake Britton; map B3, grid e1.

Campsites, facilities: There are seven primitive sites for tents or RVs up to 20 feet long and two primitive group sites that can accommodate up to 25 people each. Fire rings are provided. Vault toilets are available. Drinking water is not available. Garbage must be packed out. Leashed pets are permitted.

Reservations, fees: No reservations; $6 per night, $3 per night per extra vehicle, $7 per night per extra RV, $1 pet fee; group sites are $12 per night. Open year-round.

Directions: From Redding, drive east on Highway 299 to Burney and continue for five miles to the junction with Highway 89. At Highway 89, turn left (north) and drive 7.5 miles (past the state park entrance and over the Lake Britton Bridge) to the campground access road on the left (it will be confusing because the campground is on the right). Turn left and drive three-quarters of a mile (in the process crossing the highway) to the campground.

Contact: PG&E Building and Land Services, tel. (916) 386-5164.

7 Northshore

 8

This peaceful campground is set among the woodlands near the shore of Lake Britton, directly across the lake from McArthur-Burney Falls Memorial State Park. Boating and fishing are popular here, and once the water warms up in midsummer, swimming is also a winner. The best trout fishing in the area is on the Pit River near Powerhouse No. 3, but skilled and aggressive wading is required. A hot spring is available in Big Bend, about a 30-minute drive from camp.

Location: On Lake Britton; map B3, grid e1.

Campsites, facilities: There are 30 sites for tents or RVs up to 30 feet long. Picnic tables and fire grills are provided. Drinking water and vault toilets are available. An unimproved boat ramp is available near the camp and an improved boat ramp is available in Burney Falls State Park (about four miles away). Supplies can be obtained in Fall River Mills or Burney. Leashed pets are permitted.

Reservations, fees: No reservations; $13 per night, $1 pet fee. Open mid-May to mid-September, weather permitting.

Directions: From Redding, drive east on Highway 299 to Burney and then continue for five miles to Highway 89. Turn north (left) and drive 9.7 miles (past the state park entrance and over the Lake Britton Bridge) to Clark Creek Road. Turn left (west) and drive about a mile to the camp access road. Turn left and drive one mile to the camp.

Contact: PG&E Building and Land Services, tel. (916) 386-5164.

8 Burney Falls Trailer Resort

 5

This is a year-round RV park near Lake Britton, Burney Creek, and the Pit River. McArthur-Burney Falls Memorial State Park, with its spectacular waterfall, is within a five-minute drive. The region is loaded with adventure, with Lassen Volcanic National Park, Hat Creek, and Fall River all within a 30-minute drive.

Location: Near Lake Britton; map B3, grid e2.

Campsites, facilities: There are 28 RV sites with full hookups. Restrooms, hot showers, a coin laundry, horseshoes, modem hookups, and a swimming pool are available. Leashed pets are permitted.

Reservations, fees: Reservations are accepted; $16 per night, $1 per person per night for more than two people. Open year-round.

Directions: From Redding, drive east on Highway 299 to Burney and continue for five miles to the junction with Highway 89. At Highway 89, turn north (left) and drive four miles to Clark Creek Road. Turn left on Clark Creek

Road and drive a short distance to the campground entrance.

Contact: Burney Falls Trailer Resort, tel. (530) 335-2781; website: www.norcalis.net/bftrsbf.

Pit River

 6

Very few out-of-towners know about this hidden and primitive campground set along the Pit River. It can provide a good base camp for a fishing trip adventure. The best stretch of trout water on the Pit is near Powerhouse No. 3. In addition to fishing there are many other recreation options. A parking area and trail along Hat Creek are available where the Highway 299 bridge crosses Hat Creek. Baum Lake, Crystal Lake, and the Cassel section of Hat Creek are all within five miles of this camp.

Location: On the Pit River; map B3, grid e3.

Campsites, facilities: There are 10 sites for tents or RVs. Picnic tables and fire rings are provided. Vault toilets are available. No drinking water is available. Garbage service is provided only during summer season. There are supplies and a coin laundry in Fall River Mills. Leashed pets are permitted.

Reservations, fees: No reservations; no fee. Open year-round, weather permitting.

Directions: From Redding, drive east on Highway 299 to Burney and continue for five miles to the junction with Highway 89. At the junction, continue straight on Highway 299, cross the Pit River Bridge, and drive about three miles to Pit One Powerhouse Road on the right. Just before the powerhouse, turn right (at the bend) and drive along the river for about a mile to the campground.

Contact: Bureau of Land Management, Alturas Field Office, tel. (530) 233-4666 or fax (530) 233-5696.

10 Cassel

     8

This camp is set at 3,200 feet in the beautiful Hat Creek Valley. It is an outstanding location for a fishing trip base camp, with nearby Crystal Lake, Baum Lake, and Hat Creek (all set in the Hat Creek Valley) providing trout fishing. This section of Hat Creek is well known for its challenging fly-fishing, typically with an excellent evening hatch and surface rise. Long leaders and very small flies are critical. A good source of fishing information is Vaughn's Sporting Goods in Burney. Baum Lake is ideal for car-top boats with electric motors.

Location: On Hat Creek; map B3, grid f2.

Campsites, facilities: There are 27 sites for tents or RVs up to 30 feet long. Picnic tables and fire grills are provided. Drinking water and vault toilets are available. Leashed pets are permitted.

Reservations, fees: No reservations; $13 per night, $3 per night per extra vehicle, $7 per night per extra RV, $1 pet fee. Open mid-April through October, weather permitting.

Directions: From Redding, drive east on Highway 299 to Burney and continue for five miles to the junction with Highway 89. At the junction, continue straight on Highway 299 for two miles to Cassel Road. At Cassel Road, turn right and drive 3.6 miles to the campground entrance on the left.

Contact: PG&E Building and Land Services, tel. (916) 386-5164.

11 Hat Creek Hereford Ranch RV Park & Campground

      8

This privately operated campground is set in a working cattle ranch, so if you go for a stroll, watch where you plant your Vibrams. Fishing is available in Hat Creek or in the nearby stocked trout pond. Sight-seeing is excellent with Burney Falls, Lassen Volcanic National Park, and Subway Caves all within 30 miles.

Location: Near Hat Creek; map B3, grid g2.

Campsites, facilities: There are 40 tent sites and 40 RV sites with full or partial hookups. Restrooms, hot showers, sanitary disposal station, coin laundry, playground, modem hookups, and a grocery store are available. Some facilities are wheelchair accessible. Leashed pets are permitted.

Reservations, fees: Reservations are recommended; $15.95 to $19.95 per night, $2 per adult and $1.50 per child per night for more than two people, $.50 per night per pet. Major credit cards accepted. Open April through October.

Directions: From Redding, drive east on Highway 299 to Burney and continue for five miles to the junction with Highway 89. Turn south on Highway 89 and drive 12 miles to the second Doty Road exit and the entrance to the campground.

Contact: Hat Creek Hereford Ranch Campground, tel. (530) 335-7171; website:www.hatcreekrv.com.

12 Honn

 7

This primitive, tiny campground is set near the point where Honn Creek enters Hat Creek, at 3,400 feet elevation in Lassen National Forest. The creek is extremely pretty here, shaded by trees and flowing emerald green. The camp provides streamside access for trout fishing, though this stretch of creek is sometimes overlooked by the Department of Fish and Game in favor of stocking the creek at the more popular Cave and Bridge Campgrounds. See the entry for Cave Camp for more information.

Location: On Hat Creek in Lassen National Forest; map B3, grid h2.

Campsites, facilities: There are six tent sites. Picnic tables and fire grills are provided. Vault toilets are available. Drinking water is not available. A grocery store, coin laundry, and propane gas are also available nearby. Leashed pets are permitted.

Reservations, fees: No reservations; $8 per night. Open late April through October, weather permitting.

Directions: From Redding, drive east on High-

way 299 to Burney and continue for five miles to the junction with Highway 89. Turn south on Highway 89 and drive 15 miles to the campground entrance on the left side of the road.

Contact: Lassen National Forest, Hat Creek Ranger District, tel. (530) 336-5521 or fax (530) 335-4518.

13 Cave Camp

 7

Cave Camp is set right along Hat Creek, with both easy access off Highway 89 and an anglers' trail available along the stream. This stretch of Hat Creek is planted with rainbow trout twice per month by the Department of Fish and Game, starting with the opening of trout season on the last Saturday of April. Nearby side trips include Lassen Volcanic National Park, about a 15-minute drive to the south on Highway 89, and Subway Caves (turn left at the junction just across the road from the campground). A rare bonus at this camp is that wheelchair-accessible fishing is available.

Location: On Hat Creek in Lassen National Forest; map B3, grid h2.

Campsites, facilities: There are 46 sites for tents or RVs up to 22 feet long. Picnic tables and fire grills are provided. Drinking water, flush toilets, and vault toilets are available. Some facilities are wheelchair accessible. Supplies can be obtained in Old Station. Leashed pets are permitted.

Reservations, fees: No reservations; $13 per night. Open May through October.

Directions: From Redding, drive east on Highway 299 to Burney and continue for five miles to the junction with Highway 89. Turn right (south) on Highway 89 and drive 23 miles to the campground entrance on the right side of the road. If you reach Old Station, you have gone one mile too far.

Contact: Lassen National Forest, Hat Creek Ranger District, tel. (530) 336-5521 or fax (530) 335-4518.

14 Bridge Camp

      7

This camp is one of four along Highway 89 in the area along Hat Creek. It is set at 3,800 feet elevation, with shaded sites and the stream within very short walking distance. Trout are stocked on this stretch of the creek, with fishing access available out of camp, as well as at Rocky and Cave Camps to the south and Honn to the north. In one weekend, fishermen might hit all four. **Location:** On Hat Creek in Lassen National Forest; map B3, grid h2.

Campsites, facilities: There are 25 sites for tents or RVs up to 22 feet long. Picnic tables and fire grills are provided. Drinking water and vault toilets are available. A grocery store and propane gas are available nearby. Leashed pets are permitted.

Reservations, fees: No reservations; $11 per night. Open late April through October, weather permitting.

Directions: From Redding, drive east on Highway 299 to Burney and continue for five miles to the junction with Highway 89. Turn south on Highway 89 and drive 19 miles to the campground entrance on the right side of the road. If you reach Old Station, you have gone five miles too far.

Contact: Lassen National Forest, Hat Creek Ranger District, tel. (530) 336-5521 or fax (530) 335-4518.

15 Rocky Camp

     7

This is a small, primitive camp along Hat Creek on Highway 89. It's usually a second choice for campers if nearby Cave and Bridge Camps are full. Streamside fishing access is a plus here, with this section of stream stocked with rainbow trout. See the entry for Cave Camp for more information.

Location: On Hat Creek in Lassen National Forest; map B3, grid h2.

Campsites, facilities: There are eight tent sites. Picnic tables and grills are provided.

Vault toilets are available. No drinking water is available. A grocery store and propane gas are available nearby. Leashed pets are permitted.

Reservations, fees: No reservations; $8 per night. Open late April through October, weather permitting.

Directions: From Redding, drive east on Highway 299 to Burney and continue for five miles to the junction with Highway 89. Turn right (south) on Highway 89 and drive 20 miles to the campground entrance on the right side of the road. If you reach Old Station, you have gone four miles too far.

Contact: Lassen National Forest, Hat Creek Ranger District, tel. (530) 336-5521 or fax (530) 335-4518.

16 Hat Creek

      7

This is one in a series of Forest Service camps set beside beautiful Hat Creek, a good trout stream stocked regularly by the Department of Fish and Game. The elevation is 4,400 feet. The proximity to Lassen Volcanic National Park to the south is a big plus. Supplies are available in the little town of Old Station one mile to the north.

Location: On Hat Creek in Lassen National Forest; map B3, grid i2.

Campsites, facilities: There are 73 sites for tents or RVs up to 22 feet long and three group camp loops, each of which accommodates from 15 to 20 vehicles. Picnic tables and fire grills are provided. Drinking water, a sanitary disposal station, and vault toilets are available. A grocery store, coin laundry, and propane gas are available nearby. Leashed pets are permitted.

Reservations, fees: Reservations required for campsites 1 through 9 and for group camps at tel. (877) 444-6777 ($8.65 reservation fee) or website: www.reserveusa.com; $13 per night for family sites; $60 per night for each group camp loop. Open May through October.

Directions: From Redding, drive east on Highway 44 to the junction with Highway 89 (near the entrance to Lassen Volcanic National Park). Turn north on Highway 89 and drive about 12 miles to the campground entrance on the left side of the road. (If you reach Old Station, you have gone one mile too far.) Turn left and drive a short distance to the campground.

Contact: Lassen National Forest, Hat Creek Ranger District, tel. (530) 336-5521 or fax (530) 335-4518.

17 Big Pine Camp

     7

This campground is set on the headwaters of Hat Creek, a pretty spot amid ponderosa pines. A dirt road out of camp parallels Hat Creek, providing access for trout fishing. A great vista point is set on the highway, a mile south of the campground entrance road. It is only a 10-minute drive south to the Highway 44 entrance station for Lassen Volcanic National Park.

Location: On Hat Creek in Lassen National Forest; map B3, grid i2.

Campsites, facilities: There are 19 sites for tents or RVs up to 22 feet long. Picnic tables and fire grills are provided. Drinking water (at two hand pumps) and vault toilets are available. A sanitary disposal station, grocery store, and propane gas are available nearby. Leashed pets are permitted.

Reservations, fees: No reservations; $10 per night.

Directions: From Redding, drive east on Highway 44 to the junction with Highway 89 (near the entrance to Lassen Volcanic National Park). Turn north on Highway 89 and drive about eight miles (one mile past the vista point) to the campground entrance on the right side of the road. Turn right and drive a half mile to the campground.

Contact: Lassen National Forest, Hat Creek Ranger District, tel. (530) 336-5521 or fax (530) 335-4518.

18 North Battle Creek Reservoir

     7

This little-known lake is set at 5,600 feet in elevation, largely surrounded by Lassen National Forest. No gas engines are permitted on the lake, making it ideal for canoes, rafts, and car-top aluminum boats equipped with electric motors. When the lake level is up in early summer, it is a pretty setting with good trout fishing.

Location: On Battle Creek Reservoir; map B3, grid i0.

Campsites, facilities: There are 10 sites for tents or RVs and five walk-in tent sites. Picnic tables and fire grills are provided. Drinking water and vault toilets are available. A car-top boat launch is available nearby. Leashed pets are permitted.

Reservations, fees: No reservations; $11 per night, $3 per night per extra vehicle, $7 per night per extra RV, $1 pet fee. Open mid-May to mid-September, weather permitting.

Directions: From Redding, drive east on Highway 44 to Viola. From Viola, continue east for 3.5 miles to Forest Road 32N17. Turn left on Forest Road 32N17 and drive five miles. Turn left on Forest Road 32N31 and drive four miles. Turn right on Forest Road 32N18 and drive a half mile to the reservoir and the campground on the right side of the road.

Contact: PG&E Building and Land Services, tel. (916) 386-5164.

19 Manzanita Lake

    9

Manzanita Lake, set at 5,890 feet, is one of the prettiest lakes in Lassen Volcanic National Park and has good catch-and-release trout fishing for experienced fly fishers in prams and other non-powered boats. This is no place for a dad, mom, and a youngster to fish from shore with Power Bait. Because of the great natural beauty of the lake, the campground is often crowded. Evening walks around the lake are beautiful. A major visitor center and small store are available nearby.

Location: In Lassen Volcanic National Park; map B3, grid j0.

Campsites, facilities: There are 179 sites for tents or RVs up to 35 feet long. Picnic tables and fire grills are provided. Drinking water and flush toilets are available. Propane gas, groceries, showers, a sanitary disposal station, and a coin laundry are available nearby. A boat launch is also nearby (no motors are permitted on boats at Manzanita Lake). Some facilities are wheelchair accessible. Leashed pets are permitted at campsites only.

Reservations, fees: No reservations; $14 per night, $10 per vehicle park entrance fee. Major credit cards accepted. Open late May to late September, weather permitting.

Directions: From Redding, drive east on Highway 44 to the junction with Highway 89. Turn south on Highway 89 and drive one mile to the entrance station to Lassen Volcanic National Park (the road becomes Lassen Park Highway). Continue a short distance on Lassen Park Highway, turn right at the campground entrance road, and drive a half mile to the campground.

Contact: Lassen Volcanic National Park, tel. (530) 595-4444 or fax (530) 595-3262.

20 Crags

    8

Crags is sometimes overlooked as a prime spot at Lassen Volcanic National Park because there is no lake nearby. No problem, because even though this campground is small compared to the giant complex at Manzanita Lake, the campsites are more spacious, do not fill up as quickly, and many are backed by forest. In addition, the Emigrant Trail runs out of camp, routing east and meeting up with pretty Lost Creek after a little over a mile, a great short hike. Directly across from Crags are the towering Chaos Crags, topping out at 8,503 feet. The elevation here is 5,720 feet.

Location: In Lassen Volcanic National Park; map B3, grid i1.

Campsites, facilities: There are 45 sites for tents or RVs up to 35 feet long. Picnic tables, fire rings, and food lockers are provided. Drinking water and vault toilets are available. Leashed pets are permitted.

Reservations, fees: No reservations, $8 per night, $10 per vehicle park entrance fee. Major credit cards accepted. Open late June to early September.

Directions: From Redding, drive east on Highway 44 for 42 miles to the junction with Highway 89. At Highway 89, turn right and drive to the entrance station at Lassen Volcanic National Park (the road becomes Lassen Park Highway). Continue on Lassen Park Highway for about five miles to the campground on the left side of the road.

Contact: Lassen Volcanic National Park, tel. (530) 595-4444 or fax (530) 595-3262.

21 Summit Lake, North and South

 9

Summit Lake is a beautiful spot where deer often visit each evening on the adjacent meadow just east of the campground. The lake is small, and since trout plants were suspended, it has been just about fished out. Evening walks around the lake are perfect for families. A more ambitious trail is routed out of camp and leads past lavish wildflower displays in early summer to a series of wilderness lakes. The camps are set at an elevation of 6,695 feet.

Location: In Lassen Volcanic National Park; map B3, grid j2.

Campsites, facilities: There are 94 sites for tents or RVs up to 35 feet long. Picnic tables and fire rings are provided. Drinking water and toilets (flush toilets on the north side, vault toilets on the south side) are available. Some facilities are wheelchair accessible. Ranger programs are available in summer. Leashed pets are permitted at campsites only.

Reservations, fees: No reservations; $12 to $14 per night, $10 per vehicle park entrance fee. Major credit cards accepted. Open late-June to mid-September.

Directions: From Redding, drive east on Highway 44 to the junction with Highway 89. Turn south on Highway 89 and drive one mile to the entrance station to Lassen Volcanic National Park (where the road becomes Lassen Park Highway). Continue on Lassen Park Highway for 12 miles to the campground entrance on the left side of the road.

Contact: Lassen Volcanic National Park, tel. (530) 595-4444 or fax (530) 595-3262.

22 Butte Lake

 9

Butte Lake Camp is situated in an open, volcanic setting with a sprinkling of lodgepole pine. The contrast of the volcanics against the emerald greens of the lake is beautiful and memorable. The Cinder Cone Trail can provide an even better look. The trailhead is near the boat launch area, a strenuous hike involving a climb of 800 feet over the course of two miles to the top of the Cinder Cone. The footing is often loose because of volcanic pebbles. At the rim, you can peer inside the Cinder Cone, as well as be rewarded with lake views and a long-distance vista. Trout fishing is poor at Butte Lake, as at nearly all the lakes at this national park, because trout have not been planted for years. The elevation is 6,100 feet.

Location: In Lassen Volcanic National Park; map B3, grid j3.

Campsites, facilities: There are 42 sites for tents or RVs up to 35 feet long. No hookups. Picnic tables and fire rings are provided. Vault toilets are available. No drinking water is available. Leashed pets are permitted at campsites only. No motors are permitted on the lake.

Reservations, fees: No reservations; $10 per night, $10 per vehicle park entrance fee. Open late-June to late-September, weather permitting.

Directions: From Redding, drive east on Highway 44 to the junction with Highway 89. Bear north on Highway 89/44 and drive 13 miles to Old Station. Just past Old Station, turn right (east) on Highway 44 and drive 10 miles to Forest Road 32N21. Turn right and drive six miles to the campround.

Contact: Lassen Volcanic National Park, tel. (530) 595-4444 or fax (530) 595-3262.

23 Butte Creek

 6

This primitive, little-known spot is just three miles from the northern boundary of Lassen Volcanic National Park, set on little Butte Creek. It is a four-mile drive south out of camp on Forest Road 18 to Butte Lake in Lassen Park, as well as to the trailhead for a great hike up to the Cinder Cone (6,907 feet), with dramatic views of the Lassen wilderness.

Location: In Lassen National Forest; map B3, grid i4.

Campsites, facilities: There are 10 unimproved sites for tents or RVs up to 22 feet long. Picnic tables and fire grills are provided. Vault toilets are available. No drinking water is available. Garbage must be packed out. Leashed pets are permitted.

Reservations, fees: No reservations; no fee. Open May through October.

Directions: From Redding, drive east on Highway 44 to the junction with Highway 89 (near the entrance to Lassen Volcanic National Park). Turn north on Highway 89 and drive to Highway 44. Turn east (left) on Highway 44 and drive 11 miles to Forest Road 18. Turn right at Forest Road 18 and drive three miles to the campground on the left side of the road.

Contact: Lassen National Forest, Eagle Lake Ranger District, tel. (530) 257-4188 or fax (530) 252-5803.

24 Crater Lake

 8

This camp is set near Crater Lake at 6,800 feet in remote Lassen National Forest, just below Crater Mountain (that's it up there to the northeast at 7,420 feet). This primitive hideaway provides fishing, boating, and, if you can stand the ice-cold water, a quick dunk on warm summer days.

Location: In Lassen National Forest; map B3, grid i6.

Campsites, facilities: There are 17 sites for tents. Picnic tables and fire grills are provided. Drinking water (from a well) and vault toilets are available. Leashed pets are permitted.

Reservations, fees: No reservations; $11 per night. Open June through October.

Directions: From Redding, drive east on Highway 44 to the junction with Highway 89 (near the entrance to Lassen Volcanic National Park). Turn north on Highway 89 and drive to Highway 44. Turn east on Highway 44 (left) and drive to the Bogard Work Center and adjacent rest stop. Turn left at Forest Road 32N08 (signed Crater Lake) and drive one mile to a T intersection. Bear right and continue on Forest Road 32N08 for six miles (including two hairpin left turns) to the campground on the left side of the road.

Contact: Lassen National Forest, Eagle Lake Ranger District, tel. (530) 257-4188 or fax (530) 252-5803.

25 Rocky Knoll

 7

This is one of two camps at pretty Silver Lake, set at 6,400 feet elevation at the edge of the Caribou Wilderness. The other camp is Silver Bowl to the nearby north, which is larger and provides better access for hikers. This camp, however, is closer to the boat ramp, which is set at the south end of the lake. Silver Lake provides a good summer fishery for campers.

Location: On Silver Lake in Lassen National Forest; map B3, grid j5.

Campsites, facilities: There are seven tent sites and 11 sites for RVs up to 27 feet long. Picnic tables and fire grills are provided. Drinking water and vault toilets are available. Leashed pets are permitted.

Reservations, fees: No reservations; $11 per night. Open late May through October, weather permitting.

Directions: From Red Bluff, drive east on Highway 36 to the junction with Highway 89. Continue east on Highway 89/36 past Lake Almanor to Westwood. In Westwood, turn left on County Road A21 and drive 12.5 miles to Silver Lake Road. Turn left (west) on Silver Lake Road/County Road 110 and drive 8.5 miles north to Silver Lake. At Silver Lake, turn left and drive a short distance to the campground.

Contact: Lassen National Forest, Almanor Ranger District, tel. (530) 258-2141 or fax (530) 258-5194.

26 Silver Bowl

 7

Silver Lake is a pretty lake set at 6,400 feet elevation at the edge of the Caribou Wilderness. It is stocked with 9,000 Eagle Lake trout and 900 brown trout each year and provides a good summer fishery for campers. There is an unimproved boat ramp at the southern end of the lake. A trailhead from adjacent Caribou Lake is routed west into the wilderness, with routes available both to Emerald Lake to the northwest, and Betty, Trail, and Shotover in Lakes nearby to the southeast.

Location: On Silver Lake in Lassen National Forest; map B3, grid j5.

Campsites, facilities: There are 18 sites for tents or RVs. Picnic tables and fire grills are provided. Drinking water and vault toilets are available. Leashed pets are permitted.

Reservations, fees: No reservations; $11 per night. Open late May through October, weather permitting.

Directions: From Red Bluff, drive east on Highway 36 to the junction with Highway 89. Continue east on Highway 89/36 past Lake Almanor to Westwood. In Westwood, turn left on County Road A21 and drive 12.5 miles to Silver Lake Road. Turn left on Silver Lake Road/County Road 110 and drive 8.5 miles north to Silver Lake. At Silver Lake, turn right and drive a short distance to the campground.

Contact: Lassen National Forest, Almanor Ranger District, tel. (530) 258-2141 or fax (530) 258-5194.

27 Bogard

    6

This little camp is set along Pine Creek, which flows through Pine Creek Valley at the foot of the Bogard Buttes. It is a relatively obscure camp that gets missed by many travelers. To the nearby west is a network of Forest Service roads, and beyond is the Caribou Wilderness.

Location: In Lassen National Forest; map B3, grid j5.

Campsites, facilities: There are 13 sites for tents or RVs up to 28 feet long. Picnic tables and fire grills are provided. Drinking water and vault toilets are available. Leashed pets are permitted.

Reservations, fees: No reservations; $9 per night. Open May through September.

Directions: From Redding, drive east on Highway 44 to the junction with Highway 89 (near the entrance to Lassen Volcanic National Park). Turn north on Highway 89 and drive to Highway 44. Turn east on Highway 44 and drive to the Bogard Work Center (about seven miles past Poison Lake) and the adjacent rest stop. Continue east on Highway 44 for two miles to a gravel road on the right side of the road (Forest Road 31N26). Turn right on Forest Road 31N26 and drive two miles. Turn right on Forest Road 31N21 and drive a half mile to the campground at the end of the road.

Contact: Lassen National Forest, Eagle Lake Ranger District, tel. (530) 257-4188 or fax (530) 257-4150.

28 Christie

    9

This camp is set along the southern shore of Eagle Lake at 5,100 feet. Eagle Lake is well known for its big trout (yea) and big winds (boo). The camp offers some protection from the north winds. Its location is also good for seeing osprey with the Osprey Management Area, which covers a six-mile stretch of shoreline, just two miles to the north above Wildcat Point. A nearby resort is a bonus. The nearest boat ramp is at Aspen Grove Campground.

Location: On Eagle Lake in Lassen National Forest; map B3, grid j9.

Campsites, facilities: There are 69 sites for tents or RVs up to 50 feet long. Picnic tables and fire grills are provided. Drinking water and flush toilets are available. Some facilities are wheelchair accessible. A grocery store is nearby. A sanitary disposal station is two miles away at Merrill Campground. Leashed pets are permitted.

Reservations, fees: Reserve at (877) 444-6777 ($8.65 reservation fee) or website: www.reserveusa.com; $14 per night. Open May through September.

Directions: From Red Bluff, drive east on Highway 36 toward Susanville. Three miles before Susanville turn left on Eagle Lake Road/County Road A1 and drive 15.5 miles to County Road 231. Turn right on County Road 231 and drive four miles to the campground on the right side of the road.

Contact: Lassen National Forest, Eagle Lake Ranger District, tel. (530) 257-4188 or fax (530) 252-5803.

Note: For more campgrounds at Eagle Lake, see chapter B4.

29 Merrill

    9

This is one of the largest, most developed Forest Service campgrounds in the entire county. It is set along the southern shore of huge Eagle Lake at 5,100 feet. The nearest boat launch is adjacent to Aspen Grove Campground.

Location: On Eagle Lake in Lassen National Forest; map B3, grid j9.

Campsites, facilities: There are 180 sites for tents or RVs up to 32 feet long. Picnic tables and fire grills are provided. Drinking water, flush toilets, and a sanitary disposal station are available. Some facilities are wheelchair accessible. A grocery store and boat ramp are available nearby. Leashed pets are permitted.

Reservations, fees: Reserve at (877) 444-6777 ($8.65 reservation fee) or website: www.reserveusa.com; $14 to $15 per night. Open May through November.

Directions: From Red Bluff, drive east on Highway 36 toward Susanville. Three miles before Susanville, turn left on Eagle Lake Road/County Road A1 and drive 15.5 miles to County Road 231. Turn right on County Road 231 and drive one mile to the campground on the right side of the road.

Contact: Lassen National Forest, Eagle Lake Ranger District, tel. (530) 257-4188 or fax (530) 252-5803.

30 Aspen Grove

       9

Eagle Lake is one of the great trout lakes in California, producing the fast-growing and often huge Eagle Lake trout, which are common in the 18- to 22-inch class. This camp is one of three at the south end of the lake and is a popular choice for anglers, with a boat ramp available adjacent to the campground. The one problem with Eagle Lake is the wind, which can whip the huge but shallow lake into a froth in the early summer. It is imperative that anglers/boaters get on the water early, and then get back to camp early, with the fishing for the day often done by 10:30 a.m. There have been many days where limits of 20-inch trout are in the boat before the sun rises. A bonus here is a good chance to see bald eagles and osprey.

Location: On Eagle Lake in Lassen National Forest; map B3, grid j9.

Campsites, facilities: There are 25 tent sites. Picnic tables and fire grills are provided. Drinking water and flush toilets are available. A boat ramp is available nearby. Leashed pets are permitted

Reservations, fees: No reservations; $12 per night. Open May through September.

Directions: From Red Bluff, drive east on Highway 36 toward Susanville. Three miles before Susanville, turn left on Eagle Lake Road/County Road A1 and drive 15.5 miles to County Road 231. Turn right on County Road 231 and drive two miles to the campground on the left side of the road.

Contact: Lassen National Forest, Eagle Lake Ranger District, tel. (530) 257-4188 or fax (530) 252-5803.

31 West Eagle Group Camps

   9

If you are coming in a big group to Eagle Lake, you'd better get on the horn first and reserve this camp. Then you can have your own private slice of solitude along the southern shore of Eagle Lake. Bring your boat; the Aspen boat ramp is only about a mile away.

Location: On Eagle Lake in Lassen National Forest; map B3, grid j9.

Campsites, facilities: There are two group camps for tents and RVs up to 35 feet long. Picnic tables and fire grills are provided. Drinking water, flush toilets, and picnic areas are available. A grocery store and boat ramp are nearby. The campground capacity is limited to 100 people for camp one and 75 people for camp two. Leashed pets are permitted.

Reservations, fees: Reserve at (877) 444-6777 ($8.65 reservation fee) or website: www.reserveusa.com; $70 to $110 per night for camp one, $70 to $80 per night for camp two. Open from Memorial Day weekend to October, weather permitting.

Directions: From Red Bluff, drive east on Highway 36 toward Susanville. Three miles before Susanville, turn left on Eagle Lake Road/County Road A1 and drive 15.5 miles to County Road 231. Turn right on County Road 231 and drive a quarter mile to the campground on the left side of the road.

Contact: Lassen National Forest, Eagle Lake Ranger District, tel. (530) 257-4188 or fax (530) 252-5803.

32 Eagle

 9

Eagle is set just up the road from Aspen Grove; the latter is more popular because of the adjacent boat ramp. For information about Eagle Lake, see the entry for Aspen Grove.

Location: On Eagle Lake in Lassen National Forest; map B3, grid j9.

Campsites, facilities: There are 49 sites for tents or RVs up to 32 feet long. Picnic tables and fire grills are provided. Drinking water and flush toilets are available. Some facilities are wheelchair accessible. There is a boat launch nearby at Aspen Grove. Leashed pets are permitted.

Reservations, fees: Reserve at (877) 444-6777 ($8.65 reservation fee) or website: www.reserveusa.com; $14 per night. Open May through September.

Directions: From Red Bluff, drive east on Highway 36 toward Susanville. Three miles before Susanville, turn left on Eagle Lake Road/County Road A1 and drive 15.5 miles to County Road 231. Turn right and drive a half mile to the campground on the left side of the road.

Contact: Lassen National Forest, Eagle Lake Ranger District, tel. (530) 257-4188 or fax (530) 252-5803.

CHAPTER B4

JEFFREY PATTY

A GRAZING DOE

MAP B4

TO TRIANGLE TO HIGHWAY 140 **144** TO DAVIS CREEK TO FORT BIDWELL

1
Raker Reservoir
Thomas Reservoir

MODOC NATIONAL FOREST

Big Sage Reservoir
2

3

Upper Alkali Lake

(395)

Lake City

6
7

Cedar Pass 6,305 feet

Canby (299)

ALTURAS **4**
5

Dorris Reservoir

Cedarville (299)

MODOC NATIONAL WILDLIFE REFUGE

(447)

8

Middle Alkali Lake

(299)

9 **10**

MODOC NATIONAL FOREST

Likely

12
13

SOUTH WARNER WILDERNESS

Eagle Peak 9,906 feet

Eagleville

11

Lower Alkali Lake

14

15

MODOC NATIONAL FOREST

(447)

West Valley Reservoir

16

Sage Hen Summit 5,556 feet

17

Madeline

Tule Lake Reservoir

McDonald Peak 7,932 feet

18

(395)

Termo

Red Rock

(139)

(A1)

Ravendale

19-20
Fredonyer Peak 7,975 feet

Eagle Lake

21

Observation Peak 7,964 feet

CALIFORNIA NEVADA

(395)

TO SUSANVILLE **330** TO LITCHFIELD

TO NEWELL
TO ADIN
TO ADIN
TO PITTVILLE

TO VYA, NV
TO GERLACH, NV

222

0 1 2 3 4 5 6 7 8 9

© AVALON TRAVEL PUBLISHING, INC.

CHAPTER B4

❶ Reservoir C

    6

It is one great adventure to explore the "alphabet lakes" in the remote Devil's Garden area of Modoc County. Reservoir C and Reservoir F provide the best of the lot, but the success can go up and down like a yo-yo, just like the water levels in the lakes. Reservoir C is stocked with both Eagle Lake trout and brown trout. A sidelight to this area is the number of primitive roads that are routed through Modoc National Forest, perfect for four-wheel-drive cowboys.

Location: Near Alturas in Modoc National Forest; map B4, grid a2.

Campsites, facilities: There are six primitive sites. Picnic tables are provided. A vault toilet is available. No drinking water is available. Garbage must be packed out. Leashed pets are permitted.

Reservations, fees: No reservations; no fee. Open May through September.

Directions: From Alturas drive west on Highway 299 for three miles to Crowder Flat Road/County Road 73. Turn right on Crowder Flat Road and drive 9.5 miles to Triangle Ranch Road/Forest Road 43N18. Turn left on Triangle Ranch Road and drive seven miles to Forest Road 44N32. Turn right on Forest Road 44N32, drive a half mile, turn right on the access road for the lake and campground, and drive a half mile to the camp at the end of the road.

Contact: Modoc National Forest, Devil's Garden Ranger District, tel. (530) 233-5811 or fax (530) 233-8709.

❷ Big Sage Reservoir

 6

This is a do-it-yourself camp; that is, pick your own spot, bring your own water, and don't expect to see any Forest Service rangers or, for that matter, anybody else. This camp is set along Big Sage Reservoir—that's right, sagebrush country at 5,100 feet elevation. It is a big lake, covering 5,000 acres, and a boat ramp is adjacent to the campground. This is one of the better bass lakes in Modoc County. Catfish and crappie are also available here.

Location: In Modoc National Forest; map B4, grid a3.

Campsites, facilities: There are primitive, dispersed sites for tents or RVs of any length. Picnic tables are provided. A vault toilet is available. Some facilities are wheelchair accessible. No drinking water is available. Garbage must be packed out. A boat ramp is available nearby. Leashed pets are permitted. Supplies can be obtained in Alturas, about eight miles away.

Reservations, fees: No reservations; no fee. Open May through September.

Directions: From Alturas, drive west on Highway 299 for three miles to Crowder Flat Road/County Road 73. Turn right on Crowder Flat Road and drive about five miles to County Road 180. Turn right on County Road 180 and drive four miles. Turn left at the access road for the campground and boat ramp and drive a short distance to the camp on the left side of the road.

Contact: Modoc National Forest, Devil's Garden Ranger District, tel. (530) 233-5811 or fax (530) 233-8709.

3 Plum Valley

 7

This secluded and primitive camp is set near the South Fork of Davis Creek, at 5,600 feet elevation. Davis Creek provides for catch-and-release, barbless hook, no-bait fishing. You can, however, keep the brown trout. There are no other campgrounds within 15 miles.

Location: Near the South Fork of Davis Creek in Modoc National Forest; map B4, grid a7.

Campsites, facilities: There are 7 sites for tents or RVs up to 15 feet long. Picnic tables and fire grills are provided. A vault toilet is available. No drinking water is available. Garbage must be packed out. Supplies are available in Davis Creek, about 3.5 miles away. Leashed pets are permitted.

Reservations, fees: No reservations; no fee. Open May through September.

Directions: From Alturas drive north on U.S. 395 for 18 miles to the town of Davis Creek. Turn right on County Road 11 and drive two miles to a Y. Bear right on Forest Road 45N35 and drive one mile to the signed entrance to the campground on the left side of the road.

Contact: Modoc National Forest, Warner Mountain Ranger District, tel. (530) 279-6116 or fax (530) 279-8309.

4 Brass Rail

    4

This private RV park has easy access from the highway. The elevation is 4,400 feet. Alturas is the biggest "small town" in Modoc County and offers a nice city park with a playground, museum, old-time saloon, and just south of town, the Modoc National Wildlife Refuge. The Warner Mountains to the distant east provide a backdrop.

Location: Near Alturas; map B4, grid c4.

Campsites, facilities: There are 70 RV sites, some with full hookups, and a separate tent area. Picnic tables are provided. Hot showers, flush toilets, sanitary disposal station, coin laundry, ice, propane gas, playground, and tennis court are available. Some facilities are wheelchair accessible. Supplies can be obtained in Alturas, less than a mile away. Leashed pets are permitted.

Reservations, fees: Reservations are accepted; $8 to $14 per night, $3 to $5 per night for each extra vehicle. Major credit cards accepted. Open March through October.

Directions: In Alturas at the junction of Highway 299 and U.S. 395, turn east on U.S. 395 and drive a half mile to the signed campground entrance on the right.

Contact: Brass Rail Campground, tel. (530) 233-2906.

5 Sully's Trailer Lodge

    4

This privately operated park is next to the playground, the city park, and the Modoc County Museum, which details the history of the area. The Modoc National Wildlife Refuge is only a short drive away, either a mile southwest of town along the Pit River, or three miles east of town at Dorris Reservoir. Big Sage Reservoir provides another getaway option.

Location: Near Alturas; map B4, grid c4.

Campsites, facilities: There are 25 RV sites, including some with full hookups and five pull-through sites. Hot showers, flush toilets, coin laundry, and horseshoe pits are available. Cable TV and modem hookups are available for an extra fee. Supplies can be obtained in Alturas one block away. Leashed pets are permitted.

Reservations, fees: Reservations are accepted; $10.40 to $15.40 per night. Open year-round.

Directions: In Alturas, at the junction of Highway 299 and U.S. 395, turn south on U.S. 395 and drive a half mile (look for the steam engine) to County Road 56. Turn east on County Road 56 and drive one block to the campground.

Contact: Sully's Trailer Lodge, tel. (530) 233-5347, or fax (530) 233-2541.

6 Stowe Reservoir

 8

Stowe Reservoir looks like a large country pond where cattle might drink. You know why? Because it once actually was a cattle pond on a family ranch that has since been converted to Forest Service property. It is in the north Warner Mountains (not to be confused with the South Warner Wilderness), which features many back roads and remote four-wheel-drive routes. The camp is set at an elevation of 6,200 feet. Note that you may find this campground named "Stough Reservoir" on some maps and in previous editions of this book. The name is now officially spelled "Stowe Reservoir," after the family that originally owned the property.

Location: In Modoc National Forest; map B4, grid b7.

Campsites, facilities: There are 14 sites for tents or RVs up to 22 feet long. Picnic tables and fire grills are provided. Drinking water and vault toilets are available. Garbage must be packed out. Leashed pets are permitted.

Supplies can be obtained in Cedarville, six miles away.

Reservations, fees: No reservations; no fee. Open May to October.

Directions: From Redding, drive east on Highway 299 to Alturas. In Alturas, continue north on Highway 299/U.S. 395 for five miles. Turn right on Highway 299 and drive about 12 miles (just past Cedar Pass). Look for the signed entrance road on the left side of the road. Turn left and drive one mile to the campground on the right side of the road.

Contact: Modoc National Forest, Warner Mountain Ranger District, tel. (530) 279-6116 or fax (530) 279-8309.

7 Cedar Pass

 5

Cedar Pass is at 5,900 feet, set on the ridge between Cedar Mountain (8,152 feet) to the north and Payne Peak (7,618) to the south, high in the north Warner Mountains. Bear Creek enters Thomas Creek adjacent to the camp, both small streams, but a pretty spot.

Location: On Cedar Pass in Modoc National Forest; map B4, grid b7.

Campsites, facilities: There are 17 sites for tents or RVs up to 22 feet long. Picnic tables and fire grills are provided. Vault toilets are available. No piped water is available. Garbage must be packed out. Supplies can be obtained in Cedarville or Alturas. Leashed pets are permitted.

Reservations, fees: No reservations; no fee. Open May through September.

Directions: From Redding drive east on Highway 299 to Alturas. In Alturas continue north on Highway 299/U.S. 395 for five miles. Turn right on Highway 299 and drive about nine miles. Look for the signed entrance road on the right side of the road.

Contact: Modoc National Forest, Warner Mountain Ranger District, tel. (530) 279-6116 or fax (530) 279-8309.

8 Pepperdine

     5

This camp is outstanding for hikers planning a backpacking trip into the adjacent South Warner Wilderness. The camp is at 6,680 feet, set along the south side of tiny Porter Reservoir, with a horse corral within walking distance. A trailhead out of camp provides direct access to the Summit Trail, the best hike in the South Warner Wilderness.

Location: In Modoc National Forest; map B4, grid d7.

Campsites, facilities: There are five sites for tents or RVs up to 22 feet long. Picnic tables and fire grills are provided. Drinking water and vault toilets are available. Corrals are available with stock watering facilities. Garbage must be packed out. Supplies are available in Cedarville or Alturas. Leashed pets are permitted.

Reservations, fees: No reservations; no fee. Open July through October.

Directions: In Alturas, drive south on U.S. 395 to the southern end of town and County Road 56. Turn left on County Road 56 and drive 13 miles to the Modoc Forest boundary and the junction with Parker Creek Road. Bear left on Parker Creek Road and continue for six miles to the signed campground access road on the right. Turn right and drive a half mile to the campground on the right side of the road.

Contact: Modoc National Forest, Warner Mountain Ranger District, tel. (530) 279-6116 or fax (530) 279-8309.

9 Lower Rush Creek

    6

This is one of two obscure campgrounds set a short distance from Highway 299 on Rush Creek in southern Modoc County. Lower Rush Creek is the first camp you will come to, with flat campsites surrounded by an outer fence and set along Rush Creek. This camp is better suited for trailers than the one at Upper Rush Creek. It is little known and little used. It's set at 4,400 feet in elevation.

Location: On Rush Creek in Modoc National Forest; map B4, grid d0.

Campsites, facilities: There are 10 sites for tents and five sites for RVs up to 22 feet long. Picnic tables and fire grills are provided. Drinking water and vault toilets are available. Supplies are available in Canby. Leashed pets are permitted.

Reservations, fees: No reservations; $6 per night. Open May through September.

Directions: From Redding, turn east on Highway 299 and drive to Adin. Continue east on Highway 299 for about seven miles to a signed campground turnoff on the right side of the road. Turn right and drive to the junction with Forest Road 40N05. Turn left and drive one mile to the campground on the right.

Contact: Modoc National Forest, Big Valley Ranger District, tel. (530) 299-3215 or fax (530) 299-8409.

10 Upper Rush Creek

    8

Upper Rush Creek is a pretty campground, set along Rush Creek, a quiet, wooded spot that gets little use. It sits in the shadow of nearby Manzanita Mountain (7,036 feet elevation) to the east, where there is a Forest Service lookout for a great view. To reach the lookout, drive back toward Highway 299 and when you reach the paved road, County Road 198, turn left and drive one-half mile to Forest Road 22. Turn left on Forest Road 22 and head up the hill. One mile from the summit, turn left at a four-way junction and drive to the top. You get dramatic views of the Warm Springs Valley to the north and the Likely Flats to the east, looking across miles and miles of open country.

Location: In Modoc National Forest; map B4, grid d0.

Campsites, facilities: There are 13 sites for tents or RVs up to 22 feet long, but Lower Rush Creek is better for trailers. Picnic tables and fire grills are provided. Drinking water and vault toilets are available. Supplies can be obtained in Adin or Canby. Leashed pets are permitted.

Reservations, fees: No reservations; $6 per night. Open May through September.

Directions: From Redding, turn east on Highway 299 and drive to Adin. Continue east on Highway 299 for about seven miles to a signed campground turnoff on the right side of the road. Turn right and drive to the junction with Forest Road 40N05. Turn left and drive 2.5 miles to the campground at the end of the road.

Contact: Modoc National Forest, Big Valley Ranger District, tel. (530) 299-3215 or fax (530) 299-8409.

Ash Creek

 7

This remote camp has stark beauty and is set at 4,800 feet along Ash Creek, a stream with small trout. This region of Modoc National Forest has an extensive network of backcountry roads, popular with deer hunters in the fall. Summer comes relatively late out here, and it can be cold and wet even in early June. Stash some extra clothes, just in case. That will probably guarantee nice weather.

Location: In Modoc National Forest; map B4, grid e0.

Campsites, facilities: There are seven sites for tents or RVs up to 22 feet long. Picnic tables and fire grills are provided. Vault toilets are available. No drinking water is available. Garbage must be packed out. Supplies can be obtained in Adin. Leashed pets are permitted.

Reservations, fees: No reservations; no fee. Open May through September.

Directions: From Redding, turn east on Highway 299 and drive to Adin. In Adin, turn right on Ash Valley Road/County Road 88/527 and drive eight miles. Turn left at the signed campground turnoff and drive a mile to the campground on the right side of the road.

Contact: Modoc National Forest, Big Valley Ranger District, tel. (530) 299-3215 or fax (530) 299-8409.

Soup Springs

 8

This is a beautiful, quiet, wooded campground at a trailhead into the South Warner Wilderness. Soup Creek originates at Soup Springs in the meadow adjacent to the campground. The trailhead here is routed two miles into the wilderness, where it junctions with the Mill Creek Trail. From here, turn left for a beautiful walk along Mill Creek and into Mill Creek Meadow, an easy yet pristine stroll that can provide a serene experience. The elevation is 6,800 feet.

Location: In Modoc National Forest; map B4, grid e6.

Campsites, facilities: There are six tent sites and eight sites for tents or RVs up to 22 feet long. Picnic tables and fire grills are provided. Drinking water and vault toilets are available. Corrals are also available. Supplies can be obtained in Likely. Leashed pets are permitted.

Reservations, fees: No reservations; $6 per night. Open June through September.

Directions: From Alturas, drive south on U.S. 395 for 17 miles to the town of Likely. Turn left on Jess Valley Road/County Road 64 and drive nine miles to the fork. Bear left on West Warner Road/Forest Road 5 and go 4.5 miles to Soup Loop Road. Turn right on Soup Loop Road/Forest Road 40N24 and continue on that gravel road for six miles to the campground entrance on the right.

Contact: Modoc National Forest, Warner Mountain Ranger District, tel. (530) 279-6116 or fax (530) 279-8309.

Mill Creek Falls

 9

This nice, wooded campground is a good base camp for a backpacking trip into the South Warner Wilderness. The camp is set on Mill Creek at 5,700 feet in elevation.

To see Mill Creek Falls, take the trail out of camp and bear left at the Y. To enter the interior of the South Warner Wilderness, bear right at the Y, after which the trail passes Clear Lake, heads on to Poison Flat and Poison Creek, and then reaches a junction. Left will take you to the Mill Creek Trail, right will take you up to the Summit Trail. Take your pick. You can't go wrong.

Location: In Modoc National Forest; map B4, grid e6.

Campsites, facilities: There are 11 sites for tents and eight sites for tents or RVs up to 22 feet long. Picnic tables and fire grills are provided. Drinking water and vault toilets are available. Supplies are available in Likely. Leashed pets are permitted.

Reservations, fees: No reservations; $6 per night. Open May through October.

Directions: From Alturas drive 17 miles south on U.S. 395 to the town of Likely. Turn left on Jess Valley Road/County Road 64 and drive nine miles to the fork. Bear left on West Warner Road/Forest Road 5 for 2.5 miles, turn right on Forest Road 40N46, and proceed two miles to the campground entrance at the end of the road.

Contact: Modoc National Forest, Warner Mountain Ranger District, tel. (530) 279-6116 or fax (530) 279-8309.

14 Emerson

 6

This tiny camp is virtually unknown, nestled at 6,000 feet on the eastern boundary of the South Warner Wilderness. Big alkali lakes and miles of the Nevada flats can be seen on the other side of the highway as you drive along the entrance road to the campground. This primitive setting is used by backpackers hitting the trail, a steep, sometimes wrenching climb for 4.5 miles to North Emerson Lake (poor to fair fishing). For many, this hike is a true butt-kicker.

Location: In Modoc National Forest; map B4, grid e8.

Campsites, facilities: There are four sites for tents or RVs up to 16 feet long. Picnic ta-

bles and fire grills are provided. Vault toilets are available. No drinking water is available. Garbage must be packed out. Supplies can be obtained in Eagleville. Leashed pets are permitted.

Reservations, fees: No reservations; no fee. Open July through September.

Directions: From Alturas, drive north on U.S. 395/Highway 299 for about five miles to the junction with Highway 299. Turn right on Highway 299 and drive to Cedarville. From Cedarville, drive 15 miles south on County Road 1 to Eagleville. From Eagleville, continue one mile south on County Road 1 to County Road 40. Turn right on County Road 40 and drive three miles to the campground at the end of the road. The access road is steep and very slick in wet weather. Trailers are not recommended.

Contact: Modoc National Forest, Warner Mountain Ranger District, tel. (530) 279-6116 or fax (530) 279-8309.

15 Patterson

 7

This quiet, wooded campground is set across the road from Patterson Meadow at 7,200 feet in elevation. It's an ideal jump-off spot for a backpacking trip into the South Warner Wilderness, with a trailhead at the camp providing access to the southern wilderness boundary. A great hike from here is the East Creek Loop, a 15-miler that can be completed in a weekend, providing an encapsulated look at the amazing contrasts of the Warners, from small pristine streams to high, barren mountain rims. The camp is rarely open before July.

Location: In Modoc National Forest; map B4, grid f7.

Campsites, facilities: There are five sites for tents or RVs up to 20 feet long. Picnic tables and fire grills are provided. Drinking water and vault toilets are available. Garbage must be packed out. Supplies are available in Likely or Eagleville. Leashed pets are permitted.

Reservations, fees: No reservations; no fee.

Open late June through September, weather permitting.

Directions: From Alturas drive 17 miles south on U.S. 395 to the town of Likely. Turn left on Jess Valley Road/County Road 64 and drive nine miles to the fork. Bear right on Forest Road 64 and drive for 16 miles to the campground on the left.

Contact: Modoc National Forest, Warner Mountain Ranger District, tel. (530) 279-6116 or fax (530) 279-8309.

16 Blue Lake

 6

This is a wooded campground with some level sites near the shore of Blue Lake. The lake, which covers 160 acres, provides fishing for brown trout and rainbow trout. A 5-mph speed limit assures quiet water for small boats and canoes. A trail circles the lake and takes less than an hour to hike. The elevation is 6,000 feet. A pair of nesting bald eagles lives here; over the last several years there have been three fledged chicks. While their presence negates year-round use of six campsites otherwise available, the trade-off is an unprecedented opportunity to view the national bird.

Location: In Modoc National Forest; map B4, grid f6.

Campsites, facilities: There are 48 sites for tents or RVs up to 25 feet long. Picnic tables and fire grills are provided. Drinking water and vault toilets are available. Some facilities are wheelchair accessible, including a paved boat launch and fishing pier. Supplies are available in Likely. Leashed pets are permitted.

Reservations, fees: No reservations; $7 per night. Open June through October.

Directions: From Alturas, drive south on U.S. 395 for seven miles to the town of Likely. In Likely, turn left on Jess Valley Road/County Road 64 and drive nine miles to the fork. At the fork, bear right on Forest Road 64 and drive seven miles to Forest Road 38N60. Turn right on Forest Road 38N60 and drive two miles to the campground.

Contact: Modoc National Forest, Warner Mountain Ranger District, tel. (530) 279-6116 or fax (530) 279-8309.

17 Willow Creek

 7

This remote camp and picnic area is set at 5,200 feet along little Willow Creek amid pine, aspen, and willows. On the north side of the campground is Lower McBride Springs. To the southwest is a state game refuge, with access available by vehicle, and several four-wheel-drive routes near its border.

Location: In Modoc National Forest; map B4, grid f0.

Campsites, facilities: There are eight sites for tents or RVs up to 22 feet long. Picnic tables and fire grills are provided. Drinking water and vault toilets are available. A wheelchair-accessible toilet is at the picnic area next to the campground. Leashed pets are permitted.

Reservations, fees: No reservations; $6 per night. Open May through October.

Directions: From Redding, drive east on Highway 299 to Adin. From Adin, turn right on Highway 139 and drive 14 miles to the campground on the left side of the road.

Contact: Modoc National Forest, Big Valley Ranger District, tel. (530) 299-3215 or fax (530) 299-8409.

18 Dodge Reservoir

 6

This camp is set at 5,735 feet near Dodge Reservoir, remote and little used. The lake covers 400 acres and is stocked with Eagle Lake trout. Those who know of this lake feel like they know a secret, since the limit is two at Eagle Lake itself, yet is five here. Small boats can launch from the shoreline here, and though it can be windy, mornings are usually calm, ideal for canoes. The surrounding hillsides are sprinkled with sage and juniper. This camp is also popular with hunters who get drawn in the annual DFG lottery for tags for this zone.

Location: Near Ravendale; map B4, grid h7.

Campsites, facilities: There are 12 primitive sites for tents or RVs. Picnic tables and fire pits are provided. A vault toilet is available. No drinking water is available. There is no boat ramp, but hand-launched boats are permitted. Leashed pets are permitted. Supplies can be obtained in Alturas, about eight miles away.

Reservations, fees: No reservations; no fee, donations accepted. Open year-round, weather permitting.

Directions: From Susanville, drive north on U.S. 395 for 54 miles to Ravendale. Turn right on County Road 502 (Mail Route) and drive 12 miles to County Road 506. Turn right and drive 5.5 miles to a T intersection. Turn left on County Road 506 and continue for six miles to Dodge Reservoir access road. Turn left and drive one mile to the campground at the end of the road.

Contact: Bureau of Land Management, Eagle Lake Field Office, tel. (530) 257-0456 or fax (530) 257-4831.

dent deer can be like pets here on late summer evenings, including bucks with spectacular racks.

Location: Near Susanville; map B4, grid j0.

Campsites, facilities: There are 30 tent sites and 69 RV sites, most with full or partial hookups. There is a separate area for tents only. Picnic tables and fire grills are provided. Restrooms, showers, coin laundry, sanitary disposal station, grocery store, propane gas, RV supplies, wood, recreation room, and a boat ramp are available. Some facilities are wheelchair accessible. Leashed pets are permitted.

Reservations, fees: Reservations are recommended; $15 to $20 per night. Major credit cards accepted. Open late May to late November, weather permitting.

Directions: From Red Bluff, drive east on Highway 36 toward Susanville. Just before reaching Susanville, turn left on County Road A1 and drive to County Road 518 near Spalding Tract. Turn right on County Road 518 and drive through a small neighborhood to the lake frontage road (look for The Strand). Turn right on Palmetto Way and drive eight blocks to the store at the RV park entrance at 687-125 Palmetto Way.

Contact: Eagle Lake RV Park, tel. (530) 825-3133; website: www.eaglelakeandrv.com.

19 Eagle Lake RV Park

 7

Eagle Lake RV Park has become something of a headquarters for anglers in pursuit of Eagle Lake trout, which typically range 18 to 22 inches. A nearby boat ramp provides access to Pelican Point and Eagle Point, where the fishing is often best in the summer. In the fall, the north end of the lake provides better prospects (see North Eagle Lake Campground). This RV park has all the amenities, including a small store. That means no special trips into town, just vacation time, lounging beside Eagle Lake, maybe catching a big trout now and then. One downer: the wind typically howls here most summer afternoons. Resi-

20 North Eagle Lake

 8

This camp provides direct access in the fall to the best fishing area of huge Eagle Lake. When the weather turns cold, the population of big Eagle Lake trout migrate to their favorite haunts just outside the tules, often in water only five to eight feet deep. From shore, try fishing with inflated nightcrawlers near the lake bottom, just outside the tules. A boat ramp is located about 1.5 miles to the southwest on Stone Road. From there, troll a Needlefish along the tules, or anchor or tie up and use a nightcrawler for bait under a slip bobber. In the summer this area is quite exposed and the lake can be hammered by west winds, which typically howl from midday to sunset. The elevation is 5,100 feet.

Location: On Eagle Lake; map B4, grid j0.

Campsites, facilities: There are 20 sites for tents or RVs. Picnic tables and fire grills are provided. Drinking water and vault toilets are available. A private sanitary disposal station and boat ramp are available within 1.5 miles. Leashed pets are permitted.

Reservations, fees: No reservations; $6 per night. Open Memorial Day through mid-November.

Directions: From Red Bluff, drive east on Highway 36 to Susanville. In Susanville, turn left (north) on Highway 139 and drive 29 miles to County Road A1. Turn left at County Road A1 and drive a half mile to the campground.

Contact: Bureau of Land Management, Eagle Lake Field Office, tel. (530) 257-0456 or fax (530) 257-4831.

21 Ramhorn Springs

 3

This remote, little-known spot is set in an area with good numbers of antelope. Though being drawn for tags is nearly impossible, the lucky few hunters can use this camp for their base. It is way out in Nowhere Land, near the flank of Shinn Peak (7,562 feet). This camp is also popular with hunters lucky enough to draw a deer tag for Zone X5B, one of the most elusive of all draws in the DFG deer tag lottery. It is also popular for upland game hunters in search of sage grouse.

Location: South of Ravendale; map B4, grid j4.

Campsites, facilities: There are 12 sites for tents or RVs up to 28 feet long. Picnic tables and fire grills are provided. Vault toilets and a horse corral are available. A small spring is available for water, but BLM advises treating it before use. Leashed pets are permitted.

Reservations, fees: No reservations; no fee, donations accepted. Open year-round, weather permitting.

Directions: From Red Bluff, drive east on Highway 36 to Susanville. In Susanville, turn north on U.S. 395 and drive 45 miles to Post Camp Road. Turn right on Post Camp Road and drive 2.5 miles east to the campground.

Contact: Bureau of Land Management, Eagle Lake Field Office, tel. (530) 257-0456 or fax (530) 257-4831.

RUSSIAN GULCH

MAP CO

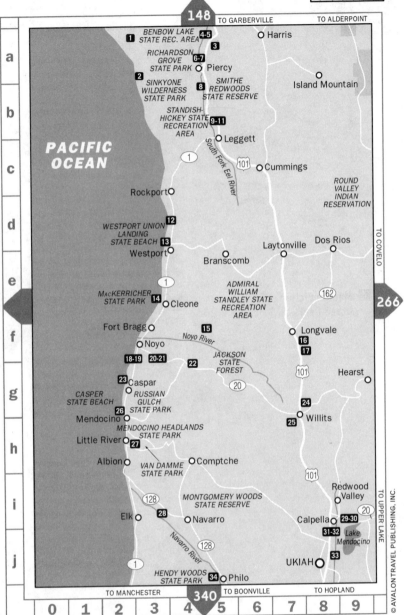

TO GARBERVILLE **TO ALDERPOINT**

148

PACIFIC OCEAN

1 BENBOW LAKE STATE REC. AREA **4-5**

Harris

3

RICHARDSON GROVE STATE PARK **6-7**

Piercy

2 SINKYONE WILDERNESS STATE PARK

SMITHE REDWOODS STATE RESERVE **8**

Island Mountain

STANDISH-HICKEY STATE RECREATION AREA **9-11**

Leggett

South Fork Eel River

101 Cummings

ROUND VALLEY INDIAN RESERVATION

Rockport

12 WESTPORT UNION LANDING STATE BEACH **13**

Westport

Branscomb

Laytonville   Dos Rios

TO COVELO

ADMIRAL WILLIAM STANDLEY STATE RECREATION AREA

162

266

MacKERRICHER STATE PARK **14**

Cleone

Fort Bragg

15

Noyo River

Longvale

16

17

Noyo

18-19 **20-21**

22

JACKSON STATE FOREST

20

Hearst

23 Caspar

CASPER STATE BEACH

RUSSIAN GULCH STATE PARK

101

24

26

Mendocino

MENDOCINO HEADLANDS STATE PARK

25 Willits

Little River **27**

Albion

VAN DAMME STATE PARK

Comptche

101

128

MONTGOMERY WOODS STATE RESERVE

Redwood Valley

TO UPPER LAKE

Elk

28 Navarro

Calpella **29-30**

20

31-32 Lake Mendocino

Navarro River

128

1

HENDY WOODS STATE PARK **34** Philo

UKIAH

33

TO MANCHESTER 340 **TO BOONVILLE** **TO HOPLAND**

© AVALON TRAVEL PUBLISHING, INC.

0   1   2   3   4   5   6   7   8   9

CHAPTER C0

Reservations, fees: No reservations; $8 p
night. Open year-round.
Directions: From U.S. 101 north of Ga
take the Redway exit, turn west
Cove Road, and drive 17 mile
Mountain Road. Turn left or
tain Road and drive o
Campground on the
Campground from
to the camp on
Contact: Bu
ta Field O
825-23

1 Nadelos & Wailaki

      7

Nadelos and Wailaki campgrounds are set a short distance apart at 1,840 feet near the South Fork Bear Creek at the southern end of the King Range National Conservation Area. This provides access to a rare geographic dynamic, where mountains and coast adjoin. Nearby Chemise Mountain, elevation 2,598 feet, is one of the highest points in California within two miles of the sea, and provides a dramatic lookout on clear days.

Location: In the King Range; map C0, grid a2.

Campsites, facilities: There are eight single tent sites at Nadelos. There are 13 sites for tents and RVs at Wailaki. Picnic tables and fire grills are provided. Drinking water and vault toilets are available. Some facilities are wheelchair accessible. Leashed pets are permitted.

...er

...rberville,
...on Shelter
...s to Chemise
...Chemise Moun-
...e mile to Nadelos
...right. To reach Wailaki
...Nadelos, continue 0.4 miles
...the right.
...eau of Land Management, Arca-
...ffice, tel. (707) 825-2300 or fax (707)
...1; website: www.ca.blm.gov/arcata.

Sinkyone Wilderness

     10

This is a great jump-off point for a backpacking trip in the Sinkyone Wilderness on the Lost Coast, one of the few wilderness areas where a trip can be made any month of the year. The terrain is primitive, steep, and often wet, but provides a rare coastal wilderness experience. Starting at the northern trailhead at Orchard Camp, or the southern trailhead at the Usal Beach campground, it's an ambitious weekend tromp of 17 miles.

Location: In Sinkyone Wilderness State Park; map C0, grid a3.

Campsites, facilities: At Usal Beach, there are 16 tent sites. Picnic tables and fire rings are provided. Pit toilets are provided. No drinking water is available. Between Bear Harbor and Jones Beach there are 25 primitive tent sites, some of which have tables, fire rings, and pit toilets. Drinking water is available at the Needle Rock Visitor Center (see directions below). Leashed pets are permitted at campsites only.

Reservations, fees: No reservations; $7 per night. Open year-round, weather permitting.

Directions: To reach the northern boundary of the Sinkyone Wilderness from U.S. 101 north of Garberville, take the Redway exit, turn west on Briceland Road, and drive 17 miles to Whitethorn. From Whitethorn continue six more miles to the four corners fork. Drive straight ahead to the middle left fork and continue six miles on a gravel road to the Needle Rock Ranger Station.

To reach the southern boundary of the Sinkyone Wilderness from Leggett on U.S. 101 turn southwest on Highway 1 (toward Fort Bragg) and drive 14.66 miles to milepost 90.88 at County Road 431. Turn right on County Road 431 (a dirt road, often unsigned) and drive six miles to the Usal Beach Campground. Note: The roads can be quite rough. Trailers and RVs are not recommended.

Contact: Sinkyone Wilderness State Park, tel. (707) 986-7711, tel. (707) 247-3318, or fax (707) 247-3300.

Madrone & Huckleberry

      8

The highway cuts a swath right through Richardson Grove State Park, and everyone slows to gawk at the tallest trees in the world, one of the most impressive groves of redwoods you can drive through in California. To explore further, there are several campgrounds available at the park, as well as a network of outstanding hiking trails. The best of these are the short Redwood Exhibit Trail, Settlers Loop, and Toumey Trail. The park is one of the prettiest and most popular state parks, making reservations a necessity from Memorial Day through Labor Day weekend.

Location: In Richardson Grove State Park; map C0, grid a5.

Campsites, facilities: At Madrone Camp, there are 40 sites for tents or RVs up to 30 feet long. At Huckleberry, there are 36 sites for tents or RVs up to 30 feet long. Picnic tables, food lockers, and fire grills are provided. Drinking water, flush toilets, and coin-operated showers are available. A mini-mart and sanitary disposal station (five miles away) are available nearby. Some facilities are wheelchair accessible. Leashed pets are permitted at campsites only.

Reservations, fees: Reserve at (800) 444-PARK (800-444-7275) or website: www.ReserveAmerica.com; $12 per night. Open year-round, but subject to occasional winter closures.

Directions: From the junction of U.S. 101 and Highway 1 in Leggett, drive north on U.S. 101 for 20 miles (past Piercy) to the park entrance along the west side of the road (note: Garberville is nine miles north on U.S. 101).

Contact: Richardson Grove State Park, tel. (707) 247-3318.

4 Benbow Lake State Recreation Area

 7

This camp is set along the South Fork of the Eel River, with easy access from U.S. 101. It gets heavy use in the summer. The river is dammed each summer, which temporarily creates Benbow Lake, an ideal spot for swimming and light boating. In the winter, this stretch of river can be quite good for steelhead fishing.

Location: On the Eel River; map C0, grid a5.

Campsites, facilities: There are 77 sites for tents or RVs up to 30 feet long; two sites have full hookups. Picnic tables, food lockers, and fire grills are provided. Drinking water, flush toilets, and coin-operated showers are available. A boat ramp (no motors) and boat rentals are available nearby. There is a sanitary disposal station at the park entrance. Supplies and a coin laundry are available in Garberville. Leashed pets are permitted at campsites only.

Reservations, fees: Reserve at (800) 444-PARK (800-444-7275) or website: www.ReserveAmerica.com; $12 to $17 per night. Open April through October, weather permitting.

Directions: From the junction of U.S. 101 and Highway 1 in Leggett, drive north on U.S. 101 past Richardson Grove State Park to the Benbow exit (two miles south of Garberville). Take that exit and drive a short distance to the park entrance.

Contact: Benbow Lake State Recreation Area, tel. (707) 923-3238.

5 Benbow Valley Resort

 7

This is an RV park set along U.S. 101 and the South Fork Eel River, with both a small golf course and little Benbow Lake providing nearby recreation. It takes on a dramatically different character in the winter, when the highway is largely abandoned, the river comes up, and steelhead migrate upstream to the stretch of water here. Cooks Valley and Benbow provide good shore fishing access. Note that fishing restrictions for steelhead are extremely severe and subject to constant change; always check with DFG before fishing for steelhead.

Location: On the Eel River; map C0, grid a5.

Campsites, facilities: There are 112 RV sites (60 drive-through) with full hookups, including nine "VIP" sites. Picnic tables are provided. Cable TV, restrooms, showers, coin laundry, grocery store, restaurant, playground, recreation room, heated swimming pool, whirlpool, RV supplies, and a nine-hole golf course are available. A boat dock and boat rentals (in summer) are available within 100 feet at Benbow Lake. Leashed pets are permitted. A doggy playground is available.

Reservations, fees: Reservations are accepted; $26 to $43 per night, $2.50 per person per night for more than two people, $2 pet fee. Major credit cards accepted. Open year-round.

Directions: From the junction of U.S. 101 and Highway 1 in Leggett, drive north on U.S. 101 past Richardson Grove State Park to the Benbow exit (two miles south of Garberville). Turn north on Benbow Drive and travel a short distance to the campground.

Contact: Benbow Valley Resort, tel. (707) 923-2777 or fax (707) 923-2821; website: www.benbowrv.com.

6 Richardson Grove Campground & RV Park

 7

This private camp provides a nearby alternative to Richardson Grove State Park, complete with cabin rentals. The state park, with its grove of giant redwoods and excellent hiking, is the primary attraction. The park is family oriented, with volleyball and basketball courts and horseshoe pits. The adjacent South Fork Eel River may look like a trickle in the summer, but there are some good swimming holes available. It also provides good steelhead fishing in January and February, especially good shore fishing access here as well as to the south in Cooks Valley (check DFG regulations before fishing).

Location: On the Eel River; map C0, grid a4.

Campsites, facilities: There are 91 sites for tents or RVs (28 drive-through), many with full or partial hookups, and six cabins. Picnic tables and fire rings are provided. Restrooms, showers, sanitary disposal station, playground, coin laundry, grocery store, LP gas, and ice are available. Leashed pets are permitted.

Reservations, fees: Reservations are recommended; $13.50 to $18 per night for individual sites, $27 per night for cabin rentals. Group rates available. Major credit cards accepted. Open year-round.

Directions: From the junction of U.S. 101 and Highway 1 in Leggett, drive north on U.S. 101 one mile past Richardson Grove State Park to the camp entrance on the west side (left) of the road.

Contact: Richardson Grove Campground, tel. (707) 247-3380, fax (707) 247-9806; website: www.heavenlywebs.com/redwoodcamp.

7 Oak Flat

 8

Oak Flat is on the eastern side of the Eel River in the shade of forest and provides easy access to the river. The campground is open only in the summer. For side trip information, see the entries for Madrone and Huckleberry.

Location: In Richardson Grove State Park; map C0, grid a4.

Campsites, facilities: There are 100 sites for tents or RVs up to 30 feet long and trailers up to 24 feet long. Picnic tables, food lockers, and fire grills are provided. Drinking water, flush toilets, and coin-operated showers are available. A grocery store and propane gas are available nearby. Leashed pets are permitted.

Reservations, fees: Reserve at (800) 444-PARK (800-444-7275) or website: www.ReserveAmerica.com; $12 per night. Open mid-June to mid-September.

Directions: From the junction of U.S. 101 and Highway 1 in Leggett, drive north on U.S. 101 for 20 miles (past Piercy) to the park entrance on the west side of the road (nine miles south of Garberville).

Contact: Richardson Grove State Park, tel. (707) 247-3318.

8 Redwood Campground

 8

This is one of three camps in Standish-Hickey State Recreation Area, and it is by far the most unusual. To reach Redwood Campground requires driving over a temporary "summer bridge," which provides access to a pretty spot along the South Fork Eel River. In early September, out comes the bridge and up comes the river. The elevation is 800 feet.

Location: On the Eel River in Standish-Hickey State Recreation Area; map C0, grid b4.

Campsites, facilities: There are 63 sites for tents or RVs up to 18 feet long. No trailers, including pop-up tent trailers, are permitted. Picnic tables and fire rings are provided. Drinking water, coin-operated showers, and flush toilets are available. Some facilities are wheelchair accessible. Leashed pets are permitted.

Reservations, fees: Reserve at (800) 444-PARK (800-444-7275) or website: www.ReserveAmerica.com; $12 per night. Open

Memorial Day weekend through Labor Day weekend.

Directions: From the junction of U.S. 101 and Highway 1 in Leggett, drive north on U.S. 101 for one mile to the park entrance.

Contact: Standish-Hickey State Recreation Area, tel. (707) 925-6482, or fax (707) 925-6402.

9 Rock Creek

 8

This is one of two main campgrounds set in a redwood grove at Standish-Hickey State Recreation Area (the other is Hickey). It is the classic state park camp, with numbered sites, flat tent spaces, picnic tables, and food lockers. Hiking is only fair in this park, but most people enjoy the short tromp down to the nearby South Fork Eel River. In the winter, steelhead migrate through the area.

Location: On the Eel River in Standish-Hickey State Recreation Area; map C0, grid b5.

Campsites, facilities: There are 36 sites for tents or RVs up to 27 feet long and trailers to 24 feet long. There is one hike-in/bike-in site that accommodates up to eight people. Picnic tables and fire rings are provided. Piped water, coin-operated showers, and flush toilets are available. Some facilities are wheelchair accessible. Leashed pets are permitted.

Reservations, fees: Reserve at (800) 444-PARK (800-444-7275) or website: www.ReserveAmerica.com; $12 per night. Hike-in, bike-in site is $1 per person per night.

Directions: From the junction of U.S. 101 and Highway 1 in Leggett, drive north on U.S. 101 for one mile to the park entrance on the west side of the road.

Contact: Standish-Hickey State Recreation Area, tel. (707) 925-6482 or fax (707) 925-6402.

10 Hickey

 8

This is an ideal layover for U.S. 101 cruisers yearning to spend a night in the redwoods. The park is best known for its campsites set amid redwoods and for the nearby South Fork Eel River with its steelhead fishing in the winter. The elevation is 800 feet.

Location: On the Eel River in Standish-Hickey State Recreation Area; map C0, grid b5.

Campsites, facilities: There are 65 sites for tents or RVs up to 27 feet long and trailers to 24 feet long. Picnic tables and fire rings are provided. Drinking water, coin-operated showers, and flush toilets are available. A grocery store is available nearby. Some facilities are wheelchair accessible. Leashed pets are permitted.

Reservations, fees: Reserve at (800) 444-PARK (800-444-7275) or website: www.ReserveAmerica.com; $12 per night.

Directions: From the junction of U.S. 101 and Highway 1 in Leggett, drive north on U.S. 101 for one mile to the park entrance on the left.

Contact: Standish-Hickey State Recreation Area, tel. (707) 925-6482 or fax (707) 925-6402.

11 Redwoods River Resort

 8

This resort is situated in a 20-acre grove of redwoods on U.S. 101. Many of the campsites are shaded. It is one in a series of both public and private campgrounds along the highway between Leggett and Garberville. Steelhead and salmon fishing are popular here in the winter, and the resort provides nearby access to state parks. The elevation is 700 feet.

Location: On the Eel River; map C0, grid b5.

Campsites, facilities: There are 14 tent sites and 27 RV sites (nine drive-through) with full hookups, eight cabins, and eight lodge rooms. Cabins and lodge rooms have fully furnished kitchenettes and private bathrooms. Lodge rooms have decks with barbecues and picnic tables. Cabins have wood-burning stoves. At campsites, picnic tables and fire rings are provided. Restrooms, hot showers, heated pool, playground, recreation room, mini-mart, coin laundry, group kitchen, sanitary disposal station, and an evening campfire are available. Some facilities are wheelchair accessible. Leashed pets are permitted.

Reservations, fees: Reservations are recommended in the summer; campsites are $17 to $26 per night, cabin rentals are $63 to $76 per night, and lodge rooms are $57 to $63 per night. Major credit cards accepted. Open year-round.

Directions: From the junction of U.S. 101 and Highway 1 in Leggett, drive north on U.S. 101 for seven miles to the campground entrance.

Contact: Redwoods River Resort, tel. (707) 925-6249 or fax (707) 925-6413; website: www.campgrounds.com/redwoodriver.

12 Westport Union Landing State Beach

 8

The northern Mendocino coast is remote, beautiful, and gets far less people pressure than the Fort Bragg area. That is the key to its appeal. The campsites are on an ocean bluff. It can get windy here, but the reward is the view.

Location: Overlooking the Pacific Ocean; map C0, grid d3.

Campsites, facilities: There are 130 primitive sites for tents or RVs up to 35 feet long. Picnic tables and fire rings are provided. Drinking water and vault toilets are available. A grocery store is nearby. Leashed pets are permitted.

Reservations, fees: No reservations; $12 per night. Open year-round.

Directions: From Fort Bragg, drive north on Highway 1 to Westport. In Westport, continue north on Highway 1 for three miles to the campground entrance.

Contact: Westport Union Landing State Beach, tel. (707) 937-5804, or fax (707) 937-2953.

13 Wages Creek Beach Campground

 8

Wages Creek Beach Campground is set above the beach near the mouth of Wages Creek, with creek-side sites available, some offering glimpses of the ocean. You will notice as you venture north from Fort Bragg that the number of vacationers in the area falls way off, providing a chance for quiet beaches and serene moments. The best nearby hiking is to the north out of the trailhead for the Sinkyone Wilderness.

Location: Overlooking the Pacific Ocean; map C0, grid d3.

Campsites, facilities: There are 129 sites for tents or RVs and 46 sites for tents only. Picnic tables and fire rings are provided. Drinking water, coin-operated showers, flush toilets, a sanitary disposal station, wood, and ice are available. Some facilities are wheelchair accessible. Leashed pets are permitted.

Reservations, fees: Reservations are accepted; $18 per vehicle per night. Open March through November.

Directions: From Fort Bragg, drive north on Highway 1 to Westport. In Westport, continue north on Highway 1 for a half mile to the campground entrance.

Contact: Wages Creek Beach Campground, tel. (707) 964-2964 or fax (707) 964-8185.

14 MacKerricher State Park

 9

MacKerricher is a beautiful park on the Mendocino coast, a great destination for adventure and exploration. The camps are set in a coastal forest, with gorgeous walk-in sites. Nearby is a small beach, great tidepools, a rocky point where harbor seals hang out in the sun, a small lake (Cleone) with trout fishing, a great bike trail, and outstanding short hikes. The short jaunt around little Cleone Lake has many romantic spots, often tunneling through vegetation, then emerging for lake views. The coastal walk to the point to see seals and tidepools is equally captivating, and if you can't get a kiss here, you're in trouble. For wheelchair users, there is a wheelchair-accessible trail to Laguna Point and also a route on a raised boardwalk that runs halfway around Cleone Lake.

Location: Overlooking the Pacific Ocean; map C0, grid e3.

Campsites, facilities: There are 142 sites for tents or RVs up to 35 feet long and 10 walk-in sites. Picnic tables, fire rings, and food lockers are provided. Drinking water, flush toilets, coin-operated showers, and a sanitary disposal station are available. Some facilities are wheelchair accessible. Leashed pets are permitted.

Reservations, fees: Reserve at (800) 444-PARK (800-444-7275) or website: www.ReserveAmerica.com; $12 per night. Open year-round.

Directions: From Fort Bragg, drive north on Highway 1 for three miles to the campground entrance on the left side of the road.

Contact: MacKerricher State Park, tel. (707) 964-9112 or (707) 937-5804, fax (707) 937-2953.

15 Jackson Demonstration State Forest, Camp 1

 6

Primitive campsites set in a vast forest of redwoods and Douglas fir are the prime attraction at Jackson Demonstration State Forest. Even though Highway 20 is a major connecting link to the coast in the summer, these camps get bypassed because they are primitive and largely unknown. Why? Because reaching them requires driving on dirt roads sometimes frequented by logging trucks, and there are no campground signs along the highway. This camp features lots of tree cover, with oaks, redwoods, and madrones. Some of the campsites are along the Noyo River, well-known among locals, but completely missed by most others. A one-mile trail circles the campground. A DFG hatchery is next to the campground, but note that no fishing is permitted in the river.

Location: Near Fort Bragg; map C0, grid f5.

Campsites, facilities: There are 50 primitive sites for tents or RVs up to 27 feet long, and one group site for up to 50 people with a minimum of 20. Picnic tables and fire pits are pro-

vided. Pit toilets are available. No drinking water is available. Leashed pets are permitted.

Reservations, fees: Reservations for group site only. For other sites, no reservations; no fee. A camping permit is required and a campground map is needed. Both can be obtained from the State Department of Forestry office at 802 North Main Street (Highway 1) in Fort Bragg, or with a reservation from the campground host in Jackson Demonstration State Forest. Open year-round, but subject to closures, especially in winter due to muddy roads. Call ahead for status.

Directions: From Willits on U.S. 101, turn west on Highway 20 and drive 27 miles to Forest Road 350 (near the 6 mile marker). Turn right and drive 1.3 miles (bear right at the forks on the road) to the campground.

Contact: Jackson Demonstration State Forest, tel. (707) 964-5674 or fax (707) 964-0941.

16 Sleepyhollow RV Park

 5

This year-round, privately operated park provides easy access off the highway. A nearby recreation option is the Skunk Train in Willits.

Location: North of Willits; map C0, grid f7.

Campsites, facilities: There are six sites for tents and 24 RV sites (six drive-through) with full or partial hookups. Picnic tables are provided. Restrooms, showers, a pond, recreation room, and a sanitary disposal station are available. Leashed pets are permitted.

Reservations, fees: Reservations are accepted; $11 to $15 per night.

Directions: From Willits on U.S. 101, drive north for eight miles to the 55.5 mile marker (two-tenths of a mile beyond the Shimmins Ridge Road sign). At the beginning of the divided four-lane highway, turn right at the signed campground access road and drive to the entrance.

Contact: Sleepyhollow RV Park, tel. (707) 459-0613.

17 Hidden Valley Campground

 5

The privately operated park is in a pretty valley, primarily oak/bay woodlands with a sprinkling of conifers. The most popular nearby recreation option is taking the Skunk Train in Willits for the ride out to the coast at Fort Bragg.

Location: North of Willits; map C0, grid f7.

Campsites, facilities: There are 50 sites for tents or RVs up to 30 feet plus towing rig. Picnic tables and fire grills are provided. Some RV sites provide modem access and full or partial hookups. Restrooms, ice, horseshoes, basketball, a coin laundry, sanitary disposal station, and showers are available. Some facilities are wheelchair accessible. Leashed pets are permitted.

Reservations, fees: Reservations are accepted; $15 to $17 per night for two campers, $2 each additional camper over four years of age; $5 per additional vehicle. Major credit cards accepted. Open year-round.

Directions: From Willits on U.S. 101, drive north for 6.5 miles on U.S. 101 to the campground on the east side (right) of the road.

Contact: Hidden Valley Campground, tel. (707) 459-2521 or fax (707) 459-3396; website: www.campgrounds.com/hiddenvalley.

18 Woodside RV Park and Campground

 7

This privately operated park is set up primarily for RVs. It covers nine acres, is somewhat wooded, and provides access to nearby Fort Bragg and the ocean.

Location: In Fort Bragg; map C0, grid f2.

Campsites, facilities: There are 18 sites for tents only and 86 sites for tents or RVs to 40 feet long with full or partial hookups. Group sites are available. Picnic tables and fire rings are provided. Restrooms, showers, recreation room, sauna, sanitary disposal station, cable TV, modem hookups, RV supplies, ice, wood, and a fish-cleaning table are available. Boat-ing and fishing access are available within one mile. Leashed pets are permitted.

Reservations, fees: Reservations are accepted; $16 to $22 per night, $9 per second vehicle, unless towed; $1 to $3 per person per night for more than two people, $1 for pets. Major credit cards accepted.

Directions: In Fort Bragg at the junction of Highway 1 and Highway 20, drive south on Highway 1 for one mile to the campground.

Contact: Woodside RV Park and Campground, tel. (707) 964-3684 or fax (707) 964-3684; website: www.infortbrag.com/woodsiderv.

19 Dolphin Isle Marina

 7

Noyo Harbor is the headquarters of Fort Bragg—the place where everything begins in this area. For vacationers that includes wharf-side restaurants, fishing trips, boat docks, and a chance for a nice stroll out to the Noyo Harbor jetty. This RV park is right at the marina, providing an ideal jump-off point for all of those adventures. Beach access is available one mile away.

Location: On the Noyo River in Fort Bragg; map C0, grid f2.

Campsites, facilities: There are 83 RV sites with full or partial hookups. Picnic tables are provided. Restrooms, hot showers (coin-operated), a sanitary disposal station, a coin laundry, modem hookups, delicatessen, propane gas, boat ramp, and a dock are available. Some facilities are wheelchair accessible. Leashed pets are permitted.

Reservations, fees: Reservations are accepted; $13 to $22 per night, $1 per person for more than two people, $6 for a second vehicle, $1 pet fee. Major credit cards accepted.

Directions: In Fort Bragg at the junction of Highway 1 and Highway 20, drive east on Highway 20 for a quarter mile to South Harbor Drive. Turn left on South Harbor Drive and drive a quarter mile to Basin Street. Turn right on Basin Street and drive one mile to the campground.

Contact: Dolphin Isle Marina, tel. (707) 964-4113, or fax (707) 964-7136.

20 Fort Bragg Leisure Time RV Park

     5

This privately operated park offers horseshoes and badminton, and a covered group picnic area. The drive from Willits to Fort Bragg on Highway 20 is always a favorite, a curving two-laner through redwoods, not too slow, not too fast, best seen from the saddle of a Harley-Davidson. At the end of it is the coast, and just three miles inland is this campground in the sunbelt, said to be out of the fog by breakfast. Within short drives are Noyo Harbor in Fort Bragg, Russian Gulch State Park, Mendocino to the south, and MacKerricher State Park to the north. In fact, there's so much in the area, you could explore for days.

Location: In Fort Bragg; map C0, grid f3.

Campsites, facilities: There are 82 sites for tents or RVs up to 40 feet long, many with full or partial hookups. Picnic tables and fire rings are provided. Restrooms, cable TV, hot showers (coin-operated), sanitary disposal station, and a coin laundry are available. Some facilities are wheelchair accessible. Leashed pets are permitted.

Reservations, fees: Reservations are accepted; $16.50 to $22.50 per night. Major credit cards accepted. Open year-round.

Directions: In Fort Bragg at the junction of Highway 1 and Highway 20, turn east on Highway 20 and drive 2.5 miles to the campground entrance on the right side of the road.

Contact: Fort Bragg Leisure Time RV Park, tel. (707) 964-5994.

21 Pomo Campground and RV Park

      7

This park covers 17 acres of lush, native vegetation near the ocean, one of several camps on the Fort Bragg and Mendocino coast. Nearby Noyo Harbor offers busy restaurants, deep-sea fishing, a boat ramp, harbor, and a nice walk out to the Noyo Harbor jetty. Huckleberry picking is also an option.

Location: In Fort Bragg; map C0, grid f3.

Campsites, facilities: There are 30 sites for tents and 94 RV sites (many quite wide) with full or partial hookups. Picnic tables and fire rings are provided. Restrooms, hot showers (coin-operated), cable TV hookups, store, wood, ice, RV supplies, modem hookups, propane gas, coin laundry, sanitary disposal station, fish-cleaning table, horseshoe pits, and large grass playing field are available. Leashed pets are permitted.

Reservations, fees: Reservations are recommended in the summer; $20 to $25 per night. Open year-round.

Directions: In Fort Bragg at the junction of Highway 1 and Highway 20, drive south on Highway 1 for one mile to Tregoning Lane. Turn left (east) and drive a short distance to the park at 17999 Tregoning Lane.

Contact: Pomo Campground and RV Park, tel. (707) 964-3373 or fax (707) 964-0619; website: www.infortbrag.com/pomorvpark.

22 Jackson Demonstration State Forest, Camp 2

    6

A highlight of Jackson Demonstration Forest is a 50-foot waterfall on Chamberlain Creek. Set in a steep canyon amid giant firs and redwoods, it can be reached with a 10-minute walk. There are also extensive logging roads that are good yet challenging for mountain biking. What to do first? Get a map from the State Forestry Department. For driving, the roads are extremely dusty in summer and muddy in winter.

Location: Near Fort Bragg; map C0, grid g4.

Campsites, facilities: There are 18 primitive sites for tents or RVs up to 27 feet long, and six equestrian sites across the road. Picnic tables and fire rings are provided. Pit toilets are available. No drinking water is available. Leashed pets are permitted.

Reservations, fees: Reservations for equestrian sites only. For other sites, no reservations; no fee. A camping permit is required and a campground map is needed. Both can be obtained from the State Department of Forestry office at 802 North Main Street (Highway 1) in Fort Bragg, or with a reservation from the campground host in Jackson Demonstration State Forest. Open year-round, but subject to closures, especially in winter due to muddy roads. Call ahead for status.

Directions: From Willits on U.S. 101, turn west on Highway 20 and drive 17 miles. At the 16.9 mile marker (just past the Chamberlain Bridge) at Road 200 turn left on Road 200 (the entrance for Jackson State Forest) and Camp 2/Dunlap. Obtain a camping permit and a map from the camp host on the premises at Camp 2.

Contact: Jackson Demonstration State Forest, tel. (707) 964-5674 or fax (707) 964-0941.

23 Caspar Beach RV Park

      8

This privately operated park has ocean frontage and opportunities for beachcombing, fishing, abalone and scuba diving, and good lookouts for whale watching. The park is somewhat wooded, with a small, year-round creek running behind it. The nearby village of Mendocino is an interesting side trip.

Location: Near Mendocino; map C0, grid g2.

Campsites, facilities: There are 23 sites for tents only and 59 RV sites with full or partial hookups. Picnic tables, barbecues and fire pits are provided. Cable TV hookups, modem hookups, flush and pit toilets, showers (coin-operated), and a sanitary disposal station are available. A store, wood, playground, video arcade, convenience store, and a coin laundry are available nearby. Some facilities are wheelchair accessible. Leashed pets are permitted.

Reservations, fees: Reservations are accepted; $20 to $28 per night, $2 pet fee. Major credit cards accepted. Open year-round.

Directions: From Mendocino on Highway 1, drive north for 3.5 miles to the Point Cabrillo exit. Turn west on Point Cabrillo Drive and continue three-quarters of a mile to the campground on the left.

From Fort Bragg on Highway 1, drive south for 4.5 miles. Turn right on Point Cabrillo Drive and continue three-quarters of a mile to the campground.

Contact: Caspar Beach RV Park, tel. (707) 964-3306 or fax (707) 964-0526; website: www.gocampingamerica.com/casparbeach.

24 Quail Meadows RV Park & Camp

    3

This is one of several RV parks in the Willits area. Nearby is Lake Emily, set near the Brook Trails development, which is stocked in the spring and early summer with trout by the Department of Fish and Game. It's like a backyard fishing hole for the folks around here. Another recreation option is the Skunk Train, which runs from Willits to Fort Bragg.

Location: In Willits; map C0, grid g7.

Campsites, facilities: There are 49 RV sites, most with full or partial hookups. There is a separate section for tents only. Picnic tables and fire grills are provided. Patios, restrooms, showers, a sanitary disposal station, coin laundry, propane gas, ice, and TV hookups are available. Leashed pets are permitted.

Reservations, fees: Reservations are accepted; $16 to $22 per night. Open year-round.

Directions: In Willits at the junction of U.S. 101 and Highway 20, drive north on U.S. 101 for one mile to the campground.

Contact: Quail Meadows Campground, tel. (707) 459-6006.

25 Willits KOA

       3

This is an ideal spot to park your RV if you plan on taking the Skunk Train west to Fort Bragg. A depot for the train is within walking distance of the campground. The campground also offers nightly entertainment. The elevation is 1,377 feet.

Location: Near Willits; map C0, grid h7.

Campsites, facilities: There are 21 sites for tents and 50 RV sites (27 drive-through) with full or partial hookups. Group sites and 12 cabins are available. Picnic tables are provided. Drinking water, flush toilets, modem hookups, showers, a playground, swimming pool, hay rides, miniature golf, basketball, volleyball, fishing pond, grocery store, RV supplies, coin laundry, and a sanitary disposal station are available. Leashed pets are permitted.

Reservations, fees: Reservations are accepted; $25 to $29 per night, $3 per person per night for more than two people. Major credit cards accepted. Open year-round.

Directions: From Willits at the junction of U.S. 101 and Highway 20, turn west on Highway 20 and drive 1.5 miles to the campground.

Contact: Willits KOA, tel. (707) 459-6179 or fax (707) 459-1489; website: www.willitskoa@pacific.net

Russian Gulch State Park

 9

Russian Gulch State Park is set near some of California's most beautiful coastline, but the camp speaks to the woods, not the water, with the campsites set in a wooded canyon. They include some of the prettiest and most secluded drive-in sites available on the Mendocino coast. There is a great hike here, an easy hour-long walk to Russian Gulch Falls, a wispy 35-foot waterfall that falls into a rock basin. While it's always pretty, it's awesome in late winter. Much of the route is accessible by bicycle, with a rack available where the trail narrows and turns to dirt.

Location: Near the Pacific Ocean; map C0, grid g2.

Campsites, facilities: There are 30 sites and one group site for tents or RVs up to 27 feet long. One hike-in/bike-in site is also available.

Picnic tables, fire grills, and food lockers are provided. Drinking water, showers, and flush toilets are available. A day-use picnic area, beach access, and recreation hall are available nearby. Some facilities are wheelchair accessible. Leashed pets are permitted.

Reservations, fees: Reserve at (800) 444-PARK (800-444-7275) or website: www.ReserveAmerica.com; $12 per night for campsites; $30 for the group site (up to 40 people); $1 per night for hike-in, bike-in site. Open mid-March to mid-October.

Directions: From Mendocino, drive two miles north on Highway 1 to the campground.

Contact: Russian Gulch State Park, tel. (707) 937-4296, tel. (707) 937-5804, or fax (707) 937-2953.

Van Damme State Park

 10

The campsites at Van Damme are extremely popular, usually requiring reservations, but with a bit of planning your reward is a base of operations in a beautiful park with redwoods and a remarkable fern understory. The hike-in sites on the Fern Canyon Trail are perfectly situated for those wishing to take one of the most popular hikes in the Mendocino area, with the trail crossing the Little River several times and weaving among old trees. Just across from the entrance of the park is a small but beautiful coastal bay with a pretty beach, ideal for launching sea kayaks.

Location: Near Mendocino; map C0, grid h2.

Campsites, facilities: There are 74 sites for tents or RVs up to 35 feet long, 10 primitive hike-in sites, and one group campsite. Picnic tables and fire grills are provided. Drinking water, flush toilets, sanitary disposal station, and showers are available. A grocery store, coin laundry, and propane gas are available nearby. Leashed pets are permitted.

Reservations, fees: Reserve at (800) 444-PARK (800-444-7275) or website: www.ReserveAmerica.com; $12 per night,

$37 per night for group site, $1 per night per person for hike-in sites. Open year-round.

Directions: From Mendocino on Highway 1, drive south for three miles to the town of Little River and the park entrance road on the left side of the road.

Contact: Van Damme State Park, tel. (707) 937-5804 or fax (707) 937-2953.

28 Paul M. Dimmick Wayside State Campground

     7

A pretty grove of redwood trees and the nearby Navarro River are the highlights of this campground. It's a nice spot but, alas, lacks any significant hiking trails that could make it an overall spectacular destination; all the trailheads along Highway 128 turn out to be just little spur routes from the road to the river.

Location: On the Navarro River in Navarro River Redwoods State Park; map C0, grid i3.

Campsites, facilities: There are 28 sites for tents or RVs up to 30 feet long. Picnic tables and fire grills are provided. Drinking water (summer only) and vault toilets are available. Leashed pets are permitted.

Reservations, fees: No reservations; $10 per night. Open March through October.

Directions: From Cloverdale on U.S. 101, drive north for two miles to Highway 128. Turn west on Highway 128 and drive 49 miles. Look for the signed campground entrance on the left side of the road.

Contact: Paul M. Dimmick Wayside Campground, tel. (707) 895-3141, tel. (707)987-5804, or fax (707) 937-2953.

29 Miti Boat-In/Hike-In

    7

One of several campgrounds on the north end of Lake Mendocino, this one has the added advantage of a boat launch facility. The north ramp (Marina Drive off Highway 20) is open 24 hours; the south ramp closes at night.

Location: On Lake Mendocino; map C0, i9.

Campsites, facilities: There are 15 sites for tents only. Picnic tables, fire rings, and lantern holders are provided. Vault toilets are available. No drinking water is available. Garbage must be packed out. Leashed pets are permitted.

Reservations, fees: No reservations; $5 per night, one-time $2 boat launch fee. Open April through September, weather permitting. (Some sites may be flooded in the spring.)

Directions: From Ukiah, drive north on U.S. 101 to the Highway 20 turnoff. For boat-in campers: Drive east on Highway 20 to Marina Drive. Turn right and drive to the north boat ramp of the lake. The campground is approximately one mile by water.

For hike-in campers: Drive five miles east on Highway 20. Just after crossing the Russian River bridge, turn left (Inlet Road) and drive approximately one mile to the Bu-Shay Ranger Station. Park and hike two miles to the campground.

Contact: U.S. Army Corps of Engineers, Lake Mendocino, tel. (707) 462-7581, or fax (707) 462-3372.

30 Bu-Shay

    7

Bu-Shay, on the northeast end of Lake Mendocino, is set on a point that provides a pretty southern exposure when the lake is full. The lake is about three miles long and one mile wide. It offers fishing for striped bass, largemouth bass, catfish, and bluegill, as well as water-skiing and power boating. A nearby visitor center features exhibits of local Native American history. The elevation is 750 feet. For more information about Lake Mendocino, see the entry for Che-Ka-Ka.

Location: At Lake Mendocino; map C0, grid i9.

Campsites, facilities: There are 164 sites for tents or RVs up to 35 feet long. There are three group sites for up to 120 people each. Picnic tables, fire rings, and lantern holders are provided. Drinking water, restrooms, showers, playground (in the adjacent day-use area), and sanitary disposal station are available. The boat ramp is two miles from camp near Ky-En Campground. Some facilities are wheelchair accessible. Leashed pets are permitted.

Reservations, fees: Reserve at tel. (877) 444-6777 ($8.65 reservation fee) or website: www.reserveusa.com; $16 per night, group sites are $110 to $190 per night. Open mid-April through September.

Directions: From Ukiah, drive north on U.S. 101 for five miles to the Highway 20 turnoff. Drive five miles east on Highway 20. Just after crossing the Russian River bridge, turn left (Inlet Road) and drive approximately one mile to the campground.

Contact: U.S. Army Corps of Engineers, Lake Mendocino, tel. (707) 462-7581, or fax (707) 462-3372.

31 Che-Ka-Ka

 7

Lake Mendocino is known for good striped bass fishing, water-skiing, and boating. Nearby, upstream of the lake, is Potter Valley and the East Fork Russian River (also called Cold Creek), which provides trout fishing in the summer. A boat ramp adjacent to the dam is a bonus. The elevation is 750 feet. This campground sits beside the dam at the south end of Lake Mendocino.

Location: At Lake Mendocino; map C0, grid j8.

Campsites, facilities: There are 22 sites for tents or RVs up to 35 feet long. Picnic tables and fire grills are provided. Drinking water, vault toilets, and lantern holders are available. A boat ramp is available nearby. Leashed pets are permitted.

Reservations, fees: Reserve at tel. (877) 444-6777 ($8.65 reservation fee) or website: www.reserveusa.com; $8 per night. Open mid-April through September.

Directions: From Ukiah, drive north on U.S. 101 to Lake Mendocino Drive. Exit right on Lake Mendocino Drive and continue to the first stoplight. Turn left on North State Street and drive to the next stoplight. Turn right (which will put you back on Lake Mendocino Drive) and drive about one mile to the signed entrance to the campground at Coyote Dam.

Contact: U.S. Army Corps of Engineers, Lake Mendocino, tel. (707) 462-7581 or fax (707) 462-3372.

32 Ky-En

 7

This camp is on the north shore of Lake Mendocino. With the access road off Highway 20 instead of U.S. 101 (as with Che-Ka-Ka), it can be overlooked by newcomers. A nearby boat ramp makes it especially attractive. For more information see the entry for Che-Ka-Ka.

Location: At Lake Mendocino; map C0, grid j8.

Campsites, facilities: There are 103 sites for tents or RVs up to 35 feet long. Picnic tables, fire grills, and lantern holders are provided. Restrooms, coin-operated showers, playground (in the adjacent day-use area), sanitary disposal station, a boat ramp, boat rentals, and limited supplies are available at the nearby marina. Some facilities are wheelchair accessible. Leashed pets are permitted.

Reservations, fees: Reserve at tel. (877) 444-6777 ($8.65 reservation fee) or website: www.reserveusa.com; $16 to $18 per night. Open year-round.

Directions: From Ukiah, drive north on U.S. 101 for five miles to the Highway 20 turnoff. Drive east on Highway 20 to Marina Drive. Turn right and drive 200 yards (past the boat ramp) to the campground.

Contact: U.S. Army Corps of Engineers, Lake Mendocino, tel. (707) 462-7581, or fax (707) 462-3372.

33 Manor Oaks RV Park

    2

Manor Oaks RV Park is a drive-in park in an urban setting for U.S. 101 motor home cruisers. Nearby Lake Mendocino provides a nearby sidetrip option, with access to boating, water-skiing, and fishing.

Location: In Ukiah; map C0, grid j8.

Campsites, facilities: There are 53 RV sites (15 drive-through) with full hookups. Picnic tables and fire grills are provided. Restrooms, showers, swimming pool (in summer), a coin laundry, and ice are available. Some facilities are wheelchair accessible. Leashed pets are permitted.

Reservations, fees: Reservations are accepted; $20 per night. Open year-round.

Directions: From U.S. 101 in Ukiah, take the Central Ukiah/Gobbi Street exit and drive east for a short distance to 700 East Gobbi Street on the left.

Contact: Manor Oaks Overnighter Park, tel. (800) 357-8772 or (707) 462-0529.

34 Hendy Woods State Park

     7

This is a remarkable setting where the flora changes from open valley grasslands and oaks to a cloaked redwood forest with old growth, as if you had waved a magic wand. The campsites are set in the forest, with a great trail routed amid the old redwoods and up to the Hermit Hut, where a hobo lived for 18 years in a few giant tree stumps covered with branches. Note: It is illegal to fish in the park's river.

Location: Near Boonville; map C0, grid j5.

Campsites, facilities: There are 92 sites for tents or RVs up to 35 feet long, and four cabins. Picnic tables, food lockers, and fire grills are provided. Drinking water, flush toilets, showers, and a sanitary disposal station are available. A grocery store and propane gas station are available nearby. Some facilities are wheelchair accessible. Leashed pets are permitted.

Reservations, fees: Reserve at (800) 444-PARK (800-444-7275) or website: www.ReserveAmerica.com; $12 per night for campsites, $20 per night for cabins. Open year-round.

Directions: From Cloverdale on U.S. 101, turn northwest on Highway 128 and drive about 35 miles to Philo Greenwood Road. Turn left on Philo Greenwood Road and drive one-half mile to the park entrance.

Contact: Hendy Woods State Park, tel. (707) 895-3141, tel. (707) 937-5804, or fax (707) 937-2953.

TOM FURRER

NO TABLE MANNERS

MAP C1

36

a

1

SHASTA-TRINITY
NATIONAL
FOREST

2

Harvey Peak
7,361 feet

YOLLA BOLLY–
MIDDLE EEL
WILDERNESS

b

TO ZENIA

c

3

Castle Peak
6,258 feet

4

MENDOCINO
NATIONAL
FOREST

Ball Rock
6,660 feet

TO RED BLUFF

ROUND
VALLEY
INDIAN
RESERVATION

7

Flournoy

d

TO DOS RIOS

Covelo

5

6

Mendocino Pass
5,000 feet

Paskenta

TO CORNING

250

e

8

Black Butte
7,448 feet

9

162

Newville

32

Black
Butte
Lake

284

f

Mount Sanhedrin
6,183 feet

MENDOCINO
NATIONAL
FOREST

Alder
Springs

g

Elk Creek

Fruto

SNOW
MOUNTAIN
WILDERNESS

Stony Gorge
Reservoir

h

Eel River

11-14

Lake
Pillsbury

17

10
Potter
Valley

15

16

162

TO WILLOW

i

TO CALPELLA

23

Fouts
Springs

18-22

Stonyford

27-28

26

24

29

East Park
Reservoir

25

20

30

31

Lodoga

Sites

TO MAXWELL

j

32-35

COW MOUNTAIN
RECREATION
AREA

29

Upper Lake

Bartlett
Springs

© AVALON TRAVEL PUBLISHING, INC.

CHAPTER C1

1 Tomhead Saddle

 4

This one is way out there in booger country. Little known and rarely visited, it's primarily a jump-off point for ambitious backpackers. The camp is on the edge of the Yolla Bolly-Middle Eel Wilderness. A trailhead here is routed to the South Fork of Cottonwood Creek, a trek that entails hiking eight miles in dry, hot terrain. The elevation is 5,700 feet.

Location: In Shasta-Trinity National Forest; map C1, grid a3.

Campsites, facilities: There are five sites for tents or RVs. Picnic tables and fire grills are provided. Vault toilets are available. No drinking water is available. Garbage must be packed out. A horse corral is also available. Leashed pets are permitted.

Reservations, fees: No reservations; no fee. Open late June to mid-September, weather permitting.

Directions: From Interstate 5 in Red Bluff, turn west on Highway 36 and drive about 13 miles. Turn left on Cannon Road and drive about five miles to Pettyjohn Road. Turn west on Pettyjohn Road, drive to Saddle

Camp, turn south on Forest Road 27N06, and drive three miles to the campground on the left. It is advisable to obtain a map of Shasta-Trinity National Forest.

Contact: Shasta-Trinity National Forest, Yolla Bolla Ranger Station, tel. (530) 352-4211 or fax (530) 352-4312.

2 White Rock

   4

There's a reason why there's no charge to camp here: usually nobody's around. It's primitive, little known, and likely to be empty. If you don't want to see anybody, you've found the right place. The big attraction here is watching the turtles swim at nearby White Rock Pond. A trailhead is available nearby out of Stuart Gap, which provides access to the North Yolla Bolly Mountains.

Location: In Shasta-Trinity National Forest; map C1, grid a6.

Campsites, facilities: There are three tent sites. Picnic tables and fire grills are provided. Vault toilets are available. No drinking water is available. Garbage must be packed out. Leashed pets are permitted.

Reservations, fees: No reservations; no fee. Open late June through mid-September, weather permitting.

Directions: From Red Bluff, drive about 45 miles west on Highway 36 to the Yolla Bolla ranger office. Continue west for about eight miles to Wild Mad River Road/Forest Road 30. Turn left on Forest Road 30 and drive nine miles to Pine Ridge Saddle Road/Forest Road 35. Turn left and drive nine miles (on a gravel road, very twisty) to the campground.

Contact: Shasta-Trinity National Forest, Yolla Bolla Ranger Station, tel. (530) 352-4211 or fax (530) 352-4312.

3 Hammerhorn Lake

      7

Obscure and hidden, this is a veritable dot of a lake, just five acres, set at 3,500 feet in Men-

docino National Forest. The lake is set near the border of the Yolla Bolly Wilderness, with the trailhead nearby to the northeast. A great side trip is the drive up to Anthony Peak and Hammerhorn Mountain Lookout.

Location: Near Covelo in Mendocino National Forest; map C1, grid c3.

Campsites, facilities: There are eight sites for tents or RVs up to 16 feet long. Picnic tables and fire grills are provided. Drinking water and vault toilets are available. Garbage must be packed out. There are two wheelchair-accessible campsites, a restroom, piers, and a trail. Supplies are available in Covelo. Leashed pets are permitted.

Reservations, fees: No reservations; $6 per night. Open May through November.

Directions: From Willits, drive north on U.S. 101 for 13 miles to Longvale and the junction with Highway 162. Turn northeast on Highway 162 and drive to Covelo. Continue east on Highway 162 to the Eel River Bridge. Turn left at the bridge on Forest Road M1 and drive about 17 miles to the campground at the north end of the lake.

Contact: Mendocino National Forest, Covelo Ranger District, tel. (707) 983-6118 or fax (707) 983-8004. For a map, send $6 to U.S. Forest Service, Attn: Map Sales, P.O. Box 587, Camino, CA 95709; tel. (530) 647-5390, fax (530) 647-5389, or website: www.r5.fs.fed.us/visitorcenter.

4 Little Doe

    5

Little Howard Lake is tucked deep in the interior of Mendocino National Forest between Espee Ridge to the south and Little Doe Ridge to the north, at elevation 3,600 feet. For a drive-to lake, it is surprisingly remote and provides fair trout fishing, primitive camping, and an opportunity for car-top boating. Side trips include Hammerhorn Lake, about six miles away, and several four-wheel-drive roads that allow you to explore the area.

Location: Near Howard Lake in Mendocino National Forest; map C1, grid c3.

Campsites, facilities: There are 13 tent sites. Fire pits are provided. No drinking water is available. All garbage must be packed out. Supplies are available in Covelo, 12 miles away. Leashed pets are permitted.

Reservations, fees: No reservations; no fee. Open May through November.

Directions: From Willits, drive north on U.S. 101 for 13 miles to Longvale and the junction with Highway 162. Turn northeast on Highway 162 and drive to Covelo. Continue east on Highway 162 to the Eel River Bridge. Turn left at the bridge on Forest Road M1 and drive about 11 miles to the campground at the north end of the lake.

Contact: Mendocino National Forest, Covelo Ranger District, tel. (707) 983-6118 or fax (707) 983-8004. For a map, send $6 to U.S. Forest Service, Attn: Map Sales, P.O. Box 587, Camino, CA 95709; tel. (530) 647-5390, fax (530) 647-5389, or website: www.r5.fs.fed.us/visitorcenter. Major credit cards accepted.

5 Eel River

 8

This is a little-known spot, set in oak woodlands at the confluence of the Middle Fork of the Eel River and Black Butte River. The elevation is 1,500 feet, and it's often extremely hot in summer. But at no cost, the price is right. Eel River, an ancient Native American campsite, is a major archaeological site. For this reason restoration has been limited and at times the camp is overgrown and weedy. Who cares, though. After all, you're camping.

Location: In Mendocino National Forest; map C1, grid d2.

Campsites, facilities: There are 16 sites for tents or RVs up to 21 feet long. Picnic tables and fire grills are provided. Drinking water and vault toilets are available. Garbage must be packed out. Leashed pets are permitted.

Reservations, fees: No reservations; $6 per night. Open May through October.

Directions: From Willits, drive north on U.S. 101 for 13 miles to Longvale and the junction with Highway 162. Turn northeast on Highway 162 and drive to Covelo. Continue east on Highway 162 for 13 miles to the campground.

Contact: Mendocino National Forest, Covelo Ranger District, tel. (707) 983-6118 or fax (707) 983-8004.

6 Wells Cabin

 6

You'll join the 5 Percent Club when you reach this spot. It is situated one mile from Anthony Peak Lookout (6,900 feet) where, on a clear day, you can get great views all the way to the Pacific Ocean and sweeping views of the Sacramento Valley to the east. This campground is hardly used during the summer and often provides a cool escape from the heat of the valley. The elevation is 6,300 feet.

Location: In Mendocino National Forest; map C1, grid d4.

Campsites, facilities: There are 25 sites for tents only. Picnic tables and fire rings are provided. Vault toilets are available. Drinking water is not available in winter. Garbage must be packed out. Leashed pets are permitted.

Reservations, fees: No reservations; no fee. Open July through October.

Directions: From Corning on Interstate 5, turn west on County Road A9 and drive 20 miles to Paskenta. In Paskenta, turn west on Forest Road 23N02 and drive to the junction with Forest Road 23N69. Turn north and drive three miles the campground.

Contact: Mendocino National Forest, Grindstone Ranger District, Corning Work Center, tel. (530) 824-5196 or fax (530) 824-6034.

7 Whitlock

     4

This obscure Forest Service camp is often empty or close to it. It is set at 4,300 feet, where conifers have taken over from the valley grasslands to the nearby east. The camp is situated amid good deer range and makes a good hunting base camp in the fall, with a network of Forest Service roads in the area. It is advisable to obtain a Forest Service map.

Location: In Mendocino National Forest; map C1, grid d6.

Campsites, facilities: There are three sites for tents or RVs up to 22 feet long. Picnic tables, fire grills, and stoves are provided. Drinking water and vault toilets are available. Garbage must be packed out. Leashed pets are permitted.

Reservations, fees: No reservations; no fee. Open June through October.

Directions: From Corning on Interstate 5, turn west onto County Road A9/Corning Road and drive 20 miles to Paskenta. Turn north (right) on Toomes Camp Road/County Road 122 and drive 14 miles to the campground on the right.

Contact: Mendocino National Forest, Grindstone Ranger District, Corning Work Center, tel. (530) 824-5196 or fax (530) 824-6034.

❽ Masterson Group Camp

 5

This is a group camp only. It is just a mile away from the Plaskett Lakes, two small lakes set at 6,000 feet and surrounded by a mixed conifer forest. No swimming or motors are permitted at either lake. It is advisable to obtain a map of Mendocino National Forest, which details nearby streams, lakes, and hiking trails. One notable trail is the Black Butte Trail. For more information see the entry for Plaskett Meadows.

Location: Near Plaskett Lakes in Mendocino National Forest; map C1, grid e4.

Campsites, facilities: This group camp can accommodate up to 100 people, with 20 tent sites. Fire grills and picnic tables are provided. Drinking water and vault toilets are available. Leashed pets are permitted.

Reservations, fees: Reservations are required; $35 group fee per night. Open mid-June through mid-October.

Directions: In Willows on Interstate 5, turn west on Highway 162 and drive toward the town of Elk Creek. Just after crossing the Stony Creek Bridge, turn north on County Road 306 and drive four miles. Turn left on Alder Springs Road/Forest Highway 7 and drive 31 miles to the camp on the right.

Contact: Mendocino National Forest, Grindstone Ranger District, Stonyford Work Center, tel. (530) 963-3128 or fax (530) 963-3173.

❾ Plaskett Meadows

 7

This is a little-known camp in the mountains near Plaskett Lakes, a pair of connected dot-size mountain lakes that form the headwaters of little Plaskett Creek. Trout fishing is best at the westernmost of the two lakes. No motors are permitted in the lakes and swimming is not recommended. The camp is set at an elevation of 6,000 feet.

Location: In Mendocino National Forest; map C1, grid e4.

Campsites, facilities: There are 32 sites for tents or RVs up to 16 feet long. Fire grills and picnic tables are provided. Drinking water and vault toilets are available. Leashed pets are permitted.

Reservations, fees: No reservations; $5 per night. Open mid-June through mid-October.

Directions: In Willows on Interstate 5, turn west on Highway 162 and drive toward the town of Elk Creek. Just after crossing the Stony Creek Bridge, turn north on County Road 306 and drive four miles. Turn left on Alder Springs Road/Forest Highway 7 and drive 31 miles to the campground on the left.

Contact: Mendocino National Forest, Grindstone Ranger District, Stonyford Work Center, tel. (530) 963-3128 or fax (530) 963-3173.

❿ Trout Creek

 7

This is a spot that relatively few campers know about. Most others looking over this area are setting up shop at nearby Lake Pillsbury to the east. But if you like to watch the water roll by, this could be your port of call since it sits at the confluence of Trout Creek and the Eel River (not far from the East Van Arsdale Reservoir). Insider's note: Nearby in Potter Valley to the south, the East Fork Russian River (Cold Creek) is stocked with trout during the summer. The elevation is 1,500 feet.

Location: Near East Van Arsdale Reservoir; map C1, grid h0.

Campsites, facilities: There are 14 sites for tents and one double site for tents or RVs. Fire grills and picnic tables are provided. Drinking water and vault toilets are available. Leashed pets are permitted.

Reservations, fees: No reservations; $10 per night, $3 per night per extra vehicle and $7 per night per extra RV, $1 dog fee. Open May through October.

Directions: From Ukiah on U.S. 101, drive north to the junction with Highway 20. Turn east (right) on Highway 20 and drive five miles. Turn northwest on East Potter Valley Road toward Lake Pillsbury. Drive 5.9 miles to the town of Potter Valley. Continue on east Potter Valley Road to Eel River Road. Turn right and drive 4.5 miles to the Eel River Bridge. From the bridge, continue two miles to the campground entrance.

Contact: PG&E Building and Land Services, tel. (916) 386-5164.

11 Pogie Point

 7

This camp is set beside Lake Pillsbury in Mendocino National Forest, in the back of a cove at the lake's northwest corner. When the lake is full, this spot is quite pretty. When the lake level is way down, well, you can't win 'em all. A boat ramp is about a quarter mile to the south, a bonus. The elevation is 1,900 feet.

Location: On Lake Pillsbury in Mendocino National Forest; map C1, grid h2.

Campsites, facilities: There are 50 sites for tents or RVs. Picnic tables and fire grills are provided. Drinking water and vault toilets are available. Some facilities are wheelchair accessible. Leashed pets are permitted.

Reservations, fees: No reservations; $10 per night, $3 per extra vehicle, $1 pet fee. Open May through October.

Directions: From Ukiah on U.S. 101, drive north to the junction with Highway 20. Turn east (right) on Highway 20 and drive five miles. Turn northwest on East Potter Valley Road toward Lake Pillsbury. Drive 5.9 miles to the town of Potter Valley. Continue on east Potter Valley Road to Eel River Road. Turn right and drive 15 miles to the Eel River Information Kiosk at Lake Pillsbury. Continue for two miles to the campground access road. Turn right and drive a short distance to the campground.

Contact: Mendocino National Forest, Upper Lake Ranger District, tel. (707) 275-2361 or fax (707) 275-0676; PG&E Building and Land Services, tel. (916) 386-5164.

12 Sunset Campground

 7

This camp is on the northeast corner of Lake Pillsbury, with a boat ramp available at the mouth of Squaw Creek Cove less than a quarter mile to the south. The adjacent designated nature trail along the shore of the lake here is another attraction. The surrounding national forest offers side trip possibilities.

Location: On Lake Pillsbury in Mendocino National Forest; map C1, grid h2.

Campsites, facilities: There are 54 sites for tents or RVs. Picnic tables and fire grills are provided. Drinking water and vault toilets are available. A boat ramp is nearby. Leashed pets are permitted.

Reservations, fees: No reservations; $10 per night, $3 per extra vehicle, $1 pet fee. Open May through October.

Directions: From Ukiah on U.S. 101, drive north to the junction with Highway 20. Turn east (right) on Highway 20 and drive five miles. Turn northwest on East Potter Valley Road toward Lake Pillsbury. Drive 5.9 miles to the town of Potter Valley. Continue on east Potter Valley Road to Eel River Road. Turn right and drive 15 miles to the Eel River Information Kiosk at Lake Pillsbury. Continue east for 4.1 miles to Lake Pillsbury and the junction with Hall Mountain Road. Turn right and drive three miles to the camp entrance.

Contact: Mendocino National Forest, Upper Lake Ranger District, tel. (707) 275-2361 or fax (707) 275-0676; PG&E Land Services, tel. (916) 386-5164.

Oak Flat

 6

This primitive camp is used primarily as an overflow area if Lake Pillsbury's other camps are full. It is set at 1,850 feet near the north shore of Lake Pillsbury in the heart of Mendocino National Forest. Nearby trails leading into the backcountry are detailed on a Forest Service map.

Location: On Lake Pillsbury in Mendocino National Forest; map C1, grid h2.

Campsites, facilities: There are 12 primitive sites for tents or RVs. Picnic tables and fire grills are provided. Vault toilets are available. No drinking water is available. Garbage must be packed out during the winter season. Leashed pets are permitted.

Reservations, fees: No reservations; no fee. Open year-round.

Directions: From Ukiah on U.S. 101, drive north to the junction with Highway 20. Turn east (right) on Highway 20 and drive five miles. Turn northwest on East Potter Valley Road toward Lake Pillsbury. Drive 5.9 miles to the town of Potter Valley. Continue on east Potter Valley Road to Eel River Road. Turn right and drive 15 miles to the Eel River Information Kiosk at Lake Pillsbury. Continue for four miles around the north end of the lake and look for the camp entrance on the right side of the road.

Contact: Mendocino National Forest, Upper Lake Ranger District, tel. (707) 275-2361 or fax (707) 275-0676.

Navy

 7

When Lake Pillsbury is full of water, this is one of the most attractive of the many camps here. It is set in the lake's north cove, sheltered from north winds. Surrounded by forest, the camp is in a pretty setting. However, when the lake level is down, as is common in the fall, it can seem like the camp is on the edge of a dust bowl.

Location: On Lake Pillsbury in Mendocino National Forest; map C1, grid h2.

Campsites, facilities: There are 20 sites for tents or RVs. Picnic tables are provided. Drinking water and vault toilets are available. A boat ramp is nearby. Some facilities are wheelchair accessible. Leashed pets are permitted.

Reservations, fees: No reservations; $8 per night, $1 pet fee. Open Memorial Day weekend through Labor Day weekend.

Directions: From Ukiah on U.S. 101, drive north to the junction with Highway 20. Turn east (right) on Highway 20 and drive five miles. Turn northwest on East Potter Valley Road toward Lake Pillsbury. Drive 5.9 miles to the town of Potter Valley. Continue on east Potter Valley Road to Eel River Road. Turn right and drive 15 miles to the Eel River Information Kiosk at Lake Pillsbury. Continue for four miles around the north end of the lake and look for the campground entrance on the right side of the road. The campground is on the north shore, just west of Oak Flat Camp.

Contact: Mendocino National Forest, Upper Lake Ranger District, tel. (707) 275-2361 or fax (707) 275-0676. For a map send $4 to Upper Lake Ranger Station, 10025 Elk Mountain Road, Upper Lake, CA 95485, and ask for Mendocino National Forest area.

15 Fuller Grove & Fuller Grove Group Camp

 7

This is one of several campgrounds bordering Lake Pillsbury, which at 2,000 acres is by far the largest lake in Mendocino National Forest. It has lakeside camping, good boat ramps, and in the spring, good fishing for trout. This camp is set along the northwest shore of the lake, with a boat ramp only about a quarter mile away to the north. There are numerous backcountry roads in the area, which provide access to a state game refuge to the north and the Snow Mountain Wilderness to the east.

Location: On Lake Pillsbury in Mendocino National Forest; map C1, grid h2.

Campsites, facilities: There are 30 sites for tents or RVs up to 22 feet long, and one group site for up to 100 people. Picnic tables and fire grills are provided. Drinking water and vault toilets are available. A boat ramp is nearby. Leashed pets are permitted.

Reservations, fees: Reservations for the group site only; call PG&E at (916) 386-5164. For individual sites, $10 per night, $3 per extra vehicle, $1 pet fee; $100 per night for group site. Open May through October.

Directions: From Ukiah on U.S. 101, drive north to the junction with Highway 20. Turn east (right) on Highway 20 and drive five miles. Turn northwest on East Potter Valley Road toward Lake Pillsbury. Drive 5.9 miles to the town of Potter Valley. Continue on East Potter Valley Road to Eel River Road. Turn right and drive 15 miles to the Eel River Information Kiosk at Lake Pillsbury. Continue for 2.2 miles to the campground access road. Turn right and drive a quarter mile to the campground.

Contact: Mendocino National Forest, Upper Lake Ranger District, tel. (707) 275-2361 or fax (707) 275-0676; PG&E Building and Land Services, tel. (916) 386-5164.

16 Lake Pillsbury Resort

 6

This is a pretty spot beside the shore of Lake Pillsbury in the heart of Mendocino National Forest. It can be headquarters for a vacation involving boating, fishing, water-skiing, or exploring the surrounding national forest. A boat ramp, small marina, and full facilities make this place a prime attraction in a relatively remote location. This is the only resort on the lake that accepts reservations, and it has some lakefront sites.

Location: On Lake Pillsbury; map C1, grid h2.

Campsites, facilities: There are 38 sites for tents or RVs, with no hookups. There are also eight cabins for rent. A snack bar, restrooms, showers, boat rentals, fuel, dock, fishing supplies, and small marina are available. Leashed pets are permitted.

Reservations, fees: Reservations are recommended; $16.50 per night. Call for cabin prices. Major credit cards accepted. Open May through November.

Directions: From Ukiah on U.S. 101, drive north to the junction with Highway 20. Turn east (right) on Highway 20 and drive five miles to East Potter Valley Road (toward Lake Pillsbury). Turn northwest on East Potter Valley Road and drive 5.9 miles to the town of Potter Valley. Continue on East Potter Valley Road to Eel River Road. Turn right and drive 15 miles to to Lake Pillsbury and Forest Road 301F. Turn right at Forest Road 301F and drive two miles to the resort.

Contact: Lake Pillsbury Resort, tel. (707) 743-1581 or fax (707) 743-2666.

17 Lower Nye

 8

This camp is on the northern border of the Snow Mountain Wilderness. It is a good jump-off point for backpackers, or a spot for folks who don't want to be bugged by anybody. It is set at 3,300 feet on Skeleton

Creek near the Eel River. It is advisable to obtain a detailed USGS topographic map.

Location: In Mendocino National Forest; map C1, grid h3.

Campsites, facilities: There are six sites for tents or RVs. Picnic tables and fire grills are provided. Vault toilets are available. No drinking water is available. Leashed pets are permitted.

Reservations, fees: No reservations; no fee. Open year-round, weather permitting.

Directions: From Ukiah on U.S. 101, drive north to the junction of Highway 20. Turn east on Highway 20 and drive to the town of Upper Lake and to Elk Mountain Road. Turn left on Elk Mountain Road (which becomes Forest Road 1N02) and drive 17 miles. Turn right on Forest Road 18N01/Bear Creek Road and drive seven miles. Turn north on Forest Road 18N04/Rice Creek Road and drive 14 miles to the campground.

Contact: Mendocino National Forest, Upper Lake Ranger District, tel. (707) 275-2361 or fax (707) 275-0676.

18 Mill Creek

 5

This tiny, pretty, secluded camp is set beside Mill Creek near Fouts Springs at the southeastern boundary of the Snow Mountain Wilderness. A nearby trailhead, a mile to the west, provides a hiking route into the wilderness that connects along Trout Creek, a great little romp. Mill Creek is quite pretty in the late spring, but by late summer the flow drops way down. The elevation is 1,700 feet. Expect heavy off-highway-vehicle use from October through May; Fouts Springs/Davis Flat is an OHV staging area.

Location: In Mendocino National Forest; map C1, grid i5.

Campsites, facilities: There are six tent sites. Picnic tables, stoves, and barbecues are provided. Vault toilets are available. No drinking water is available. Leashed pets are permitted.

Reservations, fees: No reservations; no fee. Open year-round.

Directions: From Interstate 5 at Maxwell, turn west on Maxwell-Sites Road and drive to Sites. Turn left on Sites-Lodoga Road and continue to Lodoga. Turn right on Lodoga-Stonyford Road and loop around East Park Reservoir to reach Stonyford. From Stonyford, turn west on Fouts Springs Road/Forest Road M10 and drive about 8.5 miles to the campground entrance on the right.

Contact: Mendocino National Forest, Grindstone Ranger District, Stonyford Work Center, tel. (530) 963-3128 or fax (530) 963-3173.

19 North Fork

 8

This primitive camp, quiet from June through September when motorcycle use is infrequent, is set at 1,700 feet in a grove of oak trees at the confluence of the north, south, and middle forks of Stony Creek. There are many trailheads for hiking in the area, within a few miles of the Snow Mountain Wilderness, but none at this camp. There are great views of St. John Mountain and Snow Mountain. (See entry for Mill Creek for additional information.) The elevation is 1,700 feet.

Location: On Stony Creek in Mendocino National Forest; map C1, grid i5.

Campsites, facilities: There are six tent sites. Picnic tables and stoves are provided. Vault toilets are available. No drinking water is available. Garbage must be packed out. Leashed pets are permitted.

Reservations, fees: No reservations; no fee. Open year-round.

Directions: From Interstate 5 at Maxwell, turn west on Maxwell-Sites Road and drive to Sites. Turn left on Sites-Lodoga Road and continue to Lodoga. Turn right on Lodoga-Stonyford Road and loop around East Park Reservoir to reach Stonyford. From Stonyford, turn west on Fouts Springs Road/Forest Road M10 and drive about eight miles. Turn right on Forest Road 18N03 and drive two miles to the campground on the right.

Contact: Mendocino National Forest, Grindstone Ranger District, Stonyford Work Center, tel. (530) 963-3128 or fax (530) 963-3173.

20 Fouts & South Fork

 6

These two adjoining camps are in a designated off-highway-vehicle area and are used primarily by dirt bikers. So if you're looking for quiet, these camps are not for you. They are in a brushy area shaded by gray pines near Stony Creek, Davis Flat, and Fouts Springs. Several other four-wheel-drive trails are nearby—North Fork, South Fork, and Mill Creek. To the west is the Snow Mountain Wilderness and excellent hiking trails; to the south is an extensive Forest Service road and OHV trail network that provides access for four-wheel-drive vehicles and dirt bikes. The elevation is 1,700 feet.

Location: On Stony Creek in Mendocino National Forest; map C1, grid i5.

Campsites, facilities: There are 11 dispersed sites for tents or RVs up to 16 feet long at Fouts; there are five dispersed tent sites at South Fork. Picnic tables and fire grills are provided. Vault toilets are available. Drinking water is available at Fouts, but no drinking water is available at South Fork. Some facilities are wheelchair accessible. Leashed pets are permitted.

Reservations, fees: No reservations; no fee. Open year-round.

Directions: From Interstate 5 at Maxwell, turn west on Maxwell-Sites Road and drive to Sites. Turn left on Sites-Lodoga Road and continue to Lodoga. Turn right on Lodoga-Stonyford Road and loop around East Park Reservoir to reach Stonyford. From Stonyford, turn west on Fouts Springs Road/County Road M10 and drive about eight miles. Turn right (north) on Forest Road 18N03 and drive one mile to the campgrounds on your right.

Contact: Mendocino National Forest, Grindstone Ranger District, Stonyford Work Cen-

ter, tel. (530) 963-3128 or fax (530) 963-1373.

21 Gray Pine Group Camp

 6

Similar to Fouts Campground, Gray Pine is set in an area of gray pines (surprise!) with four-wheel-drive trails nearby. It is near (but not on) Stony Creek. (See Fouts campground for additional information.)

Location: In Mendocino National Forest; map C1, grid i5.

Campsites, facilities: There is one group site that can accommodate 15 to 70 campers with tents or RVs up to 16 feet long. Picnic tables, fire rings, drinking water, a vault toilet, a group barbecue grill, and an amphitheater are available. Leashed pets are permitted.

Reservations, fees: Reservations at tel. (530) 963-3128, no fee. Open year-round.

Directions: From Interstate 5 at Maxwell, turn west on Maxwell-Sites Road and drive to Sites. Turn left on Sites-Lodoga Road and continue to Lodoga. Turn right on Lodoga-Stonyford Road and loop around East Park Reservoir to reach Stonyford. From Stonyford, turn west on Fouts Springs Road/County Road M10 and drive about eight miles. Turn right on Forest Road 18N03 and drive less than a mile to the campground on your right.

Contact: Mendocino National Forest, Grindstone Ranger District, Stonyford Work Center, tel. (530) 963-3128 or fax (530) 963-1373.

22 Davis Flat

 4

This camp is across the road from Fouts and South Fork campgrounds. All three are in a designated off-highway-vehicle area, so expect OHVers, especially in the winter. This isn't the quietest camp around, but there is some good hiking in the area to the immediate west in the Snow Mountain Wilderness. The elevation is 1,700 feet.

Location: In Mendocino National Forest; map C1, grid i5.

Campsites, facilities: There are 70 dispersed sites for tents or RVs of any length. Picnic tables and fire grills are provided. Drinking water and vault toilets are available. Leashed pets are permitted.

Reservations, fees: No reservations; no fee. Open year-round.

Directions: From Interstate 5 at Maxwell, turn west on Maxwell-Sites Road and drive to Sites. Turn left on Sites-Lodoga Road and continue to Lodoga. Turn right on Lodoga-Stonyford Road and loop around East Park Reservoir to reach Stonyford. From Stonyford, turn west on Fouts Springs Road/County Road M10 and drive about eight miles. Turn right on Forest Road 18N03 and drive one mile to the campground on your left.

Contact: Mendocino National Forest, Grindstone Ranger District, Stonyford Work Center, tel. (530) 963-3128 or fax (530) 963-3173.

23 Bear Creek Campground

    7

Bet you didn't know about this one—a primitive spot out in the boondocks of Mendocino National Forest, set at 2,000 feet. It's a pretty spot, too, set beside Bear Creek near its confluence with Blue Slides Creek. Trout fishing can be good here. It's about a 10-minute drive to the Summit Springs trailhead at the southern end of the Snow Mountain Wilderness. There are also numerous OHV roads in this region, detailed on a map of Mendocino National Forest.

Location: In Mendocino National Forest; map C1, grid i3.

Campsites, facilities: There are 16 sites for tents or small RVs. Picnic tables and fire grills are provided. Vault toilets are available. No drinking water is available. Leashed pets are permitted.

Reservations, fees: No reservations; no fee. Open year-round, weather permitting.

Directions: From Ukiah on U.S. 101, drive north to the junction with Highway 20. Turn

east on Highway 20 and drive to the town of Upper Lake. Turn left on Mendenhall Avenue (which becomes Forest Road 1N02) and drive 17 miles (the latter stretch is extremely twisty). Turn east on Forest Road 301C/Bear Creek Road and drive eight miles to the campground on the right side of the road.

Contact: Mendocino National Forest, Upper Lake Ranger District, tel. (707) 275-2361 or fax (707) 275-0676. Call for road conditions.

24 Deer Valley Campground

     4

This one is out there in booger country. It is used primarily in summer by OHV enthusiasts and in the fall by deer hunters. It is set at 3,700 feet in Deer Valley, about five miles from the East Fork of Middle Creek.

Location: In Mendocino National Forest; map C1, grid i2.

Campsites, facilities: There are 13 sites for tents or RVs. Picnic tables and fire grills are provided. Vault toilets are available. No drinking water is available. Leashed pets are permitted.

Reservations, fees: No reservations; no fee. Open year-round, weather permitting.

Directions: From Ukiah on U.S. 101, drive north to the junction of Highway 20. Turn east on Highway 20 and drive to the town of Upper Lake and to Elk Mountain Road. Turn left on Elk Mountain Road (which becomes Forest Road 1N02) and drive 12 miles (the latter section is extremely twisty). Turn right on Forest Road 16N01 and drive about three miles to the campground.

Contact: Mendocino National Forest, Upper Lake Ranger District, tel. (707) 275-2361 or fax (707) 275-0676.

25 Middle Creek Campground

   6

This camp is not widely known, but known well enough as an off-highway-vehicle staging area. It is set at 2,000 feet at the confluence of the West and East Forks of Middle Creek. This campground was refurbished in late 1997.

Location: In Mendocino National Forest; map C1, grid j2.

Campsites, facilities: There are 23 sites for tents or small RVs. Picnic tables and fire grills are provided. Drinking water and vault toilets are available. Leashed pets are permitted.

Reservations, fees: No reservations; $4 single sites, $8 double sites per night, $3 for an extra vehicle. Open year-round.

Directions: From Ukiah on U.S. 101, drive north to the junction with Highway 20. Turn east on Highway 20 and drive to the town of Upper Lake. Turn left on Mendenhall Avenue (which becomes Forest Road 1N02) and drive eight miles to the camp on the right side of the road.

Contact: Mendocino National Forest, Upper Lake Ranger District, tel. (707) 275-2361 or fax (707) 275-0676.

26 Dixie Glade Horse Camp

 6

Got a horse who likes to tromp? No? Then take a pass on this one. Yes? Then sign right up, because this is a trailhead camp for people preparing to head north by horseback into the adjacent Snow Mountain Wilderness.

Location: Near the Snow Mountain Wilderness in Mendocino National Forest; map C1, grid i5.

Campsites, facilities: This camp has single sites, or can accommodate up to 50 people in tents or RVs. Picnic tables and fire grills are provided. Vault toilets are available. No drinking water is available. Garbage must be packed out. Some facilities are wheelchair accessible. A horse corral and water in a horse trough is available. Leashed pets are permitted.

Reservations, fees: No reservations; no fee. Open year-round.

Directions: From Interstate 5 at Maxwell, turn west on Maxwell-Sites Road and drive to Sites. Turn left on Sites-Lodoga Road and continue to Lodoga. Turn right on Lodoga-Stonyford Road and loop around East Park Reservoir to reach Stonyford. From Stonyford, turn west on Fouts Springs Road/County Road M10 and drive 13 miles to the camp on the left side of the road.

Contact: Mendocino National Forest, Grindstone Ranger District, Stonyford Work Center, tel. (530) 963-3128 or fax (530) 963-3173. For a map, send $6 to U.S. Forest Service, Attn: Map Sales, P.O. Box 587, Camino, CA 95709; tel. (530) 647-5390, fax (530) 647-5389, or website: www.r5.fs.fed.us/visitorcenter. Major credit cards accepted. Ask for Mendocino National Forest.

27 Letts Lake Complex

 9

Not too many folks know about Letts Lake, a 30-acre, spring-fed lake set in a mixed conifer forest at 4,500 feet just south of the Snow Mountain Wilderness. There are four camps on the east side of the lake, so take your pick. No motors are allowed on the water, making it ideal for canoes, rafts, and float tubes. This lake is stocked with rainbow trout in the early summer and is known also for black bass and catfish. It's a designated historical landmark, the site where the homesteaders known as the Letts brothers were murdered. While that may not impress you, the views to the north of the Snow Mountain Wilderness will. In addition, there are several natural springs that can be fun to hunt up. By the way, after such a long drive to get here, don't let your eagerness cause you to stop at Lily Pond (on the left, one mile before reaching Letts Lake), because there are no trout in it.

Location: In Mendocino National Forest; map C1, grid i4.

Campsites, facilities: There are 40 sites for tents or RVs up to 20 feet long. Picnic tables and fire rings are provided. Drinking water and vault toilets are available. A wheelchair-accessible fishing pier is available. There is also an 11-unit picnic area with tables and barbecues on the left side of the lake, open during the day only. Leashed pets are permitted.

Reservations, fees: No reservations; $8 per night; 14-day limit. Open mid-April through October.

Directions: From Interstate 5 at Maxwell, turn west on Maxwell-Sites Road and drive to Sites. Turn left on Sites-Lodoga Road and continue to Lodoga. Turn right on Lodoga-Stonyford Road and loop around East Park Reservoir to reach Stonyford. From Stonyford, turn west on Fouts Springs Road/Forest Road M10 and drive about 17 miles into national forest (where the road becomes Forest Service 17N02) to the campground on the east side of Letts Lake.

Contact: Mendocino National Forest, Grindstone Ranger District, Stonyford Work Center, tel. (530) 963-3128 or fax (530) 963-3173.

28 Mill Valley

 5

This camp is set beside Lily Pond, a little, teeny guy, with larger Letts Lake just a mile away. Since Lily Pond does not have trout and Letts Lake does, this camp gets far less traffic than its counterpart. The area is crisscrossed with numerous creeks, four-wheel-drive routes, and Forest Service roads, making it a great adventure for owners of four-wheel drives. The elevation is 4,200 feet.

Location: Near Letts Lake in Mendocino National Forest; map C1, grid i4.

Campsites, facilities: There are 15 sites for tents or RVs up to 18 feet long. Picnic tables and fire stoves are provided. Vault toilets are available. Drinking water is available seasonally. Leashed pets are permitted.

Reservations, fees: No reservations; fees range from free to $5 per night, depending upon water availability. Open mid-April through October, weather permitting.

Directions: From Interstate 5 at Maxwell, turn west on Maxwell-Sites Road and drive to

Sites. Turn left on Sites-Lodoga Road and continue to Lodoga. Turn right on Lodoga-Stonyford Road and loop around East Park Reservoir to reach Stonyford. From Stonyford, turn west on Fouts Springs Road/Forest Road M10 and drive about 16 miles into national forest (where the road becomes Forest Service 17N02) to the camp access road on the left. Turn left and drive a half mile to the camp.

Contact: Mendocino National Forest, Grindstone Ranger District, Stonyford Work Center, tel. (530) 963-3128 or fax (530) 963-3173.

29 Old Mill

 5

Little known and little used, this camp is set at 3,700 feet amid a mature stand of pine and fir on Trough Spring Ridge. It's at the site of—guess what? An old mill. Expect some OHV company.

Location: Near Mill Creek in Mendocino National Forest; map C1, grid i5.

Campsites, facilities: There are eight sites for tents and two sites for tents or RVs up to 16 feet long. (However, the access road to the campground is narrow.) Picnic tables and fire stoves are provided. Vault toilets are available. No drinking water is available. All garbage must be packed out. Leashed pets are permitted.

Reservations, fees: No reservations; no fee. Open May through October.

Directions: From Interstate 5 at Maxwell, turn west on Maxwell-Sites Road and drive to Sites. Turn left on Sites-Lodoga Road and continue to Lodoga. Turn right on Lodoga-Stonyford Road and loop around East Park Reservoir to reach Stonyford. From Stonyford, turn west on Fouts Springs Road/County Road M10 and drive about six miles. Turn left on Forest Road M5/Trough Springs Road and drive 7.5 miles on a narrow road to the campground on your right.

Contact: Mendocino National Forest, Grindstone Ranger District, Stonyford Work Center, tel. (530) 963-3128 or fax (530) 963-3173.

30 Cedar Camp

 6

This camp is set at 4,300 feet elevation, just below Goat Mountain (6,121 feet), to the west about a mile away. Why did anybody decide to build a campground way out here? Because a small spring starts nearby, creating a trickle that runs into the nearby headwaters of Little Stony Creek.

Location: In Mendocino National Forest; map C1, grid j4.

Campsites, facilities: There are five sites for tents or small RVs (the access road is poor for trailers). Picnic tables and fire grills are provided. Vault toilets are available. No drinking water is available. Garbage must be packed out. Leashed pets are permitted.

Reservations, fees: No reservations; no fee. Open mid-June through mid-October.

Directions: From Interstate 5 at Maxwell, turn west on Maxwell-Sites Road and drive to Sites. Turn left on Sites-Lodoga Road and continue to Lodoga. Turn right on Lodoga-Stonyford Road and loop around East Park Reservoir to reach Stonyford. From Stonyford, turn west on Fouts Springs Road/County Road M10 and drive about six miles. Turn left on County Road M5 (Trough Springs Road) and drive 13 miles to the campground on your right.

Contact: Mendocino National Forest, Grindstone Ranger District, Stonyford Work Center, tel. (530) 963-3128 or fax (530) 963-3173.

31 Little Stony Campground

 7

This pretty spot is set in Little Stony Canyon, beside Little Stony Creek at 1,500 feet. Very few people know of the place, and you will find it is appropriately named: it is little, it is stony, and the little trout amid the stones fit right in. The camp provides streamside access and, with Goat Mountain Road running along most of the stream, it is easy to fish much of this creek in an evening. Expect heavy OHV use from fall through spring.

Location: On Little Stony Creek in Mendocino National Forest; map C1, grid j6.

Campsites, facilities: There are seven sites for tents or small RVs. Picnic tables and fire grills are provided. Vault toilets are available. No drinking water is available. Leashed pets are permitted.

Reservations, fees: No reservations; no fee. Open year-round.

Directions: From Interstate 5 at Maxwell, turn west on Maxwell-Sites Road and drive to Sites. Turn left on Sites-Lodoga Road and continue to where the road crosses Stony Creek. Just after the bridge, turn left on Goat Mountain Road and drive four miles (a rough county road) to the campground on the left.

Contact: Mendocino National Forest, Grindstone Ranger District, Stonyford Work Center, tel. (530) 963-3128 or fax (530) 963-3173.

32 Le Trianon Resort

 7

Le Trianon Resort is the biggest of the camps on the Blue Lakes, the overlooked lakes not far from giant Clear Lake. It is an angler's special with good trout fishing in spring and no water-skiing permitted. The better fishing is in Upper Blue Lake, which is stocked with 28,000 trout per year and where the water is much clearer than at the lower lake. The best fishing is in the spring, in April, May, and June. A plus at this park is a few lakeside campsites.

Location: Lower Blue Lake; map C1, grid j0.

Campsites, facilities: There are 200 sites for tents or RVs (no pull-through sites) with water and electric hookups, and 13 cabins for rent. Picnic tables are provided. Flush toilets, showers, sanitary disposal station, playground, boat ramp, boat rentals, fishing supplies, coin laundry, snack bar, and grocery store are available. Leashed pets are permitted.

Reservations, fees: No reservations; $25 per night, $5 per child. Major credit cards accepted. Open April through October.

Directions: From Ukiah, drive north on U.S. 101 for five miles to the junction with Highway 20. Turn east on Highway 20 and drive 12 miles to 5845 West Highway 20.

Contact: Le Trianon Resort, tel. (707) 275-2262 or fax (707) 275-9416.

33 Mayacmus

   5

This campground is set within the Cow Mountain Recreation Area on the slopes of Cow Mountain, the oft overlooked wild region east of Ukiah. The primitive area is ideal for hiking and horseback riding. In the fall, it is a popular hunting area as well, for the few who know of it. This section of the Rec area is quiet, with hiking on the Mayacmus Trail providing access to Willow Creek, Mill Creek, and several overlooks of Clear Lake to the south. The flora is chaparral and oak/bay grasslands, and the weather is extremely hot in the summer. By the way, off-highway vehicles frequent the southern portion of the Rec area, but not this immediate region.

Location: Near Ukiah; map C1, grid j0.

Campsites, facilities: There are nine tent sites. Picnic tables and fire grills are provided. Vault toilets are available. No drinking water is available. Garbage must be packed out. Leashed pets are permitted.

Reservations, fees: No reservations; no fee. Stay limit is 14 days. Open year-round, weather permitting.

Directions: From U.S. 101 in Ukiah, turn east on Talmage Road and drive 1.5 miles to Eastside Road. Turn right and drive a third of a mile to Mill Creek Road. Turn left and drive three miles. Just beyond Mill Creek County Park, look for the North Cow Mountain sign on the left. Make a left there and drive seven miles to a Y intersection. Bear left and drive one mile to the campground.

Contact: Bureau of Land Management, Ukiah District, tel. (707) 468-4000, or fax (707) 468-4027.

34 Pine Acres Blue Lake Resort

       8

Because of their proximity to Clear Lake, the Blue Lakes are often overlooked. But these lovely lakes offer good fishing for trout, especially in spring and early summer on Upper Blue Lake, and a decent chance the rest of the year. With a speed limit in place, quiet boating is the rule. Swimming is good here. No waterskiing is permitted.

Location: On Upper Blue Lake; map C1, grid j0.

Campsites, facilities: There are 30 RV sites, most with full or partial hookups, 12 tent sites, and 11 rooms available in cabins or hotel. Picnic tables and fire grills are provided. Flush toilets, showers, sanitary disposal station, boat rentals, boat launching, moorings, boat ramp, grocery store, fishing supplies, and lake frontage sites are available. Some facilities are wheelchair accessible. Leashed pets are permitted.

Reservations, fees: Reservations are accepted; $17 to $20 per night. Major credit cards accepted. Open year-round.

Directions: From Ukiah, drive north on U.S. 101 for five miles to the junction with Highway 20. Turn east on Highway 20 and drive about 13 miles to Irvine Street. Turn right on Irvine Street and drive one block to Blue Lakes Road. Turn right and drive two blocks to the resort.

Contact: Pine Acres Blue Lake Resort, tel. (707) 275-2811 or fax (707) 275-9549; website: www.bluelakepineacres.com.

35 Narrows Lodge Resort

       8

This is one of four campgrounds in the immediate vicinity. The Blue Lakes are often overlooked because of their proximity to Clear Lake, but they are a quiet and pretty alternative, with good trout fishing in the spring and early summer, and decent prospects year-round.

Location: On Upper Blue Lake; map C1, grid j0.

Campsites, facilities: There are 28 sites for tents or RVs, with full or partial hookups. Picnic tables are provided. Flush toilets, showers, sanitary disposal station, modem hookups, recreation room, boat rentals, pier, boat ramp, fishing supplies, propane, and ice are available. A motel and cabins are also available. Pets are allowed on leashes, but not in some motel rooms or cabins.

Reservations, fees: Reservations are accepted; $19 to $21 per night. Major credit cards accepted. Open year-round.

Directions: From Ukiah, drive north on U.S. 101 for five miles to the junction with Highway 20. Turn east on Highway 20 and drive about 11.5 miles to Blue Lakes Road. Turn right and drive to 5690 Blue Lakes Road.

Contact: Narrows Lodge Resort, tel. (707) 275-2718.

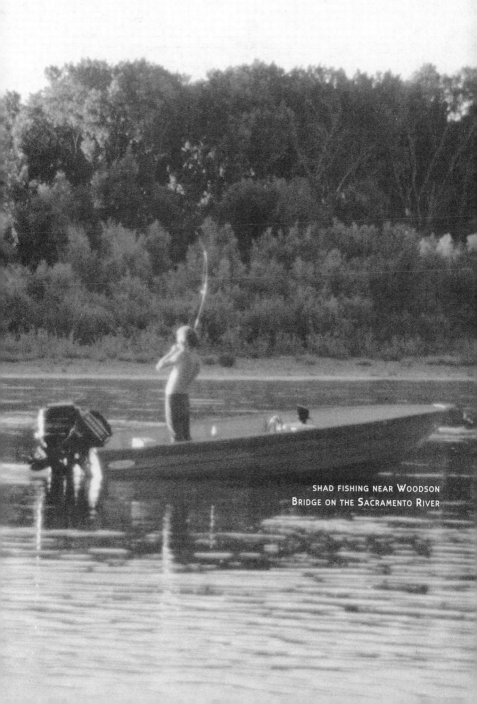

SHAD FISHING NEAR WOODSON
BRIDGE ON THE SACRAMENTO RIVER

MAP C2

TO BEEGUM

⑤
A6
Paynes Creek
Morgan Summit 5,750 feet

a

36
Dales
36
④
TO MINERAL

36

1
TEHAMA WILDLIFE AREA
STATE GAME REFUGE

2
RED BLUFF

b

TO PASKENTA

3
99
Dewitt Peak 2,064 feet
5
6
LASSEN NATIONAL FOREST

A8
Dairyville

Proberta

c

Gerber

Tehama
Los Molinos
ISHI WILDERNESS
Butte Meadows

Henleyville
WOODSON BRIDGE STATE RECREATION AREA

TO FLOURNOY

Richfield

d

A9
Corning
Deer Creek
Promontory Point 3,622 feet
7
Lomo

A9
8
Vina

9
Kirkwood
Forest Ranch
Stirling City

e

266
10 Black Butte Lake
⑤
De Sabla
294

11
12
Nord
BIDWELL MANSION STATE HISTORIC PARK

f

Orland
32
32
Magalia

Hamilton City
Paradise

45
CHICO
13

g

Artois
14

Ordbend
191
70

Durham

TO FRUTO

h

Willows
Lake Oroville
TO BERRY CREEK

162
Glenn

Nelson

15

i

SACRAMENTO NATIONAL WILDLIFE REFUGE
Butte City
99
70
16
162

162
Richvale
162
17

⑤
Afton
Oroville

Princeton

j

DELEVAN NATIONAL WILDLIFE REFUGE
45
Biggs
70
Palermo

18

TO SITES
Maxwell
Gridley
Feather River
Bangor

0 1 2 3 4 5 6 7 8 9

© AVALON TRAVEL PUBLISHING, INC.

CHAPTER C2

1 Bend RV Park and Fishing Resort

      7

Here's a spot for all you RV cruisers to tie up your horse for a while. Big Bend RV Park and Fishing Resort is open year-round and is set beside the Sacramento River. The salmon average 15 to 25 pounds in this area, and anglers typically have the best results from mid-August through October. In recent years, the Bureau of Reclamation has been raising the gates of the Red Bluff Diversion Dam in early September. When that occurs, huge numbers of salmon charge upstream from Red Bluff to Anderson, holding in each deep river hole. Expect very hot weather in July and August.

Location: On the Sacramento River; map C2, grid a2.

Campsites, facilities: There are 18 sites with full or partial hookups for RVs up to 40 feet long. In addition, there is a separate area for tents only. Picnic tables are provided. Drinking water, showers, flush toilets, grocery store, bait and tackle shop, boat ramp, boat dock, coin laundry, and a sanitary disposal station are available. Some facilities are wheelchair accessible. Leashed pets are permitted.

Reservations, fees: Reservations are accepted; $14 to $20 per night. Open year-round.

Directions: From Interstate 5 in Red Bluff, drive four miles north on Interstate 5 to the Jelly's Ferry Road exit. Turn northeast on Jelly's Ferry Road and drive 2.5 miles to the resort at 21795 Bend Ferry Road.

Contact: Bend RV Park and Fishing Resort, tel. (530) 527-6289.

2 O'Nite Park

     4

Easy access from the highway, nearby supermarkets and restaurants, and many side trips make this spot a winner. The park is only one block from the Sacramento River, which gets a big salmon run from mid-August through October. It's about a 45-minute drive east to Lassen Park. The elevation is approximately 300 feet and temperatures are typically in the 100s from mid-June through August.

Location: Near the Sacramento River; map C2, grid b2.

Campsites, facilities: There are 74 RV sites with full

hookups. Picnic tables are provided. Restrooms, showers, swimming pool, modem hookups, a coin laundry, propane gas, and ice are available. Some facilities are wheelchair accessible. Leashed pets are permitted.

Reservations, fees: Reservations are accepted; $11 to $19 per night. Open year-round.

Directions: From Interstate 5 and the junction of Highways 99 and 36 (in Red Bluff), drive west on Highway 36/Antelope Boulevard for one block to Gilmore Road. Turn south on Gilmore Road and drive one block to the camp.

Contact: O'Nite Park, tel. (530) 527-5868.

❸ Lake Red Bluff

6

Lake Red Bluff is created by the Red Bluff Diversion Dam on the Sacramento River, and water-skiing, bird-watching, hiking, and fishing are the most popular activities. It has become a backyard swimming hole for local residents in the summer when the temperatures reach the high 90s and low 100s almost every day. In early September, the Bureau of Reclamation raises the gates at the diversion dam in order to allow migrating salmon an easier course on the upstream journey, and in the process, Lake Red Bluff reverts to its former self as the Sacramento River.

Location: On the Sacramento River near Red Bluff; map C2, grid b2.

Campsites, facilities: There are 30 sites with no hookups for tents or RVs (Sycamore Camp), a group camp (Camp Discovery) with six screened cabins that can accommodate a maximum of 48 campers, and 30 picnic shelters. Drinking water, showers, vault and flush toilets, picnic areas, two boat ramps, and a fish viewing plaza are available. There are two large barbecues, electrical outlets, lockable storage, five large picnic tables, comfort station with showers and sinks, and an amphitheater in the group camp area. Some facilities are wheelchair accessible. Leashed pets are permitted.

Reservations, fees: Reservations are required only for the group camp, tel. (530) 824-5196; $10 per night for individual sites; group camp fee per night is $100 for up to 50 people, $150 for 51 to 75 people, and $200 for 76 to 100 people. Open April through October.

Directions: From Interstate 5 at Red Bluff, turn east on Highway 36 and drive 100 yards to the first turnoff at Sale Lane. Turn right (south) on Sale Lane and drive one-half mile to the campground at the end of the road.

Contact: Mendocino National Forest, Corning Work Station, tel. (530) 824-5196 or fax (530) 824-8004.

❹ Battle Creek

7

This pretty spot offers easy access and streamside camping along Battle Creek. The trout fishing can be good in May, June, and early July, when the creek is stocked by the Department of Fish and Game, which plants 23,000 rainbow trout and 2,000 smaller brook trout. Many people drive right by without knowing there is a stream here and that the fishing can be good. The elevation is 4,800 feet.

Location: On Battle Creek in Lassen National Forest; map C2, grid a9.

Campsites, facilities: There are 12 tent sites and 38 sites for tents or RVs. Picnic tables and fire grills are provided. Drinking water, flush and vault toilets, and a day-use picnic area are available. Supplies can be obtained in the town of Mineral. Leashed pets are permitted.

Reservations, fees: No reservations; $14 per night. Open late April through October, weather permitting.

Directions: From Red Bluff, turn east on Highway 36 and drive 41 miles to the campground (if you reach Mineral, you have gone two miles too far).

Contact: Lassen National Forest, Almanor Ranger District, tel. (530) 258-2141 or fax (530) 258-5194.

5 South Antelope

    6

This primitive campsite is for visitors who want to explore the Ishi Wilderness without an extensive drive (compared to other camps in the wilderness here). The South Fork of Antelope Creek runs west from the camp and provides an off-trail route for the ambitious. For easier hikes, trailheads along Ponderosa Way provide access into the eastern flank of the Ishi. The best nearby trail is the Lower Mill Creek Trail, with the trailhead eight miles south at Black Rock.

Location: Near the eastern edge of the Ishi Wilderness; map C2, grid b7.

Campsites, facilities: There are four sites for tents only. Picnic tables and fire pits are provided. A vault toilet is available. No drinking water is available. All garbage must be packed out. Leashed pets are permitted.

Reservations, fees: No reservations; no fee. Open year-round, weather permitting.

Directions: From Red Bluff, drive east on Highway 36 for about 35 miles to the town of Paynes Creek and Plum Creek Road. Turn right (south) on Plum Creek Road and drive two miles to Ponderosa Way. Turn right (south) and continue for nine miles to the campground on the right. Note: The road is rough and only vehicles with high clearance are advised. No RVs or trailers are allowed.

Contact: Lassen National Forest, Almanor Ranger District, tel. (530) 258-2141 or fax (530) 258-5194. For a map, send $6 to U.S. Forest Service, Attn: Map Sales, P.O. Box 587, Camino, CA 95709; tel. (530) 647-5390, fax (530) 647-5389, or website: www.r5.fs.fed.us/visitorcenter. Major credit cards accepted.

6 Black Rock

    7

This remote, primitive camp is set at the base of the huge, ancient Black Rock, one of the oldest geological points in Lassen National Forest. A bonus is that Mill Creek runs adjacent to the sites, providing a water source. This is the edge of the Ishi Wilderness, where remote hiking in solitude is possible without a wilderness permit and without venturing to high mountain elevations. A trailhead is available right out of the camp. The trail here is routed downstream along Mill Creek, extending five miles into the Ishi Wilderness, downhill all the way.

Location: On the eastern edge of the Ishi Wilderness; map C2, grid b7.

Campsites, facilities: There are five tent sites. Picnic tables and fire pits are provided. A vault toilet is available. No drinking water is available. Mill Creek is adjacent to the camp and is a viable water source through early summer. Leashed pets are permitted.

Reservations, fees: No reservations; $9 per night. Open year-round, weather permitting.

Directions: From Red Bluff, drive east on Highway 36 for about 35 miles to the town of Paynes Creek and Plum Creek Road. Turn right (south) on Plum Creek Road and drive two miles to Ponderosa Way. Turn right (south) and continue for 16 miles to the campground on the right. Note: The road is rough and only vehicles with high clearance are advised. No RVs or trailers are allowed.

Contact: Lassen National Forest, Almanor Ranger District, tel. (530) 258-2141 or fax (530) 258-5194. For a map, send $6 to U.S. Forest Service, Attn: Map Sales, P.O. Box 587, Camino, CA 95709; tel. (530) 647-5390, fax (530) 647-5389, or website: www.r5.fs.fed.us/visitorcenter. Major credit cards accepted.

7 Butte Meadows

    6

On hot summer days, when a cold stream sounds even better than a cold drink, Butte Meadows provides a hideout in the national forest east of Chico. This is a summer camp situated along Butte Creek, which is stocked with 5,000 rainbow trout by the Department of Fish and Game. Nearby

Doe Mill Ridge and the surrounding Lassen National Forest can provide a good side trip adventure. The camp elevation is 4,600 feet.

Location: On Butte Creek in Lassen National Forest; map C2, grid d9.

Campsites, facilities: There are 13 sites for tents or RVs. Fire grills and picnic tables are provided. Drinking water and vault toilets are available. Supplies are available in Butte Meadows. Leashed pets are permitted.

Reservations, fees: No reservations; $10 per night. Open late April through October, weather permitting.

Directions: From Chico, drive about 15 miles north on Highway 32 to the town of Forest Ranch. Continue on Highway 32 for another nine miles. Turn right on Humboldt Road and drive five miles to Butte Meadows.

Contact: Lassen National Forest, Almanor Ranger District, tel. (530) 258-2141 or fax (530) 258-5194.

8 Woodson Bridge State Recreation Area

 7

This campground features direct access to the Sacramento River, and a boat ramp makes it an ideal spot for campers with trailered boats. In June, the nearby Tehama Riffle is one of the best spots on the entire river for shad. By mid-August, salmon start arriving, en route to their spawning grounds.

Location: On the Sacramento River; map C2, grid e3.

Campsites, facilities: There are 37 sites for tents or RVs up to 31 feet long. One group site is available. Picnic tables and fire grills are provided. Drinking water, showers, flush toilets, a camp host, and boat launch (across the street) are available. Some facilities are wheelchair accessible, but the restrooms are not. Leashed pets are permitted.

Reservations, fees: Reserve at (800) 444-PARK (800-444-7275) or website: www.Re-serveAmerica.com; $10 per night, $30 for the group camp. Open year-round.

Directions: From Interstate 5 in Corning, take the South Avenue exit and drive nine miles east to the campground on the left.

Contact: Woodson Bridge State Recreation Area, tel. (530) 839-2112; Bidwell Mansion Visitor Center, tel. (530) 895-6144.

9 Buckhorn

  7

Black Butte Lake is set in the foothills of the north valley at 500 feet. It is one of the 10 best lakes in Northern California for crappie, best in spring. There can also be good fishing for largemouth, smallmouth and spotted bass, channel catfish, bluegill and sunfish. Occasionally, striped bass are even caught. Recreation options include power boating, sailboating, windsurfing, and hiking (an interpretive trail is available below the dam). For dirt bikers, an off-highway motorcycle park is available at the Buckhorn Recreation Area.

Location: On Black Butte Lake; map C2, grid e0.

Campsites, facilities: There are 92 sites for tents or RVs up to 35 feet long. Picnic tables and fire grills are provided. Drinking water, flush toilets, sanitary disposal station, showers, and a playground are available. A boat ramp, propane gas, and a grocery store are within walking distance. Some facilities are wheelchair accessible. Leashed pets are permitted.

Reservations, fees: No reservations; $14 per night. Open year-round.

Directions: From Interstate 5 in Orland, take the Black Butte Lake exit. Drive about 12 miles west on Road 200/Newville Road to Buckhorn Road. Turn left and drive a short distance to the campground on the north shore of the lake.

Contact: U.S. Army Corps of Engineers, Sacramento District, Black Butte Lake, tel. (530) 865-4781, or fax (530) 865-5283.

🔟 Orland Buttes

      7

Black Butte Lake isn't far from Interstate 5, but a lot of campers zoom right by it. The prime time to visit is in late spring and early summer, when the bass and crappie fishing can be quite good. There's a boat launch nearby. Three self-guided nature trails are in the immediate area. See entry for Buckhorn Camp for more information. Note: In late winter and early spring, this area is delightful as spring arrives. But from mid-June through August, expect very hot weather when this part of the state turns into a hellhole for campers.

Location: On Black Butte Lake; map C2, grid e0.

Campsites, facilities: There are four tent sites and 35 sites for tents or RVs up to 35 feet long. Picnic tables and fire grills are provided. Drinking water, restrooms, showers, boat ramp, a public telephone, and a sanitary disposal station are available. Leashed pets are permitted.

Reservations, fees: No reservations; $14 per night. Open April through mid-July.

Directions: From Interstate 5 in Orland, take the Black Butte Lake exit. Drive west on Road 200/Newville Road for eight miles to the east shore of the lake.

Contact: U.S. Army Corps of Engineers, Sacramento District, Black Butte Lake, tel. (530) 865-4781, or fax (530) 865-5283.

🔟🔟 Green Acres RV Park

      3

This is a layover spot near Interstate 5 in the Central Valley, set in the heart of olive and almond country. It's a restful setting, but hot in summer, at times unbearable without air conditioning. Salmon fishing is available on the nearby Sacramento River, best from mid-August through October.

Location: Near Orland; map C2, grid f1.

Campsites, facilities: There are 68 RV sites with partial or full hookups and 24 tent sites. A store, coin laundry, sanitary disposal station, barbecues, recreation room, modem hookups, swimming pool, and ice are available. Leashed pets are permitted.

Reservations, fees: Reservations are recommended; $15 to $19 per night. Open year-round.

Directions: From Orland on Interstate 5, take the Highway 32 exit and drive a half mile west to the campground.

Contact: Green Acres RV Park, 4515 County Road H, Orland, CA 95963; tel. (800) 468-9452 or (530) 865-9188.

🔟🔟 Old Orchard RV Park

     4

Most folks use this as a layover spot while on long trips up or down Interstate 5 in the Central Valley. If you're staying longer than a night, there are two side trips that have appeal for anglers. Nearby Black Butte Lake to the west, with crappie in the early summer, and the Sacramento River to the east, with salmon in the late summer and early fall, can add some spice to your trip. The elevation is 250 feet.

Location: Near Orland; map C2, grid f1.

Campsites, facilities: There are 52 sites for RVs up to 60 feet long, with partial or full hookups and a large separate site for tents only. Showers, sanitary disposal station, propane, coin laundry, modem hookups, and a store are available. Some facilities are wheelchair accessible. Leashed pets are permitted.

Reservations, fees: Reservations are accepted; $12 to $20 per night. Major credit cards accepted.

Directions: From Interstate 5 at Orland, take the Chico/Highway 32 exit, head one block west, and turn right on County Road HH. The park is one block down.

Contact: Old Orchard RV Park, 4490 County Road HH, Orland, CA 95963; tel. (877) 481-9282, tel. or fax (530) 865-5335.

Pine Ridge RV Park

5

This privately operated motor home park offers shaded sites in the pines and is set at 1,700 feet, in the transition zone where the foothill country with oak and bay grasslands starts to give way to pines and other conifers. A good side trip is to the northernmost part of the Lake Oroville State Recreation Area, the Lime Saddle Area. It offers a beach, boat ramp, concessions, and picnic area.

Location: In Paradise; map C2, grid g8.

Campsites, facilities: There are 44 RV sites with partial hookups. Drinking water, flush toilets, showers, modem hookups, and coin laundry are available. Leashed pets are permitted.

Reservations, fees: Reservations are accepted; $17 per night. Open year-round.

Directions: From Highway 191 in Paradise (at the south end of town), turn east on Pearson Road and drive two miles. Turn south on Pentz Road and go one mile to 5084 Pentz Road.

Contact: Pine Ridge RV Park, tel. (530) 877-0677, fax (530) 877-0452.

Quail Trails Village

4

This is a rural motor home campground, set near the west branch of the Feather River, with nearby Lake Oroville as the feature attraction. The Lime Saddle section of the Lake Oroville State Recreation Area is nearby, with a beach, boat launching facilities, and concessions.

Location: Near Paradise; map C2, grid g8.

Campsites, facilities: There are 20 RV sites with full hookups (all are drive-through) and five tent sites. Picnic tables are provided. Restrooms, hot showers, and coin laundry are available. Some facilities are wheelchair accessible. Leashed pets are permitted.

Reservations, fees: Reservations are accepted; $10.60 to $15.90 per night. Open year-round.

Directions: From Highway 99 in Chico, take the Paradise turnoff (Skyway). Turn right at the first signal in Paradise (Pearson Road). Go about 4.5 miles all the way to the end of the road and turn right on Pentz Magalia Highway. Drive 1.5 miles south to the park at 5110 Pentz Road.

Contact: Quail Trails Village, tel. (530) 877-6581 or fax (530) 876-0516.

Lake Oroville Boat-In and Floating Camps

10

It doesn't get any stranger than this, and for those who have tried, it doesn't get any better. We're talking about the double-decker floating camps at Lake Oroville, along with the great boat-in sites. The floating camps look like giant patio boats. They sleep 15 people and they include picnic table, sink, food locker, life jackets, garbage can, vault toilet, propane barbecue, and water (not suitable for drinking), and for $42 a night, it might be the best family camping deal in the state. There are also a series of dispersed boat-in campsites around the lake, which are particularly excellent in the spring and early summer, when the water level at the lake is high. In late summer, when the lake level drops, it can be a fair hike up the bank to the campsites, and in addition, if the water drops quickly, your boat can be left sitting on the bank; it can be quite an effort to get it back in the water. Oroville is an outstanding lake for water sports, with warm water and plenty of room, and also with excellent bass fishing, especially in the spring.

Location: On Lake Oroville; map C2, grid i8.

Campsites, facilities: There are dispersed boat-in sites, one group boat-in site (Bloomer) for up to 75 people, and 10 boat-in Floating Camps. Picnic tables, food lockers, and fire grills are provided. Vault toilets are available. No drinking water is provided. Leashed pets are permitted, except on trails or beaches; pets must be enclosed at night.

Reservations, fees: Reservations available for Floating Camps only, at tel. (800) 444-PARK (800-444-7275) or website: www.cal-parks.ca.gov; $42 per night. Individual boat-in sites are $7 per night. Group boat-in sites are $30 per night. Open year-round.

Directions: From Oroville, drive seven miles east on Highway 162 to Canyon Drive. Turn left and drive two miles to Oroville Dam. Turn left and drive over the dam to the spillway parking lot at the end of the road. Register at the entrance station. Boats can be launched from this area.

Contact: Lake Oroville State Recreation Area, tel. (530) 538-2200; Lake Oroville Visitor Center, (530) 538-2219.

16 Bidwell Canyon

 7

Bidwell Canyon is a major destination at giant Lake Oroville as the campground is near a major marina and boat ramp. It is set along the southern shore of the lake, on a point directly adjacent to the massive Oroville Dam to the west. Many campers use this spot for boating headquarters. It is popular for water-skiing, as the water is warm enough in the summer for all water sports, and there is enough room for both fishermen and water-skiers. Recent habitat work has given the bass fishing a big help, with 30- and 40-fish days possible in the spring, casting plastic worms in the backs of coves where there is floating wood debris. What a lake—there are even floating toilets here (imagine that!). It is very hot in midsummer.

Location: On Lake Oroville; map C2, grid i9.

Campsites, facilities: There are 75 sites for tents or RVs up to 40 feet long and trailers up to 31 feet long (including boat trailers), all with full hookups. Picnic tables and fire grills are provided. Drinking water, flush toilets, and showers are available. A grocery store and propane gas are available within two miles. Leashed pets are permitted, except on trails or beaches; pets must be enclosed at night.

Reservations, fees: Reserve at (800) 444-PARK (800-444-7275) or website: www.ReserveAmerica.com; $16 per night. Open year-round.

Directions: From Oroville, drive eight miles east on Highway 162. Turn north on Kelly Ridge Road and drive 1.5 miles to Arroyo Drive. Turn right and drive one-quarter mile to the campground.

Contact: Lake Oroville State Recreation Area, tel. (530) 538-2200; Lake Oroville Visitor Center, (530) 538-2219.

17 Loafer Creek Group Camps & Equestrian Camps

 7

These are three different campground areas that are linked, designed for individual use, groups, and equestrians, respectively. The camps are just across the water at Lake Oroville from Bidwell Canyon, but campers come here for more spacious sites. It's also a primary option for campers with boats, with the Loafer Creek boat ramp one mile away. So hey, this spot is no secret. Bonus here includes an extensive equestrian trail system right out of camp.

Location: On Lake Oroville; map C2, grid i9.

Campsites, facilities: There are 137 sites for tents and RVs up to 40 feet long and trailers to 31 feet long (including boat trailers), 15 equestrian sites with a two-horse limit per site. A sanitary disposal station, picnic tables, and fire grills are provided. Drinking water, flush toilets, and showers are available for campers. A tethering and feeding station is near each site for horses, and a horse washing station is provided. Some facilities are wheelchair accessible. Propane, groceries, and a boat ramp, are available nearby. Leashed pets are permitted, but not on trails or beaches.

Reservations, fees: Reserve Reserve at (800) 444-PARK (800-444-7275) or website: www. ReserveAmerica.com; $10 per night for single sites, $20 per night for group sites, $16 per night for equestrian sites. Open year-round.

Directions: From Oroville, drive east on Highway 162 about two miles past the Kelly Ridge Road turnoff to the signed campground entrance on the left.

Contact: Lake Oroville State Recreation Area, tel. (530) 538-2200; Lake Oroville Visitor Center, (530) 538-2219.

18 Dingerville USA

 3

You're right, they thought of this name all by themselves, needed no help. It is an RV park set in the Oroville foothill country—hot, dry, and sticky in the summer, but with a variety of side trips available nearby. It is adjacent to a wildlife area and the Feather River and within short range of Lake Oroville and the Thermalito Afterbay for boating, water sports, and fishing. In the fall, the Duck Club in nearby Richvale is one of the few privately owned properties that offers duck hunting on a single-day basis. The RV park is a clean, quiet campground with easy access from the highway.

Location: Near Oroville; map C2, grid j6.

Campsites, facilities: There are 29 sites for RVs with full hookups. Picnic tables are provided. Restrooms, showers, swimming pool, coin laundry, horseshoe pit, and a nine-hole executive golf course are available. Facilities are wheelchair accessible. Leashed pets are permitted.

Reservations, fees: Reservations are recommended; $20 per night. Major credit cards accepted. Open year-round.

Directions: From Oroville and north, drive south on Highway 70. Turn right at the second Pacific Heights Road turnoff and continue on Pacific Heights Road to the campground. From Highway 70 and south, turn left at Palermo-Welsh Road and continue north on Pacific Heights Road for a half mile to camp.

Contact: Dingerville USA, 5813 Pacific Heights Road, Oroville, CA 95965; tel. (530) 533-9343.

CHAPTER C3

DEER CREEK
AT ELAM CAMPGROUND

MAP C3

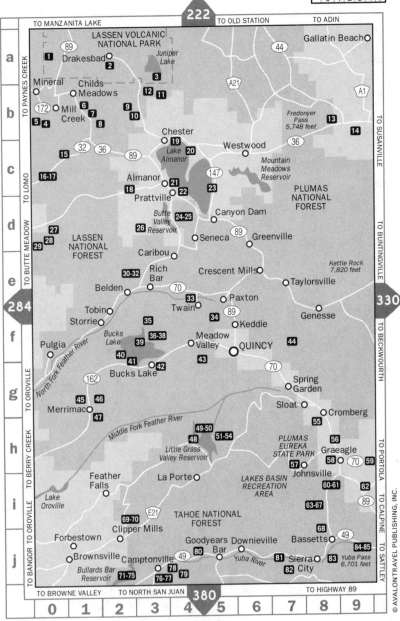

TO MANZANITA LAKE   **222**   TO OLD STATION   TO ADIN

LASSEN VOLCANIC
NATIONAL PARK

Gallatin Beach

89   Drakesbad   Juniper Lake   44

Mineral   Childs Meadows   A21   A1

172   Mill Creek   Fredonyer Pass 5,748 feet

Chester   Westwood   36

Lake Almanor   Mountain Meadows Reservoir

Almanor   147   PLUMAS NATIONAL FOREST

Prattville

Butte Valley Reservoir   Canyon Dam

LASSEN NATIONAL FOREST   Seneca   89   Greenville

Caribou   Kettle Rock 7,820 feet

Rich Bar   Crescent Mills   Taylorsville

Belden   70

Tobin   Paxton   Genesee

Storrie   Twain   89   Keddie

Bucks Lake   Meadow Valley   QUINCY

North Fork Feather River   Bucks Lake   70   Spring Garden

Pulgia   162   Sloat   Cromberg

Merrimac   Middle Fork Feather River   PLUMAS EUREKA STATE PARK   Graeagle   70

Little Grass Valley Reservoir   Johnsville

Feather Falls   La Porte   LAKES BASIN RECREATION AREA

Lake Oroville   E21   TAHOE NATIONAL FOREST   Bassetts   49

Forbestown   Clipper Mills   Goodyears Bar   Downieville   Yuba Pass 6,701 feet

Brownsville   Camptonville   49   Yuba River   Sierra City

Bullards Bar Reservoir

TO BROWNE VALLEY   TO NORTH SAN JUAN   **380**   TO HIGHWAY 89

© AVALON TRAVEL PUBLISHING, INC.

CHAPTER C3

(CONTINUED ON NEXT PAGE)

1 Southwest Walk-In

 8

Just taking the short walk required to reach this camp will launch you into an orbit beyond most of the highway cruisers visiting Lassen. In addition, the nearby trail to Bumpass Hell will put you into a different universe. The trail is about five miles north of the campground on the Lassen Park Highway on the right side of the road. The route will take you past steam vents and boiling mud pots, all set in prehistoric-looking volcanic rock. The elevation at the campground is 6,700 feet.
Location: In Lassen Volcanic National Park; map C3, grid a0.
Campsites, facilities: There are 21 walk-in tent sites. Pic-

nic tables and fire pits are provided. Drinking water and flush toilets are available in summer. Ranger-led programs are available in summer. Leashed pets are permitted.

Reservations, fees: No reservations; $12 per night, $10 per vehicle park entrance fee. Open year-round, weather permitting. Major credit cards accepted.

Directions: From Red Bluff, take Highway 36 east for 48 miles to the junction with Highway 89. Turn left on Highway 89 (becomes Lassen Park Highway) and drive to the park's entrance. Just after passing through the park entrance gate, look for the camp parking area on the right side of the road.

Contact: Lassen Volcanic National Park, tel. (530) 595-4444 or fax (530) 595-3262.

2 Warner Valley

 10

Lassen is one of the great national parks of the West, yet it gets surprisingly little use compared to Yosemite, Sequoia, and Kings Canyon National Parks. This camp gets overlooked because of its remote access out of Chester. The camp is set along Hot Springs Creek at 5,650 feet. The best hike here is the 2.5-mile walk out to the unique Devil's Kitchen Geothermal Area. Another option here is a another 2.5-mile hike, this one with an 800-foot climb to Drake Lake. It's also a good horseback riding area. The Drakesbad Resort, where reservations are about as difficult to get as finding Bigfoot, is near the campground.

Location: On Hot Springs Creek in Lassen Volcanic National Park; map C3, grid a2.

Campsites, facilities: There are 18 tent or RV sites. Trailers are not recommended due to road conditions. Picnic tables, food lockers, and fire rings are provided. Drinking water and vault toilets are available. Leashed pets are permitted.

Reservations, fees: No reservations; $12 per night, $10 per vehicle park entrance fee. Major credit cards accepted. Open June to early October, weather permitting.

Directions: From Red Bluff, take Highway 36 east for 44 miles to the junction with Highway 89 (do not turn left, or north, on Highway 89 to Lassen Volcanic National Park entrance, as signed). Continue east on Highway 36/89 to Chester. In Chester turn left (north) on Feather River Drive (Warner Valley Road). Drive three-quarters mile to County Road 312. Bear left and drive six miles to Warner Valley Road. Turn right and drive 11 miles to the campground on the right. Note: The last 3.5 miles is unpaved and there is one steep hill that can be difficult to climb if towing a trailer).

Contact: Lassen Volcanic National Park, tel. (530) 595-4444 or fax (530) 595-3262.

3 Juniper Lake

   10

This pretty spot is on the eastern shore of Juniper Lake, at an elevation of 6,792 feet. It is far distant from the busy Lassen Park Highway (Highway 89) corridor that is routed through central Lassen Volcanic National Park. From the north end of the lake, a great side trip is to make the half-mile, 400-foot climb to Inspiration Point, which provides a panoramic view of the park's backcountry. Since no piped water is provided, it is critical to bring a water purification pump or plenty of bottled water.

Location: In Lassen Volcanic National Park; map C3, grid a3.

Campsites, facilities: There are 18 sites for tents. Fire pits and food lockers are provided. Vault toilets are available. Drinking water is not available. Leashed pets are permitted.

Reservations, fees: No reservations; $10 per night, $10 per vehicle park entrance fee. Major credit cards accepted. Open late June to early October.

Directions: From Red Bluff, take Highway 36 east for 44 miles to the junction with Highway 89 (do not turn left, or north, on Highway 89 to Lassen Volcanic National Park entrance, as signed). Continue east on Highway 36/89 to Chester. In Chester, turn left (north) on Feather River Drive and drive three-quarters mile to the Y and the junction for County Road 318. Bear right (marked for Juniper Lake) on County Road 318 and drive 11 miles to the campground on the right, set along the east side of the lake. Note: This is a very rough dirt road; RVs and trailers are not recommended.

Contact: Lassen Volcanic National Park, tel. (530) 595-4444 or fax (530) 595-3262.

4 Mill Creek Resort

 7

This is a great spot, surrounded by Lassen National Forest and within close range of the southern Highway 89 entrance to Lassen Volcanic National Park. It is set at 4,800 feet along oft-bypassed Highway 172. A highlight here is Mill Creek (to reach it, turn south on the Forest Service road in town and drive to a parking area at the end of the road along the stream), where there is a great easy walk along the stream and fair trout fishing.

Location: On Mill Creek near Lassen National Forest; map C3, grid b0.

Campsites, facilities: There are 16 sites for tents or RVs up to 22 feet long, eight with full hookups. Nine one- and two-bedroom cabins are also available. Picnic tables and fire rings are provided. Drinking water and vault toilets are available. Showers, coin laundry, small grocery store, and a coffee shop are also available. Some facilities are wheelchair accessible. Leashed pets are permitted.

Reservations, fees: Reservations are accepted; $10 per night; cabins are $50 to $80 per night. Campsites are open May through October; cabins are available year-round.

Directions: From Red Bluff, drive 43 miles east on Highway 36 to the town of Mineral and the junction with Highway 172. Turn right and drive six miles to the town of Mill Creek. In Mill Creek, look for the sign for Mill Creek Resort on the right side of the road.

Contact: Mill Creek Resort, tel. (530) 595-4449.

5 Hole-In-the-Ground

     8

This is one of two campgrounds set along Mill Creek at 4,300 feet. Take your pick. The highlight here is a trail that follows along Mill Creek for many miles, which provides good fishing access. The stream is stocked with 2,000 rainbow trout each summer, joining residents and holdovers. Another option is to drive two more miles to the end of the Forest Service road, where there is a parking area for a trail that is routed downstream along Mill Creek and into a state game refuge. To keep things easy, obtain a map of Lassen National Forest that details the recreational opportunities.

Location: On Mill Creek in Lassen National Forest; map C3, grid b0.

Campsites, facilities: There are four tent sites and nine sites for tents or RVs. Picnic tables and fire grills are provided. Drinking water and vault toilets are available. Supplies are available in Mineral. Leashed pets are permitted.

Reservations, fees: No reservations; $11 per night. Open late April through October, weather permitting.

Directions: From Red Bluff, drive 43 miles east on Highway 36 to the town of Mineral and the junction with Highway 172. Turn right on Highway 172 and drive six miles to the town

of Mill Creek. In Mill Creek, turn south onto a Forest Service road (signed) and drive five miles to the campground access road. Turn left and drive a quarter mile to the camp.

Contact: Lassen National Forest, Almanor Ranger District, tel. (530) 258-2141, or fax (530) 258-5194.

6 Gurnsey Creek Group Camp

     7

This group camp is an ideal spot for a Scout troop. For more information, see the entry for the adjacent Gurnsey Creek.

Location: In Lassen National Forest; map C3, grid b1.

Campsites, facilities: This group campground can accommodate up to 100 people, with 20 sites for tents or RVs. Picnic tables and fire grills are provided. Drinking water and vault toilets are available. A large community fireplace is centrally located for group use. Supplies are available in Mineral or Chester. Leashed pets are permitted.

Reservations, fees: Reservations are required; $110 per night with a 50 percent deposit. Reserve at tel. (877) 444-6777 ($8.65 reservation fee) or website: www.reserveusa.com. The deposit is refundable if cancellation notice is given 10 days prior to the reservation date. Open May through October, weather permitting.

Directions: From Red Bluff, drive east on Highway 36 for 55 miles (five miles east of Childs Meadow). Turn left at the campground entrance road and drive a short distance to the campground.

Contact: Lassen National Forest, Almanor Ranger District, tel. (530) 258-2141 or fax (530) 258-5194.

7 Gurnsey Creek

     7

This camp is set at 5,000 feet in Lassen National Forest, with extremely easy access off Highway 36. The camp is on the headwaters of little Gurnsey Creek, a highlight of the surrounding Lost Creek Plateau. Gurnsey Creek runs downstream and pours into Deer Creek, a good trout stream with access along narrow, winding Highway 32 to the nearby south.

Location: In Lassen National Forest; map C3, grid b1.

Campsites, facilities: There are 30 sites for tents or RVs. Picnic tables and fire grills are provided. Drinking water and vault toilets are available. Supplies are available in Mineral. Leashed pets are permitted.

Reservations, fees: No reservations; $11 per night. Open May through October, weather permitting.

Directions: From Red Bluff, drive east on Highway 36 for 55 miles (five miles east of Childs Meadow). Turn left at the campground entrance road and drive a short distance to the campground.

Contact: Lassen National Forest, Almanor Ranger District, tel. (530) 258-2141 or fax (530) 258-5194.

8 Willow Springs

 6

This is a primitive, undeveloped camp set on the southwest flank of North Stover Mountain (6,035 feet), used primarily by hunters during the fall deer season and ignored the rest of the time. A network of Forest Service roads in the area provides vehicle access. Though there is no drinking water available, Lost Creek Spring to the east of camp and Lost Creek are viable water sources during wet years. The headwaters of Lost Creek run by the camp, flowing downstream into nearby Deer Creek to the south.

Location: Near Lost Creek Spring in Lassen National Forest; map C3, grid b1.

Campsites, facilities: There are 15 primitive sites for tents. Picnic tables and fire grills are provided. A vault toilet is available. Garbage must be packed out. No drinking water is available.

Reservations, fees: No reservations; $9 per night. Open late May through October, weather permitting.

Directions: From Red Bluff, drive east on Highway 36 for about 55 miles. About two miles past Childs Meadows parking area, turn left on Wilson Lake Road/Forest Road 29N19 and drive 1.5 miles to Forest Road 29N19. Turn right on Forest Road 29N19 and drive about 3.5 miles to the campground on the left side of the road.

Contact: Lassen National Forest, Almanor Ranger District, tel. (530) 258-2141 or fax (530) 258-5194. For a map, send $6 to U.S. Forest Service, Attn: Map Sales, P.O. Box 587, Camino, CA 95709; tel. (530) 647-5390, fax (530) 647-5389, or website: www.r5.fs.fed.us/visitorcenter. Major credit cards accepted.

9 Domingo Springs

 7

This camp is named after a spring adjacent to the site. It is a small fountain that pours into the headwaters of the North Fork Feather River, a good trout stream. The Pacific Crest Trail is routed from this camp north for four miles to Little Willow Lake and the southern border of Lassen Volcanic National Park. The elevation is 5,200 feet.

Location: In Lassen National Forest; map C3, grid b2.

Campsites, facilities: There are nine sites for tents and nine sites for tents or RVs. Picnic tables and fire grills are provided. Drinking water and vault toilets are available. Leashed pets are permitted.

Reservations, fees: No reservations; $11 per night. Open late May through October, weather permitting.

Directions: From Red Bluff, take Highway 36 east to Chester. In Chester, turn left on Feather River Drive and drive three-quarters mile to County Road 312. Bear left and drive five miles to the Y with County Road 311 and County Road 312. Bear left on County Road 311 and drive two miles to the campground entrance road on the left.

Contact: Lassen National Forest, Almanor Ranger District, tel. (530) 258-2141 or fax (530) 258-5194.

High Bridge

 7

This camp is set at an elevation of 5,200 feet, near where the South Cascades meets the North Sierra, and is ideal for many people. It is just far enough off pavement that it is missed by thousands of campers wishing for such a spot. The payoff includes a pretty, adjacent trout stream, the headwaters of the North Fork Feather. Trout fishing is often good here, including some rare large brown trout, a surprise considering the relatively small size of the stream. Nearby access to the Warner Valley/Drakesbad entrance of Lassen Volcanic National Park provides a must-do side trip. The area is wooded and the road dusty.

Location: On the North Fork of the Feather River in Lassen National Forest; map C3, grid b2.

Campsites, facilities: There are 12 sites for tents or RVs. Picnic tables and fire grills are provided. Drinking water and vault toilets are available. Groceries and propane gas are available nearby. Leashed pets are permitted.

Reservations, fees: No reservations; $11 per night. Open late May through October, weather permitting.

Directions: From Red Bluff, take Highway 36 east to Chester. In Chester, turn left on Feather River Drive and drive three-quarters mile to County Road 312. Bear left and drive five miles to the campground entrance road on the left.

Contact: Lassen National Forest, Almanor Ranger District, tel. (530) 258-2141 or fax (530) 258-5194.

Benner Creek

 7

Benner Creek is just outside the remote eastern border of Lassen Volcanic National Park and its stellar but primitive Juniper Lake Campground. If that national park camp is full, this provides a nearby option. For drivers of RVs, this camp is preferable to navigating the rough road to Juniper Lake. In the fall, the camp gets occasional use by deer hunters.

Location: On Benner Creek in Lassen National Forest; map C3, grid b3.

Campsites, facilities: There are nine sites for tents or RVs up to 20 feet long. Picnic tables and fire grills are provided. Vault toilets are available. No drinking water is available. Leashed pets are permitted.

Reservations, fees: No reservations; $9 per night.

Directions: In Chester on Highway 36, turn west on Feather River Drive. Drive one mile to County Road 318/Juniper Lake Road (at the fork). Bear right on Juniper Lake Road and drive seven miles to Benner Creek Campground on the right.

Contact: Lassen National Forest, Almanor Ranger District, tel. (530) 258-2141 or fax (530) 258-5194.

Warner Creek

 6

Some people find this camp by accident. They are driving to the Warner/Drakesbad entrance of Lassen Volcanic National Park and discover the small, primitive camp on the way in, always an option during crowded weekends. It is set at 5,000 feet in elevation along little Warner Creek, a tributary to the North Fork Feather River. Warner Valley is two miles to the north, and the entrance to Lassen Park is another six miles.

Location: In Lassen National Forest; map C3, grid b3.

Campsites, facilities: There are 13 sites for tents or RVs up to 22 feet long. Picnic tables and fire grills are provided. Vault toilets are available. No drinking water is available. Leashed pets are permitted.

Reservations, fees: No reservations; $9 per night. Open late May through October, weather permitting.

Directions: From Red Bluff, take Highway 36 east to Chester. In Chester, turn left on Feather River Drive and drive three-quarters mile to County Road 312. Bear left and drive 5.5 miles to a fork. Bear right (still on County Road 312) and drive one mile to the campground on the right.

Contact: Lassen National Forest, Almanor Ranger District, tel. (530) 258-2141 or tel. fax (530) 258-5194

Goumaz

 7

This camp is set beside the Susan River, adjacent to the historic Bizz Johnson Trail, a former route for a rail line that has been converted to a 25-mile trail. The trail runs from Susanville to Westwood, but this section provides access to many of its prettiest and most remote stretches as it runs in a half circle around Pegleg Mountain (7,112 feet) to the east. It is an outstanding route for biking, hiking, and horseback riding in the summer and cross-country skiing in the winter.

Location: On the Susan River in Lassen National Forest; map C3, grid b8.

Campsites, facilities: There are five sites for tents or RVs up to 30 feet long. Picnic tables and fire grills are provided. Vault toilets are available. No drinking water is available. Leashed pets are permitted.

Reservations, fees: No reservations; $6 per night. Open May through September.

Directions: From Red Bluff, drive east on Highway 36 past Lake Almanor to the junction with Highway 44. Turn west on Highway 44 and drive six miles (one mile past the Worley Ranch) to Goumaz Road/Forest Road 30N08. Turn left on Goumaz Road and drive about five miles to the campground entrance road on the right.

Contact: Lassen National Forest, Eagle Lake Ranger District, tel. (530) 257-4188 or fax (530) 252-5803.

Roxie Peconom Walk-In

 5

This small camp is set next to Willard Creek, a seasonal stream in eastern Lassen National Forest. It's shaded and quiet. The best nearby recreation is the Bizz Johnson Trail, with a trailhead on Highway 44 (two miles east) at a parking area on the left side of the highway. This is an outstanding biking and hiking route. The camp requires only about a 100-foot walk.

Location: In Lassen National Forest; map C3, grid b9.

Campsites, facilities: There are 10 tent sites. Picnic tables and fire rings are provided. Drinking water and flush toilets are available. Leashed pets are permitted.

Reservations, fees: No reservations; no fee. Open May through September.

Directions: From Red Bluff, drive east on Highway 36 past Lake Almanor and continue past Fredonyer Pass for three miles to Forest Road 29N03 on the right. Turn right and drive two miles to the campground parking area on the left. Park and walk 100 feet to the campground.

Contact: Lassen National Forest, Eagle Lake Ranger District, tel. (530) 257-4188 or fax (530) 252-5803.

Elam

 7

Of the campgrounds set on Deer Creek along Highway 32, Elam gets the most use. It is the first stopping point visitors arrive at while heading west on narrow, curvy Highway 32, and it has an excellent day-use picnic area available. The stream here is stocked with rainbow trout in late spring and early summer, with good access for fishing. It is a pretty area, set where Elam Creek enters Deer Creek. A Forest Service Information Center is nearby. If the camp has too many people to suit your style, consider other more distant and primitive camps downstream on Deer Creek. The elevation here is 4,600 feet.

Location: On Deer Creek in Lassen National Forest; map C3, grid c0.

Campsites, facilities: There are 15 sites for tents or RVs. Picnic tables and fire grills are provided. Drinking water and vault toilets are available. Leashed pets are permitted.

Reservations, fees: No reservations; $12 per night. Open mid-April through October, weather permitting.

Directions: From Red Bluff, take Highway 36 east for 44 miles to the junction with Highway 89. Continue east on Highway 36/89 to the junction with Highway 32. Turn south on Highway 32 and drive three miles to the campground on the right side of the road. Trailers are not recommended.

Contact: Lassen National Forest, Almanor Ranger District, tel. (530) 258-2141 or fax (530) 258-5194.

16 Alder

    7

Deer Creek is a great little trout stream that runs along Highway 32. Alder is one of four camps set along Highway 32 with streamside access; this one is at 3,900 feet elevation, set near where both Alder Creek and Round Valley Creek pour into Deer Creek. The stream's best stretch of trout water is from here on upstream to Elam.

Location: On Deer Creek in Lassen National Forest; map C3, grid c0.

Campsites, facilities: There are five tent sites. Picnic tables and fire grills are provided. Vault toilets are available. No drinking water is available. Leashed pets are permitted.

Reservations, fees: No reservations; $9 per night. Open late March through October, weather permitting.

Directions: From Red Bluff, take Highway 36 east for 44 miles to the junction with Highway 89. Continue east on Highway 36/89 to the junction with Highway 32. Turn south on Highway 32 and drive eight miles to the campground on the right side of the road. Trailers are not recommended.

Contact: Lassen National Forest, Almanor Ranger District, tel. (530) 258-2141 or fax (530) 258-5194.

17 Potato Patch

    7

You get good hiking and fishing at this camp. It is set beside Deer Creek, 3,400 feet elevation, with good access for trout fishing, best in May and June. In early summer, a side trip adventure is heading two miles up Highway 32 to find Deer Creek Falls.

Location: On Deer Creek in Lassen National Forest; map C3, grid c0.

Campsites, facilities: There are 20 sites for tents and 12 sites for tents or RVs. Picnic tables and fire grills are provided. Drinking water and vault toilets are available. Leashed pets are permitted.

Reservations, fees: No reservations; $11 per night. Open April through October, weather permitting.

Directions: From Red Bluff, take Highway 36 east for 44 miles to the junction with Highway 89. Continue east on Highway 36/89 to the junction with Highway 32. Turn south on Highway 32 and drive 11 miles to the campground on the right side of the road. Trailers are not recommended.

Contact: Lassen National Forest, Almanor Ranger District, tel. (530) 258-2141 or fax (530) 258-5194.

18 Soldier Creek

    7

This camp is little known and primitive and is used primarily by fishermen and hunters in season. The campsites here are shaded, set in forest on the edge of meadows, and near a stream. The latter is Soldier Creek, which is stocked with trout by the Department of Fish and Game. In the fall, early storms can drive deer through this area on their annual migration to their wintering habitat in the valley, making this a decent base camp for hunters.

However, no early storms often mean no deer.

Location: On Soldier Creek in Lassen National Forest; map C3, grid c2.

Campsites, facilities: There are 15 sites for tents or RVs. Picnic tables and fire rings are provided. Vault toilets are available. No drinking water is available. Leashed pets are permitted.

Reservations, fees: No reservations; $8 per night. Open late May through October, weather permitting.

Directions: From Chester, drive south on Highway 89 to Humboldt Road. Turn right on Humboldt Road and drive one mile, bear right at the fork, and continue five more miles to the intersection at Fanani Meadows. Turn right and drive one mile to the campground on the left.

Contact: Lassen National Forest, Almanor Ranger District, tel. (530) 258-2141 or fax (530) 258-5194.

19 Northshore Campground

 7

This large, privately developed park on the northern shoreline of beautiful Lake Almanor is primarily for RVs.

Location: On Lake Almanor; map C3, grid c4.

Campsites, facilities: There are 94 sites with partial hookups for RVs up to 40 feet long, and 34 tent sites. Picnic tables and fire rings are provided. Drinking water, showers, flush toilets, a boat ramp, and a dock are available. Leashed pets are permitted.

Reservations, fees: Reservations are accepted; $17 to $20 per night. Major credit cards accepted. Open April through October.

Directions: From Red Bluff, take Highway 36 east for 44 miles to the junction with Highway 89. Drive east on Highway 36/89; the camp is two miles past Chester.

Contact: Northshore Campground, tel. (530) 258-3376 or fax (530) 258-2838.

20 Last Chance Creek

 7

This secluded camp is set at 4,500 feet, adjacent to where Last Chance Creek empties into the north end of Lake Almanor. It is an unpublicized PG&E facility that is known primarily by locals and gets missed almost every time by out-of-towners. The adjacent lake area is a breeding ground in the spring for white pelicans, and the beauty of these birds in large flocks can be extraordinary.

Location: Near Lake Almanor; map C3, grid c4.

Campsites, facilities: There are 12 sites for tents or RVs up to 30 feet long, and 13 group campsites. Picnic tables and fire grills are provided. Drinking water and vault toilets are available. Leashed pets are permitted.

Reservations, fees: Reservations are required for the group camp, phone (916) 386-5164; $13 per night for individual sites, $20 for group sites, $1 per dog per night. Group sites require a two-night minimum stay, and a three-night stay on holidays. Open mid-May through September, weather permitting.

Directions: From Red Bluff, take Highway 36 east to Chester and continue for two miles over the causeway at the north end of Lake Almanor. About a quarter mile after crossing the causeway, turn left and drive 2.1 miles to the campground.

Contact: PG&E Building and Land Services, tel. (916) 386-5164.

21 Lake Almanor Campground

 7

What you get here is a series of four campgrounds along the southwest shore of Lake Almanor provided by PG&E as mitigation for their hydroelectric activities on the Feather River system. The camps are set upstream from the dam, with boat ramps available on each side of the dam. This is a pretty spot, with giant Almanor ringed by lodgepole pine and firs. The lake is usually full, or close to it, well into summer, with Mount Lassen set in the distance to the north—bring your camera. Though it can take a day or two to locate the fish, once that effort is made, fishing is good for large trout and salmon in the spring and fall, and for smallmouth bass in the summer.

Location: On Lake Almanor; map C3, grid c4.

Campsites, facilities: There are 131 sites for tents or RVs up to 30 feet long. Picnic tables and fire grills are provided. Drinking water, vault toilets, and a sanitary disposal station are available. Leashed pets are permitted.

Reservations, fees: No reservations; $13 per night, $3 per night per extra vehicle, $7 per night per extra RV, $1 pet fee. Open May through September.

Directions: From Red Bluff, take Highway 36 east for 44 miles to the junction with Highway 89. Continue east on Highway 36/89 to Lake Almanor and the next junction with Highway 89 (two miles before reaching Chester). Turn right on Highway 89 and drive eight miles to the southwest end of Lake Almanor. Turn left at your choice of four campground entrances.

Contact: PG&E Building and Land Services, tel. (916) 386-5164.

22 Almanor

    8

This is one of Lake Almanor's best-known and most popular Forest Service campgrounds. It is set along the western shore of beautiful Almanor, 4,519 feet elevation, directly across from the famous Almanor Peninsula. There is an excellent view of Mount Lassen to the north, along with gorgeous sunrises. A 10-mile recreation trail runs right through the campground and is excellent for biking or hiking. This section of the lake provides good fishing for smallmouth bass in the summer, best using live crickets for bait.

Location: On Lake Almanor in Lassen National Forest; map C3, grid c4.

Campsites, facilities: There are 15 sites for tents and 86 sites for tents or RVs. Picnic tables and fire grills are provided. Drinking water and vault toilets are available. A boat ramp and beach area is available nearby. Some facilities are wheelchair accessible. Leashed pets are permitted.

Reservations, fees: Reserve at tel. (877) 444-6777 ($8.65 reservation fee) or website: www.reserveusa.com, $15 per night. Open May through October, weather permitting.

Directions: From Red Bluff, take Highway 36 east for 44 miles to the junction with Highway 89. Continue east on Highway 36/89 to Lake Almanor and the next junction with Highway 89 (two miles before reaching Chester). Turn right on Highway 89 and drive six miles to County Road 310. Turn left on County Road 310 and drive one mile to the campground.

Contact: Lassen National Forest, Almanor Ranger District, tel. (530) 258-2141 or fax (530) 258-5194.

23 Lassen View Resort

   8

This is one of the few classic fishing camps in California, designed from start to finish with fishing in mind. Its location is near one of the best fishing spots on the entire lake, Big Springs, at the mouth of the Hamilton Branch. After launching a boat or renting one at Lassen View, Big Springs is just a five-minute ride, "right around the corner," as they say here. This is where salmon congregate in the spring, and big brown and rainbow trout show up in the fall to feed on the lake's huge supply of pond smelt. The camp is rustic but friendly, and the folks here can help put you on to the fish. Lake Almanor is a big, beautiful lake set at 4,600 feet, ringed by conifers, and kept full most of the year.

Location: At Lake Almanor east of Red Bluff; map C3, grid c5.

Campsites, facilities: There are 13 cabins and 59 tent and RV sites with full or partial hookups. Picnic tables and fire rings are provided. Drinking water and flush toilets are available. A small store, fishing equipment, boat rentals, boat dock, and a fish-cleaning facility are also available. A fishing guide can be hired through the store.

Reservations, fees: Reservations are recommended; $17 to $19 per night, $3 per extra vehicle, $3 per person per night for more than two people; cabins are $60 to $95. Major credit cards accepted. Open May through October.

Directions: From Red Bluff, take Highway 36 east for 44 miles to the junction with Highway 89. Continue east on Highway 36/89 to Chester and drive through Chester to the junction with County Road A13. Turn right (south) and drive about four miles to the junction with Highway 147. Turn right on Highway 147 and drive one mile to the well-signed camp entrance on the right.

Contact: Lassen View Resort, tel. (530) 596-3437 or fax (530) 596-4437.

24 Ponderosa Flat

     7

This camp is set at the north end of Butt Lake, the little brother to nearby Lake Almanor. It is a fairly popular camp, with the boat ramp a prime attraction, allowing campers/anglers a lakeside spot with easy access. Technically, Butt is the "afterbay" for Almanor, fed by a four-mile-long pipe with water from Almanor. What occurs is that pond smelt from Almanor get ground up in the Butt Lake powerhouse, providing a huge amount of feed for trout at the head of the lake; that's why the trout often get huge at Butt Lake. The one downer here is that lake drawdowns are common, exposing tree stumps.

Location: On Butt Lake; map C3, grid d4.

Campsites, facilities: There are 63 sites for tents or RVs. Picnic tables and fire grills are provided. Drinking water, vault toilets, and boat ramp are available. Leashed pets are permitted.

Reservations, fees: No reservations; $15 per night, $3 per extra vehicle per night, $7 per extra RV per night, $1 pet fee per night. Open May through October, weather permitting.

Directions: From Red Bluff, take Highway 36 east for 44 miles to the junction with Highway 89. Continue east on Highway 36/89 to Lake Almanor and the next junction with Highway 89 (two miles before reaching Chester). Turn right on Highway 89 and drive about seven miles to Butt Valley Road. Turn right on Butt Valley Road and drive 3.2 miles to the campground on the right side of the road.

Contact: PG&E Building and Land Services, tel. (916) 386-5164.

25 Cool Springs

      7

One of two camps at Butt Lake, Cool Springs is set about midway down the lake on its eastern shore, 2.5 miles south of Ponderosa Flat. Cool Springs Creek enters the lake near the camp. For more information about Butt Lake, see the entry for Ponderosa Flat.

Location: On Butt Lake; map C3, grid d4.

Campsites, facilities: There are 25 sites for tents or RVs, and five walk-in sites. Picnic tables and fire grills are provided. Drinking water, vault toilets, and a boat ramp are available. Leashed pets are permitted.

Reservations, fees: No reservations; $15 per night, $3 per extra vehicle per night, $7 per extra RV per night, $1 pet fee per night. Open May through October, weather permitting.

Directions: From Red Bluff, take Highway 36 east for 44 miles to the junction with Highway 89. Continue east on Highway 36/89 to Lake Almanor and the next junction with Highway 89 (two miles before reaching Chester). Turn right on Highway 89 and drive about seven miles to Butt Valley Road. Turn right on Butt Valley Road and drive 5.7 miles to the campground on the right side of the road.

Contact: PG&E Building and Land Services, tel. (916) 386-5164.

26 Yellow Creek

    8

Yellow Creek is one of Cal Trout's pet projects. It's a beautiful stream for fly fishers, demanding the best from skilled anglers: approaching with complete stealth, making delicate casts with long leaders and small dry flies during the evening rise. This camp is set at 4,400 feet in Humbug Valley and provides access to this stretch of water. An option is to fish Butt Creek, much easier fishing for small, planted rainbow trout, with access available along the road on the way in.

Location: In Humbug Valley; map C3, grid d3.

Campsites, facilities: There are 10 sites for tents or RVs. Picnic tables and fire grills are provided. Drinking water and vault toilets are available. Leashed pets are permitted.

Reservations, fees: No reservations; $13 per night, $3 per night per extra vehicle and $7 per night per extra RV, $1 pet fee per night. Open May through September.

Directions: From Oroville, drive north on Highway 70 to Belden. At Belden, turn left on Forest Road 26N26 and drive north about 11 miles to the campground entrance road on the left side of the road.

From Red Bluff, take Highway 36 east for 44 miles to the junction with Highway 89. Continue east on Highway 36/89 to Lake Almanor and the junction with Highway 89 (two miles before reaching Chester). Turn right on Highway 89 and drive about five miles to Humbug Road/County Road 308/309. Turn right (west) and drive 0.6 mile to the junction of County Road 308 and 309. Bear left on County Road 309 and drive 1.2 miles to the junction with County Road 307. Bear right on County Road 307 and drive 5.4 miles to a Y. Bear left at the Y and drive 1.2 miles to the campground entrance on the right. Turn right and drive 0.3 mile to the campground.

Contact: PG&E Building and Land Services, tel. (916) 386-5164.

27 Cherry Hill

 7

The camp is set along little Butte Creek at the foot of Cherry Hill, just downstream from the confluence of Colby Creek and Butte Creek. It is also on the western edge of the alpine zone in Lassen National Forest. A four-mile drive to the north, much of it along Colby Creek, will take visitors to the Colby Mountain Lookout at 6,002 feet for a dramatic view of the Ishi Wilderness to the west. Nearby to the south is Philbrook Reservoir.

Location: On Butte Creek in Lassen National Forest; map C3, grid d0.

Campsites, facilities: There are six walk-in tent sites and 19 sites for tents or RVs. Picnic tables and fire grills are provided. Drinking water and vault toilets are available. Supplies are available in the town of Butte Meadows. Leashed pets are permitted.

Reservations, fees: No reservations; $11 per night. Open May through September, weather permitting.

Directions: From Chico, drive north on Highway 32 to the junction with Humboldt Road (well past the town of Forest Ranch). Turn right and drive five miles to Butte Meadows. Continue on Humboldt Road for three miles to the campground on the right side of the road.

Contact: Lassen National Forest, Almanor Ranger District, tel. (530) 258-2141 or fax (530) 258-5194.

28 West Branch

    6

This is a small and remote campground set on the West Branch Feather River, 5,000 feet elevation, just upstream from where Philbrook Creek joins the Feather. It is set on the western edge of Lassen National Forest, with a network of backcountry roads in the area. Nearby destinations include Spring Valley Lake, Snag Lake, and Snow Mountain; several roads are accessible only to four-wheel-drive vehicles. Because of its proximity to

Philbrook Reservoir, two miles to the east, this camp is often overlooked.

Location: On the Feather River in Lassen National Forest; map C3, grid d0.

Campsites, facilities: There are eight sites for tents and seven sites for tents or RVs. Picnic tables and fire grills are provided. Drinking water and vault toilets are available. Leashed pets are permitted.

Reservations, fees: No reservations; $10 per night. Open late May through October, weather permitting.

Directions: At Orland on Interstate 5, take the Highway 32/Chico exit and drive to Chico and the junction with Highway 99. Turn south on Highway 99 and drive to Skyway Road/Paradise (in south Chico). Turn east on Skyway Road and drive through Paradise and continue for 27 miles to Humbug Summit Road. Turn right and drive two miles to Philbrook Road and the campground access road on the right. Turn right and drive a half mile to the campground.

Contact: Lassen National Forest, Almanor Ranger District, tel. (530) 258-2141 or fax (530) 258-5194.

29 Philbrook Reservoir

       7

Philbrook Reservoir is set at 5,600 feet on the western mountain slopes above Chico, on the southwest edge of Lassen National Forest. It is a pretty lake, though subject to late season drawdowns, with a scenic lookout a short distance from camp. The lake is loaded with small trout—a dink here, a dink there, a dink everywhere.

Location: In Lassen National Forest; map C3, grid d0.

Campsites, facilities: There are 20 sites for tents or RVs up to 30 feet long. Picnic tables and fire grills are provided. Drinking water and vault toilets are available. Trailer and car-top boat launches are available. Leashed pets are permitted.

Reservations, fees: No reservations; $13 per night, $3 per night for extra vehicle, $7 per night for extra RV, $1 pet fee. Open May through September.

Directions: At Orland on Interstate 5, take the Highway 32/Chico exit and drive to Chico and the junction with Highway 99. Turn south on Highway 99 and drive to Skyway Road/Paradise (in south Chico). Turn east on Skyway Road, drive through Paradise, and continue for 27 miles to Humbug Summit Road. Turn right and drive two miles to Philbrook Road. Turn right and drive 3.1 miles to the campground entrance road. Turn right and drive one-half mile to the campground.

Contact: PG&E Building and Land Services, tel. (916) 386-5164.

30 Queen Lily

     7

The North Fork Feather River is a prime destination for camping and trout fishing, especially for families. This is one of three camps along the river on Caribou Road. This stretch of river is well stocked. Insider's note: the first 150 yards of river below the dam at Caribou typically have large but elusive trout.

Location: On the North Fork of the Feather River in Plumas National Forest; map C3, grid e2.

Campsites, facilities: There are 12 sites for tents or RVs up to 16 feet long. Picnic tables and fire grills are provided. Drinking water and vault toilets are available. A grocery store and coin laundry are available within three miles. Leashed pets are permitted.

Reservations, fees: No reservations; $14 per night. Open May through September.

Directions: From Oroville, drive north on Highway 70 to Caribou Road (two miles past Belden at Gansner Ranch Ranger Station). Turn left on Caribou Road and drive about three miles to the campground on the left side of the road.

Contact: Plumas National Forest, Mount Hough Ranger District, tel. (530) 283-0555 or fax (530) 283-1821.

31 North Fork

     7

This camp is between Queen Lily to the near-by north and Gansner Bar camp to the nearby south, all three set on the North Fork Feather River. The elevation is 2,600 feet. Fishing access is good and trout plants are decent, making for a good fishing/camping trip. Note: All three camps are extremely popular on summer weekends.

Location: On the North Fork of the Feather River in Plumas National Forest; map C3, grid e2.

Campsites, facilities: There are 20 sites for tents or RVs up to 32 feet long. Picnic tables and fire grills are provided. Drinking water and vault toilets are available. A grocery store and coin laundry are available within three miles. Leashed pets are permitted.

Reservations, fees: No reservations; $14 per night. Open May through September.

Directions: From Oroville, drive north on Highway 70 to Caribou Road (two miles past Belden at Gansner Ranch Ranger Station). Turn left on Caribou Road and drive about two miles to the campground on the left side of the road.

Contact: Plumas National Forest, Mount Hough Ranger District, tel. (530) 283-0555 or fax (530) 283-1821.

32 Gansner Bar

      7

Gansner Bar is the first of three camps along Caribou Road, which runs parallel to the North Fork Feather River. Of the three, this one receives the highest trout stocks of rainbow trout in the 10- to 12-inch class. Caribou Road runs upstream to Caribou Dam, with stream and fishing access along almost all of it. The camps often fill on summer weekends.

Location: On the North Fork of the Feather River in Plumas National Forest; map C3, grid e2.

Campsites, facilities: There are 14 sites for tents or RVs up to 32 feet long. Picnic tables and fire grills are provided. Drinking water and vault toilets are available. A grocery store and coin laundry are available within one mile. Some facilities are wheelchair accessible. Leashed pets are permitted.

Reservations, fees: No reservations; $14 per night. Open April through October.

Directions: From Oroville, drive north on Highway 70 to Caribou Road (two miles past Belden at Gansner Ranch Ranger Station). Turn left on Caribou Road and drive a short distance to the campground on the left side of the road.

Contact: Plumas National Forest, Mount Hough Ranger District, tel. (530) 283-0555 or fax (530) 283-1821.

33 Hallsted

    7

Easy highway access and a pretty trout stream right alongside have made this an extremely popular campground. It typically fills on summer weekends. Hallsted is set on the East Branch North Fork River, 2,800 feet elevation. The river is stocked with trout by the Department of Fish and Game.

Location: On the North Fork of the Feather River in Plumas National Forest; map C3, grid e4.

Campsites, facilities: There are 20 sites for tents or RVs up to 22 feet long. Picnic tables and fire grills are provided. Drinking water and vault toilets are available. A grocery store is available within a quarter mile. Leashed pets are permitted.

Reservations, fees: Reserve at (877) 444-6777 ($8.65 reservation fee) or website: www.reserveusa.com; $14 per night. Open May through September.

Directions: From Oroville, drive northeast on Highway 70 to Belden. Continue past Belden for about 12 miles to the campground entrance on the right side of the road. Turn right and drive a quarter mile to the campground.

Contact: Plumas National Forest, Mount

Hough Ranger District, tel. (530) 283-0555 or fax (530) 283-1821.

34 Snake Lake

 8

Snake Lake is a rarity in the northern Sierra, a mountain lake that has bass, catfish, and bluegill. That is because it is a shallow lake, set at 4,200 feet in Plumas National Forest. The camp is on the west shore. A road that circles the lake provides a good bicycle route for youngsters. A side trip to the nearby north is Smith Lake, about a five-minute drive, with the Butterfly Valley Botanical Area bordering it.

Location: In Plumas National Forest; map C3, grid f5.

Campsites, facilities: There are seven tent sites. Picnic tables and fire grills are provided. Vault toilets are available. No drinking water is available. Garbage must be packed out. Leashed pets are permitted.

Reservations, fees: No reservations; no fee. Open May through October.

Directions: From Oroville, drive north on Highway 70 to the junction with Highway 89. Turn south on Highway 89/70 and drive 11 miles to Quincy. In Quincy, turn right at Bucks Lake Road and drive five miles to County Road 422. Turn right and drive two miles to the Snake Lake access road. Turn right and drive one mile to the campground on the right.

Contact: Plumas National Forest, Mount Hough Ranger District, tel. (530) 283-0555 or fax (530) 283-1821.

35 Silver Lake

 8

While tons of people go to Bucks Lake for the great trout fishing and lakeside camps, nearby Silver Lake gets little attention despite great natural beauty, good hiking, decent trout fishing, and a trailhead to the Bucks Lake Wilderness. The camp is at the north end of the lake, 5,800 feet elevation, a primitive and secluded spot. No powerboats (or swimming) are al-

lowed on Silver Lake, which makes it ideal for canoes and rafts. The lake has lots of small brook trout. The Pacific Crest Trail is routed on the ridge above the lake, skirting past Mount Pleasant (6,924 feet) to the nearby west.

Location: In Plumas National Forest; map C3, grid f3.

Campsites, facilities: There are eight tent sites. Picnic tables and fire grills are provided. Vault toilets are available. Garbage must be packed out. No drinking water is available. Leashed pets are permitted.

Reservations, fees: No reservations; no fee. Open May through October.

Directions: From Oroville, drive north on Highway 70 to the junction with Highway 89. Turn south on Highway 89/70 and drive 11 miles to Quincy. In Quincy, turn right at Bucks Lake Road and drive west for nine miles to Silver Lake Road. Turn right and drive seven miles to the campground at the north end of the lake

Contact: Plumas National Forest, Mount Hough Ranger District, tel. (530) 283-0555 or fax (530) 283-1821.

36 Sundew

 7

Sundew Camp is set on the northern shore of Bucks Lake, just north of Bucks Lake Dam. A boat ramp is about two miles north in the Mill Creek Cove, providing access to one of the better trout spots on the lake. You want fish? At Bucks Lake you can get fish—it's one of the state's top mountain trout lakes. Sunrises are often spectacular from this camp, with the light glowing on the lake's surface.

Location: On Bucks Lake in Plumas National Forest; map C3, grid f3.

Campsites, facilities: There are 19 sites for tents or RVs up to 22 feet long. Picnic tables and fire grills are provided. Drinking water and vault toilets are available. Leashed pets are permitted. There is a boat ramp two miles north of the camp.

Reservations, fees: No reservations; $12 per night. Open mid-May through September, weather permitting.

Directions: From Oroville, drive north on Highway 70 to the junction with Highway 89. Turn south on Highway 89/70 and drive 11 miles to Quincy. In Quincy, turn right at Bucks Lake Road and drive 17 miles to Bucks Lake and the junction with Bucks Lake Dam Road/Forest Road 33. Turn right, drive around the lake, cross over the dam, continue for a half mile, and turn right at the campground access road.

Contact: Plumas National Forest, Mount Hough Ranger District, tel. (530) 283-0555 or fax (530) 283-1821.

37 Mill Creek

      7

When Bucks Lake is full, this is one of the prettiest spots on the lake. The camp is set deep in Mill Creek Cove, adjacent to where Mill Creek enters the northernmost point of Bucks Lake. A boat ramp is a half mile away to the south, providing boat access to one of the better trout fishing spots at the lake. Unfortunately, when the lake level falls, this camp is left high and dry, some distance from the water. The elevation is 5,200 feet.

Location: At Bucks Lake in Plumas National Forest; map C3, grid f3.

Campsites, facilities: There are eight sites for tents or RVs up to 58 feet long and two walk-in tent sites. Picnic tables and fire grills are provided. Drinking water and vault toilets are available. Groceries are available within five miles. Leashed pets are permitted.

Reservations, fees: No reservations; $14 per night. Open mid-May through September, weather permitting.

Directions: From Oroville, drive north on Highway 70 to the junction with Highway 89. Turn south on Highway 89/70 and drive 11 miles to Quincy. In Quincy, turn right at Bucks Lake Road and drive 17 miles to Bucks Lake and the junction with Bucks Lake Dam Road/Forest Road 33. Turn right, drive around the lake, cross over the dam, and continue for about three miles to the campground.

Contact: Plumas National Forest, Mount Hough Ranger District, tel. (530) 283-0555 or fax (530) 283-1821.

38 Hutchins Group Camp

    6

This is a prime spot for a Scout outing or for any other large group that would like a pretty spot. An amphitheater is available. It is set at 5,200 feet near Bucks and Lower Bucks Lakes. For more information, see the entries for the following nearby campgrounds: Lower Bucks, Haskins Valley, and Sundew.

Location: Near Bucks Lake in Plumas National Forest; map C3, grid f3.

Campsites, facilities: There are three group sites for tents or RVs, each with a 25-person maximum. Picnic tables and fire grills are provided. Drinking water and vault toilets are available. A boat ramp is available. Leashed pets are permitted.

Reservations, fees: Reservations are required; $45 group fee per night. Open May through October.

Directions: From Oroville, drive north on Highway 70 to the junction with Highway 89. Turn south on Highway 89/70 and drive 11 miles to Quincy. In Quincy, turn right at Bucks Lake Road and drive 17 miles to Bucks Lake and the junction with Bucks Lake Dam Road/Forest Road 33. Turn right, drive around the lake, cross over the dam, continue for a short distance, and turn right. Drive a half mile, cross the stream (passing an intersection), and continue straight for a half mile to the campground.

Contact: Plumas National Forest, Mount Hough Ranger District, tel. (530) 283-0555 or fax (530) 283-1821.

39 Lower Bucks

      7

This camp is on Lower Bucks Lake, which is actually the afterbay for Bucks Lake, set below the Bucks Lake Dam. It is a small, primitive, and quiet spot that is often overlooked because it is not on the main lake.

Location: On Lower Bucks Lake in Plumas National Forest; map C3, grid f3.

Campsites, facilities: There are six sites for RVs only up to 26 feet long. Picnic tables and fire rings are provided. No drinking water or toilet facilities are available. Leashed pets are permitted.

Reservations, fees: No reservations; $10 per night. Open May through October.

Directions: From Oroville, drive north on Highway 70 to the junction with Highway 89. Turn south on Highway 89/70 and drive 11 miles to Quincy. In Quincy, turn right at Bucks Lake Road and drive 17 miles to Bucks Lake and the junction with Bucks Lake Dam Road/Forest Road 33. Turn right and drive four miles around the lake, cross over the dam, drive a quarter mile, and then turn left on the campground entrance road.

Contact: Plumas National Forest, Mount Hough Ranger District, tel. (530) 283-0555 or fax (530) 283-1821.

40 Grizzly Creek

      4

This is an alternative to the more developed, more crowded campgrounds at Bucks Lake. It is a small, primitive camp set near Grizzly Creek at 5,400 feet in elevation. Nearby Bucks Lake provides good trout fishing, resorts, and boat rentals.

Location: Near Bucks Lake in Plumas National Forest; map C3, grid f2.

Campsites, facilities: There are eight sites for tents or RVs up to 35 feet long. Picnic tables and fire grills are provided. Drinking water and vault toilets are available. A boat ramp is available at Bucks Lake. A grocery

store and coin laundry are available within five miles. Leashed pets are permitted.

Reservations, fees: No reservations; $14 per night. Open June through October.

Directions: From Oroville, drive north on Highway 70 to the junction with Highway 89. Turn south on Highway 89/70 and drive 11 miles to Quincy. In Quincy, turn right at Bucks Lake Road and drive 17 miles to Bucks Lake and the junction with Bucks Lake Dam Road/Forest Road 33. Turn right and drive one mile to the junction with Oroville-Quincy Road/Forest Road 36. Bear left and drive one mile to the campground on the right side of the road.

Contact: Plumas National Forest, Mount Hough Ranger District, tel. (530) 283-0555 or fax (530) 283-1821.

41 Haskins Valley

     7

This is the biggest and most popular of the campgrounds at Bucks Lake, a pretty alpine lake with excellent trout fishing and clean campgrounds. A boat ramp is available to the nearby north, along with Bucks Lodge. This camp is set deep in a cove at the extreme south end of the lake, where the water is quiet and sheltered from north winds. Bucks Lake, 5,200 feet elevation, is well documented for excellent fishing for rainbow and Mackinaw trout, with high catch rates of rainbow trout and lake records in the 16-pound class.

Location: On Bucks Lake; map C3, grid g2.

Campsites, facilities: There are 65 sites for tents or RVs. Picnic tables and fire grills are provided. Drinking water and vault toilets are available. A sanitary disposal station and boat ramp are available nearby. Leashed pets are permitted.

Reservations, fees: No reservations; $15 per night, $3 per extra vehicle per night, $7 per extra RV per night, $1 pet fee per night. Open May through October, weather permitting.

Directions: From Oroville, drive north on Highway 70 to the junction with Highway 89. Turn south on Highway 89/70 and drive 11 miles to Quincy. In Quincy, turn right at Bucks Lake Road and drive 16.5 miles to the campground entrance on the right side of the road.

Contact: PG&E Building and Land Services, tel. (916) 386-5164.

42 Whitehorse

 7

This campground is set along Bucks Creek, about two miles from the boat ramps and south shore concessions at Bucks Lake. The trout fishing can be quite good at Bucks Lake, particularly on early summer evenings. The elevation is 5,200 feet. For more information, see the entry for Haskins Valley.

Location: Near Bucks Lake in Plumas National Forest; map C3, grid g3.

Campsites, facilities: There are 20 sites for tents or RVs up to 43 feet long. Picnic tables and fire grills are provided. Drinking water and vault toilets are available. A grocery store and coin laundry are available within five miles. Leashed pets are permitted.

Reservations, fees: No reservations; $14 per night. Open June through September.

Directions: From Oroville, drive north on Highway 70 to the junction with Highway 89. Turn south on Highway 89/70 and drive 11 miles to Quincy. In Quincy, turn right at Bucks Lake Road and drive 14.5 miles to the campground entrance on the right side of the road.

Contact: Plumas National Forest, Mount Hough Ranger District, tel. (530) 283-0555 or fax (530) 283-1821.

43 Deanes Valley

 5

This secret spot is set on South Fork Rock Creek, deep in a valley at an elevation of 4,400 feet in Plumas National Forest. The trout here are very small natives. If you want a pure, quiet spot, great. If you want great fishing, not great.

The surrounding region has a network of back-country roads, including routes passable only by four-wheel-drive vehicles; to explore these roads, get a map of Plumas National Forest.

Location: On Rock Creek in Plumas National Forest; map C3, grid f4.

Campsites, facilities: There are seven sites for tents or RVs. Picnic tables and fire grills are provided. Vault toilets are available. No drinking water is available. Garbage must be packed out. Leashed pets are permitted.

Reservations, fees: No reservations; no fee. Open April through October.

Directions: From Oroville, drive north on Highway 70 to the junction with Highway 89. Turn south on Highway 89/70 and drive 11 miles to Quincy. In Quincy, turn right at Bucks Lake Road (a dirt road that is slippery when wet early in the season) and drive 3.5 miles to Forest Road 24N28. Turn left and drive seven miles to the campground on the left.

Contact: Plumas National Forest, Mount Hough Ranger District, tel. (530) 283-0555 or fax (530) 283-1821.

44 Brady's Camp

 4

Don't expect any company here. This is a tiny, little-known, primitive camp near Pine Creek, at roughly 7,000 feet in elevation. A side trip is to make the half-mile drive up to Argentine Rock (7,209 feet) for a lookout onto this remote forest country. To the east are many miles of national forest, accessible by vehicle, although there is significant logging activity in portions of the forest.

Location: On Pine Creek in Plumas National Forest; map C3, grid f7.

Campsites, facilities: There are four tent sites. Picnic tables and fire grills are provided. Vault toilets are available. No drinking water is available. Garbage must be packed out. Leashed pets are permitted.

Reservations, fees: No reservations; no fee. Open May through October.

Directions: From Oroville, drive north on Highway 70 to the junction with Highway 89. Turn south on Highway 89/70 and drive 11 miles to Quincy. In Quincy, continue on Highway 89/70 for six miles to Squirrel Creek Road. Turn left and drive seven miles (after two miles bear right at the Y) to Forest Road 25N29. Turn left and drive one mile to the campground on the right side of the road.

Contact: Plumas National Forest, Mount Hough Ranger District, tel. (530) 283-0555 or fax (530) 283-1821.

45 Rogers Cow Camp

 4

First note that the Oroville-Quincy "Highway" is actually a twisty Forest Service road, a backcountry route that connects Oroville to Quincy and passes Lake Oroville and Bucks Lake in the process. The road is paved, but it can still put you way out there in no-man's-land, set in Plumas National Forest at 4,000 feet. You want quiet, you get it. You want water, you bring it yourself. The camp is set near the headwaters of Coon Creek. There are no other natural destinations in the area, and I'm not saying Coon Creek is anything to see. It's advisable to obtain a map of Plumas National Forest, which details all backcountry roads. There has been logging activity in the area.

Location: In Plumas National Forest; map C3, grid g1.

Campsites, facilities: There are five sites for tents or RVs. Picnic tables and fire grills are provided. Vault toilets are available. No drinking water is available. Garbage must be packed out. Leashed pets are permitted.

Reservations, fees: No reservations; no fee. Open May through September.

Directions: In Oroville, drive east on Highway 162 /Oroville-Quincy Highway for 26.5 miles to the Brush Creek Work Center. Continue on Oroville-Quincy Highway for eight miles to the campground entrance road on the left side of the road. Turn left and drive a short distance to the camp.

Contact: Plumas National Forest, Feather River Ranger District, tel. (530) 534-6500 or fax (530) 532-1210.

46 Little North Fork

 7

Guaranteed quiet? You got it. This is a primitive camp in the outback that few know of. It is set along the Little North Fork of the Middle Fork of the Feather River at 4,000 feet. The surrounding backcountry of Plumas National Forest features an incredible number of roads, giving four-wheel-drive owners a chance to get so lost they'll need this camp. Instead, get a map of Plumas National Forest before venturing out.

Location: On the Middle Fork of the Feather River in Plumas National Forest; map C3, grid g1.

Campsites, facilities: There are eight sites for tents or RVs up to 16 feet long. Picnic tables and fire grills are provided. Vault toilets are available. No drinking water is available. Garbage must be packed out. Leashed pets are permitted.

Reservations, fees: No reservations; no fee. Open May through October.

Directions: From Oroville, turn east on Highway 162/Oroville-Quincy Highway and drive 26.5 miles to the Brush Creek Work Center. Continue northeast on Oroville-Quincy Highway for about six miles to Forest Road 60. Turn right and drive about eight miles to the campground entrance road on the left side of the road. Turn left and drive a quarter mile to the campground. Note: This route is long, twisty, bumpy, and narrow for most of the way.

Contact: Plumas National Forest, Feather River Ranger District, tel. (530) 534-6500 or fax (530) 532-1210.

47 Milsap Bar

Among white-water river rafters, Milsap Bar is a well-known access point to the Middle Fork Feather River. This river country features a deep canyon, beautiful surroundings, and is formally recognized as the Feather Falls Scenic Area (named after the awesome 640-foot waterfall). Note that while no commercial raft companies are permitted to run this section of the Feather, private groups or individual use is permitted. The elevation is 1,600 feet.

Location: On the Middle Fork of the Feather River in Plumas National Forest; map C3, grid g1.

Campsites, facilities: There are 20 sites for tents or RVs up to 16 feet long. Picnic tables and fire grills are provided. Vault toilets are available. No drinking water is available. Garbage must be packed out. Leashed pets are permitted.

Reservations, fees: No reservations; no fee. Open May through September.

Directions: In Oroville, drive east on Highway 162/Oroville-Quincy Highway for 26.5 miles to the Brush Creek Work Center. Turn right on Bald Rock Road and drive for about a half mile to Forest Road 22N62/Milsap Bar Road. Turn left and drive eight miles to the campground (a narrow, steep, mountainous dirt road).

Contact: Plumas National Forest, Feather River Ranger District, tel. (530) 534-6500 or fax (530) 532-1210.

48 Black Rock

This is the only campground on the west shore of Little Grass Valley Reservoir, with an adjacent boat ramp making it an attractive choice for anglers. The lake is set at 5,000 feet in Plumas National Forest and provides lakeside camping and decent fishing for rainbow trout and kokanee salmon. If you don't like the company, there are seven other camps to choose from at the lake, all on the opposite eastern shore.

Location: On Little Grass Valley Reservoir in Plumas National Forest; map C3, grid h4.

Campsites, facilities: There are 10 walk-in tent sites and 20 sites for tents or RVs up to 22 feet long. Picnic tables and fire grills are provided. Drinking water, vault toilets, and a fish-cleaning station are available. A sanitary disposal station, boat ramp, and grocery store are nearby. Leashed pets are permitted.

Reservations, fees: No reservations; $12 per night. Open June through October.

Directions: From Oroville, drive east on Highway 162 for about eight miles to the junction signed Challenge/LaPorte. Bear right and drive east past Challenge and Strawberry Valley to LaPorte. Continue two miles past LaPorte to the junction with County Road 514/Little Grass Valley Road. Turn left and drive about five miles to the campground access road on the west side of the lake. Turn right on the access road and drive a quarter mile to the campground.

Contact: Plumas National Forest, Feather River Ranger District, tel. (530) 534-6500 or fax (530) 532-1210.

49 Horse Camp

This camp is reserved for equestrians only and thus it gets low use. This is a high-country forested campground set near Little Grass Valley Reservoir, but there is no lake view because of tree cover. Several trails are accessible from the campground, including the Pacific Crest Trail and Lakeshore Trail, as well as access to Bald Mountain (6,255 feet). The elevation at camp is 5,060 feet.

Location: On Little Grass Valley Reservoir in Plumas National Forest; map C3, grid h4.

Campsites, facilities: There are 10 sites for tents or RVs up to 35 feet long available for equestrian campers only. Picnic tables and fire grills are provided. Vault toilets are available. No drinking water is available. Hitching posts are available and a wheelchair-accessible mounting rack is available. A restaurant and deli are available five miles away in LaPorte. Leashed pets are permitted.

Reservations, fees: Reservations required at tel. (877) 444-6777 ($8.65 reservation fee) or website: www.reserveusa.com; $13 per night. Credit cards accepted. Open June through September.

Directions: From Oroville, drive east on Highway 162 for about eight miles to the junction signed Challenge/LaPorte. Bear right and drive east past Challenge and Strawberry Valley to LaPorte. Continue on County Road 512 (which becomes County Road 514/Little Grass Valley Road) for three miles to Forest Road 22N57. Turn right and drive four miles (cross the bridge) to the campground on the left.

Contact: Plumas National Forest, Feather River Ranger District, tel. (530) 534-6500 or fax (530) 532-1210.

50 Peninsula Tent

This camp is exceptional in that most of the campsites provide views of Little Grass Valley Reservoir, a pretty lake set at 5,060 feet in national forest. The fishing can be excellent, especially for rainbow trout, brown trout, and kokanee salmon. The camp gets moderate use, and is a pretty site with tents sprinkled amid white fir and pine. A good family campground, tents only. A 13-mile hiking trail circles the lake.

Location: On Little Grass Valley Reservoir in Plumas National Forest; map C3, grid h5.

Campsites, facilities: There are 25 sites for tents only. Picnic tables and fire rings are provided. Drinking water and flush toilets are available. A boat launch, fishing cleaning station, and a swimming beach are available nearby. Leashed pets are permitted.

Reservations, fees: No reservations; $12 fee per night. Open Memorial Day weekend through mid-October, weather permitting.

Directions: From Oroville, drive east on Highway 162 for about eight miles to the junction signed Challenge/LaPorte. Bear right and drive east past Challenge and Strawberry Valley to LaPorte. Continue on County Road 512 (which becomes County Road 514/Little Grass Valley Road) for three miles to Forest Road 22N57. Continue on 514 for one mile to the campground entrance on right. Turn right and drive a quarter mile to the campground.

Contact: Plumas National Forest, Feather River Ranger District, tel. (530) 534-6500 or fax (530) 532-1210.

51 Running Deer

      7

Little Grass Valley Reservoir is a pretty mountain lake set at 5,060 feet in Plumas National Forest, providing lakeside camping, boating, and fishing for rainbow trout and kokanee salmon. One of seven campgrounds on the eastern shore, this one is on the far northeastern end of the lake. Looking straight north from the camp is a spectacular view, gazing across the water and up at Bald Mountain, 6,255 feet in elevation. A trailhead for the Pacific Crest Trail is available nearby at little Fowler Lake about four miles north of Little Grass Valley Reservoir.

Location: On Little Grass Valley Reservoir in Plumas National Forest; map C3, grid h5.

Campsites, facilities: There are 40 sites for tents or RVs up to 40 feet long. Picnic tables and fire rings are provided. Drinking water, flush toilets, and a fish-cleaning station are available. A boat ramp, grocery store, and sanitary disposal station are nearby. Leashed pets are permitted.

Reservations, fees: Reserve at tel. (877) 444-6777 ($8.65 reservation fee) or website: www.reserveusa.com; $13 to $15 per night. Open June through September.

Directions: From Oroville, drive east on Highway 162 for about eight miles to the junction signed Challenge/LaPorte. Bear right and drive east past Challenge and

Strawberry Valley to LaPorte. Continue on County Road 512 (which becomes County Road 514/Little Grass Valley Road) for three miles to Forest Road 22N57. Turn right and drive three miles to the campground on the left.

Contact: Plumas National Forest, Feather River Ranger District, tel. (530) 534-6500 or fax (530) 532-1210.

52 Wyandotte

 8

Of the eight camps on Little Grass Valley Reservoir, this is the favorite. It is set on a small peninsula at 5,100 foot elevation that extends well into the lake, with a boat ramp nearby. For more information, see the entry for Running Deer.

Location: On Little Grass Valley Reservoir in Plumas National Forest; map C3, grid h5.

Campsites, facilities: There are 28 sites for tents or RVs up to 22 feet long. Picnic tables and fire rings are provided. Drinking water and flush toilets are available. A sanitary disposal station, boat ramp, fish- cleaning station, and grocery store are nearby. Leashed pets are permitted.

Reservations, fees: No reservations; $13 to $22 per night. Open May through September.

Directions: From Oroville, drive east on Highway 162 for about eight miles to the junction signed Challenge/LaPorte. Bear right and drive east past Challenge and Strawberry Valley to LaPorte. Continue two miles past LaPorte to the junction with County Road 514/Little Grass Valley Road. Turn left and drive one mile to a junction. Turn left and drive one mile to the campground entrance road on the right.

Contact: Plumas National Forest, Feather River Ranger District, tel. (530) 534-6500 or fax (530) 532-1210.

53 Little Beaver

 7

This is one of eight campgrounds on Little Grass Valley Reservoir, set at 5,060 feet. Take your pick. For more information, see the entry for Running Deer.

Location: On Little Grass Valley Reservoir in Plumas National Forest; map C3, grid h5.

Campsites, facilities: There are 120 sites for tents or RVs up to 40 feet long. Picnic tables and fire rings are provided. Drinking water and flush toilets are available. A grocery store, sanitary disposal station, a fish-cleaning station, and boat ramp are nearby. Leashed pets are permitted.

Reservations, fees: No reservations; $13 to $15 per night. Open June through October.

Directions: From Oroville, drive east on Highway 162 for about eight miles to the junction signed Challenge/LaPorte. Bear right and drive east past Challenge and Strawberry Valley to LaPorte. Continue two miles past La-Porte to the junction with County Road 514/Little Grass Valley Road. Turn left and drive one mile to a junction. Turn right and drive two miles to the campground entrance road on the left.

Contact: Plumas National Forest, Feather River Ranger District, tel. (530) 534-6500 or fax (530) 532-1210.

54 Red Feather Camp

 7

This camp is well developed and popular, set on the eastern shore of Little Grass Valley Reservoir, just south of Running Deer and just north of Little Beaver. For more information, see the entry for Running Deer.

Location: On Little Grass Valley Reservoir in Plumas National Forest; map C3, grid h5.

Campsites, facilities: There are 60 sites for tents or RVs up to 22 feet long. Picnic tables and fire rings are provided. Drinking water and flush toilets are available. A sanitary disposal station, boat ramp, fish- cleaning station, and grocery store are nearby. Leashed pets are permitted.

Reservations, fees: Reserve at (877) 444-6777 ($8.65 reservation fee) or website: www.reserveusa.com; $13 to $15 per night. Open June through October.

Directions: From Oroville, drive east on Highway 162 for about eight miles to the junction signed Challenge/LaPorte. Bear right and drive east past Challenge and Strawberry Valley to LaPorte. Continue two miles past LaPorte to the junction with County Road 514/Little Grass Valley Road. Turn left and drive one mile to a junction. Turn right and drive three miles to the campground entrance road on the left.

Contact: Plumas National Forest, Feather River Ranger District, tel. (530) 534-6500 or fax (530) 532-1210.

55 Golden Coach RV Resort

    6

This is a good layover spot for RV cruisers looking to hole up for the night. The park is wooded and set near the Feather River. You'll find mostly older adults here.

Location: Near the Feather River; map C3, grid h8.

Campsites, facilities: There are 60 RV sites with full hookups. Picnic tables and fire grills are provided. Restrooms, showers, modem hookups, a coin laundry, wood, store, cafe, and LP gas are available. Leashed pets are permitted.

Reservations, fees: Reservations are recommended in July and August; $15 to $19 per night, $2 per person for more than two people. Major credit cards accepted. Open May through mid-October.

Directions: In Truckee, at the junction of Highway 80 and Highway 89, take Highway 89 north to the junction with Highway 70. Drive north on Highway 89/Highway 70 for 6.5 miles to Cromberg and look for the signed entrance to the campground at 59704 Highway 70.

Contact: Golden Coach RV Resort, tel. (800) 327-0933 or (530) 836-2426.

56 Little Bear RV Park

     7

This is a privately operated RV park set near the Feather River. Nearby destinations include Plumas-Eureka State Park and the Lakes Basin Recreation Area. The elevation is 4,300 feet.

Location: On the Feather River; map C3, grid h8.

Campsites, facilities: There are 91 RV sites, 80 with full hookups, and four cabins. Picnic tables and fire rings are provided. Drinking water, showers, flush toilets, coin laundry, grocery store, and ice are available. Leashed pets are permitted.

Reservations, fees: Reservations are accepted; $22 to $22 per night, $1 pet fee. Open mid-April through October 28th.

Directions: In Truckee, drive north on Highway 89 to Blairsden and the junction with Highway 70. Turn north and drive one mile to Little Bear Road. Turn left on Little Bear Road and drive a short distance to the campground.

Contact: Little Bear RV Park, tel. or fax (530) 836-2774.

57 Plumas-Eureka State Park

      9

Plumas-Eureka State Park is a beautiful chunk of parkland, featuring great hiking, a pretty lake, and this well-maintained campground. For newcomers to the area, Jamison Camp at the southern end of the park makes for an excellent first stop. So does the nearby hike to Grass Lake, a first-class tromp that takes about two hours and features a streamside walk along Jamison Creek, with the chance to take a five-minute cutoff to see 40-foot Jamison Falls. A historic mine, park museum, blacksmith shop, stable, and stamp mill are also available, with campers provided free admission to the museum. Other must-see destinations in the park include Eureka Lake, and from there, the 1,100-foot climb up to Eureka Peak, 7,447 feet, for a dramatic view of all the famous peaks in this region. Camp elevation is 5,200 feet.

Location: Near Graeagle; map C3, grid h7.

Campsites, facilities: There are 67 sites for tents, trailers, or RVs up to 30 feet long. Picnic tables, food lockers, and fire rings are provided. Drinking water and flush toilets are available. A sanitary disposal station is available nearby. A grocery store, coin laundry, and propane gas are available within five miles. Leashed pets are permitted.

Reservations, fees: No reservations; $12 per night, $1 pet fee. Open mid-May to mid-October, weather permitting.

Directions: In Truckee, drive north on Highway 89 to Graeagle. Just after passing Graeagle (one mile from the junction of Highway 70) turn left on County Road A14/Graeagle-Johnsville Road and drive west for about five miles to the park entrance.

Contact: Plumas-Eureka State Park, tel. (530) 836-2380 or fax (530) 836-0498.

58 Movin' West Trailer Ranch

    4

This RV area is set within a mobile home park. If that's what you want, you've found it. The elevation is 4,300 feet.

Location: In Graeagle; map C3, grid h8.

Campsites, facilities: There are 51 RV sites with full or partial hookups. Picnic tables and fire rings are provided. Drinking water, flush toilets, showers, and a coin laundry are available. Propane gas is available nearby. Leashed pets are permitted.

Reservations, fees: Reservations are accepted; $20 to $22 per night. Open May through October.

Directions: From Truckee, drive northwest on Highway 89 about 50 miles to Graeagle. Continue just past Graeagle to County Road A14. Turn left and drive a quarter mile northwest to the campground.

Contact: Movin' West Trailer Ranch, tel. (530) 836-2614.

59 Sierra Springs Trailer Resort

   5

This privately operated park is centrally located near fishing, golf, and hiking. A railroad museum is nearby in Portola. Other possible side trips include the Feather River Park, four miles away in the town of Blairsden. The elevation is 5,000 feet.

Location: Near Blairsden; map C3, grid h9.

Campsites, facilities: There are 40 RV sites, 30 with full hookups for RVs up to 40 feet. Picnic tables and fire rings are provided. Drinking water, flush toilets, a sanitary disposal station, coin laundry, cable TV, modem hookups, playground, recreation room, and volleyball net are available. Leashed pets are permitted.

Reservations, fees: Reservations are accepted; $20 per night, $2 per person per night for more than two people. Open April through October.

Directions: From Truckee, drive northwest on Highway 89 about 50 miles to Blairsden and the junction with Highway 70. Turn right and drive 3.5 miles east to Sierra Springs Drive. Turn left on Sierra Springs Drive to the resort entrance at 70099 Sierra Springs Road.

Contact: Sierra Spring Trailer Resort, tel. (530) 836-2747 or fax (530) 836-2559.

60 Lakes Basin Group Camp

      8

This is a Forest Service group camp that is ideal for Boy and Girl Scouts. It is set at 6,400 feet in elevation, just a short drive from the trailhead to beautiful Frazier Falls, and also near Gold Lake, Little Bear Lake, and some 15 lakes set below nearby Mount Elwell.

Location: In Plumas National Forest; map C3, grid i8.

Campsites, facilities: This group tent camp can accommodate up to 25 people. Picnic tables and fire grills are provided. Drinking water and vault toilets are available. Supplies are available in Graeagle. Leashed pets are permitted.

Reservations, fees: Reserve at (877) 444-6777 ($8.65 reservation fee) or website: www.reserveusa.com; $45 group fee per night. Open June through October.

Directions: From Truckee, drive north on Highway 89 toward Graeagle to the Gold Lake Highway (one mile before reaching Graeagle). Turn left on the Gold Lake Highway and drive about seven miles to the campground.

Contact: Plumas National Forest, Beckwourth Ranger District, tel. (530) 836-2575 or fax (530) 836-0493.

61 Lakes Basin

 8

Since its renovation in the late 1990s, this camp is now far more accessible to small RVs and trailers, and is a great location for a base camp to explore the surrounding Lakes Basin Recreation Area. From nearby Gold Lake or Elwell Lodge, there are many short hikes available to small pristine lakes. A must-do trip is the easy hike to Frazier Falls, only a mile round-trip to see the spectacular 176-foot waterfall, though the trail is crowded during the middle of the day. The camp elevation is 6,400 feet.

Location: In Plumas National Forest; map C3, grid i8.

Campsites, facilities: There are 24 sites for tents or small RVs. Picnic tables and fire grills are provided. Drinking water and vault toilets are available. Some facilities are wheelchair accessible. Supplies are available in Graeagle. Leashed pets are permitted.

Reservations, fees: Reserve at (877) 444-6777 ($8.65 reservation fee) or website: www.reserveusa.com; $12 per night. Open June through October.

Directions: From Truckee, drive north on Highway 89 toward Graeagle to the Gold Lake Highway (one mile before reaching Graeagle). Turn left on the Gold Lake Highway and drive about seven miles to the campground.

Contact: Plumas National Forest, Beckwourth Ranger District, tel. (530) 836-2575 or fax (530) 836-0493.

62 Clio's River's Edge RV Park

 7

This is a giant RV park set adjacent to a pretty and easily accessible stretch of the Feather River. There are many possible side trip destinations, including Plumas-Eureka State Park, Lakes Basin Recreation Area, and several nearby golf courses. The elevation is about 4,500 feet.

Location: On the Feather River; map C3, grid i9.

Campsites, facilities: There are 220 RV sites with full hookups. Picnic tables are provided. Drinking water, flush toilets, coin-operated showers, laundry room, modem hookups, and cable TV are available. Some facilities are wheelchair accessible. A grocery store is within three miles. Leashed pets are permitted.

Reservations, fees: Reservations are accepted; $22-23 per night, $3 per person (over the age of 5) for more than two people. Open mid-April through mid-October.

Directions: From Truckee, drive north on Highway 89 toward Graeagle and Blairsden. Near Clio (4.5 miles south of Highway 70 at Blairsden), look for the campground entrance.

Contact: Clio's River's Edge, tel. (530) 836-2375.

63 Diablo

 6

This is a primitive camping area set on Packer Creek, about two miles from Packer Lake. This area is extremely beautiful with several lakes nearby, including the Sardine Lakes and Packer Lake, and this camp provides an overflow area when the more developed campgrounds have filled.

Location: On Packer Creek in Tahoe National Forest; map C3, grid i8.

Campsites, facilities: This is an undeveloped, designated camping area for tents and RVs up to 40 feet long. Vault toilets are available. No drinking water is available. Supplies are available in Bassetts and Sierra City. Leashed pets are permitted.

Reservations, fees: No reservations; no fee. Open June through October.

Directions: From Truckee, turn north on Highway 89 and drive 20 miles to Sierraville. At Sierraville, turn left on Highway 49 and drive about 10 miles to the Bassetts Store. Turn right on Gold Lake Road and drive 1.5 miles to Packer Lake Road. Turn left, drive a short distance, bear right at the fork, and drive one mile to the campground on the right side of the road.

Contact: Tahoe National Forest, North Yuba/Downieville Ranger District, tel. (530) 288-3231 or fax (530) 288-0727.

64 Salmon Creek

    9

This campground is set at the confluence of Packer and Salmon Creeks, 5,800 feet in elevation, with easy access off the Gold Lakes Highway. It is on the edge of the Lakes Basin Recreation Area, with literally dozens of lakes within 15 miles, plus great hiking, fishing, and low-speed boating.

Location: In Tahoe National Forest; map C3, grid i8.

Campsites, facilities: There are 31 sites for tents or RVs up to 22 feet long. Picnic tables and fire grills are provided. Drinking water and vault toilets are available. Supplies and a coin laundry are available in Sierra City. Leashed pets are permitted.

Reservations, fees: No reservations; $12 per night. Open June through October.

Directions: From Truckee, turn north on Highway 89 and drive 20 miles to Sierraville. At Sierraville, turn left on Highway 49 and drive about 10 miles to the Bassetts Store. Turn right on Gold Lake Road and drive two miles to the campground on the left side of the road.

Contact: Tahoe National Forest, North Yuba/Downieville Ranger District, tel. (530) 288-3231 or fax (530) 288-0727.

65 Packsaddle

    6

Packsaddle is a primitive spot about a half mile from Packer Lake, with an additional 15 lakes within a five-mile radius, and one of America's truly great hiking trails available nearby. The trail to the Sierra Buttes features a climb of 2,369 feet over the course of five miles. It is highlighted by a stairway with 176 steps that literally juts out into open space, and crowned by an astounding view for hundreds of miles in all directions. Packer Lake, 6,218 feet, is at the foot of the dramatic Sierra Buttes and has lakefront log cabins, good trout fishing, and low-speed boating.

Location: Near Packer Lake in Tahoe National Forest; map C3, grid i8.

Campsites, facilities: There are 12 sites for tents or RVs. Vault toilets are available. Drinking water (hand-pumped) is available. Pack and saddle animals are permitted and corrals and hitching rails are available. Supplies are available in Bassetts and Sierra City. Leashed pets are permitted.

Reservations, fees: No reservations; $12 per night. Open June through October.

Directions: From Truckee, turn north on Highway 89 and drive 20 miles to Sierraville. At Sierraville, turn left on Highway 49 and drive about 10 miles to the Bassetts Store. Turn right on Gold Lake Road and drive 1.5 miles to Packer Lake Road. Turn left, drive a short distance, bear right at the fork, and drive 2.5 miles to the campground on the left.

Contact: Tahoe National Forest, North Yuba/Downieville Ranger District, tel. (530) 288-3231 or fax (530) 288-0727.

66 Berger Creek

    6

Berger Creek, primitive and undeveloped, provides an overflow alternative to nearby Diablo, which is also extremely primitive. On busy summer weekends, when an open campsite can be difficult to find at a premium location in the Lakes Basin Recreation Area, these two camps provide a safety valve to keep you from being stuck for the night. Nearby is Packer Lake, the trail to the Sierra Buttes, Sardine Lakes, and Sand Pond, all excellent destinations. The elevation is 5,900 feet.

Location: In Tahoe National Forest; map C3, grid i8.

Campsites, facilities: There are 10 sites for tents or RVs up to 16 feet long. Picnic tables and fire grills are provided. Vault toilets are available. No drinking water is available. Supplies are available in Bassetts and Sierra City. Leashed pets are permitted.

Reservations, fees: No reservations; no fee. Open June through October.

Directions: From Truckee, turn north on Highway 89 and drive 20 miles to Sierraville. At Sierraville, turn left on Highway 49 and drive about 10 miles to the Bassetts Store. Turn right on Gold Lake Road and drive 1.5 miles to Packer Lake Road. Turn left, drive a short distance, bear right at the fork, and drive two miles to the campground on the left.

Contact: Tahoe National Forest, North Yuba/Downieville Ranger District, tel. (530) 288-3231 or fax (530) 288-0727.

67 Snag Lake

Snag Lake is an ideal little lake for camping anglers with canoes. There are no boat ramps and you can have the place virtually to yourself. It is set at 6,600 feet in elevation, an easy-to-reach lake in the Lakes Basin Recreation Area. Trout fishing is only fair, as in fair numbers and fair size, mainly rainbow trout in the 10- to 12-inch class. This is a primitive camp, so bring everything you will need, including water.

Location: In Tahoe National Forest; map C3, grid i8.

Campsites, facilities: There are 16 sites for tents or RVs up to 16 feet long. Picnic tables

and fire grills are provided. Vault toilets are available. No drinking water is available. Only hand boat launching is allowed. Supplies are available in Bassetts and Sierra City. Leashed pets are permitted.

Reservations, fees: No reservations; no fee. Open June through October.

Directions: From Truckee, turn north on Highway 89 and drive 20 miles to Sierraville. At Sierraville, turn left on Highway 49 and drive about 10 miles to the Bassetts Store. Turn right on Gold Lake Road and drive five miles to the campground on the left.

Contact: Tahoe National Forest, North Yuba/Downieville Ranger District, tel. (530) 288-3231 or fax (530) 288-0727.

68 Sardine Lake

Lower Sardine Lake is a jewel set below the Sierra Buttes, one of the prettiest settings in California. The campground is actually about a mile east of the lake. Nearby is the beautiful Sand Pond Interpretive Trail. A great hike is routed along the shore of Lower Sardine Lake to a hidden waterfall (in spring) that feeds the lake, and ambitious hikers can explore beyond and discover Upper Sardine Lake. Trout fishing is excellent in Lower Sardine Lake, with a primitive boat ramp available for small boats. The speed limit and small size of the lake keeps boaters slow and quiet. A small marina and boat rentals are available.

Location: In Tahoe National Forest; map C3, grid j8.

Campsites, facilities: There are 29 sites for tents or RVs up to 22 feet long. Picnic tables and fire grills are provided. Drinking water and vault toilets are available. Some facilities are wheelchair accessible. There are limited supplies at the Sardine Lake Lodge or in Bassetts. Leashed pets are permitted.

Reservations, fees: No reservations; $12 per night. Open June through October.

Directions: From Truckee, drive north on Highway 89 for 20 miles to Sierraville. Turn left on Highway 49 and drive about 10 miles to the Bassetts Store. Turn right on Gold Lake Road and drive 1.5 miles to Packer Lake Road. Turn left, drive a short distance, then bear left at the fork and drive a half mile to the campground on the left.

Contact: Tahoe National Forest, North Yuba/Downieville Ranger District, tel. (530) 288-3231 or fax (530) 288-0727.

69 Strawberry

 7

Sly Creek Reservoir is a long, narrow lake set in western Plumas National Forest. There are two campgrounds on opposite ends of the lake, with different directions to each. This camp is set in the back of a cove on the lake's eastern arm at an elevation of 3,530 feet, with a nearby boat ramp available. This is a popular lake for trout fishing in the summer.

Location: On Sly Creek Reservoir in Plumas National Forest; map C3, grid i2.

Campsites, facilities: There are 27 sites for tents, trailers, or RVs. Picnic tables and fire grills are provided. Drinking water and vault toilets are available. A car-top boat launch and fish-cleaning station are available on Sly Creek Reservoir. Leashed pets are permitted.

Reservations, fees: No reservations; $12 per night. Open late May to mid-October, weather permitting.

Directions: From Oroville, drive east on Highway 162 for about eight miles to the junction signed Challenge/LaPorte. Bear right and drive east on LaPorte Road past Challenge and continue for about 14 miles to a signed turnoff on the left for Sly Creek Reservoir. Turn left and drive one mile to the campground on the eastern end of the lake.

Contact: Plumas National Forest, Feather River Ranger District, tel. (530) 534-6500 or fax (530) 532-1210.

70 Sly Creek

 7

Sly Creek Camp is set on Sly Creek Reservoir's southwestern shore near Lewis Flat, with a boat ramp about a mile to the north. Both camps are well situated for campers/anglers. This camp provides direct access to the lake's main body, with good trout fishing well upstream on the main lake arm. You get quiet water and decent fishing.

Location: On Sly Creek Reservoir in Plumas National Forest; map C3, grid i2.

Campsites, facilities: There are 21 sites for tents, trailers, or RVs up to 40 feet long. Five walk-in tent cabins are also available. Picnic tables and fire grills are provided. Drinking water and vault toilets are available. A car-top boat launch and fish-cleaning stations are available on Sly Creek Reservoir. Leashed pets are permitted.

Reservations, fees: No reservations; $14 per night. Open late May to mid-October, weather permitting.

Directions: From Oroville, drive east on Highway 162 for about eight miles to the junction signed Challenge/LaPorte. Bear right and drive east on LaPorte Road past Challenge and continue for 10 miles to Forest Road 16 (a signed turnoff on the left). Turn left and drive 4.5 miles to the campground.

Contact: Plumas National Forest, Feather River Ranger District, tel. (530) 534-6500 or fax (530) 532-1210.

71 Garden Point Boat-In

  8

Bullards Bar Reservoir is one of the few lakes in the Sierra Nevada to offer boat-in camping at developed boat-in sites and to allow boaters to create their own primitive sites anywhere along the lake's shoreline. A chemical toilet is required gear for boat-in shoreline camping. Garden Point Boat-In is on the western shore of the northern Yuba River arm. This lake provides plenty of recreation options, including good fishing for kokanee salmon, water-skiing, and many coves for playing in the water.

Location: On Bullards Bar Reservoir; map C3, grid j2.

Campsites, facilities: There are 16 sites (12 single and four double sites) accessible by boat only. Picnic tables and fire grills are provided. Vault toilets are available. No drinking water is available. You must burn or pack out your garbage. Some facilities are wheelchair accessible. Supplies are available in Emerald Cove Marina. Leashed pets are permitted.

Reservations, fees: Reservations are required from Emerald Cove Resort, tel. (530) 692-3200; $14 per night. Open mid-April to mid-October.

Directions: From Marysville, drive northeast on Highway 20 to Marysville Road. Turn north at Marysville Road (signed Bullards Bar Reservoir) and drive about 10 miles to Old Marysville Road. Turn right and drive 14 miles to reach the Cottage Creek Launch Ramp and the marina (turn left just before the dam).

To reach the Dark Day boat ramp, continue over the dam and drive four miles, turn left on Dark Day Road, and continue to the ramp. From the boat launch, continue to the campground on the northwest side.

Contact: Emerald Cove Resort and Marina, tel. (530) 692-3200. Tahoe National Forest, North Yuba/Downieville Ranger District, tel. (530) 288-3231 or fax (530) 288-0727.

72 Dark Day Walk-In

     8

Along with Schoolhouse, this is the only car-accessible camping area at Bullards Bar Reservoir with direct shoreline access. You park in a central area and then walk a short distance to the campground. The lake is a very short walk beyond that. Bullards Bar is a great camping lake, pretty and large with several lake arms and good fishing for kokanee salmon (as long as you have a boat). It is set at 2,000 feet in the foothills, like a silver dollar in a field of pennies. A bonus at Bullards Bar is that there is never a charge for day use, parking, or boat launching.

Location: On Bullards Bar Reservoir; map C3, grid j2.

Campsites, facilities: There are 16 walk-in tent sites. Picnic tables and fire pits are provided. Drinking water and flush and vault toilets are available. A boat ramp is available nearby, and supplies are available at Emerald Cove Marina. Leashed pets are permitted.

Reservations, fees: Reservations are required from Emerald Cove Resort, tel. (530) 692-3200; $14 per night. Open mid-April to mid-October.

Directions: From Marysville, drive northeast on Highway 20 to Marysville Road. Turn north at Marysville Road (signed Bullards Bar Reservoir) and drive about 10 miles to Old Marysville Road. Turn right, drive 14 miles, and continue over the dam for four miles to Dark Day Road. Turn left and drive past the boat launch to the campground on the northwest side of the lake.

Contact: Emerald Cove Resort and Marina, tel. (530) 692-3200. Tahoe National Forest, North Yuba/Downieville Ranger District, tel. (530) 288-3231 or fax (530) 288-0727.

73 Shoreline Camp Boat-In

      8

There are two boat-in campgrounds on Bullards Bar Reservoir, but another option is to throw all caution to the wind and just head out on your own, camping wherever you want. It is critical to bring a shovel to dig a flat site for sleeping, a large tarp for sun protection, and of course, plenty of water or a water purification pump. This is a big, beautiful lake, with good trolling for kokanee salmon. Note: a portable chemical toilet is required.

Location: On Bullards Bar Reservoir; map C3, grid j2.

Campsites, facilities: Boaters may choose their own primitive campsite anywhere on the shore of Bullards Bar Reservoir. Garbage must be packed out. Supplies are available at Emerald Cove Marina. Leashed pets are permitted. **Reservations, fees:** Reservations and a shoreline camping permit are required from Emerald Cove Resort, tel. (530) 692-3200; $14 per night. Open mid-April to mid-October. **Directions:** From Marysville, turn east on Highway 20 and drive 12 miles. Turn left on Marysville Road (look for the sign for Bullards Bar Reservoir) and drive 10 miles. Turn right on Old Marysville Road and drive 14 miles to the Cottage Creek Launch Ramp (turn left just before the dam). To reach the boat launch, continue to the campgrounds on the west side. **Contact:** Emerald Cove Resort and Marina, tel. (530) 692-3200. Tahoe National Forest, North Yuba/Downieville Ranger District, tel. (530) 288-3231 or fax (530) 288-0727.

74 Madrone Cove Boat-In

 8

This is one of several boat-in campgrounds at Bullards Bar Reservoir. It is set on the main Yuba River arm of the lake, along the western shore. This is a premium boat-in site. The elevation is 2,000 feet. **Location:** On Bullards Bar Reservoir; map C3, grid j2. **Campsites, facilities:** There are 10 sites, accessible by boat only. Picnic tables and fire grills are provided. Vault toilets are available. No drinking water is available. Garbage must be packed out. Supplies are available at the marina. Leashed pets are permitted. **Reservations, fees:** Reservations and a shoreline camping permit are required from Emerald Cove Resort, tel. (530) 692-3200; $14 per night. Open mid-April to mid-October. **Directions:** From Marysville, drive 12 miles east on Highway 20. Turn left at the sign for Bullards Bar Reservoir (Marysville Road). Drive 10 miles north, turn right on Old Marysville Road, and drive 14 miles to reach the Cottage Creek Launch Ramp and the marina (turn left just before the dam). To reach the ramp

continue over the dam, drive four miles, turn left on Dark Day Road, and continue to the ramp. From the boat launch, continue to the campground on the west side. **Contact:** Emerald Cove Resort and Marina, tel. (530) 692-3200. Tahoe National Forest, North Yuba/Downieville Ranger District, tel. (530) 288-3231 or fax (530) 288-0727.

75 Schoolhouse

 7

Bullards Bar Reservoir is one of the better lakes in the Sierra Nevada for camping, primarily because the lake levels tend to be higher here than at many other lakes. The camp is set on the southeast shore, with a trail available out of the camp to a beautiful lookout of the lake. Bullards Bar is known for good fishing for trout and kokanee salmon, water-skiing, and all water sports. A three-lane concrete boat ramp is to the south at Cottage Creek. Boaters should consider the special boat-in camps at the lake. The elevation is 2,200 feet. **Location:** On Bullards Bar Reservoir; map C3, grid j2. **Campsites, facilities:** There are 56 sites (one triple, 11 double, and 44 single sites) for tents or RVs. Single sites accommodate six people, double sites accommodate 12, and triple sites hold up to 18 people. Picnic tables and fire rings are provided. Drinking water and flush and vault toilets are available. A boat ramp is nearby. Supplies are available in North San Juan, Camptonville, Dobbins, and at the marina. Leashed pets are permitted. **Reservations, fees:** Reservations and a shoreline camping permit are required from Emerald Cove Resort, tel. (530) 692-3200; $14 per night. Open mid-April to mid-October. **Directions:** From Marysville, turn east on Highway 20 and drive 12 miles. Turn left on Marysville Road (look for the sign for Bullards Bar Reservoir) and drive 10 miles. Turn right on Old Marysville Road, drive 14 miles to the dam, and continue for another three miles to the campground entrance road on the left.

Contact: Emerald Cove Resort and Marina, tel. (530) 692-3200. Tahoe National Forest, North Yuba/Downieville Ranger District, tel. (530) 288-3231 or fax (530) 288-0727.

76 Fiddle Creek

     7

This camp is situated on the North Yuba River in a quiet, forested area. This is a beautiful stream, one of the prettiest to flow westward out of the Sierra Nevada, with deep pools and miniature waterfalls. It is popular for rafting out of Goodyears Bar, and if you can stand the cold water, there are many good swimming holes along Highway 49. Fiddle Bow Trail leads out from the camp to Halls Ranch Station or Indian Rock. Bring your own drinking water or a water purifier. It's set at 2,200 feet. There are a series of campgrounds on this stretch of the Yuba River.

Location: On the North Yuba River in Tahoe National Forest; map C3, grid j3.

Campsites, facilities: There are 15 tent sites. Picnic tables and fire rings are provided. Drinking water and vault toilets are available. Limited supplies are available nearby at the Indian Valley Outpost. Some facilities are wheelchair accessible, including a paved trail to the Yuba River. Leashed pets are permitted.

Reservations, fees: No reservations; $12 per night. Open year-round.

Directions: From Auburn, take Highway 49 north to Nevada City and continue (the road jogs left, then narrows) to Camptonville. Drive 9.5 miles to the campground entrance on the right.

Contact: Tahoe National Forest, North Yuba/Downieville Ranger District, tel. (530) 288-3231 or fax (530) 288-0727.

77 Carlton/Cal-Ida

     7

Carlton is on the North Yuba River, and Cal-Ida is across the road. Both are right next door to Fiddle Creek. For more information, see the entry for Fiddle Creek.

Location: On the North Yuba River in Tahoe National Forest; map C3, grid j3.

Campsites, facilities: There are two undeveloped camping areas. Picnic tables and fire grills are provided. Drinking water and vault toilets are available. Some facilities are wheelchair accessible. Some supplies are available at the Indian Valley Outpost nearby. Leashed pets are permitted.

Reservations, fees: No reservations; $12 per night. Open mid-April through November.

Directions: From Auburn, take Highway 49 north to Nevada City and continue (the road jogs left, then narrows) to Camptonville. Drive nine miles to the campground entrance. The camping area at Carlton is one mile northeast of the Highway 49 bridge at Indian Valley. The camping area at Cal-Ida is behind the Indian Valley Outpost on the Cal-Ida Road.

Contact: Tahoe National Forest, North Yuba/Downieville Ranger District, tel. (530) 288-3231 or fax (530) 288-0727.

78 Indian Valley

  7

This is an easy-to-reach spot set at 2,200 feet beside the North Yuba River. Highway 49 runs adjacent to the Yuba for miles eastward, providing easy access to the river in many areas. There are several other camps in the immediate area; see the entries for Fiddle Creek and Cal-Ida, both within a mile.

Location: On the North Yuba River in Tahoe National Forest; map C3, grid j3.

Campsites, facilities: There are nine tent sites and eight sites for RVs up to 22 feet long. Picnic tables and fire grills are provided. Drinking water and vault toilets are available. Limited supplies are available nearby at the Indian Valley Outpost. Leashed pets are permitted.

Reservations, fees: No reservations; $12 per night. Open year-round.

Directions: From Auburn, take Highway 49 north to Nevada City and continue (the road jogs left, then narrows) to Camptonville. Drive 10 miles to the camp entrance on the right.

Contact: Tahoe National Forest, North Yuba/Downieville Ranger District, tel. (530) 288-3231 or fax (530) 288-0727.

79 Rocky Rest

     7

This is one in a series of campgrounds set at streamside on the North Yuba River. The elevation is 2,200 feet. A newly constructed footbridge is now available that crosses the North Yuba and provides an outstanding seven-mile hike.

Location: On the North Yuba River in Tahoe National Forest; map C3, grid j4.

Campsites, facilities: There are 10 dispersed camping sites. Picnic tables and fire grills are provided. Drinking water and vault toilets are available. Limited supplies are available at the Indian Valley Outpost nearby. Leashed pets are permitted.

Reservations, fees: No reservations; $12 per night. Open mid-April through November.

Directions: From Auburn, take Highway 49 north to Nevada City and continue (the road jogs left, then narrows) to Camptonville. Drive 10 miles north to the campground entrance on the right.

Contact: Tahoe National Forest, North Yuba/ Downieville Ranger District, tel. (530) 288-3231 or fax (530) 288-0727.

80 Ramshorn

      7

This camp is set on Ramshorn Creek, just across the road from the North Yuba River. It's one in a series of camps on this stretch of the beautiful North Yuba River. A short distance downstream is a picnic area with a trailhead for the Hallsranch Fiddle Ridge Trail. Goodyears Bar, one mile east, is a famous access point for white-water rafting trips on the Yuba. The camp's elevation is 2,600 feet.

Location: On the North Yuba River in Tahoe National Forest; map C3, grid j4.

Campsites, facilities: There are nine tent sites and seven sites for tents or RVs up to 22 feet long. Picnic tables and fire grills are provided. Drinking water and vault toilets are available. Supplies are available in Downieville. Leashed pets are permitted.

Reservations, fees: No reservations; $12 per night. Open year-round.

Directions: From Auburn, take Highway 49 north to Nevada City and continue (the road jogs left, then narrows) to Camptonville. Drive 15 miles north to the campground entrance on the left.

Contact: Tahoe National Forest, North Yuba/Downieville Ranger District, tel. (530) 288-3231 or fax (530) 288-0727.

81 Union Flat

      8

Of all the campgrounds on the North Yuba River along Highway 49, this one has the best swimming. The camp is set near Quartz Point and Granite Mountain and has a nice swimming hole next to it if you can stand the cold. Recreational mining is also an attraction here. The elevation is 3,400 feet.

Location: On the North Yuba River in Tahoe National Forest; map C3, grid j7.

Campsites, facilities: There are 11 sites for tents or RVs up to 35 feet long. Picnic tables and fire grills are provided. Drinking water and vault toilets are available. Some facilities are wheelchair accessible. Supplies are available in Downieville. Leashed pets are permitted.

Reservations, fees: No reservations; $12 per night. Open May through October.

Directions: From Auburn, take Highway 49 north to Nevada City and continue (the road jogs left, then narrows) to Downieville. Drive six miles east to the campground entrance on the right.

Contact: Tahoe National Forest, North Yuba/ Downieville Ranger District, tel. (530) 288-3231 or fax (530) 288-0727.

82 Loganville

 8

Nearby Sierra City is only two miles away, meaning you can make a quick getaway for a prepared meal or any food or drink you may need to add to your camp. Loganville is set on the North Yuba River, elevation 4,200 feet. It offers a good stretch of water in this region for trout fishing, with many pools set below miniature waterfalls.

Location: On the North Yuba River in Tahoe National Forest; map C3, grid j7.

Campsites, facilities: There are 20 sites for tents or RVs up to 22 feet long. Picnic tables and fire grills are provided. Drinking water and vault toilets are available. Supplies and a coin laundry are available in Sierra City. Leashed pets are permitted.

Reservations, fees: No reservations; $12 per night. Open May through October.

Directions: From Auburn, take Highway 49 north to Nevada City and continue (the road jogs left, then narrows) to Downieville. Drive 12 miles east to the campground entrance on the right (two miles west of Sierra City).

Contact: Tahoe National Forest, North Yuba/ Downieville Ranger District, tel. (530) 288-3231 or fax (530) 288-0727.

83 Wild Plum

 8

This popular Forest Service camp is set on Haypress Creek at 4,400 feet. There are several hidden waterfalls in the area, which makes this a popular camp for the people who know of them. There's a scenic hike up the Haypress Trail, which goes past a waterfall to Haypress Valley. Two other nearby waterfalls are Loves Falls (on the North Yuba on Highway 49 two miles east of Sierra City) and Hackmans Falls (remote, set in a ravine one mile south of Sierra City; no road access).

Location: On Haypress Creek in Tahoe National Forest; map C3, grid j8.

Campsites, facilities: There are a total of 47 sites, 26 for tents and 21 for RVs up to 22 feet long. Picnic tables and fire grills are provided. Drinking water and vault toilets are available. Supplies and a coin laundry are available in Sierra City. Leashed pets are permitted.

Reservations, fees: No reservations; $12 per night. Open May through October.

Directions: From Auburn, take Highway 49 north to Nevada City and continue (the road jogs left, then narrows) past Downieville to Sierra City at Wild Plum Road. Turn right on Wild Plum Road and drive two miles to the campground entrance road on the right.

Contact: Tahoe National Forest, North Yuba/ Downieville Ranger District, tel. (530) 288-3231 or fax (530) 288-0727.

84 Chapman Creek

 8

This camp is set along Chapman Creek at 6,000 feet, just across the highway from where it enters the North Yuba River. A good side trip is to hike the Chapman Creek Trail, which leads out of camp to Beartrap Meadow or to Haskell Peak (8,107 feet).

Location: On the North Yuba River in Tahoe National Forest; map C3, grid j9.

Campsites, facilities: There are a total of 29 sites, 15 for tents and 14 for RVs up to 22 feet long. Picnic tables and fire grills are provided. Drinking water and vault toilets are available. Supplies are available in Bassetts. Leashed pets are permitted.

Reservations, fees: No reservations; $12 per night. Open June through October.

Directions: From Truckee, turn north on Highway 89 and drive 20 miles to Sierraville. At Sierraville, turn left on Highway 49, drive over Yuba Pass, and continue for four miles to the campground on the right.

Contact: Tahoe National Forest, North Yuba/ Downieville Ranger District, tel. (530) 288-3231 or fax (530) 288-0727.

85 Sierra

 7

This is a primitive and easy-to-reach spot set along the North Yuba River, used primarily as an overflow area from nearby Chapman Creek (a mile upstream). Nearby recreation options include the Chapman Creek Trail, several waterfalls (see Wild Plum), and the nearby Lakes Basin Recreation Area to the north off the Gold Lake Highway. The elevation is 5,600 feet.

Location: On the North Yuba River in Tahoe National Forest; map C3, grid j9.

Campsites, facilities: There are nine sites for tents and seven sites for tents or RVs up to 22 feet long. Picnic tables and fire rings are provided. Vault toilets are available. No drinking water is available. Supplies are available in Bassetts. Leashed pets are permitted.

Reservations, fees: No reservations; $10 per night. Open June through October.

Directions: From Truckee, turn north on Highway 89 and drive 20 miles to Sierraville. At Sierraville, turn left on Highway 49 and drive over Yuba Pass. Continue for five miles to the campground on the left side of the road.

Contact: Tahoe National Forest, North Yuba/Downieville Ranger District, tel. (530) 288-3231 or fax (530) 288-0727.

PATRICK RACE

PETROGLYPHS
NORTH OF HONEY LAKE

MAP C4

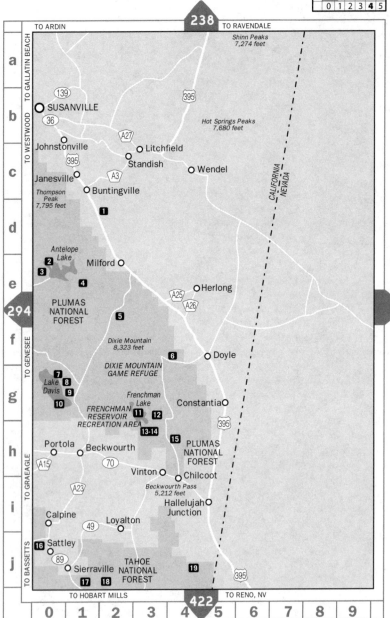

TO ARDIN **238** TO RAVENDALE

Shinn Peaks
7,274 feet

TO GALLATIN BEACH

TO WESTWOOD

(139)

SUSANVILLE
(36)

Hot Springs Peaks
7,680 feet

(395)

Johnstonville

(A27)

○ Litchfield

(395)

Standish

Janesville

(A3)

○ Wendel

Thompson
Peak
7,795 feet

○ Buntingville

1

Antelope
Lake

2
3

○ Milford

4

○ Herlong

PLUMAS
NATIONAL
FOREST

(A25)
(A26)

5

Dixie Mountain
8,323 feet

TO GENESEE

6

○ Doyle

DIXIE MOUNTAIN
GAME REFUGE

7
Lake **8**
Davis **9**

10

Frenchman
Lake

FRENCHMAN
RESERVOIR
RECREATION
AREA

11 **12**

Constantia ○

(395)

13-14

15

Portola ○
○ Beckwourth

PLUMAS
NATIONAL
FOREST

TO GRAEAGLE

(A15)

(70)

Vinton ○ ○ Chilcoot

Beckwourth Pass
5,212 feet

(A23)

Hallelujah ○
Junction

Calpine ○
○ Loyalton

(49)

TO BASSETTS

16 Sattley
(89)

TAHOE
NATIONAL
FOREST

19

○ Sierraville
17 **18**

TO HOBART MILLS **422** TO RENO, NV

CALIFORNIA
NEVADA

294

CHAPTER C4

1 Honey Lake Campground

    4

For newcomers, Honey Lake is a strange looking place—a vast, flat alkali lake with not much around. It sits in a huge basin that, from a distance, looks almost moonlike. The campground is set at 4,300 feet and covers 27 acres, most of it overlooking the lake. There are a lot of junipers and scraggly aspens nearby, and a waterfowl management area is along the north shore of the lake.

Location: Near Milford; map C4, grid d2.

Campsites, facilities: There are 50 sites for tents or RVs, most with full or partial hookups. Picnic tables are provided. Restrooms, showers, laundry room, sanitary disposal station, propane gas, grocery store, playground, ice, wood, modem hookups, and a game room are available. Some facilities are wheelchair accessible. Leashed pets are permitted.

Reservations, fees: Reservations are accepted; $12.50 to $16.50 per night, $2.50 per person per night for more than two people. Open year-round, weather permitting.

Directions: From Susanville on U.S. 395, drive 19 miles south (if you reach Milford, you have gone two miles too far) to the campground.

Contact: Honey Lake Campground, tel. (530) 253-2508.

2 Boulder Creek

    7

Antelope Lake is a pretty mountain lake circled by conifers with nice campsites and good trout fishing. It is set at 5,000 feet in remote eastern Plumas National Forest, far enough away so the marginally inclined never make the trip. Campgrounds are at each end of the lake (this one is just north of Lone Rock at the north end), with a boat ramp at Lost Cove on the east side of the lake. The lake isn't huge, but it is big enough, with 15 miles of shoreline and little islands, coves, and peninsulas to give it an intimate feel.

Location: At Antelope Lake in Plumas National Forest; map C4, grid e0.

Campsites, facilities: There are 70 sites for tents or RVs. Picnic tables and fire grills are provided. Drinking water and vault toilets are available. A sanitary disposal station, boat ramp, and grocery store are nearby. Leashed pets are permitted.

Reservations, fees: Reserve at (877) 444-6777 ($8.65 reservation fee) or website: www.reserveusa.com; $14 per night, lakeshore sites are $16 per night; $4 for an extra vehicle per night. Open May through October.

Directions: From Red Bluff, drive east on Highway 36 to Susanville and U.S. 395. Turn south on U.S. 395 and drive about 10 miles (one mile past Janesville) to County Road 208. Turn right on County Road 208 (signed Antelope Lake) and drive about 15 miles to a Y (one mile before Antelope Lake). Turn left at the Y and drive four miles to the campground entrance on the right side of the road (on the northwest end of the lake).

Contact: Plumas National Forest, Mount Hough Ranger District, tel. (530) 283-0555 or fax (530) 283-1821.

🖪 Lone Rock

      9

This camp provides an option to nearby Boulder Creek, to the immediate north at the northwest shore of Antelope Lake. For more information, see the entry for Boulder Creek. The elevation is 5,000 feet. Campfire programs are offered in the summer at the on-site amphitheater.

Location: At Antelope Lake in Plumas National Forest; map C4, grid e0.

Campsites, facilities: There are 86 sites for tents or RVs up to 45 feet long. Picnic tables and fire grills are provided. Drinking water and vault toilets are available. A sanitary disposal station, boat ramp, and grocery store are nearby. Leashed pets are permitted.

Reservations, fees: Reserve Reserve at (877) 444-6777 ($8.65 reservation fee) or website: www.reserveusa.com; $14 to $16 per night, $4 for an extra vehicle per night. Open May through October.

Directions: From Red Bluff, drive east on Highway 36 to Susanville and U.S. 395. Go south on U.S. 395 and drive about 10 miles (one mile past Janesville) to County Road 208. Turn right on County Road 208 (signed Antelope Lake) and drive about 15 miles to a Y

(one mile before Antelope Lake). Turn left at the Y and drive three miles to the campground entrance on the right side of the road (on the northwest end of the lake).

Contact: Plumas National Forest, Mount Hough Ranger District, tel. (530) 283-0555 or fax (530) 283-1821.

🖪 Long Point

    7

Long Point is a pretty camp set on a peninsula that extends well into Antelope Lake, facing Lost Cove. There are actually two camps here, with a bonus group camp set on the east side of the main campground. The lake's boat ramp is at Lost Cove, a three-mile drive around the northeast shore. Trout fishing is often good here, with a wide variety of sizes, from the little stocked Slim Jim rainbow trout on up to some large brown trout. A wheelchair-accessible nature trail and fishing pier are available.

Location: At Antelope Lake in Plumas National Forest; map C4, grid e1.

Campsites, facilities: There are 38 single sites and four group sites for tents or RVs up to 50 feet long. Picnic tables and fire grills are provided. Drinking water and vault toilets are available. A grocery store, boat ramp, and sanitary disposal station are nearby. Leashed pets are permitted.

Reservations, fees: Reserve at (877) 444-6777 ($8.65 reservation fee) or website: www.reserveusa.com; $14 to $16 per night; group sites are $40 per night. Open May through October.

Directions: From Red Bluff, drive east on Highway 36 to Susanville and U.S. 395. Go south on U.S. 395 and drive about 10 miles (one mile past Janesville) to County Road 208. Turn right on County Road 208 (signed Antelope Lake) and drive about 15 miles to a Y (one mile before Antelope Lake). Turn right at the Y and drive one mile to the campground entrance on the left side of the road.

Contact: Plumas National Forest, Greenville Work Center, Mount Hough Ranger District, tel. (530) 284-7126 or fax (530) 284-6211.

5 Conklin Park

 4

This camp is along little Willow Creek on the northeastern border of the Dixie Mountain State Game Refuge. Much of the area is recovering from a fire that burned during the summer of 1989. Although the area has greened up, there remains significant evidence of the fire. The campground is little known, primitive, rarely used, and is not likely to change any time soon. The elevation is 5,900 feet.

Location: On Willow Creek in Plumas National Forest; map C4, grid f2.

Campsites, facilities: There are nine sites for tents or RVs up to 22 feet long. Picnic tables and fire grills are provided. Vault toilets are available. No drinking water is available. Garbage must be packed out. Leashed pets are permitted.

Reservations, fees: No reservations; no fee. Open May through October.

Directions: From Susanville on U.S. 395, drive south for 24 miles to Milford. In Milford turn right (east) on County Road 336 and drive about four miles to a Y. Bear to the left on Forest Road 70/26N70 and drive three miles. Turn right at the bridge at Willow Creek, turn left on Forest Road 70 (now paved), and drive three miles to the camp entrance road on the left side.

Contact: Plumas National Forest, Beckwourth Ranger District, tel. (530) 836-2575 or fax (530) 836-0493.

6 Meadow View

 6

This little-known, primitive camp is set along the headwaters of Little Last Chance Creek, along the eastern border of the Dixie Mountain State Game Refuge. The access road contin-

ues along the creek and connects with primitive roads that enter the interior of the game refuge. Side trip options include Frenchman Lake to the south, and the drive up to Dixie Mountain, at 8,323 feet in elevation. The elevation is 6,100 feet.

Location: Near Little Last Chance Creek in Plumas National Forest; map C4, grid f4.

Campsites, facilities: There are six sites for tents or RVs up to 30 feet. Picnic tables and fire grills are provided. Vault toilets are available. No drinking water is available. Garbage must be packed out. Leashed pets are permitted.

Reservations, fees: No reservations; no fee. Open May through October.

Directions: From Reno, drive north on U.S. 395 for 43 miles to Doyle. At Doyle, turn west on Doyle Grade Road/County Road 331 (a dirt road most of the way) and drive 7.5 miles to the campground.

Contact: Plumas National Forest, Beckwourth Ranger District, tel. (530) 836-2575 or fax (530) 836-0493.

7 Lightning Tree

 7

Lake Davis is one of the top mountain lakes for fishing in California, with large rainbow trout in the early summer and fall. This camp is perfectly situated for a fishing trip. It is at Lightning Tree Point on the lake's remote northeast shore, directly across the lake from Freeman Creek, one of the better spots for big trout. This lake is famous for the botched poisoning job in the 1990s by the Department of Fish and Game, then in turn, the biggest trout plants in California history at a single lake: more than 1 million trout! A boat launch is available on the north side of the camp, a great bonus. Davis is a good-sized lake, with 30 miles of shoreline, set high in the northern Sierra at 5,775 feet, so it gets lots of snow and often freezes over in the winter.

Location: On Lake Davis in Plumas National Forest; map C4, grid g0.

Campsites, facilities: There are 38 sites for RVs up to 50 feet long. Vault toilets are available. Garbage service is provided from May through October only. No drinking water is available. Vault toilets, sanitary disposal station, and a car-top boat launch are nearby. Leashed pets are permitted.

Reservations, fees: Reserve at (877) 444-6777 ($8.65 reservation fee) or website: www.reserveusa.com; $6 per night, $10 for a double site.

Directions: From Truckee, turn north on Highway 89 and drive to Sattley and County Road A23. Turn right on County Road A23 and drive 13 miles to Highway 70. Turn left on Highway 70 and drive one mile to Grizzly Road. Turn right on Grizzly Road and drive about six miles to Lake Davis. Continue north on Lake Davis Road along the lake's east shore and drive about five miles to the campground entrance on the left side of the road.

Contact: Plumas National Forest, Beckwourth Ranger District, tel. (530) 836-2575 or fax (530) 836-0493.

8 Grasshopper Flat

 7

Grasshopper Flat provides a nearby alternative to Grizzly at Lake Davis, with the nearby boat ramp at adjacent Honker Cove a primary attraction for campers with trailered boats for fishing. The camp is on the southeast end of the lake, at 5,800 feet elevation. Lake Davis is known for its large rainbow trout that bite best in early summer and fall.

Location: On Lake Davis in Plumas National Forest; map C4, grid g0.

Campsites, facilities: There are 70 sites for tents or RVs up to 32 feet long. Picnic tables and fire grills are provided. Drinking water and vault toilets are available. A boat ramp, grocery store, and sanitary disposal station are nearby. Leashed pets are permitted.

Reservations, fees: Reservations are accepted for some sites; $13 per night. Open May through October.

Directions: From Truckee, turn north on Highway 89 and drive to Sattley and County Road A23. Turn right on County Road A23 and drive 13 miles to Highway 70. Turn left on Highway 70 and drive one mile to Grizzly Road. Turn right on Grizzly Road and drive about six miles to Lake Davis. Continue north on Lake Davis Road for a mile (just past Grizzly) to the campground entrance on the left side of the road.

Contact: Plumas National Forest, Beckwourth Ranger District, tel. (530) 836-2575 or fax (530) 836-0493.

9 Crocker

 5

Even though this camp is just four miles east of Lake Davis, it is little known and little used since there are three lakeside camps close by. This camp is set in Plumas National Forest at 5,800 feet elevation, and it is about a 15-minute drive north to the border of the Dixie Mountain State Game Refuge.

Location: In Plumas National Forest; map C4, grid g1.

Campsites, facilities: There are 10 sites for tents or RVs up to 32 feet long. Picnic tables and fire grills are provided. Vault toilets are available. No drinking water is available. Garbage must be packed out. Leashed pets are permitted.

Reservations, fees: No reservations; no fee. Open May through October.

Directions: From Reno, drive north on U.S. 395 to the junction with Highway 70. Turn west on Highway 70 and drive to Beckwourth and County Road 111/Beckwourth-Genessee Road. Turn right on County Road 111 and drive six miles to the campground on the left side of the road.

Contact: Plumas National Forest, Beckwourth Ranger District, tel. (530) 836-2575 or fax (530) 836-0493.

🔟 Grizzly

 7

This is one of the better developed campgrounds at Lake Davis and is a popular spot for camping anglers. Its proximity to the Grizzly Store, just over the dam to the south, makes getting last-minute supplies a snap. In addition, a boat ramp is to the north in Honker Cove, providing access to the southern reaches of the lake, including the island area, where trout trolling is good in early summer and fall.

Location: On Lake Davis in Plumas National Forest; map C4, grid g0.

Campsites, facilities: There are 55 sites for tents or RVs up to 32 feet long. Picnic tables and fire grills are provided. Drinking water and vault toilets are available. A boat ramp, grocery store, and sanitary disposal station are nearby. Leashed pets are permitted.

Reservations, fees: Reservations are accepted for some sites; $13 per night. Open May through October.

Directions: From Truckee, turn north on Highway 89 and drive to Sattley and County Road A23. Turn right on County Road A23 and drive 13 miles to Highway 70. Turn left on Highway 70 and drive one mile to Grizzly Road. Turn right on Grizzly Road and drive about six miles to Lake Davis. Continue north on Lake Davis Road for less than a mile to the campground entrance on the left side of the road.

Contact: Plumas National Forest, Beckwourth Ranger District, tel. (530) 836-2575 or fax (530) 836-0493.

🔟🔟 Big Cove

 7

Big Cove is one of four camps at the southeastern end of Frenchman Lake, with a boat ramp available about a mile away near the Frenchman and Spring Creek camps. See the entry for Frenchman for more information. A trail from the campground leads to the lakeshore.

Location: At Frenchman Lake in Plumas National Forest; map C4, grid g3.

Campsites, facilities: There are 38 sites for tents or RVs up to 50 feet long (19 are multiple-family units; 10 are wheelchair accessible). Picnic tables and fire rings are provided. Drinking water and flush toilets are available. Some facilities are wheelchair accessible. A boat ramp, sanitary disposal station, grocery store (seven miles away), and propane gas are available nearby. Leashed pets are permitted.

Reservations, fees: Reserve at (877) 444-6777 ($8.65 reservation fee) or website: www.reserveusa.com; $13 to $26 per night. Open May through September.

Directions: From Reno, drive north on U.S. 395 to the junction with Highway 70. Turn west on Highway 70 and drive to Chilcoot and the junction with Frenchman Lake Road. Turn right on Frenchman Lake Road and drive nine miles to the lake and to a Y. At the Y, turn right and drive two miles to Forest Road 24N01. Turn left and drive a short distance to the campground entrance on the left side of the road.

Contact: Plumas National Forest, Beckwourth Ranger District, tel. (530) 836-2575 or fax (530) 836-0493.

🔟🔟 Spring Creek

 7

Frenchman Lake is set at 5,500 feet elevation, on the edge of high desert to the east and forest to the west. This camp is on the southeast end of the lake, where there are four other campgrounds, including a group camp and a boat ramp. The lake provides good fishing for stocked rainbow trout, best in the cove near the campgrounds.

Location: On Frenchman Lake in Plumas National Forest; map C4, grid g3.

Campsites, facilities: There are 35 sites for tents or RVs up to 55 feet long. Picnic tables and fire grills are provided. Drinking water and vault toilets are available. A boat ramp and sanitary disposal station are nearby. Leashed pets are permitted.

Reservations, fees: Reserve at (877) 444-6777 ($8.65 reservation fee) or website: www.reserveusa.com; $13 per night. Open May through October.

Directions: From Reno, drive north on U.S. 395 to the junction with Highway 70. Turn west on Highway 70 and drive to Chilcoot and the junction with Frenchman Lake Road. Turn right on Frenchman Lake Road and drive nine miles to the lake and to a Y. At the Y, turn right and drive two miles to the campground on the left side of the road.

Contact: Plumas National Forest, Beckwourth Ranger District, tel. (530) 836-2575 or fax (530) 836-0493.

13 Frenchman

 7

Frenchman Lake is set at 5,500 feet in elevation, on the edge of high desert to the east and forest to the west. This camp is on the southeast end of the lake, where there are four other campgrounds, including a group camp and a boat ramp. The lake provides good fishing for stocked rainbow trout. The best fishing is in the cove near the campgrounds and the two inlets, one along the west shore and one at the head of the lake. The proximity to Reno, only 35 miles away, keeps gambling in the back of the minds of many anglers. Because of water demands downstream, the lake often drops significantly by the end of summer.

Location: On Frenchman Lake in Plumas National Forest; map C4, grid h3.

Campsites, facilities: There are 38 sites for tents or RVs. Picnic tables and fire grills are provided. Drinking water and vault toilets are available. A sanitary disposal station and boat ramp are nearby. Leashed pets are permitted.

Reservations, fees: Reserve at (877) 444-6777 ($8.65 reservation fee) or website: www.reserveusa.com; $13 per night. Open May through October.

Directions: From Reno, drive north on U.S. 395 to the junction with Highway 70. Turn west on Highway 70 and drive to Chilcoot and the junction with Frenchman Lake Road. Turn right on Frenchman Lake Road and drive nine miles to the lake and to a Y. At the Y, turn right and drive 1.5 miles to the campground on the left side of the road.

Contact: Plumas National Forest, Beckwourth Ranger District, tel. (530) 836-2575 or fax (530) 836-0493.

14 Cottonwood Springs

 7

Cottonwood Springs, elevation 5,700 feet, is largely an overflow camp at Frenchman Lake. The more popular Frenchman, Big Cove, and Spring Creek camps are along the southeast shore of the lake near a boat ramp. Cottonwood Springs is set on a creek about two miles from the dam. However, there is a great side trip here, taking Forest Road 24N52 out of camp to the southwest and driving through the Little Last Chance Canyon Scenic Area; the road dead-ends about seven miles in.

Location: Near Frenchman Lake in Plumas National Forest; map C4, grid h3.

Campsites, facilities: There are 20 sites for tents or RVs up to 50 feet long and two group camping areas which can accommodate up to 25 and 50 people, respectively. Picnic tables and fire rings are provided. Drinking water and flush toilets are available. Some facilities are wheelchair accessible. A boat ramp and sanitary disposal station are nearby. Leashed pets are permitted.

Reservations, fees: Reserve at (877) 444-6777 ($8.65 reservation fee) or website: www.reserveusa.com; $13 per night, $44 to $87 per night for groups. Open May through October.

Directions: From Reno, drive north on U.S. 395 to the junction with Highway 70. Turn west on Highway 70 and drive to Chilcoot and the junction with Frenchman Lake Road. Turn right on Frenchman Lake Road and drive nine miles to the lake and to a Y. At the Y, turn left and drive 1.5 miles to the campground on the left side of the road.

Contact: Plumas National Forest, Beckwourth Ranger District, tel. (530) 836-2575 or fax (530) 836-0493.

15 Chilcoot

 7

This small camp is set along Little Last Chance Creek at 5,400 feet in elevation, about three miles downstream from Frenchman Lake. The stream once provided excellent trout fishing, but it is now largely overgrown with brush, making fishing access very difficult.

Location: On Little Last Chance Creek in Plumas National Forest; map C4, grid h4.

Campsites, facilities: There are five walk-in sites for tents and 35 sites for tents or RVs up to 45 feet long. Two sites are wheelchair accessible. Picnic tables and fire rings are provided. Drinking water and flush toilets are available. Some facilities are wheelchair accessible. A boat ramp, grocery store, and sanitary disposal station are nearby. Leashed pets are permitted.

Reservations, fees: Reserve at (877) 444-6777 ($8.65 reservation fee) or website: www.reserveusa.com; $13 per night. Open May through October.

Directions: From Reno, drive north on U.S. 395 to the junction with Highway 70. Turn west on Highway 70 and drive to Chilcoot and the junction with Frenchman Lake Road. Turn right on Frenchman Lake Road and drive six miles to the campground on the left side of the road.

Contact: Plumas National Forest, Beckwourth Ranger District, tel. (530) 836-2575 or fax (530) 836-0493.

16 Yuba Pass

   6

This camp is set right at Yuba Pass at an elevation of 6,700 feet. In the winter, the surrounding area is a Sno-Park, which gives it an unusual look in summer. Yuba Pass is a popular bird-watching area in the summer.

Location: In Tahoe National Forest; map C4, grid j0.

Campsites, facilities: There are 20 sites for tents or RVs up to 22 feet long. Picnic tables and fire grills are provided. Drinking water and vault toilets are available. Supplies are available at Bassetts. Pets must be controlled.

Reservations, fees: No reservations; $11 per night. Open late June through October.

Directions: From Truckee, drive north on Highway 89 past Sattley to the junction with Highway 49. Turn west on Highway 49 and drive about six miles to the campground on the left side of the road.

Contact: Tahoe National Forest, Sierraville Ranger District, tel. (530) 994-3401 or fax (530) 994-3143.

17 Cottonwood Creek

      7

This camp sits beside Cottonwood Creek at 5,800 feet elevation. An interpretive trail starts at the camp and makes a short loop, and there are several nearby side trip options, including trout fishing on the Little Truckee River to the nearby south, visiting the Sierra Valley Hot Springs out of Sierraville to the nearby north, or venturing into the surrounding Tahoe National Forest.

Location: In Tahoe National Forest; map C4, grid j1.

Campsites, facilities: There are 21 sites for tents and 28 sites for tents or RVs up to 22 feet long. Picnic tables and fire grills are provided. Drinking water and vault toilets are available. Supplies are available in Sierraville. Pets must be controlled.

Reservations, fees: Reserve at (877) 444-6777 ($8.65 reservation fee) or website: www.reserveusa.com; $11 per night. Open May through October, weather permitting.

Directions: From Truckee, drive north on Highway 89 for about 20 miles to the campground entrance road on the right (a half mile past Cold Creek Camp). Turn right and drive a quarter mile to the campground.

Contact: Tahoe National Forest, Sierraville Ranger District, tel. (530) 994-3401 or fax (530) 994-3143.

18 Bear Valley

    7

The surrounding national forest land was largely burned by the historic Cottonwood Fire of 1994, but the camp itself was saved. It is set on the headwaters of Bear Valley Creek, 6,700 feet in elevation, with a spring adjacent to the campground. The road leading southeast out of camp is routed to Sardine Peak (8,134 feet), where there is a dramatic view of the burned region. There is an 18-mile loop OHV trail across the road from the campground.

Location: On Bear Valley Creek in Tahoe National Forest; map C4, grid j2.

Campsites, facilities: There are 10 tent and/or trailer sites. Picnic tables and fire grills are provided. Drinking water and vault toilets are available. Supplies are available in Sierraville. Pets must be controlled.

Reservations, fees: No reservations; no fee. Open June through October.

Directions: From Truckee, drive north on Highway 89 about 17 miles. Turn right on County Road 451 and drive northeast about six miles to the campground entrance on the right.

Contact: Tahoe National Forest, Sierraville Ranger District, tel. (530) 994-3401 or fax (530) 994-3143.

19 Lookout

    4

This primitive camp is set in remote country near the California/Nevada border at 6,700 feet. It is a former mining site, and the highlight here is a quartz crystal mine a short distance from the campground. Stampede Reservoir provides a side trip option, about 10 miles to the southwest, over the rough dirt Henness Pass Road.

Location: In Humboldt-Toiyabe National Forest; map C4, grid j4.

Campsites, facilities: There are 15 sites for tents and four sites for tents or RVs up to 22 feet long, plus a group campground that can accommodate up to 16 people. Picnic tables and fire grills are provided. Drinking water and vault toilets are available. Pets must be controlled.

Reservations, fees: No reservations; $10 per night. Open June through September.

Directions: From Truckee on Interstate 80, drive east across the state line into Nevada to Verdi. Take the Verdi exit and drive north through town to Old Dog Valley Road. Drive north on Old Dog Valley Road for 11 miles to the campground.

Contact: Humboldt-Toiyabe National Forest, Carson Ranger District, tel. (775) 882-2766, or fax (775) 884-8199.

CHAPTER DO

ON THE COAST TRAIL,
POINT REYES NATIONAL SEASHORE

MICHAEL FURNISS

MAP DO

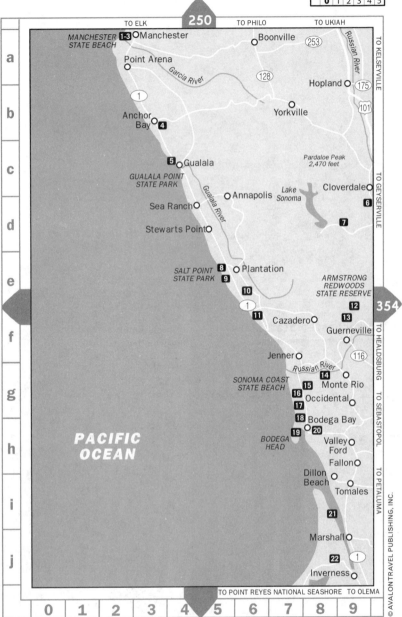

© AVALON TRAVEL PUBLISHING, INC.

CHAPTER D0

1 Manchester State Park

     8

Manchester State Park is a beautiful park on the Sonoma coast, set near the Garcia River with the town of Point Arena to the nearby north providing a supply point. If you hit it during one of the rare times when the skies are clear and the wind is down, the entire area will seem aglow in magical sunbeams. The Alder Creek Trail is a great hike here, routed north along beachfront to the mouth of Alder Creek and its beautiful coastal lagoon. This is where the San Andreas Fault heads off from land and into the sea.

Location: Near Point Arena; map D0, grid a2.

Campsites, facilities: There are 46 sites for tents or RVs up to 35 feet long, and one group site for up to 40 people and RVs up to 21 feet long. Picnic tables and fire grills are provided. Drinking water, vault toilets, and a sanitary

disposal station are available. Leashed pets are permitted.

Reservations, fees: Reservations for the group site only at tel. (800) 444-7275 or website: www.cal-parks.ca.gov; $12 per night for individual sites, $30 per night for the group site. Open year-round.

Directions: On U.S. 101 north of Santa Rosa, turn west on River Road and drive 13 miles to Guerneville and Highway 116. Turn west on Highway 116 and drive about 20 miles to Highway 1 at Jenner. Turn north on Highway 1 and drive 55 miles to Point Arena. From Point Arena. Continue north about five miles to Kinney Lane. Turn left and drive one mile to the campground entrance on the right.

Contact: Manchester State Beach, tel. (707) 937-5804, or fax (707) 937-2953.

2 Manchester Beach KOA

 7

This is a privately operated KOA park set beside Highway 1 and near the beautiful Manchester State Beach. A great plus here is the cute little log cabins, complete with electric heat. They can provide a great sense of privacy, and after a good sleep, campers are ready to explore the adjacent state park.

Location: North of Point Arena at Manchester State Beach; map D0, grid a2.

Campsites, facilities: There are 63 sites for RVs, some with full or partial hookups. There are also two cottages, 24 cabins, and 48 tent sites. Picnic tables and fire rings are provided. Drinking water, restrooms, flush toilets, showers, modem hookups, heated pool (seasonal), hot tub and spa, recreation room, playground, sanitary disposal station, a grocery store, ice, wood, a coin laundry, and propane gas are available. Some facilities are wheelchair accessible. Leashed pets are permitted.

Reservations, fees: Reservations are accepted; $28 to $36 per night for two people; each additional child (17 and under) is $3, each additional adult (18 and over) is $5. Cabins are $44 to $116 per night. Major credit cards accepted. Open year-round.

Directions: On U.S. 101 north of Santa Rosa, turn west on River Road and drive 13 miles to Guerneville and Highway 116. Turn west on Highway 116 and drive about 20 miles to Highway 1 at Jenner. Turn north on Highway 1 and drive 55 miles to Point Arena. From Point Arena, continue north about six miles to the park on the left side of the road.

Contact: Manchester Beach KOA, P.O. Box 266, Manchester, CA 95459; tel. (707) 882-2375 or fax (707) 882-3104; website: www.manchesterbeachkoa.com.

3 Rollerville Junction

 7

This privately operated campground has gone through recent renovation, and its location makes it an attractive spot, with the beautiful Manchester State Beach, Alder Creek, and Garcia River all available nearby on one of California's most attractive stretches of coastline. Point Arena Lighthouse and a fishing pier are also nearby. The elevation of the camp is 220 feet.

Location: Near Point Arena; map D0, grid a2.

Campsites, facilities: There are 51 sites for tents or RVs (12 are drive-through), 36 with full hookups. Picnic tables and fire rings are provided. Drinking water, restrooms, flush toilets, hot showers, hot tub, heated swimming pool, clubhouse with full kitchen, playground, cable TV hookups, modem hookups, sanitary disposal station, laundry facilities, small store, and propane gas are available. Some facilities are wheelchair accessible. Leashed pets are permitted.

Reservations, fees: Reservations only at (800) 910-4317; $25 to $29 per night, $3 per adult per night and $1 per child per night for more than two people. Major credit cards accepted. Open year-round.

Directions: On U.S. 101 north of Santa Rosa, turn west on River Road and drive 13 miles to Guerneville and Highway 116. Turn west on Highway 116 and drive about 20 miles to Highway 1 at Jenner. Turn north on Highway 1 and drive 55 miles to Point Arena. From Point Arena, continue north for 1.5 miles to Point Arena Lighthouse Road and the campground on the left (west side).

Contact: Rollerville Junction, tel. (707) 882-2440 or fax (707) 882-3049; website: www.campgrounds.com/rollerville.

4 Anchor Bay Campground

 8

This is a quiet and beautiful stretch of California coast. The campground is on the ocean side of Highway 1 north of Gualala, with sites set at ocean level as well as amid trees—take your pick. Nearby Gualala Regional Park provides an excellent easy hike, the headlands-to-beach loop with coastal views, a lookout of the Gualala River, and many giant cypress trees. In winter, the nearby Gualala River attracts large but elusive steelhead.

Location: Near Gualala; map D0, grid b3.

Campsites, facilities: There are 26 sites for tents or RVs, some with water and electrical hookups. Picnic tables and fire rings are provided. Drinking water, restrooms, flush toilets, hot showers, and a sanitary disposal station are available. Leashed pets are permitted.

Reservations, fees: Reservations are accepted; $25 to $27 per night. Major credit cards accepted. Open year-round.

Directions: On U.S. 101 north of Santa Rosa, turn west on River Road and drive 13 miles to Guerneville and Highway 116. Turn west on Highway 116 and drive about 20 miles to Highway 1 at Jenner. Turn north on Highway 1. Turn north on Highway 1 and drive 38 miles to Gualala. From Gualala, continue four miles north on Highway 1 to the campground on the left side of the road.

Contact: Anchor Bay Campground, tel. (707) 884-4222; website: www.abcamp.com.

5 Gualala Point Park

 8

This is a dramatic spot right on the ocean, adjacent to the mouth of the Gualala River. A trail along the bluff provides an easy hiking adventure; on the west side of the highway other trails to the beach are available.

Location: At Sonoma County Regional Park; map D0, grid c4.

Campsites, facilities: There are 19 sites for tents and RVs up to 30 feet long, six walk-in tent sites, and one hike-in/bike-in site. Picnic tables and fire rings are provided. Drinking water, restrooms, flush toilets, coin-operated showers, sanitary disposal station, and wood are available. Some facilities are wheel-

chair accessible. Leashed pets are permitted.

Reservations, fees: No reservations; $16 per night, $3 per person per night for hike-in/bike-in site, $5 per extra vehicle, $1 pet fee. Open year-round.

Directions: On U.S. 101 north of Santa Rosa, turn west on River Road and drive 13 miles to Guerneville and Highway 116. Turn west on Highway 116 and drive about 20 miles to Highway 1 at Jenner. Turn north on Highway 1 and drive 38 miles to Gualala. Turn right at the park entrance (a day-use area is on the west side of the highway).

Contact: Gualala Point, tel. (707) 785-2377.

6 Dutcher Creek RV Park and Campground

 6

This privately operated campground provides a layover for U.S. 101 cruisers. It has both native and seasonal plant displays, exceptional opportunities for native bird-watching, and the nearby Asti Vineyard provides a side trip. Lake Sonoma is seven miles to the west, with the best access provided to the south out of Dry Creek Road (see listing for Lake Sonoma). The elevation is 385 feet.

Location: Near Lake Sonoma; map D0, grid d9.

Campsites, facilities: There are six tent sites and 12 sites for RVs up to 36 feet long (two are drive-through), one with full and many with partial hookups. Picnic tables are provided. Drinking water, restrooms, flush toilets, showers, sanitary disposal station, pay phone, and coin laundry are available. Leashed pets are permitted.

Reservations, fees: Reservations are accepted; $12 to $25 per night. Open year-round.

Directions: From Santa Rosa, drive north on U.S. 101 beyond Healdsburg to the Dutcher Creek exit (just south of Cloverdale). Take the Dutcher Creek exit, drive west on Theresa Drive under the freeway, continue a half mile to the end of Theresa Drive, and follow signs to the park office at 230 Theresa Drive.

Contact: Dutcher Creek RV Park and Camp, tel. (707) 894-4829, or fax (707) 894-5744.

❼ Lake Sonoma Recreation Area

 8

Lake Sonoma is one of the best weekend vacation sites for Bay Area campers. The developed campground (Liberty Glen) is fine for car campers, but the boat-in sites are ideal for folks who desire a quiet and pretty lakeside setting. This is a big lake, extending nine miles north on the Dry Creek arm and four miles west on the Warm Springs Creek arm. There is an adjacent 8,000-acre wildlife area with 40 miles of hiking trails. The water-skier versus angler conflict has been resolved by limiting high-speed boats to specified areas. Laws are strictly enforced, making this lake excellent for either sport. The best fishing is in the protected coves of the Warm Springs and Dry Creek arms of the lake; use live minnows for bass, which are available at the Dry Creek Store on the access road south of the lake. The visitor center is adjacent to a public fish hatchery. Salmon and steelhead come to spawn from the Russian River between November and March.

Location: Near Healdsburg; map D0, grid d9.

Campsites, facilities: There are 109 primitive boat-in sites around the lake, two hike-in sites, four group sites (two of which are boat-in), and 95 tent sites and two group sites at Liberty Glen Campground 2.5 miles from the lake. Picnic tables, fire grills, and vault toilets are provided at the primitive sites, but no drinking water is available. At Liberty Glen, picnic tables and fire rings are provided, and drinking water, flush toilets, lantern holders, solar-heated showers, and a sanitary disposal station are available. A boat ramp and boat rentals are available nearby. Saturday night campfire talks are held at an amphitheater during the summer. Some facilities are wheelchair accessible. Campsites have limited facilities in winter. Leashed pets are permitted.

Reservations, fees: Reserve at tel. (877) 444-6777 ($8.65 reservation fee) or website: www.reserveusa.com; $16 per night, $10 for primitive sites, $80 per night for group campsites. A permit is required from the visitor center. Open year-round.

Directions: From Santa Rosa, drive north on U.S. 101 to Healdsburg. In Healdsburg, take the Dry Creek Road exit, turn left, and drive northwest for 11 miles. After crossing a small bridge, the visitor center will be on your right.

Contact: U.S. Army Corps of Engineers, Lake Sonoma, tel. (707) 433-9483, ext. 27, or fax (707) 431-0313.

❽ Salt Point State Park

 9

This is a gorgeous piece of Sonoma coast, highlighted by Fisk Mill Cove, inshore kelp beds, outstanding short hikes, and abalone diving. There are two campgrounds here, Gerstle Cove Campground and the much larger Woodside Campground. Great hikes include the Bluff Trail and Stump Beach Trail (great views). During abalone season, this is one of the best and most popular spots on the Northern California coast. The Kruse Rhododendron Reserve is within the park and definitely worth the stroll. This is a 317-acre conservation reserve that features second-growth redwoods, Douglas firs, tan oak, and many rhododendrons, with five miles of hiking trails. Camp reservations are advised.

Location: Near Fort Ross; map D0, grid e5.

Campsites, facilities: At Gerstle Cove Campground, there are 30 sites for tents or RVs up to 31 feet long. At Woodside Campground, there are 79 sites for tents or RVs up to 31 feet long, 20 walk-in tent sites, 10 hike-in/bike-in sites, and a group site that can accommodate up to 40 people. Picnic tables and fire rings are provided. Drinking water and flush toilets are available. Summer interpretive programs are also available; firewood is available for purchase. The picnic area and one hiking trail are wheelchair accessible.

Leashed pets are permitted, except on trails.

Reservations, fees: Reserve at (800) 444-PARK (800-444-7275) or website: www.ReserveAmerica.com; $12 per night, $1 per night for hike-in, bike-in sites; $50 for group site. Open year-round.

Directions: On U.S. 101 north of Santa Rosa, turn west on River Road and drive 13 miles to Guerneville and Highway 116. Turn west on Highway 116 and drive about 20 miles to Highway 1 at Jenner. Turn north on Highway 1 and drive about 20 miles to the park entrance; Woodside Campground on the right and Gerstle Cove on the left.

Contact: Salt Point State Park, tel. (707) 847-3221 or tel. (707) 865-2391, or fax (707) 847-3843.

🗐 Ocean Cove Campground

     8

The highlights here are the campsites on a bluff overlooking the ocean. Alas, it can be foggy during the summer. A good side trip is to Fort Ross, with a stellar easy hike available on the Fort Ross Trail, which features a walk through an old colonial fort as well as great coastal views, excellent for whale-watching. There is also excellent hiking at Stillwater Cove Regional Park, just a mile to the south off Highway 1.

Location: On the ocean five miles north of Fort Ross; map D0, grid e5.

Campsites, facilities: There are 125 sites for tents or RVs. Picnic tables and fire grills are provided. Drinking water, chemical toilets, and coin showers are available. A boat launch, grocery store, fishing supplies, and diving gear sales are available nearby. Pets are permitted.

Reservations, fees: No reservations; $12 per night per vehicle, $1 pet fee. Major credit cards accepted. Open April through November.

Directions: On U.S. 101 north of Santa Rosa, turn west on River Road and drive 13 miles to Guerneville and Highway 116. Turn west on Highway 116 and drive about 20 miles to Highway 1 at Jenner. Turn north on Highway 1

and drive 17 miles north on Highway 1 (five miles north of Fort Ross) to the campground entrance.

Contact: Ocean Cove Campground, tel. (707) 847-3422; website: www.ocean-cove.com.

🔟 Stillwater Cove Regional Park

      8

Stillwater Cove has a dramatic rock-strewn cove and sits on a classic chunk of Sonoma coast. The campground is sometimes overlooked, since it is a county-operated park and not on the state park reservation system. One of the region's great hikes is available here: the Stockoff Creek Loop, with the trailhead at the day-use parking lot. In a little over a mile, the trail is routed through forest with both firs and redwoods, and then along a pretty stream. To get beach access, you will need to cross Highway 1 and then drop down to the cove.

Location: Near Fort Ross; map D0, grid e6.

Campsites, facilities: There are 23 sites for tents or RVs up to 35 feet long, and a hike-in/bike-in site. Picnic tables and fire rings are provided. Drinking water, flush toilets, showers, firewood for purchase, and a sanitary disposal station are available. Supplies can be obtained in Ocean Cove (one mile north) and Fort Ross. Some facilities are wheelchair accessible. Leashed pets are permitted.

Reservations, fees: No reservations; $16 per night, $5 for each additional vehicle, $3 per night for the hike-in/bike-in site, $1 pet fee. Open year-round.

Directions: On U.S. 101 north of Santa Rosa, turn west on River Road and drive 13 miles to Guerneville and Highway 116. Turn west on Highway 116 and drive about 20 miles to Highway 1 at Jenner. Turn north on Highway 1 and drive 16 miles north on Highway 1 (four miles north of Fort Ross) to the park entrance.

Contact: Stillwater Cove Regional Park, Sonoma County, tel. (707) 847-3245; website: www.sonoma-county.org.

11 Fort Ross State Historic Park

       8

Fort Ross is just as it name announces: an old fort, in this case, an old Russian fort from 1812. The camp is just north of the north entrance station, less than a quarter-mile from the ocean. Some redwoods and pines provide cover, and some sites are open. The privacy and beauty of the campsites vary as much as any state park camp in California. The sites at the end of the road fill up very quickly. From camp, a trail leads down to a beach, more rocky than sandy, and a quarter-mile trail leads to the fort. As a destination site, Fort Ross is known as a popular abalone diving spot, with the best areas below the campground and also at nearby Reef Terrace. It also provides good, easy hikes amid its 3,386 acres. The park features a museum in the visitor center, which is always a must-see for campers making the tour up Highway 1.

Location: Near Fort Ross; map D0, grid f6.

Campsites, facilities: There are 21 sites for tents or RVs up to 17 feet long. No hookups. Picnic tables and fire rings are provided. Drinking water, flush toilets, showers, firewood for purchase, and a sanitary disposal station are available. Supplies can be obtained nearby. A visitor center and guided tours and programs are available. Some facilities are wheelchair accessible. Leashed pets are permitted.

Reservations, fees: No reservations; $12 per night. Open April through October.

Directions: On U.S. 101 north of Santa Rosa, turn west on River Road and drive 13 miles to Guerneville and Highway 116. Turn west on Highway 116 and drive about 20 miles to Highway 1 at Jenner. Turn north on Highway 1 and drive 10 miles north on Highway 1 to the Fort Ross State Park/Reef Campground entrance on the left.

Contact: Fort Ross State Historic Park, tel. (707) 847-3286, or (707) 847-3708.

12 Austin Creek State Recreation Area

     7

Austin Creek State Recreation Area and Armstrong Redwoods State Reserve are actually coupled, forming 5,000 acres of continuous parkland. Most visitors prefer the redwood park. The campground is called Bullfrog Pond, set near a pond with bluegill. The highlight at the recreation area is a system of hiking trails that lead to a series of small creeks: Schoolhouse Creek, Gilliam Creek, and Austin Creek. They involve pretty steep climbs, and in the summer it's hot here. There are many attractive side trip possibilities, including the adjacent Armstrong Redwoods, of course, but also canoeing on the Russian River (3.5 miles away), fishing (smallmouth bass in summer, steelhead in winter), and wine-tasting.

Location: Near the Russian River; map D0, grid f9.

Campsites, facilities: There are 23 sites for tents only and four hike-in sites. No trailers are allowed. (The access road is very narrow.) Picnic tables and fire grills are provided. Drinking water and flush toilets are available. Some facilities are wheelchair accessible. Leashed pets are permitted at the main campground only. There are also four primitive, hike-in, backcountry campsites with picnic tables, fire rings, and pit toilets, but no drinking water is available and no pets are permitted. The hike-in camps are 2.5 to 5 miles from the main campground. Obtain a backcountry camping permit from the office.

Reservations, fees: No reservations; $12 per night, $1 for hike-in sites, $1 pet fee. Open year-round.

Directions: On U.S. 101 north of Santa Rosa, turn west on River Road and drive 13 miles to Guerneville and Armstrong Woods Road. Turn right and drive 2.5 miles to the entrance of Armstrong Redwoods State Park. Continue 3.5 miles through Armstrong Redwoods to Austin Creek State Recreation Area to the campground.

Contact: Austin Creek State Recreation Area, tel. (707) 869-2015 or fax (707) 869-5629.

13 Faerie Ring Campground

     7

If location is everything, then this privately operated campground is set right in the middle of the best of it in the Russian River region. It is one-half mile north of the Russian River and less than a mile south of Armstrong Redwoods State Park.

Location: Near the Russian River; map D0, grid f9.

Campsites, facilities: There are 33 sites for tents and nine sites for RVs up to 35 feet long, with full hookups. Picnic tables and fire rings are provided. Drinking water, flush toilets, coin-operated showers, and a sanitary disposal station are available. Leashed pets are permitted.

Reservations, fees: Reservations are accepted; $20 per night (adults), $3 for kids, $2 for pets. Payment in full required in advance. Open year-round.

Directions: On U.S. 101 north of Santa Rosa, turn west on River Road and drive 13 miles to Guerneville and Armstrong Woods Road. At Armstrong Woods Road, turn right and drive 1.5 miles to the campground on the right.

Contact: Faerie Ring Campground, tel. (707) 869-2746.

14 Casini Ranch Family Campground

     8

Woods and water—this campground has both, with sites set near the Russian River in both sun-filled and shaded areas. Its location on the lower river makes a side trip to the coast easy, with the Sonoma Coast State Beach about a 15-minute drive to the nearby west.

Location: On the Russian River; map D0, grid g8.

Campsites, facilities: There are 225 sites for tents and RVs (28 drive-through), many with full or partial hookups. Picnic tables and fire grills are provided. Flush toilets, showers, playground, sanitary disposal station, coin laundry, cable TV, video arcade, game arcade, boat and canoe rentals, propane gas, and a grocery store are available. Some facilities are wheelchair accessible. Leashed pets are permitted.

Reservations, fees: Reservations are recommended; $20 to $27 per night. Major credit cards accepted. Open year-round.

Directions: On U.S. 101 north of Santa Rosa, turn west on River Road and drive 13 miles to Guerneville and Highway 116. Turn west on Highway 116 and drive to Duncan Mills. In Duncan Mills, turn southeast on Moscow Road and drive a half mile to the campground.

Contact: Casini Ranch Family Campground, tel. (707) 865-2255 or tel. (800) 451-8400 for reservations, or fax (707) 865-0147.

15 Pomo Canyon Walk-In

  10

This is a gorgeous camp, well hidden, and offering a great trailhead and nearby beach access. The camp is actually not on the coast at all, but on the east-facing slope of Pomo Canyon (just over the ridge from the coast), where the campsites are set within a beautiful second-growth redwood forest. A trail is routed through the redwoods (with many cathedral trees) and up to the ridge, where there are divine views of the mouth of the Russian River, Goat Rock, and the beautiful Sonoma coast. The trail continues for three miles, all the way to Shell Beach, where you can spend hours poking around and beachcombing. The camp's seclusion and proximity to the Bay Area make it a rare winner.

Location: In Sonoma Coast State Beach; map D0, grid g8.

Campsites, facilities: There are 21 walk-in tent sites. Picnic tables and fire grills are provided. Drinking water and pit toilets are available. No pets are permitted.

Reservations, fees: No reservations; $7 per night. Open year-round, weather permitting. Often closed from December 1 through March 31 because of weather.

Directions: In Petaluma on U.S. 101, take the East Washington exit and turn west (this street becomes Bodega Avenue). Drive west through Petaluma and continue for 10 miles to Valley Ford Road. Turn right and drive 7.5 miles to Highway 1. Turn right (north) on Highway 1 and drive nine miles to Bodega Bay. Continue north for nine miles to Willow Creek Road. Turn right on Willow Creek Road and drive about three miles to the campground. Park and walk to the campsites, requiring a one-to five-minute walk.

Contact: Sonoma Coast State Beach, tel. (707) 875-3483.

16 Wrights Beach

This state park campground is at the north end of a beach that stretches south for several miles, yet to the north it is steep and rocky. There are many excellent side trips. The best is to the north, where you can explore dramatic Shell Beach (the turnoff is on the west side of Highway 1), or take the Pomo Trail (the trailhead is on the east side of the highway, across from Shell Beach) up the adjacent foothills for sweeping views of the coast.

Location: In Sonoma Coast State Beach; map D0, grid g7.

Campsites, facilities: There are 30 sites for tents or RVs up to 27 feet long, with a limit of eight people per site. Picnic tables and fire rings are provided. Drinking water and flush toilets are available. Leashed pets are permitted.

Reservations, fees: Reserve at (800) 444-PARK (800-444-7275) or website: www.ReserveAmerica.com; $12 per night. Open year-round, weather permitting.

Directions: In Petaluma on U.S. 101, take the East Washington exit and turn west (this street becomes Bodega Avenue). Drive west through

Petaluma and continue for 10 miles to Valley Ford Road. Turn right and drive 7.5 miles to Highway 1. Turn right (north) on Highway 1 and drive nine miles to Bodega Bay. In Bodega Bay, continue six miles north to the campground entrance on the left.

Contact: Sonoma Coast State Beach, tel. (707) 875-3483.

17 Bodega Bay RV Park

Bodega Bay RV Park is one of the oldest RV parks in the state, and there are few coastal destinations better than Bodega Bay. Excellent seafood restaurants are available within five minutes, and some of the best deep-sea fishing is available out of Bodega Bay Sportfishing. In addition, there is a great view of the ocean at nearby Bodega Head to the west. What more could you want?

Location: In Bodega Bay; map D0, grid g7.

Campsites, facilities: There are 85 sites for RVs, 70 with full hookups. Picnic tables and fire rings are provided. Drinking water, flush toilets, and showers are available. Laundry, volleyball, horseshoes, boccie ball, modem hookups, and cable TV hookups are available. Some facilities are wheelchair accessible. Leashed pets are permitted.

Reservations, fees: Reservations are recommended at (800) 201-6864; $25-29 per night for two people, $2 for each additional person. Major credit cards accepted.

Directions: In Petaluma on U.S. 101, take the East Washington exit and turn west (this street becomes Bodega Avenue). Drive west through Petaluma and continue for 10 miles to Valley Ford Road. Turn right and drive 7.5 miles to Highway 1. Turn right (north) on Highway 1 and drive nine miles to Bodega Bay. In Bodega Bay, continue north for two miles past the Texaco station to the RV park on the left.

Contact: Bodega Bay RV Park, 2000 Highway 1, P.O. Box 96, Bodega Bay, CA 94923; tel. (707) 875-3701.

18 Bodega Dunes

 8

Sonoma Coast State Beach features several great campgrounds, and if you like the beach, this one rates high. It is set at the end of a beach that stretches for miles, providing stellar beach walks and excellent beachcombing during low tides. For some campers, a foghorn sounding repeatedly through the night can make sleep difficult. The quietest sites here are among the dunes. To the nearby south is Bodega Bay, including a major deep-sea sport-fishing operation with excellent salmon fishing in June and July, and outstanding prospects for rockfish and lingcod from August through November. The town of Bodega Bay offers a full marina and restaurants.

Location: In Sonoma Coast State Beach; map D0, grid h7.

Campsites, facilities: There are 98 sites for tents or RVs up to 31 feet long, with a limit of eight people per site. Picnic tables and fire grills are provided. Drinking water, flush toilets, coin showers, and a sanitary disposal station are available. Laundry facilities, supplies, and horse rentals are available within one mile. Leashed pets are permitted at the campsites only.

Reservations, fees: Reserve at (800) 444-PARK (800-444-7275) or website: www.ReserveAmerica.com; $12 per night. Open year-round, weather permitting.

Directions: In Petaluma on U.S. 101, take the East Washington exit and turn west (this street becomes Bodega Avenue). Drive west through Petaluma and continue for 10 miles to Valley Ford Road. Turn right and drive 7.5 miles to Highway 1. Turn right (north) on Highway 1 and drive nine miles to Bodega Bay. In Bodega Bay, drive one-half mile north to the campground entrance on the left.

Contact: Sonoma Coast State Beach, tel. (707) 875-3483.

19 Westside Regional Park

 7

This campground is on the west shore of Bodega Bay. One of the greatest boat launches on the coast is nearby to the south, providing access to prime fishing waters. Salmon fishing is excellent from mid-June through August. A small, protected beach (for kids to dig in the sand and wade) is available at the end of the road beyond the campground.

Location: On Bodega Bay; map D0, grid h7.

Campsites, facilities: There are 47 sites for tents or RVs. Picnic tables and fire grills are provided. Drinking water, flush toilets, showers, sanitary disposal station, fish-cleaning station, and a boat ramp are available. Supplies can be obtained in Bodega Bay, less than one mile away. Some facilities are wheelchair accessible. Leashed pets are permitted.

Reservations, fees: No reservations; $16 per night, $1 pet fee. Open year-round.

Directions: In Petaluma on U.S. 101, take the East Washington exit and turn west (this street becomes Bodega Avenue). Drive west through Petaluma and continue for 10 miles to Valley Ford Road. Turn right and drive 7.5 miles to Highway 1. Turn right (north) on Highway 1 and drive nine miles to Bodega Bay. In Bodega Bay, continue north to Bay Flat Road. Turn left on Bay Flat Road and drive two miles (looping around the bay) to the campground on the right.

Contact: Sonoma County Parks Department, tel. (707) 875-3540; website: www.sonoma-county.org.

20 Doran Regional Park

 7

This campground is set beside Doran Beach on Bodega Bay, which offers complete fishing and marina facilities. In season, it's also a popular clamming and crabbing spot. Salmon fishing is often excellent during the summer at the Whistle Buoy offshore from Bodega Head, and rockfishing is good year-round at Cordell Bank. Fishing is also available off the rock jetty in the park.

Location: On Bodega Bay; map D0, grid h8.

Campsites, facilities: There are 10 sites for tents and 124 sites for tents or RVs. Picnic tables and fire grills are provided. Drinking water, flush toilets, showers, sanitary disposal stations, fish-cleaning station, and a boat ramp are available. Some facilities are wheelchair accessible. Supplies can be obtained in Bodega Bay. Leashed pets are permitted.

Reservations, fees: No reservations; $16 per night, $1 pet fee. Open year-round.

Directions: In Petaluma on U.S. 101, take the East Washington exit and turn west (this street becomes Bodega Avenue). Drive west through Petaluma and continue for 10 miles to Valley Ford Road. Turn right and drive 7.5 miles to Highway 1. Turn right (north) on Highway 1 and drive toward Bodega Bay and look for the campground entrance on the right. If you reach the town of Bodega Bay, you have gone a mile too far.

Contact: Sonoma County Parks Department, tel. (707) 875-3540; website: www.sonoma-county.org.

21 Tomales Bay Boat-In

     10

Here is a little slice of paradise secreted away along the west shore of Tomales Bay. A series of dispersed boat-in camps are set along small, sandy coves along the bases of steep cliffs, set from just north of Indian Beach at Tomales Bay State Park on north all the way to Tomales Point. Note that boaters are required to bring chemical toilets, and that reservations are often a necessity, especially on weekends. Tomales Bay is pretty, quiet, and protected from the coastal winds, and offers outstanding sea kayaking. Note that some spots that appear gorgeous during low tides can be covered by water during high tides, so pick your spot with care.

Location: On Tomales Bay; map D0, grid i8.

Campsites, facilities: There are 20 dispersed

boat-in tent sites along the shore of Tomales Bay. Pits toilets are available only at Marshall Beach and Tomales/Kehoe Beach. No drinking water or other facilities are available. Garbage must be packed out. Boaters must bring chemical toilets. No pets are allowed.

Reservations, fees: Reservations are strongly recommended, available Monday through Friday at tel. (415) 663-8054, $10 to $30 per night. Open year-round, weather permitting.

Directions: In Petaluma on U.S. 101, take the East Washington exit and turn west (this street becomes Bodega Avenue). Drive west through Petaluma and continue for 10 miles to Valley Ford Road. Turn right and drive 7.5 miles to Highway 1. Turn left (south) and drive 3.5 miles to the Miller boat launch on the right (a half-mile before Blakes Landing). Launch your boat and drive across Tomales Bay to the boat-in campsites along the Point Reyes National Seashore.

Contact: Point Reyes National Seashore, tel. (415) 663-1092 or (415) 663-8054 (for camping information only, Monday through Friday), fax at (415) 663-1597.

22 Tomales Bay State Park Hike-In/Bike-In

 9

Few know of this tiny campground, including the many bicyclists touring Highway 1 who are looking for exactly such a spot. This camp is for hikers and bikers only. The park is on the secluded western shore of Tomales Bay, pretty, quiet, and protected from the coastal winds. The park offers good hiking and picnicking. There are several excellent hikes in this park, including the Johnstone Trail, which ranges from Heart's Desire Beach to Shell Beach and beyond, and the Indian Nature Trail. During low tides, there is an opportunity for clamming (make sure you have a fishing license) in season, though this once great spot now offers just poor to fair results.

Location: Near Inverness; map D0, grid j8.

Campsites, facilities: There are six tent sites

for hikers and bicyclists only; no vehicles permitted. Picnic tables, fire grills, and food lockers are provided. Drinking water, vault toilets, and one communal fire ring are available. No pets are allowed.

Reservations, fees: No reservations; $1 per person per night, two-night maximum stay. Open year-round, weather permitting.

Directions: From Marin on U.S. 101, take the Sir Francis Drake Boulevard exit. Turn west and drive about 20 miles to the town of Olema. Turn right on Highway 1, drive about four miles, turn left at Sir Francis Drake Boulevard, and drive north for seven miles to Pierce Point Road. Turn right and drive 1.2 miles to the access road for Tomales Bay State Park. Turn right and drive 1.5 miles to the park entrance station. Rangers will tell you where to Park. Park and hike or bike one mile to the campsites.

Contact: Tomales Bay State Park Walk-In, tel. (415) 669-1140 or fax (415) 669-1701.

"Mr. Catfish"
on Clear Lake

MAP D1

TO UPPER LAKE   TO BARTLETT SPRINGS   **266**   TO LODOGA   TO SITES

a

TO UKIAH

1 COW MOUNTAIN REC. AREA
2
3
Lakeport
4-6 Nice
7 Lucerne
Clear Lake
Indian Valley Reservoir
16
15

b

TO HOPLAND

175 Finley
17
Kelseyville
10
11
8 Glenhaven
9 Clearlake Oaks
20

c

TO CLOVERDALE

101
BOGGS LAKE PRESERVE
12-13
29
53
14 Clearlake
Cache Creek
CACHE CREEK WILDLIFE AREA
Lower Lake
16

d

TO STEWARTS POINT

18 Asti
Adams
Cobb
19
Seigler Springs
BOGGS MOUNTAIN STATE FOREST
29
21
Rumsey
Geyserville
20
175
Middletown
Knoxville
22
Guinda

e

340
TO STEWARTS POINT
Russian River
128
Mount St. Helena 4,344 feet
ROBERT LOUIS STEVENSON STATE PARK
Aetna Springs
Pope Valley
Brooks
16
374

f

TO GUERNEVILLE

23
24
Healdsburg
26 Windsor
25
27
Fulton
28
29
Calistoga
30
Angwin
31
32
Lake Berryessa
33
TO CAPAY

g

TO FREESTONE

12 SANTA ROSA
36
Sebastopol
BOTHE–NAPA VALLEY STATE PARK
SUGARLOAF RIDGE STATE PARK
BALE GRIST MILL STATE HISTORIC PARK
St. Helena
Rutherford
Oakville
34
35
128
38
TO WINTERS

h

116
101
Bloomfield
JACK LONDON STATE HISTORIC PARK
37 Kenwood
Glen Ellen
Yountville

i

TO MARSHALL

Two Rock
Rohnert Park
12
Cotati
Boyes Hot Springs
Sonoma
29
39
Napa
121
Vacaville
40
Petaluma
Soulejule Lake
12
121

j

TO PT. REYES
TO RIO VISTA

101
Stafford Lake
121
Novato
37
Nicasio Reservoir
29
12
80
680
12
Fairfield

TO SAN RAFAEL   **450**   TO VALLEJO   TO MARTINEZ

0 1 2 3 4 5 6 7 8 9

© AVALON TRAVEL PUBLISHING, INC.

TO COLUSA

TO ARBUCKLE

TO DIXON

CHAPTER D1

(CONTINUED ON NEXT PAGE)

1 Red Mountain

   3

Like Mayacmus in chapter C1, this camp is also set in the Cow Mountain area east of Ukiah. But be forewarned: It is a popular spot for off-highway motorcycles. If you don't like bikes, go to the other camp. Besides motorcycle trails, there are opportunities for hiking, horseback riding, and hunting.

Location: Near Ukiah; map D1, grid a0.

Campsites, facilities: There are 10 tent sites. Picnic tables and fire grills are provided. Drinking water and vault toilets are available. Garbage must be packed out. Leashed pets are permitted.

Reservations, fees: No reservations; no fee. Open year-round, weather permitting.

Directions: From Ukiah on U.S. 101, drive to Talmage Road. Turn east and drive 1.5 miles to Eastside Road. Turn right and drive a short distance to Mill Creek Road. Turn left and drive nine miles to the campground entrance on the right.

Contact: Bureau of Land Management, Ukiah Field Office, tel. (707) 468-4000 or fax (707) 468-4027.

2 Kelly's Family Kampground & RV Park

     6

This privately operated park is set beside Scotts Creek, within short driving range of Blue Lakes to the north on Highway 20 and the north end of Clear Lake to the south.

Location: On Scotts Creek near Clear Lake; map D1, grid a1.

Campsites, facilities: There are 75 sites for tents or RVs, many with partial hookups. Picnic tables, fire pits, and fire grills are provided. Flush toilets, showers, sanitary disposal station, coin laundry, ice, and a small camp store are available. Leashed pets are permitted.

Reservations, fees: Reservations are accepted; $18.50 to $22 per night. Open April through October.

Directions: From Ukiah on U.S. 101, drive north to the junction with Highway 20. Turn east and drive 14 miles (five miles from Upper Lake) to Scotts Valley Road. Turn south and drive to the park at 8220 Scotts Valley Road.

Contact: Kelly's Family Kampground & RV Park, tel. (707) 263-5754.

3 U-Wanna Camp

 3

Whether U-Wanna or not, this could be where you end up if you're hunting for a site on a good-weather summer weekend. The camp is set about two miles from Clear Lake, with a boat ramp at nearby Lakeport. A small fishing pond for kids here is a plus.

Location: Near Clear Lake; map D1, grid a1.

Campsites, facilities: There are 30 sites for tents or RVs (four drive-through) with partial hookups. Picnic tables and fire rings are provided. Drinking water, restrooms, flush toilets, showers, sanitary disposal station, coin laundry, and a playground are available. Leashed pets are permitted.

Reservations, fees: Reservations are accepted; $19 and up per night, $1 pet fee. Major credit cards accepted. Open year-round.

Directions: From Highway 29 in Lakeport, go to 11th Street. Turn west and drive a half mile to Riggs Road. Turn left and go 0.75 of a mile to Scotts Creek Road. Turn right and go 0.75 of a mile to 2699 Scotts Creek Road.

Contact: U-Wanna Camp, tel. (707) 263-6745; website: www.lakecounty.com (click on Blue Lakes area).

4 Sandpiper Shores

 7

Sandpiper Shores provides boating access to the northern end of Clear Lake. Fishing for catfish is good near here, both in Rodman Slough and just outside the mouth of the slough. This is where the legendary Catfish

George Powers caught 4,000 to 5,000 catfish per year, using dead minnows for bait. In addition, the old submerged pilings in this area provide good bass fishing for boaters casting spinner baits. Several beaches are also available at the north end of the lake.

Location: On Clear Lake; map D1, grid a2.

Campsites, facilities: There are 30 RV sites with full or partial hookups. Picnic tables are provided. Drinking water, restrooms, flush toilets, showers, and coin laundry are available. Moorings, pier, and boat ramp are available nearby. Leashed pets are permitted.

Reservations, fees: Reservations are accepted; $17 to $21 per night, $3 for second car, $3 per person for more than two adults, $2 per child. Major credit cards accepted. Open year-round.

Directions: From Ukiah on U.S. 101, drive north to the junction with Highway 20. Turn east on Highway 20 and drive to the town of Nice and Hammond Avenue. Turn right on Hammond and drive a half mile to Lakeshore Boulevard. Turn left and drive to 2630 Lakeshore Boulevard.

Contact: Sandpiper Shores, tel. (707) 274-4448.

5 North Shore Resort and Marina

 7

This is one of a half dozen privately run parks in the immediate vicinity.

Location: On Clear Lake; map D1, grid a2.

Campsites, facilities: There are 10 sites with full or partial hookups for tents or RVs. Picnic tables and fire grills are provided. Restrooms, showers, coin laundry, boat ramp, pier, and a bookstore are available. Leashed pets are permitted.

Reservations, fees: Reservations are accepted; $18 per night. Major credit cards accepted. Open year-round.

Directions: From Ukiah on U.S. 101, drive north to the junction with Highway 20. Turn east on Highway 20 and drive toward the town of Nice to Hammond Avenue. Turn right on Hammond Avenue and drive a half mile to Lakeshore Boulevard. Turn right and drive to 2345 Lakeshore Boulevard.

Contact: North Shore Resort and Marina, tel. (707) 274-7771.

6 Holiday Harbor RV Park & Marina

 7

This is one of the most popular resorts at the north end of Clear Lake. It is ideal for boaters, with marina gas and a major docking complex. Fishing for bass is good in this area, along old docks and submerged pilings. Water-skiing just offshore is also good, with the north end of the lake often more calm than the water to points south. The elevation is about 2,000 feet.

Location: On Clear Lake; map D1, grid a2.

Campsites, facilities: There are 30 RV sites with full or partial hookups. Picnic tables are provided. Restrooms, showers, recreation room, modem hookups, a sanitary disposal station, a coin laundry, and ice are available. An enclosed marina with 150 boat slips, boat ramp, and an adjacent beach are available nearby. Leashed pets are permitted.

Reservations, fees: Reservations are accepted; $16 to $17.50 per night, $2.50 per person per night for more than two people. Open year-round.

Directions: From north of Ukiah on U.S. 101, drive north to the junction with Highway 20. Turn east on Highway 20 and drive toward the town of Nice to Hammond Avenue. Turn left on Hammond Avenue and drive 200 feet to 3605 Lakeshore Boulevard.

Contact: Holiday Harbor RV Park, tel. (707) 274-1136; website: www.sojourner2000.com/clc/hh.

7 Arrow RV Park and Marina

 7

Lucerne is known for its harbor and its long stretch of well-kept public beaches along the shore of Clear Lake. The town offers a shopping district, restaurants, and cafes. In summer, crappie fishing is good at night from the boat docks, as long as there are bright lights to attract gnats, which in turn attract minnows, the prime food for crappie.

Location: On Clear Lake; map D1, grid a3.

Campsites, facilities: There are 24 sites for RVs, many with full or partial hookups. Restrooms, showers, coin laundry, moorings, fishing supplies, boat ramp, beer, wine, and ice are available. Some facilities are wheelchair accessible. Leashed pets are permitted.

Reservations, fees: Reservations are accepted; $18 per night. Open year-round.

Directions: From north of Ukiah on U.S. 101, or from Williams on Interstate 5, turn on Highway 20 and drive to Clear Lake and the town of Lucerne. Look for the campground at 6720 East Highway 20.

Contact: Arrow RV Park and Marina, P.O. Box 1735, Lucerne, CA 95458; tel. (707) 274-7715.

8 Glenhaven Beach Camp and Marina

 7

This makes a good base camp for all boaters, water-skiers, and anglers. It is set on a peninsula on the eastern shore of Clear Lake, with nearby Indian Beach providing a good recreation and water-play spot. In addition, it is a short boat ride out to Anderson Island, Weekend Island, and Buckingham Point, where bass fishing can be excellent along shaded tules.

Location: On Clear Lake; map D1, grid b3.

Campsites, facilities: There are 21 sites with full or partial hookups for RVs up to 26 feet long. Picnic tables and fire rings are provided. Drinking water, restrooms, showers, flush toilets, modem hookups, and a recreation room are available. A boat ramp and boat rentals are available nearby. Some facilities are wheelchair accessible. Leashed pets are permitted.

Reservations, fees: Reservations are accepted; $16 to $18 per night. Major credit cards accepted. Open February through November.

Directions: From north of Ukiah on U.S. 101, or Interstate 5 at Williams, turn on Highway 20 and drive to Clear Lake and the town of Glenhaven (four miles northwest of Clearlake Oaks). In Glenhaven, drive to the camp at 9625 East Highway 20.

Contact: Glenhaven Beach Camp and Marina, tel. (707) 998-3406; website: www.glenhaven-beach.ohgolly.com.

9 M & M Campgrounds

 7

This park has a unique setting on an island in the shaded lagoons and waterways that lead from Clear Lake into the town of Clearlake Oaks. That means the boat ramp is extremely sheltered from wakes. Fishing for bass and catfish is good in the immediate area, with an excellent catfish hole off nearby Rattlesnake Island.

Location: On Clear Lake; map D1, grid b4.

Campsites, facilities: There are 36 RV sites. Flush toilets, showers, and a boat ramp are available. A pay phone is available at park office. Boat rentals and a grocery store are available within a quarter mile. Leashed pets are allowed.

Reservations, fees: Reservations are required; $12.50 per night, $5 launch fee. Open year-round.

Directions: From north of Ukiah on U.S. 101, or at Williams on Interstate 5, turn on Highway 20 and drive to Clearlake Oaks and Island Drive. Turn south (the only way you can turn) on Island Drive and drive two blocks to 13050 Island Drive.

Contact: M & M Campgrounds, tel. (707) 998-9943.

10 Clear Lake State Park

 9

If you have fallen in love with Clear Lake and its surrounding oak woodlands, it is difficult to find a better spot than at Clear Lake State Park. It is set on the western shore of Clear Lake, and though the oak woodlands flora means you can seem quite close to your camping neighbors, the proximity to quality boating, water sports, and fishing makes the lack of privacy worth it. Reservations are a necessity in summer. That stands to reason, with excellent bass fishing from boats beside a tule-lined shoreline near the park and good catfishing in the sloughs that run through the park. Some campsites have water frontage. A few short hiking trails are also available. Rangers here are friendly, helpful, and provide reliable fishing information. Junior ranger programs and guided walks for bird and flower identification are also available. The elevation is 2,000 feet.

Location: In Kelseyville; map D1, grid b3.

Campsites, facilities: There are 147 sites for tents or RVs up to 35 feet long in four campgrounds, and two hike-in/bike-in sites. Picnic tables and fire rings are provided. Drinking water, restrooms, showers, flush toilets, and sanitary disposal station are available. A boat ramp, dock, fish-cleaning station, and swimming beach are available nearby. A grocery store, coin laundry, propane gas, restaurant, and gas station are available within three miles. The boat ramp, picnic area, and some campsites are wheelchair accessible. Leashed pets are permitted.

Reservations, fees: Reserve at (800) 444-PARK (800-444-7275) or website: www.ReserveAmerica.com; $12 per night, $1 per night for hike-in/bike-in sites. Open year-round.

Directions: From Vallejo, drive north on Highway 29 to Lower Lake. Turn left on Highway 29 and drive seven miles to Soda Bay Road. Turn right on Soda Bay Road and drive 11 miles to the park entrance on the right side of the road.

From Kelseyville on Highway 29, take the Kelseyville exit and turn north on Main Street. Drive a short distance to State Street. Turn right and drive one-quarter mile to Gaddy Lane. Turn right on Gaddy Lane and drive about two miles to Soda Bay Road. Turn right and drive one mile to the park entrance on the left.

Contact: Clear Lake State Park, tel. (707) 279-4293.

11 Edgewater Resort and RV Park

 7

Soda Bay is one of Clear Lake's prettiest and most intimate spots, and this camp provides excellent access. Both water-skiing and fishing for bass and bluegill are excellent in this part of the lake, sheltered from north winds for quiet water, with a tule-lined shore from Henderson Point all the way around to Dorn Bay—nearly three miles of prime fishing territory. This resort specializes in groups and gatherings.

Location: On Clear Lake; map D1, grid b3.

Campsites, facilities: There are 61 RV sites with full hookups and eight cabins (sleep 4 to 12 people) with air conditioning and heat, kitchenettes, color TV, and cable. Picnic tables and fire grills are provided. Restrooms, showers, modem hookups, game room, general store, laundry, swimming pool, horseshoes, volleyball and Ping-Pong are available. A swimming beach, boat ramp, fishing pier, boat docking, and watercraft rentals are available nearby. Wood is available for purchase. Leashed pets are permitted. There is a dog run at the beach.

Reservations, fees: Reservations are accepted; $25 to $35 per night, $5 per person per night for more than two people, $85 to $300 for cabins. Major credit cards accepted. Open year-round.

Directions: In Kelseyville on Highway 29, take the Merritt Road exit and drive on Merritt for two miles (it becomes Gaddy Lane) to Soda Bay Road. Turn right on Soda Bay Road and drive three miles to the campground entrance on the left.

Contact: Edgewater Resort and RV Park, tel. (800) 396-6224 or (707) 279-0208 or fax (707) 279-0138; website: www.edgewaterresort.net.

12 Shaw's Shady Acres

      7

This is one of several privately operated campgrounds set beside Cache Creek, just south of Clear Lake. The fishing for catfish is often quite good on summer nights in Cache Creek, a deep green, slow-moving water that looks more like a slough in a Mississippi bayou than a creek. Waterfront campsites with scattered walnut, ash, and oak trees are available. Clear Lake is a short drive to the north.

Location: On Cache Creek; map D1, grid c4.

Campsites, facilities: There are 13 sites for tents or RVs up to 38 feet, many sites with partial or full hookups. Picnic tables and fire grills are provided. Restrooms, showers, sanitary disposal station, pier, boat rentals, boat ramp, coin laundry, swimming pool, recreation patio, beer and wine bar, fishing supplies, and a grocery store are available. Some facilities are wheelchair accessible. Pets must be leashed and may not be left unattended in camp.

Reservations, fees: Reservations are recommended; $16 per night, $2 per person per night for more than two people, $.50 pet fee.

Directions: From the town of Lower Lake, drive north on Highway 53 for 1.3 miles to Old Highway 53. Turn left (a frontage road) and drive a quarter mile to the park entrance.

Contact: Shaw's Shady Acres, tel. (707) 994-2236.

13 Garners' Resort

     7

This is one of several privately operated parks near the mouth of Cache Creek at the southern end of Clear Lake. The park offers sites for tents as well as RVs, many near Cache Creek, which actually looks more like a slough—deep, wide, green, and slow moving.

Location: On Clear Lake; map D1, grid c4.

Campsites, facilities: There are 25 sites for tents and 40 full-hookup RV sites. Flush toilets, showers, sanitary disposal station, boat rentals, pier, boat ramp, recreation room, swimming pool, wading pool, fishing supplies, coin laundry, and a store are available. Some facilities are wheelchair accessible. Leashed pets are permitted.

Reservations, fees: Reservations are accepted; $15 to $20 per night, $2 per person per night for more than two people. Major credit cards accepted. Open year-round.

Directions: From the town of Lower Lake, drive north on Highway 53 for 1.3 miles to Old Highway 53. Turn left (a frontage road) and drive 1.5 miles to the resort entrance on the left.

Contact: Garners' Resort, tel. (707) 994-6267 or fax (707) 994-3470; website: www.garnersresort.com.

14 Aztec RV Park

    7

This is an adults-only RV park set near Cache Creek, just south of Clear Lake.

Location: On Cache Creek; map D1, grid c5.

Campsites, facilities: There are 30 sites with full or partial hookups for RVs up to 40 feet long (no pop-outs), and six tent sites. This is an "adult park" (no children allowed). Restrooms, showers, pier, boat ramp, coin laundry, and river frontage sites are available. Some facilities are wheelchair accessible. Propane gas is available within 1.5 miles. Small, leashed pets are permitted.

Reservations, fees: Reservations are recommended; $17 per night, $5 per person per night for more than two people. Open year-round.

Directions: From the town of Lower Lake, drive north on Highway 29 for a mile to Dam Road. Turn right and drive across the bridge.

Turn left on Tish-a-Tang Road and continue to the campground at 16150 Tish-a-Tang Road. **Contact:** Aztec RV Park, tel. (707) 994-4377.

15 Blue Oak

 7

Indian Valley Reservoir is kind of like an ugly dog that you love more than anything because inside beats a heart that will never betray you. The camp is out in the middle of nowhere in oak woodlands, about a mile from the dam. It is primitive and little known. For many, that kind of isolation is perfect. While there are good trails nearby, it is the outstanding fishing for bass and bluegill at the lake every spring and early summer that is the key reason to make the trip. In addition, in the spring, there is a great variety of wildflowers in and around the campground.

Location: At Indian Valley Reservoir; map D1, grid b6.

Campsites, facilities: There are six sites for tents or RVs. Picnic tables and fire grills are provided. Drinking water and vault toilets are available. Leashed pets are permitted.

Reservations, fees: No reservations; no fee; 14-day stay limit. Open year-round, weather permitting.

Directions: From Williams on Interstate 5, turn west on Highway 20 and drive 25 miles into the foothills to Walker Ridge Road. Turn north (right) on Walker Ridge Road (a dirt road) and drive north for about four miles to a "major" intersection of two dirt roads. Turn left and drive about 2.5 miles toward the Indian Valley Dam. The Blue Oak campground is just off the road to your right, about 1.5 miles from Indian Valley Reservoir.

Contact: Bureau of Land Management, Ukiah Field Office; tel. (707) 468-4000, or fax (707) 478-4027. A detailed map is available from the BLM.

16 Wintun

 6

If you want to feel like you are out in the middle of nowhere without being out in the middle of nowhere, then this camp answers your call. Wintun is the smallest and most obscure camp anywhere, set at an elevation of 3,000 feet, about a 20-minute drive from the north end of Indian Valley Reservoir (which has outstanding bass fishing). Note: Summer temperatures can burn you into a crispy chimichanga, so bring a tarp that you can rig for shade cover.

Location: Near Indian Valley Reservoir; map D1, grid a7.

Campsites, facilities: There is a primitive tent site. A picnic table and a fire ring are provided. Drinking water is available. Garbage must be packed out. Leashed pets are permitted.

Reservations, fees: No reservations; no fee. Open year-round, weather permitting.

Directions: From Williams on Interstate 5, turn west on Highway 20 and drive 25 miles into the foothills to Walker Ridge Road. Turn north on Walker Ridge Road (a dirt road) and drive north for about four miles to a "major" intersection of two dirt roads. Continue straight on Walker Ridge Road for another five miles. At the sign for Wintun, turn left and drive about a mile on a spur road that dead-ends at the campground. Note: To reach Indian Valley Reservoir from Wintun, you must backtrack a mile, turn left on Walker Ridge Road, and drive eight or nine miles to the north end of the lake.

Contact: Bureau of Land Management, Ukiah Field Office; tel. (707) 468-4000, or fax (707) 478-4027. A detailed map is available from the BLM.

17 Sheldon Creek

 3

Only the locals know about this spot, and hey, there aren't a lot of locals around. The camp is set amid rolling hills, grasslands, and oaks along little Sheldon Creek. It is pretty and quiet in the spring when the hills have greened up, but hot in the summer. Recreational possibilities include hiking, and in the fall, hunting.

Location: Near Hopland; map D1, grid b0.

Campsites, facilities: There are four sites for tents. Picnic tables and fire grills are provided. Vault toilets are available. No drinking water is available. Garbage must be packed out. Leashed pets are permitted.

Reservations, fees: No reservations; no fee. Open year-round, weather permitting.

Directions: From Santa Rosa on U.S. 101, drive north to Hopland and the junction with Highway 175. Turn east on Highway 175 and drive three miles to Old Toll Road. Turn right on Old Toll Road and drive eight miles to the camp.

Contact: Bureau of Land Management, Ukiah Field Office; tel. (707) 468-4000, or fax (707) 478-4027.

⓲ Cloverdale KOA

 7

This KOA campground is set just above the Russian River in the Alexander Valley wine country, just south of Cloverdale. Since new owners took over in the mid-1990s, the place has undergone considerable renovation and is now both rustic and tidy, with adorable little camping cabins a great bonus. In addition, a fishing pond is stocked with largemouth bass, bluegill, catfish, and, when water temperatures are cool enough, trout. The nearby Russian River is an excellent beginner's route in an inflatable kayak or canoe. The nearby winery in Asti makes for a popular side trip.

Location: Near the Russian River; map D1, grid c0.

Campsites, facilities: There are 47 sites for tents, 104 RV sites (11 drive-through), most with full hookups, and 14 cabins. Picnic tables and fire grills are provided. Flush toilets, showers, modem hookups, swimming pool, playground, sanitary disposal station, coin laundry, recreation room, mini-golf, nature trails, catch-and-release fishpond, nightly entertainment on weekends in the summer, and a grocery and gift store are available. Leashed pets are permitted.

Reservations, fees: Reservations are accepted; $26 for tent sites, $32 for RV sites, cabins are $46 to $56 per night. Major credit cards accepted. Open year-round.

Directions: From Cloverdale on U.S. 101, take the Central Cloverdale exit, which puts you on Asti Road. Drive straight on Asti Road to First Street. Turn right (east) and drive a short distance to River Road. Turn right (south) and drive four miles to KOA Road. Turn left and drive to the campground entrance.

In summer/fall: South of Cloverdale on U.S. 101, take the Asti exit and drive east a block to Asti Road. Turn right (south) and drive 1.5 miles to Washington School Road. Turn left (east) and drive 1.5 miles to KOA Road. Turn right and drive to the campground entrance. (Note: This route is open May 15 to December 15, when a seasonal bridge is in place.) Both routes are well signed.

Contact: Cloverdale KOA, tel. (707) 894-3337. Reserve at tel. (800) 368-4558.

⓳ Yogi Bear Beaver Creek Campground

 7

This camp has a trout creek, a pond with canoes and kayaks in summer, plus plenty of hiking and bird-watching opportunities. In addition, horseback riding and hot air balloon rides are available nearby. This camp is set near Highway 175 between Middletown and Clear Lake, and while there is a parade of vacation traffic on Highway 29, relatively few people take the longer route on Highway 175. Cobb Mountain looms nearby.

Location: Near Cobb Mountain; map D1, grid d2.

Campsites, facilities: There are 10 tent sites and 97 sites for RVs up to 40 feet long, four cabins, and two tepees. Most sites are pull-through, and all have full hookups. Picnic tables and fire rings are provided. Drinking water, restrooms, showers, group area, coin laundry, modem hookups, pool, kayaks and paddleboats, boating pond, playground, horseshoes, recreation hall, and a store are available. Some facilities are wheelchair accessible. Leashed pets are permitted.

Reservations, fees: Reservations are recommended; $19 to $22 per night, $2 per person per night for more than two people. Tepees are $25 per night. Cabins are $39 to $45 per night. Major credit cards accepted.

Directions: From Vallejo, drive north on Highway 29 past Calistoga to Middletown and the junction with Highway 175. Turn north on Highway 175 and drive 8.5 miles to Bottle Rock Road. Turn left and drive three miles to the campground entrance on the left side of the road.

Contact: Beaver Creek RV Park, 14417 Bottle Rock Road, P.O. Box 49, Cobb Mountain, CA 95426; tel. (707) 928-4322, tel. (800) 307-CAMP (800-307-2267), from California only, or fax (707) 928-5341; website: www.campyogi.com.

20 Cache Creek Canyon Regional Park

      7

This is the best campground in Yolo County, yet it's known by few out-of-towners. It is set at 1,300 feet beside Cache Creek, which is the closest river to the Bay Area that provides white-water rafting opportunities. This section of river features primarily Class I and II water, ideal for inflatable kayaks and overnight trips. One rapid, Big Mother, is sometimes considered Class III, though that might be a stretch. Occasionally, huge catfish are caught in this area.

Location: Near Rumsey; map D1, grid d3.

Campsites, facilities: There are 45 sites for tents or RVs and three group sites that can accommodate 20 to 30 people. Picnic tables and fire rings are provided. Drinking water, flush toilets, and a sanitary disposal station are available. Some facilities are wheelchair accessible. Leashed pets are permitted.

Reservations, fees: No reservations; $13 to $15 per night, $2 fee for pets. Open year-round.

Directions: From Vacaville on Interstate 80, turn north on Interstate 505 and drive 21 miles to Madison and the junction with Highway 16. Turn north on Highway 16 and drive northwest for about 45 miles to the town of Rumsey. From Rumsey, continue west on Highway 16 for five miles to the park entrance.

Contact: Cache Creek Canyon Regional Park, tel. (530) 666-8115 or fax (530) 666-8728.

21 Boggs Mountain Demonstration State Forest

    5

This overlooked spot is set in a state forest that covers 3,000 acres of pine and fir. There are two adjoining campgrounds here. This is a popular destination for the region's equestrians. There are numerous trails for horses, hikers, and bikers, and there have been some trail conflicts between the groups. Remembers: Equestrians have the right of way over hikers and bikers, and hikers have the right of way over bikers. Got it? Apparently not, because too many mountain bikers are not yielding out here, and there have been some shouting matches over close calls. Note that in early fall, this area is open to deer hunting, and everybody yields to the guys with rifles.

Location: Near Middletown; map D1, grid d7.

Campsites, facilities: There are 20 sites for tents or RVs up to 22 feet long. Picnic tables and fire pits are provided. Vault toilets are available. No drinking water is available. Garbage must be packed out. Coin laundry, pizza parlor, and gas station are available within two miles. Horses are permitted. Leashed pets are permitted.

Reservations, fees: No reservations; no fee. Open year-round.

Directions: From Vallejo, drive north on Highway 29 past Calistoga to Middletown and the junction with Highway 175. Turn left (north) on Highway 175 and drive seven miles to Cobb and Foresty Road 500. Turn right and drive one mile to the campgrounds on the left.

Contact: Boggs Mountain Demonstration State Forest, tel. (707) 928-4378.

22 Lower Hunting Creek

 4

This little-known camp might seem like it's out in the middle of nowhere for the folks who wind up here accidentally (like we did), and it turns out that it is. If you plan on spending a few days here, it's advisable to get information or a map of the surrounding area from the Bureau of Land Management prior to your trip. There are some 25 miles of trails for off-highway-vehicle exploration on the surrounding lands. In the fall, the area provides access for deer hunting with generally poor to fair results.

Location: Near Lake Berryessa; map D1, grid e7.

Campsites, facilities: There are five sites for tents or RVs. Picnic tables and fire grills are provided. Drinking water, shade shelters, and vault toilets are available. Garbage must be packed out. Leashed pets are permitted.

Reservations, fees: No reservations; no fee. Open year-round.

Directions: In Lower Lake on Highway 29, turn southeast on Morgan Valley Road/Berryessa-Knoxville Road and drive 15 miles to Devilhead Road. Turn south and drive two miles to the campground.

Contact: Bureau of Land Management, Ukiah District, tel. (707) 468-4000, or fax (707) 468-4027.

23 Burke's Canoe Trips

 7

Burke's is the long-established canoe rental service and campground on the Russian River.

The favorite trip is the 10-miler from Burke's in Forestville to Guerneville, which is routed right through the heart of the area's redwoods, about a 3.5-hour paddle trip with plenty of time in the day for sunbathing, swimming, or anything else you can think of. The cost is $39, including a return by shuttle. Many other trips are available.

Location: On the Russian River; map D1, grid e0.

Campsites, facilities: There are 60 sites for tents or RVs. Picnic tables and fire rings are provided. Flush toilets, showers, wood, and canoe rentals are available. Pets are not allowed.

Reservations, fees: Reservations are required; $16 per night, $8 per person per night for more than two people. Open May through mid-October.

Directions: From the Bay Area, drive north on U.S. 101 to the junction with Highway 116 West. Take Highway 116 West and drive 15 miles to Forestville and Mirabel Road (at the gas station). Turn right and drive 1.5 miles until it dead-ends at Burke's and the Russian River.

Contact: Burke's Canoe Trips, tel. (707) 887-1222.

24 Schoolhouse Canyon Campground

 6

This campground comprises 210 acres and features a mile of river access along the Russian River, campsites in a grove of large redwoods, and a park-like setting on land originally homesteaded in the 1850s. A one-mile scenic hiking trail is available, routed up to a ridge for some nice views of the countryside. Touring the adjacent Korbel Winery is a popular side trip.

Location: In the Russian River Valley; map D1, grid f0.

Campsites, facilities: There are 65 sites for tents or RVs up to 27 feet long, some with partial hookups. Picnic tables and fire grills are provided. Drinking water, flush toilets, showers, and wood are available. Some facilities are wheelchair accessible. Leashed pets are permitted.

Reservations, fees: Reservations are accepted; $23 to $25 per night for two people, $5 for each additional person, $4 pet fee. Open May through October.

Directions: From Santa Rosa, drive north on U.S. 101 about 2.5 miles and take the River Road/Guerneville exit. Drive to the stop sign, turn left on River Road, and drive 12.5 miles to the campground entrance.

Contact: Schoolhouse Canyon Campground, tel. (707) 869-2311.

25 Mirabel Trailer Park and Camp

     7

The big attraction here during the summer is swimming and paddling around in canoes or kayaks. The campsites are shaded by redwood, pine, and bay trees. This privately operated park is set near the Russian River, but in the summer the "river" is actually a series of small lakes, with temporary dams stopping most of the water flow. In winter, out come the dams, up comes the water, and in come the steelhead, migrating upstream past this area. Armstrong Redwoods State Park just north of Guerneville provides a nearby side trip.

Location: On the Russian River; map D1, grid f0.

Campsites, facilities: There are 125 sites for tents or RVs up to 35 feet, many sites with full or partial hookups. Picnic tables and fire grills are provided. Flush toilets, showers, playground, coin laundry, sanitary disposal station, horseshoes, shuffleboard, a small video arcade, and canoe and kayak rentals are available. Some facilities are wheelchair accessible. Leashed pets, except pit bulls (which are prohibited), are allowed.

Reservations, fees: Reservations are recommended; $16 to $19 per night, $2 per person per night for more than two people, $3 per additional vehicle per night, $2 pet fee. Open March through October.

Directions: North of Santa Rosa on U.S. 101, take the River Road exit and head west. Drive eight miles to the campground at 7600 River Road.

Contact: Mirabel Trailer Park and Camp, tel. or fax (707) 887-2383.

26 Windsorland RV Park

     3

This developed park is close to the Russian River, the wine country to the east, redwoods to the west, and Lake Sonoma to the northwest. But with a swimming pool, playground, and recreation room, many visitors are content to stay right here, spend the night, then head out on their vacation.

Location: Near Santa Rosa; map D1, grid f0.

Campsites, facilities: There are 55 sites with full hookups for RVs up to 35 feet long. Patios are provided. Flush toilets, showers, swimming pool, sanitary disposal station, coin laundry, recreation room, and a playground are available. Some facilities are wheelchair accessible. Leashed pets are permitted.

Reservations, fees: Reservations are accepted; $24 to $27 per night. Open year-round.

Directions: From Santa Rosa on U.S. 101, drive north for nine miles to Windsor. Take the Windsor exit, turn north on Old Redwood Highway, and drive a half mile to 9290 Old Redwood Highway.

Contact: Windsorland RV Park, tel. (800) 864-3407 or (707) 838-4882.

27 Hilton Park Family Campground

      6

This lush, wooded park is set on the banks of the Russian River, with a choice of open or secluded sites. The highlight of the campground is a large, beautiful beach that offers access for swimming, fishing, and canoeing. The folks here are very friendly, and you get a choice of many recreation options in the area.

Location: On the Russian River; map D1, grid f0.

Campsites, facilities: There are 20 tent sites and five sites for RVs up to 33 feet long, with no hookups. Picnic tables and fire rings are provided. Restrooms, showers, coin laundry, dishwashing area, arcade, playground, firewood, and ice are available. A beach is available nearby. Canoe rentals are available within three miles. Leashed pets are permitted.

Reservations, fees: Reservations are recommended; $20 to $25 per night, $5 per person per night for more than three people. Pets $5 per night. Major credit cards accepted. Open year-round.

Directions: From U.S. 101 north of Santa Rosa, take the River Road/Guerneville exit. Drive west for 11.5 miles (one mile after the metal bridge) to the campground on the left side of the road (just before the Russian River Pub).

Contact: Hilton Park, tel. (707) 887-9206.

28 Napa County Fairgrounds

     2

What this really is, folks, is just the county fairgrounds, converted to an RV park for 11 months each year. It is closed to camping from mid-June through mid-July, but what the heck, you can stick around and try to win a stuffed animal. What is more likely, of course, is that you have come here for the health spas, with great natural hot springs, mud baths, and assorted goodies at the health resorts in Calistoga. Nearby parks for hiking include Bothe-Napa Valley and Robert Louis Stevenson State Parks.

Location: In Calistoga; map D1, grid f3.

Campsites, facilities: There are 50 RV sites (some drive-through and with hookups) and a lawn area for tents. Group sites are available by reservation only. Restrooms, showers, and a sanitary disposal station are available. No fires are permitted. A nine-hole golf course is adjacent to the campground area. Some facilities are wheelchair accessible. Leashed pets are permitted.

Reservations, fees: No reservations (except for groups); $10-20 per night, $1 per person per night for more than four people.

Directions: From Napa on Highway 29, drive north to Calistoga, turn right on Lincoln Avenue, and drive four blocks to Fairway. Turn left and drive to the end of the road to the campground.

Contact: Napa County Fairgrounds, tel. (707) 942-5111 or fax (707) 942-5125.

29 Bothe-Napa Valley State Park

    7

It's always a stunner for newcomers to discover this beautiful park with redwoods and a pretty stream so close to the Napa Valley wine and spa country. Though the campsites are relatively exposed, they are set beneath a pretty oak/bay/madrone forest, with trailheads for hiking nearby. One trail is routed south from the day-use parking lot for 1.1 mile to the restored Bale Grist Mill, a giant partially-restored waterwheel on a pretty creek. Another, more scenic, route heads up Ritchey Canyon, amid redwoods and along Ritchey Creek, beautiful and intimate. The park covers 2,000 acres.

Location: Near Calistoga; map D1, grid f3.

Campsites, facilities: There are 40 sites for tents or RVs up to 31 feet long, and one group tent site for up to 30 people. Picnic tables and fire grills are provided. Drinking water, flush toilets, coin-operated showers, and a swimming pool in the summer are available. Some facilities are wheelchair accessible. Supplies can be obtained in Calistoga or St. Helena, seven miles away. Leashed pets are permitted.

Reservations, fees: Reserve at (800) 444-PARK (800-444-7275) or website: www.ReserveAmerica.com; $12, and $22 for the group site. $1 pool fee, free for children 16 and under. Open year-round.

Directions: From Napa on Highway 29, drive north to St. Helena and continue north for five miles (one mile past the entrance to Bale Grist Mill State Park) to the park entrance road on the left.

Contact: Bothe-Napa Valley State Park, tel. (707) 942-4575.

30 Calistoga Ranch Campground

      4

This is a large, privately run camp set in the heart of the wine country, about a 15-minute drive from the famous Calistoga spas and mud baths. The elevation is 400 feet.

Location: Near Calistoga; map D1, grid f4.

Campsites, facilities: There are 60 sites for tents, 84 sites for RVs up to 45 feet long with full or partial hookups, four cabins, and two trailers. There is a limit of four people per site. Picnic tables are provided. Flush toilets, showers, sanitary disposal station, coin laundry, lake, swimming pool, and a snack bar are available. Some sites have barbecues. No wood burning fires permitted. Leashed pets are permitted with RV campers only.

Reservations, fees: Reservations are accepted; $20 to $27 per night, $54 per night for cabins, $98 per night for trailers, $2 pet fee. Major credit cards accepted. Open year-round.

Directions: From Napa on Highway 29, drive north through St. Helena and continue for about five miles to Larkmead Lane. Turn right and drive a short distance to the Silverado Trail. Turn left and drive about 200 yards to Lommel Road. Turn right and drive a quarter mile to the campground.

Contact: Calistoga Ranch Campground, tel. (707) 942-6565 or fax (707) 942-6902.

31 Rancho Monticello Resort

      7

This is a fully developed, privately operated park set on the shore of Lake Berryessa. Berryessa is the third largest man-made lake in Northern California, smaller than only Shasta and Oroville. It is a popular spot for water-skiing and fishing for trout and bass. The elevation is 475 feet. A bonus is a nearby day park with picnic tables and barbecues set near the lake.

Location: On Lake Berryessa; map D1, grid f7.

Campsites, facilities: There are 57 sites for tents and 10 RV sites with full hookups (including five wired for 220 volt). Picnic tables and fire grills are provided. Restrooms, drinking water, showers, snack bar, complete marina facilities, ice, propane gas, and groceries are available. Leashed pets are permitted.

Reservations, fees: Reservations recommended; $14 to $27 per night per vehicle. Major credit cards accepted. Open year-round.

Directions: From Vallejo, drive north on Interstate 80 to the Suisun Valley Road exit. Take Suisun Valley Road north to Highway 121. Turn north on Highway 121 and drive five miles to Highway 128. Turn north on Highway 128, drive five miles to Berryessa-Knoxville Road, and continue 10 miles to 6590 Knoxville Road.

Contact: Rancho Monticello Resort, tel. (707) 966-2188 or fax (707) 963-2440; website: www.ranchomonticelloresort.com.

32 Putah Creek Resort

     7

This campground is set at 400 feet elevation on the northern end of Lake Berryessa. The Putah Creek arm provides very good bass fishing in the spring and trout trolling in the summer. The north end of the lake has a buoy line that keeps powerboats out, but it can still be explored by paddling a canoe, which allows you to fish in relatively untouched waters and see deer during the evening on the eastern shore. In the fall, usually by mid-October, the trout come to the surface and provide excellent fishing at the mouth of Pope Creek or Putah Creek for anglers drifting live minnows. The resort also has a small, rustic motel.

Location: On Lake Berryessa; map D1, grid f7.

Campsites, facilities: There are 200 tent and 55 RV sites, many with full or partial hookups for RVs up to 40 feet. Restrooms, showers, sanitary disposal station, coin laundry, boat ramp, rowboat rentals, snack bar, motel, cocktail lounge, restaurant, propane gas, ice, and groceries are available. Leashed pets are permitted.

Reservations, fees: Reservations at tel. (707) 966-0794; $21 to $26 per night, $21 for a second vehicle, $2 pet fee. Major credit cards accepted. Open year-round.

Directions: From Vallejo, drive north on Interstate 80 to the Suisun Valley Road exit. Take Suisun Valley Road and drive north to Highway 121. Turn north on Highway 121 and drive five miles to Highway 128. Turn left on Highway 128, drive five miles to Berryessa-Knoxville Road, and continue 13 miles to 7600 Knoxville Road.

Contact: Putah Creek Park, tel. (707) 966-2116 or tel. (707) 966-0794, or fax (707) 966-0593.

33 Lake Berryessa Marina Resort

      7

Lake Berryessa is the Bay Area's backyard water recreation headquarters, the number one lake (in the greater Bay Area) for water-skiing, loafing, and fishing. This resort is set on the west shore of the main lake, one of several resorts at the lake.

Location: On Lake Berryessa; map D1, grid g7.

Campsites, facilities: There are 73 sites for tents and 45 sites for RVs up to 40 feet, with water and electrical hookups, and five cabins. Flush toilets, showers, sanitary disposal station, coin laundry, snack bar, complete marina facilities, RV supplies, and groceries are available. Some facilities are wheelchair accessible. Leashed pets are permitted at RV sites (prohibited at tent sites).

Reservations, fees: Reservations are recommended; $15 to $24 per night, $1 pet fee. Cabins $75 to $100 per night. Major credit cards accepted. Open year-round.

Directions: From Vallejo, drive north on Interstate 80 to the Suisun Valley Road exit. Take Suisun Valley Road and drive north to Highway 121. Turn north on Highway 121 and drive five miles to Highway 128. Turn left on Highway 128, drive five miles to Berryessa-Knoxville Road, turn right, and continue nine miles to 5800 Knoxville Road.

Contact: Lake Berryessa Marina Resort, tel. (707) 966-2161 or fax (707) 966-0761; website: www.lakeberryessa.com.

34 Spanish Flat Resort

      7

This is one of several lakeside camps at Lake Berryessa. This is one of the most popular because many of the sites are on the waterfront. That makes it a natural gathering place for water-skiers and power boaters, and on summer weekends, particularly holidays, it can get rowdy here. Berryessa, considered the Bay Area's backyard fishing hole, is the third largest man-made lake in Northern California (Lakes Shasta and Oroville are larger). Trout fishing is good, trolling deep in the summer in Skier's Cove from dawn to mid-morning, or drifting with minnows in fall and winter. The elevation is approximately 500 feet.

Location: On Lake Berryessa; map D1, grid g7.

Campsites, facilities: There are 120 sites for tents or RVs up to 37 feet, a few sites with partial hookups, and two yurts. Picnic tables and fire grills are provided. Restrooms, drinking water, flush toilets, showers, boat launch, complete marina facilities, boat rentals, and groceries are available. A deli and grill is open on summer weekends. Coin laundry, restaurant, post office, and RV supplies are available within 1.5 miles. Some facilities are wheelchair accessible. Leashed pets are permitted.

Reservations, fees: Reservations are accepted; $21 to $26 per night, $60 per night for yurts, $5 for boat launching, $1 pet fee. Major credit cards accepted. Open year-round.

Directions: From Vallejo, drive north on Interstate 80 to the Suisun Valley Road exit. Take Suisun Valley Road and drive north to Highway 121. Turn north on Highway 121 and drive five miles to Highway 128. Turn north on Highway 128 and drive five miles. Turn right on Berryessa-Knoxville Road and continue four miles to 4290 Knoxville Road.

Contact: Spanish Flat Resort, tel. (707) 966-7700 or fax (707) 966-7704; website: www.spanishflatresort.com.

35 Pleasure Cove Resort

     7

Pleasure Cove is set on the south end of Lake Berryessa, an excellent area for trout and bass fishing. Top spots that are nearby include the Monticello Dam, the narrows, Skier's Cove for trout, and the back of the coves of the Markley Cove arm for bass. This park is family oriented.

Location: On Lake Berryessa; map D1, grid h8.

Campsites, facilities: There are 105 sites for tents or RVs (20 have water and electrical hookups). Picnic tables and fire grills are provided. Restrooms, showers, ice, restaurant, bar, boat ramp, propane gas, and groceries are available. Some facilities are wheelchair accessible. Pets are not permitted.

Reservations, fees: Reservations are accepted; $20 to $24 per night per vehicle. Major credit cards accepted. Open year-round.

Directions: From Vallejo, drive north on Interstate 80 about 10 miles to the Suisun Valley Road exit. Take Suisun Valley Road and drive north another 10 miles to Highway 121. Turn north right on Highway 121 and drive about eight miles to the end of Highway 121 and the junction with Highway 128. Bear southeast on Highway 128 and proceed four miles to Wragg Canyon Road. Turn left and continue three miles to the resort entrance.

Contact: Pleasure Cove Resort, tel. (707) 966-2172 or fax (707) 966-0320.

36 Spring Lake Regional Park

 6

Spring Lake is one of the few lakes in the greater Bay Area that provides lakeside camping. Not only that, Spring Lake is stocked twice each month in late winter and spring with rainbow trout by the Department of Fish and Game. Only nonpowered boats are permitted on this small, pretty lake, which keeps things fun and quiet for everybody. An easy trail along the west shore of the lake to the dam, then into adjoining Howarth Park, provides a pleasant evening stroll. This little lake is where a 24-pound world-record bass was reportedly caught, a story now taken as a hoax by nearly all anglers.

Location: At Spring Lake near Santa Rosa; map D1, grid g2.

Campsites, facilities: There are 30 sites for tents or RVs up to 44 feet long. Picnic tables, fire grills, and piped water are provided. Flush toilets, showers, sanitary disposal station, boat ramp (no gas-powered motorboats), summer boat rentals, and bike paths are available. Some facilities are wheelchair accessible. A grocery store, coin laundry, wood, and propane gas are available within five minutes. Leashed pets are permitted with proof of rabies vaccination.

Reservations, fees: Reservations are accepted; reserve at tel. (707) 539-8082 on Mondays, Tuesdays and Wednesdays 10 days in advance; $16 per night, $1 pet fee and proof of rabies vaccination, $5 for the second vehicle. Note: The limit is eight people and two vehicles per campsite. Major credit cards accepted. Open daily from mid-May through mid-September and on weekends and holidays only during off-season.

Directions: From Santa Rosa on U.S. 101, turn east on Highway 12 (it will become Hoen Avenue) and continue to Newanga Avenue. Turn left and drive to the park at the end of the road.

Contact: Spring Lake Regional Park, tel. (707) 539-8082 or (707) 539-8092.

37 Sugarloaf Ridge State Park

 5

Sugarloaf Ridge State Park is a perfect example of a place that you can't make a final judgment about from your first glance. Your first glance will lead you to believe that this is just hot foothill country, with old ranch roads set in oak woodlands for horseback riding and sweaty hiking or biking. A little discovery here, however, is that a half-mile walk off the Canyon Trail will lead you to 25-foot waterfall, beautifully set in a canyon, complete with a redwood canopy. A shortcut to this waterfall is available off the south side of the park's entrance road. Otherwise, it can be a long, hot, and challenging hike. In all, there are 21 miles of trail here, and hikers planning for a day of it should leave early, wear a hat, and bring plenty of water. Rangers report that some unprepared hikers have suffered heat stroke, and many others have just plain suffered.

Location: Near Santa Rosa; map D1, grid h3.

Campsites, facilities: There are 49 sites for tents or RVs up to 27 feet long, and one group site for tents only for up to 50 people. Picnic tables and fire grills are provided. Drinking water and flush toilets are available. Leashed pets are permitted in campsites only.

Reservations, fees: Reserve at (800) 444-PARK (800-444-7275) or website: www.ReserveAmerica.com; $12 per night, $37 per night for group site. Open year-round.

Directions: From Santa Rosa on U.S. 101, turn east on Highway 12 and drive seven miles to Adobe Canyon Road. Turn left (north) and drive 3.5 miles to the park entrance.

Contact: Sugarloaf Ridge State Park, tel. (707) 833-5712.

38 Lake Solano County Park

 6

Lake Solano provides a low-pressure option to nearby Lake Berryessa. It is a long, narrow lake set below the outlet at Monticello Dam at Lake Berryessa, technically called the after-bay. Compared to Berryessa, life here moves at a much slower pace and some people prefer it. The lake has fair trout fishing in the spring. The camp can also be used as an overflow area if the camps at Berryessa fill on popular weekends. No motors, including electric motors, are permitted on boats at the lake.

Location: Near Lake Berryessa; map D1, grid h9.

Campsites, facilities: There are 90 sites for tents or RVs up to 38 feet long, 40 sites with full hookups. Picnic tables and fire grills are provided. Drinking water, flush toilets, a sanitary disposal station, showers, boat ramp, and boat rentals are available. A grocery store is within walking distance, and firewood and ice are sold on the premises. Some facilities are wheelchair accessible. Leashed pets are accepted with proof of vaccination.

Reservations, fees: Reservations are accepted; $15 to $18 per night, $5 for second vehicle, $1 pet fee. Major credit cards accepted. Open year-round.

Directions: In Vacaville, turn north on Interstate 505 and drive 11 miles to the junction of Highway 128. Turn west on Highway 128 and drive about five miles (past Winters) to Pleasant Valley Road. Turn left on Pleasant Valley Road and drive to the park at 8685 Pleasant Valley Road.

Contact: Lake Solano County Park, tel. (530) 795-2990 or fax (530) 795-1408.

39 Napa Town and Country Fairgrounds

 2

This RV Park is actually the parking area for the Napa Fairgrounds. When the fair is in operation in early August, it is closed temporarily. The rest of the year it is simply a large parking lot near Napa.

Location: In Napa; map D1, grid i6.

RV facilities: There are 100 RV sites, many with electrical and water hookups, and an open area with space for 400 self-contained units. Restrooms, showers, coin laundry, and a sanitary disposal station are available. A grocery store and restaurant are within walking distance. Leashed pets are permitted.

Reservations, fees: No reservations except for groups of 15 or more; $18 per night.

Directions: From Napa on Highway 29, drive to the Napa/Lake Berryessa exit. Turn east and drive to Third Street. Turn right and drive to Burnell Street and the campground entrance.

Contact: Napa Town and Country Fairgrounds, tel. (707) 253-4900 or fax (707) 253-4943; website: www.napavalleyexpo.com.

40 San Francisco North/Petaluma KOA

 3

This campground is less than a mile from U.S. 101, yet it has a rural feel. It's a good base camp for folks who require some quiet mental preparation before heading south to the Bay Area or to the nearby wineries, redwoods, and the Russian River. The big plus here is that this KOA has the cute log cabins called "Kamping Kabins," providing privacy for those who want it.

Location: Near Petaluma; map D1, grid i2.

Campsites, facilities: There are 312 sites for tents or RVs (161 drive-through), many with full or partial hookups, and 34 cabins. Picnic tables and fire grills are provided. Flush toilets, showers, cable TV hookups, modem hookups, sanitary disposal station, playground, recreation rooms, swimming pool, whirlpool, petting zoo, shuffleboard, coin laundry, propane gas, and a grocery store are available. Some facilities are wheelchair accessible. Leashed pets are permitted.

Reservations, fees: Reservations are recommended; $29 to $40 per night, cabins are $29.95 to $47 per night. Major credit cards accepted. Open year-round.

Directions: From Petaluma on U.S. 101, take the Penngrove exit and drive west for a quarter mile on Petaluma Boulevard to Stony Point Road. Turn right (north) on Stony Point Road and drive to Rainsville Road. Turn left (west) on Rainsville Road and drive to 20 Rainsville Road.

Contact: San Francisco North/Petaluma KOA, tel. (707) 763-1492 or fax (707) 763-2668; website: www. koakampgrounds.com.

Visit historic Sutter's Fort
if you're staying at
Sacramento-Metro KOA.

MAP D2

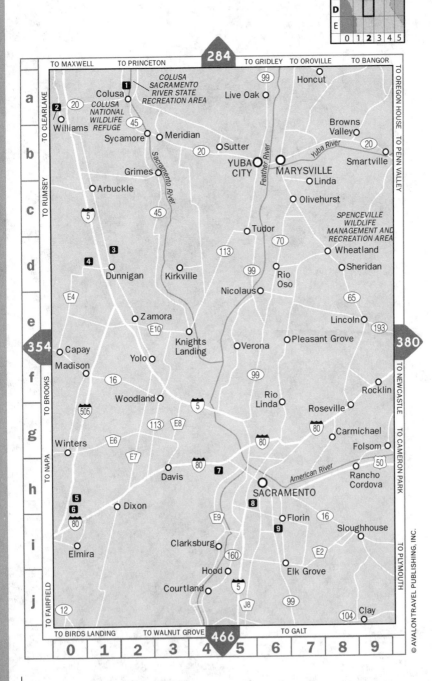

CHAPTER D2

1 Colusa-Sacramento River State Recreation Area

 5

This region of the Sacramento Valley is well known as a high-quality habitat for birds. Nearby Delevan and Colusa National Wildlife Refuges are outstanding destinations for wildlife viewing, and provide good duck hunting in December. In summer the nearby Sacramento River is a bonus with shad fishing in June and July, salmon fishing from August through October, sturgeon fishing in the winter, and striped bass fishing in the spring.

Location: Near Colusa; map D2, grid a2.

Campsites, facilities: There are 14 sites for tents or RVs up to 30 feet long, and one group site for a minimum of 10 people and maximum of 40 people. Picnic tables and fire rings are provided. Drinking water, flush toilets, hot showers, and sanitary disposal station are available. Some facilities are wheelchair accessible. A grocery store, restaurant, gas station, tackle shop, and coin laundry are nearby (within three blocks). A boat ramp is available. Leashed pets are permitted.

Reservations, fees: Reserve at (800) 444-PARK (800-444-7275) or website: www.ReserveAmerica.com; $10 per night, $30 per night for the group site. Open year-round.

Directions: In Williams, at the junction of Interstate 5 and Highway 20, drive east on Highway 20 for 10 miles to the town of Colusa. Turn north (straight ahead) on 10th Street and drive two blocks, just over the levee, to the park.

Contact: Colusa-Sacramento River State Recreation Area, tel. and fax (530) 458-4927 or tel. (530) 538-2200.

2 Almond Grove Mobile Home Park

 1

The town of Williams is set in the middle of the Sacramento Valley, a popular spot to stop and grab a bite at its outstanding delicatessen (Granzella's), where there is a gigantic stuffed polar bear.

Location: In Williams; map D2, grid a0.

Campsites, facilities: There are seven pull-through RV sites with full hookups. Picnic tables are provided. Restrooms, showers, cable TV (included with hookup), and a coin laundry are available. Some facilities are wheelchair accessible. A store is nearby (within six blocks). Leashed pets are permitted.

Reservations, fees: Reservations are accepted; $14 per night. Open year-round.

Directions: From the Central Valley on Interstate 5, drive to Williams and the Central Williams exit. Take that exit and drive west on E Street for eight blocks. Turn left on 12th Street and drive three blocks to the entrance at 880 12th Street.

Contact: Almond Grove Mobile Home Park, tel. (530) 473-5620.

3 Happy Time RV Park

 1

If you are cruising Interstate 5 and are exhausted, or need to take a deep breath before hitting the Bay Area or Sacramento, this private park can provide a respite and, to be honest, not a whole lot more. Restaurants are available in nearby Dunnigan.

Location: Near Dunnigan; map D2, grid d1.

Campsites, facilities: There are eight tent sites and 43 RV sites (28 drive-through) with full hookups. Picnic tables are provided. Restrooms, flush toilets, showers, modem hookups, playground, coin laundry, and a swimming pool are available. Some facilities are wheelchair accessible. Leashed pets are permitted.

Reservations, fees: Reservations are accepted; $18 to $20 per night. Major credit cards accepted. Open year-round.

Directions: From Interstate 5 near the Interstate 505 intersection, take the County Road 8 exit. Drive east on County Road 8 for a short distance to Road 99W. Turn left on Road 99W and drive to the first driveway (less than one block) and camp entrance on the left.

Contact: Happy Time RV Park, tel. (530) 724-3336.

4 Campers Inn & Golf Course

 1

This private park has a rural valley atmosphere and provides a layover for drivers cruising Interstate 5. The Sacramento River to the east is the closest body of water, but this section of river is hardly a premium side trip destination. There are no nearby lakes.

Location: Near Dunnigan; map D2, grid d1.

Campsites, facilities: There are 13 tent sites and 72 RV sites (44 drive-through) with full or partial hookups. Picnic tables are provided. Restrooms, flush toilets, showers, modem hookups, heated pool, clubhouse, horseshoes, nine-hole golf course, coin laundry, propane gas, ice, and groceries are available. Some facilities are wheelchair accessible. Leashed pets are permitted.

Reservations, fees: Reservations are accepted; $15 to $21 per night. $2 per person per night for more than four people. Major credit cards accepted. Open year-round.

Directions: From Interstate 5, take the Dunnigan exit (just north of the Interstate 505 cutoff). Drive west on County Road E-4 for a mile to County Road 88. Turn north and drive for 1.5 miles to the park.

Contact: Campers Inn, tel. (800) 79-GOLF3 or (530) 724-3350, or fax (530) 724-3110; website: www.campersinnrv.com.

5 Neil's Vineyard RV Park

 2

This is one of two privately operated parks in the area set up primarily for RVs. It is in a eucalyptus grove, with clean, well-kept sites. If you are heading to the Bay Area, it is late in the day, and you don't have your destination set, this spot offers a chance to hole up for the night and formulate your travel plans.

Location: In Vacaville; map D2, grid h0.

Campsites, facilities: There are 10 tent sites and 110 sites (20 drive-through) with full hookups for RVs up to 40 feet. Picnic tables are provided. Restrooms, flush toilets, showers, modem hookups, swimming pool, coin laundry, sanitary disposal station, putting green, pay phones, and ice are available. Some facilities are wheelchair accessible. Leashed pets are permitted.

Reservations, fees: Reservations are recommended; $25 per night, $2 per person per night for more than two people, $1 pet fee. Major credit cards accepted. Open year-round.

From Vacaville on Interstate 80, turn north on Interstate 505 and drive three miles to Midway Road. Turn right (east) on Midway Road and travel a half mile to the second campground on the left.

Contact: Neil's Vineyard RV Park, 4985 Midway Road, Vacaville, CA 95688; tel. (707) 447-8797.

6 Gandy Dancer RV Park

   2

This layover spot for RV cruisers is near Vacaville. Six Flags Marine World in Vallejo is within a half-hour drive.

Location: Near Vacaville; map D2, grid h0.

Campsites, facilities: There are 51 RV sites, all drive-through with full hookups. Picnic tables are provided. Flush toilets, showers, modem hookups, swimming pool, children's pool, and coin laundry are available. Leashed pets are permitted.

Reservations, fees: Reservations are recommended; $20 per night ($18 for seniors). Major credit cards accepted. Open year-round.

Directions: From Vacaville on Interstate 80, turn north on Interstate 505 and drive three miles to Midway Road. Turn east (right) on Midway Road and travel a quarter mile to the campground.

Contact: Gandy Dancer, tel. (707) 446-7679.

7 Sacramento-Metro KOA

      1

This is the choice of car and RV campers touring California's capital and looking for a layover spot. It is in downtown Sacramento near the Capitol building and the railroad museum.

Location: West of Sacramento; map D2, grid h4.

Campsites, facilities: There are 27 tent sites and 95 sites with full or partial hookups for RVs up to 40 feet long. Ten cabins are also available. Restrooms, flush toilets, showers, modem hookups, playground, swimming pool, coin laundry, propane gas, and groceries are available. Some facilities are wheelchair accessible. Leashed pets are permitted.

Reservations, fees: Reservations are recommended; $23 to $29 per night, cabins are $36 per night. Major credit cards accepted. Open year-round.

Directions: From Sacramento, drive west on Interstate 80 about four miles to the West Capitol Avenue exit. Exit and turn left onto West Capitol Avenue, going under the freeway to the first stoplight and the intersection with Lake Road. Turn left onto Lake Road and continue a half block to the camp on the left at 3951 Lake Road.

Contact: Sacramento-Metro KOA, tel. (916) 371-6771 or tel. (800) 545-KAMP (800-545-5267); website: www.koakampgrounds.com.

8 Stillman Trailer Park

    1

This is an adults-only RV park in downtown Sacramento near the Capitol and the railroad museum. It's a popular layover spot in summer.

Location: In Sacramento; map D2, grid h5.

Campsites, facilities: There are 67 RV sites with full hookups. Restrooms, flush toilets, showers, modem hookups, coin laundry, clubhouse, and a swimming pool are available. Some facilities are wheelchair accessible. Adults only. Small leashed pets are permitted.

Reservations, fees: Reservations are accepted; $30 per night. Major credit cards accepted. Open year-round.

Directions: In Sacramento on Highway 99, take the 47th Avenue West exit and go to the first light, turn right and drive 200 yards to Stillman Park Circle. Turn right and the park will be just ahead at 3880 Stillman Park Circle.

Contact: Stillman Trailer Park, tel. (800) 570-6562 or (916) 392-2820.

9 99 Laguna Village

   2

This is a popular RV park for folks touring Sacramento because it's about a five-minute drive from the city. Most of the sites are tree shaded and that's a good thing, since Sacramento does a good job of imitating a furnace in the summer. Maybe it's all the hot air emanating from the mouths of politicians. Side trips include all the sights of California's capital city, of course, and the nearby Consumnes River.

Location: Near Sacramento; map D2, grid i6.

Campsites, facilities: There are 26 RV sites with full hookups, including phone. There are no restroom facilities. Some facilities are wheelchair accessible. Weekly residents preferred. A grocery store and propane gas are within 300 feet. Leashed pets are permitted.

Reservations, fees: Reservations are accepted; $18 per night. Open year-round.

Directions: From Sacramento, drive south on Highway 99 to the Sheldon Road exit. Turn right and drive onto Stockton Boulevard (frontage road). Drive a short distance to the park.

Contact: 99 Trailer Park, tel. (916) 423-4078.

CHAPTER D3

AT MALAKOFF DIGGINS
STATE HISTORIC PARK

MAP D3

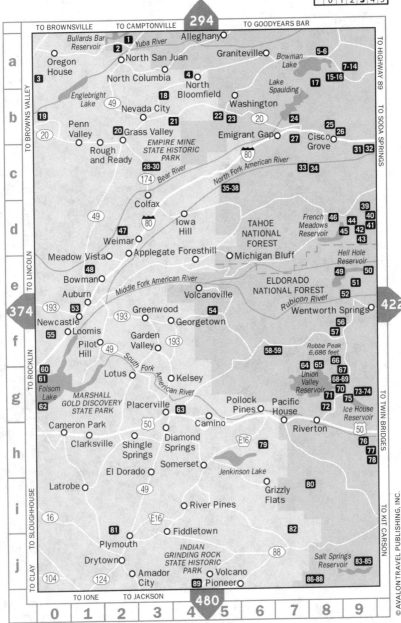

CHAPTER D3

(CONTINUED ON NEXT PAGE)

1 Hornswoggle Group Camp

      7

This camp is designed for group use. A three-lane concrete boat ramp is two miles north at the Dark Day Picnic Area. For information about family campgrounds and boat-in sites, see the listings for Bullards Bar Reservoir in chapter C3.

Location: On Bullards Bar Reservoir in Tahoe National Forest; map D3, grid a2.

Campsites, facilities: There are five 25-person group sites and one 50-person group site for tents or RVs up to 50 feet long. Picnic tables and fire grills are provided. Drinking water, flush and vault toilets are available. A boat ramp is nearby. Supplies are available at the marina. Leashed pets are permitted.

Reservations, fees: Reservations are required; phone Emerald Cove Marina, tel. (530) 692-3200; $50 to $100 per night. Open April to mid-October.

Directions: From Auburn, drive north on Highway 49 to Nevada City and continue for 17 miles through the town of North San Juan. Continue on Highway 49 for approximately eight miles to Marysville Road. Turn left on Marysville Road and drive approximately five miles to the campground on the left.

Contact: Tahoe National Forest, North Yuba/Downieville Ranger District, tel. (530) 288-3231 or fax (530) 692-3200.

2 Moonshine Campground

     7

This campground features shaded sites and a swimming hole on the nearby Middle Fork Yuba River. Both are needed, with the weather hot here in the summer, at 1,430 feet in the Sierra foothills. It's a seven-mile drive to a three-lane boat ramp at Dark Day Picnic Area at Bullards Bar Reservoir, the feature side trip.

Location: Near the Yuba River and Bullards Bar Reservoir; map D3, grid a2.

Campsites, facilities: There are 25 sites for tents or RVs up to 30 feet, all with partial hookups. Picnic tables and fire rings are provided. Drinking water, vault toilets, modem hookups, ice, and firewood are available. Some facilities are wheelchair accessible. A grocery store and propane gas are available about three miles away in North San Juan. Leashed pets are permitted.

Reservations, fees: Reservations are required; $20 to $25 per night, $2 per person per night for more than five people. Open May through October 5.

Directions: From Auburn, drive north on Highway 49 to Nevada City and continue for 17 miles through the town of North San Juan. Continue on Highway 49 and cross a bridge over the Middle Fork Yuba to Moonshine Road. Turn left on Moonshine Road and drive three-quarters of a mile to the campground.

Contact: Moonshine Campground, tel. (530) 288-3585; website: www.oro.net/~wmoonshine.

3 Collins Lake Recreation Area

      8

Collins Lake is set in the foothill country east of Marysville at 1,200 feet in elevation, ideal for the camper, boater, and angler. This lake is becoming known as an outstanding destination for trophy size trout, especially in late spring through early summer, though fishing is often good year-round for know-hows. The lake has 12 miles of shoreline and is quite pretty. In summer, warm water makes the lake exceptional for water-skiing (permitted from May 15 through Sept. 30). There is a marina adjacent to the campground, and farther south is a swimming beach and boat ramp. Bonuses for anglers: No personal watercraft are allowed on the lake. A weekly fishing report is available the camp's website.

Location: Near Marysville on Collins Lake; map D3, grid a0.

Campsites, facilities: There are 159 sites for tents or RVs (29 drive-through), many with partial hookups (52 are along the lakefront). A large overflow camping area is also nearby, which requires no reservations and has drinking water and chemical toilets. There are also three group picnic areas. Picnic tables and fire grills are provided. Restrooms, drinking water, flush toilets, sanitary disposal station, coin-operated showers, boat ramp, boat rentals, sandy swimming beach, volleyball, marina, grocery store, coin laundry, wood, ice, and propane gas are available. Some facilities are wheelchair accessible. Leashed pets are permitted.

Reservations, fees: Reservations are recommended; $15 to $26 per night, $8 per night for a second vehicle. Major credit cards accepted. Open year-round.

Directions: From Marysville, drive east on Highway 20 for about 12 miles to Marysville Road. Turn north and drive approximately eight miles to the recreation area entrance road on the right. Turn right, drive a mile to the entrance station, and then continue to the campground on the left side of the road.

Contact: Collins Lake Recreation Area, tel. (800) 286-0576 or (530) 692-1600, or fax (530) 692-1607; website: www.collinslake.com.

4 Malakoff Diggins State Historic Park

 7

This camp is set near a small lake in the park, but the main attraction of the area is the gold mining history. Tours of the numerous historic sites are available during the summer. The elevation is 3,400 feet.

Location: Near Nevada City; map D3, grid a4.

Campsites, facilities: There are 30 sites for tents or RVs up to 24 feet long, three cabins, and one group tent site for up to 50 people. Picnic tables and fire grills are provided. Drinking water and flush toilets (except mid-November through February) are available. Pets must be controlled.

Reservations, fees: Reserve at (800) 444-PARK (800-444-7275) or website: www.ReserveAmerica.com, Memorial Day through Labor Day; $10 per night, $37 for group site. Open year-round.

Directions: From Auburn, drive north on Highway 49 to Nevada City and continue 11 miles to the junction of Tyler Foote Crossing Road (it will become Cruzon Grade). Turn right and drive 16 miles (the last two are quite steep) to the entrance on the right.

Contact: California State Parks, Goldrush District, tel. or fax (530) 265-2740.

5 Jackson Creek

 7

This primitive campground is at 5,600 feet, adjacent to Jackson Creek, a primary feeder stream to Bowman Lake to the nearby west. There are several lakes within a five-mile radius, including Bowman Lake, Jackson Meadow Reservoir, Sawmill Lake (private), and Faucherie Lake. A trailhead is available a mile south (on the right side of the road) at the north end of Sawmill Lake. The trail is routed to a series of pretty Sierra lakes to the west of Haystack Mountain (7,391 feet).

Location: Near Bowman Lake in Tahoe National Forest; map D3, grid a8.

Campsites, facilities: There are 14 primitive tent sites. Picnic tables and fire grills are provided. Vault toilets are available. No drinking water is available. Garbage must be packed out. Leashed pets are permitted.

Reservations, fees: No reservations; no fee. Open June through September, weather permitting.

Directions: From Sacramento, drive east on Interstate 80 past Emigrant Gap to Highway 20. Head west on Highway 20 and drive to Bowman Road/Forest Road 18. Turn right and drive about 16 miles to Bowman Lake (much of the road is quite rough), then continue for four miles east of the lake to the campground.

Contact: Tahoe National Forest, Nevada City Ranger District, tel. (530) 265-4531 or fax (530) 478-6109.

6 Bowman Lake

 8

Bowman is a sapphire jewel set in Sierra granite at 5,568 feet, extremely pretty and ideal for campers with car-top boats. There is no boat ramp (you wouldn't want to trailer a boat on the access road anyway), but there are lots of small rainbow trout that are eager to please during the evening bite. The camp is set on the eastern end of the lake, just below where Jackson Creek pours in. The lake is flanked by Bowman Mountain (7,392 feet) and Red Hill (7,075 feet) to the south and Quartz Hill (7,025 feet) to the north.

Location: In Tahoe National Forest; map D3, grid a8.

Campsites, facilities: There are seven primitive tent sites. Vault toilets are available. No drinking water is available. Garbage must be packed out. Leashed pets are permitted.

Reservations, fees: No reservations; no fee. Open June through October.

Directions: From Sacramento, drive east on Interstate 80 past Emigrant Gap to Highway 20. Head west on Highway 20 and drive to Bowman Road/Forest Road 18. Turn right and drive about 16 miles (much of the road is quite rough) to Bowman Lake and the campground on the right side of the road at the head of the lake.

Contact: Tahoe National Forest, Nevada City Ranger District, tel. (530) 265-4531 or fax (530) 478-6109.

7 Silver Tip Group Camp

This group camp is set on the southwest edge of Jackson Meadow Reservoir at 6,200 feet, in a pretty area with pine forest, high meadows, and the trademark granite look of the Sierra Nevada. A boat ramp and swimming beach are nearby at Woodcamp. For more information, see the entry for Woodcamp.

Location: At Jackson Meadow Reservoir in Tahoe National Forest; map D3, grid a9.

Campsites, facilities: There are two 25-person group sites for tents or RVs up to 22 feet long. Picnic tables and fire grills are provided. Drinking water and vault toilets are available. Obtain supplies in Truckee or Sierraville. A boat ramp is nearby. Leashed pets are permitted.

Reservations, fees: Reserve at (877) 444-6777 ($8.65 reservation fee) or website: www.reserveusa.com; $55 group fee per night. Open June through October.

Directions: From Truckee, drive north on Highway 89 for 17.5 miles to Forest Road 7. Turn left on Forest Road 7 and drive 16 miles to Jackson Meadow Reservoir. At the lake, continue across the dam around the west shoreline and then turn left at the campground access road. The entrance is on the right just before the Woodcamp boat ramp.

Contact: Tahoe National Forest, Sierraville Ranger District, tel. (530) 944-3401 or fax (530) 994-3143.

8 Woodcamp

Woodcamp and Pass Creek are the best camps for boaters at Jackson Meadow Reservoir because each is directly adjacent to a boat ramp. That is critical because fishing is far better by boat here than from shore, with a good mix of both rainbow and brown trout. The camp is set at 6,100 feet along the lake's southwest shore, in a pretty spot with a swimming beach and short interpretive hiking trail nearby. This is a beautiful lake in the Sierra Nevada, complete with pine forest and a classic granite backdrop.

Location: At Jackson Meadow Reservoir in Tahoe National Forest; map D3, grid a9.

Campsites, facilities: There are 10 sites for tents and 10 sites for tents or RVs up to 22 feet long. Picnic tables and fire grills are provided. Drinking water and vault toilets are available. Supplies are available in Truckee or Sierraville. A boat ramp is adjacent to the camp. Leashed pets are permitted.

Reservations, fees: Reservations are accepted; $13 per night, $5 for each additional vehicle. Open June through October.

Directions: From Truckee, drive north on Highway 89 for 17.5 miles to Forest Road 7. Turn left on Forest Road 7 and drive 16 miles to Jackson Meadow Reservoir. At the lake, continue across the dam around the west shoreline and then turn left at the campground access road. The entrance is on the right just before the Woodcamp boat ramp.

Contact: Tahoe National Forest, Sierraville Ranger District, tel. (530) 944-3401 or fax (530) 994-3143.

9 Pass Creek

This is the premium campground at Jackson Meadow Reservoir, a developed site with water, concrete boat ramp, swimming beach nearby at Aspen Creek

Picnic Area, and access to the Pacific Crest Trail a half mile to the east (you'll pass it on the way in). This lake has the trademark look of the high Sierra, and the bonus here is that lake levels are often kept higher than at other reservoirs on the western slopes of the Sierra Nevada. Trout stocks are excellent, with 85,000 rainbow and brown trout planted each summer after ice-out. The elevation is 6,100 feet.

Location: At Jackson Meadow Reservoir in Tahoe National Forest; map D3, grid a9.

Campsites, facilities: There are 15 sites for tents and 15 sites for RVs up to 22 feet long. Picnic tables and fire grills are provided. Drinking water, vault toilets, and a sanitary disposal station are available. A boat ramp is nearby. Supplies are available in Truckee or Sierraville. Leashed pets are permitted.

Reservations, fees: Reserve Reserve at (877) 444-6777 ($8.65 reservation fee) or website: www.reserveusa.com; $13 per night, $3 for an extra vehicle. Open June through October.

Directions: From Truckee, drive north on Highway 89 for 17.5 miles to Forest Road 7. Turn left on Forest Road 7 and drive 16 miles to Jackson Meadow Reservoir; the campground is on the left at the north end of the lake.

Contact: Tahoe National Forest, Sierraville Ranger District, tel. (530) 944-3401 or fax (530) 994-3143.

10 Fir Top

 7

Jackson Meadow is a great destination for a short vacation, and that's why there are so many campgrounds available; it's not exactly a secret. This camp is set on a cove on the lake's southwest shore, less than a mile from a boat ramp near Woodcamp. See the entries for Woodcamp and Pass Creek for more information. The elevation is 6,200 feet.

Location: At Jackson Meadow Reservoir in Tahoe National Forest; map D3, grid a9.

Campsites, facilities: There are 12 sites for tents or RVs up to 22 feet long. Picnic tables and fire grills are provided. Drinking water, vault toilets, and a sanitary disposal station (on the east side) are available. Supplies are available in Truckee or Sierraville. A boat ramp is nearby. Some facilities are wheelchair accessible. Leashed pets are permitted.

Reservations, fees: Reserve at (877) 444-6777 ($8.65 reservation fee) or website: www.reserveusa.com; $12 per night. Open June through November.

Directions: From Truckee, drive north on Highway 89 for 17.5 miles to Forest Road 7. Turn left on Forest Road 7 and drive 16 miles to Jackson Meadow Reservoir. Continue across the dam and around the lake to the west side. Turn left at the campground access road. The campground entrance is on the right across from the entrance to the Woodcamp Picnic Area.

Contact: Tahoe National Forest, Sierraville Ranger District, tel. (530) 944-3401 or fax (530) 994-3143.

11 Findley

 7

Findley is set near Woodcamp Creek, a quarter mile from where it pours into Jackson Meadow Reservoir. Though it is not a lakeside camp, it is quite pretty just the same, and within a half mile of the boat ramp near Woodcamp. It is set at 6,200 feet. This is one of several camps at the lake.

Location: At Jackson Meadow Reservoir in Tahoe National Forest; map D3, grid a9.

Campsites, facilities: There are 15 sites for tents or RVs up to 22 feet long. Picnic tables and fire grills are provided. Drinking water and vault toilets are available. Supplies are available in Truckee or Sierraville. A boat ramp is nearby. Some facilities are wheelchair accessible. Leashed pets are permitted.

Reservations, fees: Reserve at (877) 444-6777 ($8.65 reservation fee) or website: www.reserveusa.com; $13 per night. Open late June through October.

Directions: From Truckee, drive north on Highway 89 for 17.5 miles to Forest Road 7. Turn left on Forest Road 7 and drive 16 miles to Jackson Meadow Reservoir. Continue across the dam around the lake to the west side. Turn left at the campground access road and drive about a quarter mile to the entrance on the left.

Contact: Tahoe National Forest, Sierraville Ranger District, tel. (530) 944-3401 or fax (530) 994-3143.

12 Jackson Point Boat-In

 10

This is one of the few boat-in camps available anywhere in the high Sierra. The gorgeous spot is situated on the end of a peninsula that extends from the east shore of Jackson Meadow Reservoir. Small and primitive, it's the one place at the lake where you can gain entry into the 5 Percent Club. From the point, there is a spectacular view of the Sierra Buttes. Because the lake levels are kept near full all summer, this boat-in camp is doubly appealing. The elevation is 6,100 feet.

Location: At Jackson Meadow Reservoir in Tahoe National Forest; map D3, grid a9.

Campsites, facilities: There are 10 tent sites. Picnic tables and fire grills are provided. Vault toilets are available. No drinking water is available. Garbage must be packed out. Supplies are available in Truckee or Sierraville. Leashed pets are permitted.

Reservations, fees: No reservations; no fee. Open June through September.

Directions: From Truckee, drive north on Highway 89 for 17.5 miles to Forest Road 7. Turn left on Forest Road 7 and drive 16 miles to Jackson Meadow Reservoir. Drive to Pass Creek and boat launch (on the left at the north end of the lake). Launch your boat and cruise a half mile south to Jackson Point and the boat-in campsites.

Contact: Tahoe National Forest, Sierraville Ranger District, tel. (530) 944-3401 or fax (530) 994-3143.

13 East Meadow

 7

This camp is in a beautiful setting on the east side of Jackson Meadow Reservoir, on the edge of a sheltered cove. The Pacific Crest Trail passes right by camp, providing access for a day trip, though no stellar destinations are on this stretch of the PCT. The nearest boat ramp is at Pass Creek, two miles away. The elevation is 6,100 feet.

Location: At Jackson Meadow Reservoir in Tahoe National Forest; map D3, grid a9.

Campsites, facilities: There are 20 tent sites and 26 sites for tents or RVs. (Some sites can accommodate RVs 40 feet in length, most can accommodate 22 feet). Picnic tables and fire grills are provided. Drinking water and vault toilets are available. A sanitary disposal station and boat ramp are available at Pass Creek. Supplies are available in Truckee or Sierraville. Some facilities are wheelchair accessible. Leashed pets are permitted.

Reservations, fees: Reserve at (877) 444-6777 ($8.65 reservation fee) or website: www.reserveusa.com; $13 per night, $3 for an extra vehicle. Open June through October.

Directions: From Truckee, drive north on Highway 89 for 17.5 miles to Forest Road 7. Turn left on Forest Road 7 and drive 15 miles to the campground entrance road on the left (if you reach Pass Creek, you have gone too far). Turn left and drive a mile to the campground on the right.

Contact: Tahoe National Forest, Sierraville Ranger District, tel. (530) 944-3401 or fax (530) 994-3143.

14 Aspen Group Camp

 7

A boat ramp and easy access to adjacent Jackson Meadow Reservoir make this a premium group camp. The elevation is 6,100 feet.

Location: At Jackson Meadow Reservoir in Tahoe National Forest; map D3, grid a9.

Campsites, facilities: There are two 25-person group sites and a 50-person group site for tents or RVs up to 22 feet long. Picnic tables and fire grills are provided. Drinking water, vault toilets, a sanitary disposal station and a campfire circle are available. There is a boat ramp nearby at Pass Creek. Supplies are available in Truckee or Sierraville. Leashed pets are permitted.

Reservations, fees: Reserve at (877) 444-6777 ($8.65 reservation fee) or website: www.reserveusa.com; $55 to $110 group fee per night. Open June through October.

Directions: From Truckee, drive north on Highway 89 for 17.5 miles to Forest Road 7. Turn left on Forest Road 7 and drive 16 miles (a mile past Pass Creek) to the campground entrance on the right.

Contact: Tahoe National Forest, Sierraville Ranger District, (530) 944-3401 or fax (530) 994-3143.

15 Faucherie Lake Group Camp

     7

Faucherie Lake is the kind of place that most people believe can only be reached by long, difficult hikes with a backpack. Guess again: here it is, set in Sierra granite at 6,100 feet in elevation, quiet and pristine, a classic alpine lake. It is ideal for car-top boating and has decent fishing for both rainbow and brown trout. This is a group camp on the lake's northern shore, a prime spot, with the outlet creek nearby. Note: Road washouts may require four-wheel drive.

Location: Near Bowman Lake in Tahoe National Forest; map D3, grid a8.

Campsites, facilities: There is a large group camp for tents or RVs up to 22 feet long. The camp accommodates up to 25 campers. Picnic tables and fire grills are provided. Vault toilets are available. No drinking water is available. Garbage must be packed out. Leashed pets are permitted.

Reservations, fees: Reserve at (877) 444-6777 ($8.65 reservation fee) or website: www.reserveusa.com; $30 per night. Open June through October.

Directions: From Sacramento, drive east on Interstate 80 past Emigrant Gap to Highway 20. Head west on Highway 20 and drive to Bowman Road/Forest Road 18. Turn right and drive about 16 miles (much of the road is quite rough) to Bowman Lake and continue four miles to a Y. Bear right at the Y and drive about three miles to the campground at the end of the road.

Contact: Tahoe National Forest, Nevada City Ranger District, tel. (530) 265-4531 or fax (530) 478-6109.

16 Canyon Creek

   6

This pretty spot is at 6,000 feet in Tahoe National Forest, a mile from Sawmill Lake (which you pass on the way in) and a mile from pretty Faucherie Lake. It is set along Canyon Creek, the stream that connects those two lakes. Of the two, Faucherie provides better fishing and, because of that, there are fewer people at Sawmill. Take your pick. A trailhead is available at the north end of Sawmill Lake with a hike to several small alpine lakes, a great day or overnight backpacking trip.

Location: Near Faucherie Lake in Tahoe National Forest; map D3, grid a8.

Campsites, facilities: There are 20 sites for tents. Picnic tables and fire grills are provided. Vault toilets are available. No drinking water is available. Garbage must be packed out. Leashed pets are permitted.

Reservations, fees: No reservations; no fee. Open June through October.

Directions: From Sacramento, drive east on Interstate 80 to Emigrant Gap. Take the off-ramp and head north on the short connector road to Highway 20. Turn west on Highway 20 and drive four miles to Bowman Road/Forest Road 18. Turn right and drive about 16 miles (nine of these miles are paved, but the rest is quite rough) to Bowman Lake and continue four miles to a Y. Bear right at the Y and drive about two miles to the campground on the right side of the road.

Contact: Tahoe National Forest, Nevada City Ranger District, tel. (530) 265-4531 or fax (530) 478-6109.

🔢 Grouse Ridge

 6

Grouse Ridge is set at 7,400 feet at the gateway to some beautiful hiking country filled with small high Sierra lakes. The camp is primarily used as a trailhead and jump-off point, not as a destination itself. The closest hike is the half-mile tromp up to the Grouse Ridge Lookout, 7,707 feet, which provides a spectacular view to the north of this area and its many small lakes. Hiking north, the trail passes Round Lake (to the left) in the first mile and Middle Lake (on the right) two miles later, with opportunities to take cutoff trails on either side of the ridge to visit numerous other lakes.

Location: Near Bowman Lake in Tahoe National Forest; map D3, grid a8.

Campsites, facilities: There are nine sites for tents only. Picnic tables and fire grills are provided. Vault toilets are available. No drinking water is available. Garbage must be packed out. Leashed pets are permitted.

Reservations, fees: No reservations; no fee. Open June through October.

Directions: From Sacramento, drive east on Interstate 80 past Emigrant Gap to Highway 20. Turn west on Highway 20 and drive to Bowman Road/Forest Road 18. Turn north on Bowman Road and drive five miles to Grouse Ridge Road. Turn right on Grouse Ridge Road and drive six miles on rough gravel to the campground.

Contact: Tahoe National Forest, Nevada City Ranger District, tel. (530) 265-4531 or fax (530) 478-6109.

🔢 South Yuba

 7

This little-known BLM camp is set next to where little Kenebee Creek enters the Yuba River. The Yuba is about a mile away, with some great swimming holes and evening trout fishing spots to explore. The 12-mile long South Yuba Trail begins at the state park and features outstanding spring wildflower blooms. A good side trip is to nearby Malakoff Diggins State Historic Park and the town of North Bloomfield (about a 10-minute drive to the northeast on North Bloomfield Road), which is being completely restored to its 1850s character. Hopefully, that does not include the food. The elevation is 2,600 feet.

Location: Near the Yuba River; map D3, grid b4.

Campsites, facilities: There are 16 sites for tents or RVs up to 27 feet long. Picnic tables and fire grills are provided. Drinking water and vault toilets are available. Some facilities are wheelchair accessible. Leashed pets are permitted.

Reservations, fees: No reservations; $5 per night. Open April through October, weather permitting.

Directions: From Auburn, turn north on Highway 49, drive to Nevada City, then continue a short distance to North Bloomfield Road. Turn right and drive 10 miles to the one-lane bridge at Edward's Crossing. Cross the bridge and continue 1.5 miles to the campground on the right side of the road (the road gets quite rough).

Alternate route for RVs or vehicles with trailers: From Auburn turn north on Highway 49 to Nevada City and continue to Tyler Foote Crossing Road. Turn right and drive to Grizzly Hills Road (just past North Columbia). Turn right and drive three miles to North Bloomfield Road. Turn left and drive to the campground on the right.

Contact: The Bureau of Land Management, Folsom Field Office, tel. (916) 985-4474, or fax (916) 985-3259.

19 Englebright Lake Boat-In

 8

Englebright Lake is an outstanding destination for boat-in camping, fishing, and water-skiing. Remember this place. It always seems to have plenty of water, and there are more developed boat-in campsites along its 24 miles of shoreline than at any other lake in California. The lake looks like a huge water snake, long and narrow, set in the Yuba River Canyon at 520 feet in elevation. In summer, it is a water-skiing mecca, with warm and calm water. Trout fishing is good on the upper end of the lake, where water-skiing is prohibited year-round.

Location: Near Marysville; map D3, grid b0.

Campsites, facilities: There are 100 boat-in sites along the shores of Englebright Lake and a group camping area that accommodates 50 people (by reservation only). Picnic tables, fire grills, and lantern hangers are provided. Vault toilets are available. Two boat ramps are available on either side of Skippers Cove (and more boat-in campsites). Drinking water is available at each boat launch and at the marina. Boat rentals (including houseboats), mooring, fuel dock, and groceries are available. Leashed pets are permitted.

Reservations, fees: Group reservations only, tel. (530) 639-2342; $10 per night for boat-in sites, $25-50 per night for group site. Open year-round.

Directions: From Auburn, drive north on Highway 49 to Grass Valley and the junction with Highway 20. Turn west on Highway 20 and drive to Mooney Flat Road (if you reach Smartville, you have gone a mile too far). Turn right on Mooney Flat and drive three miles to a fork. Turn left at the fork and drive a mile to park headquarters and the boat ramp just east of the dam.

Contact: U.S. Army Corps of Engineers, Sacramento District, Englebright Lake, tel. (530) 639-2342 or fax (530) 639-2175; Skippers Cove concessionaire, tel. (530) 639-2272.

20 Nevada County Fairgrounds

 6

The motto here is "California's Most Beautiful Fairgrounds," and they're right. The area is set at 2,300 feet in the Sierra foothills, with a good number of pines sprinkled about. The park is adjacent to the fairgrounds, and even though the fair runs for a week every summer, the park is open year-round. A caretaker at the park is available to answer any questions. Kids can fish at a small lake nearby.

Location: At the fairgrounds near Grass Valley; map D3, grid b2.

Campsites, facilities: There are 120 sites for RVs, 15 with hookups. Two sanitary disposal stations, showers, and flush toilets are available. A modem is available in park office. Some facilities are wheelchair accessible. Leashed pets are permitted.

Reservations, fees: Reservations are accepted; $17 to $20 per night. A 14-day limit is enforced. Major credit cards accepted. Open year-round.

Directions: From Auburn, drive north on Highway 49 to Grass Valley. Take either the McKnight Way or Empire Street exit and follow the signs to the Nevada County Fairgrounds.

Contact: Nevada County Fairgrounds, 11228 McCourtney Road, Grass Valley, CA 95945; tel. (530) 273-6217 or fax (530) 273-1146; website: www.nevadacountyfair.com.

21 Scotts Flat Lake Recreation Area

 8

Scotts Flat Reservoir (at 3,100 feet in elevation) is shaped like a large teardrop, one of the prettier lakes in the Sierra foothills, with 7.5 miles of shoreline circled by forest. The camp is set on the lake's north shore, largely protected from spring winds and within short range of the marina and one of the lake's two boat launches. Trout fishing is good here in the spring and early summer. When the lake heats up, water-skiing and powerboating become more popular.

Location: Near Grass Valley; map D3, grid b4.

Campsites, facilities: There are 187 sites for tents or RVs up to 35 feet long. Restrooms, showers, and a sanitary disposal station are provided. A general store, bait and tackle shop, boat rentals, boat ramp, and a playground are also available. Most facilities are wheelchair accessible. Leashed pets are permitted.

Reservations, fees: Reservations are recommended in the summer; $18 to $23 per night, $5 per night for a second vehicle, $1 per person per night for more than four people. Major credit cards accepted. Open year-round, weather permitting.

Directions: From Auburn, drive north on Highway 49 to Nevada City and the junction with Highway 20. Turn right and drive five miles to Scotts Flat Road. Turn right and drive four miles to the camp entrance road on the right (on the north shore of the lake).

Contact: Scotts Flat Lake Recreation Area, tel. (530) 265-5302.

22 White Cloud

 5

This camp is set along the historic Pioneer Trail, which has turned into one of the top mountain bike routes in the Sierra Nevada, easy and fast. The trail traces the route of the first wagon road opened by emigrants and gold seekers in 1850. It is best suited for mountain biking, with a lot of bikers taking the one-way downhill ride (with an extra car for a shuttle ride) from Bear Valley to Lone Grave. The Omega Overlook is the highlight, with dramatic views of granite cliffs and the Yuba River. The elevation is 4,200 feet.

Location: In Tahoe National Forest; map D3, grid b5.

Campsites, facilities: There are 46 sites for tents or RVs up to 26 feet long. Picnic tables and fire grills are provided. Drinking water

and vault toilets are available. Leashed pets are permitted.

Reservations, fees: Reserve at (877) 444-6777 ($8.65 reservation fee) or website: www.reserveusa.com; $12 per night, $6 per extra vehicle. Open June through October.

Directions: From Sacramento, drive east on Interstate 80 to Emigrant Gap. Take the off-ramp and then head north on the short connector road to Highway 20. Turn west on Highway 20 and drive about 15 miles to the campground entrance on the left.

Contact: Tahoe National Forest, Nevada City Ranger District, tel. (530) 265-4531 or fax (530) 478-6109; Sierra Recreation Managers, tel. (209) 295-4512.

23 Skillman Group Camp

 5

Skillman Group Camp is set at 4,400 feet, on a loop access road just off of Highway 20, and the historic Pioneer Trail runs right through it. See the entry for White Cloud for more information.

Location: In Tahoe National Forest; map D3, grid b5.

Campsites, facilities: This group campsite can accommodate up to 75 people. Picnic tables and fire grills are provided. Vault toilets are available. No drinking water is available. Horse corrals, tie rails, troughs and stock water are available. Leashed pets are permitted.

Reservations, fees: Reserve at tel. (209) 295-4512; $13 to $30 per night. Open May through November, weather permitting.

Directions: From Sacramento, drive east on Interstate 80 past Emigrant Gap to Highway 20. Turn west on Highway 20 and drive 12 miles to the campground entrance on the left.

Contact: Tahoe National Forest, Nevada City Ranger District, tel. (530) 265-4531 or fax (530) 478-6109; Sierra Recreation Managers, tel. (209) 295-4512.

24 Lake Spaulding

 8

Lake Spaulding is set at 5,000 feet in the Sierra Nevada, complete with huge boulders and a sprinkling of conifers. Its clear, pure, very cold water has startling effects on swimmers. The lake is extremely pretty, with the Sierra granite backdrop looking as if it has been cut, chiseled, and smoothed. Just one problem. There's no lake view from the campground. The drive here is nearly a straight shot up Interstate 80, the boat ramp is fine for small aluminum boats, and if there is any problem here, it is that there will be plenty of company at the campground. Fishing for kokanee salmon and rainbow trout is often good, as well as fishing for trout at the nearby South Fork Yuba River. There are many other lakes set in the mountain country to the immediate north that can make for excellent side trips, including Bowman, Weaver, and Faucherie Lakes.

Location: Near Emigrant Gap; map D3, grid b7.

Campsites, facilities: There are 25 sites for tents or RVs up to 20 feet long. Picnic tables and fire grills are provided. Drinking water and vault toilets are available. A boat ramp is available. Supplies are available in Nevada City. Leashed pets are permitted.

Reservations, fees: No reservations; $13 per night, $3 per night per extra vehicle, $7 per night per extra RV, $1 pet fee. Open mid-May through September, weather permitting.

Directions: From Sacramento, drive east on Interstate 80 past Emigrant Gap to Highway 20. Drive west on Highway 20 for 2.3 miles to Lake Spaulding Road. Turn right on Lake Spaulding Road and drive one-half mile to the campground (the lake is an additional one-half mile).

Contact: PG&E Building and Land Services, tel. (916) 386-5164.

25 Indian Springs

 7

The camp is easy to reach from Interstate 80, yet is in a beautiful setting at 5,600 feet along the South Fork Yuba River. This is a gorgeous stream, running deep blue-green and pure through a granite setting, complete with giant boulders and beautiful pools. Trout fishing is fair. There is a small beach nearby where you can go swimming, though the water is cold. There are also several lakes in the vicinity.

Location: Near the Yuba River in Tahoe National Forest; map D3, grid b8.

Campsites, facilities: There are 35 sites for tents or RVs up to 25 feet long. Picnic tables and fire grills are provided. Drinking water and vault toilets are available. A grocery store and propane gas are available nearby. Leashed pets are permitted.

Reservations, fees: No reservations; $12 per night, $6 for each additional vehicle. Open May through October.

Directions: From Sacramento, drive east on Interstate 80 to Yuba Gap and continue for about three miles to the Eagle Lakes exit. Head north on Eagle Lakes Road for a mile to the campground on the left side of the road.

Contact: Tahoe National Forest, Nevada City Ranger District, tel. (530) 265-4531 or fax (530) 478-6109; Sierra Recreation Managers, tel. (209) 295-4512.

26 Woodchuck

 8

This small camp is only a few miles from Interstate 80, but it is quite obscure and little known to most travelers. It is set on Rattlesnake Creek at 6,300 feet in Tahoe National Forest, at the threshold of some great backcountry and four-wheel-drive roads that lead to many beautiful lakes. To explore, a map of Tahoe National Forest is a must.

Location: On Rattlesnake Creek in Tahoe National Forest; map D3, grid b8.

Campsites, facilities: There are eight sites for tents or RVs up to 16 feet long. Picnic tables and fire grills are provided. Vault toilets are available. No drinking water is available. Garbage must be packed out. A grocery store and propane gas are available nearby. Leashed pets are permitted.

Reservations, fees: No reservations; no fee. Open June through October.

Directions: From Sacramento, drive east on Interstate 80 to Yuba Gap and continue for about four miles to the Cisco Grove exit north. Take that exit, turn left on the frontage road, and drive a short distance onto Rattlesnake Road (just prior to reaching Thousand Trails). Turn right and continue on Rattlesnake Road (gravel, steep, and curvy; trailers not recommended) and drive three miles to the campground on the right.

Contact: Tahoe National Forest, Nevada City Ranger District, tel. (530) 265-4531 or fax (530) 478-6109.

27 Lodgepole

      8

Lake Valley Reservoir is set at 5,786 feet and covers 300 acres. It is gorgeous when full, its shoreline sprinkled with conifers and boulders. The lake provides decent results for anglers, who have the best luck while trolling. A speed limit prohibits water-skiing and personal watercraft, and that keeps the place quiet and peaceful. The camp is about a quarter mile from the lake's southwest shore and two miles from the boat ramp on the north shore. A trailhead from camp leads south up Monumental Ridge and to Monumental Creek (three miles, one way) on the northwestern flank of Quartz Mountain (6,931 feet).

Location: On Lake Valley Reservoir in Tahoe National Forest; map D3, grid b7.

Campsites, facilities: There are 18 sites for tents or RVs up to 20 feet long. Picnic tables and fire grills are provided. Drinking water and vault toilets are available. A boat ramp is available nearby. Supplies can be obtained off Interstate 80. Leashed pets are permitted.

Reservations, fees: No reservations; $13 per night, $3 per night per extra vehicle, $7 per night per extra RV, $1 pet fee. Open late May through September, weather permitting.

Directions: From Interstate 80, take the Yuba Gap exit and drive south for 0.4 mile to Lake Valley Road. Turn right on Lake Valley Road and drive for 1.2 miles until the road forks. Bear right and continue for 1.5 miles to the campground entrance road to the right on another fork.

Contact: PG&E Building and Land Services, tel. (916) 386-5164.

28 Long Ravine

   7

Long Ravine is one of three campgrounds at Rollins Lake, a popular lake for fishing (bass and trout) and water-skiing. The lake, in the Sierra foothills at 2,100 feet, has two extensive lake arms covering 26 miles of shoreline. It also has long stretches of open water near the lower end of the lake, making it excellent for water-skiing, with water surface temperatures ranging from 75 to 80 degrees in the summer.

Location: On Rollins Lake near Colfax; map D3, grid c3.

Campsites, facilities: There are 84 sites for tents or RVs. Flush toilets, picnic tables, and barbecues or fire pits are provided. Hot showers, parking pads, hiking trails, and a sanitary disposal station are available. A full-service marina with floating gas dock, stores, restaurant (breakfast and lunch), and boat rentals, and a water slide are nearby. Some facilities are wheelchair accessible. Pets must be controlled.

Reservations, fees: Reservations are recommended; $20 to $25 per night. Open year-round. Major credit cards accepted.

Directions: From Auburn, drive northeast on Interstate 80 for about 20 miles. Turn north on Highway 174 (a winding, two-lane road) and drive about two miles. Turn right on Rollins Lake Road and drive to the campground at 26909 Rollins Lake Road.

Contact: Long Ravine, tel. (530) 346-6166; website: longravineresort.com.

29 Orchard Springs

 7

Orchard Springs is set on the shore of Rollins Lake in the Sierra Nevada foothills among pine, oak, and cedar trees. The summer heat makes the lake excellent for water-skiing, boating, and swimming, and the spring and fall are great for trout and bass fishing.

Location: On Rollins Lake; map D3, grid c3.

Campsites, facilities: There are 19 sites with full hookups for tents or RVs, and 90 tent sites. Picnic tables, fire rings, and barbecues are provided. Drinking water, restrooms, flush toilets, showers, launch ramp, boat rentals, gas, dock space rentals, swimming beach, group picnic area, and a store are available. A restaurant nearby overlooks Collins Lake. Some facilities are wheelchair accessible. Leashed pets are permitted.

Reservations, fees: Reservations are accepted; $18 to $28 per night, $2 pet fee. Major credit cards accepted. Open year-round.

Directions: From Auburn, drive northeast on Interstate 80 for about 20 miles to Colfax and Highway 174. Turn north on Highway 174 (a winding, two-lane road) and drive 3.7 miles (bear left at Giovanni's Restaurant) to Orchard Spring Road. Turn right on Orchard Springs Road and drive a half mile to the road's end. Turn right at the gatehouse and continue to the campground.

Contact: Orchard Springs, P.O. Box 270, Colfax, CA 95713; tel. (530) 346-2212.

30 Peninsula Campground

 8

Peninsula Campground is set on a point that extends into Rollins Lake, flanked on each side by two sprawling lake arms. If you like boating, water-skiing, or swimming, you'll definitely like this place in the summer. If you want trout, prospects are best in April and May. After that the fast boats take over, though there is a good bass bite at dawn and dusk.

Location: On Rollins Lake; map D3, grid c3.

Campsites, facilities: There are 78 sites for tents or RVs up to 38 feet long. Picnic tables and fire rings are provided. Restrooms with flush toilets and hot showers, drinking water, modem hookups, sanitary disposal station, boat rentals, boat launch ramp, swim beach, and a country store are available. No RV hookups. Leashed pets are permitted.

Reservations, fees: Reservations are accepted; $19 to $23 per night with a maximum of six campers and a vehicle per site. Major credit cards accepted. Open year-round.

Directions: From Auburn, drive northeast on Interstate 80 for about 20 miles. Turn north on Highway 174 (a winding, two-lane road) and drive about six miles. Turn right on You Bet Road, drive 4.3 miles (turning right again to stay on You Bet Road), and continue another 3.1 miles to the campground entrance at 21597 You Bet Road.

Contact: Peninsula Campground, P.O. Box 344, Chicago Park, CA 95712; tel. (530) 477-9413; website: www.penresort.com.

31 Hampshire Rocks

 8

This camp sits along the South Fork of the Yuba River at 5,900 feet in elevation, with easy access off Interstate 80 and a nearby Forest Service visitor information center. Fishing for trout is fair. There are some swimming holes, but the water is often very cold. Nearby lakes that can provide side trips include Sterling and Fordyce Lakes (drive-to) to the north, and the Loch Leven Lakes (hike-to) to the south.

Location: On the Yuba River in Tahoe National Forest; map D3, grid c9.

Campsites, facilities: There are 31 sites for tents or RVs up to 22 feet long. Picnic tables and fire grills are provided. Drinking water and vault toilets are available. A grocery store, restaurant, and propane gas are available nearby. Leashed pets are permitted.

Reservations, fees: Reserve at (877) 444-6777 ($8.65 reservation fee) or website: www.reserveusa.com; $12 per night, $6 per night for each extra vehicle. Open May through October.

Directions: From Sacramento, drive east on Interstate 80 to Cisco Grove and continue for a mile to the Big Bend exit. Take that exit (remaining just south of the highway), then turn left on the frontage road and drive east for 1.5 miles to the campground.

Contact: Tahoe National Forest, Nevada City Ranger District, tel. (530) 265-4531 or fax (530) 478-6109.

Kidd Lake Group Camp

    7

Kidd Lake is one of four lakes bunched in a series along the access road just south of Interstate 80. It is set in the northern Sierra's high country, at 6,750 feet, and gets loaded with snow every winter. In late spring and early summer, always call ahead for conditions on the access road. The fishing is frustrating, consisting of a lot of tiny brook trout. Only cartop boats are permitted on Kidd Lake. The camp is set just northeast of the lake, within walking distance of the shore.

Location: West of Truckee; map D3, grid c9.

Campsites, facilities: This group site will accommodate up to 100 people in tents only. Picnic tables and fire grills are provided. Drinking water, restrooms and vault toilets are available. An unimproved boat ramp is available. Supplies are available in Truckee. Leashed pets are permitted.

Reservations, fees: Reservations are required, tel. (916) 386-5164; $18 to $23 per night, $100 per night at group camp (two night minimum except for three night minimum on holidays), $1 pet fee. Open June to mid-September, weather permitting.

Directions: From Sacramento, drive east on Interstate 80 toward Truckee. Take the Norden/Soda Springs exit, drive a short distance, turn south on Soda Springs Road, and drive 0.8 mile to Pahatsi Road. Turn right and drive two miles. When the road forks, bear right and drive a mile to the campground entrance road on the left.

Contact: PG&E Building and Land Services, tel. (916) 386-5164.

⬛ North Fork

 7

This is gold mining country, and this camp is set along the Little North Fork of the North Fork American River at 4,400 feet in elevation, where you might still find a few magic gold flecks. Unfortunately, they are probably fool's gold, not the real stuff. This feeder stream is small and pretty, and the camp is fairly remote and overlooked by most. It is set on the edge of a network of backcountry Forest Service roads. To explore them, a map of Tahoe National Forest is a must.

Location: On the North Fork of the American River in Tahoe National Forest; map D3, grid c7.

Campsites, facilities: There are 17 sites for tents or RVs up to 16 feet long. Picnic tables and fire grills are provided. Drinking water and vault toilets are available. Supplies are available at Emigrant Gap, Cisco Grove, and Soda Springs. Leashed pets are permitted.

Reservations, fees: No reservations; $11 per night, $6 per night for each extra vehicle. Open May through October.

Directions: From Sacramento, drive east on Interstate 80 to the Emigrant Gap exit. Take that exit and drive south for a quarter mile to Texas Hill Road/Forest Road 19. Turn right and drive about five miles to the camp on the right.

Contact: Tahoe National Forest, Nevada City Ranger District, tel. (530) 265-4531 or fax (530) 478-6109.

34 Tunnel Mill Group Camp

      7

This is a good spot for a Boy or Girl Scout camp out. It's a rustic, quiet group camp set all by itself along the (take a deep breath) East Fork of the North Fork of the North Fork of the American River (whew). (See North Fork for more recreation information.) The elevation is 4,400 feet.

Location: On the North Fork of the American River in Tahoe National Forest; map D3, grid c8.

Campsites, facilities: There are two group sites for tents or RVs up to 16 feet long. Each camp can accommodate up to 30 people. Picnic tables and fire grills are provided. Vault toilets are available. No drinking water is available. Supplies are available at the Nyack exit of Emigrant Gap. Leashed pets are permitted.

Reservations, fees: Reserve at (877) 444-6777 ($8.65 reservation fee) or website: www.reserveusa.com; call for fees. Open from June through October.

Directions: From Sacramento, drive east on Interstate 80 to the Emigrant Gap exit. Drive south for a quarter mile to Texas Hill Road/Forest Road 19. Turn right and drive about seven miles to the campground on the right side of the road.

Contact: Tahoe National Forest, Nevada City Ranger District, tel. (530) 265-4531 or fax (530) 478-6109.

35 Forbes Creek Group Camp

    7

The boat launch is nearby, but note: a 10-mph speed limit is the law. That makes for quiet water, perfect for anglers, canoeists, and other small boats. A paved trail circles the lake. For more information see Giant Gap entry. **Location:** On Sugar Pine Reservoir in Tahoe National Forest; map D3, grid c5.

Campsites, facilities: There are two group campsites, Madrone and Rocky Ridge, each

of which can accommodate up to 50 people in tents or RVs up to 45 feet long. Picnic tables and fire grills are provided. Drinking water, vault toilets, and a camp host are available. Some facilities are wheelchair accessible. A campfire circle, central parking area, sanitary disposal station, and a boat ramp are available nearby. Supplies can be obtained in Foresthill. Leashed pets are permitted.

Reservations, fees: Reserve at (877) 444-6777 ($8.65 reservation fee) or website: www.reserveusa.com; $55 per night. Open May through mid-October.

Directions: From Sacramento, drive east on Interstate 80 to the north end of Auburn and the Foresthill Road exit. Take that exit and drive east for 20 miles to Foresthill. Drive through Foresthill (road changes to Foresthill Divide Road) and continue for eight miles to Sugar Pine Road/Forest Road 10. Turn left and drive five miles to the lake and campground.

Contact: Tahoe National Forest, Foresthill Ranger District, tel. (530) 367-2224 or fax (530) 367-2992.

36 Giant Gap

    7

This is a lakeside spot along the western shore of Sugar Pine Reservoir at 3,500 feet in elevation in Tahoe National Forest. For boaters, there is a ramp on the south shore. Note that a 10-mph speed limit is the law, making this lake ideal for anglers in search of quiet water. Other recreation notes: There's a little less than a mile of paved trail which goes through the day-use area. Big Reservoir, five miles to the east, is the only other lake in the region and also has a campground. The trout fishing at Sugar Pine is fair, not usually great, not usually bad.

Location: On Sugar Pine Reservoir in Tahoe National Forest; map D3, grid c5.

Campsites, facilities: There are 30 sites for tents or RVs up to 30 feet long. Picnic tables and fire grills are provided. Drinking water, vault toilets, and a camp host are available. Some facilities are wheelchair accessible. A sanitary disposal station and boat ramp are available on the south shore. Supplies can be obtained in Foresthill. Leashed pets are permitted.

Reservations, fees: Reserve at (877) 444-6777 ($8.65 reservation fee) or website: www.reserveusa.com; $11 for a single, $22 for a double, per night. Open May through mid-October.

Directions: From Sacramento, drive east on Interstate 80 to the north end of Auburn and the Foresthill Road exit. Take that exit and drive east for 20 miles to Foresthill. Drive through Foresthill (road changes to Foresthill Divide Road) and continue for eight miles to Sugar Pine Road. Turn left and drive five miles to a fork. Turn right and drive one mile to the campground.

Contact: Tahoe National Forest, Foresthill Ranger District, tel. (530) 367-2224 or fax (530) 367-2992.

③⑦ Big Reservoir

   7

Here's a quiet lake where no boat motors are allowed. That makes it ideal for canoeists, row boaters, and tube floaters who don't like the idea of having to dodge water-skiers. The lake is stocked with rainbow trout. Big Reservoir is quite pretty and a nice beach is available not far from the resort. The elevation is 3,500 feet.

Location: On Big Reservoir in Tahoe National Forest; map D3, grid c5.

Campsites, facilities: There are 100 sites for tents or RVs up to 25 feet long. Picnic tables and fire grills are provided. Drinking water and vault toilets are available. Firewood is limited. There is a small store near the campground and supplies are also available in Foresthill. Leashed pets are permitted.

Reservations, fees: Reservations are accepted, tel. (530) 367-2129; $15 per night. Open May through October.

Directions: From Sacramento, drive east on Interstate 80 to the north end of Auburn and

the Foresthill Road exit. Take that exit and drive east for 20 miles to Foresthill. Drive through Foresthill (road changes to Foresthill Divide Road) and continue for eight miles to Sugar Pine Road. Turn left and drive about three miles to Forest Road 24 (signed Big Reservoir). Bear right on Forest Road 24 and drive about five miles to the campground entrance road on the right.

Contact: Tahoe National Forest, Foresthill Ranger District, tel. (530) 367-2224 or fax (530) 367-2992.

③⑧ Shirttail Creek

   7

This camp is set near the little creek that feeds into the north end of Sugar Pine Reservoir. The boat ramp is all the way around the south side of the lake (near Forbes Creek Group Camp). For recreation information, see the entry for Giant Gap.

Location: On Sugar Pine Reservoir in Tahoe National Forest; map D3, grid c5.

Campsites, facilities: There are 30 sites for tents or RVs up to 30 feet long (double and triple sites are available). Picnic tables and fire grills are provided. Drinking water, vault toilets, and a camp host are available. Some facilities are wheelchair accessible. A sanitary disposal station and boat ramp are available on the south shore. Supplies can be obtained in Foresthill. Leashed pets are permitted.

Reservations, fees: Reserve at (877) 444-6777 ($8.65 reservation fee) or website: www.reserveusa.com; $11 for single sites, $22 for double sites, $33 for triples sites, per night. Open May through mid-October.

Directions: From Sacramento, drive east on Interstate 80 to the north end of Auburn and the Foresthill Road exit. Take that exit and drive east for 20 miles to Foresthill. Drive through Foresthill (road changes to Foresthill Divide Road) and continue for eight miles to Sugar Pine Road. Turn left and drive five miles to the campground access road. Turn right (signed) and drive to the campground.

Contact: Tahoe National Forest, Foresthill Ranger District, tel. (530) 367-2224 or fax (530) 367-2992.

39 Talbot

 7

Talbot camp is set at 5,600 feet along the Middle Fork of the American River, primarily used as a trailhead camp for backpackers heading into the Granite Chief Wilderness. The trail is routed along the Middle Fork American River, turning south into Picayune Valley, flanked by Needle Peak (8,971 feet), Granite Chief (9,886 feet), and Squaw Peak to the east, then beyond to connect with the Pacific Crest Trail. The nearby trailhead has 10 stalls for horses and pack stock trailer parking. Hitching rails are available at the trailhead. No horses are allowed at the campground.

Location: On the Middle Fork of the American River in Tahoe National Forest; map D3, grid d9.

Campsites, facilities: There are five tent sites. Picnic tables and fire grills are provided. Vault toilets are available. No drinking water is available. Supplies are available in Foresthill. The camp is within a state game refuge and no firearms are permitted. Leashed pets are permitted.

Reservations, fees: No reservations; no fee. Open June through October, weather permitting.

Directions: From Sacramento, drive east on Interstate 80 to the north end of Auburn and the Foresthill Road exit. Take that exit and drive east to Foresthill and Mosquito Ridge Road (Forest Road 96). Turn right (east) and drive 40 miles (curvy) to Anderson Dam and to a junction. Turn left (still Mosquito Ridge Road) and then continue along the southern shoreline of French Meadows Reservoir for four miles (road turns into dirt) and continue four more miles to the campground.

Contact: Tahoe National Forest, Foresthill Ranger District, tel. (530) 367-2224 or fax (530) 367-2992.

40 Ahart

 7

This camp is a mile north of French Meadows Reservoir near where the Middle Fork of the American River enters the lake. It is on the Middle Fork, and is primarily used for campers who would rather camp near this river than French Meadows Reservoir. Note: This is bear country in the summer.

Location: Near French Meadows Reservoir in Tahoe National Forest; map D3, grid d9.

Campsites, facilities: There are 12 sites for tents or RVs up to 22 feet long. Picnic tables and fire grills are provided. Vault toilets are available. No drinking water is available. Supplies are available in Foresthill. Leashed pets are permitted.

Reservations, fees: No reservations; $8 per night. Open June through October.

Directions: From Sacramento, drive east on Interstate 80 to the north end of Auburn and the Foresthill Road exit. Take that exit and drive east to Foresthill and Mosquito Ridge Road (Forest Road 96). Turn right (east) and drive 40 miles (curvy) to Anderson Dam and to a junction. Turn left (still Mosquito Ridge Road) and then continue along the southern shoreline of French Meadows Reservoir for seven miles.

Contact: Tahoe National Forest, Foresthill Ranger District, tel. (530) 367-2224 or fax (530) 367-2992.

41 Gates Group Camp

 7

This group camp is well secluded along the North Fork American River, just upstream from where it pours into French Meadows Reservoir. For recreation options, see the entries for French Meadows, Lewis and Coyote Group Camp.

Location: On the North Fork of the American River in Tahoe National Forest; map D3, grid d9.

Campsites, facilities: There are two 25-person group sites and a 75-person group site for tents or RVs up to 35 feet long. Picnic tables and fire grills are provided. Drinking water, vault toilets, central parking, and a campfire circle are available. Obtain supplies in Foresthill. Leashed pets are permitted.

Reservations, fees: Reserve at (877) 444-6777 ($8.65 reservation fee) or website: www.reserveusa.com; $45 to $60 fee per night. Open May through October.

Directions: From Sacramento, drive east on Interstate 80 to the north end of Auburn and the Foresthill Road exit. Take that exit and drive east to Foresthill and Mosquito Ridge Road (Forest Road 96). Turn right (east) and drive 40 miles (curvy) to Anderson Dam and to a junction. Turn left (still Mosquito Ridge Road) and continue along the southern shoreline of French Meadows Reservoir for five miles to a fork at the head of the lake. Bear left at the fork (Forest Road 68) and drive a mile to the camp at the end of the road.

Contact: Tahoe National Forest, Foresthill Ranger District, tel. (530) 367-2224 or fax (530) 367-2992; L & L, Inc., tel. (800) 342-2267.

42 Coyote Group Camp

      6

This group camp is set right at the head of French Meadows Reservoir, at 5,300 feet in elevation. A boat ramp is two miles to the south, just past Lewis on the lake's north shore. For recreation options, see the entries for Poppy Hike-In/Boat-In and French Meadows.

Location: On French Meadows Reservoir, in Tahoe National Forest; map D3, grid d9.

Campsites, facilities: There are three 25-person group sites and a 50-person group site for tents or RVs up to 35 feet long. Picnic tables and fire grills are provided. Drinking water and vault toilets are available. A campfire circle and central parking area are also available. Supplies are available in Foresthill. Leashed pets are permitted.

Reservations, fees: Reserve at (877) 444-6777 ($8.65 reservation fee) or website: www.reserveusa.com; $45 to $60 group fee per night or $1 per person. Open May through October.

Directions: From Sacramento, drive east on Interstate 80 to the north end of Auburn and the Foresthill Road exit. Take that exit and drive east to Foresthill and Mosquito Ridge Road (Forest Road 96). Turn right (east) and drive 40 miles (curvy) to Anderson Dam and to a junction. Turn left (still Mosquito Ridge Road) and then continue along the southern shoreline of French Meadows Reservoir for five miles along the southern shoreline to French Meadows Reservoir and a fork at the head of the lake. Bear left at the fork and drive a half mile to the camp on the left side of the road.

Contact: Tahoe National Forest, Foresthill Ranger District, tel. (530) 367-2224 or fax (530) 367-2992.

43 French Meadows

   7

The nearby boat launch makes this choice for boating campers. The camp is on French Meadows Reservoir at 5,300 feet. It is set on the lake's southern shore, with the boat ramp about a mile to the south (you'll see the entrance road on the way in). This is a big lake set in remote Tahoe National Forest in the North Fork American River Canyon with good trout fishing. The lake level often drops in late summer, then a lot of stumps and boulders start poking through the lake surface. This creates navigational hazards for boaters, but it also makes it easier for the fishermen to know where to find the fish. If the fish don't bite here, boaters should make the nearby side trip to pretty Hell Hole Reservoir to the south.

Location: On French Meadows Reservoir in Tahoe National Forest; map D3, grid d9.

Campsites, facilities: There are 75 sites for tents or RVs up to 35 feet long. Picnic tables and fire grills are provided. Drinking water and vault toilets are available. Some facilities are wheelchair accessible. A concrete boat ramp is nearby. Supplies are available in Foresthill. Leashed pets are permitted.

Reservations, fees: Reserve at (877) 444-6777 ($8.65 reservation fee) or website: www.re-serveusa.com; $11 per night. Open June through October.

Directions: From Sacramento, drive east on Interstate 80 to the north end of Auburn and the Foresthill Road exit. Take that exit and drive east to Foresthill and Mosquito Ridge Road (Forest Road 96). Turn right (east) and drive 40 miles (curvy) to Anderson Dam and to a junction. Turn left (still Mosquito Ridge Road) and then continue along the southern shoreline of French Meadows Reservoir for four miles to the campground.

Contact: Tahoe National Forest, Foresthill Ranger District, tel. (530) 367-2224 or fax (530) 367-2992; L & L, Inc., tel. (800) 342-2267.

44 Lewis

 7

This camp is not right at lakeside but is just across the road from French Meadows Reservoir. It is still quite pretty, set along a feeder creek near the lake's northeast shore. A boat ramp is available only a half mile to the south, and the adjacent McGuire Picnic Area has a trailhead that is routed along the lake's northern shoreline. This lake is big (2,000 acres) and pretty, created by a dam on the Middle Fork American River, with good fishing for rainbow trout.

Location: On French Meadows Reservoir in Tahoe National Forest; map D3, grid d9.

Campsites, facilities: There are 40 sites for tents or RVs up to 35 feet long. Picnic tables and fire grills are provided. Drinking water and vault toilets are available. A concrete boat ramp is nearby. Supplies are available in Foresthill. Leashed pets are permitted.

Reservations, fees: Reserve at (877) 444-6777 ($8.65 reservation fee) or website: www.re-serveusa.com; $11 per night. Open May through October.

Directions: From Sacramento, drive east on Interstate 80 to the north end of Auburn and the Foresthill Road exit. Take that exit and drive east to Foresthill and Mosquito Ridge Road (Forest Road 96). Turn right (east) and drive 40 miles (curvy) to Anderson Dam and to a junction. Turn left (still Mosquito Ridge Road) and then continue along the southern shoreline of French Meadows Reservoir for five miles along the southern shoreline to French Meadows Reservoir and a fork at the head of the lake. Bear left at the fork and drive a half mile to the camp on the right side of the road.

Contact: Tahoe National Forest, Foresthill Ranger District, tel. (530) 367-2224 or fax (530)367-2992.

45 Poppy Hike-In/Boat-In

 10

This camp is on the north side of French Meadows Reservoir, about midway along the lake's shore. It can be reached only by boat or on foot, supplying a great degree of privacy compared to the other camps on this lake. A trail that is routed along the north shore of the reservoir runs right through the camp, providing two different trailhead access points, as well as a good side trip hike. The lake is quite big, covering nearly 2,000 acres when full, at 5,300 feet in elevation on a dammed-up section of the Middle Fork American River. It is stocked with rainbow trout but also has prime habitat for brown trout, and big ones are sometimes caught by surprise.

Location: On French Meadows Reservoir in Tahoe National Forest; map D3, grid d9.

Campsites, facilities: There are 12 tent sites, accessible by boat or by a mile-long foot trail from McGuire Boat Ramp. Picnic tables and fire grills are provided. Vault toilets are available. No drinking water is available. Garbage must be packed out. Supplies are available in Foresthill. Leashed pets are permitted.

Reservations, fees: No reservations; no fee.

Directions: From Sacramento, drive east on Interstate 80 to the north end of Auburn and the Foresthill Road exit. Take that exit and drive east to Foresthill and Mosquito Ridge Road (Forest Road 96). Turn right (east) and drive 40 miles (curvy) to French Meadows Reservoir Dam and to a junction. Turn left (still Mosquito Ridge Road) and continue for three miles to the lake and campground. Note: If the gate is locked early or late in the season, an option is to drive around the lake and hike in a mile from the McGuire Picnic Area.

Contact: Tahoe National Forest, Foresthill Ranger District, tel. (530) 367-2224 or fax (530) 367-2992.

46 Robinson Flat

   5

This camp is set at 6,800 feet in remote Tahoe National Forest, on the eastern flank of Duncan Peak (7,116 feet), with a two-mile drive south to Duncan Peak Lookout (7,182 feet). A trail out of camp follows along a small stream, a fork to Duncan Creek, in Little Robinsons Valley. French Meadows Reservoir is 15 miles southeast.

Location: Near French Meadows Reservoir in Tahoe National Forest; map D3, grid d8.

Campsites, facilities: There are five tent sites. Picnic tables and fire grills are provided. Vault toilets are available. No drinking water is available. Garbage must be packed out. Supplies are available in Foresthill. Leashed pets are permitted.

Reservations, fees: No reservations; no fee. Open mid-May through October, weather permitting.

Directions: From Sacramento, drive east on Interstate 80 to the north end of Auburn and the Foresthill Road exit. Take that exit, Foresthill Divide Road, and drive east to Foresthill and continue northeast (the road is narrow and curvy) for 27 miles to the junction

with County Road 43. The campground is at the junction.

Contact: Tahoe National Forest, Foresthill Ranger District, tel. (530) 367-2224 or fax (530) 367-2992.

47 Bear River Park

 7

This RV park is set in the Sierra foothills at 1,800 feet, near Bear River, featuring riverfront campsites. The park covers 200 acres, offers five miles of hiking trails, and is set right on the Placer and Nevada county lines. Wow! (Hey, try writing 1,600 of these). It fills up on weekends and is popular with both locals and out-of-towners. In the spring, when everything is greened up, it can be a gorgeous landscape. Fishing is OK for trout, noncommercial gold panning is permitted, and some rafting is popular on the river.

Location: Near Colfax on Bear River; map D3, grid d2.

Campsites, facilities: There are 25 sites for tents or RVs, and one group site for up to 100 people. Picnic tables and fire rings are provided. Drinking water and pit toilets are available. Supplies are available within five miles in Colfax or Bowman. Leashed pets are permitted.

Reservations, fees: Group reservations at tel. (530) 889-7750 ($5 reservation fee); $10 per night, $2 for each additional vehicle, $1 pet fee, $40 to $75 for group site. Open year-round.

Directions: From Sacramento, drive east on Interstate 80 east of Auburn to West Weimar Crossroads exit. Take that exit on to Weimar Cross Road and drive north for 1.5 miles to Placer Hills Road. Turn right and drive 2.5 miles to Plum Tree Road. Turn left and drive one mile to the campground. The access road is steep and narrow, and trailers and RVs are not recommended.

Contact: Bear River Park, tel. (530) 889-7750, or fax (530) 889-6809; website: www.placer.ca.gov.

48 Auburn KOA

     4

This year-round KOA park is set at 1,250 feet and has all the amenities. Hey, a swimming pool is always a bonus in Auburn.

Location: Near Auburn; map D3, grid e1.

Campsites, facilities: There are 10 tent sites and 66 sites for RVs up to 40 feet, all with hookups. There are also two cabins and a rental trailer. Picnic tables and fire rings are provided. Restrooms, drinking water, flush toilets, showers, sanitary disposal station, a playground, swimming pool, whirlpool, recreation room, fishing pond, badminton, horseshoes, volleyball, grocery store, coin laundry, and propane gas are available. Some facilities are wheelchair accessible. Leashed pets are permitted.

Reservations, fees: Reservations are accepted; $22 to $32.50 per night, $39.50 per night for a cabin and $50 per night for the trailer. Major credit cards accepted. Open year-round.

Directions: From Auburn, drive north on Highway 49 for 3.5 miles to Rock Creek Road (one block past Bell Road). Turn right on Rock Creek Road and follow the signs to 3550 KOA Way.

Contact: Auburn KOA, tel. (530) 885-0990.

49 Big Meadows

      7

This camp sits on a meadow near the ridge above Hell Hole Reservoir (which is about two miles away). For more information, see the entry for Hell Hole.

Location: Near Hell Hole Reservoir in Eldorado National Forest; map D3, grid e9.

Campsites, facilities: There are 54 sites for tents or RVs up to 22 feet long. Picnic tables and fire grills are provided. Drinking water, flush and vault toilets are available. One wheelchair accessible campsite and toilet are available. Supplies are available in Georgetown. Leashed pets are permitted.

Reservations, fees: No reservations; $8 per night. Open May through October.

Directions: From Sacramento, drive east on Interstate 80 to the north end of Auburn. Take the Elm Avenue exit and turn left at the first stoplight onto Elm Avenue. Drive 0.1 mile, turn left on High Street, and continue through the signal where High Street merges with Highway 49. Travel on Highway 49 for about 3.5 miles, turn right over the bridge, and drive about 2.5 miles into the town of Cool. Turn left on Georgetown Road/Highway 193 and drive about 14 miles into Georgetown. At the four-way stop turn left on Main Street (which becomes Wentworth Springs/Forest Road 1) and drive about 25 miles. Turn left on Forest Road 2 and drive 21 miles to the campground on the left.

Contact: Eldorado Information Center, (530) 644-6048; Eldorado National Forest, Georgetown Ranger District, tel. (530) 333-4312 or fax (530) 333-5522.

50 Upper Hell Hole Walk-In

     10

This is a beautiful spot, set on the southern shore at the upper end of Hell Hole Reservoir in remote national forest seen by relatively few people. Getting here requires a 3.5-mile walk on a trail routed along the southern edge of the lake overlooking Hell Hole. The trail's short rises and falls can tire you out on a hot day—bring plenty of water. You arrive at this little trail camp, ready to explore onward the next day into the Granite Chief Wilderness, or just do nothing except enjoy adjacent Buck Meadow, the lake's headwaters, and the paradise you have discovered.

Location: On Hell Hole Reservoir in Eldorado National Forest; map D3, grid e9.

Campsites, facilities: There are 15 tent sites, accessible by trail or boat only. Picnic tables and fire grills are provided. Vault toilets are available. No drinking water is available. Garbage must be packed out. A boat launch is available at the reservoir and the camp can be reached by boat, but low water levels during August and September can make passage difficult or impossible. Supplies can be obtained in Georgetown. Leashed pets are permitted.

Reservations, fees: No reservations; no fee. Open May through October.

Directions: From Sacramento, drive east on Interstate 80 to the north end of Auburn. Take the Elm Avenue exit and turn left at the first stoplight onto Elm Avenue. Drive 0.1 of a mile, turn left on High Street, and continue through the signal where High Street merges with Highway 49. Travel on Highway 49 for about 3.5 miles, turn right over the bridge, and drive about 2.5 miles into the town of Cool. Turn left on Georgetown Road/Highway 193 and drive about 14 miles into Georgetown. At the four-way stop turn left on Main Street (which becomes Wentworth Springs/Forest Road 1) and drive about 25 miles. Turn left on Forest Road 2 and drive about 23 miles (a mile past the Hell Hole Campground access road) to the parking area at the boat ramp. From the trailhead hike 3.5 miles to the camp.

Contact: Eldorado National Forest, Georgetown Ranger District, tel. (530) 333-4312 or fax (530) 333-5522.

51 Hell Hole

    8

Hell Hole is a mountain temple with sapphire blue water. For the most part, there is limited bank access because of its granite-sculpted shore, and that's why there are no lakeside campsites. This is the closest drive-to camp at Hell Hole Reservoir, about a mile away with a boat launch nearby. Be sure to bring a boat and then enjoy the scenery while you troll for kokanee salmon, brown trout, Mackinaw trout, and a sprinkling of rainbow trout. This is a unique fishery compared to the put-and-take rainbow trout at so many other lakes. The lake elevation is 4,700 feet; the camp elevation is 5,200 feet.

Location: Near Hell Hole Reservoir in Eldorado National Forest; map D3, grid e9.

Campsites, facilities: There are 10 sites for tents or RVs. Picnic tables and fire grills are

provided. Drinking water and vault toilets are available. Supplies can be obtained in Georgetown. A boat launch is available nearby at the reservoir. Leashed pets are permitted.

Reservations, fees: No reservations; $8 per night in the summer season. Open May through mid-November, weather permitting.

Directions: From Sacramento, drive east on Interstate 80 to the north end of Auburn. Take the Elm Avenue exit and turn left at the first stoplight onto Elm Avenue. Drive 0.1 mile, turn left on High Street, and continue through the signal where High Street merges with Highway 49. Travel on Highway 49 for about 3.5 miles, turn right over the bridge, and drive about 2.5 miles into the town of Cool. Turn left on Georgetown Road/Highway 193 and drive about 14 miles into Georgetown. At the four-way stop turn left on Main Street (which becomes Wentworth Springs/Forest Road 1) and drive about 25 miles. Turn left on Forest Road 2 and drive about 22 miles to the campground on the left.

Contact: Eldorado Information Center, (530) 644-6048; Eldorado National Forest, Georgetown Ranger District, tel. (530) 333-4312 or fax (530) 333-5522.

52 Middle Meadows Group Camp

    7

This group camp is within range of several adventures. To the nearby east is Hell Hole Reservoir (you'll need a boat here to do it right), and to the nearby north is French Meadows Reservoir (you'll drive past the dam on the way in). Unfortunately, there isn't a heck of a lot to do at this camp other than watch the water flow by on adjacent Long Canyon Creek.

Location: On Long Canyon Creek in Eldorado National Forest; map D3, grid e9.

Campsites, facilities: There are two group sites for tents or small RVs. Picnic tables and fire grills are provided. Drinking water and flush and vault toilets are available. Supplies can be obtained in Foresthill. Leashed pets are permitted.

Reservations, fees: Reserve at (877) 444-6777 ($8.65 reservation fee) or website: www.reserveusa.com; $25 to $50 per night. Open June through September.

Directions: From Sacramento, drive east on Interstate 80 to the north end of Auburn. Take the Elm Avenue exit and turn left at the first stoplight onto Elm Avenue. Drive 0.1 mile, turn left on High Street, and continue through the signal where High Street merges with Highway 49. Travel on Highway 49 for about 3.5 miles, turn right over the bridge, and drive about 2.5 miles into the town of Cool. Turn left on Georgetown Road/Highway 193 and drive about 14 miles into Georgetown. At the four-way stop turn left on Main Street (which becomes Wentworth Springs/Forest Road 1) and drive about 25 miles. Turn left on Forest Road 2 and drive 19 miles to the campground on the right.

Contact: Eldorado Information Center, (530) 644-6048; Eldorado National Forest, Georgetown Ranger District, tel. (530) 333-4312 or fax (530) 333-5522.

53 Auburn State Recreation Area

     8

This 42,000-acre state park is a jewel in the valley foothill country, at 1,200 feet in elevation. It is in the scenic American River Canyon, just far enough out of Sacramento to make visitors feel like they're escaping the city treadmill. There are two drive-in campgrounds, Mineral Bar and Rucky-A-Chucky, and two boat-in campgrounds at Lake Clementine. The American River runs through the park, offering visitors opportunities to fish, boat, and raft. In addition, there are over 100 miles of hiking and horseback riding trails. Lake Clementine offers fishing (not stocked) and water-skiing, with a boat limit of 25 boats per day; the quota is reached every day on summer weekends.

Location: Near Auburn; map D3, grid e1.

Campsites, facilities: Mineral Camp provides 17 campsites. Rucky-A-Chucky provides six campsites. There are two boat-in campgrounds with 20 boat-in sites. Picnic tables and fire grills are provided. Pit toilets are available. No drinking water is available. Garbage must be packed out. Leashed pets are permitted.

Reservations, fees: Reserve at (800) 444-PARK (800-444-7275) or website: www.ReserveAmerica.com, $7 per night, $10 per night for premium boat-in sites at Lake Clementine. Tent sites open year-round. Boat-in sites open Memorial Day weekend through Labor Day weekend.

Directions to Mineral Bar Camp: From Interstate 80 in Auburn, drive east for 15 miles to Colfax. Take the Colfax exit and turn right on the frontage road and drive one-half mile to Iowa Hill Road. Turn left and drive 2.5 miles to the campground on the left.

Directions to Rucky-A-Chucky Camp: From Interstate 80 in Auburn, take the Foresthill Road exit on to Foresthill Road. Continue on Foresthill Road for seven miles to Drivers Flat Road. Turn right and drive 2.8 miles (becomes Rucky-A-Chucky Road) to the campground on the right.

Directions to Lake Clementine boat-in camps: From Interstate 80 at Auburn, take the Foresthill exit on to Foresthill Road. Continue northeast on Foresthill Road for two miles to Lake Clementine Road. Turn left and drive 2.5 miles to the boat launch. After launching, cruise by boat 1.5 miles northeast to the campgrounds.

Contact: Auburn State Recreation Area, tel. (530) 885-4527, or fax (530) 885-2798.

54 Dru Barner Equestrian Camp

      7

This camp, set at 3,200 feet in an area of pine and fir, is ideal for horses; there are miles of equestrian trails. For more information see the entries for Stumpy Meadows and Black Oak Group Camp.

Location: Near Georgetown in Eldorado National Forest; map D3, grid f5.

Campsites, facilities: There are 48 sites for tents or RVs up to 35 feet long. Picnic tables and fire grills are provided. Drinking water and vault toilets are available. Two stock troughs are also available. Garbage must be packed out. Leashed pets are permitted.

Reservations, fees: No reservations; $6 per night. Open year-round.

Directions: From Sacramento on Interstate 80, drive east to the north end of Auburn. Turn left on Elm Avenue and drive about 0.1 mile. Turn left on High Street and drive through the signal that marks the continuation of High Street as Highway 49. Drive 3.5 miles on Highway 49, turn right over the bridge, and drive 2.5 miles into the town of Cool. Turn left on Georgetown Road/Highway 193 and drive 14 miles into Georgetown. At the four-way stop, turn left on Main Street, which becomes Georgetown-Wentworth Springs Road/Forest Road 1, and drive 5.5 miles. Turn left on Bottle Hill Bypass Road and drive about a mile to the campground on the left.

Contact: Eldorado Information Center, (530) 644-6048; Eldorado National Forest, Georgetown Ranger District, tel. (530) 333-4312 or fax (530) 333-5522.

55 Loomis KOA

 2

This KOA park is set in the Sierra foothills, which are known for hot summer weather. The sites are on level gravel and some are shaded. The elevation is 600 feet.

Location: In Loomis; map D3, grid f0.

Campsites, facilities: There are 74 sites for RVs up to 40 feet long, many with hookups, a separate tent area, and two one-room cabins. Picnic tables and fire grills are provided. Drinking water, restrooms, flush toilets, showers, a sanitary disposal station, a playground, swimming pool, recreation room, volleyball, horseshoes, grocery store, coin laundry, and propane gas are available. Some facilities are wheel-chair accessible. Leashed pets are permitted.

Reservations, fees: Tel. (800) 562-3312. Reservations are accepted; $21 to $28 per night, $34 cabin fee per night. Major credit cards accepted. Open year-round.

Directions: From Sacramento, drive east on Interstate 80 to Loomis and the junction of Sierra College Boulevard. Drive north on Sierra College Boulevard for a half mile to Taylor Road. Turn east and drive a half block to the camp.

Contact: Loomis KOA, tel. (916) 652-6737.

56 Gerle Creek

 7

This is a small, pretty, but limited spot set along the northern shore of little Gerle Creek Reservoir at 5,231 feet in elevation. The lake is ideal for canoes or other small boats because no motors are permitted and no boat ramp is available. That makes for quiet water. It is set in the Gerle Creek Canyon, which feeds into the South Fork Rubicon River. No trout plants are made at this lake, and fishing is correspondingly poor. A network of Forest Service roads to the north can provide great exploring. A map of Eldorado National Forest is a must.

Location: On Gerle Creek Reservoir in Eldorado National Forest; map D3, grid f8.

Campsites, facilities: There are 50 sites for tents or RVs up to 22 feet long. Picnic tables and fire grills are provided. Drinking water and vault toilets are available. Wheelchair-accessible trails and fishing pier are available nearby. Leashed pets are permitted.

Reservations, fees: Reserve at (877) 444-6777 ($8.65 reservation fee) or website: www.reserveusa.com; $13 per night. Open late May to early September.

Directions: From Sacramento, drive east on U.S. 50 to Riverton and the junction with Ice House Road/Soda Springs-Riverton Road. Turn north and drive 27 miles (past Union Valley Reservoir) to a fork with

Forest Road 30. Turn left, drive two miles, bear left on the campground entrance road, and drive a mile to the campground.

Contact: Eldorado Information Center, (530) 644-6048; Eldorado National Forest, Pacific Ranger District, tel. (530) 644-2349 or fax (530) 647-5405.

57 South Fork

 8

This primitive national forest camp sits alongside the South Fork Rubicon River, just over a mile downstream from the outlet at Gerle Creek Reservoir. Trout fishing is fair, the water tastes extremely sweet (always pump filter with a water purifier), and there are several side trips available. These include Loon Lake (eight miles to the northeast), Gerle Creek Reservoir (to the nearby north), and Union Valley Reservoir (to the nearby south).

Location: On the South Fork of the Rubicon River in Eldorado National Forest; map D3, grid f8.

Campsites, facilities: There are 17 sites for tents or RVs up to 22 feet long. Picnic tables and fire grills are provided. Vault toilets are available. No drinking water is available. Leashed pets are permitted.

Reservations, fees: No reservations; no fee. Open June through October.

Directions: From Sacramento, drive east on U.S. 50 Riverton and the junction with Ice House Road/Soda Springs-Riverton Road. Turn north and drive about 25 miles to the junction with Forest Road 13N28 (3.5 miles past Union Valley Reservoir). Bear left on Forest Road 13N28 and drive two miles to the campground entrance on the right.

Contact: Eldorado Information Center, (530) 644-6048; Eldorado National Forest, Pacific Ranger District, tel. (530) 644-2349 or fax (530) 647-5405.

58 Black Oak Group Camp

 7

This group camp is set directly adjacent to Stumpy Meadows Campground. For more information, see the entry for Stumpy Meadows. The boat ramp for the lake is just south of the Mark Edson Dam, near the picnic area. The elevation is 4,400 feet.

Location: Near Stumpy Meadows Lake in Eldorado National Forest; map D3, grid f6.

Campsites, facilities: There are three group sites for tents and one group site for RVs up to 16 feet long. Picnic tables and fire grills are provided. Drinking water and vault toilets are available. A boat ramp is nearby. Leashed pets are permitted.

Reservations, fees: Reserve at (877) 444-6777 ($8.65 reservation fee) or website: www.reserveusa.com; $50 group-use fee. Open April through September.

Directions: From Sacramento on Interstate 80, drive east to the north end of Auburn. Turn left on Elm Avenue and drive about 0.1 of a mile. Turn left on High Street and drive through the signal that marks the continuation of High Street as Highway 49. Drive 3.5 miles on Highway 49, turn right over the bridge, and drive 2.5 miles into the town of Cool. Turn left on Georgetown Road/Highway 193 and drive 14 miles into Georgetown. At the four-way stop, turn left on Main Street, which becomes Georgetown-Wentworth Springs Road/Forest Road 1. Drive about 18 miles to Stumpy Meadows Lake, and then continue for two miles to the north shore of the lake and the campground entrance road on the right.

Contact: Eldorado Information Center, (530) 644-6048; Eldorado National Forest, Georgetown Ranger District, tel. (530) 333-4312 or fax (530) 333-5522.

59 Stumpy Meadows

 7

This is the camp of choice for visitors to Stumpy Meadows Lake. The first thing visitors notice is the huge ponderosa pine trees, noted for their distinctive mosaic-like bark. The lake is set at 4,400 feet in Eldorado National Forest and covers 320 acres with water that is cold and clear. The lake has both rainbow and brown trout, and in the fall provides good fishing for big browns (they move up into the head of the lake, near where Pilot Creek enters).

Location: On Stumpy Meadows Lake in Eldorado National Forest; map D3, grid f6.

Campsites, facilities: There are 40 sites for tents or RVs up to 16 feet long. Two of the sites are double units. Picnic tables and fire grills are provided. Drinking water and vault toilets are available. A boat ramp is nearby. Leashed pets are permitted.

Reservations, fees: Reserve at (877) 444-6777 ($8.65 reservation fee) or website: www.reserveusa.com; $13 per night, $26 for double-unit sites. Open April through October.

Directions: From Sacramento on Interstate 80, drive east to the north end of Auburn. Turn left on Elm Avenue and drive about 0.1 of a mile. Turn left on High Street and drive through the signal that marks the continuation of High Street as Highway 49. Drive 3.5 miles on Highway 49, turn right over the bridge, and drive 2.5 miles into the town of Cool. Turn left on Georgetown Road/Highway 193 and drive 14 miles into Georgetown. At the four-way stop, turn left on Main Street, which becomes Georgetown-Wentworth Springs Road/Forest Road 1. Drive about 18 miles to Stumpy Meadows Lake. Continue about a mile and turn right into Stumpy Meadows campground.

Contact: Eldorado Information Center, (530) 644-6048; Eldorado National Forest, Georgetown Ranger District, tel. (530) 333-4312 or fax (530) 333-5522.

60 Negro Bar Group Camp

Lake Natoma is the afterbay for Folsom Lake, but it is nothing like Folsom Lake. Natoma is comparatively small (500 acres),

very narrow instead of wide, with cold water instead of warm. This camp is set at the head of the lake on the northern shore, with an adjacent boat ramp available. Negro Bar used to have family sites but these were eliminated when the bridge crossing at Lake Natoma was built. Beal's Point increased its family sites in compensation.

Location: In Folsom Lake State Recreation Area; map D3, grid g0.

Campsites, facilities: There are three group sites that can accommodate from 25 to 50 people each. Picnic tables and fire grills are provided. Drinking water, restrooms and flush toilets are available. A bike path is available nearby. Boat rentals, moorings, snack bar, ice, and bait and tackle are available at the Folsom Lake Marina. Leashed pets are permitted.

Reservations, fees: Reserve at (800) 444-PARK (800-444-7275) or website: www.ReserveAmerica.com from May through September. Reserve at (916) 988-0205 from October through April; $18 to $37 per night. Open year-round.

Directions: From Interstate 80 north of Sacramento, take the Douglas Boulevard exit and head east for five miles to Auburn-Folsom Road. Turn right on Auburn-Folsom Road and drive south for six miles until the road dead-ends into Greenback Lane. Turn right on Greenback Lane and merge immediately into the left lane. The park entrance is approximately 0.2 mile on the left.

Contact: Folsom Lake State Recreation Area, tel. (916) 988-0205, or fax (916) 988-9062.

61 Beal's Point

Folsom Lake is Sacramento's backyard vacation spot, a huge lake covering some 12,000 acres with 75 miles of shoreline, which means plenty of room for boating, water-skiing, fishing, and sun-tanning. This camp is set on the lake's southwest side, just north of the dam, with a boat ramp nearby at Granite Bay. The lake has a productive trout fishery in the spring, a fast-growing population of kokanee salmon, and good prospects for bass in late spring and early summer. By summer water-skiers usually take over the lake each day by about 10 a.m. One problem with this lake is that a minor water drawdown can cause major amounts of shoreline to become exposed on its upper arms.

Location: In Folsom Lake State Recreation Area; map D3, grid g0.

Campsites, facilities: There are 69 sites for tents or RVs up to 31 feet long. Picnic tables and fire grills are provided. Drinking water, flush toilets, showers, and sanitary disposal station are available. A bike path and horseback riding facilities are available nearby. Camping, picnicking, and fishing areas are wheelchair accessible. There are boat rentals, moorings, summer snack bar, ice, and bait and tackle available at the Folsom Lake Marina. Leashed pets are permitted.

Reservations, fees: Reserve at (800) 444-PARK (800-444-7275) or website: www.ReserveAmerica.com, April through September; $12 per night. Open year-round.

Directions: From Sacramento, drive east on U.S. 50 to the Folsom Boulevard exit. Turn left at the stop sign and continue on Folsom Boulevard for 3.5 miles, following the road as it curves onto Leidesdorff Street. Head east on Leidesdorff Street for a half mile, dead-ending into Riley Street. Turn left onto Riley Street and proceed over the bridge, turning right on Folsom-Auburn Road. Head north on Folsom-Auburn Road for 3.5 miles to the park entrance on the right.

Contact: Folsom Lake State Recreation Area, tel. (916) 988-0205, or fax (916) 988-9062.

62 Peninsula

6

This is one of the big camps at Folsom Lake, but it is also more remote than the other camps, requiring a circuitous drive. It is set on the peninsula on the northeast shore, right where the North Fork American River arm of the lake enters the main lake area. A nearby boat ramp, marina, and boat rentals make this a great weekend spot. Fishing for bass and trout is often quite good in spring and early summer, and water-skiing is popular in the hot summer.

Location: In Folsom Lake State Recreation Area; map D3, grid g0.

Campsites, facilities: There are 100 sites for tents or RVs. Picnic tables and fire grills are provided. Drinking water, restrooms, flush toilets and showers are available. A bike path is available nearby. Boat rentals, moorings, snack bar, ice, and bait and tackle are available at the Folsom Lake Marina. Leashed pets are permitted.

Reservations, fees: Reserve at (800) 444-PARK (800-444-7275) or website: www.ReserveAmerica.com; $12 per night. Open year-round.

Directions: From Placerville, drive east on U.S. 50 to the Spring Street/Highway 49 exit. Turn north on Highway 49 (toward the town of Coloma) and continue 8.3 miles into the town of Pilot Hill and Rattlesnake Bar Road. Turn left on Rattlesnake Bar Road and drive nine miles to the end of the road and the park entrance.

Contact: Folsom Lake State Recreation Area, tel. (916) 988-0205, or fax (916) 988-9062.

63 Placerville KOA

7

This is a classic KOA campground, complete with the cute little log cabins KOA calls "Kamping Kabins." The location of this camp is ideal for many, set near U.S. 50 in the Sierra foothills, the main route up to South Tahoe. Nearby is Apple Hill, where from September to November it is a popular tourist attraction, when the local ranches and orchards sell produce and crafts, often with live music. In addition, the Marshall Gold Discovery Site is 10 miles north, where gold was discovered in 1848, setting off the 1849 gold rush. Whitewater rafting and gold panning are popular on the nearby American River.

Location: Near Placerville; map D3, grid g4.

Campsites, facilities: There are 70 sites for RVs, 43 with full hookups and 27 with partial hookups, 14 tent sites (eight with electricity), 20 sites for tents or RVs, and eight cabins. Picnic tables and barbecues are provided. Restrooms, drinking water, flush toilets, showers, sanitary disposal station, phone, cable TV, modem hookups, recreation room, swimming pool, spa, playground, video arcade, basketball courts, 19-hole miniature golf course, convenience store, snack bar, dog run, petting zoo, fishing pond, bike rentals, pavilion cooking facilities, volleyball court, and horseshoe pits are available. Some facilities are wheelchair accessible. Leashed pets are permitted.

Reservations, fees: Reservations at (800) 562-4197; $24 to $35 for RV sites, $22 to $25 for tent sites, $40 to $48 for cabins, $3 per person per night for more than two people. Major credit cards accepted. Open year-round.

Directions: From US 50 west of Placerville, take the Shingle Springs Drive exit (and not the Shingle Springs/Ponderosa Road exit). Drive one block to Rock Barn Road. Turn left and drive one-half mile to the campground at the end of the road.

Contact: Placerville KOA, tel. (530) 676-2267; website: www.koa-placerville.com.

64 Wolf Creek

 9

Wolf Creek Camp is on the north shore of Union Valley Reservoir. Listen up? Notice that it's quieter? Yep. That's because there are not as many water-skiers in the vicinity. Why? There's no boat ramp in the immediate area. This camp opened in the summer of 1998 and was an immediate hit—hey, maybe it's time to create a major low-speed zone for this lake.

The view of the Crystal Range from the campground is drop-dead gorgeous. The elevation is 4900 feet.

Location: On Union Valley Reservoir in Eldorado National Forest; map D3, grid g7.

Campsites, facilities: There are 42 sites for tents or RVs up to 50 feet long, and four double sites. Picnic tables and fire grills are provided. Drinking water and vault toilets are available. Some facilities are wheelchair accessible. A boat ramp is three miles away at the campground at Yellowjacket. Leashed pets are permitted.

Reservations, fees: Reserve at (877) 444-6777 ($8.65 reservation fee) or website: www.reserveusa.com; $13 for a single site per night, $20 for a double, $5 for a third vehicle. Open early-May through October, weather permitting.

Directions: From Sacramento, drive east on U.S. 50 to Riverton and the junction with Ice House Road/Soda Springs-Riverton Road. Turn left and drive 21 miles to Union Valley Road (at the head of Union Valley Reservoir). Turn left and drive 2.5 miles to the campground.

Contact: Eldorado Information Center, (530) 644-6048; Eldorado National Forest, Pacific Ranger District, tel. (530) 644-2349 or fax (530) 647-5405.

65 Camino Cove

 10

Camino Cove Camp opened in the summer of 2000, and right off, it is the nicest spot at Union Valley Reservoir, a slam dunk. It is set at the north end of the lake on a peninsula, absolutely beautiful, a tree-covered landscape and yet with sweeping views of the Crystal Basin. The nearest boat ramp is 1.5 miles to the west at West Point. If this camp is full, there is a small camp at West Point, with just eight sites. The elevation is 4900 feet.

Location: On Union Valley Reservoir in Eldorado National Forest; map D3, grid g8.

Campsites, facilities: There are 32 sites for tents or RVs up to 25 feet long. Fire rings are provided. Vault toilets are available. No drinking water is available. A swimming beach is nearby and a boat ramp is 1.5 miles away at the campground at West Point. Leashed pets are permitted.

Reservations, fees: No reservations; no fee. Open early-May through October, weather permitting.

Directions: From Sacramento, drive east on U.S. 50 to Riverton and the junction with Ice House Road/Soda Springs-Riverton Road. Turn north on Ice House Road and drive seven miles to Peavine Ridge Road. Turn left and drive three miles to Bryant Springs Road. Turn right and drive five miles north past the West Point boat ramp, and continue 1.5 miles east to the campground entrance on the right.

Contact: Eldorado Information Center, (530) 644-6048; Eldorado National Forest, Pacific Ranger District, tel. (530) 644-2349 or fax (530) 647-5405.

66 Yellowjacket

 8

The camp, set at 4,900 feet, is on the north shore of the reservoir. A boat launch adjacent to the camp makes this an ideal destination for trout-angling campers with boats. Union Valley Reservoir, a popular weekend destination for campers from the Central Valley, is stocked with brook trout and rainbow trout by the Department of Fish and Game.

Location: On Union Valley Reservoir in Eldorado National Forest; map D3, grid g8.

Campsites, facilities: There are 40 sites for tents or RVs up to 22 feet long. Picnic tables and fire rings are provided. Drinking water and vault toilets are available. A boat ramp is nearby. Leashed pets are permitted.

Reservations, fees: Reserve at (877) 444-6777 ($8.65 reservation fee) or website: www.reserveusa.com; $13 for a single site per night,

$20 for a double, $5 for a third vehicle. Open Memorial Day weekend through Labor Day weekend.

Directions: From Sacramento, drive east on U.S. 50 to Riverton and the junction with Ice House Road/Soda Springs-Riverton Road. Turn left and drive 21 miles to Union Valley Road (at the head of Union Valley Reservoir). Turn left and drive a mile to the campground entrance road. Turn left and drive a mile to the campground.

Contact: Eldorado Information Center, (530) 644-6048; Eldorado National Forest, Pacific Ranger District, tel. (530) 644-2349 or fax (530) 647-5405.

67 Wench Creek

 7

Wench Creek is on the northeast shore of Union Valley Reservoir. For more information, see the entries for Jones Fork and Sunset. The elevation is 4900 feet.

Location: On Union Valley Reservoir in Eldorado National Forest; map D3, grid g8.

Campsites, facilities: There are 100 sites for tents or RVs up to 22 feet long. There are also two group sites. Picnic tables and fire grills are provided. Drinking water and vault toilets are available. A boat ramp is three miles away at the campground at Yellowjacket. Leashed pets are permitted.

Reservations, fees: No reservations for family sites; $13 for a single site per night, $20 for a double, $5 for a third vehicle. Reserve group sites at (877) 444-6777 ($8.65 reservation fee) or website: www.reserveusa.com; $60 group fee. Open mid-May through September.

Directions: From Sacramento, drive east on U.S. 50 to Riverton and the junction with Ice House Road/Soda Springs-Riverton Road. Turn left and drive 19 miles to the campground entrance road (four miles past the turnoff for Sunset Camp). Turn left and drive a mile to the campground at the end of the road.

Contact: Eldorado Information Center, (530) 644-6048; Eldorado National Forest, Pacific

Ranger District, tel. (530) 644-2349 or fax (530) 647-5405.

Azalea Cove Hike-In/Boat-In

 7

On the shores of Union Valley Reservoir at 4,900 feet in elevation, there is access to 4.5 miles of bike trail in addition to boating and fishing activities. The distance to the campsite is less than a half mile by boat or by trail. For additional information, see the entries for Wench Creek and Peninsula Recreation Area.

Location: On Union Valley Reservoir in Eldorado National Forest; map D3, grid g8.

Campsites, facilities: There are 10 sites for tents only. Picnic tables and fire grills are provided. Vault toilets are available. No drinking water is available. Garbage must be packed out. Leashed pets are permitted.

Reservations, fees: No reservations; no fee. Open June through September.

Directions: From Sacramento, drive east on U.S. 50 to Riverton and the junction with Ice House Road/Soda Springs-Riverton Road. Turn left and drive about 17 miles to the campground entrance road (three miles past the turnoff for Sunset Camp). Park and then hike or boat less than one mile to the campground.

Contact: Eldorado Information Center, (530) 644-6048; Eldorado National Forest, Pacific Ranger District, tel. (530) 644-2349 or fax (530) 647-5405.

Big Silver Group Camp

 7

This camp was built along the Union Valley bike trail, less than a mile from Union Valley Reservoir. The paved bike trail stretches for miles both north and south of the campground and is wheelchair accessible. It's a classic Sierra forest setting, with plenty of ponderosa pine on the north side of Big Silver Creek.

Location: On Big Silver Creek in Eldorado

National Forest; map D3, grid g8.

Campsites, facilities: There is a large group site for tents or RVs up to 22 feet in length. Picnic tables and fire grills are provided. Vault toilets are available. No drinking water is available. Garbage must be packed out. There is also a group kitchen area with pedestal grills. Some facilities are wheelchair accessible. Leashed pets are permitted.

Reservations, fees: Reserve at (877) 444-6777 ($8.65 reservation fee) or website: www.reserveusa.com; $50 per night. Open late May to mid-October.

Directions: From Sacramento, drive east on U.S. 50 to Riverton and the junction with Ice House Road/Soda Springs-Riverton Road. Turn left and drive about 17 miles to the campground entrance road (three miles past the turnoff for Sunset Camp).

Contact: Eldorado Information Center, (530) 644-6048; Eldorado National Forest, Pacific Ranger District, tel. (530) 644-2349 or fax (530) 647-5405.

Peninsula Recreation Area

8

The two campgrounds here, Sunset and Fashoda, are the prettiest of all the camps at Union Valley Reservoir, set at the eastern tip of the peninsula that juts out into the lake at the mouth of Jones Fork. A nearby boat ramp (you'll see it on the left on the way in) is a big plus, along with a picnic area and beach. The lake has decent trout fishing, with brook trout, brown trout, rainbow trout, mackinaw, kokanee salamon, and smallmouth bass. The place is gorgeous, set at 4,900 feet in the Sierra Nevada.

Location: On Union Valley Reservoir in Eldorado National Forest; map D3, grid g8.

Campsites, facilities: There are 131 sites for tents or RVs up to 22 feet long at Sunset Camp and 30 walk-in tent sites at Fashoda Camp. Picnic tables, fire rings, and fire grills are provided. Drinking water and vault toilets are available. A boat ramp and sanitary disposal station are available. Some facilities are wheelchair accessible. Leashed pets are permitted.

Reservations, fees: Reserve at (877) 444-6777 ($8.65 reservation fee) or website: www.reserveusa.com; $13 for a single site per night, $20 for a double, $5 for a third vehicle. Open late May to early September.

Directions: From Sacramento, drive east on U.S. 50 to Riverton and the junction with Ice House Road/Soda Springs-Riverton Road. Turn left and drive 15 miles to the campground entrance road (a mile past the turnoff for Jones Fork Camp). Turn left and drive 1.5 miles to the campground at the end of the road.

Contact: Eldorado Information Center, (530) 644-6048; Eldorado National Forest, Pacific Ranger District, tel. (530) 644-2349 or fax (530) 647-5405.

71 Jones Fork

 7

The Crystal Basin Recreation Area is the most popular backcountry region for campers from the Sacramento area, and Union Valley Reservoir is the centerpiece. The area gets its name from the prominent granite Sierra ridge, which looks like crystal when it is covered with frozen snow. This is a big lake, set at 4,900 feet in elevation, with 10 lakeside campgrounds and three boat ramps providing access. This is the first camp you will arrive at, set at the mouth of the Jones Fork Cove.

Location: On Union Valley Reservoir in Eldorado National Forest; map D3, grid g8.

Campsites, facilities: There are 10 sites for tents or RVs up to 25 feet long. Picnic tables and fire rings are provided. Vault toilets are available. No drinking water is available. Leashed pets are permitted.

Reservations, fees: No reservations; $5 per night, $5 for a third vehicle. Open June through October.

Directions: From Sacramento, drive east on U.S. 50 to Riverton and the junction with Ice House Road/Soda Springs-Riverton Road.

Turn left and drive 14 miles to the campground entrance road on the left (at the south end of Union Valley Reservoir). Turn left and drive a half mile to the campground.

Contact: Eldorado Information Center, (530) 644-6048; Eldorado National Forest, Pacific Ranger District, tel. (530) 644-2349 or fax (530) 647-5405.

72 Silver Creek

 5

Silver Creek might be a pretty spot at 5,200 feet in elevation, but it is rarely the destination of campers. Rather, it is primarily used as an overflow spot if the camps at nearby Ice House Reservoir are full. Ice House is only two miles north, and Union Valley Reservoir is four miles north. Note: Not recommended for RVs or trailers.

Location: Near Ice House Reservoir in Eldorado National Forest; map D3, grid g8.

Campsites, facilities: There are 12 tent sites. Picnic tables and fire grills are provided. Vault toilets are available. No drinking water is available. Leashed pets are permitted.

Reservations, fees: No reservations; $6. Open June through October.

Directions: From Sacramento, drive east on U.S. 50 to Riverton and the junction with Ice House Road/Soda Springs-Riverton Road. Turn left and drive about seven miles to the campground entrance road on the left (if you reach the junction with Forest Road 3, you have gone a quarter mile too far). Turn left and drive a quarter mile to the campground.

Contact: Eldorado Information Center, (530) 644-6048; Eldorado National Forest, Pacific Ranger District, tel. (530) 644-2349 or fax (530) 647-5405.

73 Northwind

 7

This camp sits on the north shore of Ice House Reservoir. It is slightly above the reservoir, offering prime views. See the entry for Ice House for more information.

Location: On Ice House Reservoir in Eldorado National Forest; map D3, grid g9.

Campsites, facilities: There are nine sites for tents or RVs up to 25 feet long, and one double site. Picnic tables and fire grills are provided. Vault toilets are available. No drinking water is available. Leashed pets are permitted.

Reservations, fees: No reservations; $5 per night, $5 for a third vehicle. Open June through October.

Directions: From Sacramento, drive east on U.S. 50 to Riverton and the junction with Ice House Road/Soda Springs-Riverton Road. Turn left and drive about 11 miles to the junction with Forest Road 3 and Ice House Road. Turn right on Ice House Road and drive about three miles (two miles past the boat ramp) to the campground access road on the right.

Contact: Eldorado National Forest, Pacific Ranger District, tel. (530) 644-2349 or fax (530) 647-5405.

74 Strawberry Point

 7

This camp is one of two free camps on the north shore of Ice House Reservoir, 5,400 feet in elevation. For more information, see the entry for Ice House.

Location: On Ice House Reservoir in Eldorado National Forest; map D3, grid g9.

Campsites, facilities: There are 10 sites for tents or RVs up to 25 feet long. Picnic tables and fire grills are provided. Vault toilets are available. No drinking water is available. Leashed pets are permitted.

Reservations, fees: No reservations; $5 per night, $5 for a third vehicle. Open March through December, weather permitting.

Directions: From Sacramento, drive east on U.S. 50 to Riverton and the junction with Ice House Road/Soda Springs-Riverton Road. Turn left and drive about 11 miles to the junc-

tion with Forest Road 3 and Ice House Road. Turn right on Ice House Road and drive about four miles (three miles past the boat ramp) to the campground access road on the right.

Contact: Eldorado Information Center, (530) 644-6048; Eldorado National Forest, Pacific Ranger District, tel. (530) 644-2349 or fax (530) 647-5405.

75 Ice House

 8

Along with Loon Lake and Union Valley Reservoir, Ice House Reservoir is a feature destination in the Crystal Basin Recreation Area. Ice House gets most of the fishermen and Union Valley gets most of the campers. The camp here is set on the lake's northwestern shore, 5,500 feet in elevation, just up from the dam and adjacent to the lake's boat ramp. The lake was created by a dam on South Fork Silver Creek and covers 650 acres, with the deepest spot about 130 feet deep. It is stocked with rainbow trout, brook trout, and brown trout.

Location: On Ice House Reservoir in Eldorado National Forest; map D3, grid g9.

Campsites, facilities: There are 17 sites for tents and 66 sites for tents or RVs up to 22 feet long. Three sites are wheelchair accessible. Picnic tables and fire grills are provided. Drinking water, vault toilets, boat ramp, and sanitary disposal station are available. Leashed pets are permitted.

Reservations, fees: Reserve at (877) 444-6777 ($8.65 reservation fee) or website: www.reserveusa.com; $13 for a single site per night, $20 for a double, $5 for a third vehicle. Open June through October.

Directions: From Sacramento, drive east on U.S. 50 to Riverton and the junction with Ice House Road/Soda Springs-Riverton Road. Turn left and drive about 11 miles to the junction with Forest Road 3 and Ice House Road. Turn right on Ice House Road and drive two miles to the campground access road on the right.

Contact: Eldorado Information Center, (530) 644-6048; Eldorado National Forest, Pacific Ranger District, tel. (530) 644-2349 or fax (530) 647-5405.

76 Sand Flat

 7

This first-come, first-served campground often gets filled up by U.S. 50 travelers. And why not? You get easy access, a well-signed exit, and a nice setting on the South Fork of the American River. The elevation is 3,900 feet. The river is very pretty here, but fishing is often poor. In winter the snow level usually starts just a few miles uphill.

Location: On the South Fork of the American River in Eldorado National Forest; map D3, grid h9.

Campsites, facilities: There are 29 sites for tents or RVs up to 22 feet long. Picnic tables and fire grills are provided. Drinking water and vault toilets are available. Groceries, restaurant, and gas are available nearby. Leashed pets are permitted.

Reservations, fees: No reservations; $11 per night, $5 per night for each extra vehicle. Open year-round.

Directions: From Sacramento, drive east on U.S. 50 to Placerville and then continue 28 miles to the campground on the right.

Contact: Eldorado Information Center, tel., (530) 644-6048. Eldorado National Forest, Placerville Ranger District, tel. (530) 644-6048 or fax (530) 295-5994.

77 China Flat

 7

China Flat sits across the road from the Silver Fork American River, with a nearby access road that is routed along the river for a mile. This provides access for fishing, swimming, gold panning, and exploring. The camp feels far off the beaten path, even though it is only five minutes from that parade of traffic on U.S. 50.

Location: On the Silver Fork of the American River in Eldorado National Forest; map D3, grid h9.

Campsites, facilities: There are 18 sites and one double site for tents or RVs up to 22 feet long. Picnic tables and fire grills are provided. Drinking water and vault toilets are available. Some facilities are wheelchair accessible. Leashed pets are permitted.

Reservations, fees: No reservations; $11 per night, $22 per night for the double site, $5 per night for each extra vehicle. Open May through October.

Directions: From Sacramento, drive east on U.S. 50 to Kyburz and Silver Fork Road. Turn right and drive three miles to the campground on the left side of the road.

Contact: Eldorado Information Center, tel., (530) 644-6048. Eldorado National Forest, Placerville Ranger District, tel. (530) 644-6048 or fax (530) 295-5994.

78 Silver Fork

 7

The tons of vacationers driving U.S. 50 along the South Fork American River always get frustrated when they try to fish or camp, because there are precious few opportunities for either, with about zero trout and camps alike. But, just 10 minutes off the beaten path, you can find both at Silver Fork Camp. The access road provides many fishing opportunities and is stocked with rainbow trout by the state. The camp is set right along the river, at 5,500 feet in elevation, in Eldorado National Forest.

Location: On the Silver Fork of the American River in Eldorado National Forest; map D3, grid h9.

Campsites, facilities: There are 35 sites for tents or RVs up to 22 feet long and four double-family sites. Picnic tables and fire grills are provided. Drinking water and vault toilets are available. Some of the facilities are wheelchair accessible. Leashed pets are permitted.

Reservations, fees: No reservations; $11 per night, $22 for double-family sites. Open May through October.

Directions: From Sacramento, drive east on U.S. 50 to Kyburz and Silver Fork Road. Turn right and drive eight miles to the campground on the right side of the road.

Contact: Eldorado Information Center, tel., (530) 644-6048; Eldorado National Forest, Placerville Ranger District, tel. (530) 644-6048 or fax (530) 295-5994.

79 Sly Park Recreation Area

    7

Jenkinson Lake is set at 3,500 feet in elevation in the lower reaches of Eldorado National Forest, with a climate that is perfect for water-skiing and fishing. Participants of both sports get along, with most water-skiers motoring around the lake's main body, while anglers head upstream into the Hazel Creek arm of the lake for trout (in the spring) and bass (in the summer). Good news for anglers: No personal watercraft are permitted. More good news: This is one of the better lakes in the Sierra for brown trout. The boat ramp is in a cove on the southwest end of the lake, about two miles from the campground. The area also has several hiking trails, and the lake is good for swimming. A group camp is available for visitors with horses, complete with riding trails, hitching posts, and corrals. An equestrian trail circles the 640-acre lake.

Location: On Jenkinson Lake; map D3, grid h6.

Campsites, facilities: There are 159 sites with no hookups for tents or RVs up to 32 feet long. Picnic tables and fire grills are provided. Drinking water and vault toilets are available. Two boat ramps are available nearby. Some facilities are wheelchair accessible. There are five group sites that can accommodate 50 to 100 people and an equestrian camp called Black Oak, which has 15 sites and two youth-group sites. A grocery store, snack bar, bait, and propane gas are available nearby. Firewood is sold on site. Leashed pets are permitted.

Reservations, fees: Reservations are recommended; tel. (530) 644-2792; $15 to $20 per night; $110 minimum group fee for the first 50 people, $1.50 for each additional camper, $2.50 pet fee, $9 for each additional vehicle, $6 boat-launch fee. Checkin and checkout by 2 p.m. Open year-round.

Directions: From Sacramento, drive east on U.S. 50 to Pollock Pines and take the exit for Sly Park Road. Drive south for five miles to Jenkinson Lake and the campground access road. Turn left and drive a half mile to the campground on the left.

Contact: Sly Park Recreation Area, tel. (530) 644-2545.

80 Capps Crossing

 7

Here's a candidate for the 5 Percent Club. It's set out in the middle of nowhere along the North Fork of the Cosumnes River. It's a primitive spot that doesn't get much use. This camp is in the western reaches of a vast number of backcountry Forest Service roads. A map of Eldorado National Forest is a must to explore them. The elevation is 5,200 feet.

Location: On the North Fork of the Consumes River in Eldorado National Forest; map D3, grid i8.

Campsites, facilities: There are 11 tent sites. Picnic tables and fire grills are provided. Drinking water and vault toilets are available. Leashed pets are permitted.

Reservations, fees: No reservations; $11 per night. Open June through October.

Directions: From Sacramento, drive east on U.S. 50 to Placerville and continue for 12 miles to the Sly Park Road exit. Turn right and drive about six miles to the Mormon Emigrant Trail/Forest Road 5. Turn left on Mormon Emigrant Trail and drive about 13 miles to North-South Road/Forest Road 6. Turn right (south) on North-South Road and drive about six miles to the campground on the left side of the road.

Contact: Eldorado Information Center, tel. (530) 644-6048; Eldorado National Forest, Placerville Ranger District, tel. (530) 644-6048 or fax (530) 295-5994.

81 Far Horizons 49er Trailer Village

      4

This is the granddaddy of RV parks, set in the heart of the gold country 40 miles east of Stockton and Sacramento. It is rarely crowded and offers warm pools, a huge spa, and a friendly staff.

Location: In Plymouth; map D3, grid i2.

Campsites, facilities: There are 329 sites for RVs only, with full hookups. Flush toilets, showers, sanitary disposal station, playground, two swimming pools, hot tub, recreation room, pool room, TV lounge, modem hookups, coin laundry, delicatessen, propane gas, and a general store are available. Some facilities are wheelchair accessible. Leashed pets are permitted.

Reservations, fees: Reservations are recommended; $25 to $33 per night. Major credit cards accepted. Open year-round.

Directions: From Sacramento, drive east on U.S. 50 to Watt Ave. Turn south on Watt Ave and drive to Highway 16. Turn east on Highway 16 and drive to Highway 49. Turn north on Highway 49 and drive a mile to the campground on the left side of the road at 18265 Highway 49. Note: This is a mile south of Main Street in Plymouth.

Contact: Far Horizons 49er Trailer Village, tel. (209) 245-6981 or tel. (800) 339-6981; website: www.49ervillage.com.

82 PiPi

       7

This place is far enough out of the way to get missed by most campers. It is beside the Middle Fork of the Cosumnes River at 4,100 feet.

There are some good swimming holes in the area, but the water is cold in early summer (after all, it's snowmelt). A trail/boardwalk along the river is wheelchair accessible. Several sites border a pretty meadow in the back of the camp. This is also a gateway to a vast network of Forest Service roads to the north in Eldorado National Forest.

Location: On the Middle Fork of the Cosumnes River in Eldorado National Forest; map D3, grid i7.

Campsites, facilities: There are 51 sites for tents or RVs up to 50 feet long (three double-family sites). Picnic tables and fire grills are provided. Drinking water and vault toilets are available. There is wheelchair access to some camping areas, restrooms, and pathways. Leashed pets are permitted.

Reservations, fees: Some sites can be reserved, tel. (877) 444-6777 ($8.65 reservation fee) or website: www.reserveusa.com; $11 per night. Open May through mid-November, weather permitting.

Directions: From Jackson, drive east on Highway 88 to Pioneer and continue for nine miles to Omo Ranch Road. Turn left and drive a 0.8 mile to North-South Road/Forest Road 6. Turn right and drive 5.9 miles to the campground on the left side of the road.

Contact: Eldorado Information Center, tel., (530) 644-6048; Eldorado National Forest, Amador Ranger District, tel. (209) 295-4251 or fax (209) 295-5994.

83 South Shore

      7

Bear River Reservoir is set at 5,900 feet, which means it becomes ice-free earlier in the spring than its uphill neighbors to the east, Silver Lake and Caples Lake. It is a good-sized lake—725 acres—and cold and deep, too. It gets double-barreled trout stocks, receiving fish from the state and from the operator of the lake's marina and lodge. This campground is on the lake's southern shore, just east of the dam. Explorers can drive south for five miles to Salt Springs Reservoir, which has a trailhead and parking area on the north side of the dam for a great day hike along the lake.

Location: On Bear River Reservoir in Eldorado National Forest; map D3, grid j9.

Campsites, facilities: There are 13 sites for tents and nine sites for tents or RVs. There are four two-family sites. Picnic tables and fire grills are provided. Drinking water and vault toilets are available. A boat ramp, grocery store, boat rentals, and propane gas are available at nearby Bear River Lake Resort. Leashed pets are permitted.

Reservations, fees: No reservations; $11 per night, $22 per night for two-family sites. Open June through October.

Directions: From Stockton, drive east on Highway 88 for about 80 miles to the lake entrance on the right side of the road. Turn right and drive four miles (past the dam) to the campground entrance on the right side of the road.

Contact: Eldorado Information Center, tel. (530) 644-6048; Eldorado National Forest, Amador Ranger District, tel. (209) 295-4251 or fax (209) 295-5994.

84 Bear River Group Camp

      6

This is a group camp set near Bear River Reservoir, a pretty lake that provides power boating and trout fishing. See the entry for South Shore, which is just a mile from this camp.

Location: On Bear River Reservoir in Eldorado National Forest; map D3, grid j9.

Campsites, facilities: There are three group sites for tents; two sites can accommodate 25 people each and one site can accommodate 50 people. Picnic tables and fire grills are provided. Drinking water, vault toilets, and wash racks are available. A grocery store, boat ramp, boat rentals, and propane gas are available nearby. Leashed pets are permitted.

Reservations, fees: Reservations are required at tel. (209) 295-4512; $50 to $100 per night. Open mid-June through mid-September, weather permitting.

Directions: From Stockton, drive east on Highway 88 for about 80 miles to the lake entrance on the right side of the road. Turn right and drive five miles (past the dam) to the campground entrance on the left side of the road.

Contact: Eldorado Information Center, tel. (530) 644-6048; Eldorado National Forest, Amador Ranger District, tel. (209) 295-4251 or fax (209) 295-5994.

85 Bear River Lake Resort

    8

Bear River Lake Resort is a complete vacation service lodge, with everything you could ask for. A lot of people have been asking in recent years, making this a popular spot that often requires a reservation. The resort also sponsors fishing derbies in the summer, and sweetens the pot considerably by stocking exceptionally large rainbow trout. The resort is set at 6,000 feet. The lake freezes over in the winter. For more information about Bear River Reservoir, see the entry for South Shore.

Location: On Bear River Reservoir; map D grid j9.

Campsites, facilities: There are 127 sites for tents or RVs, all with partial hookups, and eight lodging units. Picnic tables and fire grills are provided. Restrooms, drinking water, showers, sanitary disposal station, boat ramp, boat rentals, firewood, ice, propane gas, coin laundry, post office, telephone, restaurant and cocktail lounge, and a grocery store are available. Some facilities are wheelchair accessible. Leashed pets are permitted at campsites. No pets in lodging units.

Reservations, fees: Reservations are recommended; $20 per night for campsites, $82.50 for lodging units, two-night minimum. Major credit cards accepted. Open year-round (call for access in winter).

Directions: From Stockton, drive east on Highway 88 for about 80 miles to the lake entrance on the right side of the road. Turn right and drive 2.5 miles to a junction (if you pass the dam, you have gone a quarter mile too far). Turn left and drive a half mile to the campground entrance on the right side of the road.

Contact: Bear River Reservoir, tel. (209) 295-4868 or fax (209) 295-4585; website: www.bear-riverlake.com.

86 White Azalea

    7

Out here in the remote Mokelumne River Canyon are three primitive camps set on the Mokelumne's North Fork. White Azalea, 3,500 feet in elevation, is the closest of the three to Salt Springs Reservoir, the prime recreation destination. It's about a three-mile drive to the dam and an adjacent parking area for a wilderness trailhead for the Mokelumne Wilderness. This trail makes a great day hike, routed for four miles along the north shore of Salt Springs Reservoir to Blue Hole at the head of the lake.

Location: On the Mokelumne River in Eldorado National Forest; map D3, grid j8.

Campsites, facilities: There are six tent sites. Vault toilets are provided. No drinking water is available. Garbage must be packed out. Leashed pets are permitted.

Reservations, fees: No reservations; no fee. Open year-round, weather permitting.

Directions: From Jackson, drive east on Highway 88 to Pioneer and then continue for 18 miles to Ellis Road/Forest Road 92 (78 miles from Jackson), at a signed turnoff for Lumberyard Campground. Turn right on Ellis Road and drive 12 miles to Salt Springs Road (Forest Road 9). Turn left, cross Bear River, and continue for three miles to the campground on the right. The road is steep, narrow and curvy in spots, not good for RVs or trailers.

Contact: Eldorado Information Center, tel., (530) 644-6048. Eldorado National Forest, Amador Ranger District, tel. (209) 295-4251 or fax (209) 295-5994.

87 Moore Creek

    7

This camp is set at 3,200 feet elevation on little Moore Creek, a feeder stream to the nearby North Fork Mokelumne River. It's one of three primitive camps within two miles. See the entry for White Azalea for more information.

Location: On the Mokelumne River in Eldorado National Forest; map D3, grid j8.

Campsites, facilities: There are eight tent sites. Vault toilets are provided, and some sites have picnic tables. No drinking water is available. Garbage must be packed out. Leashed pets are permitted.

Reservations, fees: No reservations; no fee. Open year-round, weather permitting.

Directions: From Jackson, drive east on Highway 88 to Pioneer and then continue for 18 miles to Ellis Road/Forest Road 92 (78 miles from Jackson), at a signed turnoff for Lumberyard Campground. Turn right on Ellis Road and drive 12 miles to Salt Springs Road (Forest Road 9). Turn right and drive 2.5 miles, cross the bridge over the Mokelumne River, and turn right on the campground entrance road. Drive a quarter mile to the campground on the right. The road is steep, narrow, and winding in spots—not good for RVs or trailers.

Contact: Eldorado Information Center, tel. (530) 644-6048; Eldorado National Forest, Amador Ranger District, tel. (209) 295-4251 or fax (209) 295-5994.

88 Mokelumne

    7

This primitive spot is set beside the Mokelumne River at 3,200 feet in elevation, one of three primitive camps in the immediate area. See the entry for White Azalea for more information. There are some good swimming holes nearby. Fishing is fair, with trout on the small side.

Location: On the Mokelumne River in Eldorado National Forest; map D3, grid j8.

Campsites, facilities: There are five tent

sites and eight sites for tents or RVs. Vault toilets are provided. No drinking water is available. Garbage must be packed out (it is occasionally serviced in summer). Leashed pets are permitted.

Reservations, fees: No reservations; no fee. Open year-round, weather permitting.

Directions: From Jackson, drive east on Highway 88 to Pioneer and then continue for 18 miles to Ellis Road/Forest Road 92 (78 miles from Jackson), at a signed turnoff for Lumberyard Campground. Turn right on Ellis Road and drive 12 miles to Salt Springs Road (Forest Road 9). Turn right and drive 2.5 miles to the campground on the left side of the road (at the Mokelumne River).

Contact: Eldorado Information Center, tel. (530) 644-6048; Eldorado National Forest, Amador Ranger District, tel. (209) 295-4251 or fax (209) 295-5994.

89 Indian Grinding Rock State Historic Park

     7

Visiting this park, about 10 miles from Jackson, is like entering a time machine. It offers a reconstructed Miwok village with petroglyphs, bedrock mortars, a cultural center, a two-mile nature trail, and interpretive talks for groups, by reservation. One unique element is that you will discover *Chaw-fe* (grinding rock) signs about the park. The camp is set at 2,500 feet in the Sierra foothills.

Location: Near Jackson; map D3, grid j4.

Campsites, facilities: There are 23 sites for tents or RVs, some up to 27 feet long. Picnic tables and fire grills are provided. Drinking water, flush toilets, and coin-operated hot showers are available. Some facilities are wheelchair accessible. Leashed pets are permitted.

Reservations, fees: No reservations; $12 per night. Open year-round.

Directions: From Jackson, drive east on Highway 88 for 11 miles to Pine Grove-Volcano Road. Turn left on Pine Grove-Volcano Road and drive 1.5 miles to the park on the left

Contact: Indian Grinding Rock State Historic Park, tel. (209) 296-7488.

CHAPTER D4

BEAUTIFUL DONNER LAKE

MAP D4

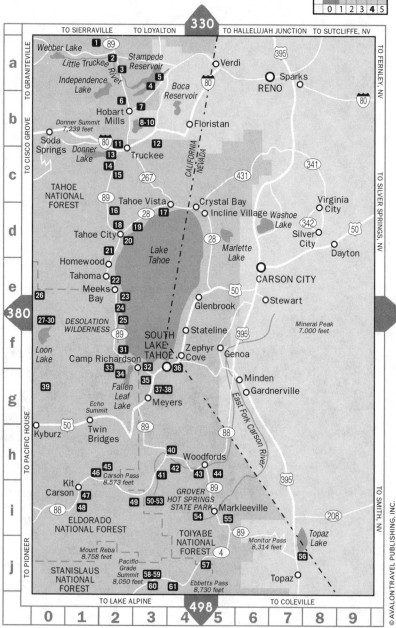

TO GRANITEVILLE
TO CISCO GROVE
TO PACIFIC HOUSE
TO PIONEER

TO FERNLEY, NV
TO SILVER SPRINGS, NV
TO SMITH, NV

380

Webber Lake
Little Truckee River
Independence Lake
Stampede Reservoir
Verdi
Sparks
RENO
395
80
Boca Reservoir
Hobart Mills
Floristan
Donner Summit 7,239 feet
Soda Springs
Donner Lake
Truckee
CALIFORNIA NEVADA
341
431
Crystal Bay
Incline Village
Washoe Lake
Virginia City
342
Silver City
Dayton
50
TAHOE NATIONAL FOREST
Tahoe Vista
28
Tahoe City
Lake Tahoe
Marlette Lake
CARSON CITY
Homewood
Tahoma
Meeks Bay
Glenbrook
Stewart
Mineral Peak 7,000 feet
DESOLATION WILDERNESS
Loon Lake
Stateline
SOUTH LAKE TAHOE
Zephyr Cove
Genoa
Camp Richardson
Minden
Gardnerville
Fallen Leaf Lake
Meyers
Echo Summit
East Fork Carson River
Kyburz
50
Twin Bridges
89
88
395
Woodfords
Carson Pass 8,573 feet
Kit Carson
88
GROVER HOT SPRINGS STATE PARK
89
Markleeville
208
ELDORADO NATIONAL FOREST
TOIYABE NATIONAL FOREST
4
Monitor Pass 8,314 feet
Topaz Lake
Mount Reba 8,758 feet
STANISLAUS NATIONAL FOREST
Pacific Grade Summit 8,050 feet
Ebbetts Pass 8,730 feet
Topaz

© AVALON TRAVEL PUBLISHING, INC.

CHAPTER D4

(CONTINUED ON NEXT PAGE)

1 Cold Creek

 8

There are four small campgrounds along Highway 89 between Sierraville and Truckee, all within close range of side trips to Webber Lake, Independence Lake, and Campbell Hot Springs in Sierraville. Cold Creek is set just downstream of the confluence of Cottonwood Creek and Cold Creek, at 5,800 feet in elevation.

Location: In Tahoe National Forest; map D4, grid a1.

Campsites, facilities: There are 13 sites for tents or RVs up to 22 feet long. Picnic tables and fire grills are provided. Drinking water and vault toilets are available. Supplies are available in Sierraville. Leashed pets are permitted.

Reservations, fees: Reserve at (877) 444-6777 ($8.65 reservation fee) or website: www.reserveusa.com; $10 per night, $5 for an extra vehicle. Open May through October.

Directions: From Truckee, drive north on Highway 89 for about 20 miles to the campground on the left side of the road. If you reach Sierraville, you have gone five miles too far.

Contact: Tahoe National Forest, Truckee Ranger District, tel. (530) 587-3558 or fax (530) 587-6914; California Land Management, tel. (530) 544-0426.

2 Upper Little Truckee

      7

This camp is set along the Little Truckee River at 6,100 feet, two miles from Stampede Reservoir. The Little Truckee is a pretty trout stream, with easy access not only from this campground, but also from another three miles northward along Highway 89, then from another seven miles to the west along Forest Road 7, the route to Webber Lake. It is only about a 10-minute drive from this camp to reach Stampede Reservoir to the east or Independence Lake to the west.

Location: On the Little Truckee River in Tahoe National Forest; map D4, grid a2.

Campsites, facilities: There are 26 sites for tents or RVs up to 22 feet long. Picnic tables and fire grills are provided. Drinking water and vault toilets are available. Supplies are available in Sierraville. Leashed pets are permitted.

Reservations, fees: Reserve at (877) 444-6777 ($8.65 reservation fee) or website: www.reserveusa.com; $10 per night, $5 for an extra vehicle. Open May through October.

Directions: From Truckee, drive north on Highway 89 for about 11 miles to the campground on the left, a short distance beyond Lower Little Truckee Camp.

Contact: Tahoe National Forest, Truckee Ranger District, tel. (530) 587-3558 or fax (530) 587-6914; California Land Management, tel. (530) 544-0426.

3 Lower Little Truckee

   7

This pretty camp is set along Highway 89 and the Little Truckee River at 6,000 feet, about two miles from Stampede Reservoir and about a quarter mile from Lower Little Truckee. For more information, see the entry for Upper Little Truckee.

Location: On the Little Truckee River in Tahoe National Forest; map D4, grid a2.

Campsites, facilities: There are 15 sites for tents or RVs up to 22 feet long. Picnic tables and fire grills are provided. Drinking water and vault toilets are available. Supplies are available in Sierraville. Leashed pets are permitted.

Reservations, fees: Reserve at (877) 444-6777 ($8.65 reservation fee) or website: www.reserveusa.com; $10 per night, $5 for an extra vehicle. Open May through October.

Directions: From Truckee, drive north on Highway 89 for about 12 miles to the campground on the left. If you reach Upper Little Truckee Camp, you have gone a halfmile too far.

Contact: Tahoe National Forest, Truckee Ranger District, tel. (530) 587-3558 or fax (530) 587-6914; California Land Management, tel. (530) 544-0426.

4 Logger

    7

Stampede is a huge lake by Sierra standards, covering 3,400 acres, the largest lake in the region after Lake Tahoe. It is set at 6,000 feet, surrounded by classic Sierra granite and pines, and is big and beautiful. The campground is also huge, set along the lake's southern shore, a few minutes drive from the Captain Roberts Boat Ramp. This camp is ideal for campers, boaters, and anglers. The lake is becoming one of the top fishing lakes in California for kokanee salmon (catchable only by trolling), and also has some large Mackinaw trout and a sprinkling of planter-sized rainbow trout. One problem at Stampede is receding water levels from midsummer through fall, a real pain, which puts the campsites some distance from the lake. However, the boat ramp has been extended to assist boaters during drawdowns.

Location: At Stampede Reservoir in Tahoe National Forest; map D4, grid a3.

Campsites, facilities: There are 252 sites for tents or RVs up to 32 feet long. Picnic tables and fire rings are provided. Drinking water, flush toilets, and a sanitary disposal station are available. A concrete boat ramp is available one mile from camp. A grocery store is within seven miles. Some facilities are wheelchair accessible. Leashed pets are permitted.

Reservations, fees: Reserve at (877) 444-6777 ($8.65 reservation fee) or website: www.reserveusa.com; $13 per night, $5 for an extra vehicle. Open May through October.

Directions: From Truckee, drive east on Interstate 80 for seven miles to the Boca-Hirschdale/County Road 270 exit. Take that exit and drive north on County Road 270 for about seven miles (past Boca Reservoir) to the junction with County Road S261 on the left. Turn left and drive 1.5 miles to the campground on the right.

Contact: Tahoe National Forest, Truckee Ranger District, tel. (530) 587-3558 or fax (530) 587-6914; California Land Management, tel. (530) 544-0426.

5 Emigrant Group Camp

    7

Emigrant Group Camp is set at a beautiful spot on Stampede Reservoir, near a point along a cove on the southeastern corner of the lake. There is a beautiful view of the lake from the point, and a boat ramp is two miles to the east. Elevation is 6,000 feet. See the entry for Logger for more information.

Location: At Stampede Reservoir in Tahoe National Forest; map D4, grid a3.

Campsites, facilities: There are two 25-person group sites and two 50-person group sites for tents or RVs up to 32 feet long. Picnic tables and fire grills are provided. Drinking water and vault toilets are available. Bring your own firewood. A three-lane concrete boat ramp is available. Some facilities are wheelchair accessible. Leashed pets are permitted.

Reservations, fees: Reserve at (877) 444-6777 ($8.65 reservation fee) or website: www.reserveusa.com; $55 to $110 group fee per night. Open May through September.

Directions: From Truckee, drive east on Interstate 80 for seven miles to the Boca-Hirschdale/County Road 270 exit. Take that exit and drive north on County Road 270 for about seven miles (past Boca Reservoir) to the junction with County Road S261 on the left. Turn left and drive 1.5 miles to the campground access road on the right. Turn right and drive one mile to the camp on the left.

Contact: Tahoe National Forest, Truckee Ranger District, tel. (530) 587-3558 or fax (530) 587-6914; California Land Management, tel. (530) 544-0426.

6 Sagehen Creek

  7

This is a small, primitive camp set at 6,500 feet beside little Sagehen Creek, just north of a miniature mountain range called the Sagehen Hills, which tops out at 7,707 feet. It is popular with hunters and with campers who want to avoid the crowds. Sagehen Creek is primarily used as an overflow site on popular weekends when the camps along Highway 89 and at Stampede, Boca, and Prosser Creek have filled.

Location: In Tahoe National Forest; map D4, grid b2.

Campsites, facilities: There are 10 sites for tents or RVs up to 16 feet long. Vault toilets are available. No drinking water is available. Garbage must be packed out. Leashed pets are permitted.

Reservations, fees: No reservations; no fee. Open June through October.

Directions: From Truckee, drive 8.5 miles north on Highway 89 to Sagehen Summit Road on the left. Turn left and drive four miles to the campground. A gate on the road a short distance from the camp is sometimes locked early and late in the season.

Contact: Tahoe National Forest, Truckee Ranger District, tel. (530) 587-3558 or fax (530) 587-6914.

7 Lakeside

  7

This primitive camp is in a deep cove in the northwestern end of Prosser Creek Reservoir, near the lake's headwaters. It is a gorgeous lake, set at 5,741 feet, and a 10-mph speed limit keeps the fast boats out. The adjacent shore is decent for hand-launched, car-top boats, providing the lake level is up, and a concrete boat ramp is a mile down the road. Lots of trout are stocked here every year, including 100,000 rainbow trout fingerlings added in an experiment by the Department of Fish and Game to see how fast they will grow. The trout fishing is often quite good after the ice breaks up in late spring; the lake is also popular with ice fishermen in the winter. Sound perfect? Unfortunately for many, the Prosser ORV Park is nearby and can be noisy.

Location: On Prosser Creek Reservoir in Tahoe National Forest; map D4, grid b3.

Campsites, facilities: There are 30 sites for tents or RVs up to 33 feet long and one group site. Drinking water and vault toilets are available. A boat ramp is available nearby. Leashed pets are permitted.

Reservations, fees: No reservations; $8 per night. Open June through October.

Directions: From Truckee, drive north on Highway 89 for three miles to the campground entrance road on the right. Turn right and drive less than a mile to the campground.

Contact: Tahoe National Forest, Truckee Ranger District, tel. (530) 587-3558 or fax (530) 587-6914; California Land management, (530) 544-0426.

8 Boyington Mill

     7

Boyington Mill is a little Forest Service camp set between Boca Reservoir to the nearby south and Stampede Reservoir to the nearby north, along a small inlet creek to the adjacent Little Truckee River. It is used as an overflow camp when lakeside campsites at Boca, Stampede, and Prosser have already filled. The elevation is 5,700 feet.

Location: On the Little Truckee River in Tahoe National Forest; map D4, grid b3.

Campsites, facilities: There are 10 sites for tents or RVs up to 32 feet long. Picnic tables are provided. Vault toilets are available. No drinking water is available. Leashed pets are permitted.

Reservations, fees: No reservations; $10 per night, $5 for an extra vehicle. Open May through October.

Directions: From Truckee, go east on Interstate 80 for seven miles. Take the Boca-Hirschdale exit and drive north on County Road 270 for four miles (past Boca Reservoir) to the campground.

Contact: Tahoe National Forest, Truckee Ranger District, tel. (530) 587-3558 or fax (530) 587-6914; California Land Management, tel. (530) 544-0426.

9 Boca Rest Campground

      7

The Boca Dam faces Interstate 80, so the lake is out of sight of the zillions of highway travelers who would otherwise certainly stop here. Those who do stop find that the lake is very pretty, set at 5,700 feet in elevation and covering 1,000 acres with deep, blue water. This camp is on the lake's northeastern shore, not far from the inlet to the Little Truckee River. The boat ramp is some distance away.

Location: On Boca Reservoir in Tahoe National Forest; map D4, grid b3.

Campsites, facilities: There are 31 sites for tents or RVs up to 22 feet long. Picnic tables and fire grills are provided. Drinking water and vault toilets are available. A hand-launch boat ramp is also available. A concrete boat ramp is three miles away on the southwest shore of Boca Reservoir. Truckee is the nearest place for telephones and supplies. Leashed pets are permitted.

Reservations, fees: No reservations; $8 per night, $5 for an extra vehicle. Open May through October.

Directions: From Truckee, travel east on Interstate 80 for seven miles to the Boca-Hirschdale exit. Take that exit and drive north on County Road 270 for about 2.5 miles to the campground on the right side of the road.

Contact: Tahoe National Forest, Truckee Ranger District, tel. (530) 587-3558 or fax (530) 587-6914; California Land Management, tel. (530) 544-0426.

10 Boca

     7

Boca Reservoir is known as a "big fish factory," with some huge but rare brown trout and rainbow trout sprinkled among a growing fishery for kokanee salmon. The lake is set at 5,700 feet, a Sierra gem within a few miles of Interstate 80. The camp is the best choice for anglers/boaters, with a launch ramp set just down from the campground.

Location: On Boca Reservoir in Tahoe National Forest; map D4, grid b3.

Campsites, facilities: There are 22 sites for tents or RVs up to 16 feet long. Picnic tables and fire grills are provided. Vault toilets are available. No drinking water is available. A concrete boat ramp is north of the campground on Boca Reservoir. Truckee is the nearest place for telephones and supplies. Leashed pets are permitted.

Reservations, fees: No reservations; $10 per night, $5 for an extra vehicle. Open May through October.

Directions: From Truckee, travel east on Interstate 80 for seven miles to the Boca-

Hirschdale exit. Take that exit and drive north for a short distance to County Road 73 and continue for one mile to the campground on the right side of the road.

Contact: Tahoe National Forest, Truckee Ranger District, tel. (530) 587-3558 or fax (530) 587-6914; California Land Management, tel. (530) 544-0426.

11 Coachland RV Park

 6

Truckee is the gateway to recreation at North Tahoe. Within minutes are Donner Lake, Prosser Creek Reservoir, Boca Reservoir, Stampede Reservoir, and the Truckee River. Squaw Valley is a short distance to the south off Highway 89, and Northstar is just off Highway 267. The park is set in a wooded area near the junction of Interstate 80 and Highway 89, providing easy access. The downtown Truckee area (with restaurants) is nearby. This is one of the only parks in the area that is open year-round. The elevation is 6,000 feet.

Location: In Truckee; map D4, grid b2.

Campsites, facilities: There are 131 sites for trailers or RVs up to 40 feet long. Picnic tables, restrooms, showers, coin laundry, cable TV, modem hookups, and propane are available. Some facilities are wheelchair accessible. Leashed pets are permitted.

Reservations, fees: Reservations are recommended; $25 per night, $1 per night for each extra vehicle. Major credit cards accepted. Open year-round.

Directions: From Truckee, drive north on Highway 89 for a short distance to the park at 10500 Highway 89 on the left side of the road.

Contact: Coachland RV Park, tel. (530) 587-3071 or fax (530) 587-6976.

12 Martis Creek Lake

 7

If only this lake weren't so often windy in the afternoon, it would be heaven to fly fishers in float tubes, casting out with sinking lines and leech patterns, using a strip retrieve. To some it's heaven anyway, with Lahontan cutthroat trout ranging to 25 inches here. This is a special catch-and-release fishery where anglers are permitted to use only artificial lures with single, barbless hooks. The setting is somewhat sparse and open, a small lake on the eastern edge of the Martis Valley. No motors are permitted at the lake, making it ideal (when the wind is down) for float tubes or prams. The lake level can fluctuate daily, which along with the wind, can be frustrating for those who show up expecting automatic perfection; that just isn't the way it is out there. The elevation is 5,800 feet.

Location: Near Truckee; map D4, grid b3.

Campsites, facilities: There are 25 sites for tents or RVs up to 30 feet long. Picnic tables and fire grills are provided. Drinking water, vault toilets, tent pads, and pay phones are available. Some facilities are wheelchair accessible. Supplies are available six minutes away in Truckee. Leashed pets are permitted.

Reservations, fees: No reservations except for wheelchair-accessible sites; $10 per night. Open May through mid-November.

Directions: From Truckee, drive south on Highway 267 for about three miles (past the airport) to the entrance road to the lake on the left. Turn left and drive another 2.5 miles to the campground at the end of the road.

Contact: U.S. Army Corps of Engineers, Sacramento District, tel. (530) 639-2342 or fax (530) 639-2175.

13 Donner Memorial State Park

 9

The remarkable beauty of Donner Lake often evokes a deep, heartfelt response. The lake is big, three miles long and three-quarters of a mile wide, gemlike blue, and set near the Sierra crest at 5,900 feet. The area is well developed, with a number of cabins and access roads, and this state park is the feature destination. Located along the southeastern end of the lake, it is extremely pretty. Fishing is good here (typically only in the early morning), trolling for kokanee salmon or rainbow trout, with big Mackinaw and brown trout providing wild cards. In the summer a wind often comes up in the early afternoon. In the winter a good cross-country ski trail is available. Campers get free admission to Emigrant Trail Museum.

Location: On Donner Lake; map D4, grid c2.

Campsites, facilities: There are 147 sites for tents or RVs up to 28 feet long and trailers up to 24 feet long, and two hike-in/bike-in sites. Picnic tables and fire grills are provided. Drinking water and vault toilets are available. Supplies are available about one mile away in Truckee. Facilities are wheelchair accessible. Leashed pets are permitted.

Reservations, fees: Reserve at (800) 444-PARK (800-444-7275) or website: www.ReserveAmerica.com; $12 per night, $1 per person for hike-in or bike-in sites. Open mid-May to mid-October, weather permitting.

Directions: From Auburn, drive east on Interstate 80 just past Donner Lake to the Donner State Park exit. Turn south on Donner Pass Road and drive a half mile to the park entrance and the southeast end of the lake.

Contact: Donner Memorial State Park, tel. (530) 582-7892, tel. (530) 582-7894 or fax (530) 583-7893.

14 Granite Flat

 6

This camp is set along the Truckee River at 5,800 feet, in an area known for a ton of traffic on adjacent Highway 89, as well as decent trout fishing and, in the spring and early summer, rafting. It is about a 15-minute drive to Squaw Valley or Lake Tahoe. A bike route is also available along the Truckee River out of Tahoe City.

Location: On the Truckee River in Tahoe National Forest; map D4, grid c2.

Campsites, facilities: There are 68 sites for tents or RVs and seven walk-in tent sites. Picnic tables and fire grills are provided. Drinking water and vault toilets are available. Some facilities are wheelchair accessible. Leashed pets are permitted.

Reservations, fees: Reserve at (877) 444-6777 ($8.65 reservation fee) or website: www.reserveusa.com; $12 per night, $5 for an extra vehicle. Open May through October.

Directions: From Truckee, drive south on Highway 89 for 1.5 miles to the campground entrance on the right.

Contact: Tahoe National Forest, Truckee Ranger District, tel. (530) 587-3558 or fax (530) 587-6914; California Land Management, tel. (530) 544-0426.

15 Goose Meadows

    6

There are three campgrounds set along the Truckee River off Highway 89 between Truckee and Tahoe City. Goose Meadows provides good fishing access with decent prospects, despite the high number of vehicles roaring past on the adjacent highway. This stretch of river is also popular for rafting. The elevation is 5,800 feet.

Location: On the Truckee River in Tahoe National Forest; map D4, grid c2.

Campsites, facilities: There are 24 sites for tents or RVs up to 30 feet long. Picnic tables and fire grills are provided. Drinking water (hand-pumped) and vault toilets are available. Supplies are available in Truckee and Tahoe City. Leashed pets are permitted.

Reservations, fees: Reserve at (877) 444-6777 ($8.65 reservation fee) or website: www.reserveusa.com; $10 per night, $5 for an extra vehicle. Open May through October, weather permitting.

Directions: From Truckee, drive south on Highway 89 for four miles to the campground entrance on the left (river) side of the highway.

Contact: Tahoe National Forest, Truckee Ranger District, tel. (530) 587-3558 or fax (530) 587-6914; California Land Management, tel. (530) 544-0426.

16 Silver Creek

     8

This pretty campground is set near where Deer Creek enters the Truckee River. The trout fishing is often good in this area, and side trips include a good hike up the trail that runs along Deer Creek, with the trailhead right at the camp. This is one of three campgrounds along Highway 89 and the Truckee River, between Truckee and Tahoe City. The elevation is 5,800 feet.

Location: On the Truckee River in Tahoe National Forest; map D4, grid d2.

Campsites, facilities: There are 21 sites for tents or RVs up to 40 feet long and seven walk-in sites. Picnic tables and fire grills are provided. Drinking water and vault toilets are available. Supplies are available in Truckee and Tahoe City. Leashed pets are permitted.

Reservations, fees: Reserve at (877) 444-6777 ($8.65 reservation fee) or website: www.reserveusa.com; $10 per night, $5 for an extra vehicle. Open June through September.

Directions: From Truckee, drive south on Highway 89 for six miles to the campground entrance on the river side of the highway.

Contact: Tahoe National Forest, Truckee Ranger District, tel. (530) 587-3558 or fax (530) 587-6914. California Land Management, tel. (530) 544-0426.

17 Sandy Beach Campground

       8

Sandy Beach Campground is set at 6,200 feet near the northwest shore of Lake Tahoe. A nearby boat ramp provides access to one of the better fishing areas of the lake for Mackinaw trout. The water in Tahoe is always cold, and though a lot of people will get suntans on beaches next to the lake, swimmers need to be members of the Polar Bear Club. A short drive to the east will take you past the town of Kings Beach and into Nevada, where there

are some small casinos near the shore of Crystal Bay.

Location: On Lake Tahoe; map D4, grid d3.

Campsites, facilities: There are 44 sites with full or partial hookups for tents or RVs up to 40 feet long. Picnic tables and barbecues are provided. Drinking water, showers, flush toilets, and laundry room are available. A free public boat ramp is available half a block away. A grocery store and propane gas are available nearby. Leashed pets are permitted.

Reservations, fees: Reservations are accepted; $20 to $25 per night up to six people with two vehicles, two dog limit. Major credit cards accepted. Open May through October.

Directions: From Truckee, drive south on Highway 267 to Highway 28. Turn right and drive one mile to the park on the right side of the road (entrance well signed).

Contact: Sandy Beach Campground, P.O. Box 6868, Tahoe City, CA 96145; tel. (530) 546-7682.

18 Tahoe State Recreation Area

     9

This is a popular summer-only campground at the northwest side of Lake Tahoe. The Tahoe State Recreation Area covers a large area just west of Highway 28 near Tahoe City. There are opportunities for hiking and horseback riding nearby (though not right at the park). A boat ramp is two miles to the northwest at nearby Lake Forest, and bike rentals are available in Tahoe City for rides along Highway 89 near the shore of the lake.

Location: On Lake Tahoe; map D4, grid d2.

Campsites, facilities: There are 38 sites for tents or RVs up to 24 feet long. Picnic tables, food lockers, barbecues, and fire pits are provided. Drinking water, vault toilets, and coin-operated showers are available. Firewood, other supplies, and a coin laundry are available within walking distance. Leashed pets are permitted.

Reservations, fees: Reserve at (800) 444-PARK (800-444-7275) or website: www.ReserveAmerica.com; $12 per night. Open May through October, weather permitting.

Directions: From Truckee, drive south on Highway 89 through Tahoe City. Turn north on Highway 28 and drive 0.9 mile to the campground entrance on the right side of the road.

Contact: Tahoe State Recreation Area, tel. (530) 583-3074 or tel. (530) 525-7232.

19 Lake Forest Campground

      8

The northwest shore of Lake Tahoe provides beautiful lookouts and excellent boating access. The latter is a highlight of this camp, with a boat ramp nearby. From here it is a short cruise to Dollar Point and around the corner north to Carnelian Bay, one of the better stretches of water for trout fishing. The elevation is 6,200 feet.

Location: On Lake Tahoe; map D4, grid d3.

Campsites, facilities: There are 20 sites for tents or RVs up to 20 feet long. Picnic tables and fire grills are provided. Drinking water and vault toilets are available. Some facilities are wheelchair accessible. A grocery store, coin laundry, and propane gas are available within 2.5 miles.

Reservations, fees: No reservations; $15 per night. Major credit cards accepted. Open April through October.

Directions: From Truckee, drive south on Highway 89 through Tahoe City. Turn north on Highway 28 and drive two miles to the campground entrance road (Lake Forest Road).

Contact: Tahoe City Public Utility District, Parks & Rec, tel. (530) 583-3796, ext. 29, or fax (530) 583-1475.

20 William Kent

    8

William Kent camp is a little pocket of peace set near the busy traffic of Highway 89 on the western shore corridor. It is on the west side of the highway, meaning visitors have to cross the highway in order to get lakeside access.

The elevation is 6,300 feet, and the camp is wooded with primarily lodgepole pines. The drive here is awesome or ominous, depending on how you look at it, with the view of incredible Lake Tahoe to the east, the deepest blue in the world. But you often have a lot of time to look at it, since traffic rarely moves quickly.

Location: Near Lake Tahoe in the Lake Tahoe Basin; map D4, grid d2.

Campsites, facilities: There are 55 tent sites and 40 sites for RVs up to 57 feet long. Picnic tables and fire grills are provided. Drinking water, flush toilets, and sanitary disposal station are available. A grocery store, coin laundry, and propane gas are available nearby. Leashed pets are permitted.

Reservations, fees: Reserve at (877) 444-6777 ($8.65 reservation fee) or website: www.reserveusa.com; $14 per night, $5 per night for each extra vehicle. Open June through September.

Directions: From Truckee, drive south on Highway 89 to Tahoe City. Turn south on Highway 89 and drive three miles to the campground entrance on the right side of the road.

Contact: Lake Tahoe Basin Management Unit, Visitors Center, tel. (530) 573-2674, or fax (530) 573-2693; California Land Management, tel. (530) 583-3642.

21 Sugar Pine Point State Park

    10

This is one of three beautiful and popular state parks on the west shore of Lake Tahoe. It is just north of Meeks Bay on General Creek, with almost two miles of lake frontage available, though the campground is on the opposite side of Highway 89. A pretty trail is routed four miles along the creek up to Lost Lake, just outside the northern boundary of the Desolation Wilderness. The elevation is 6,200 feet.

Location: On Lake Tahoe; map D4, grid d2.

Campsites, facilities: There are 175 sites for tents or RVs up to 32 feet long and trailers up to 26 feet long. There are also 10 group sites available. Picnic tables and fire rings are provided. Drinking water, restrooms, flush toilets, coin-operated showers (except in winter), and sanitary disposal station are available. A grocery store, coin laundry, and propane gas are available nearby. Some facilities are wheelchair accessible. Leashed pets are permitted.

Reservations, fees: Reserve at (800) 444-PARK (800-444-7275) or website: www.ReserveAmerica.com; $12 per night, $37 per night group sites. Open year-round.

Directions: From Truckee, drive south on Highway 89 through Tahoe City. Continue south on Highway 89 and drive 9.3 miles to the campground (signed) on the right (west) side of the road.

Contact: Sugar Pine Point State Park, tel. (530) 525-7982 or tel. (530) 525-7232.

22 Kaspian

 7

As gorgeous and as huge as Lake Tahoe is, there are relatively few camps or even restaurants with lakeside settings. This is one of the few. Kaspian is set along the west shore of the lake at 6,235 feet in elevation, near the little town of Tahoe Pines. A Forest Service road (03) is available adjacent to the camp on the west side of Highway 89, routed west into national forest (becoming quite rough) to a trailhead. From there you can hike up to Barker Peak (8,166 feet) for incredible views of Lake Tahoe, as well as access to the Pacific Crest Trail.

Location: On Lake Tahoe; map D4, grid e2.

Campsites, facilities: There are 10 sites for tents. RVs up to 20 feet long may use the parking lot on a space-available basis. Picnic tables and fire grills are provided. Drinking water and vault toilets are available. A grocery store, coin laundry, and propane gas are available nearby. Leashed pets are permitted.

Reservations, fees: Reserve at (877) 444-6777 ($8.65 reservation fee) or website: www.reserveusa.com.; $12 per night, $5 per night for each extra vehicle (unless towed). Open May through September.

Directions: From Truckee, drive south on Highway 89 to Tahoe City. Turn south on Highway 89 and drive four miles to the campground (signed) on the east side of the road.

Contact: Lake Tahoe Basin Management Unit, Visitors Center, tel. (530) 573-2674, or fax (530) 573-2693; California Land Management, tel. (530) 583-3642.

23 Meeks Bay

 9

Meeks Bay is a beautiful spot along the western shore of Lake Tahoe. A bicycle trail is available nearby and is routed along the lake's shore, but it requires occasionally crossing busy Highway 89.

Location: On Lake Tahoe; map D4, grid e2.

Campsites, facilities: There are 40 sites for tents or RVs up to 20 feet long. Picnic tables and fire grills are provided. Drinking water and vault toilets are available. Coin laundry and groceries are available nearby. Leashed pets are permitted.

Reservations, fees: Reserve at (877) 444-6777 ($8.65 reservation fee) or website: www.reserveusa.com; $14 to $16 per night, $5 per night for each extra vehicle (if not towed). Open May through September.

Directions: In South Lake Tahoe at the junction of Highway 89 and U.S. 50, turn north on Highway 89 and drive 17 miles to the campground.

Contact: Lake Tahoe Basin Management Unit, Visitors Center, tel. (530) 573-2674, or fax (530) 573-2693; California Land Management, tel. (530) 583-3642.

24 Meeks Bay Resort & Marina

    7

Prime access for boating makes this a camp of choice for the boater/camper at Lake Tahoe. A boat launch is not only nearby, but access to Rubicon Bay and beyond to breathtaking Emerald Bay is possible, a six-mile trip one way for boats large enough and fast enough to make it. The resort is adjacent to a 20-mile paved bike trail.

Location: On Lake Tahoe; map D4, grid e2.

Campsites, facilities: There are 28 sites for RVs, 10 with full hookups. Showers, flush toilets, picnic tables, and fire grills are provided. Coin laundry, snack bar, gift shop, and groceries are available. A boat ramp and boat slips are also available. No pets are allowed.

Reservations, fees: Reservations are accepted at tel. (877) 326-3357; $25 to $30 per night, $5 day-use fee, $20 per night for boat slips. Major credit cards accepted. Open June through September.

Directions: In South Lake Tahoe at the junction of Highway 89 and U.S. 50, turn north on Highway 89 and drive 17 miles to the campground.

Contact: Meeks Bay Resort & Marina, tel. (530) 525-6946 or tel. (877) 326-3357.

25 D. L. Bliss State Park

     10

D. L. Bliss State Park is set on one of Lake Tahoe's most beautiful stretches of shoreline, from Emerald Point at the mouth of Emerald Bay on northward to Rubicon Point, spanning some three miles. The camp is at the north end of the park, the sites nestled amid pine trees, with 80 percent of the campsites within a half mile to mile of the beach. A trail from the camp is routed south to Emerald Point (6,232 feet), where there is a beautiful view of the lake and beyond to the surrounding mountain rim, an awesome sight in early summer when it is still covered with snow.

One great hike for youngsters is the Balancing Rock Trail, where after about 40 yards, you arrive at this 130-ton, oblong-shaped granite boulder that is set on a tiny perch, and the whole thing seems to defy gravity. Some day it has to fall, right? Not yet. Another fantastic hike is the Rubicon Trail, a meandering path just above the southwest shore of Lake Tahoe, wandering through pine, cedars, and firs, with occasional breaks for panoramas of the lake. Don't be surprised if you are joined by a chipmunk circus, many begging, sitting upright, hoping for their nut for the day. The Rubicon Trail runs all the way past Emerald Point to Emerald Bay.

Location: On Lake Tahoe; map D4, grid f2.

Campsites, facilities: There are 168 sites for tents or RVs up to 18 feet long and trailers up to 15 feet long, and a group site for up to 50 people. Picnic tables, fire grills, and food lockers are provided. Restrooms, drinking water, showers, and flush toilets are available. Leashed pets are permitted at campsites only.

Reservations, fees: Reserve at (800) 444-PARK (800-444-7275) or website: www.ReserveAmerica.com; $12 per night, $37 per night for group site. Open May through mid-October, weather permitting.

Directions: In South Lake Tahoe at the junction of Highway 89 and U.S. 50, turn north on Highway 89 and drive 10.5 miles to the state park turnoff on the right side of the road. Turn right (east) and drive to the park entrance.

Contact: D. L. Bliss State Park, tel. (530) 525-7277 or tel. (530) 525-7232.

26 Wentworth Springs 4-wheel-drive

    7

There is one reason people come here: to set up a base camp for an OHV adventure, whether they are the owners of four-wheel drives, all-terrain vehicles, or dirt bikes. A network of roads lead from this camp, passable only by these vehicles, roads that would flat-out destroy your average car. The camp is set deep in Eldorado National Forest, at 6,200 feet in elevation. While the north end of Loon Lake is a mile to the east, the road there is extremely rough (perfect, right?). The road is gated along the lake, preventing access to this camp for those who drive directly to Loon Lake.

Location: Near Loon Lake in Eldorado National Forest; map D4, grid e0.

Campsites, facilities: There are eight tent sites. Picnic tables and fire grills are provided. Vault toilets are available. No drinking water is available. Garbage must be packed out. Leashed pets are permitted.

Reservations, fees: No reservations; no fee. Open June through October.

Directions: From Sacramento, drive east on U.S. 50 to Riverton and the junction with Ice House Road/Soda Springs-Riverton Road on the left. Turn left and drive 30 miles to the junction with Forest Road 30. Bear left and drive 3.5 miles to Forest Road 33. Turn right and drive seven miles to the campground on the left side of the road. (The access road is suitable for four-wheel-drive vehicles and off-highway motorcycles only.)

Contact: Eldorado Information Center, (530) 644-6048; Eldorado National Forest, Pacific Ranger District, tel. (530) 644-2349 or fax (530) 644-5405.

Red Fir Group Camp

 6

This is a pretty, wooded camp, ideal for medium-sized groups. It is across the road from the water, offering a secluded, quiet spot. Lake access is a short hike away. See the entry for Loon Lake Northshore for more information. The elevation is 6,500 feet.

Location: On Loon Lake in Eldorado National Forest; map D4, grid f0.

Campsites, facilities: This group site will accommodate up to six vehicles and 25 people. Drinking water, vault toilets, fire rings,

and grills are provided. Leashed pets are permitted.

Reservations, fees: Reserve at (877) 444-6777 ($8.65 reservation fee) or website: www.reserveusa.com; $35 per night, $5 for an extra vehicle. Open June through September.

Directions: From Sacramento, drive east on U.S. 50 to Riverton and the junction with Ice House Road/Soda Springs-Riverton Road on the left. Turn left and drive 34 miles to a fork at the foot of Loon Lake. Turn left and drive three miles to the campground (just beyond the Loon Lake Northshore Camp).

Contact: Eldorado Information Center, tel. (530) 644-6048; Eldorado National Forest, Pacific Ranger District, tel. (530) 644-2349 or fax (530) 644-5405.

28 Loon Lake Northshore

 8

This camp is for tents only, where the waterfront sites provide an extremely pretty setting on the northwestern shore of Loon Lake, even though there are few facilities and no boat ramp. (The boat ramp is near the Loon Lake campground and picnic area at the south end of the lake.) For more information about Loon Lake, see the entries for Pleasant Hike-In/Boat-In and Loon Lake.

Location: On Loon Lake in Eldorado National Forest; map D4, grid f0.

Campsites, facilities: There are 15 sites for tents or self-contained RVs. Picnic tables, fire rings, and grills are provided. Vault toilets are available. No drinking water is available. Leashed pets are permitted.

Reservations, fees: No reservations; $5 per night, $5 for an extra vehicle. Open June through September.

Directions: From Sacramento, drive east on U.S. 50 to Riverton and the junction with Ice House Road/Soda Springs-Riverton Road on the left. Turn left and drive 34 miles to a fork at the foot of Loon Lake. Turn left and drive three miles to the campground.

Contact: Eldorado Information Center, (530) 644-6048; Eldorado National Forest, Pacific Ranger District, tel. (530) 644-2349 or fax (530) 644-5405.

29 Pleasant Hike-In/Boat-In

      9

This premium Sierra camp, hike-in or boat-in only, is set on the remote northeast shore of Loon Lake at 6,378 feet in elevation. In many ways this makes for a perfect short vacation. After reaching the camp a trail is available routed east for four miles past Buck Island Lake (6,436 feet) and Rockbound Lake (6,529 feet), set just inside the northern border of the Desolation Wilderness. When the trail is clear of snow, this makes for a fantastic day hike; a wilderness permit is required if staying overnight inside the wilderness boundary.

Location: On Loon Lake in Eldorado National Forest; map D4, grid f0.

Campsites, facilities: There are 10 boat-in or hike-in tent sites. Picnic tables and fire rings are provided. Vault toilets are available. No drinking water is available. Garbage must be packed out. The camp is accessible by boat or trail only. Leashed pets are permitted.

Reservations, fees: No reservations; no fee. Open June through October.

Directions: From Sacramento, drive east on U.S. 50 to Riverton and the junction with Ice House Road/Soda Springs-Riverton Road on the left. Turn left and drive 34 miles to a fork at the foot of Loon Lake. Turn right and drive a mile to the Loon Lake Picnic Area or boat ramp. Either hike or boat 2.5 miles to the campground on the northeast shore of the lake.

Contact: Eldorado Information Center, (530) 644-6048; Eldorado National Forest, Pacific Ranger District, tel. (530) 644-2349 or fax (530) 644-5405.

30 Loon Lake

    9

Loon Lake is set near the Sierra crest at 6,400 feet, covering 600 acres with depths up to 130 feet. This is the lake's primary campground, and it is easy to see why, with a picnic area, beach (includes a small unit to change your clothes in), and boat ramp adjacent to the camp. The lake provides good trout fishing, and once the access road is clear of snow, the lake can be stocked every week of summer. Afternoon winds drive anglers off the lake but are cheered by sailboarders. An excellent trail is also available here, with the hike routed along the lake's eastern shore to Pleasant Hike-In/Boat-In where there's a trailhead for the Desolation Wilderness.

Location: In Eldorado National Forest; map D4, grid f0.

Campsites, facilities: There are 53 sites for tents or RVs up to 22 feet long. Picnic tables and fire grills are provided. Drinking water and vault toilets are available. A boat ramp and swimming beach are nearby. Some facilities are wheelchair accessible. Leashed pets are permitted.

Reservations, fees: Reserve at (877) 444-6777 ($8.65 reservation fee) or website: www.reserveusa.com; $13 per night (single), $20 per night (double), $5 for a third vehicle. Open June through early September.

Directions: From Sacramento, drive east on U.S. 50 to Riverton and the junction with Ice House Road/Soda Springs-Riverton Road on the left. Turn left and drive 34 miles to a fork at the foot of Loon Lake. Turn right and drive one mile to the Loon Lake Picnic Area or boat ramp.

Contact: Eldorado Information Center, (530) 644-6048; Eldorado National Forest, Pacific Ranger District, tel. (530) 644-2349 or fax (530) 644-5405.

31 Emerald Bay State Park and Boat-In

    10

This is one of the most beautiful and popular state parks on the planet. The campground is set at Eagle Point, near the mouth of Emerald Bay on Lake Tahoe, a place of rare, divine beauty. Although the high number of people at Lake Tahoe, and at this park in particular, present inevitable problems, the 20 boat-in sites provide a remarkable solution. There may be no more beautiful place anywhere to run a boat than in Emerald Bay, with its deep cobalt-blue waters, awesome surrounding ridgelines, glimpses of Lake Tahoe out the mouth of the bay, and even a little island. The park also has several short hiking trails.

Location: On Lake Tahoe; map D4, grid f2.

Campsites, facilities: There are 100 sites for tents or RVs up to 21 feet long and trailers up to 18 feet long. Picnic tables and fire grills are provided. Drinking water, restrooms, flush toilets, and coin-operated showers are available. There are also 22 boat-in sites available on the north side of the bay with water and toilets provided. Leashed pets are permitted except on the beach.

Reservations, fees: Reserve at (800) 444-PARK (800-444-7275) or website: www.ReserveAmerica.com; $12 per night. No reservations for boat-in sites; $10 per night. Open late May through early September.

Directions: In South Lake Tahoe at the junction of Highway 89 and U.S. 50, turn north on Highway 89 and drive 6.5 miles to the state park entrance turnoff on the right side of the road.

Contact: Emerald Bay State Park, tel. (530) 541-3030, or tel. (530) 525-7277.

32 Camp Richardson Resort

    7

Camp Richardson Resort is within minutes of boating, biking, gambling and, in the winter, skiing. It's a take-your-pick deal. With cabins and a hopping restaurant and nightclub also on the property, this is a place that offers one big package. The campsites are set in the woods, not on the lake itself. From here you can gain access to an excellent bike route that runs for three miles, then loops around by the lake for another three miles, most of it flat and easy, all of it beautiful. Expect company. The elevation is 6,300 feet.

Location: On Lake Tahoe; map D4, grid f3.

Campsites, facilities: There are 223 sites for tents and 112 sites for RVs up to 35 feet, some with full or partial hookups. Picnic tables and fire pits are provided. Restrooms, drinking water, showers, flush toilets, modem hookups, sanitary disposal station, and playground are available. A boat ramp, boat rentals, groceries, and propane gas are available nearby. Some facilities are wheelchair accessible. No pets are allowed.

Reservations, fees: Reservations are recommended at tel. (800) 544-1801; $17 to $25 per night. Major credit cards accepted. Open June through October.

Directions: In South Lake Tahoe at the junction of Highway 89 and U.S. 50, turn north on Highway 89 and drive 2.5 miles to the resort on the right side of the road.

Contact: Camp Richardson Resort, tel. (800) 544-1801 or (530) 541-1801 or fax. (530) 541-1802; website: www.camprichardson.com.

33 Camp Shelley

       7

This privately owned campground is set near South Lake Tahoe, within close range of an outstanding bicycle trail. Nearby to the west is the drive to Inspiration Point and the incredible lookout of Emerald Bay, as well as the parking area for the short hike to Eagle Falls. Nearby to the east are Fallen Leaf Lake and the south shore of Lake Tahoe.

Location: Near Lake Tahoe in the Lake Tahoe Basin; map D4, grid f2.

Campsites, facilities: There are 26 sites for tents or RVs up to 22 feet long. Picnic tables and fire grills are provided. Drinking water and vault toilets are available. Some facilities are wheelchair accessible. A boat ramp, groceries, and propane gas are available nearby at Camp Richardson. Leashed pets are permitted.

Reservations, fees: Reservations can be made in person, Monday through Friday, 9 a.m. to 4 p.m. at the Livermore Recreation and Park District Office, 71 Trevarno Road, Livermore, CA 94550. Reservations can also be made at the campground office, which is intermittently staffed during the season; $25 fee per night, ($18 for Livermore residents). Major credit cards accepted. Open mid-June through Labor Day.

Directions: In South Lake Tahoe at the junction of U.S. 50 and Highway 89, turn north on Highway 89, drive 2.5 miles to Camp Richardson, and then continue for 1.3 miles to the sign for Mount Tallac. Turn left on Mount Tallac Trailhead Road and drive to the campground on the right.

Contact: Livermore Area Recreation and Park District, tel. (925) 373-5700.

34 Fallen Leaf Campground

     7

This is a large "tent city" near the north shore of Fallen Leaf Lake, set at 6,337 feet. The lake is almost as deep blue as nearby Lake Tahoe. It's a big lake, three miles long, and also quite deep, 430 feet at its deepest point. The campground is operated by the concessionaire, which provides a variety of recreational opportunities, including a boat ramp and horseback riding rentals. Fishing is best in the fall for kokanee salmon. Because Fallen Leaf Lake is circled by forest and much of it is private property, you will need a boat to fish or ex-plore the lake. A visitor center is available north of the Fallen Leaf Lake turnoff on Highway 89.

Location: In the Lake Tahoe Basin; map D4, grid g2.

Campsites, facilities: There are 75 sites for tents and 130 sites for tents or RVs up to 40 feet long. Picnic tables and fire grills are provided. Drinking water and vault toilets are available. A boat ramp, coin laundry, and supplies are available nearby. Leashed pets are permitted.

Reservations, fees: Reserve at (877) 444-6777 ($8.65 reservation fee) or website: www.reserveusa.com; $15 per night, $5 per night for each extra vehicle (unless towed). Open May through October, weather permitting.

Directions: In South Lake Tahoe at the junction of U.S. 50 and Highway 89, turn north on Highway 89 and drive two miles to the Fallen Leaf Lake turnoff. Turn left and drive 1.5 miles to the campground.

Contact: Lake Tahoe Basin Management Unit, Visitors Center, tel. (530) 573-2674, or fax (530) 573-2693; California Land Management, tel. (530) 544-0426.

35 Chris Haven Mobile Home and RV Park

   5

This is an RV-only park that is set within the boundaries of a mobile home park, within close range of the casinos to the east.

Location: Near South Lake Tahoe; map D4, grid g3.

Campsites, facilities: There are 30 sites with full hookups for RVs up to 40 feet. Patios, restrooms, showers, modem hookups, and a coin laundry are available. Some facilities are wheelchair accessible. Leashed pets are permitted.

Reservations, fees: Reservations are recommended; $26 per night. Major credit cards accepted. Open year-round.

Directions: Entering South

Lake Tahoe on U.S. 50, drive east to E Street (a half mile south of the junction of U.S. 50 and Highway 89). Turn left on E Street and drive one block to the park on the right.

Contact: Chris Haven Mobile Home and RV Park, tel. (530) 541-1895 or fax (530) 541-0525; website: www.chrishaven.com

Campground by the Lake

    5

This city-operated campground at South Lake Tahoe is set at 6,200 feet and is primarily designed for RV drivers on tour.

Location: Near Lake Tahoe; map D4, grid g4.

Campsites, facilities: There are 170 sites for tents or RVs up to 32 feet long. No hookups are available. Picnic tables and fire grills are provided. Drinking water, flush toilets, showers, sanitary disposal station, playground, and a boat ramp are available. Some facilities are wheelchair accessible. Supplies and a coin laundry are nearby. Pets are permitted with proof of vaccinations.

Reservations, fees: Reservations are accepted; $11 to $20 per night (two-night minimum on holidays), $2 for a second vehicle, $11 for trailers, $1 pet fee. Major credit cards accepted. Open April through September.

Directions: Entering South Lake Tahoe on U.S. 50, drive east on U.S. 50 to Rufus Allen Boulevard. Turn right and drive a quarter mile to the campground on the right side of the road.

Contact: Campground by the Lake, tel. (530) 542-6096 or tel. (530) 542-6055; website:www.ci. south-lake-tahoe.ca.us.

KOA South Lake Tahoe

     5

Like so many KOA camps, this one is on the outskirts of a major destination area, in this case, South Lake Tahoe. It is within close range of gambling, fishing, hiking, and bike rentals. The camp is set at 6,300 feet.

Location: Near Lake Tahoe; map D4, grid g3.

Campsites, facilities: There are 16 sites for tents and 52 sites with full hookups for RVs up to 30 feet long. Picnic tables and fire grills are provided. Restrooms, showers, sanitary disposal station, recreation room, swimming pool, cable TV, and a playground are available, weather permitting. Coin laundry, groceries, RV supplies, and propane gas are also available. Pets are permitted.

Reservations, fees: Reservations are recommended; $26 to $34 per night, $3.50 pet fee. Open April through October 15.

Directions: From Sacramento, take U.S. 50 and drive east over the Sierra Nevada past Echo Summit to Meyers. As you enter Meyers, it will be the first campground on the right. Turn right and enter the campground.

Contact: KOA South Lake Tahoe, tel. (800) 562-3477, (530) 577-3693; website: www.laketahoekoa.com.

Tahoe Valley Campground

    5

This is a massive, privately operated park near South Lake Tahoe. The nearby attractions include five golf courses, horseback riding, casinos and, of course, "The Lake."

Location: Near Lake Tahoe; map D4, grid g3.

Campsites, facilities: There are 77 sites for tents and 305 sites with full or partial hookups for RVs. Picnic tables and grills are provided. Restrooms, modem hookups, sanitary disposal station, coin laundry, heated swimming pool, playground, tennis courts, grocery store, RV supplies, propane gas, ice, firewood, cable TV, and a recreation room are available. Some facilities are wheelchair accessible. Leashed pets are permitted (limit of two animals).

Reservations, fees: Reservations are recommended; $24 to $33 per night, $2 pet fee. Major credit cards accepted. Open year-round.

Directions: Entering South Lake Tahoe on U.S. 50, drive east on U.S. 50 to Meyers. Continue on U.S. 50 about five miles beyond Meyers to the signed entrance on the right.

Contact: Tahoe Valley Campground, tel. (530) 541-2222, or fax (530) 541-1825.

39 Wrights Lake

       9

This high mountain lake (7,000 feet) has shoreline camping and good fishing and hiking. There is no boat ramp, plus rules do not permit motors, so it is ideal for canoes, rafts, prams, and people who like quiet. Fishing is fair for both rainbow trout and brown trout. It is a classic alpine lake, though small (65 acres), with a trailhead for the Desolation Wilderness at its north end. From here it is only a three-mile hike to the beautiful Twin Lakes and Island Lake, set on the western flank of Mount Price (9,975 feet).

Location: In Eldorado National Forest; map D4, grid g0.

Campsites, facilities: There are 35 sites for tents and 36 sites for tents or RVs up to 22 feet long. Picnic tables and fire grills are provided. Drinking water and vault toilets are available. Leashed pets are permitted.

Reservations, fees: Reserve at (877) 444-6777 ($8.65 reservation fee) or website: www.reserveusa.com; $13 per night (single), $20 per night (double), $5 for a third vehicle. Open late June to early October, weather permitting.

Directions: From Sacramento, drive east on U.S. 50 about 20 miles beyond Placerville. Turn left on Ice House Road and drive north 11.5 miles to Ice House Reservoir. Turn east on Road 32 and drive 10 miles. Turn left on Wrights Lake Road and drive two miles to the campground on the right side of the road.

Contact: Eldorado Information Center, tel. (530) 644-6048; Eldorado National Forest, Pacific Ranger District, (530) 644-2349, or fax (530) 644-5405.

40 Kit Carson

    8

This is one in a series of pristine, high Sierra camps set along the West Fork of the Carson River. There's good trout fishing, thanks to regular stocks from the Department of Fish and Game. This is no secret, however, and the area from the Highway 89 bridge on downstream gets a lot of fishing pressure. The elevation is 6,900 feet.

Location: On the West Fork of the Carson River in Humboldt-Toiyabe National Forest; map D4, grid h4.

Campsites, facilities: There are 12 sites for tents or RVs up to 22 feet long. Picnic tables and fire grills are provided. Drinking water and vault toilets are available. Leashed pets are permitted.

Reservations, fees: No reservations; $9 per night. Open late-May through mid-September.

Directions: From Sacramento, drive east on U.S. 50 to the junction with Highway 89. Turn south on Highway 89 and drive over Luther Pass to the junction with Highway 88. Turn left and drive a mile to the campground on the left side of the road.

From Jackson, drive east on Highway 88 over Carson Pass and to the junction with Highway 89 and then continue for a mile to the campground on the left side of the road.

Contact: Humboldt-Toiyabe National Forest, Carson Ranger District, tel. (775) 882-2766, or fax (775) 884-8199.

41 Hope Valley

     7

The West Fork of the Carson River runs right through Hope Valley, a pretty trout stream with a choice of four streamside campgrounds. Trout stocks are made near the campgrounds during summer. The campground at Hope Valley is just east of Carson Pass, at 7,300 feet in elevation, in a very pretty area. A trailhead for the Pacific Crest Trail is three miles south of the campground. The primary nearby destination is Blue Lakes, about a 10-minute drive away. An insider's note is that little Tamarack Lake, set just beyond the turnoff for Lower Blue Lake, is excellent for swimming.

Location: Near the Carson River in Humboldt-Toiyabe National Forest; map D4, grid h3.

Campsites, facilities: There are 20 sites for tents or RVs up to 22 feet long and a group area for up to 16 people. Picnic tables and fire grills are provided. Drinking water and vault toilets are available. Leashed pets are permitted.

Reservations, fees: Reserve at (877) 444-6777 ($8.65 reservation fee) or website: www.reserveusa.com; $9 per night, $16 group camp fee per night. Open June through September.

Directions: From Sacramento, drive east on U.S. 50 to the junction with Highway 89. Turn south on Highway 89 and drive over Luther Pass to the junction with Highway 88. Turn right (west) and drive two miles to Blue Lakes Road. Turn left (south) and drive 1.5 miles to the campground on the right side of the road.

From Jackson, drive east on Highway 88 over Carson Pass and continue east for five miles to Blue Lakes Road. Turn right (south) and drive 1.5 miles to the campground on the right side of the road.

Contact: Humboldt-Toiyabe National Forest, Carson Ranger District, tel. (775) 882-2766 or fax (775) 884-8199.

42 Snowshoe Springs

 8

Take your pick of this or the other three streamside camps on the West Fork of the Carson River. This one is at 6,600 feet. Trout are plentiful but rarely grow very large.

Location: On the West Fork of the Carson River in Humboldt-Toiyabe National Forest; map D4, grid h4.

Campsites, facilities: There are 13 tent sites. Picnic tables and fire grills are provided. Drinking water and vault toilets are available. Leashed pets are permitted.

Reservations, fees: No reservations; $9 per night. Open June through September.

Directions: From Sacramento, drive east on U.S. 50 to the junction with Highway 89. Turn south on Highway 89 and drive over Luther Pass to the junction with Highway 88. Turn left

(east) and drive two miles to the campground on the right side of the road.

From Jackson, drive east on Highway 88 over Carson Pass to the junction with Highway 89 and continue for two miles to the campground on the right side of the road.

Contact: Humboldt-Toiyabe National Forest, Carson Ranger District, tel. (775) 882-2766 or fax (775) 884-8199.

43 Crystal Springs

 8

For many people, this camp is an ideal choice. It is set at an elevation of 6,000 feet, right alongside the West Fork of the Carson River. This stretch of water is stocked with trout by the Department of Fish and Game. Crystal Springs is easy to reach, just off Highway 88, and supplies can be obtained in nearby Woodfords or Markleeville. Grover Hot Springs State Park makes a good side trip destination.

Location: On the West Fork of the Carson River in Humboldt-Toiyabe National Forest; map D4, grid h4.

Campsites, facilities: There are 20 sites for tents or RVs up to 22 feet long. Picnic tables and fire grills are provided. Drinking water and vault toilets are available. Leashed pets are permitted.

Reservations, fees: No reservations; $9 per night. Open late April through September.

Directions: From Sacramento, drive east on U.S. 50 to the junction with Highway 89. Turn south on Highway 89 and drive over Luther Pass to the junction with Highway 88. Turn left (east) and drive 4.5 miles to the campground on the right side of the road.

From Jackson, drive east on Highway 88 over Carson Pass to the junction with Highway 89 and continue for 4.5 miles to the campground on the right side of the road.

Contact: Humboldt-Toiyabe National Forest, Carson Ranger District, tel. (775) 882-2766 or fax (775) 884-8199.

Turtle Rock Park

 5

This pretty, wooded campground, set at 6,000 feet, gets missed by a lot of folks. That's because it is administered at the county level and also because most vacationers want the more pristine beauty of the nearby camps along the Carson River. (If it snows, they close, so call ahead if you're planning an autumn visit.) Nearby side trips include Grover Hot Springs and the hot springs in Markleeville.

Location: Near Woodfords; map D4, grid h5.

Campsites, facilities: There are 28 sites for tents or RVs up to 35 feet long. Picnic tables and fire grills are provided. Drinking water and vault toilets are available. Coin laundry, groceries, and propane gas are available within two miles. Leashed pets are permitted.

Reservations, fees: No reservations; $8 per night, senior discounts, $3 for each additional vehicle. Open May to mid-October, weather permitting.

Directions: From Sacramento, drive east on U.S. 50 to the junction with Highway 89. Turn south on Highway 89 and drive over Luther Pass to the junction with Highway 88. Turn left (east) and drive to Woodfords and the junction with Highway 89. Turn south and drive 4.5 miles to the park entrance on the right side of the road.

Contact: Alpine County Parks, tel. (530) 694-2140.

Caples Lake

 8

Caples Lake, here in the high country at 7,800 feet, is a pretty lake right along Highway 88. It covers 600 acres, has a 10-mph speed limit, and provides good trout fishing and excellent hiking terrain. The camp is set across the highway (a little two-laner) from the lake, with the Caples Lake Resort and boat rentals nearby. There is a parking area at the west end of the lake, and from here you can begin a great 3.5-mile hike to Emigrant Lake, in the

Mokelumne Wilderness on the western flank of Mount Round Top (10,310 feet).

Location: In Eldorado National Forest; map D4, grid h2.

Campsites, facilities: There are 20 sites for tents and 15 sites for tents or RVs up to 22 feet long. Picnic tables and fire grills are provided. Drinking water and vault toilets are available. Groceries, propane gas, boat ramp, and boat rentals are nearby. Leashed pets are permitted.

Reservations, fees: No reservations; $12 per night, $24 per night for a double site. Open June through October.

Directions: From Jackson, drive east on Highway 88 for 63 miles (one mile past the entrance road to Kirkwood Ski Area) to the camp entrance road on the left.

Contact: Eldorado Information Center, (530) 644-6048; Eldorado National Forest, Amador Ranger District, tel. (209) 295-4251 or fax (209) 295-5994.

Kirkwood Lake

    8

Little Kirkwood Lake is in a beautiful Sierra setting, with good shoreline access, fishing for small rainbow trout, and quiet water. Despite that, it is often overlooked in favor of nearby Silver Lake and Caples Lake along Highway 88. Nearby Kirkwood Ski Resort stays open all summer and offers excellent opportunities for horseback riding, hiking, and meals. The elevation is 7,600 feet.

Location: In Eldorado National Forest; map D4, grid h1.

Campsites, facilities: There are 12 tent sites. Picnic tables and fire grills are provided. Drinking water and vault toilets are available. Leashed pets are permitted.

Reservations, fees: No reservations; $11 per night. Open June through October.

Directions: From Jackson, drive east on Highway 88 for 60 miles (four miles past Silver Lake) to the campground entrance road on the left (if you reach the sign for Kirkwood Ski Resort, you have gone a half mile too far). Turn left and drive a quarter mile (road not suitable for trailers or RVs) to the campground on the left.

Contact: Eldorado Information Center, (530) 644-6048; Eldorado National Forest, Amador Ranger District, tel. (209) 295-4251 or fax (209) 295-5994.

47 Silver Lake West

 9

The Highway 88 corridor provides access to three excellent lakes: Lower Bear River Reservoir, Silver Lake, and Caples Lake. Silver Lake is difficult to pass by, with cabin rentals, pretty campsites, decent trout fishing, and excellent hiking. Note that the gate for this camp is locked each night, guaranteeing privacy. The lake is set at 7,200 feet in a classic granite cirque just below the Sierra ridge. This camp is on the west side of Highway 88, across the road from the lake. A great hike starts at the trailhead on the east side of the lake, a two-mile tromp to little Hidden Lake, one of several nice hikes in the area.

Location: On Silver Lake; map D4, grid i1.

Campsites, facilities: There are 37 sites for tents or RVs up to 30 feet long. Picnic tables and fire pits are provided. Vault toilets are available. No drinking water is available. Leashed pets are permitted.

Reservations, fees: No reservations; $13 per night, $9 per night for each extra vehicle. Open mid-May through October, weather permitting.

Directions: From Jackson, drive east on Highway 88 for 50 miles (to the north end of Silver Lake) to the campground entrance road on the left.

Contact: Eldorado Irrigation District, tel. (530) 644-1960, or fax (530) 644-5155.

48 East Silver Lake

 7

Silver Lake is an easy-to-reach alpine lake set at 7,200 feet, which provides a beautiful setting, good trout fishing, and hiking. This camp is on the northeast side of the lake, with a boat ramp nearby. See the entry for Silver Lake West for more information.

Location: In Eldorado National Forest; map D4, grid i1.

Campsites, facilities: There are 28 sites for tents and 34 sites for tents or RVs. Picnic tables and fire grills are provided. Drinking water and vault toilets are available. A grocery store, boat rentals, boat ramp, and propane gas are nearby. Leashed pets are permitted.

Reservations, fees: Reserve at (877) 444-6777 ($8.65 reservation fee) or website: www.reserveusa.com; $12 per night. Open June through October.

Directions: From Jackson, drive east on Highway 88 for 50 miles (to the north end of Silver Lake) to the campground entrance road on the right.

Contact: Eldorado Information Center, (530) 644-6048; Eldorado National Forest, Amador Ranger District, tel. (209) 295-4251 or fax (209) 295-5994.

49 Woods Lake

 9

Woods Lake is only two miles from Highway 88, yet it can provide campers the feeling of visiting a far-off land. It is a small but beautiful lake in the granite backdrop of the high Sierra, set at 8,200 feet near Carson Pass. Boats with motors are not permitted, making it ideal for canoes and rowboats. Trout fishing is fair. A great trailhead is available here, a three-mile loop hike to little Round Top Lake and Winnemucca Lake (twice the size of Woods Lake) and back. They are set on the northern flank of Mount Round Top (10,310 feet).

Location: In Eldorado National Forest; map D4, grid i2.

Campsites, facilities: There are 25 tent sites and a multiple-family unit. Picnic tables and fire rings are provided. Drinking water (hand-pumped) and vault toilets are available. Groceries and propane gas are available within five miles. Leashed pets are permitted.

Reservations, fees: No reservations; $11 per night. Open June through October, weather permitting.

Directions: From Jackson, drive east on Highway 88 to Caples Lake and continue for a mile to the Woods Lake turnoff on the right (two miles west of Carson Pass). Turn south and drive a mile to the campground on the right (trailers and RVs are not recommended).

Contact: Eldorado Information Center, (530) 644-6048; Eldorado National Forest, Amador Ranger District, tel. (209) 295-4251 or fax (209) 295-5994.

50 Lower Blue Lake

   7

This is the high country, 8,200 feet, where the terrain is stark and steep and edged by volcanic ridgelines, and where the deep blue-green hue of lake water brightens the landscape. Lower Blue Lake provides a popular trout fishery, with rainbow trout, brook trout, and cutthroat trout all stocked regularly. The boat ramp is adjacent to the campground. The access road crosses the Pacific Crest Trail, providing a route to a series of small, pretty, hike-to lakes just outside the edge of the Mokelumne Wilderness.

Location: Near Carson Pass; map D4, grid i3.

Campsites, facilities: There are 16 sites for tents or RVs to 30 feet. Picnic tables and fire grills are provided. Drinking water and vault toilets are available. Leashed pets are permitted.

Reservations, fees: No reservations; $15 per night, $1 pet fee, 14-day occupancy limit. Open mid-May through October, weather permitting.

Directions: From Sacramento, drive east on U.S. 50 to the junction with Highway 89. Turn south on Highway 89 and drive over Luther Pass to the junction with Highway 88. Turn right and drive two miles to Blue Lakes Road. Turn left and drive 11 miles to a junction at the south end of Lower Blue Lake. Turn right and drive a short distance to the campground on the left side of the road.

From Jackson, drive east on Highway 88 over Carson Pass and continue east for five miles to Blue Lakes Road. Turn right (south) and drive 11 miles (five paved, seven gravel) to a junction at the south end of Lower Blue Lake. Turn right and drive a short distance to the campground on the left.

Contact: El Dorado Irrigation District, tel. (530) 644-1960, or fax (530) 647-5155.

51 Middle Creek

     7

This is a tiny, captivating spot set along the creek that connects Upper and Lower Blue Lakes, providing a take-your-pick deal for anglers. See the entry for Lower Blue Lake for more information. The elevation is 8,200 feet.

Location: Near Carson Pass and Blue Lakes; map D4, grid i3.

Campsites, facilities: There are five sites for tents or RVs. Picnic tables and fire grills are provided. Drinking water and vault toilets are available. Leashed pets are permitted.

Reservations, fees: No reservations; $15 per night, $3 per night for each extra vehicle, $7 per night for each extra RV, $1 pet fee. Open June through September, weather permitting.

Directions: From Sacramento, drive east on U.S. 50 to the junction with Highway 89. Turn south on Highway 89 and drive over Luther Pass to the junction with Highway 88. Turn right and drive 2.5 miles to Blue Lakes Road. Turn left and drive 11 miles to a junction at the south end of Lower Blue Lake. Turn right and drive 1.5 miles to the campground on the left side of the road.

From Jackson, drive east on Highway 88 over Carson Pass

and continue east for five miles to Blue Lakes Road. Turn right (south) and drive 11 miles (five paved, seven gravel) to a junction at the south end of Lower Blue Lake. Turn right and drive 1.5 miles to the campground on the left side of the road.

Contact: PG&E Building and Land Services, tel. (916) 386-5164.

52 Upper Blue Lake

      7

This is one of two camps set along Upper Blue Lake and one of four camps in the immediate area. The trout fishing is usually quite good here in early summer. See the entry for Lower Blue Lake for more information. The elevation is 8,200 feet.

Location: Near Carson Pass; map D4, grid i3.

Campsites, facilities: There are 32 sites for tents. Picnic tables and fire grills are provided. Drinking water and vault toilets are available. Leashed pets are permitted.

Reservations, fees: No reservations; $15 per night, $3 per night for each extra vehicle, $7 per night for each extra RV, $1 pet fee. Open June through September, weather permitting.

Directions: From Sacramento, drive east on U.S. 50 to the junction with Highway 89. Turn south on Highway 89 and drive over Luther Pass to the junction with Highway 88. Turn right and drive 2.5 miles to Blue Lakes Road. Turn left and drive 11 miles to a junction at the south end of Lower Blue Lake. Turn right and drive three miles to the campground on the left side of the road.

From Jackson, drive east on Highway 88 over Carson Pass and continue east for five miles to Blue Lakes Road. Turn right (south) and drive 11 miles (five paved, seven gravel) to a junction at the south end of Lower Blue Lake. Turn right and drive three miles to the campground on the left side of the road.

Contact: PG&E Building and Land Services, tel. (916) 386-5164.

53 Upper Blue Lake Dam

     8

This is one of four camps at the Blue Lakes, at 8,200 feet in elevation south of Carson Pass. A boat ramp is near this camp. For recreation options, see the entry for Lower Blue Lake.

Location: Near Carson Pass; map D4, grid i3.

Campsites, facilities: There are 25 tent sites. Picnic tables and fire grills are provided. Drinking water and vault toilets are available. Leashed pets are permitted.

Reservations, fees: No reservations; $15 per night, $3 per night for each extra vehicle, $7 per night for each extra RV, $1 pet fee. Open June through September, weather permitting.

Directions: From Sacramento, drive east on U.S. 50 to the junction with Highway 89. Turn south on Highway 89 and drive over Luther Pass to the junction with Highway 88. Turn right and drive 2.5 miles to Blue Lakes Road. Turn left and drive 11 miles to a junction at the south end of Lower Blue Lake. Turn right and drive two miles to the campground next to the dam.

From Jackson, drive east on Highway 88 over Carson Pass and continue east for five miles to Blue Lakes Road. Turn right and drive 11 miles (five paved, seven gravel) to a junction at the south end of Lower Blue Lake. Turn right and drive two miles to the campground next to the dam.

Contact: PG&E Building and Land Services, tel. (916) 386-5164.

54 Grover Hot Springs State Park

    8

This is a famous spot for folks who like the rejuvenating powers of a hot spring. Some say they feel a glow about them for weeks. When touring the South Tahoe/Carson Pass area, many vacationers take part of a day to make the trip to the hot springs. Side trip options include a nature trail in the park and driving to the Carson River (where the water is a mite cooler) and fishing for trout. The elevation is 5,800 feet.

Location: Near Markleeville; map D4, grid i4.

Campsites, facilities: There are 26 sites for tents, 50 sites for tents or RVs up to 26 feet long and trailers up to 24 feet long. Picnic tables, fire rings, and food lockers are provided. Restrooms, drinking water, flush toilets, coin-operated showers (except in the winter), hot springs pool with wheelchair access, and swimming pool are available. A grocery store and coin laundry are nearby. Leashed pets are permitted.

Reservations, fees: Reserve at (800) 444-PARK (800-444-7275) or website: www.ReserveAmerica.com; $12 per night; pool fees are $2 per adult, $1 per child 16 or under. Open year-round.

Directions: From Sacramento, drive east on U.S. 50 to the junction with Highway 89. Turn south on Highway 89 and drive over Luther Pass to the junction with Highway 88. Turn left and drive to Woodfords and the junction with Highway 89. Turn right (south) and drive six miles to Markleeville and the junction with Hot Springs Road. Turn right and drive four miles to the park entrance.

Contact: Grover Hot Springs State Park, tel. (530) 694-2248, for fax (530) 694-2502, or tel. (530) 525-7232.

55 Markleeville

 7

This is a pretty, streamside camp set at 5,500 feet along Markleeville Creek, a mile from the East Fork of the Carson River. The trout here are willing, but alas, are dinkers. This area is the transition zone where high mountains to the west give way to the high desert to the east. The hot springs in Markleeville and Grover Hot Springs State Park provide good side trips.

Location: On Markleeville Creek in Humboldt-Toiyabe National Forest; map D4, grid i5.

Campsites, facilities: There are 10 sites for tents or RVs up to 20 feet long. Trailers are prohibited due to road conditions. Picnic tables and fire grills are provided. Drinking water and vault toilets are available. A grocery store and restaurant are nearby. Leashed pets are permitted.

Reservations, fees: No reservations; $9 per night. Open late April through September.

Directions: From Sacramento, drive east on U.S. 50 to the junction with Highway 89. Turn south on Highway 89 and drive over Luther Pass to the junction with Highway 88. Turn left and drive to Woodfords and the junction with Highway 89. Turn south, drive six miles to Markleeville, and continue for a half mile to the campground on the left side of the highway.

Contact: Humboldt-Toiyabe National Forest, Carson Ranger District, tel. (775) 882-2766 or fax (775) 884-8199.

56 Topaz Lake RV Park

 6

Topaz Lake, set at 5,000 feet, is one of the hidden surprises for California anglers. The surprise is the size of the rainbow trout, with one of the highest rates of 15- to 18-inch trout of any lake in the mountain country. The setting is hardly pretty, a good-sized lake on the edge of barren high desert which also serves as the border between California and Nevada. Wind is a problem for small boats, especially in the early summer.

Location: On Topaz Lake, near Markleeville; map D4, grid j7.

Campsites, facilities: There are 54 RV sites. Full hookups, cable TV, and picnic tables are provided. Restrooms, showers, coin laundry, propane gas, small grocery store, and modem hookups are available. A 40-boat marina with courtesy launch and boat trailer storage is available at lakeside. Some facilities are wheelchair accessible. Leashed pets are permitted.

Reservations, fees: Reservations are accepted; $20 to $22 per night. Major credit cards accepted. Open March through mid-October, weather permitting; owners request a call prior to visits in the off-season.

Directions: From Carson City, drive south on U.S. 395 for 45 miles to Topaz Lake and the campground on the left side of the road.

From Bridgeport, drive north on U.S. 395 for 45 miles to the campground on the right side of the road.

Contact: Topaz Lake RV Park, tel. (530) 495-2357 or fax (530) 495-2118.

57 Silver Creek

 6

This pretty spot, set near Silver Creek, has easy access from Highway 4 and, in years without washouts, good fishing in early summer for small trout. It is in the remote high Sierra, east of Ebbetts Pass. A side trip to Ebbetts Pass features Kinney Lake, PCT access, and a trailhead at the north end of the lake (on the west side of Highway 4) for a mile hike to Lower Kinney Lake. No bikes are permitted on the trails. The elevation is 6,800 feet.

Location: In Humboldt-Toiyabe National Forest; map D4, grid j5.

Campsites, facilities: There are 22 sites for tents or RVs up to 22 feet long. Picnic tables and fire grills are provided. Drinking water and vault toilets are available. Leashed pets are permitted.

Reservations, fees: Reserve at (877) 444-6777 ($8.65 reservation fee) or website: www.reserveusa.com; $9 per night. Open late June to early September.

Directions: From Angels Camp, drive east on Highway 4 all the way over Ebbetts Pass and continue for about six miles to the campground.

From Markleeville, drive south on Highway 89 to the junction with Highway 4. Turn west on Highway 4 (steep and winding) and drive about five miles to the campground.

Contact: Humboldt-Toiyabe National Forest,

Carson Ranger District, tel. (775) 882-2766 or fax (775) 884-8199.

58 Hermit Valley

 8

This tiny, remote, little-known spot is set near the border of the Mokelumne Wilderness near where Grouse Creek enters the Mokelumne River, at 7,500 feet in elevation. Looking north, there is a good view into Deer Valley. A primitive road, a half mile west of camp, is routed through Deer Valley north for six miles to the Blue Lakes. On the opposite (south) side of the road from the camp there is a little-traveled hiking trail that is routed up Grouse Creek to Milk Ranch Meadow at the border of the Carson-Iceberg Wilderness.

Location: In Stanislaus National Forest; map D4, grid j3.

Campsites, facilities: There is a large area for dispersed camping. Vault toilets are available. No drinking water is available. Leashed pets are permitted.

Reservations, fees: No reservations; no fee. A free campfire permit is required from the district office. Open June through September.

Directions: From Angels Camp, drive east on Highway 4 to Lake Alpine and continue for about nine miles to the campground on the left side of the road (just east of the Mokelumne River Bridge).

Contact: Stanislaus National Forest, Calaveras Ranger District, tel. (209) 795-1381 or fax (209) 795-6849. For a map, send $6 to U.S. Forest Service, Attn: Map Sales, P.O. Box 587, Camino, CA 95709; tel. (530) 647-5390, fax (530) 647-5389, or website: www.r5.fs.fed.us/visitorcenter. Major credit cards accepted.

59 Mosquito Lake

 10

Mosquito Lake is in a pristine Sierra setting at 8,260 feet, presenting remarkable beauty for a place that can be reached by car. Most people believe that Mosquito Lake is for day-use only, and that's why they get crowded into nearby Alpine Campground. But it's not just for day-use, and this camp is often overlooked because it is about a mile west of the little lake, and on the opposite side of the road. The lake is small, a pretty emerald green, and even has a few small trout in it.

Location: At Mosquito Lake in Stanislaus National Forest; map D4, grid j3.

Campsites, facilities: There are a few primitive, undesignated sites for tents. Picnic tables and fire grills are provided. Vault toilets are available. No drinking water is available. Garbage must be packed out. Leashed pets are permitted.

Reservations, fees: No reservations; $5 per night. A free campfire permit is required from the district office.

Directions: From Angels Camp, drive east on Highway 4 to Lake Alpine and continue for about six miles to the campground on the left side of the road.

Contact: Stanislaus National Forest, Calaveras Ranger District, tel. (209) 795-1381 or fax (209) 795-6849. For a map, send $6 to U.S. Forest Service, Attn: Map Sales, P.O. Box 587, Camino, CA 95709; tel. (530) 647-5390, fax (530) 647-5389, or website: www.r5.fs.fed.us/visitorcenter. Major credit cards accepted.

60 Pacific Valley

 7

This is a do-it-yourself special; that is, more of a general area for camping than a campground, set up for backpackers heading out on expeditions into the Carson-Iceberg Wilderness to the south. It is set at 7,600 feet along Pacific Creek, a tributary to the Mokelumne River. The landscape here is an open lodgepole forest with nearby meadow and a small stream. The trail from camp is routed south and reaches three forks within two miles. The best is routed deep into the wilderness, flanking Hiram Peak (9,760 feet), Airola Peak (9,938 feet), and Iceberg Peak (9,720 feet).

Location: Overlooking Pacific Creek in Stanislaus National Forest; map D4, grid j3.

Campsites, facilities: There are 15 sites for tents and a large area for dispersed camping. Trailers are not recommended due to road conditions. Picnic tables and fire grills are provided. Vault toilets are available. No drinking water is available. Leashed pets are permitted.

Reservations, fees: No reservations; no fee. A free campfire permit is required from the district office. Open June through September.

Directions: From Angels Camp, drive east on Highway 4 to Lake Alpine and continue for eight miles to a dirt road. Turn east and drive about a half mile to the campground.

Contact: Stanislaus National Forest, Calaveras Ranger District, tel. (209) 795-1381 or fax (209) 795-6849. For a map, send $6 to U.S. Forest Service, Attn: Map Sales, P.O. Box 587, Camino, CA 95709; tel. (530) 647-5390, fax (530) 647-5389, or website: www.r5.fs.fed.us/visitorcenter. Major credit cards accepted.

61 Bloomfield

 7

This is a primitive and little-known camp set at 7,800 feet near Ebbetts Pass. The North Fork Mokelumne River runs right by the camp, with good stream access for about a mile on each side of the camp. The access road continues south to Highland Lakes, a destination that provides car-top boating, fair fishing, and trailheads for hiking into the Carson-Iceberg Wilderness.

Location: In Stanislaus National Forest; map D4, grid j4.

Campsites, facilities: There are 20 sites for tents or RVs. Trailers are not recommended due to road conditions. Picnic tables and fire rings are provided. Drinking water and vault toilets are available. A grocery store, propane gas, and coin laundry are available nearby. Leashed pets are permitted.

Reservations, fees: No reservations; $8 per night. A free campfire permit is required from the district office. Open June through October.

Directions: From Angels Camp, drive east on Highway 4 to Lake Alpine and continue for about 15 miles to Forest Road 8N01 on the right side of the road (1.5 miles west of Ebbetts Pass). Turn right and drive two miles to the campground on the right side of the road.

Contact: Stanislaus National Forest, Calaveras Ranger District, tel. (209) 795-1381 or fax (209) 795-6849. For a map, send $6 to U.S. Forest Service, Attn: Map Sales, P.O. Box 587, Camino, CA 95709; tel. (530) 647-5390, fax (530) 647-5389, or website: www.r5.fs.fed.us/visitor center. Major credit cards accepted.

TOM STIENSTRA

HARDWOOD FOREST ALONG THE
SKYLINE-TO-THE-SEA TRAIL

MAP E1

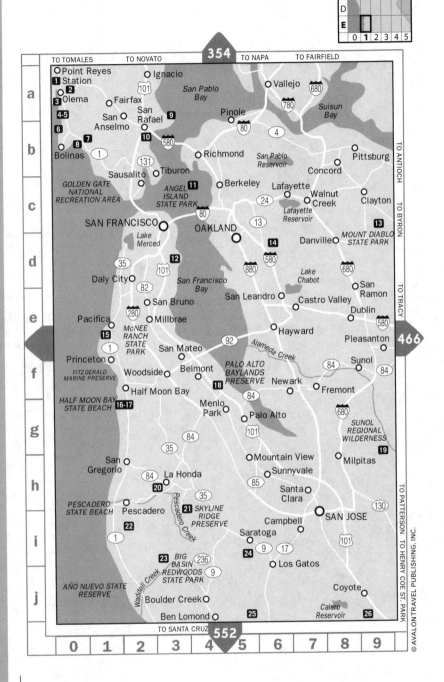

TO TOMALES   TO NOVATO   **354**   TO NAPA   TO FAIRFIELD

a
Point Reyes
1 Station
2
3 Olema
4-5
6
Bolinas **8 7**

Ignacio
101
San Pablo Bay
Vallejo
680
Fairfax
780
Suisun Bay

San Rafael **9**
San Anselmo
Pinole
80
4

b
131   Richmond
San Pablo Reservoir
Pittsburg
580
Sausalito   Tiburon
Concord

c
GOLDEN GATE NATIONAL RECREATION AREA
ANGEL ISLAND STATE PARK **11**
Berkeley
Lafayette
24   Walnut Creek
Clayton
13
Lafayette Reservoir
SAN FRANCISCO
OAKLAND
13
MOUNT DIABLO STATE PARK

d
Lake Merced
12
14
Danville
Lake Chabot
35
101
880 580
680
San Ramon

Daly City
82
San Bruno
San Francisco Bay
San Leandro
Castro Valley
Dublin

e
Pacifica
280
Millbrae
McNEE RANCH STATE PARK
580
466
15
1   San Mateo
92
Hayward
Pleasanton

f
Princeton
FITZGERALD MARINE PRESERVE
Woodside   Belmont
Alameda Creek
84
Sunol
84
PALO ALTO BAYLANDS PRESERVE
Newark   Fremont
Half Moon Bay   **18**
84
680
HALF MOON BAY STATE BEACH **16-17**

g
Menlo Park
84
Palo Alto
101
SUNOL REGIONAL WILDERNESS
19
35

h
San Gregorio
84   La Honda
20
35
Mountain View
Sunnyvale
85
Santa Clara
Milpitas
130

i
PESCADERO STATE BEACH   Pescadero
SKYLINE RIDGE PRESERVE
21
Campbell
SAN JOSE
22
1
Saratoga
24   9   17
101

j
AÑO NUEVO STATE RESERVE
23
BIG BASIN REDWOODS STATE PARK
236
9
Los Gatos
Coyote
Boulder Creek
Ben Lomond   **25**
Calero Reservoir   **26**

TO SANTA CRUZ   **552**

0 1 2 3 4 5 6 7 8 9

CHAPTER E1

1 Olema Ranch Campground

4

If location is everything, then this park should be rated a 10. It is set in Olema, in a valley amid Marin's coastal foothills, an ideal jumpoff spot for a Point Reyes adventures. It borders the Point Reyes National Seashore to the west and the Golden Gate National Recreation Area to the east, with Tomales Bay to the nearby north. There are several excellent trailheads available within a 10-minute drive along Highway 1 to the south. The campsites are small, tightly placed, and we have received complaint letters about the ambiance of the place. In the past, when such problems are noted, we have found they are often quickly addressed.

Location: In Olema; map E1, grid a0.

Campsites, facilities: There are 225 sites for tents or RVs, some with full or partial hookups. Picnic tables are provided. Drinking water, restrooms, showers, fire pits, sanitary disposal station, coin laundry, modem hookups, arcade, and a recreation hall (for groups of 25 or more only) are available. Some facilities are wheelchair accessible. Leashed pets are permitted.

Reservations, fees: Reservations are accepted, tel. (800) 655-CAMP; $20 to $28 per night, $2 for second vehicle, $3 per person for more than two people. Major credit cards accepted. Open year-round.

Directions: From U.S. 101 in Marin, take the San Anselmo/Sir Francis Drake Boulevard exit and drive west for about 20 miles to Highway 1 at Olema. Turn north (right) on Highway 1 and drive a half mile to the campground on the left.

Contact: Olema Ranch Campground, tel. (415) 663-8001 or fax (415) 663-8832; website: www.campgrounds.com/olemaranch.

☑ Samuel P. Taylor State Park

      9

This is a beautiful park, with campsites set amid redwoods, complete with a babbling brook running nearby. Hikers will find 20 miles of hiking trails, a hidden waterfall, and some good mountain biking routes on service roads. The paved bike path that runs through the park and parallels Sir Francis Drake Boulevard is a terrific, easy ride.

Location: Near San Rafael; map E1, grid a0.

Campsites, facilities: There are 25 sites for tents and 35 sites for tents or RVs up to 27 feet long, two group sites for 25 and 50 people, and three equestrian sites with corrals at Devil's Gulch Horse Camp. Picnic tables, food lockers, and fire grills are provided. Drinking water and flush toilets are available. There is a small store and cafe two miles away in Lagunitas. Some facilities are wheelchair accessible. Leashed pets are permitted in campsites only.

Reservations, fees: Reserve at (800) 444-PARK (800-444-7275) or website: www.ReserveAmerica.com; $12 per night, group sites are $18 to $37 per night, equestrian camp $12 per night. Open year-round.

Directions: From U.S. 101 in Marin, take the Sir Francis Drake Boulevard exit and drive west for about 15 miles to the park entrance on the left side of the road.

Contact: Samuel P. Taylor State Park, tel. (415) 488-9897, or fax (415) 488-4315; California State Parks, Marin District, tel. (415) 893-1580 or fax (415) 893-1583.

☒ Sky Camp Hike-In

  7

Sky Camp is set on the western flank of Mount Wittenberg on Inverness Ridge at 1,025 feet, right at the edge of the area in Point Reyes National Seashore that burned in the fall 1995 wildfire. In fact, this hike-in camp was right at the edge of the firebreak and was partially burned. To reach the camp, take the Bear Valley Trail from park headquarters and walk 0.2 mile to the Mount Wittenberg Trail. Turn right (north) on the Mount Wittenberg Trail and hike 2.2 miles to the Sky Trail. Turn right and hike 0.6 mile to the campground. From here you get a dramatic view of the burned area and the adjacent Marin coast. No open fires and no pets are permitted. You must have a backcountry permit from the Bear Valley Visitor Center to camp here.

Location: In Point Reyes National Seashore; map E1, grid a0.

Campsites, facilities: There are 11 individual sites and a group site (walk-in only) which can accommodate up to six campers. Pit toilets and fire grills (charcoal only, no wood fires) are provided. Piped water is available, but it must be treated before use. Garbage must be packed out. No vehicles or pets are allowed.

Reservations, fees: Reservations are required, tel. (415) 663-8054, Monday through Friday, or fax (415) 663-1597, or in person; $10 per night, $10 to $30 per night for the group site (maximum of 25 people); four-day maximum stay. Open year-round.

Directions: From U.S. 101 in Marin, take the Sir Francis Drake Boulevard exit and drive west for about 20 miles to Highway 1 at Olema. Turn north on Highway 1 and drive a very short distance. Turn left on Bear Valley Road and drive north for 0.7 mile. Turn left at the "Seashore Information" sign and drive to the visitors center parking lot and the Bear Valley Trailhead.

Contact: Point Reyes National Seashore, tel. (415) 663-1092; camping information only at (415) 663-8054; fax at (415) 663-1597.

4 Coast Camp Hike-In

  7

This is a classic ocean-bluff setting, a hike-in camp set just above Santa Maria Beach on the Point Reyes National Seashore, providing an extended tour into a land of charm. It is a 2.8-mile hike to get here, the northernmost camp on the Coast Trail. (The complete Coast Trail is a 19-mile trip that is one of the best hikes in the Bay Area.) From Coast Camp, the trail contours south along the bluffs above the beach for 1.4 miles to Sculptured Beach, where there is a series of odd geologic formations, including caves, tunnels, and sea stacks. A backcountry permit is required. Note: This camp is set on the edge of the area that burned in the fall 1995 wildfire.

Location: In Point Reyes National Seashore; map E1, grid a0.

Campsites, facilities: There are 12 individual and two group hike-in sites. Picnic tables and fire grills are provided. Vault toilets are available. Piped water is available, but it must be treated before use. Charcoal or gas stoves are allowed, with backpacking stoves recommended for cooking. No wood fires permitted. Garbage must be packed out. No vehicles or pets are permitted.

Reservations, fees: Reservations are recommended and permits required at tel. (415) 663-8054; $10 per night, four-day maximum stay; $10 to $30 per night for group sites. Open year-round.

Directions: From U.S. 101 in Marin, take the Sir Francis Drake Boulevard exit and drive about 20 miles to Highway 1 at Olema. Turn right on Highway 1 and drive a very short distance. Turn left at Bear Valley Road and drive north for two miles to Limantour Road. Turn left at Limantour Road and drive six miles to the access road for the Point Reyes Hostel. Turn left and drive 0.2 mile to the trailhead on the right side of the road. A parking area is a short distance ahead and to the right.

Contact: Point Reyes National Seashore, tel. (415) 663-1092; camping information only at (415) 663-8054; fax at (415) 663-1597.

5 Wildcat Camp Hike-In

   10

This backpack camp sits in a grassy meadow near a small stream that flows to the ocean, just above remote Wildcat Beach. From the Palomarin Trailhead, getting to this camp takes you on a fantastic 5.6-mile hike that crosses some of the Bay Area's most beautiful wildlands. The trail is routed along the ocean for about a mile, heads up in the coastal hills, turns left, and skirts past Bass Lake, Crystal Lake, and Pelican Lake and, ultimately, heads past Alamere Creek to this beautiful camp set on an ocean bluff. A fantastic side trip is to hike along the beach from Wildcat Camp on south, where you can get a full frontal view of Alamere Falls. It is a dramatic 40-foot freefall, one of the rare ocean bluff waterfalls anywhere.

Location: In Point Reyes National Seashore; map E1, grid a0.

Campsites, facilities: There are five individual and three group hike-in sites. Picnic tables and fire grills are provided. Vault toilets are available. Piped water is available, but it must be treated before use. Charcoal or gas stoves are allowed, with backpacking stoves recommended for cooking. No wood fires permitted. Garbage must be packed out. No vehicles or pets are permitted.

Reservations, fees: Reservations are recommended and permits required at tel. (415) 663-8054; $10 per night, group sites $10 to $30 per night; four-day maximum stay. Open year-round.

Directions: From U.S. 101 in Marin, take the Sir Francis Drake Boulevard exit and drive west for about 20 miles to Highway 1 at Olema. Turn south on Highway 1 and drive about 10 miles south to Olema-Bolinas Road (the sign is often missing; stolen regularly). Turn right and drive 2.1 miles to Mesa

Road. Turn right and drive 5.8 miles to the Palomarin Trailhead. It is a 5.6-mile hike to the campground on the Coast Trail.

Contact: Point Reyes National Seashore, tel. (415) 663-1092; camping information only at (415) 663-8054; fax at (415) 663-1597.

6 Glen Camp Hike-In

  9

Glen Camp Hike-In is set in the coastal foothills of Point Reyes National Seashore and is surrounded by forest. The hike to it starts at the Bear Valley Visitor Center, where you can obtain your backcountry permits and hiking information, and is routed on the popular Bear Valley Trail, a wide road made out of compressed rock. It is 1.6 miles to Divide Meadow, with a modest 215-foot climb, then another 1.6 miles through Bear Valley to the Glen Trail. Turn left on Glen Loop Trail and hike 1.4 miles, with the trail lateralling in and out of two canyons to reach the camp. It is secluded and quiet. Get a map, a permit, and bring everything you need.

Location: In Point Reyes National Seashore; map E1, grid b0.

Campsites, facilities: There are 12 hike-in sites. Picnic tables and fire grills are provided. Pit toilets are available. Water is usually available (check before arranging trip), but it must be treated before use. Charcoal or gas stoves are allowed, with backpacking stoves recommended for cooking. No wood fires permitted. Garbage must be packed out. No vehicles or pets are permitted.

Reservations, fees: Reservations recommended and permits are required at tel. (415) 663-8054; $10 per night, group sites $10 to $30 per night; four-day maximum stay. Open year-round.

Directions: From U.S. 101 in Marin, take the Sir Francis Drake Boulevard exit and drive about 20 miles to Highway 1 at Olema. Turn north on Highway 1 and drive a very short distance. Turn left on Bear Valley Road and drive north for 0.7 mile. Turn left at the "Seashore Information" sign and drive to the park head-

quarters parking lot and the Bear Valley Trailhead. It is a 4.6-mile hike to the camp.

Contact: Point Reyes National Seashore, tel. (415) 663-1092; camping information only at (415) 663-8054; fax at (415) 663-1597.

7 Pantoll Campground Walk-in & Alice Eastwood Group Camps

    8

When camping at Pantoll, you are within close range of the divine, including some of the best hiking, best lookouts, and just plain best places to be anywhere in the Bay Area. The camp is set in the woods on the western slopes of Mount Tamalpais, which some say is a place of special power. The Steep Ravine Trail is routed out of camp to the west into a wondrous gorge filled with redwoods and a stream with miniature waterfalls. It is best seen after a good rain, when everything is dripping with moisture. Another great hike from this camp is on the Matt Davis/Coast Trail, provides beautiful views of the coast. Another must is the nearby drive to the East Peak Lookout, where the entire world seems within reach.

Location: In Mount Tamalpais State Park; map E1, grid b1.

Campsites, facilities: There are 16 walk-in tent sites, and two group sites for 10 to 75 people. Picnic tables, food lockers, and fire grills are provided. Drinking water and vault toilets are available. Firewood is available to purchase. Leashed pets are permitted at campsites only.

Reservations, fees: Reservations for groups only; individual sites $7 per night, group sites $18 to $37 per night. Open year-round.

Directions: From U.S. 101 in Marin, take the Stinson Beach/Highway 1 exit. Drive west to the stoplight at the T intersection (Highway 1). Turn left and drive about four miles uphill to the Panoramic Highway. Bear to the right on Panoramic Highway and continue for 5.5 miles to the Pantoll parking area. Turn left at the Pantoll parking area and ranger station. A 100-

foot walk is required to reach the campground. To reach the group site, directions and the combination to the gate lock will be provided when reservations are made.

Contact: Pantoll Campground, tel. (415) 388-2070; California State Parks, Marin District, tel. (415) 893-1580 or fax (415) 388-2968.

8 Steep Ravine Environmental Campsites

 10

This is one of the most remarkable spots on the California coast, with primitive cabin/wood shacks set on a bluff on Rocky Point overlooking the ocean. It is primitive but dramatic, with passing ships, fishing boats, lots of marine birds, occasionally even whales, and a chance for heart-stopping sunsets. There is an easy walk to the north down to Redrock Beach, which is secluded, and just across the road (with a short jog to the right) is a trailhead for the Steep Ravine Trail on the slopes of Mount Tamalpais. After a while you'll feel like you're a million miles from civilization.

Location: In Mount Tamalpais State Park; map E1, grid b0.

Campsites, facilities: There are six walk-in sites for tents and 10 primitive cabins, each with a wood stove, picnic table, and a flat wood surface for sleeping. Pit toilets, fire grills, and tables are provided. Drinking water is nearby, and wood is available to purchase. No pets are permitted.

Reservations, fees: Reserve by phoning (800) 444-PARK (800-444-7275) or website: www.cal-parks.ca.gov; $15 per night, one vehicle per cabin, five people maximum per site. Open year-round.

Directions: From U.S. 101 in Marin, take the Stinson Beach/Highway 1 exit. Drive west to the stoplight at the T intersection (Highway 1). Turn left and drive north on Highway 1 about 11 miles to the gated access road on the left side of the highway. (The gate lock combination will be provided when reservations are made.)

Contact: Steep Ravine Environmental Campsites, tel. (415) 388-2070; California State Parks, tel. (415) 893-1580 of fax (415) 388-2968.

9 China Camp State Park Walk-In

 10

This is one of the Bay Area's prettiest campgrounds. It is set in woodlands with a picturesque creek running past. The camps are shaded and sheltered. Directly adjacent to the camp is a meadow, marshland, and then San Pablo Bay. Deer can seem as tame as chipmunks. Hiking is outstanding here, either taking the Shoreline Trail for a pretty walk near the edge of San Pablo Bay, or the Bay View Trail for the climb up the ridge that borders the park, in the process gaining spectacular views of the bay and miles of charm.

Location: On San Pablo Bay near San Rafael; map E1, grid a3.

Campsites, facilities: There are 30 walk-in tent sites and one bike-in site. Picnic tables, food lockers, and fire grills are provided. Drinking water, showers, and a restroom are available. Leashed pets are permitted at campsites only.

Reservations, fees: Reserve at (800) 444-PARK (800-444-7275) or website: www.ReserveAmerica.com; $1 per person per night. Open year-round, weather permitting.

Directions: From San Francisco, drive north on U.S. 101 to San Rafael and take the North San Pedro Road exit. Drive east on North San Pedro Road for five miles to the park entrance station at Back Ranch Meadows. Shortly after passing through the entrance station, bear right and drive a short distance to the campground parking lot. Reaching the sites requires a one- to five-minute walk.

Contact: China Camp State Park Walk-In, tel. (415) 456-0766, or fax (415) 456-1743; California State Parks, Marin District, tel. (415) 893-1580.

10 Marin Park, Inc.

 2

For out-of-towners with RVs, this can make an ideal base camp for Marin County adventures. To the west are Mount Tamalpais State Park, Muir Woods National Monument, Samuel P. Taylor State Park, and Point Reyes National Seashore. To the nearby east is the Loch Lomond Marina on San Pablo Bay, where fishing trips can be arranged for striped bass and sturgeon; phone (415) 456-0321. The park offers complete sight-seeing information and easy access to buses and ferry service to San Francisco.

Location: In Greenbrae; map E1, grid b2.

Campsites, facilities: There are 89 RV sites with full hookups. Showers, coin laundry, modem hookups, swimming pool, and RV supplies are available. Some facilities are wheelchair accessible. Pets are permitted.

Reservations, fees: Reservations advised at tel. (415) 461-5199; $31 per night, $2 per person per night for more than two people. Six people maximum per site. Major credit cards accepted. Open year-round.

Directions from the south: From the Golden Gate Bridge, drive north on U.S. 101 for 10 miles to Lucky Drive (south of San Rafael). Exit and turn left on Redwood Highway (no sign) and drive three blocks north to the park entrance.

Directions from the north: From San Rafael, drive south on U.S. 101 to the Lucky Drive exit. Take that exit to the first light at Tamal Vista. Turn left and drive to Wornum. Turn left at Wornum and drive under the freeway to Redwood Highway (frontage road). Turn left and drive four blocks north to the park entrance.

Contact: Marin Park, Inc., tel. (415) 461-5199; website: www.campground.com.

11 Angel Island State Park Walk-In

 10

Camping at Angel Island is one of the unique adventures in the Bay Area; the only catch is that getting to the campsites requires a walk of up to two miles. The payoff comes at 4:30 p.m., when all of the park's day visitors depart for the mainland, leaving the entire island to you. From start to finish, it's a great trip, featuring a ferry boat ride, a great hike in, and a private campsite, often with spectacular views of San Francisco Bay. The tromp up to 781-foot Mount Livermore includes a short, very steep stretch, but in return furnishes one of the most spectacular urban lookouts in America. Be ready for cold, foggy weather at night in mid-summer.

Location: On Angel Island; map E1, grid c4.

Campsites, facilities: There are nine hike-in/bike-in sites. Picnic tables and fire grills are provided. Drinking water and vault toilets are available. No pets are permitted. A seasonal cafe is available on the island.

Reservations, fees: Reserve at (800) 444-PARK (800-444-7275) or website: www.ReserveAmerica.com; $7 per night (limit eight people per site). Open year-round, with limited ferry service in winter.

Directions: Angel Island is in northern San Francisco Bay and can be reached by ferry from San Francisco, Vallejo and Oakland/Alameda, for schedule information, call (415) 705-5555; and from Tiburon, for schedule information, call (415) 435-2131.

Contact: Angel Island State Park, tel. (415) 435-1915; California State Parks, Marin District, tel. (415) 893-1580 or fax (415) 893-1583.

12 Candlestick RV Park

 6

This RV park is set adjacent to Candlestick Park, or 3Com Park on one side (that will always sound ridiculous) and the Candlestick State Recreation Area on the other. The location is four miles from downtown San Francisco. It is an ideal destination for out-of-towners who want to explore the city without having to drive, because the park offers tours and inexpensive shuttles to the downtown area. In addition, there are good hiking opportunities along the shoreline of the Bay. On summer afternoons, when the wind howls at 20 to 30 mph here, windsurfers rip by at 50 mph.

Location: In San Francisco; map E1, grid d3.

Campsites, facilities: There are 160 sites for trailers or RVs, all with full hookups. Restrooms, showers, coin laundry, modem hookups, grocery store, game room, and propane are available. Shuttles and bus tours are also available. Some facilities are wheelchair accessible. A security officer is posted at the entry station at night. Small leashed pets are permitted.

Reservations, fees: Reservations are recommended; phone (800) 888-2267; $42 to $45 per night, $10 per night for each extra vehicle, $2 per person per night for more than two people. Major credit cards accepted. Open year-round.

Directions: From San Francisco on U.S. 101 south, take the Candlestick Park (3COM) exit. Turn east on the stadium entrance road and drive around the parking lot to the far end of the stadium (Gate 4).

Contact: Candlestick RV Park, tel. (415) 822-2299 or fax (415) 822-7638.

🔢 Mount Diablo State Park

🚶 🐕 ♿ 🚐 ⛺ 6

Mount Diablo, elevation 3,849 feet, provides one of the most all-encompassing lookouts anywhere in America. On crystal clear days you can see the Sierra Nevada and its white, snowbound crest. With binoculars, some claim to have seen Half Dome in Yosemite. The drive to the summit is a must-do trip, and the interpretive center right on top of the mountain is one of the best in the Bay Area. The camps at Mount Diablo are set in foothill/oak grassland country, with some shaded sites. Winter and spring are good times to visit, when the weather is still cool enough for good hiking trips. Most of the trails require long hikes, often including significant elevation gains and losses. In late summer the park is sometimes closed

to camping due to fire danger. No alcohol is permitted in the park.

Location: East of Oakland; map E1, grid c9.

Campsites, facilities: There are 64 sites for tents or RVs up to 24 feet long (in three campgrounds), five group sites for 20 to 50 people, one group site is accessible for equestrian use with hitching posts and a water trough. Picnic tables and fire grills are provided. Drinking water and flush toilets are available. Leashed pets are permitted.

Reservations, fees: Reserve at (800) 444-PARK (800-444-7275) or website: www.ReserveAmerica.com; $12 per night, group sites are $15 to $22 per night. Open year-round.

Directions: From Danville on Interstate 680, take the Diablo Road exit. Turn east on Diablo Road and drive three miles to Mount Diablo Scenic Boulevard. Turn left and continue 3.5 miles to the park entrance station (the road becomes South Gate Road). Register at the kiosk, obtain a park map, and drive to the designated campground.

Contact: Mount Diablo State Park, tel. (925) 837-2525 or tel. (415) 330-6300.

🔢 Anthony Chabot Regional Park

The campground at Chabot Regional Park is set on a hilltop sheltered by eucalyptus, with good views and trails available. The best campsites are the walk-in units, requiring a walk of only a minute or so. Several provide views of Lake Chabot to the south a half mile away. The lake provides good trout fishing in the winter and spring, and a chance for huge but elusive largemouth bass. The Huck Trail is routed down from the campground (near walk-in site 20) to the lake at Honker Bay, a good fishing area. There is also a good 12-mile bike ride around the lake. Boat rentals at a small marina are available.

Location: Near Castro Valley; map E1, grid d6.

Campsites, facilities: There are 65 tent and RV sites, some with partial hookups, and 10 walk-in tent sites. Picnic tables and fire grills are provided. Restrooms, drinking water, flush toilets, showers, and a sanitary disposal station are available. Leashed pets are permitted.

Reservations, fees: Reservations are accepted; phone (510) 562-2267 ($6 reservation fee); $15 to $20 per night, $6 per night for each additional vehicle, $1 pet fee. Major credit cards accepted. Open year-round.

Directions: From Interstate 580 in the Oakland hills, take the 35th Avenue exit. Turn east on 35th Avenue and drive up the hill and straight across Skyline Boulevard, where 35th Avenue becomes Redwood Road. Continue on Redwood Road for eight miles to the park and campground entrance on the right.

Contact: Anthony Chabot Regional Park, tel. (510) 639-4751, (510) 639-4752, Regional Park Headquarters at (510) 635-0135, ext. 2200, or fax (510) 636-0751.

credit cards accepted. Open year-round.

Directions: From San Francisco, drive south on Highway 280 to Highway 1. Bear west on Highway 1 and drive into Pacifica and the Manor Drive exit. Take that exit and drive to the stop sign (you will be on the west side of the highway). Continue straight ahead (the road becomes Palmetto Avenue) for about two blocks and look for the entrance to the park on the right side of the road at 700 Palmetto.

From the south, drive north on Highway 1 into Pacifica. Take the Manor Drive exit. At the stop sign, turn left on the frontage road (you will be on the east side of the highway) and drive a block to another stop sign. Turn left, drive a short distance over the highway to a stop sign at Manor/Palmetto, and turn left. Drive about two blocks to the park on the right.

Contact: Pacific Park RV Resort, tel. (800) 992-0554 or fax (650) 355-7102; website: www.sanfranciscorv.com.

15 Pacific Park RV Resort

 8

This has become the best RV park in the Bay Area. It is set on the bluffs just above the Pacific Ocean, complete with beach access, nearby fishing pier, and sometimes excellent surf fishing. There is also a nearby golf course and the chance for dramatic ocean sunsets. The park is relatively new, kept clean and in good shape, and though there is too much asphalt, the proximity to the beach overcomes it. It is only 20 minutes from San Francisco.

Location: In Pacifica; map E1, grid e1.

Campsites, facilities: There are 257 RV sites with full hookups. Restrooms, showers, heated swimming pool, spa, a group-only recreation room, cable TV, grocery store, coin laundry, and propane gas are available. Some facilities are wheelchair accessible. Leashed pets are permitted.

Reservations, fees: Reservations are recommended; $38 to $69 per night, $2 per person for more than two people, $2 pet fee. Major

16 Half Moon Bay State Beach Northern California

 7

In summer, this park often fills to capacity with campers touring Highway 1. The campground has level, grassy sites for tents, a clean parking area for RVs, and a state beach available just a short walk away. Side trips include Princeton and Pillar Point Marina, seven miles north on Highway 1, where fishing and whale-watching trips are possible.

Location: At Half Moon Bay; map E1, grid g1.

Campsites, facilities: There are 54 sites for tents or RVs up to 36 feet long, four hike-in or bike-in sites, and one group site two miles north of the main campground. Picnic tables, food lockers, and fire grills are provided. Restrooms, drinking water, flush toilets, and a sanitary disposal station are available. Leashed pets are permitted in campsites only. They are not permitted on the beach.

Reservations, fees: No reservations; $12 per night, $1 per person per night for hike-in or bike-in sites, $37 per night for group site. Open year-round.

Directions: In Half Moon Bay, at the junction of Highway 1 and Highway 92, turn south on Highway 1 and drive one block to Kelly Avenue. Turn right on Kelly Avenue and drive one-half mile to the park entrance.

Contact: Half Moon Bay State Beach, tel. (650) 726-8820 or tel. (415) 330-6300.

17 Pelican Point RV Park

 7

This park is in a rural setting on the southern outskirts of the town of Half Moon Bay, set on an extended bluff near the ocean. All facilities are available nearby, with restaurants available in Half Moon Bay and 10 miles north in Princeton at Pillar Point Harbor. The harbor has an excellent boat launch, a fish-cleaning station, party boat trips for salmon and rockfish and, in the winter, whale-watching trips.

Location: In Half Moon Bay; map E1, grid g1.

Campsites, facilities: There are 75 RV sites with full hookups and patios. Picnic tables are provided. Restrooms, showers, coin laundry, propane gas, small store, clubhouse, and a sanitary disposal station are available. Leashed pets are permitted.

Reservations, fees: Reservations are recommended; $30 to $34 per night, $2 per night for each extra vehicle, $3 per person per night for more than two people, $1 pet fee. Major credit cards accepted. Open year-round.

Directions: In Half Moon Bay, at the junction of Highway 1 and Highway 92, turn south on Highway 1 and drive 2.5 miles to Miramontes Point Road. Turn right and drive a short distance to the park entrance.

Contact: Pelican Point RV Park, tel. (650) 726-9100.

18 Trailer Villa

 6

The Peninsula can seem like a zoo on parade when driving the "Bayshore Freeway," but a short drive to Trailer Villa provides a quick return to some semblance of sanity. It is near the Redwood City Harbor, a pretty spot adjacent to the unusual Leslie Salt site on the shore of the Bay, where there is often an unbelievably high pile of salt. A boat launch is available at the harbor, providing access to South San Francisco Bay.

Location: In Redwood City; map E1, grid f4.

Campsites, facilities: There are 115 RV sites with full hookups. Restrooms, showers, coin laundry, and a sanitary disposal station are available. A modem hookup is available in park office. Leashed pets are permitted.

Reservations, fees: Reservations are required at tel. (800) 366-7880; $23 to $26 per night, $2 per person per night for more than two people, $2 for a second vehicle. Some facilities are wheelchair accessible. Major credit cards accepted. Open year-round.

Directions: In Redwood City on U.S. 101, take the Seaport Boulevard exit east. Drive a short distance to East Bayshore Road. Turn right and drive a mile to 3401 East Bayshore Road.

Contact: Trailer Villa, tel. (650) 366-7880 or fax (650) 366-7948.

19 Sunol Regional Wilderness

 7

This is a very primitive camp set in the Sunol Regional Wilderness, an outstanding park for off-season hiking and camping. In the spring and early summer, it is one of the best of the 250 parks in the Bay Area to see wildflowers. It is also the home of more nesting golden eagles than anywhere else in the world, with a chance to see falcons and hawks as well. In addition, Alameda Creek in Little Yosemite forms several miniature pool-and-drop waterfalls in the spring and early summer. The park is set in rolling oak/bay grasslands. Some sites require hikes of 3.4 miles or longer, with access to the Ohlone Wilderness trail. It is extremely quiet and secluded, with a nearby spring developed to provide drinking water. No alcohol is permitted in the park, and it is subject to temporary closures in late summer due to fire danger.

Location: South of Sunol; map E1, grid g9.

Campsites, facilities: There are four primitive tent sites requiring hikes of 3.4 miles and longer, and two sites for horses requiring rides of 10 miles. Picnic tables and fire grills are provided. Drinking water and vault toilets are available. No dogs are permitted in wilderness.

Reservations, fees: Reservations are required at tel. (510) 562-2267; ($5 reservation fee); $11 per night, $1 pet fee. Major credit cards accepted. Open year-round, weather permitting.

Directions: In the East Bay on Interstate 680, drive to Sunol and the Calaveras Road exit. Turn south on Calaveras and drive four miles to Geary Road. Turn left on Geary Road and drive two miles to the park entrance.

Contact: Sunol Regional Wilderness, tel. (510) 862-2244; East Bay Regional Park District, tel. (510) 635-0135, ext. 2200.

20 Memorial County Park

   8

This beautiful redwood park is set on the western slopes of the Santa Cruz Mountains, tucked in a pocket between the tiny towns of La Honda and Loma Mar. The campground features access to a nearby network of 50 miles of trails, with the best hike along the headwaters of Pescadero Creek. In late winter, it is sometimes possible to see steelhead spawn (no fishing permitted, of course). The trails link up with others in nearby Portola State Park and Sam McDonald County Park, providing access to a vast recreation land. The camp is often filled on summer weekends, but the sites are spaced so it won't cramp your style.

Location: Near La Honda; map E1, grid h3.

Campsites, facilities: There are 156 sites for tents or RVs up to 35 feet long. Picnic tables and fire grills are provided. Drinking water, showers, and flush toilets are available. A sanitary disposal station is available from May through October. No pets are allowed.

Reservations, fees: No reservations; $15 per night, $5 for each additional vehicle. Open year-round.

Directions: In Half Moon Bay, at the junction of Highway 1 and Highway 92, drive south on Highway 1 for 18 miles to the Pescadero Road exit. Turn left on Pescadero Road and drive about 10 miles to the park entrance.

Contact: Memorial County Park, San Mateo County Parks and Recreation, tel. (650) 363-4021.

21 Portola Redwoods State Park

    9

Portola State Park is very secluded, since visitors are required to travel on an extremely slow and winding series of roads to reach it. The park features redwoods and a mixed evergreen and hardwood forest on the western slopes of the Santa Cruz Mountains, the headwaters of Pescadero Creek, and 18 miles of hiking trails. A four-mile hike links up to nearby Memorial Park. At times in the summer, a low fog will move in along the San Mateo coast, and from lookouts near Skyline, visitors can peer to the west at what seems like a pearlescent sea with little islands (hilltops) poking through.

Location: Near Skyline Ridge; map E1, grid i3.

Campsites, facilities: There are 53 sites for tents or RVs up to 24 feet long, four hike-in/bike-in sites, and four group sites for 25 to 50 people. Picnic tables and fire grills are provided. Drinking water, flush toilets, coin-operated showers, ice, and firewood are available. There are nature hikes and campfire programs scheduled on weekends from Memorial Day through Labor Day. The nearest gas is 13 miles away. Leashed pets are permitted on paved surfaces only.

Reservations, fees: Reserve at (800) 444-PARK (800-444-7275) or website: www.ReserveAmerica.com; $12 per night, $37 to $75 per night for group sites. Open March through November.

Directions: From Palo Alto on Interstate 280, turn west on Page Mill Road and drive (slow and twisty) to Skyline Boulevard/Highway 35. Cross Skyline and continue west on Alpine Road (very twisty) for about three miles to Portola State Park Road. Turn left on Portola State Park Road and drive about three miles to the park entrance.

Contact: Portola Redwoods State Park, tel. (650) 948-9098 or fax (650) 948-0137; California State Parks, Santa Cruz District, tel. (831) 429-2850 or fax (831) 429-2876.

22 Butano State Park

 9

The campground at Butano is set in a redwood forest, so pretty and with such good hiking that it has become popular enough to make reservations a must. The reason for its popularity is a series of exceptional hikes, including one to the A-o Nuevo Lookout (well, the lookout is now blocked by trees, but there are glimpses of the ocean elsewhere along the way), the Mill Ox Loop and, for the ambitious, the 11-mile Butano Rim Loop. The latter has a backpack camp in the park's most remote area, where no water is available.

Location: Near Pescadero; map E1, grid i2.

Campsites, facilities: There are 21 sites for tents or RVs and 18 walk-in sites with pit toilets. Picnic tables, food lockers, and fire grills are provided. Restrooms, drinking water, and flush toilets are available. Leashed pets are permitted in campsites.

Reservations, fees: Reserve at (800) 444-PARK (800-444-7275) or website: www.ReserveAmerica.com; $12 per night, $37 to $75 per night for group sites. Open year-round.

Directions: In Half Moon Bay, at the junction of Highway 1 and Highway 92, drive south on Highway 1 for 18 miles to the Pescadero Road exit. Turn left on Pescadero Road and drive past the town of Pescadero to Cloverdale Road. Turn right and drive 4.5 miles to the park entrance on the left.

Contact: Butano State Park, tel. (650) 879-

2040; California State Parks, Bay Area District, tel. (415) 330-6300 or fax (415) 330-6312.

23 Big Basin Redwoods State Park

 10

Big Basin is one of the best state parks in California, featuring giant redwoods near the park headquarters, secluded campsites set in forest, and rare opportunities to stay in a tent cabin or a backpacking trail site. It is a great park for hikers, with two waterfalls, one close and one far, making for stellar destinations. The close one is Sempervirens Falls, a long, narrow, silvery stream, an easy 1.5-hour round trip on the Sequoia Trail. The far one is the famous Berry Creek Falls, a spectacular 70-foot cascade set in a beautiful canyon, framed by redwoods. For hikers in good condition, figure two hours (4.7 miles) to reach Berry Creek Falls, five hours for the round-trip in-and-out, and six hours for the complete loop (12 miles) that extends into the park's most remote areas. There is also an easy nature loop trail near the park headquarters in the valley floor that is routed past several mammoth redwoods.

Location: Near Santa Cruz; map E1, grid i3.

Campsites, facilities: There are 31 sites for tents or RVs up to 27 feet long, 74 sites for tents only, 38 walk-in sites, 41 tent cabins (reservations required), 40 hike-in campsites, and four group sites for 40 to 50 people. Picnic tables, food lockers, and fire grills are provided. Restrooms, drinking water, flush toilets, coin-operated showers, sanitary disposal station, and groceries are available. Some facilities are wheelchair accessible. Leashed pets are allowed in campsites and on paved roads only.

Reservations, fees: Reserve at (800) 444-PARK (800-444-7275) or website: www.Reserve America.com; $12 for family sites, $60 to $75 per night for group sites. Reserve tent cabins at (800) 874-8368, $35 to $49. Open year-round.

Directions: From Santa Cruz, turn north on Highway 9 and drive 12 miles to Boulder Creek. Turn west on Highway 236 and drive nine miles to the park headquarters.

Contact: Big Basin Redwoods State Park, tel. (831) 338-8861, or fax (831) 338-8863; California State Parks, Santa Cruz District, tel. (831) 429-2851 or fax (831) 429-2876.

Sanborn-Skyline County Park

 8

This is a pretty camp set in redwood forest, semi-primitive, but like a world in a different orbit compared to the asphalt of San Jose and the rest of the Santa Clara Valley. These campgrounds get heavy use on summer weekends, of course. This is headquarters for a 3,600-acre park that stretches from the foothills of Saratoga up to the Skyline Ridge. Many hiking trails are available, including a trailhead at camp, in all 15 miles of trails. Most explore lush wooded slopes, with redwoods and tan oak.

Location: Near Pescadero; map E1, grid i5.

Campsites, facilities: There are 15 sites for RVs up to 30 feet long with full hookups, and a separate walk-in campground with 33 sites for tents. Picnic tables and fire pits are provided. Drinking water and flush toilets are available. A youth science center and one-mile nature trail gate closes 30 minutes after sunset. Some facilities are wheelchair accessible. Leashed pets are permitted in RV campground only.

Reservations, fees: Reservations for RV sites required, no reservations for walk-in sites; $25 per night, $8 per night for walk-in, $1 pet fee. Major credit cards accepted. RV sites open year-round, walk-in sites open April to mid-October.

Directions: From Highway 17 in San Jose, drive south for six miles to Highway 9/Saratoga Avenue. Turn west and drive to Saratoga, then continue on Highway 9 for two miles to Sanborn Road. Turn left and drive one mile to

the park on the right. Walk-in sites require a 0.1 to 0.5-mile walk from the parking area.

Contact: Sanborn-Skyline County Park, tel. (408) 867-9959; website: www.parkhere.org.

Carbonero Creek Trailer Park

 5

This camp is just a short hop from Santa Cruz and the shore of Monterey Bay. There are many side trip options, making this a prime location for vacationers cruising the California coast. In Santa Cruz there are several quality restaurants, plus fishing trips and boat rentals at Santa Cruz Wharf, as well as the famous Santa Cruz Boardwalk and amusement park. Note: Open fires are prohibited in the campground.

Location: Near Scotts Valley; map E1, grid j5.

Campsites, facilities: There are 10 sites for tents and 104 RV sites with full or partial hookups. Restrooms, showers, cable TV, coin laundry, modem hookups, recreation room, hot tub, whirlpool, and a seasonal swimming pool are available. Leashed pets are permitted at the RV sites only.

Reservations, fees: Reservations are recommended; $22 to $29 per night, $10 per night for each extra vehicle. Major credit cards accepted. Open year-round.

Directions: From Santa Cruz, at the junction of Highways 1 and 17 north, turn east on Highway 17 north and drive four miles to the Mount Hermon/Big Basin exit. Take that exit north onto Mount Hermon Road and drive to Scotts Valley Drive. Turn right and drive to Disc Drive. Turn right and continue to 917 Disc Drive.

Contact: Carbonero Creek Trailer Park, tel. (831) 438-1288, tel. (800) 546-1288, or fax (831) 438-2877; website: www.campersworld.com.

Parkway Lakes RV Park

 3

This RV park provides a spot to park on the southern outskirts of the San Francisco Bay

Area. It gets its name from nearby Parkway Lake, a pay-to-fish lake where for $12 you get a chance to catch rainbow trout up to 10 pounds in the winter and spring, and catfish and sturgeon in the summer. There are several other reservoirs in the nearby foothills, including Coyote, Anderson, Chesbro, Uvas, and Calero. The best nearby source for fishing and recreation is Coyote Discount Bait and Tackle at tel. (408) 463-0711.

Location: Near Morgan Hill; map E1, grid j9.

Campsites, facilities: There are 113 RV sites with electricity. Restrooms, drinking water, showers, sanitary disposal station, heated swimming pool, modem hookups, coin laundry, and a recreation room are available. Some facilities are wheelchair accessible. Leashed pets are permitted.

Reservations, fees: Reservations are required; $25 to $27 per night. Major credit cards accepted. Open year-round.

Directions: From San Jose, drive south about 12 miles on U.S. 101 to the Cochrane-Monterey Road exit. Turn right on Cochrane Road and continue about 1.5 miles to the Monterey Highway turnoff. Drive south (right) on Monterey Highway about 3.5 miles to Ogier Road. Turn right on Ogier Road and drive to 100 Ogier Road on the right.

Contact: Parkway Lakes RV Park, tel. (408) 779-0244 or fax (408) 778-7647.

Note: For Del Valle Regional Park, Joseph Grant County Park, and Henry W. Coe State Park, see chapter E2.

TANGLING WITH A DELTA STURGEON

MAP E2

374

TO DIXON   TO COURTLAND   TO SACRAMENTO

a
(113)
🏴 **1**
Rio Vista
🏴 **3**
Walnut Grove
🏴 **2**
Thornton
Galt
Birds Landing
🏴 **4-5**
Isleton
(99)
(5)

b
🏴 **7** (160)
🏴 **6**
Webb Tract
(12)
🏴 **8** 🏴 **9**
Lodi
Lockeford
Clements
Antioch
Jersey Island
Bethel Island
San Joaquin River

c
Contra Loma Reservoir
Oakley
🏴 **10** 🏴 **11**
(4)
Knightsen
(J8)
(J3)
(88)
(J5)
Waterloo
Bellota
🏴 **12**
🏴 **13**
(26)
Linden
Brentwood

d
Discovery Bay
(4)
Byron
BETHANY RESERVOIR STATE RECREATION AREA
(J4)
STOCKTON
(99)
(4)
Farmington
🏴 **14**

e
(580)
(205)
Bethany
Tracy
🏴 **15**
Manteca
(J3)
(120)
Escalon
(J7)
(J6)

450   **480**

f
Livermore
(J2)
Del Valle Reservoir
🏴 **16**
(580)
🏴 **17**
🏴 **18**
Vernalis
🏴 **19**
CASWELL MEMORIAL STATE PARK
Stanislaus River
Ripon
(106)
Riverbank
(99)
MODESTO
(5)

g
OHLONE REGIONAL WILDERNESS
Westley
(33)
(132)
Tuolumne River
(J16)
Ceres

h
🏴 **20**
Patterson
Keyes
(J17)
Turlock

i
🏴 **21**
(130)
Mount Hamilton 4,208 feet
LICK OBSERVATORY
(5)
Crows Landing
🏴 **22**
🏴 **23**
Merced River
Hilmar
(165)

j
HENRY W. COE STATE PARK
🏴 **24**
(101)
Newman
Stevinson
KESTERSON NATIONAL WILDLIFE REFUGE
Gustine
(140)

TO CONCORD
TO HAYWARD
TO PLEASANTON
TO SAN JOSE
TO IONE
TO SPRING VALLEY
TO COPPEROPOLIS
TO OAKDALE
TO WATERFORD
TO SNELLING
TO LIVINGSTON
TO MERCED

568
TO SANTA NELLA   TO LOS BANOS

© AVALON TRAVEL PUBLISHING, INC.

0 1 2 3 4 5 6 7 8 9

CHAPTER E2

1 Snug Harbor Marina and RV Camp/Park

       6

This year-round resort is an ideal resting place for families who enjoy water-skiing, boating, biking, swimming, and fishing. Anglers will find good prospects for striped bass, black bass, blue gill, and catfish. The waterfront sites with docks give Snug Harbor the feel of a Louisiana bayou.

Location: Near Rio Vista; map E2, grid a3.

Campsites, facilities: There are 45 waterfront sites for RVs or tents with docks and full hookups and 15 inland sites with water hookups only. There are also five rental cabins. Restrooms, hot showers, sanitary disposal station, convenience store, barbecue, swimming beach, children's play area, boat launch, paddle boat rentals, propane gas, and a full-service marina are available. Some facilities are wheelchair accessible.

Reservations, fees: Reservations recommended; $27 to $30 per night, $4 per night for each extra vehicle, $4 per person per night for more than four people. Major credit cards accepted. Open year-round.

Directions: From Sacramento, drive 26 miles south on Interstate 5 to Highway 12. Drive west on Highway 12 about 20 miles to Rio Vista and then turn north on Route 84 for two miles to the Real McCoy Ferry to Ryer Island. Take the ferry across the

Sacramento River (cars are allowed). On Ryer Island, drive four miles on the levee road to Snug Harbor.

Contact: Snug Harbor Marina and RV Camp/Park, tel. (916) 775-1455 or fax (916) 775-1594; website: www.snugharbor.net.

2 Brannan Island State Recreation Area

 7

This state park is perfectly designed for boaters, set in the heart of the Delta's vast waterways. You get year-round adventure: water-skiing and fishing for catfish are popular in the summer, and in the winter the immediate area is often good for striped bass fishing. The proximity of the campgrounds to the boat launch deserves a medal. What many people do is tow a boat here, launch it, and keep it docked, then return to their site and set up; this allows them to come and go as they please, boating, fishing, and exploring in the Delta.

Location: On the Sacramento River; map E2, grid a4.

Campsites, facilities: There are 102 sites for tents or RVs up to 36 feet long, and six group sites for up to 30 people each. Picnic tables and fire grills are provided. Drinking water, restrooms, showers (at the boat launch site), boat berths, sanitary disposal station, and a boat launch are available. Some facilities are wheelchair accessible. Supplies can be obtained three miles away in Rio Vista. Leashed pets are permitted.

Reservations, fees: Reserve at (800) 444-PARK (800-444-7275) or website: www.ReserveAmerica.com; $12 per night, $22 per night for group sites. Open year-round.

Directions: In Fairfield on Interstate 80, take the Highway 12 exit, drive 14 miles southeast to Rio Vista, and continue to Highway 160 (at the signal before the bridge). Turn right on Highway 160 and drive three miles to the park entrance on the left.

Contact: Brannan Island State Recreation Area, tel. (916) 777-6671; Goldrush District Office, tel. (916) 445-7373.

3 Sandy Beach County Park

 6

This is a surprisingly little-known park, especially considering it provides beach access to the Sacramento River. It is a popular spot for sunbathers in hot summer months, but in winter, it is one of the few viable spots where you can fish from the shore for sturgeon. It also provides outstanding boating access to the Sacramento River, including one of the best fishing spots for striped bass in the fall, the Rio Vista Bridge.

Location: On the Sacramento River; map E2, grid a2.

Campsites, facilities: There are 42 sites for tents or RVs. Picnic tables and fire grills are provided. Electricity, drinking water, flush toilets, showers, sanitary disposal station, and a boat ramp are available. Some facilities are wheelchair accessible. Supplies can be obtained nearby (within a mile). Pets are permitted with proof of rabies vaccination.

Reservations, fees: Reservations are accepted; $12 to $15 per night, $5 per night for each extra vehicle, maximum 10 people per site, senior discounts, $1 pet fee. Major credit cards accepted. Open year-round.

Directions: From Interstate 80 in Fairfield, take the Highway 12 exit and drive southeast for 25 miles to Rio Vista and the intersection with Main Street. Turn right on Main Street and drive a short distance to Second Street. Turn right and drive a half mile to Beach Drive. Continue on Beach Drive to the park.

Contact: Solano County Parks, tel. (707) 374-2097 or fax (707) 374-4972.

4 Duck Island RV Park

 6

This pleasant rural park, set up for adults only, has riverside access that provides an opportunity for bank fishing on the Sacramento

River. A boat ramp is available at the end of Main Street in Rio Vista. Both Hap's and The Trap provide reliable fishing information as well as all gear needed for fishing.

Location: On the Sacramento River; map E2, grid a2.

Campsites, facilities: There are 51 RV sites with full hookups. Picnic tables are provided. A laundry and recreation room with a kitchen are available. Some facilities are wheelchair accessible. A small store is available, with propane, bait, and RV supplies. Other supplies can be obtained in Rio Vista. Adults only. Leashed pets are permitted.

Reservations, fees: Reservations are accepted; $20 per night. Reservation and deposit are required for groups. Major credit cards accepted. Open year-round.

Directions: In Fairfield on Interstate 80, take the Highway 12 exit and drive 14 miles southeast to Rio Vista and continue to Highway 160 (at the signal before the bridge). Turn right on Highway 160 and drive just under a mile to the RV park.

Contact: Duck Island RV Park, tel. (800) 825-3898 or (916) 777-6663.

5 Delta Marina RV Resort

     6

This is a prime spot for boat campers. Summers are hot and breezy, and water-skiing is popular on the nearby Sacramento River. From November to March, the striped bass fishing is quite good, often as close as just a half mile upriver at the Rio Vista Bridge. The boat launch at the harbor is a bonus.

Location: On the Sacramento River Delta; map E2, grid a2.

Campsites, facilities: There are 25 RV sites with full hookups. Picnic tables and fire grills are provided. Restrooms, showers, coin laundry, playground, boat ramp, ice, and propane gas are available. Some facilities are wheelchair accessible. Leashed pets (one pet per vehicle) are permitted.

Reservations, fees: Reservations are ac-

cepted; $18 to $25 per night. Major credit cards accepted. Open year-round.

Directions: From Fairfield on Interstate 80, take the Highway 12 exit and drive southeast for 14 miles to Rio Vista and the intersection with Main Street. Take the Main Street exit, drive a short distance, turn right on Second Street, left on Marina Drive, and continue another short distance to the harbor.

Contact: Delta Marina RV Resort, tel. (707) 374-2315 or fax (707) 374-6471.

6 Eddo's Harbor and RV Park

     6

This is an ideal spot for campers with boats. Eddo's is set on the San Joaquin River, upstream of the Antioch Bridge, in an outstanding region for fishing, powerboating, and water-skiing. In summer, boaters have access to 1,000 miles of Delta waterways, with the best of them in a nearby spider web of rivers and sloughs off the San Joaquin to False River, Frank's Tract, and Old River. Hot weather and sheltered sloughs make this ideal for water-skiing. In the winter, a nearby fishing spot called Eddo's Bar, as well as the mouth of the False River, attract striped bass.

Location: On the San Joaquin River Delta; map E2, grid a2.

Campsites, facilities: There are 20 sites with full hookups for RVs and three tent sites. Picnic tables are provided. Flush toilets, hot showers, launch ramp, boat storage, fuel dock, coin laundry, modem hookups, and a small grocery store are available. Some facilities are wheelchair accessible. Leashed pets are permitted.

Reservations, fees: Reservations are recommended; $19 to $22 per night. Major credit cards accepted. Open year-round.

Directions: In Fairfield on Interstate 80, take the Highway 12 exit and drive 14 miles southeast to Rio Vista and continue three miles to Highway 160 (at the signal before the bridge). Turn left on Highway 160 and drive five miles to the campground along the San Joaquin River. Note: If arriving by boat, the camp is adjacent to Light 21.

Contact: Eddo's Harbor and RV Park, tel. (925) 757-5314 or fax (925) 757-6246; website: www.eddosresort.com.

⑦ New Hope Landing

 6

New Hope Landing is a privately operated resort set along the Mokelumne River in the upper San Joaquin Delta. There's a marina available, which provides access to 1,000 miles of Delta waterways via the Mokelumne River. The Lower Mokelumne is often an excellent area to troll for striped bass in April, and to water-ski in summer. In late summer, water hyacinth is sometimes a problem farther upstream.

Location: On the Mokelumne River north of Stockton; map E2, grid b1.

Campsites, facilities: There are 12 sites for tents and 52 sites for RVs with full hookups. Restrooms, showers, ice, bait, propane gas, and a marina are available. Some facilities are wheelchair accessible. Leashed pets are permitted.

Reservations, fees: Reservations are accepted; $15 to $22.50 per night for two people, $3 for each additional person. Open year-round.

Directions: From Stockton on Interstate 5, drive north for 25 miles to the Thornton exit. Take that exit, turn west on Walnut Grove Road, and drive 3.3 miles to the campground entrance on the left.

Contact: New Hope Landing, tel. or fax (209) 794-2627.

⑧ Tower Park Marina and Resort

 6

This huge resort is ideal for boat-in campers who desire a full-facility marina. The camp is set on Little Potato Slough near the Mokelumne River. In the summer, this is a popular water-skiing area. Some hot weekends are like a continuous party.

Location: Near Stockton; map E2, grid b5.

Campsites, facilities: There are 500 sites for tents or RVs, most with full hookups (tent sites are closed in the winter). Park-model rentals are also available. Picnic tables and barbecues are provided. Restrooms, showers, sanitary disposal station, pavilion, boat rentals, overnight boat slips, double boat launch, playground, restaurant, coin laundry, gift shop, grocery store, and propane gas are available. Some facilities are wheelchair accessible. Leashed pets are permitted.

Reservations, fees: Reservations are recommended; $14 to $26 per night, maximum six people per site, $2 pet fee per night; park models rent for $60 per night or $295 per week. Major credit cards accepted. Open year-round.

Directions: In Stockton, head north on Interstate 5 for 14 miles to the Lodi/Highway 12 exit. Turn west on Highway 12 and drive about five miles to Tower Park Way (turn left before first bridge). Turn left and drive a short distance to the park.

Contact: Tower Park Marina and Resort, tel. (209) 369-1041 or fax (209) 943-5656.

⑨ Westgate Landing County Park

 6

Summer temperatures typically reach the high 90s and low 100s here, and this county park provides a little shade and boating access to the South Fork Mokelumne River. On hot summer nights, some campers will stay up late and night fish for catfish. Between storms in winter, the area typically gets smothered in dense fog.

Location: In the San Joaquin River Delta near Stockton; map E2, grid b5.

Campsites, facilities: There are 14 sites for tents or RVs. Picnic tables and barbecues are provided. Drinking water and flush toilets are available. Groceries and propane gas are nearby. There are 24 boat slips available. Leashed pets are permitted.

Reservations, fees: Reservations available at least three weeks in advance; $9 per night, $3 per night for each extra vehicle, boat slips are $10, $1 pet fee. Open year-round.

Directions: In Stockton at the junction of Interstate 5 and Highway 4, head north on Interstate 5 for 14 miles to the Lodi/Highway 12 exit. Turn left (west) on Highway 12 and drive about five miles to Glasscock Road. Turn right and drive about a mile to the park.

Contact: County Parks Department, tel. (209) 953-8800.

🔟 Island Park

    5

This privately operated RV park is set on the edge of the San Joaquin Delta's boating paradise, with more than 1,000 miles of waterways available. Frank's Tract, Old River, False River, and the lower Mokelumne River are all spots that provide good water-skiing in the summer. Nearby Frank's Tract has become one of the best fishing spots for largemouth bass in North America.

Location: On the San Joaquin River Delta; map E2, grid c2.

Campsites, facilities: There are 80 RV sites with full hookups. Restrooms, showers, coin laundry, recreation room, cable TV, and a swimming pool are available. Some facilities are wheelchair accessible. Small leashed pets are permitted.

Reservations, fees: No reservations; $20 per night. Open year-round.

Directions: From Antioch, turn east on Highway 4 and drive to Oakley and Cypress Road. Turn left on Cypress Road, drive over the Bethel Island Bridge, and continue a half mile to Gateway Road. Turn right and drive a half mile to Island Park.

Contact: Island Park, tel. (925) 684-2144 or fax (925) 684-0889.

🔢 Lundborg Landing

     5

This park is set on Bethel Island in the heart of the San Joaquin Delta. The boat ramp here provides immediate access to an excellent area for water-skiing, and it turns into a playland on hot summer days. In the fall and winter, the area often provides good striper fishing at nearby Frank's Tract, False River, and San Joaquin River. The fishing for largemouth bass at Frank's Tract is rated among the best in North America. Catfishing in surrounding slough areas is also good year-round. The Delta Sportsman Shop at Bethel Island has reliable fishing information. Live web camera pictures of Frank's Tract available on website.

Location: On the San Joaquin River Delta; map E2, grid c2.

Campsites, facilities: There are 76 RV sites with full hookups. Cabins are available. Restrooms, laundry room, showers, sanitary disposal station, propane gas, playground, boat ramp, and full restaurant and bar are available. Some facilities are wheelchair accessible. Leashed pets are permitted.

Reservations, fees: Reservations and deposit are required; $16 to $20 per night, $97 weekly rate. Open year-round.

Directions: From Antioch, turn east on Highway 4 and drive to Oakley and Cypress Road. Turn left on Cypress Road, drive over the Bethel Island Bridge, and continue a half mile to Gateway Road. Turn right on Gateway Road, drive two miles, then turn left into the park at the large sign and tugboat.

Contact: Lundborg Landing, P.O. Box 220, Bethel Island, CA 94511; tel. (925) 684-9351; website: www.lundborglanding.com.

🔢 Stockton-Lodi KOA

      1

This KOA camp is in the heart of the San Joaquin Valley. The proximity to Interstate 5 and Highway 99 makes it work for long-distance vacationers looking for a spot to park the rig for the night. The San Joaquin Delta is 15 miles to the west, with best access provided off Highway 12 to Isleton and Rio Vista; it's also a pretty drive.

Location: In Lodi; map E2, grid c6.

Campsites, facilities: There are 102 sites for tents or RVs, many with full hookups. There are two cabins available. Picnic tables are provided. Restrooms, showers, sanitary disposal station, grocery store, propane gas, coin laundry, modem hookups, recreation room, swimming pool, and a playground are available. Some facilities are wheelchair accessible. Leashed pets are permitted.

Reservations, fees: Reservations only at tel. (800) 562-1229; $19 to $25 per night for tent and RV sites, $34 per night for cabins, four person maximum. Major credit cards accepted. Open year-round.

Directions: From Stockton on Interstate 5 north, drive five miles north to Eight Mile Road. Turn east and drive five miles to the campground at 2851 East Eight Mile Road.

Contact: Stockton-Lodi KOA, tel. (209) 941-2573, tel. (209) 334-0309, or fax (209) 941-2573.

13 Sahara Mobile Court

     1

They play Bingo every Tuesday night here, and that should tell you everything you need to know about this spot.

Location: In Stockton; map E2, grid c6.

Campsites, facilities: There are 27 RV sites with full hookups. Restrooms, showers, cable TV, phone hookups, recreation room, swimming pool (seasonal), and coin laundry are available. Some facilities are wheelchair accessible. A playground and grocery store can be found within several miles. Small leashed pets are permitted.

Reservations, fees: Reservations are accepted; $20 per night, $85 weekly rate, $270 monthly rate. Open year-round.

Directions: In Stockton on Highway 99 north, take the Cherokee Lane exit. Turn right and

three miles to Sanguinetti Lane. Turn right and drive a mile to 2340 Sanguinetti Lane.

Contact: Sahara Mobile Park, tel. or fax (209) 464-9392.

14 Oakwood Lake Resort & Manteca Waterslides

     2

This is a huge, privately operated "water theme" park that covers 375 acres and offers a wide array of water-related recreation activities. It is a great place for families to cool off and have fun on hot summer days, with youngsters lining up for trips down the water slides.

Location: Near Stockton; map E2, grid d5.

Campsites, facilities: There are 111 tent sites, 74 tent or RV sites with partial hookups, and 196 RV-only sites with full hookups. Picnic tables are provided. Electrical connections and sewer hookups are provided at most sites. Restrooms, showers, sanitary disposal station, grocery store, coin laundry, propane gas, swimming lagoon, water slides, organized activities, and a stocked 75-acre lake are available. The facilities are wheelchair accessible. Leashed pets are permitted.

Reservations, fees: Reservations are accepted; $25 to $29 per night, $11.99 per person per night for more than four people (age 5 and under are free), $2 pet fee. Open year-round.

Directions: In Manteca, turn east on Highway 120 and drive two miles to Airport Way. Turn south and drive a half mile to Woodward Way. Turn right and drive two miles to the park entrance.

Contact: Oakwood Lake Resort, tel. (209) 239-9566 or fax (209) 239-2060; website: www.oakwoodlake.com.

15 Dos Reis County Park

      6

This is a 90-acre county park that has a quarter mile of San Joaquin River frontage, boat ramp, and nearby access to the eastern Delta near Stockton. The sun gets scalding hot here in the summer, branding everything in sight. That's why boaters make quick work of getting in the water, then cooling off with water sports. In the winter, this area often has zero visibility from tule fog.

Location: On the San Joaquin River near Stockton; map E2, grid ee.

Campsites, facilities: There are 26 tent and RV sites with full hookups. Picnic tables and fire grills are provided. Restrooms, showers, and a boat ramp are available. A grocery store, coin laundry, and propane gas can be found within several miles. Leashed pets are permitted.

Reservations, fees: Reservations are accepted and must be made at least three weeks in advance; $13 per night, $1 pet fee. Open year-round.

Directions: From Stockton on Interstate 5, drive a short distance to the Lathrop exit. Turn northwest on Lathrop and drive a mile to Dos Reis Road. Turn toward the San Joaquin River and drive to the park on the east side of the river.

Contact: San Joaquin County Parks Department, tel. (209) 953-8800.

16 Del Valle Regional Park

 7

Of the 50 parks in the East Bay Regional Park District, it is Del Valle that provides the greatest variety of recreation at the highest quality. Del Valle Reservoir is the centerpiece, a long narrow lake that fills a canyon, providing a good boat launch for powerboating and fishing for trout, striped bass, and catfish. The sites are somewhat exposed due to the grassland habitat, but they fill anyway on most weekends and three-day holidays. A trailhead south of the lake provides access to the Ohlone Wilderness Trail, and for the well conditioned, there is the 5.5-mile butt-kicker of a climb to Murietta Falls, gaining 1,600 feet in 1.5 miles. Murietta Falls is the Bay Area's highest waterfall, 100 feet tall, though its thin, silvery wisp is difficult to view directly and rarely

evokes much emotional response after such an intense climb.

Location: Near Livermore; map E2, grid f0.

Campsites, facilities: There are 150 sites for tents or RVs, 21 with partial hookups. Picnic tables and fire grills are provided. Drinking water, flush toilets, hot showers, a sanitary disposal station, full marina, and a boat launch are available. Pets are permitted.

Reservations, fees: Reservations are required; phone (510) 562-2267 ($6 reservation fee); $15 to $18 per night, $1 pet fee. Major credit cards accepted. Open year-round.

Directions: On Interstate 580, drive to Livermore and the North Livermore Avenue exit. Turn south and drive on North/South Livermore Road (this will turn into Tesla Road) to Mines Road. Turn right and drive south for three miles to Del Valle Road. Turn right and drive for three miles to the entrance to the park.

Contact: East Bay Regional Park District, tel. (510) 635-0135, ext. 2200; Del Valle Regional Park, tel. (925) 373-0332.

17 Carnegia State Vehicular Rec Area

 2

This is a major state-run OHV area, with mainly dirt bikes. Don't show up without one, or its equivalent. This area is barren and ugly, and extremely noisy on weekends. It can get hot, windy, and dusty as well. But that's just what dirt bikers want, and they have it all to themselves. There is an overflow area, so no one need fear being turned away, but the main campsite almost never fills.

Location: Carenegia State Vehicular Rec Area near Tracy; map E2, grid f3.

Campsites, facilities: There are 18 tent and RV sites with no length limit. No hookups. Picnic tables and fire rings are provided. Restrooms, drinking water, flush toilets, and outdoor cold showers are available, but note that the drinking water (high in iron) tastes terrible, and you are advised to bring bottled water. Nearest supplies are 10 miles away. Leashed pets are permitted.

Reservations, fees: No reservations; $6 fee per night. Open year-round, weather permitting.

Directions: From Interstate 580 (south of Tracy), drive to Corral Hollow Road. Take that exit, and drive southwest for six miles to the campground on the left.

Contact: Carnegia State Vehicular Rec Area, tel. (925) 447-9027 or (925) 447-0426.

18 Orchard RV Park

    5

The huge swimming pool and water slides here make this a popular campground for families. Temperatures in the 100-degree range in the summer keep both in constant use. This privately operated park is set up primarily for owners of RVs. Its location near Interstate 5 makes it a winner for many of them.

Location: Near Stockton; map E2, grid f5.

Campsites, facilities: There are 12 tent sites and 88 drive-through RV sites with full hookups. Picnic tables and fire grills are provided. Restrooms, showers, laundry room, sanitary disposal station, swimming pool, restaurant, and horseshoe pits are available. The facilities are wheelchair accessible. Groceries and a weekend flea market can be found within walking distance (less than a mile). Leashed pets are permitted.

Reservations, fees: Reservations are accepted; $20 per night. Open year-round.

Directions: From Interstate 5 in Vernalis, turn east on Highway 132 and drive three miles to the signed campground entrance at 2701 East Highway 132.

Contact: Orchard RV Park, tel. (209) 836-2090.

19 Caswell Memorial State Park

       7

Caswell Memorial State Park features shoreline frontage along the Stanislaus River, along with an additional 250 acres of parkland. The Stanislaus provides shoreline fishing for catfish on summer nights. Other recreation options here include a visitor center, an interpretive nature trail, and swimming.

Location: On the Stanislaus River near Stockton; map E2, grid f6.

Campsites, facilities: There are 64 sites for tents or RVs up to 24 feet long, and one group site for up to 50 people. Picnic tables, food lockers, and fire grills are provided. Drinking water, flush toilets, showers, wood, a swimming beach, nature trail and exhibits are available. Some facilities, including the exhibits, are wheelchair accessible. Weekend interpretive programs are available in the summer. Leashed pets are permitted.

Reservations, fees: Reserve at (800) 444-PARK (800-444-7275) or website: www.ReserveAmerica.com; $12 per night; groups with up to 12 vehicles, $37 per night. Open year-round.

Directions: From Manteca, drive south on Highway 99 for 1.5 miles to the Austin Road exit. Turn south and drive four miles to the park entrance.

Contact: Caswell Memorial State Park, tel. (209) 599-3810; California State Parks, Four Rivers District, tel. (209) 826-1196 or fax (209) 826-0284.

20 Frank Raines Regional Park

      4

This park is primarily a riding area for folks with dirt bikes and three- and four-wheel OHVs, who take advantage of the rough-terrain riding course available here. A side trip option is to visit Minniear Park, directly to the east, which is a day-use wilderness park with hiking trails and a creek. This area is very pretty in the spring when the foothills are still green and many wildflowers are blooming.

Location: Near Modesto; map E2, grid h5.

Campsites, facilities: There are 34 tent or RV sites. Fire grills and picnic tables are provided. Restrooms, drinking water, showers, electrical connections, sewer hookups, and a playground are available. Some facilities are wheelchair accessible. Pets are permitted.

Reservations, fees: No reservations; $12 to $16 per night, $6 to $8 per night for each extra vehicle, $2 pet fee, $2 fee for rough-terrain vehicles. Disabled vets can camp 15 days for free, others with disabilities get a 50 percent camp discount. Open year-round.

Directions: On Interstate 5 (south of the junction of Interstate 5 and Interstate 580), drive to the Patterson exit. Turn west and drive to Del Puerto Canyon Road. Turn west and drive 16 miles to the park.

Contact: Frank Raines Regional Park, tel. (408) 897-3127, or fax (408) 897-3127.

21 Joseph Grant County Park
 7

Grant Ranch is a great, wild playland covering 9,000 acres in the foothills of nearby Mount Hamilton to the east. It features 40 miles of hiking trails (horses permitted), 20 miles of old ranch roads that are perfect for mountain biking, a pretty lake (Grant Lake), and miles of foothills, canyons, and grasslands. The campground is set amid oak grasslands, is shaded, and can be used as a base camp for planning the day's recreation. The best hikes are to Halls Valley, especially in the winter and spring when there are many secret little creeks and miniature waterfalls in hidden canyons, the Hotel Trail, and Cañada de Pala Trail, which drops down to San Felipe Creek, the prettiest stream in the park. A great side trip is the slow, curvy drive east to Lick Observatory for great views of the Santa Clara Valley.

Location: Near San Jose; map E2, grid i0.

Campsites, facilities: There are 40 sites for tents or RVs up to 28 feet long. Picnic tables and fire grills are provided. Drinking water, hot showers, sanitary disposal station, and toilets are available. Pets are permitted.

Reservations, fees: Reservations for group sites only at tel. (408) 358-3751; $15 per night for individual sites, $6 per night for each extra

vehicle, eight person maximum per campsite, $1 pet fee. Check-in required before sunset; gates locked. Open weekends in March, then daily from April through November.

Directions: In San Jose at the junction of Interstate 680 and U.S. 101, take Interstate 680 north to the Alum Rock Avenue exit. Turn east and drive four miles to Mount Hamilton Road. Turn right and drive eight miles to the park headquarters entrance on the right side of the road.

Contact: Santa Clara County Parks Department, tel. (408) 274-6121 or fax (408) 270-4808; website: www.parkhere.org.

22 Fisherman's Bend River Camp
   5

This small, privately operated campground is set along the San Joaquin River on the southern outskirts of the San Joaquin Delta country. The park offers shaded sites and direct river access for boaters. This section of river provides fishing for catfish on hot summer nights.

Location: On the San Joaquin River; map E2, grid i7.

Campsites, facilities: There are 20 sites for tents only and 38 RV sites with full hookups. Picnic tables and fire grills are provided. Drinking water, restrooms, showers, sanitary disposal station, laundry room, modem hookups, boat ramp, fish-cleaning station, swimming pool, playground, and horseshoe pits are available. Some facilities are wheelchair accessible. Leashed pets are permitted.

Reservations, fees: Reservations are accepted at (800) 862-3731; $18 to $26 per night, $3 per person per night for more than three people. Major credit cards accepted. Open year-round.

Directions: South of the junction of Interstate 5 and Interstate 580, take Interstate 5 south to the Newman/Stuhr

Road exit. Turn left (east) on County Road J18/Stuhr Road and drive 6.5 miles to Hills Ferry Road. Turn left and drive a mile to River Road. Turn left on River Road and drive to 26836 River Road.

Contact: Fisherman's Bend River Camp, tel. (209) 862-3731, or fax (209) 862-1684.

George J. Hatfield State Recreation Area

    5

This is a small state park set in the heart of the San Joaquin Valley, near the confluence of the Merced River and the San Joaquin River, well known for hot summer days and foggy winter nights. Fishing is good for catfish in the summer here, and some folks will stay up late hoping a big channel catfish will take their bait. During the peak migration from late fall through winter and early spring, there can also be a good number of striped bass in the area.

Location: Near Newman; map E2, grid j8.

Campsites, facilities: There are 21 family sites and a large group site for tents or RVs. The group site has an electrical hookup and can accommodate up to 40 people. Picnic tables and fire grills are provided. Drinking water and flush toilets are available. Supplies can be obtained in Newman, five miles away. Leashed pets are permitted.

Reservations, fees: Call ahead for group reservations; $12 per night for family sites, $15 to $30 per night for the group site. Open year-round.

Directions: South of the junction of Interstate 5 and Interstate 580, take Interstate 5 south to the Newman/Stuhr Road exit. Turn east on County Road J18/Stuhr Road and drive to Newman and the junction with Highway 33. Turn right and drive a short distance to Hills Ferry Road. Turn left and drive five miles to the park entrance on the right.

Contact: George J. Hatfield State Recreation Area, tel. (209) 632-1852 or (209) 826-1196.

24 Henry W. Coe State Park

 8

This is the Bay Area's backyard wilderness, with 100,000 acres of wildlands. All of it is networked by 100 miles of ranch roads and 300 miles of hiking trails—providing access to 140 ponds and small lakes, hidden streams, and a habitat that is paradise for fish, wildlife, and wild flora. While there are drive-in campsites at park headquarters, set at a hilltop and ideal for stargazing and watching meteor showers, it is the wilderness hike-in and bike-in sites where you will get the full flavor of the park. Before setting out for the outback, always consult with the rangers here—the ambitious plans of many hikers cause them to suffer dehydration and heatstroke. For wilderness trips, the best jump-off point is Coyote Creek trailhead upstream of Coyote Reservoir near Gilroy. The park has excellent pond-style fishing, but requires extremely long hikes (typically 10- to 25-mile round trips) to reach the best lakes, including Mustang Pond, Jackrabbit Lake, Coit Lake, and Mississippi Lake. Expect hot weather in the summer; spring and early summer are the prime times. Even though the park may appear to be 120 square miles of oak foothills, the terrain is often steep, and making ridges often involves climbs of 1,500 feet. There are many great secrets to be discovered here, including Rooster Comb and Coyote Creek. At times on spring days, wild pigs seem to be everywhere. Golden eagles are also abundant. Bring a water purifier for hikes because there is no drinking water in the outback.

Location: Near Gilroy; map E2, grid j1.

Campsites, facilities: There are 10 sites for tents and 10 sites for tents or RVs. There are also six equestrian campsites, 82 hike-in/bike-in sites, and 10 group sites for 10 to 50 people. At the drive-in site at park headquarters, picnic tables and fire grills are provided. Drinking water and vault toilets are available. Leashed pets are permitted. At the horse camps, corrals and water troughs are available. At hike-in/bike-in sites, vault toilets are provided, but no drinking water is available. Garbage must be packed out.

Reservations, fees: Reserve at (800) 444-PARK (800-444-7275) or website: www.ReserveAmerica.com; $10 per night. Reservations for group site at tel. (408) 779-2728, $25 per night. No reservation for hike-in/bike-in or horse sites, $12 per night for horse sites, $3 for hike-in/bike-in sites. For hike-in/bike-in or horse sites, a wilderness permit is required from park headquarters. Open year-round.

Directions: From Morgan Hill on U.S. 101, take the East Dunne Avenue exit. Turn east and drive 13 miles (including over the bridge at Anderson Lake, then very twisty) to the park entrance.

Contact: Henry W. Coe State Park, tel. (408) 779-2728 or tel. (408) 848-4006; California State Parks, Four Rivers District, tel. (209) 826-1196; website: www.coepark.parks.ca.gov.

TOM STIENSTRA

CHAPTER E3

REBEL IN THE SOUTH FORK
TUOLUMNE RIVER, STANISLAUS NATIONAL FOREST

MAP E3

TO DRYTOWN   **380**   TO PIONEER

a

Ione
Buena Vista 104 Lake Amador Jackson Pine Grove 26 STANISLAUS NATIONAL FOREST

88 **1** **2** Mokelumne River **3**

Camanche Reservoir Pardee Reservoir Mokelumne Hill CALAVERAS BIG TREES STATE PARK **4**

b

12 Wallace **4** Valley Springs **5** San Andreas **8-9** **10**

Burson 28 **6** Arnold

7 New Hogan Reservoir Sheep Ranch North Fork Stanislaus River Middle Fork

c

Jenny Lind 49 Murphys South Fork Stanislaus River

d

Milton Angels Camp Vallecito **11** Mi-Wuk Village

J14 Copperopolis **12** Melones **14** **15**

4 **13** New Melones Lake Columbia Twain Harte

4 Eugene Tuttletown 108 **16**

e

17 Jamestown Sonora Tuolumne

Woodward Reservoir **19** Tulloch Reservoir

J14

f

Oakdale Stanislaus River **18** Knights Ferry Chinese Camp Tuolumne River

108 J59 49 **22** Groveland Buck Meadow

g

20 Big Oak Flat 120 **23**

Modesto Reservoir **21** Don Pedro Reservoir **24**

Waterford **25** 132 **26** La Grange **28** Coulterville

h

Hickman **27** **29**

Turlock Lake **30** Lake McClure

i

J17 J16 J59 **31** Merced River

Snelling Merced Falls Bear Valley

Delhi J17 Merced River **32** J16 49 Mount Bullion

j

99 **33** 59 Hornitos Catheys Valley 140 Mariposa

Livingston Winton

Atwater

TO MERCED   **576**   TO MERCED

0 1 2 3 4 5 6 7 8 9

TO CLEMENTS TO BELLOTA TO FARMINGTON 466 TO ESCALON TO MODESTO TO STEVENSON TO TURLOCK

TO BEAR VALLEY TO SONORA PASS 498 TO CRANE FLAT/YOSEMITE TO YOSEMITE

© AVALON TRAVEL PUBLISHING, INC.

CHAPTER E3

1 Lake Amador Recreation Area

 7

Lake Amador is set in the foothill country east of Stockton at an elevation of 485 feet, covering 425 acres with 13 miles of shoreline. Everything here is set up for fishing, with large trout stocks from winter through late spring and the chance for huge bass; plus, water-skiing and personal watercraft are prohibited. The largest two-man bass limit in California was caught here (80 pounds), and the lake record weighed 15 pounds, 13 ounces. The Carson Creek arm and Jackson Creek arm are the top spots.

Location: Near Stockton; map E3, grid a1.

Campsites, facilities: There are 150 sites for tents or RVs, 72 with full hookups, and 12 group sites. Picnic tables and fire grills are provided. Drinking water, restrooms, showers, sanitary disposal station, boat ramp, boat rentals, fishing supplies (including bait and tackle), restaurant, grocery store, propane gas, swimming pond, and a playground are available. Some facilities are wheelchair accessible. Leashed pets are permitted.

Reservations, fees: Reservations are accepted seven days in advance in the summer; $18 per vehicle to $23 per night, $1 per person per night for more than two people. Major credit cards accepted. Open year-round.

Directions: From Stockton, turn east on Highway 88 and drive 24 miles to Clements. Just east of Clements, continue straight on Highway 12 and drive 11 miles to Jackson Valley Road. Turn right (well signed) and drive 4 miles to Lake Amador Drive. Turn right and drive over the dam to the campground office.

Contact: Lake Amador Recreation Area, tel. (209) 274-4739; website: www.lakeamador.com.

2 Lake Pardee Marina

 7

Many people feel that Pardee is the prettiest lake in the Mother Lode country, a big lake covering 2,257 acres with 37 miles of shoreline. It is a beautiful sight in the spring when the lake is full and the surrounding hills are green and glowing. Water-skiing, personal watercraft, and swimming are prohibited at the lake; it is set up expressly for fishing, with high catch rates for rainbow trout and kokanee salmon. During hot weather, attention turns to bass, both smallmouth and largemouth, as well as catfish.

Location: On Pardee Reservoir; map E3, grid a2.

Campsites, facilities: There are 99 sites for tents or RVs without hookups and 12 RV sites with full hookups. Picnic tables and fire grills are provided. Drinking water, restrooms, showers (in the RV section), sanitary disposal station, boat ramp, boat rentals, coin laundry, modem hookups, grocery store, propane gas, RV and boat storage, wading pool, and a swimming pool are available. Some facilities are wheelchair accessible. Leashed pets are permitted.

Reservations, fees: Reservations are accepted for full-hookup RV sites only; $15 to $21 per night, $7.50 per night for each extra vehicle, $1 pet fee. Major credit cards accepted. Open February through October.

Directions: From Stockton, drive east on Highway 88 for 24 miles to the town of Clements. Just east of Clements, turn left on Highway 88 and drive 11 miles to Jackson Valley Road. Turn right and drive to a four-way stop sign at Buena Vista. Turn right and drive for three miles to Stony Creek Road on the left. Turn left and drive a mile to the campground.

Contact: Pardee Recreation Area, tel. (209) 772-1472 or fax (209) 772-0985; website: www.lakepardee.com.

3 Golden Pines RV Resort and Camp

 6

This is a privately operated park set at 5,800 feet on the slopes of the Sierra Nevada near Stanislaus National Forest, the North Stanislaus River, and Calaveras Big Trees State Park (three miles away). The latter features 150 giant sequoias, along with the biggest stump you can imagine, and two easy hikes, one routed through the North Grove, another through the South Grove.

Location: Near Arnold; map E3, grid a9.

Campsites, facilities: There are 40 tent sites, 62 RV sites with full hookups, and four with partial hookups. Fire pits, barbecues, and picnic tables are provided. Drinking water, restrooms, showers, sanitary disposal station, recreation room, swimming pool, playground, grocery store, laundry room, and propane gas are available. Some facilities are wheelchair accessible. Pets are permitted.

Reservations, fees: Reservations are recommended; $16 to $25 per night, $2 per person per night for more than four people, $1 per night for each extra vehicle. Major credit cards accepted. Open year-round.

Directions: From Angels Camp, turn northeast on Highway 4 and drive 22 miles to

Arnold. Continue for seven miles to the campground entrance.

Contact: Golden Pines RV Resort and Camp, tel. (209) 795-2820 or fax (209) 795-7432; website: www.angelfire.com/biz/goldenpines/index/html.

4 Lake Camanche North

The sites at North Shore feature grassy spots with picnic tables set above the lake, and though there are few trees and the sites seem largely exposed, the lake view is quite pretty. The lake will beckon you for water sports and is excellent for boat owners. The warm, clean waters make for good water-skiing (in specified areas), and fishing for trout in spring, bass in early summer, and crappie, bluegill, and catfish in summer.

Location: On Camanche Reservoir; map E3, grid b1.

Campsites, facilities: There are 219 sites for tents or RVs, all without hookups. There are also 12 cottages and some motel rooms. Picnic tables and fire grills are provided. Restrooms, drinking water, showers, sanitary disposal station, boat ramp, boat rentals, laundry room, grocery store, coffee shop/restaurant, and a playground are available. Some facilities are wheelchair accessible. Leashed pets are permitted.

Reservations, fees: Reservations taken only on holidays and for cottages, tel. (209) 763-5121. RV or tent sites are $16 per night, cottages are $77 to $98 per night, and motel rooms are $36 to $65 per night; $8 per night for each extra vehicle; $6 boat launch fee. Major credit cards accepted. Open year-round.

Directions: From Stockton, drive east on Highway 88 for 24 miles to Clements. Just east of Clements, bear left on Highway 88 and drive six miles to Camanche Parkway. Turn right and drive seven miles to the Camanche North Shore entrance gate.

Contact: Lake Camanche North, (209) 763-5121 or fax (209) 763-5789; website: www.norcalfishing.com.

5 Lake Camanche South

Camanche Reservoir is a huge, multifaceted facility, covering 7,700 acres with 53 miles of shoreline, set in the foothills east of Lodi at 325 feet in elevation. It is the No. 1 recreation lake for water-skiing and personal watercraft (in specified areas), as well as swimming. In the spring and summer, it provides outstanding fishing for bass, trout, crappie, bluegill, and catfish. There are two campgrounds at the lake, and both have boat ramps nearby and full facilities. This one at South Shore has a large, but exposed, overflow area for camping, a way to keep from getting stuck for a spot on popular weekends.

Location: On Camanche Reservoir; map E3, grid b1.

Campsites, facilities: There are 330 sites for tents or RVs, 120 with full hookups. There are also seven cottages. Picnic tables and fire grills are provided. Drinking water, restrooms, showers, sanitary disposal station, trout pond, boat ramp, boat rentals, coin laundry, snack bar, and a grocery store are available. Some facilities are wheelchair accessible. Leashed pets are permitted.

Reservations, fees: Reservations are required for group RV sites and cottages; RV site reservations are recommended, and tent site reservations accepted for holidays only at tel. (209) 763-5178. RV sites are $22 per night, cottages $77 to $98 per night, $8 per night for each extra vehicle. Major credit cards accepted. Open year-round.

Directions: From Stockton, drive east on Highway 88 for 24 miles to Clements. Just east of Clements continue east on Highway 12 and drive six miles to South Camanche Parkway. Turn left and drive six miles to the entrance gate.

Contact: Lake Camanche South, tel. (209) 763-5178 or fax (209) 763-5724; website: www.norcalfishing.com

6 Oak Knoll

 7

This is one of three camps at New Hogan Reservoir and is primarily used for overflow camping. The reservoir was created by an Army Corps of Engineers dam project on the Calaveras River. See the entry for Acorn West and Acorn East for more information.

Location: At New Hogan Reservoir; map E3, grid b2.

Campsites, facilities: There are 50 sites for tents or RVs. Fire grills and picnic tables are provided. Drinking water and vault toilets are available. Groceries, propane gas, sanitary disposal station, and a four-lane boat ramp are available nearby. Leashed pets are permitted.

Reservations, fees: Reserve at (877) 444-6777 ($8.65 reservation fee) or website: www.reserveusa.com; $10 per night. Open May to early September.

Directions: From Stockton, drive east on Highway 26 for about 35 miles to Valley Springs and Hogan Dam Road. Turn right and drive 1.5 miles to Hogan Parkway. Turn left and drive one mile to South Petersburg Road. Turn left and drive one-half mile to the campground on the right (adjacent to Acorn campgrounds).

Contact: Goldstrike Harbor Marina, tel. (209) 772-1462; U.S. Army Corps of Engineers, Sacramento District, tel. (209) 772-1343.

7 Acorn West & Acorn East

 7

New Hogan is a big lake in the foothill country, at an elevation of 680 feet, set east of Stockton, covering 4,000 acres with 50 miles of shoreline. Acorn West and Acorn East are two campgrounds on the lake operated by the Army Corps of Engineers. Boaters might also consider boat-in sites near Deer Flat on the eastern shore. Boating and water-skiing are popular here. Fishing for largemouth bass is off-and-on, best in the spring up the Bear Creek and Whiskey Creek arms, and again in the fall when the striped bass come to life, chasing bait fish on the surface. Fishing for largemouth bass can be exceptional in spring and summer. An interpretive trail below the dam is worth checking out.

Location: At New Hogan Reservoir; map E3, grid b2.

Campsites, facilities: There are 58 sites for tents or RVs at Acorn West and 69 sites for tents or RVs at Acorn East. Fire pits and picnic tables are provided. Drinking water, flush toilets, showers, pay telephones, fish-cleaning station, and a sanitary disposal station are available. A four-lane, paved boat ramp is in Acorn East Campground. Groceries, a restaurant, and propane gas are available within three miles. Leashed pets are permitted.

Reservations, fees: Reserve at (877) 444-6777 ($8.65 reservation fee) or website: www.reserveusa.com; $12 to $16 per night. Major credit cards accepted.

Directions: From Stockton, drive east on Highway 26 for about 35 miles to Valley Springs and Hogan Dam Road. Turn right and drive 1.5 miles to Hogan Parkway. Turn left and drive one mile to South Petersburg Road. Turn left and drive one-quarter mile to the campground on the right.

Contact: Goldstrike Harbor Marina, tel. (209) 772-1462; U.S. Army Corps of Engineers, Sacramento District, tel. (209) 772-1343.

8 North Grove

 7

This is one of two campgrounds at Calaveras Big Trees State Park, the state park known for its two groves of giant sequoias (mountain redwoods). The trailhead for a hike on the North Grove Loop is available here, an easy one-mile walk that is routed among 150 sequoias, where the sweet fragrance of the huge trees fills the air. These trees are known for their massive diameter, not for their height, as is the case with coastal redwoods. Another hike, a five-miler, is available in the South Grove, where the park's two largest sequoias (the Agassiz Tree and the Palace Hotel Tree) can be seen on a spur trail. A visitor center is open during peak periods, offering exhibits on the giant sequoia and natural history. The North Fork Stanislaus River runs near Highway 4, providing trout fishing access. The Stanislaus (near the bridge) and Beaver Creek (about 10 miles away) are stocked with trout in late spring and early summer. In the winter this is a popular spot for cross-country skiing and snowshoeing. The elevation is 4,800 feet.

Location: In Calaveras Big Trees State Park; map E3, grid b8.

Campsites, facilities: There are 27 sites for tents, 30 sites for RVs up to 22 feet long, three hike-in sites and two sites designed for wheelchair use. Two group sites are also available for 40 to 60 people each. Fire grills, food lockers, and picnic tables are provided. Drinking water, flush toilets, firewood for purchase, coin-operated showers, and a sanitary disposal station are available. Some facilities are wheelchair accessible, including a nature trail and exhibits. No bicycles are allowed on the paths, but they are permitted on fire roads and paved roads. Leashed pets are permitted, but not on trails.

Reservations, fees: Reserve at (800) 444-PARK (800-444-7275) or website: www.ReserveAmerica.com; $12 per night, $30 to $45 group fee, and $11 for hike-in sites. Open year-round.

Directions: From Angels Camp, drive east on Highway 4 for 23 miles to Arnold and then continue another four miles to the park entrance on the right.

Contact: Calaveras Big Trees State Park, tel. (209) 795-2334 or Columbia State Park, tel. (209) 532-0150.

9 Oak Hollow

 7

This is one of two campgrounds at Calaveras Big Trees State Park. See the entry for North Grove for recreation information.

Location: In Calaveras Big Trees State Park; map E3, grid b8.

Campsites, facilities: There are 23 sites for tents only, 18 sites for RVs up to 22 feet long. Picnic tables, fire rings, and food lockers are provided. Drinking water, flush toilets, and coin-operated showers are available. A sanitary disposal station is available four miles away at North Grove. You can buy supplies in Dorrington. Some facilities are wheelchair accessible, including a nature trail and exhibits. Leashed pets are permitted, except on trails.

Reservations, fees: Reserve at (800) 444-PARK (800-444-7275) or website: www.ReserveAmerica.com; $12 per night. Open May through September.

Directions: From Angels Camp, drive east on Highway 4 for 23 miles to Arnold and then continue another four miles to the park entrance on the right. Continue another four miles to the campground on the right.

Contact: Calaveras Big Trees State Park, tel. (209) 795-2334 or Columbia State Park, tel. (209) 532-0150.

10 Boards Crossing

 8

One of the oldest campgrounds in the Western U.S., Boards Crossing is near a historic one-way bridge that crosses the North Fork Stanislaus River. It is a small, primitive camp set along the river at 3,800 feet in elevation, with Beaver Creek three miles to the east (continue on the access road after crossing the bridge). This place is just far enough off Highway 4 to be overlooked by most campers.

Location: On the North Fork of the Stanislaus River in Stanislaus National Forest; map E3, grid b9.

Campsites, facilities: There are five tent sites. Picnic tables and fire rings are provided. Vault toilets are available. No drinking water is available. Garbage must be packed out. You can buy groceries and propane gas nearby. Leashed pets are permitted.

Reservations, fees: No reservations; no fee; campfire permits required (free). Open June through September.

Directions: From Angels Camp, drive east on Highway 4 and pass Arnold to Dorrington and Boards Crossing Road on the right. Turn right and drive about two miles to the campground entrance road on the right. Turn right and drive about a mile to the campground on the right.

Contact: Stanislaus National Forest, Calaveras Ranger District, tel. (209) 795-1381 or fax (209) 795-6849.

11 49er RV Ranch

This historic ranch/campground was originally built in 1852 as a dairy farm. Several original barns are still standing. The place has been brought up to date, of course, with a small store on the property providing last-minute supplies. Location is a plus, with the Columbia State Historic Park only a half mile away, and the Stanislaus River arm of New Melones Lake within a five-minute drive. The elevation is 2,100 feet.

Location: Near Columbia; map E3, grid d6.

Campsites, facilities: There are 45 sites for trailers and RVs, all with full hookups. Picnic tables and barbecues are provided. Restrooms, drinking water, hot showers, laundry room, store, sanitary disposal station, cable TV, modem hookups, propane gas, and a large barn for group or club activities are available. Some facilities are wheelchair accessible. Leashed pets are permitted.

Reservations, fees: Reservations are accepted; $22.85 to $26.50 per night, $2.50 for each additional person. Group rates are available. Open year-round.

Directions: From Sonora, turn north on Highway 49 for 2.5 miles to Parrots Ferry Road. Turn right and drive 1.7 miles to Columbia Street. Turn right and drive 0.4 mile to Pacific Street. Turn left and drive a block to Italian Bar Road. Turn right and drive a half mile to the campground on the right.

Contact: 49er RV Ranch, tel. (209) 532-4978 or fax (209) 532-4978; website: www.49rv.com.

12 Glory Hole

 7

Glory Hole encompasses both Big Oak and Ironhorse campgrounds. This is one of two major camping areas on New Melones Lake in the Sierra Nevada foothills, a popular spot with a boat ramp nearby for access to outstanding water-skiing and fishing. See the entry for Tuttletown Recreation Area.

Location: At New Melones Lake; map E3, grid d5.

Campsites, facilities: Big Oak has 55 sites for tents or RVs, Ironhorse has 89 sites for tents or RVs; 20 sites at Glory Hole are for tents only. Picnic tables and fire grills are provided. Drinking water, flush toilets, sanitary disposal station, showers, marina, boat rentals, volleyball net, baseball diamond, and a playground are available. Some facilities are wheelchair accessible. Leashed pets are permitted.

Reservations, fees: No reservations; $14 per night. Open year-round.

Directions: From Sonora, drive north on Highway 49 for about 15 miles (Glory Hole Market will be on the left side of the road) to Glory Hole Road. Turn left and drive five miles to the campground, with sites on both sides of the road.

Contact: U.S. Department of Reclamation, tel. (209) 536-9094, or fax (209) 536-9652.

13 Tuttletown Recreation Area

 7

Here is mammoth camping area set on the giant New Melones Lake in the Sierra Nevada foothills. Tuttletown encompasses three campgrounds (Acorn, Manzanita and Chamise) and two group camping areas (Oak Knoll and Fiddleneck). New Melones is a huge reservoir that covers 12,250 acres and offers 100 miles of shoreline and good fishing. Water-skiing is permitted in specified areas; a boat ramp is near camp. Although the lake's main body is huge, the better fishing is well up the lake's Stanislaus River arm (for trout) and in its coves (for bass and bluegill), where there are submerged trees providing perfect aquatic habitat. Trolling for kokanee salmon also has become popular. The lake level often drops dramatically in the fall.

Location: At New Melones Lake; map E3, grid e5.

Campsites, facilities: At Acorn there are 69 sites, at Chamise there are 35 sites, and at Manzanita there are five sites for tents or RVs. Among these are 68 tent-only sites. Two group sites accommodate 100 people (Oak Knoll) and 60 people (Fiddleneck) each. Picnic tables and fire grills are provided. Drinking water, flush toilets, sanitary disposal station, showers, playground, and a boat ramp are available. Some facilities are wheelchair accessible. Leashed pets are permitted.

Reservations, fees: No reservations; $14 per night. Group reservations only; $84 to $140 per night. Open year-round.

Directions: From Sonora, drive north on Highway 49 to Reynolds Ferry Road. Turn left and drive about two miles to the entrance road to the campgrounds.

Contact: U.S. Department of Reclamation, tel. (209) 536-9094, or fax (209) 536-9652.

14 Marble Quarry RV Park

 6

This RV park is set at 2,100 feet in the Mother Lode country, within nearby range of several adventures. Columbia State Historic Park is within walking distance, and the Stanislaus River arm of New Melones Lake is only five miles away.

Location: Near Columbia; map E3, grid d6.

Campsites, facilities: There are 85 sites for RVs (36 have full hookups, 49 have partial hookups), including a small area for tents. Drinking water and picnic tables are provided. Restrooms, showers, swimming pool, coin laundry, modem hookups, store, sanitary disposal station, playground, two clubhouses, lounge, two full kitchens, satellite TV, and propane gas are available. Some facilities are wheelchair accessible. Leashed pets are permitted.

Reservations, fees: Reservations are accepted; $19 to $26.75 per night. Major credit cards accepted. Open year-round.

Directions: From Sonora, turn north on Highway 49 for 2.5 miles to Parrotts Ferry Road. At the stop sign, bear right on Columbia Street and drive to Jackson Street. Turn right on Jackson Street and drive a quarter mile (becomes Yankee Hill Road) to the campground at 11551 Yankee Hill Road.

Contact: Marble Quarry RV Park, tel. (800) 446-1333, ext. 350, or (209) 532-9539; website: www.marblequarry.com.

15 Sugarpine RV Park

 5

Twain Harte is a beautiful little town, right at the edge of the winter snow line, where pines take over the alpine landscape. This park is at the threshold of mountain country, with Pinecrest, Dodge Ridge, and Beardsley Reservoir nearby. Note: Heading east out of Twain Harte, beware of the unannounced hairpin turn at the town of

Confidence. Some drivers are caught off guard by the turn and cross over into oncoming traffic.

Location: In Twain Harte; map E3, grid d9.

Campsites, facilities: There are 13 tent sites and 13 RV sites with full hookups. Picnic tables are provided. Restrooms, showers, playground, pool, video games in summer, laundry room, guest lounge, and a store are available. Some facilities are wheelchair accessible. Leashed pets are permitted.

Reservations, fees: Reservations are accepted; $20 to $25 per night. Open year-round.

Directions: From Sonora, drive east on Highway 108 for 17 miles to the park on the right side of the road.

Contact: Sugarpine RV Park, tel. (800) 326-9014 or (209) 586-4631.

16 River Ranch Campground

 7

This pretty spot, at 2,700 feet, is right where conifers begin to take over from the valley foothill grasslands. The campground is placed near Basin Creek as it enters the Tuolumne River, adding a peaceful element for campers, as well as a chance for trout fishing.

Location: On the Tuolumne River; map E3, grid e9.

Campsites, facilities: There are 50 sites for tents or RVs. Picnic tables and fire rings are provided. Restrooms and showers are available. A grocery store, coin laundry, and propane gas are nearby. Leashed pets are permitted.

Reservations, fees: Group reservations are accepted; $14 per night, $3 per person per night for more than four people. Open year-round.

Directions: From Sonora, drive east on Highway 108 and exit right at Tuolumne Road. Drive to the end of Tuolumne Road and turn left on Carter Street. Drive four blocks and turn right on Buchanon Road. Drive another four miles and continue straight on Fish Hatchery Road for two miles to the campground exit on the right.

Contact: River Ranch Campground, tel. (209) 928-3708 or fax (209) 928-1606.

17 Woodward Reservoir County Park

 7

Woodward Reservoir is a large lake covering 2,900 acres with 23 miles of shoreline, set in the rolling foothills just north of Oakdale. It is a good lake for both water-skiing and bass fishing, with minimal conflict between the two sports. Alas, just when peace was at hand, rentals of personal watercraft are now available here. Two large coves on the south and east ends of the lake, as well as the area behind Whale Island, are for low-speed boats only. That makes for good fishing, while the speedboats have the main lake body to let 'er rip.

Location: Near Oakdale; map E3, grid e0.

Campsites, facilities: There are 155 sites for tents or RVs, 115 with partial hookups, 40 with full hookups, and some equestrian facilities. Picnic tables and fire grills are provided. Drinking water, flush toilets, showers, sanitary disposal station, groceries, three boat ramps, mooring, dry boat storage, bait, and fishing licenses are available. Some facilities are wheelchair accessible. Leashed pets are permitted.

Reservations, fees: No reservations; $12 to $16 per night, $5 boat launch fee, $2 pet fee. Open year-round.

Directions: From Manteca, drive east on Highway 120 (it becomes Highway 108) for 20 miles to Oakdale and the junction with County Road J14/26 Mile Road. Turn left and drive four miles to 14528 26 Mile Road at Woodward Reservoir.

Contact: Woodward Reservoir County Park, tel. (209) 847-3304 or tel. (209) 525-6750; website: www.co.stanislaus.ca.us.

18 Knights Ferry Resort

 8

This is a privately run resort in the small historic town of Knights Ferry. Side trips include tours of the covered bridge ("the longest west of the Mississippi") and several historic buildings and homes, all within walking distance of the park. River access and hiking trails are available at the east end of town. Raft and canoe rentals are also available nearby.

Location: On the Stanislaus River; map E3, grid f2.

Campsites, facilities: There are 21 sites for tents or RVs. A community fire pit, restrooms, showers, and a restaurant are available. Some facilities are wheelchair accessible. Leashed pets are permitted.

Reservations, fees: Reservations are accepted with deposit; $20 to $23 per night, $3 pet fee. There is a two-night minimum stay on weekends and a three-night minimum on holidays. Major credit cards accepted. Open year-round.

Directions: From Manteca, drive east on Highway 120 (it becomes Highway 108) for about 35 miles to Knights Ferry and Kennedy Road. Turn left, drive to a bridge, cross the bridge, and continue a short distance to Sonora Road/Main Street. Turn left and drive to the Knights Ferry Restaurant at the entrance to the campground.

Contact: Knights Ferry Resort, tel. (209) 881-3349.

19 Lake Tulloch RV Camp and Marina

 8

Unlike so many reservoirs in the foothill country, this one is nearly always full of water. In addition, it is one of the rare places where fishermen and water-skiers live in harmony. That is due to the many coves and a six-mile-long arm with an enforced 5-mph speed limit. It's a big lake, shaped like a giant "X" with extended lake arms adding up to 55 miles of shoreline. The campground features mature oak trees that provide shade to most of the developed sites. In addition, 51 of the sites for RVs provide lake frontage. A secret at Tulloch is that fishing is also good for crawdads. The elevation is 500 feet.

Location: On the south shore of Lake Tulloch; map E3, grid f3.

Campsites, facilities: There are 120 sites for tents or RVs, 51 with hookups and boat sites, 45 with electricity and water. There are 10 waterfront cabins with electricity; each sleeps six and each has its own dock or swimming beach. An additional large area is available for lakefront tent camping and self-contained-unit camping. Picnic tables and fire grills are provided. Drinking water, flush toilets, showers, laundry room, store, sanitary disposal station, propane gas, playground, restaurant, volleyball, horseshoes, tetherball, ping pong, marina, boat rentals, boat launch, and a boat ramp are available. Some facilities are wheelchair accessible, including three cabins. Group sites and rates are available. Leashed pets are permitted.

Reservations, fees: Reservations are accepted; $17.50 to $27.50 per night for tent and RV sites, cabins are $75 per night or $400 per week, $100 deposit required. No boat berth charge for campers. Credit cards accepted. Open year-round.

Directions: From Manteca, drive east on Highway 120 (it becomes Highway 108) for about 35 miles to Tulloch Road. Turn left and drive 4.6 miles to the campground entrance at the south shore of Lake Tulloch.

Contact: Lake Tulloch RV Camp and Marina, 14448 Tulloch Dam Road, Jamestown, CA 95327; tel. or fax (209) 881-0107; website: www.laketullochcampground.com.

20 Blue Oaks

Blue Oaks is between the dam at Don Pedro Reservoir and Fleming Meadows. The on-site boat ramp to the east is a big plus here. See the entries for Fleming Meadows and Moccasin Point for more information.

Location: At Don Pedro Reservoir; map E3, grid g4.

Campsites, facilities: There are 117 sites for tents and RVs, including 29 RV sites with electricity and water. Picnic tables, food lockers, and barbecue units are provided. Drinking water, flush toilets, showers, and sanitary disposal station are available. Some facilities are wheelchair accessible. A grocery store, coin laundry, and propane gas are nearby at Fleming Meadows Marina. Campfires are prohibited. No pets are permitted.

Reservations, fees: Reservations are accepted; $15 to $20 per night, $5 per night for more than one vehicle. Major credit cards accepted. Open Memorial Day weekend through Labor Day weekend.

Directions: From Modesto, drive east on Highway 132 to La Grange. Turn left on La Grange/J59 and drive five miles. Turn right on Bonds Flat Road and drive one-half mile to the campground on the left along the shoreline.

Contact: Blue Oaks, tel. (209) 852-2396; website: www.donpedrolake.com.

21 Fleming Meadows

Fleming Meadows is set on the shore of Don Pedro Reservoir at its extreme south end, just east of the dam. A boat ramp is available in the campground on the southeast side of the dam. This is a big camp at the foot of a giant lake, where hot weather, warm water, waterskiing, and bass fishing make for weekend vacations. Don Pedro has many extended lake arms, providing 160 miles of shoreline and nearly 13,000 surface acres when full.

Location: On Don Pedro Reservoir; map E3, grid g4.

Campsites, facilities: There are 173 sites for tents or RVs, and 89 RV sites with full hookups. Picnic tables, food lockers, and fire grills are provided. Restrooms, drinking water, flush toilets, showers, and sanitary disposal station are available. A coin laundry, store, ice, snack bar, restaurant, tackle and bait, motorboat and houseboat rentals, boat ramp, berths, engine repairs, and propane gas are nearby. Some facilities are wheelchair accessible. Campfires are prohibited. No pets are permitted.

Reservations, fees: Reservations are accepted; $14 to $20 per night, $5 per night for more than one vehicle. Major credit cards accepted. Open year-round.

Directions: From Modesto, drive east on Highway 132 to La Grange. Turn left on La Grange/J59 and drive five miles. Turn right on Bonds Flat Road and drive two miles to the campground.

Contact: Fleming Meadows, tel. (209) 852-2396; website: www.donpedrolake.com.

22 Moccasin Point

This camp is at the north end of Don Pedro Reservoir, adjacent to a boat ramp. Moccasin Point juts out well into the lake, directly across from where the major Tuolumne River arm enters the lake. Don Pedro is a giant lake, with nearly 13,000 surface acres and 160 miles of shoreline, but is subject to drawdowns from midsummer through early fall. At different times, fishing is excellent for salmon, trout, or bass. Houseboating and boat-in camping (bring sunscreen) provide options.

Location: At Don Pedro Reservoir; map E3, grid g6.

Campsites, facilities: There are 65 sites for tents and 15 sites with full hookups for RVs. Picnic tables, food lockers, and barbecue units are provided at all sites. Drinking water, restrooms, showers, store, sanitary disposal station, propane gas, ice, snack bar, boat ramp, motorboat and houseboat rentals, fuel, moorings, and bait and tackle are available. Some facilities are wheelchair accessible. Campfires are prohibited. No pets are permitted.

Reservations, fees: Reservations are accepted; $15 to $22 per night, $5 per night for each extra vehicle. Major credit cards accepted. Open year-round.

Directions: From Manteca, drive east on Highway 120 (it becomes Highway 108) for 30 miles to the Highway 120/Yosemite exit. Bear right on Highway 120 and drive 11 miles. Turn left on Jacksonville Road and drive a short distance to the campground on the right.

Contact: Moccasin Point, tel. (209) 852-2396 or fax (209) 857-2780; website: www.donpedrolake.com

23 The Pines

   4

The Pines Camp is set at 3,200 feet in elevation on the western edge of Stanislaus National Forest, only a half mile from the Groveland District Office and about five miles from the Tuolumne River (see Lumsden, chapter E4). A Forest Service road is routed south of camp for two miles, climbing to Smith Peak Lookout (3,877 feet) and providing sweeping views to the west of the San Joaquin Valley foothills.

Location: In Stanislaus National Forest; map E3, grid g9.

Campsites, facilities: There are 12 sites for tents or RVs up to 22 feet long. Picnic tables and fire grills are provided. Drinking water (May through October only) and vault toilets are available. A grocery store is nearby. Leashed pets are permitted.

Reservations, fees: Reservations for group site only; individual sites no reservations, $10 per night, $50 per night for group site. Open year-round.

Directions: From Groveland, drive east on Highway 120 for nine miles (about a mile past the County Road J132 turnoff) to the signed campground entrance road on the right. Turn

right onto the campground entrance road and drive a short distance to the camp.

Contact: Stanislaus National Forest, Groveland Ranger District, tel. (209) 962-7825 or fax (209) 962-6406.

24 Moore Creek Group Camp

  6

This group camp is set at 2,800 feet, just past where the Sierra alpine zone takes over from foothill oak woodlands. It is near the access route (Highway 120) to the Crane Flat entrance station of Yosemite National Park.

Location: In Stanislaus National Forest; map E3, grid g9.

Campsites, facilities: There is a group campsite. Picnic tables and fire grills are provided. Vault toilets are available. No drinking water is available. Garbage must be packed out. Leashed pets are permitted.

Reservations, fees: Reservations are recommended; no fee. Open year-round, weather permitting.

Directions: From Groveland, drive east on Highway 120 about 12 miles to Forest Road 2S95. Turn right and drive 1.5 miles to the campground on the right.

Contact: Stanislaus National Forest, Groveland Ranger District, tel. (209) 962-7825 or fax (209) 962-6406.

25 Big Bear Water Park

 7

Big Bear Water Park is set at 2,500 feet in the foothill country east of Modesto. The park welcomes families with young children. The Tuolumne River runs right alongside the campground. Nearby side trips include Modesto Reservoir, Turlock Lake, and Don Pedro Reservoir.

Location: On the Tuolumne River near Modesto; map E3, grid g1.

Campsites, facilities: There are 96 sites for tents and 116 RV sites, most with full hookups.

Drinking water, restrooms, showers, sanitary disposal station, coin laundry, modem hookups, propane, ice, small store, three clubhouses, arcade, and a playground are available. Some facilities are wheelchair accessible. A miniature train ride and a water slide operate from May to September. Leashed pets are permitted (RV section only).

Reservations, fees: Reservations are accepted; $19 to $23 per night, four campers per site. Major credit cards accepted. Open year-round.

Directions: From Modesto, drive east on Highway 132 for 12 miles to the town of Waterford (where the road becomes Yosemite Boulevard) and drive to the park at 13400 Yosemite Boulevard.

Contact: Camping information at tel. (209) 874-4000; Big Bear Water Park, tel. (209) 874-1984 or fax (209) 874-4544; website: www.campgrounds.com/bigbear.

26 Modesto Reservoir Regional Park

     7

Modesto Reservoir is not well known, but it is a surprisingly big lake, at 2,700 acres with 31 miles of shoreline, set in the hot foothill country. It is one of the first recreation lakes in the Central Valley to advertise "MTBE-free waters." To keep it that way, boaters must buy gas that does not contain MTBE. Some gas stations provide gas that does not contain MBTE. You must show proof that the gas in your boat has been purchased from such a station. Water-skiing is excellent in the main lake body. Anglers head to the southern shore of the lake, which is loaded with submerged trees and coves and is also protected by a 5-mph speed limit. Fishing for bass is good, though the fish are often small.

Location: On Modesto Reservoir; map E3, grid h3.

Campsites, facilities: There are 150 sites for RVs with full hookups and 38 tent sites. Picnic tables and fire grills are provided. Drinking water, flush toilets, sanitary disposal station, showers, two boat ramps, marina, and a store are available. Some facilities are wheelchair accessible. Propane gas is available within four miles. No pets are allowed.

Reservations, fees: No reservations; $12 to $16 per night, $2 surcharge per vehicle on holidays. Open year-round.

Directions: From Modesto, drive east on Highway 132 for 16 miles past Waterford to Reservoir Road. Turn left and drive to the campground at 18139 Reservoir Road.

Contact: Modesto Reservoir Regional Park, tel. (209) 874-9540 or fax (209) 874-4513; website: www.co.stanislaus.ca.us.

27 Turlock Lake State Recreation Area

    6

Turlock Lake warms to 65 to 74 degrees in the summer, cooler than many Central Valley reservoirs, since the water entering this lake is released from the bottom of New Melones Reservoir. It often seems just right for boating and all water sports on hot summer days. The lake covers 3,500 acres and offers 26 miles of shoreline. A boat ramp is available near the camp, making it ideal for boaters/campers. Bass fishing is fair in the summer. In the late winter and spring, the lake is quite cold, fed by snowmelt from the Tuolumne River. Trout fishing is good year-round as a result. **Location:** East of Modesto; map E3, grid h3.

Campsites, facilities: There are 15 sites for tents and 51 sites for tents or RVs up to 27 feet long. Picnic tables, fire grills, and food lockers are provided. Drinking water, flush toilets, coin showers, a swimming beach, and a boat ramp are available. The boat facilities are wheelchair accessible. Leashed pets are permitted.

Reservations, fees: Reserve at (800) 444-PARK (800-444-7275) or website: www.ReserveAmerica.com; $12 per night. Open year-round.

Directions: From Modesto, go east on Highway 132 for 14 miles to Waterford. Continue eight miles on Highway 132 to Roberts Ferry Road. Turn right and drive one mile to Lake Road. Turn left and drive two miles to the campground on the left.

Contact: Turlock Lake State Recreation Area, tel. (209) 874-2008, tel. (209) 874-2056, or fax (209) 874-2611.

28 Lake McClure/Horseshoe Bend Recreation Area

       7

Lake McClure is a unique, horseshoe-shaped lake in the foothill country west of Yosemite. It adjoins smaller Lake McSwain, connected by the Merced River. McClure is shaped like a giant "H," with its lake arms providing 81 miles of shoreline, warm water for water-skiing, and fishing for bass (on the left half of the "H" near Cotton Creek) and for trout (on the right half of the "H"). There is a boat launch adjacent to the campground. It's one of four lakes in the immediate area; the others are Don Pedro Reservoir to the north and Modesto Reservoir and Turlock Lake to the west. The elevation is 900 feet.

Location: On Lake McClure; map E3, grid h7.

Campsites, facilities: There are 110 sites for tents or RVs, 35 with partial hookups. Picnic tables are provided. Restrooms, showers, sanitary disposal station, and a boat ramp are available. Some facilities are wheelchair accessible. A grocery store and coin laundry are nearby. Leashed pets are permitted.

Reservations, fees: Reservations are required, phone (800) 468-8889; $14 to $18 per night, $8 per night for each extra vehicle, $2 pet fee. Major credit cards accepted. Open year-round.

Directions: From Modesto, drive east on Highway 132 for 31 miles to La Grange and then continue for about 17 miles (toward Coulterville) to the north end of Lake McClure and the campground entrance road on the right side of the road. Turn right and drive a half

mile to the campground.

Contact: Horseshoe Bend Recreation Area, tel. (209) 878-3452 or fax (209) 378-2519; website: www.lakemcclure.com.

29 McClure Point Recreation Area

      7

McClure Point Recreation Area is the campground of choice for campers/boaters coming from the Turlock and Merced areas. It is a well-developed facility with an excellent boat ramp that provides access to the main body of Lake McClure. This is the best spot on the lake for water-skiing.

Location: On Lake McClure; map E3, grid h6.

Campsites, facilities: There are 100 sites for tents or RVs up to 40 feet long. Picnic tables are provided. Drinking water and electrical connections are provided at many sites. Restrooms, showers, boat ramp, and a laundry room are available. A grocery store is nearby. Leashed pets are permitted.

Reservations, fees: Reservations are accepted; $14 to $18 per night, $2 pet fee. Open year-round.

Directions: From Turlock, drive east on County Road J16 for 19 miles to the junction with Highway 59. Continue east on Highway 59/County Road J16 for 4.5 miles to Snelling and bear right at Lake McClure Road. Drive seven miles to Lake McSwain Dam and continue for seven miles to the campground at the end of the road.

Contact: McClure Point Recreation Area, tel. (800) 468-8889 or tel. (209) 378-2521, or fax (209) 378-2519; website: www.lakemcclure.com.

30 Barrett Cove Recreation Area

    7

Lake McClure is shaped like a giant "H," with its lake arms providing 81 miles of shoreline.

This camp is on the left side of the "H," that is, on the western shore, within a park that provides a good boat ramp. This is the largest in a series of camps on Lake McClure. See Horseshoe Bend Recreation Area, McClure Point Recreation Area, and Bagby Recreation Area for more information.

Location: On Lake McClure; map E3, grid h6.

Campsites, facilities: There are 275 sites for tents or RVs. Picnic tables are provided. Drinking water, electrical connections, and sewer hookups are provided at some sites. Restrooms, showers, boat ramps, sanitary disposal station, swimming lagoon, and playground are available. A grocery store, coin laundry, boat and houseboat rentals, and propane gas are also available on site. Some facilities are wheelchair accessible. Leashed pets are permitted.

Reservations, fees: Reservations are accepted; $14 to $18 per night, $8 per night for each extra vehicle, $2 pet fee. Major credit cards accepted. Open year-round.

Directions: From Modesto, drive east on Highway 132 for 31 miles to La Grange and then continue for about 11 miles (toward Coulterville) to Merced Falls Road. Turn right and drive three miles to the campground entrance on the left. Turn left and drive a mile to the campground on the left side of the road.

Contact: Barrett Cove Recreation Area, tel. (800) 468-8889 or tel. (209) 378-2521, or fax (209) 378-2519; website: www.lakemcclure.com.

31 Bagby Recreation Area

 7

This is the most distant and secluded camp on Lake McClure. It is set near the Merced River as it enters the lake, way up adjacent to the Highway 49 Bridge, nearly an hour's drive from the dam. Trout fishing is good in the area, and it makes sense; when the lake heats up in summer, the trout naturally congregate near the cool incoming flows of the Merced River.

Location: On upper Lake McClure; map E3, grid i8.

Campsites, facilities: There are 25 tent sites and several RV sites with partial hookups available. Drinking water, restrooms with flush toilets and hot showers, small store, and a boat ramp are available. Leashed pets are permitted.

Reservations, fees: Reservations are accepted; $13 to $17 per night, $2 pet fee. Open year-round.

Directions: From Modesto, drive east on Highway 132 for 31 miles to La Grange and then continue for 20 miles to Coulterville and the junction with Highway 49. Turn south on Highway 49, drive about 12 miles, cross the bridge, and look for the campground entrance on the left side of the road. Turn left and drive a quarter mile to the campground.

Contact: Bagby Recreation Area, tel. (800) 468-8889 or tel. (209) 378-2521, or fax (209) 378-2519; website: www.lakemcclure.com.

32 Lake McSwain Recreation Area

 7

Lake McSwain is actually the afterbay for adjacent Lake McClure, and this camp is near the McSwain Dam on the Merced River. If you have a canoe or car-top boat, this lake is preferable to Lake McClure because waterskiing is not allowed. In terms of size, McSwain is like a puddle compared to the giant McClure, but unlike McClure, the water levels are kept up almost year-round at McSwain. The water is cold here and trout stocks are good in the spring.

Location: Near McSwain Dam on the Merced River; map E3, grid i6.

Campsites, facilities: There are 112 sites for tents or RVs up to 40 feet long. Picnic tables and electrical connections are provided. Drinking water, sanitary disposal station, restrooms, showers, boat ramp, boat rentals, coin laundry, and a playground are available. A grocery store, boat rentals, and propane gas are available nearby. Leashed pets are permitted.

Reservations, fees: Reservations are accepted; $14 to $18 per night, $2 pet fee. Open year-round.

Directions: From Turlock, drive east on County Road J16 for 19 miles to the junction with Highway 59. Continue east on Highway 59/County Road J16 for 4.5 miles to Snelling and bear right at Lake McClure Road. Drive seven miles to the campground turnoff on the right.

Contact: Lake McSwain Recreation Area, tel. (800) 468-8889 or tel. (209) 378-2521, or fax (209) 378-2519; website: www.lakemcclure.com.

33 McConnell State Recreation Area

     6

The weather gets scorching hot around these parts in the summer, and a lot of out-of-towners would pay a bunch for a little shade and a river to sit next to. That's what this park provides, with the Merced River flowing past, along with occasional mermaids on the beach. In high-water years the Merced River attracts salmon (in the fall).

Location: On the Merced River; map E3, grid j1.

Campsites, facilities: There are 20 sites for tents, one site for RVs up to 18 feet long, and two group sites for tents only. Picnic tables, fire grills, and food lockers are provided. Drinking water, flush toilets, coin showers, and a swimming beach are available. One group site has an electrical hookup. Firewood is available for purchase. Supplies can be obtained in Delhi, three miles away. Leashed pets are permitted.

Reservations, fees: Reserve at (800) 444-PARK (800-444-7275) or website: www.ReserveAmerica.com; $12 per night for family sites, $18 to $37 per night for group site. Open year-round.

Directions: From Modesto or Merced, drive on Highway 99 to Delhi and the Shanks Road exit. Turn east on El Capitan Way and drive five miles to Pepper Street. Turn right and drive one-quarter mile to the park.

Contact: McConnell State Recreation Area at tel. (209) 394-7755; Four Rivers District, California State Parks, tel. (209) 826-1196.

CATHEDRAL LAKE,
YOSEMITE NATIONAL PARK,
MIRRORS CATHEDRAL PEAK

MAP E4

Lake Alpine
Lake Alpine [2-5]
[1]
Coleville
NEVADA
CALIFORNIA

[6-10]
[4]
Bear Valley
Walker
TO ARNOLD
North Fork
Stanislaus River
[11]
[12]
STANISLAUS
NATIONAL
FOREST
TOIYABE
NATIONAL
FOREST
395

[13]
[14]
[15-16]
[17-19]
Dardanelle
[20]
[21]
Donnell
Reservoir
[25]
[28] [29] [30]
[31]
108
22
Devil's Gate
Summit
7,519 feet
[33]
[32]
[26] [27]
23
Middle Fork
Stanislaus R.
Kennedy
Meadows
Sonora Pass
9,624 feet
24
108
Beardsley
Reservoir
[34]
Pinecrest
Lake
Hanna Mountain
11,846 feet
395
TO BRIDGEPORT
[38]
[35-37]
Pinecrest
40

Long
[39]
Relief Peak
10,808 feet
Eagle Peak
11,845 feet
[41-44]
TO U.S. 395

45

[46]
YOSEMITE
NATIONAL
PARK
Excelsior Mountain
12,446 feet
Twin
Lakes
47
480
Cherry
Lake
48
538

Lake
Eleanor
GRAND CANYON
OF THE TUOLUMNE
TO BUCK MEADOWS
[49-52]
Tuolumne River

Mather
Hetch Hetchy
Reservoir
Tuolumne River
55
[53]
54
56
[57-64]
120
65
68
120
69
Tuolumne
Meadows
Tioga
Pass
9,946
feet
TO LEE VINING
66
70
67
Crane Flat
71
Amelia Earhart
11,952 feet
Merced River
72
Yosemite
Village
Tenaya
Lake
INYO
NATIONAL
FOREST
76
El Portal
[73-74]
75
Half Dome
8,842 feet
YOSEMITE
VALLEY
Glacier
Point
140
Chinquapin
Mount Lyell
13,114 feet
Briceburg
41
SIERRA NATIONAL
FOREST
78
Mount Ansel Adams
11,760 feet

77
Badger Pass
7,300 feet
TO MARIPOSA
Midpines
80
Merced Peak
11,726 feet
Mount
Ritter
79
Wawona
49
81
82
Fish Camp
MARIPOSA GROVE
OF BIG TREES
[83-89]

TO OAKHURST
580

© AVALON TRAVEL PUBLISHING, INC.

CHAPTER E4

(CONTINUED ON NEXT PAGE)

1 Upper and Lower Highland Lakes

     9

This camp is set between Upper and Lower Highland Lakes, two beautiful alpine ponds that offer good fishing for small brook trout as well as spectacular panoramic views. Hiram Peak (9,760 feet) looms to the nearby south. A trail that starts at the north end of Highland Lakes (a parking area is available) is routed east for two miles to Wolf Creek Pass, where it connects with the Pacific Crest Trail; from there, turn left or right—you can't lose.
Location: In Stanislaus National Forest; map E4, grid a3.

Campsites, facilities: There are 35 sites for tents or RVs, including five sites for equestrians. Picnic tables and fire grills are provided. Drinking water and vault toilets are available. Leashed pets are permitted.
Reservations, fees: No reservations; $8 per night. Open mid-June through September.
Directions: From Angels Camp, drive east on Highway 4 to Arnold, past Lake Alpine, and continue for 14.5 miles to Forest Road 8N01 (one mile west of Ebbetts Pass). Turn right and drive 7.5 miles to the campground on the right side of the road. Trailers are not recommended.
Contact: Stanislaus National Forest, Calaveras Ranger District, tel. (209) 795-1381 or fax (209) 795-6849.

2 Pine Marten

 8

Lake Alpine is a beautiful Sierra lake surrounded by granite and pines and set at 7,320 feet, just above where the snowplows stop in winter. This camp is on the northeast side, about a quarter mile from the shore. Fishing for rainbow trout is good in May and early June, prior to the summer crush. Despite the long drive to get here, the lake is becoming better known for its beauty, camping, and hiking. A trailhead out of nearby Silver Valley Camp provides a two-mile hike to pretty Duck Lake and beyond into the Carson-Iceberg Wilderness.

Location: Near Lake Alpine in Stanislaus National Forest; map E4, grid a2.

Campsites, facilities: There are 33 sites for tents or RVs up to 22 feet long. Picnic tables and fire grills are provided. Restrooms, drinking water, flush toilets, showers, and a boat ramp are available. A grocery store, propane gas, and coin laundry are nearby. Leashed pets are permitted.

Reservations, fees: No reservations; $15 per night. A free campfire permit is required. Open June to mid-October.

Directions: From Angels Camp, drive east on Highway 4 to Arnold and continue for 29 miles to Lake Alpine. Drive to the northeast end of the lake to the campground entrance on the right side of the road.

Contact: Stanislaus National Forest, Calaveras Ranger District, tel. (209) 795-1381 or fax (209) 795-6849.

3 Silver Valley

 8

This is one of four camps at Lake Alpine. Silver Valley is on the northeast end of the lake at 7,400 feet in elevation, with a trailhead nearby that provides access to the Carson-Iceberg Wilderness. For recreation information, see the entry for Pine Marten.

Location: On Lake Alpine in Stanislaus National Forest; map E4, grid a2.

Campsites, facilities: There are 25 sites for tents or RVs up to 22 feet long. Picnic tables and fire grills are provided. Drinking water and vault toilets are available. A boat launch is available. Some facilities are wheelchair accessible. A grocery store, propane gas, and a coin laundry are nearby. Leashed pets are permitted.

Reservations, fees: No reservations; $15 per night. A free campfire permit is required. Open June through mid-October.

Directions: From Angels Camp, drive east on Highway 4 to Arnold and continue for 29 miles to Lake Alpine. Drive to the northeast end of the lake to the campground entrance on the right side of the road. Turn right and drive a half mile to the campground.

Contact: Stanislaus National Forest, Calaveras Ranger District, tel. (209) 795-1381 or fax (209) 795-6849.

4 Alpine Campground

 8

This is the campground that is in the greatest demand at Lake Alpine, and it is easy to see why. It is very small, a boat ramp is adjacent to the camp, you can get supplies at a small grocery store within walking distance, and during the evening rise you can often see the jumping trout from your campsite. Lake Alpine is one of the prettiest lakes you can drive to, set at 7,320 feet amid pines and Sierra granite. A trailhead out of nearby Silver Valley Camp provides a two-mile hike to pretty Duck Lake and beyond into the Carson-Iceberg Wilderness.

Location: On Lake Alpine in Stanislaus National Forest; map E4, grid a2.

Campsites, facilities: There are five tent sites and 22 sites for RVs up to 22 feet long. Picnic tables and fire grills are provided. Restrooms, drinking water, flush and vault toilets, showers, and a boat launch are available. A grocery store, propane gas, and a coin laundry are nearby. Some facilities are wheelchair accessible. Leashed pets are permitted.

Reservations, fees: No reservations; $15 per night. Open June through October.

Directions: From Angels Camp, drive east on Highway 4 to Arnold and continue for 29 miles to Lake Alpine. Just before reaching the lake turn right and drive a quarter mile to the campground on the left.

Contact: Stanislaus National Forest, Calaveras Ranger District, tel. (209) 795-1381 or fax (209) 795-6849.

5 Silver Tip

 6

This camp is about two miles from the shore of Lake Alpine at an elevation of 7,350 feet. Why then would anyone camp here when there are campgrounds right at the lake? Two reasons: One, those lakeside camps are often full on summer weekends. Two, Highway 4 is snowplowed to this campground entrance, but not beyond. So in big snow years when the road is still closed in late spring and early summer, you can park your rig here to camp, then hike in to the lake. It also makes a good base camp for hunters. See the entry for Alpine Campground for more information.

Location: Near Lake Alpine in Stanislaus National Forest; map E4, grid a2.

Campsites, facilities: There are 24 sites for tents or RVs up to 22 feet long. Picnic tables and fire grills are provided. Restrooms, drinking water, and flush toilets are available. A boat launch is about a mile away. A grocery store, propane gas, a coin laundry, and coin showers are nearby. Leashed pets are permitted.

Reservations, fees: No reservations; $15 per night. Open July through September, weather permitting.

Directions: From Angels Camp, drive east on Highway 4 to Arnold and continue for 29 miles to Lake Alpine. A mile before reaching the lake (adjacent to the Bear Valley/Mount Reba turnoff), turn right at the campground entrance on the right side of the road.

Contact: Stanislaus National Forest, Calaveras Ranger District, tel. (209) 795-1381 or fax (209) 795-6849.

6 Big Meadows Group Camp

 5

Big Meadows Group Camp is set at 6,460 feet on the western slopes of the Sierra Nevada. There are a number of recreation attractions nearby, the most prominent being the North Fork Stanislaus River two miles to the south in national forest (see Sand Flat), with access available from a four-wheel-drive road just east of camp, or on Spicer Reservoir Road (see Stanislaus River). Lake Alpine, a pretty, popular lake for trout fishing, is nine miles east on Highway 4.

Location: In Stanislaus National Forest; map E4, grid a0.

Campsites, facilities: There is a group campsite for tents or RVs. Picnic tables and fire grills are provided. Drinking water and vault toilets are available. Groceries, a coin laundry, and propane gas are nearby. Leashed pets are permitted.

Reservations, fees: Reserve at (877) 444-6777 ($8.65 reservation fee) or website: www.reserveusa.com; $50 per group of 25 people per night, $2 per additional camper. Open May through September.

Directions: From Angels Camp on Highway 49, turn east on Highway 4 and drive about 30 miles (three miles past Ganns Meadows) to the campground on the right.

Contact: Stanislaus National Forest, Calaveras Ranger District, tel. (209) 795-1381 or fax (209) 795-6849.

7 Sand Flat

 7

This one is for four-wheel-drive cowboys who want to carve out a piece of the Sierra Nevada wildlands for themselves. It is set at 5,900 feet on the North Fork Stanislaus River, where there is decent fishing for small trout, with the fish often holding right where white water runs into pools. The tiny, primitive camp, where you won't get bugged by anyone, was named for the extensive sandy flat on the south side of the river.

Location: On the Stanislaus River in Stanislaus National Forest; map E4, grid a0.

Campsites, facilities: There are four tent sites. Picnic tables and fire rings are provided. Vault toilets are available. No drinking water is available. Garbage must be packed out. Leashed pets are permitted.

Reservations, fees: No reservations; no fee. Free campfire permits are required. Open June through August.

Directions: From Angels Camp on Highway 49, turn east on Highway 4, drive about 30 miles (3.5 miles past Ganns Meadows), and then continue a half mile past Big Meadows Group Camp to a dirt/gravel road on the right. Turn right and drive two miles on a steep, unimproved road (four-wheel drive required).

Contact: Stanislaus National Forest, Calaveras Ranger District, tel. (209) 795-1381 or fax (209) 795-6849.

8 Stanislaus River

 8

As you might figure from its name, this camp provides excellent access to the adjacent North Fork Stanislaus River, but it is also the closest drive-in campground to Utica Reservoir, Union Reservoir, and Spicer Reservoir, all within seven miles to the east. Of the three, Spicer has the best trout fishing. The elevation is 6,200 feet, with timbered sites and the river just south of camp.

Location: In Stanislaus National Forest; map E4, grid a0.

Campsites, facilities: There are 25 sites for tents or RVs up to 16 feet long. Fire grills and picnic tables are provided. Drinking water and vault toilets are available. Supplies are available in Tamarack. Leashed pets are permitted.

Reservations, fees: No reservations; $8 per night. Open June through September.

Directions: From Angels Camp on Highway 49, turn east on Highway 4 and drive about 32 miles (five miles past Ganns Meadows) to Spicer Reservoir Road on the right. Turn right and drive four miles to the campground on the right side of the road.

Contact: Stanislaus National Forest, Calaveras Ranger District, tel. (209) 795-1381 or fax (209) 795-6849.

9 Big Meadow

 5

Big Meadow is set at 6,460 feet and features a number of nearby recreation options. The most prominent is the North Fork Stanislaus River, with access available at Sand Flat and Stanislaus River campgrounds. In addition, Lake Alpine is nine miles to the east, and three mountain reservoirs, Spicer, Utica, and Union, are all within a 15-minute drive. Big Meadow is also a good base camp for hunters.

Location: Near the Stanislaus River in Stanislaus National Forest; map E4, grid a0.

Campsites, facilities: There are 42 sites for tents and 23 sites for RVs up to 27 feet long. Picnic tables and fire grills are provided. Drinking water and vault toilets are available. Groceries, a coin laundry, and propane gas are nearby. Leashed pets are permitted.

Reservations, fees: Reserve at (877) 444-6777 ($8.65 reservation fee) or website: www.reserveusa.com; $11 per night. Open June through October.

Directions: From Angels Camp on Highway 49, turn east on Highway 4 and drive about 30 miles (three miles past Ganns Meadows) to the campground on the right.

Contact: Stanislaus National Forest, Calaveras Ranger District, tel. (209) 795-1381 or fax (209) 795-6849.

10 Wa Ka Luu Hep Yoo

 8

This is a riverside Forest Service campground that provides good trout fishing on the Stanislaus River and a put-in for white-water rafting. The highlight for most is the fishing, one of the best spots on the Stanislaus, stocked monthly by Fish and Game, and good for rainbow, brook, and brown trout. It is four miles downstream of Dorrington, first opened in 1999 as part of the Sourgrass Recreation Complex. There are cultural sites and preserved artifacts, such as grinding rocks. It is a pretty streamside spot, with ponderosa pine and black oak providing good screening. A wheelchair-accessible trail is available along the stream. The camp is set at an elevation of 3,900 feet, but it feels higher.

Location: On the Stanislaus River in Stanislaus National Forest; map E4, grid a0.

Campsites, facilities: There are 49 sites for tents or RVs up to 40 feet long. No RV hookups. Picnic tables and fire grills are provided. Restrooms, drinking water, showers, and flush and vault toilets are available. A camp host is on-site in summer. Some facilities are wheelchair accessible. Leashed pets are permitted.

Reservations, fees: No reservations; $13 per night. Free campfire permits are required. Open Memorial Day weekend through September, weather permitting.

Directions: From Angels Camp, drive east on Highway 4, past Arnold to Dorrington and Boards Crossing Road. Turn right and drive four miles to the campground on the left (just before the bridge that crosses the Stanislaus River.

Contact: Stanislaus National Forest, Calaveras Ranger District, tel. (209) 795-1381, or fax (209) 795-6849.

11 Union Reservoir Walk-In

 10

Union Reservoir is set in Sierra granite at 6,850 feet, a beautiful and quiet lake that is kept that way with rules that mandate a 5-mph speed limit and walk-in camping only. Most of the sites provide lakeside views. Fishing is often good, trolling for kokanee salmon, but you need a boat. The setting is great, especially for canoes or other small boats. This camp was once a secret, but now it fills up quickly on weekends. Those who visit usually keep the noise down so everybody can enjoy a pristine experience.

Location: Northeast of Arnold in Stanislaus National Forest; map E4, grid a1.

Campsites, facilities: There are 15 primitive walk-in tent sites. A vault toilet is available, along with a signboard explaining lake rules and camp policies. No drinking water is available. Garbage must be packed out. A boat ramp is available nearby.

Reservations, fees: No reservations; no fee. Open June through September, weather permitting.

Directions: From Angels Camp, drive east on Highway 4 for about 32 miles to Spicer Reservoir Road. Turn right and travel east for about seven miles to Forest Road 7N75. Turn left and drive three miles to Union Reservoir. There are four designated parking areas for the walk-in camps along the road.

Contact: Stanislaus National Forest, Calaveras Ranger District, tel. (209) 795-1381 or fax (209) 795-6849. For a map, send $6 to U.S. Forest Service, Attn: Map Sales, P.O. Box 587, Camino, CA 95709; tel. (530) 647-5390, fax (530) 647-5389, or website: www.r5.fs.fed.us/visitorcenter. Major credit cards accepted.

12 Spicer Reservoir Group Camp

 7

Set at 6,418 feet, Spicer Reservoir isn't big by reservoir standards, covering only 227 acres, but it is quite pretty from a boat and is surrounded by canyon walls. The beauty is compounded by good trout fishing. A boat ramp is available near the campground. A trail that leads around the reservoir has recently been completed. Note: This area can really get hammered with snow in big winters, so in the spring and early summer, always check for access conditions before planning a trip.

Location: Near Spicer Reservoir in Stanislaus National Forest; map E4, grid a2.

Campsites, facilities: There is one group site that can accommodate up to 50 people. Picnic tables and fire grills are provided. Drinking water, vault toilets, food preparation area, primitive amphitheater, and a group parking area are available. A boat ramp is available a mile away. Some facilities are wheelchair accessible. Leashed pets are permitted.

Reservations, fees: Reservations are required; phone (877) 444-6777 ($8.65 reservation fee); $90 per night. Open June through September, weather permitting.

Directions: From Angels Camp, drive east on Highway 4 for about 32 miles to Spicer Reservoir Road/Forest Road 7N01. Turn right, drive seven miles, bear right at a fork with a sharp right turn, and drive a mile to the campground at the west end of the lake.

Contact: Stanislaus National Forest, Calaveras Ranger District, tel. (209) 795-1381 or fax (209) 795-6849. For a map, send $4 to the USDA Forest Service, U.S. Forest Map Sales, 1323 Club Drive, Vallejo, CA 94592.

13 Clark Fork & Clark Fork Horse

     8

Clark Fork borders the Clark Fork of the Stanislaus River and is used both by drive-in vacationers and backpackers. A trailhead for hikers is a quarter mile away on the north side of Clark Fork Road (a parking area is available here). From here the trail is routed up along Arnot Creek, skirting between Iceberg Peak on the left and Lightning Mountain on the right, for eight miles to Wolf Creek Pass and the junction with the Pacific Crest Trail. For another nearby trailhead, see the entry for Sand Flat.

Location: On the Clark Fork of the Stanislaus River in Stanislaus National Forest; map E4, grid b4.

Campsites, facilities: There are 88 sites for tents or RVs up to 22 feet long, and at an adjacent area, 14 equestrian sites with water troughs. Picnic tables and fire grills are provided. Drinking water, flush toilets, and a sanitary disposal station are available. At the equestrian site, no drinking water is available. Some facilities are wheelchair accessible. You can buy supplies in Dardanelle. Leashed pets are permitted.

Reservations, fees: No reservations; $10 to $11 per night for family sites, horse camp fee is $5 per night, $5 for an extra vehicle. Open May through mid-October, weather permitting.

Directions: From Sonora, drive east on Highway 108 past the town of Strawberry to Clark Fork Road. Turn left, drive five miles, turn right again, and drive a half mile to the campground entrance on the right side of the road.

Contact: Stanislaus National Forest, Summit Ranger District, tel. (209) 965-3434 or fax (209) 965-3372. For a map, send $6 to U.S. Forest Service, Attn: Map Sales, P.O. Box 587, Camino, CA 95709; tel. (530) 647-5390, fax (530) 647-5389, or website: www.r5.fs.fed.us/visitorcenter. Major credit cards accepted.

14 Sand Flat

      7

Sand Flat Campground, at 6,200 feet, is only three miles (by vehicle on Clark Fork Road) from an outstanding trailhead for the Carson-Iceberg Wilderness. The camp is used primarily by late-arriving backpackers who camp for the night, get their gear in order, then head off on the trail. The trail is routed out of Iceberg Meadow, with a choice of heading north to Paradise Valley (unbelievably green and loaded with corn lilies along a creek) and onward to the Pacific Crest Trail, or east to Clark Fork and upstream to Clark Fork Meadow below Sonora Peak. Two choices, both winners.

Location: On the Clark Fork of the Stanislaus River in Stanislaus National Forest; map E4, grid b4.

Campsites, facilities: There are 53 sites for tents or RVs and 15 walk-in sites. Picnic tables and fire grills are provided. Drinking water and vault toilets are available. You can buy supplies in Dardanelle. Leashed pets are permitted.

Reservations, fees: No reservations; $7 per night per vehicle. Open May through September.

Directions: From Sonora, drive east on Highway 108 past the town of Strawberry to Clark Fork Road. Turn left on Clark Fork Road and drive six miles to the campground entrance on the right side of the road.

Contact: Stanislaus National Forest, Summit Ranger District, tel. (209) 965-3434 or fax (209) 965-3372.

15 Spicer Reservoir

 8

Spicer Reservoir, set at 6,418 feet, isn't big by reservoir standards, covering 227 acres, but it is surrounded by canyon walls and is quite pretty from a boat. The beauty is compounded by good trout fishing, sometimes even excellent trout fishing. A boat ramp is available near the campground. A trail that leads around the reservoir has recently been completed. Note: This area can really get hammered with snow in big winters, so in the spring and early summer, always check for access conditions before planning a trip.

Location: Near Spicer Reservoir in Stanislaus National Forest; map E4, grid b2.

Campsites, facilities: There are 60 family sites, two double-family sites, and a triple-family site, all suitable for tents or RVs. Picnic tables and fire grills are provided. Drinking water, vault toilets, and a phone are available. Some facilities are wheelchair accessible. A boat ramp is available nearby. Leashed pets are permitted.

Reservations, fees: No reservations; $12 per night. Open June through September, weather permitting.

Directions: From Angels Camp, drive east on Highway 4 for about 32 miles to Spicer Reservoir Road/Forest Road 7N01. Turn right, drive seven miles, bear right at a fork with a sharp right turn, and drive a mile to the campground at the west end of the lake.

Contact: Stanislaus National Forest, Calaveras Ranger District, tel. (209) 795-1381 or fax (209) 795-6849. For a map, send $6 to U.S. Forest Service, Attn: Map Sales, P.O. Box 587, Camino, CA 95709; tel. (530) 647-5390, fax (530) 647-5389, or website: www.r5.fs.fed.us/visitorcenter. Major credit cards accepted.

16 Fence Creek

 4

Fence Creek is a feeder stream to Clark Fork, which runs a mile downstream and joins with the Middle Fork Stanislaus River en route to Donnells Reservoir. The camp sits along little Fence Creek, 5,600 feet in elevation. Fence Creek Road continues east for another nine miles to an outstanding trailhead at Iceberg Meadow on the edge of the Carson-Iceberg Wilderness.

Location: Near the Middle Fork of the Stanislaus River in Stanislaus National Forest; map E4, grid b2.

Campsites, facilities: There are 34 sites for tents or RVs up to 22 feet long. Picnic tables and fire grills are provided. Vault and pit toilets are available. No drinking water is available. You can buy supplies in Pinecrest about 10 miles away. Leashed pets are permitted.

Reservations, fees: No reservations; $5 per night. Open May through mid-October, weather permitting.

Directions: From Sonora, drive east on Highway 108 about 49 miles to Clark Ford Road.

Turn left and drive a mile to Forest Road 6N06. Turn left again and drive a half mile to the campground on the right.

Contact: Stanislaus National Forest, Summit Ranger District, tel. (209) 965-3434 or fax (209) 965-3372.

17 Boulder Flat

 7

You want camping on the Stanislaus River? Driving east on Highway 108, this is the first in a series of campgrounds along the Middle Fork Stanislaus. Boulder Flat is set at 5,600 feet and offers easy access off the highway. Here's another bonus: this stretch of river is stocked with trout.

Location: Near the Middle Fork of the Stanislaus River in Stanislaus National Forest; map E4, grid b3.

Campsites, facilities: There are 20 sites for tents or RVs up to 22 feet long, and one double site. Picnic tables and fire grills are provided. Drinking water and vault toilets are available. You can buy supplies in Dardanelle. Leashed pets are permitted.

Reservations, fees: No reservations; $12 per night, $15 per night for a double site, $5 for an extra vehicle. Open May through September.

Directions: From Sonora, drive east on Highway 108 past the town of Strawberry to Clark Fork Road. At Clark Fork Road, continue east on Highway 108 for a mile to the campground on the left side of the road.

Contact: Stanislaus National Forest, Summit Ranger District, tel. (209) 965-3434 or fax (209) 965-3372.

18 Brightman Flat

 7

This camp is on the Middle Fork of the Stanislaus River at 5,600 feet elevation, a mile east of Boulder Flat and two miles west of Dardanelle. For recreation options, see the entry for Pigeon Flat.

Location: On the Middle Fork of the Stanislaus River in Stanislaus National Forest; map E4, grid b3.

Campsites, facilities: There are 33 sites for tents or RVs up to 22 feet long. Picnic tables and fire grills are provided. Vault toilets are available. No drinking water is available. You can buy supplies in Dardanelle. Leashed pets are permitted.

Reservations, fees: No reservations; $9 per night, $5 per night for each extra vehicle. Open May through mid-October, weather permitting.

Directions: From Sonora, drive east on Highway 108 past the town of Strawberry to Clark Fork Road. From Clark Fork Road continue driving east on Highway 108 for two miles to the campground entrance on the left side of the road.

Contact: Stanislaus National Forest, Summit Ranger District, tel. (209) 965-3434 or fax (209) 965-3372.

19 Dardanelle

 7

This Forest Service camp is within walking distance of supplies in Dardanelle and is also right alongside the Middle Fork Stanislaus River. This section of river is stocked with trout by the Department of Fish and Game. The trail to see Columns of the Giants is just 1.5 miles to the east out of Pigeon Flat.

Location: On the Middle Fork of the Stanislaus River in Stanislaus National Forest; map E4, grid b3.

Campsites, facilities: There are 28 sites for tents or RVs up to 22 feet long, and three double sites. Picnic tables and fire grills are provided. Drinking water and vault toilets are available. You can buy supplies in Dardanelle. Leashed pets are permitted.

Reservations, fees: No reservations; $14 per night for single sites, $19 per night for double sites, $5 for an extra vehicle. Open May through October, weather permitting.

Directions: From Sonora, drive east on Highway 108 past

Strawberry to Dardanelle and the campground on the left side of the road.

Contact: Stanislaus National Forest, Summit Ranger District, tel. (209) 965-3434 or fax (209) 965-3372.

20 Bootleg

   6

Location is always a key, and easy access off U.S. 395, the adjacent West Walker River, and good trout stocks in summer make this a popular spot. See the entries for Chris Flat and Sonora Bridge for more information. Note that this camp is on the west side of the highway, and that anglers will have to cross the road in order to gain fishing access (which makes Chris Flat a better choice). The elevation is 6,600 feet.

Location: On the Walker River in Humboldt-Toiyabe National Forest; map E4, grid b7.

Campsites, facilities: There are 63 paved sites for tents or RVs up to 45 feet long. Picnic tables and fire grills are provided. Drinking water and flush toilets are available. Leashed pets are permitted.

Reservations, fees: No reservations; $10 per night. Open late April to mid-September.

Directions: From Carson City, drive south on U.S. 395 to Coleville and then continue south for 13 miles to the campground on the west side of the highway (six miles north of the junction of U.S. 395 and Highway 108).

Contact: Humboldt-Toiyabe National Forest, Bridgeport Ranger District, tel. (760) 932-7070, or fax (760) 932-1299.

21 Chris Flat

     7

This is one of two campgrounds set along U.S. 395 next to the West Walker River, a pretty trout stream with easy access and good stocks of rainbow trout. The plants are usually made at two campgrounds, resulting in good prospects here at Chris Flat, and west on Highway 108 at Sonora Bridge. The elevation is 6,600 feet.

Location: On the Walker River in Humboldt-Toiyabe National Forest; map E4, grid b8.

Campsites, facilities: There are 15 sites for tents or RVs up to 40 feet long. Picnic tables and fire grills are provided. Drinking water and vault toilets are available. Leashed pets are permitted.

Reservations, fees: No reservations; $10 per night. Open late April through October.

Directions: From Carson City, drive south on U.S. 395 to Coleville and then continue south for 15 miles to the campground on the east side of the road (four miles north of the junction of U.S. 395 and Highway 108).

Contact: Humboldt-Toiyabe National Forest, Bridgeport Ranger District, tel. (760) 932-7070 or fax (760) 932-1299.

22 Sonora Bridge

    7

The West Walker River is a pretty stream, flowing over boulders and into pools, and each year this stretch of river is well stocked with rainbow trout by the Department of Fish and Game. One of several campgrounds near the West Walker, Sonora Bridge is set at 6,800 feet, about a half mile from the river. The setting is in the transition zone from high mountains to high desert on the eastern edge of the Sierra Nevada.

Location: Near the Walker River in Humboldt-Toiyabe National Forest; map E4, grid b7.

Campsites, facilities: There are 23 sites for tents or RVs up to 40 feet long. Picnic tables and fire grills are provided. Drinking water and vault toilets are available. Leashed pets are permitted.

Reservations, fees: No reservations; $10 per night. Open May through mid-October.

Directions: From north of Bridgeport, at the junction of U.S. 395 and Highway 108, turn west on Highway 108 and drive two miles to the campground.

Contact: Humboldt-Toiyabe National Forest, Bridgeport Ranger District, tel. (760) 932-7070 or fax (760) 932-1299.

23 Leavitt Meadows

 9

While Leavitt Meadows sits right aside Highway 108, a little winding two-laner, there are several nearby off-pavement destinations that make this camp a winner. The camp is set in the high eastern Sierra, east of Sonora Pass at 7,000 feet in elevation, where Leavitt Creek and Brownie Creek enter the West Walker River. There is a pack station for horseback riding nearby. For four-wheel-drive owners, the most popular side trip is driving four miles west on Highway 108, then turning south and driving four miles to Leavitt Lake, where the trout fishing is sometimes spectacular, trolling a gold Cripplure.

Location: On the Walker River in Humboldt-Toiyabe National Forest; map E4, grid c6.

Campsites, facilities: There are 16 sites for tents or RVs up to 40 feet long. Picnic tables and fire grills are provided. Drinking water and vault toilets are available. Leashed pets are permitted.

Reservations, fees: No reservations; $9 per night. Open mid-April to mid-October, weather permitting.

Directions: From the junction of Highway 108 and U.S. 395 north of Bridgeport, turn west on Highway 108 and drive seven miles to the campground on the left side of the road.

Contact: Humboldt-Toiyabe National Forest, Bridgeport Ranger District, tel. (760) 932-7070 or fax (760) 932-1299.

24 Obsidian

 6

This primitive, little-known camp at 7,800 feet in elevation is set up for backpackers, with an adjacent trailhead providing a jump-off point into the wilderness. The trail here is routed up the Molybdenite Creek drainage and into the Hoover Wilderness.

Location: On Molybdenite Creek in Humboldt-Toiyabe National Forest; map E4, grid c8.

Campsites, facilities: There are 14 sites for tents or RVs up to 30 feet long. Picnic tables and fire grills are provided. Vault toilets are available. No drinking water is available. Garbage must be packed out. Leashed pets are permitted.

Reservations, fees: No reservations; $5 per night. Open early June to mid-October.

Directions: At the junction of U.S. 395 and Highway 108 (12 miles north of Bridgeport), drive south a short distance on U.S. 395 to an improved dirt road and a sign that says "Forest Service Campground." Turn west and drive four miles to the campground.

Contact: Humboldt-Toiyabe National Forest, Bridgeport Ranger District, tel. (760) 932-7070, or fax (760) 932-1299.

25 Niagara Creek Off-Highway Vehicle

 6

This small, primitive camp along Niagara Creek is designed primarily for people with off-highway vehicles. Got it? It is set on Niagara Creek near Donnells Reservoir. The elevation is 6,600 feet.

Location: On Niagara Creek in Stanislaus National Forest; map E4, grid b2.

Campsites, facilities: There are 10 sites for tents or RVs up to 22 feet long and two double sites. Picnic tables and fire grills are provided. A vault toilet is available. No drinking water is available. You can buy supplies in Pinecrest about 10 miles away. Leashed pets are permitted.

Reservations, fees: No reservations; no fee. Open May through mid-October, weather permitting.

Directions: From Sonora, drive east on Highway 108 to Strawberry and continue for about 15 miles to Eagle Meadows Road/Forest Road 5N01 on the right. Turn right and drive 1.5 miles to the campground on the left (just after crossing the bridge at Niagara Creek).

Contact: Stanislaus National Forest, Summit Ranger District, tel. (209) 965-3434 or fax (209) 965-3372.

26 Mill Creek

 7

This pretty little camp is set along Mill Creek at 6,200 feet in elevation, high in Stanislaus National Forest, near a variety of outdoor recreation options. The camp is near the Middle Fork Stanislaus River, which is stocked with trout near Donnells. For hiking, there is an outstanding trailhead at Kennedy Meadow (east of Donnells). For fishing, both Beardsley Reservoir (boat necessary) and Pinecrest Lake (shoreline prospects fair) provide two nearby alternatives.

Location: On Mill Creek in Stanislaus National Forest; map E4, grid b2.

Campsites, facilities: There are 17 sites for tents or RVs. Picnic tables and fire grills are provided. Vault toilets are available. No drinking water is available.

Reservations, fees: No reservations; $5 per night. Open May through mid-October, weather permitting.

Directions: From Sonora, drive east on Highway 108 to Strawberry. From Strawberry continue east on Highway 108 about 13 miles; turn right on Forest Road 5N21 and drive 0.1 mile to the campground access road (Forest Road 5N26) on the left.

Contact: Stanislaus National Forest, Summit Ranger District, tel. (209) 965-3434 or fax (209) 965-3372.

27 Niagara Creek

 6

This camp is set beside Niagara Creek at 6,600 feet, high in Stanislaus National Forest on the western slopes of the Sierra with direct access to roads in national forest, including routes to Double Dome Rock and Eagle Meadows. So if you have a four-wheel-drive vehicle or dirt bike, this is the place to come.

Location: In Stanislaus National Forest; map E4, grid b2.

Campsites, facilities: There are six sites for tents, five sites for RVs up to 22 feet long, and four walk-in sites. Picnic tables and fire grills are provided. A vault toilet is available. No drinking water is available. You can buy supplies in Pinecrest about 10 miles away. Leashed pets are permitted.

Reservations, fees: No reservations; $5 per night. Open May through mid-October, weather permitting.

Directions: From Sonora, drive east on Highway 108 to the town of Strawberry and continue for about 15 miles to Eagle Meadows Road/Forest Road 5N01 on the right. Turn right and drive one-half mile to the campground on the left.

Contact: Stanislaus National Forest, Summit Ranger District, tel. (209) 965-3434 or fax (209) 965-3372.

28 Pigeon Flat

 7

The prime attraction at Pigeon Flat is the short trail to Columns of the Giants, a rare example of columnar hexagonal rock, similar to the phenomenon at Devils Postpile near Mammoth Lakes. In addition, the camp is adjacent to the Middle Fork Stanislaus River; trout are small here and get fished hard. Supplies are available within walking distance in Dardanelle. The elevation is 6,000 feet.

Location: On the Middle Fork of the Stanislaus River in Stanislaus National Forest; map E4, grid b3.

Campsites, facilities: There are seven walk-in tent sites. Picnic tables and fire grills are provided. Vault toilets are available. No drinking water is available. You can buy supplies in Dardanelle. Leashed pets are permitted.

Reservations, fees: No reservations; $8 per night, $5 for an extra vehicle. Open May through October, weather permitting.

Directions: From Sonora, drive east on Highway 108 past the town of Strawberry to Dardanelle. Continue 1.5 miles east to the campground on the right side of the road, next to the Columns of the Giants Interpretive Site. **Contact:** Stanislaus National Forest, Summit Ranger District, tel. (209) 965-3434 or fax (209) 965-3372.

Eureka Valley

    8

There are some half-dozen campgrounds on this stretch of the Middle Fork Stanislaus River near Dardanelle, at 6,100 feet in elevation. The river runs along two side of this campground, making it quite pretty. This stretch of river is planted with trout by the Department of Fish and Game, but it is hit pretty hard despite its relatively isolated location. A good short and easy hike is to Columns of the Giants, accessible on a quarter-mile-long trail out of Pigeon Flat, a mile to the west.

Location: On the Middle Fork of the Stanislaus River in Stanislaus National Forest; map E4, grid b3.

Campsites, facilities: There are 28 sites for tents or RVs up to 30 feet long. Picnic tables and fire grills are provided. Drinking water and vault toilets are available. You can buy supplies in Dardanelle. Leashed pets are permitted.

Reservations, fees: No reservations; $12 per night, $5 for an extra vehicle. Open May through mid-October, weather permitting.

Directions: From Sonora, drive east on Highway 108 past the town of Strawberry to Dardanelle. Continue three miles east to the campground on the right.

Contact: Stanislaus National Forest, Summit Ranger District, tel. (209) 965-3434 or fax (209) 965-3372.

Baker

    7

Baker lies at the turnoff for the well-known and popular Kennedy Meadow trailhead for the Emigrant Wilderness. The camp is set along the Middle Fork Stanislaus River, 6,200 feet elevation, downstream a short way from the confluence with Deadman Creek. The trailhead, with a nearby horse corral, is another two miles farther on the Kennedy Meadow access road. From here it is a 1.5-mile hike to a fork in the trail; right will take you two miles to Relief Reservoir, 7,226 feet, and left will route you up Kennedy Creek for five miles to pretty Kennedy Lake, just north of Kennedy Peak (10,716 feet).

Location: On the Middle Fork of the Stanislaus River in Stanislaus National Forest; map E4, grid b4.

Campsites, facilities: There are 44 sites for tents or RVs up to 22 feet long. Picnic tables and fire grills are provided. Drinking water and vault toilets are available. You can buy supplies in Dardanelle. Leashed pets are permitted.

Reservations, fees: No reservations; $10 per night, $4 for an extra vehicle. Open May to mid-October, weather permitting.

Directions: From Sonora, drive east on Highway 108 past Strawberry to Dardanelle. From Dardanelle, continue 5.5 miles east to the campground on the right side of the road at the turnoff for Kennedy Meadow.

Contact: Stanislaus National Forest, Summit Ranger District, tel. (209) 965-3434 or fax (209) 965-3372.

Deadman

    7

This is a popular trailhead camp and an ideal jump-off point for backpackers heading into the adjacent Emigrant Wilderness. The camp is a short distance from Baker; see the entry for Baker for hiking destinations.

Location: On the Middle Fork of the Stanislaus River in Stanislaus National Forest; map E4, grid b4.

Campsites, facilities: There are 17 sites for tents or RVs up to 22 feet long. Picnic tables and fire grills are provided. Drinking water and vault toilets are available. You can buy supplies in Dardanelle. Leashed pets are permitted.

Reservations, fees: No reservations; $10 per night, $4 for an extra vehicle. Open May through mid-October, weather permitting.

Directions: From Sonora, drive east on Highway 108 past the town of Strawberry to Dardanelle. From Dardanelle, continue 5.5 miles east to the Kennedy Meadow turnoff. Drive a mile on Kennedy Meadow Road to the campground, which is opposite the parking area for the Kennedy Meadow Trail.

Contact: Stanislaus National Forest, Summit Ranger District, tel. (209) 965-3434 or fax (209) 965-3372.

32 Cascade Creek

  6

This campground is set along Cascade Creek at an elevation of 6,000 feet. A Forest Service road about a quarter mile west of camp on the south side of the highway provides a side trip three miles up to Pikes Peak, at 7,236 feet.

Location: In Stanislaus National Forest; map E4, grid b1.

Campsites, facilities: There are 14 sites for tents or RVs up to 22 feet long. Picnic tables and fire rings are provided. Pit and vault toilets are available. No drinking water is available. Supplies are available in Dardanelle. Leashed pets are permitted.

Reservations, fees: No reservations; $5 per night. Open May through mid-October.

Directions: From Sonora, drive east on Highway 108 to Strawberry and continue for 11 miles to the campground on the left side of the road.

Contact: Stanislaus National Forest, Summit Ranger District, tel. (209) 965-3434 or fax (209) 965-3372.

33 Beardsley

      6

For years people wondered why there was no campground at Beardsley Reservoir. In fact, some started parking their campers and creating their own. Well, that's why this primitive site is here, used primarily as a base camp for people fishing for trout at Beardsley Reservoir. It is often an outstanding fishery early in the season for brown trout, and then once planted, good for limits of hatchery fish during the evening bite. In winter and spring, as soon as they open the gate to the boat ramp access road, the fishing is best when the wind blows, believe it or not; let it push your boat while you drift half a nightcrawler behind a set of Half Fast Flashers. The wind always comes up here out of the west, but this is what gets the fish biting. The camp is set at 3,400 feet, but because it is near the bottom of the lake canyon, it actually feels much higher in elevation. Bonus: There is more fishing nearby on the Middle Fork of the Stanislaus.

Location: At Beardsley Lake in Stanislaus National Forest; map E4, grid c0.

Campsites, facilities: There are 26 sites for tents or RVs up to 22 feet long. Picnic tables and fire rings are provided. Vault toilets are available. No drinking water is available. Leashed pets are permitted.

Reservations, fees: No reservations; no fee. Open year-round, weather permitting (the road is often gated at the top of the canyon, when the boat ramp road at lake level is iced over).

Directions: From Sonora, drive east on Highway 108 for about 25 miles to Strawberry and the turnoff for Beardsley Reservoir/Forest Road 52. Turn left and drive seven miles to Beardsley Dam. Continue for a quarter mile past the dam to the campground.

Contact: Stanislaus National Forest, Summit Ranger District, tel. (209) 965-3434 or fax (209) 965-3372.

34 Herring Reservoir

   8

This is a pretty little spot, a rustic campground set near Herring Creek as it enters Herring Lake, set at an elevation of 7,350 feet. There is no boat ramp, but hand-launched boats, such as canoes, rafts, prams, and float tubes, are ideal. The lake is shallow, with fair fishing for brook trout and rainbow trout. No horses are permitted here.

Location: At Herring Lake in Stanislaus National Forest; map E4, grid c1.

Campsites, facilities: There are 49 sites for tents and RVs. Picnic tables and fire rings are provided. Vault toilets are available. No drinking water is available. Leashed pets are permitted.

Reservations, fees: No reservations; no fee, donations accepted. Open May through October, weather permitting.

Directions: From Sonora, drive east on Highway 108 for about 25 miles to Strawberry. Continue past Strawberry for two miles to Herring Creek Road/Forest Road 4N12. Turn right and drive 7 miles to Hamill Canyon Road/Forest Road 4N12. Bear right and drive a quartermile to Herring Creek Reservoir. Continue another quarter mile (cross the bridge) and turn right to the campground. The road is rough and not recommended for RVs or low-clearance vehicles.

Contact: Stanislaus National Forest, Summit Ranger District, tel. (209) 965-3434 or fax (209) 965-3372.

35 Meadowview

     7

No secret here, folks. This camp is one mile from Pinecrest Lake, a popular weekend vacation area (and there's a trail that connects the camp with the town). Pinecrest Lake is set at 5,621 feet, covers 300 acres, is stocked with rainbow trout, and has a 20-mph speed limit for boaters. This is a family-oriented vacation center, and a popular walk is the easy hike around the lake. If you want something more ambitious, there is a cutoff on the north side of the lake that is routed one mile up to little Catfish Lake. The Dodge Ridge Ski Area is nearby, with many privately owned cabins in the area.

Location: Near Pinecrest Lake in Stanislaus National Forest; map E4, grid c1.

Campsites, facilities: There are 100 sites for tents or RVs up to 22 feet long. Picnic tables and fire grills are provided. Drinking water and flush toilets are available. A grocery store, coin laundry, boat ramp, pay showers (in summer only), and propane gas are nearby. Leashed pets are permitted.

Reservations, fees: No reservations; $13 per night. Open May to mid-October.

Directions: From Sonora, drive east on Highway 108 for about 30 miles to the signed road for Pinecrest Lake. Turn right at the sign and drive a half mile to Pinecrest/Dodge Ridge Road. Turn right and drive about 200 yards to the campground entrance on the left side of the road.

Contact: Stanislaus National Forest, Summit Ranger District, tel. (209) 965-3434 or fax (209) 965-3372.

36 Pioneer Trail Group Camp

    8

If you're going to Pinecrest Lake with a Scout troop, this is the spot, since it is set up specifically for groups. You get beautiful creek and canyon views, with the camp set at an elevation of 5,800 feet. For recreation information, see the entry for nearby Meadowview.

Location: Near Pinecrest Lake in Stanislaus National Forest; map E4, grid c1.

Campsites, facilities: There are three group sites for 50 to 100 people. Picnic tables and fire grills are provided. Drinking water and vault toilets are available. A grocery store, coin laundry, boat ramp, pay showers (in summer only), and propane gas are nearby. Leashed pets are permitted.

Reservations, fees: Reserve at (877) 444-6777 ($8.65 reservation fee) or website: www.reserveusa.com; $50 to $65 group fee per night. Open May to mid-October, weather permitting.

Directions: From Sonora, drive east on Highway 108 for about 30 miles to the signed road for Pinecrest Lake. Turn right at the sign and drive one-half mile to the signed road for Pinecrest/Dodge Ridge Road. Turn right and drive about a mile to the campground entrance on the left.

Contact: Stanislaus National Forest, Summit Ranger District, tel. (209) 965-3434 or fax (209) 965-3372.

37 Pinecrest

      7

This monster-sized Forest Service camp is set near Pinecrest Lake. In early summer, there is good fishing for stocked rainbow trout. A launch ramp is available, and a 20-mph speed limit is enforced on the lake. A trail circles the lake and also branches off to nearby Catfish Lake. The elevation is 5,600 feet. Winter camping is allowed near the Pinecrest Day-Use Area.

Location: Near Pinecrest Lake in Stanislaus National Forest; map E4, grid c1.

Campsites, facilities: There are 200 sites for tents or RVs up to 22 feet long. Picnic tables and fire grills are provided. Drinking water and toilets are available. There are two winterized rest-rooms with flush toilets and sinks. A grocery store, coin laundry, pay showers (in summer only), boat ramp, and propane gas are nearby. Leashed pets are permitted.

Reservations, fees: Reservations required from mid-May to mid-September at tel. (877) 444-6777 ($8.65 reservation fee) or website: www.reserveusa.com.; $15.50 per night. Open April to mid-October, weather permitting.

Directions: From Sonora, drive east on Highway 108 for about 25 miles. Turn right at the sign for Pinecrest Lake. Go about 100 yards past the turnoff for Pinecrest and turn right on the access road for Pinecrest Camp.

Contact: Stanislaus National Forest, Summit Ranger District, tel. (209) 965-3434 or fax (209) 965-3372.

38 Fraser Flat

   7

This camp is set along the South Fork of the Stanislaus River. If the fish aren't biting, a seven-mile side trip via Forest Service roads will route you north into the main canyon of the Middle Fork Stanislaus. A map of Stanislaus National Forest is required for this adventure. Fraser Flat also provides an overflow area if the camps at Pinecrest Lake near Strawberry are filled.

Location: On the South Fork of the Stanislaus River in Stanislaus National Forest; map E4, grid d0.

Campsites, facilities: There are 32 sites for tents or RVs up to 22 feet long. Picnic tables and fire grills are provided. Drinking water and vault toilets are available. Some facilities are wheelchair accessible. A grocery store and propane gas are nearby. A camping and fishing site for wheelchair use is provided. Leashed pets are permitted.

Reservations, fees: No reservations; $12 per night, $5 per night for each extra vehicle for more than two vehicles. Open April through October.

Directions: From Sonora, drive east on Highway 108 to Long Barn. Continue east for six miles to the campground entrance road on the left. Turn left and drive two miles to the campground on the left side of the road.

Contact: Stanislaus National Forest, Mi-Wok Ranger District, tel. (209) 586-3234 or fax (209) 586-0643.

39 Hull Creek

    7

This obscure camp borders little Hull Creek (too small for trout fishing), at 5,600 feet elevation in Stanislaus National Forest. This is a good spot for those wishing to test out four-wheel-drive vehicles, with an intricate set of Forest Service roads available to the east. To explore that area, a map of Stanislaus National Forest is essential.

Location: In Stanislaus National Forest; map E4, grid d0.

Campsites, facilities: There are 20 sites for tents or RVs up to 22 feet long. Picnic tables and fire grills are provided. Drinking water and vault toilets are available. Leashed pets are permitted.

Reservations, fees: No reservations; $5 per night. Open May through October, weather permitting.

Directions: From Sonora, drive east on Highway 108 to Long Barn. Turn right and drive nine miles east on Road 31/Road 3N01 to the campground on the left side of the road.

Contact: Stanislaus National Forest, Mi-Wok Ranger District, tel. (209) 586-3234 or fax (209) 586-0643.

40 Buckeye

 8

Here's a little secret: A two-mile hike out of camp heads to the undeveloped Buckeye Hot Springs. That is what inspires campers to bypass the fishing at nearby Robinson Creek (three miles away) and Twin Lakes (six miles away). The camp feels remote and primitive, set at 7,000 feet on the eastern slope of the Sierra near Buckeye Creek. Another secret is that brook trout are planted at the little bridge that crosses Buckeye Creek near the campground. A trail that starts near camp is routed through Buckeye Canyon and into the Hoover Wilderness.

Location: Near Buckeye Creek in Humboldt-Toiyabe National Forest; map E4, grid d8.

Campsites, facilities: There are 65 paved sites for tents or RVs up to 30 feet long. There is one group site available. Picnic tables and fire grills are provided. Drinking water and flush toilets are available. Leashed pets are permitted.

Reservations, fees: Group site reservations at (877) 444-6777 ($8.65 reservation fee) or website: www.reserveusa.com; $40 per night. No reservations for individual sites; $10 per night. Open early May to mid-October.

Directions: On U.S. 395, drive to Bridgeport and the junction with Twin Lakes Road. Turn west and drive seven miles to Buckeye Road. Turn north on Buckeye Road (dirt, often impassable when wet) and drive 3.5 miles to the campground.

Contact: Humboldt-Toiyabe National Forest, Bridgeport Ranger District, tel. (760) 932-7070, fax (760) 932-1299.

41 Honeymoon Flat

 8

The camp is set beside Robinson Creek at 7,000 feet in elevation, in the transition zone between the Sierra Nevada range to the west and the high desert to the east. It is easy to reach on the access road to Twin Lakes, only three miles farther. The lake is famous for occasional huge brown trout. However, the fishing at Robinson Creek is also often quite good, thanks to the more than 50,000 trout planted each year by the Department of Fish and Game.

Location: On Robinson Creek in Humboldt-Toiyabe National Forest; map E4, grid d9.

Campsites, facilities: There are 35 sites for tents or RVs up to 45 feet long. Picnic tables and fire grills are provided. Drinking water and vault toilets are available. Leashed pets are permitted.

Reservations, fees: Reserve at (877) 444-6777 ($8.65 reservation fee) or website: www.reserveusa.com; $10 per night. Open mid-April through October.

Directions: On U.S. 395, drive to Bridgeport and the junction with Twin Lakes Road. Turn west and drive eight miles to the campground.

Contact: Humboldt-Toiyabe National Forest, Bridgeport Ranger District, tel. (760) 932-7070 or fax (760) 932-1299.

42 Paha

 8

This is one in a series of camps near Robinson Creek and within close range of Twin Lakes. The elevation at the camp is 7,000 feet. See the entries for Lower Twin Lake and Honeymoon Flat for more information.

Location: Near Twin Lakes in Humboldt-Toiyabe National Forest; map E4, grid d9.

Campsites, facilities: There are 22 paved sites for tents or RVs up to 40 feet long. Picnic tables and fire grills are provided. Drinking water and flush toilets are available. A boat launch, store, showers, and a coin laundry are available nearby. Leashed pets are permitted.

Reservations, fees: Reserve at (877) 444-6777 ($8.65 reservation fee) or website: www.reserveusa.com; $10 per night. Open early May to late October, weather permitting.

Directions: On U.S. 395, drive to Bridgeport and the junction with Twin Lakes Road. Turn west and drive 10 miles to the campground.

Contact: Humboldt-Toiyabe National Forest, Bridgeport Ranger District, tel. (760) 932-7070 or fax (760) 932-1299.

43 Robinson Creek

 9

This campground, one of a series in the area, is set at 7,000 feet on Robinson Creek, not far from Twin Lakes. For recreation options, see the entries for Lower Twin Lake and Honeymoon Flat.

Location: Near Twin Lakes in Humboldt-Toiyabe National Forest; map E4, grid d9.

Campsites, facilities: There are 54 paved sites for tents or RVs up to 45 feet long. Picnic tables and fire grills are provided. Drinking water, flush and vault toilets are available. Some facilities are wheelchair accessible. An amphitheater is nearby. Leashed pets are permitted.

Reservations, fees: Reserve at (877) 444-6777 ($8.65 reservation fee) or website: www.reserveusa.com; $10 per night. Open mid-April through October.

Directions: On U.S. 395, drive to Bridgeport and the junction with Twin Lakes Road. Turn west and drive 10 miles to the campground.

Contact: Humboldt-Toiyabe National Forest, Bridgeport Ranger District, tel. (760) 932-7070 or fax (760) 932-1299.

44 Crags Campground

 8

Crags Camp is set at 7,000 feet in the Sierra, one of a series of campgrounds along Robinson Creek near Lower Twin Lake. While this camp does not offer direct access to Lower Twin, home of giant brown trout, it is very close. See the entries for Lower Twin Lake and Honeymoon Flat.

Location: On Robinson Creek in Humboldt-Toiyabe National Forest; map E4, grid d9.

Campsites, facilities: There are 27 sites for tents or RVs up to 45 feet long. Picnic tables and fire grills are provided. A lighted restroom, drinking water, and flush toilets are available. Some facilities are wheelchair accessible. A boat launch (at Lower Twin Lake), store, a coin laundry, and showers are within a half mile. Leashed pets are permitted.

Reservations, fees: Reserve at (877) 444-6777 ($8.65 reservation fee) or website: www.reserveusa.com; $10 per night. Open early May to mid-October, weather permitting.

Directions: On U.S. 395, drive to Bridgeport and the junction with Twin Lakes Road. Turn west and drive 11 miles to a road on the left (just before reaching Lower Twin Lake). Turn left and drive over the bridge at Robinson Creek to another road on the left. Turn left and drive a short distance to the campground.

Contact: Humboldt-Toiyabe National Forest, Bridgeport Ranger District, tel. (760) 932-7070 or fax (760) 932-1299.

45 Lower Twin Lake

      9

The Twin Lakes are actually two lakes, set high in the eastern Sierra at 7,000 feet. The best of the two is Lower Twin, where a full resort, marina, boat ramp, and some of the biggest brown trout in the West can be found. The state record brown was caught here, 26.5 pounds and, in 1991, 11-year-old Micah Beirle of Bakersfield caught one that weighed 20.5 pounds, one of the great fish catches by a youngster anywhere in America. Of course, most of the trout are your typical 10- to 12-inch planted rainbow trout, but nobody seems to mind, with the chance of a true monster-sized fish always in the back of the minds of anglers. An option for campers is an excellent trailhead for hiking near Mono Village at the head of Upper Twin Lake. Here you will find the Barney Lake Trail, which is routed up the headwaters of Robinson Creek, steeply at times, to little Barney Lake, an excellent day hike.

Location: In Humboldt-Toiyabe National Forest; map E4, grid d8.

Campsites, facilities: There are 15 paved sites for tents or RVs up to 40 feet long. Picnic tables and fire grills are provided. Drinking water and flush toilets are available. A boat launch, store, showers, and a coin laundry are available nearby. Leashed pets are permitted.

Reservations, fees: Reserve at (877) 444-6777 ($8.65 reservation fee) or website: www.reserveusa.com; $10 per night. Open early May to mid-October, weather permitting.

Directions: On U.S. 395, drive to Bridgeport and the junction with Twin Lakes Road. Turn west and drive 11 miles to the campground.

Contact: Humboldt-Toiyabe National Forest, Bridgeport Ranger District, tel. (760) 932-7070 or fax (760) 932-1299.

46 Cherry Valley

       8

Cherry Lake is a mountain lake surrounded by national forest at 4,700 feet in elevation, just outside the western boundary of Yosemite National Park. It is much larger than most people anticipate and provides much better trout fishing than anything in Yosemite. The camp is on the southwest shore of the lake, a very pretty spot, about a mile ride to the boat launch on the west side of the Cherry Valley Dam. The lake is bordered to the east by Kibbie Ridge; just on the other side is Yosemite Park and Lake Eleanor.

Location: On Cherry Lake in Stanislaus National Forest; map E4, grid e1.

Campsites, facilities: There are 46 sites for tents or RVs of any length. Picnic tables and fire grills are provided. Drinking water and vault toilets are available. A boat ramp is nearby. Leashed pets are permitted.

Reservations, fees: No reservations; $12 per night, $24 for double sites. Open April through October.

Directions: From Groveland, drive east on Highway 120 for about 15 miles to Forest Road 1N07/Cherry Lake Road on the left side of the road. Turn left and drive 18 miles to the south end of Cherry Lake and the campground access road on the right. Turn right and drive one mile to the campground.

Contact: Stanislaus National Forest, Groveland Ranger District, tel. (209) 962-7825 or fax (209) 962-6406.

47 Green Creek

     7

This camp is ideal for backpackers or campers who like to fish for trout in streams. That is because it is set at 7,500 feet, with a trailhead that leads into the Hoover Wilderness and to several high mountain lakes, including Green Lake, West Lake, and East Lake; the ambitious can hike beyond in remote northeastern Yosemite National Park. The camp is set along Green Creek, a fair trout stream with small rainbow trout.

Location: In Humboldt-Toiyabe National Forest; map E4, grid e9.

Campsites, facilities: There are 11 sites for tents or RVs up to 22 feet long and two group sites for up 20 and 25 people. Picnic tables and fire grills are provided. Drinking water and vault toilets are available. Leashed pets are permitted.

Reservations, fees: Reserve at (877) 444-6777 ($8.65 reservation fee) or website: www.reserveusa.com; $10 per night per individual site. Open mid-May to early October, weather permitting.

Directions: From Bridgeport, drive south on U.S. 395 for four miles to Green Lakes Road (dirt). Turn right and drive seven miles to the campground.

Contact: Humboldt-Toiyabe National Forest, Bridgeport Ranger District, tel. (760) 932-7070 or fax (760) 932-1299.

48 Trumbull Lake

     8

This is a high-mountain camp (9,500 feet) at the gateway to a beautiful Sierra basin. Little Trumbull Lake is the first lake on the north side of Virginia Lakes Road, with Virginia Lakes set nearby, along with the Hoover Wilderness and access to many other small lakes by trail. A trail is available that is routed just north of Blue Lake, then leads west to Frog Lake, Summit Lake, and beyond into a remote area of Yosemite National Park. If you don't want to rough it, cabins, boat rentals, and a restaurant are available at Virginia Lakes Resort.

Location: In Humboldt-Toiyabe National Forest; map E4, grid f9.

Campsites, facilities: There are 45 sites for tents or RVs up to 45 feet long. Picnic tables and fire grills are provided. Drinking water and vault toilets are available. A store is nearby at the resort. Leashed pets are permitted.

Reservations, fees: Reserve at (877) 444-6777 ($8.65 reservation fee) or website: www.reserveusa.com; $10 per night. Open mid-June to mid-October, weather permitting.

Directions: From Bridgeport, drive south on U.S. 395 for 13.5 miles to Virginia Lakes Road. Turn right on Virginia Lakes Road and drive 6.5 miles to the campground entrance road.

Contact: Humboldt-Toiyabe National Forest, Bridgeport Ranger District, tel. (760) 932-7070 or fax (760) 932-1299.

49 Lumsden

   7

This is one of the great access points for white-water rafting on the wild and scenic Tuolumne River and its premium stretch between Hetch Hetchy Reservoir in Yosemite and Don Pedro Reservoir in the Central Valley foothills. Unless you are an expert rafter, you are advised to attempt running this stretch of river only with a professional rafting company. The camp is set at 1,500 feet, just across the road from the river. The access road down the canyon is steep and bumpy. There are two other camps within a mile, South Fork and Lumsden Bridge.

Location: On the Tuolumne River in Stanislaus National Forest; map E4, grid f0.

Campsites, facilities: There are 11 tent sites. Picnic tables and fire grills are provided. Vault toilets are available. No drinking water is available. Leashed pets are permitted.

Reservations, fees: No reservations; no fee. Open April through October.

Directions: From Groveland, drive east on Highway 120 for about eight miles (just under a mile beyond County Road J132) to Ferretti Road. Turn left on Ferretti and drive to a Forest Service road intersection. Jog left, then right, and continue for four miles to the camp on the left side of the road.

Contact: Stanislaus National Forest, Groveland Ranger District, tel. (209) 962-7825 or fax (209) 962-6406. For a map, send $6 to U.S. Forest Service, Attn: Map Sales, P.O. Box 587, Camino, CA 95709; tel. (530) 647-5390, fax (530) 647-5389, or website: www.r5.fs.fed.us/visitorcenter. Major credit cards accepted.

50 Lumsden Bridge

  7

This is one of three camps along this immediate stretch of the Tuolumne River, one of the best white-water rafting rivers in California. The camp is set at 1,500 feet on the north side of the river, accessible just after crossing the Lumsden Bridge, hence the name. See the entry for Lumsden for more information.

Location: On the Tuolumne River in Stanislaus National Forest; map E4, grid f0.

Campsites, facilities: There are nine tent sites. Picnic tables and fire grills are provided. Vault toilets are available. No drinking water is available. Garbage must be packed out. Leashed pets are permitted.

Reservations, fees: No reservations; no fee. Open April through October.

Directions: From Groveland, drive east on Highway 120 for about eight miles (just under a mile beyond County Road J132) to Ferretti Road. Turn left on Ferretti and drive to a Forest Service road intersection. Jog left, then right, and continue for 5.5 miles to the camp on the left side of the road.

Contact: Stanislaus National Forest, Groveland Ranger District, tel. (209) 962-7825 or fax (209) 962-6406. For a map, send $6 to U.S. Forest Service, Attn: Map Sales, P.O. Box 587, Camino, CA 95709; tel. (530) 647-5390, fax (530) 647-5389, or website: www.r5.fs.fed.us/visitorcenter. Major credit cards accepted.

51 South Fork

 6

South Fork Camp is a half mile upstream from Lumsden and about a mile downstream from Lumsden Bridge. Why do we say "upstream" and "downstream" instead of east and west? Because this is a camp for white-water rafters, featuring the spectacular Tuolumne River and access to its most exciting stretches. You should only attempt to run this river with a professional rafting company. The elevation is 1,500 feet.

Location: Near the Tuolumne River in Stanislaus National Forest; map E4, grid f0.

Campsites, facilities: There are eight tent sites. Picnic tables and fire grills are provided. Vault toilets are available. No drinking water is available. Leashed pets are permitted.

Reservations, fees: No reservations; no fee. Open April through October.

Directions: From Groveland, drive east on Highway 120 for about eight miles (just under a mile beyond County Road J132) to Ferretti Road. Turn left on Ferretti and drive to a Forest Service road intersection. Jog left, then right, and continue for five miles to the camp on the left side of the road.

Contact: Stanislaus National Forest, Groveland Ranger District, tel. (209) 962-7825 or fax (209) 962-6406. For a map, send $6 to U.S. Forest Service, Attn: Map Sales, P.O. Box 587, Camino, CA 95709; tel. (530) 647-5390, fax (530) 647-5389, or website: www.r5.fs.fed.us/visitorcenter. Major credit cards accepted.

52 Lost Claim

   4

This is one in a series of easy-access camps off Highway 120 that provide overflow areas when all the sites are taken in Yosemite National Park to the east. A feeder stream to the Tuolumne River runs by the camp. The elevation is 3,100 feet.

Location: Near the Tuolumne River in Stanislaus National Forest; map E4, grid f0.

Campsites, facilities: There are 10 sites for tents or small RVs. Picnic tables and fire grills are provided. Vault toilets and drinking water are available. A grocery store is nearby. Leashed pets are permitted.

Reservations, fees: No reservations; $9 per night. Open May through Labor Day.

Directions: From Groveland, drive east on Highway 120 for 14 miles (1.5 miles past the Groveland District Office) to the campground on the left side of the road.

Contact: Stanislaus National Forest, Groveland Ranger District, tel. (209) 962-7825 or fax (209) 962-6406.

53 Sweetwater

 4

This camp is set at 3,000 feet, near the South Fork Tuolumne River, one of several camps along Highway 120 that provides a safety valve for campers who can't find space in Yosemite National Park to the east.

Location: Near the South Fork of the Tuolumne River in Stanislaus National Forest; map E4, grid g0.

Campsites, facilities: There are 13 sites for tents or RVs up to 22 feet long. Picnic tables and fire grills are provided. Drinking water and vault toilets are available. A grocery store is nearby. Leashed pets are permitted.

Reservations, fees: No reservations; $11 per night. Open April through October.

Directions: From Groveland, drive east on Highway 120 for about 18 miles (four miles past the Groveland District Office) to the campground on the left side of the road.

Contact: Stanislaus National Forest, Groveland Ranger District, tel. (209) 962-7825 or fax (209) 962-6406.

54 White Wolf

 8

This is one of Yosemite National Park's prime mountain camps for people who like to hike, either for great day hikes in the immediate area and beyond, or for overnight backpacking trips. The day hike to Lukens Lake is an easy two-mile trip, the payoff being this pretty little alpine lake set amid a meadow, pines, and granite. Just about everybody who camps at White Wolf makes the trip. Backpackers can make the overnight trip into the Ten Lakes Basin, set below Grand Mountain and Colby Mountain. Bears are common at this camp, so be certain to secure your food in the bearproof lockers. The elevation is 8,000 feet.

Location: In Yosemite National Park; map E4, grid g3.

Campsites, facilities: There are 87 sites for tents or RVs up to 30 feet long. Picnic tables and fire grills are provided. Drinking water and flush toilets are available. Evening ranger programs are also available. A grocery store is nearby. Leashed pets are permitted in the campground, but not on trails.

Reservations, fees: No reservations; $10 per night, plus $20 park entrance fee. Open June through mid-September.

Directions: From Merced, drive east on Highway 140 to the El Portal entrance station at Yosemite National Park. Continue east on Highway 140 to the junction with Highway 120/Tioga Road (just before entering the valley). Turn left and drive to the junction with Highway 120. Turn right and drive 15 miles to White Wolf Road on the left. Turn left and drive a mile to the campground entrance road on the right.

Contact: Yosemite National Park, tel. (209) 372-0200 for a recorded message, tel. (209) 372-0265, or fax (209) 372-0371.

55 Saddlebag Lake

 10

This camp is set in spectacular high country above tree line, the highest drive-to camp and lake in California, with Saddlebag Lake at 10,087 feet. The camp is about a quarter mile from the lake, within walking range of the little store, boat rentals, and a one-minute drive for launching a boat at the ramp. The scenery is stark; everything is granite, ice, or water, with only a few lodgepole pines managing precarious toeholds, sprinkled across the landscape on the access road. An excellent trailhead is available for hiking, with the best hike routed out past little Hummingbird Lake to Lundy Pass. Note that with the elevation and the high mountain pass, it can be windy and cold here, and some people find it difficult to catch their breath on simple hikes. In addition, RV users should note that level sites are extremely hard to come by.

Location: In Inyo National Forest; map E4, grid f8.

Campsites, facilities: There are 20 sites for tents or RVs up to 30 feet long. One group site can accommodate up to 25 people. Drinking water, fire grills, and picnic tables are provided. Vault toilets, boat rentals, and a boat launch are available. A grocery store is nearby. Leashed pets are permitted.

Reservations, fees: Reservations for the group site only at tel. (877) 444-6777 ($8.65 reservation fee) or website: www.reserve usa.com; $11 per night for single sites, $20 per night for the group site. Open July through September, weather permitting.

Directions: On U.S. 395, drive one-half mile south of Lee Vining and the junction with Highway 120. Turn west and drive about 11 miles to Saddlebag Lake Road. Turn right and drive two miles to the campground on the right.

From Merced, turn east on Highway 140, drive into Yosemite National Park, and continue toward Yosemite Valley to the junction with Highway 120. Turn north and drive about 65 miles through the Tioga Pass entrance station. Continue two miles to Saddlebag Lake Road. Turn left and drive three miles to the campground.

Contact: Inyo National Forest, Visitor Information, tel. (760) 873-2408; Mono Lake Ranger District, tel. (760) 647-3044 or fax (760) 647-3046.

56 Junction

    7

Which way do you go? From Junction any way you choose, you can't miss. Two miles to the north is Saddlebag Lake, the highest drive-to lake (10,087 feet) in California. Directly across the road is Ellery Lake, and a mile to the south is Tioga Lake, two beautiful, pristine waters with trout fishing. To the east is Mono Lake, and to the west is Yosemite National Park. From camp, it is a one-mile hike to Bennetville, a historic camp. Take your pick. Camp elevation is 9,600 feet.

Location: Near Ellery and Tioga Lakes in Inyo National Forest; map E4, grid g8.

Campsites, facilities: There are 13 sites for tents or RVs up to 30 feet long. Picnic tables and fire grills are provided. Vault toilets are available. No drinking water is available. Leashed pets are permitted.

Reservations, fees: No reservations; $6 per night. Open June to October, weather permitting.

Directions: On U.S. 395, drive to just south of Lee Vining and the junction with Highway 120. Turn west on highway 120 and drive about 10 miles to Saddlebag Road and the campground on the right side of the road.

From Merced, turn east on Highway 140, drive into Yosemite National Park, and continue toward Yosemite Valley to the junction with Highway 120/Tioga Road. Turn north and drive about 65 miles through the Tioga Pass entrance station. Continue four miles to Saddlebag Road and the campground on the left side of the road.

Contact: Inyo National Forest, Visitor Information, tel. (760) 873-2408, or Mono Lake Ranger District, tel. (760) 647-3044 or fax (760) 647-3046.

57 Lower Lee Vining Camp

   7

This camp and its neighboring camps—Cattleguard, Moraine, Aspen, Big Bend and Boulder—can be a godsend for vacationers who show up at Yosemite National Park and make the discovery that there are no sites left, a terrible experience for some late-night arrivals. But these county campgrounds provide a great safety valve, even if they are extremely primitive, on the edge of timber. Lee Vining Creek is the highlight, flowing right past the campgrounds along Highway 120, bound for Mono Lake to the nearby east. It is stocked weekly during the fishing season. A must-do side trip is venturing to the south shore of Mono Lake to walk amid the bizarre yet beautiful tufa towers. There is good rock climbing and hiking in the area. Although sunshine is the norm, be prepared for all kinds of weather: It can snow every month of the year here. Short but lively thunderstorms are common in early summer. Other nearby trips are available to Mammoth, June Lake, and Bodie State Park.

Location: Near Lee Vining; map E4, grid g9.

Campsites, facilities: There are 59 sites for tents or RVs up to 40 feet long. Pit and portable toilets are available. No drinking water is available. You can buy supplies in Lee Vining (about two miles away). Leashed pets are permitted.

Reservations, fees: No reservations; $7 per night. Open May through October, weather permitting.

Directions: On U.S. 395, drive to just south of Lee Vining and the junction with Highway 120. Turn west on Highway 120 and drive about 2.5 miles. Turn left into the campground entrance.

Contact: Mono County Building and Parks Department, tel. (760) 932-5451 or fax (760) 932-5458.

58 Cattleguard Camp

    7

This camp is an alternative to Yosemite National Park. Though primitive, it has several advantages: It is quiet, gets more sun than the three neighboring camps (Lower Lee Vining, Moraine, and Boulder), and provides the best views of Dana Plateau. For more information, see the entry for Lower Lee Vining Camp.

Location: Near Lee Vining; map E4, grid g9.

Campsites, facilities: There are 16 sites for tents or RVs up to 30 feet long in four separate campgrounds next to each other. Portable toilets are available. No drinking water is available. You can buy supplies in Lee Vining (about two miles away). Leashed pets are permitted.

Reservations, fees: No reservations; $7 per night. Open May through October.

Directions: On U.S. 395, drive to just south of Lee Vining and the junction with Highway 120.

Turn west on Highway 120 and drive about three miles. Turn left into the campground entrance.

Contact: Mono County Building and Parks Department, tel. (760) 932-5451 or fax (760) 932-5458.

59 Moraine Camp

    7

This camp provides an alternative to Yosemite National Park. For more information, see the entry for Lower Lee Vining Camp.

Location: Near Lee Vining; map E4, grid g9.

Campsites, facilities: There are 30 sites for tents or RVs up to 30 feet long in four separate campgrounds next to each other. Portable toilets are available. There is no drinking water, so bring your own. You can buy supplies in Lee Vining (about two miles away). Leashed pets are permitted.

Reservations, fees: No reservations; $7 per night, limited to two vehicles and six persons per site. Open May through October.

Directions: On U.S. 395, drive to just south of Lee Vining and the junction with Highway 120. Turn west on Highway 120 and drive 3.5 miles to Poole Power Plant Road. Exit left onto Poole Power Plant Road and drive a quarter mile to the campground entrance at the end of the road.

Contact: Mono County Building and Parks Department, tel. (760) 932-5451 or fax (760) 932-5458.

60 Boulder Camp

    7

This camp provides an alternative to Yosemite National Park. For more information, see the entry for Lower Lee Vining.

Location: Near Lee Vining; map E4, grid g9.

Campsites, facilities: There are 22 sites for tents or RVs up to 30 feet long in four separate campgrounds next to each other. Portable toilets are available. No drinking water is available. You can buy supplies in Lee Vining (about two miles away). Leashed pets are permitted.

Reservations, fees: No reservations; $7 per night, limited to two vehicles and six persons per site. Open May through October.

Directions: On U.S. 395, drive to just south of Lee Vining and the junction with Highway 120. Turn west on Highway 120 and drive three miles to Poole Power Plant Road. Exit left and then make a quick right on Poole Power Plant Road and drive a half mile to the campground entrance on the left.

Contact: Mono County Building and Parks Department, tel. (760) 932-5451, or fax (760) 932-5458.

61 Big Bend

    8

This camp is set in sparse but beautiful country along Lee Vining Creek at 7,800 feet elevation. It is an excellent bet for an overflow camp if Tuolumne Meadows in nearby Yosemite is packed. The view from the camp to the north features Mono Dome (10,614 feet) and Lee Vining Peak (11,691 feet).

Location: On Lee Vining Creek in Inyo National Forest; map E4, grid g9.

Campsites, facilities: There are 16 sites for tents or RVs up to 30 feet long. Picnic tables and fire grills are provided. Drinking water and vault toilets are available. Leashed pets are permitted.

Reservations, fees: No reservations; $11 per night. Open May to mid-October, weather permitting.

Directions: On U.S. 395, drive to just south of Lee Vining and the junction with Highway 120. Turn west on Highway 120 and drive about 3.5 miles to a county road. Turn right and drive three miles west to the campground access road on the left. Turn left and drive a short distance to the camp.

Contact: Inyo National Forest, Visitor Information, tel., (760) 873-2408, or Mono Lake Ranger District, tel. (760) 647-3044 or fax (760) 647-3046.

62 Aspen Grove

    8

This high-country, primitive camp is set along Lee Vining Creek at 7,500 feet, on the eastern slopes of the Sierra just east of Yosemite National Park. Take the side trip to moonlike Mono Lake, best seen at the south shore's Tufa State Reserve.

Location: On Lee Vining Creek; map E4, grid g9.

Campsites, facilities: There are 58 sites for tents or RVs up to 40 feet long. Pit and portable toilets are available. Drinking water is available from a wellhead at the entrance to the camp. You can buy supplies in Lee Vining. Leashed pets are permitted.

Reservations, fees: No reservations; $7 per night, limit two vehicles and six people per site. Open May through October, weather permitting.

Directions: On U.S. 395, drive to just south of Lee Vining and the junction with Highway 120. Turn west on Highway 120 and drive about 3.5 miles. Exit onto Poole Power Plant Road. Turn left and drive about 4 miles west to the campground on the left.

Contact: Mono County Building and Parks Department, tel. (760) 932-5451, or fax (760) 932-5458; or Inyo National Forest, Mono Lake Ranger District, tel. (760) 647-3044 or fax (760) 647-3046.

63 Tioga Lake

    9

Tioga Lake is a dramatic sight, with gemlike blue waters encircled by Sierra granite at 9,700 feet in elevation. Together with adjacent Ellery Lake, it makes up a pair of gorgeous waters with near-lake camping, trout fishing (stocked with rainbow trout), and access to Yosemite National Park and Saddlebag Lake. The only downers: It can get windy here (no foolin'!) and the camps fill quickly from the overflow crowds at Tuolumne

Meadows. See the entry for Ellery Lake for more information.

Location: In Inyo National Forest; map E4, grid g9.

Campsites, facilities: There are 13 sites for tents or RVs up to 30 feet long. Picnic tables and fire grills are provided. Drinking water and vault toilets are available. Leashed pets are permitted.

Reservations, fees: No reservations; $11 per night. Open June through September, weather permitting.

Directions: On U.S. 395, drive to just south of Lee Vining and the junction with Highway 120. Turn west on Highway 120 and drive about 11 miles (just past Ellery Lake) to the campground on the left side of the road.

From Merced, turn east on Highway 140, drive into Yosemite National Park, and continue toward Yosemite Valley to the junction with Highway 120/Tioga Road. Turn north and drive about 65 miles through the Tioga Pass entrance station. Continue one mile to the campground on the right side of the road.

Contact: Inyo National Forest, Visitor Information, tel., (760) 873-2408, or Mono Lake Ranger District, tel. (760) 647-3044 or fax (760) 647-3046.

64 Ellery Lake

 9

Ellery Lake offers all the spectacular beauty of Yosemite but is two miles outside park borders. That means it is stocked with trout by the Department of Fish and Game (no lakes in Yosemite are planted, hence the lousy fishing. Just like neighboring Tioga Lake, here are deep-blue waters set in rock in the 9,500-foot elevation range, one of the most pristine highway-access lake settings anywhere. Nearby Saddlebag Lake is a common side trip, the highest drive-to lake in California. Whenever Tuolumne Meadows fills in Yosemite, this camp fills shortly thereafter. Camp elevation is 9,600 feet.

Location: In Inyo National Forest; map E4 grid g9.

Campsites, facilities: There are 12 sites for tents or RVs up to 30 feet long. Picnic tables and fire grills are provided. Drinking water and flush toilets are available. A grocery store is nearby. Leashed pets are permitted.

Reservations, fees: No reservations; $11 per night. Open June through September, weather permitting.

Directions: On U.S. 395, drive to just south of Lee Vining and the junction with Highway 120. Turn west on Highway 120 and drive about 10 miles to the campground on the left side of the road.

From Merced turn east on Highway 140, drive into Yosemite National Park, and continue toward Yosemite Valley to the junction with Highway 120/Tioga Road. Turn north and drive about 65 miles through the Tioga Pass entrance station. Continue four miles to the campground on the right side of the road.

Contact: Inyo National Forest, Visitor Information, tel., (760) 873-2408, or Mono Lake Ranger District, tel. (760) 647-3044 or fax (760) 647-3046.

65 Dimond "O"

  7

Dimond "O" is set at 4,400 feet in elevation on the eastern side of Stanislaus National Forest—just two miles from the Yosemite National Park border.

Location: In Stanislaus National Forest; map E4, grid g2.

Campsites, facilities: There are 38 sites suitable for trailers and RVs up to 33 feet long. Picnic tables and fire grills are provided. Drinking water and vault toilets are available. Some facilities are wheelchair accessible. Leashed pets are permitted.

Reservations, fees: No reservations; $13 per night. Open April through October.

Directions: From Groveland, drive east on Highway 120 for 25 miles. Turn left on Evergreen Road and drive six miles to the campground.

Contact: Stanislaus National Forest, Groveland Ranger District, tel. (209) 962-7825 or fax (209) 962-6406.

66 Hodgdon Meadow

   7

Hodgdon Meadow is on the outskirts of Yosemite, just inside the park's borders at the Highway 120 entrance station, at 4,900 feet in elevation. It is near a small feeder creek to the South Fork Tuolumne River. It is about a 20-minute drive on Highway 120 to a major junction, where a left turn takes you on Tioga Road and to Yosemite's high country, including Tuolumne Meadows, and a right turn routes you toward Yosemite Valley (25 miles from the camp).

Location: In Yosemite National Park; map E4, grid g1.

Campsites, facilities: There are 105 family sites for tents or RVs up to 35 feet long. There are also four group sites for 13 to 30 people. Picnic tables and fire rings are provided. Drinking water and flush toilets are available. A grocery store and propane gas are available nearby. Leashed pets are permitted in the campground, but not on trails.

Reservations, fees: Reserve at (800) 436-PARK (800-436-7275) or website: reservations .nps.gov/. Reservations are required May through October; $15 per night May through October, $10 remainder of year, group campsite is $35 per night, plus $20 park entrance fee per car. Open year-round.

Directions: From Groveland, drive east on Highway 120 to the Big Oak Flat entrance station for Yosemite National Park. Just after passing the entrance station, turn left and drive a short distance to the campground on the right.

Contact: Yosemite National Park, tel. (209) 372-0200 for a recorded message, tel. (209) 372-0265, or fax (209) 372-0371.

67 Crane Flat

   6

Crane Flat is within a five-minute drive of the Tuolumne Grove of Big Trees, as well as the Merced Grove to the nearby west. This is the feature attraction in this part of Yosemite National Park, set near the western border in close proximity to the Highway 120 entrance station. The elevation is 6,200 feet. Yosemite Valley is about a 25-minute drive away.

Location: Near Tuolumne Grove of Big Trees in Yosemite National Park; map E4, grid h2.

Campsites, facilities: There are 166 sites for tents or RVs up to 35 feet long. Picnic tables and fire rings are provided. Drinking water, flush toilets, groceries, propane gas, and evening ranger programs are available. A gas station is nearby.

Reservations, fees: Reserve at (800) 436-PARK (800-436-7275) or website: reservations .nps.gov/; $15 per night, plus $20 park entrance fee. Open June through September.

Directions: From Groveland, drive east on Highway 120 to the Big Oak Flat entrance station for Yosemite National Park. After passing through the entrance station, drive about 10 miles to the campground entrance road on the right. Turn right and drive a half mile to the campground.

Contact: Yosemite National Park, tel. (209) 372-0200 for a recorded message, tel. (209) 372-0265, or fax (209) 372-0371.

68 Yosemite Creek

    9

This is the most remote drive-to camp in Yosemite National Park, a great alternative to camping in the valley or at Tuolumne Meadows, and the rough, curvy access road keeps many out-of-state tourists away. It is set along Yosemite Creek at 7,659 feet, with poor trout fishing but a trailhead for a spectacular hike. If you arrange a shuttle ride, you can make a great one-way trip down to the north side of the Yosemite Canyon rim, skirting past the top of Yosemite Falls (a side trip to Yosemite Point is a must!), then tackling the unbelievable descent into the valley, emerging at Camp 4 Walk-In. Note: The narrow entrance road is a remnant of "Old Tioga Road."

Location: On Yosemite Creek in Yosemite National Park; map E4, grid g4.

Campsites, facilities: There are 75 tent sites. Picnic tables and fire grills are provided. Pit toilets are available. No drinking water is available. Leashed pets are permitted.

Reservations, fees: No reservations; $6 to $8 per night, plus $20 park entrance fee. A 14-day stay limit is enforced. Open June through September.

Directions: From Merced, drive east on Highway 140 to the Yosemite National Park entrance and continue toward Yosemite Valley to the junction with Highway 120/Tioga Road. Turn north and drive about 30 miles (just beyond the White Wolf turnoff on the left) to Yosemite Creek Campground Road on the right. Turn right (RVs and trailers are not recommended) and drive five miles to the campground at the end of the road.

Contact: Yosemite National Park, tel. (209) 372-0200 for a recorded message, tel. (209) 372-0265, or fax (209) 372-0371.

69 Porcupine Flat

   6

Porcupine Flat, set at 8,100 feet, is southwest of Mount Hoffman, one of the prominent nearby peaks along Tioga Road in Yosemite National Park. The trailhead for a hike to May Lake, set just below Mount Hoffman, is about five miles away on a signed turnoff on the north side of the road. There are several little peaks above the lake where hikers can gain great views, including one of the back side of Half Dome.

Location: Near Yosemite Creek in Yosemite National Park; map E4, grid g5.

Campsites, facilities: There are 52 sites for tents or RVs up to 35 feet long. There is limited RV space. Picnic tables and fire rings are provided. Pit toilets are available. No drinking water is available. No pets are allowed.

Reservations, fees: No reservations; $6 per night, plus $20 park entrance fee. Open June through September.

Directions: From Merced, drive east on Highway 140 to the El Portal entrance station at Yosemite National Park. Continue east on Highway 140 to the junction with Highway 120/Tioga Road (just before entering the valley). Turn left and drive to the junction with Highway 120. Turn right and drive about 25 miles to the campground on the left side of the road (16 miles west from Tuolumne Meadows).

Contact: Yosemite National Park, tel. (209) 372-0200 for a recorded message, tel. (209) 372-0265, or fax (209) 372-0371.

70 Tuolumne Meadows

    8

This is Yosemite's biggest camp, and for the variety of nearby adventures, it might also be the best. It is set in the high country, at 8,600 feet, and can be used as a base camp for fishing, hiking, and horseback riding, or as a jump-off point for a backpacking trip (wilderness permits required). There are two outstanding and easy day hikes from here, one heading north on the Pacific Crest Trail for the near-level walk to Tuolumne Falls, the other heading south up Lyell Fork, with good fishing for small brook trout. With a backpack, either route can be extended for as long as desired into remote and beautiful country. The campground is huge, and neighbors are guaranteed, but it is well wooded and feels somewhat secluded even with all the RVs and tents. There are lots of food-raiding bears in the area, so use of the food lockers is required.

Location: In Yosemite National Park; map E4, grid g7.

Campsites, facilities: There are 304 sites for tents or RVs up to 35 feet long. Picnic tables and fire grills are provided. There are also an additional 25 hike-in sites available for backpackers (no parking is available for back-packer campsites, usually reserved for those hiking the Pacific Crest Trail, for which a wilderness permit is required), and seven group sites that can accommodate 30 people each. Drinking water, flush toilets, and a sanitary disposal station are available. No RV hookups are available. Showers and groceries are nearby. Leashed pets are permitted.

Reservations, fees: Reserve at (800) 436-PARK (800-436-7275) or website: reservations.nps.gov/; half of the sites are available through reservations; the other half are first come, first served. There is a $15 fee per night for family sites, $3 per night per person for walk-in sites, and $35 per night for group sites, plus a $20 per vehicle park entrance fee. Open June through mid-September.

Directions: From Merced, drive east on Highway 140 to the El Portal entrance station at Yosemite National Park. Continue east on Highway 140 to the junction with Highway 120/Tioga Road (just before entering the valley). Turn left and drive to the junction with Highway 120. Turn right and drive 46 miles to the campground on the right side of the road.

From just south of Lee Vining at the junction of U.S. 395 and Highway 120, turn west and drive to the Tioga Pass entrance station for Yosemite National Park. Continue for about 10 miles to the campground entrance on the left.

Contact: Yosemite National Park, tel. (209) 372-0200 for a recorded message, tel. (209) 372-0265, or fax (209) 372-0371.

71 Tamarack Flat

  7

The road to this campground looks something like the surface of the moon. Then you arrive and find one of the few primitive drive-to camps in Yosemite National Park, 6,300 feet in elevation. From the trailhead at camp, you can link up with the El Capitan Trail and then hike across Ribbon Meadow on up to the north valley rim at El Capitan, 7,569 feet in elevation. This is the largest single piece of granite

in the world, and standing atop it for both the sensation and the divine view is a breathtaking experience. From camp, Yosemite Valley is 23 miles away.

Location: On Tamarack Creek in Yosemite National Park; map E4, grid h3.

Campsites, facilities: There are 52 sites for tents or small RVs up to 24 feet long (note difficult access road). Picnic tables and fire grills are provided. Vault toilets are available. No drinking water is available. No pets are allowed.

Reservations, fees: No reservations; $6 per night, plus $20 park entrance fee. Open June through September.

Directions: From Merced, drive east on Highway 140 to the El Portal entrance station at Yosemite National Park. Continue east on Highway 140 to the junction with Highway 120/Tioga Road (just before entering the Valley). Turn left and drive to the junction with Highway 120. Turn right on Tioga Road and drive three miles to the campground entrance on the right side of the road. Turn right and drive 2.5 miles to the campground at the end of the road. Trailers and RVs are not advised.

Contact: Yosemite National Park, tel. (209) 372-0200 for a recorded message, tel. (209) 372-0265, or fax (209) 372-0371.

72 Camp 4

  8

The concept at Camp 4 was to provide a climber's bivuoac near the base of El Capitan, and so it is. It has also worked as a walk-in alternative to drive-in camps that sometimes resemble combat zones. The sites here are jammed together, and six people will be placed in your site, whether you know them or not. Regardless, the camp is in a great location, within walking distance of Yosemite Falls. It has a view of Leidig Meadow and the southern valley rim, with Sentinel Rock directly across the valley. A trail is routed from camp to Lower Yosemite Falls.

In addition, the trailhead for the Yosemite Falls Trail is a short distance away, a terrible, butt-kicking climb up Columbia Rock to the rim adjacent to the top of the falls, but providing one of most incredible views in all the world. Note: this camp was once named Sunnyside walk-in, but renamed. After all, the El Capitan climbers had been calling it Camp 4 for years.

Location: In Yosemite Valley in Yosemite National Park; map E4, grid h4.

Campsites, facilities: There are 35 walk-in tent sites. Six people are placed in each campsite, regardless of the number of people in each party. Picnic tables and fire pits are provided. Drinking water and flush toilets are available. A parking area, showers, groceries, and a coin laundry are nearby. No pets are allowed.

Reservations, fees: No reservations; $3 per person per night, plus $20 park entrance fee. There is a seven-day limit.

Directions: After entering Yosemite Valley, drive past the chapel and turn left at the first stop sign. Cross Sentinel Bridge, drive about a quarter mile, and then turn left at the next stop sign (at the sign for Yosemite Lodge). Drive a half mile past the base of Yosemite Falls and look for the large sign marking the parking area for Camp 4 Walk-in on the right.

Contact: Yosemite National Park, tel. (209) 372-0200 for a recorded message, tel. (209) 372-0265, or fax (209) 372-0371.

73 Upper Pines

 9

Of the campgrounds in Yosemite Valley, Upper Pines is closest to the jump-off to paradise, providing you can get a campsite at the far south end of the camp. From here it is a short walk to the Happy Isles trailhead and with it the chance to hike to Vernal Falls on the Mist Trail (steep), or beyond to Nevada Falls (very steep) at the foot of Liberty Cap. But crowded this camp is, and you'd best expect it. People come from all over the world to camp here. Sometimes it appears as if they are from other worlds as well. The elevation is 4,000 feet.

Location: In Yosemite Valley in Yosemite National Park; map E4, grid h5.

Campsites, facilities: There are 238 sites for tents or RVs up to 40 feet long. Fire rings and picnic tables are provided. Drinking water, flush toilets, and a sanitary disposal station are available. A grocery store, coin laundry, propane gas, recycling center, and bike rentals are available nearby. Leashed pets are permitted in the campground, but not on trails.

Reservations, fees: Reserve at (800) 436-PARK (800-436-7275) or website: reservations .nps.gov/; $15 per night, plus $20 park entrance fee. Open year-round.

Directions: After entering Yosemite Valley, drive past Curry Village (on the right) and Stoneman Meadow (on the left) to the campground entrance on the right side of the road (just before Clarks Bridge).

Contact: Yosemite National Park, tel. (209) 372-0200 for a recorded message, tel. (209) 372-0265, or fax (209) 372-0371.

74 North Pines

 9

North Pines is set along the Merced River. A trail out of camp heads east and links up the paved road/trail to Mirror Lake, a virtual parade of people. If you continue hiking past Mirror Lake you will get astounding views of Half Dome and then leave the masses behind as you enter Tenaya Canyon. The elevation is 4,000 feet.

Location: In Yosemite Valley in Yosemite National Park; map E4, grid h5.

Campsites, facilities: There are 80 sites for tents or RVs up to 40 feet long. Picnic tables and fire grills are provided. Drinking water and flush toilets are available. A grocery store, coin laundry, recycling center, propane gas, and bike rentals are available nearby. Leashed pets are allowed.

Reservations, fees: Reserve at (800) 436-PARK (800-436-7275) or website: reservations .nps.gov/; $15 per night, plus $20 park entrance fee. Open April through September.

Directions: After entering Yosemite Valley, drive past Curry Village (on the right) and Stoneman Meadow (on the left). Continue past Upper and Lower Pines Campgrounds, drive over Clarks Bridge, turn left (at the horse stables), and drive a short distance to the campground on the right.

Contact: Yosemite National Park, tel. (209) 372-0200 for a recorded message, tel. (209) 372-0265, or fax (209) 372-0371.

75 Lower Pines

 9

For combat-style camping, this is a pretty good place. Lower Pines sits right along the Merced River, quite pretty, in the center of Yosemite Valley. Of course, the tents and RVs are jammed in quite close together. Within walking distance is the trail to Mirror Lake (a zoo on parade), as well as the trailhead at Happy Isles for the hike up to Vernal Falls and Nevada Falls. The park's shuttle bus picks up riders near the camp entrance.

Location: In Yosemite Valley in Yosemite National Park; map E4, grid h4.

Campsites, facilities: There are 60 sites for tents or RVs up to 40 feet long. Fire rings and picnic tables are provided. Drinking water and flush toilets are available. A grocery store, coin laundry, propane gas, recycling center, and horse, bike, and cross-country ski rentals are available nearby. Leashed pets are allowed.

Reservations, fees: Reserve at (800) 436-PARK (800-436-7275) or website: reservations.nps.gov/; $15 per night, plus $20 park entrance fee. Open April through October, weather permitting.

Directions: After entering Yosemite Valley, drive past Curry Village (on the right) and Stoneman Meadow (on the left) to the campground entrance on the left side of the road (just before Clarks Bridge).

Contact: Yosemite National Park, tel. (209) 372-0200 for touch-tone menu, or tel. (209) 372-0265, or fax (209) 372-0371.

76 Merced Recreation Area

 8

What a spot: The campsites are along one of the prettiest sections of the Merced River, where you can enjoy great hiking, swimming, and fishing, all on the same day. There are three campgrounds here: McCabe Flat, Willow Placer, and Railroad Flat. The access road out of camp leads downstream to the Yosemite Railroad Grade, which has been converted into a great trail. One of the best wildflower blooms anywhere in the Sierra foothills is found near here at Red Hills (just outside Chinese Camp), best usually in April. If you don't mind the cold water, swimming in the Merced River's pools can provide relief from summer heat. Evening fly-fishing is good in many of the same spots through July.

Location: On the Merced River east of Briceburg; map E4, grid i0.

Campsites, facilities: There are 21 walk-in tent sites and nine sites for tents or RVs up to 18 feet long. Picnic tables and fire grills are provided. Vault and pit toilets are available. No drinking water is available (drinking water is available across from the Briceburg Bridge). Some facilities are wheelchair accessible. Leashed pets are permitted. Supplies are available in Mariposa.

Reservations, fees: No reservations; $10 per night. There is a 14-day limit. Open April to mid-October, weather permitting.

Directions: From Merced, drive south on Highway 99 for just a few miles to its junction with Highway 140. Turn east on Highway 140 and drive 40 miles to Mariposa and continue another 15 miles to Briceburg. At the Briceburg Visitor Center, turn left at a road that is signed "BLM Camping Areas" (the road remains paved for about 150 yards). Drive over the Briceburg suspension bridge and turn left, traveling downstream on the road, parallel to the river. Drive 2.5 miles to Mc-Cabe Flat, 3.8 miles to Willow Placer and 4.8 miles to Railroad Flat.

Contact: Bureau of Land Management, Folsom Field Office; tel. (916) 985-4474, or fax (916) 985-3259.

77 Yosemite-Mariposa KOA

 7

A little duck pond, cute log cabins, swimming pool, and proximity to Yosemite National Park make this one a winner. The RV sites are lined up along the entrance road, edged by grass. A 10 p.m. "quiet time" helps ensure a good night's sleep. It's a one-hour drive to Yosemite Valley, and your best bet is to get there early to enjoy the spectacular beauty before the park is packed with people.

Location: Near Mariposa; map E4, grid i0.

Campsites, facilities: There are 26 tent sites and 51 RV sites, 30 with full hookups and 20 with partial hookups, plus 12 cabins. Picnic tables and barbecues are provided. Restrooms, showers, sanitary disposal station, modem hookups, coin laundry, store, propane gas, recreation room, swimming pool, and a playground are available. Leashed pets are permitted.

Reservations, fees: Reservations are accepted; $27 to $37 per night, $47 per night for cabins. Major credit cards accepted. Open year-round.

Directions: From Merced, drive east on Highway 140 to Mariposa. Continue on Highway 140 for six miles to Midpines and 6323 Highway 140. Turn left at the campground entrance.

Contact: Yosemite-Mariposa KOA, tel. (209) 966-2201 or tel. (800) 562-9391 (reservations only); website: www.koa.com.

of Yosemite's wilderness backcountry. This is the closest camp to Glacier Point's drive-to vantage point, but it is also the closest camp to the best day hikes in the entire park. Along Glacier Point Road are trailheads to Sentinel Dome (incredible view of Yosemite Falls) and Taft Point (breathtaking drop, incredible view of El Capitan), and McGurk Meadow (one of the most pristine and romantic spots on Earth). At 7,200 feet, the camp is more than 3,000 feet higher than Yosemite Valley. A good day hike out of camp leads you to Ostrander Lake, just below Horse Ridge.

Location: Near Glacier Point in Yosemite National Park; map E4, grid i4.

Campsites, facilities: There are 74 sites for tents and RVs up to 35 feet long. Picnic tables and fire grills are provided. Drinking water and flush toilets are available. Leashed pets are permitted.

Reservations, fees: No reservations; $10 per night, plus $20 park entrance fee. A 14-day stay limit is enforced. Open June through September, weather permitting.

Directions: In Yosemite, drive toward Yosemite Valley and the junction of Highway 140 and Highway 41. Turn right on Highway 41/Wawona Road and drive about 10 miles to Glacier Point Road. Turn left on Glacier Point Road and drive about 25 miles (a few miles past Badger Pass Ski Area) to Peregoy Meadow and the campground access road on the right. Turn right and drive a short distance to the campground.

Contact: Yosemite National Park, tel. (209) 372-0200 for a recorded message, tel. (209) 372-0265, or fax (209) 372-0371.

78 Bridalveil Creek

 10

There may be no better view in the world than the one from Glacier Point, looking down into Yosemite Valley, where Half Dome stands like nature's perfect sculpture. Then there are the perfect views of Yosemite Falls, Nevada Falls, Vernal Falls, and several hundred square miles

79 Jerseydale

 5

This little camp gets overlooked by many visitors shut out of nearby Yosemite National Park simply because they don't realize it exists. Jerseydale is set southwest of the national park in Sierra National Forest, with two good side trips nearby. If you continue north on Jerseydale Road to its end (about six miles), you will come to a gated Forest Service road/trailhead that provides access east for miles along the South Fork of the Merced River, where there is often good fishing, swimming, and rafting. In addition, a dirt road from the camp is routed east for many miles into the Chowchilla Mountains.

Location: In Sierra National Forest; map E4, grid j1.

Campsites, facilities: There are eight tent sites and two sites for tents or RVs up to 22 feet long. Picnic tables and fire grills are provided. Drinking water and vault toilets are available. Garbage must be packed out. Leashed pets are permitted.

Reservations, fees: No reservations; no fee. Open May through November.

Directions: From Mariposa, drive northeast on Highway 140 for about five miles to Triangle Road (if you reach Midpines, you have gone 1.5 miles too far). Turn right on Triangle Road and drive about six miles to Darrah and Jerseydale Road. Turn left and drive three miles to the campground on the left side of the road (adjacent to the Jerseydale Ranger Station).

Contact: Sierra National Forest, Mariposa-Minarets Ranger District, tel. (559) 877-2218, or fax (559) 877-3108.

North Wawona. It's a 45-minute drive to either Glacier Point or Yosemite Valley.

Location: On the South Fork of the Merced River in Yosemite National Park; map E4, grid j3.

Campsites, facilities: There are 93 sites for tents or RVs up to 35 feet long and one group campsite. Picnic tables and fire grills are provided. Drinking water and flush toilets are available. A grocery store, propane gas, and horseback riding facilities are available nearby. Pets are permitted on leashes in the campground, but not on trails. There are also some stock handling facilities for camping with pack animals; call for further information.

Reservations, fees: Reserve at (800) 436-PARK (800-436-7275) or website: http://reservations.nps.gov/; $15 per night, plus $20 park entrance fee. A seven-day camping limit is enforced. Open year-round.

Directions: From Oakhurst, drive north on Highway 41 to the Wawona entrance to Yosemite National Park. Continue north on Highway 41 past Wawona (golf course on the left) and drive one mile to the campground entrance on the left.

Contact: Yosemite National Park, tel. (209) 372-0200 for a recorded message, tel. (209) 372-0265, or fax (209) 372-0371.

80 Wawona

 9

Wawona Camp is an attractive alternative to the packed camps in Yosemite Valley, providing you don't mind the relatively long drives to the best destinations. The camp is pretty, set along the South Fork Merced River, with the sites more spacious than at most other drive-to camps in the park. The nearest attraction is the Mariposa Grove of giant sequoias, but get your visit in early and be out by 9 a.m. because after that it turns into a zoo, complete with shuttle train. The best nearby hike is a strenuous eight-mile round-trip to Chilnualna Falls, the prettiest sight in the southern region of the park, with its trailhead at the east end of the Redwoods in

81 Summit Camp

 5

The prime attraction of tiny Summit Camp is its proximity to the Wawona entrance of Yosemite National Park. It sits along a twisty Forest Service road, perched in the Chowchilla Mountains at 5,800 feet, about three miles from Big Creek. It's a little-known alternative when the park campgrounds at Wawona are packed.

Location: In Sierra National Forest; map E4, grid j2.

Campsites, facilities: There are six tent sites. Picnic tables and fire grills are provided. Vault toilets are available. No drinking water is available. Garbage must be packed out. Leashed pets are permitted.

Reservations, fees: No reservations; no fee. Open June through October.

Directions: From Oakhurst, drive north on Highway 41 toward the town of Fish Camp and the gravel Forest Road 5S09X a mile before Fish Camp on the left. Turn left and drive six twisty miles to the campground on the left side of the road.

Contact: Sierra National Forest, Minarets Ranger District, tel. (559) 877-2218, or fax (559) 877-3108.

82 Summerdale

     7

You can't get much closer to Yosemite National Park. This camp is within a mile of the Wawona entrance to Yosemite, about a five-minute drive to the Mariposa Grove. If you don't mind its proximity to the highway, this is a pretty spot in its own right, set along Big Creek, a feeder stream to the South Fork Merced River. Some good swimming holes are in this area. The elevation is 5,000 feet.

Location: On the South Fork of the Merced River in Sierra National Forest; map E4, grid j3.

Campsites, facilities: There are 30 tent sites and nine sites for tents or RVs up to 22 feet long. Picnic tables and fire grills are provided. Drinking water and vault toilets are available. A grocery store is nearby (within one mile). Leashed pets are permitted.

Reservations, fees: No reservations, but this camp usually fills by noon on Fridays; $14 per night. Open May through September.

Directions: From Oakhurst, drive north on Highway 41 to Fish Camp and continue for one mile to the campground entrance on the left side of the road.

Contact: Sierra National Forest, Minarets Ranger District, tel. (559) 877-2218, or fax (559) 877-3108.

83 Minaret Falls

    8

This camp has one of the prettiest settings of the series of camps along the Upper San Joaquin River and near Devils Postpile National Monument. It is set at 7,700 feet near Minaret Creek, across from where beautiful Minaret Falls pours into the San Joaquin River. Devils Postpile National Monument, one of the best examples in the world of hexagonal, columnar jointed rock, is less than a mile from camp, where there is also a trail to awesome Rainbow Falls. The Pacific Crest Trail runs right through this area as well, and if you hike to the south, there is excellent streamside fishing access.

Location: On the San Joaquin River in Inyo National Forest; map E4, grid j9.

Campsites, facilities: There are 27 sites for tents or RVs, most of which can accommodate RVs up to 47 feet long and some up to 55 feet. Picnic tables and fire grills are provided. Drinking water and vault toilets are available. Chemical toilets and horseback riding facilities are available nearby. You can buy limited supplies at the Red's Meadow Store, or all supplies in Mammoth Lakes. Leashed pets are permitted.

Reservations, fees: No reservations; $14 per night. Open mid-June to late September.

Directions: On U.S. 395, drive to Mammoth Junction/Highway 203. Turn west on Highway 203 and drive four miles, through the town of Mammoth Lakes to Minaret Road (still Highway 203). Turn right and drive 4.5 miles to the Devils Postpile entrance kiosk (past the Mammoth Mountain Ski Area). Continue for six miles to the campground entrance road on the right. Turn right and drive a quarter mile to the campground.

Access note: Noncampers arriving between 7:30 a.m. and 5:30 p.m. are required to take a shuttle bus ($5 to $9 per person, with many price levels and exceptions) from the Mammoth Mountain Ski Area to this area.

Contact: Inyo National Forest, Mammoth Lakes Ranger District, tel. (760) 924-5500 or fax (760) 924-5537.

84 Devils Postpile National Monument

     9

Devils Postpile is a spectacular and rare example of hexagonal, columnar jointed rock that looks like posts, hence the name. The camp is set at 7,600 feet in elevation and provides nearby access for the easy hike to the Postpile. If you keep walking, it is a 2.5-mile walk to Rainbow Falls, a breathtaking 101-foot cascade that produces rainbows in its floating mist seen only from the trail alongside the waterfall looking downstream. The camp is also adjacent to the Middle Fork San Joaquin River and the Pacific Crest Trail.

Location: Near the San Joaquin River; map E4, grid j9.

Campsites, facilities: There are 21 sites for tents or RVs. Picnic tables and fire grills are provided. Drinking water and flush toilets are available. Leashed pets are permitted.

Reservations, fees: No reservations; $12 per night. Open mid-June to late October, weather permitting.

Directions: On U.S. 395, drive to Mammoth Junction/Highway 203. Turn west on Highway 203 and drive four miles, through the town of Mammoth Lakes to Minaret Road (still Highway 203). Turn right and drive 4.5 miles to the entrance kiosk (across from the Mammoth Mountain Ski Area). Continue for nine miles to the campground entrance road on the right.

Access note: Noncampers arriving between 7:30 a.m. and 5:30 p.m. are required to take a shuttle bus ($5 to $9 per person, with many price levels and exceptions) from the Mammoth Mountain Ski Area to this area.

Contact: Devil Postpile National Monument, tel. or fax (760) 934-2289.

85 Red's Meadow

     6

Red's Meadow has long been established as one of the best outfitters for horseback riding trips. To get the feel of it, three-mile round-trip rides are available to Rainbow Falls. Multi-day trips into the Ansel Adams Wilderness on the Pacific Crest Trail are also available. A small restaurant is a bonus here, always a must-stop for long-distance hikers getting a shot to chomp their first hamburger in weeks, something like a bear finding a candy bar, quite a sight for the drive-in campers. The nearby Devils Postpile National Monument, Rainbow Falls, Minaret Falls, and San Joaquin River provide recreation options.

Location: In Inyo National Forest; map E4, grid j9.

Campsites, facilities: There are 56 sites for tents or RVs, most of which can accommodate RVs 30 feet in length and some up to 55 feet. Picnic tables and fire grills are provided. Drinking water and flush toilets are available. Natural hot springs, shower house, and horseback riding facilities are also available. You can buy limited supplies at a small store. Leashed pets are permitted.

Reservations, fees: No reservations; $14 per night. Open mid-June to late October.

Directions: On U.S. 395, drive to Mammoth Junction/Highway 203. Turn west on Highway 203 and drive four miles, through the town of Mammoth Lakes to Minaret Road (still Highway 203). Turn right and drive 4.5 miles to the entrance kiosk (adjacent to the Mammoth Mountain Ski Area). Continue for 7.4 miles to the campground entrance on the left.

Access note: Noncampers arriving between 7:30 a.m. and 5:30 p.m. are required to take a shuttle bus ($5 to $9 per person, with many price levels and exceptions) from the Mammoth Mountain Ski Area to this area.

Contact: Inyo National Forest, Mammoth Lakes Ranger District, tel. (760) 924-5500 or fax (760) 924-5537.

86 Pumice Flat

 8

Pumice Flat (7,700 feet in elevation) provides roadside camping within short range of several adventures. A trail out of camp links with the Pacific Crest Trail, where you can hike along the Upper San Joaquin River for miles, providing excellent access for fly-fishing, and head north into the Ansel Adams Wilderness. Devils Postpile National Monument is just two miles south, along with the trailhead for Rainbow Falls.

Location: On the San Joaquin River in Inyo National Forest; map E4, grid j9.

Campsites, facilities: There are 17 sites for tents or RVs, most of which can accommodate RVs 47 feet in length and some up to 55 feet. Picnic tables and fire grills are provided. Drinking water, flush toilets, and horseback riding facilities are available. Limited supplies are available at a small store, or full supplies in Mammoth Lakes. Leashed pets are permitted.

Reservations, fees: No reservations; $14 per night. Open mid-June to late September.

Directions: On U.S. 395, drive to Mammoth Junction/Highway 203. Turn west on Highway 203 and drive four miles, through the town of Mammoth Lakes to Minaret Road (still Highway 203). Turn right and drive 4.5 miles to the entrance kiosk (adjacent to the Mammoth Mountain Ski Area). Continue for 5.1 miles to the campground on the right side of the road.

Access note: Noncampers arriving between 7:30 a.m. and 5:30 p.m. are required to take a shuttle bus ($5 to $9 per person, with many price levels and exceptions) from the Mammoth Mountain Ski Area to this area.

Contact: Inyo National Forest, Mammoth Lakes Ranger District, tel. (760) 924-5500 or fax (760) 924-5537.

87 Upper Soda Springs

 8

This is a premium location within earshot of the Upper San Joaquin River and within minutes of many first-class recreation options. The river is stocked with trout at this camp, with several good pools within short walking distance. Farther upstream, accessible by an excellent trail, are smaller wild trout that provide good fly-fishing prospects. Devils Postpile National Monument, a massive formation of ancient columnar jointed rock, is only three miles to the south. The Pacific Crest Trail passes right by the camp, providing a trailhead for access to numerous lakes in the Ansel Adams Wilderness. The elevation is 7,700 feet.

Location: On the San Joaquin River in Inyo National Forest; map E4, grid j9.

Campsites, facilities: There are 29 sites for tents or RVs, most of which can accommodate RVs 36 feet in length and some up to 55 feet. Picnic tables and fire grills are provided. Drinking water, flush toilets, and horseback riding facilities are available. You can buy supplies at Red's Meadows. Leashed pets are permitted.

Reservations, fees: No reservations; $14 per night. Open mid-June to late September.

Directions: On U.S. 395, drive to Mammoth Junction/Highway 203. Turn west on Highway 203 and drive four miles, through the town of Mammoth Lakes to Minaret Road (still Highway 203). Turn right and drive 4.5 miles to the entrance kiosk (adjacent to the Mammoth Mountain Ski Area). Continue for five miles to the campground entrance road on the right. Turn right and drive a quarter mile to the campground.

Access note: Noncampers arriving between 7:30 a.m. and 5:30 p.m. are required to take a shuttle bus ($5 to $9 per person, with many price levels and exceptions) from the Mammoth Mountain Ski Area to this area.

Contact: Inyo National Forest, Mammoth Lakes Ranger District, tel. (760) 924-5500 or fax (760) 924-5537.

88 Agnew Meadows

 9

This is a perfect camp to use as a launching pad for a backpacking trip or day of fly-fishing for trout. It is set along the Upper San Joaquin River at 8,400 feet, with a trailhead for the Pacific Crest Trail available near the camp. From here you can hike seven miles to the gorgeous Thousand Island Lake, a beautiful lake sprinkled with islands set below Banner and Ritter Peaks in the spectacular Minarets. For day hikes, another choice is walking the River Trail, which is routed from Agnew Meadows along the San Joaquin, providing excellent fishing, though the trout are small.

Location: In Inyo National Forest; map E4, grid j9.

Campsites, facilities: There are 21 sites for tents or RVs, most of which can accommodate RVs 46 feet in length and some up to 55 feet. A group camp is also available (reservations required for the group camp). Picnic tables and fire grills are provided. Drinking water, chemical toilets, and horseback riding facilities are available (three family sites have hitching racks where horse camping is permitted). Supplies can be obtained at Red's Meadows. Leashed pets are permitted.

Reservations, fees: No reservations; $14 per night. For group camp and horse camping sites, reserve at (877) 444-6777 ($8.65 reservation fee) or website: www.reserveusa.com; $15 to $30 per night. Open mid-June to early October.

Directions: On U.S. 395, drive to Mammoth Junction/Highway 203. Turn west on Highway 203 and drive four miles, through the town of Mammoth Lakes to Minaret Road (still Highway 203). Turn right and drive 4.5 miles to the entrance kiosk (adjacent to the Mammoth Mountain Ski Area). Continue for 2.6 miles to the campground entrance road on the right. Turn right and drive just under a mile to the campground.

Access note: Noncampers arriving between 7:30 a.m. and 5:30 p.m. are required to take a shuttle bus ($5 to $9 per person, with many price levels and exceptions) from the Mammoth Mountain Ski Area to this area.

Contact: Inyo National Forest, Mammoth Lakes Ranger District, tel. (760) 924-5500 or fax (760) 924-5537.

89 Pumice Flat Group Camp

     6

Pumice Flat Group Camp is set at 7,700 feet in elevation near the Upper San Joaquin River, adjacent to Pumice Flat. For recreation information, see the entry for Pumice Flat.

Location: On the San Joaquin River in Inyo National Forest; map E4, grid j9.

Campsites, facilities: There are four group sites for tents or RVs (check with ranger for information regarding acceptable RV lengths). Picnic tables and fire grills are provided. Drinking water, flush toilets, and horseback riding facilities are available. You can buy supplies in Mammoth Lakes. Leashed pets are permitted.

Reservations, fees: Reserve at (877) 444-6777 ($8.65 reservation fee) or website: www.reserveusa.com; $40 to $100 per night per group. Open mid-June to late September.

Directions: On U.S. 395, drive to Mammoth Junction/Highway 203. Turn west on Highway 203 and drive four miles, through the town of Mammoth Lakes to Minaret Road (still Highway 203). Turn right and drive 4.5 miles to the entrance kiosk (adjacent to the Mammoth Mountain Ski Area). Continue for 5.1 miles to the campground on the left side of the road.

Access note: Noncampers arriving between 7:30 a.m. and 5:30 p.m. are required to take a shuttle bus ($5 to $9 per person, with many price levels and exceptions) from the Mammoth Mountain Ski Area to this area.

Contact: Inyo National Forest, Mammoth Lakes Ranger District, tel. (760) 924-5500 or fax (760) 924-5537.

JEFFREY PATTY

THE HIGH SIERRA

MAP E5

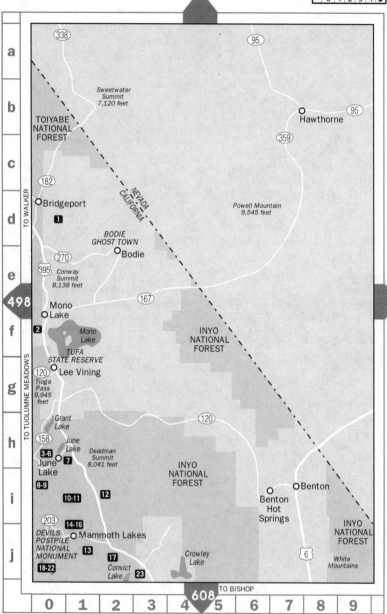

A
B
C
D
E
0 1 2 3 4 **5**

(338)

(95)

Sweetwater
Summit
7,120 feet

(95)

TOIYABE
NATIONAL
FOREST

Hawthorne

(359)

(182)

○ Bridgeport

1

Powell Mountain
9,545 feet

TO WALKER

BODIE
GHOST TOWN

(270)

○ Bodie

(395)

Conway
Summit
8,138 feet

(167)

498

Mono
○ Lake

2

Mono
Lake

INYO
NATIONAL
FOREST

TUFA
STATE RESERVE

(120)

○ Lee Vining

Tioga
Pass
9,945
feet

(120)

TO TUOLUMNE MEADOWS

Grant
Lake

(158)

June
Lake

3-6

○

7

Deadman
Summit
8,041 feet

INYO
NATIONAL
FOREST

June
Lake

8-9

10-11

12

(203)

14-16

○ Benton

Benton

DEVILS
POSTPILE
NATIONAL
MONUMENT

13

○ Mammoth Lakes

Benton
Hot
Springs

INYO
NATIONAL
FOREST

17

18-22

Convict
Lake

23

Crowley
Lake

(6)

White
Mountains

NEVADA
CALIFORNIA

608 TO BISHOP

0 1 2 3 4 5 6 7 8 9

© AVALON TRAVEL PUBLISHING, INC.

CHAPTER E5

1 Willow Springs Trailer Park

  6

Willow Springs Trailer Park is set at 6,800 feet along U.S. 395, which runs along the eastern Sierra from Carson City south to Bishop and Independence. The country is stark here on the edge of the high Nevada desert, but there are many side trips that give the area life. The most popular destinations are to the nearby south: Mono Lake with its tufa towers and incredible populations of breeding gulls and waterfowl, and the ghost town of Bodie. For trout fishing, there's Bridgeport Reservoir to the north (good trolling) and downstream to the East Walker River (fly-fishing), both excellent destinations, as well as Twin Lakes to the west (huge brown trout). Ken's Sporting Goods in Bridgeport provides excellent information.
Location: Near Bridgeport; map E5, grid d0.
Campsites, facilities: There are 25 RV sites. Picnic tables and full hookups are provided. Restrooms, showers, trout pond, coin laundry, and nightly campfires are available. A restaurant is within walking distance. Leashed pets are permitted.
Reservations, fees: Reservations are accepted; $20 per night, $4 per person per night for more than two people. Open May through October.
Directions: From Bridgeport on U.S. 395, drive five miles south to the park.
Contact: Willow Springs Trailer Park, tel. (760) 932-7725, or fax (760) 932-1145.

2 Lundy Canyon Campground

      7

This camp is set high in the eastern Sierra at 7,800 feet in elevation along pretty Lundy Creek, the mountain stream that feeds Lundy Lake and then runs downhill, eventually joining other creeks on its trip to nearby Mono Lake. Nearby Lundy Lake is a long, narrow lake with good fishing for rainbow trout and brown trout. There is a trailhead just west of the lake that is routed steeply up into the Hoover Wilderness to several small pretty lakes, passing two waterfalls about two miles in. A must-do side trip is visiting Mono Lake and its spectacular Tufa Towers, best done at the Mono Lake Tufa State Reserve along the southern shore of the lake.

Location: Near Lundy Lake; map E5, grid f0.

Campsites, facilities: There are 50 sites for tents or RVs up to 24 feet long. Pit toilets are available. No drinking water is available. You can buy supplies in Lee Vining, 8.5 miles away. Leashed pets are permitted.

Reservations, fees: No reservations; $7 per night, with a limit of two vehicles and six persons per site. Open May through October.

Directions: From Lee Vining, drive north on U.S. 395 for seven miles to Lundy Lake Road. Turn left and drive a short distance to the campground.

Contact: Mono County Building and Parks Department, tel. (760) 932-5252, or fax (760) 932-5458.

3 Pine Cliff Resort

 7

This camp is in a pretty setting along the north shore of June Lake (7,600 feet in elevation), the feature lake among four in the June Lake Loop. The campsites are nested in pine trees, designed so each site accommodates different size rigs and families, and the campground is set about a quarter-mile from June Lake. This is the only camp at June Lake Loop that has a swimming beach available. The landscape is a pretty one, with the lake set below snowcapped peaks. The bonus is that June Lake gets large numbers of trout plants each summer, making it extremely popular with anglers. Of the lakes in the June Lake Loop, this is the one that has the most of everything—the most beauty, the most fish, the most developed accommodations and, alas, the most people.

Location: At June Lake; map E5, grid h0.

Campsites, facilities: There are 55 sites for tents and small trailers (18 feet or less) only, 17 partial-hookup sites for tents or RVs, and 154 RV sites with full or partial hookups. Picnic tables and fire rings are provided. Restrooms, flush toilets, showers, drinking water, coin laundry, basketball, volleyball, tetherball and horseshoes, store, and propane gas are available. Some facilities are wheelchair accessible. A primitive boat ramp, boat and tackle rentals, fish cleaning facilities, and fuel are available within two miles. Leashed pets are permitted.

Reservations, fees: Reservations are recommended; $10 to $18 per night. Open mid-April through October.

Directions: From Lee Vining, drive south on U.S. 395 (passing the first Highway 158 North/June Lake Loop turnoff) for 20 miles (six miles past Highway 158 North) to June Lake Junction (a sign is posted for "June Lake Village") and Highway 158 South. Turn right (west) on Highway 158 South and drive a mile to North Shore Drive (a sign is nearby for Pine Cliff Resort). Turn right and drive one-half mile to Pine Cliff Road. Turn left and drive one-half mile to the resort store on the right (route is well signed).

Contact: Pine Cliff Resort, tel. (760) 648-7558, or fax (760) 648-7428.

4 Silver Lake

 9

Silver Lake is set at 7,600 feet, an 80-acre lake in the June Lake Loop with Carson Peak looming in the background. Boat rentals, fishing for trout at the lake, a beautiful trout stream (Rush Creek) next to the camp, and a nearby trailhead for wilderness hiking and horseback riding (rentals available) are the highlights. The camp is largely exposed and vulnerable to winds, the only downer. Within walking distance to the south is Silver Lake, always a pretty sight, especially when afternoon winds cause the lake surface to sparkle in crackling silvers. Just across the road from the camp is a great trailhead for the Ansel Adams Wilderness, with a two-hour hike available that climbs up to pretty Agnew Lake overlooking the June Lake basin.

Location: In Inyo National Forest; map E5, grid h0.

Campsites, facilities: There are 63 sites for tents or RVs up to 40 feet long. Picnic tables and fire grills are provided. Drinking water, flush toilets, and horseback riding facilities are available. A grocery store, coin laundry, motorboat rentals, boat ramp, bait, snack bar, boat fuel, and propane gas are available nearby. Leashed pets are permitted.

Reservations, fees: No reservations; $12 per night. Open May through September.

Directions: From Lee Vining on U.S. 395, drive south for six miles to the first Highway 158 North/June Lake Loop turnoff. Turn west (right) and drive nine miles (past Grant Lake) to Silver Lake. Just as you arrive at Silver Lake (a small store is on the right), turn left at the campground entrance.

Contact: Inyo National Forest, Visitor Information, tel. (760) 873-2408; Mono Lake Ranger District, tel. (760) 647-3044 or fax (760) 647-3046.

5 June Lake

      9

There are three campgrounds at pretty June Lake; this is one of the two operated by the Forest Service (the other is Oh! Ridge). This one is on the northeast shore of the lake at 7,600 feet in elevation, a pretty spot with all supplies available just two miles to the south in the town of June Lake. The nearest boat launch is north of town. This is a good lake for trout fishing, receiving nearly 100,000 stocked trout per year.

Location: In Inyo National Forest; map E5, grid h0.

Campsites, facilities: There are 28 sites for tents or RVs up to 20 feet long. Picnic tables and fire grills are provided. Drinking water, flush toilets, and a boat ramp are available. A grocery store, coin laundry, boat and tackle rentals, moorings, and propane gas are available nearby. Leashed pets are permitted.

Reservations, fees: Reserve at (877) 444-6777 ($8.65 reservation fee) or website: www.reserveusa.com; $12 per night. Open mid-April through October.

Directions: From Lee Vining, drive south on U.S. 395 (passing the Highway 158 North) for 20 miles (six miles past Highway 158 North) to June Lake Junction (a sign is posted for "June Lake Village") and Highway 158 South. Turn west (right) on Highway 158 North and drive two miles to June Lake. Turn right (signed) and drive a short distance to the campground.

Contact: Inyo National Forest, Visitor Information, tel. (760) 873-2408; Mono Lake Ranger District, tel. (760) 647-3044 or fax (760) 647-3046.

6 Oh! Ridge

      8

This is the largest of the campgrounds on June Lake. However, it is not the most popular since it is not right on the lakeshore, but back about a quarter mile or so from the north end of the lake. Regardless, it has the best views of the lake, with the ridge of the high Sierra providing a backdrop. The lake is a good one for trout fishing. The elevation is 7,600 feet.

Location: On June Lake in Inyo National Forest; map E5, grid h0.

Campsites, facilities: There are 148 sites for tents or RVs up to 40 feet long. Picnic tables and fire grills are provided. Drinking water, flush toilets, and a playground are available. A grocery store, coin laundry, boat ramp, boat and tackle rentals, swimming beach, moorings, and propane gas are available nearby. Leashed pets are permitted.

Reservations, fees: Reserve at (877) 444-6777 ($8.65 reservation fee) or website: www.reserveusa.com; $12 per night. Open mid-April through October.

Directions: From Lee Vining, drive south on U.S. 395 (past the first Highway 158/June Lake Loop turnoff) to June Lake Junction (a gas station/store is on the west side of the road) and Highway 158 South. Turn west on Highway 158 South and drive two miles to Oh! Ridge Road. Turn right and drive a mile to the campground access road (signed). Turn left and drive to the campground.

Contact: Inyo National Forest, Visitor Information, tel. (760) 873-2408; Mono Lake Ranger District, tel. (760) 647-3044 or fax (760) 647-3046.

⁷ Hartley Springs

    8

Even though this camp is only a five-minute drive from U.S. 395, those five minutes will take you into another orbit. It is set in a forest of Jeffrey pine, and has the feel of a remote, primitive camp, set in a high-mountain environment at an elevation of 8,400 feet. About two miles to the immediate north at elevation 8,611 feet is Obsidian Dome "Glass Flow," a craggy geologic formation that some people enjoy scrambling around and exploring; pick your access point carefully.

Location: In Inyo National Forest; map E5, grid h1.

Campsites, facilities: There are 20 sites for tents or RVs up to 40 feet long. Picnic tables and fire grills are provided. Vault toilets are available. No drinking water is available. Leashed pets are permitted.

Reservations, fees: No reservations; no fee. Open June to mid-September.

Directions: From Lee Vining, drive south on U.S. 395 (passing the first Highway 158/June Lake Loop turnoff) for 10 miles to June Lake Junction. Continue south on U.S. 395 for six miles to Glass Creek Road (a dirt road on the west side of the highway). Turn west (right) and drive two miles to the campground entrance road on the left.

Contact: Inyo National Forest, Visitor Information, tel. (760) 873-2408; Mono Lake Ranger District, tel. (760) 647-3044 or fax (760) 647-3046.

⁸ Reversed Creek

     6

This camp is set at 7,600 feet near pretty Reversed Creek, the only stream in the region that flows toward the mountains, not away from them. It is a small, tree-lined stream that provides decent trout fishing. The campsites are sheltered and set in a grove of aspen, but close enough to the road so you can still hear highway traffic. There are also cabins available for rent near here. Directly opposite the camp, on the other side of the road, is Gull Lake and the boat ramp. Two miles to the west, on the west side of the road, is the trailhead for the hike to Fern Lake on the edge of the Ansel Adams Wilderness, a little butt-kicker of a climb.

Location: In Inyo National Forest; map E5, grid i0.

Campsites, facilities: There are 17 sites for tents or RVs up to 30 feet long. Picnic tables and fire grills are provided. Drinking water and flush toilets are available. A grocery store, coin laundry, and propane gas are nearby. Boating is available at nearby Silver Lake, two miles away. Leashed pets are permitted.

Reservations, fees: No reservations; $12 per night. Open May through September.

Directions: From Lee Vining, drive south on U.S. 395 (past the first Highway 158/June Lake Loop turnoff) to June Lake Junction (a gas station/store is on the west side of the road) and Highway 158 South. Turn west on Highway 158 South and drive three miles to the campground on the left side of the road (across from Gull Lake).

Contact: Inyo National Forest, Visitor Information, tel. (760) 873-2408; Mono Lake Ranger District, tel. (760) 647-3044 or fax (760) 647-3046.

⁹ Gull Lake

      8

Little Gull Lake, just 64 acres, is the smallest of the lakes on the June Lake Loop, but to many it is the prettiest. It is set at 7,600 feet, just west of June Lake and, with Carson Peak looming on the Sierra crest to the west, it is a dramatic and intimate setting. The lake is stocked with nearly 50,000 trout each summer, providing good fishing. A boat ramp is on the lake's southwest corner.

Location: In Inyo National Forest; map E5, grid i0.

Campsites, facilities: There are 11 sites for tents or RVs up to 30 feet long. Drinking water, fire grills, and picnic tables are provided, and flush toilets are available. A grocery store, coin laundry, boat ramp, and propane gas are available nearby. Leashed pets are permitted.

Reservations, fees: No reservations; $12 per night. Open May through October.

Directions: From Lee Vining, drive south on U.S. 395 (past the first Highway 158/June Lake Loop turnoff) to June Lake Junction (a gas station/store is on the west side of the road) and Highway 158. Turn west on Highway 158 and drive three miles to the campground entrance on the right side of the road.

Contact: Inyo National Forest, Visitor Information, tel. (760) 873-2408; Mono Lake Ranger District, tel. (760) 647-3044 or fax (760) 647-3046.

🔟 Glass Creek

 5

This primitive camp is set along Glass Creek at 7,600 feet, about a mile from Obsidian Dome to the nearby west. A trail follows Glass Creek past the southern edge of the dome, a craggy, volcanic formation that tops out at 8,611 feet in elevation. That trail continues along Glass Creek, climbing to the foot of San Joaquin Mountain for a great view of the high desert to the east. Insider's note: The Department of Fish and Game stocks Glass Creek with trout just once each June, right at the camp.

Location: In Inyo National Forest; map E5, grid i1.

Campsites, facilities: There are 50 sites for tents or RVs up to 40 feet long. Picnic tables and fire grills are provided. Vault toilets are

available. No drinking water is available. Leashed pets are permitted.

Reservations, fees: No reservations; no fee. Open mid-May through October.

Directions: From Lee Vining, drive south on U.S. 395 (past the first Highway 158/June lake Loop turnoff) for 11 miles to June Lake Junction. Continue south on US 395 for six miles to a Forest Service road (Glass Creek Road). Turn west (right) and drive a quarter mile to the camp access road on the right. Turn right and continue a half mile to the main camp at the end of the road. Two notes: 1. A primitive area with large RV sites can be used as an overflow area on the right side of the access road. 2. If arriving from the south on U.S. 395, a direct left turn to Glass Creek Road is impossible. Heading north you will pass the Cal-Trans Crestview Maintenance Station on the right. Continue north, make a U-turn when possible, and follow the above directions.

Contact: Inyo National Forest, Visitor Information, tel. (760) 873-2408; Mono Lake Ranger District, tel. (760) 647-3044 or fax (760) 647-3046.

11 Deadman

 5

This little-known camp is set at 7,800 feet along little Deadman Creek. It is primitive and dusty in the summer, cold in the early summer and fall. From camp, hikers can drive west for three miles to the headwaters of Deadman Creek and to a trailhead for a route that runs past San Joaquin Mountain and beyond to little Yost Lake, a one-way hike of four miles.

Location: On Deadman Creek in Inyo National Forest; map E5, grid i1.

Campsites, facilities: There are 30 sites for tents or RVs up to 40 feet long. A group camp, Obsidian Flat, is also available (reservations required). Picnic tables and fire grills are provided. Vault toilets are available. No drinking water is available. Leashed pets are permitted.

Reservations, fees: Reservations are required for group

sites only. Reserve at (877) 444-6777 ($8.65 reservation fee) or website: www.reserve usa.com; $20 per night per group site, no fee for individual sites. Open May to mid-October.

Directions: From Lee Vining, drive south on U.S. 395 (past the first Highway 158/June lake Loop turnoff) to June Lake Junction. Continue south for 6.5 miles to a Forest Service road (Deadman Creek Road) on the west (right) side of the road. Turn west (right) and drive two miles to the camp access road on the right. Turn right and drive a half mile to the camp. Note: If you are arriving from the south on U.S. 395 and you reach the CalTrans Crestview Maintenance Station on the right, you have gone one mile too far; make a U-turn when possible and return for access.)

Contact: Inyo National Forest, Visitor Information, tel. (760) 873-2408; Mono Lake Ranger District, tel. (760) 647-3044 or fax (760) 647-3046.

12 Big Springs

 5

Big Springs, at 7,300 feet, is set on the edge of the high desert on the east side of U.S. 395. The main attractions are Deadman Creek, which runs right by the camp, and Big Springs, which is set just on the opposite side of the river. There are several hot springs in the area, best reached by driving south on U.S. 395 to the Mammoth Lakes Airport and turning left on Hot Creek Road.

Location: On Deadman Creek in Inyo National Forest; map E5, grid i2.

Campsites, facilities: There are 26 sites for tents or RVs up to 40 feet long. Picnic tables and fire grills are provided. Vault toilets are available. No drinking water is available. Leashed pets are permitted.

Reservations, fees: No reservations; no fee. Open May through September.

Directions: From Lee Vining, drive south on U.S. 395 (past the first Highway 158/June lake Loop turnoff) to June Lake Junction. Continue

south for about seven miles to Owens River Road. Turn east (left) and drive two miles to a fork. Bear left at the fork and drive a quarter mile to the camp on the left side of the road.

Contact: Inyo National Forest, Visitor Information, tel. (760) 873-2408; Mono Lake Ranger District, tel. (760) 647-3044 or fax (760) 647-3046.

13 Mammoth Mountain RV Park

 6

This RV park is just across the street from the Forest Service Visitor Center. Got a question? They've got an answer. This camp is open year-round, making it a great place to stay for a ski trip.

Location: Near Mammoth Lakes; map E5, grid j1.

Campsites, facilities: There are 185 sites for tents and RVs, some with full hookups. Fire grills are provided. Restrooms, drinking water, showers, electricity, picnic tables, cable TV hookups, modem hookups, sanitary disposal station, coin laundry, swimming pool, RV supplies, and a whirlpool are available. Some facilities are wheelchair accessible. Supplies can be obtained in Mammoth Lakes, a quarter-mile away. Leashed pets are permitted.

Reservations, fees: Reservations are accepted; $18 to 28 per night, $2 per night for each extra vehicle. Major credit cards accepted. Open year-round.

Directions: From Lee Vining on U.S. 395, drive south for 25 miles to Mammoth Junction and Highway 203. Turn west on Highway 203 and drive three miles to the park.

From Bishop, drive 40 miles north on Highway 395 to Mammoth Lakes exit. Turn west on Highway 203, go under the overpass, and drive three miles to the park.

Contact: Mammoth Mountain RV Park, tel. (760) 934-3822 or fax (760) 934-1896; website: www.campgrounds.com/mammoth.

Pine Glen

   6

This is a well-located base camp for several side trips. The most popular is the trip to Devils Postpile National Monument, with a shuttle ride from the Mammoth Ski Area. Other nearby trips include exploring Inyo Craters, Mammoth Lakes, and the hot springs near Mammoth Lakes Airport. The elevation is 7,800 feet. **Location:** In Inyo National Forest; map E5, grid j1.

Campsites, facilities: There are 11 family sites (used as overflow from Old Shady Rest and New Shady Rest campgrounds) and six group sites for tents or RVs. Most family sites will accommodate RVs up to 51 feet in length and some up to 55 feet. Check with the ranger for RV length limits in the group sites. Picnic tables and fire grills are provided. Drinking water, flush toilets, and a sanitary disposal station are available. A grocery store, coin laundry, propane gas, and horseback riding facilities are nearby in Mammoth Lakes. Leashed pets are permitted.

Reservations, fees: Reservations are required for group sites only. Reserve at (877) 444-6777 ($8.65 reservation fee) or website: www.reserveusa.com; $35 to $50 for group sites, $12 per night for family sites. Open late May through September.

Directions: From Lee Vining on U.S. 395, drive south for 25 miles to Mammoth Junction and Highway 203/Minaret Summit Road. Turn west on Highway 203 and drive about three miles to the Forest Service Visitor Center. Just past the visitor center, turn right and drive a short distance to the campground.

Contact: Inyo National Forest, Mammoth Lakes Ranger District, tel. (760) 924-5500 or fax (760) 924-5537.

New Shady Rest

    6

This easy-to-reach camp is set at 7,800 feet, not far from the Mammoth Mountain Ski Area.

The surrounding Inyo National Forest provides many side trip opportunities, including Devils Postpile National Monument (shuttles available from Mammoth), Upper San Joaquin River, and the Inyo National Forest backcountry trails, streams, and lakes. The camp is open for walk-in, tent-only camping during the winter. **Location:** In Inyo National Forest; map E5, grid j1.

Campsites, facilities: There are 94 sites for tents or RVs, most of which will accommodate RVs up to 38 feet in length and some up to 55 feet. Picnic tables and fire grills are provided. Drinking water and flush toilets are available. A sanitary disposal station, playground, grocery store, coin laundry, and propane gas are available nearby. Leashed pets are permitted.

Reservations, fees: No reservations; $12 per night; 14-day limit. Open late May to mid-October, weather permitting.

Directions: From Lee Vining on U.S. 395, drive south for 25 miles to Mammoth Junction and Highway 203/Minaret Summit Road. Turn west on Highway 203 and drive about three miles to the Forest Service Visitor Center. Just past the visitor center, turn right and drive a short distance to the campground.

Contact: Inyo National Forest, Mammoth Lakes Ranger District, tel. (760) 924-5500 or fax (760) 924-5537.

Old Shady Rest

    6

Names like "Old Shady Rest" are usually reserved for mom-and-pop RV parks. The Forest Service respected tradition in officially naming this park what the locals have called it all along. Like New Shady Rest, this camp is near the Mammoth Visitor Center, with the same side trips available. It is one of three camps in the immediate vicinity. The elevation is 7,800 feet. **Location:** In Inyo National Forest; map E5, grid j1.

Campsites, facilities: There are 51 sites for tents or RVs, most of which can accommodate RVs up to 40 feet in length and some up to 55 feet. Picnic tables and fire grills are provided. Drinking water and flush toilets are available. A sanitary disposal station, playground, grocery store, coin laundry, and propane gas are available nearby. Leashed pets are permitted.

Reservations, fees: No reservations; $12 per night; 14-day limit. Open mid-June through early September.

Directions: From Lee Vining on U.S. 395, drive south for 25 miles to Mammoth Junction and Highway 203/Minaret Summit Road. Turn west on Highway 203 and drive about three miles to the Forest Service Visitor Center. Just past the visitor center turn right and drive 0.3 mile to the campground.

Contact: Inyo National Forest, Mammoth Lakes Ranger District, tel. (760) 924-5500 or fax (760) 924-5537.

17 Sherwin Creek

    7

This camp is set along little Sherwin Creek, at 7,600 feet in elevation, a short distance from the town of Mammoth Lakes. If you drive a mile east on Sherwin Creek Road, then turn right at the short spur road, you will find a trailhead for a hike that is routed up six miles to Valentine Lake in the John Muir Wilderness, set on the northwest flank of Bloody Mountain.

Location: In Inyo National Forest; map E5, grid j2.

Campsites, facilities: There are 87 sites for tents or RVs, most of which can accommodate RVs up to 34 feet in length and some up to 50 feet, and 15 walk-in sites for tents only. Picnic tables and fire grills are provided. Drinking water and flush toilets are available. Leashed pets are permitted.

Reservations, fees: Reservations are accepted for 58 sites, including the 15 walk-in sites; $12 per night; 21-day limit. Open mid-May through mid-September.

Directions: From Lee Vining on U.S. 395, drive south for 25 miles to Mammoth Junction and Highway 203/Minaret Summit Road. Turn west on Highway 203 and drive about three miles to the Forest Service Visitor Center and continue a short distance to Old Mammoth Road. Turn left and drive about a mile to Sherwin Creek. Turn south and drive two miles on largely unpaved road to the campground on the left side of the road.

Contact: Inyo National Forest, Mammoth Lakes Ranger District, tel. (760) 924-5500 or fax (760) 924-5537.

18 Twin Lakes

    8

From Twin Lakes, you can look west and see pretty Twin Falls, a wide cascade that runs into the head of upper Twin Lake. There are actually two camps here, one on each side of the access road, at 8,600 feet. Lower Twin Lake is a favorite for fly fishers in float tubes.

Location: In Inyo National Forest; map E5, grid j0.

Campsites, facilities: There are 95 sites for tents and RVs, most of which can accommodate RVs up to 38 feet long and some up to 55 feet. Picnic tables and fire grills are provided. Drinking water, flush toilets, boat launch, and horseback riding facilities are available. A grocery store, coin laundry, coin showers, and propane gas are available nearby. Some facilities are wheelchair accessible. Leashed pets are permitted.

Reservations, fees: No reservations; $13 per night, seven-day limit. Open mid-May to late October.

Directions: From Lee Vining on U.S. 395, drive south for 25 miles to Mammoth Junction and Highway 203/Minaret Summit Road. Turn west on Highway 203 and drive four miles to Lake Mary Road. Continue straight through the intersection and drive 2.3 miles to Twin Lakes Loop Road. Turn right and drive a half mile to the campground.

Contact: Inyo National Forest, Mammoth Lakes Ranger District, tel. (760) 924-5500 or fax (760) 924-5537.

19 Lake George

 8

The sites here have views of Lake George, a beautiful lake in a rock basin set below the spectacular Crystal Crag. Lake George is at 9,000 feet in elevation, a small lake fed by creeks coming from both Crystal Lake and TJ Lake. Both of the latter make excellent short hiking trips; TJ Lake is only about a 20-minute walk from the campground. Trout fishing at Lake George is decent—not great, not bad, but decent.

Location: In Inyo National Forest; map E5, grid j0.

Campsites, facilities: There are 16 sites for tents or RVs, most of which can accommodate RVs up to 18 feet long and some up to 25 feet. Picnic tables and fire grills are provided. Drinking water and flush toilets are available. A grocery store, coin laundry, coin showers, and propane gas are available nearby. Leashed pets are permitted.

Reservations, fees: No reservations; $13 per night; seven-day limit. Open mid-June to mid-September.

Directions: From Lee Vining on U.S. 395, drive south for 25 miles to Mammoth Junction and Highway 203/Minaret Summit Road. Turn west on Highway 203 and drive four miles to Lake Mary Road. Continue straight through the intersection and drive four miles to Lake Mary Loop Drive. Turn left and drive one-third of a mile to Lake George Road. Turn right and drive a half mile to the campground.

Contact: Inyo National Forest, Mammoth Lakes Ranger District, tel. (760) 924-5500 or fax (760) 924-5537.

20 Lake Mary

 9

Lake Mary is the star of the Mammoth Lakes region. Of the 11 lakes in the area, this is the largest. It provides a resort, boat ramp, and boat rentals, and it receives the highest number of trout stocks. It is set at 8,900 feet in a place of incredible natural beauty, one of the few spots that literally has it all. Of course, that often includes quite a few other people. If there are too many for you, an excellent trailhead is available at nearby Coldwater camp.

Location: In Inyo National Forest; map E5, grid j0.

Campsites, facilities: There are 48 sites for tents or RVs up to 30 feet long. Picnic tables and fire grills are provided. Drinking water and flush toilets are available. A grocery store, coin laundry, and propane gas are nearby. Leashed pets are permitted.

Reservations, fees: No reservations; $13 per night; 14-day limit. Open mid-June to mid-September.

Directions: From Lee Vining on U.S. 395, drive south for 25 miles to Mammoth Junction and Highway 203/Minaret Summit Road. Turn west on Highway 203 and drive four miles to Lake Mary Road. Continue straight through the intersection and drive four miles to Lake Mary Loop Drive. Turn left and drive a quarter mile to the campground entrance.

Contact: Inyo National Forest, Mammoth Lakes Ranger District, tel. (760) 924-5500 or fax (760) 924-5537.

21 Pine City

 7

This camp is at the edge of Lake Mary at an elevation of 8,900 feet. This camp is popular for both families and fly fishers with float tubes.

Location: Near Lake Mary in Inyo National Forest; map E5, grid j0.

Campsites, facilities: There are 10 sites for tents or RVs, most of which can accommodate RVs up to 40 feet in length and some up to 50 feet. Picnic tables and fire grills are provided. Drinking water and flush toilets are available. A grocery store, a coin laundry, and propane gas are available nearby. Some facilities are wheelchair accessible. Leashed pets are permitted.

Reservations, fees: No reservations; $13 fee per night. Open late June to mid-September.

Directions: From Lee Vining on U.S. 395, drive south for 25 miles to Mammoth Junction and Highway 203/Minaret Summit Road. Turn west on Highway 203 and drive four miles to Lake Mary Road. Continue straight through the intersection and drive 3.6 miles to Lake Mary Loop Drive. Turn left and drive a quarter mile to the campground.

Contact: Inyo National Forest, Mammoth Lakes Ranger District, tel. (760) 924-5500 or fax (760) 924-5537.

22 Coldwater

    7

While this camp is not the first choice of many simply because there is no lake view, it has a special attraction all its own. First, it is a two-minute drive from the campground to Lake Mary, where there is a boat ramp, rentals, and good trout fishing. Second, at the end of the campground access road is a trailhead for two outstanding hikes. From the Y at the trailhead, if you head right, you will be routed up Coldwater Creek to Emerald Lake, a great little hike. If you head to the left, you will have a more ambitious trip to Arrowhead, Skelton, and Red Lakes, all within three miles. The elevation is 8,900 feet.

Location: On Coldwater Creek in Inyo National Forest; map E5, grid j0.

Campsites, facilities: There are 77 sites for tents or RVs, most of which can accommodate RVs up to 37 feet in length and some up to 50 feet. Picnic tables and fire grills are provided. Drinking water, flush toilets, and horse facilities are available. You can buy supplies in Mammoth Lakes. Leashed pets are permitted.

Reservations, fees: No reservations; $13 per night; 14-day limit. Open mid-June to late September.

Directions: From Lee Vining on U.S. 395, drive south for 25 miles to Mammoth Junction and Highway 203/Minaret Summit Road. Turn west on Highway 203 and drive four miles to Lake Mary Road. Continue straight through the intersection and drive 3.6 miles to Lake Mary Loop Drive. Turn left and drive six-tenths of a mile to the camp entrance road.

Contact: Inyo National Forest, Mammoth Lakes Ranger District, tel. (760) 924-5500 or fax (760) 924-5537.

23 Convict Lake

     7

After driving in the stark desert on U.S. 395 to get here, it is always astonishing to clear the rise and see Convict Lake (7,583 feet) and its gemlike waters set in a mountain bowl beneath a back wall of high, jagged wilderness peaks. The camp is right beside Convict Creek, about a quarter mile from Convict Lake. Both provide very good trout fishing, including some rare monster-size brown trout below the Convict Lake outlet. Fishing is often outstanding in Convict Lake, with a chance of hooking a 10- or 15-pound trout. A bonus is an outstanding resort with a boat launch, boat rentals, cabin rentals, small store, restaurant, and bar. Horseback rides and hiking are also available, with a trail routed along the north side of the lake, then along upper Convict Creek (a stream crossing is required about three miles in), and into the John Muir Wilderness. This is the most popular camp in the Mammoth area and is frequently full. While the lake rates a 10 for scenic beauty, the camp itself is in a stark desert setting, out of sight of the lake; plus it can get windy and cold here because of the exposed sites.

Location: In Inyo National Forest; map E5, grid j3.

Campsites, facilities: There are 88 sites for tents or RVs, most of which can accommodate RVs up to 41 feet in length and some up to 55 feet. Rental cabins are also available through the Convict Lake Store. Picnic tables and fire grills are provided. Drinking water and flush toilets are available. A sanitary disposal station, boat ramp, store, restaurant, and horseback riding facilities are available nearby. Leashed pets are permitted.

Reservations, fees: No reservations; $10 per night; seven-day limit. For cabins, reservations advised, tel. (800) 992-2260, $85 to $500 per night, depending on number of beds. Open late April through October.

Directions: From Lee Vining on U.S. 395, drive south for 31 miles (5 miles past Mammoth Junction) to Convict Lake Road (adjacent to Mammoth Lakes Airport). Turn west (right) on Convict Lake Road and drive two miles to Convict Lake. Cross the dam and drive a short distance to the campground entrance road on the left. Turn left and drive a quarter mile to the campground.

Contact: Inyo National Forest, Mammoth Lakes Ranger District, tel. (760) 924-5500 or fax (760) 924-5537; Convict Lake Resort & Cabins, (800) 992-2260.

CENTRAL CALIFORNIA
CHAPTER F1

LAKE WITH ROLLING HILLS

MAP F1

One inch equals approximately 11 miles.

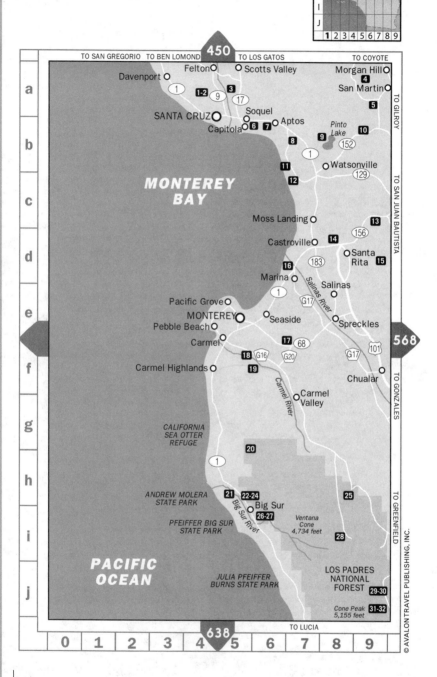

MONTEREY BAY

PACIFIC OCEAN

TO SAN GREGORIO   TO BEN LOMOND   **450**   TO LOS GATOS   TO COYOTE

Davenport○
Felton○
Scotts Valley○
Morgan Hill○
San Martin○

SANTA CRUZ○
Soquel○
Aptos○
Pinto Lake

Capitola○
Watsonville○

Moss Landing○
Castroville○
Santa Rita○
Marina○
Salinas
Pacific Grove○
MONTEREY○
Seaside○
Spreckles○
Pebble Beach○
Carmel○
Chualar
Carmel Highlands○

CALIFORNIA SEA OTTER REFUGE

Carmel Valley

ANDREW MOLERA STATE PARK
Big Sur
Ventana Cone 4,734 feet
PFEIFFER BIG SUR STATE PARK

JULIA PFEIFFER BURNS STATE PARK

LOS PADRES NATIONAL FOREST
Cone Peak 5,155 feet

TO LUCIA   **638**

© AVALON TRAVEL PUBLISHING, INC.

CENTRAL CALIFORNIA

CHAPTER F1

1 Cotillion Gardens RV Park

 6

This is a pretty place with several possible side trips. It is set on the edge of the Santa Cruz Mountain redwoods, near Henry Cowell Redwoods State Park and the San Lorenzo River. Monterey Bay is only about a 10-minute drive from the park. Other side trips include the steam engine ride along the San Lorenzo River out of Roaring Camp Train Rides in Felton, and visiting Loch Lomond Reservoir near Ben Lomond for hiking, boat rentals, or fishing.

Location: Near Santa Cruz; map F1, grid a4.

Campsites, facilities: There are three sites for tents and 80 for RVs, many with full hookups, and five camping cabins. Picnic tables and fire grills are provided. Restrooms, showers, cable TV hookups, recreation room, swimming pool, and a small store are available. Some facilities are wheelchair accessible. Leashed pets are permitted.

Reservations, fees: Reservations are recommended; $30 to $32 per night, $3 per person per night for more than two people with a maximum of six, cabins $65 to $85 per night. Major credit cards accepted. Open year-round.

Directions: From Los Gatos, drive west on Highway 17 for 20 miles toward Santa Cruz to the Mount Hermon Road exit/Scotts Valley (second exit in Scotts Valley). Take Mount Hermon Road exit to the stoplight. Turn right on Mount Hermon Road and drive 3.5 miles to Felton and Graham Hill Road. Turn right on Graham Hill Road and drive 50 feet to Highway 9. Turn left on Highway 9 and drive 1.5 miles to the park.

Contact: Cotillion Gardens RV Park, 300 Old Big Trees, Felton, CA 95018; tel. (831) 335-7669.

2 Smithwoods RV Park

    6

You get a pretty redwood setting at this privately operated park with its many side trip possibilities. Henry Cowell Redwoods State Park (good) and Big Basin Redwoods State Park (better) are two nearby parks that provide hiking opportunities. The narrow-gauge train ride through the area is fun, too; it is in Felton at Roaring Camp Train Rides.

Location: Near Felton; map F1, grid a4.

Campsites, facilities: There are 142 RV sites with full hookups. No tent camping is allowed. Picnic tables and fire pits are provided. Restrooms, showers, a recreation room, a swimming pool, a playground, modem hookups, and a small store are available. Some facilities are wheelchair accessible. Leashed pets are permitted.

Reservations, fees: Reservations are recommended; $30 per night (two people), $1 for each additional person.

Directions: From Los Gatos, drive west on Highway 17 for 20 miles toward Santa Cruz to the Mount Hermon Road exit/Scotts Valley (second exit in Scotts Valley). Take Mount Hermon Road exit to the stoplight. Turn right on Mount Hermon Road and drive 3.5 miles to Felton and Graham Hill Road. Turn right on Graham Hill Road and drive 50 feet to Highway 9. Turn left on Highway 9 and drive 1.5 miles to the park.

Contact: Smithwoods RV Park, tel. (831) 335-4321.

3 Henry Cowell Redwoods State Park

      8

This is a quality redwood state park near Santa Cruz with good hiking, including a 15-minute walk to a great lookout over Santa Cruz and the Pacific Ocean; the trailhead is near campsite 49. Another good hike is the Eagle Creek Trail, a three-mile walk that heads along Eagle Creek and the San Lorenzo River, running through a classic redwood canyon.

Location: Near Santa Cruz; map F1, grid a5.

Campsites, facilities: There are 112 sites for tents or RVs up to 40 feet long, including two sites for RVs up to 65 feet long. Picnic tables and fire grills are provided. Drinking water, flush toilets, and coin-operated showers are available. Some facilities are wheelchair accessible. Leashed pets are permitted.

Reservations, fees: The reservation service is closed from November through mid-March, but reservations are advisable the rest of the year. Reserve at (800) 444-PARK (800-444-7275) or website: www.ReserveAmerica.com; $12 per night (maximum of eight people). Open mid-February through November.

Directions: In Scotts Valley on Highway 17, take the Mount Hermon Road exit and drive west toward Felton. Turn left on Lockwood Lane and drive about one mile. Turn left on Graham Hill Road and continue a half mile to the campground on the right.

Contact: Henry Cowell Redwoods State Park, tel. (831) 335-4598, tel. (831) 438-2396.

4 Oak Dell

  2

A highlight of this park is the relative proximity of two lakes, Anderson Dam (20-minute drive) and Coyote Lake (30-minute drive), on the east side of the Santa Clara Valley near Morgan Hill. Anderson (accessible from Dunne Avenue or Cochran Road off U.S. 101) is a large, beautiful lake, nearly 1,000 acres, providing water-skiing, fishing for bass, bluegill, crappie, and catfish, swimming, and general relief on the hot summer days here. Coyote Reservoir is Anderson's little brother to the south, a long, narrow lake that is stocked with trout in late winter and provides good bass fishing in early spring.

Location: Near Morgan Hill; map F1, grid a9.

Campsites, facilities: There are 57 RV sites, most with full hookups. Picnic tables and fire grills are provided. Drinking water and flush toilets are available. Leashed pets are permitted.

Reservations, fees: Reservations are accepted; $30 per night for two people, $2 per night for each additional person. Major credit cards accepted. Open year-round.

Directions: From U.S. 101 in Morgan Hill, take the Tennant Road exit and drive west for a mile to Monterey Road. Turn left onto Monterey Road and drive a short distance to Watsonville Road. Turn right on Watsonville Road and drive 3.5 miles to the RV park on the left.

Contact: Oak Dell, tel. (408) 779-7779; 12790 Watsonville Road, Morgan Hill, CA 95037.

5 Uvas Canyon County Park

      6

This county park has a stunning array of waterfalls that can be reached with short hikes, including Triple Falls, Black Rock Falls, and several others, making for stellar hikes in winter and spring. But Uvas is even better known for its lake, Uvas Reservoir, which provides some of the better black bass and crappie fishing in the Bay Area. Prospects are best by far during the spring, when the lake is also stocked with rainbow trout. Call Coyote Discount Bait and Tackle at tel. (408) 463-0711 for the latest fishing tips. Note that the gate to the campground is locked at sunset.

Location: Near Morgan Hill; map F1, grid a9.

Campsites, facilities: There are 25 sites for tents only. There is a youth group area with five tent sites. Picnic tables and fire grills (charcoal fires only) are provided. Drinking water and flush toilets are available. There is a boat ramp at the reservoir six miles away. Some facilities are wheelchair accessible. Leashed pets are permitted.

Reservations, fees: No reservations for individual sites; phone (831) 358-3751 to reserve the youth group area; $15 per night, $6 for each additional vehicle, $1 pet fee.

Directions: From U.S. 101 in San Jose, drive west on Bernal Avenue and then south on Santa Teresa Boulevard to Bailey Avenue. Drive west on Bailey Avenue to McKean Road. Go south on McKean Road, which becomes Uvas Road. Continue on Uvas Road to Croy Road. Turn right on Croy Road and drive 4.5 miles to the park.

Contact: Uvas Canyon County Park, tel. (408) 779-9232 or fax (408) 779-3315; website: www.parkhere.org.

6 New Brighton State Beach

      10

This is one in a series of state park camps set on the bluffs overlooking Monterey Bay. They are among the most popular and in-demand state campgrounds in California. Reservations are a necessity. The summer is often foggy and cool, especially in the morning. Beachcombing and surf fishing for perch provide recreation options, and skiff rentals are available at the nearby Capitola Wharf. The San Lorenzo River enters the ocean nearby.

Location: Near Santa Cruz; map F1, grid b6.

Campsites, facilities: There are 112 sites for tents or RVs up to 36 feet long. Picnic tables, fire grills, and food lockers are provided. Drinking water, coin-operated showers, and flush toilets are available. A sanitary disposal station, propane gas, groceries, coin laundry, restaurant, and gas station are available within 2.5 miles. Leashed pets are permitted in the campground but not on the beach.

Reservations, fees: Reservations are recommended from mid-March through October. Reserve at (800) 444-PARK (800-444-7275) or website: www.ReserveAmerica.com; $12 per night. Open year-round, weather permitting.

Directions: From Santa Cruz, drive south on Highway 1 for about five miles to the Bay Avenue/New Brighton Beach exit. The park is just off the highway.

Contact: New Brighton State Beach, tel. (831) 464-6330 or (831) 464-6329; California State Parks, Santa Cruz District, tel. (831) 429-2851 or fax (831) 429-2876.

◼ Seacliff State Beach

    10

Here is a very pretty spot on a beach along Monterey Bay. Beach walks are great, especially on clear evenings for dramatic sunsets. A structure named the "old cement ship" nearby provides some fascination, but visitors are no longer allowed to walk on it. Fishing is often good adjacent to the ship. An interpretive center is available in the summer. This is a popular layover for vacationers touring Highway 1 in the summer, but the best weather is from mid-August to early October.

Location: Near Santa Cruz; map F1, grid b6.

Campsites, facilities: There are 26 sites with hookups for RVs up to 40 feet long, and an overflow area for RVs up to 30 feet long. Picnic tables and fire grills are provided. Restrooms, drinking water, flush toilets, and coin-operated showers are available. Propane gas, groceries, and a coin laundry are available nearby. Some facilities are wheelchair accessible. Leashed pets are permitted in the camping area and on the beach.

Reservations, fees: Reserve at (800) 444-PARK (800-444-7275) or website: www.ReserveAmerica.com; $18 per night, and $12 per night for overflow site. Open year-round.

Directions: From Santa Cruz, drive south on Highway 1 about six miles to State Park Drive/Seacliff Beach exit. Turn west and drive to the park entrance.

Contact: Seacliff State Beach, tel. (831) 685-6500; California State Parks, Santa Cruz District, tel. (831) 429-2851 or fax (831) 429-2876.

◼ Santa Cruz KOA

    8

Bike rentals and nearby access to Manresa State Beach make this KOA campground a winner. The little log cabins are quite cute, and security is first class. For those who have been here, it is a popular layover spot and weekend vacation destination. The only downer is the amount of asphalt, with everything paved right up to your cabin doorstep.

Location: Near Watsonville; map F1, grid b7.

Campsites, facilities: There are eight sites for tents only and 213 RV sites with full or partial hookups. There are also 50 camping cabins. Picnic tables and fire grills are provided. Restrooms, showers, sanitary disposal station, modem hookups, swimming pool, hot tub, wading pool, playground, recreation room, bicycle rentals, miniature golf, store, and propane gas are available. Some facilities are wheelchair accessible. Leashed pets are permitted.

Reservations, fees: Reservations are accepted; $34.95-67.95 per two adult campers per night, $3 each child and $6 each additional adult. Major credit cards accepted. Open year-round.

Directions: From Santa Cruz, drive 12 miles southeast on Highway 1. Take the San Andreas Road exit and head southwest for 3.5 miles to 1186 San Andreas Road.

Contact: Santa Cruz KOA, tel. (831) 722-0551 or fax (831) 722-0989.

9 Pinto Lake Park

     7

Pinto Lake can be a real find. Of the seven lakes in the nine Bay Area counties that offer camping, it is the only one where the RV campsites are actually near the lake. For the few who know about it, it's an offer that can't be refused. But note that no tent camping is permitted. From winter to early summer, the Department of Fish and Game stocks the lake twice a month with rainbow trout. A 5-mph speed limit has been established for boaters, and no swimming is permitted.

Location: Near Watsonville; map F1, grid b8.

Campsites, facilities: There are 28 RV sites with full hookups. Drinking water, sewer hookups, modem hookups, and electricity are available. A boat ramp and boat rentals are available nearby in the summer. Leashed pets are permitted. Some facilities are wheelchair accessible.

Reservations, fees: Reservations are accepted; $20 per night, $2 per child and per additional car, $2 pet fee.

Directions: From Santa Cruz, drive 17 miles south on Highway 1 to the Watsonville/Highway 152 exit and immediately turn left on Green Valley Road. Drive three miles (a half mile past Holbhan intersection) to the campground on the lake.

From Monterey, drive north on Highway 1, take a right at the Green Valley Road exit, and drive three miles (a half mile past the Holbhan intersection) to the campground on the lake.

Contact: Pinto Lake Park, tel. (831) 722-8129; website: www.pintolake.com.

10 Mount Madonna County Park

     7

It's a twisty son-of-a-gun road to reach the top of Mount Madonna, but the views on clear days of Monterey Bay to the west and Santa Clara Valley to the east always make it worth the trip. In addition, a small herd of white deer are kept protected in a pen near the parking area for a rare chance to see unique wildlife. There are many good hiking trails in the park; the best is the Bayview Loop. Elevation in the park reaches 1,896 feet.

Location: Between Watsonville and Gilroy; map F1, grid b9.

Campsites, facilities: There are 117 sites for tents or RVs. Picnic tables and fire grills are provided. Drinking water, showers, and vault toilets are available. Some facilities are wheelchair accessible. Leashed pets are permitted.

Reservations, fees: No reservations; $15 to $25 per night, $6 per night for each extra vehicle, $1 pet fee. Major credit cards accepted. Open year-round.

Directions: From U.S. 101 in Gilroy, take the Hecker Pass Highway/Highway 152 exit west. Drive approximately seven miles west to the park entrance.

From Highway 1 in Watsonville, turn east onto Highway 152 and drive about 12 miles to the park entrance.

Contact: Call Mount Madonna County Park, tel. (408) 842-2341 or fax (408) 842-6642; website: www.parkhere.org.

11 Manresa State Beach

    10

This is a beautiful and extremely popular state park, with the campground set on uplands overlooking the Pacific Ocean. Many sites have ocean views; others are set back in a secluded grove of pine and cypress trees. There is beach access for fishing, swimming, or beachcombing. Santa Cruz and Monterey are each a short drive away and offer endless recreation possibilities.

Location: On the Pacific Ocean; map F1, grid b6.

Campsites, facilities: There are 64 walk-in tent sites. Picnic tables and fire grills are provided. Restrooms, drinking water, flush toilets, and coin-operated showers are available. Some facilities are wheelchair accessible. Leashed pets are permitted.

Reservations, fees: Reserve at (800) 444-PARK (800-444-7275) or website: www.ReserveAmerica.com; $12 per night. Open April through October.

Directions: From Santa Cruz, drive 12 miles southeast on Highway 1 to the San Andreas Road exit. Drive five miles south on San Andreas Road to Sand Dollar Drive and follow the signs to the park entrance. The parking area is about 1,000 yards from the camping area. A 20-minute unloading zone is available within 20 to 150 yards of the sites.

Contact: Manresa Beach State Park, tel. (831) 761-1795; California State Parks, Santa Cruz District, tel. (831) 429-2851 or fax (831) 429-2876.

12 Sunset State Beach

 9

On clear evenings, the sunsets here look like they are imported from Hawaii. The camp is set on a bluff overlooking Monterey Bay, making it a short traipse for a beautiful beach walk. It was once a good spot for clamming, but they're just about been fished out. The best weather is in late summer and fall. Spring can be windy here, and early summer is often foggy. Reservations are often needed well in advance to secure a spot.

Location: Near Watsonville; map F1, grid c7.

Campsites, facilities: There are 90 sites for tents or RVs up to 31 feet long and one group site for up to 50 people. Picnic tables, food lockers, and fire grills are provided. Restrooms, drinking water, flush toilets, and coin-operated showers are available. Some facilities are wheelchair accessible. Firewood is available for purchase. Leashed pets are permitted, except on the beach.

Reservations, fees: Reserve at (800) 444-PARK (800-444-7275) or website: www.ReserveAmerica.com; $12 per night, $75 per night for group site. Open year-round.

Directions: From Highway 1 near Watsonville, take the Riverside Drive exit toward the ocean to Beach Road. Drive 3.5 miles on Beach Road to the San Andreas Road exit. Turn right on San Andreas Road and drive about three miles to the beach on the left.

Contact: Sunset State Beach, tel. (831) 763-7063; California State Parks, Santa Cruz District, tel. (831) 429-2851 or fax (831) 429-2876.

13 Monterey Vacation RV Park

 5

This RV park has an ideal location for many vacationers. It's a 10-minute drive to San Juan Bautista, 30 minutes to the Monterey Bay Aquarium, and 40 minutes to Monterey's Fisherman's Wharf. It's set in an attractive spot with some trees, but the nearby attractions are what make it a clear winner. The park is well landscaped.

Location: Near San Juan Bautista; map F1, grid c9.

Campsites, facilities: There are 88 sites for RVs with full hookups and a few tent sites. Flush toilets, showers, hot tub, swimming pool, coin laundry, modem hookups (in office) and propane gas are available. Some facilities are wheelchair accessible. Leashed pets are permitted.

Reservations, fees: Reservations are recommended for three-day holiday weekends; $23 per night. Major credit cards accepted (except on discounts).

Directions: The park is between Gilroy and Salinas, at 1400 Highway 101 (two miles south of the Highway 156/San Juan Bautista exit).

Contact: Monterey Vacation RV Park, tel. (831) 726-9118 or fax (831) 726-1841.

14 Cabana Holiday

 2

If Big Sur, Monterey, and Carmel are packed, this spot provides some overflow space. It's about a half-hour drive from the Monterey area. Facilities are limited in the winter.

Location: Near Salinas; map F1, grid d8.

Campsites, facilities: There are 96 RV sites with full or partial hookups. Picnic tables are provided. Restrooms, showers, recreation room, swimming pool, playground, coin laundry, and a snack bar are available. Leashed pets are permitted. Some facilities are wheelchair accessible.

Reservations, fees: Reservations are recommended at tel. (800) 541-0085; $28.95 per night. Major credit cards accepted.

Directions: From Salinas, drive north on U.S. 101 for seven miles to the junction with Highway 156. This park is at the intersection at 8710 Prunedale North Road, which runs parallel to U.S. 101.

Contact: Cabana Holiday, tel. (800) 541-0085 or (831) 663-2886, or fax (831) 663-1660.

15 Fremont Peak State Park

    7

Most vacationers in this region are heading to Monterey Bay and the surrounding environs. That's why Fremont Peak State Park is missed by a lot of folks. It is on a ridge (2,900 feet) with great views of Monterey Bay available on the trail going up Fremont Peak. An observatory at the park is open to the public on specified Saturdays. Note: There is no access from this park to the adjacent Hollister Hills State Vehicular Recreation Area.

Location: Near San Juan Bautista; map F1, grid d9.

Campsites, facilities: There are 25 primitive sites for tents or RVs up to 26 feet long and trailers up to 18 feet long, and one group site for up to 25 people. Picnic tables and fire grills are provided. Drinking water and vault toilets are available. Some facilities are wheelchair accessible. Leashed pets are permitted.

Reservations, fees: No reservations; $7 per night, group site $1 per person with $10 minimum. Open year-round.

Directions: From Highway 156 in San Juan Bautista, turn south on San Juan Canyon Road and drive 11 miles to the park.

Contact: Fremont Peak State Park, tel. (831)

623-4255, or fax (831) 623-4612; Monterey District Office, tel. (831) 649-2836, or fax (831) 649-2847.

16 Marina Dunes RV Park

     5

This is a popular park for RV cruisers who are touring Highway 1 and want a layover spot near Monterey. This place fills the bill, open all year and in Marina, just a short drive from the many side trip opportunities available in Monterey and Carmel. It is set in the sand dunes, about 300 yards from the ocean.

Location: Near Monterey Bay; map F1, grid d6.

Campsites, facilities: There are 65 RV sites, many with full or partial hookups, and 10 sites for tents. Picnic tables are provided. Restrooms, drinking water, showers, laundry room, cable TV (some RV sites), modem hookups, recreation room, and groceries are available. Leashed pets are permitted. Some facilities are wheelchair accessible.

Reservations, fees: Reservations are recommended; $21 to $36 per night, $1 pet fee. Major credit cards accepted.

Directions: From Highway 1 in Marina, take the Reservation Road exit and drive one block west to Dunes Drive. Bear right onto Dunes Drive and drive to 3330 Dunes Drive on the right.

Contact: Marina Dunes RV Park, tel. (831) 384-6914 or fax (831) 384-0285.

17 Laguna Seca Recreation Area

      5

This campground is just minutes away from the sights in Monterey and Carmel. It is situated in oak woodlands overlooking the world-famous Laguna Seca Raceway.

Location: Near Monterey; map F1, grid f7.

Campsites, facilities: There are 175 sites for tents or RVs, many with partial hookups. Picnic tables and fire grills are provided. Restrooms, showers, sanitary disposal station, pond, rifle and pistol range, clubhouse, and group camping facilities are available. Some facilities are wheelchair accessible. Leashed pets are permitted.

Reservations, fees: Reservations are accepted, phone (831) 755-4899 or (888) 588-2267; $18 to $22 per night, $1 pet fee. Major credit cards accepted. Open year-round.

Directions: From Monterey, drive nine miles east on Highway 68 to the entrance.

Contact: Laguna Seca Recreation Area, tel. (831) 758-3604, tel., or fax (831) 755-6818; website: www.co.monterey.ca.us/parks.

18 Carmel by the River RV Park

 8

Location, location, location. That's what vacationers want. Well, this park is set on the Carmel River, minutes away from Carmel, Cannery Row, the Monterey Bay Aquarium, golf courses, and the beach. Each RV site is separated by hedges and flowers.

Location: On the Carmel River; map F1, grid f5.

Campsites, facilities: There are 35 RV sites with full hookups and cable TV. Restrooms, showers, modem hookups, recreational cabana, game room with pool tables, barbecue area, horseshoes, basketball courts, and a river beach are available. A grocery store, coin laundry, and propane gas are nearby. Some facilities are wheelchair accessible. Leashed pets are permitted.

Reservations, fees: Reservations are accepted for two or more nights; $40-45 per night for two people, $13 each additional camper over 14 years old, $1 pet fee. Open year-round.

Directions: In Carmel on Highway 1, take Carmel Valley Road and drive southeast for 4.5 miles to Schulte Road. Turn right and drive to the end of the road (27680 Schulte Road).

Contact: Carmel by the River RV Park, tel. (831) 624-9329 or fax (831) 624-8416.

19 Saddle Mountain Recreation Park

 6

This pretty park is set about 100 yards from the Carmel River amid a grove of oak trees. The park offers hiking trails, and if you want to make a buyer's swing into Carmel, it's only a five-mile drive. Note: The Carmel River is reduced to a trickle most of the year.

Location: Near the Carmel River; map F1, grid f5.

Campsites, facilities: There are 25 tent sites and 25 full-hookup sites for RVs. Picnic tables, food lockers, and fire grills are provided. Restrooms, drinking water, flush toilets, and showers are available. A swimming pool, playground, horseshoe pits, volleyball net, basketball court, and a game room are available nearby. Some facilities are wheelchair accessible. Leashed pets are permitted in the RV area only.

Reservations, fees: Reservations are accepted weekends only; $25 to $40 per night. Open year-round.

Directions: In Carmel, on Highway 1 take Carmel Valley Road and drive southeast 4.5 miles to Schulte Road. Turn right and drive to the park at the end of the road.

Contact: Saddle Mountain Recreation Park, tel. (831) 624-1617 or fax (831) 624-4470.

20 Bottcher's Gap Walk-In

 6

Here is a surprise for all the Highway 1 cruisers who never leave the highway. Just inland is this little-known camp, set in beautiful Palo Colorado (redwood) Canyon. It's a good jump-off spot for a hiking trip; the trail leading out of camp is routed all the way into the Ventana Wilderness. Compared to the RV parks near Monterey and Carmel, this place is truly a world apart. The elevation is 2,100 feet.

Location: In Los Padres National Forest; map F1, grid h5.

Campsites, facilities: There are 11 walk-in sites. Picnic tables and fire grills are provided. Vault toilets are available. No drinking water is available. Leashed pets are permitted.

Reservations, fees: No reservations; $10 per night. Open year-round.

Directions: From Carmel, drive south on Highway 1 for about 10 miles to Palo Colorado Road/County Road 5012. Turn left and drive nine miles to the campground.

Contact: Los Padres National Forest, Monterey Ranger District, tel. (831) 385-5434 or fax (831) 385-0628; Parks Management Company at tel. (805) 434-1996.

21 Andrew Molera State Park Walk-In

     7

Considering the popularity and grandeur of Big Sur, some campers might find it hard to believe that any primitive campgrounds are available. Believe it. This park offers walk-in sites amid some beautiful coastal terrain. One of the highlights is a great trail that leads one mile to a beautiful beach. Park rangers often have a one-page flyer available on the best places to spot sea otters. One downer: The campsites are too close together, and if you don't like your neighbor, you're in for a long night.

Location: In Big Sur; map F1, grid h5.

Campsites, facilities: There is a 10-acre meadow with undesignated, primitive, walk-in sites. Picnic tables and fire grills are provided. Drinking water and vault toilets are available. Bring your own wood. Leashed pets are permitted.

Reservations, fees: No reservations; $1 per night per person. There is a three-day limit. Open year-round, weather permitting.

Directions: From Carmel, drive 21 miles south on Highway 1 to the park camping lot on the right. Park and walk 150 yards to the camp.

Contact: Andrew Molera State Park, tel. (831) 667-2315; California State Parks, Monterey District, tel. (831) 649-2836.

22 Fernwood Park

     7

This motor home park is on the banks of the Big Sur River in the redwoods of the beautiful Big Sur coast. You can crown your trip with a first-class dinner at Nepenthe or the Ventana Inn (bring your bank with you).

Location: On the Big Sur River; map F1, grid h5.

Campsites, facilities: There are 38 sites for tents only and 28 RV sites with partial hookups. Fire grills and picnic tables are provided. Restrooms with showers, grocery store, restaurant, and a bar are available. Leashed pets are permitted.

Reservations, fees: Reservations are accepted; $24 to $27 per night, $5 per night for each extra vehicle, $3 pet fee. Major credit cards accepted.

Directions: From Carmel, drive 26 miles south on Highway 1 to the campground on the right.

Contact: Fernwood Park, tel. (831) 667-2422.

23 Big Sur Campground and Cabins

   8

This camp is in the redwoods near the Big Sur River. Campers can stay in the redwoods, hike on great trails through the forest at nearby state parks, or explore nearby Pfeiffer Beach. Nearby Los Padres National Forest and Ventana Wilderness in the mountains to the east provide access to remote hiking trails with ridge-top vistas. Cruising Highway 1 south to Lucia and back offers endless views of breathtaking coastal scenery.

Location: On the Big Sur River; map F1, grid h6.

Campsites, facilities: There are 40 RV sites with water and electrical hookups, 40 sites for tents or RVs, and 13 cabins. Picnic tables and fire grills are provided. Restrooms, drinking water, flush toilets, showers, sanitary disposal station, playground, small store, and a laundry room are available. Some facilities are wheelchair accessible. Leashed pets are permitted, except in the cabins.

Reservations, fees: Reservations are recommended; $26 to $29 per night, $6 per night for each extra vehicle, $3 pet fee. Cabin fees are $80 to $160 for two people and $12 for each additional person. Major credit cards accepted.

Directions: From Carmel, drive 27 miles south on Highway 1 to the campground on the right side of the road.

Contact: Big Sur Campground and Cabins, tel. (831) 667-2322 or fax (831) 667-0456.

24 Riverside Campground & Cabins

 8

This is one in a series of privately operated camps designed for Highway 1 cruisers touring the Big Sur area. This camp is set amid redwoods. Side trips include expansive beaches with sea otters playing on the edge of kelp beds (Andrew Molera State Park), redwood forests and waterfalls (Julia Pfeiffer Burns State Park), and several quality restaurants, including Nepenthe for those on a budget, and the Ventana Inn for those who can light cigars with $100 bills.

Location: On the Big Sur River; map F1, grid h6.

Campsites, facilities: There are 46 sites for tents or RVs, some with water and electrical hookups. Picnic tables and fire grills are provided. Restrooms and showers are available. Leashed pets are permitted.

Reservations, fees: Reservations are recommended ($3 reservation fee) at tel. (831) 667-2414; $26 to $38 per night, $6 per night for each extra vehicle, $3 per person per night for more than two people, $3 pet fee. Major credit cards accepted. Open year-round, weather permitting.

Directions: From Carmel, drive 25 miles south on Highway 1 to the campground on the right.

Contact: Riverside Campground, tel. or fax (831) 667-2414.

25 White Oaks

 7

This camp is set at 4,200 feet, near Anastasia Creek, and there's a surprisingly remote feel to the area despite its relative proximity to Carmel Valley. You can get some unexpected adventures around here. On one trip, I kept meeting these bald guys and asking them about the hiking possibilities. They just shook their heads. Turns out they were from a religious group on a one-week vigil of silence. Either that or they wanted to keep their favorite hikes secret. Well, there is a good one that starts about a mile from the camp and is routed into the Ventana Wilderness. Several backcountry trail camps are also available.

Location: On Chews Ridge in Los Padres National Forest; map F1, grid h8.

Campsites, facilities: There are eight tent sites. There is no drinking water. Picnic tables and fire grills are provided. Vault toilets are available. Leashed pets are permitted.

Reservations, fees: No reservations; a $5 day-use Adventure Pass (or $30 annual fee) is required.

Directions: From Highway 1 in Carmel, turn east on Carmel Valley Road and drive about 22 miles. Turn right (south) on Tassajara Road/County Road 5007 and drive eight miles to the campground on the left.

Contact: Los Padres National Forest, Monterey Ranger District, tel. (831) 385-5434 or fax (831) 385-0628.

26 Ventana Campgrounds

 10

This rustic camp has wooded sites and is set in an ideal location for many. The campsites are private and extremely beautiful, set in the redwoods with a small creek running through camp, with a few small waterfalls nearby. Premium side trips are available, highlighted by the beautiful beach at Andrew Molera State Park (a one-mile hike is necessary), the majestic redwoods, a creek hike, and a bluff-top waterfall in Julia Pfeiffer Burns State Park.

Location: In Big Sur; map F1, grid i6.

Campsites, facilities: There are 75 sites for tents or RVs up to 22 feet. Picnic tables and fire grills are provided. A restroom, drinking water, showers, and flush toilets are available. A small grocery store is nearby. Some facilities are wheelchair accessible. Leashed pets are permitted.

Reservations, fees: Reservations are accepted; $25 to $30 per night, $5 per person per night for more than two people, $5 per night for each extra vehicle, $5 pet fee. Three-day minimum stay on holidays. Major credit cards accepted. Open year-round.

Directions: From Carmel, drive 28 miles south on Highway 1 to the campground, on the left in Big Sur.

Contact: Ventana Campgrounds, tel. (831) 667-2688; P.O. Box 206, Big Sur, CA 93920; website: www.ventanabigsur.com.

27 Pfeiffer Big Sur State Park

    10

This stretch of coast is one of the most beautiful anywhere and this is one of the most popular state parks in California, and it's easy to see why. You can have it all: fantastic coastal vistas along Highway 1, redwood forests and waterfalls in the Julia Pfeiffer Burns State Park (11.5 miles to the south), expansive beaches with sea otters playing on the edge of kelp beds in the Andrew Molera State Park (4.5 miles north), great restaurants like the Nepenthe and Ventana Inn (a few miles south), and private, patrolled sites. Reservations are a necessity.

Location: In Big Sur; map F1, grid i6.

Campsites, facilities: There are 218 sites for tents or RVs up to 32 feet long, some primitive hike-in or bike-in sites, and two group sites for up to 50 people. Picnic tables and fire grills

are provided. Restrooms, drinking water, showers, and flush toilets are available. Groceries and propane gas are available nearby. Some facilities are wheelchair accessible. Leashed pets are permitted in the campground only.

Reservations, fees: Reserve at (800) 444-PARK (800-444-7275) or website: www.ReserveAmerica.com; $12 per night, $26 per night for group sites, $1 for hike-in or bike-in sites. Open year-round, weather permitting.

Directions: From Carmel, drive 26 miles south on Highway 1 to the park on the left.

Contact: Pfeiffer Big Sur State Park, tel. (831) 667-2315, or fax (831) 667-2886; California State Parks, Monterey District, tel. (831) 649-2836.

28 China Camp

   6

A lot of folks might find it difficult to believe that a spot that feels so remote can be so close to the manicured Carmel Valley. But here it is, one of two camps on Tassajara Road. This one has a trail out of camp that is routed into the Ventana Wilderness. Tassajara Hot Springs is seven miles away at the end of Tassajara Road. And keep a lookout for the gents with shaved heads. They're good at keeping secrets; they never tell you the good hiking spots. The elevation is 4,300 feet.

Location: On Chews Ridge in Los Padres National Forest; map F1, grid i8.

Campsites, facilities: There are six sites for tents only. Picnic tables and fire grills are provided. Vault toilets are available. No drinking water is available. Leashed pets are permitted.

Reservations, fees: No reservations; a $5 day-use Adventure Pass (or $30 annual fee) is required. Open April through November, weather permitting.

Directions: From Highway 1 in Carmel, turn east on Carmel Valley Road and drive about 22 miles. Turn right (south) on Tassajara Road/County Road 5007 and drive 10 miles to the campground on the right.

Contact: Los Padres National Forest, Monterey Ranger District, tel. (831) 385-5434 or fax (831) 385-0628.

29 Arroyo Seco

     8

This pretty spot near Arroyo Seco River (900-foot elevation) is just outside the northern border of the Ventana Wilderness. Arroyo Seco Group Camp is available to keep the pressure off this campground.

Location: Along Arroyo Seco River in Los Padres National Forest; map F1, grid j9.

Campsites, facilities: There are 49 sites for tents or RVs up to 26 feet long. Picnic tables and fire grills are provided. Restrooms, drinking water, flush toilets, and coin-operated showers are available. Leashed pets are permitted.

Reservations, fees: No reservations; $10 to $16 per night, $16 per night for multi-family sites. Open year-round.

Directions: From U.S. 101 in the town of Greenfield, turn west on Greenfield-Arroyo Seco Road/County Roads G16 and 3050 and drive 19 miles to the camp at the end of the road.

Contact: Los Padres National Forest, Monterey Ranger District, tel. (831) 385-5434 or fax (831) 385-0628.

30 Arroyo Seco Group Camp

     8

If you have a larger group, give the folks at Arroyo Seco a break and use this adjoining spot instead. That way you'll get the privacy you desire. This camp is in a pretty spot, set near Arroyo Seco Creek near the northern border of the Ventana Wilderness.

Location: In Los Padres National Forest; map F1, grid j9.

Campsites, facilities: There is a group campsite for tents or RVs up to 26 feet long. Picnic tables and fire grills are provided. Drinking water and vault toilets are available. Leashed pets are permitted.

Reservations, fees: Reserve at (877) 444-6777 ($8.65 reservation fee) or website: www.reserveusa.com; $50 group fee per night. Open year-round.

Directions: From U.S. 101 at the town of Greenfield, turn west on Greenfield-Arroyo Seco Road/County Roads G16 and 3050 and drive 19 miles to the camp.

Contact: Los Padres National Forest, Monterey Ranger District, tel. (831) 385-5434 or fax (831) 385-0628.

31 Memorial Park

   5% 6

This is one of two backcountry camps in the area. The camp has a trailhead that provides access to the Ventana Wilderness trail network. The elevation is 2,000 feet, which gives hikers a nice head start on the climb. Be sure to pack plenty of drinking water for the trail and, even in spring, expect warm, dry conditions.

Location: In Los Padres National Forest; map F1, grid j9.

Campsites, facilities: There are eight tent sites. Picnic tables and fire grills are provided. Vault toilets are available. No drinking water is available. Leashed pets are permitted.

Reservations, fees: No reservations; $9 per night. Open year-round.

Directions: From U.S. 101 in King City, turn south on County Route G14 and drive 18 miles. Turn north on Mission Road and drive six miles. Turn left on Del Venturi-Milpitas Road/County Road 4050 and drive 16 miles to the campground on the right.

Contact: Los Padres National Forest, Monterey Ranger District, tel. (831) 385-5434 or fax (831) 385-0628.

32 Escondido

 6

This is a prime jump-off spot for backpackers heading into the Ventana Wilderness. The camp is set at 900 feet at a trailhead that connects to a network of other trails. The only catch is you have to plan on walking up, steeply at times, for a climb of more than a thousand feet to reach the ridge.

Location: In Los Padres National Forest; map F1, grid j9.

Campsites, facilities: There are nine tent sites. Picnic tables and fire grills are provided. Vault toilets are available. No drinking water is available. Leashed pets are permitted.

Reservations, fees: No reservations; $9 per night. Open April through November.

Directions: From U.S. 101 in King City, turn south on County Route G14 and drive 18 miles. Turn north on Mission Road and drive six miles. Turn left on Del Venturi-Milpitas Road/Indian Road and drive 20 miles to the campground on the left.

Contact: Los Padres National Forest, Monterey Ranger District, tel. (831) 385-5434 or fax (831) 385-0628.

CHAPTER F2

HOPING FOR A BITE
ON A HOT DAY

MAP F2

TO MADRONE   **466**   TO NEWMAN   TO STEVINSON

a

Anderson
Reservoir
HENRY W. COE
STATE PARK
1 Coyote
Reservoir
Gilroy
Hot Springs
101
TO WATSONVILLE

Gustine
5
33
KESTERSON
NATIONAL
WILDLIFE
REFUGE
SAN LUIS
NATIONAL
WILDLIFE
REFUGE
165

b

GILROY
Bell Station
152
2
San Felipe
25
SAN LUIS RESERVOIR
STATE RECREATION AREA
San Luis
Reservoir
3 **5** **4**
Santa Nella
Volta
Los
Banos
33
TO RED TOP

c

156
Laveaga Peak
3,801 feet
San Juan
Bautista
6-7
G1
156 HOLLISTER
8
165

d

9
FREMONT PEAK
STATE PARK
Tres Pinos
5
TO FIREBAUGH
TO SALINAS

e

552
Paicines
Mount Johnson
3,453 feet
J1
576

f

25
Mercey Hot
Springs
J1
5
TO MENDOTA I-5 SOUTH

g

Gonzales
PINNACLES
NATIONAL
MONUMENT
10
Soledad
146
Panoche
TO SALINAS

h

G17
TO CARMEL VALLEY

i

Paraiso
Springs
Greenfield
101 G15
G13
25
New Idria
San Benito
Mountain
5,248 feet

j

LOS
PADRES
Junipero
Serra Peak
5,844 feet
NATIONAL
FOREST
11 King City
SOUTH TO JOLON

TO SAN LUCAS   **644**   TO PRIEST VALLEY   TO COALINGA

0   1   2   3   4   5   6   7   8   9

© AVALON TRAVEL PUBLISHING, INC.

CHAPTER F2

❶ Coyote Lake County Park

 7

Coyote Lake is a pretty surprise to newcomers, a long, narrow lake set in a canyon just over the ridge east of U.S. 101. It covers 688 acres and is stocked with a total of 24,000 trout on a biweekly basis from late winter through spring; the lake also provides a decent fishery for bass. The campground is nestled in oaks, furnishing some much-needed shade. Note: If you continue east about four miles on the access road that runs past the lake to the Coe State Park Hunting Hollow entrance, you'll come to two outstanding trailheads (one at a parking area, one at the Coyote Creek gate) into that park's wildlands. Wildlife is abundant, including deer and wild turkey.

Location: Near Gilroy; map F2, grid a0.

Campsites, facilities: There are 74 sites for tents. Picnic tables and fire grills are provided. Drinking water, flush toilets, and a boat ramp are available. A visitor's center and firewood for sale are also available. Some facilities are wheelchair accessible. Leashed pets are permitted.

Reservations, fees: No reservations; $15 per night, $6 for a second vehicle. Major credit cards accepted. Open year-round.

Directions: From U.S. 101 in Gilroy, drive east on Leavesley Road to New Avenue. Turn left on New Avenue and drive to Roop Road. Turn right on Roop Road and drive to Coyote Lake Road. Turn left on Coyote Lake Road and drive to the campground. The park is a total of 5.5 miles from Gilroy.

Contact: Coyote Lake County Park, tel. (408) 842-7800 or fax (408) 842-6439; website: www.parkhere.org.

❷ Casa De Fruta Orchard Resort

 1

This 80-acre RV park has a festival-like atmosphere to it, with country music and dancing every weekend in the summer and barbecues on Sundays. Huge, but sparse, San Luis Reservoir is 20 miles to the east.

Location: Near Pacheco Pass; map F2, grid b2.

Campsites, facilities: There are 300 RV sites, all with water and electric hookups (some also have sewer connections). Picnic tables and fire grills are provided. Flush toilets, showers, sanitary disposal station, cable TV, satellite TV, coin laundry, playground, swimming pool, wading pool, outdoor dance floor, horseshoes, volleyball courts, baseball diamonds, wine and cheese tasting room, candy factory, bakery, fruit stand, petting zoo, 24-hour restaurant, gift shop, and a mini-mart are available. Leashed pets are permitted. Some facilities are wheelchair accessible.

Reservations, fees: Reservations are accepted; $24 to $26 per night, $2 per person per night for more than two people. Major credit cards accepted. Open year-round.

Directions: From Gilroy, drive 13 miles east on Highway 152. Take the Casa De Fruta Parkway exit. You will see the entrance at 10031 Pacheco Pass Highway.

Contact: Casa De Fruta Orchard Resort, tel. (408) 842-9316 or fax (831) 848-3793.

❸ Basalt

 5

San Luis Reservoir is a huge, man-made lake, covering 13,800 acres with 65 miles of shoreline, developed among stark foothills to provide a storage facility along the California Aqueduct. It fills by late winter and is used primarily by anglers, water-skiers, and windsurfers. When the Sacramento River Delta water pumps take the water, they also take the fish, filling this lake up with both. Striped bass fishing is best in the fall when the stripers chase schools of bait fish on the lake surface. Spring and early summer can be quite windy, but that makes for good windsurfing. The adjacent O'Neill Forebay is the best recreation bet because of the developed marina and often good fishing. The elevation is 575 feet.

Location: On San Luis Reservoir; map F2, grid b5.

Campsites, facilities: There are 79 sites for tents or RVs. Picnic tables and fire grills are provided. Drinking water, flush toilets, coin showers, sanitary disposal station, and a boat ramp are available. A grocery store, coin laundry, gas station, restaurant, and propane gas are nearby (about 1.5 miles away). Some facilities are wheelchair accessible. Leashed pets are permitted.

Reservations, fees: Reservations accepted; reserve at tel. (800) 444-PARK (444-7275) or website: www.reserveamerica.com; $12 per night. Open year-round.

Directions: From Los Banos, drive 12 miles west on Highway 152 to the entrance road. Turn left and drive 2.5 miles to the campground on the left.

Contact: San Luis Reservoir State Recreation Area, tel. (209) 826-1196 or fax (209) 826-0284.

❹ Madeiros

 5

This is a vast, primitive campground set on the stark expanse of foothill country near San Luis Reservoir. See the entry for Basalt for more information. It is best known for wind in the spring, hot weather in the summer, and low water levels in the fall. Striped bass fishing is best in the fall when the wind is down and stripers will corral schools of bait fish near the lake surface. The elevation is 225 feet.

Location: On San Luis Reservoir; map F2, grid b6.

Campsites, facilities: There are 350 primitive sites for tents or RVs. Some shaded ramadas with fire grills and picnic tables are available. Drinking water and chemical toilets are available. A boat ramp is nearby. Leashed pets are permitted.

Reservations, fees: No reservations; $7 per night. Open year-round.

Directions: From Los Banos, drive 12 miles west on Highway 152 to the intersection with Highway 33. Turn north (right) on Highway 33 and drive one-quarter mile to the campground entrance on the left.

Contact: San Luis Reservoir State Recreation Area, tel. (209) 826-1196 or fax (209) 826-0284.

5 San Luis Creek

 5

San Luis Campground is on Los Banos Creek near San Luis Reservoir. It is one in a series of camps operated by the state in the San Luis Reservoir State Recreation Area, adjacent to the reservoir and O'Neill Forebay, home of the biggest striped bass in California, including the world record for landlocked stripers.

Location: On San Luis Reservoir; map F2, grid b6.

Campsites, facilities: There are 53 sites for tents or RVs with electrical and water hookups, and two group sites for up to 30 to 60 people. Picnic tables and fire pits are provided. Drinking water and pit toilets are available. A sanitary disposal station is nearby at Basalt Camp. Leashed pets are permitted.

Reservations, fees: Reserve at (800) 444-PARK (800-444-7275) or website: www.ReserveAmerica.com; $15 per night, $20 to $45 per night for group sites.

Directions: From Los Banos, drive 15 miles west on Highway 152 to the signed entrance on the right. Turn right and drive two miles to the campground on the left.

Contact: San Luis Reservoir State Recreation Area, tel. (209) 826-1196 or fax (209) 826-0284.

6 Mission Farm RV Park

 5

The primary appeal of this RV park is that it is within easy walking distance of San Juan Bautista. The park is set beside a walnut orchard.

Location: Near San Juan Bautista; map F2, grid d0.

Campsites, facilities: There are four sites for tents and 165 RV sites with full hookups and picnic tables. Flush toilets, showers, barbecue area, sanitary disposal station, coin laundry, and propane gas are available. Leashed pets are permitted; a dog run is available.

Reservations, fees: Reservations are recommended; $25 to $28 per night, $5 per night for each extra vehicle, $6 per person per night for more than two people, $1 pet fee. Major credit cards accepted. Open year-round.

Directions: From U.S. 101, drive three miles east on Highway 156. Turn right on The Alameda and drive a block. Turn left on San Juan-Hollister Road and drive a quarter mile to the campground at 400 San Juan-Hollister Road.

Contact: Mission Farm RV Park, tel. (831) 623-4456.

7 McAlpine Lake and Park

 5

This is the only privately operated campground in the immediate region that has any spots for tenters. The two camping cabins here look like miniature log cabins, quite cute and comfortable. In addition, the park has a 40-foot deep lake stocked with trout and catfish. Other highlights of the park are its proximity to Mission San Juan Bautista and the relatively short drive to the Monterey-Carmel area.

Location: Near San Juan Bautista; map F2, grid d0.

Campsites, facilities: There are 17 sites for tents only, 27 sites with partial hookups for tents or RVs, and 14 RV sites with full hookups. Two cabins are also available. Picnic tables and fire grills are provided. Flush toilets, showers, sanitary disposal station, recreation room, swimming pool, coin laundry, propane gas, and groceries are available. Some facilities are wheelchair accessible. Leashed pets are permitted.

Reservations, fees: Reservations are accepted; $21 to $26 per night, $4 for each additional adult, $5 per night for each extra vehicle, $35 per night for cabin rentals, Major credit cards accepted.

Directions: From U.S. 101, take the Highway 129 exit west and drive 100 feet. Turn left onto Searle Road (frontage road) and drive to the stop sign. Turn left again on Anzar and drive under the freeway to 900 Anzar Road.

Contact: McAlpine Lake and Park, tel. (831) 623-4263, or fax (831) 623-4559; website: www.mcalpinelakeandpark.aol.com.

8 Los Banos Creek Reservoir

 6

Los Banos Creek Reservoir is set in a long, narrow valley, covering 410 surface acres with 12 miles of shoreline. It provides a smaller, more low-key setting (a 5- mph speed limit is enforced) compared to the nearby giant, San Luis Reservoir. In spring, it can be quite windy and is a popular spot for sailboarding. The elevation is 400 feet.

Location: Near Los Banos; map F2, grid c7.

Campsites, facilities: There are 25 sites for tents or RVs up to 30 feet long. Picnic tables and fire grills are provided. Vault toilets are available. No drinking water is available. A boat ramp is available nearby. Leashed pets are permitted.

Reservations, fees: No reservations; $7 per night. Open year-round.

Directions: From Los Banos, go five miles west on Highway 152. Turn south (left) on Volta Road and drive about a mile. Turn left on Pioneer Road and drive a mile. Turn south (right) onto Canyon Road and drive about five miles to the park.

Contact: San Luis Reservoir State Recreation Area, tel. (209) 826-1196 or fax (209) 826-0284.

9 Hollister Hills State Vehicular Recreation Area

 4

This unique park was designed for off-highway-vehicle enthusiasts. It provides 80 miles of trails for motorcycles and 40 miles of trails for four-wheel-drive vehicles. Some of the trails are accessible directly from the campground. All trails close at sunset. Note that there is no direct access to the Fremont Peak State Park, bordering directly to the west. The elevation is about 1,500 feet.

Location: Near Hollister; map F2, grid d1.

Campsites, facilities: There are 125 sites for tents or RVs, and group sites for up to 300 people. Picnic tables and fire rings are provided. Drinking water, flush toilets, showers, and a camp store are available. Leashed pets are permitted.

Reservations, fees: No reservations; $7 per night, group site $200. Open year-round.

Directions: From Highway 156 northwest of Hollister, turn south on Union Road and drive three miles. Turn left (south) on Cienega Road and drive five miles to the park on the right.

Contact: Hollister Hills State Vehicular Recreation Area, tel. (831) 637-3874, tel. (831) 637-8186 or fax (831) 637-4725.

10 Pinnacles Campground

 7

This is the only camp at the Pinnacles National Monument; a once-great hike-in site was closed by flooding. This private one has always received a lot more use—it has more facilities, the access road is in better shape, and the campground is closer to Bear Gulch Caves, a prime destination. The jagged pinnacles for which the park was named were formed by the erosion of an ancient volcanic eruption. The Pinnacles National Monument is like a different planet. It's a 16,000-acre park with volcanic clusters and strange caves, all great for exploring. In addition, expansion is imminent. If you are planning to stay a weekend in the spring, arrive early on Friday evening to be sure you get a campsite. In the summer, beware of temperatures in the 90s and 100s.

Location: Near Pinnacles National Monument; map F2, grid g3.

Campsites, facilities: There are 36 RV sites, 78 sites for tents or RVs, and 13 group sites. Picnic tables and fire grills are provided. Drinking water, flush toilets, electricity, modem hookups, sanitary disposal station, showers, store, and a swimming pool are available. Bring your own firewood or buy it at the campground. Some facilities are wheelchair accessible. Leashed pets are permitted, except on trails.

Reservations, fees: Reservations available at website: www.co.monterey.ca.us/parks, and required for group sites; $7 per night per person for a family site, $6 per night per person for a group site with a $60 minimum, and a $10 leash deposit per pet. Major credit cards accepted. Open year-round, weather permitting.

Directions: From Hollister, drive 32 miles south on Highway 25. Turn at the sign for the Pinnacles/Highway 146 and drive about 2.5 miles to the campground.

Contact: Pinnacles Campground, tel. (831) 389-4462 or fax (831) 637-2337; website: www.pinncamp.com.

11 San Lorenzo County Park

 3

A lot of folks cruising up and down the state on U.S. 101 can underestimate their travel time and find themselves caught out near King City, a small city about midpoint between Northern and Southern California. Well, don't sweat it, because San Lorenzo County Park offers a spot to overnight. It's set near the Salinas River, which isn't exactly the Mississippi, but it'll do. A museum and visitor center capture the rural agricultural life of the valley. The park covers 200 acres, featuring a playground and ball fields.

Location: In King City; map F2, grid j2.

Campsites, facilities: There are 99 sites for tents or RVs with partial hookups. Tables and fire grills are provided. A sanitary disposal station, restrooms, and showers are available. Leashed pets are permitted.

Reservations, fees: Reservations are accepted at tel. (888) 588-2267; $16 to $21 per night, maximum of one vehicle, eight people per site. Open year-round.

Directions: From King City on U.S. 101, turn left at the Broadway exit and drive to the park at 1160 Broadway.

Contact: San Lorenzo County Park, tel. (831) 385-5964.

TUNDRA SWANS

MAP F3

TO STEVINSON   TO ATWATER   TO HORNITOS   **480**   TO MARIPOSA

a

MERCED NATIONAL
WILDLIFE REFUGE

(140) ○ **MERCED**
Tuttle ○
○ Planada

Ben Hur ○

b

(59)

(99)

○ Le Grand

Eastman
Lake

El Nido ○

San Joaquin River

TO LOS BANOS

c

(33) (152)   Red Top ○

(233)   Chowchilla ○

Fairmead ○

1
Raymond ○

TO AHWAHNEE

d

South
Dos
Palos ○

Dos Palos ○

Dairyland ○

Berenda ○

2

Hensley
Lake

(33)

Madera ○

(145)

3

TO I-5

e

Firebaugh ○

568

(145)   (99)

TO HIGHWAY 41

580

San Joaquin River

Ripperdan ○

f

(J1)

Mendota ○

Herndon ○
Pinedale ○

Highway City ○

g

TO PANOCHE

MENDOTA
WILDLIFE
PRESERVE

Kings River

(180)

Kerman ○

Rolinda ○

FRESNO ○

TO CLOVIS

(5)

(33)

Tranquillity ○

h

San Joaquin ○

Raisin ○

Easton ○

Helm ○

(41)

i

Caruthers ○

Burrell ○

j

(5)

Five Points ○

Lanare ○

Layton ○

(145)

Riverdale ○

Hub ○

TO COALINGA TO KETTLEMAN CITY   **656**   TO LEMOORE

0   1   2   3   4   5   6   7   8   9

© AVALON TRAVEL PUBLISHING, INC.

TO HIGHWAY 43

CHAPTER F3

1 Cordorniz Recreation Area

 5

Many people stopped going to Eastman Lake because of a problem with hydrilla, an invasive weed that was choking off the lake. Well, word is getting out that the problem has been largely solved, the lake is open, and people are beginning to return. Hey, Eastman Lake may not look like paradise, but it is treated just the same by people seeking relief on your typical 100-degree summer day out here. It is tucked in the foothills of the San Joaquin Valley at an elevation of 650 feet and covers 1,800 surface acres. The DFG has established a trophy bass program here. It makes a nice tub to take a dunk in, a favorite for water-skiing, swimming and, in the spring, fishing for big bass. Check fishing regulations, posted on all bulletin boards. The lake is also a designated "Watchable Wildlife" site with 163 species of birds, and it is home to a nesting pair of bald eagles. The upper end of the lake is closed to boating to protect bald eagle habitat.

Location: On Eastman Lake; map F3, grid c9.

Campsites, facilities: There are 62 sites for tents or RVs, 15 with full hookups, three group sites for up to 200 people, and three equestrian sites. Picnic tables and fire grills are provided. Drinking water, flush toilets, showers, sanitary disposal station, and a boat ramp are available. An equestrian staging area is available for overnight use, and there are seven miles of hiking, biking, and equestrian trails. Leashed pets are permitted.

Reservations, fees: Reserve at tel. (877) 444-6777 ($8.65 reservation fee) or website: www.reserveusa.com.; $14 to $20 per night, group sites $35 to $75 per night, equestrian sites $8 to $25 per night. Open year-round.

Directions: From Chowchilla, on Highway 99 take the Avenue 26 exit. Drive 17 miles east on Avenue 26. Turn left (north) on County Road 29 and drive eight miles to the lake.

Contact: U.S. Army Corps of Engineers, Sacramento District, Eastman Lake, tel. (559) 689-3255 or fax (559) 689-3408.

2 Hidden View

 5

Hensley Lake is one of two lakes just east of Madera (the other is Millerton Lake). Hensley covers 1,500 surface acres with 24 miles of shoreline and, as long as water levels are maintained, makes for a wonderful water playland. Swimming is good, with two beaches to choose from; the best spot is at Buck Ridge on the east side of the lake, where there are picnic tables and trees for shade. The reservoir was created by a dam on the Fresno River. A nature trail is available. The elevation is 500 feet.

Location: North of Fresno on Hensley Lake; map F3, grid d9.

Campsites, facilities: There are 55 sites for tents or RVs, some with electric hookups, and two group sites for 25 to 100 people. Picnic tables and fire grills are provided. Restrooms, drinking water, flush toilets, showers, sanitary disposal station, playground, and a boat ramp are available. Leashed pets are permitted.

Reservations, fees: Reservations accepted, recommended for groups; reserve at tel. (877) 444-6777 ($8.65 reservation fee) or website: www.reserveusa.com; $14-20 per night for individual sites, $50 for group sites, $2 boat launch fee. Groups can also reserve the Wakalumi Primitive Area at tel. (559) 673-5151. Open year-round.

Directions: From Madera, drive northeast on Highway 145 for about six miles. Bear left on County Road 400 and left again on County Road 603 below the dam. Drive about two miles on County Road 603, turn right on County Road 407, and drive a half mile to the campground at the reservoir.

Contact: U.S. Army Corps of Engineers, Sacramento District, Hensley Lake, tel. (559) 673-5151 or fax (559) 673-2044.

❸ Country Living Mobile Home and RV Park

 1

It can be a dry piece of life driving this country on a hot summer afternoon, when you're ready to stop but know of nowhere to go. This RV park gives you an option, one of the scant few on Highway 99 in this region of the San Joaquin Valley. The ambiance of the place has been helped by the planting of 34 trees in spring of 2000, along with the removal of 64 dead trees (killed by bug infestation).

Location: In Madera; map F3, grid e7.

Campsites, facilities: There are 49 sites for RVs, many with electrical connections and sewer hookups. Picnic tables are provided. Restrooms, drinking water, showers, and coin laundry are available. A swimming pool and hot tub are open in the summer only. A store is available within 1.5 miles. Leashed pets are permitted.

Reservations, fees: Reservations are accepted; $12 to $20 per night, $1 per person per night for more than two people. Open year-round.

Directions: In Madera, take the Avenue 16 exit west from Highway 99 and drive a quarter mile to the camp on the right at 24833 Avenue 16.

Contact: Country Living Mobile Home and RV Park, phone or fax (559) 674-5343.

TOM STIENSTRA

GRAZING BUCK

MAP F4

CHAPTER F4

(CONTINUED ON NEXT PAGE)

1 Big Sandy

 7

It's only six miles from the highway and just eight miles from the southern entrance to Yosemite National Park. Add that up: right, when Wawona is full in southern Yosemite, this camp provides a much-needed option. It's a pretty camp set on Big Creek in the Sierra National Forest, one of two camps in the immediate area. The elevation is 5,800 feet. If you head into Yosemite for the tour of giant sequoias in Wawona, get there early, by 7:30 or 8:30 a.m., when the grove is still quiet and cool, and you will have the old, mammoth trees practically to yourself.

Location: On Big Creek in Sierra National Forest; map F4, grid a3.

Campsites, facilities: There are 14 sites for tents only and four sites for tents or RVs up to 16 feet long. Picnic tables and fire grills are provided. Vault toilets are available. No drinking water is available. Leashed pets are permitted.

Reservations, fees: No reservations; $12 per night, $5 for each additional vehicle. Open from June through October.

Directions: From Oakhurst on Highway 41, turn right on Jackson Road/Forest Road 6507 and drive about five miles north. Go northeast on County Road 632 for about 20 miles to the camp.

Contact: Sierra National Forest, Mariposa-Minarets Ranger District, tel. (559) 877-2218 or fax (559) 877-3108.

2 Texas Flat Group Camp

 1

If you are on your honeymoon, this definitely ain't the place. Unless you like the smell of horses, that is. It's a pretty enough spot, set along the North Fork of Willow Creek, but the camp is primitive and designed for groups with horses. This camp is 15 miles from the south entrance of Yosemite National Park and 15 miles north of Bass Lake. The elevation is 5,500 feet.

Location: On the North Fork of Willow Creek in Sierra National Forest; map F4, grid a4.

Campsites, facilities: There are four sites for tents or RVs up to 22 feet long. Fire grills and picnic tables are provided. Vault toilets and stock handling facilities are available. No drinking water is available. Leashed pets are permitted.

Reservations, fees: Reservations are ac-cepted; reserve at tel. (877) 444-6777 ($8.65 reservation fee) or website: www. reserve usa.com for reservations and fees. Open June through November.

Directions: From Fresno, drive about 52 miles north on Highway 41. Turn east on Sky Ranch Road/County Road 632 and drive approxi-mately five miles. Turn right on Forest Road 6540 and drive about three-quarters of a mile. Turn left on Forest Road 6538 and drive 2.5 miles to the campground.

Contact: Sierra National Forest, Mariposa-Minarets Ranger District, tel. (559) 877-2218 or fax (559) 877-3108.

3 Clover Meadow

 8

This is one of two excellent jump-off camps in the area for backpackers; the other is Granite Creek. The camp is set at 7,000 feet, adjacent to the Clover Meadow Ranger Station, where backcountry information is available. While a trail is available from camp heading east into the Ansel Adams Wilderness, most hikers drive about three miles farther northeast on Minarets Road to a trailhead for a five-mile hike to Cora Lakes.

Location: In Sierra National Forest; map F4, grid a7.

Campsites, facilities: There are seven sites for tents or RVs up to 16 feet long. Picnic tables and fire grills are provided. Drinking water and vault toilets are available. Leashed pets are permitted.

Reservations, fees: No reservations; no fee. Open June through September.

Directions: From the town of North Fork (south of Bass Lake), drive east and south on Mammoth Pool Road/County Road 225, which becomes Minarets Road/ Forest Road 4S81 and which will veer left (north) to the campground entrance road. The camp is adjacent to the Clover Meadow Ranger Station. The total distance from North Fork to the entrance road is about 63 miles—20 miles north of Mammoth Pool Reservoir on Minarets Road.

Contact: Sierra National Forest, Mariposa-Minarets Ranger District, tel. (559) 877-2218 or fax (559) 877-3108.

4 Granite Creek

     6

This camp is a good jump-off point for backpackers since a trail from camp leads north for five miles to Cora Lakes in the Ansel Adams Wilderness, with the option of continuing onward to more remote wilderness. Note that nearby Clover Meadow may be more desirable because it has both drinking water to tank up your canteens and a ranger station to obtain the latest trail information. In addition, one-half of this campground is available for equestrians. The elevation is 6,900 feet.

Location: In Sierra National Forest; map F4, grid a7.

Campsites, facilities: There are 20 tent sites, half available for equestrian use. Picnic tables and fire grills are provided. Vault toilets and a horse corral are available. No drinking water is available. Garbage must be packed out. Leashed pets are permitted.

Reservations, fees: No reservations; no fee. Open June through September.

Directions: From the town of North Fork (south of Bass Lake), drive east and south on Mammoth Pool Road/County Road 225, which becomes Minarets Road/Forest Road 4S81. Veer left on Minarets Road/Forest Road 4S81 and drive to the campground entrance road, which goes to the Clover Meadow Ranger Station. (The total distance from North Fork to the entrance road is about 61 miles—18 miles north of Mammoth Pool Reservoir on Minarets Road.) Drive 3.5 miles to the campground.

Contact: Sierra National Forest, Mariposa-Minarets Ranger District, tel. (559) 877-2218 or fax (559) 877-3108.

5 Upper Chiquito

   7

Upper Chiquito is set at 6,800 feet on a major access road to Sierra National Forest and the western region of the Ansel Adams Wilderness, about 15 miles to the east. The camp is set on Upper Chiquito Creek. About a mile down the road (southwest) is a Forest Service spur road (turn north) that provides access to a trail that is routed up Chiquito Creek for three miles to gorgeous Chiquita Lake (another route with a longer drive and shorter hike is available out of Fresno Dome).

Location: On Chiquito Creek in Sierra National Forest; map F4, grid a5.

Campsites, facilities: There are 10 sites for tents only and 10 sites for tents or RVs up to 22 feet long. Picnic tables and fire grills are provided. Vault toilets are available. No drinking water is available. Garbage must be packed out. Leashed pets are permitted.

Reservations, fees: No reservations; no fee. Open from June through September.

Directions: From Fresno, drive 50 miles north on Highway 41 to Yosemite Forks. Turn right onto County Road 222 and drive six miles to Pines Village. Turn left onto Beasore Road and drive 16 miles to the campground.

Contact: Sierra National Forest, Mariposa-Minarets Ranger District, tel. (559) 877-2218 or fax (559) 877-3108.

6 Fresno Dome

 7

This camp is named after nearby Fresno Dome to the east, at 7,540 feet the dominating feature in the surrounding landscape. The trailhead for a mile hike to its top is two miles curving down the road to the east. This camp is set at 6,400 feet on Big Creek in Sierra National Forest, a good option to nearby Yosemite National Park.

Location: On Big Creek in Sierra National Forest; map F4, grid a4.

Campsites, facilities: There are 15 sites for tents or RVs up to 22 feet long. Picnic tables and fire grills are provided. Pit toilets are available. No drinking water is available. Garbage must be packed out. Leashed pets are permitted.

Reservations, fees: No reservations; $12 per night, $5 for each additional vehicle. Open June through mid-October.

Directions: From Fresno, drive north on Highway 41 about 60 miles to Jackson Road/Forest Road 6507. Turn right and drive six miles to the campground on the left.

Contact: Sierra National Forest, Mariposa-Minarets Ranger District, tel. (559) 877-2218 or fax (559) 877-3108.

7 Grey's Mountain

 7

This is a small, primitive campground to keep in mind when all the campgrounds are filled at nearby Bass Lake. It is one of a series of campgrounds on Willow Creek. The elevation is 5,200 feet, set just below Sivels Mountain to the east at 5,813 feet.

Location: On Willow Creek in Sierra National Forest; map F4, grid a4.

Campsites, facilities: There are 26 sites for tents and RVs up to 22 feet long. Picnic tables and fire grills are provided. Vault toilets are available. No drinking water is available. Leashed pets are permitted.

Reservations, fees: No reservations; $12 per night, $5 for each additional vehicle. Open June through October.

Directions: From Fresno, drive north on Highway 41 about 60 miles to Jackson Road/Forest Road 6507. Turn right and drive four miles to the campground on the right.

Contact: Sierra National Forest, Mariposa-Minarets Ranger District, tel. (559) 877-2218 or fax (559) 877-3108.

8 Kelty Meadow

 6

This primitive campground is often used by campers with horses. It is located at Kelty Meadow by Willow Creek. Side trip options feature nearby Fresno Dome, the Nelder Grove of giant sequoias and, of course, the southern entrance to nearby Yosemite National Park. The elevation is 5,800 feet.

Location: On Willow Creek in Sierra National Forest; map F4, grid a4.

Campsites, facilities: There are 11 sites for tents and RVs up to 22 feet long. Fire grills and picnic tables are provided. Vault toilets and stock handling facilities are available. No drinking water is available. Leashed pets are permitted.

Reservations, fees: Reservations are required for equestrians; reserve via phone at tel. (877) 444-6777 ($8.65 reservation fee) or website: www.reserveusa.com; $10 per night, $5 for each additional vehicle. Open June through October.

Directions: From Oakhurst on Highway 41, drive five miles north to Sky Ranch Road/

County Road 632. Drive northeast on County Road 632 about 10 miles to the campground.

Contact: Sierra National Forest, Mariposa-Minarets Ranger District, tel. (559) 877-2218 or fax (559) 877-3108.

9 Soquel

 7

Soquel is at 5,400 feet in elevation on the North Fork of Willow Creek, an alternative to nearby Grey's Mountain in Sierra National Forest. When the camps are filled at Bass Lake, these two camps provide overflow areas as well as more primitive settings for those who are looking for more of a wilderness experience.

Location: On the North Fork of Willow Creek in Sierra National Forest; map F4, grid a4.

Campsites, facilities: There are 11 sites for tents and RVs up to 22 feet long. Picnic tables and fire grills are provided. Vault toilets are available. No drinking water is available. Leashed pets are permitted.

Reservations, fees: Reserve via phone at tel. (877) 444-6777 ($8.65 reservation fee) or website: www.reserveusa.com; $12 per night, $5 for each additional vehicle. Open June through October.

Directions: From Fresno, drive about 52 miles north on Highway 41 to Sky Ranch Road/County Road 632. Turn east on County Road 632 and drive about five miles. Turn right on Forest Road 6540 and drive about three-quarters of a mile to the campground.

Contact: Sierra National Forest, Mariposa-Minarets Ranger District, tel. (559) 877-2218 or fax (559) 877-3108.

10 Nelder Grove

 7

Nelder Grove is a primitive spot, also pretty, yet a camp that is often overlooked. It is set amid the Nelder Grove of giant sequoias, the majestic mountain redwoods. Since the southern entrance to Yosemite National Park is just 10 miles away, Nelder Grove is overshadowed by Yosemite's Wawona Grove. The elevation is 5,300 feet. A good option.

Location: In Sierra National Forest; map F4, grid a4.

Campsites, facilities: There are seven sites for tents or RVs up to 22 feet long. Picnic tables and fire grills are provided. Vault toilets are available. No drinking water is available. Garbage must be packed out. Leashed pets are permitted.

Reservations, fees: No reservations; no fee. Open May through September.

Directions: From Fresno, drive 46 miles north on Highway 41 to the town of Oakhurst. Continue north on Highway 41 for five miles to Sky Ranch Road/County Road 632. Drive northeast about eight miles to the campground.

Contact: Sierra National Forest, Mariposa-Minarets Ranger District, tel. (559) 877-2218 or fax (559) 877-3108.

11 Lower Chiquito

 7

Lower Chiquito is a small, little-known, primitive camp in Sierra National Forest, about eight miles from Mammoth Pool Reservoir. The elevation is 4,900 feet, with a very warm climate here in summer. Note that Lower Chiquito is a long distance (a twisting, 30- to 40-minute drive) from Upper Chiquito, despite the similarity in names and streamside settings along the same creek.

Location: On Chiquito Creek in Sierra National Forest; map F4, grid a5.

Campsites, facilities: There are seven sites for tents or RVs up to 22 feet long. Picnic tables and fire grills are provided. Vault toilets are available. No drinking water is available. Leashed pets are permitted.

Reservations, fees: No reservations; $10 per night, $5 for each additional vehicle. Open May through September.

Directions: From the town of North Fork (south of Bass Lake), drive east and south on Mammoth Pool Road/County Road

225, which becomes Minarets Road/Forest Road 4S81. Veer left (north) on Minarets Road/Forest Road 4S81. The drive is about 38 miles from North Fork. Turn left onto Forest Road 6S71 and drive three miles to the campground.

Contact: Sierra National Forest, Mariposa-Minarets Ranger District, tel. (559) 877-2218 or fax (559) 877-3108.

12 Chilkoot

 7

A lot of people have heard of Bass Lake, but only the faithful know about Chilcoot Creek. That's where this camp is, but it's just two miles from Bass Lake. It provides a primitive option to use either as an overflow area for Bass Lake or for folks who don't want to get jammed into one of the Bass Lake campgrounds on a popular weekend.

Location: Near Bass Lake in Sierra National Forest; map F4, grid b4.

Campsites, facilities: There are 14 sites for tents and RVs up to 22 feet long. Picnic tables and fire grills are provided. Vault toilets are available. No drinking water is available. Groceries and a coin laundry are available at Bass Lake. Leashed pets are permitted.

Reservations, fees: Reserve via phone at tel. (877) 444-6777 ($8.65 reservation fee) or website: www.reserveusa.com; $12 per night, $5 for each additional vehicle. Open May through August.

Directions: From Fresno, drive 50 miles north on Highway 41 to Yosemite Forks. Turn right onto County Road 222 and drive six miles to the town of Bass Lake. Turn left onto Beasore Road and drive 4.5 miles to the campground.

Contact: Sierra National Forest, Mariposa-Minarets Ranger District, tel. (559) 877-2218 or fax (559) 877-3108.

13 Gaggs Camp

 7

The masses are not exactly beating a hot trail to this camp. It's a small, remote, and primitive

spot, set along a little creek at 5,800 feet, deep in the interior of Sierra National Forest. A Forest Service map is advisable. With that in hand, you can make the three-mile drive to Little Shuteye Pass, where the road is often gated in the winter (the gate is open when the look-out station is staffed); from here it is a three-mile trip to Shuteye Peak, 8,351 feet, where there is a drop-dead gorgeous view of the surrounding landscape.

Location: In Sierra National Forest; map F4, grid b5.

Campsites, facilities: There are 12 sites for tents or RVs up to 16 feet long. Picnic tables and fire grills are provided. Vault toilets are available. No drinking water is available. Garbage must be packed out. Leashed pets are permitted.

Reservations, fees: No reservations; $12 per night, $5 per night for each extra vehicle. Open June through October, weather permitting.

Directions: From the town of North Fork (south of Bass Lake), drive 4.5 miles north on Malum Ridge Road/County Road 274. Turn right onto Central Camp Road (a narrow, winding road) and drive 11.5 miles to the campground on the right.

Contact: Sierra National Forest, Mariposa-Minarets Ranger District, tel. (559) 877-2218 or fax (559) 877-3108.

14 Soda Springs

 7

Soda Springs is set at 4,400 feet on West Fork Chiquito Creek, about five miles from Mammoth Pool Reservoir, and is used primarily as an overflow area if the more developed camps with drinking water have filled up. As long as you remember that the camp is primitive, it is a good overflow option.

Location: On the West Fork of Chiquito Creek in Sierra National Forest; map F4, grid b5.

Campsites, facilities: There are 18 sites for tents or RVs up to 25 feet long. Picnic tables and fire grills are provided. Vault toilets are available. No drinking water is available. A grocery store and boat ramp are nearby. Leashed pets are permitted.

Reservations, fees: No reservations; $12 per night, $5 per night for each extra vehicle. Open April through October, weather permitting.

Directions: From the town of North Fork (south of Bass Lake), drive east and south on Mammoth Pool Road/County Road 225, which will become Minarets Road/ Forest Road 4S81 and will veer north to the campground. The total distance from North Fork is about 37 miles on narrow, winding roads.

Contact: Sierra National Forest, Mariposa-Minarets Ranger District, tel. (559) 877-2218 or fax (559) 877-3108.

15 Forks

      8

Bass Lake is set in a canyon. It's a long, narrow, deep lake that is popular for fishing in the spring and water-skiing in the summer. It's a pretty spot, set at 3,400 feet in the Sierra National Forest. This is one of several camps at the lake. Boats must be registered at the Bass Lake observation tower after launching. Note that the only camp on Bass Lake that is open year-round is Lupine-Cedar.

Location: On Bass Lake in Sierra National Forest; map F4, grid b3.

Campsites, facilities: There are 25 sites for tents only and six sites for tents or RVs up to 22 feet long. Picnic tables and fire grills are provided. Drinking water and flush toilets are available. A grocery store and coin laundry are nearby. Leashed pets are permitted.

Reservations, fees: From Memorial Day through Labor Day, reserve via phone at tel. (877) 444-6777 ($8.65 reservation fee) or website: www.reserveusa.com; $16 per night, $5 for each additional vehicle. Open May through September.

Directions: From Fresno, drive 50 miles north on Highway 41 to Yosemite Forks. Turn right onto County Road 222 and drive six miles, keeping right at each of two Ys in the road, to the campground on Bass Lake.

Contact: Sierra National Forest, Mariposa-Minarets Ranger District, tel. (559) 877-2218 or fax (559) 877-3108.

16 Crane Valley Group and Recreation Point

      8

Bass Lake is a long, narrow, mountain lake set in the Sierra foothills at 3,400 feet. It's especially popular in the summer for water-skiers.

Location: On Bass Lake in Sierra National Forest; map F4, grid b3.

Campsites, facilities: There are four sites that hold 30 to 50 people each at Recreation Point Group Camp and seven sites that hold 30 to 50 people each at Crane Valley Camp. At Recreation Point, picnic tables and fire grills are provided. Drinking water and flush toilets are available. At Crane Valley, picnic tables and fire grills are provided. Vault toilets are available. No drinking water is available. A grocery store is nearby. Leashed pets are permitted.

Reservations, fees: Reserve via phone at tel. (877) 444-6777 ($8.65 reservation fee); $20 to $50 per night, $5 for each additional vehicle. Open year-round.

Directions: From Fresno, drive 50 miles north on Highway 41 to Yosemite Forks. Turn right onto County Road 222 and drive six miles to Bass Lake.

Contact: Sierra National Forest, Mariposa-Minarets Ranger District, tel. (559) 877-2218 or fax (559) 877-3108.

17 Lupine-Cedar Bluffs

    8

This is the camping headquarters at Bass Lake and the only camp open year-round. Bass Lake is a popular vacation spot, a pretty lake, long and narrow, covering 1,200 acres when full and surrounded by national forest. Most of the campgrounds are filled on weekends and three-day holidays. Fishing is best in the spring for rainbow trout and largemouth bass, and by mid-June water-skiers have usually taken over. Boats must be registered at the Bass Lake observation tower after launching.

Location: On Bass Lake in Sierra National Forest; map F4, grid b3.

Campsites, facilities: There are 113 sites for tents or RVs up to 40 feet long, and several double-family sites. Picnic tables and fire grills are provided. Drinking water and flush toilets are available. Some facilities are wheelchair accessible. Groceries and a boat ramp are available nearby. Leashed pets are permitted.

Reservations, fees: Reserve via phone at tel. (877) 444-6777 ($8.65 reservation fee) or website: www.reserveusa.com; $16 per night, $30 per night for double-family sites, $5 for each additional vehicle. Open year-round.

Directions: From Fresno, drive 50 miles north on Highway 41 to Yosemite Forks. Turn right onto County Road 222 and drive six miles, keeping to the right at each of two Ys in the road, to the campground on Bass Lake.

Contact: Sierra National Forest, Mariposa-Minarets Ranger District, tel. (559) 877-2218 or fax (559) 877-3108.

18 Spring Cove

 8

This is one of the several camps beside Bass Lake, a long, narrow reservoir in the Sierra foothill country. Expect hot weather in the summer. Boats must be registered at the Bass Lake observation tower after launching. The elevation is 3,400 feet.

Location: On Bass Lake in Sierra National Forest; map F4, grid b3.

Campsites, facilities: There are 54 sites for tents only and 11 sites for RVs up to 30 feet long. Picnic tables and fire grills are provided. Drinking water and flush toilets are available. Groceries and a boat ramp are available nearby. Leashed pets are permitted.

Reservations, fees: From Memorial Day

through Labor Day, reserve via phone at tel. (877) 444-6777 ($8.65 reservation fee) or website: www.reserveusa.com; $16 per night. Open May through August.

Directions: From Fresno, drive 50 miles north on Highway 41 to Yosemite Forks. Turn right onto County Road 222 and drive six miles, bearing right at each Y, to the campground on Bass Lake.

Contact: Sierra National Forest, Mariposa-Minarets Ranger District, tel. (559) 877-2218 or fax (559) 877-3108.

19 Wishon Point

 9

This camp on Wishon Point is the smallest, and many say the prettiest, of the camps at Bass Lake. The elevation is 3,400 feet.

Location: On Bass Lake in Sierra National Forest; map F4, grid b3.

Campsites, facilities: There are 47 sites for tents or RVs up to 30 feet long and several double-family sites. Picnic tables and fire grills are provided. Drinking water and flush toilets are available. Groceries and a boat ramp are nearby. Leashed pets are permitted.

Reservations, fees: From Memorial Day through Labor Day, reserve via phone at tel. (877) 444-6777 ($8.65 reservation fee) or website: www.reserveusa.com; $16 per night, $30 per night for double-family sites. Open June through September.

Directions: From Fresno, drive 50 miles north on Highway 41 to Yosemite Forks. Turn right onto County Road 222 and drive six miles, bearing right at each Y, to the campground on Bass Lake.

Contact: Sierra National Forest, Mariposa-Minarets Ranger District, tel. (559) 877-2218 or fax (559) 877-3108.

20 Mammoth Pool

 7

Mammoth Pool was created by a dam in the San Joaquin River gorge, a steep canyon, resulting in a long, narrow lake with steep, high walls. The lake seems much higher than its official elevation of 3,330 feet, but that is because of the high ridges. This is the only drive-in camp at the lake, though there is a boat-in camp, China Camp, on the lake's upper reaches. Trout fishing can be good in the spring and early summer, with water-skiing dominant during warm weather. Get this: Water sports are restricted from May 1 to June 15 due to deer migrating across the lake—that's right, swimming—but the campgrounds here are still open.

Location: Near Mammoth Pool Reservoir in Sierra National Forest; map F4, grid b6.

Campsites, facilities: There are 18 sites for tents only, 29 sites for tents or RVs up to 22 feet long, and five multi-family sites. Picnic tables and fire grills are provided. Drinking water and vault toilets are available. A grocery store and boat ramp are within a mile. Leashed pets are permitted.

Reservations, fees: No reservations; $12 per night, $24 multi-family site fee, $5 for each additional vehicle. Open May through October.

Directions: From the town of North Fork (south of Bass Lake), drive southeast on County Road 225, which becomes Minarets Road/Forest Road 4S81 and will veer north to the campground. The total distance from North Fork is about 42 miles on narrow, winding roads.

Contact: Sierra National Forest, Mariposa-Minarets Ranger District, tel. (559) 877-2218 or fax (559) 877-3108.

21 Placer

This little camp is just three miles from Mammoth Pool Reservoir. With Forest Road and a pretty setting along Chiquito Creek, it is one of the better campgrounds used as an overflow area for Mammoth Pool visitors. The elevation is 4,100 feet. For more information, see the entry for Mammoth Pool.

Location: Near Mammoth Pool Reservoir on Chiquito Creek in Sierra National Forest; map F4, grid b6.

Campsites, facilities: There are seven tent sites. Picnic tables and fire grills are provided. Vault toilets are available. No drinking water is available. Leashed pets are permitted.

Reservations, fees: No reservations; $12 per night. Open April through October.

Directions: From the town of North Fork (south of Bass Lake), drive east and south on Mammoth Pool Road/County Road 225, which becomes Minarets Road/Forest Road 4S81 and will veer north to the campground. The total distance from North Fork is about 39 miles on narrow, winding roads.

Contact: Sierra National Forest, Mariposa-Minarets Ranger District, tel. (559) 877-2218 or fax (559) 877-3108.

22 Sweetwater

 6

Sweetwater is small and primitive, but if the camp at Mammoth Pool Reservoir is filled up, this spot provides an alternative. It is set on Chiquito Creek, just a mile from the lake. The elevation is 3,800 feet. See the entry for Mammoth Pool for more information.

Location: Near Mammoth Pool Reservoir on Chiquito Creek in Sierra National Forest; map F4, grid b6.

Campsites, facilities: There are five sites for tents only and five sites for RVs up to 16 feet long. Picnic tables and fire grills are provided. Vault toilets are available. No drinking water is available. A grocery store and boat ramp are within 1.5 miles. Leashed pets are permitted.

Reservations, fees: No reservations; $12 per night. Open April through October.

Directions: From the town of North Fork (south of Bass Lake), drive southeast on County Road 225, which becomes Minarets Road/ Forest Road 4S81 and will veer north to the campground. The total distance from North Fork is about 41 miles on narrow, winding roads.

Contact: Sierra National Forest, Mariposa-Minarets Ranger District, tel. (559) 877-2218 or fax (559) 877-3108.

23 Sample Meadow

   7

This is a pretty, secluded spot set at 7,800 feet along Kaiser Creek, with nearby trailheads available for backpackers. While there is a trail out of camp, most will drive a mile down Forest Road 80 to the Rattlesnake Parking Area. From here, one trail is routed three miles southwest to Kaiser Ridge and Upper and Lower Twin Lakes in the Kaiser Wilderness, a great hike. Another trail heads north for three miles to Rattlesnake Creek, then enters the western slopes of the Ansel Adams Wilderness, with this portion featuring a series of canyons, streams, and very few people.

Location: On Kaiser Creek in Sierra National Forest; map F4, grid b8.

Campsites, facilities: There are 16 sites for tents or small RVs up to 16 feet long. Picnic tables and fire grills are provided. Vault toilets are available. No drinking water is available. Garbage must be packed out. Leashed pets are permitted.

Reservations, fees: No reservations; no fee. Open June through September.

Directions: From the town of Shaver Lake, drive 21 miles north on Highway 168. Turn northeast on Kaiser Pass Road /Forest Road 80 and drive nine miles. Turn north on the entrance road (dirt) and drive five miles to the campground.

Contact: Sierra National Forest, Pineridge Ranger District, tel. (559) 855-5360 or fax (559) 855-5375.

24 Portal Forebay

      8

This small, primitive camp is set along the shore of little Forebay Lake at 7,200 feet. The camp is pretty and provides a good hiking option, with a trailhead near the camp that is routed up Camp 61 Creek and then to Mono Creek, with a ford of Mono Creek required about two miles in. Another side trip is visiting Mono Hot Springs about five miles to the east, just off the road to Lake Edison.

Location: On Forebay Lake in Sierra National Forest; map F4, grid b9.

Campsites, facilities: There are 14 sites for tents or small RVs up to 16 feet long. Picnic tables and fire grills are provided. Vault toilets are available. No drinking water is available. Garbage must be packed out. Groceries are available nearby at Mono Hot Springs. Leashed pets are permitted.

Reservations, fees: No reservations; $8 per night, $5 per night for each extra vehicle. Open June through September.

Directions: From the town of Shaver Lake, drive 21 miles north on Highway 168 to the town of Lakeshore. From Lakeshore, drive northeast on Kaiser Pass Road/Forest Road 80 for about 13.5 miles to the campground entrance.

Contact: Sierra National Forest, Pineridge Ranger District, tel. (559) 855-5360 or fax (559) 855-5375.

25 Rock Creek

    6

Drinking water is the big bonus here. It's easier to live with than the no-water situation at Fish Creek, the other camp in the immediate area. It is also why this camp tends to fill up on weekends. A side trip is the primitive road that heads southeast out of camp, switchbacks as its heads east, and drops down the canyon near where pretty Aspen Creek feeds into Rock Creek. The elevation at camp is 4,300 feet. Note that the best camp in the immediate region is at Mammoth Pool.

Location: In Sierra National Forest; map F4, grid c6.

Campsites, facilities: There are 18 sites for tents or RVs up to 32 feet long. Picnic tables and fire grills are provided. Drinking water and vault toilets are available. Leashed pets are permitted.

Reservations, fees: Reservations at website:www.reserveusa.com; $13 per night. Open April through October, weather permitting.

Directions: From the town of North Fork (south of Bass Lake), drive east and south on Mammoth Pool Road/County Road 225, which becomes Minarets Road/Forest Road 4S81 and will veer north to the campground. The total distance from North Fork is about 27 miles.

Contact: Sierra National Forest, Mariposa-Minarets Ranger District, tel. (559) 877-2218 or fax (559) 877-3108.

26 Catavee

Catavee Camp is one of three camps in the immediate vicinity, set on the north shore at the eastern end of Huntington Lake. The camp sits near where Bear Creek enters the lake. Huntington Lake is a scenic, high Sierra lake at 7,000 feet, where visitors can enjoy fishing, hiking, and sailing. Sailboat regattas take place here regularly during the summer. Nearby resorts offer boat rentals and guest docks, and a boat ramp is nearby. Tackle rentals and bait are also available. A trailhead near camp accesses the Kaiser Wilderness.

Location: On Huntington Lake in Sierra National Forest; map F4, grid c8.

Campsites, facilities: There are 26 sites for tents or RVs up to 25 feet long. Picnic tables and fire grills are provided. Drinking water and vault toilets are available. Horseback riding facilities and a small grocery store are nearby. Some facilities are wheelchair accessible. Leashed pets are permitted.

Reservations, fees: Reserve via phone at tel. (877) 444-6777 ($8.65 reservation fee) or website: www.reserveusa.com; $15 to $17 per night, $5 per night for each extra vehicle. Open June through October.

Directions: From the town of Shaver Lake, drive 21 miles north on Highway 168. Turn left on Huntington Lake Road and drive a half mile to the campground.

Contact: Sierra National Forest, Pineridge Ranger District, tel. (559) 855-5360 or fax (559) 855-5375.

27 Kinnikinnick

Flip a coin; there are three camps in the immediate vicinity of Huntington Lake and, with a boat ramp nearby, they are all favorites. Kinnikinnick is on the lake's north shore at the eastern end, set between Catavee and Deer Creek campgrounds. The elevation is 7,000 feet.

Location: On Huntington Lake in Sierra National Forest; map F4, grid c8.

Campsites, facilities: There are 35 sites for tents or RVs up to 22 feet long. Picnic tables and fire grills are provided. Drinking water and flush toilets are available. Horseback riding facilities and a grocery store are available nearby. Some facilities are wheelchair accessible. Leashed pets are permitted.

Reservations, fees: Reserve via phone at tel. (877) 444-6777 ($8.65 reservation fee) or website: www.reserveusa.com; $15 to $17 per night, $5 per night for each extra vehicle. Open June through August.

Directions: From the town of Shaver Lake, drive 21 miles north on Highway 168. Turn left on Huntington Lake Road and drive a half mile to the campground.

Contact: Sierra National Forest, Pineridge Ranger District, tel. (559) 855-5360 or fax (559) 855-5375.

28 Deer Creek

This is one of the best camps at Huntington Lake, set near lakeside with a boat ramp nearby. It is on the north shore of the lake's eastern end. Huntington Lake is four miles long and a half mile wide, with 14 miles of shoreline, five resorts, boat rentals, and a trailhead for hiking into the Kaiser Wilderness.

Location: On Huntington Lake in Sierra National Forest; map F4, grid c8.

Campsites, facilities: There are 34 sites for tents or RVs up to 22 feet long. Picnic tables and fire grills are provided. Drinking water and flush toilets are available. Some facilities are wheelchair accessible. A grocery store and propane gas are nearby. Leashed pets are permitted.

Reservations, fees: Reserve via phone at tel. (877) 444-6777 ($8.65 reservation fee) or website: www.reserveusa.com; $15 to $17 per night, $5 per night for each extra vehicle. Open June through September.

Directions: From the town of Shaver Lake, drive 21 miles north on Highway 168. Turn left on Huntington Lake Road and drive a half mile to the campground.

Contact: Sierra National Forest, Pineridge Ranger District, tel. (559) 855-5360 or fax (559) 855-5375.

29 College

 7

College is a beautiful site along the shore of the northeastern end of Huntington Lake, at 7,000 feet elevation.

Location: On Huntington Lake in Sierra National Forest; map F4, grid c8.

Campsites, facilities: There are 11 sites for tents or RVs up to 22 feet long. Picnic tables and fire grills are provided. Drinking water and vault toilets are available. Horseback riding facilities, grocery store, and propane gas are available nearby. Leashed pets are permitted.

Reservations, fees: Reserve via phone at tel. (877) 444-6777 ($8.65 reservation fee) or website: www.reserveusa.com; $14 to $16 per night, $5 per night for each extra vehicle. Open June through September.

Directions: From the town of Shaver Lake, drive 21 miles north on Highway 168. Turn left on Huntington Lake Road and drive a half mile to the campground.

Contact: Sierra National Forest, Pineridge Ranger District, tel. (559) 855-5360 or fax (559) 855-5375.

30 Bolsillo

 4

This tiny camp has many first-class bonuses, including Forest Road. It is set at 7,400 feet along Bolsillo Creek, just three miles by car to Mono Hot Springs and seven miles to Lake Edison. A trailhead out of camp provides the chance for a three-mile hike south, climbing along Bolsillo Creek and up to small, pretty Corbett Lake on the flank of nearby Mount Givens, 10,648 feet.

Location: On Bolsillo Creek in Sierra National Forest; map F4, grid c9.

Campsites, facilities: There are three tent sites. Picnic tables and fire grills are provided. Drinking water and vault toilets are available. Garbage must be packed out. You can buy supplies in Mono Hot Springs. Leashed pets are permitted.

Reservations, fees: No reservations; no fee. Open June through September.

Directions: From the town of Shaver Lake, drive 21 miles north on Highway 168. Turn northeast on Kaiser Pass Road/Forest Road 80 and drive for 15 miles to the campground entrance on the right.

Contact: Sierra National Forest, Pineridge Ranger District, tel. (559) 855-5360 or fax (559) 855-5375.

31 Upper & Lower Billy Creek

 8

Huntington Lake is at an elevation of 7,000 feet in the Sierra Nevada, and this is one of several camps here. The lake is four miles long and a half-mile wide, with 14 miles of shoreline, five resorts, boat rentals, and a trailhead for hiking into the Kaiser Wilderness. This camp is on the north side of the lake's western end, where Billy Creek feeds the lake. Of the camps at the lake, this one is closest to town. Lower Billy Creek, just across the road, is smaller than Upper Billy and has lakeside sites available.

Location: On Huntington Lake in Sierra National Forest; map F4, grid c7.

Campsites, facilities: Upper Billy has 57 sites for tents only and 20 sites for tents or RVs up to 25 feet long. Lower Billy has 11 sites for tents or RVs. Picnic tables and fire grills are provided. Drinking water and flush toilets are available. A small grocery store is nearby. Leashed pets are permitted.

Reservations, fees: Reserve via phone at tel. (877) 444-6777 ($8.65 reservation fee) or website: www.reserveusa.com; $14 to $16 per night, $5 per night for each extra vehicle. Open June through September.

Directions: From the town of Shaver Lake, drive 21 miles north on Highway 168. Turn left on Huntington Lake Road and drive about five miles west to the campground.

Contact: Sierra National Forest, Pineridge Ranger District, tel. (559) 855-5360 or fax (559) 855-5375.

32 Fish Creek
    6

This is a small, primitive camp set along Fish Creek at 4,600 feet in the Sierra National Forest. It's a nearby option to Rock Creek, both set on the access road to Mammoth Pool Reservoir.

Location: In Sierra National Forest; map F4, grid c6.

Campsites, facilities: There are seven sites for tents or RVs up to 16 feet long. Picnic tables and fire grills are provided. Vault toilets are available. No drinking water is available. Leashed pets are permitted.

Reservations, fees: Reservations at website:www.reserveusa.com; $12 per night. Open April through October, weather permitting.

Directions: From the town of North Fork (south of Bass Lake), drive east and south on Mammoth Pool Road/County Road 225, which becomes Minarets Road/Forest Road 4S81 and will veer north to the campground. The total distance from North Fork is about 23 miles.

Contact: Sierra National Forest, Mariposa-Minarets Ranger District, tel. (559) 877-2218 or fax (559) 877-3108.

33 Rancheria
     8

This is the granddaddy of the camps at Huntington Lake, and some say the best in the area. It is along the shore of the lake's eastern end. A bonus here is the nearby Rancheria Falls National Recreation Trail, which provides access to beautiful Rancheria Falls. Another side trip is the 15-minute drive to Bear Butte (the access road is across from the campground entrance) at 8,598 feet, providing a sweeping view of the lake below. The elevation at camp is 7,000 feet.

Location: Near Huntington Lake in Sierra National Forest; map F4, grid c8.

Campsites, facilities: There are 150 sites for tents or RVs up to 22 feet long. Picnic tables and fire grills are provided. Drinking water and flush toilets are available. A grocery store and propane gas are available nearby. Leashed pets are permitted.

Reservations, fees: Reserve via phone at tel. (877) 444-6777 ($8.65 reservation fee) or website: www.reserveusa.com; $14 to $16 per night, $5 per night for each extra vehicle. Open year-round.

Directions: From the town of Shaver Lake, drive 20 miles north on Highway 168 to the campground.

Contact: Sierra National Forest, Pineridge Ranger District, tel. (559) 855-5360 or fax (559) 855-5375.

34 Badger Flat Group Camp
   7

Badger Flat is a primitive site along Rancheria Creek at 8,200 feet, about five miles east of Huntington Lake. It is a popular horse camp and a good jump-off spot for wilderness trekkers. A trail that passes through camp provides two options: Head south for three miles to enter the Dinkey Lakes Wilderness, or head north for two miles to enter the Kaiser Wilderness.

Location: On Rancheria Creek in Sierra National Forest; map F4, grid c9.

Campsites, facilities: This campground will accommodate groups of up to 100 people in tents or RVs up to 25 feet long. Picnic tables and fire grills are provided. Vault toilets and horseback riding facilities are available. No drinking water is available. A grocery store is nearby. Leashed pets are permitted.

Reservations, fees: Reserve via phone at tel. (877) 444-6777 ($8.65 reservation fee) or website: www.reserveusa.com; $150 per night per group. Open June through September.

Directions: From the town of Shaver Lake, drive 21 miles north on Highway 168. Turn northeast on Kaiser Pass Road/Forest Road 80 and drive six miles to the campground.

Contact: Sierra National Forest, Pineridge Ranger District, tel. (559) 855-5360 or fax (559) 855-5375.

35 Badger Flat

   7

This camp is a good launching pad for backpackers. It is set at 8,200 feet along Rancheria Creek. The trail leading out of the camp is routed into the Kaiser Wilderness to the north and Dinkey Lakes Wilderness to the south.

Location: On Rancheria Creek in Sierra National Forest; map F4, grid c9.

Campsites, facilities: There are 15 sites for tents or RVs up to 22 feet long. Fire grills and picnic tables are provided. Vault toilets and horseback riding facilities are available. No drinking water is available. Leashed pets are permitted.

Reservations, fees: No reservations; $8 per night, $5 per night for each extra vehicle. Open June through September.

Directions: From the town of Shaver Lake, drive 21 miles north on Highway 168. Turn northeast on Kaiser Pass Road/Forest Road 80 and drive seven miles to the campground.

Contact: Sierra National Forest, Pineridge Ranger District, tel. (559) 855-5360 or fax (559) 855-5375.

36 Smalley Cove

       7

Kerckhoff Reservoir can get so hot that it might seem you could fry an egg on the rocks. Campers should be certain to have some kind of tarp they can set up as a sun screen. The lake is small and remote, and the use of motors on boats is prohibited. Most campers bring rafts or canoes, and there is a good swimming beach near the picnic area and campground.

Location: On Kerckhoff Reservoir near Madera; map F4, grid c3.

Campsites, facilities: There are five sites for tents or RVs. Picnic tables and fire grills are provided. Drinking water and vault toilets are available. Five group picnic sites are available. You can buy supplies in Auberry. Leashed pets are permitted.

Reservations, fees: No reservations; $10 per night, $3 per night for each extra vehicle, $7 per night for extra RV, $1 pet fee per night. Open year-round.

Directions: From Highway 99 in Madera, drive 19 miles east on Highway 145. Turn right (south) on County Road 206 to Friant. From Friant, drive 19 miles northeast on Millerton Road and Auberry Road to Auberry. From Auberry, drive 8.5 miles north on Powerhouse Road to the camp.

Directions: From Highway 168 in Clovis, drive 20 miles northeast to Auberry Road. Turn left and drive 2.8 miles to Powerhouse Road. Turn left and drive 8.4 miles to the camp.

Contact: PG&E Building and Land Services, tel. (916) 386-5164.

37 Squaw Leap Walk-In

    8

Not many folks know about this spot. It's a primitive setting, but it has some bonuses. For one thing, there's access to the San Joaquin River if you drive to the fishing access trailhead at the end of the road. From there, you get great views of the San Joaquin River Gorge. The camp is a trailhead for two excellent hiking and equestrian trails. Beautiful wildflower displays are available in the late winter and spring.

Location: On the San Joaquin River near Madera; map F4, grid d3.

Campsites, facilities: There are five family sites and two group sites for tents. All are walk-in sites. Fire grills and picnic tables are provided. Vault toilets and a hitching post are available. No drinking water is available. You can buy supplies in Auberry. Leashed pets are permitted.

Reservations, fees: No reservations; no fee. Open year-round.

Directions: From Highway 99 in Madera, drive 19 miles east on Highway 145. Go right on Road 206 to the town of Friant. From Friant, drive 19 miles northeast on Millerton/Auberry Road to Auberry. From Auberry, drive two miles north on Powerhouse Road. Turn left at the Squaw Leap Management Area sign at Smalley Road. Drive four miles to the campground on the right.

Contact: Bureau of Land Management, Bakersfield Field Office, tel. (661) 391-6000 or fax (661) 391-6040.

38 Millerton Lake State Recreation Area

    6

As the temperature gauge goes up in the summer, the value of Millerton Lake increases at the same rate. The lake is set at 578 feet in the foothills of the San Joaquin Valley, and the water is like gold here. The campground and recreation area are set on a peninsula along the north shore of the lake; there are sandy beach areas on both sides of the lake with boat ramps available near the campgrounds. It's a big lake, with 43 miles of shoreline, from a narrow lake inlet extending to an expansive main lake body. The irony at Millerton is that when the lake is filled to the brim, the beaches are covered, so ideal conditions are actually when the lake level is down a bit, typically from early summer on.

Location: Near Madera; map F4, grid d1.

Campsites, facilities: There are 138 sites for tents or RVs up to 31 feet long, with full hookups available at 26 sites, and two group sites for 45 to 75 people. Picnic tables and fire grills are provided. Drinking water, flush toilets, coin-operated showers, sanitary disposal station, and boat ramps are available. Some facilities are wheelchair accessible. You can buy supplies in Friant. Leashed pets are permitted.

Reservations, fees: From March 10 through September 10, reserve at tel. (800) 444-PARK (800-444-7275) or website: www.reserveamerica.com; $12 to $18 per night, $30 to $56 for group sites. Open year-round.

Directions: From Highway 99 in Madera, drive 22 miles east on Highway 145 (six miles past the intersection with Highway 41) to the campground on the right.

Contact: Millerton Lake State Recreation Area, tel. (559) 822-2332 or fax (559) 822-2319.

39 Camp Edison

      7

Camp Edison is the best camp at Shaver Lake, set on a peninsula along the lake's western shore, with a boat ramp nearby. The lake is at 5,370 feet in the Sierra, a pretty area that has become popular for its calm, warm days and cool water. Boat rentals and bait and tackle are available at the nearby marina.

Newcomers with youngsters will discover that the best area for swimming and playing in the water is on the east side of the lake. Though more distant, this part of the lake offers sandy beaches rather than rocky drop-offs.

Location: On Shaver Lake; map F4, grid d6.

Campsites, facilities: There are 252 sites for tents or RVs, 43 with full hookups. Picnic tables, fire rings, and barbecues are provided. Restrooms, drinking water, flush toilets, cable TV, electrical connections, coin showers, sanitary disposal station, coin laundry, marina, boat ramp, and horseback riding facilities are available. In winter, a minimum of 25 sites are kept open. Some facilities are wheelchair accessible. Leashed pets are permitted.

Reservations, fees: Reservations are accepted; $18 to $35 per night, $4 per night for each extra vehicle with a maximum of eight people per site, $4 per night for a boat, $3 pet fee per night. Open year-round with limited winter services.

Directions: From the town of Shaver Lake, drive a mile north on Highway 168 to the campground entrance road.

Contact: Camp Edison, tel. (559) 841-3134 or fax (559) 841-3193; website: www.campedison.com.

40 Dorabelle

      7

This is one of the few Forest Service camps in the state that is set up more for RVers than for tenters. Shaver Lake is a popular lake for vacationers, and it is well stocked with trout during the summer. Boat rentals and bait and tackle are available at the nearby marina. This is also a popular snow-play area in the winter. The elevation is 5,400 feet.

Location: On Shaver Lake in Sierra National Forest; map F4, grid d6.

Campsites, facilities: There are 68 sites for tents or RVs up to 30 feet long. Picnic tables and fire grills are provided. Drinking water and vault toilets are available. A grocery store is nearby. Leashed pets are permitted.

Reservations, fees: Reserve at tel. (877) 444-6777 ($8.65 reservation fee) or website:

www.reserveusa.com; $14 per night, $5 per night for each extra vehicle. Open May through September.

Directions: From Highway 168 south of the town of Shaver Lake, turn east onto County Road N257/Dorabelle Road and drive a half mile to the campground.

Contact: Sierra National Forest, Pineridge Ranger District, tel. (559) 855-5360 or fax (559) 855-5375.

41 Swanson Meadow

   4

This is the smallest and most primitive of the camps near Shaver Lake; it is used primarily as an overflow area if lakeside camps are full. It is about two miles from Shaver Lake at an elevation of 5,600 feet.

Location: Near Shaver Lake in Sierra National Forest; map F4, grid d6.

Campsites, facilities: There are 12 sites for tents or RVs up to 22 feet long. Picnic tables and fire grills are provided. Vault toilets are available. No drinking water is available. A grocery store is nearby. Leashed pets are permitted.

Reservations, fees: No reservations; $10 per night, $5 per night for each extra vehicle. Open May through October.

Directions: From Highway 168 just south of the town of Shaver Lake, drive three miles east on Dinkey Creek Road to the campground.

Contact: Sierra National Forest, Pineridge Ranger District, tel. (559) 855-5360 or fax (559) 855-5375.

42 Dinkey Creek

     7

This is a huge Forest Service camp set along Dinkey Creek at 5,700 feet. It is a popular camp for anglers who take the trail and hike upstream along the creek for small-trout fishing in a pristine setting. Backpackers occasionally lay over here before driving on to the Dinkey

Lakes Parking Area, for hikes to Mystery Lake, Swede Lake, South Lake, and others in the nearby Dinkey Lakes Wilderness.

Location: In Sierra National Forest; map F4, grid e8.

Campsites, facilities: There are 128 sites for tents or RVs up to 30 feet long. Picnic tables and fire grills are provided. Drinking water, flush toilets, showers, and horseback riding facilities are available nearby. You can buy supplies in Dinkey Creek. Leashed pets are permitted.

Reservations, fees: From Memorial Day through Labor Day, reserve at tel. (877) 444-6777 ($8.65 reservation fee) or website: www.reserveusa.com; $14 per night; 14-day stay limit. Open from May through September.

Directions: From Highway 168 just south of the town of Shaver Lake, turn east on Dinkey Creek Road and drive 14 miles to the campground.

Contact: Sierra National Forest, Kings River Ranger District, tel. (559) 855-5360 or fax (559) 855-5375.

43 Trapper Springs

  8

Courtright Reservoir is a great destination, with excellent camping, boating, fishing, and hiking into the nearby John Muir Wilderness. The lake is set at an elevation of 8,200 feet, with a 15-mph speed limit making the lake ideal for fishing, canoeing, and rafting. This camp is on the west side of the lake. A trailhead a mile north of camp by car heads around the north end of the lake to a fork; to the left is routed into the Dinkey Lakes Wilderness, and to the right is routed to the head of the lake, then follows Dusy Creek in a long climb into spectacular country in the John Muir Wilderness.

Location: On Courtright Reservoir in Sierra National Forest; map F4, grid e9.

Campsites, facilities: There are 75 sites for tents or RVs up to 22 feet long. Picnic tables and fire grills are provided. Drinking water and vault toilets are available. A boat ramp is nearby. Some facilities are wheelchair accessible. Leashed pets are permitted.

Reservations, fees: No reservations; $15 per night, $3 per night for each extra vehicle, $1 pet fee. Open June through September.

Directions: From Highway 168 just south of the town of Shaver Lake, turn east onto Dinkey Creek Road and drive 12 miles. Turn right on McKinley Grove Road and drive 14 miles. Turn north onto Courtright Road and drive 12 miles to the campground.

Contact: Sierra National Forest, Kings River Ranger District, tel. (559) 855-5360 or fax (559) 855-5375.

44 Marmot Rock Walk-In

 8

Courtright Reservoir is in the high country at 8,200 feet. Marmot Rock Walk-In is set at the southern end of the lake, with a boat ramp nearby. This is a pretty Sierra lake that provides options for boaters and hikers. Trout fishing can also be good here. Boaters must observe a 15-mph speed limit, which makes for quiet water.

Location: On Courtright Reservoir in Sierra National Forest; map F4, grid e9.

Campsites, facilities: There are 14 walk-in sites for tents only. Picnic tables and fire grills are provided. Vault toilets are available. No drinking water is available, but water is available three miles away at Trapper Springs Campground. A boat ramp is available nearby. Leashed pets are permitted.

Reservations, fees: No reservations; $15 per night, $3 per night for each extra vehicle, $1 pet fee. Open June through September.

Directions: From Highway 168 just south of the town of Shaver Lake, turn east onto Dinkey Creek Road and drive 12 miles. Turn right (east) on McKinley Grove Road and drive 14 miles. Turn north on Courtright Reservoir Road and drive 10 miles to the campground on the south shore.

Contact: Sierra National Forest, Kings River Ranger District, tel. (559) 855-5360, or fax (559) 855-5375; PG&E Building and Land Services, tel. (916) 386-5164 or fax (916) 386-5388;

45 Gigantea

    7

This primitive campground is set along Dinkey Creek adjacent to the McKinley Grove Botanical Area, which features a little-known grove of giant sequoias. The campground is set on a short loop spur road, and day visitors are better off stopping at the McKinley Grove Picnic Area. The elevation is 6,500 feet.

Location: On Dinkey Creek in Sierra National Forest; map F4, grid e8.

Campsites, facilities: There are 10 sites for tents or RVs up to 16 feet long. Picnic tables and fire grills are provided. Vault toilets are available. No drinking water is available. You can buy supplies in Dinkey Creek. Leashed pets are permitted.

Reservations, fees: No reservations; $10 per night. Open June through September.

Directions: From Highway 168 just south of Shaver Lake, turn east on Dinkey Creek Road and drive about 12 miles. Turn right on McKinley Grove Road and drive six miles to the campground.

Contact: Sierra National Forest, Kings River Ranger District, tel. (559) 855-5360, or fax (559) 855-5375.

46 Buck Meadow

    7

This is one of the three little-known, primitive camps in the area. It's set at 6,800 feet along Deer Creek, about seven miles from Wishon Reservoir, a more popular destination.

Location: On Deer Creek in Sierra National Forest; map F4, grid f8.

Campsites, facilities: There are five sites for tents only and five sites for tents or RVs up to 22 feet long. Picnic tables and fire grills are provided. Vault toilets are available. No drink-

ing water is available. Leashed pets are permitted.

Reservations, fees: No reservations; $13 per night. Open June through September.

Directions: From Highway 168 just south of Shaver Lake, turn east on Dinkey Creek Road and drive about 12 miles. Turn right on McKinley Grove Road and drive eight miles to the campground.

Contact: Sierra National Forest, Kings River Ranger District, tel. (559) 855-5360, or fax (559) 855-5375.

47 Upper Kings River Group Camp

    8

Wishon Reservoir is a great place for a camping trip. When the lake is full, which is not often enough, the place has great natural beauty, set at 6,500 feet and surrounded by national forest. The fishing is fair enough on summer evenings, and a 15-mph speed limit keeps the lake quiet. A side trip option is hiking from the trailhead at Woodchuck Creek, which within the span of a one-day hike takes you into the John Muir Wilderness and past three lakes— Woodchuck, Chimney, and Marsh.

Location: On Wishon Reservoir; map F4, grid f9.

Campsites, facilities: There is a group site that will accommodate up to 50 people. Picnic tables and fire grills are provided. Drinking water and vault toilets are available. Leashed pets are permitted.

Reservations, fees: Reservations are required; $125 per night with a two-night minimum, $1 pet fee per night. Open May through October, weather permitting.

Directions: On Highway 168 just south of the town of Shaver Lake, turn east on Dinkey Creek Road and drive 12 miles. Turn right on McKinley Grove Road and continue to the Wishon Dam. The campground is near the base of the dam.

Contact: Sierra National Forest, Kings River Ranger District, tel. (559) 855-5360, or fax (559)

855-5375. PG&E Building and Land Services, tel. (916) 386-5164 or fax (916) 386-5388.

Lily Pad

      7

This is the smallest of the three camps at Wishon Reservoir. It is set along the southwest shore at 6,500 feet, about a mile from both the lake and a good boat ramp. A 15-mph speed limit ensures quiet water, making this an ideal destination for families with canoes or a raft.

Location: Near Wishon Reservoir in Sierra National Forest; map F4, grid f9.

Campsites, facilities: There are six sites for tents only and 10 sites for tents or RVs up to 16 feet long. Picnic tables and fire grills are provided. Drinking water and vault toilets are available. Groceries, boat rentals, boat ramp, and propane gas are available nearby. Some facilities are wheelchair accessible. There is also a group campsite nearby called Upper Kings River for up to 50 people. Leashed pets are permitted.

Reservations, fees: No reservations for single sites; $15 per night, $3 per night for each extra vehicle, $1 pet fee. Open May through October, weather permitting.

Directions: From Highway 168 south of the town of Shaver Lake, turn east on Dinkey Creek Road and drive 12 miles. Turn right (east) on McKinley Grove Road and drive 16 miles to the campground.

Contact: Sierra National Forest, Kings River Ranger District, tel. (559) 855-5360 or fax (559) 855-5375; PG&E Land Services at (916) 386-5164.

49 Wishon Village

      7

This privately operated mountain park is set on the North Fork of the Kings River near the shore of Wishon Reservoir. Trout stocks often make for good fishing in early summer, and anglers with boats love the 15-mph speed limit

which keeps personal watercraft off the water. Backpackers and hikers can find a great trailhead at the south end of the lake at Coolidge Meadow, where a trail awaits that is routed to the Woodchuck Creek drainage and numerous lakes in the John Muir Wilderness. The elevation is 6,500 feet.

Location: Near Wishon Reservoir; map F4, grid e9.

Campsites, facilities: There are 26 sites for tents only and 96 RV sites with full hookups. Picnic tables and fire pits are provided. Restrooms, drinking water, showers, electrical connections, and sewer hookups are available. Coin laundry, country store, ice, boat ramp, motorboat rentals, bait and tackle, and propane gas are available nearby. Leashed pets are permitted.

Reservations, fees: Reservations are recommended; $14 to $23 per night for two people, $2 for each additional person up to a six-camper limit per site. Open May through October.

Directions: From Highway 168 just south of the town of Shaver Lake, turn east onto Dinkey Creek Road and drive 12 miles. Turn right on McKinley Grove Road and drive about 15 miles to 66500 McKinley Grove Road.

Contact: Wishon Village, tel. (559) 865-5361, or fax (559) 865-2000; website: www.wishonvillage.com.

50 Black Rock

   7

Little Black Rock Reservoir is a little-known spot that can provide a quiet respite compared to the other big-time lakes and camps in the region. The camp is set near the outlet stream on the west end of the lake, created from a small dam on the North Fork Kings River at 4,200 feet elevation.

Location: On Black Rock Reservoir in Sierra National Forest; map F4, grid f9.

Campsites, facilities: There are seven sites for tents only and a trailer site. Picnic tables and fire grills are provided. Drinking water and vault toilets are available. Garbage must be packed out. Leashed pets are permitted.

Reservations, fees: No reservations; $10 per night. Open May through September.

Directions: From Trimmer, drive east on Trimmer Springs Road for about 20 miles. Turn northwest onto Black Road and drive 10 miles to the campground.

Contact: Sierra National Forest, Kings River Ranger District, tel. (559) 855-5360 or fax (559) 855-5375.

51 Kirch Flat

 6

Kirch Flat is on the Kings River, about five miles from the head of Pine Flat Lake. This campground is a popular take-out spot for rafters running the Middle Kings, putting in at Garnet Dike dispersed camping area and then making the 10-mile run downstream to Kirch Flat, a Class III run. The camp is set in the foothill country at 1,100 feet in elevation, where the temperatures are often hot and the water cold.

Location: On the Kings River in Sierra National Forest; map F4, grid f7.

Campsites, facilities: There are 17 sites for tents or RVs up to 22 feet long and a group camp that will accommodate up to 50 people. Picnic tables and fire grills are provided. Vault toilets are available. No drinking water is available. Leashed pets are permitted.

Reservations, fees: No reservations, no fee for family camping. To reserve the group site, call the Trimmer Ranger Station, tel. (209) 855-8321; group camp fee is $25 per night, with a 50-person maximum. Open year-round.

Directions: From Trimmer, drive 18 miles east on Trimmer Springs Road to the campground entrance.

Contact: Sierra National Forest, Kings River Ranger District, tel. (559) 855-5360 or fax (559) 855-5375.

52 Pine Flat Recreation Area

  7

This is a county park that is open all year, set below the dam of Pine Flat Lake, actually not on the lake at all. As a county park campground, it is often overlooked by out-of-towners.

Location: On Pine Flat Lake; map F4, grid g5.

Campsites, facilities: There are 52 sites for tents or RVs. Drinking water, fire grills, and picnic tables are provided. Flush toilets, sanitary disposal station, playground, and a wheelchair-accessible fishing area are available. A grocery store, coin laundry, and propane gas are nearby (within a mile). Leashed pets are permitted.

Reservations, fees: No reservations; $11 per night. Open year-round.

Directions: From Fresno, take Belmont Avenue east; it will merge with Trimmer Springs Road. Continue on Belmont/Trimmer Springs to Pine Flat Road. Turn right on Pine Flat Road and drive three miles to the signed campground entrance on the right.

Contact: Fresno County Parks Department, tel. (559) 488-3004, or fax (559) 488-1988.

53 Island Park & Deer Creek Point Group

 7

These are two of four Army Corp of Engineer campgrounds available at Pine Flat Lake, a popular lake set in the foothill country east of Fresno. When Pine Flat Lake is full, or close to full, it is very pretty, set in the foothills east of Fresno at 961 feet elevation. The lake is 21 miles long with 67 miles of shoreline and 4,270 surface acres. Right: a big lake with unlimited potential. Because the temperatures get warm in spring here, then smoking hot in summer, the lake is like Valhalla for boating and water sports. The fishing for white bass is often excellent in late winter and early spring and, after that, conditions are ideal for water sports. The elevation is 1,000 feet.

Location: On Pine Flat Lake; map F4, grid g5.

Campsites, facilities: There are 52 designated sites for tents or RVs and 60 overflow sites (at Island Park), and two group sites for 50 people each for tents or RVs. Picnic tables and fire grills are provided. Restrooms, drinking water, flush toilets, coin showers, pay telephone, boat ramp, fish-cleaning station, and sanitary disposal station are available. Some facilities are wheelchair accessible. There is a seasonal store at the campground entrance. Boat rentals are available within five miles. Leashed pets are permitted.

Reservations, fees: Reservations for Island Park available at tel. (877) 444-6777 ($8.65 reservation fee) or website: www.reserve usa.com.; reservations for group sites required at tel. (559) 787-2589; $10 to $16 per night, $60 for group sites, $2 boat launch fee. Open year-round.

Directions: From Fresno, take Belmont Avenue east. Belmont Avenue will merge into Trimmer Springs Road. Continue on Belmont/Trimmer Springs approximately eight miles past the community of Piedra. Look for the Island Park sign on the right. Turn right at the sign and continue about a quarter mile to the signed park entrance.

Contact: U.S. Army Corps of Engineers, Sacramento District, Pine Flat Field Office, tel. (559) 787-2589 or fax (559) 787-2773.

54 Lakeridge Camping and Boating Resort

 7

Pine Flat Lake is a big lake with seemingly unlimited recreation potential. It is in the foothills east of Fresno at 961 feet elevation, covering 4,270 surface acres with 67 miles of shoreline. The lake's proximity to Fresno has made it a top destination for boating and water sports. Fishing for white bass can also be excellent in the spring and early summer.

Note: The one downer is that there are only a few sandy beaches.

Location: On Pine Flat Lake; map F4, grid g5.

Campsites, facilities: There are 108 sites for tents or RVs up to 32 feet long. Picnic tables, restrooms, showers, modem hookups, coin laundry, convenience store, ice, pay phone, petting zoo, and houseboat rentals are available.

Reservations, fees: Reservations are recommended at tel. (877) 787-2260; $20 per night for tent sites and $25 per night for RV sites with hookups (for two people), $2.50 per person for more than two people, $2.50 per day for pets. Major credit cards accepted.

Directions: From Fresno, drive east on Belmont Avenue (it will merge with Trimmer Springs Road). Continue on Trimmer Springs Road to Sunnyslope Road. Drive southeast on Sunnyslope Road to the resort at 30547 Sunnyslope Road.

Contact: Lakeridge Camping and Boating Resort, P.O. Box 250, Piedra, CA 93649; tel. or fax (559) 787-2260.

55 Camp 4 1/2

 7

We found five sites here, not "four and a half." This campground is small, primitive, and usually hot. It is one in a series of camps just east of Pine Flat Lake along the Kings River, primarily used for rafting access. See the entries for Kirch Flat and Mill Flat for more information.

Location: On the Kings River in Sequoia National Forest; map F4, grid g8.

Campsites, facilities: There are five sites for tents only. Picnic tables and fire grills are provided. Vault toilets are available. No drinking water is available. Garbage must be packed out. Leashed pets are permitted.

Reservations, fees: No reservations; no fee. Open year-round.

Directions: From Trimmer, drive about 17 miles east on Trimmer Springs Road/ Forest Road 11S12. Cross the river and drive a mile along the south side of the Kings River on Forest Road 12S01. At the junction with the second bridge, turn right onto a dirt road (Forest Road 12S01) and drive about 0.7 of a mile to the campground. Trailers are not recommended.

Contact: Sequoia National Forest, Hume Lake Ranger District, tel. (559) 338-2251 or fax (559) 338-2131.

56 Camp 4

    7

This is one in a series of camps set on the Kings River upstream from Pine Flat Lake, a popular access point for rafters. The weather gets so hot that many take a dunk in the river on purpose; nonrafters better bring a cooler stocked with ice and drinks. See the entry for Mill Flat for information on a great hike to Garlic Falls.

Location: On the Kings River in Sequoia National Forest; map F4, grid g8.

Campsites, facilities: There are five sites for tents only. Picnic tables and fire grills are provided. Vault toilets are available. No drinking water is available. Garbage must be packed out. Leashed pets are permitted.

Reservations, fees: No reservations; no fee. Open year-round.

Directions: From Trimmer, drive about 17 miles east on Trimmer Springs Road/Forest Road 11S12. Cross the river and drive a mile along the south side of the Kings River on Forest Road 12S01. At the junction with the second bridge, turn right onto a dirt road/Forest Road 12S01 and drive about 1.5 miles to the campground on the south side of the river. Camp 4 is a mile from Mill Flat. Trailers are not recommended.

Contact: Sequoia National Forest, Hume Lake Ranger District, tel. (559) 338-2251 or fax (559) 338-2131.

57 Mill Flat

    7

This camp is on the Kings River at the confluence of Mill Flat Creek. It's a small, primitive spot that gets very hot in the summer. Rafters sometimes use this as an access point for trips down the Kings River. A side trip from this camp is driving east on the Forest Service access road for five miles to its end point at the Kings River National Recreational Trail, then making the challenging seven-mile hike to the overlook of spectacular Garlic Falls. Try it in the spring, when temperatures are still cool and snowmelt from the high country is underway.

Location: On the Kings River in Sequoia National Forest; map F4, grid g8.

Campsites, facilities: There are five sites for tents only. Picnic tables and fire grills are provided. Vault toilets are available. No drinking water is available. Garbage must be packed out. Leashed pets are permitted.

Reservations, fees: No reservations; no fee. Open year-round.

Directions: From Trimmer, drive about 17 miles east on Trimmer Springs Road/Forest Road 11S12. Cross the river and drive a mile along the south side of the Kings River on Forest Road 11S12, parallel to the Keller Ranch. At the junction with the second bridge, turn right onto a dirt road (Forest Road 12S01) and drive about 2.5 miles to the campground on the south side of the river. Trailers are not recommended.

Contact: Sequoia National Forest, Hume Lake Ranger District, tel. (559) 338-2251 or fax (559) 338-2131.

58 Princess

    7

This mountain camp is at 5,900 feet. It is popular because of its proximity to both Hume Lake and the star attractions at Kings Canyon National Park. Hume Lake is just four miles from the camp and the Grant Grove entrance to Kings Canyon National Park is only six miles away to the south, while continuing on Highway 180 to the east will take you into the heart of Kings Canyon.

Location: On Princess Meadow in Giant Sequoia National Monument; map F4, grid h9.

Campsites, facilities: There are 50 tent sites and 40 sites for tents or RVs up to 22 feet long. Picnic tables and fire grills are provided. Drinking water and vault toilets are available. A grocery store is nearby in Hume Lake (four miles away). Leashed pets are permitted.

Reservations, fees: Reserve via phone at tel. (877) 444-6777 ($8.65 reservation fee) or website: www.reserveusa.com; $12 for a single site per night, $14 for a double site, $5 per night for each extra vehicle. Open May through September.

Directions: From Fresno, drive east on Highway 180 for about 60 miles to the fork of Highway 180 north. Bear left and drive six miles on Highway 180 north to the campground on the right.

Contact: Sequoia National Forest, Hume Lake Ranger District, tel. (559) 338-2251 or fax (559) 338-2131.

59 Sunset

7

This is the biggest of the camps that are just inside the Kings Canyon National Park boundaries at Grant Grove Village, 6,600 feet in elevation. The nearby General Grant Grove of Giant Sequoias is the main attraction, with many short, easy walks among the sequoias, each breathtakingly beautiful. They include the Big Stump Trail, Sunset Trail, North Grove Loop, General Grant Tree, Manzanita and Azalea Loop, and Panoramic Point and Park Ridge Trail. Seeing the General Grant Tree is a rite of passage for newcomers; after a half-hour walk you arrive at a sequoia that is 1,800 years old, 107 feet in circumference, and 267 feet tall.

Location: In Kings Canyon National Park; map F4, grid h9.

Campsites, facilities: There are 200 sites for tents or RVs up to 30 feet long. Picnic tables and fire grills are provided. Drinking water, flush toilets, and horseback riding facilities are available. Some facilities are wheelchair accessible. In the summer, evening ranger programs are often available. A grocery store

is nearby. Showers are available in Grant Grove Village. Leashed pets are permitted, except on trails.

Reservations, fees: No reservations; $14 per night, $10 per vehicle park entrance fee. Open late May to mid-September.

Directions: From Grant Grove Village in Kings Canyon National Park, drive a half mile north on Highway 180 to the campground entrance.

Contact: Kings Canyon National Park, tel. (559) 565-3341.

60 Azalea

7

This camp is tucked just inside the western border of Kings Canyon National Park. It is set at 6,600 feet near the General Grant Grove of giant sequoias. For information on several short, spectacular hikes among the giant sequoias, see the entry for Sunset. Nearby Sequoia Lake is privately owned; no fishing, no swimming, no trespassing. To see the spectacular Kings Canyon, one of the deepest gorges in North America, reenter the park on Highway 180.

Location: In Kings Canyon National Park; map F4, grid h9.

Campsites, facilities: There are 113 sites for tents or RVs up to 30 feet long. Picnic tables and fire grills are provided. Drinking water, flush toilets, sanitary disposal station, and horseback riding facilities are available. Evening ranger programs are often available in the summer. Some facilities are wheelchair accessible. A grocery store is nearby. Showers are available in Grant Grove Village. Leashed pets are permitted, except on trails.

Reservations, fees: No reservations; $14 per night, $10 per vehicle park entrance fee. Open year-round.

Directions: From the Kings Canyon National Park, entrance drive 3.3 miles north on Highway 180 to the campground.

Contact: Kings Canyon National Park, tel. (559) 565-3341.

61 Crystal Springs

    5

Directly to the south of this camp is the General Grant Grove and its giant sequoias. But continuing on Highway 180 provides access to the interior of Kings Canyon National Park, and this camp makes an ideal jump-off point. From here you can drive east, passing Cedar Grove, cruising along the Kings River, and finally coming to a dead-end loop, taking in the drop-dead gorgeous landscape of one of the deepest gorges in North America. One of the best hikes, but also the most demanding, is the 13-mile round-trip to Lookout Peak, out of the Cedar Grove area of Highway 180. It involves a 4,000-foot climb to 8,531 feet, and with it, a breathtaking view of Sierra ridges, Cedar Grove far below, and Kings Canyon.

Location: In Kings Canyon National Park; map F4, grid h9.

Campsites, facilities: There are 67 sites for tents or RVs up to 22 feet long. Picnic tables and fire grills are provided. Drinking water, flush toilets, sanitary disposal station, and horseback riding facilities are available. Evening ranger programs are often available in the summer. Some facilities are wheelchair accessible. A grocery store is nearby. Showers are available in Grant Grove Village. Leashed pets are permitted, except on trails.

Reservations, fees: No reservations; $14 per night, $10 per vehicle park entrance fee. Open mid-May to late September.

Directions: From Grant Grove Village in Kings Canyon National Park, drive three-quarters of a mile north on Highway 180 to the campground.

Contact: Kings Canyon National Park, tel. (559) 565-3341.

62 Sierra Lake Campground

      7

This secluded, privately managed, 106-acre park offers a 10-acre lake stocked with trout. The park is about a 30-minute drive from Kings Canyon and Sequoia National Parks and has three restaurants within three miles of the camp.

Location: Near Visalia; map F4, grid i8.

Campsites, facilities: There are 10 sites for tents only and 25 RV sites, 12 with full hookups. Picnic tables and fire grills are provided. Restrooms, drinking water, flush toilets, showers, electrical connections, a laundry room, store, sanitary disposal station, and a full-service restaurant are available. Some facilities are wheelchair accessible. Leashed pets are permitted.

Reservations, fees: Reservations are recommended; $12 to $22 per night, $1 pet fee. Open April through October.

Directions: From Highway 99, drive east on Highway 198 through Visalia to the town of Lemon Cove. Turn left on Highway 216 and go a half mile. Turn right (north) on Dry Creek Road and drive 16 miles to Mountain Road 453/Stagecoach Drive. Turn right and drive 1.5 miles to the campground on the right.

Contact: Sierra Lake Campground, 49320 Stagecoach Drive, Badger, CA 93603; tel. (559) 337-2520; website: www.rvcampingcalifornia.com.

63 Eshom Creek

    7

The campground at Eshom Creek is just two miles outside the boundaries of Sequoia National Park, an ideal alternative to the camps in the park. It is set along Eshom Creek, at an elevation of 4,800 feet. Most Eshom Creek campers head straight into the national park, with a trailhead at Redwood Saddle (just inside the park boundary) providing a route to see the Redwood Mountain Grove, Fallen Goliath, Hart Tree, and Hart Meadow in a sensational loop hike.

Location: On Eshom Creek in Giant Sequoia National Monument; map F4, grid i8.

Campsites, facilities: There are 17 sites for tents or RVs up to 22 feet long and seven multi-family units. Picnic tables and fire grills

are provided. Drinking water and vault toilets are available. Leashed pets are permitted.
Reservations, fees: No reservations; $10 to $16 per night. Open May through September.
Directions: From Highway 99, drive east on Highway 198 through Visalia to Highway 245. Turn left (north) on Highway 245 and drive to Badger. From Badger drive eight miles northeast on County Road 465 to the campground.
Contact: Sequoia National Forest, Hume Lake Ranger District, tel. (559) 338-2251 or fax (559) 338-2131.

THE MUIR HUT
AT MUIR PASS
(11,965 FEET)
PROTECTS HIKERS
FROM LIGHTNING BOLTS.

MAP F5

CHAPTER F5

(CONTINUED ON NEXT PAGE)

1 McGee Creek RV Park

 6

This is a popular layover spot for folks visiting giant Crowley Lake. Crowley Lake is still one of the better lakes in the Sierra for trout fishing, with good prospects for large rainbow trout and brown trout, though the 20-pound brown trout that once made this lake famous are now mainly a legend. Beautiful Convict Lake provides a nearby side trip option. The elevation is 7,000 feet.

Location: Near Crowley Lake; map F5, grid a3.

Campsites, facilities: There are 30 sites for tents or RVs, many with partial or full hookups. Picnic tables and fire pits are provided. Restrooms, drinking water, showers, and flush toilets are available. Leashed pets are permitted.

Reservations, fees: Reservations are accepted; $13.50 to $16.50 per night. Open late April through mid-October.

Directions: From the junction of U.S. 395 and Highway 203 (the Mammoth Lakes turnoff), drive south on U.S. 395 for nine miles to the turnoff for McGee Creek Road. Take that exit and you'll see the park entrance on the left.

Contact: McGee Creek RV Park, tel. (760) 935-4233.

2 Tuff

 5

Easy access off U.S. 395 makes this camp a winner, though it is not nearly as pretty as those up Rock Creek Road to the west of Tom's Place. The fact that you can get in and out of here quickly makes it ideal for campers planning fishing trips to nearby Crowley Lake. The elevation is 7,000 feet.

Location: Near Crowley Lake in Inyo National Forest; map F5, grid a4.

Campsites, facilities: There are 15 sites for tents only and 19 sites for tents or RVs up to 22 feet long. Picnic tables and fire grills are provided. Drinking water and flush toilets are available. Leashed pets are permitted.

Reservations, fees: Reserve at (877) 444-6777 ($8.65 reservation fee) or website: www.reserveusa.com; $12 per night. Open late April through mid-October.

Directions: From the junction of U.S. 395 and Highway 203 (the Mammoth Lakes turnoff), drive 15.5 miles south on U.S. 395 (one mile north of Tom's Place) to Rock Creek Road. Turn left on Rock Creek Road and drive one mile to the campground.

Contact: Inyo National Forest, White Mountain Ranger District, tel. (760) 873-2500 or fax (760) 873-2563.

❸ McGee Creek

      7

This is a Forest Service camp at elevation 7,600 feet set along little McGee Creek, a good location for fishing and hiking. The stream is stocked with trout, and a trailhead is available just up the road. From here you can hike along upper McGee Creek and into the John Muir Wilderness.

Location: In Inyo National Forest; map F5, grid a3.

Campsites, facilities: There are 28 sites for tents or RVs up to 22 feet long. Picnic tables and fire grills are provided. Drinking water and flush toilets are available. Some facilities are wheelchair accessible. Leashed pets are permitted.

Reservations, fees: Reserve at (877) 444-6777 ($8.65 reservation fee) or website: www.reserveusa.com; $12 per night. Open May through September.

Directions: From the junction of U.S. 395 and Highway 203 (the Mammoth Lakes turn off), drive south on U.S. 395 for 6.5 miles to the turnoff for the frontage road that runs parallel to the west side of U.S. 395. Continue south on that road for about two miles to McGee Creek Road. Turn right (southwest) and drive 1.5 miles to the campground.

Contact: Inyo National Forest, White Mountain Ranger District, tel. (760) 873-2500 or fax (760) 873-2563.

❹ Crowley Lake

      5

This large BLM camp is across U.S. 395 from the south shore of Crowley Lake. Crowley is the trout-fishing capital of the eastern Sierra, with the annual opener (the last Saturday in April) a great celebration. Though the trout fishing can go through a lull in midsummer, it can become excellent again in the fall when the lake's population of big brown trout heads up to the top of the lake and the mouth of the

Owens River. The surroundings are fairly stark; the elevation is 6,800 feet.

Location: Near Crowley Lake; map F5, grid a4.

Campsites, facilities: There are 47 sites for tents or RVs. Picnic tables and fire grills are provided. Vault toilets are available. No drinking water is available. A grocery store and boat ramp are nearby on Crowley Lake. Leashed pets are permitted.

Reservations, fees: No reservations; no fee. Open late April through October, weather permitting.

Directions: From Bishop, drive north on U.S. 395 for 21 miles to the Crowley Lake Road exit. Turn left on Crowley Lake Road and drive northwest for 5.5 miles (past Tom's Place) to the campground entrance on the left (well signed).

Contact: Bureau of Land Management, Bishop Field Office, tel. (760) 872-4881 or fax (760) 872-2894.

❺ French Camp

    5

French Camp is just a short hop from U.S. 395 and Tom's Place, right where the high Sierra turns into high plateau country. Side trip opportunities include boating and fishing on giant Crowley Lake and, to the west on Rock Creek Road, visiting little Rock Creek Lake 10 miles away. The elevation is 7,500 feet.

Location: On Rock Creek near Crowley Lake in Inyo National Forest; map F5, grid a4.

Campsites, facilities: There are six sites for tents only and 80 sites for tents or RVs up to 22 feet long. Picnic tables and fire grills are provided. Drinking water, flush toilets, and a sanitary disposal station are available. You can buy groceries nearby. Leashed pets are permitted.

Reservations, fees: Reservations are accepted for sites 1-30 and 73-86; reserve at (877) 444-6777 ($8.65 reservation fee) or website: www.reserveusa.com; $12 per night. Open late April through October.

Directions: From the junction of U.S. 395 and Highway 203 (the Mammoth Lakes turnoff), drive 15 miles south on U.S. 395 to Tom's Place. Turn south on Rock Creek Road and drive a quarter mile to the campground on the right.

Contact: Inyo National Forest, White Mountain Ranger District, tel. (760) 873-2500 or fax (760) 873-2563.

6 Holiday

      5

During peak weekends, this campground is used as an overflow area. It is near Rock Creek, not far from Crowley Lake. The elevation is 7,500 feet, with surroundings far more stark than the camps to the west on Rock Creek Road.

Location: Near Crowley Lake in Inyo National Forest; map F5, grid a4.

Campsites, facilities: There are 35 sites for tents or RVs up to 22 feet long. Picnic tables and fire grills are provided. Drinking water and flush toilets are available. You can buy groceries nearby. Leashed pets are permitted.

Reservations, fees: No reservations; $12 per night. Opened as necessary.

Directions: From the junction of U.S. 395 and Highway 203 (the Mammoth Lakes turnoff), drive 15 miles south on U.S. 395 to Tom's Place. Turn south on Rock Creek Road and drive a half mile to the campground on the left.

Contact: Inyo National Forest, White Mountain Ranger District, tel. (760) 873-2500 or fax (760) 873-2563.

7 Iris Meadow

     5

Iris Meadow, at 8,600 feet elevation on the flank of Red Mountain (11,472 feet), is the first in a series of five Forest Service camps set near Rock Creek Canyon on the road leading from Tom's Place up to pretty Rock Creek Lake. Rock Creek is stocked with trout, and nearby Rock Creek Lake also provides fishing and boating for hand-launched boats. This camp also has access to a great trailhead for wilderness exploration.

Location: Near Crowley Lake in Inyo National Forest; map F5, grid a4.

Campsites, facilities: There are 14 sites for tents or RVs up to 22 feet long. Picnic tables and fire grills are provided. Drinking water and flush toilets are available. You can buy supplies in Tom's Place, three miles away. Leashed pets are permitted.

Reservations, fees: No reservations; $12 per night. Open late June through early September.

Directions: From the junction of U.S. 395 and Highway 203 (the Mammoth Lakes turnoff), drive 15 miles south on U.S. 395 to Tom's Place. Turn south on Rock Creek Road and drive three miles to the campground.

Contact: Inyo National Forest, White Mountain Ranger District, tel. (760) 873-2500 or fax (760) 873-2563.

8 Aspen Group Camp

    7

This small group campground set on Rock Creek is used primarily as a base camp for anglers and campers heading to nearby Crowley Lake or venturing west to Rock Creek Lake. The elevation at the camp is 8,100 feet.

Location: Near Crowley Lake in Inyo National Forest; map F5, grid a4.

Campsites, facilities: There is one group camp for tents or RVs up to 16 feet long. Picnic tables and fire grills are provided. Drinking water and flush toilets are available. You can buy supplies in Tom's Place, three miles away. Leashed pets are permitted.

Reservations, fees: Reserve Reserve at (877) 444-6777 ($8.65 reservation fee) or website: www.reserveusa.com; $40 group fee per night. Open mid-May through mid-October.

Directions: From the junction of U.S. 395 and Highway 203 (the Mammoth Lakes turnoff), drive 15 miles south on U.S. 395 to Tom's Place. Turn south on Rock Creek Road and drive three miles to the campground.

Contact: Inyo National Forest, White Mountain Ranger District, tel. (760) 873-2500 or fax (760) 873-2563.

9 Big Meadow

 7

This is a smaller, quieter camp in the series of campgrounds along Rock Creek. Giant Crowley Lake and tiny Rock Creek Lake provide nearby side trips. The elevation is 8,600 feet.

Location: Near Crowley Lake in Inyo National Forest; map F5, grid a4.

Campsites, facilities: There are five sites for tents only and six sites for tents or RVs up to 22 feet long. Picnic tables and fire grills are provided. Drinking water and flush toilets are available. You can buy supplies in Tom's Place, four miles away. Leashed pets are permitted.

Reservations, fees: No reservations; $12 per night. Open late June through early September.

Directions: From the junction of U.S. 395 and Highway 203 (the Mammoth Lakes turnoff), drive 15 miles south on U.S. 395 to Tom's Place. Turn south on Rock Creek Road and drive four miles to the campground.

Contact: Inyo National Forest, White Mountain Ranger District, tel. (760) 873-2500 or fax (760) 873-2563.

10 Palisade

 7

This shoe might just fit. Palisade, a tiny campground, provides a pretty spot along Rock Creek at 8,600 feet in elevation, with many side trip options. The closest is fishing for small trout on Rock Creek, with Crowley Lake toward the high plateau country to the east and pretty Rock Creek Lake up the road to the west.

Location: Near Crowley Lake in Inyo National Forest; map F5, grid a4.

Campsites, facilities: There are two sites for tents only and three sites for tents or RVs up to 22 feet long. Picnic tables and fire grills are provided. Drinking water and flush toilets are available. Horseback riding facilities

are available nearby. You can buy supplies in Tom's Place, five miles away. Leashed pets are permitted.

Reservations, fees: No reservations; $12 per night. Open from late June through early September.

Directions: From the junction of U.S. 395 and Highway 203 (the Mammoth Lakes turnoff), drive 15 miles south on U.S. 395 to Tom's Place. Turn south on Rock Creek Road and drive five miles to the campground.

Contact: Inyo National Forest, White Mountain Ranger District, tel. (760) 873-2500 or fax (760) 873-2563.

11 East Fork

 8

This is a beautiful, popular campground set along East Fork Rock Creek at 9,000 feet elevation. The camp is only three miles from Rock Creek Lake, where there's an excellent trailhead.

Location: Near Crowley Lake in Inyo National Forest; map F5, grid a4.

Campsites, facilities: There are 133 sites for tents or RVs up to 22 feet long. Picnic tables and fire grills are provided. Drinking water and flush toilets are available. You can buy supplies in Tom's Place and at Rock Creek Lake Resort. Leashed pets are permitted.

Reservations, fees: Reservations are accepted for sites 16-57 and 102-127; reserve Reserve at (877) 444-6777 ($8.65 reservation fee) or website: www.reserveusa.com; $12 per night. Open mid-May through October.

Directions: From the junction of U.S. 395 and Highway 203 (the Mammoth Lakes turnoff), drive 15 miles south on U.S. 395 to Tom's Place. Turn south on Rock Creek Road and drive five miles to the campground access road on the left.

Contact: Inyo National Forest, White Mountain Ranger District, tel. (760) 873-2500 or fax (760) 873-2563.

12 Pine Grove

Pine Grove is one of the smaller camps in the series of campgrounds along Rock Creek. Of the five camps in this canyon, this one is the closest to Rock Creek Lake, just a two-mile drive away. The elevation is 9,300 feet.

Location: Near Crowley Lake in Inyo National Forest; map F5, grid b4.

Campsites, facilities: There are five sites for tents only and six sites for tents or RVs up to 22 feet long. Picnic tables and fire grills are provided. Drinking water and flush toilets are available. Horseback riding facilities are available nearby. You can buy supplies in Tom's Place and at the Rock Creek Lake Resort. Leashed pets are permitted.

Reservations, fees: No reservations; $12 per night. Open mid-May through mid-October.

Directions: From the junction of U.S. 395 and Highway 203 (the Mammoth Lakes turnoff), drive 15 miles south on U.S. 395 to Tom's Place. Turn right (south) on Rock Creek Road and drive seven miles to the campground.

Contact: Inyo National Forest, White Mountain Ranger District, tel. (760) 873-2500 or fax (760) 873-2563.

13 Rock Creek Lake

 9

Rock Creek Lake, set at an elevation of 9,600 feet, is a small but beautiful lake that features cool, clear water, small trout, and a great trailhead for access to the adjacent John Muir Wilderness. The setting is drop-dead beautiful, hence the high rating for scenic beauty, but note that the campsites are set closely together, side by side, in a paved parking area. For a more classic setting, choose instead the nearby East Fork Mosquito Flat walk-in only campground. Note that at times, especially afternoons in the early summer, winds out of the west can be cold and pesky at the lake.

Location: In Inyo National Forest; map F5, grid b4.

Campsites, facilities: There are 28 sites for tents or RVs up to 22 feet long, and one group site for up to 50 people. Picnic tables and fire grills are provided. Drinking water and flush toilets are available. You can buy supplies in Tom's Place and at the Rock Creek Lake Resort. Leashed pets are permitted.

Reservations, fees: Reservations for group site only; $12 per night for family sites, $40 per night for group site. Open mid-May through October.

Directions: From the junction of U.S. 395 and Highway 203 (the Mammoth Lakes turnoff), drive 15 miles south on U.S. 395 to Tom's Place. Turn right (south) on Rock Creek Road and drive seven miles to the campground.

Contact: Inyo National Forest, White Mountain Ranger District, tel. (760) 873-2500 or fax (760) 873-2563.

14 Vermillion

 8

Lake Edison is a premium vacation destination. The 15-mph speed limit on the lake guarantees quiet water, and trout fishing is often quite good in early summer. A day trip option is to hike the trail from the camp which travels along the north shore of Lake Edison for five miles to Quail Meadows, where it intersects with the Pacific Crest Trail in the John Muir Wilderness. The elevation is 7,700 feet.

Location: On Lake Edison in Sierra National Forest; map F5, grid b0.

Campsites, facilities: There are 11 tent sites and 20 sites for tents or RVs up to 16 feet. Picnic tables and fire grills are provided. Drinking water and vault toilets are available. A boat ramp and horseback riding facilities are nearby. You can buy supplies in Mono Hot Springs. Leashed pets are permitted.

Reservations, fees: Reserve at (877) 444-6777 ($8.65 reservation fee) or website: www.reserveusa.com; $14 per night, $5 per night for each extra vehicle. Open June through September.

Directions: From the town of Shaver Lake,

drive 21 miles north on Highway 168 to Kaiser Pass Road. Go northeast on Kaiser Pass Road/Forest Road 80; it becomes Edison Lake Road at Mono Hot Springs. Continue north on Kaiser Pass/Edison Lake Road for five miles past Mono Hot Springs to the campground on the west shore of Lake Edison.

Contact: Sierra National Forest, Pineridge Ranger District, tel. (559) 855-5360 or fax (559) 855-5375.

15 Mono Hot Springs

 8

How well do you speak horse? Yep, don't be surprised if you meet Mr. Ed at this camp which is used primarily by horses, not people, to carry vacationers into the adjacent backcountry. The campground is set in the Sierra at 6,500 feet in elevation along the San Joaquin River directly adjacent to the Mono Hot Springs Resort. There is a trail from the camp that forks either to Lake Edison or into the backcountry of the Ansel Adams Wilderness. It's a good idea to bring an apple along with you to this camp. Horsies like that.

Location: On the San Joaquin River in Sierra National Forest; map F5, grid b0.

Campsites, facilities: There are four tent sites and 26 sites for trailers, tents, or RVs, with horse pastures across from the campground. Picnic tables and fire grills are provided. Drinking water and vault toilets are available. You can buy supplies in Mono Hot Springs. For those heading into the wilderness, there is also a free campground at the Mono Creek Trailhead for overnight horse camping.

Leashed pets are permitted.

Reservations, fees: Reserve at (877) 444-6777 ($8.65 reservation fee) or website: www.reserveusa.com; $14 per night, $5 per night for each extra vehicle. Open May through September.

Contact: Sierra National Forest, Pineridge

Ranger District, tel. (559) 855-5360 or fax (559) 855-5375.

Directions: From the town of Shaver Lake, drive 21 miles north on Highway 168. Turn northeast on Kaiser Pass Road/Forest Road 80; it becomes Edison Lake Road at Mono Hot Springs. Continue north beyond Mono Hot Springs about three miles to the campground entrance sign on the left.

16 Mono Creek

 5

Here's a beautiful spot along Mono Creek that offers a good alternative to nearby Lake Edison. The camp, set at 7,400 feet, is about a mile upstream from the dam at Lake Edison and has good evening trout fishing. For side trips, the Mono Hot Springs Resort is three miles away, and there are numerous trails nearby into the backcountry.

Location: Near Lake Edison in Sierra National Forest; map F5, grid b0.

Campsites, facilities: There are 14 sites for tents or RVs up to 16 feet long. Picnic tables and fire grills are provided. Drinking water and vault toilets are available. Horseback riding facilities and a boat ramp are nearby. You can buy supplies in Mono Hot Springs. Leashed pets are permitted.

Reservations, fees: Reserve at (877) 444-6777 ($8.65 reservation fee) or website: www.reserveusa.com; $14 per night, $5 per night for each extra vehicle. Open June through August.

Directions: From the town of Shaver Lake, drive 21 miles north on Highway 168. Drive northeast on Kaiser Pass Road/Forest Road 80; it becomes Edison Lake Road at Mono Hot Springs. Continue north on Edison Lake Road, three miles past Mono Hot Springs to the campground.

Contact: Sierra National Forest, Pineridge Ranger District, tel. (559) 855-5360 or fax (559) 855-5375.

Jackass Meadow

    7

Jackass Meadow is a pretty spot adjacent to Florence Lake, near the Upper San Joaquin River. There are good canoeing, rafting, and float-tubing possibilities, all high-Sierra style. The elevation is 7,200 feet.

Location: On Florence Lake in Sierra National Forest; map F5, grid c0.

Campsites, facilities: There are 44 sites for tents or RVs up to 16 feet long. Picnic tables and fire grills are provided. Drinking water and vault toilets are available. A wheelchair-accessible fishing pier is available nearby. Leashed pets are permitted.

Reservations, fees: Reserve at (877) 444-6777 ($8.65 reservation fee) or website: www.reserveusa.com; $14 per night, $5 per night for each extra vehicle. Open June through September.

Directions: From the town of Shaver Lake, drive 21 miles north on Highway 168. Turn northeast on Kaiser Pass Road/Forest Road 80 and drive to Florence Lake Road (two miles south of the town of Mono Hot Springs). Turn south and drive five miles to the campground.

Contact: Sierra National Forest, Pineridge Ranger District, tel. (559) 855-5360 or fax (559) 855-5375.

18 Highlands RV Park

   3

This is a privately operated RV park near Bishop that is set up for U.S. 395 cruisers. Possible side trips include the Indian Cultural Center in Bishop or Pleasant Valley Reservoir, about 10 miles northwest. The elevation is 4,300 feet.

Location: Near Bishop; map F5, grid b7.

Campsites, facilities: There are 103 RV sites with full hookups. Picnic tables are provided. Restrooms, drinking water, flush toilets, showers, a sanitary disposal station, cable TV, propane gas, and coin laundry are available. You can buy groceries nearby (about three

blocks away). Leashed pets are permitted.

Reservations, fees: Reservations are recommended; $24 per night. Open year-round.

Directions: From Bishop, drive two miles north on U.S. 395/North Sierra Highway to the campground on the right at 2275 North Sierra Highway.

Contact: Highlands RV Park, tel. (760) 873-7616.

19 Pleasant Valley County Park

   7

This county park is set adjacent to long, narrow Pleasant Valley Reservoir, created by the Owens River. It is east of the Sierra range in the high desert plateau country; the elevation is 4,200 feet. That makes it available for year-round fishing.

Location: Near Pleasant Valley Reservoir; map F5, grid c6.

Campsites, facilities: There are 200 sites for tents or RVs. Picnic tables and fire grills are provided. Drinking water (hand-pumped well water) and pit toilets are available. Leashed pets are permitted. No hookups.

Reservations, fees: No reservations; $6 per night. Open year-round.

Directions: From Bishop, drive seven miles north on U.S. 395. Turn right on the campground entrance road. Or seven miles northwest of Bishop on U.S. 395 go north on Pleasant Valley Road and drive a mile to the campground on the right.

Contact: Inyo County Parks Department, tel. (760) 878-0272 or tel. (800) 447-4696.

20 Horton Creek

    7

This is a little-known, primitive BLM camp set along Horton Creek, northwest of Bishop. It can make a good base camp for hunters in the fall, with wild, rugged country to the west. The Inyo Mono Ecology Center is nearby. The elevation is 4,975 feet.

Location: Near Bishop; map F5, grid c6.

Campsites, facilities: There are 53 sites for tents or RVs. Picnic tables and fire grills are provided. Pit toilets and a dumpster are available. No drinking water is available. Leashed pets are permitted.

Reservations, fees: No reservations; no fee. Open May through October, weather permitting.

Directions: From Bishop, drive 8.5 miles north on U.S. 395 to Sawmill Road. Turn west on Sawmill Road and drive 100 feet to Round Valley Road. Turn right and drive five miles to the campground on the left.

Contact: Bureau of Land Management, Bishop Field Office, tel. (760) 872-4881 or fax (760) 872-2894.

21 Brown's Millpond Campground

      6

This privately operated camp is adjacent to the Millpond Recreation Area which offers ball fields, playgrounds, and a swimming lake. There is also the opportunity for sailing, archery, tennis courts, horseshoe games, and fishing.

Location: Near Bishop; map F5, grid c6.

Campsites, facilities: There are 100 sites for tents or RVs, many with water and electric hookups. Picnic tables and fire grills are provided. Restrooms, drinking water, flush toilets, showers, and coin laundry are available. A concession stand is available nearby. Leashed pets are permitted.

Reservations, fees: Reservations are accepted; $12 to $15 per night. Open March through November.

Directions: From Bishop, drive 6.5 miles north on U.S. 395. Turn west at the Millpond Recreation Area sign and drive a mile to the campground on the left.

Contact: Brown's Millpond Campground, tel. (760) 873-5342.

22 Brown's Town Schober Lane Camp

   5

This privately operated campground, one of several in the vicinity of Bishop, is the only one in the area that accepts tents. It's all shade and grass, and it's next to the golf course.

Location: Near Bishop; map F5, grid c7.

Campsites, facilities: There are 150 sites for tents or RVs, many with water and electric hookups. Picnic tables are provided. Restrooms, drinking water, flush toilets, showers, cable TV, museum, store, and a snack bar are available. Leashed pets are permitted.

Reservations, fees: Reservations are accepted; $14 to $19 per night, limited to one vehicle per site. Major credit cards accepted. Open March through November.

Directions: From Bishop, drive a mile south on U.S. 395 to Schober Lane and exit left to the campground entrance. The campground is virtually at the corner of U.S. 395 and Schober Lane.

Contact: Brown's Town Schober Lane Camp, tel. (760) 873-8522; website: www.sierraweb.com.

23 Shady Rest Trailer Park

   3

This is an option for folks who want to find a layover in the Bishop area without going to much trouble to find it. Possible side trips include the Indian Cultural Center in Bishop and the Pleasant Valley Reservoir, about a 15-minute drive from Shady Rest.

Location: In Bishop; map F5, grid c7.

Campsites, facilities: There are 25 sites for tents or RVs with full hookups. Restrooms, drinking water, flush toilets, showers, cable TV, and coin laundry are available. Leashed pets are permitted.

Reservations, fees: Reservations are recommended; $16 to $18 per night for two people, $2 for each additional camper. Open year-round.

Directions: In Bishop on U.S. 395 heading north, turn right on Yaney Street and drive three-quarters of a mile to the campground at 399 East Yaney Street.

Contact: Shady Rest Trailer Park, tel. (760) 873-3430.

24 Grandview

 6

This is a primitive and little-known camp, and the folks who find this area earn their solitude. It is in the White Mountains east of Bishop at 8,600 feet along White Mountain Road. The road borders the Ancient Bristle Cone Pine Forest to the east and leads north to jump-off spots for hikers heading up Mount Barcroft (13,023 feet) or White Mountain (14,246 feet, the third highest mountain in California). A trail out of the camp leads up to an old mining site.

Location: Near Big Pine in Inyo National Forest; map F5, grid c9.

Campsites, facilities: There are 26 sites for tents or RVs up to 22 feet long. Picnic tables and fire grills are provided. Vault toilets are available. No drinking water is available. Leashed pets are permitted.

Reservations, fees: No reservations; $5 per night. Open May through October.

Directions: From Big Pine on U.S. 395, turn east on Highway 168 and drive 13 miles. Turn north on Forest Road 4S01/White Mountain Road and drive 5.5 miles to the campground.

Contact: Inyo National Forest, White Mountain Ranger District, tel. (760) 873-2500 or fax (760) 873-2563.

25 Big Trees

 8

This is a small Forest Service camp on Bishop Creek at 7,500 feet in elevation. This section of the stream is stocked with small trout by the Department of Fish and Game. Both South Lake and Lake Sabrina are about 10 miles away.

Location: On Bishop Creek in Inyo National Forest; map F5, grid c5.

Campsites, facilities: There are nine sites for tents or RVs. Picnic tables and fire grills are provided. Drinking water and flush toilets are available. You can buy supplies in Bishop. Leashed pets are permitted.

Reservations, fees: No reservations; $12 per night. Open late April through September.

Directions: From Bishop on U.S. 395, turn west on Highway 168 and drive 11 miles to the campground access road on the left. Turn left and drive two miles on a dirt road to the campground.

Contact: Inyo National Forest, White Mountain Ranger District, tel. (760) 873-2500 or fax (760) 873-2563.

26 North Lake

 8

This prime trailhead camp in the high country (9,500 feet) takes care of a lot of the "up" that hikers usually have to contend with when entering the nearby John Muir Wilderness. The camp is set on the North Fork of Bishop Creek near North Lake and close to a trailhead that accesses numerous lakes in the John Muir Wilderness and eventually connects with the Pacific Crest Trail.

Location: On Bishop Creek near North Lake in Inyo National Forest; map F5, grid c4.

Campsites, facilities: There are 11 tent sites. Picnic tables and fire grills are provided. Drinking water and vault toilets are available. Horseback riding facilities are available nearby. You can buy supplies in Bishop. Leashed pets are permitted.

Reservations, fees: No reservations; $12 per night. Open mid-May through September.

Directions: From Bishop on U.S. 395, turn west on Highway 168 and drive 17 miles. Turn north on Forest Road 8S02 and continue for two miles to the campground.

Contact: Inyo National Forest, White Mountain Ranger District, tel. (760) 873-2500 or fax (760) 873-2563.

27 Sabrina

 8

You get the best of both worlds at this camp. Set at 9,000 feet on Bishop Creek, the trails that are available here are routed into the high country of the John Muir Wilderness, and you're also just a half mile from Lake Sabrina, a beautiful high Sierra lake. Take your pick. Whatever your choice, it's a good one.

Location: Near Lake Sabrina in Inyo National Forest; map F5, grid d4.

Campsites, facilities: There are 18 sites for tents or RVs. Picnic tables and fire grills are provided. Drinking water and vault toilets are available. A boat ramp and boat rentals are available nearby. You can buy supplies in Bishop. Leashed pets are permitted.

Reservations, fees: No reservations; $12 per night. Open mid-May through October.

Directions: From Bishop on U.S. 395, drive 17 miles west on Highway 168 to the campground.

Contact: Inyo National Forest, White Mountain Ranger District, tel. (760) 873-2500 or fax (760) 873-2563.

28 Forks

 6

After a visit here, it's no mystery how the Forest Service named this camp. It is at the fork in the road, which gives you two options: you can turn south on South Lake Road and drive along the South Fork of Bishop Creek up to pretty South Lake, or you can keep driving on Highway 168 to another beautiful lake, Lake Sabrina, where hikers will find a trailhead that accesses the John Muir Wilderness. The elevation is 7,800 feet.

Location: Near South Lake in Inyo National Forest; map F5, grid d4.

Campsites, facilities: There are eight sites for tents or RVs. Picnic tables and fire grills are provided. Drinking water and flush toilets are available. Horseback riding facilities are available at North Lake. You can buy supplies in Bishop. Leashed pets are permitted.

Reservations, fees: No reservations; $12 per night. Open mid-April through October.

Directions: From Bishop on U.S. 395, drive 13 miles west on Highway 168 to the campground.

Contact: Inyo National Forest, White Mountain Ranger District, tel. (760) 873-2500 or fax (760) 873-2563.

29 Creekside RV Park

 3

This privately operated park in the high country is set up primarily for RVs. A lot of folks are surprised to find it here. North, Sabrina, and South Lakes are in the area. The elevation is 8,400 feet.

Location: On the South Fork of Bishop Creek; map F5, grid d4.

Campsites, facilities: There are four sites for tents only and 45 sites for RVs with full or partial hookups. Restrooms, drinking water, flush toilets, showers, coin laundry, grocery store, fish-cleaning facilities, and propane gas are available. Leashed pets are permitted.

Reservations, fees: A deposit is required with each reservation; $20 to $28 per night, $1 pet fee. Open May through October. Major credit cards accepted.

Directions: From Bishop on U.S. 395, turn west on Highway 168 and drive 15 miles. Turn left (south) on South Lake Road and drive two miles to the campground on the left at 1949 South Lake Road.

Contact: Creekside RV Park, tel. (760) 873-4483 or fax (760) 872-1966.

30 Bishop Park

 6

Bishop Park Camp is one in a series of camps along Bishop Creek. This one is set just behind the summer community of Aspendell. It is about two miles from Lake Sabrina, an ideal jump-off spot for a backpacking expedition into the John Muir Wilderness. The elevation is 8,400 feet.

Location: Near Lake Sabrina in Inyo National Forest; map F5, grid d4.

Campsites, facilities: There are 20 family sites and a group campsite for tents or RVs up to 22 feet long. Picnic tables and fire grills are provided. Drinking water and flush toilets are available. Horseback riding facilities are available at North Lake. You can buy supplies in Bishop. Leashed pets are permitted.

Reservations, fees: No reservations; $12 per night, $42 group fee per night. Open mid-April through mid-October.

Directions: From Bishop on U.S. 395, turn west on Highway 168 and drive 15 miles to the campground.

Contact: Inyo National Forest, White Mountain Ranger District, tel. (760) 873-2500 or fax (760) 873-2563.

31 Intake

      7

This small camp, set at 8,200 feet at a tiny reservoir on Bishop Creek, is about three miles from Lake Sabrina where a trailhead leads into the John Muir Wilderness. Nearby North Lake and South Lake provide side trip options.

Location: On Sabrina Creek in Inyo National Forest; map F5, grid d4.

Campsites, facilities: There are seven walk-in sites for tents only and eight sites for tents or RVs. Picnic tables and fire grills are provided. Drinking water and flush toilets are available. You can buy supplies in Bishop. Leashed pets are permitted.

Reservations, fees: No reservations; $12 per night. The walk-in sites are open year-round. Drive-in sites are open mid-April through October.

Directions: From Bishop on U.S. 395, turn west on Highway 168 and drive 14 miles to the campground entrance.

Contact: Inyo National Forest, White Mountain Ranger District, tel. (760) 873-2500 or fax (760) 873-2563.

32 Four Jeffrey

     8

The camp is set on the South Fork of Bishop Creek at 8,100 feet, about four miles from South Lake. If you can arrange a trip in the fall, make sure you visit this camp. The fall colors are spectacular, with the aspen trees exploding in yellows and oranges. It is also the last camp on South Lake Road to be closed in the fall, and though nights are cold, it is well worth the trip. This is by far the largest of the Forest Service camps in the vicinity. There are three lakes in the area: North Lake, Lake Sabrina, and South Lake.

Location: Near South Lake in Inyo National Forest; map F5, grid d5.

Campsites, facilities: There are 106 sites for tents or RVs up to 22 feet long. Picnic tables and fire grills are provided. Drinking water, vault toilets, and a sanitary disposal station are available. Some facilities are wheelchair accessible. You can buy supplies in Bishop. Leashed pets are permitted.

Reservations, fees: No reservations; $12 per night. Open mid-April through October.

Directions: From Bishop on U.S. 395, turn west on Highway 168 and drive 13 miles. Turn south on South Lake Road and drive a half mile to the campground.

Contact: Inyo National Forest, White Mountain Ranger District, tel. (760) 873-2500 or fax (760) 873-2563.

33 Baker Creek County Campground

    4

Because this is a county-operated RV park, it is overlooked by many who usually consider only camps on reservations systems. That makes this a good option for cruisers touring the eastern Sierra on U.S. 395. It's ideal for a quick overnighter, with easy access from Big Pine. The camp is set along Baker Creek at 4,000 feet in the high plateau country of the eastern Sierra. An option is fair trout fishing during the evening bite on the creek.

Location: Near Big Pine; map F5, grid e7.

Campsites, facilities: There are 70 sites for tents or RVs. Picnic tables and fire grills are provided. Pit toilets are available. No drinking water is available, but the stream can be hand-pumped with a water filter. You can buy supplies about 1.5 miles away in Big Pine. Leashed pets are permitted.

Reservations, fees: No reservations; $5 per night.

Directions: From Big Pine, drive a half mile north on U.S. 395. Turn left on Baker Creek Road and drive a mile to the campground on the left.

Contact: Inyo County Parks Department, tel. (760) 878-0272 or fax (760) 873-2241.

34 Glacier View County Campground

   4

This is one of two county camps near the town of Big Pine, providing U.S. 395 cruisers with two options. The camp is set along the Big Pine Canal at 3,900 feet.

Location: Near Big Pine; map F5, grid e8.

Campsites, facilities: There are 40 sites for tents or RVs. Picnic tables and fire grills are provided. Drinking water and flush toilets are available. You can buy supplies in Big Pine. Leashed pets are permitted.

Reservations, fees: No reservations; $5 per night. Open April through October.

Directions: From Big Pine, drive a half mile north on U.S. 395 to the campground on the right.

Contact: Inyo County Parks Department, tel. (760) 878-0272 or fax (760) 873-2241.

35 Palisade Group Camp

    8

This trailhead camp at 7,600 feet is popular for groups planning to rock climb the Palisades. This climbing trip is for experienced mountaineers only; it's a dangerous expedition where risk of life can be included in the bargain. Safer options include exploring the surrounding John Muir Wilderness.

Location: On Big Pine Creek in Inyo National Forest; map F5, grid e6.

Campsites, facilities: There is one group site for tents or RVs. Picnic tables and fire grills are provided. Drinking water and vault toilets are available. Leashed pets are permitted.

Reservations, fees: Reserve at (877) 444-6777 ($8.65 reservation fee) or website: www.reserveusa.com; $32 per night. Open mid-April to mid-October.

Directions: From U.S. 395 in Big Pine, turn west on Glacier Lodge Road and drive 8.5 miles to the campground.

Contact: Inyo National Forest, White Mountain Ranger District, tel. (760) 873-2500 or fax (760) 873-2563.

36 Sage Flat

     8

This camp, like the others in the immediate vicinity, is set up primarily for backpackers who are getting ready to head out on multiday expeditions into the nearby John Muir Wilderness. Your hike from here will begin with a steep climb from the trailhead at 7,400 feet elevation. The camp is set along Big Pine Creek, which is stocked with small trout.

Location: On Big Pine Creek near Big Pine in Inyo National Forest; map F5, grid e6.

Campsites, facilities: There are 28 sites for tents or RVs. Picnic tables and fire grills are provided. Drinking water and vault toilets are available. Some facilities are wheelchair accessible. Leashed pets are permitted.

Reservations, fees: Reserve at (877) 444-6777 ($8.65 reservation fee) or website: www.reserveusa.com; $11 per night. Open mid-April through October.

Directions: From U.S. 395 in Big Pine, turn west on Glacier Lodge Road and drive 8.5 miles to the campground.

Contact: Inyo National Forest, White Mountain Ranger District, tel. (760) 873-2500 or fax (760) 873-2563.

37 Upper Sage Flat

 8

This is one in a series of Forest Service camps in the area set up primarily for backpackers taking off on wilderness expeditions. Several trails are available near the camp that lead into the John Muir Wilderness. Even starting at 7,600 feet, expect a steep climb.

Location: On Big Pine Creek in Inyo National Forest; map F5, grid e6.

Campsites, facilities: There are 21 sites for tents or RVs. Picnic tables and fire grills are provided. Drinking water and vault toilets are available. Leashed pets are permitted.

Reservations, fees: Reserve at (877) 444-6777 ($8.65 reservation fee) or website: www.reserveusa.com; $11 per night. Open mid-April through October.

Directions: From U.S. 395 in Big Pine, turn west on Glacier Lodge Road and drive 8.5 miles to the campground.

Contact: Inyo National Forest, White Mountain Ranger District, tel. (760) 873-2500 or fax (760) 873-2563.

38 First Falls Hike-In Camp

 10

This high country hike-in camp is the first step for backpackers heading into the John Muir Wilderness. It is set at 8,300 feet on the South Fork of Big Pine Creek, with nearby Mount Alice (11,630 feet) looming to the west.

Location: In Inyo National Forest; map F5, grid e5.

Campsites, facilities: There are five tent sites. Picnic tables and fire grills are provided. Pit toilets are available. Garbage must be packed out. No drinking water is available. Leashed pets are permitted.

Reservations, fees: No reservations; no fee. Open May to mid-October.

Directions: From U.S. 395 in Big Pine, turn west onto Glacier Lodge Road and drive 8.5 miles. Park and hike two miles to the campground.

Contact: Inyo National Forest, White Mountain Ranger District, tel. (760) 873-2500 or fax (760) 873-2563.

39 Big Pine Creek

 8

This is another good spot for backpackers to launch a multi-day trip. The camp is set along Big Pine Creek at 7,700 feet, with trails near the camp that are routed to the numerous lakes in the high country of the John Muir Wilderness.

Location: In Inyo National Forest; map F5, grid e5.

Campsites, facilities: There are five sites for tents only and 25 sites for tents or RVs. Picnic tables and fire grills are provided. Drinking water and vault toilets are available. Some facilities are wheelchair accessible. Leashed pets are permitted.

Reservations, fees: Reserve at (877) 444-6777 ($8.65 reservation fee) or website: www.reserveusa.com; $11 per night. Open early May through October.

Directions: From U.S. 395 in Big Pine, turn west on Glacier Lodge Road and drive nine miles to the campground.

Contact: Inyo National Forest, White Mountain Ranger District, tel. (760) 873-2500 or fax (760) 873-2563.

40 Taboose Creek County Campground

 4

The eastern Sierra is stark country, but this little spot provides a stream (Taboose Creek) and some trees near the campground. There is an opportunity for trout fishing, fair, not spectacular. The easy access off U.S. 395 is a bonus. The elevation is 3,900 feet.

Location: Near Big Pine; map F5, grid f8.

Campsites, facilities: There are 55 sites for tents or RVs. Picnic tables and fire grills are provided. Drinking water (hand-pumped from a well) and pit toilets are available. You can buy supplies in Big Pine or Independence. Leashed pets are permitted.

Reservations, fees: No reservations; $5 per night. Open year-round.

Directions: From Big Pine, drive 11 miles south on U.S. 395. Turn left on Taboose Creek Road and drive 2.5 miles to the campground.

Contact: Inyo County Parks Department, tel. (760) 878-0272 or fax (760) 873-2241.

41 Tinemaha Creek County Park

This primitive, little-known (to out-of-towners) county park campground is on Tinemaha Creek at 4,400 feet.

Location: Near Big Pine; map F5, grid f8.

Campsites, facilities: There are 55 sites for tents or RVs. Picnic tables and fire grills are provided. Pit toilets are available. No drinking water is available. There is no piped water. Stream water is available to be hand-pumped with filters. Leashed pets are permitted.

Reservations, fees: No reservations; $5 per vehicle per night. Open year-round.

Directions: From Independence, drive 19.5 miles north on U.S. 395. Turn left on Fish Springs Road and drive a half mile. Turn right on Tinemaha Road and drive two miles to the campground on the left.

Contact: Inyo County Parks Department, tel. (760) 878-0272 or fax (760) 873-2241.

42 Goodale Creek

 6

This obscure BLM camp is set along little Goodale Creek at 4,000 feet. It is a good lay-over spot for U.S. 395 cruisers heading north.

Location: Near Independence; map F5, grid f7.

Campsites, facilities: There are 62 sites for tents or RVs. Picnic tables and fire rings are

provided. Pit toilets and a trash bin are available. No drinking water is available. Leashed pets are permitted.

Reservations, fees: No reservations; no fee. Open mid-April through October.

Directions: From Independence, drive 12 miles north on U.S. 395. Turn left on Aberdeen Road and drive two miles to the campground on the left.

Contact: Bureau of Land Management, Bishop Field Office, tel. (760) 872-4881 or fax (760) 872-2894.

43 Hume Lake

 8

For newcomers, Hume Lake is a surprise: a pretty lake, small enough to hike around, with good trout fishing, especially near the dam. Another surprise is the adjacent religious camp center. The nearby entrances to Kings Canyon National Park add a bonus. The elevation is 5,200 feet.

Location: In Giant Sequoia National Monument; map F5, grid g0.

Campsites, facilities: There are 60 tent sites and 14 sites for tents or RVs up to 22 feet long. Picnic tables and fire grills are provided. Drinking water and flush toilets are available. A grocery store is nearby. Leashed pets are permitted.

Reservations, fees: Reservations are recommended for weekends and holidays; Reserve at (877) 444-6777 ($8.65 reservation fee) or website: www.reserveusa.com; $14 per night, $5 per night for each extra vehicle. Open May through August.

Directions: From Fresno, drive east on Highway 180 for about 60 miles to the Y at Highway 180 north. Bear left on Highway 180 north and drive six miles to the Hume Lake Road junction. Turn south and drive three miles to Hume Lake.

Contact: Sequoia National Forest, Hume Lake Ranger District, tel. (559) 338-2251 or fax (559) 338-2131.

44 Aspen Hollow Group Camp

    6

This large group camp is set at 5,200 feet, near Hume Lake. It was reconstructed in 1999 and early 2000. Entrances to Kings Canyon National Park are nearby.

Location: Near Hume Lake in Sequoia National Forest; map F5, grid g0.

Campsites, facilities: This is a group campsite for up to 75 people. Picnic tables and fire grills are provided. Drinking water and vault toilets are available. A grocery store is nearby. Leashed pets are permitted.

Reservations, fees: Reserve at (877) 444-6777 ($8.65 reservation fee) or website: www.reserveusa.com; $112.50 per night. Open May through August.

Directions: From Fresno, drive east at Highway 180 for about 60 miles to the Y at Highway 180 north. Bear left on Highway 180 north and drive six miles to the Hume Lake Road junction. Turn south and drive about three miles to the Aspen Hollow Group Camp entrance, 1.5 miles past the campground at Hume Lake.

Contact: Sequoia National Forest, Hume Lake Ranger District, tel. (559) 338-2251 or fax (559) 338-2131.

45 Logger Flat Group Camp

  7

This is the group site alternative to Landslide. For more information, see the entry for Landslide,

Location: On Ten Mile Creek in Giant Sequoia National Monument; map F5, grid g0.

Campsites, facilities: This is one group campsite for up to 50 people. Picnic tables and fire grills are provided. Vault toilets are available. No drinking water is available. A grocery store is nearby. Leashed pets are permitted.

Reservations, fees: Reserve at (877) 444-6777 ($8.65 reservation fee) or website: www.reserveusa.com; $75 per night.

Directions: From Grant Grove in Kings Canyon National Park, drive six miles north on Highway 180 to the Hume Lake Road junction. Turn south and drive about seven miles around Hume Lake and up Ten Mile Road to the campground.

Contact: Sequoia National Forest, Hume Lake Ranger District, tel. (559) 338-2251 or fax (559) 338-2131.

46 Landslide

     7

If you want quiet, you got it; few folks know about this camp. If you want a stream nearby, you got it; Landslide Creek runs right beside the camp. If you want a lake nearby, you got it; Hume Lake is about two miles away. If you want a national park nearby, you got it; Kings Canyon National Park is nearby. Add it up: You got it. The elevation is 5,800 feet.

Location: On Ten Mile Creek in Giant Sequoia National Monument; map F5, grid h1.

Campsites, facilities: There are six sites for tents only and three sites for tents or RVs up to 16 feet long. Picnic tables and fire grills are provided. Vault toilets are available. No drinking water is available. A grocery store is nearby. Leashed pets are permitted.

Reservations, fees: No reservations; no fee. Open May through September.

Directions: From Grant Grove in Kings Canyon National Park, drive six miles north on Highway 180 to the Hume Lake Road junction. Turn south and drive seven miles around Hume Lake and up Ten Mile Road to the campground. Landslide is on the right, 1.5 miles beyond Ten Mile Campground.

Contact: Sequoia National Forest, Hume Lake Ranger District, tel. (559) 338-2251 or fax (559) 338-2131.

47 Sentinel

     8

This camp provides a nearby alternative to Sheep Creek. They both tend to fill up quickly in the summer. It's a short walk to Cedar Grove

Village, the center of activity in the park. The elevation is 4,600 feet.

Location: In Kings Canyon National Park; map F5, grid h2.

Campsites, facilities: There are 82 sites for tents or RVs up to 30 feet long. Picnic tables and grills are provided. Restrooms, drinking water, flush toilets, showers, and a sanitary disposal station are available. Some facilities are wheelchair accessible. A grocery store, coin laundry, restaurant, and horseback riding facilities are nearby. Leashed pets are permitted.

Reservations, fees: No reservations; $14 per night, $10 per vehicle park entrance fee. Open April through October, weather permitting.

Directions: From Cedar Grove Village in Kings Canyon National Park, drive west on Highway 180 about a quarter mile to the campground.

Contact: Kings Canyon National Park, tel. (559) 565-3341.

48 Sheep Creek

 8

This is one of the camps that always fills up quickly on summer weekends. It's a pretty spot and just a short walk from Cedar Grove Village. The camp is set along Sheep Creek at 4,600 feet.

Location: In Kings Canyon National Park; map F5, grid h2.

Campsites, facilities: There are 111 sites for tents or RVs up to 30 feet long. Picnic tables and fire grills are provided. Restrooms, drinking water, flush toilets, showers, and a sanitary disposal station are available. A grocery store, coin laundry, restaurant, and horseback riding facilities are available nearby. Leashed pets are permitted.

Reservations, fees: No reservations; $14 per night, $10 per vehicle park entrance fee. Open June through September.

Directions: From Cedar Grove Village in Kings Canyon National Park, drive a half mile west on Highway 180 to the campground.

Contact: Kings Canyon National Park, tel. (559) 565-3341.

49 Canyon View Group Camp

 8

If it weren't for this spot, large groups wishing to camp together in Kings Canyon National Park would be out of luck. Reservations are a must. The elevation is 4,600 feet.

Location: In Kings Canyon National Park; map F5, grid h2.

Campsites, facilities: There are four group sites for tents accommodating a minimum of 20 people and a maximum of 40 people per site. Picnic tables and fire grills are provided. Drinking water, flush toilets, and a sanitary disposal station are available. A grocery store, coin laundry, showers, restaurant, and horseback riding facilities are nearby (within 1.5 miles). Leashed pets are permitted.

Reservations, fees: Reservations are required by mail at Canyon View Group Sites, P.O. Box 926, Kings Canyon National Park, CA 93633, or by fax at tel. (559) 565-0314 May through October, or by fax at (559) 565-4391 November through April; $29 per night for up to 20 people, $1 per person per night for more than 20 people, plus a $10 per vehicle park entrance fee. Open June through September, weather permitting.

Directions: From Cedar Grove Village in Kings Canyon National Park, drive east on Highway 180 to the campground (a half mile past the ranger station).

Contact: For group camp information only, phone (559) 565-3792 May through October, (559) 565-4335 November through April; Kings Canyon National Park, tel. (559) 565-3341.

50 Canyon View

 8

This is another of several camps in the Cedar Grove Village area of the Kings Canyon National Park. The access road leads to dramatic views of the deep Kings River Canyon, one of the deepest gorges in North America. The elevation is 4,600 feet.

Location: In Kings Canyon National Park; map F5, grid h2.

Campsites, facilities: There are 37 sites for tents. Picnic tables and fire grills are provided. Drinking water and flush toilets are available. Showers, horseback riding facilities, grocery store, restaurant, and a coin laundry are nearby. Leashed pets are permitted.

Reservations, fees: No reservations; $14 per night, $10 per vehicle park entrance fee. Open June through September, weather permitting.

Directions: From Cedar Grove Village in Kings Canyon National Park, drive east on Highway 180 to the campground (a half mile past the ranger station).

Contact: Kings Canyon National Park, tel. (559) 565-3341.

51 Moraine

    8

This is one in a series of camps in the Cedar Grove Village area of Kings Canyon National Park. This camp is used only as an overflow area. Hikers should drive past the Cedar Grove Ranger Station to the end of the road at Copper Creek, a prime jump-off point for a spectacular hike. The elevation is 4,600 feet.

Location: In Kings Canyon National Park; map F5, grid h2.

Campsites, facilities: There are 120 sites for tents or RVs. Picnic tables and fire grills are provided. Drinking water and flush toilets are available. Showers, horseback riding facilities, grocery store, restaurant, and a coin laundry are nearby. Leashed pets are permitted.

Reservations, fees: No reservations; $14 per night, $10 per vehicle park entrance fee. Open June through September, weather permitting.

Directions: From Cedar Grove Village in Kings Canyon National Park, drive east on Highway 180 to the campground (one mile past the ranger station).

Contact: Kings Canyon National Park, tel. (559) 565-3341.

52 Ten Mile

    7

This is one of three small, primitive campgrounds along Ten Mile Creek above Hume Lake. This one is about four miles from the lake at 5,800 feet in elevation. It provides an alternative to camping in nearby Kings Canyon National Park.

Location: On Ten Mile Creek in Giant Sequoia National Monument; map F5, grid h0.

Campsites, facilities: There are 10 sites for tents or RVs up to 22 feet long. Picnic tables and fire grills are provided. Vault toilets are available. No drinking water is available. Leashed pets are permitted.

Reservations, fees: No reservations; no fee. Open May through September.

Directions: From Grant Grove in Kings Canyon National Park, drive six miles north on Highway 180 to the Hume Lake Road junction. Turn south and drive about seven miles around Hume Lake and up Ten Mile Road to the campground.

Contact: Sequoia National Forest, Hume Lake Ranger District, tel. (559) 338-2251 or fax (559) 338-2131.

53 Big Meadows

    7

This primitive, high mountain camp (7,600 feet) is beside little Big Meadows Creek. Backpackers can use this as a launching pad, with the nearby trailhead (one mile down the road to the west) leading to the Jennie Lake Wilderness. Kings Canyon National Park, only a 12-mile drive away, is a nearby side trip.

Location: On Big Meadows Creek in Giant Sequoia National Monument; map F5, grid h1.

Campsites, facilities: There are numerous sites along Big Meadows Creek and Big Meadows Road for tents or RVs up to 22 feet long. Picnic tables and fire grills are provided. Vault toilets are available. No drinking water is available. Leashed pets are permitted.

Reservations, fees: No reservations; no fee. Open June through September.

Directions: From Grant Grove, drive seven miles southeast on Generals Highway. Turn left on Big Meadows Road/Forest Road 14S11 and drive five miles to the camp.

Contact: Sequoia National Forest, Hume Lake Ranger District, tel. (559) 338-2251 or fax (559) 338-2131.

54 Buck Rock

 4

This is a remote camp that provides a little-known option to nearby Sequoia and Kings Canyon National Parks. If the national parks are full and you're stuck, this camp provides an insurance policy. The elevation is 7,500 feet.

Location: Near Big Meadows Creek in Giant Sequoia National Monument; map F5, grid h0.

Campsites, facilities: There are five primitive sites for tents or RVs up to 16 feet long. Picnic tables and fire grills are provided. Vault toilets are available. No drinking water is available. Leashed pets are permitted.

Reservations, fees: No reservations; no fee. Open June through September.

Directions: From Grant Grove in Kings Canyon National Park, drive seven miles southeast on Generals Highway. Turn left on Big Meadows Road/Forest Road 14S11 and drive four miles to the camp.

Contact: Sequoia National Forest, Hume Lake Ranger District, tel. (559) 338-2251 or fax (559) 338-2131.

55 Dorst

Things that go bump in the night swing through Dorst all summer long. That's right, Mr. Bear, a whole bunch of them, make food raids like UPS drivers on pick-up routes. There are so many bears raiding food here that some years rangers keep a running tally posted on the bulletin board. That's why keeping your food in a bear-proof locker is not only a must, it's the law. The camp is set on Dorst Creek at 6,700 feet, near a trail that is routed into the backcountry and through Muir Grove. It is one in a series of big, popular camps in Sequoia National Park.

Location: On Dorst Creek in Sequoia National Park; map F5, grid h0.

Campsites, facilities: There are 204 family sites for tents or RVs up to 30 feet long and five group sites. Picnic tables and fire grills are provided. Drinking water, flush toilets, a sanitary disposal station, and evening ranger programs are available. Some facilities are wheelchair accessible. A grocery store and a coin laundry are nearby. Leashed pets are permitted.

Reservations, fees: Reserve via phone at (800) 365-CAMP (800-365-2267), or website: reservations.nps.gov/; $16 per night (includes reservation fee) for family sites, $38 to $57 for group sites; plus a $10 per vehicle park entrance fee. Open June through September.

Directions: From Lodgepole Village in Sequoia National Park, drive nine miles northwest on Generals Highway. Note: Due to steep curves on Generals Highway, vehicles over 22 feet are not advised on this road between Giant Forest and Potwisha Camp. An alternate route is to take Highway 180 into Kings Canyon National Park, and then turn south on Generals Highway just after entering the park.

Contact: Sequoia National Park, tel. (559) 565-3341.

56 Stony Creek

Stony Creek Camp provides a good option if the national park camps are filled. It is set at creekside at 6,400 feet elevation. Sequoia and Kings Canyon National Parks are nearby.

Location: In Giant Sequoia National Monument; map F5, grid i0.

Campsites, facilities: There are 49 sites for tents and RVs up to 22 feet long. Picnic tables and fire grills are provided.

Drinking water and flush toilets are available. A grocery store and coin laundry are nearby. Leashed pets are permitted.

Reservations, fees: Reserve at (877) 444-6777 ($8.65 reservation fee) or website: www.reserveusa.com; $14 per night, $5 per night for each extra vehicle. Open June through August.

Directions: From Grant Grove in Kings Canyon National Park, drive 13 miles southeast on Generals Highway to the campground on the right.

Contact: Sequoia National Forest, Hume Lake Ranger District, tel. (559) 338-2251 or fax (559) 338-2131.

57 Lodgepole

    8

This giant, pretty camp on the Marble Fork of the Kaweah River is typically crowded. A bonus here is an excellent trailhead nearby that leads into the backcountry of Sequoia National Park. The elevation is 6,700 feet.

Location: On the Marble Fork of the Kaweah River in Sequoia National Park; map F5, grid i1.

Campsites, facilities: There are 214 sites for tents or RVs up to 40 feet long. Picnic tables and fire grills are provided. Restrooms, drinking water, flush toilets, pay showers, sanitary disposal station, horseback riding facilities, gift shop, and evening ranger programs are available. A grocery store, deli, and a coin laundry are nearby. Leashed pets are permitted.

Reservations, fees: Reserve via phone at (800) 365-CAMP (800-365-2267), or website: reservations.nps.gov/; $16 per night (includes reservation fee) for family sites, plus a $10 per vehicle park entrance fee. Open year-round, with limited winter services.

Directions: From Lodgepole Village in Sequoia National Park, continue on Lodgepole Village access road for one-quarter mile (beyond Lodgepole Village) to the campground. Note: This campground is not on Generals Highway.

Contact: Sequoia National Park, tel. (559) 565-3341.

58 Fir Group Campground

    6

This is the second of two large group camps in the area set along Stony Creek.

Location: Near Stony Creek in Giant Sequoia National Monument; map F5, grid i0.

Campsites, facilities: This is a group campsite for up to 100 people. Picnic tables and fire grills are provided. Drinking water and vault toilets are available. A grocery store and coin laundry are nearby. Leashed pets are permitted.

Reservations, fees: Reserve at (877) 444-6777 ($8.65 reservation fee) or website: www.reserveusa.com; $75 per night. Open June through August.

Directions: From Grant Grove in Kings Canyon National Park, drive 14 miles southeast on Generals Highway to the campground on the left.

Contact: Sequoia National Forest, Hume Lake Ranger District, tel. (559) 338-2251 or fax (559) 338-2131.

59 Cove Group Camp

    6

This large group camp is beside Stony Creek. The elevation is 6,500 feet.

Location: Near Stony Creek in Giant Sequoia National Monument; map F5, grid i0.

Campsites, facilities: This is a group campsite for up to 50 people. Picnic tables and fire grills are provided. Drinking water and vault toilets are available. A grocery store and coin laundry are available nearby. Leashed pets are permitted.

Reservations, fees: Reserve at (877) 444-6777 ($8.65 reservation fee) or website: www.reserveusa.com; $50 per night. Open June through August.

Directions: From Grant Grove in Kings Canyon National Park, drive 14 miles southeast on Generals Highway to the campground on the left.

Contact: Sequoia National Forest, Hume Lake Ranger District, tel. (559) 338-2251 or fax (559) 338-2131.

60 Onion Valley

 8

Onion Valley is one of the best trailhead camps for backpackers in the Sierra. The camp is set at 9,200 feet, and from here it's a 2,600-foot climb over the course of about three miles to awesome Kearsage Pass (11,823 feet). From there you can camp at the Kearsage Lakes, explore the Kearsage Pinnacles, or join up with the John Muir Trail and venture to your choice of many high Sierra lakes. A $6 Forest Service map and a free wilderness permit (if obtained from the ranger station) are your passports to the high country from this camp. Note: Bears frequent this camp most every night of summer.

Location: In Inyo National Forest; map F5, grid i6.

Campsites, facilities: There are 29 sites for tents only. Picnic tables and fire grills are provided. Drinking water and vault toilets are available. Leashed pets are permitted.

Reservations, fees: Reservations are accepted at (877) 444-6777 ($8.65 reservation fee) or website: www.reserveusa.com; $11 per night. Open mid-June through September.

Directions: From U.S. 395 in Independence, drive 15 miles west on Onion Valley Road to the campground at the road's end.

Contact: Inyo National Forest, Mount Whitney Ranger District, tel. (760) 876-6200 or fax (760) 876-6202.

61 Oak Creek

 6

Oak Creek is in a series of little-known camps west of Independence that provide a jump-off spot for backpackers. This camp is set at 5,000 feet, with a trail from camp that is routed west (and up) into the California Bighorn Sheep Zoological Area, a rugged, stark region well above the tree line. Caution: Plan on a terrible, long, butt-kicker of a climb up to the Sierra crest; stay on trail.

Location: In Inyo National Forest; map F5, grid h7.

Campsites, facilities: There are 22 sites for tents or RVs. Picnic tables and fire grills are provided. Drinking water and flush toilets are available. Some facilities are wheelchair accessible. Supplies and a coin laundry are available in Independence. Leashed pets are permitted.

Reservations, fees: Reservations accepted; tel. (877) 444-6777; $11 per night. Open mid-April through mid-October.

Directions: From Independence, drive two miles north on U.S. 395. Turn left (west) on North Oak Creek Drive and drive three miles to the campground on the right.

Contact: Inyo National Forest, Mount Whitney Ranger District, tel. (760) 876-6200 or fax (760) 876-6202.

62 Independence Creek County Campground

 7

This unpublicized county park is often overlooked among U.S. 395 cruisers. It is set at 3,900 feet along Independence Creek. Trout fishing provides an opportunity here.

Location: In Independence; map F5, grid h8.

Campsites, facilities: There are 25 sites for tents or RVs. Picnic tables are provided. Drinking water and pit toilets are available. Some facilities are wheelchair accessible. Supplies and a coin laundry are available in Independence. Leashed pets are permitted.

Reservations, fees: No reservations; $5 per night. Open year-round.

Directions: In Independence, drive west on Market Street to the campground about half a mile outside the town limits.

Contact: Inyo County Parks Department, tel. (760) 878-0272 or fax (760) 873-2241.

63 Gray's Meadow

     6

Gray's Meadow is one of two adjacent camps set along Independence Creek, which is stocked with small trout by the Department of Fish and Game. The highlight in the immediate area is the trailhead at the end of the road at Onion Valley Camp. For U.S. 395 cruisers looking for a spot, this is a pretty alternative to the camps in Bishop.

Location: On Independence Creek in Inyo National Forest; map F5, grid i7.

Campsites, facilities: There are 52 sites for tents or RVs. Picnic tables and fire grills are provided. Drinking water and flush toilets are available. Supplies and a coin laundry are available in Independence. Leashed pets are permitted.

Reservations, fees: Reservations are accepted at (877) 444-6777 ($8.65 reservation fee) or website: www. reserveusa.com; $11 per night. Open April through October.

Directions: From U.S. 395 in Independence, turn west on Onion Valley Road and drive five miles to the campground on the right.

Contact: Inyo National Forest, Mount Whitney Ranger District, tel. (760) 876-6200 or fax (760) 876-6202.

64 Potwisha

     7

This pretty spot on the Marble Fork of the Kaweah River is one of Sequoia National Park's smaller drive-to campgrounds. From Buckeye Flat, a few miles east of the camp, a trail runs along Paradise Creek. Hike with plenty of water here; it can be very hot and dry in the summer.

Location: On the Marble Fork of the Kaweah River in Sequoia National Park; map F5, grid j0.

Campsites, facilities: There are 42 sites for tents or RVs up to 30 feet long. Picnic tables and fire grills are provided. Drinking water, flush toilets, a sanitary disposal station, and evening ranger programs are available. Restrooms and some campsites are wheelchair accessible. Leashed pets are permitted.

Reservations, fees: No reservations; $14 per night, plus a $10 per vehicle park entrance fee. Open year-round.

Directions: From Visalia, drive east on Highway 198 to the Foothills Visitor Center at Ash Mountain Park Headquarters. Turn northeast on Generals Highway and drive four miles to the campground entrance. Vehicles of 22 feet or longer are not advised on Generals Highway from Potwisha to Giant Forest Village.

Contact: Sequoia National Park, tel. (559) 565-3341.

65 Buckeye Flat

   8

In any big, popular national park like Sequoia, the smaller the campground, the better. Well, Buckeye Flat is one of the smaller ones here, set on the Middle Fork of the Kaweah River with a trail just south of camp that runs beside pretty Paradise Creek.

Location: On the Middle Fork of the Kaweah River in Sequoia National Park; map F5, grid j0.

Campsites, facilities: There are 28 tent sites. Picnic tables and fire grills are provided. Drinking water and flush toilets are available. Leashed pets are permitted.

Reservations, fees: No reservations; $14 per night, plus a $10 per vehicle park entrance fee. Open April through Labor Day weekend, weather permitting.

Directions: From Visalia, drive east on Highway 198 to the Foothills Visitor Center at Ash Mountain Park Headquarters and then drive six miles northeast on Generals Highway. Vehicles of 22 feet or longer are not advised on Generals Highway from Potwisha to Giant Forest Village.

Contact: Sequoia National Park, tel. (559) 565-3341.

66 Whitney Trailhead Hike-In

   9

If Whitney Portal is full (common for this world-class trailhead), this camp provides a hike-in option, backpacking in a quarter-mile to an elevation of 8,300 feet. Reservations for the summit hike are required. That accomplished, this hike-in camp is an excellent choice for spending a day to become acclimated to the high altitude. The trailhead to the Mount Whitney summit (14,495 feet) is nearby. Mount Whitney is the beginning of the 211-mile John Muir Trail, which ends in Yosemite Valley.

Location: In Inyo National Forest; map F5, grid j7.

Campsites, facilities: There are 10 tent sites at this walk-in campground. Picnic tables and fire grills are provided. Drinking water and pit toilets are available. Supplies are available in Lone Pine. Leashed pets are permitted.

Reservations, fees: No reservations; $6 per night. Stays are limited to one night only. Open late-May to mid-October.

Directions: From Lone Pine, drive 13 miles west on Whitney Portal Road and then hike a quarter mile to the camp.

Contact: Inyo National Forest, Mount Whitney Ranger District, tel. (760) 876-6200 or fax (760) 876-6202.

67 Lone Pine and Lone Pine Group

     8

This is an alternative for campers preparing to hike Mount Whitney or start the John Muir Trail. It is set at 6,000 feet, 2,000 feet below Whitney Portal (the hiking jump-off spot), providing a lower elevation location for hikers to acclimate themselves to the altitude. The camp is set on Lone Pine Creek, with decent fishing and spectacular views of Mount Whitney.

Location: Near Mount Whitney in Inyo National Forest; map F5, grid j7.

Campsites, facilities: There are 43 sites for tents or RVs, and one group site. Picnic ta-

bles and fire grills are provided. Drinking water and flush toilets are available. Supplies are available in Lone Pine. Leashed pets are permitted.

Reservations, fees: Reservations are accepted for 60 percent of the sites. Reserve at (877) 444-6777 ($8.65 reservation fee) or website: www.reserveusa.com; $10 per night, $30 for a group site. Stays are limited to 14 days. Open April through mid-October.

Directions: From Lone Pine, drive six miles west on Whitney Portal Road to the campground on the left.

Contact: Inyo National Forest, Mount Whitney Ranger District, tel. (760) 876-6200 or fax (760) 876-6202.

68 Whitney Portal and Whitney Portal Group

     9

This camp is home to a world-class trailhead, regarded as the number one jump-off spot for the hike to the top of Mount Whitney (at 14,495 feet the highest spot in the Continental U.S.), as well as the start of the 211-mile John Muir Trail from Mount Whitney to Yosemite Valley. Hikers planning to scale the summit must have a wilderness permit, available at the Forest Service office in Lone Pine. The camp is at 8,000 feet, and virtually everyone staying here plans to make the trek to the Whitney summit, a climb of 6,500 feet over the course of 10 miles. The trip includes an ascent over 100 switchbacks (often snow-covered in early summer) to top Wotan's Throne and reach Trail Crest (13,560 feet). Here you turn right and take the Summit Trail, where the ridge is cut by huge notch windows providing a view down more than 10,000 feet to the little town of Lone Pine and the Owens Valley. When you sign the logbook on top, don't be surprised if you see my name in the registry.

Location: Near Mount Whitney in Inyo National Forest; map F5, grid j7.

Campsites, facilities: There are 43 sites for tents or RVs up to 16 feet long, and three group sites. Picnic tables and fire grills are provided. Drinking water and flush toilets are available. Some facilities are wheelchair accessible. Supplies are available in Lone Pine. Leashed pets are permitted.

Reservations, fees: Reservations are accepted for 60 percent of the sites. Reserve at (877) 444-6777 ($8.65 reservation fee) or website: www.reserveusa.com; $12 per night, $30 for group sites. Stays are limited to seven days. Open late May to mid-October.

Directions: From Lone Pine, drive 13 miles west on Whitney Portal Road to the campground on the left.

Contact: Inyo National Forest, Mount Whitney Ranger District, tel. (760) 876-6200 or fax (760) 876-6202.

69 Portagee Joe County Campground

   4

This small, little-known county park provides an option for both Mount Whitney hikers and U.S. 395 cruisers. It is about five miles from Diaz Lake (see Chapter G5), set on a small creek at 3,750 feet. Very few out-of-towners know about this spot, a nice insurance policy if you find yourself stuck for a campsite in this region. Trout fishing provides an opportunity.

Location: Near Lone Pine; map F5, grid j8.

Campsites, facilities: There are 15 sites for tents or RVs. Picnic tables and fire grills are provided. Vault toilets are available. There is no drinking water, but water from the stream can be hand-pumped with a filter. Supplies and a coin laundry are available in Lone Pine. Leashed pets are permitted.

Reservations, fees: No reservations; $5 per night. Open year-round.

Directions: In Lone Pine, drive a half mile west on Whitney Portal Road to Tuttle Creek Road. At Tuttle Creek Road turn south and drive 0.1 of a mile to the campground.

Contact: Inyo County Parks Department, tel. (760) 878-0272 or fax (760) 873-2241.

CHAPTER F6

JEFFREY PATTY

IN THE MOUNTAINS

MAP F6

TO COALDALE JUNCTION, NV

○ Dyer

INYO NATIONAL FOREST

266

Oasis ○

NEVADA
CALIFORNIA

168

Gilbert Summit
6,374 feet

Lida Summit
7,400 feet

Lida ○ 266

Magruder Mountain
9,046 feet

TO I-95

Westgard Pass
7,271 feet

1-4

TO BIG PINE

608

EUREKA SAND DUNES

TO SCOTTY'S JUNCTION, NV

DEATH VALLEY NATIONAL PARK

Scotty's Castle ○ 267

Ubehebe Crater

Dry Mountain
8,726 feet

Saline Valley

5

Grapevine Mountains

TO FURNACE CREEK RANCH

692

TO PANAMINT SPRINGS

0 1 2 3 4 5 6 7 8 9

© AVALON TRAVEL PUBLISHING, INC.

CHAPTER F6

1 Piñon Group Camp

 5

Piñon Group Camp is the first of four group camps set in the immediate area along Highway 168. It is a remote and stark setting, 7,200 feet in elevation, at the foot of the White Mountains on the east side of the Owens Valley. Most campers here will head to the Ancient Bristle Cone Pine Forest (turn north on White Mountain Road and drive eight miles to Schulman Picnic Area), where the oldest tree in the world, about 4,000 years old, has been documented. (It is unmarked so some idiot won't cut it down.) The road up here, by the way, provides sweeping views to the west of the Sierra. Hikers can get a similar view by taking the trail out of Cedar Flat to Black Mountain (9,038 feet), about a five-mile tromp one way, with the trail quite faint, often invisible, over the last mile.
Location: Near Big Pine in Inyo National Forest; map F6, grid d0.
Campsites, facilities: There are five sites for tents or RVs. Picnic tables are provided. Vault toilets are available. No drinking water is available. Leashed pets are permitted.
Reservations, fees: Reserve at (877) 444-6777 ($8.65 reservation fee) or web-site www.re-serveusa.com; $20 group fee per night. Open year-round.
Directions: From Big Pine on U.S. 395, head east on Highway 168 for 13 miles to the camp.
Contact: Inyo National Forest, White Mountain Ranger District, tel. (760) 873-2500 or fax (760) 873-2563.

2 Poleta Group Camp

 5

This is one of four camps in the immediate area, so take your pick. For side trip possibilities, see the entry for Piñon Group Camp.
Location: Near Big Pine in Inyo National Forest; map F6, grid d0.
Campsites, facilities: There are eight sites for tents or RVs. Picnic tables are provided. Vault toilets are available. No drinking water is available. Leashed pets are permitted.
Reservations, fees: Reserve at (877) 444-6777 ($8.65 reservation fee) or website: www.re-serveusa.com; $20 group fee per night. Open year-round.
Directions: From Big Pine on U.S. 395, turn east on Highway 168 and drive 13 miles to the campground.
Contact: Inyo National Forest, White Mountain Ranger District, tel. (760) 873-2500 or fax (760) 873-2563.

3 Juniper Group Camp

 5

Juniper Camp is a nearby option to Poleta Camp for group campers. See the entry for Piñon Group Camp for side trip details.
Location: Near Big Pine in Inyo National Forest; map F6, grid d0.
Campsites, facilities: There are five sites for tents or RVs. Picnic tables are provided. Vault toilets are available. No drinking water is available. Leashed pets are permitted.
Reservations, fees: Reserve at (877) 444-6777 ($8.65 reservation fee) or website: www.re-serveusa.com; $20 group fee per night. Open year-round.
Directions: From Big Pine on U.S. 395, head east on Highway 168 for 13 miles to the camp.
Contact: Inyo National Forest, White Mountain Ranger District, tel. (760) 873-2500 or fax (760) 873-2563.

4 Fossil Group Camp

   5

Fossil Group Camp is a primitive Forest Service group camp set at 7,220 feet in elevation, one of four in the immediate vicinity. See the entry for Piñon Group Camp for side trip options.

Location: Near Big Pine in Inyo National Forest; map F6, grid d0.

Campsites, facilities: There are 11 sites for tents or RVs. Picnic tables are provided. Vault toilets are available. No drinking water is available. Leashed pets are permitted.

Reservations, fees: Reserve at (877) 444-6777 ($8.65 reservation fee) or website: www.reserveusa.com; $20 group fee per night. Open year-round.

Directions: From Big Pine on U.S. 395, head east on Highway 168 and drive 13 miles to the campground.

Contact: Inyo National Forest, White Mountain Ranger District, tel. (760) 873-2500 or fax (760) 873-2563

5 Mesquite Spring

    7

Mesquite Spring is the northernmost and often the prettiest campground in Death Valley, providing you time it right. If you are a lover of desert beauty, then you must make this trip in late winter or early spring, when all kinds of tiny wildflowers can bring the stark valley floor to life. The key is soil moisture, courtesy rains in November and December.

Location: In Death Valley National Park; map F6, grid h8.

Campsites, facilities: There are 30 sites for tents or RVs. Picnic tables and fire grills are provided. Drinking water, flush toilets, and a sanitary disposal station are available. Some facilities are wheelchair accessible. Leashed pets are permitted.

Reservations, fees: No reservations; $10 per night, plus a $10 park entrance fee. Visitors may pay entrance fee and obtain a park brochure at the Furnace Creek, Grapevine, Stovepipe Wells, or Beatty Ranger Stations.

Directions:

Contact: Death Valley National Park, tel. (760) 786-2331 or (760) 786-3244, or fax (760) 786-3283.

ELEPHANT SEALS

KIM WEIR

MAP G1

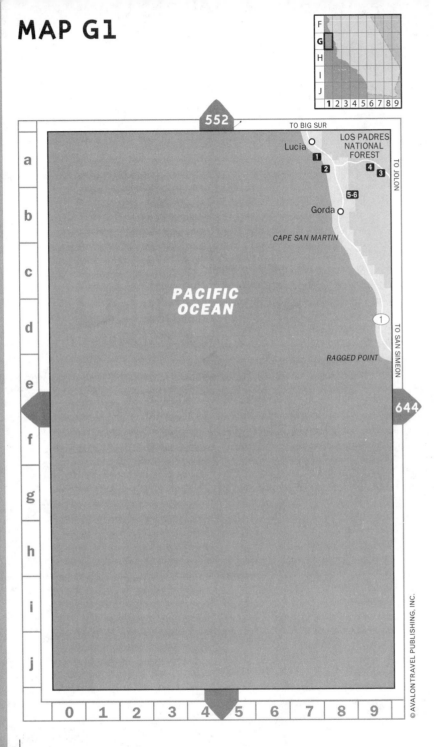

552

TO BIG SUR

Lucia ○

LOS PADRES
NATIONAL
FOREST

1

2

4

3

TO JOLON

5-6

Gorda ○

CAPE SAN MARTIN

**PACIFIC
OCEAN**

1

TO SAN SIMEON

RAGGED POINT

644

a
b
c
d
e
f
g
h
i
j

0 1 2 3 4 5 6 7 8 9

© AVALON TRAVEL PUBLISHING, INC.

CHAPTER G1

1 Limekiln State Park

 9

This camp provides a great layover spot in the Big Sur area of Highway 1, with drive-in campsites set up both near the beach and the redwoods, take your pick. Several hiking trails are available, including one that is routed past some historic lime kilns, which were used in the late 1800s to make cement and bricks. Want more? A short rock hop on a spur trail (just off the main trail) leads to dramatic 100-foot Limekiln Falls, a gorgeous waterfall. This camp was originally called Limekiln Beach Redwoods and was privately operated. It became a state park in 1995.

Location: On the Pacific Ocean; map G1, grid a7.

Campsites, facilities: There are 28 sites for tents or RVs up to 24 feet long, 15 sites for tents, and 3 hike-in/bike-in sites. Picnic tables and fire grills are provided. Restrooms, drinking water, showers, flush toilets, sanitary disposal station, small store, bait, and firewood are available. Leashed pets are allowed, except on trails.

Reservations, fees: Reservations at tel. (800) 444-PARK (444-7275) or website: www.reserveamerica.com; $12 per night, $1 per person per night for hike-in/bike-in sites. Major credit cards accepted. Open year-round.

Directions: From Big Sur, drive 26 miles south on Highway 1 to the park on the left.

Contact: Limekiln State Park (under California Land Management), tel. (831) 667-2403; California State Parks, Monterey District, tel. (831) 649-2836.

2 Kirk Creek

 8

This pretty camp is set along Kirk Creek as it empties into the Pacific Ocean. A trail from camp branches north through the Ventana Wilderness, which is sprinkled with little-used, hike-in, backcountry campsites. For gorgeous scenery without all the work, a quaint little cafe in Lucia provides open-air dining on a cliff-top deck, with a dramatic sweeping lookout over the coast.

Location: Near the Pacific Ocean in Los Padres National Forest; map G1, grid a8.

Campsites, facilities: There are 33 sites for tents or RVs up to 26 feet long. Picnic tables and fire grills are provided. Drinking water and flush toilets are available. Leashed pets are permitted.

Reservations, fees: No reservations; $16 per night, $5 per night for bicyclists. Open year-round.

Directions: From the little town of Lucia, drive four miles south on Highway 1 to the campground on the right.

Contact: Parks Management Company, tel. (805) 434-1996; Los Padres National Forest, Monterey Ranger District; tel. (831) 385-5434 or fax (831) 385-0628.

3 Ponderosa

 4

As soon as you turn off Highway 1, you leave behind the crowds and enter a land that is largely unknown to people. This camp is set at 1,500 feet elevation in Los Padres National Forest, not far from the border of the Ventana Wilderness (good hiking and backpacking) and the Hunter Liggett Military Reservation (wild pig hunting is allowed there with a permit). It is one in a series of small camps on Nacimiento-Ferguson Road.

Location: In Los Padres National Forest; map G1, grid a9.

Campsites, facilities: There are 23 sites for tents or RVs up to 32 feet long. Picnic tables and fire grills are provided. Vault toilets are available. No drinking water is available. Leashed pets are permitted.

Reservations, fees: No reservations; $12 per night. Open year-round.

Directions: From Highway 1 four miles south of Lucia, turn left on Nacimiento-Ferguson Road and drive about 12 miles to the campground on the right.

Contact: Parks Management Company, tel. (805) 434-1996; Los Padres National Forest, Monterey Ranger District, tel. (831) 385-5434 or fax (831) 385-0628.

4 Nacimiento

 5

This little-known spot is set near the Nacimiento River at 1,600 feet elevation. Most campers will head up Nacimiento-Ferguson Road to camp on a Friday night and get up Saturday morning to head off on a hiking or backpacking trip in the nearby Ventana Wilderness.

Location: In Los Padres National Forest; map G1, grid a9.

Campsites, facilities: There are nine sites for tents and eight sites for tents or RVs up to 24 feet long. Picnic tables and fire grills are provided. Vault toilets are available. No drinking water is available. Leashed pets are permitted.

Reservations, fees: No reservations; $5 per night. Open year-round.

Directions: From the little town of Lucia, drive four miles south on Highway 1 to Nacimiento Road. Turn east (left) and drive 11 winding miles to the campground on the right.

Contact: Parks Management Company, tel. (805) 434-1996; Los Padres National Forest,

Monterey Ranger District, tel. (831) 385-5434 or fax (831)385-0628.

5 Plaskett Creek

 8

This is a premium coastal camp for Highway 1 cruisers, set at 200 feet elevation along little Plaskett Creek above the Pacific Ocean. It gets overlooked by many for two reasons: it is not listed with a reservation service, and it is farther south of Big Sur than most are willing to drive. A little cafe in Lucia provides open-air dining with a dramatic lookout over the coast.

Location: Overlooking the Pacific Ocean in Los Padres National Forest; map G1, grid b8.

Campsites, facilities: There are 43 sites for tents or RVs up to 26 feet long. Picnic tables and fire grills are provided. Drinking water and flush toilets are available. Leashed pets are permitted.

Reservations, fees: No reservations; $16 per night, $5 for bicyclists. Open year-round.

Directions: From the town of Lucia, drive 9.5 miles south on Highway 1 to the campground on the left.

Contact: Parks Management Company, tel. (805) 434-1996; Los Padres National Forest, Monterey Ranger District, tel. (831) 385-5434 or fax (831) 385-0628.

6 Plaskett Creek Group Camp

 8

This is one of two prime coastal camps in the immediate area along Highway 1, which is one of the prettiest drives in the West. The camp is for small groups and is set beside little Plaskett Creek. For a premium day trip, drive north five miles to Nacimiento-Ferguson Road, turn east, and drive into Los Padres National Forest and to the border of the Ventana Wilderness. Coastal views and hikes are first-class.

Location: Overlooking the Pacific Ocean in Los Padres National Forest; map G1, grid b8.

Campsites, facilities: There are three group

sites for tents or RVs up to 26 feet long. Picnic tables and fire grills are provided. Drinking water and vault toilets are available. Leashed pets are permitted.

Reservations, fees: Reserve at (877) 444-6777 ($8.65 reservation fee) or website: www.reserveusa.com; $60 group fee per night. Open year-round.

Directions: From the little town of Lucia, drive 9.5 miles south on Highway 1 to the campground on the left.

Contact: Parks Management Company, tel. (805) 434-1996; Los Padres National Forest, Monterey Ranger District, tel. (831) 385-5434 or fax (831) 385-0628.

CHAPTER G2

SAND DUNES

MAP G2

TO KING CITY

568

| a | | San Lucas | Priest Valley |

G14 | 198 |

TO HIGHWAY 1

Jolon

San Ardo

b | LOS PADRES NATIONAL FOREST | Lockwood

101

G14 | **1**

G18

LAKE SAN ANTONIO RECREATION AREA | **2** | Lake San Antonio | Bradley

c

Lake Nacimiento

G19

d

HEARST SAN SIMEON HISTORICAL MONUMENT | LAKE NACIMIENTO RECREATION AREA | **3**

San Simeon | San Miguel

WILLIAM R. HEARST MEMORIAL STATE BEACH | Adelaida | Estrella

e | **4** | Cambria Pines

Cambria | 1

101

PASO ROBLES

Whitley Gardens | 46

638 | 656

Shandon

TO GORDA | TO PARKFIELD | TO COALINGA

Harmony | 46

f | Templeton | 41

CAYUCOS STATE BEACH

Cayucos | Atascadero | Creston

MORRO STRAND STATE BEACH | **5**

g | **6** **7** | 229

8 | 41

58

9 | Morro Bay

MORRO BAY STATE PARK

h | Baywood Park | Santa Margarita | **11** | **12**

Los Osos | **10** | **13**

MONTANA DE ORO STATE PARK | Santa Margarita Lake | Pozo

i | **14** | SAN LUIS OBISPO | LOS PADRES NATIONAL FOREST | **15**

227

Avila Beach

101 | Edna

j | **16** | **17** | Lopez Lake | **20**

Shell Beach | **18**

PACIFIC OCEAN | Pismo Beach | **19**

Grover City | Arroyo Grande

700

TO GUADALUPE TO NIPOMO

0 1 2 3 4 5 6 7 8 9

© AVALON TRAVEL PUBLISHING, INC.

TO CHOLAME

TO CALIFORNIA VALLEY

CHAPTER G2

1 North Shore San Antonio

     7

Lake San Antonio makes a great year-round destination for adventure. It is a big, warm-water lake, long and narrow, set at an elevation of 775 feet in the foothills north of Paso Robles. The camp features four miles of shoreline camping, with the bonus of primitive sites along Pleyto Points. The lake is 16 miles long, covers 5,500 surface acres, and has 60 miles of shoreline and average summer water temperatures in the 70s, making it an ideal place for fun in the sun. It is one of the top lakes in California for bass fishing, best in spring and early summer. It is also good for striped bass, catfish, crappie, sunfish, and bluegill. It also provides the best wintering habitat in the region for bald eagles, and eagle-watching tours are available from the south shore of the lake. Of course, the size of the lake, along with hot temperatures all summer, make water-skiing and water sports absolutely first-class.

Location: On Lake San Antonio; map G2, grid c3.

Campsites, facilities: There are 285 sites for tents or RVs, some with full or partial hookups, and more than 500 primitive sites for tents and RVs. Mobile homes are also available for rent. Fire grills and tables are provided. Restrooms, drinking water, showers, sanitary disposal station, boat ramp, boat rentals, stables, playground, recreation room, laundry facilities, a grocery store, and fishing licenses are available. Leashed pets are permitted.

Reservations, fees: Reservations are accepted at tel. (888) 588-2267; $20 to $22 per night, $2 pet fee; numerous additional fees. Major credit cards accepted. Open year-round.

Directions: On U.S. 101 (just north of King City), take the Jolon Road/G-14 exit. Turn south on Jolon Road and drive

27 miles to Pleyto Road (curvy road). Turn right and drive 3 miles to the North Shore entrance of the lake. Note: When arriving from the south or east on U.S. 101 near Paso Robles, it is faster to take G-18/Jolon Road exit.
Contact: North Shore, tel. (805) 472-2311; website: www.co.monterey.ca.us/parks.

2 South Shore San Antonio

 7

Harris Creek, Redondo Vista, and Lynch are the three campgrounds set near each other along the south shore of Lake San Antonio, a 16-mile reservoir that provides good bass fishing in the spring and water-skiing in the summer. There are also 26 miles of good biking and hiking trails available nearby. There is a museum and visitor center available at the park's administration building. In the winter, the Monterey County Department of Parks offers a unique eagle watch program here which includes boat tours. See the entry for North Shore for more details about the lake.
Location: On Lake San Antonio; map G2, grid c3.
Campsites, facilities: There are three campgrounds here: Redondo has 173 sites for tents and 86 for RVs with full hookups. Lynch has 52 sites for tents and 54 for RVs with full hookups. Harris Creek has 91 sites for tents and 26 for RVs with full hookups. Cabin and mobile home rentals are also available. Picnic tables and fire grills are provided. Drinking water and flush toilets are available. Restrooms, showers, sanitary disposal station, boat ramp, boat rentals, stables, playground, recreation room, laundry facilities, a grocery store, and fishing licenses are available nearby. Leashed pets are permitted.
Reservations, fees: Reservations are accepted at tel. (888) 588-2267; $18 to $22 per night, $2 pet fee. Open year-round.
Directions from the north: On U.S. 101 (just north of King City), take the Jolon Road/G-14 exit. Turn south on Jolon Road and drive 20 miles to Lockwood and Interlake Road (G-14). Turn right and drive 13 miles to San Antonio Lake Road. Turn left and drive 3 miles to the South Shore entrance of the lake.
Directions from the south: On U.S. 101 at Paso Robles, take the 24th Street exit (G-14 West) and drive 14 miles to Lake Nacimiento Drive. Turn right and drive across Lake Nacimiento Dam to Interlake Road. Turn left and drive seven miles to Lake San Antonio Road. Turn right and drive three miles to South Shore entrance.
Contact: South Shore, tel. (805) 472-2311; website: www.co.monterey.ca.us/parks.

3 Lake Nacimiento Resort

 8

This is the only game in town at Nacimiento, and they play it well. It's an outstanding operation, with headquarters for a great fishing or water sports trip. The fishing for white bass can be incredible, catching dozens, vertical jigging a Horizon jig. And the water play is also great, with such a big lake, 70-degree temperatures, and some of the best water-skiing in California. The lake has 165 miles of shoreline with an incredible number of arms and lakes, many ideal for bass fishing. Nacimiento hosts 25 fishing tournaments per year. Not only is bass fishing good, but there are also opportunities for trout (in cool months) and bluegill and catfish (in warm months). The resort has a great restaurant with a lake view, and the campsites provide limited tree cover with pines and oaks. Two camps are on the lake's shore, the rest are set back about three-quarters of a mile from the lake. Lakeview lodging is also available.
Location: At Lake Nacimiento; map G2, grid d4.
Campsites, facilities: There are 297 campsites at a series of campgrounds operated by the resort at the southeast end of the lake, 17 lodges, RV rental, mobile home rental, and 10 group sites for 15 to 40 people. Oak Knoll

Camp has 40 sites with full hookups for RVs. Picnic tables and fire grills are provided. Drinking water and flush toilets are available. Restrooms, showers, sanitary disposal station, boat ramp, boat docks, boat rentals, stables, playground, swimming pool, restaurant, recreation room, laundry facilities, a grocery store, and fishing licenses are available nearby. Swimming beaches, basketball and volleyball courts, and horseshoe pits are also available. Leashed pets are permitted.

Reservations, fees: Reservations are accepted at tel. (800) 323-3839, ext. 1, or (805) 238-3256, ext. 1; $14 to $27 per vehicle per night, lodges are $95 to $385, RVs rent for $70 to $95, mobile homes $130 to $275, pets $5 per night. Major credit cards accepted. Open year-round.

Directions: From U.S. 101 in Paso Robles, take the 24th Street/Lake Nacimiento exit. Turn west on 24th Street (becomes Lake Nacimiento Road/G-14) and drive for nine miles. Bear right on Lake Nacimiento road for seven miles to the resort entrance on the left. Note: If you cross the Lake Nacimiento dam, you've gone too far.

Contact: Lake Nacimiento Resort, tel. (800) 323-3839 or (805) 238-3256; website: www. nacimientoresort.com.

4 San Simeon State Park

 9

Hearst Castle is only five miles northeast, so San Simeon Creek is a natural for visitors planning to take the tour; for a tour reservation, phone (800) 444-4445 ($10 per adult and $5 per child tour fee). San Simeon Creek Campground is set across the highway from the ocean, with easy access under the highway to the beach. San Simeon Creek, while not exactly the Mississippi, runs through the campground and adds a nice touch. Washburn Campground provides an option at this park, and while providing better views, the sites are exposed and can be windy. The best hike in the area is from Leffingwell Landing to Moonstone Beach, featuring sweeping views of the coast from ocean-top bluffs and a good chance to see passing whales.

Location: In San Simeon State Park; map G2, grid e1.

Campsites, facilities: At San Simeon Creek Camp, there are 133 sites for tents or RVs up to 35 feet long. At Washburn Camp, there are 70 sites for tents or RVs up to 31 feet long. Picnic tables and fire grills are provided. Drinking water, flush toilets, coin-operated showers, and a sanitary disposal station are available. Some facilities are wheelchair accessible. A grocery store, coin laundry, gas station, restaurants, and propane gas can be found nearby in Cambria. Leashed pets are permitted.

Reservations, fees: Reserve at tel. (800) 444-PARK (444-7275) or website: www.reserve america.com; $12 per night at San Simeon Creek, $7 per night at Washburn. Open year-round.

Directions: From Cambria, drive three miles north on Highway 1 to the park entrance.

Contact: San Simeon Creek, tel. (805) 927-2035 or tel. (805) 927-2020.

5 Cerro Alto

 7

This camp is set near Morro Creek, which runs most of the year but which in dry years can disappear in late summer. In addition, some sites are along the creek, nicely spaced, with sycamore and bay trees peppering the hillside. There are numerous hiking and mountain biking trails. The best of these is the Cerro Alto Trail, which is accessible from camp and then is routed four miles up to Cuesta Ridge for sweeping views of Morro Bay.

Location: Near San Luis Obispo; map G2, grid g4.

Campsites, facilities: There are 20 sites for tents or RVs up to 25 feet long. No hookups. Picnic tables and grills are provided. Drinking water and vault toilets are available. A camp host, amphitheater, and public phone are nearby. Some facilities are wheelchair accessible. Leashed pets permitted.

Reservations, fees: No reservations; $16 per night. Open year-round, weather permitting.

Directions: From U.S. 101 at Atascadero, take the Highway 41 West exit. Drive eight miles west to the campground on the left.

Contact: Los Padres National Forest, Santa Lucia Ranger District, tel. (805) 925-9538, or fax (805) 681-2781.

6 Morro Strand State Beach

 7

A ton of Highway 1 cruisers plan to stay overnight at this state park. And why not? It is set along the ocean near Morro Bay, right on the beach, a pretty spot year-round. Side trips include the Morro Bay Wildlife Refuge, the Museum of Natural History, or an ocean fishing trip out of Morro Bay. See the entry for Morro Bay State Park for more information.

Location: Near Morro Bay; map G2, grid g3.

Campsites, facilities: There are 75 sites for tents or RVs up to 24 feet long. Picnic tables and fire grills are provided. Drinking water and flush toilets are available. Cold, outdoor showers are also available. Supplies and a coin laundry are available in Morro Bay. Leashed pets are permitted.

Reservations, fees: Reserve at tel. (800) 444-PARK (800-444-7275) or website: www.reserve-america.com; $12 per night. Open year-round.

Directions: On Highway 1, drive to Morro Bay. Take the Yerba Buena Street/Morro Strand State Beach exit. Turn west on Yerba Buena Street and drive one block to the campground.

Contact: Morro Strand State Beach, tel. (805) 772-8812 or fax (805) 772-7434; California State Parks, San Luis Obispo District, tel. (805) 549-3312 or fax (805) 541-4799.

7 Rancho Colina RV Park

 6

This privately operated RV park is one of several camping options in the Morro Bay area.

Folks who park here typically stroll the boardwalk, exploring the little shops. For recreation activities, see the entry for Morro Bay State Park.

Location: In Morro Bay; map G2, grid g4.

Campsites, facilities: There are 57 RV sites with full hookups. Picnic tables are provided. Restrooms, showers, laundry facilities, and a recreation room are available. You can buy supplies nearby. Leashed pets are permitted.

Reservations, fees: Reservations are accepted; $23 per night. Major credit cards accepted. Open year-round.

Directions: From Morro Bay on Highway 1, drive one mile east on Atascadero Road/Highway 41 to 1045 Atascadero Road.

Contact: Rancho Colina RV Park, tel. (805) 772-8420.

8 Morro Dunes Trailer Park and Camp

 6

A wide array of side trip possibilities and great natural beauty make Morro Bay an attractive destination. Most visitors will walk the boardwalk, try at least one of the coastal restaurants, and then head to Morro Bay State Park for hiking or sea kayaking. Other folks will head straight to the port for fishing, or just explore the area before heading north to San Simeon for the Hearst Castle tour. See the entry for Morro Bay State Park for more information.

Location: In Morro Bay; map G2, grid g4.

Campsites, facilities: There are 43 sites for tents and 139 RV sites with full hookups. Picnic tables and fire grills are provided. Restrooms, drinking water, showers, electrical connections, cable TV, modem hookups, laundry facilities, store, wood, ice, and a sanitary disposal station are available. Propane gas can be obtained nearby. Leashed pets are permitted. Some facilities are wheelchair accessible.

Reservations, fees: Reservations are accepted; $16 to $24 per night, pets $1 per night. Major credit cards accepted. Open year-round.

Directions: From Highway 1 in Morro Bay,

drive west on Atascadero Road/Highway 41 for a half mile to 1700 Embarcadero/Atascadero Road.

Contact: Morro Dunes Trailer Park and Camp, tel. (805) 772-2722 or fax (805) 772-5319; website: www.campgrounds.com/morrodunes/.

🟨9 Morro Bay State Park

     9

Reservations are strongly advised at this popular campground. This is one of the premium stopover spots for folks cruising north on Highway 1. The park offers a wide range of activities and exhibits covering the natural and cultural history of the area. Activities include beach walks, kayaking in Morro Bay, fishing the nearby ocean on a party boat, touring Hearst Castle, or visiting the Morro Bay Wildlife Refuge. A "morro" is a small volcanic peak, and there are nine of them along the local coast. The top hike at the park climbs one of them, Black Hill, and rewards hikers with sensational coastal views.

Location: In Morro Bay; map G2, grid h3.

Campsites, facilities: There are 30 RV sites with water and electrical connections, 95 sites for tents or RVs up to 31 feet long, and two group sites for 30 to 50 people. Picnic tables, food lockers, and fire rings are provided. Restrooms, drinking water, flush toilets, coin-operated showers, sanitary disposal station, museum exhibits, and nature walks and programs are available. A coin laundry, grocery store, propane gas, boat ramp, mooring, rentals, gas stations and food service are available in Morro Bay. The museum and food service areas are wheelchair accessible. Leashed pets are permitted.

Reservations, fees: Reserve at tel. (800) 444-PARK (444-7275) or website: www.reserveamerica.com; $12-18 per night, group sites $22 to $37 per night. Open year-round.

Directions: On Highway 1, drive to Morro Bay and take the South Bay Boulevard/Morro Bay State Park exit. Turn south and drive one mile to State Park Road. Turn right and drive one mile to the park entrance on the right.

Contact: Morro Bay State Park, tel. (805) 772-7434 or fax (805) 772-5760; California State Parks, San Luis Obispo District, tel. (805) 549-3312 or fax (805) 541-4799.

🟨10 El Chorro Regional Park

     6

North of Morro Bay on the way to San Simeon and Hearst Castle, this can be a prime spot for RV travelers. Note that the campground isn't in the state park reservation system, which means there are times when coastal state parks can be jammed full and this regional park may still have space. Morro Bay, six miles away, provides many possible side trips. The park has full recreational facilities, including volleyball, horseshoe pits, softball, hiking trails, and botanical gardens. A golf course is nearby. Note that there's a men's prison about one mile away. For some people, this can be a real turnoff.

Location: Near San Luis Obispo; map G2, grid h5.

Campsites, facilities: There are 42 sites for tents or RVs with full hookups and some undesignated overflow sites. Fire grills and picnic tables are provided. Restrooms, drinking water, flush toilets, showers, and recreational facilities are available. Supplies and a coin laundry are nearby in San Luis Obispo. Leashed pets are permitted.

Reservations, fees: No reservations; $18 to $22 per night, $2 pet fee. Groups may reserve six or more sites three weeks prior to arrival, $18 per night per site. Major credit cards accepted. Open year-round.

Directions: From San Luis Obispo, drive 4.5 miles north on Highway 1 to the park entrance on the right side of the highway.

Contact: El Chorro Regional Park, tel. (805) 781-5930; website: www.slocountyparks.com.

ⅠⅠ Santa Margarita KOA

      6

Santa Margarita Lake should have a sign at its entrance that proclaims, "Fishing Only!"That's because the rules here do not allow water-skiing or any water contact, including swimming, wading, using float tubes, and windsurfing. The excellent prospects for bass fishing, along with the prohibitive rules, make this lake a favorite among anglers. Santa Margarita Lake covers nearly 800 acres, most of it long and narrow and set in a dammed-up valley in the foothill country at an elevation of 1,300 feet, just below the Santa Lucia Mountains. On weekends, this place can turn into another world: Paintball war games are often held here, and on Saturday afternoons, a BMX track is popular.

Location: Near Santa Margarita Lake; map G2, grid h7.

Campsites, facilities: There are 54 sites for tents or RVs, some with electrical connections and sewer hookups. There are also 11 cabins. Picnic tables and fire grills are provided. Restrooms, drinking water, flush toilets, showers, modem hookups, swimming pool, playground, coin laundry, store, sanitary disposal station, and propane gas are available. Leashed pets are permitted.

Reservations, fees: Reservations at (800) 562-5619; $20 to $26 per night, $3 to $4 (depending on age) per person per night for more than two people, $34 to $42 per cabin per night. Major credit cards accepted. Open year-round.

Directions: From San Luis Obispo, drive eight miles north on U.S. 101 to the Highway 58/Santa Margarita exit. Drive through the town of Santa Margarita and turn right on Entrada. Within one mile, Entrada turns into Pozo Road. Continue six miles on Pozo Road to Santa Margarita Lake Road. Turn left and drive a half mile to the campground on the right.

Contact: Santa Margarita KOA, tel. (805) 438-5618; website: www.koacampgrounds.com.

ⅠⅡ Selby

    6

The Carrizo Plain is California's largest nature preserve, but due to its remote location, primitive setting, and lack of recreational lakes and streams, it remains largely unknown and is explored by few people. The feature attraction is to visit Soda Lake in the winter to see flocks of the endangered sandhill crane; the lake is a nesting area for the huge bird with a seven-foot wingspan. Selby is a primitive camping area at the base of the Caliente Mountain Range, known for its scorching hot (hey, after all, "Caliente") temperatures during the summer. The top hiking destination in the region is Painted Rock, a 55-foot rock with Indian pictographs.

Location: At the Carrizo Plain, northeast of San Luis Obispo; map G2, grid h9.

Campsites, facilities: This is a primitive camping area with no designated sites. Picnic tables and fire pits are provided. A pit toilet is available. No drinking water is available. Garbage must be packed out. Leashed pets are permitted.

Reservations, fees: No reservations; no fee. Open year-round.

Directions: From Bakersfield, take Highway 58 west for about 30 miles to McKittrick (where Highway 33 merges with Highway 58). Stay on Highway 58/33 for about another 10 miles, turn west on Seven-Mile Road, and drive seven miles (six miles will be on gravel road). Turn left on Soda Lake Road and drive about six miles to the Selby camping area on your right.

Contact: Bureau of Land Management, Bakersfield Field Office; tel. (661) 391-6000, or fax (661) 391-6040.

ⅠⅢ KCL

     6

KCL is the name of the old ranch headquarters in the Carrizo, of which remains an old broken-down barn, a water wagon, and not much else. At least there are some trees here (in comparison, there are none at nearby Selby camp). The Carrizo Plain is best known for providing a habitat for many rare species of plants, in addition to furnishing the winter nesting sites at Soda Lake for the awesome migration of giant sandhill cranes. Occasionally these huge birds will fly down the valley and are visible here.

Location: At the Carrizo Plain, northeast of San Luis Obispo; map G2, grid h9.

Campsites, facilities: This is a primitive camping area with no designated sites. Picnic tables and fire pits are provided. A pit toilet and corrals are available. No drinking water is available. Garbage must be packed out. Leashed pets are permitted.

Reservations, fees: No reservations; no fee. Open year-round.

Directions: From Bakersfield, take Highway 58 west for about 30 miles to McKittrick (where Highway 33 merges with Highway 58). Stay on Highway 58/33 for another 10 to 12 miles, turn west on Seven-Mile Road, and drive seven miles. Turn left on Soda Lake Road and drive six miles to the entrance of the Carrizo Plains Natural Area. Continue about 15 miles to the KCL camping area on your right.

Contact: Bureau of Land Management, Bakersfield Field Office; tel. (661) 391-6000, or fax (661) 391-6040.

🔢14 Montaña de Oro State Park

    9

This sprawling chunk of primitive land includes coastline, 8,500 acres of foothills, and Valencia Peak at 1,345 feet in elevation. But there's no water—and that stops a lot of people from ever venturing here. The camp is perched near a bluff, and while there are no sweeping views from campsites, they await nearby. The Bluffs Trail is one of the best easy coastal walks anywhere, offering stunning views of the ocean and cliffs and, in the spring, tons of wildflowers over the course of just 1.5 miles. Another hiking option at the park is to climb Valencia Peak, a little butt-kicker of an ascent

that tops out at 1,373 feet, providing more panoramic coastal views. These are the two best hikes among 50 miles of trails for horses and hikers, with trails accessible right out of the campground.

Location: Near Morro Bay; map G2, grid i2.

Campsites, facilities: There are 50 sites for tents or RVs up to 27 feet long, four walk-in environmental sites, four equestrian sites and two group equestrian sites for up to 50 people and 25 horses. Picnic tables and fire grills are provided. Vault toilets are available. Drinking water is available only at the main campground. There is limited corral space and single site equestrian camps with two stalls each. Garbage from equestrian and environmental sites must be packed out. Supplies and a coin laundry are available five miles away in Los Osos. Leashed pets are permitted.

Reservations, fees: Reserve at tel. (800) 444-PARK (444-7275) or website: www.reserve america.com; $7 per night, $12 for equestrian sites, $25 for group sites. Open year-round.

Directions: From Morro Bay, drive two miles south on Highway 1. Turn on South Bay Boulevard and drive four miles to Los Osos. Turn right on Los Osos Valley Road and drive five miles (it becomes Pecho Valley Road) to the park.

Contact: Montaña de Oro State Park, tel. (805) 528-0513 or tel. (805) 549-3312.

🔢15 Hi Mountain

    4

At an elevation of 2,800 feet, this is the highest point in the Santa Lucia Wilderness. A mile west you can drive to the Hi Mountain Lookout, with awesome 360-degree views from the 3,180-foot summit. A mile to the east is a primitive road; turn south and drive to its end for a trailhead. From here, you can hike along Trout Creek for six miles to a little-known backpack camp called Buckeye.

Location: In Los Padres National Forest; map G2, grid i8.

Campsites, facilities: There are 11 sites for tents or RVs up to 16 feet long (trailers not recommended). Picnic tables and fire grills are provided. Vault toilets are available. No drinking water is available. Leashed pets are permitted.

Reservations, fees: No reservations; no camping fee, $5 per day per parked vehicle or Adventure Pass ($30 annual fee). Open year-round (road may be closed during heavy rains).

Directions: From San Luis Obispo, drive eight miles north on U.S. 101. Turn east on Highway 58 and drive four miles (four miles past Santa Margarita). Turn southeast on Pozo Road and drive for 16 miles to the town of Pozo. Turn on Hi Mountain Road and drive four miles to the campground.

Contact: Los Padres National Forest, Santa Lucia Ranger District at tel. (805) 925-9538 or fax (805) 681-2781.

16 Avila Valley Hot Springs Spa and RV Park

 6

The hot mineral pool here is a featured attraction. A pizza kitchen and snack bar are available as well. Nearby recreation options include Avila State Beach and Pismo State Beach.

Location: On San Luis Obispo Bay; map G2, grid j4.

Campsites, facilities: There are 25 sites for tents and 50 RV spaces, many with full or partial hookups. Picnic tables and fire grills (at some spots) are provided. Restrooms, showers, swimming pool, hot mineral pool, spa, cable TV, sanitary disposal station, recreation room, arcade, massage service, golf course, grocery store, snack bar, and group barbecue pits are available. Leashed pets are permitted. Some facilities are wheelchair accessible.

Reservations, fees: Reserve at tel. (800) 332-2359; $18 to $28 per night, $5 per night for each extra vehicle. There is an extra charge for use of the pool and spa facilities. Open year-round. Major credit cards accepted.

Directions: From San Luis Obispo, drive nine miles south on U.S. 101 to the Avila Beach Drive exit. Continue to 250 Avila Beach Drive.

Contact: Avila Valley Hot Springs Spa and RV Park, tel. (805) 595-2359 or fax (805) 595-2060; website: www.avilahotsprings.com.

17 Pismo Coast Village RV Resort

 7

This big-time RV park gets a lot of use by Highway 1 cruisers. Its location is a plus, set near the ocean. Pismo Beach is famous for its clamming, sand dunes, and beautiful coast.

Location: In Pismo Beach; map G2, grid j5.

Campsites, facilities: There are 400 RV sites with full hookups. Picnic tables and fire grills are provided. Restrooms, showers, satellite TV, modem hookups, playgrounds, swimming pools, laundry facilities, store, firewood, ice, recreation room, propane gas, recreation programs, restaurant, and a miniature golf course are available. Leashed pets are permitted. Some facilities are wheelchair accessible.

Reservations, fees: Reserve at (888) RV BEACH (888-782-3224); $26 to $37 per night. Open year-round. Major credit cards accepted.

Directions: In Pismo Beach, drive to 165 South Dolliver Street/Highway 1.

Contact: Pismo Coast Village, tel. (805) 773-1811, or fax (805) 773-1507; website: www.pismocoastvillage.com.

18 North Beach

 7

The adjacent dune area makes for great walks or, for kids, great rolls. The clamming on minus low tides is legendary. OHV use is popular nearby. Plan on needing a reservation and having plenty of company when you come to North Beach. This is an exceptionally popular state beach, as an ultimate destination or as a stopover for folks cruising Highway 1.

Location: In Pismo State Beach; map G2, grid j5.

Campsites, facilities: There are 103 sites for tents or RVs up to 31 feet long, and one hike-in/bike-in site. Fire grills, food lockers, and picnic tables are provided. Restrooms, drinking water, showers, flush toilets, and a sanitary disposal station are available. Horseback riding facilities, grocery store, restaurants, coin laundry, and propane gas are nearby. Some facilities are wheelchair accessible. Leashed pets are permitted.

Reservations, fees: Reserve at tel. (800) 444-PARK (444-7275) or website: www.reserve america.com; $12-18 per night. Hike-in site is $1 per person per night. Open year-round.

Directions: On Highway 1 in Pismo Beach, take the North Beach/State Campground exit (well signed) and drive to the park entrance.

Contact: California State Parks, San Luis Obispo District, tel. (805) 773-2334, or (805) 549-3312.

19 Le Sage Riviera

     4

This is a year-round RV park that can serve as headquarters for folks who are interested in visiting several nearby attractions, including neighboring Pismo State Beach and Lopez Lake, 10 miles to the east.

Location: Near Pismo State Beach; map G2, grid j5.

Campsites, facilities: There are 60 RV sites, many with hookups. No tent camping is permitted. Picnic tables are provided. Restrooms, drinking water, showers, and laundry facilities are available. Stores, restaurants, and golf courses are nearby. Some facilities are wheelchair accessible. Leashed pets are permitted.

Reservations, fees: Reservations are accepted; $23 to $32 per night. Open year-round.

Directions: From Pismo Beach, drive two miles south on Grand Avenue or Dolliver Street to 319 North Highway 1.

Contact: Le Sage Riviera, tel. (805) 489-5506 or fax (805) 489-2103

20 Lopez Lake Recreation Area

     7

Lopez Lake has become an example of how to do something right, with special marked areas set aside exclusively for water-skiing, personal watercraft, and windsurfing, and the rest of the lake designated for fishing and low-speed boating. There are also reserved areas for swimming. That makes it perfect for just about everyone and, with good bass fishing, the lake has become very popular, especially on spring weekends when the bite is on. Lopez Lake is set amid oak woodlands southeast of San Luis Obispo. The lake is shaped something like a horseshoe, has 940 surface acres with 22 miles of shoreline when full, and gets excellent weather most of the year.

Location: Near Arroyo Grande; map G2, grid j8.

Campsites, facilities: There are 354 sites for tents or RVs of any length, many with full or partial hookups, and a group site is available. Picnic tables and fire rings are provided. Restrooms, showers, playground, laundry facilities, store, ice, snack bar, marina, boat ramp, mooring, boat fuel, tackle, boat rentals, and a water slide are available. Some facilities are wheelchair accessible. Leashed pets are permitted.

Reservations, fees: Reservations are accepted; phone (805) 489-8019; $14 to $22 per night, $2 pet fee, $5 boat launch fee, $5 per night for each extra vehicle, group camp $72 to $144. Major credit cards accepted. Open year-round.

Directions: From Arroyo Grande on U.S. 101, take the Grand Avenue exit. Turn east and drive through Arroyo Grande. Turn northeast on Lopez Drive and drive 10 miles to the park.

Contact: Lopez Lake Recreation Area, tel. (805) 788-2381; website: www.slocountyparks.com.

POPPIES ON ROLLING HILLS

MAP G3

TO LOS BANOS **576** TO FIVE POINTS TO HUB

198

5 O Huron

O Coalinga

198 269

O Stratford 41

O Lemoore 198

TO HANFORD

TO GUERNSEY

Avenal O **1** O Kettleman City

33

41

KETTLEMAN STATE RECREATION AREA

TO CORCORAN

Parkfield O

5

TO SAN MIGUEL

Cholame O

46 Devils Den O

KERN NATIONAL WILDLIFE REFUGE

660

644

Shandon O

TO PASO ROBLES

Blackwells Corner O 46 **2**

Lost Hills

TO SANTA MARGARITA

33

5

TO WASCO

TO SHAFFER

3

LOS PADRES NATIONAL FOREST

TO POZO

58 Buttonwillow O

California Valley O

58

TO WHEELER RIDGE

McKittrick O

706 TO DERBY

© AVALON TRAVEL PUBLISHING, INC.

CHAPTER G3

1 Kettleman City RV Park

 2

Being stuck in Kings County looking for a place to park an RV is no picnic. Unless, that is, you are lucky enough to know about Kettleman City RV Park. The spaces are wide open with long-distance views of the Sierra. It's literally the "only game in town"; in fact, it's the only camp in the entire county. Another claim to fame: it's eight hours to the Mexican border. Visitors will find access to miles of open paths and roads for hiking or running.

Location: Near Kettleman City; map G3, grid c5.

Campsites, facilities: There are 65 RV sites with full or partial hookups and an overflow area with unlimited tent sites. Picnic tables are provided. Eight RV sites have telephone hookups. Restrooms, showers, playgrounds, video game room, swimming pool, meeting room, coin laundry, store, sanitary disposal station, dog run, restaurant, snack bar, horseshoeing services, horseback riding, and propane gas are available. There is also a two-acre RV sales lot at the park. Leashed pets are permitted. Some facilities are wheelchair accessible.

Reservations, fees: Reservations at (800) 258-0537; $12 to $20 per night. Note: Overnight campers receive a 10 percent discount at the camp restaurant. Open year-round. Major credit cards accepted.

Directions: From Interstate 5 near Kettleman City, take the Highway 41 exit. Drive a half mile north on Highway 41. Turn left on Hubert Way, then right on Cyril Place to 452 Cyril Place.

Contact: Kettleman City RV Park, tel. (559) 386-4000.

2 Lost Hills KOA

 4

The pickings can get slim around these parts when you're cruising north on Interstate 5 so if it's late, you'll likely be happy to find this KOA camp. The nearby Kern National Wildlife Refuge, about a 15-minute drive away, offers a side trip possibility. It's a waterfowl reserve that attracts ducks, geese, and other waterfowl in the fall and winter.

Location: Near Kern National Wildlife Refuge; map G3, grid g8.

Campsites, facilities: There are 15 sites for tents only, 79 RV sites with full hookups, 20 overflow spots with no hookups, and one cabin. Picnic tables are provided. Restrooms, drinking water, showers, satellite TV, swimming pool, laundry facilities, store, video room, and propane gas are available. Some facilities are wheelchair accessible. Restaurants are nearby. Leashed pets are permitted.

Reservations, fees: Reserve at tel. (800) 562-2793; $22 to $26 per night; $36 per night cabin fee. Major credit cards accepted. Open year-round.

Directions: Drive to the junction of Interstate 5 and Highway 46. If you are coming from the south, make a left turn on Highway 46 into the park entrance. Coming from the north, make a right turn on Highway 46 into the park entrance (three blocks off I-5 behind Carl's Jr.).

Contact: Lost Hills KOA, tel. (661) 797-2719; website: www.koacampgrounds.com.

3 La Panza

 3

This primitive spot is at 2,400 feet in the La Panza Range, an oak woodland area that is crisscrossed by numerous trails and streams. From camp, if you drive west on the access road for one mile to a junction, turn left on Road M3093, and drive three miles to Pozo Summit, you will arrive at one of the better trailheads for the Maghesna Mountain Wilderness to the south. From here, the trail is routed on a ridge for two miles to the wilderness boundary, then heads east across Pine Mountain and Castle Crags. Water is scarce.

Location: In Los Padres National Forest; map G3, grid i0.

Campsites, facilities: There are 16 sites for tents or RVs up to 16 feet long. Picnic tables and fire grills are provided. Vault toilets are available. No drinking water is available. Leashed pets are permitted.

Reservations, fees: No reservations; an Adventure Pass ($30 annual fee) or a $5 daily fee per parked vehicle is required. Open year-round.

Directions: From San Luis Obispo, drive eight miles north on U.S. 101. Turn east on Highway 58 and drive four miles (two miles past Santa Margarita). Turn southeast on Pozo Road and drive for 16 miles to the town of Pozo. Continue 11.5 miles east past Pozo on County Road M3093 to the campground.

Contact: Los Padres National Forest, Santa Lucia Ranger District, tel. (805) 925-9538 or fax (805) 681-2781.

TULE ELK

MAP G4

TO SELMA · TO WILSONIA
580

TO LEMOORE · TO STRATFORD · TO I-5 · TO LOST HILLS · TO HIGHWAY 33 · TO MCKITTRICK

TO GIANT FOREST VILLAGE · TO CAMP NELSON · TO WOFFORD HEIGHTS · TO MIRACLE HOT SPRINGS

Hanford · Goshen · **1**
VISALIA
Woodlake · **216** · Lake Kaweah · **198**
Ivanhoe · Lemon Cove · Three Rivers · **3**
198 · **245** · **2**
Guernsey
Farmersville · Exeter
43 · **99** · **63** · **198**
137
Tulare
Waukena · **4**
Lindsay
Corcoran · **137**
J15 · **J27**
Strathmore
Tipton · Woodville
Lake Success · Springville
J26 · **J26**
190 · Porterville
Angiola · Poplar
Pixley · **190** · **5** · **6**
PIXLEY NATIONAL WILDLIFE REFUGE
Terra Bella
J42
TULE RIVER INDIAN RESERVATION
Alpaugh · **99** · **65**
Allensworth · **7**
COLONEL ALLENSWORTH STATE HISTORIC PARK
J22
Earlimart · Ducor · Fountain Springs
43 · **J22**
J44 · Richgrove
White River
Delano · **155**
Pond
McFarland · Woody · Glennville
46
Wasco · Famoso
65
Shafter · **8**
SEQUOIA NATIONAL FOREST
43 · **99**
Rosedale · Oildale · **9**
TULE ELK STATE RESERVE · **58** · **178**
BAKERSFIELD
TO WHEELER RIDGE
724

656 · **666**

© AVALON TRAVEL PUBLISHING, INC.

CHAPTER G4

1 Visalia/Fresno South KOA

     1

This is a layover spot for Highway 99 cruisers. If you're looking for a spot to park your rig for the night, you can't get too picky around these parts.

Location: West of Visalia; map G4, grid a3.

Campsites, facilities: There are 30 sites for tents only, 48 RV sites with full or partial hookups, and 38 sites for tents or RVs. Restrooms, showers, swimming pool, laundry facilities, playground, recreation room, store, sanitary disposal station, and propane gas are available. Leashed pets are permitted.

Reservations, fees: Reservations at (800) 562-0544; $19 to $26 per night. Major credit cards accepted. Open year-round.

Directions: From Visalia, drive five miles west on Highway 198 to the Plaza exit. Turn right on Plaza and drive five miles to Goshen Road. Turn left on Goshen Road and drive a quarter mile to Road 76. Turn right and drive to the camp entrance (well signed).

Contact: Visalia-Fresno KOA, tel. (559) 651-0544; website: ww.explorekoa.com.

2 Lemon Cove-Sequoia

      5

This is a privately run, year-round campground set on the outskirts of Visalia, about eight miles off Highway 99. It may not be the most beautiful spot on earth, but if you're stuck looking for a spot for the night and find this campground, it will look like paradise. Lake Kaweah is 17 miles east on Highway 198.

Location: Near Lake Kaweah; map G4, grid a7.

Campsites, facilities: There are 55 sites for tents or RVs, as well as group camping facilities. Picnic tables, drinking water, and full or partial hookups are provided. Restrooms, showers, playground, swimming pool, laundry facilities, recreation room, cable TV, store, sanitary disposal station, and propane gas are available. Leashed pets are permitted.

Reservations, fees: Reservations are accepted; $16-22 per night. Open year-round. Major credit cards accepted.

Directions: From Visalia, drive east on Highway 198 for 22 miles to the campground at Lake Kaweah.

Contact: Lemon Cove-Sequoia, tel. (559) 597-2346; website: www.lemoncovesequoia.com.

3 Horse Creek

    6

Lake Kaweah is a big lake, covering nearly 2,000 acres with 22 miles of shoreline. In the spring when the lake is full and the surrounding hills are green, you may even think you have found Valhalla. With such hot weather in the San Joaquin Valley, it's a boater's heaven, ideal for water-skiers, with good bass fishing in the coves and enough room for personal watercraft to stay clear. The camp is set on the southern shore of the lake. One problem is that the water level drops a great deal during late summer, as thirsty farms suck up every drop they can get, killing prospects of developing beaches for swimming and wading. The elevation is 300 feet.

Location: On Lake Kaweah; map G4, grid a8.

Campsites, facilities: There are 80 sites for tents or RVs. Picnic tables and fire grills are provided. Restrooms, drinking water, flush toilets, showers, paved boat ramp, playground, and a sanitary disposal station are available. Some facilities are wheelchair accessible. A grocery store, coin laundry, boat and water-ski rentals, ice, snack bar, restaurant, gas station, and propane gas are available nearby. Leashed pets are permitted.

Reservations, fees: Reserve at tel. (877) 444-6777 ($8.65 reservation fee) or website: www.reserveusa.com; $16 per night. Major credit cards accepted. Open year-round.

Directions: From Visalia, drive 25 miles east on Highway 198 to Lake Kaweah's south shore and the camp on the left.

Contact: U.S. Army Corps of Engineers, tel. (559) 597-2301, or fax (559) 597-2468.

4 Sun and Fun RV Park

 1

This RV park is just off Highway 99, exactly halfway between San Francisco and Los Angeles. Are you having fun yet? Anybody making the long drive up or down the state on Highway 99 will learn what a dry piece of life the San Joaquin Valley can seem. That's why the swimming pool at this RV park can be a lifesaver.

Location: Near Tulare; map G4, grid c3.

Campsites, facilities: There are 60 RV sites. Picnic tables, fire grills, and full hookups are provided. Restrooms, drinking water, showers, modem hookups, sanitary disposal station, playground, swimming pool, spa, laundry facilities, and a recreation room are available. Some facilities are wheelchair accessible. A golf course, restaurant, and store are nearby. Leashed pets are permitted.

Reservations, fees: Reservations are accepted; $23 per night. Open year-round.

Directions: From Tulare, drive three miles south on Highway 99 to the Avenue 200 exit west. Drive a short distance to 1000 Avenue 200. From Tipton, drive 10 miles north on Highway 99. Exit on Avenue 200, bearing right over the freeway to the campground entrance.

Contact: Sun and Fun RV Park, tel. (559) 686-5779.

5 Eagle's Nest Roost

     4

This campground is in a park-like setting with trees and flowers. It is two miles from Lake Success. A small, stocked fishing pond is available, and pet geese and ducks are often wandering around. For information on Lake Success, see the entry for Tule Recreation Area.

Location: Near Lake Success; map G4, grid d8.

Campsites, facilities: There are 250 sites for tents or RVs, 50 with full or partial hookups. Picnic tables and, in some cases, fire grills are provided. Restrooms, showers, recreation room, playground, swimming pool, fishing facilities, laundry room, store, sanitary disposal station, firewood, dog-walking area, and propane gas are available. Quiet, well-mannered, leashed pets are permitted.

Reservations, fees: Reservations are accepted; $14 to $28 per night. Major credit cards accepted. Open year-round.

Directions: From Porterville on Highway 65, turn east on Highway 190 and drive five miles to 27798 Highway 190 on left.

Contact: Eagle's Nest Roost, tel. (559) 784-3948.

6 Tule Recreation Area

    7

Lake Success is a big lake with many arms, providing 30 miles of shoreline and making the place seem like a dreamland for boaters on hot summer days. The lake is set in the foothill country, at an elevation of 650 feet, where day after day of 100-degree summer temperatures are common. That is why boating, water-skiing, and personal watercraft are so popular—anything to get wet. In the winter and spring, trout fishing and bass fishing are also big. No beaches are developed for swimming due to fluctuating water levels, though the day-use area has a decent sloped stretch of shore that is good for swimming. The wildlife area along the west side of the lake is worth exploring, and there is a nature trail below the dam.

Location: On Lake Success; map G4, grid d8.

Campsites, facilities: There are 104 sites for tents or RVs up to 30 feet long. Picnic tables and fire grills are provided. Restrooms, flush toilets, sanitary disposal station, and a playground are available. A grocery store, marina, boat ramp, boat and water-ski rentals, bait, tackle, propane gas, restaurant, and gas station are available nearby. Leashed pets are permitted.

Reservations, fees: Reserve at tel. (877) 444-6777 ($8.65 reservation fee) or website: www.reserveusa.com; $16 per night. Open year-round.

Directions: From Porterville, drive eight miles east on Highway 190 to Lake Success and look for the campground entrance on the left.

Contact: U.S. Army Corps of Engineers, Sacramento District, tel. (559) 784-0215 or fax (559) 784-5469; Success Marina, (559) 781-2078.

❼ Colonel Allensworth State Historic Park

   3

What you have here is the old town of Allensworth, which has been restored as a historical park dedicated to the African-American pioneers who founded it with Colonel Allen Allensworth, the highest ranking army chaplain of his time. One museum is available at the school here and another at the colonel's house with a 30-minute movie on the history of Allensworth. One frustrating element here is

that railroad tracks run alongside the park and it can be disruptive. There can be other problems: Very hot weather in the summer, and since it is an open area, the wind can blow dust and sand. Are we having fun yet?

Location: Near Earlimart; map G4, grid e1.

Campsites, facilities: There are 15 sites for tents or RVs up to 35 feet long. Picnic tables and fire grills are provided. Restrooms, drinking water, flush toilets, coin showers, sanitary disposal station, and a visitor center are available. A grocery store and coin laundry are 12 miles away in Delano. Leashed pets are permitted.

Reservations, fees: Reserve at tel. (800) 444-PARK (800-444-7275) or website: www.reserve america.com; $8 per night. Open year-round.

Directions: From Fresno, drive south on Highway 99 about 60 miles to Earlimart and the Alpaugh Road Exit. Take that exit and drive to Avenue 56. Turn right (west) on Avenue 56 and drive eight miles to the Highway 43 turnoff. Turn left on Highway 43 and drive two miles to Palmer Avenue. Turn right (and drive over the railroad tracks) to the park entrance.

Contact: Colonel Allensworth State Historic Park, tel. (661) 634-3795 or (661) 849-3433.

❽ KOA Bakersfield

     1

If you're stuck in the southern valley and the temperature feels like you're sitting in a cauldron, well, this spot provides a layover for the night near the town of Shafter. It's not exactly a hotbed of excitement.

Location: North of Bakersfield; map G4, grid i3.

Campsites, facilities: There are 12 tent sites and 62 RV sites with full or partial hookups. Picnic tables are provided. Restrooms, drinking water, showers, swimming pool (summer only), laundry room, store, sanitary disposal station, and propane gas are available. Leashed pets are permitted. Some facilities are wheelchair accessible.

Reservations, fees: Reservations at (800) 562-1633; $23 to $28 per night, cabins $36 per night, $4 per person per night for more than two people. Major credit cards accepted. Open year-round.

Directions: From Bakersfield, drive 12 miles north on Highway 99 to the Shafter-Lerdo Highway exit. Drive a mile west on Lerdo Highway to 5101 Lerdo Highway in Shafter.

Contact: KOA Bakersfield, tel. (661) 399-3107; website: www.explorekoa.com.

9 Kern River

      7

Lake Ming is a little lake covering just 205 surface acres, and with the weather so hot, the hot jet boats can make it a wild affair here. It's become a popular spot for southern valley residents, only a 15-minute drive from Bakersfield. It is so popular for water sports that every year the lake is closed to the public one weekend per month for private boat races and water-skiing competitions. Sailing and windsurfing are permitted on the second weekend of every month and on Tuesday and Thursday afternoons. All motorized boating, including water-skiing, is permitted on the remaining days. All boats are required to have a permit; boaters may buy one at the park. Swimming is not allowed. The elevation is 450 feet.

Location: At Lake Ming; map G4, grid j6.

Campsites, facilities: There are 50 sites for tents or RVs up to 28 feet long. Picnic tables and fire rings are provided. Restrooms, drinking water, flush toilets, coin showers, sanitary disposal station, playground, and a boat ramp are available. Some facilities are wheelchair accessible. A grocery store is nearby. Leashed pets are permitted.

Reservations, fees: No reservations; $15 per night, $8 per night for each extra vehicle (15 person maximum per site), $3 pet fee. Open year-round.

Directions: From Bakersfield, drive east on Highway 178. Turn left (north) on Alfred Harrell Highway and follow the signs to Lake Ming Road. Turn right on Lake Ming Road and follow the signs to the campground on the right.

Contact: Kern County Parks Department, tel. (661) 868-7000 or tel. (661) 872-3179.

TOM STIENSTRA

LIGHTING
THE CAMPFIRE

MAP G5

608

TO LONE PINE

TO THREE RIVERS

a
2 3
Mineral King
1

SEQUOIA
NATIONAL PARK

4

5 (136)

b
Florence Peak
12,405 feet

INYO
NATIONAL
FOREST

6

(395)

c
7
8
9
10 11
13 12

Olancha Peak
12,123 feet

Cartago
Olancha (190)

d
14
(190)
Camp
Nelson 15
16 17
Quaking
18 Aspen

SEQUOIA
NATIONAL
FOREST

21

e
660
TULE RIVER
INDIAN
RESERVATION
Parker Pass
6,400 feet
19
20
Johnsondale
23
24
25
26 Roads
End 28
27

22

Sherman Pass
9,200 feet

Kennedy
Meadows
29

692

f
TO SPRINGVILLE
TO FOUNTAIN SPRINGS
California
Hot Springs 30 Fairview
31
32
33

Sirretta Peak
9,977 feet

g
Posey
34
35
36
37 38

Big
Meadow

(J41)

Little Lake

39 40

h
TO GLENVILLE
Sunday Peak
9,875 feet
(155)
41
42 43
Wofford
Heights
45 44
49
46
47-48
50-52
53 54
56

Kernville
Isabella
Lake

Onyx
Weldon

(178)

(395)

Pearsonville

i
TO BAKERSFIELD
(178)
Kern River
Lake
Isabella
55

Miracle
58
Hot 59
Springs
Bodfish

SEQUOIA
NATIONAL
FOREST

Walker Pass
5,250 feet
57

(178) Inyokern

j
Havilah
60 Breckenridge
Mountain
7,544 feet

SEQUOIA
NATIONAL
FOREST

Freeman
Junction
(14)

TO JOHANNESBURG

TO CALIENTE

738

TO MOJAVE

0 1 2 3 4 5 6 7 8 9

© AVALON TRAVEL PUBLISHING, INC.

CHAPTER G5

(CONTINUED ON NEXT PAGE)

1 South Fork

   7

The smallest developed camp in Sequoia National Park might just be what you're looking for. It is set at 3,650 feet on the South Fork of the Kaweah River, just inside the southwestern border of Sequoia National Park. A trail heads east from the camp and traverses Dennison Ridge, eventually leading to Hockett Lakes, a long, demanding overnight trip. This is black bear habitat so proper food storage is required.

Location: On the South Fork of the Kaweah River in Sequoia National Park; map G5, grid a0.

Campsites, facilities: There are 10 sites for tents only. Picnic tables and fire grills are provided. Vault toilets are available. No drinking water is available. Leashed pets are permitted, except on trails.

Reservations, fees: No reservations; $8 per night from May through October, no fee in other months, $10 per vehicle park entrance fee.

Directions: From Visalia, drive to Three Rivers on Highway 198. Turn east on South Fork Road and drive 13 miles to the campground.

Contact: Sequoia National Park, tel. (559) 565-3341.

2 Atwell Mill

  8

This small, pretty camp in Sequoia National Park is on Atwell Creek near the East Fork of the Kaweah River, at an

Chapter G5 **667**

elevation of 6,650 feet. A trail at camp is routed south for a mile down to the Kaweah River, then climbs out of the canyon and along Deer Creek for another two miles through the East Fork Grove, an outstanding day hike.

Location: On Atwell Creek in Sequoia National Park; map G5, grid a1.

Campsites, facilities: There are 21 tent sites; no trailers are permitted. Picnic tables and fire grills are provided. Drinking water and pit toilets are available. A small grocery store is nearby. Leashed pets are permitted.

Reservations, fees: No reservations; $8 per night, $10 per vehicle park entrance fee. Open from May to September (depending on road and weather conditions).

Directions: From Visalia, take Highway 198 to Three Rivers. Continue north for three miles on Highway 198. Turn right on Mineral King Road and drive 20 miles on a steep and winding road to the campground. Mineral King Road is quite rough-RVs and trailers are not recommended.

Contact: Sequoia National Park, tel. (559) 565-3341.

3 Cold Springs

  9

This high country camp at Sequoia National Park is set at 7,500 feet on the East Fork of the Kaweah River. There is a stellar hiking trail from here, with the trailhead just west of the camp. The hike is routed south along Mosquito Creek, climbing over the course of about three miles to the pretty Mosquito Lakes, a series of four small, beautiful lakes set on the north flank of Hengst Peak (11,127 feet elevation).

Location: On the East Fork of the Kaweah River in Sequoia National Park; map G5, grid a2.

Campsites, facilities: There are 40 tent sites; no trailers are permitted. Picnic tables and fire grills are provided. Drinking water and vault toilets are available. A grocery store is nearby. Leashed pets are permitted.

Reservations, fees: No reservations; $8 per night, $10 per vehicle park entrance fee. Open from May to September.

Directions: From Visalia, take Highway 198 to Three Rivers. Continue to drive three miles north on Highway 198. Turn right on steep and winding Mineral King Road and drive 25 miles to the campground.

Contact: Sequoia National Park, tel. (559) 565-3341.

4 Tuttle Creek

     4

This primitive BLM camp is set at the base of Mount Whitney along Tuttle Creek at 5,120 feet and is shadowed by several impressive peaks (Mount Whitney, Lone Pine Peak, and Mount Williamson). It is often used as an overflow area if the camps farther up Whitney Portal Road are full.

Location: Near Mount Whitney; map G5, grid a8.

Campsites, facilities: There are 85 sites for tents or RVs and one group picnic area. Picnic tables and fire rings are provided. Pit toilets are available. No drinking water is available. Supplies are available in Lone Pine. Leashed pets are permitted.

Reservations, fees: No reservations; no fee. Open from early March through October.

Directions: From Lone Pine, drive 3.5 miles west on Whitney Portal Road. Turn south on Horseshoe Meadow Road and drive 1.5 miles. Turn west on Tuttle Creek Road (a winding, dirt road) and drive directly into the campground.

Contact: Bureau of Land Management, Bishop Field Office, tel. (760) 872-4881 or fax (760) 872-2894.

5 Diaz Lake

      6

Diaz Lake is set at 3,650 feet in the Owens Valley, where it is often overlooked by visitors to nearby Mount Whitney. It's a small lake, just 85 acres, and it is popular for trout fishing in the spring, when a speed limit of 15 mph is enforced. In summer when hot weather takes over and the speed limit is bumped to 35 mph, you can say adios to the anglers and hola to water-skiers. It also becomes a good spot for swimming in the shallows. A 20-foot limit is enforced for boats.

Location: Near Lone Pine; map G5, grid a9.

Campsites, facilities: There are 200 sites for tents or RVs, some sites with hookups. Picnic tables and fire grills are provided. Restrooms, drinking water, flush toilets, solar shower, and a boat ramp are available. Supplies and a coin laundry are available in Lone Pine. Leashed pets are permitted.

Reservations, fees: Reservations are accepted; $7 per night. Open year-round.

Directions: From Lone Pine, drive two miles south on U.S. 395 to the entrance on the right.

Contact: Inyo County Parks Department, tel. (760) 876-5656.

6 Horseshoe Meadow

   8

Horseshoe Meadow features three trailhead camps, remote and obscure, for backpackers heading into the adjacent John Muir Wilderness and Golden Trout Wilderness. The three camps are Cottonwood Pass walk-in, Cottonwood Lakes walk-in, and Horseshoe Meadow Equestrian. The camps are set at 10,000 feet near the wilderness border, with several trails leading out of camp. The best heads west through Horseshoe Meadow and along a creek, then rises steeply for four miles to Cottonwood Pass where it intersects with the Pacific Crest Trail. From here backpackers can hike north on the PCT for one mile to Chicken Spring Lake to set up camp, a demanding but rewarding overnighter.

Location: Near the John Muir Wilderness in Inyo National Forest; map G5, grid b7.

Campsites, facilities: Cottonwood Pass has 18 walk-in sites,

Cottonwood Lakes walk-in has 12 sites, and Horseshoe Meadow Equestrian has 10 sites. Picnic tables and fire grills are provided. Drinking water and vault toilets are available. A pack station and horseback riding facilities are also available at the equestrian camp. Leashed pets are permitted.

Reservations, fees: No reservations; $6 per night for walk-in sites, $12 for equestrians. Open from late May through mid-October.

Directions: From Lone Pine, drive 3.5 miles west on Whitney Portal Road. Turn left on Horseshoe Meadows Road and drive 19 miles to the end of the road.

Contact: Inyo National Forest, Mount Whitney Ranger District, tel. (760) 876-6200 or fax (760) 876-6202.

7 Hidden Falls Walk-in

    7

This small, quiet camp, set at 6,000 feet along the Tule River near Hidden Falls, is one of the prettier camps in Mountain Home State Forest. It is remote and overlooked by all but a handful of insiders who know its qualities.

Location: On the Tule River in Mountain Home State Forest; map G5, grid b1.

Campsites, facilities: There are eight walk-in sites for tents only. Picnic tables and fire grills are provided. Drinking water and pit toilets are available. Leashed pets are permitted.

Reservations, fees: No reservations; no fee. Open from June to October.

Directions: From Porterville, drive 19 miles east on Highway 190 (a mile past the town of Springville). Turn left (north) onto Balch Park Road and drive about 23 miles to the Mountain Home State Forest sign on the right. Continue on Balch Road, following the signs to the State Forest Headquarters where free forest maps are available. The campgrounds are well signed from this point. The total trip from the Highway 190/Balch Road turnoff to the campground is about 45 miles. Alternate route: After driving three miles on Balch Park Road,

turn right (east) on Bear Creek Road and drive 25 miles to the campground. This is not a good road for trailers and RVs.

Contact: Mountain Home State Forest, tel. (559) 539-2321 (summer) or tel. (559) 539-2855 (winter).

8 Moses Gulch

    7

Obscure Moses Gulch sits in a canyon below Moses Mountain (9,331 feet) to the nearby north. Mountain Home State Forest is surrounded by Sequoia National Forest. A trailhead at the eastern end of the state forest provides access both north and south along the North Fork of the Middle Fork Tule River for a scenic hike. The cost? Free.

Location: On the Tule River in Mountain Home State Forest; map G5, grid b1.

Campsites, facilities: There are 10 sites for tents. Picnic tables and fire grills are provided. Drinking water and vault toilets are available. Leashed pets are permitted.

Reservations, fees: No reservations; no fee. Open mid-May to early November, weather permitting.

Directions: From Porterville, drive 19 miles east on Highway 190 (a mile past the town of Springville). Turn left (north) onto Balch Park Road and drive about 23 miles to the Mountain Home State Forest sign on the right. Continue on Balch Road, following the signs to the State Forest Headquarters where free forest maps are available. (The campgrounds are well signed from this point.) The total trip from the Highway 190/Balch Road turnoff to the campground is about 31 miles. Alternate route: After driving three miles on Balch Park Road, turn right (east) on Bear Creek Road and drive 26 miles to the campground. This is not a good road for trailers and RVs.

Contact: Mountain Home State Forest, tel. (559) 539-2321 (summer) or tel. (559) 539-2855 (winter).

9 Frazier Mill

    5

The prime attractions here are the obscurity, remoteness and abundance of old-growth giant sequoias. The Wishon Fork of the Tule River is the largest of the several streams that pass through this forest. You can't beat the price.

Location: In Mountain Home State Forest; map G5, grid c1.

Campsites, facilities: There are 46 sites for tents and a few sites for small RVs. Picnic tables and fire grills are provided. Drinking water and vault toilets are available. Leashed pets are permitted.

Reservations, fees: No reservations; no fee. Open from June to October.

Directions: From Porterville, drive 19 miles east on Highway 190 (a mile past the town of Springville). Turn left (north) onto Balch Park Road and drive about 23 miles to the Mountain Home State Forest sign on the right. Continue on Balch Road, following the signs to the State Forest Headquarters where free forest maps are available. (The campgrounds are well signed from this point.) The total trip from the Highway 190/Balch Road turnoff to the campground is about 35 miles. Alternate route: After driving three miles on Balch Park Road, turn right (east) on Bear Creek Road and drive 17 miles to the campground. This is not a good road for trailers and RVs.

Contact: Mountain Home State Forest, tel. (559) 539-2321 (summer) or tel. (559) 539-2855 (winter).

10 Shake Camp

    6

This is a little-known spot for horseback riding. Horses can be rented for the day, hour, or night. The camp is set at 6,500 feet and there's a trailhead here for trips into the adjoining Sequoia National Forest and beyond to the east into the Golden Trout Wilderness. Hikers should note that the Balch Park Pack Station,

a commercial outfitter, is nearby, so you can expect horse traffic on the trail.

Location: In Mountain Home State Forest; map G5, grid c1.

Campsites, facilities: There are 11 sites for tents or small RVs. Picnic tables and fire grills are provided. Drinking water and vault toilets are available. A public pack station with corrals is nearby. Leashed pets are permitted.

Reservations, fees: No reservations; no fee. Open from June to October.

Directions: From Porterville, drive 19 miles east on Highway 190 (a mile past the town of Springville). Turn left (north) onto Balch Park Road and drive about 23 miles to the Mountain Home State Forest sign on the right. Continue on Balch Road, following the signs to the State Forest Headquarters where free forest maps are available. (The campgrounds are well signed from this point.) The total trip from the Highway 190/Balch Road turnoff to the campground is about 36 miles. Alternate route: After driving three miles on Balch Park Road, turn right (east) on Bear Creek Road and drive 21 miles to the campground. This is not a good road for trailers and RVs.

Contact: Mountain Home State Forest, tel. (559) 539-2321 (summer) or tel. (559) 539-2855 (winter).

11 Hedrick Pond

     6

Mountain Home State Forest is highlighted by giant sequoias, and Hedrick Pond provides a fishing opportunity, as it's stocked occasionally in summer with rainbow trout. This camp is set at 6,200 feet, one of five campgrounds in the immediate region. See Methuselah Group Camp for recreation options.

Location: In Mountain Home State Forest; map G5, grid c1.

Campsites, facilities: There are 14 sites for tents or RVs. Picnic tables and grills are provided. Drinking water and vault toilets are available. Leashed pets are permitted.

Reservations, fees: No reservations; no fee. Open from June through October.

Directions: From Porterville, drive 19 miles east on Highway 190 (a mile past the town of Springville). Turn left (north) onto Balch Park Road and drive about 23 miles to the Mountain Home State Forest sign on the right. Continue on Balch Road, following the signs to the State Forest Headquarters where free forest maps are available. (The campgrounds are well signed from this point.) The total trip from the Highway 190/Balch Road turnoff to the campground is about 35 miles. Alternate route: After driving three miles on Balch Park Road, turn right (east) on Bear Creek Road and drive 16 miles to the campground. This is not a good road for trailers and RVs.

Contact: Mountain Home State Forest, tel. (559) 539-2321 (summer) or tel. (559) 539-2855 (winter).

12 Methuselah Group Camp

    6

This is one of the few group campgrounds anywhere in California that is free to users. But hey: Remember to bring water. The elevation is 5,900 feet. Mountain Home State Forest is best known for its remoteness, old-growth giant sequoias (hence the name of this camp, Methuselah), trails that provide access to small streams, and horseback trips into the surrounding Sequoia National Forest.

Location: In Mountain Home State Forest; map G5, grid c1.

Campsites, facilities: This group site can accommodate 20 to 100 people in tents or RVs. Fire grills and some picnic tables are provided. Vault toilets are available. No drinking water is available. Leashed pets are permitted. Garbage must be packed out.

Reservations, fees: Reservations are required; no fee. Open from June to October.

Directions: From Porterville, drive 19 miles east on Highway 190 (a mile past the town of Springville). Turn left (north) onto Balch Park Road and drive about 23 miles to the Mountain Home State Forest sign on the right. Continue on Balch Road, following the signs to the State Forest Headquarters where free forest maps are available. (The campgrounds are well signed from this point.) The total trip from the Highway 190/Balch Road turnoff to the campground is about 40 miles. Alternate route: After turning north onto Balch Park Road, drive 40 miles to the campground.

Contact: Mountain Home State Forest, tel. (559) 539-2321 (summer) or tel. (559) 539-2855 (winter).

13 Balch Park

     6

Balch Park is surrounded by Mountain Home State Forest and Sequoia National Forest. A nearby grove of giant sequoias is a featured attraction. The elevation is 6,500 feet.

Location: Near Mountain Home State Forest; map G5, grid c1.

Campsites, facilities: There are 71 sites for tents or RVs up to 30 feet long. Picnic tables and fire grills are provided. Drinking water and flush toilets are available. Some facilities are wheelchair accessible. Leashed pets are permitted.

Reservations, fees: Reservations required at tel. (559) 733-6291; $12 per night, $1 per night for each extra vehicle, $1 pet fee. Open from May to October 25.

Directions: From Porterville, drive 19 miles east on Highway 190 (a mile past the town of Springville). Turn left (north) onto Balch Park Road and drive three miles to Bear Creek Road. Turn east (right) and drive 15 miles to the campground (trailers not recommended). Alternate route: After turning north onto Balch Park Road, drive 40 miles to the park.

Contact: Balch Park, Tulare County, tel. (559) 733-6291.

14 Wishon

 8

Wishon Camp is set at 4,000 feet on the Middle Fork of the North Fork Tule River, just west of the Doyle Springs Summer Home Tract. Just down the road to the east, on the left side, is a parking area for a trailhead. The hike here is routed for a mile to the Tule River and then runs along the stream for several miles, including four miles to Mountain Home State Forest.

Location: On the Tule River in Giant Sequoia National Monument; map G5, grid d1.

Campsites, facilities: There are nine sites for tents only and 26 sites for tents or RVs up to 22 feet long. Picnic tables and fire grills are provided. Drinking water and vault toilets are available. Leashed pets are permitted.

Reservations, fees: Reserve at (877) 444-6777 ($8.65 reservation fee) or website: www.reserveusa.com; $12 per night, $5 per night for each extra vehicle. Open year-round.

Directions: From Porterville, drive 25 miles east on Highway 190. Turn left on County Road 208/Wishon Drive and drive 3.5 miles. This camp is at the bottom of a canyon.

Contact: Giant Sequoia National Monument, Tule River/Hot Springs Ranger District, tel. (559) 539-2607 or fax (559) 539-2067.

15 Belknap

 7

The groves of sequoias in this area are a highlight wherever you go. This camp is set on the South Middle Fork of Tule River near McIntyre Grove and Belknap Camp Grove, and a trail from camp is routed east for three miles through Wheel Meadow Grove to the junction with the Summit National Recreation Trail at Quaking Aspen Camp. The elevation is 5,000 feet.

Location: On the South Middle Fork of Tule River in Giant Sequoia National Monument; map G5, grid d2.

Campsites, facilities: There are 15 sites for tents or RVs up to 22 feet long. Trailers are prohibited in this area. Picnic tables and fire grills are provided. Drinking water and vault toilets are available. A grocery store is nearby. Leashed pets are permitted.

Reservations, fees: Reserve at (877) 444-6777 ($8.65 reservation fee) or website: www.reserveusa.com; $12 per night, $5 for an extra vehicle. Open from mid-April through mid-November.

Directions: From Porterville, drive 34 miles east on Highway 190 to Camp Nelson. Turn right on Nelson Drive and drive a mile to the camp.

Contact: Giant Sequoia National Monument, Tule River/Hot Springs Ranger District, tel. (209) 539-2607 or fax (209) 539-2067.

16 Coy Flat

 4

Coy Flat is set near Bear Creek, a small fork of the Tule River at 5,000 feet in elevation. The road out of camp is routed five miles to the Black Mountain Grove of redwoods, with some giant sequoias set just inside the border of the neighboring Tule River Indian Reservation. From camp, a hiking trail (Forest Trail 31S31) is routed east for two miles through the Belknap Camp Grove of sequoias and then turns and heads south for four miles to Slate Mountain, where it intersects with the Summit National Recreation Trail, a steep butt-kicker of a hike that tops out at over 9,000 feet.

Location: In Giant Sequoia National Monument; map G5, grid d2.

Campsites, facilities: There are 20 sites for tents or RVs up to 22 feet long. Picnic tables and fire grills are provided. Drinking water and vault toilets are available. Leashed pets are permitted.

Reservations, fees: Reserve at (877) 444-6777 ($8.65 reservation fee) or website: www.reserveusa.com; $10 per night, $5 per night for each additional vehicle. Open from mid-April through mid-November.

Directions: From Porterville, drive 34 miles east on Highway 190 to Camp Nelson. Turn right on Coy Flat Road and drive one mile.

Contact: Giant Sequoia National Monument, Tule River/Hot Springs Ranger District, tel. (559) 539-2607 or fax (559) 539-2067.

17 Quaking Aspen Group Camp

 6

For groups, here is an alternative to nearby Peppermint. See the entry for Peppermint for recreation options. The elevation is 7,000 feet.

Location: At the headwaters of the South Middle Fork Tule River in Giant Sequoia National Monument; map G5, grid d2.

Campsites, facilities: There are three group sites for up to 12 people, two group sites for up to 25 people, and two group sites for up to 50 people, suitable for tents only. Picnic tables and fire grills are provided. Drinking water and vault toilets are available. A lodge with limited supplies is nearby. Leashed pets are permitted.

Reservations, fees: Reserve at (877) 444-6777 ($8.65 reservation fee) or website: www.reserveusa.com; $18 to $75 group fee per night, depending on group size. Open from mid-May to mid-November.

Directions: From Porterville, drive 34 miles east on Highway 190 to Camp Nelson. Continue about 11 miles east on Highway 190 to the campground.

Contact: Giant Sequoia National Monument, Tule River/Hot Springs Ranger District, tel. (559) 539-2607 or fax (559) 539-2067.

18 Quaking Aspen

 6

Quaking Aspen sits at a junction of Forest Service roads at 7,000 feet in elevation, near the headwaters of Freeman Creek. A trailhead for the Summit National Recreation Trail runs right through camp, a popular trip on horseback, heading deep into Sequoia National For-

est. Another trail, ideal for day hikes, is routed east along Freeman Creek and reaches the Freeman Grove of sequoias in four miles.

Location: In Giant Sequoia National Monument; map G5, grid d2.

Campsites, facilities: There are 32 sites for tents or RVs up to 22 feet long. Picnic tables and fire grills are provided. Drinking water and vault toilets are available. A grocery store is nearby. Leashed pets are permitted. Some facilities are wheelchair accessible.

Reservations, fees: Reserve at (877) 444-6777; $12 per night, $5 per night per extra vehicle. Open from May to mid-November, weather permitting.

Directions: From Porterville, drive 34 miles east on Highway 190 to Camp Nelson. Continue 11 miles east of Camp Nelson on Highway 190 to the campground.

Contact: Giant Sequoia National Monument, Tule River/Hot Springs Ranger District, tel. (559) 539-2607 or fax (559) 539-2067.

19 Peppermint

 7

This is one of two primitive camps at Peppermint Creek, but the two are not directly connected by a road. Several backcountry access roads snake throughout the area, as detailed on a Forest Service map, and exploring them can make for some self-styled fortune hunts. For the ambitious, hiking the two-mile trail at the end of nearby Forest Road 21S05 can lead to a fantastic lookout at The Needles (8,245 feet). The camp elevation is 7,100 feet.

Location: On Peppermint Creek in Giant Sequoia National Monument; map G5, grid e2.

Campsites, facilities: There is dispersed camping for tents or RVs up to 22 feet long. Picnic tables are provided. Vault toilets are available. No drinking water is available. A lodge with limited supplies is nearby. Leashed pets are permitted.

Reservations, fees: No reservations; no fee. A fire permit is required. Open from May to October.

Directions: From Porterville, drive 34 miles east on Highway 190 to Camp Nelson. Continue about 15 miles southeast on Highway 190 to the entrance road.

Contact: Giant Sequoia National Monument, Tule River/Hot Springs Ranger District, tel. (559) 539-2607 or fax (559) 539-2067.

20 Lower Peppermint

 7

This is a little-known camp in Sequoia National Forest, set along Peppermint Creek at 5,300 feet. This area has a vast network of backcountry roads, which are detailed on a Forest Service map.

Location: In Giant Sequoia National Monument; map G5, grid e2.

Campsites, facilities: There are 17 sites for tents or RVs up to 40 feet long. Picnic tables and fire grills are provided. Drinking water and vault toilets are available. Leashed pets are permitted.

Reservations, fees: No reservations; $12 per night. Open from June to October.

Directions: From the town of Lake Isabella, drive 35 miles north on Burlando Road and Sierra Way to the town of Johnsondale. Turn right on Forest Road 22S82/Lloyd Meadow Road and drive about 10.5 miles on a paved road to the campground.

Contact: Giant Sequoia National Monument, Tule River/Hot Springs Ranger District, tel. (559) 539-2607 or fax (559) 539-2067.

21 Troy Meadows

 7

Obscure? Yes, but what the heck, it gives you an idea of what is possible out in the boondocks. The camp is set at 7,800 feet right along Fish Creek. An information station is available two miles northwest. You are advised to stop there prior to any backcountry trips. Note that off-highway vehicles (OHVs) are allowed in this area. Also note that the Jackass National Recreation Trail is available a short drive to the east; it runs north aside Jackass Creek to its headwaters just below Jackass Peak (9,245 feet).

Location: On Fish Creek in Sequoia National Forest; map G5, grid e5.

Campsites, facilities: There are 10 sites for RVs up to 30 feet long and 63 sites for tents or RVs up to 22 feet long. Picnic tables and fire grills are provided. Drinking water and vault toilets are available. Garbage must be packed out. Leashed pets are permitted.

Reservations, fees: No reservations; $5 per night. Open from May to November.

Directions: From the town of Pearsonville on U.S. 395, drive four miles north to Nine Mile Canyon Road. Turn left (west) on Nine Mile Canyon Road and drive 31 miles northwest (the road becomes Sherman Pass Road) to the campground.

Contact: Sequoia National Forest, Cannell Meadow Ranger District, tel. (760) 376-3781 or fax (760) 376-3795.

22 Fish Creek

 8

This is a pretty spot set at the confluence of Fish Creek and Jackass Creek. The elevation is 7,400 feet. The nearby trails are used by off-highway vehicles and can make this a noisy campground during the day.

Location: In Sequoia National Forest; map G5, grid e5.

Campsites, facilities: There are 27 sites for tents and 12 sites for RVs up to 30 feet long. Picnic tables and fire grills are provided. Drinking water and vault toilets are available. Garbage must be packed out. A grocery store is nearby. Leashed pets are permitted.

Reservations, fees: No reservations; $5 per night. Open from May to November.

Directions: From U.S. 395 15 miles north of China Lake, turn left on Nine Mile Canyon Road and drive 28 miles northwest (the road becomes Sherman Pass Road) to the campground.

Contact: Sequoia National Forest, Cannell Meadow Ranger District, tel. (760) 376-3781 or fax (760) 376-3795.

Long Meadow Group Camp

    8

Long Meadow is set on little Long Meadow Creek at an elevation of 6,500 feet, within a mile of the remote Cunningham Grove of redwoods one mile to the east. Note that Redwood Meadow is just one mile to the west, where the Trail of the Hundred Giants is a feature attraction.

Location: In Giant Sequoia National Monument; map G5, grid e2.

Campsites, facilities: One group site for tents or RVs up to 16 feet long can accommodate up to 36 people. Picnic tables and fire grills are provided. Vault toilets are available. No drinking water is available. Leashed pets are permitted.

Reservations, fees: Reservations required at tel. (877) 444-6777 ($8.65 reservation fee) or website: www.reserveusa.com; $24 per night. Open from June to September.

Directions: From Highway 99 in Earlimart, take the County Road J22/Avenue 56 exit and drive east for 39 miles to the town of California Hot Springs. Turn left on County Road M50/Parker Pass Road and drive 12 miles. Turn left on County Road M107/Western Divide Highway and drive north for four miles to the entrance.

Contact: Giant Sequoia National Monument, Tule River/Hot Springs Ranger District, tel. (559) 539-2607 or fax (559) 539-2067.

Redwood Meadow

    7

The highlight here is the half-mile Trail of the Hundred Giants, which is routed through a grove of giant sequoias and is accessible for wheelchair hikers. This is the site where President Clinton proclaimed the Giant Sequoia National Monument in 2000. The camp is set near Parker Meadow Creek at 6,500 feet elevation. This is a popular place, so get here early.

Location: Near Parker Meadow Creek in Giant Sequoia National Monument; map G5, grid f2.

Campsites, facilities: There are 15 sites for tents or RVs up to 16 feet long. Picnic tables and fire grills are provided. Drinking water and vault toilets are available. Leashed pets are permitted.

Reservations, fees: Reserve at (877) 444-6777 ($8.65 reservation fee) or website: www.reserveusa.com; $12 per night, $5 per night for each extra vehicle. Open from June to September.

Directions: From Highway 99 in Earlimart, take the County Road J22/Avenue 56 exit and drive east for 39 miles to the town of California Hot Springs. Turn north left on County Road M50/Parker Pass Road and drive 12 miles. Turn left on County Road M107/Western Divide Highway and drive north three miles to the entrance.

Contact: Giant Sequoia National Monument, Tule River/Hot Springs Ranger District, tel. (559) 539-2607 or fax (559) 539-2067.

Limestone

   8

Set deep in the Sequoia National Forest at 3,800 feet, Limestone is a small campground along the Kern River, fed by snowmelt from Mount Whitney. This stretch of the Kern is extremely challenging and sensational for white-water rafting, with cold water and many of the rapids rated Class IV and Class V, for experts with guides only. The favored put-in is at the Johnsondale Bridge, and from here it's a 21-mile run to Kernville, where the river pours into Lake Isabella a few miles later. Two sections are unrunnable: Fairview Dam (mile 2.5) and Salmon Falls (mile 8). For non-rafters, South Creek Falls provides a side trip, one mile to the west.

Location: On the Kern River in Sequoia National Forest; map G5, grid f2.

Campsites, facilities: There are 12 sites for tents only and 10 sites for tents or RVs up to

30 feet long. Picnic tables and fire grills are provided. Vault toilets are available. No drinking water is available. Supplies and a coin laundry are available in Kernville. Leashed pets are permitted.

Reservations, fees: Reserve at (877) 444-6777 ($8.65 reservation fee) or website: www.reserveusa.com; $10 per night, $5 for an extra vehicle. Open from April through November.

Directions: From Kernville, drive 19 miles north on Kern River Highway/Sierra Way Road to the campground entrance.

Contact: Sequoia National Forest, Cannell Meadow Ranger District, tel. (760) 376-3781 or fax (760) 376-3795.

26 Fairview

 9

Fairview is one of six campgrounds set on the upper Kern River above Lake Isabella and adjacent to the Kern River, one of the prime rafting rivers in California. This camp sits at 3,500 feet. Many of the rapids are rated Class IV and Class V, for experts with guides only. The favored put-in is at the Johnsondale Bridge, and from here it's a 21-mile run to Kernville, where the river pours into Lake Isabella a few miles later. Two sections are unrunnable, Fairview Dam (mile 2.5) and Salmon Falls (mile eight).

Location: On the Kern River in Sequoia National Forest; map G5, grid f2.

Campsites, facilities: There are 55 sites for tents or RVs up to 45 feet long. Picnic tables and fire grills are provided. Drinking water and vault toilets are available. Some facilities are wheelchair accessible. Supplies and a coin laundry are available in Kernville. Leashed pets are permitted.

Reservations, fees: Reserve at (877) 444-6777 ($8.65 reservation fee) or website: www.reserveusa.com; $12 to $14 per night, $5 for an extra vehicle. Open from May to October.

Directions: From Kernville, drive 16 miles north on Kern River Highway/Sierra Road to the town of Fairview. The campground is at the north end of town.

Contact: Sequoia National Forest, Cannell Meadow Ranger District, tel. (760) 376-3781 or fax (760) 376-3795.

27 Holey Meadow

 7

Holey Meadow is set at 6,400 feet on the western slopes of the Sierra, near Redwood and Long Meadow. Parker Pass is a mile to the west, and if you drive on the Forest Service road over the pass, continue southwest (four miles from camp) to Cold Springs Saddle, and then turn east on the Forest Service spur road, it will take you two miles to Starvation Creek and the Starvation Creek Grove.

Location: On Double Bunk Creek in Giant Sequoia National Monument; map G5, grid f1.

Campsites, facilities: There are 10 sites for tents or RVs up to 16 feet long, and a group site for up to 60 people. Drinking water, fire grills, and picnic tables are provided. Vault toilets are available. Leashed pets are permitted.

Reservations, fees: Reserve group site at tel. (877) 444-6777 ($8.65 reservation fee) or website: www.reserveusa.com; $10 per night, $75 for group site. Open from June to October.

Directions: From Highway 99 in Earlimart, take the County Road J22/Avenue 56 exit and drive east for 39 miles to the town of California Hot Springs. Turn left on County Road M50/Parker Pass Road and drive 12 miles. Turn left (north) on County Road M107/Western Divide Highway and drive a half mile to the entrance.

Contact: Giant Sequoia National Monument, Tule River/Hot Springs Ranger District, tel. (559) 539-2607 or fax (559) 539-2067.

28 Horse Meadow

 8

This is a little-known spot set along Salmon Creek at 7,600 feet. It is a region known for big meadows, forests, backcountry roads, and plenty of horses. It is just west of the Dome Land Wilderness, and there is a series of three public pastures for horses in the area, as well as trails ideal for horseback riding. From camp, one such trail follows along Salmon Creek to the west to Salmon Falls, a favorite for the few who know of it. A more popular overnight trip is to head to a trailhead about five miles east, which provides a route to Manter Meadows in the Dome Lands.

Location: On Salmon Creek in Sequoia National Forest; map G5, grid f3.

Campsites, facilities: There are 26 sites for tents only and 15 sites for tents or RVs up to 22 feet long. Picnic tables and fire grills are provided. Drinking water and vault toilets are available. Garbage must be packed out. Leashed pets are permitted.

Reservations, fees: No reservations; $5 per night. Open from June to November.

Directions: From Kernville, drive north on Sierra Way for about 20 miles to the sign that says "Highway 395/Black Rock Ranger Station." Make a sharp right on Sherman Pass Road and drive about 6.5 miles to Cherry Hill Road/Forest Road 22512. There is a green gate with a sign that says "Horse Meadow/Big Meadow." Turn right and drive for about four miles. The road becomes dirt and continues for about another three miles (follow the signs) to the campground entrance road.

Contact: Sequoia National Forest, Cannell Meadow Ranger District, tel. (760) 376-3781 or fax (760) 376-3795.

29 Kennedy Meadow

 8

This is a pretty Forest Service camp set amid pinon pine and sage country, with the Pacific Crest Trail running by the camp. That makes it a great trailhead camp, as well as a refreshing stopover for PCT-through hikers. A highlight is the nearby South Fork Kern River, which provides fishing for rainbow trout. The camp gets moderate use.

Location: On the South Fork of the Kern River in Sequoia National Forest; map G5, grid f6.

Campsites, facilities: There are 38 sites for tents or RVs up to 35 feet long. Picnic tables and fire rings are provided. Drinking water (seasonal) and vault toilets are available. Garbage must be packed out. Leashed pets are permitted.

Reservations, fees: No reservations; $5 fee per night. Open year-round, weather permitting.

Directions: From Pearsonville on U.S. 395, drive four miles north to Nine Mile Canyon Road. Turn left (west) and drive 21 miles. Bear right at the store (still Nine Mile Canyon Road) and continue for three miles to the campground.

Contact: Sequoia National Forest, Cannell Meadow Ranger District, tel. (760) 376-3781 or fax (760) 376-3795.

30 Frog Meadow

 6

This small, primitive camp, set near Tobias Creek at 7,500 feet, is in the center of a network of Forest Service roads that explore the surrounding Sequoia National Forest. The nearby feature destination is the Tobias Peak Lookout (8,284 feet), two miles directly south of the camp.

Location: In Giant Sequoia National Monument; map G5, grid f2.

Campsites, facilities: There are 10 sites for tents or RVs up to 16 feet long. Picnic tables and fire grills are provided. Vault toilets are available. No drinking water is available. Leashed pets are permitted. Garbage must be packed out.

Reservations, fees: No reservations; no fee. Open from June to October, weather permitting.

Directions: From Highway 155 just west of Glennville, turn north on Linns Valley Road/County Road M3 and drive about four miles. Turn left onto County Road M9 and drive 4.5 miles to Guernsey Mill/Sugarloaf Lodge. Continue on Sugarloaf Road/Forest Road 23S16 for about seven miles. Turn left on Forest Road 24S50 (dirt road) to Frog Meadow and the campground.

Contact: Giant Sequoia National Monument, Tule River/Hot Springs Ranger District, tel. (559) 539-2607 or fax (559) 539-2067.

31 Leavis Flat

 7

Leavis Flat is just inside the western border of Sequoia National Forest along Deer Creek, at an elevation of 3,100 feet. The highlight here is the adjacent California Hot Springs.

Location: On Deer Creek in Giant Sequoia National Monument; map G5, grid f0.

Campsites, facilities: There are five sites for tents only and four sites for RVs up to 16 feet long. Picnic tables and fire grills are provided. Drinking water and vault toilets are available. A grocery store, coin laundry, and propane gas can be found nearby. Leashed pets are permitted.

Reservations, fees: Reserve at (877) 444-6777; $10 per night, $5 per night for each extra vehicle. Open year-round.

Directions: From Highway 99 in Earlimart, take the County Road J22/Avenue 56 exit and drive east for 39 miles to the campground. Or from Highway 65 follow the California Hot Springs Resort signs from Ducor.

Contact: Giant Sequoia National Monument, Tule River/Hot Springs Ranger District, tel. (559) 539-2607 or fax (559) 539-2067.

32 White River

 7

White River is set at 4,000 feet, on the White River near where little Dark Canyon Creek enters it. A trail from camp follows downstream along the White River to the west for three miles, dropping into Ames Hole and Cove Canyon. The region's hot springs are about a 10-minute drive away to the north.

Location: In Giant Sequoia National Monument; map G5, grid g0.

Campsites, facilities: There are eight sites for tents and four sites for RVs up to 16 feet long. Picnic tables and fire grills are provided.

Drinking water and vault toilets are available. Leashed pets are permitted.

Reservations, fees: Reserve at (877) 444-6777 ($8.65 reservation fee) or website: www.reserveusa.com; $10 per night, $5 per night for each extra vehicle. Open from May to October.

Directions: From Highway 155 just west of Glennville, turn north on Linns Valley Road and drive about 2.5 miles. Turn left on County Road M10 and drive through Idylwild. Continue northeast on Forest Road 24S05 (dirt road) for six more miles.

Contact: Giant Sequoia National Monument, Tule River/Hot Springs Ranger District, tel. (559) 539-2607 or fax (559) 539-2067.

33 Gold Ledge

 7

This is another in the series of camps on the Kern River north of Lake Isabella. This one is set at 3,200 feet.

Location: On the Kern River in Sequoia National Forest; map G5, grid f2.

Campsites, facilities: There are 37 sites for tents or RVs up to 30 feet long. Picnic tables and fire grills are provided. Drinking water and vault toilets are available. Supplies and a coin laundry are available in Kernville. Leashed pets are permitted.

Reservations, fees: Reserve at (877) 444-6777 ($8.65 reservation fee) or website: www.reserveusa.com; $12 to $14 per night, $5 for an extra vehicle. Open from May to September.

Directions: From Kernville, drive 10 miles north on Kern River Highway/Sierra Way Road to the campground.

Contact: Sequoia National Forest, Cannell Meadow Ranger District, tel. (760) 376-3781 or fax (760) 376-3795.

34 Panorama

 7

This pretty spot is set at 7,200 feet in elevation in a region of Sequoia National Forest filled with a network of backcountry roads. This camp is set in an inconspicuous spot and is easy to miss. A good side trip is to drive two miles south, turn left, and continue a short distance to a trailhead on the right side of the road for Portuguese Peak (a Forest Service map is strongly advised). From here, it's a one-mile butt-kicker to the top of Portuguese Peak, 7,914 feet in elevation.

Location: In Giant Sequoia National Monument; map G5, grid g1.

Campsites, facilities: There are 10 sites for tents or RVs up to 40 feet long. Picnic tables and fire grills are provided. Vault toilets are available. No drinking water is available. Garbage must be packed out. Leashed pets are permitted.

Reservations, fees: No reservations; no fee. Open from June to September.

Directions: From Highway 155 just west of Glennville, turn north on Linns Valley Road/County Road M3 and drive about four miles. Turn left onto County Road M9 and drive about 4.5 miles to Guernsey Mill/Sugarloaf Lodge, and then continue on Sugarloaf Road 23S16 for about six miles to the campground (paved all the way).

Contact: Giant Sequoia National Monument, Tule River/Hot Springs Ranger District, tel. (559) 539-2607 or fax (559) 539-2067.

35 Hospital Flat

      8

It's kind of like the old shell game, trying to pick the best of the camps along the North Fork of the Kern River. This one is seven miles north of Lake Isabella. The elevation is 2,800 feet. For information on rafting on the Kern River, see the entry for Fairview.

Location: On the North Fork of the Kern River in Sequoia National Forest; map G5, grid g2.

Campsites, facilities: There are 40 sites for tents or RVs up to 30 feet long. Picnic tables and fire grills are provided. Drinking water and vault toilets are available. Some facilities are wheelchair accessible. Supplies and a coin

laundry are available in Kernville. Leashed pets are permitted.

Reservations, fees: Reserve at (877) 444-6777 ($8.65 reservation fee) or website: www.reserveusa.com; $12 to $14 per night, $5 for an extra vehicle. Open from May to September.

Directions: From Kernville, drive seven miles north on Kern River Highway/Sierra Way Road to the campground.

Contact: Sequoia National Forest, Cannell Meadow Ranger District, tel. (760) 376-3781 or fax (760) 376-3795.

36 Camp 3

     9

This is the second in a series of camps along the Kern River north of Lake Isabella (in this case, five miles north of the lake). If you don't like this spot, Hospital Flat is just two miles upriver and Headquarters is just one mile downriver. The camp elevation is 2,800 feet.

Location: On the North Fork of the Kern River in Sequoia National Forest; map G5, grid g2.

Campsites, facilities: There are 52 sites for tents or RVs up to 30 feet long. Picnic tables and fire grills are provided. Drinking water and vault toilets are available. Supplies and a coin laundry are available in Kernville. Leashed pets are permitted.

Reservations, fees: Reserve at (877) 444-6777 ($8.65 reservation fee) or website: www.reserveusa.com; $12 to $14 per night, $5 for an extra vehicle. Open from May to September.

Directions: From Kernville, drive five miles north on Kern River Highway/Sierra Way Road to the campground.

Contact: Sequoia National Forest, Cannell Meadow Ranger District, tel. (760) 376-3781 or fax (760) 376-3795.

37 Headquarters

      8

As you head north from Lake Isabella on Sierra Way, this is the first in a series of Forest Service campgrounds that you have your pick of, all of them set along the North Fork of the Kern River. The North Fork Kern is best known for offering prime white water for rafting. The elevation is 2,700 feet.

Location: On the North Fork of the Kern River in Sequoia National Forest; map G5, grid h2.

Campsites, facilities: There are 44 sites for tents or RVs up to 27 feet long. Picnic tables and fire grills are provided. Drinking water and vault toilets are available. Some facilities are wheelchair accessible. Supplies and a coin laundry are available in Kernville. Leashed pets are permitted.

Reservations, fees: Reserve at (877) 444-6777 ($8.65 reservation fee) or website: www.reserveusa.com; $12 to $14 per night, $5 for an extra vehicle. Open year-round.

Directions: From Kernville, drive three miles north on Kern River Highway/Sierra Way Road to the campground.

Contact: Sequoia National Forest, Cannell Meadow Ranger District, tel. (760) 376-3781 or fax (760) 376-3795.

38 Rivernook Campground

 7

This is a large, privately operated park set near Lake Isabella a few miles from the head of the lake. Boat rentals are available at one of the nearby marinas. An optional side trip is to visit Keysville, the first town to become established on the Kern River during the gold rush days. The elevation is 2,665 feet.

Location: On the North Fork of the Kern River; map G5, grid h3.

Campsites, facilities: There are 39 sites for tents or RVs without hookups, 56 with partial hookups, and 30 RV sites with full hookups. Picnic tables and drinking water are provided. Restrooms, showers, sanitary disposal station, and cable TV and modem hookups are available. Leashed pets are permitted. Some facilities are wheelchair accessible.

Reservations, fees: Reservations are accepted to secure site; $17 to $23 per night.

Major credit cards accepted. Open year-round.

Directions: From Kernville, drive a half mile north to 14001 Sierra Way.

Contact: Rivernook Campground, tel. (760) 376-2705, or fax (760) 376-2595; website: www.campgrounds.com/rivernook.

39 Long Valley

 5

This one is way out there in booger country. It's set at road's end in Long Valley, a mile from the border of the Dome Land Wilderness to the east, and the camp is used primarily as a jump-off spot for hikers. A trail from camp leads 2.5 miles west, climbing along a small stream and reaching the South Fork of the Kern River, in rugged and remote country. The elevation is 5,200 feet.

Location: Near the Dome Land Wilderness; map G5, grid h6.

Campsites, facilities: There are 13 tent sites. Picnic tables and fire grills are provided. Pit toilets are available. No drinking water is available. Garbage must be packed out. Leashed pets are permitted.

Reservations, fees: No reservations; no fee, donations encouraged. Open year-round.

Directions: From north of San Bernardino, drive north on U.S. 395 to the junction of U.S. 395 and Highway 14. Continue north for 11 miles to Pearsonville. At Pearsonville continue two miles north to Nine Mile Canyon Road (at the Kennedy Meadows sign). Turn left and drive 11 miles to the BLM Work Station. Turn left on Cane Brake Road (the dirt road opposite the station) and drive six miles to Long Valley Road. Turn right and drive eight miles to the campground entrance road on the left. Turn left and drive one mile to the campground.

Contact: Bureau of Land Management, Bakersfield Field Office, tel. (661) 391-6000 or fax (661) 391-6040.

40 Chimney Creek

 5

This BLM camp is set at 5,900 feet along the headwaters of Chimney Creek, on the southern flank of Chimney Peak (7,990 feet) two miles to the north. This is a trailhead camp for the Pacific Crest Trail, one of its relatively obscure sections. The PCT heads north from camp and in 10 miles it skirts the eastern border of Dome Land Wilderness.

Location: On the Pacific Crest Trail; map G5, grid h7.

Campsites, facilities: There are 36 sites for tents or RVs up to 25 feet long. Picnic tables and fire grills are provided. Vault toilets are available. No drinking water is available. Garbage must be packed out. Leashed pets are permitted.

Reservations, fees: No reservations, no fee. Open year-round.

Directions: From north of San Bernardino, drive north on U.S. 395 to the junction of U.S. 395 and Highway 14, continue north for 11 miles to Pearsonville. At Pearsonville, continue two miles north to Nine Mile Canyon Road (at the Kennedy Meadows sign). Turn left and drive 11 miles to the BLM Work Station. Turn left on Cane Brake Road (the dirt road opposite the station) and drive three miles to the camp on the left.

Contact: Bureau of Land Management, Bakersfield Field Office, tel. (661) 391-6000 or fax (661) 391-6040.

41 Cedar Creek

 7

This is a little-known Forest Service camp set at 4,800 feet on the southwest flank of Sequoia National Forest, right along little Cedar Creek, with easy access off Highway 155. Greenhorn Mountain Park and Alder Creek provide nearby alternatives.

Location: In Sequoia National Forest; map G5, grid h1.

Campsites, facilities: There are 10 sites for tents only. Picnic tables and fire grills are provided. Drinking water (from May to October only) and vault toilets are available. Garbage must be packed out. Leashed pets are permitted.

Reservations, fees: No reservations; no fee. Open year-round.

Directions: From Glennville on Highway 155, drive nine miles east on Highway 155 to the campground. Or from Wofford Heights (on the west shore of Lake Isabella), drive 11 miles west on Highway 155 to the campground.

Contact: Sequoia National Forest, Greenhorn Ranger District, tel. (760) 379-5646 or fax (760) 379-8597.

42 Alder Creek

 7

This primitive camp is just inside the western border of Sequoia National Forest, an obscure spot that requires traversing a very twisty and, at times, rough road. It is set at 3,900 feet, just a quarter of a mile upstream from where Alder Creek meets Slick Rock Creek. There is a trail out of the camp that runs north for two miles along Slick Rock Creek.

Location: In Sequoia National Forest; map G5, grid h1.

Campsites, facilities: There are 12 sites for tents or RVs up to 20 feet long. Picnic tables and fire grills are provided. Vault toilets are available. No drinking water is available. Garbage must be packed out. Leashed pets are permitted.

Reservations, fees: No reservations; no fee. Open from May to November.

Directions: From Glennville, drive about eight miles east on Highway 155. Turn right on Alder Creek Road and drive three miles to the campground.

Contact: Sequoia National Forest, Greenhorn Ranger District, tel. (760) 379-5646 or fax (760) 379-8597.

43 Greenhorn Mountain Park

    7

This county campground is near the Shirley Meadows Ski Area, a small ski park open on weekends in winter when there is sufficient snow. Greenhorn Mountain Park covers 160 acres, set at 6,000 feet in elevation. The region is filled with a spider-web network of Forest Service roads, detailed on a map of Sequoia National Forest. Lake Isabella is a 15-minute drive to the east.

Location: Near Shirley Meadows; map G5, grid h1.

Campsites, facilities: There are 70 sites for tents or RVs up to 24 feet long. Picnic tables and fire grills are provided. Drinking water and flush toilets are available. Leashed pets are permitted.

Reservations, fees: Reservations are accepted for groups only; $8 per night, $3 pet fee. Major credit cards accepted. Open spring through fall, weather permitting, closed in winter due to snow.

Directions: From Wofford Heights (on the west shore of Lake Isabella), drive 10 miles west on Highway 155 to the park on the left side of the highway.

Contact: For group reservations, phone Kern County Parks Department, tel. (661) 868-7000; website: www.co.kern.ca.us/parks/index.htm. For area information, phone the Sequoia National Forest, Greenhorn Ranger District, tel. (760) 379-5646 or fax (760) 379-8597.

44 Camp 9

      8

This campground is primitive and sparsely covered, but it has several bonus features. It is set along the northwest shore of Lake Isabella, known for good boating, water-skiing in the summer, and fishing in the spring. Other options include great rafting waters along the North Fork of the Kern River (north of the lake), a good bird-watching area at the South Fork Wildlife Area (along the northeast corner of the lake), and an off-highway-motorcycle park across the road from this campground. The elevation is 2,650 feet.

Location: On Lake Isabella; map G5, grid h2.

Campsites, facilities: There are 109 primitive sites for tents or RVs. Drinking water, flush toilets, sanitary disposal station, boat launch, and a fish-cleaning station are available. Supplies and a coin laundry are available nearby in Kernville. Leashed pets are permitted.

Reservations, fees: No reservations; $8 per night, $5 for each additional vehicle. Open year-round.

Directions: From Kernville, drive six miles south on Sierra Way to the northeast shore of Lake Isabella and the campground entrance on the right.

Contact: Sequoia National Forest, Greenhorn Ranger District, tel. (760) 379-5646 or fax (760) 379-8597.

45 Live Oak North and South

      8

This is one of two camps set in the immediate area on Lake Isabella's northwest side; the other is Tillie Creek. Live Oak is on the west side of the road, Tillie Creek on the eastern, lake side of the road. For recreation information, see the entry for Tillie Creek.

Location: On Lake Isabella; map G5, grid h2.

Campsites, facilities: There are 150 family sites and a group site for tents or RVs up to 30 feet long. Picnic tables and fire grills are provided. Drinking water, showers, and flush toilets are available. Supplies and a coin laundry are available in nearby Wofford Heights. Leashed pets are permitted.

Reservations, fees: Reservations are required for group sites; Reserve at (877) 444-6777 ($8.65 reservation fee) or website: www.reserveusa.com; $14 per night for family sites, $5 for an extra vehicle; $150 per night for group site. Open from May through September.

Directions: From Wofford Heights on the west side of Lake Isabella, drive a half mile south on Highway 155 to the campground entrance road on your right.

Contact: Sequoia National Forest, Greenhorn Ranger District, tel. (760) 379-5646 or fax (760) 379-8597.

46 Evans Flat

   4

Evans Flat is an obscure campground in the southwest region of Sequoia National Forest, about 10 miles west of Lake Isabella, with no other camps in the vicinity. You have to earn this one, but if you want solitude, Evans Flat can provide it. It is set at 6,200 feet, with Woodward Peak a half mile to the east. A natural spring is east of camp within walking distance.

Location: In Sequoia National Forest; map G5, grid h0.

Campsites, facilities: There are 20 sites for tents or RVs up to 16 feet long. Fire grills and picnic tables are provided. A portable restroom is available. No drinking water is available. Garbage must be packed out. Four corrals with water troughs (though water for the troughs is not always available) and a pasture area are provided for horses. Leashed pets are permitted.

Reservations, fees: No reservations; no fee. Open from May to October.

Directions: From Greenhorn Summit on Highway 155, turn south on Rancheria Road (paved, then dirt) and drive 8.3 miles to the campground.

Contact: Sequoia National Forest, Greenhorn Ranger District, tel. (760) 379-5646 or fax (760) 379-8597.

47 Hungry Gulch

       9

Hungry Gulch is on the western side of Lake Isabella, but across the road from the shore. Nearby Boulder Gulch, directly across the road, is an option. There are no boat ramps in

the immediate area. For details about Lake Isabella, see the entry for Pioneer Point.

Location: On Lake Isabella, in Sequoia National Forest; map G5, grid h1.

Campsites, facilities: There are 78 sites for tents, RVs, or trailers up to 30 feet long. Picnic tables and fire grills are provided. Restrooms, drinking water, showers, and flush toilets are available. A playground is available nearby. Supplies and a coin laundry are available in Lake Isabella. Leashed pets are permitted.

Reservations, fees: Reserve at (877) 444-6777 ($8.65 reservation fee) or website: www.reserve usa.com; $14 per night, $5 for each additional vehicle. Open from April through September.

Directions: From the town of Lake Isabella, drive four miles north on Highway 155 to the campground.

Contact: Sequoia National Forest, Greenhorn Ranger District, tel. (760) 379-5646 or fax (760) 379-8597.

48 Pioneer Point

       9

Lake Isabella is the largest freshwater lake in Southern California, covering 11,400 acres, and with it comes a dynamic array of campgrounds, marinas, and facilities. It is set at 2,605 feet in the foothills east of Bakersfield, fed by the Kern River, and dominated by boating sports of all kinds. This camp is at the lake's southwest corner, between the spillway and the main dam, with a boat ramp available a mile to the east. Another camp is nearby, Main Dam. Isabella is a first-class lake for water-skiing, but in the spring and early summer windsurfing is also excellent, best just east of the Auxiliary Dam. Boat rentals of all kinds are available at several marinas.

Location: On Lake Isabella, in Sequoia National Forest; map G5, grid h1.

Campsites, facilities: There are 78 sites for tents, RVs, or trailers up to 30 feet long. Picnic tables and fire grills are provided. Restrooms, drinking water, showers, and flush toilets are available. A playground and a fish-cleaning station are available nearby. A boat ramp is three miles from camp. Supplies and a coin laundry are available in the town of Lake Isabella. Leashed pets are permitted.

Reservations, fees: Reserve at (877) 444-6777 ($8.65 reservation fee) or website: www.reserveusa.com; $14 per night, $5 for each additional vehicle. Open year-round.

Directions: From the town of Lake Isabella, drive 2.5 miles north on Highway 155 to the campground.

Contact: Sequoia National Forest, Greenhorn Ranger District, tel. (760) 379-5646 or fax (760) 379-8597.

49 Tillie Creek

 9

This is one of two camps (the other is Live Oak) near where Tillie Creek enters Lake Isabella, set on the northwest shore of the lake near the town of Wofford Heights. Lake Isabella is the largest freshwater lake in Southern California, covering 11,400 acres, and with it comes a dynamic array of campgrounds, marinas, and facilities. It is set at 2,605 feet in the foothills east of Bakersfield, fed by the Kern River, and dominated by boating sports of all kinds.

Location: On Lake Isabella; map G5, grid h2.

Campsites, facilities: There are 155 family sites and four group sites for tents or RVs up to 45 feet long. Picnic tables and fire grills are provided. Restrooms, drinking water, showers, and flush toilets are available. A sanitary disposal station, playground, amphitheater, and a fish-cleaning station are available nearby. Some facilities are wheelchair accessible. Supplies and a coin laundry are nearby in Wofford Heights. Leashed pets are permitted.

Reservations, fees: Reservations are required for group sites; Reserve at (877) 444-6777 ($8.65 reservation fee) or website: www.reserveusa.com; $14 per night for family sites, $5 for an extra vehicle; $75 to $120 per night for group sites. Open year-round.

Directions: From Wofford Heights on the west side of Lake Isabella, drive one mile southwest on Highway 155 to the campground.

Contact: Sequoia National Forest, Greenhorn Ranger District, tel. (760) 379-5646 or fax (760) 379-8597.

50 French Gulch Group Camp

 9

This is a large group camp on Lake Isabella at the southwest end of the lake about two miles north of Pioneer Point and the spillway. For recreation information, see the entry for Pioneer Point. The elevation is 2,700 feet.

Location: On Lake Isabella; map G5, grid h2.

Campsites, facilities: There is one large group campsite for up to 100 people with tents or RVs. Picnic tables and fire grills are provided. Drinking water, flush toilets, and solar-heated showers are available. A grocery store, coin laundry, and propane gas are nearby. Leashed pets are permitted.

Reservations, fees: Reserve at (877) 444-6777 ($8.65 reservation fee) or website: www.reserveusa.com; $60 group fee per night. Open year-round.

Directions: From the town of Lake Isabella, drive three miles north on Highway 155 to the campground entrance on the right.

Contact: Sequoia National Forest, Greenhorn Ranger District, tel. (760) 379-5646 or fax (760) 379-8597.

51 Boulder Gulch

 8

Boulder Gulch lies fairly near the western shore of Lake Isabella, across the road from Hungry Gulch. Take your pick. Isabella is the biggest lake in Southern California and a prime destination point for Bakersfield area residents. Fishing for trout and bass is best in the spring. By the dog days of summer, when people are bow-wowin' at the heat, water-skiers take over, along with folks just looking to cool off. Like a lot of lakes in the valley, Isabella is subject to drawdowns. The elevation is 2,650 feet. For more information, see the entry for Pioneer Point.

Location: On Lake Isabella; map G5, grid h2.

Campsites, facilities: There are 78 sites for tents, trailers, or RVs up to 45 feet long. Picnic tables and fire grills are provided. Restrooms, drinking water, flush toilets, showers, playground, and a fish-cleaning station are available. Some facilities are wheelchair accessible. Supplies and a coin laundry are available in the town of Lake Isabella. Leashed pets are permitted.

Reservations, fees: Reserve at (877) 444-6777 ($8.65 reservation fee) or website: www.reserveusa.com; $14 per night, $5 for each additional vehicle. Open from April through September.

Directions: From the town of Lake Isabella, drive four miles north on Highway 155 to the campground entrance.

Contact: Sequoia National Forest, Greenhorn Ranger District, tel. (760) 379-5646 or fax (760) 379-8597.

52 Main Dam

      8

This camp is on the south shore of Lake Isabella, just east of Pioneer Point and within a mile of a boat ramp. For recreation information, see the entry for Pioneer Point.

Location: On Lake Isabella; map G5, grid h2.

Campsites, facilities: There are 82 sites for tents, trailers, or RVs up to 30 feet long. Picnic tables and fire grills are provided. Drinking water and flush toilets are available. A sanitary disposal station is available nearby. Supplies and a coin laundry are available in the town of Lake Isabella. Leashed pets are permitted with proof of shots.

Reservations, fees: Reserve at (877) 444-6777 ($8.65 reservation fee) or website: www.reserveusa.com; $12 per night, $5 for each additional vehicle. Open May to September.

Directions: From the town of Lake Isabella, drive 1.5 miles northwest on Highway 155 to the campground.

Contact: Sequoia National Forest, Greenhorn Ranger District, tel. (760) 379-5646 or fax (760) 379-8597.

53 Auxiliary Dam

      8

This primitive camp was designed to be an overflow area if other camps at Lake Isabella are packed. It's the only camp directly on the shore of the lake, and many people like it. In addition, a boat ramp is just a mile north for good lake access, and the windsurfing prospects adjacent to the campground are the best of the entire lake. The winds come up and sail right over the dam, creating a steady breeze in the afternoon that is not gusty.

Location: On Lake Isabella; map G5, grid i2.

Campsites, facilities: There are a number of primitive, undesignated sites for tents or RVs. Drinking water and flush toilets are available. Supplies and a coin laundry are available in the town of Lake Isabella. Leashed pets are permitted.

Reservations, fees: No reservations; no fee. Open year-round.

Directions: From the town of Lake Isabella, drive a mile northeast on Highway 178 to the campground entrance.

Contact: Sequoia National Forest, Greenhorn Ranger District, tel. (760) 379-5646 or fax (760) 379-8597.

54 Paradise Cove

      6

Paradise Cove is on the southeast shore of Lake Isabella. A boat ramp is about two miles away to the east, near the South Fork Picnic Area. While the camp is not directly at the lakeshore, it does overlook the broadest expanse of the lake. This part of the lake is relatively undeveloped compared to the areas near Wofford Heights and the dam.

Location: On Lake Isabella; map G5, grid i2.

Campsites, facilities: There are 58 sites for tents or RVs, some with picnic tables and fire grills. Flush toilets, showers, and a fish-cleaning station are available. Some facilities are wheelchair accessible. Supplies, sanitary disposal station, and a coin laundry are available in Mountain Mesa. Leashed pets are permitted.

Reservations, fees: Reserve at (877) 444-6777 ($8.65 reservation fee) or website: www.reserveusa.com; $6 to $14 per night, $5 for each additional vehicle. Open year-round.

Directions: From the town of Lake Isabella, drive six miles northeast on Highway 178 to the campground entrance.

Contact: Sequoia National Forest, Greenhorn Ranger District, tel. (760) 379-5646 or fax (760) 379-8597.

55 KOA Lake Isabella

     4

This KOA camp provides a good, clean option to the Forest Service camps on the southern end of Lake Isabella, Southern California's largest lake. It is set in South Fork Valley (elevation 2,600 feet), east of the lake off Highway 178. The nearest boat ramp is at South Fork Picnic Area (about a five-minute drive to the west), where there is also a good view of the lake.

Location: On Lake Isabella; map G5, grid i3.

Campsites, facilities: There are 104 sites for tents or RVs with full or partial hookups. Picnic tables are provided. Restrooms, drinking water, flush toilets, showers, playground, swimming pool, laundry facilities, store, sanitary disposal station, and propane gas are available. Leashed pets are permitted.

Reservations, fees: Reservations are accepted; $20 to $25 per night. Major credit cards accepted. Open year-round.

Directions: From the town of Lake Isabella, drive 10 miles east on Highway 178 and look for the KOA sign on the left.

Contact: KOA Lake Isabella, tel. (760) 378-2001.

56 Lake Isabella RV Resort

     7

This quiet, privately operated park set up for RVs is across the street from Lake Isabella. It is one of many camps at the lake, so plan on plenty of company. There is a free public boat ramp 200 yards away within Sequoia National Forest and a full-service marina with watercraft rentals two miles west of the resort. For details on the immediate area, see the entry for the nearby Forest Service camps, Auxiliary Dam and Paradise Cove. The elevation is 2,600 feet.

Location: Near Lake Isabella; map G5, grid i3.

Campsites, facilities: There are 91 RV sites with full hookups. Picnic tables and barbecues are provided. Restrooms, showers, swimming pool, modem hookups, clubhouse, billiards, cable TV, laundry facilities, and a fish-cleaning station are available. Some facilities are wheelchair accessible. Leashed pets are permitted.

Reservations, fees: Reservations are accepted; $22 to $25 per night. Major credit cards accepted. Open year-round.

Directions: From the town of Lake Isabella, drive six miles northeast on Highway 178 to the signed entrance on the right.

Contact: Lake Isabella RV Resort, tel. (800) 787-9920; website: www.lakeisabellarv.com.

57 Walker Pass Walk-In

    6

Long-distance hikers on the Pacific Crest Trail treat this camp as if they were arriving at Valhalla. That's because it is set right on the trail and, better yet, drinking water is available. Out here in the desert there aren't many places where you can act like a camel and suck up all the liquid you can hold. The camp is set at 5,200 feet, southwest of Death Valley National Park. If you guessed it was named for Joe Walker, the West's greatest trailblazer and one of my heroes, well, right you are. If you arrive by car instead of on the PCT, use this spot as a base camp. Because of its desert remoteness very few hikers start trips from this location.

Location: On the Pacific Crest Trail southwest of Death Valley National Park; map G5, grid i7.

Campsites, facilities: There are two sites for tents and RVs with limited parking and 11 walk-in sites for tents only. Picnic tables and fire rings are provided. Drinking water (spring through fall) and pit toilets are available. Hitching racks and corrals are available. Garbage must be packed out.

Reservations, fees: No reservations; no fee. A 14-day stay limit is enforced. Open year-round.

Directions: From Lake Isabella, drive east on Highway 178 and continue 14 miles past Onyx. At Walker Pass look for the campground on the right side of the road, where a sign is posted for the Pacific Crest Trail. It is a quarter-mile walk from the parking area to the campground.

Contact: Bureau of Land Management, Bakersfield Field Office; tel. (661) 391-6000, or fax (661) 391-6040.

58 Sandy Flat

 6

This camp was opened in the mid-1990s as an overflow camp in case Hobo was filled. It is about a mile from Hobo. It is a low-use campground, with less shade than Hobo; some sites shaded, others, well, nope. It is used primarily as a boat launch area for kayakers and rafters. Fishing is fair for catfish, bass, and rainbow trout. The river is stocked with trout in the summer.

Location: On the Kern River in Sequoia National Forest; map G5, grid i1.

Campsites, facilities: There are 38 sites for tents and for RVs. Fire rings and picnic tables are provided. Water is provided some of the time; call ahead for details. Vault toilets are available. Some facilities are wheelchair accessible. Leashed pets are permitted.

Reservations, fees: Reservations are recommended; reserve at (877) 444-6777 ($8.65 reservation fee) or website: www. reserveusa.com; $14 per night for the first vehicle, $5 per night for each additional vehicle. There is no fee when there is no water at the camp. Open from May through September.

Directions: From the town of Lake Isabella, drive five miles southwest on Highway 178. Turn left on Borel Road and drive south for about a third of a mile to the intersection of Old Kern Road. Turn right and drive one mile to the campground on your right.

Contact: Sequoia National Forest, Greenhorn Ranger District, tel. (760) 379-5646 or fax (760) 379-8597.

59 Hobo

 7

The secret is out about Hobo: It is set adjacent to a mineral hot springs, that is, an open-air springs, with room for about 10 people at once. The camp is also situated along the lower Kern River, about 10 miles downstream of the dam at Lake Isabella. Rafters sometimes use this camp as a put-in spot for an 18-mile run to the takeout at Democrat Picnic Area, a challenging Class IV run. The elevation is 2,300 feet.

Location: On the Kern River in Sequoia National Forest; map G5, grid j1.

Campsites, facilities: There are 25 sites for tents and 10 sites for RVs up to 16 feet long. Fire grills and picnic tables are provided. Water is provided some of the time; call ahead for details. Vault toilets and showers are available. Leashed pets are permitted. Some facilities are wheelchair accessible.

Reservations, fees: Reservations are recommended; reserve at (877) 444-6777 ($8.65 reservation fee) or website: www. reserve usa.com; $13 per night for the first vehicle, $5 per night for each additional vehicle. There is no fee when there is no water at the camp. Open from May through September.

Directions: From the town of Lake Isabella, drive five miles southwest on Highway 178. Turn left on Borel Road and drive south for about a third of a mile to the intersection of Old Kern Road. Turn right and drive about two miles to the campground on your right.

Contact: Sequoia National Forest, Greenhorn Ranger District, tel. (760) 379-5646 or fax (760) 379-8597.

60 Breckenridge

  7

This is a popular spot for people to visit with sport utility vehicles. It is a tiny, primitive camp set at 7,100 feet near Breckenridge Mountain (a good lookout here) in a little-traveled southwest sector of the Sequoia National Forest. From camp, it's a two-mile drive south up to the lookout, with sweeping views afforded in all directions. There are no other camps in the immediate area.

Location: In Sequoia National Forest; map G5, grid j0.

Campsites, facilities: There are eight tent sites. Picnic tables and fire grills are provided. A portable toilet is available. No drinking water is available. Garbage must be packed out. Leashed pets are permitted.

Reservations, fees: No reservations; no fee. Open from May to October.

Directions: From the town of Lake Isabella, on Highway 178 turn south on Caliente Bodfish Road and drive about 12 miles to the town of Havilah. Continue south on Caliente Bodfish Road for two miles. Turn right on Forest Road 28S06 and drive 10 miles to the campground.

Contact: Sequoia National Forest, Greenhorn Ranger District, tel. (760) 379-5646 or fax (760) 379-8597.

RARE BIGHORN SHEEP

MAP G6

TO BIG PINE **634** TO SCOTTY'S CASTLE

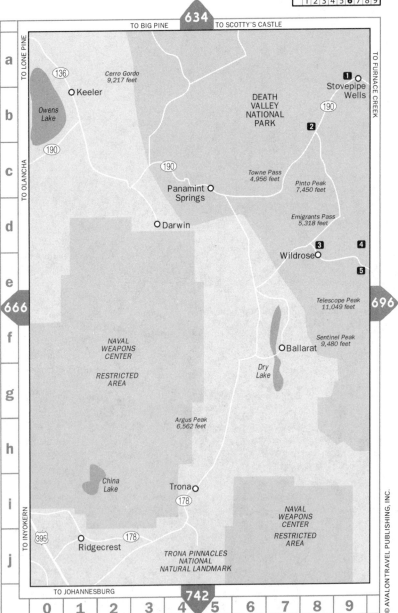

TO LONE PINE
TO OLANCHA
TO INYOKERN
TO FURNACE CREEK
TO JOHANNESBURG

(136)

Cerro Gordo
9,217 feet

O Keeler

Owens
Lake

(190)

(190)

DEATH
VALLEY
NATIONAL
PARK

❶ O
Stovepipe
Wells

(190)

❷

Towne Pass
4,956 feet

Pinto Peak
7,450 feet

Panamint O
Springs

Emigrants Pass
5,318 feet

O Darwin

❸ ❹

WildroseO

❺

Telescope Peak
11,049 feet

NAVAL
WEAPONS
CENTER

RESTRICTED
AREA

Sentinel Peak
9,480 feet

O Ballarat

Dry
Lake

Argus Peak
6,562 feet

China
Lake

Trona O
(178)

(395)

O
Ridgecrest

(178)

TRONA PINNACLES
NATIONAL
NATURAL LANDMARK

NAVAL
WEAPONS
CENTER

RESTRICTED
AREA

666

696

742

© AVALON TRAVEL PUBLISHING, INC.

CHAPTER G6

1 Stovepipe Wells

 4

Stovepipe Wells is on the major highway through Death Valley. The RV sites consist of an enormous asphalt area with sites simply marked on it. There is no shelter or shade. But note: Get fuel here because prices are usually lower than at Furnace Creek. An unusual trail is available off the highway within a short distance; look for the sign for the Mosaic Canyon Trail parking area. From here you can take the easy one-mile walk up a beautiful canyon, where the walls are marble and seem as if they are polished. Rock scramblers can extend the trip for another mile. The elevation is at sea level on the edge of a large expanse of Death Valley below sea level.

Location: In Death Valley National Park; map G6, grid a9.

Campsites, facilities: There are 18 sites for tents only and 200 sites for RVs. Drinking water, flush toilets, sanitary disposal station, swimming pool, camp store, and gasoline are available. Evening ranger programs are available on winter weekends. Some facilities are wheelchair accessible. Leashed pets are permitted at campsites only.

Reservations, fees: No reservations; $10 per night, plus a $10 park entrance fee per vehicle. Open May through October.

Directions: In Stovepipe Wells Village, drive west on Highway 190 through town to the signed entrance (just before the general store) on the right.

Contact: Death Valley National Park, tel. (760) 786-2331, or (760) 786-3244, or fax (760) 786-3283.

2 Emigrant

 4

The key here is the elevation, and Emigrant, at 2,100 feet, is out of the forbidding subzero elevations of Death Valley. That makes it one of the more habitable camps. From the camp a good side trip is to drive south 21 miles on Emigrant Canyon Road, then turn east on Upper Wildrose Canyon Road for seven miles, the last two miles a rough dirt road. That done, you come to the trailhead for Wildrose Peak, on the left side of the road at the parking area for Charcoal Kilne. The trail here climbs 4.2 miles to the peak, with awesome views in the last two miles; the last mile is a butt-kicker.

Location: In Death Valley National Park; map G6, grid b8.

Campsites, facilities: There are 10 sites for tents or RVs. Picnic tables are provided. Drinking water and flush toilets are available. Leashed pets are permitted at campsites only.

Reservations, fees: No reservations; no camping fee, however, there is a $10 park entrance fee per vehicle. Open May through October.

Directions: In Stovepipe Wells Village, drive eight miles southwest on Highway 190 to the campground on the right.

Contact: Death Valley National Park, tel. (760) 786-2331, or fax (760) 786-3283.

3 Wildrose

 4

Wildrose is set on the road that heads out to the primitive country of the awesome Panamint Range, eventually within range of

Telescope Peak, the highest point in Death Valley National Park (11,049 feet). The elevation at the camp is 4,100 feet.

Location: In Death Valley National Park; map G6, grid d8.

Campsites, facilities: There are 30 sites for tents or RVs up to 25 feet long. Picnic tables are provided. Drinking water (April through November only) and pit toilets are available. Leashed pets are permitted at campsites only.

Reservations, fees: No reservations; no camping fee, however, there is a $10 park entrance fee per vehicle. Open year-round.

Directions: From Stovepipe Wells Village, drive 30 miles south on Highway 190 to Wildrose Canyon Road. Turn left and drive to the signed campground entrance road.

Contact: Death Valley National Park, tel. (760) 786-2331 or (760) 786-3244, or fax (760) 786-3283.

4 Thorndike 4-wheel-drive

    4

This is one of Death Valley National Park's little-known camps. It is set in the high country at 7,500 feet. It's free, of course. Otherwise they'd have to actually send somebody out to tend to the place. Nearby are century-old charcoal kilns that were built by Chinese laborers and tended by Shoshone Indians. The trailhead that serves Telescope Peak (11,049 feet), the highest point in Death Valley, can be found in nearby Mahogany Flat. (For more camps in Death Valley National Park, see chapter G7.)

Location: In Death Valley National Park; map G6, grid d9.

Campsites, facilities: This backcountry campground is accessible only by foot or four-wheel-drive vehicle and has eight campsites for tents. Picnic tables and pit toilets are available. No drinking water is available. Leashed pets are permitted at campsites only.

Reservations, fees: No reservations; no camping fee, however, there is a $10 park entrance fee per vehicle.

Directions: From Stovepipe Wells Village, drive 37 miles south on Highway 190 to Wildrose Canyon Road, turn left, and drive to the end of the road and the camp. (The road becomes extremely rough; four-wheel drive is required.)

Contact: Death Valley National Park, tel. (760) 786-2331 or (760) 786-3244, or fax (760) 786-3283.

5 Mahogany Flat 4-wheel drive

 5

This is one of two primitive, hard-to-reach camps (the other is Thorndike) set in the Panamint Range high country. It is one of the few shaded camps, offering beautiful piñon pines and junipers. What makes it popular, however, is the trail to Telescope Peak leading out from camp. Only the ambitious and well conditioned should attempt the climb, a seven-mile trip one way with breathtaking (literally) views of both Panamint Valley and Death Valley. The elevation at the campground is 8,200 feet and Telescope Peak summits out at 11,049 feet, which translates to a climb of 2,849 feet.

Location: In Death Valley National Park; map G6, grid e9.

Campsites, facilities: There are 10 sites for tents only. Picnic tables are provided. Pit toilets are available. No drinking water is available. The campground is accessible only by foot or four-wheel-drive vehicle. Leashed pets are permitted at campsites only.

Reservations, fees: No reservations; no camping fee, however, there is a $10 park entrance fee per vehicle. Open year-round, weather permitting.

Directions: From Stovepipe Wells Village, drive 38 miles south on Highway 190 to Wildrose Canyon Road, turn left, and drive to the end of the road and the camp.

Contact: Death Valley National Park, tel. (760) 786-2331, or (760) 786-3244, or fax (760) 786-3283.

KIM WEIR

MOUNTAINS AROUND
DEATH VALLEY

MAP G7

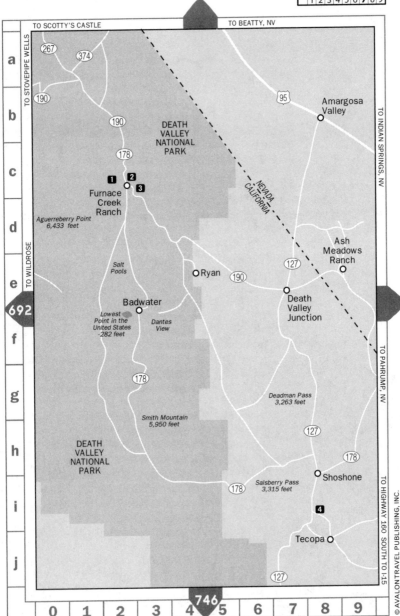

TO SCOTTY'S CASTLE   TO BEATTY, NV

TO STOVEPIPE WELLS

267
374
190

190
178

DEATH VALLEY NATIONAL PARK

95

Amargosa Valley

TO INDIAN SPRINGS, NV

1
2
3

Furnace Creek Ranch

Aguerreberry Point 6,433 feet

NEVADA
CALIFORNIA

TO WILDROSE

Salt Pools

Ryan

190

127

Ash Meadows Ranch

Badwater

Lowest Point in the United States -282 feet

Dantes View

Death Valley Junction

692

178

TO PAHRUMP, NV

Deadman Pass 3,263 feet

Smith Mountain 5,950 feet

127

DEATH VALLEY NATIONAL PARK

178

178

Salsberry Pass 3,315 feet

178

Shoshone

4

TO HIGHWAY 160 SOUTH TO I-15

Tecopa

127

746

© AVALON TRAVEL PUBLISHING, INC.

CHAPTER G7

1 Furnace Creek

 5

This is a well-developed national park site that provides a good base camp for exploring Death Valley, especially for newcomers. The nearby visitor center includes Death Valley Museum and offers maps and suggestions for hikes and drives in this unique wildland. The elevation is 190 feet below sea level. This camp offers shady sites, a rarity in Death Valley. It's open all year, but keep in mind that the daytime summer temperatures commonly exceed 120 degrees, making this area virtually uninhabitable in the summer.

Location: In Death Valley National Park; map G7, grid c2.

Campsites, facilities: There are 136 sites for tents or RVs. Picnic tables are provided. Drinking water, flush toilets, sanitary disposal station, and evening ranger programs are available. Some facilities are wheelchair accessible. Leashed pets are permitted at campsites only.

Reservations, fees: Reservations are recommended mid-October through mid-April at tel. (800) 365-CAMP (800-365-2267); website: reservationsnps.gov; $16 per night (includes reservation fee), plus a $10 park entrance fee. Open year-round.

Directions: From Furnace Creek Ranch, drive one mile north on Highway 190 to the signed campground entrance on the left.

Contact: Death Valley National Park, (760) 786-2331 or (760) 786-3244, or fax (760) 786-3283.

2 Sunset

 4

This is one of several options for campers in the Furnace Creek area of Death Valley, with an elevation of 190 feet below sea level. It is advised to make your first stop at the nearby visitor center for maps and suggested hikes (according to your level of fitness) and drives. Don't forget your canteen—and if you're backpacking, never set up a wilderness camp closer than 100 yards to water in Death Valley.

Location: In Death Valley National Park; map G7, grid c2.

Campsites, facilities: There are 1,000 sites for RVs. Drinking water, flush toilets, and a sanitary disposal station are available. Some facilities are wheelchair accessible. Leashed pets are permitted at campsites.

Reservations, fees: No reservations for individual sites, $10 per night fee, plus a $10 park entrance fee per vehicle. Open October through April.

Directions: From Furnace Creek Ranch, turn south on Highway 190 and drive a quarter mile to the signed campground entrance and turn left into the campground.

Contact: Death Valley National Park, (760) 786-2331 or (760) 786-3244, or fax (760) 786-3283.

3 Texas Spring

 2

This camp is another enormous section of asphalt where the campsites consist of white lines as borders. There's no shade and no shelter. The nearby visitor center, which features the Death Valley Museum, offers maps and suggestions for hikes and drives. The lowest point in the U.S., Badwater, set 282 feet below sea level, is to the southwest. This camp has one truly unique feature: bathrooms that are listed on the National Historic Register.

Location: In Death Valley National Park; map G7, grid c3.

Campsites, facilities: There are 92 sites for tents or RVs, and two group sites for up to 10 vehicles and 40 people each. Picnic tables are provided. Drinking water, flush toilets, and a sanitary disposal station are available. Some facilities are wheelchair accessible. Leashed pets are permitted.

Reservations, fees: No reservations for individual sites, $10 per night fee, plus a $10 park entrance fee per vehicle. Reservations are required for group camp at tel. (800) 365-CAMP (800-365-2267) or website: reservationsnps.gov; $50 per night (includes reservation fee), plus a $10 park entrance fee per vehicle. Open October through March.

Directions: From Furnace Creek Ranch, drive south on Highway 190 for a quarter mile to the signed campground entrance on the left.

Contact: Death Valley National Park, (760) 786-2331 or (760) 786-3244, or fax (760) 786-3283

◪ Tecopa Hot Springs County Campground

    3

This one is out there in no-man's-land, and if it weren't for the hot springs and the good rockhounding, all you'd see around here is a few skeletons. Regardless, it's quite an attraction in the winter, when the warm climate is a plus and the nearby mineral baths are worth taking a dunk in. Rockhounds will enjoy looking for amethysts, opals, and petrified wood in the nearby areas. The elevation is 1,500 feet. Nobody gets here by accident.

Location: North of Tecopa; map G7, grid i8.

Campsites, facilities: There are 340 sites for tents or RVs, some with electrical hookups. Picnic tables and fire grills are provided. Drinking water, flush toilets, showers, and a sanitary disposal station are available. Some facilities are wheelchair accessible. Coin laundry, groceries, and propane gas are available nearby. Leashed pets are permitted.

Reservations, fees: No reservations; $6.50 to $8 per night. Open year-round.

Directions: From Shoshone, drive south on State Highway 127 for five miles to County Road. Turn southwest on County Road and drive three miles to the park entrance.

Contact: Inyo County Parks Department, tel. (760) 852-4264.

THE HILLS OF
THE CENTRAL COAST

MAP H2

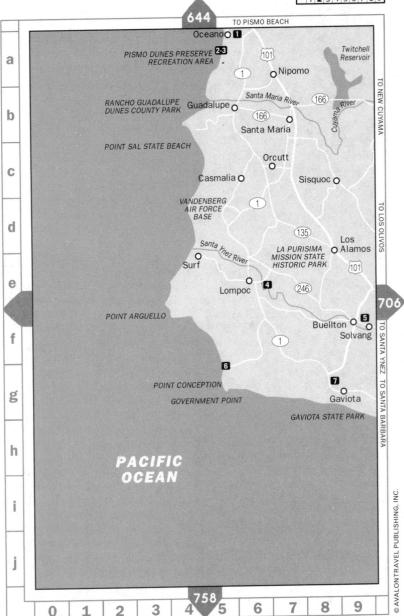

644

TO PISMO BEACH

Oceano **1**

PISMO DUNES PRESERVE **2-3**
RECREATION AREA

(101)

Twitchell
Reservoir

(1) Nipomo

TO NEW CUYAMA

Santa Maria River

(166)

RANCHO GUADALUPE
DUNES COUNTY PARK   Guadalupe

(166)

Santa Maria

POINT SAL STATE BEACH

Orcutt

Casmalia   Sisquoc

TO LOS OLIVOS

VANDENBERG
AIR FORCE
BASE

(1)

(135)

Los
Alamos

Santa Ynez River

LA PURISIMA
MISSION STATE
HISTORIC PARK

(101)

Surf

706

Lompoc   **4**   (246)

POINT ARGUELLO

Buellton **5**
Solvang

(1)

6

POINT CONCEPTION

GOVERNMENT POINT

7
Gaviota

GAVIOTA STATE PARK

TO SANTA YNEZ   TO SANTA BARBARA

PACIFIC
OCEAN

© AVALON TRAVEL PUBLISHING, INC.

758

| 0 | 1 | 2 | 3 | 4 | 5 | 6 | 7 | 8 | 9 |

CHAPTER H2

1 Oceano Memorial Campground

    7

This county park often gets overlooked because it isn't on the state reservation system. That's other folks' loss and your gain. The location is a bonus, set near Pismo State Beach, the site of great sand dunes, clamming, and wide-open ocean frontage.

Location: Near Arroyo Grande; map H2, grid a6.

Campsites, facilities: There are 22 sites for tents or RVs up to 40 feet, with full hookups, and a group site. Picnic tables and fire grills are provided. Drinking water and flush toilets are available. A playground, coin laundry, grocery store, and propane gas are available nearby. Leashed pets are permitted with proof of vaccinations.

Reservations, fees: No reservations for individual sites. Reservation for group site only; individual sites $18 to $22 per night, $2 pet fee. Open year-round.

Directions: From Pismo Beach, drive south on U.S. 101. Take the Arroyo-Grande Avenue exit west to Highway 1. Drive south on Highway 1 for 1.5 miles, turn right on Pier Avenue, and drive about half a block. Turn left on Per-shing Avenue and continue to the campground on the right at 414 Pershing Avenue.

Contact: Oceano Memorial Campground, tel. (805) 781-5930 or fax (805) 781-1102; website: www.slocountyparks.com.

2 Oceano Dunes State Vehicular Recreation Area

      6

This is "National Headquarters" for all-terrain vehicles (ATVs)—you know, those three- and four-wheeled motorcycles that turn otherwise normal people into lunatics. The camps are along one to three miles of beach and 1,500 acres of open sand dunes, and since not many make the walk to the campsites, four-wheel drives or ATVs are needed for access. High tides can limit access. A beach towing service for RVs and trailers is available. They roam wild on the dunes here; that's the law, so don't go planning a quiet stroll. If you don't like 'em, you are strongly advised to go elsewhere. If this is your game, have fun and try to keep from killing yourself. Each fall, the "National Sand Drags" are held here each fall. More than 1 million people visit here each year.

Location: South of Pismo Beach; map H2, grid a5.

Campsites, facilities: There are 1,000 primitive sites for off-highway vehicles. Vault toilets are provided. No drinking water is available at campsites. Drinking water, horseback riding facilities, grocery store, coin laundry, restaurants, gas stations, and a sanitary disposal station are available nearby. Leashed pets are permitted.

Reservations, fees: Reserve at tel. (800) 444-PARK (444-7275) or website: www.reserve america.com; $6 per night, $1 per person per night for hike-in sites. Open year-round.

Directions: Heading north on U.S. 101 in Arroyo Grande, take the Grand Avenue exit. Make a left at the signal and drive west on Grand Avenue for about four miles until the road ends at the North Entrance beach camping area (the South Entrance is one mile south; from Highway 1, take Pier Avenue).

Contact: Oceano Dunes, tel. (805) 473-7230 or fax (805) 473-7234.

❸ Oceano

 6

This is a prized state beach campground, with Pismo Beach and its sand dunes and coastal frontage a centerpiece for the state park system. Its location on the central coast on Highway 1, as well as its beauty and recreational opportunities, makes it extremely popular. It fills to capacity most nights, and reservations are usually a necessity. Poaching has devastated the clamming here, with no legal clams taken for years.

Location: In Pismo State Beach; map H2, grid a5.

Campsites, facilities: There are 82 sites for tents, trailers, or RVs up to 31 feet long, 42 with partial hookups for trailers and RVs up to 36 feet long. There is also one primitive hike-in/bike-in site. Picnic tables, food lockers, and fire grills are provided. Restrooms, drinking water, flush toilets, and coin-operated showers are available. Horseback riding facilities, grocery store, coin laundry, sanitary disposal station, restaurants, and gas stations are nearby. Leashed pets are permitted.

Reservations, fees: Reserve at tel. (800) 444-PARK (444-7275) or website: www.reserve america.com; $12 to $18 per night, $1 per night per person for hike-in/bike-in sites. Open year-round.

Directions: From Pismo Beach, drive two miles south on Highway 1 to Pier Avenue. Turn right and drive 0.2 mile to the campground entrance.

Contact: Oceano, tel. (805) 489-1869 or (805) 473-7220.

❹ River Park

 4

Before checking in here you'd best get a lesson in how to pronounce Lompoc. It's "Lom-Poke." If you arrive and say, "Hey, it's great to be in Lom-Pock," they might just tell ya to get on back to Nebraska with the other cowpokes. The camp is set near the lower Santa Ynez River, which looks quite a bit different than it does up in Los Padres National Forest. A small fishing lake within the park is stocked regularly with trout. Side trip possibilities include the nearby La Purisima Mission State Historic Park.

Location: In Lompoc; map H2, grid e6.

Campsites, facilities: There 36 RV sites with full hookups and a large open area for tents. Restrooms, drinking water, flush toilets, showers, sanitary disposal station, fishing pond, and a playground are available. Supplies and a coin laundry are nearby. Leashed pets are permitted.

Reservations, fees: Reservations are accepted for groups only; $15 per night, $4 per night for hike-in/bike-in sites, $2 for disposal station use, and $1 pet fee. Open year-round.

Directions: In Lompoc, drive to the junction of Highway 246 and Sweeney Road at the southwest edge of town and continue to the park at 401 East Highway 246.

Contact: Lompoc Parks & Recreation Department, tel. (805) 736-6565 or fax (805) 736-5195; website: www.ci.lompoc.ca.us.

❺ Flying Flags RV Park

 3

This is one of the few privately operated parks in the area that welcomes tenters as well as RVers. Nearby side trips include the Santa Ynez Mission, just east of Solvang. The town of Solvang is of interest, originally a small Danish settlement that has expanded since the 1920s yet managed to keep its cultural heritage intact over the years. The town is spotless, no trash of any kind in sight, and an example of how to do something right.

Location: Near Solvang; map H2, grid f9.

Campsites, facilities: There are 100 sites for tents and 256 RV sites with full or partial hookups. Picnic tables are provided. Restrooms, showers, playground, swimming pool, two hot therapy pools, laundry room, store, sanitary disposal station, ice, recreation room, modem hookups, arcade, five clubhouses, and propane gas are available. Some facilities are wheelchair accessible. A nine-hole golf course is nearby. Leashed pets are permitted.

Reservations, fees: Reservations are recommended; $18 to $26 per night for one or two people, $3 for each additional camper, $1 pet fee. Open year-round. Major credit cards accepted.

Directions: From Santa Barbara, drive 45 miles north on U.S. 101 to its intersection with Highway 246. Turn west (left) on Highway 246 and drive about a half mile to the four-way stop. Turn left on Avenue of the Flags and drive about one block to the campground entrance on the left at 180 Avenue of the Flags.

Contact: Flying Flags RV Park, tel. (805) 688-3716 or fax (805) 688-9245; website: www.flyingflags.com.

6 Jalama Beach County Park

 8

This is a pretty spot set where Jalama Creek empties into the ocean, about five miles north of Point Conception and just south of Vandenberg Air Force Base. The area is known for its sunsets and beachcombing, with occasional lost missiles washing up on the beach. The camp is so popular that a waiting list is common in summer.

Location: Near Lompoc on the Pacific Ocean; map H2, grid g5.

Campsites, facilities: There are 110 sites for tents or RVs up to 35 feet long, including several group sites. Some sites have electrical hookups, but there are no water hookups. Picnic tables and fire grills are provided. Rest-

rooms, drinking water, flush toilets, showers, sanitary disposal station, and a grocery store are available. Note: the nearest gas station is 20 miles away. Leashed pets are permitted. Some facilities are wheelchair accessible.

Reservations, fees: No reservations except for groups; $15 to $21 per night, $8 for an extra vehicle (two-vehicle maximum per site); group reservation at tel. (805) 934-2611 ($25 reservation fee), $2 pet fee. Major credit cards accepted. Open year-round.

Directions: From Lompoc, drive about five miles south on Highway 1. Turn southwest on Jalama Road and drive 14 miles to the park.

Contact: Jalama Beach County Park, tel. (805) 736-6316 or fax (805) 736-8020 or tel. (805) 736-3504; website: www.slocountyparks.com.

7 Gaviota State Park

 10

This is the granddaddy, the biggest of the three state beaches along U.S. 101 northwest of Santa Barbara. Spectacular and beautiful, the park covers 2,700 acres, providing trails for hiking and horseback riding, as well as a mile-long stretch of stunning beach frontage. The ambitious can hike the beach to get more seclusion. Trails to Gaviota Overlook (1.5 miles) and Gaviota Peak (3.2 miles one way) provide lookouts with drop-dead gorgeous views. Want more? There is also a half-mile trail to the hot springs.

Location: Near Santa Barbara; map H2, grid g8.

Campsites, facilities: There are 42 sites for tents and RVs up to 27 feet long, and an area with hike-in/bike-in sites. Picnic tables and fire grills are provided. Restrooms, drinking water, flush toilets, coin showers, summer lifeguard service, and a boat hoist are available. Some facilities are wheelchair accessible. A convenience store (open summer only) is nearby. Leashed pets are permitted at campsites.

Reservations, fees: No reservations; $12 per night, $1 per person per night for hike-in or bike-in sites. Open year-round.

Directions: From Santa Barbara, drive 33 miles north on U.S. 101 to the Gaviota State Beach exit. Turn west and drive a short distance to the park entrance.

Contact: Gaviota State Park, Channel Coast District, tel. (805) 968-1033 or tel. (805) 899-1400.

KIM WEIR

Don't miss the
Queen of the Missions
if you're camping near
Santa Barbara.

MAP H3

TO SANTA MARIA

TO SISQUOC

Derby
Acres ○
(33)

Fellows ○   (119)

Ford City ○

Taft ○

TO OLD RIVER

TO MARICOPA

1

2 **3**

Cuyama River

(166)

4

New Cuyama ○

Cuyama ○

(166)

Manzanita Mountain
3,125 feet

McPherson Peak
5,947 feet   **5**

Grocer
Grade
2,968 feet

(33)

8

Zaca Peak
4,220 feet

9   **10**

6   **7**

Ventucopa ○

LOS PADRES
NATIONAL
FOREST

Los Olivos ○
(154)

Solvang ○

11

Cuyama Peak
5,875 feet

700

(246) ○ Santa Ynez

Santa Ynez River

12

Lake
Cachuma

724

TO FRAZIER PARK

13

14

Gibraltar
Reservoir

15
16

San Marcos Pass
2,225 feet

17-21

(154)

Pine Mountain
Summit
5,084 feet

TO GAVIOTA

22

25 **26**   Monte Arido
6,003 feet

(101)   **23**

(192)

27

REFUGIO
STATE BEACH

24

Wheeler
Springs

29

30

EL CAPITAN
STATE BEACH

Goleta ○

28

SANTA
BARBARA ○

Montecito ○

○ Summerland

(33)

TO SANTA PAULA

**PACIFIC
OCEAN**

Carpinteria ○

CARPINTERIA
STATE BEACH

33

(150)

31   **32**

Lake
Casitas

Oak
View ○

34-36

(33)

37

38

EMMA K. WOOD
STATE BEACH

Ventura ○

TO CAMARILLO

© AVALON TRAVEL PUBLISHING, INC.

762

CHAPTER H3

1 Wagon Flat

 6

Not many folks know about this obscure spot, and if it's a hot, late summer day, they're probably better off for it. The camp is set at an elevation of 1,400 feet, pretty in spring, but in summer often a hot, dry region of Los Padres National Forest. The bright spot is little La Brea Creek, which runs by the camp.

Location: On the North Fork of La Brea Creek in Los Padres National Forest; map H3, grid b1.

Campsites, facilities: There are three sites for tents. Picnic tables and fire grills are provided. Vault toilets are available. No drinking water is available. Garbage must be packed out. Leashed pets are permitted.

Reservations, fees: No reservations; no camping fee. An Adventure Pass ($30 annual fee) or $5 daily pass per parked vehicle is required. Open year-round, but access roads may be closed during and after heavy rains.

Directions: From U.S. 101 in Santa Maria, take the Betteravia Road exit. Drive eight miles southeast on Foxen Canyon Road. Bear left at the fork and continue southeast on

Santa Maria Mesa Road. Turn left on Tepusquet Road and drive 6.5 miles. Turn right on Colson Canyon Road/Forest Road 11N04 and drive 10 more miles to the campground. Colson Canyon Road can be impassable when wet.

Contact: Los Padres National Forest, Santa Lucia Ranger District, tel. (805) 925-9538 or fax (805) 681-2781.

2 Colson

 6

Colson is set just a mile from the western border of Los Padres National Forest, making it far easier to reach than other Forest Service camps in this region. The camp is named after the canyon in which it sits, Colson Canyon. This area really has just two seasons when you should visit, spring and fall. In the summer, it's hot and dry, with no water available, and is scarcely fit for habitation. The elevation is 2,100 feet.

Location: In Los Padres National Forest; map H3, grid b0.

Campsites, facilities: There are five tent sites. Picnic tables and fire grills are provided. A pit toilet is available. No drinking water is available. Garbage must be packed out. Leashed pets are permitted.

Reservations, fees: No reservations; no camping fee. An Adventure Pass ($30 annual fee) or $5 daily pass per parked vehicle is required. Open year-round.

Directions: From U.S. 101 in Santa Maria, take the Betteravia Road exit. Drive eight miles southeast on Foxen Canyon Road. Bear left at the fork and continue southeast on Santa Maria Mesa Road. Turn left on Tepusquet Road and drive 6.5 miles. Turn right on Colson Canyon Road/Forest Road 11N04 and drive four miles to the campground. Colson Canyon Road can be impassable when wet.

Contact: Los Padres National Forest, Santa Lucia Ranger District, tel. (805) 925-9538 or fax (805) 681-2781.

3 Barrel Springs

 7

This small, primitive camp sits at 1,000 feet in elevation along La Brea Creek and is shaded by the oaks in La Brea Canyon. It is named after nearby Barrel Springs, which forms a small creek and feeds into La Brea Creek.

Location: In Los Padres National Forest; map H3, grid b1.

Campsites, facilities: There are six tent sites. Picnic tables and fire grills are provided. Vault toilets are available. No drinking water is available. Garbage must be packed out. Leashed pets are permitted.

Reservations, fees: No reservations; no camping fee. An Adventure Pass ($30 annual fee) or $5 daily pass per parked vehicle is required. Open year-round, but access roads may be closed during and after heavy rains.

Directions: From Santa Maria on U.S. 101, take the Betteravia Road exit. Drive eight miles southeast on Foxen Canyon Road. Bear left at the fork and continue southeast on Santa Maria Mesa Road. Turn left on Tepusquet Road and drive 6.5 miles. Turn right on Colson Canyon Road/Forest Road 11N04 and drive eight miles to the campground. Colson Canyon Road can be impassable when wet.

Contact: Los Padres National Forest, Santa Lucia Ranger District, tel. (805) 925-9538 or fax (805) 681-2781.

4 Bates Canyon

 7

This camp is on the northeast flank of the Sierra Madre Mountains, along a small stream in Bates Canyon, at 2,900 feet in elevation. Note that the primitive access road out of camp to the south is often gated; it leads to the Sierra Madre Ridge, where a road contours right along the ridge on the border of the San Rafael Wilderness, passing from peak to peak.

Location: In Los Padres National Forest; map H3, grid c3.

Campsites, facilities: There are six tent sites. Picnic tables and fire grills are provided. Vault toilets are available. No drinking water is available. Garbage must be packed out. Leashed pets are permitted.

Reservations, fees: No reservations; no camping fee. An Adventure Pass ($30 annual fee) or $5 daily pass per parked vehicle is required. Open year-round. Note that access roads can be closed during and after heavy rains.

Directions: From Santa Maria, drive 50 miles east on Highway 166. Turn right on Cottonwood Canyon Road and drive 7.5 miles southwest to the campground.

Contact: Los Padres National Forest, Santa Lucia Ranger District, tel. (805) 925-9538 or fax (805) 681-2781.

5 Aliso Park

 6

This primitive, quiet camp is set at the foot of the Sierra Madre Mountains at 3,200 feet, directly below McPherson Peak (5,749 feet). It is just inside the northeast boundary of Los Padres National Forest, making it easily accessible from Highway 166.

Location: In Los Padres National Forest; map H3, grid d5.

Campsites, facilities: There are 10 sites for tents or RVs up to 22 feet long. Picnic tables and fire grills are provided. Pit toilets are available. No drinking water is available. Garbage must be packed out. Leashed pets are permitted.

Reservations, fees: No reservations; no camping fee. An Adventure Pass ($30 annual fee) or $5 daily pass per parked vehicle is required. Open year-round.

Directions: From Santa Maria, drive east on Highway 166 for 59 miles to Aliso Canyon Road/Forest Road 10N04. Turn right and drive south about six miles to the campground at the end of the road.

Contact: Los Padres National Forest, Mount Piños Ranger District, tel. (661) 245-3731 or fax (661) 245-1526.

6 Ballinger

 3

Ballinger Camp is right inside the boundary of Los Padres National Forest in the Mount Piños Ranger District, just six miles east of Highway 33. During the week, this camp receives very little use. On weekends, it gets moderate, even heavy use at times, from OHV owners. The camp is set at an elevation of 3,000 feet.

Location: In Los Padres National Forest; map H3, grid d8.

Campsites, facilities: There are 20 sites for tents or RVs up to 32 feet long. Picnic tables and fire grills are provided. Vault toilets are available. No drinking water is available. Garbage must be packed out. Leashed pets are permitted.

Reservations, fees: No reservations; no camping fee. An Adventure Pass ($30 annual fee) or $5 daily pass per parked vehicle is required. Open year-round.

Directions: From Maricopa, drive southwest on Highway 166 about 14 miles to Highway 33. Turn south and drive about 3.5 miles to Ballinger Canyon Road/Forest Road 9N10. Turn left (east) and drive three miles to the campground.

Contact: Los Padres National Forest, Mount Piños Ranger District, tel. (661) 245-3731 or fax (661) 245-1526.

7 Valle Vista

 8

The view of the southern San Joaquin Valley and the snow-capped Sierra is the highlight of this primitive camp. It is set at 4,800 feet, near the boundary of Los Padres National Forest. Visitors have an opportunity to view condors here, and you can usually spot a few buzzards, er, turkey vultures, circling around. If you don't bring your own water, they might just start circling you. Little-known fact: this camp sits exactly on the border of Kern County and Ventura County. Wow.

Location: In Los Padres National Forest; map H3, grid d9.

Campsites, facilities: There are seven sites for tents or RVs up to 22 feet long. Picnic tables and fire grills are provided. Pit toilets are available. No drinking water is available. Garbage must be packed out. Leashed pets are permitted.

Reservations, fees: No reservations; no camping fee. An Adventure Pass ($30 annual fee) or $5 daily pass per parked vehicle is required. Open year-round.

Directions: From Maricopa, drive south on Highway 166 about nine miles to Cerro Noroeste Road. Turn left and drive 12 miles to the campground on the left.

Contact: Los Padres National Forest, Mount Piños Ranger District, tel. (661) 245-3731 or fax (661) 245-1526.

8 Nira

 8

Nira is a premium jump-off spot for backpackers, set at 2,100 feet along Manzana Creek, on the border of the San Rafael Wilderness. A primary wilderness trailhead is available, routed east into the San Rafael Wilderness through Lost Valley, along Fish Creek, and to Manzana Creek (and beyond), all in just six miles, with a series of hike-in camps available as the trail enters the wilderness interior. Today's history lesson? This camp was originally an NRA (National Recovery Act) camp during the Depression, hence the name Nira.

Location: On Manzana Creek in Los Padres National Forest; map H3, grid d3.

Campsites, facilities: There are 11 sites for tents or RVs up to 16 feet long. Picnic tables and fire grills are provided. Vault toilets and horse hitching posts are available. No drinking water is available. Garbage must be packed out. Leashed pets are permitted.

Reservations, fees: No reservations; no camping fee. An Adventure Pass ($30 annual fee) or $5 daily pass per parked vehicle is required. Open year-round, but access roads may be closed during and after heavy rains.

Directions: From U.S. 101 in Santa Barbara, drive 22 miles northeast on Highway 154. Turn right on Armour Ranch Road and drive 1.5 miles. Turn right on Happy Canyon Road and drive 11 miles to Cachuma Saddle. Continue straight (north) on Sunset Valley/Cachuma Road/Forest Road 8N09 for six miles to the campground.

Contact: Los Padres National Forest, Santa Lucia Ranger District, tel. (805) 925-9538 or fax (805) 681-2781.

9 Figueroa

 7

This is one of the more attractive camps in Los Padres National Forest. It is set at 4,000 feet beneath an unusual stand of oak and huge manzanita trees, and offers a view of the Santa Ynez Valley. Nearby attractions include the Piño Alto Picnic Area, 2.5 miles away, offering a panoramic view of the adjacent wildlands with a half-mile, wheelchair-accessible nature trail. An exceptional view is also available from the nearby Figueroa fire lookout. Though it requires a circuitous 10-mile ride around Figueroa Mountain to get there, Nira to the east provides the best trailhead for the San Rafael Wilderness in this area.

Location: In Los Padres National Forest; map H3, grid e2.

Campsites, facilities: There are 33 sites for tents. Picnic tables and fire grills are provided. Drinking water and vault toilets are available. Garbage must be packed out. Leashed pets are permitted.

Reservations, fees: No reservations; no camping fee. An Adventure Pass ($30 annual fee) or $5 daily pass per parked vehicle is required. Open year-round.

Directions: From Los Olivos on Highway 154, turn northeast on Figueroa Mountain Road and drive 12.5 miles to the campground.

Contact: Los Padres National Forest, Santa Lucia Ranger District, tel. (805) 925-9538 or fax (805) 681-2781.

10 Davy Brown

 7

This is a pretty spot, set along little Davy Brown Creek at 4,000 feet, deep in Los Padres National Forest. The border of the San Rafael Wilderness and an excellent trailhead are just two miles down the road (along Davy Brown Creek) to the northeast at Nira (see for hiking options).

Location: On Davy Brown Creek in Los Padres National Forest; map H3, grid d2.

Campsites, facilities: There are 13 sites for tents and RVs up to 18 feet long. Picnic tables and fire grills are provided. Vault toilets are available. No drinking water is available. Garbage must be packed out. Leashed pets are permitted.

Reservations, fees: No reservations; no camping fee. An Adventure Pass ($30 annual fee) or $5 daily fee per parked vehicle is required. Open year-round.

Directions: From U.S. 101 in Santa Barbara, drive 22 miles northeast on Highway 154. Turn right on Armour Ranch Road and drive 1.5 miles. Turn right on Happy Canyon Road/County Route 3350 and drive 11 miles to Cachuma Saddle. Continue straight (north) on Sunset Valley/Cachuma Road/Forest Road 8N09 for four miles to the campground.

Contact: Los Padres National Forest, Santa Lucia Ranger District, tel. (805) 925-9538 or fax (805) 681-2781.

11 Cachuma

 6

This camp is set at 2,200 feet, along one of the major streams that feeds Lake Cachuma, just 10 miles downstream. A dirt road south of the camp follows the creek to the lake.

Location: Near Cachuma Creek in Los Padres National Forest; map H3, grid e3.

Campsites, facilities: There are five tent sites. Picnic tables and fire grills are provided. Vault toilets are available. No drinking water is available. Garbage must be packed out.

Leashed pets are permitted.

Reservations, fees: No reservations; no camping fee. An Adventure Pass ($30 annual fee) or $5 daily pass per parked vehicle is required. Open year-round.

Directions: From U.S. 101 in Santa Barbara, drive 22 miles northeast on Highway 154. Turn right on Armour Ranch Road and drive 1.5 miles. Turn right on Happy Canyon Road/County Route 3350 and drive 9.5 miles to the campground.

Contact: Los Padres National Forest, Santa Barbara Ranger District, tel. (805) 967-3481 or fax (805) 967-7312.

12 Lake Cachuma Recreation Area

 7

Cachuma has become one of the best lakes in America for fishing big bass, and the ideal climate makes it a winner for camping as well. Cachuma is set at 600 feet in the foothills northwest of Santa Barbara, a big, beautiful lake covering 3,200 acres. The rules are perfect for fishing: no water-skiing, personal watercraft, swimming, canoeing, kayaking, or windsurfing is permitted; for fishing boats there is a 5-mph speed limit in the coves and a 40-mph limit elsewhere. Yeah, let it rip on open water, then quiet down to sneak-fish the coves.

Location: Near Santa Barbara; map H3, grid f2.

Campsites, facilities: There are 500 sites for tents or RVs, some with full hookups, and yurts are also available. Picnic tables and fire pits are provided. Restrooms, drinking water, flush toilets, and showers are available. Playground, general store, propane gas, swimming pool, boat ramp, mooring, boat fuel, boat rentals, bicycle rentals, ice, and a snack bar are available nearby. Watercraft under 10 feet are prohibited on the lake. Leashed pets are permitted, but must be kept at least 50 feet from the lake.

Reservations, fees: No reservations; $15 to $21 per night, $8 for a second vehicle, $1 pet fee. Group reservations available. Open year-round.

Directions: From Santa Barbara, drive 20 miles north on Highway 154 to the campground entrance on the right.

Contact: Lake Cachuma, tel. (805) 688-4658 or tel. (805) 686-5053.

13 Ozena

     7

This camp is set at 3,660 feet, about a mile from Reyes Creek and about 3.5 miles from Reyes Creek, the premium campground in this area. This camp gets light use and is known primarily by the locals. A Forest Service map is recommended.

Location: In Los Padres National Forest; map H3, grid f9.

Campsites, facilities: There are 10 sites for tents or RVs up to 22 feet long. Picnic tables and fire grills are provided. Vault toilets are available. No drinking water is available. Garbage must be packed out. You can buy groceries and propane gas about 30 minutes away in Ojai or Frazier Park. Leashed pets are permitted.

Reservations, fees: No reservations; no camping fee. An Adventure Pass ($30 annual fee) or $5 daily pass per parked vehicle is required. Open year-round.

Directions: From Ojai, drive 36 miles north on Highway 33. Turn right on Lockwood Valley Road and drive 1.5 miles to the campground on the right.

Contact: Los Padres National Forest, Mount Piños Ranger District, tel. (661) 245-3731 or fax (661) 245-1526. For a map, ask for Los Padres and send $4 to USDA Forest Service, Attn: Map Sales, 4260 Eight Mile Road, Camino, CA 95709, tel. (530) 647-5390 or fax (530) 647-5311. Major credit cards accepted.

14 Reyes Creek

    7

This developed Forest Service camp sits at the end of an old spur, Forest Road 7N11. The camp is set at 3,960 feet along Reyes Creek, which is stocked with trout in early summer. A trail is routed out of camp to the south and climbs three miles to Upper Reyes backpack camp, and beyond, up a ridge and down to Beartrap Creek and several trail camps along that creek.

Location: In Los Padres National Forest; map H3, grid f9.

Campsites, facilities: There are 24 sites for tents and six sites for tents or RVs up to 22 feet long. Picnic tables and fire grills are provided. Pit toilets and a corral are available. No drinking water is available. Garbage must be packed out. A small store, bar, and cafe are nearby. Leashed pets are permitted.

Reservations, fees: No reservations; no camping fee. An Adventure Pass ($30 annual fee) or $5 daily pass per parked vehicle is required. Open year-round.

Directions: From Ojai, drive 36 miles north on Highway 33. Turn right on Lockwood Valley Road (Ozena Road) and drive about 3.5 miles to Forest Road 7N11. Turn right and drive about 1.5 miles to the village of Camp Scheideck. Bear left at the T intersection and drive one-quarter mile to the campground.

Contact: Los Padres National Forest, Mount Piños Ranger District, tel. (661) 245-3731 or fax (661) 245-1526.

15 Pine Mountain

   6

Pine Mountain, along with nearby Reyes Peak Campground (a quarter mile to the east), is a tiny, primitive campground in a pretty setting with a few trailheads close at hand. The two best nearby hikes lead to springs. A trail is routed out of camp and into Boulder Canyon for a mile down the mountain, where it meets another trail that turns left and heads a quarter mile to McGuire Spring Trail Camp (piped spring water is available there). It's advisable to obtain a Forest Service map. The elevation is 6,700 feet.

Location: In Los Padres National Forest; map H3, grid g9.

Campsites, facilities: There are eight tent sites. Picnic tables and fire grills are provided. Pit toilets are available. No drinking water is available. Garbage must be packed out. Leashed pets are permitted.

Reservations, fees: No reservations; no camping fee. An Adventure Pass ($30 annual fee) or $5 daily pass per parked vehicle is required. Open April through November, weather permitting (closed after first winter snow).

Directions: From Ojai, drive 33 miles north on Highway 33. Turn right on Reyes Peak Road and drive 2.5 miles to the campground on the left.

Contact: Los Padres National Forest, Ojai Ranger District, tel. (805) 646-4348 or fax (805) 646-0484.

16 Reyes Peak

 6

Reyes Peak is a primitive camp set at 6,800 feet. Three short hikes in the immediate vicinity lead to trail camps. The closest is from a trailhead just to the west of camp, which provides an easy, half-mile hike north to Raspberry Spring (a backcountry camp is available there). Nearby Pine Mountain Campground provides an alternative.

Location: In Los Padres National Forest; map H3, grid g9.

Campsites, facilities: There are seven tent sites. Picnic tables and fire grills are provided. Vault toilets are available. No drinking water is available. Garbage must be packed out. Leashed pets are permitted.

Reservations, fees: No reservations; no camping fee. An Adventure Pass ($30 annual fee) or $5 daily pass per parked vehicle is required. Open April through October.

Directions: From Ojai, drive 33 miles north on Highway 33. Turn right on Reyes Peak Road and drive five miles to the campground.

Contact: Los Padres National Forest, Ojai Ranger District, tel. (805) 646-4348 or fax (805) 646-0484.

17 Fremont

 7

Traveling west to east, Fremont is the first in a series of Forest Service campgrounds near the Santa Ynez River. This one is just inside the boundary of Los Padres National Forest at 900 feet in elevation, nine miles east of Lake Cachuma to the west.

Location: Near Santa Ynez River in Los Padres National Forest; map H3, grid g4.

Campsites, facilities: There are 15 sites for tents or RVs up to 16 feet long. Picnic tables and fire grills are provided. Drinking water and flush toilets are available. Some facilities are wheelchair accessible. Groceries are available within one mile and propane gas is available at Lake Cachuma nine miles away. Leashed pets are permitted.

Reservations, fees: No reservations; $12 per night, $4 for a second vehicle. Open April through September.

Directions: From Santa Barbara, drive about 10 miles northwest on Highway 154. Turn right on Paradise Road/Forest Road 5N18 and drive 2.5 miles to the campground on the right.

Contact: Los Padres National Forest, Santa Barbara Ranger District, tel. (805) 967-3481 or fax (805) 967-7312.

18 Los Prietos

 7

Los Prietos is set across from the Santa Ynez River at an elevation of 1,000 feet, just upstream from nearby Fremont campground to the west. There are several nice hiking trails nearby; the best starts near the Los Prietos Ranger Station, heading south for two miles to Wellhouse Falls (get specific directions and a map at the ranger station).

Location: Near Santa Ynez River in Los Padres National Forest; map H3, grid g4.

Campsites, facilities: There are 37 sites for tents or RVs up to 22 feet long. Picnic tables and fire grills are provided. Drinking water and flush toilets are available. Some facilities are wheelchair accessible. Leashed pets are permitted.

Reservations, fees: No reservations; $12 per night, $4 for a second vehicle. Open April through September.

Directions: From Santa Barbara, drive about 10 miles north on Highway 154. Turn right on Paradise Road/Forest Road 5N18 and drive 3.8 miles to the campground.

Contact: Los Padres National Forest, Santa Barbara Ranger District, tel. (805) 967-3481 or fax (805) 967-7312.

19 Upper Oso

 7

This is one of the Forest Service campgrounds in the Santa Ynez Recreation Area. It is set in Oso Canyon at 1,100 feet, one mile from the Santa Ynez River. Note that at high water this campground can become inaccessible. A mile north of camp, the Santa Cruz Trailhead is available for a hike that is routed north up Oso Canyon for a mile, then three miles up to Happy Hollow, and beyond that to a trail camp just west of Little Pine Mountain, elevation 4,508 feet. A trailhead into the San Rafael Wilderness is nearby, and once on the trail, you'll find many primitive sites in the backcountry.

Location: Near the Santa Ynez River in Los Padres National Forest; map H3, grid g4.

Campsites, facilities: There are 28 sites for tents or RVs up to 22 feet long. Picnic tables and fire grills are provided. Drinking water and flush toilets are available. Some facilities are wheelchair accessible. Horse corrals are also available. Leashed pets are permitted.

Reservations, fees: No reservations; $12 per night, $4 for a second vehicle. Open year-round, weather permitting.

Directions: From Santa Barbara, drive about 10 miles north on Highway 154. Turn right on Paradise Road/Forest Road 5N18 and drive six miles. Turn left on Upper Oso Road and drive one mile to the campground at the end of the road.

Contact: Los Padres National Forest, Santa Barbara Ranger District, tel. (805) 967-3481 or fax (805) 967-7312.

20 Paradise

 7

Here is yet another option among the camps along the Santa Ynez River. As you drive east it is the second camp you will come to, just after Fremont. The best hiking trailheads nearby are at Upper Oso Camp and the Sage Hill Group Campground. Lake Cachuma is six miles to the west.

Location: Near Santa Ynez River in Los Padres National Forest; map H3, grid g4.

Campsites, facilities: There are 15 sites for tents or RVs up to 22 feet long. Picnic tables and fire grills are provided. Drinking water and flush toilets are available. Some facilities are wheelchair accessible. Groceries are available nearby. Leashed pets are permitted.

Reservations, fees: Reserve at (877) 444-6777 ($8.65 reservation fee) or website: www.reserveusa.com; $12 per night, $4 for a second vehicle. Open year-round.

Directions: From Santa Barbara, drive about 10 miles north on Highway 154. Turn right on Paradise Road/Forest Road 5N18 and drive three miles to the campground on the right.

Contact: Los Padres National Forest, Santa Barbara Ranger District, tel. (805) 967-3481 or fax (805) 967-7312.

21 Sage Hill Group Camp

 7

This is another in the series of camps along the Santa Ynez River in Los Padres National Forest. This one, set at 2,000 feet, was designed for large groups. A 3.5-mile loop trail starts at the back end of Sage Hill Group Camp. The first mile is a self-guided interpretive trail.

Location: On the Santa Ynez River in Los Padres National Forest; map H3, grid g4.

Campsites, facilities: There are five group areas with sites for tents or RVs up to 32 feet long. Picnic tables and fire grills are provided. Drinking water and flush toilets are available. Horse corrals are in one group site. Leashed pets are permitted.

Reservations, fees: Reservations are required; reserve at (877) 444-6777 ($8.65 reservation fee) or website: www.reserveusa.com; $50 to $60 per group of 25 to 50 per night. Open year-round, weather permitting.

Directions: From Santa Barbara, drive about 10 miles north on Highway 154. Turn right on Paradise Road/Forest Road 5N18 and drive five miles to the ranger station. Turn left and drive a half mile to the campground.

Contact: Los Padres National Forest, Santa Barbara Ranger District, tel. (805) 967-3481 or fax (805) 967-7312.

22 Refugio State Beach

     9

Refugio State Beach is the smallest of the two beautiful state beaches along U.S. 101 north of Santa Barbara. The other is El Capitan, which also has a campground. This is a great spot for family campers with bikes, with a paved two-mile bike trail connecting Refugio campground with El Capitan. As with all state beaches and private camps on the Coast Highway, reservations are strongly advised and often a necessity throughout the vacation season.

Location: Near Santa Barbara; map H3, grid g0.

Campsites, facilities: There are 85 sites for tents or RVs up to 30 feet long, and five hike-in/bike-in sites. There is one group site that can accommodate 80 tent or RV campers. Picnic tables and fire grills are provided. Restrooms, drinking water, flush toilets, coin-operated showers, summer lifeguard service and summer convenience store, and food services are available. Some facilities are wheelchair accessible. Leashed pets are permitted at campsites.

Reservations, fees: Reserve at tel. (800) 444-PARK (444-7275) or website: www.reserve america.com; $12 per night, $1 per night per person for hike-in/bike-in sites, $60 per night for the group site. Open year-round, weather permitting.

Directions: From Santa Barbara, drive 23 miles northwest on U.S. 101 to the Refugio State Beach exit. Turn west (left) and drive a short distance to campground entrance.

Contact: Refugio State Beach, tel. (805) 968-1033, or Channel Coast District, tel. (805) 899-1400.

23 El Capitan Canyon

   8

El Capitan Canyon, on 65 acres in the coastal foothills north of Santa Barbara, offers campers the best of both worlds: There are 2,200 acres of public land near the camp with backcountry hiking and mountain biking trails, or for those who prefer the sand and surf, beach access is within walking distance and ocean kayaking and deep-sea fishing trips can be booked at the resort. In the summer live entertainment is available, including a concert series and the "Blues and Barbecue" event every Saturday night.

Location: Near Goleta; map H3, grid g2.

Campsites, facilities: There are 150 sites with partial hookups for tents or RVs and 85 tent sites. Picnic tables and fire pits are provided. Bottled water is recommended. Restrooms, flush toilets, showers, swimming pool, children's playground, live music (on Saturday nights), volleyball, horseshoes, small store, and firewood are available. Some facilities are wheelchair accessible. Leashed pets are permitted.

Reservations, fees: Reservations are recommended; $20 to $25 per night, $5 per night for each extra vehicle, $5 per person per night for more than four people, $5 pet fee. Major credit cards accepted. Open year-round.

Directions: From Santa Barbara, drive about 20 miles northwest on U.S. 101 to the El Capitan State Beach exit. Go straight on the frontage road paralleling the freeway for about 100 yards. Turn right at the sign for El Capitan Canyon on the mountain side of the freeway.

Contact: El Capitan Canyon, 11560 Calle Real, Goleta, CA 93117; tel. (805) 685-3887 or fax (805) 968-6772; website: www.elcapitan-canyon.com.

24 El Capitan State Beach

    10

This is one in a series of beautiful state beaches along the Santa Barbara coast. The water is warm, the swimming good. A paved, two-mile bicycle trail is routed to Refugio State Beach, a great family trip. This is a perfect layover for Coast Highway vacationers, and reservations are usually required to assure a spot. Refugio State Beach to the north is another camping option.

Location: Near Santa Barbara; map H3, grid g1.

Campsites, facilities: There are 142 sites for tents or RVs up to 30 feet long, seven hike-in/bike-in sites, and group sites for 50 to 125 people. Picnic tables, food lockers, and fire grills are provided. Restrooms, drinking water, flush toilets, coin-operated showers, sanitary disposal station, summer lifeguard service, and a summer convenience store are available. Leashed pets are permitted at campsites. Some facilities are wheelchair accessible.

Reservations, fees: Reserve at tel. (800) 444-PARK (444-7275) or website: www.reserve america.com; $12 per night; $1 per person for hike-in/bike-in sites, from $37 to $93 per night for group sites. Open year-round, weather permitting.

Directions: From Santa Barbara, drive 20 miles northwest on U.S. 101 to the El Capitan State Beach exit. Turn west (left) and drive a short distance to the campground entrance.

Contact: El Capitan State Beach, tel. (805) 968-1033 or tel. (805) 899-1400.

25 Mono Hike-In

      7

Not many folks know about this spot. The camp is small and primitive, at elevation 1,500 feet on little Mono Creek, complete with a great swimming hole. Also note that Little Caliente Hot Springs is one mile northeast of the campground. Mono Creek is a feeder to Gibralter Reservoir, a long, narrow lake with no direct access available.

Location: On Mono Creek in Los Padres National Forest; map H3, grid g6.

Campsites, facilities: There are five tent sites. Picnic tables and fire grills are provided. Vault toilets are available. No drinking water is available. Garbage must be packed out. Leashed pets are permitted.

Reservations, fees: No reservations; no camping fee. An Adventure Pass ($30 annual fee) or $5 daily pass per parked vehicle is required. Open year-round, weather permitting.

Directions: From U.S. 101 in Santa Barbara, drive eight miles north on Highway 154. Turn right on East Camino Cielo/Forest Road 5N12 and drive 18 miles to the end of the paved road at Camuesa Road/Forest Road 5N15, which is a dirt road. Continue on Camuesa Road for five miles to Juncal Campground (closed). Turn left (still on Forest Road 5N15) and drive seven miles to Mono Hike-In.

Contact: Los Padres National Forest, Santa Barbara Ranger District, tel. (805) 967-3481 or fax (805) 967-7312.

26 P-Bar Flat

    7

The best thing or the worst thing, depending on how you look at it, about P-Bar Flat is a trailhead that is routed north into the remote wildlands of Los Padres National Forest. The camp is very small and primitive, set at 1,800 feet along the Santa Ynez River. The trail starts by heading up Horse Canyon along a creek, but eventually is routed 10 miles to Hildreth Peak, elevation 8,066 feet, a 6,000-foot butt-kicker of a climb. A lot of guys in prison get less punishment.

Location: On the Santa Ynez River in Los Padres National Forest; map H3, grid g7.

Campsites, facilities: There are four tent sites. Picnic tables and fire grills are provided. Vault toilets are available. No drinking water is available. Garbage must be packed out. Leashed pets are permitted.

Reservations, fees: No reservations; no camping fee. An Adventure Pass ($30 annual fee) or $5 daily pass per parked vehicle is required. Open year-round, weather permitting.

Directions: From U.S. 101 in Santa Barbara, drive eight miles north on Highway 154. Turn right on East Camino Cielo/Forest Road 5N12 and drive 18 miles to the end of the paved road at Camuesa Road/Forest Road 5N15, which is a dirt road. Continue on Camuesa Road for five miles to Juncal Campground (closed campground). Turn left and drive four miles to P-Bar Flat.

Contact: Los Padres National Forest, Santa Barbara Ranger District, tel. (805) 967-3481 or fax (805) 967-7312.

27 Middle Santa Ynez

   7

There are four camps bordering the Santa Ynez River between Gibraltar Reservoir to the west and little Jameson Lake to the east. Look 'em over and pick the one you like best. This one is set at an elevation 1,500 feet, about a half mile east of P-Bar Flat; see the entry for a trailhead there.

Location: On the Santa Ynez River in Los Padres National Forest; map H3, grid g7.

Campsites, facilities: There are nine tent sites. Picnic tables and fire grills are provided.

Vault toilets are available. No drinking water is available. Garbage must be packed out. Leashed pets are permitted.

Reservations, fees: No reservations; no camping fee. An Adventure Pass ($30 annual fee) or $5 daily pass per parked vehicle is required. Open year-round, weather permitting.

Directions: From U.S. 101 in Santa Barbara, drive eight miles north on Highway 154. Turn right on East Camino Cielo/Forest Road 5N12 and drive 18 miles to the end of the paved road at Camuesa Road/Forest Road 5N15, which is a dirt road. Continue on Camuesa Road for five miles to Juncal Campground (closed campground). Turn left and drive three miles to Middle Santa Ynez.

Contact: Los Padres National Forest, Santa Barbara Ranger District, tel. (805) 967-3481 or fax (805) 967-7312.

28 Santa Barbara Sunrise RV Park

   3

Motor home cruisers get a little of two worlds here. For one thing, the park is close to the beach; for another, the downtown shopping area isn't too far away, either. This is the only RV park in Santa Barbara.

Location: In Santa Barbara; map H3, grid h4.

Campsites, facilities: There are 33 sites for RVs with full hookups and patios and two tent sites. Restrooms, showers, cable TV, and laundry facilities are available. A grocery store, golf course, tennis courts, and propane gas are nearby. Leashed pets are permitted.

Reservations, fees: Reservations are recommended; $25 to $35 per night for two people, $5 per night for each extra vehicle. Major credit cards accepted. Open year-round.

Directions: In Santa Barbara on U.S. 101, take the Salinas Street exit going north or the Milpas Street exit going south and follow the blue camper signs to 516 South Salinas Street.

Contact: Santa Barbara Sunrise RV Park, tel. (805) 966-9954, tel. (800) 345-5018, or fax (805) 966-7950; website: www.campgrounds.com/santabarbara.

29 Holiday Group Camp

 7

This group site, set at 2,000 feet, is near the North Fork of the Matilija. It's only three miles uphill from Matilija Reservoir.

Location: On Matilija Creek in Los Padres National Forest; map H3, grid h9.

Campsites, facilities: There are eight sites for tents or RVs up to 22 feet long. Picnic tables and fire grills are provided. Drinking water and vault toilets are available. Leashed pets are permitted.

Reservations, fees: Reservations are required; reserve at (877) 444-6777 ($8.65 reservation fee) or website: www. reserveusa.com; $50 group fee per night. Open year-round.

Directions: From Ojai, drive nine miles northwest on Highway 33 to the campground entrance on the right.

Contact: Los Padres National Forest, Ojai Ranger District, tel. (805) 646-4348 or fax (805) 646-0484.

30 Wheeler Gorge

 7

This developed Forest Service camp is set at 2,000 feet and is one of the more popular spots in the area. The North Fork of the Matilija runs beside the camp and provides some fair trout fishing in the spring and good swimming holes in early summer.

Location: On Matilija Creek in Los Padres National Forest; map H3, grid h9.

Campsites, facilities: There are 73 sites for tents or RVs up to 16 feet long. Picnic tables and fire grills are provided. Drinking water and pit toilets are available. Garbage must be packed out. Leashed pets are permitted. Some facilities are wheelchair accessible.

Reservations, fees: Reserve at (877) 444-6777 ($8.65 reservation fee) or website: www.reserveusa.com; $12 per night. Open year-round.

Directions: From Ojai, drive 8.5 miles northwest on Highway 33 to the campground on the right.

Contact: Los Padres National Forest, Ojai Ranger District, tel. (805) 646-4348 or fax (805) 646-0484.

31 Lake Casitas Recreation Area

 7

Lake Casitas is known as one of Southern California's world-class fish factories, with more 10-pound bass produced here than anywhere, including the former state record, a bass that weighed 21 pounds, three ounces. The ideal climate in the foothill country (560 feet elevation) gives the fish a nine-month growing season, as well as providing excellent weather for camping. Casitas is north of Ventura at an elevation of 285 feet in the foothills bordering Los Padres National Forest. The lake has 32 miles of shoreline with a huge number of sheltered coves, covering 2,700 acres. The lake is managed primarily for anglers. Water-skiing, personal watercraft, and swimming are not permitted, and only boats between 11 and 24 feet are allowed on the lake.

Location: North of Ventura; map H3, grid i8.

Campsites, facilities: There are 400 sites for tents or RVs up to 50 feet long, 150 with partial hookups and 14 with full hookups. Picnic tables and fire grills are provided. Restrooms, drinking water, flush toilets, showers, two sanitary disposal stations, seven playgrounds, grocery store, propane gas, ice, snack bar, water playground for children 12 and under, and a full-service marina (including boat ramps, boat rentals, slips, fuel, tackle, and bait) are available. Some facilities are wheelchair accessible. Leashed pets are permitted.

Reservations, fees: Reservations should be made at least 14 days in advance and must be made 72 hours before arrival; reserve at (805) 649-1122; $14 to $39 per night, $9.50 per night for each extra vehicle, $2 pet fee. Open year-round. Major credit cards accepted.

Directions: From Ventura, drive 11 miles north on Highway 33. Turn west on Highway 150 and drive about four miles to the campground entrance at 11311 Santa Ana Road.

Contact: Lake Casitas Recreation Area, tel. (805) 649-2233.

32 Camp Comfort Park

    2

This park gets missed by many. It's set in a residential area in the foothill country at 1,000 feet along San Antonio Creek in the Ojai Valley. Lake Casitas Recreation Area is 10 miles away.

Location: On San Antonio Creek; map H3, grid i9.

Campsites, facilities: There are 43 sites for tents or RVs up to 34 feet long. Picnic tables and fire grills are provided. Restrooms, drinking water, flush toilets, showers, and a playground are available. Supplies and a coin laundry are nearby. Leashed pets are permitted.

Reservations, fees: Reservations are accepted; $10 to $12 per night, $3 for a second vehicle, $1 pet fee.

Directions: From Ventura, take Highway 33 north to Highway 150. Turn west on Highway 150 and drive three miles to Creek Road. Turn right and drive one mile to the park.

Contact: Camp Comfort Park, tel. (805) 646-2314.

33 Carpinteria State Beach

     8

First, plan on reservations, and then, plan on plenty of neighbors. This state beach is one pretty spot, and a lot of folks cruising up the coast like the idea of taking off their cowboy boots here for awhile. This is an urban park; that is, it is within walking distance of downtown, restaurants, and shopping. You can love it or hate it, but this camp is almost always full. Other state beaches to the nearby north are El Capitan State Beach and Refugio State Beach, both with campgrounds.

Location: Near Santa Barbara; map H3, grid i6.

Campsites, facilities: There are 82 sites for tents, 60 sites with full or partial hookups for RVs up to 21 feet long, and 119 sites for tents or RVs up to 30 feet long. There are also two group sites for a maximum of 40 and 65 campers. Picnic tables and fire grills are provided. Restrooms, drinking water, flush toilets, and coin-operated showers are available. A convenience store, coin laundry, restaurants, and propane gas are nearby. Some areas are wheelchair accessible. Leashed pets are permitted, except on the beach.

Reservations, fees: Reserve at tel. (800) 444-PARK (444-7275) or website: www.reserve america.com; $12-18 per night, $50 for group sites. Open year-round.

Directions: From Santa Barbara, drive 12 miles south on U.S. 101 to the Casitas Pass exit. Turn right on Casitas Pass Road and drive about a block to Carpinteria Avenue. Turn right and drive a short distance to Palm Avenue. Turn left and drive about three blocks to the campground at the end of Palm Avenue.

Contact: Carpinteria State Beach, tel. (805) 684-2811, or (805) 968-1033.

34 Rincon Parkway

    5

This is basically an RV park near the ocean, where the sites are parking end-to-end along old Highway 1. It is not quiet. Passing trains across the highway vie for noise honors with the surf. Emma Wood State Beach, San Buenaventura State Beach, and McGrath State Beach are all within 10 miles.

Location: On the Pacific Ocean north of Ventura; map H3, grid i7.

Campsites, facilities: There are 127 RV sites for self-contained vehicles up to 34 feet long. A sanitary disposal station and supplies are available nearby. Leashed pets are allowed, but not on the beach.

Reservations, fees: No reservations; $18 per night, $1 pet fee. Open year-round.

Directions: From Ventura, drive six miles northwest on U.S. 101 to the State Beaches exit. Turn north on West Pacific Highway and drive 4.5 miles to the campground on the left. **Contact:** Ventura County Parks Department, tel. (805) 654-3951; website: www.ventura. org/gsa/c-srv.htm.

35 Hobson County Park

     6

This county park is at the end of Rincon Parkway, kind of like a crowded cul-de-sac, with easy access to the beach and many side trip possibilities. Emma Wood State Beach, San Buenaventura State Beach, and McGrath State Beach are all within 11 miles of the park. **Location:** On the Pacific Ocean north of Ventura; map H3, grid i7.

Campsites, facilities: There are 31 sites for tents or RVs up to 34 feet long. Picnic tables and fire grills are provided. Restrooms, drinking water, flush toilets, coin-operated showers, and a snack bar are available. Leashed pets are permitted, but not on the beach.

Reservations, fees: Reservations are accepted; $22 to $30 per night, $1 pet fee. Open year-round.

Directions: From Ventura, drive six miles northwest on U.S. 101 to the State Beaches exit. Turn north on West Pacific Highway and drive five miles to the campground on the left **Contact:** Ventura County Parks Department, tel. (805) 654-3951; website: www.ventura.org/gsa/c-srv.htm.

36 Faria County Park

     7

This county park provides a possible base of operations for beach adventures. It is set along the ocean, with Emma Wood State Beach, San Buenaventura State Beach, and McGrath State Beach all within 10 miles of the park. **Location:** On the Pacific Ocean north of Ventura; map H3, grid i7.

Campsites, facilities: There are 42 sites for tents or RVs up to 34 feet long. Picnic tables and fire grills are provided. Restrooms, drinking water, flush toilets, coin-operated showers, playground, and a snack bar are available. Pets are permitted.

Reservations, fees: Reservations are accepted; $22 to $30 per night, $1 pet fee. Open year-round.

Directions: From Ventura, drive six miles north on U.S. 101 to the State Beaches exit. Turn north on West Pacific Highway and drive four miles to the campground. **Contact:** Ventura County Parks Department, tel. (805) 654-3951; website: www.ventura.org/gsa/c-srv.htm.

37 Ventura River Group Camp

    2

This is an extremely noisy area and the campsites are also downright ugly. It is set near the freeway and railroad tracks, and you get a lot of noise from both. It's not popular either. **Location:** On the Pacific Ocean near Ventura; map H3, grid j8.

Campsites, facilities: There are four group tent sites for up to 30 people each, and one group RV site, which accommodates 50 people. Picnic tables and fire rings are provided. Drinking water (limited), chemical toilets, and cold showers are available. Cold showers are available nearby. Leashed pets are permitted. All conveniences are within one mile.

Reservations, fees: Reserve at tel. (800) 444-PARK (444-7275) or website: www.reserve america.com; $22 to $62 per night. Open year-round.

Directions: On U.S. 101 in Ventura, take the Main Street exit and turn west. Drive one mile on Main Street to the campground on the left. **Contact:** Ventura River Group Camp, tel. (805) 643-7532, or Channel Coast State Park District, tel. (805) 899-1400.

38 Emma Wood State Beach

 8

This is more of a camping "area" than a campground with individual sites. And oh, what a place to camp: It is set along the ocean, a pretty spot with tidepools full of all kinds of little marine critters waiting to be discovered. It is also just a short drive from the town of Ventura and the Mission San Buenaventura.

Location: On the Pacific Ocean north of Ventura; map H3, grid j8.

Campsites, facilities: There are 94 primitive sites for tents and RVs. Chemical toilets are available. No drinking water is available. Supplies and a coin laundry are three miles away. Leashed pets are permitted.

Reservations, fees: No reservations; $12 fee per night. Open year-round.

Directions: From Ventura drive two miles north on U.S. 101 to the State Beaches exit. Take that exit, drive under the freeway, and continue to the park entrance on the left.

Contact: Emma Wood State Beach Group Camp, tel. (805) 648-4807, or Channel Coast State Park District, tel. (805) 899-1400.

THE BLACK-NECKED STILT

MAP H4

TO BUTTONWILLOW **660** TO BAKERSFIELD

a

Edison

(119) Lake Webb (99) (204)

Old River (119)

TO FORD CITY

1 Buena Vista Lake

Lamont (58) Caliente

b

Weed Patch

(33)

Arvin (223) Keene

Maricopa

Bear Mountain 6,895 feet

TO VENTUCOPA TO HIGHWAY 166 TO CUYAMA

(166)

(5) (99) (184)

c

Cummings Mountain 7,753 feet (202)

2 **3**

d

Wheeler Ridge

4
5

6

FORT TEJON STATE HISTORIC PARK

7 Mount Abel 8,286 feet **8**

TO HIGHWAY 33

e

9 Mount Pinos 8,831 feet **10**
11

Frazier Park

706 **738**

Lebec

Tejon Pass 4,144 feet Gorman

f

Frazier Mountain 8,026 feet (138)

12 **13**

TO LANCASTER

g

Reyes Peak 7,510 feet

14

ANGELES NATIONAL FOREST N2

16 **15** LOS PADRES NATIONAL FOREST

17

18
19

Thorn Point 6,935 feet

Pyramid Lake

Sawtooth Mountain 5,175 feet

h

(33)

20

21

Topatopa Mountain 6,210 feet

Lake Castaic

Green Valley **23**

TO PALMDALE

22 Lake Piru

24

i

Ojai (150)

Castaic **25**

TO OAK VIEW

27 **26** Fillmore

(5)

j

28

TO VENTURA

(126) Santa Paula (23) Piru (126)

Saugus

Saticoy

Valencia **29**

Montalvo (118) Moorpark (14)

TO CAMARILLO TO SIMI VALLEY **768** TO BURBANK

TO SIMI VALLEY

TO VINCENT

© AVALON TRAVEL PUBLISHING, INC.

TO TEHACHAPI

TO HAVILAH

0 1 2 3 4 5 6 7 8 9

CHAPTER H4

1 Buena Vista Aquatic Recreation Area

        6

Buena Vista is actually two connected lakes fed by the West Side Canal, little Lake Evans to the west and larger Lake Webb to the east. Be certain to know the difference between the two: Lake Webb (875 acres) is open to all boating including personal watercraft, and fast boats towing skiers is a common sight in designated ski areas. The speed limit is 45 mph. Lake Evans (85 acres) is small, quiet, and has a strictly enforced 5-mph speed limit, an ideal lake for family water play and fishing. The elevation is 330 feet on the outskirts of Bakersfield.

Location: Near Bakersfield; map H4, grid a2.

Campsites, facilities: There are 112 sites for tents or RVs, many with full hookups. Picnic tables and fire grills are provided. Restrooms, drinking water, flush toilets, showers, playground, three boat ramps, store, sanitary disposal station, and propane gas are available. Two swimming lagoons, marina, snack bar, fishing supplies, and groceries are available nearby. A PGA-rated golf course is two miles west. Leashed pets are permitted.

Reservations, fees: Reservations accepted at tel. (661) 868-7050, Monday through Friday; $18 to $26 per night, $10 per night for each extra vehicle, $3 pet fee. Major credit cards accepted. Open year-round.

Directions: From Interstate 5 just south of Bakersfield, drive two miles west on Highway 119.

Turn left (south) on Highway 43 and drive two miles to the campground at road's end.

Contact: Buena Vista Aquatic Recreation Area, tel. (661) 763-1526; website: www.co.kern. ca.us/parks/index.htm.

2 Brite Valley Aquatic Recreation Area

   7

Brite Valley Lake is a speck of a water hole (90 acres) on the northern flanks of the Tehachapi Mountains, at an elevation of 4,000 feet. No gas motors are permitted on the lake, so it's perfect for canoes, kayaks, or inflatables. That makes the campground and lake ideal for a family camping experience. No swimming is permitted. Fishing is fair for trout in the spring, catfish in the summer.

Location: At Brite Lake; map H4, grid c9.

Campsites, facilities: There are 12 RV sites with water and electric connections, as well as several designated tent sites without hookups. Picnic tables and fire grills are provided. Restrooms, drinking water, flush toilets, showers, sanitary disposal station, playground, three pavilions with electricity and tables, and a fish-cleaning station are available. Supplies are available about eight miles away in Tehachapi. Leashed pets are permitted.

Reservations, fees: No reservations; $9 to $12 per night for each vehicle. Open late April to late October.

Directions: From Highway 58 near Tehachapi, take the Tucker Road (to Highway 202) exit and drive a short distance to Highway 202. Turn west on Highway 202 and drive 3.5 miles to Banducci Road. Turn left on Banducci Road and follow the signs for about a mile to the park on the right.

Contact: Brite Valley Aquatic Recreation Area, tel. (661) 822-3228.

3 Indian Hill Ranch Campground

     7

This is a unique park with five ponds, all stocked with trout and catfish. The campground is open year-round and offers spacious, private sites with oak trees and a view of Brite Valley. The elevation is 5,000 feet.

Location: Near Tehachapi; map H4, grid c9.

Campsites, facilities: There are 225 sites for tents or RVs, 46 with full hookups and some with water and electric connections. Picnic tables and fire pits are provided. Flush toilets, showers, sanitary disposal station, modem hookups, and five stocked fishing ponds are available. Leashed pets are permitted.

Reservations, fees: Reservations are accepted; $12 to $21 per night, $3 per person per night for more than four people. Major credit cards accepted. Open year-round.

Directions: From Highway 58 near Tehachapi, take the Highway 202 exit. Head west on Highway 202 for 3.5 miles to Banducci Road. Turn left and drive a mile to Indian Hill/Arosa Road. Turn left and drive 1.5 miles to the campground.

Contact: Indian Hill Ranch Campground, tel. (661) 822-6613 or tel. (800) 882-6613; website: www.ihrcamp.com.

4 Caballo

   4

Caballo is set at 5,850 feet on a small creek that is the headwaters for Santiago Creek, on the northern flank of Mount Abel. The creek only flows about 10 days a year, usually before the opening of the campground, so do not count on it for water. It is one of several primitive camps in the immediate area—a take-your-pick offer. But it's an offer not many folks even know about.

Location: In Los Padres National Forest; map H4, grid e1.

Campsites, facilities: There are six sites for tents or RVs up to 16 feet long. Picnic tables and fire grills are provided. Pit toilets are available. No drinking water is available. Garbage must be packed out. Leashed pets are permitted.

Reservations, fees: No reservations; no camping fee. An Adventure Pass ($30 annual fee) or $5 daily fee per parked vehicle is required. Open May through October.

Directions: From Interstate 5 just south of Lebec take the Frazier Park exit and drive west on Frazier Mountain Road to the town of Lake of the Woods and Cuddy Valley Road. Turn right on Cuddy Valley Road and drive six miles to Mil Potrero Highway (signs says Pine Mountain Club). Turn right and drive 10 miles to Forest Road 9N27. Turn right and drive a short distance to the campground. Note: To reach Marian campground, continue for another mile.

Contact: Los Padres National Forest, Mount Piños Ranger District, tel. (661) 245-3731 or fax (661) 245-1526.

5 Marian

   4

Marian is extremely primitive, set on the outskirts of Los Padres National Forest at 6,600 feet in elevation, between Brush Mountain to the immediate northwest and San Emigdio Mountain to the immediate southeast. A primitive route out of camp leads three miles to the San Emigdio summit, 7,495 feet in elevation. A network of Forest Service roads provides access to a number of other camps in the area, as well as Mount Abel (8,286 feet) and Mount Piños (8,831 feet). If the access gate is locked, reaching this camp requires a two-mile hike; nearby Toad Spring and Caballo are smaller, but more easily accessible. This camp is popular with deer hunters in the fall.

Location: In Los Padres National Forest; map H4, grid e1.

Campsites, facilities: There are five sites for tents or RVs up to 16 feet long. Picnic tables and fire grills are provided. Pit toilets are available. No drinking water is available.

Garbage must be packed out. Leashed pets are permitted.

Reservations, fees: No reservations; no camping fee. An Adventure Pass ($30 annual fee) or $5 daily fee per parked vehicle is required. Open May through October.

Directions: From Interstate 5 just south of Lebec take the Frazier Park exit and drive west on Frazier Mountain Road to the town of Lake of the Woods and Cuddy Valley Road. Turn right on Cuddy Valley Road and drive six miles to Mil Potrero Highway (signs says Pine Mountain Club). Turn right and drive 10 miles to Forest Road 9N27. Turn right and drive one mile (passing Caballo Campground) to the camp.

Contact: Los Padres National Forest, Mount Piños Ranger District, tel. (661) 245-3731 or fax (661) 245-1526.

6 Toad Springs

    8

Toad Springs is set at 5,700 feet near Apache Saddle, on the northwest flank of Mount Abel (8,286 feet). It is at the head of Quatal Canyon, with a spectacular badlands landscape. Note that a landslide destroyed a primitive trail (about a mile out of camp) that once was routed south out of camp for six miles to Mesa Springs and a trail camp. It is considered too dangerous for use.

Location: In Los Padres National Forest; map H4, grid e1.

Campsites, facilities: There are five sites for tents or RVs up to 16 feet long. Picnic tables and fire grills are provided. Pit toilets are available. No drinking water is available. Garbage must be packed out. Leashed pets are permitted.

Reservations, fees: No reservations; no camping fee. An Adventure Pass ($30 annual fee) or $5 daily fee per parked vehicle is required. Open May through October.

Directions: From Interstate 5 just south of Lebec take the Frazier Park exit and drive west on Frazier Mountain Road to the town of Lake of the Woods and Cuddy Valley Road. Turn right on Cuddy Valley Road and drive six miles to Mil Potrero Highway (signs says Pine Mountain Club). Turn right and drive 10 miles to the campground on the left.

Contact: Los Padres National Forest, Mount Piños Ranger District, tel. (661) 245-3731 or fax (661) 245-1526.

⑦ Nettle Springs

 4

This remote camp borders the Chumash Wilderness, set near the end of a Forest Service road in Apache Canyon. A mile east of camp, via the access road, is a primitive trailhead on the left side. This trail is routed four miles to Mesa Springs and a trail camp. The elevation is 4,400 feet.

Location: In Los Padres National Forest; map H4, grid e0.

Campsites, facilities: There are seven sites for tents only and four sites for tents or RVs up to 22 feet long. Picnic tables and fire grills are provided. Pit toilets are available. No drinking water is available. Garbage must be packed out. Leashed pets are permitted.

Reservations, fees: No reservations; no camping fee. An Adventure Pass ($30 annual fee) or $5 daily fee per parked vehicle is required. Open year-round.

Directions: From Maricopa, drive 14 miles south on Highway 166 to the Highway 33 exit. Turn south on Highway 33 and drive about 13 miles to Apache Canyon Road (Forest Road 8N06). Turn left and drive about 10 miles to the campground. Note: The last 10 miles is rough and high-clearance vehicles are advised.

Contact: Los Padres National Forest, Mount Piños Ranger District, tel. (661) 245-3731 or fax (661) 245-1526.

⑧ Mil Potrero Park

 5

This is one of the rare RV parks that provides equal billing for tents. It is set at 5,300 feet,

with national forest generally surrounding the area. Nearby side trips worth noting are to the Big Trees of Pleito Canyon, and also the drive on Forest Service roads to the summit of Frazier Mountain at 8,013 feet, where there is a lookout with drop-dead gorgeous 360-degree views.

Location: Near Mount Piños; map H4, grid e2.

Campsites, facilities: There are 43 sites for tents or RVs. Picnic tables and fire grills are provided. Restrooms, drinking water, flush toilets, showers, and horse corrals are available. Leashed pets are permitted.

Reservations, fees: Reservations are recommended; $15 per night, 10 person maximum per site. Open year-round.

Directions: From Interstate 5, take the Frazier Park exit (just south of Lebec) and drive 6.5 miles on Frazier Mountain Park Road. Bear right on Cuddy Valley Road and drive five miles to Mil Potrero Highway. Turn right and drive 5.5 miles to Pine Mountain Village Center. Continue 1.3 miles to the park entrance on the left.

Contact: Mil Potrero Park, tel. (661) 763-4246.

⑨ Campo Alto

 6

Campo Alto means "High Camp," and you'll find that the name fits when you visit here. The camp is set high (8,250 feet) on Cerro Noroeste/Mount Abel in Los Padres National Forest. Don't show up thirsty, as there's no drinking water. About half a mile from camp there is a trailhead on the southeast side of the road. From here, you can hike two miles to Grouse Mountain, and in another mile, reach remote, hike-in Sheep Camp.

Location: In Los Padres National Forest; map H4, grid e1.

Campsites, facilities: There are 17 sites for tents or RVs up to 22 feet long. Picnic tables and fire grills (stoves) are provided. Pit toilets are available. No drinking water is available. Garbage must be packed out. Leashed pets are permitted.

Reservations, fees: No reservations; no camping fee. An Adventure Pass ($30 annual fee) or $5 daily fee per parked vehicle is required. Open May through October.

Directions: From Interstate 5 just south of Lebec take the Frazier Park exit and drive west on Frazier Mountain Road to the town of Lake of the Woods and Cuddy Valley Road. Turn right on Cuddy Valley Road and drive six miles to Mil Potrero Highway (signs says Pine Mountain Club). Turn right and drive nine miles to Cerro Noroeste Road (Forest Road 9N07). Turn left and drive nine miles to the campground.

Contact: Los Padres National Forest, Mount Piños Ranger District, tel. (661) 245-3731 or fax (661) 245-1526.

10 McGill

 6

The camp is set at 7,400 feet, about four miles from the top of nearby Mount Piños. Although the road is closed to the top of Mount Pinos, there are numerous hiking and biking trails in the area that provide spectacular views. On clear days, there are vantage points to the high Sierra, the San Joaquin Valley, and Antelope Valley.

Location: Near Mount Piños in Los Padres National Forest; map H4, grid e3.

Campsites, facilities: There are 73 family sites for tents or RVs up to 16 feet long, and two group sites for 60 and 80 people. Picnic tables and fire grills are provided. Drinking water and flush toilets are available. Leashed pets are permitted. A note of caution: the water wells have been known to run dry in the summer, so bring your own water during the summer. Some facilities are wheelchair accessible.

Reservations, fees: Reservations are required for group sites; reserve via phone at tel. (877) 444-6777 ($8.65 group reservation fee); $8 per night for family sites, $75 for a group site. Open late May through October.

Directions: From Interstate 5 just south of Lebec take the Frazier Park exit and drive west

on Frazier Mountain Road to the town of Lake of the Woods and Cuddy Valley Road. Turn right on Cuddy Valley Road and drive about six miles to Mount Pinos Highway. Turn left and drive about four miles to the campground on the right.

Contact: Los Padres National Forest, Mount Piños Ranger District, tel. (661) 245-3731 or fax (661) 245-1526.

11 Mount Piños

   7

This camp is set at 7,800 feet, one of three camps on the eastern flank of Mount Piños (8,831 feet). This is one of the few places on earth where it is possible to see California condors flying, the largest bird in North America. Note that a once popular drive to the top of Mount Piños for beautiful and sweeping views is now closed after being recognized as a Chumash holy site. There's access to the Mount Piños summit trail 2.5 miles away on Mil Potrero Highway at the Chula Vista parking area. From there it's about 1.5 miles to the summit, which is a designated botanical area. July and August usually are the best months for wildflower displays. McGill provides a nearby camping alternative.

Location: In Los Padres National Forest; map H4, grid e3.

Campsites, facilities: There are 19 sites for tents or RVs up to 16 feet long. Picnic tables and fire grills are provided. Drinking water and pit toilets are available. Leashed pets are permitted. A note of caution: the water wells have been known to run dry in the summer, so bring your own water during the summer.

Reservations, fees: No reservations; $8 per night. Open late May through September.

Directions: From Interstate 5 just south of Lebec take the Frazier Park exit and drive west on Frazier Mountain Road to the town of Lake of the Woods and Cuddy Valley Road. Turn right on Cuddy Valley Road and drive about six miles to Mount Pinos Highway.

Bear left and drive four miles to the campground.

Contact: Los Padres National Forest, Mount Piños Ranger District, tel. (661) 245-3731 or fax (661) 245-1526.

12 Pine Springs

 6

This primitive camp is set at 5,800 feet in elevation on a short spur road that dead-ends on the east flank of San Guillermo Mountain (6,569 feet). Pine Springs feeds the tiny headwaters of Guillermo Creek at this spot. This is a quiet spot. It gets little use, primarily in the fall by hunters.

Location: Near San Guillermo Mountain in Los Padres National Forest; map H4, grid f2.

Campsites, facilities: There are 12 sites for tents or RVs up to 22 feet long. Picnic tables and fire grills are provided. Pit toilets are available. No drinking water is available. Garbage must be packed out. Leashed pets are permitted.

Reservations, fees: No reservations; no camping fee. An Adventure Pass ($30 annual fee) or $5 daily fee per parked vehicle is required. Open May through September.

Directions: From Interstate 5 just south of Lebec take the Frazier Park exit and drive west on Frazier Mountain Road to the town of Lake of the Woods and Lockwood Valley Road. Turn left on Lockwood Valley Road (take the left fork) and drive about 12 miles to Grade Valley Road (Forest Road 7N03). Turn left and drive 3.5 miles to Forest Road 7N03A. Turn right and drive one mile to the campground.

Contact: Los Padres National Forest, Mount Piños Ranger District, tel. (661) 245-3731 or fax (661) 245-1526.

13 Kings

 5

The Hungry Valley State Vehicular Recreation Area is just five miles to the east. Figure it out: right, this is a primitive but well-placed camp for four-wheel-drive and off-highway vehicles. The camp is near Piru Creek, off a short spur road, so it feels remote yet is close to one of California's top off-road areas.

Location: Near Piru Creek in Los Padres National Forest; map H4, grid f4.

Campsites, facilities: There are seven sites for tents or RVs up to 16 feet long. Picnic tables and fire grills are provided. Vault toilets are available. No drinking water is available. Garbage must be packed out. Leashed pets are permitted.

Reservations, fees: No reservations; no camping fee. An Adventure Pass ($30 annual fee) or $5 daily fee per parked vehicle is required. Open year-round.

Directions: From Interstate 5, south of Gorman take the Gorman-Hungry Valley Road exit (the northern exit for the Hungry Valley Recreation Area). Turn south on Hungry Valley Road (Forest Road 8N01) and drive six miles to Gold Hill Road (Forest Road 8N01). Turn right and drive six miles to Forest Road 18N01A. Turn left and drive three-quarters mile to the campground.

Contact: Los Padres National Forest, Mount Piños Ranger District, tel. (661) 245-3731 or fax (661) 245-1526.

14 Twin Pines & Dutchman

 6

Twin Pines Camp is set at 6,600 feet on Alamo Mountain, a small, remote, and primitive spot. Dutchman Campground is nearby at 6,800 feet. These spots are best known by four-wheel-drive cowboys rumbling around the area. The big attraction here is access to the Miller Jeep Trail, a gnarly black-diamond route which can bend metal and alter minds. This camp also provides an alternative to the Hungry Valley State Vehicular Recreation Area to the nearby northeast.

Location: On Alamo Mountain in Los Padres National Forest; map H4, grid g4.

Campsites, facilities: There are five tent sites at Twin Pines and eight primitive sites at

Dutchman. Picnic tables and fire grills are provided. Pit toilets are available. No drinking water is available. Garbage must be packed out. Leashed pets are permitted.

Reservations, fees: No reservations; no camping fee. An Adventure Pass ($30 annual fee) or $5 daily fee per parked vehicle is required. Open May through October.

Directions: From Interstate 5 south of Gorman, take the Gorman-Hungry Valley Road exit (the northern exit for the Hungry Valley Recreation Area). Turn south on Hungry Valley Road (Forest Road 8N01) and drive six miles to Gold Hill Road (Forest Road 8N01). Turn right and drive 13 miles to Twin Pines campground. To reach Dutchman, at Twin Pines campground, turn right at Forest Road 7N01 and drive three miles to the campground.

Contact: Los Padres National Forest, Mount Piños Ranger District, tel. (661) 245-3731 or fax (661) 245-1526.

15 Half Moon

 7

Half Moon is a primitive camp set along Piru Creek at 4,700 feet. Adjacent to camp, Forest Road 7N13 follows the creek for a few miles, then dead-ends at a trailhead that continues along more remote stretches of this little stream. Hikers should also consider the trail to nearby Thorn Point for a beautiful lookout; see the entry for Thorn Meadows for more information.

Location: Near Piru Creek in Los Padres National Forest; map H4, grid g3.

Campsites, facilities: There are 10 sites for tents or RVs up to 22 feet long. Picnic tables and grills are provided. Pit toilets are available. No drinking water is available. Garbage must be packed out. Leashed pets are permitted.

Reservations, fees: No reservations; no camping fee. An Adventure Pass ($30 annual fee) or $5 daily fee per parked vehicle is required. Open May through October.

Directions: From Interstate 5 just south of Lebec take the Frazier Park exit and drive west

on Frazier Mountain Road to the town of Lake of the Woods and Lockwood Valley Road. Turn left on Lockwood Valley Road and drive about 12 miles to Mutau Flat Road (Forest Road 7N03). Turn left and drive 11 miles to the campground on the left. Four-wheel-drive vehicles are recommended.

Contact: Los Padres National Forest, Mount Piños Ranger District, tel. (661) 245-3731 or fax (661) 245-1526.

16 Thorn Meadows

 7

The reward at Thorn Meadows is a small, quiet spot along Piru Creek at 5,000 feet, deep in Los Padres National Forest. A trail out of camp leads three miles up to Thorn Point, a magnificent 6,935-foot lookout. It is by far the best view in the area, worth the 2,000-foot climb, and on a clear day you can see the Channel Islands.

Location: On Piru Creek in Los Padres National Forest; map H4, grid g2.

Campsites, facilities: There are five sites for tents or RVs up to 16 feet long. Picnic tables and fire grills are provided. Pit toilets and a corral are available. No drinking water is available. Garbage must be packed out. Leashed pets are permitted.

Reservations, fees: No reservations; no camping fee. An Adventure Pass ($30 annual fee) or $5 daily fee per parked vehicle is required. Open May through October.

Directions: From Interstate 5 just south of Lebec take the Frazier Park exit and drive west on Frazier Mountain Road to the town of Lake of the Woods and Lockwood Valley Road. Turn left on Lockwood Valley Road and drive about 12 miles to Mutau Flat Road (Forest Road 7N03). Turn left and drive seven miles to Forest Road 7N03B. Turn right and drive one mile to the campground.

Contact: Los Padres National Forest, Mount Piños Ranger District, tel. (661) 245-3731 or fax (661) 245-1526.

17 Los Alamos

 4

Los Alamos is set at an elevation of 2,600 feet near the southern border of the Hungry Valley State Vehicular Recreation Area and about 2.5 miles north of Pyramid Lake. Pyramid Lake is a big lake, covering 1,300 acres with 20 miles of shoreline, and is extremely popular for water-skiing and fast boating, as well as for windsurfing (best at the northern launch point), fishing (best in the spring and early summer and in the fall for striped bass), and swimming (best at boat-in picnic sites).

Location: Near Pyramid Lake in Angeles National Forest; map H4, grid g6.

Campsites, facilities: There are 93 family sites and several group sites for tents or RVs. Picnic tables and fire pits are provided. Drinking water and flush toilets are available. A boat ramp is at the Emigrant Landing Picnic Area. Leashed pets are permitted. Some facilities are wheelchair accessible.

Reservations, fees: For group reservations, phone (661) 248-6575; $10 per night for family sites, $50 per night for group sites. Open April through October.

Directions: From Gorman, drive eight miles south on Interstate 5. Take the Smokey Bear Road exit. Drive west about three-quarters of a mile and follow the signs to the campground.

Contact: Angeles National Forest, Santa Clara/Mojave Rivers Ranger District, tel. (661) 296-9710 or fax (661) 296-5847.

18 Sawmill

 7

This is a classic hiker's trailhead camp. It is set at 5,200 feet, right on the Pacific Crest Trail and just one mile from the junction with the Burnt Peak Canyon Trail. For a good day hike, head southeast on the Pacific Crest Trail for one mile to the Burnt Peak Canyon Trail, turn right (southwest), and hike just over a mile to Burnt Peak, elevation 5,788 feet. Note that this camp is inaccessible after the first snow.

Nearby Upper Shake provides an alternative.

Location: On the Pacific Crest Trail in Angeles National Forest; map H4, grid g8.

Campsites, facilities: There are eight sites for tents or RVs up to 16 feet long. Picnic tables and fire pits are provided. Vault toilets are available. No drinking water is available. Garbage must be packed out. Leashed pets are permitted.

Reservations, fees: No reservations; no camping fee. An Adventure Pass ($30 annual fee) or $5 daily pass per parked vehicle is required. Open May through October, weather permitting.

Directions: From Castaic, turn northeast on Lake Hughes Road and drive 27 miles to the town of Lake Hughes. Turn left on Pine Canyon Road and drive 10 miles to Bushnell Summit Road. Turn left and drive two miles to the campground on the left.

Contact: Angeles National Forest, Santa Clara/Mojave Rivers Ranger District, tel. (661) 296-9710 or fax (661) 296-5847.

19 Upper Shake

 7

Upper Shake, like nearby Sawmill, is right on the Pacific Crest Trail. The elevation is 4,300 feet. Hikers who plan on heading to Burnt Peak are better off departing from Sawmill (less than two miles to the west). This camp is used primarily as a jump-off point for those heading east on the PCT; Lake Hughes is the nearest destination, less than four miles away, and a mile after that is Lake Elizabeth. The camp is inaccessible after the first snow.

Location: Near the Pacific Crest Trail in Angeles National Forest; map H4, grid g8.

Campsites, facilities: There are 18 sites for tents or RVs up to 22 feet long. Picnic tables and fire pits are provided. Vault toilets are available. No drinking water is available. Garbage must be packed out. Leashed pets are permitted.

Reservations, fees: No reservations; no camping fee. An Adventure Pass ($30 annual fee) or $5 daily fee per parked vehicle is required. Open May through October, weather permitting.

Directions: From Castaic, turn northeast on Lake Hughes Road and drive 27 miles to the town of Lake Hughes. Turn left on County Road N2/Pine Canyon Road and drive about 5.5 miles to the entrance road on the left.

Contact: Angeles National Forest, Santa Clara/Mojave Rivers Ranger District, tel. (661) 296-9710 or fax (661) 296-5847.

20 Rose Valley

 8

The short walk to Rose Valley Falls, a 300-foot waterfall that provides a happy surprise, makes this camp a sure-thing winner in late winter and spring. The walk to the waterfall is just a half-mile round-trip; note that there are two views of it, a long-distance view of the entire waterfall, and then at the base, a view of just the lower tier. It is one of the scenic highlights in this section of Los Padres National Forest. The camp is set at 3,400 feet next to Rose Valley Creek, about two miles from Sespe Creek.

Location: In Los Padres National Forest; map H4, grid h1.

Campsites, facilities: There are nine sites for tents or RVs up to 16 feet long. Picnic tables and fire grills are provided. Drinking water and vault toilets are available. Horseback riding facilities are available nearby. Garbage must be packed out. Some facilities are wheelchair accessible. Leashed pets are permitted.

Reservations, fees: No reservations; no camping fee. An Adventure Pass ($30 annual fee) or $5 daily pass per parked vehicle is required. Open year-round, weather permitting.

Directions: From Ojai, drive about 15 miles north on Highway 33. Turn right on Sespe River Road/Rose Valley Road and drive 5.5 miles to the campground entrance.

Contact: Los Padres National Forest, Ojai Ranger District, tel. (805) 646-4348 or fax (805) 646-0484.

21 Oak Flat

 3

Oak Flat is just a short drive from Pyramid Lake, at 2,800 feet near the southwestern border of Angeles National Forest. Pyramid is surrounded by national forest, quite beautiful, and is a favorite destination for folks with powerboats, especially those towing water-skiers. The lake covers 1,300 acres and has 20 miles of shoreline. Fishing for striped bass can be good in the spring and fall, but in summer warfare can practically break out between low-speed fishermen and high-speed skiers. For more information on Pyramid Lake, see the entry for Los Alamos.

Location: Near Pyramid Lake in Angeles National Forest; map H4, grid h6.

Campsites, facilities: There are 27 sites for tents or RVs up to 32 feet long. Picnic tables and fire pits are provided. Vault toilets are available. No drinking water is available. Leashed pets are permitted.

Reservations, fees: No reservations; no camping fee. An Adventure Pass ($30 annual fee) or $5 daily fee per parked vehicle is required. Open year-round.

Directions: From Castaic, drive six miles north on Interstate 5. Turn left on Templin Highway, driving under the freeway, and continue northwest for three more miles to the campground.

Contact: Angeles National Forest, Santa Clara/Mojave Rivers Ranger District, tel. (661) 296-9710 or fax (661) 296-5847.

22 Lake Piru Recreation Area

 7

Things can get crazy at Lake Piru, but it's usually a happy crazy, not an insane crazy. This is a lake set up for water-skiing, with lots of fast boats. All others be forewarned: the rules prohibit boats under 12 feet and personal watercraft. The lake, shaped something like a teardrop, covers 1,200 acres when full and is set at an elevation of 1,055 feet. Bass fishing can be quite good in the spring before the water-skiers take over.

Location: On Lake Piru; map H4, grid h5.

Campsites, facilities: There are 235 sites for tents or RVs with electrical hookups. Five additional RV sites have full hookups. Fire pits and picnic tables are provided. Restrooms, drinking water, flush toilets, showers, sanitary disposal station, snack bar, ice, bait, boat ramp, temporary mooring, boat fuel, motorboat rentals, and tackle are available. Some facilities are wheelchair accessible. Leashed pets are permitted.

Reservations, fees: Reservations can be made Monday through Thursday from 8 a.m. to 4 p.m., seven days in advance; $22 to $32 per night, $22 per night for each extra vehicle, $2 pet fee. Major credit cards accepted. Open year-round.

Directions: From Ventura, drive east on Highway 126 for about 30 miles to the Piru Canyon Road exit. Drive northeast on Piru Canyon Road for about six miles to the campground at the end of the road.

Contact: Lake Piru Recreation Area, tel. (805) 521-1500; website: www.lake-piru.org.

23 Cottonwood

    5

Cottonwood Camp is set at 2,680 feet in remote Angeles National Forest along a small stream. The camp is on the north flank of Warm Springs Mountain. A great side trip is to the Warm Springs Mountain Lookout (4,023 feet), about a five-mile drive. Drive south on Forest Road 7N09 for three miles, turn right (west) on Forest Road 6N32, and drive for 1.5 miles to Forest Road 7N13. Turn left (south) and drive a mile to the summit.

Location: Near the Warm Springs Mountain Lookout in Angeles National Forest; map H4, grid h9.

Campsites, facilities: There are 22 sites for tents or RVs up to 22 feet long. Picnic tables and fire pits are provided. Vault toilets are

available. No drinking water is available. Supplies are less than four miles away in the town of Lake Hughes. Leashed pets are permitted.

Reservations, fees: No reservations; no camping fee. An Adventure Pass ($30 annual fee) or $5 daily fee per parked vehicle is required. Open year-round.

Directions: From Castaic, turn northeast on Lake Hughes Road and drive 25 miles to the campground on the right.

Contact: Angeles National Forest, Santa Clara/Mojave Rivers Ranger District, tel. (661) 296-9710 or fax (661) 296-5847.

24 Spunky

   7

Spunky Camp is set at 3,000 feet elevation amid good tree cover, much of it large oaks. The campsites are open, a peaceful setting. The highlight is hiking, with the Pacific Crest Trail passing just 1.5 miles east of the camp. In addition, many campers will hike up the canyon behind the campground. The creek runs during the winter. Nearby Elizabeth Lake, 10 miles to the west, provides swimming, fishing, sailing and low-speed power boating, with a 10-horsepower maximum on motors.

Location: In Angeles National Forest; map H4, grid i9.

Campsites, facilities: There are eight tent sites. Picnic tables and fire pits are provided. Pit toilets are available. A camp host is often available. No drinking water is available. A restaurant, gas station, and mini mart are available one mile away in Green Valley. Leashed pets are permitted.

Reservations, fees: No reservations; no camping fee. An Adventure Pass ($30 annual fee) or $5 daily fee per parked vehicle is required. Open year-round.

Directions: On Interstate 5 at Santa Clarita, take the Valencia Boulevard exit east and drive five miles to Bouquet Canyon Road. Turn left on Bouquet Canyon Road and drive 19 miles to Spunky Canyon Road. Turn left and drive four miles to the campground on the right.

Contact: Angeles National Forest, Santa Clara/Mojave Rivers Ranger District, tel. (661) 296-9710 or fax (661) 296-5847.

25 Streamside

   7

Streamside Camp is one of three Forest Service camps (Big Oak and Bouquet are the others) clustered along pretty Bouquet Canyon Creek at elevation 2,300 feet. This stream is typically stocked with trout twice a month in late spring and early summer. The creek and campgrounds are just downstream of Bouquet Reservoir, which provides stream flows in warm weather. Do not drink the water from Bouquet Canyon Creek under any circumstances. Note that this camp was closed in 2000 due to damage from mudslides. Check status before planning trip.

Location: On Bouquet Canyon Creek in Angeles National Forest; map H4, grid i9.

Campsites, facilities: There are nine tent sites. Picnic tables and fire pits are provided. Vault toilets are available. No drinking water is available. Leashed pets are permitted.

Reservations, fees: No reservations; no camping fee. An Adventure Pass ($30 annual fee) or $5 daily fee per parked vehicle is required. Open April through September.

Directions: On Interstate 5 at Santa Clarita, take the Valencia Boulevard exit east and drive five miles to Bouquet Canyon Road. Turn left on Bouquet Canyon Road and drive about 14 miles to the campground on the left.

Contact: Angeles National Forest, Santa Clara/Mojave Rivers Ranger District, tel. (661) 296-9710 or fax (661) 296-5847.

26 Kenney Grove

    4

A lot of folks miss this spot, a park tucked away among orchards and eucalyptus groves. It's just far enough off the highway to allow for some privacy. Note that groups are given priority over family and individual campers.

Location: Near Fillmore; map H4, grid i3.

Campsites, facilities: There are 19 sites for tents and 33 RV sites with partial hookups. Picnic tables and fire grills are provided. Drinking water, flush toilets, and a playground are available. Supplies and a coin laundry are nearby. Leashed pets are permitted.

Reservations, fees: Reservations required at (805) 524-0750; $13 to $16 per night, $2 for a second vehicle, $1 pet fee. Open year-round.

Directions: From Ventura, drive east on Highway 126 for 22 miles to Old Telegraph Road (before the town of Fillmore). Take the Old Telegraph Road exit and turn left and drive to Seventh Street. Turn left and drive to Oak. Turn right on Oak and drive to the park on the left.

Contact: Kenney Grove, tel. (805) 524-0750.

27 Far West Resort at Steckel County Park

     7

You either know about this spot or you don't. You either have this book or you don't. Other than the locals, few people are familiar with this park. It is a pretty spot set along little Santa Paula Creek in the foothill country. For those who want a well-developed park with a lot of amenities, the shoe fits.

Location: On Santa Paula Creek; map H4, grid i2.

Campsites, facilities: There are 72 sites for tents or RVs, 15 with full hookups, the rest with partial hookups, three group sites for RVs, and a group tent site for up to 400 people. Picnic tables and fire grills are provided. Restrooms, drinking water, flush toilets, coin laundry, modem hookups, sanitary disposal station, clubhouse, and a playground are available. Supplies and a coin laundry are nearby. Leashed pets are permitted.

Reservations, fees: Reservations are recommended at tel. (877) FAR-WEST; $14 to $26 per night for three people, $3 per person per night for more than three people, $2 pet fee. Major credit cards accepted. Open year-round for RVs and group tent site; individual tent sites closed from November through March.

Directions: From Ventura, drive 14 miles east on Highway 126, turn northwest on Highway 150, and drive four miles to the park on the right (take the second entrance to Steckel County Park).

Contact: Far West Resort, tel. (805) 933-3200; Ventura County Parks Department, tel. (805) 654-3951; website: www.farwestresort.com.

Mountain View RV Park
 3

The town of Santa Paula is known for its excellent weather and nearby recreation options. They include Steckel County Park, Los Padres National Forest, and the beaches at Ventura. Lake Casitas and Lake Cachuma, both known for big Florida bass, are within reasonable driving range.

Location: In Santa Paula; map H4, grid j1.

Campsites, facilities: There are 31 sites for self-contained vehicles. Cable TV and a swim spa are available. A coin laundry, restaurant, and shopping center are nearby. Leashed pets are permitted.

Reservations, fees: Call for available space; $23 to $25 per night. Open year-round.

Directions: From Ventura, drive 11 miles east on Highway 126. Take the Peck Drive exit and drive a short distance to Harvard Boulevard. Turn right and drive to 714 West Harvard Boulevard.

Contact: Mountain View RV Park, tel. (805) 933-1942.

29 Valencia Travel Village
 6

This huge RV park is in the scenic San Fernando foothills, just five minutes from Six Flags Magic Mountain. Lake Piru and Lake Castaic are only 15 minutes away. The camp was built on a 65-acre horse ranch.

Location: In Valencia; map H4, grid j8.

Campsites, facilities: There are 280 RV sites with full hookups, plus 200 tent sites. Fire pits are provided. A market and deli, two swimming pools, spa, lounge, video and games arcade, playground, shuffleboard, horseshoes, volleyball courts, laundry facilities, modem hookups, propane, and a sanitary disposal station are available. Some facilities are wheelchair accessible.

Reservations, fees: Reservations are recommended at tel. (888) LUV-TORV (888-588-8678); $20 to $25 per night, $2 per person per night for more than two people for RV sites, $4 per person per night for more than two people at tent sites. Weekly and monthly rates are available. Major credit cards accepted. Open year-round.

Directions: From Los Angeles, take Interstate 405 to Interstate 5, pass Magic Mountain Parkway, and exit at Highway 126. Turn left (north) and drive about one mile to the camp on the left.

Contact: Valencia Travel Village, 27946 Henry Mayo Road (Highway 126), Valencia, CA 91384; tel. (661) 257-3333; website: www.valencia-travelvillage.com.

CALIFORNIA DEPARTMENT
OF PARKS AND RECREATION

Hikers should watch out
for rattlers.

MAP H5

TO HAVILAH   TO WELDON   666   TO FREEMAN JUNCTION

a

Harper Peak
5,784 feet

SEQUOIA
NATIONAL
FOREST

Butterbread Peak
6,000 feet

(14)   Black Mountain
5,259 feet

Loraine ○

1

RED ROCK
CANYON
STATE PARK

Garlock ○

TO BAKERSFIELD

b

TO RANDSBURG

Cross Mountain
5,192 feet

Cantil ○

Koehn
Lake

c

(58)

(202)

Tehachapi ○

2

Cache Peak
6,708 feet

(14)

TO RED MOUNTAIN

○ Monolith

Tehachapi Summit
4,064 feet

d

Double Mountain
7,988 feet

○ Mojave

California
City ○

TO BORON

e

(58)

North
Edwards ○

724   **742**

f

Willow
Springs ○

Edwards ○

Rogers Dry
Lake

Rosamond ○

EDWARDS
AIR FORCE
BASE

g

(138)

Antelope Valley
○

Rosamond
Dry Lake

TO I-5

h

Lake
Hughes ○

Quartz
Hill ○

○ Lancaster

(N5)

Bouquet
Reservoir

(N2)

3

SADDLEBACK
BUTTE STATE PARK

i

ANGELES
NATIONAL
FOREST

Palmdale ○

(138)

El Mirage ○

TO VICTORVILLE

TO SAUGUS

j

(14)

Soledad Pass
3,179 feet

Littlerock ○
○ Pearblossom

Acton ○   ○ Vincent

Ravenna ○

(N6)

ANGELES
NATIONAL
FOREST

(N3)

Valyermo ○

(N4) (138) (18)

TO PASADENA   776   TO WRIGHTWOOD

© AVALON TRAVEL PUBLISHING, INC.

0 1 2 3 4 5 6 7 8 9

CHAPTER H5

1 Red Rock Canyon State Park

 8

This unique state park is one of the prettiest spots in the region year-round. What makes it worthwhile in any season is the chance to see wondrous geologic formations, most of them tinted red. A great, easy hike is the two-mile walk to Red Cliffs Natural Preserve, where there are awesome 300-foot cliffs and columns, painted red by the iron in the soil (this area is closed from February through June to protect nesting raptors). For those who don't hike, a must is driving up Jawbone Canyon Road to see Jawbone and Last Chance Canyons. Hikers have it better. The elevation is 2,600 feet.

Location: Near Mojave; map H5, grid a7.

Campsites, facilities: There are 50 sites for tents or RVs up to 30 feet long. Picnic tables and fire grills are provided. Drinking water, pit toilets, sanitary disposal station, exhibits, and a nature trail are available. In spring and fall, nature walks led by rangers are available. Some facilities are wheelchair accessible. Leashed pets are permitted.

Reservations, fees: No reservations; $10 per night. Open year-round.

Directions: From Highway 58 in the town of Mojave, turn northeast on Highway 14 and drive 24 miles to the park on the left.

Contact: Red Rock Canyon State Park, Mojave Desert Information Center, tel. (661) 942-0662, or fax (661) 940-7327.

2 Tehachapi Mountain Park

 5

This county park is overlooked by most out-of-towners. It is a pretty spot covering 570 acres, set on the slopes of the Tehachapi Mountains, with elevations in the park ranging from 5,500 to 7,000 feet. The roads to the campgrounds are steep, the sites are flat, and each site has its own toilet, a rarity (yes, it's really true—61 toilets). Trails for equestrians are available. This park is not only popular in spring, but also in winter, with the elevations sometimes high enough to get snow, offering a chance at winter sports (chains often required for access).

Location: Southwest of Tehachapi; map H5, grid c0.

Campsites, facilities: There are 61 sites for tents or RVs, a group campsite, and 10 cabins with 10 beds each. Picnic tables and fire grills are provided. Restrooms, drinking water (natural spring), pit and vault toilets are available. Some facilities are wheelchair accessible. Leashed pets are permitted.

Reservations, fees: Reservations for group site and cabins at (661) 868-7000; individual sites $8 per night, $2 pet fee, and cabins $200 per night with $400 deposit. Open year-round.

Directions: In Tehachapi on Tehachapi Boulevard, take the Cury Street exit south and drive about three miles. Turn right on Highline Road and drive two miles. Turn left on Water Canyon Road and drive three miles to the park.

Contact: Kern County Parks Department, Info line, tel. (661) 822-4632; website: www.co.kern.ca.us/parks/index.htm.

3 Saddleback Butte State Park

 8

This 3,000-acre park was originally established to preserve ancient Joshua trees. In fact, it used to be called Joshua Tree

State Park, but folks kept getting it confused with Joshua Tree National Park, so it was renamed. The terrain is sparsely vegetated and desert-like, with excellent hiking trails up the nearby buttes. The best hike is the Saddleback Loop, a five-mile trip that features a 1,000-foot climb to Saddleback Summit at 3,651 feet. On rare clear days, there are fantastic views in all directions, including the Antelope Valley California Poppy Preserve, the surrounding mountains, and the Mojave Desert. On the typical hazy day, the poppy reserve might as well be on the moon; you can't even come close to seeing it. The elevation is 2,700 feet.

Location: Near Lancaster; map H5, grid h6.

Campsites, facilities: There are 50 sites for tents, trailers, or self-contained RVs up to 30 feet long. A group camp is available for up to 30 people. Picnic tables and fire grills are provided. Drinking water, flush toilets, and a sanitary disposal station are available. A visitor center is nearby. Some facilities are wheelchair accessible. Leashed pets are permitted.

Reservations, fees: No reservations for single sites; the group camp may be reserved at tel. (800) 444-PARK (444-7275) or website: www.reserveamerica.com; $10 per night for individual sites, $22 per night for the group site. Open year-round.

Directions: From Highway 14 at Lancaster, turn east on Avenue J and drive 17 miles to the park entrance on the right (note: If driving westbound, turn north on 170th Street and drive to Avenue J. Then turn east on Avenue J and drive 17 miles to the park entrance.).

Contact: Saddleback Butte State Park, Mojave Desert Information Center, tel. (661) 942-0662 or fax (661) 940-7327.

THE MINE AT CALICO

CALICO GHOST TOWN

MAP H6

692

TO INYOKERN   TO WESTEND

395

O Searles

178

U.S.
NAVAL
WEAPONS
CENTER

TO GARLOCK

Randsburg O
O Johannesburg
O Red Mountain

O Atolia

TO CALIFORNIA CITY

FORT
IRWIN
MILITARY
RESERVE

Cuddleback
Lake

395

TO NORTH EDWARDS

Fremont Peak
4,584 feet

Opal Mountain
3,950 feet

TO FORT IRWIN

738

58

Boron O

RAINBOW
BASIN
NATURAL
AREA

746

EDWARDS
AIR FORCE
BASE

Harper
Lake

❶

58   O Hinkley

BARSTOW ❷

Lenwood   15 ❸ Yermo
O

TO BAKER

Hodge O

O Daggett

TO NEWBERRY SPRINGS

Helendale O

15

40

395

TO EL MIRAGE

GEORGE AIR
FORCE BASE   Oro
O Grande

247

TO LITTLEROCK

Adelanto O

❹

18

Victorville O

18

O Apple Valley

TO SAN BERNARDINO   TO LUCERNE VALLEY

798

0   1   2   3   4   5   6   7   8   9

© AVALON TRAVEL PUBLISHING, INC.

CHAPTER H6

1 Owl Canyon

 3

The primary attraction of Owl Canyon camp is that the surrounding desert is sprinkled with exposed fossils of ancient animals. Guess they couldn't find any water, heh, heh. Well, if people try hiking here without a full canteen, there may soon be some human skeletons out here, too. The sparse BLM land out here is kind of like an ugly dog you learn to love: after a while, when you look closely, you learn it has a heart of gold. This region is best visited in the spring and fall, of course, when hiking allows a fresh, new look at what may appear to some as a wasteland. The beauty is in the detail of it—tiny critters and tiny flowers seen against the unfenced vastness, with occasional fossils yet to be discovered. The elevation is 2,600 feet.

Location: Near Barstow; map H6, grid f6.

Campsites, facilities: There are 31 sites for tents or RVs. Picnic tables and fire grills are provided. Drinking water (limited) and vault toilets are available. Leashed pets are permitted.

Reservations, fees: No reservations; $6 per night. Open year-round.

Directions: From Barstow on Interstate 15, take the First Street exit and drive north (crossing the Mojave River Bridge) for 0.75 miles to Fort Irwin Road. Turn left and drive to Old Highway 58. Turn north and drive eight miles to Fossil Bed Road. Turn left and drive two miles to the campground on the right.

Contact: Bureau of Land Management, Barstow Field Office, (760) 252-6000, or fax (760) 252-6099.

2 Calico Ghost Town Regional Park

  4

Let me tell you about this ghost town: There are probably more people here now than there have ever been. In the 1880s and 1890s it was a booming silver mine town, and there are still remnants of that. Alas, it now has lots of restaurants and shops. Recreation options include riding on a narrow gauge railroad, touring a silver mine, and watching an old-style play with villains and heroes. Whatever you do, don't take any artifacts you may come across, such as an old nail, a jar, or anything; you will be doomed with years of bad luck. No foolin'.

Location: Near Barstow; map H6, grid g8.

Campsites, facilities: There are 247 sites for tents or RVs, 47 with full hookups. Cabins and a bunkhouse are also available. Fire grills are provided. Restrooms, drinking water, flush toilets, showers, and a sanitary disposal station are available. Groceries, propane gas, and laundry facilities are available 10 miles away. Leashed pets are permitted.

Reservations, fees: Reservations are requested at (800) To-CALICO; $18 to $22 per night for tent or RV sites (scout camping is available at $3 per night). The cabin fee is $28 per night with a refundable $25 deposit, the bunkhouse fee is $5 per camper per night ($60 minimum), $1 fee for off-highway vehicles. Major credit cards accepted. Open year-round.

Directions: From Barstow, drive seven miles northeast on Interstate 15. Take the Ghost Town Road exit and drive north for three miles to the park on the left.

Contact: Calico Ghost Town Regional Park, San Bernardino County, tel. (760) 254-2122; website: www.calicotown.com.

3 Barstow Calico KOA

 3

Don't blame us if you end up way out here. Actually, for vacationers making the long-distance grind of a drive on Interstate 15, this KOA can seem like the promised land. It's clean, and a nightly quiet time ensures that you have a chance to get rested. But hey, as long as you're here, you might as well take a side trip to the Calico Ghost Town, about 10 miles to the northeast at the foot of the Calico Mountains. Rockhounding and hiking are other nearby options. The elevation is 1,900 feet.

Location: Near Barstow; map H6, grid g8.

Campsites, facilities: There are 78 sites for tents or RVs, many with full or partial hookups. Picnic tables and fire grills are provided. Restrooms, drinking water, flush toilets, showers, sanitary disposal station, modem hookups, playground, swimming pool, recreation room, grocery store, propane gas, ice, and laundry room facilities are available. Some facilities are wheelchair accessible. Leashed pets are permitted.

Reservations, fees: Reservations accepted at (800) KOA-0059; $18 to $25 per night, $1 for each additional vehicle. Major credit cards accepted. Open year-round.

Directions: From Barstow, drive seven miles northeast on Interstate 15 north. Take the Ghost Town Road exit, drive left under the freeway, and then immediately turn left again onto the frontage road. Drive about a quarter mile to the campground on the right.

Contact: Barstow Calico KOA, tel. (760) 254-2311 or fax (760) 254-2247; website: www.koa.com.

4 Shady Oasis Victorville KOA

3

Most long-distance trips on Interstate 15 are grueling endurance tests with drivers making the mistake of trying to get a decent night's sleep at a roadside rest stop. Why endure the torture, especially with a KOA way out here, in Victorville of all places? Where the heck is Victorville? If you are exhausted and lucky enough to find the place, you won't be making any jokes about it. By the way, if you visit, keep your eyes open for the ghost of Roy Rogers, the legendary cowboy singer. He lived just minutes away from this park, where he sat happily in his living room with his horse, Trigger, which he had stuffed. Happy trails to you, until we meet again.

Location: Near Victorville; map H6, grid j3.

Campsites, facilities: There are 136 sites for tents or RVs, many with full or partial hookups. Picnic tables and fire grills are provided. Restrooms, drinking water, flush toilets, showers, recreation room, swimming pool, playground, modem hookups, grocery store, propane gas, and a laundry room are available. Some facilities are wheelchair accessible. Leashed pets are permitted.

Reservations, fees: Reservations at (800) KOA-3319; $19 to $24 per night, $2 per person per night for more than two people, $1 per night for each extra vehicle, cabins $35 per night. Major credit cards accepted. Open year-round.

Directions: From Victorville, drive north on Interstate 15 to Stoddard Wells Road. Turn south and drive a short distance to the campground at 16530 Stoddard Wells Road.

Contact: Shady Oasis Victorville KOA, tel. (760) 245-6867, or fax (760) 243-2108; website: www.koa.com.

KIM WEIR

SIGHTS ALONG THE ROADSIDE

MAP H7

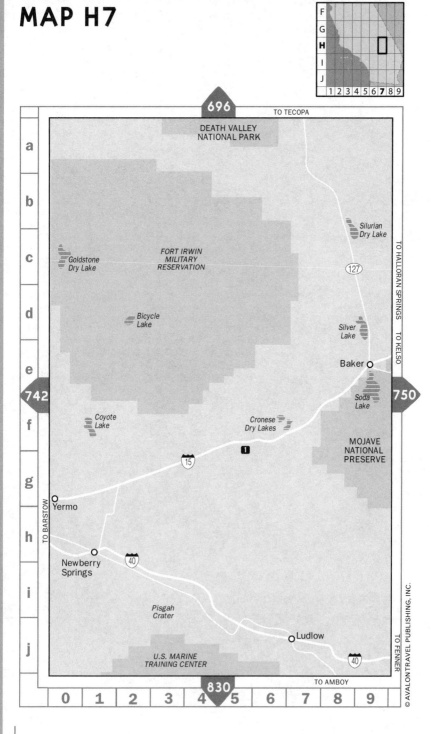

696

TO TECOPA

DEATH VALLEY
NATIONAL PARK

Silurian
Dry Lake

Goldstone
Dry Lake

FORT IRWIN
MILITARY
RESERVATION

127

TO HALLORAN SPRINGS

Bicycle
Lake

Silver
Lake

TO KELSO

Baker

742

Coyote
Lake

Cronese
Dry Lakes

Soda
Lake

750

MOJAVE
NATIONAL
PRESERVE

1

15

Yermo

TO BARSTOW

Newberry
Springs

40

Pisgah
Crater

Ludlow

TO FENNER

U.S. MARINE
TRAINING CENTER

830

40

TO AMBOY

© AVALON TRAVEL PUBLISHING, INC.

a b c d e f g h i j

0 1 2 3 4 5 6 7 8 9

CHAPTER H7

■ Afton Canyon

 6

This camp is set at 1,400 feet elevation in a desert riparian habitat along the Mojave River. This is one of several Bureau of Land Management tracts in the East Mojave National Scenic Area. Side trip options include the Rainbow Basin Natural Area, Soda Springs, and the Calico Early Man Site. Remember, rivers in the desert are not like rivers in cooler climates. There are no fish worth eating.

Location: Near Barstow in the East Mojave National Scenic Area; map H7, grid f5.

Campsites, facilities: There are 22 sites for tents or RVs. Picnic tables and fire rings are provided. Drinking water (limited) and vault toilets are available. Leashed pets are permitted.

Reservations, fees: No reservations; $6 per night. Open year-round.

Directions: From Barstow, drive 40 miles east on Interstate 15 to Afton Road. Turn right and drive three miles to the campground on the left.

Contact: Bureau of Land Management, Barstow Field Office, tel. (760) 252-6000 or fax (760) 252-6099.

KIM WEIR

DESERT SCENE

MAP H8

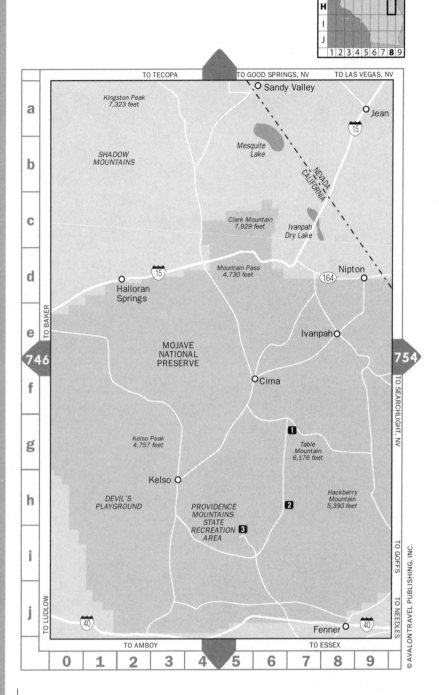

TO TECOPA — TO GOOD SPRINGS, NV — TO LAS VEGAS, NV

Sandy Valley

Jean
15

Kingston Peak
7,323 feet

SHADOW
MOUNTAINS

Mesquite
Lake

NEVADA
CALIFORNIA

Clark Mountain
7,929 feet

Ivanpah
Dry Lake

15

Mountain Pass
4,730 feet

164 Nipton

Halloran
Springs

TO BAKER

746

MOJAVE
NATIONAL
PRESERVE

Ivanpah

754

TO SEARCHLIGHT, NV

Cima

Kelso Peak
4,757 feet

1

Table
Mountain
6,176 feet

Kelso

DEVIL'S
PLAYGROUND

2

Hackberry
Mountain
5,390 feet

PROVIDENCE
MOUNTAINS
STATE
RECREATION
AREA

3

TO GOFFS

TO LUDLOW

TO NEEDLES

40

Fenner

40

TO AMBOY — TO ESSEX

© AVALON TRAVEL PUBLISHING, INC.

CHAPTER H8

Mid Hills

 5

This is a primitive campground set among the junipers and piñon trees in a mountainous area at 5,300 feet. It is one of two little-known camps in the vast desert that is now managed by the National Park Service. The primary attraction here is the remoteness, as well as the nearby Providence Mountains State Recreation Area and winter hikes to obscure landmarks. The best hike in the region is to Teutonia Peak, elevation 5,755 feet, a four-mile round-trip that tops out on the rounded dome-like top and provides 360-degree views across this vast desert landscape.

Location: In the Mojave National Preserve; map H8, grid g7.

Campsites, facilities: There are 26 sites for tents or RVs up to 22 feet long. Picnic tables and fire grills are provided. Drinking water and vault toilets are available. Leashed pets are permitted.

Reservations, fees: No reservations; $10 per night. Open year-round.

Directions: From Interstate 40 near Essex, take the Essex Road exit and drive 10 miles north to Black Canyon Road. Turn north and drive about nine miles on pavement and 10 miles on rough, dirt road to the campground on the right.

Contact: Mojave National Preserve, tel. (760) 733-4040, or fax (760) 733-4027.

Hole-In-The-Wall and Black Canyon Group & Horse Campground

 5

This is the largest and best-known of the camps in the vast Mojave National Preserve; the campgrounds are set at 4,300 feet in elevation, with a family camp, group camp, and equestrian camp situated across the road from each other. An interesting side trip is to the Mitchell Caverns and Winding Stair Caverns in the nearby Providence Mountains State Recreation Area. To get there, go back to Essex Road, turn right, and continue northeast for about six miles to the end of Essex Road. For group reservations for the Mitchell Cavern tour, tel. (661) 942-0662.

Location: In the Mojave National Preserve; map H8, grid h7.

Campsites, facilities: There are 35 sites for tents or RVs, one group site for up to 70 people, and an equestrian camp. Picnic tables and fire grills are provided. Drinking water, sanitary disposal station, and vault toilets are available. Leashed pets are permitted.

Reservations, fees: No reservations; $10 to $20 per night, $20 per night for horses. Open year-round.

Directions: From Highway 40 near Essex, take the Essex Road exit. Turn north and drive 10 miles to Black Canyon Road. Turn north and drive 9 miles to the campgrounds.

Contact: Mojave National Preserve, tel. (760) 733-4040, or fax (760) 733-4027.

Providence Mountains State Recreation Area

 8

This remote desert park, set at 4,300 feet, offers guided tours of Mitchell Caverns ($1-3 tour fee, discounts available) every day from early September through late May, and on weekends from late May to early September. It's a good idea to make a reservation for the tour; phone (760) 928-2586. The cavern tours are the reason most people visit and camp at this park, but there are additional recreational opportunities. From the campground the Nina Mora Overlook Trail is a short (quarter-mile) walk to a lookout of the Marble Mountains and the valley below. Another short hike with a great view is the steep, one-mile hike on the Crystal Springs Trail. But the best hike here is the Mary Beale, an interpretive trail accessible from the visitor center, a one-mile loop.

Location: Near Mitchell Caverns; map H8, grid i5.

Campsites, facilities: There are six sites for tents. RVs up to 32 feet long can park in the parking lot, and primitive walk-in sites that require a 100-foot walk are available. Picnic tables and fire grills are provided. Drinking water and vault toilets are available. A pay telephone is available nearby. Leashed pets are permitted.

Reservations, fees: No reservations; $12 per night. Open year-round.

Directions: From Interstate 40 near the town of Essex, turn northwest on Essex Road and drive 16 miles to the park at road's end.

Contact: Providence Mountains State Recreation Area, tel. (760) 928-2586, or Mojave Desert Information Center, tel. (661) 942-0662 or fax (661) 940-7327.

CENTURY PLANTS

KIM WEIR

MAP H9

TO LAS VEGAS, NV

95

TO NIPTON

164

Searchlight

Cottonwood
Cove

Cal Nev Ari

Hart Peak
5,543 feet

ARIZONA
NEVADA

Colorado River

NEVADA
CALIFORNIA

TO IVANPAH

EAST
MOJAVE
NATIONAL
SCENIC
AREA

163

DAVIS DAM

Laughlin   Bullhead City

95

ARIZONA
CALIFORNIA

Goffs

TO FENNER

40

1
2
3

FORT
MOJAVE
INDIAN
RESERVATION

Needles

TO VIDAL JUNCTION

TO TOPOCK, AZ

840

© AVALON TRAVEL PUBLISHING, INC.

CHAPTER H9

Rainbo Beach Resort and Marina

 6

The big bonus here is the full marina, making this resort on the Colorado River the headquarters for boaters and water-skiers. And headquarters it is, with tons of happy folks who are extremely well lubed, both inside and out. For boating details, see the entry for Needles Marina Park.

Location: On the Colorado River; map H9, grid j5.

Campsites, facilities: There are 70 RV sites with full hookups and picnic tables. Restrooms with showers, coin laundry, swimming pool, hot tub, recreation room, and a beer bar are available. A boat dock with gas is available nearby. Leashed pets are permitted.

Reservations, fees: Reservations are accepted; $26 to $31 per night. Open year-round. Major credit cards accepted.

Directions: From Interstate 40 in Needles, drive 1.5 miles north on River Road to the resort on the right.

Contact: Rainbo Beach Resort and Marina, tel. (760) 326-3101 or fax (760) 326-5085; website: www.rainbowbeachresort.wazzu.com.

Needles Marina Park

      6

Bring your suntan lotion and a beach towel. This section of the Colorado River is a big tourist spot where the body oil and beer can flow faster than the river. There are a ton of hot bodies and hot boats, and water-skiing dominates the adjacent calm water section of the Colorado River. However, note that upstream of the Needles-area put-in is the prime area for water-skiing. Downstream is the chance for canoeing or kayaking. Meanwhile, there's also an 18-hole golf course adjacent to the camp, but most folks head for the river. Compared to the surrounding desert, this park is almost a golden paradise.

Location: On the Colorado River; map H9, grid j5.

Campsites, facilities: There are 190 sites for RVs with full hookups and picnic tables. There are also six cabins. Restrooms, drinking water, flush toilets, showers, heated pool, whirlpool, recreation room, modem hookups, swimming pool, playground, boat ramp, boat slips, grocery store, gas, and laundry facilities are available. Leashed pets are permitted.

Reservations, fees: Reservations are accepted; $25 to $27 per night, $6.50 per person per night for more than three people, $57 per night for cabins. Major credit cards accepted. Open year-round.

Directions: From Interstate 40 in Needles, take the J Street exit to Broadway. Turn left on Broadway and drive three-quarters of a mile to Needles Highway. Turn right on Needles Highway, and drive a half mile to the park on the left.

Contact: Needles Marina Park, tel. (760) 326-2197 or fax (760) 326-4125; website: www.needlesmarina.com.

Needles KOA

 2

At least you've got the Needles KOA out here, complete with swimming pool, where you can get a new start. Side trips include venturing to the nearby Colorado River or heading north to Lake Mead. Of course, you could always go to Las Vegas. Nah.

Location: Near the Colorado River; map H9, grid j5.

Campsites, facilities: There are 101 sites for tents or RVs, 30 with water and electric connections, and 63 with full hookups. Restrooms, drinking water, flush toilets, showers, recreation room, swimming pool, playground, grocery store, snack bar, propane gas, and laundry facilities are available. Some facilities are wheelchair accessible. Leashed pets are permitted.

Reservations, fees: Reservations accepted at (800) 562-3407; $17.95 to $23.95 per night, $2 per night for more than two people. Major credit cards accepted. Open year-round.

Directions: In Needles on Interstate 40, take the West Broadway exit, turning left on Needles Highway. Drive a short distance, turn left on National Old Trails Highway, and drive to the park on the right at 5400 National Old Trails Highway.

Contact: Needles KOA, tel. (760) 326-4207 or fax (760) 326-6329; website: www.koa.com.

SOUTHERN CALIFORNIA
CHAPTER 12

SEAGULL IN FLIGHT

MAP 12

One inch equals approximately 11 miles.

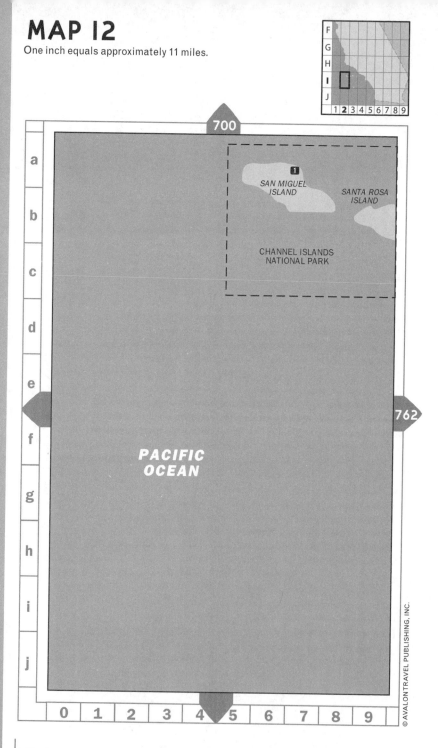

SAN MIGUEL
ISLAND

SANTA ROSA
ISLAND

CHANNEL ISLANDS
NATIONAL PARK

**PACIFIC
OCEAN**

700

762

© AVALON TRAVEL PUBLISHING, INC.

SOUTHERN CALIFORNIA

CHAPTER 12

1 San Miguel Island Hike-In

 10

There is no camping trip like this one anywhere in America. It starts with a five-hour boat ride, after which you arrive at San Miguel Island, the most unusual of the five Channel Islands. It is small, distant, and extremely rugged, and is home to unique birds and much wildlife, including elephant seals and the largest sea lion rookery in California (on the south side of the island). Only rarely do people take advantage of this island paradise, limited to no more than 30 people at any one time on the entire island. To reach the campground start from Cuyler Harbor, where you will be dropped off, and then hike up Nidever Canyon and take the left fork. Bring plenty of water, warm clothes, and be prepared for the chance of fog and wind; the boat typically will not return to pick you up for several days. That's why camping here is like staking out your own personal island wilderness.

Location: In Channel Islands National Park; map 12, grid a7.

Campsites, facilities: There are nine primitive tent sites. Picnic tables and food lockers are provided. Pit toilets and windbreaks are available. No drinking water is available, and garbage must be packed out. No open fires are allowed; bring a camp stove for cooking. No pets are permitted.

Reservations, fees: Reserve by calling Island Packers at tel. (805) 642-1393 or Truth Aquatics at Sea Landing in Santa Barbara at tel. (805) 963-3564. After arranging transportation, you must obtain a camping reservation at tel. (800) 365-CAMP (800-365-2267) or website: reservations.nps .gov/. Camping is $2.60 (reservation fee) per night; round-trip boat transportation varies in cost, generally in the $100 range. Open year-round, weather permitting.

Directions: On U.S. 101 in Ventura, drive south to the Seaward exit. Take that exit and turn west on Seaward Avenue for one mile to Harbor Boulevard. Bear left on Harbor and drive about two miles to Spinnaker Drive. Turn right and drive a short distance to the harbor. The boat ride is about five hours each way.

Contact: For camping information, phone the park visitor center at tel. (805) 658-5730.

THE ENDEARING SEA OTTER

MAP 13

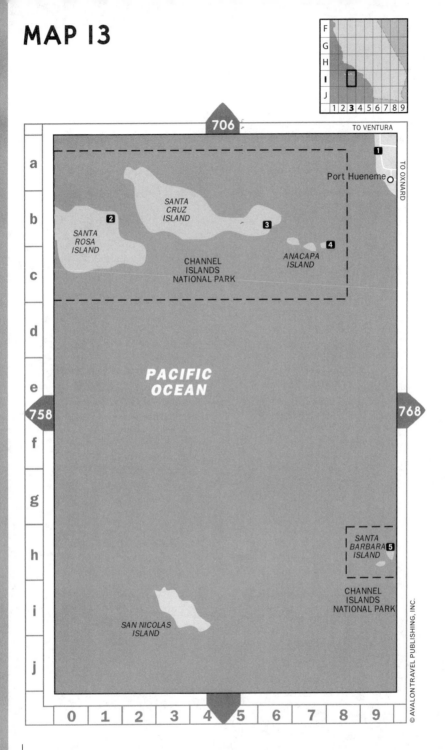

TO VENTURA

1

Port Hueneme ○

TO OXNARD

SANTA CRUZ ISLAND

2

SANTA ROSA ISLAND

3

CHANNEL ISLANDS NATIONAL PARK

ANACAPA ISLAND

4

PACIFIC OCEAN

706

758

768

SANTA BARBARA ISLAND **5**

CHANNEL ISLANDS NATIONAL PARK

SAN NICOLAS ISLAND

© AVALON TRAVEL PUBLISHING, INC.

CHAPTER 13

1 McGrath State Beach

 9

This is a pretty spot just south of Ventura Harbor. The north tip of the park borders the Santa Clara River Estuary Natural Preserve, where the McGrath State Beach Nature Trail provides an easy walk along the Santa Clara River as it feeds into the estuary and then into the ocean. Ventura Harbor and the Channel Islands National Park Visitor Center are nearby side trips. Note: During summer, plan on making a camping reservation or don't plan to visit this park.

Location: On the Pacific Ocean south of Ventura; map I3, grid a9.

Campsites, facilities: There are 174 sites for tents or RVs up to 34 feet long (29 of the sites can be used as group sites), and a hike-in/bike-in site. Picnic tables and fire grills are provided. Restrooms, drinking water, flush toilets, coin-operated showers, sanitary disposal station, horseshoes, and a visitor center are available. A lifeguard service is provided in summer. Supplies and a coin laundry are nearby. Leashed pets are permitted in campsites only.

Reservations, fees: Reserve at tel. (800) 444-PARK (444-7275) or website: www.reserve america.com; $12 per night, $1 per person for hike-in/bike-in sites. Open year-round. Some facilities are wheelchair accessible.

Directions: On U.S. 101 in Ventura, drive south to the Seaward exit. Take that exit and turn west on Seaward Avenue for one mile to Harbor Boulevard. Bear left on Harbor and drive four miles to the park (signed).

Contact: McGrath State Beach, tel. (805) 654-4744 or (805) 648-4127; Channel Coast State Park District, (805) 899-1400.

2 Santa Rosa Island

 10

Santa Rosa, the second largest of the Channel Islands (the largest is Santa Cruz), is 10 miles wide and 15 miles long, and it holds many mysteries and adventures. A camping trip to Santa Rosa Island, available Friday through Sunday, will be an unforgettable experience even for those who think they've seen it all. The "Painted Caves" of Santa Rosa makes this a world-class trip for kayakers. The island is beautiful in the spring, when its grasslands turn emerald green and are sprinkled with wildflowers. There are many good hikes, the best the Cherry Canyon Trail into the island's interior with the likely chance of seeing wild goats, and the Lobo Canyon Trail descending to a Chumash village site and tidepools. Because the boat ride to Santa Rosa is approximately four hours, longer than the trip to Santa Cruz, this island often receives fewer visitors than its nearby neighbor, which makes it even more special. Bring plenty of fresh water and, because of the chance of fog and wind, warm clothes.

Location: In Channel Islands National Park; map I3, grid b1.

Campsites, facilities: There are 15 primitive tent sites. Picnic tables and windbreaks are provided. Pit toilets are available. No open fires are allowed; bring a camp stove for cooking. Garbage must be packed out. No pets are permitted.

Reservations, fees: Reserve by calling Island Packers at tel. (805) 642-1393 or Truth Aquatics at Sea Landing in Santa Barbara at tel. (805) 963-3564. After arranging transportation, you must obtain a camping reservation at tel. (800) 365-CAMP (800-365-2267) or website: reservations.nps .gov/. Camping is $2.60 (reservation fee) per night; round-trip boat transportation varies in cost, generally in the $80 range. Open year-round, weather permitting.

Directions: On U.S. 101 in Ventura, drive south to the Seaward exit. Take that exit and turn west on Seaward Avenue for one mile to Harbor Boulevard. Bear left on Harbor and drive about two miles to Spinnaker Drive. Turn right and drive a short distance to the harbor. The boat ride is about four hours each way.

Contact: For camping information, phone the park visitor center at tel. (805) 658-5730.

3 Santa Cruz Island

     10

This is the largest of the Channel Islands, perfect for camping and multi-day visits. It covers 96 square miles, features a 2,450-foot mountain (Devil's Peak), and boasts an incredible array of flora and fauna, sheltered canyons, and sweeping ocean views. The camp is set in a eucalyptus grove in a valley, with trailheads near camp that hikers can take to the surrounding ridgeline. A great hike is from Pelican Bay to Prisoner's Harbor, a three-miler that is routed through the interior of the island to a beautiful beach. Kayaking through sea caves is outstanding.

Location: In the Channel Islands; map I3, grid b6.

Campsites, facilities: There are 35 primitive campsites. Picnic tables, and fire rings are provided. Pit toilets are available. No drinking water is available. Garbage must be packed out. No pets are permitted.

Reservations, fees: Reserve by calling Island Packers at tel. (805) 642-1393 or Truth Aquatics at Sea Landing in Santa Barbara at tel. (805) 963-3564. After arranging transportation, you must obtain a camping reservation at tel. (800) 365-CAMP (800-365-2267) or website: reservations.nps.gov/. Camping is $2.60 (reservation fee) per night; round-trip boat transportation

varies in cost, generally in the $45 range. Open year-round, weather permitting.

Directions: On U.S. 101 in Ventura, drive south to the Seaward exit. Take that exit and turn west on Seaward Avenue for one mile to Harbor Boulevard. Bear left on Harbor and drive about two miles to Spinnaker Drive. Turn right and drive a short distance to the harbor. The boat ride is about 1.5 hours each way.

Contact: For camping information, phone the park visitor center at tel. (805) 658-5730.

4 Anacapa Island

      10

Little Anacapa, long and narrow, is known for its awesome caves, cliffs, and sea lion rookeries that range near huge kelp beds. After landing on the island, you face a 154-step staircase trail that leaves you perched on an ocean bluff. The trails from there, as well as from Inspiration Point and Cathedral Cove, provide vast views of the channel. The inshore waters are an ecological preserve loaded with marine life and seabirds and, with the remarkably clear water, this island makes a great destination for snorkeling and sea kayaking. Of the Channel Islands, the boat ride here is the shortest, only 75 minutes.

Location: In Channel Islands National Park; map I3, grid c8.

Campsites, facilities: There are seven primitive tent sites. Picnic tables are provided. Pit toilets are available. No drinking water is available. Garbage must be packed out. No open fires are allowed; bring a camp stove for cooking. No pets are permitted.

Reservations, fees: Reserve by calling Island Packers at tel. (805) 642-1393 or Truth Aquatics at Sea Landing in Santa Barbara at tel. (805) 963-3564. After arranging transportation, you must obtain a camping reservation at tel. (800) 365-CAMP (800-365-2267) or website: reservations.nps.gov/. Camping is $2.60 (reservation fee) per night; round-trip boat transportation varies in cost, generally in the $45 range. Open year-round, weather permitting.

Directions: On U.S. 101 in Ventura, drive south to the Seaward exit. Take that exit and turn west on Seaward Avenue for one mile to Harbor Boulevard. Bear left on Harbor and drive about two miles to Spinnaker Drive. Turn right and drive a short distance to the harbor. The boat ride is about 75 minutes each way.

Contact: For camping information, phone the park visitor center at tel. (805) 658-5730.

5 Santa Barbara Island

      10

This is a veritable dot of an island, well to the south of the four others that make up the Channel Islands. It is best known for its five miles of hiking trails, solitude, snorkeling, swimming, and excellent viewing of marine mammals. It is a breeding ground for elephant seals, with dolphins, sea lions, and whales (in the winter), all common in the area. The snorkeling can be wonderful, as you dive amid playful seals. The only negative is the long boat ride, five hours from the mainland.

Location: In Channel Islands National Park; map I3, grid h9.

Campsites, facilities: There are eight primitive tent sites. Picnic tables are provided. Pit toilets are available. No drinking water is available. Garbage must be packed out. No open fires are allowed; bring a camp stove for cooking. No pets are permitted.

Reservations, fees: Reserve by calling Island Packers at tel. (805) 642-1393 or Truth Aquatics at Sea Landing in Santa Barbara at tel. (805) 963-3564. After arranging transportation, you must obtain a camping reservation at tel. (800) 365-CAMP (800-365-2267) or website: reservations.nps.gov/. Camping is $2.60 (reservation fee) per night; round-trip boat transportation varies in cost, generally in the $50 to $75 range. Open year-round, weather permitting.

Directions: On U.S. 101 in Ventura, drive south to the Seaward exit. Take that exit and turn west on Seaward Avenue for one mile to Harbor Boulevard. Bear left on Harbor and drive about two miles to Spinnaker Drive. Turn right and drive a short distance to the harbor. The boat ride is about five hours each way.

Contact: For camping information, phone the park visitor center at tel. (805) 658-5730.

OFFICER'S LATRINE

CHAPTER 14

*M*A*S*H* SET IN
MALIBU CREEK STATE PARK

MAP 14

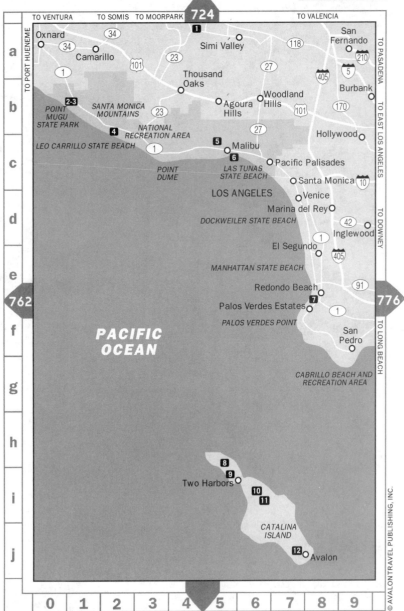

1

Oxnard

34

34

Camarillo

Simi Valley

San Fernando

118

27

210

101

23

Thousand Oaks

5

405

Burbank

2-3

SANTA MONICA MOUNTAINS

23

Agoura Hills

Woodland Hills

170

POINT MUGU STATE PARK

101

4

NATIONAL RECREATION AREA

27

Hollywood

LEO CARRILLO STATE BEACH

1

5 Malibu

6

Pacific Palisades

POINT DUME

LAS TUNAS STATE BEACH

Santa Monica

10

LOS ANGELES

Venice

Marina del Rey

DOCKWEILER STATE BEACH

42

Inglewood

El Segundo

1

MANHATTAN STATE BEACH

405

91

Redondo Beach

762

PACIFIC OCEAN

Palos Verdes Estates

7

1

776

PALOS VERDES POINT

San Pedro

CABRILLO BEACH AND RECREATION AREA

TO PORT HUENEME

TO PASADENA

TO EAST LOS ANGELES

TO DOWNEY

TO LONG BEACH

8

9

Two Harbors

10

11

CATALINA ISLAND

© AVALON TRAVEL PUBLISHING, INC.

12 Avalon

0   1   2   3   4   5   6   7   8   9

CHAPTER 14

1 Oak Park

 3

One of the frustrations of trying to find a camp for the night is that so many state and national park campgrounds are full from advance reservations, especially the state beaches. The county parks often provide a safety valve, and Oak Park certainly applies. But not always, and that's the catch. This is an oft-overlooked county park set in the foothill country of Simi Valley. The park has many trails offering good hiking possibilities. The camp is somewhat secluded, more so than many expect. The catch? Sometimes the entire campground is rented to a single group. Note: Gates close at dusk and re-open at 7 a.m.

Location: In Simi Valley near Moorpark; map 14, grid a4.

Campsites, facilities: There is a large group tent area for up to 140 people, 16 sites for RVs with partial hookups, and an RV group area for up to 22 RVs. Picnic tables and fire grills are provided. Restrooms, drinking water, flush toilets, and a sanitary disposal station are available. Horsehoe pits, a playground, and basketball and volleyball courts are available nearby. Supplies and a coin laundry are within one mile. Leashed pets are permitted.

Reservations, fees: Reservations are accepted; $12 to $17 per night, $5 per person per night for more than two people, $1 pet fee. Open year-round, except Christmas Day.

Directions: From Ventura, drive south on U.S. 101 to Highway 23. Drive north on Highway 23 (which becomes Highway 118) for about three miles to the Collins Street exit. Turn right (east) on Old Los Angeles Avenue and drive about 1.5 miles to Quimisa Drive. Turn left into the park.

Contact: Oak Park, Ventura County, tel. (805) 527-6886, or Ventury County Parks Department, (805) 654-3951.

2 Big Sycamore Canyon

 6

While this camp is across the highway from the ocean, it is also part of Point Mugu State Park, which covers 14,980 acres. That gives you plenty of options. One of the best is taking the Big Sycamore Canyon Loop, a long hiking route with great views that starts right at the camp. In all, it's a 9.5-mile loop that climbs to a ridge top and offers beautiful views of nearby canyons and long-distance vistas of the coast. Note: Front gate closes at 10 p.m. and re-opens at 8 a.m.

Location: In Point Mugu State Park; map I4, grid b1.

Campsites, facilities: There are 54 sites for tents or RVs up to 31 feet long (up to eight campers per site), and one hike-in/bike-in site. Picnic tables and fire grills are provided. Restrooms, drinking water, flush toilets, coin showers, and a sanitary disposal station are available. Supplies can be obtained nearby. Some facilities are wheelchair accessible. Leashed pets are permitted at campsites.

Reservations, fees: Reserve at tel. (800) 444-PARK (800-444-7275) or website: www.reserveamerica.com; $12 per night, $1 per person per night for hike-in/bike-in site. Open year-round.

Directions: From Oxnard, drive 16 miles south on Highway 1 to the camp on the left.

Contact: Big Sycamore Canyon, tel. (818) 880-0350 or fax (818) 880-6165.

3 Thornhill Broome State Beach & La Jolla Group

 7

Of the two campgrounds at Point Mugu State Park, this one is more attractive to those touring Highway 1 because it is on the ocean side of the highway (the other is on the east side of the highway). While the beachfront is pretty and you can always just lie there in the sun and pretend you're a beached whale, the park's expanse on the east side of the highway in the Santa Monica Mountains provides more recreation. That includes two stellar hikes, the 9.5-mile Big Sycamore Canyon Loop and the seven-mile La Jolla Valley Loop. In all, the park covers 14,980 acres, far more than the obvious little strip of beachfront.

Location: In Point Mugu State Park; map I4, grid b1.

Campsites, facilities: There are 88 primitive sites for tents or RVs up to 31 feet long, and one group site for up to 50 people. Picnic tables and fire rings are provided. Drinking water and vault toilets are available. La Jolla Group Camp also has a restroom and coin showers available. Supplies can be obtained

nearby. Leashed pets are permitted.

Reservations, fees: Reserve at tel. (800) 444-PARK (800-444-7275) or website: www.reserveamerica.com; $7 per night, $12 per night for site designed for physically challenged, $37 per night for group site. Open year-round.

Directions: From Oxnard, drive 15 miles south on Highway 1 to the camp entrance; on the right for Thornhill Broome, on the left for La Jolla Group.

Contact: Thornhill Broome State Beach, tel. (818) 880-0350 or fax (818) 880-6165.

4 Leo Carrillo State Park

 8

The camping area at this state park is set in a nearby canyon. Reservations are essential for the canyon sites during the summer. The Nicholas Flat Trail provides an excellent hike to the Willow Creek Overlook for beautiful views of the beach. In addition, a pedestrian tunnel is available that provides access to a wonderful coastal spot with sea caves, tunnels, and patches of beach. In the summer, lifeguards are posted at the beach. Many will remember a beach camp that was once popular here. Well, that sucker is gone, wiped out by a storm in the late 1990s.

Location: North of Malibu; map I4, grid b2.

Campsites, facilities: There are 127 sites for tents or RVs up to 31 feet long, one hike-in/bike-in site for up to 24 people, and one group tent site. Picnic tables and fire rings are provided. Restrooms, drinking water, flush toilets, coin showers, a sanitary disposal station, summer programs, and a summer convenience store are available. Some facilities are wheelchair accessible. Leashed pets are permitted. Front gates close at 10 p.m. and reopen at 8 a.m.

Reservations, fees: Reserve at tel. (800) 444-PARK (800-444-7275) or website: www.reserveamerica.com; $12 per night, $1 per person per night for hike-in/bike-in site, $37 for group tent site. Open year-round.

Directions: From Santa Monica, drive 28 miles north on Highway 1 to the park on the right. Or from Oxnard, drive 20 miles south on Highway 1 to the signed park exit on the left. Exit directly into the park.

Contact: Leo Carrillo State Beach, tel. (818) 880-0350 or fax (818) 880-6165.

5 Malibu Beach RV Park

 7

This is one of the few privately developed RV parks that provides some sites for tent campers as well. It's one of the nicer spots in the area, set on a bluff overlooking the Pacific Ocean, near both Malibu Pier (for fishing) and Paradise Cove. Each site has a view of either the ocean or adjacent mountains. Get this: Hollywood is 10 miles to the east.

Location: In Malibu; map I4, grid c5.

Campsites, facilities: There are 50 tent sites and 140 RV sites with full or partial hookups. Picnic tables and barbecue grills are provided. Restrooms, showers, hot tub, recreation room, playground, coin laundry, modem hookups, propane gas, ice, cable TV, sanitary disposal station, and a grocery store are available. Some facilities are wheelchair accessible. Leashed pets are permitted, except in the tent area.

Reservations, fees: Reservations are recommended at (800) 622-6052; $15 to $45 per night, $3 per person per night for more than two people. Major credit cards accepted. Open year-round.

Directions: In Malibu at the intersection of Pacific Coast Highway/Highway 1 and Malibu Canyon Road, drive north on Pacific Coast Highway two miles to the RV park on the right.

Contact: Malibu Beach RV Park, tel. (310) 456-6052 or fax (310) 456-2532; website: www.malibubeachrv.com.

6 Malibu Creek State Park

9

If you plan on staying here, be sure to get your reservation in early. This 6,600-acre state park is just a few miles out of Malibu between Highway 1 and U.S. 101, two major thoroughfares for vacationers. Despite its popularity, the park manages to retain a natural setting, with miles of trails for hiking, biking, and horseback riding, and inspiring scenic views. It is an ideal spot for a break on a coastal road trip.

Location: Near Malibu; map I4, grid c5.

Campsites, facilities: There are 63 sites for tents or self-contained RVs up to 24 feet long, and a group tent site for up to 50 people. Picnic tables are provided. No wood fires are permitted, but propane or charcoal barbecues are allowed. Restrooms, drinking water, flush toilets, and coin showers are available. Some facilities are wheelchair accessible. Leashed pets are permitted, but only in the campground area.

Reservations, fees: Reserve at tel. (800) 444-PARK (800-444-7275) or website: www.reserveamerica.com; $12 per night, $45 per night for group site. Open year-round.

Directions: From U.S. 101 northeast of Malibu, take the Las Virgenes exit. Drive south on Las Virgenes Canyon Road for four miles to the park entrance on the right. If you're coming from Highway 1 in Malibu, turn east on Malibu Canyon Road and drive about five miles to the park entrance on the left.

Contact: Malibu Creek State Park, tel. (818) 880-0350 or fax (818) 880-6165.

7 Dockweiler Beach RV Park

 6

This layover spot for coast cruisers is just a hop from the beach and the Pacific Ocean. A 26-mile-long bike path runs between the park and the beach.

Location: On the Pacific Ocean near Manhattan Beach; map I4, grid f8.

Campsites, facilities: There are 117 sites for RVs up to 35 feet long, 82 with full hookups. Picnic tables and barbecue grills are provided. Flush toilets, hot showers, sanitary disposal station, and coin laundry are available. Some facilities are wheelchair accessible. You can buy supplies nearby. Leashed pets are permitted.

Reservations, fees: Reserve at tel. (800) 950-7275 ($7 reservation fee), $12 to $25 per night, $5-6 for more than one vehicle. Open year-round. Major credit cards accepted.

Directions: From Santa Monica, drive 12 miles south on Interstate 405 to the Imperial Highway West exit. Drive about 4 miles west on Imperial Highway to Vista del Mar and the park on the left.

Contact: Dockweiler Beach, Los Angeles County, tel. (800) 950-7275 or tel. (310) 322-4951.

❽ Parson's Landing Hike-In

    10

This primitive campground is one of five on Catalina Island. It is set on the island's northern end, seven miles from the island's isthmus and the village of Two Harbors. If you want to try and avoid the crowds, this is the area to visit; forget Avalon and head instead to Two Harbors.

Location: On Catalina Island; map I4, grid h5.

Campsites, facilities: There are eight tent sites, each for up to six campers. Picnic tables, barbecue and fire rings, and a locker with firewood and 2 gallons of drinking water are provided. Chemical toilets are available. Pets are not permitted.

Reservations, fees: Reservations are required at (310) 510-2800; $6 to $12 per person per night. Open year-round, weather permitting. Check in at the visitor information booth to validate your camping permit and obtain locker key for water and wood. A round-trip ferry ride costs $38, $28.50 for children under 12. Open year-round, weather permitting.

Directions: A direct ferry boat ride is available from San Pedro to Two Harbors. From Two Harbors travel by shore boat (check schedule) to Emerald Bay. Hike 1.5 miles to the campground. Or from Two Harbors, hike seven miles to campsites.

Contact: For ferry information, camp reservations, or general information, phone (310) 510-2800 or tel. (310) 510-0303; website: www.catalina.com/camping.

❾ Two Harbors

   10

This campground is only a quarter mile away from the village of Two Harbors. Nearby attractions include the Two Harbors Dive Station with snorkeling equipment, paddleboard rentals, and scuba tank fills to 3,000 psi. There are guided tours of the island and a scheduled bus service between Two Harbors and Avalon; the bus stops at all the interior campgrounds. An excellent hike is the nine-mile round-trip from Two Harbors to Emerald Bay, featuring a gorgeous coast and pretty valleys. A quarter-mile hike is required to reach this campground.

Location: On Catalina Island; map I4, grid i5.

Campsites, facilities: There are 36 sites, two of which can accommodate up to 25 people, and 13 tent cabins for up to six people. Picnic tables and fire grills are provided. Drinking water, sun shades, cold showers, and chemical toilets are available. Firewood, charcoal, and propane are sold at the ranger station by advance order. A general store, restaurant and saloon, snack bar, tennis courts, volleyball, coin laundry, and hot showers are available in the town of Two Harbors. Pets are not permitted.

Reservations, fees: Reservations are required at (310) 510-2800; $6 to $12 per person per night, $30 for tent cabins. Open year-round, weather permitting. Check in at the visitor information booth to validate your camping permit. A round-trip ferry ride costs $38, $28.50 for children under 12. Open year-round.

Directions: A direct ferry boat ride is available from San Pedro to Two Harbors. If you are at Avalon, take the bus to Two Harbors. From Two Harbors, after checking in with rangers, hike one-quarter mile to campground.

Contact: For ferry information, camp reservations, or general information, phone (310) 510-2800 or tel. (310) 510-0303; website: www.catalina.com/camping.

Black Jack Hike-In

 7

This camp is named after Mount Black Jack (2,008 feet) and is a great place to hunker down for a spell. It's also the site of the old Black Jack Mine. This is the least-popular campground on the island, viewed by most as a stopover site, not a base camp. From Black Jack Junction (accessible by shuttle bus), it is a one-mile hike to the camp. The camp is set at 1,500 feet in elevation. If you stand in just the right spot, you can see the mainland, but L.A. will seem like a million miles away.

Location: On Catalina Island; map I4, grid i6.

Campsites, facilities: There are 11 tent sites with a maximum of six campers per site. Drinking water, picnic tables, fire pits, cold showers, and a locker with firewood are provided. Chemical toilets are available. A phone is available nearby. Propane, charcoal, and other rental equipment are not available November through March. Pets are not permitted.

Reservations, fees: Reservations are required at (310) 510-2800; $6 to $12 per person per night. Open year-round, weather permitting. Check in at the visitor information booth to validate your camping permit and obtain locker key for water and wood. A round-trip ferry ride costs $38, $28.50 for children under 12. Open year-round, weather permitting.

Directions: From San Pedro, Newport Beach, Long Beach, Dana Point, or Long Beach, a ferry is available to Avalon on Catalina Island.

From Avalon, take the shuttle bus to Black Jack Junction and then hike one mile to the campground.

Contact: For ferry information, camp reservations, or general information, phone (310) 510-2800 or tel. (310) 510-0303; website: www.catalina.com/camping.

Little Harbor Hike-In

 10

There is plenty to do: You can swim, dive, fish, or go for day hikes. There are two sandy beaches near this camp, both great for swimming and snorkeling. A Native American historic site is nearby. Two Harbors has several excellent hikes, including the nine-mile excursion to Emerald Bay. Of course, you could always take the shuttle bus. Many folks consider this to be the pick of the campgrounds on the island. It is a gorgeous place—small wonder that some big Hollywood flicks have been shot here.

Location: On Catalina Island; map I4, grid i6.

Campsites, facilities: There are 16 tent sites. Picnic tables and fire rings are provided. Drinking water, cold showers, sun shades, pay telephone, shuttle bus service, and chemical toilets are available. A phone is available nearby. Wood, charcoal, and propane can be ordered in advance from the ranger station. Pets are not permitted.

Reservations, fees: Reservations are required at (310) 510-2800; $6 to $12 per person per night. Open year-round, weather permitting. A round-trip ferry ride costs $38, $28.50 for children under 12.

Directions: A direct ferry boat ride is available from San Pedro to Two Harbors. From Two Harbors, take the shuttle bus to Little Harbor. A short hike is required.

Contact: For ferry information, camp reservations, or general information, phone (310) 510-2800 or tel. (310) 510-0303; website: www. catalina.com/camping.

12 Hermit Gulch

 10

This is the closest campground to the town of Avalon, the gateway to Catalina. Reaching the camp requires a 1.25-mile hike up Avalon Canyon. If you're making a tourist trip, there are a ton of things to do here: Visit Avalon's underwater city park, play the nine-hole golf course, rent a bicycle, or visit the famous casino. Fishing can be excellent, including angling for white seabass, yellowtail, and, in the fall, even marlin. The best hiking experience in the Avalon area is found by taking the shuttle bus to the Airport in the Sky and from there hiking along Empire Landing Road. The route traces the island's curving, hilly northern shore, providing great views of secluded beaches, coves, and rock formations, and a chance to see wildlife, at times even buffalo.

Location: On Catalina Island; map I4, grid j7.

Campsites, facilities: There are 84 tent sites, seven tent cabins, and six tepees. Picnic tables, fire rings, and barbecue pits are provided. Restrooms, drinking water, flush toilets, showers, ice, lockers, playground, coin microwave, vending machines, and a public phone are available. Some camping equipment is available for rent. Pets are not permitted.

Reservations, fees: Reservations are required at (310) 510-2800; $6 to $12 per person per night, tent cabins and tepees $30. Open year-round, weather permitting. Check in at the visitor information booth to validate your camping permit. A round-trip ferry ride costs $38, $28.50 for children under 12. Open year-round, weather permitting.

Directions: A direct ferry boat ride is available from San Pedro, Newport Beach, Dana Point, or Long Beach to Avalon. From Sumner Avenue in Avalon, walk up Avalon Canyon (follow the "Avalon Canyon Road" sign) for 1.25 miles to the campground. The camp is across from the picnic grounds.

Contact: For ferry information, camp reservations, or general information, phone (310) 510-2800 or tel. (310) 510-0303; website: www.catalina.com/camping.

CHAPTER 15

NEAR
LAGUNA BEACH

MAP 15

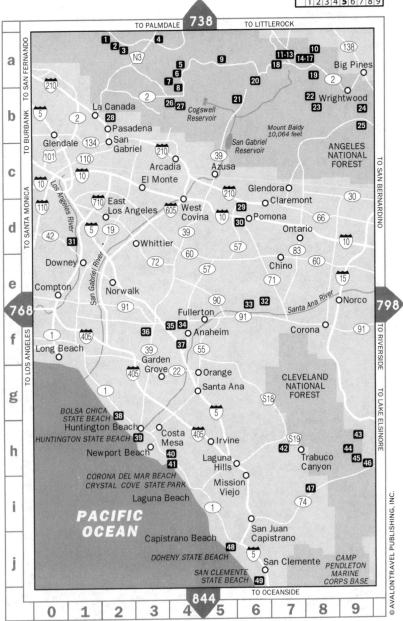

TO SAN FERNANDO

TO BURBANK

TO SANTA MONICA

TO LOS ANGELES

1 **2** **3** N3 **4**

5

6

7

8

26 **27**

138

11-13 **10**

14-17

18 **19** Big Pines

9 2

20 Wrightwood

21 **22** **23** **24**

Cogswell
Reservoir

Mount Baldy
10,064 feet

San Gabriel
Reservoir

25

La Canada 2

28

Pasadena

Glendale 134 San
Gabriel

101 110 210

Arcadia Azusa

El Monte

ANGELES
NATIONAL
FOREST

39

TO SAN BERNARDINO

10 10

710 East
Los Angeles

605 West
Covina

Glendora

Claremont

29 Pomona

30 Ontario

30

66

42 19

31

5

Whittier

39

60

57

83

60

10

TO SAN BERNARDINO

Downey

Compton

72

Chino

Norwalk

57

71

15

91

90

33 **32**

Santa Ana River

Norco

TO RIVERSIDE

TO LAKE ELSINORE

768

Fullerton 91

798

Corona 91

35 **34**

36

37

Anaheim

55

1 405

Long Beach

39 Garden
Grove 405 22

Orange

Santa Ana

CLEVELAND
NATIONAL
FOREST

1

S18

BOLSA CHICA
STATE BEACH **38**

Huntington Beach

HUNTINGTON STATE BEACH **39**

Costa
Mesa

S19

43

42

44

45 **46**

Newport Beach 405 Irvine

Trabuco
Canyon

40

41

Laguna
Hills

CORONA DEL MAR BEACH
CRYSTAL COVE STATE PARK

Laguna Beach

Mission
Viejo

47

74

**PACIFIC
OCEAN**

1

Capistrano Beach

San Juan
Capistrano

48

5

DOHENY STATE BEACH

San Clemente

CAMP
PENDLETON
MARINE
CORPS BASE

SAN CLEMENTE
STATE BEACH **49**

© AVALON TRAVEL PUBLISHING, INC.

TO OCEANSIDE

844

0 1 2 3 4 5 6 7 8 9

CHAPTER 15

(CONTINUED ON NEXT PAGE)

1 Messenger Flats

   7

Messenger Flats is an ideal camp for many, located a half mile east of Mount Gleason (6,502 feet). The Pacific Crest Trail is routed through this camp, featuring a one-mile hike with a climb of 600 feet to reach Gleason's summit. The camp is at 5,500 feet, set in a flat area about a quarter mile east of an electronic transmitter at Messenger Peak.

Location: Near Mount Gleason in Angeles National Forest; map I5, grid a2.

Campsites, facilities: There are 10 tent sites. Picnic tables and fire grills are provided. Drinking water and vault toilets are available. Two horse corrals are also available. Leashed pets are permitted.

Reservations, fees: No reservations; $5 per night. Open April through November, weather permitting.

Directions: From Interstate 210 north of Pasadena, take the Angeles Crest Highway/ Highway 2 exit and drive nine miles north. Turn left onto Angeles Forest Highway/County Road N3 and drive about 12 miles to the intersection with Santa Clara Divide Road. Turn left and drive 11 miles to the campground.

Contact: Angeles National Forest, Los Angeles River Ranger District, tel. (818) 899-1900 or fax (818) 896-6727.

2 Lightning Point Group Camp

 8

Lightning Point is set at 6,200 feet, high on the southwest flank of Mount Gleason, just a mile from the summit (6,502 feet). This camp offers a one-mile interpretive trail and is also near a trailhead at Messenger Flats for a short hike to the top of Mount Gleason.

Location: Near Mount Gleason in Angeles National Forest; map I5, grid a2.

Campsites, facilities: There are six group sites and 26 horse corrals. Picnic tables and fire pits are provided. Drinking water and flush toilets are available. Leashed pets are permitted.

Reservations, fees: Reservations are required; reserve at tel. (818) 899-1900. The entire camp can accommodate 230 campers and is available for a fee of $240 per night. Open late April through October.

Directions: From Interstate 210 north of Pasadena, take the Angeles Crest Highway/Highway 2 exit and drive north for nine miles. Turn left onto Angeles Forest Highway/County Road N3 and drive about 12 miles to the Santa Clara Divide Road intersection. Turn left and drive 10 miles to the campground entrance road on the left.

Contact: Angeles National Forest, Los Angeles River Ranger District, tel. (818) 899-1900 or fax (818) 896-6727.

3 Mount Pacifico

   7

This is one of the great primitive camps in Angeles National Forest. It is set near the top of Mount Pacifico at an elevation of 7,134 feet, with the Pacific Crest Trail running right through the camp. The views are outstanding, especially to the north of the sparse Antelope Valley and beyond. From here, the PCT is routed through a series of ravines and draws and up short ridges, pleasant but not inspiring.

Location: On the Pacific Crest Trail in Angeles National Forest; map I5, grid a2.

Campsites, facilities: There are 7 tent sites. Picnic tables and fire grills are provided. Vault toilets are available. No drinking water is available. Garbage must be packed out. Leashed pets are permitted.

Reservations, fees: No reservations; an Adventure Pass ($30 annual fee) or $5 daily pass per parked vehicle is required. Open mid-May through mid-November.

Directions: From Interstate 210 north of

Pasadena, drive north on the Angeles Crest Highway/Highway 2 for 29 miles. Turn left on Angeles Forest Highway/County Road N3 and drive about 12 miles. At the intersection with Santa Clara Divide Road/County Road 3N17, look for the Mill Creek Summit sign. Turn right and drive about five miles to Mount Pacifico Road. Turn left on the dirt road and drive four miles to the campground.

Note that at Mill Creek Summit, the gate is locked from November 15 to May 15 and it will be necessary to walk from the gate. When Santa Clara Divide Road is impassable due to weather conditions, it will be necessary to walk from Alder Saddle.

Contact: Angeles National Forest, Los Angeles River Ranger District, tel. (818) 790-1151 or fax (818) 790-5392.

◘ Monte Cristo

 7

This is a Forest Service camp on Mill Creek at 3,600 feet, just west of Iron Mountain. The camp is situated under sycamore trees, which provide great color in the fall. In most years Mill Creek flows eight months out of the year.

Location: On Mill Creek in Angeles National Forest; map I5, grid a3.

Campsites, facilities: There are 19 sites for tents or RVs up to 30 feet long. Picnic tables and fire grills are provided. Drinking water and vault toilets are available. Some facilities are wheelchair accessible. Leashed pets are permitted.

Reservations, fees: No reservations except for wheelchair sites; $8 per night, $2 for each additional vehicle. Open year-round.

Directions: From Interstate 210 north of Pasadena, take the Angeles Crest Highway/Highway 2 exit and drive north for nine miles. Turn left onto Angeles Forest Highway/County Road N3 and drive about nine miles to the campground.

Contact: Angeles National Forest, Los Angeles River Ranger District, tel. (818) 899-1900 or fax (818) 896-6727.

◘ Chilao & Coulter Group

 6

These popular trailhead camps get a lot of use. And it's easy to see why, with the Chilao Visitor Center (have any questions? Here's where you ask.) nearby and a national recreation trail running right by the camp. Coulter Group Camp is within Chilao and will accommodate up to 50 people. Access to the Pacific Crest Trail is two miles north at Three Points, and parking is available there. The elevation is 5,300 feet.

Location: Near the San Gabriel Wilderness in Angeles National Forest; map I5, grid a4.

Campsites, facilities: There are 110 sites for tents or RVs up to 22 feet long, and a group site for up to 50 people. Picnic tables and fire rings are provided. Drinking water and vault toilets are available. A sanitary disposal station is available at Charlton Flat Picnic Area. Leashed pets are permitted.

Reservations, fees: Reservations required for group site at (818) 899-1900; $12 per night for individual sites, $30 per night for reserved double sites, $100 per night for group site. Open May through October.

Directions: From Interstate 210 north of Pasadena, take the Angeles Crest Highway/Highway 2 exit and drive 26 miles northeast to the signed campground entrance road on the left.

Contact: Angeles National Forest, Los Angeles River Ranger District, tel. (818) 790-1151 or fax (818) 790-5392.

◘ Sulphur Springs Group Camp

 6

This group camp is on the South Fork of Little Rock Creek, a short distance from a trailhead for the Pacific Crest Trail. It's set at 5,300 feet amid pines and is a popular jump-off point for group hikes. The nearby Chilao Visitor Center is a must-stop for newcomers.

Location: Near the Pacific Crest Trail in Angeles National Forest; map I5, grid a4.

Campsites, facilities: This is essentially a group camp available for tents or RVs up to 16 feet long. If reserved for a group, the campground will hold up to 80 people. Picnic tables and stoves are provided. Drinking water and pit toilets are available. A water trough is available for horses. Leashed pets are permitted.

Reservations, fees: No reservations for individual sites; reservations are required for groups at (818) 899-1900; $6 per night for individual sites, $100 group fee per night (maximum of 80 people). Open April through November.

Directions: From Interstate 210 north of Pasadena, take the Angeles Crest Highway/Highway 2 exit and drive north for 28 miles to the intersection with Santa Clara Divide Road at Three Points (there is a sign). Turn left and drive five miles to the campground entrance road on the right (it will seem like the continuation of the road you're on).

Contact: Angeles National Forest, Los Angeles River Ranger District, tel. (818) 790-1151 or fax (818) 790-5392.

❼ Horse Flats

 7

This is one of four options in the immediate area: Chilao, Bandido Group Camp, and Coulter Group Camp are the other three. Horse Flats is set at 5,700 feet along a national recreation trail and is close to the Chilao Visitor Center. Several trails into the San Gabriel Wilderness are nearby.

Location: Near the San Gabriel Wilderness in Angeles National Forest; map I5, grid a4.

Campsites, facilities: There are 25 sites for tents or RVs up to 36 feet long. Picnic tables and fire pitss are provided. Vault toilets, hitching rails, and horse corrals are available. No drinking water is available. A grocery store is nearby. Leashed pets are permitted.

Reservations, fees: No reservations; $10 per night. Open April through November.

Directions: From Interstate 210 north of Pasadena, take the Angeles Crest Highway/Highway 2 exit and drive north for 29 miles to the intersection with Santa Clara Divide Road at Three Points (there is a sign). Turn left and drive three miles to the signed campground.

Contact: Angeles National Forest, Los Angeles River Ranger District, tel. (818) 790-1151 or fax (818) 790-5392.

❽ Bandido Group Camp

    6

This is a base camp for groups preparing to hike off into the surrounding wilderness. A trail out of the camp heads north and intersects with the Pacific Crest Trail a little over one mile away at Three Points, a significant PCT junction. Before heading out most visitors check in with the rangers at nearby Chilao Visitor Center, two miles west of Three Points on Highway 2. The elevation is 5,840 feet.

Location: Near the Pacific Crest Trail in Angeles National Forest; map I5, grid b4.

Campsites, facilities: There are 25 sites for tents or RVs up to 16 feet long. The camp will accommodate up to 120 people. Picnic tables and fire rings are provided. Drinking water, vault toilets, corrals and water troughs are available. Leashed pets are permitted.

Reservations, fees: Reservations are required at (818) 899-1900; $25 per night per site. Groups can reserve half the campground for $100 per night (60-person maximum) or the entire campground for $175 per night (120-person maximum). Open April through November.

Directions: From Interstate 210 north of Pasadena, take the Angeles Crest Highway/Highway 2 exit and drive north for 28 miles to the intersection with Santa Clara Divide Road at Three Points (there is a sign). Turn left and drive two miles to the campground on the left.

Contact: Angeles National Forest, Los Angeles River Ranger District, tel. (818) 790-1151 or fax (818) 790-5392.

🟨 Buckhorn

 9

This is a prime jump-off spot for backpackers in Angeles National Forest. The camp is set at 6,300 feet among huge pine and cedar trees, along a small creek near Mount Waterman (8,038 feet). A great day hike begins here, a tromp down to Cooper Canyon and the PCT; hikers will be rewarded by beautiful Cooper Falls on this three-hour round-trip. Want a weekend trip? Got it: The High Desert National Recreational Trail leads north from camp into the backcountry, over Burkhart Saddle, and west around Devil's Punchbowl County Park to South Fork Campground. Then it heads south to the Islip Trailhead, east past Eagle's Roost, and south again for the last mile back to Buckhorn. It's a 20-mile hike, with the South Fork Camp situated 10 miles out, perfect for a weekend trip.

Location: Near Snowcrest Ridge in Angeles National Forest; map I5, grid a5.

Campsites, facilities: There are 38 sites for tents or RVs up to 20 feet long. Picnic tables and fire pits are provided. Drinking water, vault toilets, and a camp host are available. Leashed pets are permitted.

Reservations, fees: No reservations; $12 per night. Open May through November.

Directions: From Interstate 210 north of Pasadena, take the Angeles Crest Highway/Highway 2 exit and drive 34 miles northeast to the signed campground entrance.

Contact: Angeles National Forest, Los Angeles River Ranger District, tel. (818) 790-1151 or fax (818) 790-5392.

🔟 Table Mountain

 6

This is a family campground that accommodates both tents and RVs. The road leading in is a paved two-lane county road, easily accessible by any vehicle. The nearby Big Pines Visitor Information Center, one mile to the south, can provide maps and information on road conditions. The camp elevation is 7,200 feet. A rough road for four-wheel-drive rigs is available out of camp that leads north along the Table Mountain Ridge.

Location: In Angeles National Forest; map I5, grid a8.

Campsites, facilities: There are 115 sites for tents or RVs up to 32 feet long. Picnic tables and fire pitss are provided. Drinking water and vault toilets are available. Leashed pets are permitted.

Reservations, fees: Reserve at tel. (877) 444-6777 ($8.65 reservation fee) or website: www.reserveusa.com; $12 per night. Open May through September.

Directions: From Interstate 15 near Cajon, take Highway 138 west. Turn west on Angeles Crest Highway/Highway 2 and drive five miles to Wrightwood. Continue for three miles to Big Pines. Turn right on Table Mountain Road and drive one mile to the campground.

Contact: Angeles National Forest, Santa Clara/Mojave Rivers Ranger District, tel. (661) 944-2187 or fax (661) 944-4698.

🔢 Big Rock

 7

This is a good spot for four-wheel-drive cowboys. It is a primitive Forest Service camp set at the head of Fenner Canyon along Big Rock Creek. Forest Road 4N11 to the southeast is a four-wheel-drive road that connects to a network of backcountry roads and hiking trails. A Forest Service map is essential. The elevation is 5,550 feet.

Location: On Big Rock Creek in Angeles National Forest; map I5, grid a7.

Campsites, facilities: There are eight sites for tents. Picnic tables and fire pits are provided. Vault toilets are available. No drinking water is available. Leashed pets are permitted.

Reservations, fees: No reservations; Adventure Pass ($30 annual fee) or a $5 daily fee per parked vehicle is required. Open year-round.

Directions: In Pearblossom on Highway 138, turn south on Longview Road and left on Avenue W/Valyermo Road and drive about 20 miles. Drive past the ranger station, turn right on Big Rock Road, and continue up the canyon (past the turnoff for South Fork Camp and past Camp Fenner) to the campground entrance road on the right.

Contact: Angeles National Forest, Santa Clara/Mojave Rivers Ranger District, tel. (661) 944-2187 or fax (661) 944-4698.

12 Sycamore Flat

   7

Sycamore Flat is a developed camp just inside the northern boundary of Angeles National Forest, set at 4,300 feet on the southwest flank of Piñon Ridge. While there are no trails leading out from this camp, a trailhead is available at South Fork, which is two miles to the south.

Location: On Big Rock Creek in Angeles National Forest; map I5, grid a7.

Campsites, facilities: There are 11 sites for tents or RVs up to 22 feet long. Picnic tables and fire grills are provided. Drinking water and vault toilets are available. Leashed pets are permitted.

Reservations, fees: No reservations; Adventure Pass ($30 annual fee) or a $5 daily fee per parked vehicle is required. Open year-round.

Directions: In Pearblossom on Highway 138, turn south on Longview Road and left on Avenue W/Valyermo Road and drive about 20 miles. Drive past the ranger station, turn right on Big Rock Road, and continue about two miles to the campground entrance.

Contact: Angeles National Forest, Santa Clara/Mojave Rivers Ranger District, tel. (661) 944-2187 or fax (661) 944-4698.

13 South Fork

     7

This is an excellent trailhead camp set at 4,500 feet along South Fork Creek. One trail climbs 2.2 miles to the west to Devils Punchbowl County Park, topping out at Devils Chair (the trail includes a steep descent and climb). There are two other options. You can hike south along Big Rock Creek, and another hike heads east on the High Desert National Recreation Trail (also called the Manzanita Trail).

Location: On Big Rock Creek in Angeles National Forest; map I5, grid a7.

Campsites, facilities: There are 21 sites for tents or RVs up to 16 feet long. Picnic tables and fire rings are provided. Vault toilets are available. No drinking water is available. Leashed pets are permitted.

Reservations, fees: No reservations; Adventure Pass ($30 annual fee) or a $5 daily fee per parked vehicle is required. Open May to November.

Directions: In Pearblossom on Highway 138, turn south on Longview Road and left on Avenue W/Valyermo Road and drive about 20 miles. Drive past the ranger station, turn right on Big Rock Road, and continue about four miles up the canyon past the Sycamore Flat campground entrance to the South Fork campground entrance.

Contact: Angeles National Forest, Santa Clara/Mojave River Ranger District, tel. (661) 944-2187 or fax (661) 944-4698.

14 Apple Tree

  6

This is one of four camps set on Big Pines "Highway" near Jackson Lake. This "lake" is more of a pond and is about a half mile to the west, just up the road. Lake and Peavine camps are between Apple Tree and Jackson Lake, while Mountain Oak is just beyond the lake. Any questions? Rangers can answer them at the nearby Big Pines Visitor Information Center and ski complex. The elevation is 6,200 feet.

Location: Near Jackson Lake in Angeles National Forest; map I5, grid a7.

Campsites, facilities: There are eight tent

sites. Picnic tables and fire rings are provided. Drinking water and vault toilets are available. Leashed pets are permitted.

Reservations, fees: No reservations; Adventure Pass ($30 annual fee) or a $5 daily fee per parked vehicle is required. Open year-round.

Directions: From Interstate 15 near Cajon, take Highway 138 west. Turn west on Angeles Crest Highway/Highway 2 and drive five miles to Wrightwood. Continue for three miles to Big Pines. Bear right on Big Pines Highway/County Road N4 and drive two miles to the campground.

Contact: Angeles National Forest, Santa Clara/Mojave Rivers Ranger District, tel. (661) 944-2187 or fax (661) 944-4698.

🔢15 Mountain Oak

 4

This is one of four camps within a mile of little Jackson Lake on Big Pines Highway. The others are Lake, Peavine, and Apple Tree. This camp is about a quarter mile northwest of the lake. The elevation is 6,200 feet.

Location: Near Jackson Lake in Angeles National Forest; map I5, grid a8.

Campsites, facilities: There are 17 sites for tents or RVs up to 18 feet long. Picnic tables and fire pits are provided. Drinking water and flush toilets are available. Groceries and propane gas are nearby. Leashed pets are permitted.

Reservations, fees: Reserve at tel. (877) 444-6777 ($8.65 reservation fee) or website: www.reserveusa.com; $10 per night. Open May through September.

Directions: From Interstate 15 near Cajon, take Highway 138 west. Turn west on Angeles Crest Highway/Highway 2 and drive five miles to Wrightwood. Continue for three miles to Big Pines. Bear right on Big Pines Highway/County Road N4 and drive three miles to the campground.

Contact: Angeles National Forest, Santa Clara/Mojave Rivers Ranger District, tel. (661) 944-2187 or fax (661) 944-4698.

🔢16 Lake

 8

This is a pretty setting on the southeast shore of little Jackson Lake. Of the four camps within a mile, this is the only one right beside the lake. The elevation is 6,100 feet.

Location: On Jackson Lake in Angeles National Forest; map I5, grid a8.

Campsites, facilities: There are eight sites for tents or RVs up to 18 feet long. Picnic tables and fire pits are provided. Drinking water and vault toilets are available. Leashed pets are permitted. Some facilities are wheelchair accessible.

Reservations, fees: Reserve at tel. (877) 444-6777 ($8.65 reservation fee) or website: www.reserveusa.com; $10 per night. Open May through October.

Directions: From Interstate 15 near Cajon, take Highway 138 west. Turn west on Angeles Crest Highway/Highway 2 and drive five miles to Wrightwood. Continue for three miles to Big Pines. Bear right on Big Pines Highway/County Road N4 and it's 2.5 miles to the campground.

Contact: Angeles National Forest, Santa Clara/Mojave Rivers Ranger District, tel. (661) 944-2187 or fax (661) 944-4698.

🔢17 Peavine

 4

This tiny camp is one of four in the immediate area, just a half mile east of little eight-acre Jackson Lake. The elevation is 6,100 feet.

Location: Near Jackson Lake in Angeles National Forest; map I5, grid a8.

Campsites, facilities: There are four tent sites. Picnic tables and fire pits are provided. Drinking water and vault toilets are available. A grocery store and propane gas are nearby. Leashed pets are permitted.

Reservations, fees: No reservations; Adventure Pass ($30 annual fee) or a $5 daily fee per parked vehicle is required. Open May through October.

Directions: From Interstate 15 near Cajon, take Highway 138 west. Turn west on Angeles Crest Highway/Highway 2 and drive five miles to Wrightwood. Continue for three miles to Big Pines. Bear right on Big Pines Highway/County Road N4 and drive 2.5 miles to the campground.

Contact: Angeles National Forest, Santa Clara/Mojave Rivers Ranger District, tel. (661) 944-2187 or fax (661) 944-4698.

18 Jackson Flat Group Camp Walk-In

   4

This is a good spot for a group to overnight, assess themselves, and get information prior to heading out into the surrounding wildlands. The camp is set in the Angeles National Forest high country at 7,500 feet, near the end of a short spur road. Reaching it requires about a 200-yard walk. The Pacific Crest Trail passes just north of camp and can be reached by a short connecting link trail.

Location: Near the Pacific Crest Trail in Angeles National Forest; map I5, grid a7.

Campsites, facilities: There are five group sites that will accommodate 40 to 50 people each. Picnic tables and fire pits are provided. Drinking water and vault toilets are available. Leashed pets are permitted.

Reservations, fees: Reservations requested at tel. (877) 444-6777 ($8.65 reservation fee) or website: www.reserveusa.com; $70 to $85 per night. Open June through September.

Directions: From Interstate 15 near Cajon, take Highway 138 west. Turn west on Angeles Crest Highway/Highway 2 and drive five miles to Wrightwood. Continue for three miles to Big Pines. Bear left and continue on Angeles Crest Highway for two miles. Turn right opposite the sign for Grassy Hollow Campground and drive one mile to the campground parking lot. Walk 200 yards to the campground.

Contact: Angeles National Forest, Santa Clara/Mojave Rivers Ranger District, tel. (661) 944-2187 or fax (661) 944-4698.

19 Blue Ridge

   8

Blue Ridge is set high in Angeles National Forest at 8,000 feet and makes a jump-off spot for a multi-day backpacking trip. The Pacific Crest Trail runs right alongside the camp. Guffy, also aside the PCT, provides an option two miles to the southeast, but it takes a four-wheel-drive vehicle to get there. There are a number of primitive four-wheel-drive routes in the area.

Location: On the Pacific Crest Trail in Angeles National Forest; map I5, grid a8.

Campsites, facilities: There are eight sites for tents or RVs up to 16 feet long. Picnic tables and fire rings are provided. Vault toilets are available. No drinking water is available. Leashed pets are permitted.

Reservations, fees: No reservations; Adventure Pass ($30 annual fee) or a $5 daily fee per parked vehicle is required. Open June through September.

Directions: From Interstate 15 near Cajon, take Highway 138 west. Turn west on Angeles Crest Highway/Highway 2 and drive five miles to Wrightwood. Continue for three miles to Big Pines. Bear left and continue on Angeles Crest Highway for 1.5 miles. Turn left (opposite Inspiration Point) on Blue Ridge Road and drive three miles to the campground.

Contact: Angeles National Forest, Santa Clara/Mojave Rivers Ranger District, tel. (661) 944-2187 or fax (661) 944-4698.

20 Deer Flats Group Camp

   6

This is an ideal spot to bring a troop of Boy or Girl Scouts. It is about a mile from little Crystal Lake, a small lake with decent shoreline bait-dunking for trout. A nearby trail leads north from camp and in two miles intersects with the Pacific Crest Trail, though most just make it to the junction of the PCT, enjoy the views, and return. The Crystal Lake Recreation Area has a network of excellent trails.

Location: Near Crystal Lake in Angeles National Forest; map I5, grid a6.

Campsites, facilities: There are nine group sites for tents or RVs up to 22 feet long, for up to 65 campers each, a total capacity of 300. Picnic tables and fire grills are provided. Drinking water and vault toilets are available. A visitor information center is nearby. Leashed pets are permitted.

Reservations, fees: Reservations required at tel. (877) 444-6777 ($8.65 reservation fee) or website: www.reserveusa.com; $40 per night for a single site, $600 per night for all nine sites. Open mid-May to late September, weather permitting.

Directions: From Interstate 210, take the Azusa Canyon exit. Drive 25 miles north on San Gabriel Canyon Road/Highway 39 to the Crystal Lake Recreation Area and the campground.

Contact: Angeles National Forest, San Gabriel Ranger District, tel. (626) 335-1251 or fax (626) 914-3790.

21 Coldbrook

    7

This roadside camp is set along the North Fork San Gabriel River, with little Crystal Lake to the north. A secret waterfall is hidden off the road, about three miles north on Soldier Creek. To find it, park at the deep bending turn in the road at Soldier Creek, then hike uphill for less than a mile. It's just like a treasure hunt, and it's always a welcome surprise to find the waterfall. The elevation is 3,300 feet.

Location: On the North Fork of the San Gabriel River in Angeles National Forest; map I5, grid b6.

Campsites, facilities: There are 22 sites for tents or RVs up to 22 feet long. Picnic tables and fire rings are provided. Drinking water and vault toilets are available. Leashed pets are permitted.

Reservations, fees: No reservations; $8 per night, $3 for each additional vehicle. Open year-round.

Directions: From Interstate 210, take the Azusa Canyon exit. Drive 18 miles north on San Gabriel Canyon Road/Highway 39 to the campground entrance.

Contact: Angeles National Forest, San Gabriel River Ranger District, tel. (626) 335-1251 or fax (626) 914-3790.

22 Lupine

    7

This little-known, hard-to-reach camp, set at 6,500 feet along Prairie Fork Creek, is used most often by campers with four-wheel-drive rigs. A challenging butt-kicker hike on a primitive trail starts here. The trail is routed from the camp over Pine Mountain Ridge, down into a canyon, and then winds to the east up Dawson Peak—long, difficult, and completed by few.

Location: On Prairie Fork Creek in Angeles National Forest; map I5, grid b8.

Campsites, facilities: There are 11 tent sites. Picnic tables and fire pits are provided. Vault toilets are available. No drinking water is available. Leashed pets are permitted.

Reservations, fees: No reservations; Adventure Pass ($30 annual fee) or a $5 daily fee per parked vehicle is required. Open June through September.

Directions: From Interstate 15 near Cajon, take Highway 138 west. Turn west on Angeles Crest Highway/Highway 2 and drive five miles to Wrightwood. Continue for three miles to Big Pines. Bear left and continue on Angeles Crest Highway/Highway 2 for 1.5 miles. Turn left (opposite Inspiration Point) on Blue Ridge Road (it's a rough, dirt road after the first three miles) and drive 10 miles to the camp.

Contact: Angeles National Forest, Santa Clara/Mojave Rivers Ranger District, tel. (661) 944-2187 or fax (661) 944-4698.

23 Cabin Flat

    7

It takes a four-wheel drive to get here, but that done, you're guaranteed solitude along little Prairie Fork Creek, deep in the Angeles National Forest. To get here, you will pass several other camps, including Guffy and Lupine. A short trail runs beside the stream for about a quarter mile. The elevation is 5,400 feet.

Location: On Prairie Fork Creek in Angeles National Forest; map I5, grid b8.

Campsites, facilities: There are 12 tent sites. Picnic tables, fire pits, and vault toilets are provided. There is no drinking water, so bring your own. Leashed pets are permitted.

Reservations, fees: No reservations; Adventure Pass ($30 annual fee) or a $5 daily fee per parked vehicle is required. Open June through September.

Directions: From Interstate 15 near Cajon, take Highway 138 west. Turn west on Angeles Crest Highway/Highway 2 and drive five miles to Wrightwood. Continue for three miles to Big Pines. Bear left and continue on Angeles Crest Highway for 1.5 miles. Turn left (opposite Inspiration Point) on Blue Ridge Road and drive 12 miles to the campground (the road becomes a rough, dirt road after the first three miles).

Contact: Angeles National Forest, Santa Clara/Mojave Rivers Ranger District, tel. (661) 944-2187 or fax (661) 944-4698.

24 Guffy

    7

A short trail right out of this camp connects with the Pacific Crest Trail, making Guffy a backpacker's special. The area is also popular for campers with four-wheel-drive rigs, with a number of primitive roads in the area. The elevation is 8,300 feet.

Location: On the Pacific Crest Trail in Angeles National Forest; map I5, grid b9.

Campsites, facilities: There are six tent sites. Picnic tables and fire rings are provided. Vault toilets are available. No drinking water is available. Leashed pets are permitted.

Reservations, fees: No reservations; Adventure Pass ($30 annual fee) or a $5 daily fee per parked vehicle is required. Open June through September.

Directions: From Interstate 15 near Cajon, take Highway 138 west. Turn west on Angeles Crest Highway/Highway 2 and drive five miles to Wrightwood. Continue for three miles to Big Pines. Bear left and continue on Angeles Crest Highway for 1.5 miles. Turn left (opposite Inspiration Point) on Blue Ridge Road and drive six miles to the campground (it's a rough, dirt road after the first three miles).

Contact: Angeles National Forest, Santa Clara/Mojave Rivers Ranger District, tel. (661) 944-2187 or fax (661) 944-4698.

25 Manker Flats

   7

This camp is best known for its proximity to Mount Baldy, as well as the nearby trailhead to reach San Antonio Falls. The trail to San Antonio Falls starts at an elevation of 6,160 feet, three-tenths of a mile up the road on the left. From here, it's a 1.5-mile saunter on a ski park maintenance road to the waterfall, a pretty 80-footer. The wild and ambitious can continue six more miles and climb to the top of Mount Baldy (10,064 feet) for breathtaking 360-degree views. Making this all-day butt-kicker is like a baptism for Southern California hikers.

Location: Near Mount Baldy in Angeles National Forest; map I5, grid b9.

Campsites, facilities: There are 21 sites for tents or RVs up to 16 feet long. Picnic tables and fire grills are provided. Drinking water and vault toilets are available. Leashed pets are permitted.

Reservations, fees: No reservations are taken; $12 per night, $4 for each additional vehicle, discounts with Adventure Pass. Open May through September.

Directions: From Ontario, drive six miles north on Highway 83 to Mount Baldy Road.

Drive nine miles north on Mount Baldy Road to the campground.

Contact: Angeles National Forest, San Gabriel River Ranger District, tel. (626) 335-1251 or fax (626) 914-3790.

26 West Fork Walk-In

   8

It takes a circuitous drive and a 4.5- to 6-mile hike to reach this camp, but for backpackers it is worth it. The camp is on the West Fork of the San Gabriel River amid pine woodlands, with two national recreation trails intersecting just south of here. The canyon is deep and the river is beautiful. The elevation is 3,100 feet.

Location: On the West Fork of the San Gabriel River in Angeles National Forest; map I5, grid b4.

Campsites, facilities: There are seven tent sites. Picnic tables and fire rings are provided. Vault toilets are available. No drinking water is available, but stream water is available for use with a filter. Garbage must be packed out. Leashed pets are permitted.

Reservations, fees: No reservations; no camping fee, however, an Adventure Pass ($30 annual fee) or $5 daily fee per parked vehicle is required. Open year-round.

Directions: From Interstate 210 north of Pasadena, take the Angeles Crest Highway/Highway 2 and drive about 14 miles to Mount Wilson Road. Park in the lot there, walk in through the gate (on Red Box-Rincon Road) to the dirt road (not the paved one), and walk six miles to the camp or use the rock stairway on the east side of the parking lot and take that trail to the campground.

Contact: Angeles National Forest, Los Angeles River Ranger District, tel. (818) 790-1151 or fax (818) 790-5392.

27 Valley Forge Walk-In

     8

Valley Forge is a good camp for anglers or hikers who are looking for a short backpacking trip. For hikers, a national recreation trail passes close to the camp. For fishermen, there are small but feisty trout. The elevation is 3,500 feet.

Location: On the San Gabriel River in Angeles National Forest; map I5, grid b4.

Campsites, facilities: There are 12 tent sites. Picnic tables and fire rings are provided. Vault toilets are available. No drinking water is available, but stream water is available for use with a filter. Garbage must be packed out. Leashed pets are permitted.

Reservations, fees: No reservations; Adventure Pass ($30 annual fee) or $5 daily fee per parked vehicle is required. Open year-round, weather permitting.

Directions: From Interstate 210 north of Pasadena, take the Angeles Crest Highway/Highway 2 and drive about 14 miles to Mount Wilson Road. Park in the lot there, walk in through the gate (on Red Box-Rincon Road) to the dirt road (not the paved one), and walk three miles to the campground.

Contact: Angeles National Forest, Los Angeles River Ranger District, tel. (818) 790-1151 or fax (818) 790-5392.

28 Millard

   8

This tiny, pretty camp, set near a creek amid oak and alder woodlands, is best known as the launching point for some excellent hikes. The best is the half-mile hike to Millard Falls, where you actually rock hop your way upstream to the 60-foot waterfall, a drop-dead beautiful sight. On weekends, there can be lots of foot traffic through the campground with hikers on their way to the falls. Another trail out of camp leads to Inspiration Point and continues farther to San Gabriel Peak.

Location: Near Millard Falls in Angeles National Forest; map I5, grid b2.

Campsites, facilities: There are five tent sites. Picnic tables and fire pits are provided.

Vault toilets are available. No drinking water is available. Leashed pets are permitted.

Reservations, fees: No reservations; Adventure Pass ($30 annual fee) or $5 daily fee per parked vehicle is required. Open year-round.

Directions: From Interstate 210 north of Pasadena, take the Lake Avenue exit north to Loma Alta Drive. Turn west on Loma Alta Drive and drive to Chaney Trail Road (at the flashing yellow light). Follow the signs to the camp. It is a walk of several hundred feet from the parking lot to the campground.

Contact: Angeles National Forest, Los Angeles River Ranger District, tel. (818) 790-1151 or fax (818) 790-5392.

29 East Shore RV Park

      7

Considering how close Puddingstone Lake is to so many people, the quality of fishing and water-skiing might be a surprise to newcomers. The lake covers 250 acres and is an excellent recreation facility. For the most part, rules permit water-skiing between 10 a.m. and 4 p.m., making it an excellent lake for fishing for bass and trout (in season) during the morning and evening. In addition, even days are set for water-skiing and boating (but no personal watercraft), and odd days for personal watercraft. A ski beach is available on the north shore, and there is a large, sandy swimming beach on the southwest shore. The lake is just south of Raging Waters in San Dimas, and is bordered to the south by Bonelli Regional County Park.

Location: At Puddingstone Lake; map I5, grid d6.

Campsites, facilities: There are 25 walk-in tent sites and 519 RV sites, many with hookups. Restrooms, showers, recreation room, swimming pool, modem hookups, cable TV, grocery store, propane gas delivery, and coin laundry are available. Leashed pets are permitted. Some facilities are wheelchair accessible.

Reservations, fees: Reservations are accepted; $27 to $29 per night, $2 per person for more than two people, $2 pet fee. Major credit cards accepted. Open year-round.

Directions: From Pomona, drive five miles west on Interstate 10. Take the Fairplex exit north to the first traffic light. Turn left on Via Verde and drive to the first stop sign. Turn right on Campers View and drive into the park.

Contact: East Shore RV Park, tel. (909) 599-8355, tel. (800) 809-3778, or fax (909) 592-7481.

30 Fairplex RV Park

    4

This is what you might call an urban RV park. Then again, the L.A. County Fairgrounds are right across the street, and there's something going on there every weekend. Fishing at Bonelli Park is only 15 minutes away.

Location: In Pomona; map I5, grid d6.

Campsites, facilities: There are 185 pull-through sites for RVs, 158 with full hookups and 27 with water and electric hookups. Restrooms, showers, heated pool and spa, convenience store, sanitary disposal station, and coin laundry are available. Some facilities are wheelchair accessible.

Reservations, fees: Reservations are accepted; $32.45 per night, $1 per night for each extra vehicle, $4 per person per night for more than two people. Major credit cards accepted. Open year-round.

Directions: From Interstate 10 in Pomona, take the Fairplex exit and go left. At the bottom of the hill, turn right on McKinley Avenue. Take McKinley all the way to White Avenue and then turn left. The RV park is at 2200 North White Avenue.

Contact: Fairplex RV Park, 2200 North White Avenue, Pomona, CA 91768; tel. (909) 865-4318 or tel. (909) 593-8915; website: www.fairplex.com.

31 Del Rio Mobile Home and RV Park

    1

This privately operated, urban RV park is about 15 minutes from downtown Los Angeles and 20 minutes from Long Beach.

Location: Near Los Angeles; map I5, grid d1.

Campsites, facilities: There are 30 RV sites with full hookups. Restrooms, drinking water, flush toilets, showers, recreation room, swimming pool, hot tub, and coin laundry are available. Leashed pets are permitted.

Reservations, fees: Reservations are accepted; $20 for two people per night, $1 for each additional camper (maximum of $24 for six or more people). Open year-round.

Directions: From Interstate 710/Long Beach Freeway, take the Florence Avenue exit. Drive west on Florence Avenue to 5246 East Florence Avenue.

Contact: Del Rio Mobile Home and RV Park, tel. (323) 560-2895.

32 Prado Regional Park

     6

Prado Park Lake is the centerpiece of a 2,000-acre recreation-oriented park that features an equestrian center, athletic fields, shooting range, and a golf course. The lake is small and used primarily for paddling small boats and fishing, which is best in the winter and early spring when trout are planted, and then in early summer for catfish and bass.

Location: On Prado Park Lake near Corona; map I5, grid e6.

Campsites, facilities: There are 35 sites for RVs with full hookups, 15 tent sites, and 25 group sites. Picnic tables and fire pits are provided. Restrooms, coin laundry, showers, snack bar, picnic area, playing fields, boat ramp, and boat rentals are available. Leashed pets are permitted. Some facilities are wheelchair accessible.

Reservations, fees: Reservations are accepted at (909) 597-4260 ($2 reservation fee); $16 per night, $1 pet fee. Weekly, monthly, and senior rates are available. Group rates are $11 per unit, with a maximum of two units per site. (There is also a $10 reservation fee for groups.) Proof of insurance for all vehicles is required. Open year-round. Major credit cards accepted.

Directions: From Riverside, take Highway 91 west to Highway 71. Turn north on Highway 71 and proceed four miles to Highway 83/Euclid Avenue. Turn right on Euclid Avenue and drive a mile to the park entrance on the right.

Contact: Prado Regional Park, tel. (909) 597-4260; website: www.san-bernardino.ca.us/parks/prado.

33 Canyon RV Park

    4

In the mad rush to find a spot to park an RV in the area, this Orange County regional park is often overlooked. It is near the Santa Ana River. Side trip possibilities include Chino Hills State Park to the north, Cleveland National Forest to the south, and Lake Matthews to the southeast. The park is also close to Disneyland and Knott's Berry Farm.

Location: Near Disneyland; map I5, grid e6.

Campsites, facilities: There are 110 sites for RVs up to 40 feet long, all with water and electricity. Some tent sites are available. Picnic tables and fire grills are provided. Restrooms, flush toilets, hot showers, modem hookups, sanitary disposal station, seasonal swimming pool, and a playground are available. A convenience store, coin laundry, and propane are also available. Restaurants are nearby. Leashed pets are permitted; no Rottweilers or pit bulls. Some facilities are wheelchair accessible.

Reservations, fees: Reservations are accepted; $25 to $30 per night, $5 for each additional vehicle, $1 per person for more than two people, $1 pet fee. Major credit cards accepted. Open year-round.

Directions: From Interstate 5 in Anaheim, drive east on Highway 91 for 13 miles. Turn left on Gypsum Canyon Road, go under the freeway, and drive about one block to the park entrance on the left.

Contact: Canyon RV, tel. (714) 637-0210 or fax (714) 637-9317; website: www.canyonrvpark.com.

Orangeland RV Park

 1

This park is about five miles east of Disneyland. If the RV parks on West Street near Disneyland are filled, this is a viable alternative.

Location: Near Disneyland; map I5, grid f4.

Campsites, facilities: There are 212 RV sites with picnic tables, fire grills, and full hookups provided. Restrooms, showers, playground, swimming pool, therapy pool, exercise room, coin laundry, store, modem hookups, car wash, shuffleboard court, billiards, sanitary disposal station, ice, and a recreation room are available. Some facilities are wheelchair accessible. Leashed pets are permitted.

Reservations, fees: Reservations are encouraged; $35 per night, $2 for each additional person, $1 pet fee. Major credit cards accepted. Open year-round.

Directions: In Anaheim on Interstate 5, turn east on Katella Avenue and drive two miles, passing Anaheim Stadium and the Santa Ana River, to the park at 1600 West Struck Avenue.

Contact: Orangeland RV Park, tel. (714) 633-0414 or fax (714) 633-9012; website: www.campgrounds.com/orangeland.

35 C. C. Camperland

 1

Camperland is nine blocks south of Disneyland, and that right there is the number-one appeal. Knott's Berry Farm is also close by.

Location: Near Disneyland; map I5, grid f4.

Campsites, facilities: There are 90 sites for tents or RVs. Picnic tables and full hookups are provided. Restrooms, showers, solar-heated swimming pool, coin laundry, sanitary disposal station, and ice are available. Some facilities are wheelchair accessible. Leashed pets are permitted, except in the tent area.

Reservations, fees: Call ahead for available space; $20 to $28 per night for one or two people, $2 for each additional person. Major credit cards accepted. Open year-round.

Directions: From Interstate 5 in Garden Grove, drive south for 1.5 miles on Harbor Boulevard to the campground on the left at 12262 Harbor Boulevard.

Contact: C. C. Camperland, tel. (714) 750-6747.

36 Destiny Anaheim Vacation Park

 1

Some of the most popular RV parks in America are in this area, and it's easy to see why. Knott's Berry Farm is within walking distance (five blocks) and Disneyland is nearby. Plus, where else are you going to park your rig? The park has a western theme.

Location: Near Knott's Berry Farm; map I5, grid f3.

Campsites, facilities: There are 215 RV sites with full hookups for RVs up to 42 feet long and trailers up to 40 feet, and seven tent sites. Restrooms, showers, spa, satellite TV, phone and modem hookups, swimming pool, coin laundry, store, recreation room, and propane gas are available. The tent sites have barbecues. A round-trip shuttle service is available to Disneyland for $2. A grocery store is nearby. Leashed pets are permitted.

Reservations, fees: Reservations are accepted at (800)772-3636; $25 for tent sites, $33 to $45 for RV sites, $2.50 per person per night for more than two people. Major credit cards accepted. Open year-round.

Directions: From Interstate 5 in Anaheim, take the Beach Boulevard exit. Drive south on Beach Boulevard for two miles to the park on the right.

Contact: Destiny Anaheim Vacation Park, tel. (714) 821-4311; website: www.destinyrv.com.

37 Travelers World RV Park

 1

This is one of the most popular RV parks for visitors to Disneyland and other nearby attractions. It is easy to see why, with the park just a half mile from Disneyland. A shuttle service is a great bonus, with buses to Knott's

Berry Farm, the Wax Museum, Universal Studios, Marineland, and the Queen Mary.

Location: Near Disneyland; map I5, grid f4.

Campsites, facilities: There are 335 sites for tents or RVs with full hookups. Picnic tables and fire grills are provided. Restrooms, showers, playground, adult lounge/game room, swimming pool, coin laundry, store, sanitary disposal station, ice, recreation room, RV wash rack, and propane gas are available. Leashed pets are permitted. Some facilities are wheelchair accessible.

Reservations, fees: Call for available space; $30 to $34 per night, $3 per person for more than two people, $2 pet fee. Major credit cards accepted. Open year-round.

Directions: Heading south into Anaheim on Interstate 5, take a left at the Ball Road exit and drive to East Vermont Street. Make a right and proceed to Lemon Street. Make another right on Lemon Street and a right again at Ball Road and continue half a block to the campground on the right at 333 West Ball Road.

Contact: Travelers World RV Park, tel. (714) 991-0100 or fax (714) 991-4939; website: www.travel.to/rv.

38 Bolsa Chica State Beach

 7

This is basically a beachfront parking lot, but a popular one at that. A great little walk is available at the adjacent Bolsa Chica State Reserve, a 1.5-mile loop that provides an escape from the parking lot and entry into the 530-acre nature reserve, complete with egrets, pelicans, and many shorebirds. Lifeguard service is available during the summer. This camp has a seven-day maximum stay during the summer, and a 14-day maximum stay during the winter. This beach camp was remodeled in fall of 2000.

Location: Near Huntington Beach; map I5, grid g2.

Campsites, facilities: There are RV sites with partial hookups available in a parking lot configuration for RVs up to 48 feet long. Fire rings are provided. Restrooms, drinking water, flush toilets, coin showers, sanitary disposal station, picnic areas, bicycle trail, and food service are available. Some facilities are wheelchair accessible, including a paved ramp for wheelchair access to the beach. Leashed pets are permitted at campsites.

Reservations, fees: Reservations at tel. (800) 444-PARK (444-7275) or website: www.reserve america.com; $18 per night. Open year-round.

Directions: From Huntington Beach, drive north on Highway 1 for 1.5 miles to the park.

Contact: Bolsa Chica State Beach, tel. (714) 846-3460 or tel. (714) 492-0802.

39 Huntington City Beach

 7

This is the other of the two popular beachside camps in the immediate area, both prime layovers for Highway 1 cruisers. Bolsa Chica State Beach provides an alternative if this camp is full. The best nearby adventure is the short loop walk at Bolsa Chica State Reserve; see the entry for Bolsa Chica State Beach for more information.

Location: On the Pacific Ocean; map I5, grid h3.

Campsites, facilities: There are 160 sites for RVs up to 30 feet long. Fire rings are provided. Drinking water, flush toilets, and a sanitary disposal station are available. Supplies are available within a mile. No pets are allowed.

Reservations, fees: Reservations are accepted in the winter only; $15 per night. Open November through April.

Directions: From Interstate 405 in Huntington Beach, take the Beach Boulevard exit and drive to Highway 1/Pacific Coast Highway. Turn north, drive to the intersection with First Street, and turn left into the campground parking area.

Contact: Huntington City Beach, tel. (714) 536-5280.

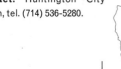

40 Newport Dunes Resort

 9

This privately operated park is set in a pretty spot on the bay, with a beach, boat ramp, and storage area providing bonuses. It is situated on 100 acres of Newport Bay beach, beautiful and private, without public access. That is why this RV park is the most expensive in the Western U.S. Corona del Mar State Beach to the west and Crystal Cove State Park to the south provide possible side trips. The park is five minutes' walking distance from Balboa Island, and is next to the largest estuary in California, the Upper Newport Bay Ecological Reserve.

Location: In Newport Beach; map I5, grid h4.

Campsites, facilities: There are 406 sites for tents or RVs, all with full hookups, and 46 sites for RVs up to 50 feet long. Picnic tables and fire grills are provided. Restrooms, showers, swimming pool and spa, waveless saltwater lagoon, 450-slip marina, satellite TV, planned activities, beach volleyball, coin laundry, grocery store, waterfront restaurant, fitness room, and marina with boat launch ramp are available. Some facilities are wheelchair accessible. Kayaking, windsurfing, and sailing lessons and rentals are also available. Leashed pets are permitted (no Rottweilers or pit bulls).

Reservations, fees: Reserve at tel. (800) 765-7661; $30 to $145 per night, $7 per night for each additional vehicle. Major credit cards accepted. Open year-round.

Directions: From Laguna Hills, take Interstate 405 north to the Highway 55 exit. Turn south on Highway 55 and drive to the junction with Highway 73. Turn south on Highway 73 and drive three miles to Jamboree Road exit. Take that exit and drive south on Jamboree Road for five miles to Back Bay Drive. Turn right and drive a short distance to the resort on the left.

Contact: Newport Dunes Resort, tel. (949) 729-3863 or fax (949) 729-1133; website: www. newportdunes.com.

41 Crystal Cove State Park Hike-In and Horse Camp

 9

This is a gorgeous park that covers 2,200 acres, featuring 3.5 miles of coast and a 1,140-acre underwater park that is popular with scuba divers and snorkelers. The two Moro camps are the most popular. Deer Canyon Camp is sheltered by a grove of oaks, and offers privacy, but no views. The two Moro camps have a ridgetop vantage point and beautiful views of the ocean. El Moro Canyon is shady and tree-lined. Note that El Moro Creek flows only in the wet season. The camps are rarely full. Most of the park's backcountry is grass hills.

Location: On the Pacific Ocean; map I5, grid h4.

Campsites, facilities: There are 32 hike-in/bike-in and equestrian sites at three environmental campgrounds, Lower Moro, Upper Moro, and Deer Canyon, although horses are not allowed at Lower Moro. Picnic tables are provided. Vault toilets are available. No drinking water is available. No fires are permitted. Bring a backpacking stove for cooking. No pets are permitted.

Reservations, fees: No reservations; $7 per night. Registration at visitor center is required. Open year-round.

Directions: On Highway 1 at Corona del Mar, drive south on Highway 1 for three miles to the park entrance on the left (east side of highway). Register at the visitor center. The Moro camps require a 3.5- to 4-mile walk. The Deer Canyon Camp requires a 4.5-mile walk.

Contact: Crystal Cove State Park, (949) 494-3539, or San Clemente District, (949) 492-0802.

42 O'Neill Regional Park

 6

This park is just far enough off the main drag to get missed by most of the RV cruisers on Interstate 5. It is set near Trabuco Canyon, adjacent to Cleveland National Forest to the east. About 70 percent of the campsites are set under a canopy of sycamore and oak. Several roads near this park lead to trailheads into Cleveland National Forest. The elevation is 1,000 feet.

Location: Near Cleveland National Forest; map I5, grid h7.

Campsites, facilities: There are 85 sites for tents or RVs up to 35 feet long, including eight pull-through sites, six equestrian sites for up to three horses per site, and two group camping areas for up to 150 people. Picnic tables and fire rings are provided. Restrooms, drinking water, flush toilets, showers, playground, and a sanitary disposal station are available. Horse corral, water troughs, and an arena are available at equestrian sites. Firewood is sold on site. A nature center is open on weekends. A grocery store is nearby. Leashed pets are permitted. Some facilities are wheelchair accessible.

Reservations, fees: Reservations for group sites only at (949) 858-9365 ($10 reservation fee); individual sites $12 per night, group site prices vary, $4 per night for each extra vehicle, $2 pet fee, $3 per horse. Open year-round.

Directions: From Interstate 5 in Laguna Hills, take the County Road S18/El Toro Road exit and drive east (past El Toro) for 7.5 miles. Turn right onto Live Oak Canyon Road/County Road S19 and drive about three miles to the park on the right.

Contact: O'Neill Regional Park, Orange County, tel. (949) 858-9365; website: www.oc.ca. gov/pfrd/hbp/.

43 Upper San Juan

    6

Two seasonal creeks run through this camp, set under an oak canopy in Cleveland National Forest at an elevation of 1,800 feet. Unfortunately, not all is sanguine. It is close enough to the highway that you can not only hear cars, but see them. Numerous hiking trails save the day. The San Juan Loop Trail is accessible from the campground. It runs 2.2 miles. That trail intersects with the Chiquito Trail, which

extends 8.5 miles into national forest land.

Location: In Long Canyon in Cleveland National Forest; map I5, grid h9.

Campsites, facilities: There are 15 sites for tents or RVs up to 18 feet long. Picnic tables and fire pits are provided. Drinking water and vault toilets are available. A small store is one mile away. Leashed pets are permitted. Some facilities are wheelchair accessible.

Reservations, fees: No reservations; $15 per night with a two-vehicle maximum. Open year-round, weather permitting.

Directions: From Interstate 15 in Lake Elsinore, take the Central exit on to Highway 74 west. Drive west on Highway 74 for 12 miles to Forest Road 6S05 (North Main Divide Road). Turn right and drive five miles to a Y junction with Long Canyon Road. Bear to the left on Long Canyon Road and drive 0.9 miles to the campground entrance on the right.

Contact: Cleveland National Forest, Trabuco Ranger District, tel. (909) 736-1811 or fax (909) 736-3002.

44 Falcon Group Camp

    4

At an elevation of 3,300 feet, Falcon is near the trailheads for the San Juan and Chiquito Trails, which both lead into the backcountry wilderness and the Santa Ana Mountains.

Location: In the Santa Ana Mountains in Cleveland National Forest; map I5, grid h9.

Campsites, facilities: There are three group campsites for tents or RVs. Sage Camp accommodates 30 people and RVs up to 40 feet, Lupine Camp accommodates 40 people and RVs up to 20 feet, and Yarrow Camp accommodates 70 people and RVs up to 30 feet. Picnic tables and fire rings are provided. Drinking water and pit toilets are available. A grocery store is within five miles. Leashed pets are permitted.

Reservations, fees: Reserve at tel. (877) 444-6777 ($8.65 reservation fee) or website: www.reserveusa.com; $35 to

$80 per group per night. Open year-round, weather permitting.

Directions: From Interstate 15 in Lake Elsinore, take the Highway 74 exit and drive 12 miles west. Turn right on Forest Road 6S05 and drive about seven miles to the campground entrance on your left.

Contact: Cleveland National Forest, Trabuco Ranger District, tel. (909) 736-1811 or fax (909) 736-3002.

45 Blue Jay

    4

The few hikers who know of this spot like it and keep coming back, provided they time their hikes when temperatures are cool (nearby Upper San Juan Campground is also set near a great trailhead). The trailheads to the San Juan Trail and the Chiquito Trail, both of which lead into the backcountry wilderness and the Santa Ana Mountains, are adjacent to the camp. A Forest Service map is strongly advised. The elevation is 3,400 feet.

Location: In the Santa Ana Mountains in Cleveland National Forest; map I5, grid h9.

Campsites, facilities: There are 12 sites for tents only and 43 sites for tents or RVs up to 20 feet long. Picnic tables and fire rings are provided. Drinking water and vault toilets are available. A grocery store is within five miles. Leashed pets are permitted.

Reservations, fees: No reservations; $15 per night with a two-vehicle maximum. Open year-round, weather permitting.

Directions: From Interstate 15 at Lake Elsinore, take the Highway 74 exit and drive 12 miles west. Turn right on Forest Road 6S05 and drive about seven miles to the campground entrance on your left.

Contact: Cleveland National Forest, Trabuco Ranger District, tel. (909) 736-1811 or fax (909) 736-3002.

46 El Cariso North Campground

   5

This pretty, shaded spot at 2,600 feet is just inside the border of Cleveland National Forest with Lake Elsinore to the east. On the drive in there are great views to the east, looking down at Lake Elsinore and across the desert country. Hikers should head west to the Upper San Juan Campground.

Location: Near Lake Elsinore in Cleveland National Forest; map I5, grid h9.

Campsites, facilities: There are 24 sites for tents or RVs up to 22 feet long. Picnic tables and fire rings are provided. Drinking water and vault toilets are available. Leashed pets are permitted.

Reservations, fees: No reservations; $15 per night with a two-vehicle maximum. Open year-round, weather permitting.

Directions: From Interstate 5 in San Juan Capistrano, drive 24 miles northeast on Highway 74/Ortega Highway. Or from Interstate 15 in Lake Elsinore, drive 12 miles west on Highway 74 to the campground.

Contact: Cleveland National Forest, Trabuco Ranger District, tel. (909) 736-1811 or fax (909) 736-3002.

47 Caspers Wilderness Park

     6

Highway 74 provides easy access to this regional park. It is a popular spot for picnics and day hikes, and since the campground is not listed with any of the computer-based reservation services, it is overlooked by most out-of-town travelers. A highlight is 30 miles of trails. It is bordered to the south by the San Juan Creek and to the east by the Cleveland National Forest and the San Mateo Canyon Wilderness.

Location: On the San Juan Creek; map I5, grid i8.

Campsites, facilities: There are 42 sites for tents or RVs, 30 additional sites for equestrian campers, six group sites, and 10 RV sites in an overflow area. Picnic tables and barbecues are provided. Drinking water, flush toilets, showers, sanitary disposal station, corrals, stables, museum with interpretive programs, and a playground are available. Pets are not allowed. Some facilities are wheelchair accessible.

Reservations, fees: Reservations are accepted for groups only; $12 per night, $4 per extra vehicle, $3 for each horse per night, group fees vary. Open year-round.

Directions: From San Juan Capistrano, drive 7.5 miles northeast on Highway 74 to the signed park entrance on the left.

Contact: Caspers Wilderness Park, Orange County, tel. (949) 728-0235.

48 Doheny State Beach

  8

It's right in town, but you should still make a reservation to guarantee a site at this popular campground. It is set at the entrance to Dana Point Harbor, a pretty spot with easy access off the highway. A lifeguard service is available in the summer, and campfire and junior ranger programs are also available. San Juan Capistrano provides a nearby side trip.

Location: On Dana Point Harbor; map I5, grid j5.

Campsites, facilities: There are 120 sites for tents or RVs, and one hike-in/bike-in site. No hookups are provided. Picnic tables and fire grills are provided. Restrooms, drinking water, flush toilets, coin showers, sanitary disposal station, exhibits, and food service (summer only) are available. Propane gas is nearby. Some facilities are wheelchair accessible. Leashed pets are permitted in campground only, not on the beach.

Reservations, fees: Reserve at tel. (800) 444-PARK (800-444-7275) or website: www.reserve-america.com; $12 per night, $1 per person for hike-in/bike-in site. Open year-round.

Directions: From San Juan Capistrano, drive three miles south on Interstate 5 to the Pacific Coast Highway/Doheny State Beach exit. Turn left at the second light onto Dana Point Harbor Drive. Drive one block and go left onto Park Lantern. The park entrance is one block away.

Contact: Doheny State Beach, tel. (949) 496-6172 or tel. (949) 492-0802.

49 San Clemente State Beach

  8

Of the three local state beaches that provide easy access and beachfront camping, this one offers full hookups. The others are Doheny State Beach to the north and San Onofre State Beach to the south. A feature at this park is a two-mile long interpretive trail, along with hike-in/bike-in campsites. Surfing camp is held here during the summer. The park was renovated in 2000.

Location: Near San Clemente; map I5, grid j6.

Campsites, facilities: There are 157 sites for tents or RVs, 72 with full hookups, and 12 hike-in/bike-in sites. Picnic tables and fire grills are provided. Flush toilets, coin showers, summer lifeguard service, and summer programs are available. A grocery store, coin laundry, and propane gas are nearby. Some facilities are wheelchair accessible. Leashed pets are permitted.

Reservations, fees: Reserve at tel. (800) 444-PARK (444-7275) or website: www.reserve america.com; $12-18 per night, $1 per person for hike-in/bike-in sites. Open year-round.

Directions: From Interstate 5 in San Clemente, take the Avenida Calafia exit. Drive west for a short distance to the park entrance on the left.

Contact: California State Parks, Orange Coast District, tel. (949) 492-3281 or tel. (949) 492-0802.

BIG BEAR LAKE IS GREAT
FOR WATER-SKIING

MAP 16

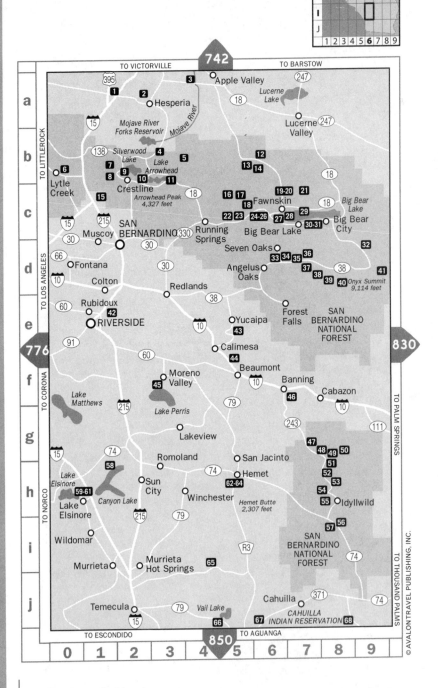

a

395
1   **2**
Apple Valley   247
Hesperia   Lucerne Lake
18   Lucerne Valley   247

b

TO LITTLEROCK
15   Mojave River Forks Reservoir
138   Silverwood Lake   **4**   **5**   **12**
7   Lake Arrowhead   **13**   **14**
8   **9**   **10**   **11**
6   Crestline   18
Lytle Creek   Arrowhead Peak 4,327 feet
15

c

15   **16** **17**   **19-20**   **21**
215   **18**   Fawnskin   18   Big Bear Lake
SAN BERNARDINO   **22** **23**   **24-26**   **27** **28**   **29**
Muscoy   330   Running Springs   **30-31**   Big Bear City
30   30   Big Bear Lake   **32**

d

TO LOS ANGELES
66   30   Seven Oaks   **33** **34** **35** **36**
Fontana   Angelus Oaks   **37**   38   **41**
10   Colton   **38** **39**   **40**   Onyx Summit 9,114 feet
Redlands   38

e

60   Rubidoux
42   Forest Falls   SAN BERNARDINO NATIONAL FOREST
RIVERSIDE   10   Yucaipa
91   **43**

f

TO CORONA
60   Calimesa
44   Beaumont
Moreno Valley   10   Banning   Cabazon
45   **46**   10
Lake Matthews   215   Lake Perris   79   243   111

g

15   Lakeview   **47**
74   Romoland   San Jacinto   **48** **49** **50**
58   74   **51**
Lake Elsinore   Hemet   **52**
Sun City   **62-64**   **53**
59-61   Canyon Lake   Winchester   **54**
Lake Elsinore   Hemet Butte 2,307 feet   **55**   Idyllwild

i

TO NORCO
Wildomar   215   79   **57** **56**
Murrieta   SAN BERNARDINO NATIONAL FOREST   74
Murrieta Hot Springs   R3
65

j

Temecula   79   Vail Lake   Cahuilla   371   74
15   **66**   **67**   CAHUILLA INDIAN RESERVATION   **68**
TO ESCONDIDO   TO AGUANGA

TO PALM SPRINGS   TO THOUSAND PALMS

© AVALON TRAVEL PUBLISHING, INC.

CHAPTER 16

(CONTINUED ON NEXT PAGE)

1 Desert Willow RV Park

    2

This is an RV park for Interstate 15 cruisers looking to make a stop. Silverwood Lake, a 1,000-acre recreation lake with fishing, boating, and water sports, is 16 miles to the south. The elevation is 3,200 feet.

Location: In Hesperia; map I6, grid a1.

Campsites, facilities: There are 176 RV sites with full hookups. Restrooms, hot showers, cable TV hookups, convenience store, groceries, ice, coin laundry, propane gas, swimming pool, indoor spa, recreation room, library, and cable TV are on the premises. Some facilities are wheelchair accessible. Leashed pets are permitted.

Reservations, fees: Reservations at (800) 900-8114; $20 to $22 per night, $2 pet fee. Major credit cards accepted. Open year-round, with limited winter facilities.

Directions: In Hesperia on Interstate 15, take the Main Street exit and drive west to 12624 Main Street West on the right.

Contact: Desert Willow RV Park, tel. (760) 949-0377 or fax (760) 949-4334.

2 Hesperia Lake Campground

      5

This is a slightly more rustic alternative to Desert Willow RV Park in Hesperia. There is a small lake/pond for recreational fishing and there is a small fishing fee, but no fishing license is required. No boating or swimming is allowed, but youngsters usually get a kick out of feeding the ducks and geese that live at the pond.

Location: In Hesperia; map I6, grid a2.

Campsites, facilities: There are 50 sites for tents, trailers, or RVs, 30 with electrical hookups, and two tent-only group sites. Picnic tables and fire pits are provided. Restrooms, drinking water, flush toilets, showers, a playground, horseshoe pits, and a fishing pond are available. Some facilities are wheelchair accessible. Leashed pets are permitted in the camp, but not around the lake.

Reservations, fees: No reservations; $12 to $15 per night, $1 per person per night for more than six people, $2 pet fee. Major credit cards accepted. Open year-round.

Directions: From Interstate 15 in Hesperia, take the Main Street exit and drive 9.5 miles east (the road curves around and becomes Arrowhead Lake Road); the park is on the left.

Contact: Hesperia Lake Campground, tel. (800) 521-6332 or (760) 244-5951.

3 Mojave Narrows Regional Park

 6

Almost no one except the locals knows about this little county park. It is set at 2,000 feet and provides a few recreation options, including a stocked pond for fishing, horseback riding facilities, and trails. The river level fluctuates here, almost disappearing in some years in summer and early fall. Note: The gate closes each evening.

Location: On the Mojave River; map I6, grid a4.

Campsites, facilities: There are 110 sites for tents or RVs, 38 with full hookups. Picnic tables and barbecue grills are provided. Restrooms, drinking water, flush toilets, showers, sanitary disposal station, snack bar, bait house, boat rentals, horse rentals, and horseback riding facilities are available. A grocery store, propane gas, and coin laundry are available three miles from the campground. Leashed pets are permitted.

Reservations, fees: Reservations are accepted for full hookups; $10 to $15 per night, $2 per person per night for more than six people, $1 pet fee. Fishing fees are charged when the river is stocked ($2 to $4). A fishing permit

is required for $3. Major credit cards accepted. Open year-round.

Directions: From Interstate 15 south of Victorville, take the Bear Valley exit and drive east for six miles. Turn left on Ridgecrest, drive three miles, and make a left into the park.

Contact: Mojave Narrows Regional Park, tel. (760) 245-2226; website: www.co.sanbernardino.ca.us/ccr/parks/mojave.htm.

4 Mojave River Forks Regional Park

 5

The bonus here is the full hookups for RVs and the park's proximity to Silverwood Lake, which is only 15 minutes away but does not have any sites with hookups. The sites here are well spaced, but the nearby "river" is usually dry. The elevation is 3,000 feet.

Location: Near Silverwood Lake; map I6, grid b3.

Campsites, facilities: There are 30 sites for tents only, 25 RV sites with full hookups, and 25 sites for tents or RVs. Four group sites are also available. Picnic tables and fire grills are provided. Restrooms, drinking water, flush toilets, showers, and a sanitary disposal station are available. Leashed pets are permitted with proof of shots and/or current license.

Reservations, fees: Reservations are accepted for RV sites only; $15 to $22 per night, $10 per night for each extra vehicle, $3 pet fee. Open year-round.

Directions: From San Bernardino, drive north on Interstate 215/Interstate 15 to the Highway 138 exit. Drive nine miles east to Highway 173. Stay to the left and drive seven miles to the park on the right. From Hesperia on Interstate 15, take the Hesperia exit and drive four miles east to Hesperia. Continue southeast on Highway 173 for nine miles to the park entrance on the left.

Contact: Mojave River Forks Regional Park, tel. (760) 389-2322.

5 Dogwood

 6

So close, but yet so far—that's the paradox between Lake Arrowhead and Dogwood. The lake is just a mile away, but no public boating or swimming is permitted and only extremely limited access for shore fishing is permitted, with the lake ringed by gated trophy homes, each worth millions. The elevation is 5,600 feet. Any questions? The rangers at the Arrowhead Ranger Station, about 1.5 miles down the road to the east, can answer them.

Location: Near Lake Arrowhead in San Bernardino National Forest; map I6, grid b4.

Campsites, facilities: There are 93 sites for tents or RVs up to 22 feet long. Picnic tables and fire grills are provided. Drinking water, flush toilets, and a sanitary disposal station are available. Some facilities are wheelchair accessible. A grocery store and coin laundry are nearby. Leashed pets are permitted.

Reservations, fees: Reserve at tel. (877) 444-6777 ($8.65 reservation fee) or website: www.reserveusa.com; $15 per night, $20 for multifamily units, $5 per night for each extra vehicle. Open May through October.

Directions: From San Bernardino, drive about 15 miles north on Highway 18 to Rimforest. Continue east on Highway 18 for 0.2 mile to Daley Canyon Road. Turn left on Daley Canyon Road, make an immediate right on the Daley Canyon access road, and turn left into the campground.

Contact: San Bernardino National Forest, Mountaintop Ranger Station, tel. (909) 337-2444 or fax (909) 337-1104.

6 Apple White

 5

Nothing like a little insiders' know-how, especially at this camp, set at 3,300 feet near Lytle Creek. You can reach the Middle Fork of Lytle Creek by driving north from Fontana via Serra Avenue to the Lytle Creek area. To get to the stretch of water that is stocked with trout by the Department of Fish and Game, turn west on Middle Fork Road, which is 1.5 miles before the campground at Apple White. The first mile upstream is stocked in early summer.

Location: Near Lytle Creek in San Bernardino National Forest; map I6, grid b0.

Campsites, facilities: There are 42 sites for tents or RVs up to 30 feet long. Picnic tables and fire grills are provided. Restrooms, drinking water, flush toilets, and showers are available. A grocery store is nearby. Leashed pets are permitted. Some facilities are wheelchair accessible.

Reservations, fees: No reservations; $10 per night, $3 per night for each extra vehicle, $15 for double sites. Open year-round.

Directions: From Los Angeles, take Interstate 10 past Ontario to the Interstate 15 north interchange. Drive 11 miles north on Interstate 15 to the Sierra Avenue exit. Turn left, go under the freeway, and continue north for about nine miles to the campground on the right.

Contact: San Bernardino National Forest, Lytle Creek Ranger Station, tel. (909) 887-2576 or fax (909) 887-8197.

7 Mesa

 6

This state park campground is on the west side of Silverwood Lake at 3,355 feet in elevation, bordered by San Bernardino National Forest to the south and high desert to the north. The hot weather and proximity to San Bernardino make it a winner with boaters, who have 1,000 surface acres of water and 13 miles of shoreline to explore. It's a great lake for water-skiing (35-mph speed limit) and water sports (5- mph speed limit in coves), and fair for fishing (trout or bass, according to season) and windsurfing, with afternoon winds usually strong in the spring and early summer. The park has a modest trail system with both nature and bike trails. A bonus is that there are also some hike-in/bike-in campsites.

Location: On Silverwood Lake; map I6, grid b1.

Campsites, facilities: There are 131 sites for tents or RVs up to 32 feet long (with a few for RVs up to 60 feet long), and 15 hike-in/bike-in sites. Picnic tables and fire rings are provided. Restrooms, drinking water, flush toilets, showers, sanitary disposal station, boat ramp, and boat rentals are available. Some facilities are wheelchair accessible. Leashed pets are permitted.

Reservations, fees: Reserve at tel. (800) 444-PARK (800-444-7275) or website: www.reserve america.com; $8 per night, $1 per night per camper for hike-in/bike-in sites. Open year-round.

Directions: From San Bernardino, drive north on Interstate 215/Interstate 15. Continue north on Interstate 15 to the Highway 138 exit in Cajon. Turn right and drive 13 miles east on Highway 138 to the park on the right.

Contact: Silverwood Lake State Recreation Area, tel. (760) 389-2303 or tel. (760) 389-2281.

8 West Fork Group Camps

       6

There are three group camps at this site, Barranca, Rio, and Valle. This is a group camping option at Silverwood Lake (see the entry for Mesa Campground).

Location: At Silverwood Lake; map I6, grid b1.

Campsites, facilities: There are three group camps here for up to 80 people each, and one equestrian site for up to 4 horses and 20 people. Picnic tables and fire rings are provided. Restrooms, drinking water, flush toilets, and coin showers are available. Some facilities are wheelchair accessible. A corral is available at the equestrian site. Picnic areas, fishing, hiking, swimming, boating, food service, and a grocery store are available nearby. A sanitary disposal station is available at Mesa Campground. Leashed pets are permitted.

Reservations, fees: Reserve at tel. (800) 444-PARK (800-444-7275) or website: www.reserve-america.com; $37 group fee per night. Open April through October.

Directions: From San Bernardino, drive north on Interstate 215/Interstate 15. Continue north on Interstate 15 to the Highway 138 exit in Cajon. Turn right and drive 13 miles east on Highway 138 to the park on the right.

Contact: Silverwood Lake State Recreation Area, tel. (760) 389-2303 or tel. (760) 389-2281.

9 Miller Canyon Group

    6

This group camp at Silverwood Lake is about a half mile from the lake. It is set in a pine and redwood forest, with good hiking and biking trails out of camp. The Pacific Crest Trail (no bikes permitted) runs nearby, ideal for hiking and horses. Silverwood Lake is set at 3,355 feet in elevation, bordered by San Bernardino National Forest to the south and high desert to the north.

Location: At Silverwood Lake; map I6, grid b2.

Campsites, facilities: There are three group sites for up to 80 people in each. Picnic tables and fire grills are provided. Restrooms, drinking water, flush toilets, showers, corral, snack bar, and convenience store are available. Some facilities are wheelchair accessible. Leashed pets are permitted.

Reservations, fees: Reserve at tel. (800) 444-PARK (800-444-7275) or website: www.reserve-america.com; $20 per night. Open April through October.

Directions: From San Bernardino, drive north on Interstate 215/Interstate 15. Continue north on Interstate 15 to the Highway 138 exit in Cajon. Turn right and drive about 15 miles east on Highway 138 to the exit for Miller Canyon Campground. Turn right and drive a short distance to the campground.

Contact: Silverwood Lake State Recreation Area, tel. (760) 389-2303 or tel. (760) 389-2281.

10 Camp Switzerland

 7

Well, it really doesn't look much like Switzerland, but this camp is set in a wooded canyon at 4,500 feet below the dam at little Lake Gregory. There are no lake views or even much of a sense that the lake is nearby. Surrounded by the San Bernardino National Forest, Lake Gregory covers just 120 acres, and while no privately owned boats are permitted here, boats can be rented at the marina. No gas motors are permitted, but electric motors are OK. A large swimming beach is available on the south shore (about three-quarter mile away) with a water slide and dressing rooms.

Location: Adjacent to Lake Gregory; map I6, grid b2.

Campsites, facilities: There are 10 sites for tents, 30 sites for RVs with full hookups, and two cabins. Picnic tables are provided. Restrooms, drinking water, flush toilets, coin showers, and propane gas are available nearby. Leashed pets are permitted.

Reservations, fees: Reservations are accepted; individual sites $18 to $22 per night, $5 per night for each extra vehicle, cabins start at $55 per night, $3 pet fee. Open year-round, weather permitting.

Directions: From San Bernardino, drive 14 miles north on Highway 18 to the Crestline/Highway 138 exit. Drive two miles north on Highway 138, turn right on Lake Drive, and continue three miles to the signed campground entrance at the north end of Lake Gregory.

Contact: Camp Switzerland, P.O. Box 967, Crestline, CA 92325; tel. (909) 338-2731.

11 North Shore

 8

Of the two camps at Lake Arrowhead, this one is preferable. It is set at 5,300 feet near the northeastern shore of the lake, which provides decent trout fishing in the spring and early summer. To the nearby north, Deep Creek in San Bernardino National Forest is well worth

exploring; a hike along the stream to fish for small trout or see a unique set of small waterfalls is highly recommended.

Location: On Lake Arrowhead in San Bernardino National Forest; map I6, grid b3.

Campsites, facilities: There are 27 sites for tents or RVs up to 22 feet long. Picnic tables and fire rings are provided. Drinking water and flush toilets are available. Some facilities are wheelchair accessible. A grocery store and a coin laundry are nearby. Leashed pets are permitted.

Reservations, fees: Reserve one at tel. (877) 444-6777 ($8.65 reservation fee) or website: www.reserveusa.com; $12 per night, $5 per night for each extra vehicle. Open May through November.

Directions: From San Bernardino, drive about 17 miles north on Highway 18 to Highway 173. Turn left on Highway 173 and drive north for 1.6 miles to the stop sign. Turn right (still on Highway 173) and drive 2.9 miles to Hospital Road. Turn right and continue 0.1 mile to the top of the small hill. Turn left just past the hospital entrance and you will see the campground.

Contact: San Bernardino National Forest, Mountaintop Ranger Station, tel. (909) 337-2444 or fax (909) 337-1104.

12 Big Pine Flats

 6

This is a favorite staging area for OHV users, with many OHV trails nearby. It is a pretty spot set at 6,800 feet in San Bernardino National Forest and provides a little of both worlds: you are surrounded by wildlands near Redondo Ridge, yet you're not a long drive from Big Bear Lake to the south. Any questions? The firefighters at Big Pine Flats Fire Station, just across the road, can answer them.

Location: In San Bernardino National Forest; map I6, grid b6.

Campsites, facilities: There are 17 sites for tents or RVs up to 32 feet long. Picnic tables and fire grills are provided. Vault toilets are available. No drinking water is available. Leashed pets are permitted.

Reservations, fees: No reservations; $12 per night. Open mid-May to mid-November.

Directions: From San Bernardino, take Highway 30 (the sign says "Mountain Resorts") to Highway 330. Drive about 35 miles on Highway 330 to the dam on Big Bear Lake. Take the left fork (Highway 38) and drive about four miles to the town of Fawnskin. Turn left on Rim of the World Road (it becomes Forest Road 3N14, a dirt road, after a half mile) and drive seven miles to Big Pine Flats Fire Station and the campground on the right.

Contact: San Bernardino National Forest, Big Bear Discovery Center, tel. (909) 866-3437 or fax (909) 866-1781.

13 Big Pine Horse Camp

 3

You might want to bring an apple or a carrot, or maybe some nose plugs. That's because this is a camp for the horse packers adjacent to the Big Pine Flats Fire Station. A trailhead for the Pacific Crest Trail is about two miles to the southeast of the camp via Forest Road 3N14. The elevation is 6,700 feet.

Location: In San Bernardino National Forest; map I6, grid b5.

Campsites, facilities: This camp is expressly for equestrians. There is one group camp that can accommodate up to 60 people and 15 cars or RVs up to 32 feet, and stock. Picnic tables and fire grills are provided. Vault toilets are available. No drinking water is available, but water is available for livestock. Leashed pets are permitted.

Reservations, fees: Reservations are required; reserve at tel. (877) 444-6777 ($8.65 reservation fee) or website: www. reserveusa.com; $50 group fee per night.

Directions: From San Bernardino, take Highway 30 (the sign says "Mountain Resorts") to Highway 330. Drive about 35 miles on Highway 330 to the dam on Big Bear Lake. Take the

left fork (Highway 38) and drive about four miles to the town of Fawnskin. Turn left on Rim of the World Road (it becomes Forest Road 3N14, a dirt road, after a half mile) and drive seven miles. Turn left on Forest Road 3N16 and drive one-quarter mile to the campground on the right.

Contact: San Bernardino National Forest, Big Bear Discovery Center, tel. (909) 866-3437 or fax (909) 866-1781.

14 Ironwood Group Camp

  7

This is a primitive and isolated group camp. It is set at 6,700 feet, nestled in huge pines amid an old-growth forest, and also close to a creek near a meadow. The last two miles of the access road can be rough going for cars.

Location: In San Bernardino National Forest; map I6, grid b6.

Campsites, facilities: There is one group camp that can accommodate up to 25 people and five cars (no trailers or RVs). Picnic tables and fire grills are provided. Vault toilets are available. No drinking water is available. Leashed pets are permitted.

Reservations, fees: Reservations are required; reserve at tel. (877) 444-6777 ($8.65 reservation fee) or website: www. reserve usa.com; $50 group fee per night. Open June through September.

Directions: From San Bernardino, take Highway 30 (the sign says "Mountain Resorts") to Highway 330. Drive about 35 miles on Highway 330 to the dam on Big Bear Lake. Take the left fork (Highway 38) and drive about four miles to the town of Fawnskin. Turn left on Rim of the World Road (it becomes Forest Road 3N14, a dirt road, after a half mile) and drive six miles. Turn left on Forest Road 3N97 and drive two miles to the campground.

Contact: San Bernardino National Forest, Big Bear Discovery Center, tel. (909) 866-3437 or fax (909) 866-1781.

15 San Bernardino- Cable Canyon KOA

      5

This KOA camp provides space for tents as well as RVs. It is set at 2,200 feet and is virtually surrounded by national forest. Silverwood Lake to the east provides a nearby side trip. For information on Silverwood Lake, see the entry for Mesa Campground.

Location: Near Silverwood Lake; map I6, grid c1.

Campsites, facilities: There are 155 tent and RV sites with full or partial hookups, and two camping cabins. Picnic tables are provided. Restrooms, drinking water, flush toilets, showers, coin laundry, modem hookups, playground, swimming pool, recreation room, grocery store, and propane gas are available. Some facilities are wheelchair accessible. Leashed pets are permitted.

Reservations, fees: Reservations accepted at (800) KOA-4155; $19 to $42 per couple per night, cabins are $39 per night, $2 to $4 per extra camper per night. Open year-round. Major credit cards accepted.

Directions: From San Bernardino, drive 16 miles north on Interstate 215. Take the Devore exit, turn right on Devore Road, and drive to Santa Fe Road. Turn right and drive one block. Turn right on Dement Road (which becomes Cable Canyon Road) and continue to 1707 Cable Canyon Road.

Contact: San Bernardino-Cable Canyon KOA, tel. (909) 887-4098; website: www.koacampgrounds.com.

16 Crab Flats

    4

Four-wheel-drive cowboys and dirt-bike enthusiasts often make this a base camp, known as a staging area for off-highway vehicles. It is a developed Forest Service camp set at a fork in the road at 6,200 feet. A challenging jeep road and motorcycle trail is available from here, heading west into Deep Creek Canyon.

Note that Tent Peg Group Camp is just a half mile to the west on Forest Road 3N34 (hiking trails are available there).

Location: Near Crab Creek in San Bernardino National Forest; map I6, grid c5.

Campsites, facilities: There are 29 sites for tents or RVs up to 15 feet long. Drinking water, vault toilets, picnic tables, and fire rings are provided. Leashed pets are permitted.

Reservations, fees: Reserve at tel. (877) 444-6777 ($8.65 reservation fee) or website: www.reserveusa.com; $10 per night, $5 per night for each extra vehicle. Open mid-May through October.

Directions: From San Bernardino, take Highway 30 to Highway 330 and continue on Highway 330 to Running Springs. Drive east on Highway 18 (two miles east of the town of Running Springs). Turn left on Green Valley Road and drive three miles to Forest Road 3N16 (a dirt road). Turn left and drive four miles. You will cross two creeks which vary in depth depending on season; high clearance is recommended but is not necessary if you are careful. After four miles, bear left at the intersection, and you'll see the campground entrance on your right.

Contact: San Bernardino National Forest, Mountaintop Ranger Station, tel. (909) 337-2444 or fax (909) 337-1104.

17 Green Valley

     7

This camp sits along pretty Green Valley Creek at an elevation of 7,000 feet. Little Green Valley Lake is a mile to the west. The lake is stocked with trout by the Department of Fish and Game and is also a good spot to take a flying leap and belly flop.

Location: Near Green Valley Lake in San Bernardino National Forest; map I6, grid c5.

Campsites, facilities: There are 37 sites for tents or RVs up to 22 feet long. Picnic tables and grills are provided. Drinking water and flush toilets are available. A grocery store and coin laundry are nearby. Leashed pets are permitted.

Reservations, fees: Reservations may be made at tel. (877) 444-6777 ($8.65 reservation fee) or website: www.reserveusa.com; $12 per night, $5 per night for each extra vehicle. Open May through September.

Directions: From San Bernardino, take Highway 30 to Highway 330; continue on Highway 330 to Running Springs. Drive east on Highway 18 to Green Valley Road. Turn left and go four miles up the road to the campground (one mile past town of Green Valley Lake).

Contact: San Bernardino National Forest, Mountaintop Ranger Station, tel. (909) 337-2444 or fax (909) 337-1104.

Shady Cove Group Walk-In

 7

The highlight here is the adjacent short looped trail that is routed through the Children's Forest. The camp is excellent for Boy Scout and Girl Scout troops. The elevation is 7,500 feet.

Location: Near the Children's Forest in San Bernardino National Forest; map I6, grid c5.

Campsites, facilities: There are two group campsites which can accommodate a maximum of 30 at one site and 70 at the other. When reserved together, the two sites are allowed a maximum of 100 people with a limit of 15 cars (no trailers or RVs). Picnic tables and fire grills are provided. Drinking water and flush toilets are available. Note: The camp is gated for safety; groups are given a key. Leashed pets are permitted.

Reservations, fees: Reservations are required; reserve at tel. (877) 444-6777 ($8.65 reservation fee) or website: www. reserve usa.com; $30 to $100 per night. Open May through September.

Directions: From San Bernardino, drive about 17 miles north on Highway 18 to the Mountaintop Ranger Station. Continue east on Highway 18 for seven miles (past the town of Running Springs). Turn south (right) on Keller Peak Road (just past Deer Lick Fire Station) and drive four miles to the Children's Forest.

Bear left to the parking area. The sites are 100 yards from the parking area.

Contact: San Bernardino National Forest, Mountaintop Ranger Station, tel. (909) 337-2444 or fax (909) 337-1104.

Hanna Flat

 8

This is one of the largest, best maintained, and most popular of the Forest Service camps in the Big Bear Lake District (Serrano Campground is the most popular). All the trees and vegetation provide seclusion for individual sites. There is great forest scenery with many hardwood trees, including oak and mountain mahogany. The camp is set at 7,000 feet on the slopes on the north side of Big Bear Lake, just under three miles from the lake. Big Bear is a beautiful mountain lake covering over 3,000 acres, with 22 miles of shoreline and often excellent trout fishing and water-skiing. A trailhead for the Pacific Crest Trail is a mile by road north of the camp.

Location: Near Big Bear Lake in San Bernardino National Forest; map I6, grid c6.

Campsites, facilities: There are 69 sites for tents and 19 sites for tents or RVs up to 32 feet long. Picnic tables and fire grills are provided. Drinking water and flush toilets are available. Some facilities are wheelchair accessible. Leashed pets are permitted.

Reservations, fees: Reservations are accepted at tel. (877) 444-6777 ($8.65 reservation fee) or website: www.reserveusa.com; $15 per night, $5 per night for a second vehicle. Open May through September.

Directions: From San Bernardino, take Highway 30 (the sign says "Mountain Resorts") to Highway 330. Drive about 35 miles on Highway 330 to the dam on Big Bear Lake. Take the left fork (Highway 38) and drive about four miles to the town of Fawnskin. Turn left on Rim of the World Road (it becomes Forest Road 3N14, a dirt road, after a half mile) and drive three miles to the campground on the left.

Contact: San Bernardino National Forest, Big Bear Discovery Center, tel. (909) 866-3437 or fax (909) 866-1781.

20 Gray's Peak Group Camp

 4

The appeal of this primitive group camp is its proximity to Big Bear Lake, with the camp just three miles northwest of the lake, set at 7,200 feet. Gray's Peak (7,952 feet) is about a mile south of the camp, but there is no direct access to the peak. The drive is not recommended for trailers or large RVs.

Location: Near Big Bear Lake in San Bernardino National Forest; map I6, grid c7.

Campsites, facilities: There is one group campsite that will accommodate up to 40 people and eight cars (limited use of trailers and RVs up to 32 feet). Picnic tables and fire grills are provided. Vault toilets are available. No drinking water is available. Leashed pets are permitted.

Reservations, fees: Reservations are accepted at tel. (877) 444-6777 ($8.65 reservation fee) or website: www.reserveusa.com; $50 per night. Open June through September.

Directions: From San Bernardino, take Highway 30 (the sign says "Mountain Resorts") to Highway 330. Drive about 35 miles on Highway 330 to the dam on Big Bear Lake. Take the left fork (Highway 38) and drive about four miles to the town of Fawnskin. Turn left on Rim of the World Road (it becomes Forest Road 3N14, a dirt road, after a half mile) and drive 1.2 miles to Forest Road 2N13. Turn left and drive about a mile to the campground on the right.

Contact: San Bernardino National Forest, Big Bear Discovery Center, tel. (909) 866-3437 or fax (909) 866-1781.

21 Tanglewood Group Camp

 4

This primitive group camp is off an old spur road with the Pacific Crest Trail trailhead the primary highlight. It is set at 7,400 feet in a flat but wooded area northeast of Big Bear Lake. It is about a 10- to 15-minute drive from Big Bear City.

Location: On the Pacific Crest Trail in San Bernardino National Forest; map I6, grid c7.

Campsites, facilities: There is one group campsite that will accommodate up to 40 people and eight cars (limited use of trailers or RVs up to 32 feet long). Picnic tables and fire grills are provided. Pit toilets are available. No drinking water is available. Leashed pets are permitted.

Reservations, fees: Reservations are required; reserve at tel. (877) 444-6777 ($8.65 reservation fee) or website: www.reserveusa.com; $50 group fee per night. Open June through September.

Directions: From San Bernardino, take Highway 30 (the sign says "Mountain Resorts") to Highway 330. Drive about 35 miles on Highway 330 to the dam on Big Bear Lake. Take the left fork (Highway 38) and drive about 10 miles. Turn left on Van Dusen Canyon Road/Forest Road 3N09 and drive on the dirt road for four miles. Turn right on Forest Road 3N16, drive 1.7 miles, turn right on Forest Road 3N79, and drive one-half mile to the campground. Trailers are not recommended.

Contact: San Bernardino National Forest, Big Bear Discovery Center, tel. (909) 866-3437 or fax (909) 866-1781.

22 Tent Peg Group

 10

This camp would be a lot easier to reach with a helicopter than a vehicle. But that's why Tent Peg is a well-loved camp for the few who book it: a primitive camp for groups at 5,400 feet, complete with trailhead. A rough jeep road heads out of camp to the west and down into Deep Creek. In addition, there is a trailhead for a three-mile hike down the canyon to the south to Fisherman's Hike-In Group Campground, set along Deep Creek. The trout are small but willing, in a beautiful setting.

Location: Near the Pacific Crest Trail in San Bernardino National Forest; map I6, grid c5.

Campsites, facilities: There is one group camp that will accommodate 10 to 30 people and five cars. Picnic tables and fire grills are provided. Vault toilets are available. No drinking water is available. A grocery store and coin laundry are five miles away. Leashed pets are permitted.

Reservations, fees: Reservations are required; reserve at tel. (877) 444-6777 ($8.65 reservation fee) or website: www. reserve usa.com; $50 per night. Open mid-May through October.

Directions: From San Bernardino, take Highway 30 to Highway 330 and continue on Highway 330 to Running Springs. Drive east on Highway 18 (past the town of Running Springs), turn left on Green Valley Road, and drive three miles to Forest Road 3N16 (a dirt road). Turn left and drive four miles. You will cross two creeks which vary in depth depending on season; high clearance is recommended but not necessary if you are careful. After four miles, you will come to an intersection. Bear left on Forest Road 3N34 and drive west for one mile; the campground is on the left.

Contact: San Bernardino National Forest, Mountaintop Ranger Station, tel. (909) 337-2444 or fax (909) 337-1104.

23 Fisherman's Hike-In Group Camp

     10

Get here and you join the 5 Percent Club. Fisherman's Hike-In Group Camp is a secluded, wooded campground set deep in San Bernardino National Forest at 5,400 feet. Deep Creek runs alongside providing stream trout fishing and a beautiful setting. It's worth the significant effort required to get here. Once here, you will find a primitive route along the creek (which looks more like a deer trail than a hiking trail) that anglers use to tromp along the stream. The trout are small but well col-

ored, and the first cast into the head of a pool often results in a strike.

Location: On Deep Creek in San Bernardino National Forest; map I6, grid c5.

Campsites, facilities: There are four group campsites that will accommodate 10 to 30 people. Picnic tables and fire grills are provided. Vault toilets are available. No drinking water is available. Garbage must be packed out. Leashed pets are permitted.

Reservations, fees: Reservations are required; reserve at tel. (877) 444-6777 ($8.65 reservation fee) or website: www. reserve usa.com; $10 per site. Open mid-May to mid-October, weather permitting.

Directions: From San Bernardino, take Highway 30 to Highway 330; continue on Highway 330 to Running Springs. Drive east on Highway 18 (two miles east of the town of Running Springs), turn left on Green Valley Road, and drive three miles to Forest Road 3N16 (a dirt road). Turn left and drive four miles. You will cross two creeks which vary in depth depending on season; high clearance is recommended but not necessary if you are careful. After four miles, you will come to an intersection. Bear left on Forest Road 3N34 and drive west for 1.3 miles to Forest Service Trail 2W07 on your left. Park and follow this hiking trail southwest for 2.5 miles to Deep Creek; the campground is on the other side of the creek.

Contact: San Bernardino National Forest, Mountaintop Ranger Station, tel. (909) 337-2444 or fax (909) 337-1104.

24 Siberia Creek Hike-In Group Camp

    7

This is a primitive area that requires a fairly steep three-mile hike. Your reward is solitude at a camp that will hold up to 40 people. The camp is set near the confluence of Siberia Creek and larger Bear Creek. The latter is the major feeder stream into Big

Bear Lake, and both provide a good opportunity to try sneak-fishing techniques for small rainbow trout. The elevation is 4,800 feet.

Location: In San Bernardino National Forest; map I6, grid c6.

Campsites, facilities: There is one group campsite that will accommodate up to 40 people. Fire rings are provided, but that's all. No drinking water is available. Garbage must be packed out. Leashed pets are permitted.

Reservations, fees: Reservations at (909) 866-3437; no camping fee. Adventure Pass ($30 annual fee) or a $5 daily fee per parked vehicle is required.

Directions: From San Bernardino, take Highway 30 (the sign says "Mountain Resorts") to Highway 330. Drive about 20 miles on Highway 330 to just past Snow Valley Ski Area. Take the Camp Creek Trail turnoff and follow the signs to the trailhead. Park and hike three miles to the camp.

Contact: San Bernardino National Forest, Big Bear Discovery Center, tel. (909) 866-3437 or fax (909) 866-1781.

Bluff Mesa Group Camp

 7

Bluff Mesa Group Camp is one of several camps south of Big Bear Lake. A highlight here is the trailhead (signed on the access road on the way in) for the half-mile walk to the Champion Lodgepole Pine, the largest lodgepole pine in the world: 400 years old, 112 feet tall, with a circumference of 20 feet. Many Forest Service roads are available nearby for self-planned side trips. The elevation is 7,600 feet.

Location: Near Big Bear Lake in San Bernardino National Forest; map I6, grid c6.

Campsites, facilities: There is one group campsite that will accommodate up to 40 people and eight cars. Picnic tables and fire grills are provided. Pit toilets are available. No drinking water is available. Leashed pets are permitted.

Reservations, fees: Reservations are requested; reserve at tel. (877) 444-6777 ($8.65

reservation fee) or website: www.reserve usa.com; $50 group fee per night. Open June through September.

Directions: From San Bernardino, take Highway 30 (the sign says "Mountain Resorts") to Highway 330. Drive about 35 miles on Highway 330 to the dam on Big Bear Lake. Bear right at the dam on Highway 18 and drive about four miles. Turn right on Mill Creek Road and drive about 1.5 miles to the sign at the top of the hill. Turn right on Forest Road 2N10 and drive three miles on the dirt road. Turn right on Forest Road 2N86 and drive a quarter mile to the campground.

Contact: San Bernardino National Forest, Big Bear Discovery Center, tel. (909) 866-3437 or fax (909) 866-1781.

Boulder Group Camp

  6

This is a primitive camp at 7,500 feet elevation, just far enough away from some prime attractions to make you wish you could move the camp to a slightly different spot. The headwaters of Metcalf Creek are hidden in the forest on the other side of the road, tiny Cedar Lake is about a half-mile drive north, and Big Bear Lake is about two miles north. You get the idea.

Location: Near Big Bear Lake in San Bernardino National Forest; map I6, grid c6.

Campsites, facilities: There is one group campsite that will accommodate up to 40 people and eight cars (limited use of trailers and RVs up to 32 feet). Picnic tables and fire grills are provided. Pit toilets are available. No drinking water is available. A grocery store and coin laundry are nearby. Leashed pets are permitted.

Reservations, fees: Reservations are required; reserve at tel. (877) 444-6777 ($8.65 reservation fee) or website: www. reserve usa.com; $50 group fee per night. Open June through September.

Directions: From San Bernardino, take Highway 30 (the sign says "Mountain Resorts") to

Highway 330. Drive about 35 miles on Highway 330 to the dam on Big Bear Lake. Bear right at the dam on Highway 18 and drive about four miles to Mill Creek Road. Turn right on Forest Road 2N10 and drive about two miles. Turn right on Forest Road 2N10B and drive to the camp.

Contact: San Bernardino National Forest, Big Bear Discovery Center, tel. (909) 866-3437 or fax (909) 866-1781.

27 Holcomb Valley

    7

This camp is set near the Holcomb Valley Historic Area, 7,400 feet, in the mountains about four miles north of Big Bear Lake. On the way in on Van Dusen Canyon Road you will pass a trailhead for the Pacific Crest Trail (two miles southeast of the camp.) From here you can make the two-mile climb southwest to Bertha Peak, 8,198 feet, overlooking Big Bear to the south.

Location: Near the Pacific Crest Trail in San Bernardino National Forest; map I6, grid c6.

Campsites, facilities: There are 19 sites for tents or RVs up to 32 feet long. Picnic tables and fire grills are provided. Pit toilets are available. No drinking water is available. Garbage service provided only in summer. Leashed pets are permitted.

Reservations, fees: No reservations; $10 per night. Open year-round, weather permitting.

Directions: From San Bernardino, take Highway 30 (the sign says "Mountain Resorts") to Highway 330. Drive about 35 miles on Highway 330 to the dam on Big Bear Lake. Take the left fork (Highway 38) and drive about 10 miles. Turn left on Van Dusen Canyon Road/Forest Road 3N09 (a dirt road) and drive three miles. Turn left on Forest Road 3N16 to the campground on the right.

Contact: San Bernardino National Forest, Big Bear Discovery Center, tel. (909) 866-3437 or fax (909) 866-1781.

28 Holloway's Marina and RV Park

     6

This privately operated RV park (no tent sites) is a good choice at Big Bear Lake with boat rentals, ramp, and full marina available. Big Bear is the jewel of Southern California's lakes, covering over 3,000 surface acres with 22 miles of shoreline. Its cool waters make for excellent trout fishing, and yet, by summer, it has heated up enough to make for superb water-skiing. A bonus in the summer is that a breeze off the lake keeps the temperature in the mid-80s.

Location: On Big Bear Lake; map I6, grid c7.

Campsites, facilities: There are 100 RV sites with full hookups, two with partial hookups, and seven with no hookups. No tent sites are available. Picnic tables and fire grills are provided. Restrooms, drinking water, flush toilets, showers, sanitary disposal station, cable TV, convenience store, ice, propane gas, coin laundry, playground, and a full marina with boat rentals are on the premises. Leashed pets are permitted.

Reservations, fees: Reservations are suggested; $25 to $40 per night, $5 per night for each extra vehicle. Major credit cards accepted. Open year-round, weather permitting.

Directions: From San Bernardino, take Highway 30 (the sign says "Mountain Resorts") to Highway 330. Drive about 17 miles to Highway 18 and bear right on Highway 18. Drive another 17 miles to the dam. Three miles past the dam, turn left on Edgemoor Road and drive one-half mile to the park on the left.

Contact: Holloway's Marina and RV Park, tel. (909) 866-5706 or tel. (800) 448-5335.

29 Serrano

       8

This campground opened in the 1990s and became the first National Forest campground to offer state-of-the-art restrooms and hot showers. That is why it costs so much to camp here. Regardless, it has since become the most popular campground in the region. Location is also a big plus, as this is one of the few camps at Big Bear within walking distance of the lakeshore. Another bonus is a paved trail that is wheelchair accessible. Want more? Big Bear is the jewel of Southern California lakes, the Lake Tahoe of the South, with outstanding trout fishing and water-skiing. A trailhead for the Pacific Crest Trail is nearby, and Canada is only 2,200 miles away. The elevation is 7,000 feet.

Location: On Big Bear Lake in San Bernardino National Forest; map I6, grid c7.

Campsites, facilities: There are 132 sites for tents or RVs up to 36 feet long, including 30 sites that offer full hookups. Picnic tables and fire rings are provided. Restrooms, drinking water, flush toilets, showers, and a sanitary disposal station are available. Some facilities are wheelchair accessible. A store is nearby. Leashed pets are permitted.

Reservations, fees: Reserve at tel. (877) 444-6777 ($8.65 reservation fee) or website: www.reserveusa.com; $17 per night, double tents sites are $34, RV sites are $27. Open mid-April to mid-November.

Directions: From San Bernardino, take Highway 30 (the sign says "Mountain Resorts") to Highway 330. Drive about 33 miles on Highway 330 to the dam on Big Bear Lake. Take the left fork (Highway 38), drive about 2.5 miles east of Fawnskin, and watch for the Serrano Campground signs. The campground entrance is off North Shore Lane.

Contact: San Bernardino National Forest, Big Bear Discovery Center, tel. (909) 866-3437 or fax (909) 866-1781.

30 Pineknot

     6

This popular, developed Forest Service camp is set just east of Big Bear Lake Village (on the southern shore of the lake) about two miles from the lake. It is a popular spot for mountain biking, with several ideal routes available. Of the camps at Big Bear, this is the closest to supplies. The elevation is 7,000 feet.

Location: Near Big Bear Lake in San Bernardino National Forest; map I6, grid c7.

Campsites, facilities: There are 52 sites for tents and RVs up to 45 feet long. Picnic tables and fire grills are provided. Drinking water and flush toilets are available. Some facilities are wheelchair accessible. A grocery store and coin laundry are nearby. Leashed pets are permitted.

Reservations, fees: Reservations are accepted at tel. (877) 444-6777 ($8.65 reservation fee) or website: www.reserveusa.com; $15 per night. Open mid-May through September.

Directions: From San Bernardino, take Highway 30 (the sign says "Mountain Resorts") to Highway 330. Drive about 35 miles on Highway 330 to the dam on Big Bear Lake. Bear right at the dam on Highway 18 and drive about six miles to Summit Boulevard. Turn right, drive through the parking area, and make a left just before the gate to the ski area. Drive one-quarter mile to the campground on the right.

Contact: San Bernardino National Forest, Big Bear Discovery Center, tel. (909) 866-3437 or fax (909) 866-1781.

31 Buttercup Group Camp

   5

This is a forested camp designed for large groups looking for a developed site near Big Bear Lake. It is about four miles from the southeast side of the lake, just outside the Snow Summit Ski Area. The elevation is 7,000 feet.

Location: Near the town of Big Bear Lake in San Bernardino National Forest; map I6, grid c7.

Campsites, facilities: There is one group campsite that will accommodate up to 40 people and eight cars (limited use of trailers or RVs up to 32 feet long). Picnic tables and fire rings are provided. Drinking water and portable toilets are available. A grocery store and coin laundry are nearby. Leashed pets are permitted.

Reservations, fees: Reservations are requested; reserve at tel. (877) 444-6777 ($8.65 reservation fee) or website: www. reserve usa.com; $75 group fee per night. Open June through September.

Directions: From San Bernardino, take Highway 30 (the sign says "Mountain Resorts") to Highway 330. Drive about 35 miles on Highway 330 to the dam on Big Bear Lake. Bear right at the dam on Highway 18 and drive about six miles to Summit Boulevard. Turn right, drive through the parking area, and make a left just before the gate to the ski area. Drive one-half mile (past Pineknot Camp) to the campground on the right.

Contact: San Bernardino National Forest, Big Bear Discovery Center, tel. (909) 866-3437 or fax (909) 866-1781.

32 Juniper Springs Group Camp

   3

This is a little-known group camp, set at 7,700 feet in a desert-like area about 10 miles east of Big Bear Lake. It is little known because there are not a lot of reasons to camp here. You need to be creative. Got a Scrabble game? Want to watch the junipers grow? Or maybe watch the features of the land change colors as the day passes? You get the idea.

Location: In San Bernardino National Forest; map I6, grid d9.

Campsites, facilities: There is one group camp that will accommodate up to 40 people and eight cars (limited use of trailers and RVs up to 32 feet long). Picnic tables and fire grills are provided. Pit toilets are available. No drinking water is available. Leashed pets are permitted.

Reservations, fees: Reservations are required; reserve at tel. (877) 444-6777 ($8.65 reservation fee) or website: www. reserve usa.com; $50 per night. Open June through September.

Directions: From Interstate 10 in Redlands, drive about 40 miles east on Highway 38 (1.5 miles past Onyx Summit) to the campground entrance road (Forest Road 2N01) on the right. Turn in on the dirt road and drive three miles. Make a right (opposite the sign that says 2N04 on your left) and drive into the campground.

Contact: San Bernardino National Forest, Big Bear Discovery Center, tel. (909) 866-3437 or fax (909) 866-1781.

33 Council Group Camp

  5

This is a group camp in a pretty wooded area across the road from little Jenks Lake (there is a nice, easy walk around the lake) and a few miles north of the northern border of the San Gorgonio Wilderness. There are several other camps in the area.

Location: Near the San Gorgonio Wilderness in San Bernardino National Forest; map I6, grid d6.

Campsites, facilities: There is one group campsite for tents only that will accommodate up to 50 people and 10 cars (no trailers or RVs). Picnic tables and fire rings are provided. Drinking water and vault toilets are available. Leashed pets are permitted.

Reservations, fees: Reserve at tel. (877) 444-6777 ($8.65 reservation fee) or website: www. reserveusa.com; $100 group fee per night. Open May through November.

Directions: From Interstate 10 in Redlands, drive 26 miles east on Highway 38 to the campground on the left.

Contact: San Bernardino National Forest, Mill Creek Ranger Station, tel. (909) 794-1123 or fax (909) 794-1125.

34 Barton Flats

    7

This is one of the more developed Forest Service camps in San Bernardino National Forest. The camp is set at 6,300 feet near the northwest end of Jenks Lake, a small, pretty lake with good hiking and a picnic area. Barton Creek, a small stream, runs nearby although it may be waterless in late summer. The San Gorgonio Wilderness, one mile to the south, is accessible via Forest Service roads to the wilderness area trailhead. Permits are required for overnight camping within the wilderness boundaries and are available at Forest Service ranger stations. For those driving in on Highway 38, stop at the Mill Creek Ranger Station in Redlands.

Location: Near Jenks Lake in San Bernardino National Forest; map I6, grid d7.

Campsites, facilities: There are 47 sites for RVs up to 45 feet long. Picnic tables and fire grills are provided. Drinking water and flush toilets are available. Some facilities are wheelchair accessible. Leashed pets are permitted.

Reservations, fees: Reserve at tel. (877) 444-6777 ($8.65 reservation fee) or website: www.reserveusa.com; $20 per night, $30 for multifamily sites, $5 per night for each additional vehicle. Open mid-May through October.

Directions: From Interstate 10 in Redlands, drive 27.5 miles east on Highway 38 to the campground on the left.

Contact: San Bernardino National Forest, Mill Creek Ranger Station, tel. (909) 794-1123 or fax (909) 794-1125.

35 San Gorgonio

 7

San Gorgonio is one in a series of Forest Service camps along Highway 38 near Jenks Lake. See the entry for Barton Flats for details.

Location: Near the San Gorgonio Wilderness in San Bernardino National Forest; map I6, grid d7.

Campsites, facilities: There are 55 sites for RVs up to 43 feet long. Picnic tables and fire grills are provided. Restrooms, drinking water, flush toilets, and showers are available. Leashed pets are permitted. Some facilities are wheelchair accessible.

Reservations, fees: Reserve at tel. (877) 444-

6777 ($8.65 reservation fee) or website: www. reserveusa.com; $20 per night, $30 for multifamily sites, $5 per night for each additional vehicle. Open mid-May through October.

Directions: From Interstate 10 in Redlands, drive 28 miles east on Highway 38 to the campground.

Contact: San Bernardino National Forest, Mill Creek Ranger Station, tel. (909) 794-1123 or fax (909) 794-1125.

36 Oso & Lobo Group

 6

Oso and Lobo Group Camps are set directly adjacent to each other at 6,600 feet elevation. The camps are about three-quarters of a mile from the Santa Ana River. Little Jenks Lake is two miles away to the west, and the northern border of the San Gorgonio Wilderness is just a few miles to the south.

Location: Near the San Gorgonio Wilderness in San Bernardino National Forest; map I6, grid d7.

Campsites, facilities: Oso will accept up to 100 people and 20 cars (limited use of trailers and RVs), and Lobo accepts up to 75 people and 15 cars. Picnic tables and fire grills are provided. Drinking water and flush toilets are available. Leashed pets are permitted.

Reservations, fees: Reserve at tel. (877) 444-6777 ($8.65 reservation fee) or website: www.reserveusa.com; $150 per night for Lobo, $200 per night for Oso. Open April through October, weather permitting.

Directions: From Interstate 10 in Redlands, drive 29 miles east on Highway 38 to the campground entrance road on the left.

Contact: San Bernardino National Forest, Mill Creek Ranger Station, tel. (909) 794-1123 or fax (909) 794-1125.

37 South Fork

 7

This is an easy-access Forest Service camp just off Highway 38, set at 6,400 feet near the headwaters of the South Fork Santa Ana River. It is part of the series of camps in the immediate area, just north of the San Gorgonio Wilderness. This one is a four-mile drive from little Jenks Lake. See the entry for Barton Flats for more details.

Location: Near the Santa Ana River in San Bernardino National Forest; map I6, grid d7.

Campsites, facilities: There are 24 sites for tents or RVs up to 30 feet long. Picnic tables and fire rings are provided. Drinking water and vault toilets are available. Leashed pets are permitted.

Reservations, fees: No reservations; $15 per night, $5 per night for each additional vehicle. Open mid-May through mid-October.

Directions: From Interstate 10 in Redlands, drive 29.5 miles east on Highway 38 to the campground entrance road.

Contact: San Bernardino National Forest, Mill Creek Ranger Station, tel. (909) 794-1123 or fax (909) 794-1125.

⏳ Skyline Group Camp

 6

Skyline Group Camp is set at an elevation of 6,900 feet near Big Meadows. A trailhead at the end of a short spur road about a half mile to the north off the main road provides access to a great butt-kicker of a trail about eight or nine miles (one way) that runs along Wildhorse Creek and up to Sugarloaf Mountain, elevation 9,952 feet. Insider's note: A trail camp is set on Wildhorse Creek, just past the midway point on the trail to Sugarloaf Mountain.

Location: In San Bernardino National Forest; map I6, grid d7.

Campsites, facilities: There is one group campsite that will accommodate up to 25 people. Picnic tables and fire rings are provided. Drinking water and vault toilets are available. Leashed pets are permitted.

Reservations, fees: Reserve at tel. (877) 444-6777 ($8.65 reservation fee) or website: www.reserveusa.com; $50 group fee per night. Open May through November.

Directions: From Redlands on Interstate 10, turn east on Highway 38 and drive 33.5 miles to Forest Road 1N02. Turn right and drive a mile to the campground, just behind Heart Bar.

Contact: San Bernardino National Forest, Mill Creek Ranger Station, tel. (909) 794-1123 or fax (909) 794-1125.

⏳ Heart Bar Family Camp

 4

It's a good thing there is drinking water at this camp. Why? Because Heart Bar Creek often isn't much more than a trickle and can't be relied on for water. The camp is set at 6,900 feet near Big Meadows, the location of the Heart Bar Fire Station. A challenging butt-kicker of a hike has a trailhead about a half mile away to the north off a spur road, midway between the camp and the fire station. The trail here is routed along Wildhorse Creek to Sugarloaf Mountain (9,952 feet, about eight or nine miles one way to the top). Insider's note: Just past the midway point on the trail to Sugarloaf Mountain is a trail camp on Wildhorse Creek.

Location: In San Bernardino National Forest; map I6, grid d8.

Campsites, facilities: There are 94 sites for tents or RVs up to 50 feet long. Picnic tables and fire grills are provided. Drinking water and vault toilets are available. Some facilities are wheelchair accessible. Leashed pets are permitted.

Reservations, fees: Reserve at tel. (877) 444-6777 ($8.65 reservation fee) or website: www.reserveusa.com; $15 per night for single family sites, $25 for multifamily sites. Open May through November.

Directions: From Interstate 10 in Redlands, drive 33.5 miles east on Highway 38 to Forest Road 1N02. Turn right and drive a mile to the campground.

Contact: San Bernardino National Forest, Mill Creek Ranger Station, tel. (909) 794-1123 or fax (909) 794-1125.

40 Heart Bar Equestrian Group & Wild Horse Equestrian

   5

You might not meet Mr. Ed here, but bring an apple anyway. Heart Bar is a horse camp on Heart Bar Creek, less than a mile east of Heart Bar Family Camp. Wild Horse is just one-tenth of a mile down the road. A good trail that leads into the San Gorgonio Wilderness starts four miles down the road at Fish Creek Meadows. It is routed west for three miles to Fish Creek and then up Grinnell Mountain to the north peak of the Ten Thousand Foot Ridge. A wilderness permit is required. The elevation is 7,000 feet.

Location: In San Bernardino National Forest; map I6, grid d8.

Campsites, facilities: Heart Bar has one group campsite with 46 corrals for up to 65 people and 21 cars (limited use of trailers and RVs). Wild Horse has 11 equestrian sites. Picnic tables and fire grills are provided. Flush toilets are available. No drinking water is available. Water is available for horses. Leashed pets are permitted.

Reservations, fees: Reserve at tel. (877) 444-6777 ($8.65 reservation fee) or website: www.reserveusa.com; $20 per night for family equestrian sites, $200 per night for group sites. At Wild Horse, $5 per night for each extra vehicle. Open May through November.

Directions: From Interstate 10 in Redlands, drive 33.5 miles east on Highway 38 to Forest Road 1N02. Turn right and drive one mile to the Heart Bar campground on the right. For Wild Horse Campground, continue for 0.1 mile to the camp on the left.

Contact: San Bernardino National Forest, Mill Creek Ranger Station, tel. (909) 794-1123 or fax (909) 794-1125.

41 Coon Creek Cabin Group Camp

   4

Backpackers call this the "Coon Creek jump-off" because it is set on the Pacific Crest Trail at 8,200 feet and provides a "jump-off" for a trek on the PCT. The camp is set on Coon Creek, but the creek often runs dry by summer. Note that in the off-season the access road, Forest Road 1N02, can be gated; campers must hike or cross-country ski to the camp.

Location: On the Pacific Crest Trail in San Bernardino National Forest; map I6, grid d9.

Campsites, facilities: There is one group camp that will accommodate up to 40 people and 14 cars (no trailers or RVs). Picnic tables and fire grills are provided. Vault toilets are available. No drinking water is available. Leashed pets are permitted.

Reservations, fees: Reserve at tel. (877) 444-6777 ($8.65 reservation fee) or website: www.reserveusa.com; $50 group fee per night. Open year-round.

Directions: From Interstate 10 in Redlands, drive 33.5 miles east on Highway 38 to Forest Road 1N02. Turn right and it's five miles to the campground. (The access road is a dirt road.)

Contact: San Bernardino National Forest, Big Bear Discovery Center, tel. (909) 866-3437 or fax (909) 866-1781.

42 Rancho Jurupa County Park

      4

Lord, it gets hot in the summertime, but there is shade and grass here. In the cooler weather during spring, this county park stocks a fishing pond. That is also the best time to explore the park's hiking and equestrian trails. Summer visitors will find that the nearest lake for swimming and water sports is Lake Perris, about a 20-minute drive away. The elevation is 780 feet.

Location: Near Riverside; map I6, grid e1.

Campsites, facilities: There are 72 sites for

tents or RVs, 12 with full hookups. Picnic tables and fire grills are provided. Drinking water, flush toilets, showers, and a sanitary disposal station are available. Some facilities are wheelchair accessible. Leashed pets are permitted.

Reservations, fees: Reservations are accepted at tel. (800) 234-7275; $16 to $18 per night, $4 per night for each extra vehicle, $5-per-rod fishing fee, $2 pet fee. Major credit cards accepted. Open year-round.

Directions: From Interstate 215 in Riverside, turn east on Highway 60. Drive east on Highway 60 for about seven miles to Rubidoux Boulevard. Turn right on Rubidoux Boulevard and drive a half mile to Mission Boulevard. Turn left on Mission Boulevard and drive about a mile to Crestmore Road. Turn right and drive 1.5 miles to the park gate on the left.

Contact: Rancho Jurupa County Park, tel. (909) 684-7032.

43 Yucaipa Regional Park

      7

This is a great family-oriented county park, complete with water slides and paddleboats for the kids and fishing access and hiking trails for adults. Three lakes are stocked weekly with catfish in the summer and trout in the winter, the closest thing around to an insurance policy for anglers. Spectacular scenic views of the Yucaipa Valley, the San Bernardino Mountains, and Mount San Gorgonio are possible from the park. Two museums are also nearby.

Location: Near Redlands; map I6, grid e5.

Campsites, facilities: There are nine tent sites and 26 sites for trailers or RVs, 11 with full hookups. Picnic tables and fire rings are provided. Restrooms, drinking water, flush toilets, and showers are available. A swimming lagoon, fishing ponds, water slides, and paddleboat rentals are available nearby. Some facilities

are wheelchair accessible. The water slide is open Memorial Day weekend through Labor Day weekend. Leashed pets are permitted.

Reservations, fees: Reservations are accepted; $10 to $18 per night. Major credit cards accepted. Additional fees are charged for fishing, swimming, and use of the water slide. Open year-round.

Directions: From Redlands, drive east on Interstate 10 to the Yucaipa exit. Drive north on Yucaipa Boulevard to Oak Glen Road. Turn left and continue two miles to the park on the left.

Contact: Yucaipa Regional Park, tel. (909) 790-3127; website: www.co.san-bernardino.ca.us/parks.

44 Bogart County Park

 4

This county park is overlooked by many vacationers on Interstate 10, and it is as pretty as it gets for this area. There are two miles of horse trails and some hiking trails for a recreation option during the cooler months. The elevation is 2,800 feet.

Location: In Cherry Valley; map I6, grid f5.

Campsites, facilities: There are 40 sites for tents or RVs and a group camping area. Fire grills and picnic tables are provided. Drinking water, flush toilets, and a playground are available. Supplies are available in Beaumont. Leashed pets are permitted.

Reservations, fees: Reservations are required for groups only; reserve at tel. (800) 234-7275 ($6.50-12 reservation fee is charged); $12 per night, $4 per night for each extra vehicle, $2 for pets. Open year-round.

Directions: From Interstate 10 in Beaumont, drive four miles north on Beaumont Avenue to 14th and Cherry Avenue; the park is located at 9600 Cherry Avenue on the right.

Contact: Bogart County Park, tel. (909) 845-3818.

45 Lake Perris State Recreation Area

7

Lake Perris is a great recreation lake with first-class fishing for spotted bass and, in the summer, it's an excellent destination for boating and water sports. It is set at 1,500 feet in Moreno Valley, just southwest of the Badlands foothills. The lake has a roundish shape, covering 2,200 acres, with an island that provides a unique boat-in picnic site. There are large ski beaches on the northeast and southeast shores and a designated sailing cove on the northwest side, an ideal spot for windsurfing and sailing. Swimming is also excellent, but allowed only at the developed beaches a short distance from the campground. The Recreation Area covers 8,300 acres, and includes 11 miles of paved bike trails, including a great route that circles the lake, 15 miles of equestrian trails, and five miles of hiking trails. Summer campfire and junior ranger programs are available.

Location: On Lake Perris; map I6, grid f3.

Campsites, facilities: There are 177 sites for tents only, 254 sites with partial hookups for tents or RVs up to 31 feet long, seven primitive horse camps with corrals and water troughs, six group sites for 25 to 85 people each, and one hike-in/bike-in site. There are no hookups in the group area. Picnic tables, fire grills, electric connections, and drinking water are provided. Restrooms, flush toilets, coin-operated showers, sanitary disposal station, playground, convenience store, two swimming beaches, boat launch, mooring, and boat rentals are available. Some facilities are wheelchair accessible. Leashed pets are permitted, except near the water.

Reservations, fees: Reserve at tel. (800) 444-PARK (444-7275) or website: www.reserve america.com for individual sites, (909) 657-0676 for group and equestrian sites; $8 to $14 per night, $60 per night for group sites, $12 per night for equestrian sites, $1 per person per night for hike-in/bike-in site. Open year-round.

Directions: From Riverside, drive east on Highway 215/60 for about five miles to the 215/60 split. Bear south on 215 at the split and drive six miles to Ramona Expressway. Turn left (east) and drive 3.5 miles to Lake Perris Drive. Turn left and drive three-quarters mile to the park entrance.

Contact: Lake Perris State Park, tel. (909) 657-0676 or tel. (909) 940-5603.

46 Stagecoach RV Park

      2

Banning may not seem like a hotbed of civilization at first glance, but this clean, comfortable park is a good spot to make camp while exploring some of the area's hidden attractions, including Agua Caliente Indian Canyons and the Lincoln Shrine. It is set at 2,400 feet, 22 miles from Palm Springs. A good side trip is to head south on curving "Highway" 240 up to Vista Point in the San Bernardino National Forest.

Location: In Banning; map I6, grid f7.

Campsites, facilities: There are 106 sites for tents or RVs, many with full hookups. Picnic tables and fire grills are provided. Cable TV, restrooms, showers, playground, swimming pool, coin laundry, modem hookups, store, sanitary disposal station, ice, recreation room, horseshoes, video arcade, and propane gas are available. Leashed pets are permitted.

Reservations, fees: Reservations are accepted; $14 to $19.50 per night. Major credit cards accepted. Open year-round.

Directions: From Interstate 10 in Banning, take the Highway 243 exit and drive one block south on 8th Avenue. Turn left on Lincoln and drive two blocks. Turn right on San Gorgonio and drive a mile to the park at 1455 South San Gorgonio Avenue.

Contact: Stagecoach RV Park, tel. (909) 849-7513 or fax (909) 849-7998.

47 Black Mountain Group Camp

    6

This is a beautiful scenic area, particularly to the north on the edge of the San Jacinto Wilderness and to the east of Mount San Jacinto State Park. The camp is set at 7,500 feet, and is within a mile of a trailhead for the Pacific Crest Trail. Here you can turn southeast and hike along Fuller Ridge for another mile to the border of Mount San Jacinto State Park. Note that Black Mountain Lookout is just a two-mile drive, close to Boulder Basin Camp.

Location: Near Mount San Jacinto in San Bernardino National Forest; map I6, grid g7.

Campsites, facilities: There is one group camp with tent sites for up to 100 people and 20 vehicles. Picnic tables and fire rings are provided. Drinking water and vault toilets are available. Leashed pets are permitted.

Reservations, fees: Reserve at tel. (877) 444-6777 ($8.65 reservation fee) or website: www.reserveusa.com; $60 to $130 per night. Open May through September.

Directions: From Idyllwild, drive nine miles north on Highway 243. Turn right on Forest Road 4S01 (a narrow dirt road) and drive eight miles to the campground on the right. Because of the rough road, trailers and RVs are not recommended.

Contact: San Bernardino National Forest, San Jacinto Ranger District, tel. (909) 659-2117 or fax (909) 659-2107.

48 Boulder Basin

    8

This camp is on the top of the world for these parts, 7,300 feet, adjacent to the Black Mountain Fire Lookout with great views in all directions and highlighted by Tahquitz Peak (8,828 feet) 10 miles to the southeast. Boulder Basin is also near the San Jacinto Wilderness (to the northeast) and makes a good trailhead camp for hikers. A trail starting at Black Mountain Lookout leads west, dropping steeply into a canyon and also into a designated scenic area.

Location: Near the San Jacinto Wilderness in San Bernardino National Forest; map I6, grid g8.

Campsites, facilities: There are 34 sites for tents or RVs up to 22 feet long (trailers are not recommended). Picnic tables and fire rings are provided. Drinking water and vault toilets are available. Leashed pets are permitted.

Reservations, fees: Reservations are accepted for half of the sites; reserve at tel. (877) 444-6777 ($8.65 reservation fee) or website: www.reserveusa.com; $10 per night. Open May to mid-October.

Directions: From Idyllwild, drive nine miles north on Highway 243. Turn right on Forest Road 4S01 (a very narrow dirt road) and drive six miles to the campground on the right.

Contact: San Bernardino National Forest, San Jacinto Ranger District, tel. (909) 659-2117, or fax (909) 659-2107.

49 Dark Canyon

     7

This pretty setting is on the slopes of the San Jacinto Mountains at 5,800 feet in elevation. Hikers can drive to the Seven Pines Trailhead less than a mile north of camp at the end of Forest Road 4S02. The trail leads east for three miles into Mount San Jacinto State Park to Deer Springs, where there is a trail camp and a junction with the Pacific Crest Trail. A wilderness permit is required.

Location: In the San Jacinto Mountains in San Bernardino National Forest; map I6, grid g8.

Campsites, facilities: There are 21 sites for tents or RVs up to 22 feet long. Picnic tables and fire grills are provided. Drinking water and vault toilets are available. Leashed pets are permitted.

Reservations, fees: Reservations are accepted for half of the sites; reserve at tel. (877) 444-6777 ($8.65 reservation fee)

or website: www.reserveusa.com; $12 per night. Open May to mid-October.

Directions: From Idyllwild, drive seven miles north on Highway 243. Turn right on Forest Road 4S02 and drive three more miles on a narrow paved road to the camp.

Contact: San Bernardino National Forest, San Jacinto Ranger District, tel. (909) 659-2117, or fax (909) 659-2107.

50 Round Valley & Tamarack Valley Tram & Walk-in

  10

This is one of the most spectacular getaways in the Western U.S. It includes a tram ride that will take you from 2,643 feet to 8,516 feet, with stunning views across the desert, especially heart-breaking sunsets. On clear days, you can see the Salton Sea 50 miles to the south. From the tram, you then hike 2 or 2.5 miles to one of the two camps, set at 9,100 feet, an ideal launch point for the hike to the Mount San Jacinto summit, at 10,804 feet, the second-highest peak in Southern California. From Round Valley Camp, it is a 7.5-mile round trip (just add another mile round-trip from Tamarack Valley). On clear days from the summit, you can see 100 miles, including the Channel Islands, Mexico, and Nevada.

Location: Near Mount San Jacinto; map I6, grid g8.

Campsites, facilities: There are 28 tent sites at Round Valley and 12 tent sites at Tamarack Valley. Pit toilets are available. No drinking water is available (Round Valley Camp has stream water). No campfires are permitted. Bring a camp stove for cooking. Garbage must be packed out. Pets are not permitted.

Reservations, fees: Camping permit required, no fee, by mail at Mount San Jacinto State Park, P.O. Box 308, Idyllwild, CA 92549, or at website: www.sanjac.statepark.org. A required tram ride costs $20 for adults, $12 for children under 12 (prices subject to change). Open May through September.

Directions: From Banning, drive east on Interstate 10 for 12 miles to the Highway 111/Palm Springs exit. Take that exit to Highway 111 and drive south nine miles to Tramway Road. Turn right and drive three miles to the parking area for Palm Springs Aerial Tramway. Ride the tram to Mountain Station. Hike two miles to Round Valley Camp, or continue from Round Valley Camp for another half-mile to Tamarack Valley Camp.

Contact: Mount San Jacinto State Park, tel. (909) 659-2607; website: www.sanjac.state park.org. Palm Springs Aerial Tramway, tel. (760) 325-1391; website: www.pstramway.com.

51 Marion Mountain

   7

You get good lookouts and a developed campground at this spot. Nearby Black Mountain is a good side trip, including a drive-to scenic lookout point. In addition, there are several trailheads in the area. The best one starts near this camp and heads up the slopes to Marion Mountain and east into adjacent Mount San Jacinto State Park. The elevation is 6,400 feet.

Location: In San Bernardino National Forest; map I6, grid h8.

Campsites, facilities: There are 24 sites for tents or RVs up to 15 feet long. Picnic tables and fire grills are provided. Drinking water and vault toilets are available.

Reservations, fees: Reservations are accepted for half of the sites; reserve at tel. (877) 444-6777 ($8.65 reservation fee) or website: www.reserveusa.com; $10 per night. Open May to mid-October.

Directions: From Idyllwild, drive seven miles north on Highway 243. Turn right on Forest Road 4S02 and drive two miles to the campground.

Contact: San Bernardino National Forest, San Jacinto Ranger District, tel. (909) 659-2117 or fax (909) 659-2107.

52 Fern Basin

    7

This is a nearby alternative to Stone Creek (you'll pass it on the way in) and Dark Canyon (another three miles in). The Marion Mountain Trailhead is accessible within one-half mile of the campground by driving east on Forest Road 4S02.

Location: Near Mount San Jacinto State Park in San Bernardino National Forest; map I6, grid h8.

Campsites, facilities: There are 22 sites for tents or RVs up to 15 feet long. Picnic tables and fire rings are provided. Drinking water and vault toilets are available. Leashed pets are permitted.

Reservations, fees: Reservations are accepted for half of the sites; reserve at tel. (877) 444-6777 ($8.65 reservation fee) or website: www.reserveusa.com; $10 per night. Open May through September.

Directions: From Idyllwild, drive seven miles north on Highway 243. Turn right on Forest Road 4S02 and drive one mile to the campground on the left.

Contact: San Bernardino National Forest, San Jacinto Ranger District, tel. (909) 659-2117 or fax (909) 659-2107.

53 Stone Creek

     7

This is a wooded camp, 5,900 feet in elevation, one-quarter mile off the main road along Stone Creek just outside the national forest boundary. It is less than a mile from Fern Basin and less than three miles from Dark Canyon. The best trailhead in the immediate area is the Seven Pines Trail out of Marion Mountain Camp, one-half mile from this camp.

Location: In Mount San Jacinto State Park; map I6, grid h8.

Campsites, facilities: There are 10 tent sites and 40 sites for tents or RVs up to 24 feet long. Picnic tables and fire rings are provided. Drinking water and vault toilets are available. Some

facilities are wheelchair accessible. Supplies and coin laundry are three miles away in Pine Cove. Leashed pets are permitted.

Reservations, fees: Reserve at tel. (800) 444-PARK (800-444-7275) or website: www.reserve-america.com; $7 per night, $12 for sites designed for the physically challenged. Open year-round.

Directions: From Idyllwild, drive six miles north on Highway 243 to the park entrance on the right.

Contact: Mount San Jacinto State Park, tel. (909) 659-2607, or website: www.sanjac.state park.org; Colorado Desert District Office, or tel. (760) 767-5311.

54 Idyllwild County Park

     6

This park is set at 5,300 feet, surrounded by Mount San Jacinto State Park, San Jacinto Wilderness, and the San Bernardino National Forest lands. That provides plenty of options for visitors. The top hike in the region is the ambitious climb up the western slopes to the top of Mount San Jacinto (10,804 feet), a terrible challenge of a butt-kicker that provides one of the most astounding views in all the land. (The best route, however, is out of Palm Springs, taking the aerial tramway, which will get you to 8,516 feet in elevation before hiking out the rest.)

Location: Near San Bernardino National Forest; map I6, grid h8.

Campsites, facilities: There are 90 sites for tents or RVs up to 34 feet long (30 for RVs only). Fire grills and picnic tables are provided. Restrooms, drinking water, flush toilets, and showers are available. A grocery store, coin laundry, and propane gas are nearby. Leashed pets are permitted. Some facilities are wheelchair accessible.

Reservations, fees: Reservations are accepted at (800) 234-PARK (800-234-7275) ($6.50 reservation fee); $15 per night, six person per site maximum. Open year-round. Major credit cards accepted.

Directions: From Highway 243 in Idyllwild, drive a half mile west on Riverside County Playground Road (follow the signs) to the campground on the left.

Contact: Idyllwild County Park, tel. (909) 659-2656.

55 Idyllwild

     8

This is a prime spot for hikers and one of the better jump-off points for trekking in the area, set at 5,400 feet. There are no trails from this campground. But a half-mile north is the Deer Spring Trail, which is connected with the Pacific Crest Trail and then climbs on to Mount San Jacinto (10,804 feet) and its astounding lookout.

Location: In Mount San Jacinto State Park; map I6, grid h8.

Campsites, facilities: There are 11 sites for tents only, 22 sites for tents or RVs up to 24 feet long, and one hike-in/bike-in site. Fire grills and picnic tables are provided. Piped water, flush toilets, and showers are available. Supplies and coin laundry (100 yards) are nearby. Leashed pets are permitted. Some facilities are wheelchair accessible.

Reservations, fees: Reserve at tel. (800) 444-PARK (800-444-7275) or website: www.reserve-america.com; $12 per night, $1 per person for hike-in/bike-in site. Open year-round.

Directions: In Idyllwild, drive to the north end of town on Highway 243 to the park entrance on the left (next to the fire station).

Contact: Mount San Jacinto State Park, tel. (909) 659-2607, or website: www.sanjac.state park.org; Colorado Desert District Office, or tel. (760) 767-5311.

56 Hurkey Creek County Park

      5

This large county park is just east (across the road) of Lake Hemet, beside Hurkey Creek (which runs in winter and spring). The highlight, of course, is the nearby lake, known for good fishing in the spring. No swimming is permitted. The camp elevation is 4,800 feet.

Location: Near Lake Hemet; map I6, grid i8.

Campsites, facilities: There are 107 family sites and 105 group sites for tents or RVs up to 35 feet long. Fire grills and picnic tables are provided. Drinking water, flush toilets, and showers are available. Some facilities are wheelchair accessible. A sanitary disposal station is available for a fee at nearby Lake Hemet. Leashed pets are permitted.

Reservations, fees: Reservations are recommended; reserve at (800) 234-PARK, (800-234-7275) (a reservation fee is charged); $15 per night, $2 pet fee. Major credit cards accepted. Open year-round.

Directions: From Palm Desert, drive about 32 miles southwest on Highway 74 to the campground entrance on your right.

Contact: Hurkey Creek County Park, tel. (909) 659-2050.

57 Lake Hemet

     7

Lake Hemet covers 420 acres, is set at 4,335 feet, and sits near San Bernardino National Forest just west of Garner Valley. It provides a good camping/fishing destination, with stocks of 75,000 trout each year, a lot for a lake this size, and yep, catch rates are good. The lake also has bass, bluegill, and catfish. Boating rules prohibit boats under 10 feet, canoes, sailboats, inflatables, and swimming.

Location: Near Hemet; map I6, grid i8.

Campsites, facilities: There are 300 sites for tents or RVs with full hookups, and 200 sites for tents or RVs with partial hookups. Picnic tables and fire rings are provided. Restrooms, drinking water, flush toilets, showers, sanitary disposal station, playground, pond, boat ramp, boat rentals, grocery store, coin laundry, and propane gas are available. Some facilities are wheelchair accessible. Leashed pets are permitted.

Reservations, fees: No reservations; $13 to $16.25 per vehicle per night, $1 pet fee. Major credit cards accepted. Open year-round.

Directions: From Palm Desert, drive 32 miles southwest on Highway 74 to the camp entrance on the left.

Contact: Lake Hemet, tel. (909) 659-2680; website: www.lakehemet.com.

58 Palm View RV Park

      5

This privately operated RV park is in a quiet valley between Lake Perris and Lake Elsinore at 700 feet elevation. The sites are fairly rustic, with some shade trees. The park's recreation area offers basketball, volleyball, horseshoes, tetherball, and a playground, which should tell you everything you need to know. For you wonderful goofballs, bungy jumping and parachuting are available in the town of Perris.

Location: Near Lake Elsinore; map I6, grid h1.

Campsites, facilities: There are 45 sites for tents or RVs, some with full hookups. Restrooms, fire rings, sanitary disposal station, recreation area, modem hookups, swimming pool, pond, laundry facilities, store, ice, and firewood are available. Leashed pets are permitted.

Reservations, fees: Reservations are accepted; $18 to $20 per night, $3 per person per night for more than four people. Open year-round.

Directions: From the Los Angeles area, travel south on Interstate 15 and exit at the Highway 74/Central Avenue turnoff. Drive east on Highway 74 for four miles to River Road. Drive south (right) on River Road about one mile to the park at 22200 River Road on the left.

Contact: Palm View RV Park, tel. (909) 657-7791; website: www.palmviewrvpark.com.

59 Lake Elsinore Marina & RV Resort

      7

This privately operated RV park is just a half mile from Lake Elsinore. A nearby alternative RV park is Roadrunner, which used to be owned by the same folks. For information about Lake Elsinore, see the entry for Lake Elsinore Recreation Area.

Location: On Lake Elsinore; map I6, grid h0.

Campsites, facilities: There are 195 sites for tents or RVs with full hookups. Picnic tables are provided. Restrooms, showers, sanitary disposal station, horseshoe pit, clubhouse, convenience store, telephone hookups, cable TV hookups, and a boat ramp are available. Some facilities are wheelchair accessible. Leashed pets are permitted.

Reservations, fees: Reservations are accepted; $27.50 per night. Major credit cards accepted. Open year-round.

Directions: From Interstate 15 in Lake Elsinore, take Highway 74 and drive four miles west to the park at 32700 Riverside Drive.

Contact: Elsinore West Marina, tel. (909) 678-1300 or tel. (800) 328-6844.

60 Roadrunner RV Park

     7

The Roadrunner, a privately operated park, features 600 feet of lakefront property along Lake Elsinore. This lake is best known for water-skiing, with hot weather to match, but only poor to fair fishing, with some bluegill, crappie, and catfish. Boat ramps are at both the north and south ends of the lake.

Location: On Lake Elsinore; map I6, grid h1.

Campsites, facilities: There are 20 sites for RVs with full hookups and 21 sites for tents only. Picnic tables are provided. Restrooms, drinking water, flush toilets, showers, cable television, clubhouse, telephone hookups, coin laundry, sanitary disposal station, and boat ramp are available. Leashed pets are permitted.

Reservations, fees: Reservations required at (909) 674-4900; $25 per night, $7 per person per night for more than four people, $3 for more than one vehicle (six-person maximum per site). Major credit cards accepted. Open year-round.

Directions: From Lake Elsinore on Interstate 15, turn west on

Highway 74 and drive about four miles. Look for Roadrunner on the left side of the road, just a half mile past the city park.
Contact: Roadrunner, tel. (909) 674-4900.

61 Lake Elsinore Recreation Area

     7

The weather is hot and dry enough in this region to make the water in Lake Elsinore more valuable than gold. Elsinore is a huge, wide lake, where water-skiers, personal watercraft, and windsurfers can find a slice of heaven. This camp is set along the north shore, where there are also several trails for hiking, biking, and horseback riding. There is a designated area near the campground for swimming and water play, with a gently sloping lake bottom a big plus here. If you like thrill sports, hang gliding and parachuting are also available at the lake and, as you scan across the water, you can often look up and see these daredevils soaring overhead. The recreation area covers 3,300 acres. It was once operated as a state facility, but operations are now run by the City of Lake Elsinore.
Location: On Lake Elsinore; map I6, grid h1.
Campsites, facilities: There are 400 sites for tents or RVs up to 40 feet long, many with hookups. Picnic tables (not all sites) and fire pits are provided. Restrooms, drinking water, flush toilets, showers, sanitary disposal station, playground, coin laundry, and a grocery store are available. Some facilities are wheelchair accessible. Leashed pets are permitted.
Reservations, fees: No reservations; $15 to $20 per night, $5 for more than one vehicle. Open year-round.
Directions: From Interstate 15 in Lake Elsinore, drive three miles west on Highway 74 to the park entrance.
Contact: Elsinore Campground, (909) 471-1212; The City of Lake Elsinore, tel. (909) 674-3124 or fax (909) 245-9308.

62 Golden Village Palms RV Resort

    5

This RV resort is for those aged 55 and over. It is the biggest RV park in Southern California, with major renovation planned for completion in 2003. The grounds are lush, with gravel pads for RVs. It is set near Diamond Valley Lake, about 10 miles south, a new lake which will become the largest reservoir in California. A golf course is nearby, Lake Hemet is 20 miles east, and winery tours are available in Temecula, a 30-minute drive.
Location: In Hemet; map I6, grid h5.
Campsites, facilities: There are 998 sites for RVs up to 40 feet long, including 60 pull-through sites. No tent sites. Restrooms, drinking water, flush toilets, showers, cable TV, modem hookups, telephones, sewer hookups, three swimming pools, recreation room, fitness center, billiard room, three spas, coin laundry, large clubhouse, banquet and meeting rooms, tennis courts, shuffleboard, nine-hole putting green, volleyball courts, and horseshoe pits are available. A day-use area with propane barbecues is also available. Leashed pets are permitted.
Reservations, fees: Reservations at (800) 323-9610; $30 per night, $10 per person for more than two people, $187 per week. Open year-round.
Directions: From Interstate 215 south of Perris, turn east on Highway 74 and drive about 18 miles to Hemet (the highway becomes Florida Avenue in Hemet). The resort is on the left.
Contact: Golden Village Palms RV Resort, tel. (909) 925-2518.

63 Casa del Sol RV Resort

    3

Hemet is a retirement town, so if you want excitement, the three lakes in the area are the best place to look for it: Lake Perris to the northwest, Lake Skinner to the south, and Lake Hemet to the east.

Location: In Hemet; map I6, grid h5.

Campsites, facilities: There are 358 RV sites. Restrooms, drinking water, flush toilets, showers, cable TV, telephones, sewer hookups, swimming pool, recreation room, exercise room, billiard room, hot tub, and coin laundry are available. Leashed pets are permitted.

Reservations, fees: Reservations are accepted at (888) 925-2516; $23 per night, $15 per night for each extra vehicle, $2.50 per person per night for more than two people. Open year-round.

Directions: From Interstate 215 south of Perris, turn east on Highway 74 and drive about 18 miles to Hemet (the highway becomes Florida Avenue in Hemet). Turn right (south) on Kirby Avenue and drive one-half block to the resort at 2750 West Acacia Avenue.

Contact: Casa del Sol RV Resorts, tel. (909) 925-2515.

64 Mountain Valley RV Park

 3

This is one of three RV parks in the Hemet area. Three lakes in the area provide side trip possibilities: Lake Perris to the northwest, Lake Skinner to the south, and Lake Hemet to the east.

Location: In Hemet; map I6, grid h5.

Campsites, facilities: There are 171 RV sites, many with hookups. Restrooms, drinking water, flush toilets, showers, a fireside room, swimming pool, enclosed hot tub, coin laundry, satellite TV, recreation room, and telephone hookups are available. Some facilities are wheelchair accessible. A grocery store and propane gas are nearby. Leashed pets are permitted.

Reservations, fees: Reservations at (800) 926-5593; $25 per night, $2 pet fee. Major credit cards accepted. Open year-round.

Directions: From Interstate 215 south of Perris, turn east on Highway 74 and drive about 18 miles to Hemet (the highway becomes Florida Avenue in Hemet). Turn right on Lyon Avenue and drive to 235 South Lyon Avenue. The park is at the corner of Lyon and South Acacia Avenues.

Contact: Mountain Valley RV Park, tel. (909) 925-5812; website: www.mountainvalleyrvpark.com.

65 Lake Skinner Recreation Area

 7

Lake Skinner is set within a county park at an elevation of 1,470 feet in sparse foothill country, where the water can sparkle, and covers 1,200 surface acres. There is a speed limit of 10 mph. Unlike nearby Lake Elsinore, which is dominated by fast boats and water-skiers, no water contact sports are permitted here; hence no water-skiing, no swimming, no windsurfing. Afternoon winds make for great sailing, there is good fishing for trout or striped bass in the spring, and the recreation area provides hiking and horseback riding trails.

Location: On Lake Skinner; map I6, grid i4.

Campsites, facilities: There are 257 sites for tents or RVs, many with full hookups. Picnic tables and fire grills are provided. Restrooms, drinking water, flush toilets, showers, playground, grocery store, ice, bait, sanitary disposal station, swimming pool (in the summer), boat ramp, mooring, boat rentals, and propane gas are available. Leashed pets are permitted. Some facilities are wheelchair accessible.

Reservations, fees: Reservations at (800) 234-7275; $15 to $18 per night, $4 per night for each additional vehicle, six-person maximum per site, $2 pet fee. Open year-round. Major credit cards accepted.

Directions: From Interstate 15 in Temecula, take the Rancho California exit and drive 9.5 miles northeast to the park entrance on the right.

Contact: Lake Skinner Recreation Area, tel. (909) 926-1541.

66 Dripping Springs

    7

This is one of the premium Forest Service camps available, set just inside the national forest border near Vail Lake and adjacent to the Agua Tibia Wilderness. The Dripping Springs Trail is routed south out of camp, starting at 1,600 feet and climbing near the peak of Agua Tibia Mountain, 4,779 feet.

Location: Near the Agua Tibia Wilderness in Cleveland National Forest; map I6, grid j4.

Campsites, facilities: There are 24 sites for tents or RVs up to 32 feet long. Picnic tables and fire rings are provided. Drinking water and vault toilets are available. Supplies are available nearby in Temecula. Leashed pets are permitted.

Reservations, fees: No reservations; $12 per night, $2 for each additional vehicle. Open July through March. Closed April through June for protection of endangered species, the Arroyo Southwestern toad.

Directions: From Interstate 15 in Temecula, drive 11 miles east on Highway 79 to the campground.

Contact: Cleveland National Forest, Palomar Ranger District, tel. (760) 788-0250 or fax: tel. (760) 788-6130.

67 Oak Springs RV Resort

     6

This campground is set on 250 acres in an ideal location for hiking, biking, and fishing. A trailhead at the camp leads into 200,000 acres of wilderness in the neighboring San Bernardino National Forest. There is also a stocked lake, giving anglers the chance to catch trophy-size bass, bluegill, and catfish. The nearby Temecula wine country makes a good side trip.

Location: Near Temecula; map I6, grid j6.

Campsites, facilities: There are 30 tent sites, 60 sites with full hookups, and 20 sites with partial hookups for RVs up to 45 feet long. A bunkhouse and a tepee are also available.

Picnic tables and barbecues are provided. Restrooms, drinking water, flush toilets, coin-operated hot showers, sanitary disposal station, propane gas, coin laundry, modem hookups, heated swimming pool (seasonal), children's playground, miniature golf, volleyball, basketball, baseball, horseshoes, shuffleboard, badminton, Ping-Pong, exercise room, horse corrals, private lake, and a small store are available. Paddleboat, kayak, and bicycle rentals are also available. Some facilities are wheelchair accessible. Leashed pets are permitted.

Reservations, fees: Reservations are recommended; $18 to $23 per night. Group and monthly rates are available. Open year-round. Major credit cards accepted.

Directions: From Temecula, drive southwest on Highway 79 for 17.5 miles. Turn left on Highway 371 and drive three miles to Wilson Valley Road. Turn left and drive three miles to Reed Valley Road. Turn right and drive four miles to the resort at the end of the road.

Contact: Oak Springs RV Resort, 38901 Reed Valley Road, Aguanga, CA 92536; tel. (909) 767-1636, tel. (888) 787-7275, or fax (909) 767-1612; website: www.oakspringspark.net.

68 Kamp Anza RV Resort

     4

This is a year-round RV park set at 4,100 feet, with many nearby recreation options. Lake Hemet is 11 miles away, with hiking, motorbiking, and jeep trails nearby in San Bernardino National Forest. Pacific Crest Trail hikers are welcome to clean up, and arrange for food and mail pick-up.

Location: Near Anza; map I6, grid j8.

Campsites, facilities: There are 116 sites for tents or RVs, many with full hookups. Equestrian facilities are available. Picnic tables and fire grills are provided. Restrooms, showers, playground, fishing pond, hot tub, horseshoe pits, coin laundry, store, sanitary disposal station, ice, recreation room, modem hookups, and propane gas are available.

Reservations, fees: Reservations are accepted; $12 to $18 per night, $17.50 per night per horse site. Open year-round.

Directions: From Palm Desert, drive west on Highway 74 for 24 miles. Turn left on Highway 371 and drive west to the town of Anza and Kirby Road. Turn left on Kirby Road and drive 3.5 miles to the campground on the left at Terwilliger Road (Look for the covered wagon out front).

Contact: Kamp Anza RV Resort, tel. (909) 763-4819, or fax (909) 763-0619.

JOSHUA TREES

MAP 17

746
TO LUDLOW
TO AMBOY

F
G
H
I
J
1 2 3 4 5 6 7 8 9

a

BULLION
MOUNTAINS

Amboy
Crater

TO LUCERNE VALLEY

b

MARINE CORPS
TRAINING
CENTER

c

(247)

SAN
BERNARDINO
NATIONAL
FOREST

d

Yucca
Valley

Joshua Tree

e

(62)

798

Morongo
Valley

Twentynine
Palms

840
TO RICE

(62)

1

f

2

(62)

3

TO CABAZON

Desert Hot
Springs

4

5

6

7 **8**

g

(10)

9

10

(111)

Keys View
5,185 feet

JOSHUA
TREE
NATIONAL
PARK

h

PALM SPRINGS

11

Thousand
Palms

12

13

(10)

Cathedral
City

i

Rancho Mirage

Palm Desert

Indian Wells

14 (111) **15**

Indio

La Quinta

Coachella **16**

17

TO DESERT CENTER

j

(74)

18

Lake
Cahuilla

19

(86)

Thermal

(111)

(10)

SAN
BERNARDINO
NATIONAL
FOREST

TO CAHUILLA

20

Mecca

TO DESERT SHORES
870
TO NILAND

0 1 2 3 4 5 6 7 8 9

© AVALON TRAVEL PUBLISHING, INC.

CHAPTER 17

1 Indian Cove Campground

    4

This is one of the campgrounds near the northern border of Joshua Tree National Park. The vast desert park, covering 1,238 square miles, is best known for its unique granite formations and scraggly looking trees. If you had to withstand the summer heat here, you'd look scraggly too. Drinking water is available at the Indian Cove Ranger Station.

Location: In Joshua Tree National Park; map 17, grid e4.

Campsites, facilities: There are 101 sites for tents or RVs up to 40 feet long. Adjacent to this campground is a group camp with 13 tent-only sites that will accommodate 15 to 60 people each. Drinking water is available at the Indian Cove Ranger Station. Pit toilets, picnic tables, and fire grills are provided. Gas, groceries, and laundry services are available in Joshua Tree, which is about 10 miles from camp. Leashed pets are permitted, but not on trails.

Reservations, fees: Reserve at (800) 365-CAMP (800-365-2267) or website: reservations.nps.gov; $10 per night for family sites, $20 to $35 per night for group sites, plus $10 per vehicle park entrance fee. Open year-round.

Directions: From Joshua Tree, drive about nine miles east on Highway 62 to Indian Cove Road. Turn right and drive three miles to the campground.

Contact: Joshua Tree National Park, tel. (760) 367-5500 or fax (760) 367-6392.

2 Black Rock Canyon & Horse Camp

    4

This is the fanciest darn campground this side of the desert. Why, they actually have drinking water. Course, they charge you for it. The camp is set at the mouth of Black Rock Canyon, 4,000 feet elevation, which provides good winter hiking possibilities amid unique (in other words, weird) rock formations. Show up in summer and you'll trade your gold for a sip of water. The camp is set near the excellent Black Rock Canyon Visitor Center and a trailhead for a four-mile round-trip hike to a rock wash. If you scramble onward, the route continues all the way to the top of Eureka Peak, 5,518 feet, an 11-mile round-trip. But hey, why not just drive there?

Location: In Joshua Tree National Park; map I7, grid f3.

Campsites, facilities: There are 100 sites for tents or RVs up to 40 feet long, and 15 equestrian sites for up to six people and four horses per site. Picnic tables and fire grills are provided. Drinking water, flush toilets, and a sanitary disposal station are available. Some facilities are wheelchair accessible. The horse camp has hitching posts and a water faucet and no tents are allowed. Leashed pets are permitted, but not on backcountry trails.

Reservations, fees: Reserve at (800) 365-CAMP (800-365-2267) or website: reservations .nps.gov; $10 per night, plus $10 park entrance fee per vehicle. Open year-round, weather permitting.

Directions: From the junction of Interstate 10 and Highway 62, drive about 22.5 miles north on Highway 62 to Yucca Valley. Turn right (south) on Joshua Lane and drive about five miles to the campground.

Contact: Joshua Tree National Park, tel. (760) 367-5500 or fax (760) 367-6392, or Black Rock Nature Center, tel. (760) 365-9585.

3 Sheep Pass Group Camp

 4

Several campgrounds are in this stretch of high desert. Ryan campground is just a couple miles down the road from this one with an excellent trailhead for a trek to Ryan Mountain, the best hike in the park (see the entry for Ryan). For details on this area, see the entry for White Tank. Temperatures are routinely over 100 degrees here in the summer.

Location: In Joshua Tree National Park; map I7, grid f5.

Campsites, facilities: There are six sites for tents. Picnic tables and fire grills are provided. Pit toilets are available. No drinking water is available. Leashed pets are permitted.

Reservations, fees: Reserve at (800) 365-CAMP (800-365-2267) or website: reservations .nps.gov; $20 to $35 per night, plus $10 park entrance fee per vehicle. Open year-round.

Directions: From Twentynine Palms, drive south on Utah Trail for about 16 miles to the campground on the south (left) side of the road.

Contact: Joshua Tree National Park, tel. (760) 367-5500 or fax (760) 367-6392.

4 Belle

 4

This camp is at 3,800 feet in rocky high country. It is one of six camps in the immediate area. For more details, see the entry for White Tank.

Location: In Joshua Tree National Park; map I7, grid f7.

Campsites, facilities: There are 18 sites for tents or RVs up to 40 feet long. Picnic tables and fire grills are provided. Pit toilets are available. No drinking water is available. Leashed pets are permitted.

Reservations, fees: No reservations; no camp fee, $10 park entrance fee per vehicle. Open year-round.

Directions: From Twentynine Palms, drive eight miles south on Utah Trail to Cottonwood Springs Road. Turn left on Cottonwood Springs Road (heading toward Interstate 10) and drive about 1.5 miles to the campground on the left.

Contact: Joshua Tree National Park, tel. (760) 367-5500 or fax (760) 367-6392.

5 Hidden Valley

 7

This is one of California's top campgrounds for rock climbers. Set at 4,200 feet in the high desert country, this is one of several camping options in the area. A trailhead is available two miles from camp at Barker Dam, an easy one-mile loop that features the Wonderland of Rocks. The hike takes you next to a small lake with magical reflections of rock formations off its surface. The RV sites here are snatched up quickly and this campground fills almost daily with rock climbers.

Location: In Joshua Tree National Park; map I7, grid g5.

Campsites, facilities: There are 39 sites for tents or RVs up to 40 feet long. Picnic tables and fire grills are provided. Pit toilets are available. No drinking water is available. Leashed pets are permitted.

Reservations, fees: No reservations; no camp fee, $10 park entrance fee per vehicle. Open year-round.

Directions: From Joshua Tree on Highway 62, turn south on Park Boulevard and drive 14 miles southeast to the campground on the left.

Contact: Joshua Tree National Park, tel. (760) 367-5500 or fax (760) 367-6392.

6 Ryan

   4

This is one of the high desert camps in the immediate area (see also Jumbo Rocks). Joshua Tree National Park is a forbidding paradise: huge, hot, and waterless (most of the time). The unique rock formations look like some great artist made them with a chisel. The elevation is 4,300 feet. The best hike in the park starts here, a three-mile round-trip to Ryan Mountain, a 1,000-foot climb to the top at 5,470 feet. The view is simply drop-dead gorgeous, not only of San Jacinto, Tahquitz, and San Gorgonio peaks, but of several beautiful rock-studded valleys as well as the Wonderland of Rocks.

Location: In Joshua Tree National Park; map I7, grid g5.

Campsites, facilities: There are 31 sites for tents or RVs up to 40 feet long. Picnic tables and fire grills are provided. Pit toilets are available. No drinking water is available. Hitching

posts are available (bring water for the horses). Leashed pets are permitted.

Reservations, fees: No reservations; no camp fee, $10 park entrance fee per vehicle. Open year-round.

Directions: From Twentynine Palms, drive south on Utah Trail about 20 miles to the signed campground entrance on the left.

Contact: Joshua Tree National Park, tel. (760) 367-5500 or fax (760) 367-6392.

7 Jumbo Rocks

    4

Joshua Tree National Park covers more than 1,238 square miles. It is striking high desert country with unique granite formations that seem to change color at different times of the day. This camp is one of the higher ones in the park at 4,400 feet, with adjacent boulders and rock formations that look as if they have been strewn about by an angry giant. It is a popular site for rock climbing.

Location: In Joshua Tree National Park; map I7, grid g6.

Campsites, facilities: There are 125 sites for tents or RVs up to 40 feet long. Picnic tables and fire grills are provided. Pit toilets are available. No drinking water is available. Leashed pets are permitted.

Reservations, fees: No reservations; no camp fee, $10 park entrance fee per vehicle. Open year-round.

Directions: From Twentynine Palms, drive south on Utah Trail for about nine miles to the campground on the left (south) side of the road.

Contact: Joshua Tree National Park, tel. (760) 367-5500 or fax (760) 367-6392.

8 White Tank

    4

Joshua Tree National Park is a unique area where the high and low desert meet. Winter is a good time to explore the beautiful boulder piles and rock formations amid scraggly Joshua trees. There are several trails in the area, with the best near Black Rock Campground, Hidden Valley, and Cottonwood. The elevation is 3,800 feet.

Location: In Joshua Tree National Park; map I7, grid g7.

Campsites, facilities: There are 15 sites for tents or RVs up to 25 feet long. Picnic tables and fire grills are provided. Pit toilets are available. No drinking water is available. Leashed pets are permitted.

Reservations, fees: No reservations; no camp fee, $10 park entrance fee per vehicle. Open year-round.

Directions: From Twentynine Palms, drive eight miles south on Utah Trail to the intersection with Cottonwood Springs Road. Turn left on Cottonwood Road (heading toward Interstate 10) and drive three miles to the campground on the left.

Contact: Joshua Tree National Park, tel. (760) 367-5500 or fax (760) 367-6392.

9 Sam's Family Spa

 3

Hot mineral pools attract swarms of winter vacationers to the Palm Springs area. This park, set 10 miles outside of Palm Springs, provides an alternative to the more crowded spots. The elevation of Sam's Family Spa is 1,000 feet. For information on the tramway ride to Desert View west of Palm Springs, or the hike to Mount San Jacinto, see the entry for Sky Valley East and West.

Location: Near Palm Springs; map I7, grid g2.

Campsites, facilities: There are 180 RV sites with full hookups and picnic tables. There is a separate area with fire grills. Restrooms, showers, playground, swimming pool, wading pool, four hot mineral pools, sauna, coin laundry, and a store are available. Some facilities are wheelchair accessible. Leashed pets are permitted.

Reservations, fees: No reservations; $35 per night, $6 for more than two people per site.

Major credit cards accepted. Open year-round.

Directions: From Interstate 10, take the Palm Drive exit and travel three miles north on Palm Drive. Turn right (east) on Dillon Road and drive 4.5 miles to 70-875 Dillon Road on the right.

Contact: Sam's Family Spa, tel. (760) 329-6457 or fax (760) 329-8267; website: samsfamilyspa.com.

10 Sky Valley Parks

 2

This park is a wonderful spot for family fun and relaxation. One of the best adventures in California is just west of Palm Springs, taking the tramway up from Chino Canyon to Desert View, a ride/climb of 2,600 feet for remarkable views to the east across the desert below. An option from there is hiking the flank of Mount San Jacinto, including making the ascent to the summit (10,804 feet), a round-trip butt-kicker of nearly 12 miles.

Location: Near Palm Springs; map I7, grid g2.

Campsites, facilities: There are 614 RV sites with hookups for cable TV, electrical connections, and sewer. Restrooms, showers, four swimming pools, nine natural hot mineral whirlpools, two laundry rooms, two large recreation rooms, modem hookups, social director, shuffleboard, tennis, horseshoes, crafts room, and walking paths are available. A grocery store and propane gas are nearby. Some facilities are wheelchair accessible. Leashed pets are permitted.

Reservations, fees: Reservations at (888) 893-7727; $31 to $33 per night, $3 per person per night for more than two people. Open year-round.

Directions: From Interstate 10, take the Palm Drive exit and travel three miles north on Palm Drive. Turn right on Dillon Road and drive 8.5 miles to 74-711 Dillon Road on the right.

Contact: Sky Valley Parks, tel. (760) 329-2909 or fax (760) 329-9473; website: www.skyvalleyresort.com.

11 Outdoor Resort of Palm Springs

    1

This is the RV park that was voted the "Most Likely to Succeed As a City." It's huge, it's flat, and it offers many activities. If you still can't think of anything to do, you can always compare tires. The park is four miles from Palm Springs. One of the best adventures in California is just west of Palm Springs, taking the tramway up from Chino Canyon to Desert View, a ride/climb of 2,600 feet for remarkable views to the east across the desert below. An option from there is hiking the flank of Mount San Jacinto, including making the ascent to the summit (10,804 feet), a round-trip butt-kicker of nearly 12 miles.

Location: Near Palm Springs; map I7, grid h1.

Campsites, facilities: There are 1,213 RV sites with full hookups. Restrooms, showers, eight swimming pools, 14 tennis courts, 10 whirlpools, a 27-hole golf course, two clubhouses, a health club with three saunas, a snack bar, a beauty salon, coin laundry, modem hookups, store, shuffleboard, and planned activities are available. Some facilities are wheelchair accessible. Leashed pets are permitted.

Reservations, fees: Reservations at (800) 843-3131 (California only); $45 to $60 per night (six person maximum per site), pets $1 per night (two pet maximum). Major credit cards accepted. Open year-round.

Directions: From Cathedral City, drive two miles north on Date Palm Drive to Ramon Road. Turn left and drive to 69-411 Ramon Road on the right.

Contact: Outdoor Resorts, tel. (760) 324-4005, ext. 2, or tel. (800) 843-3131, ext. 2 (California only); website: www.outdoorresorts.com.

12 Happy Traveler RV Park

    1

Are we having fun yet? They are at Happy Traveler, which is within walking distance of Palm Springs shopping areas.

Location: In Palm Springs; map I7, grid h0.

Campsites, facilities: There are 139 RV sites with full hookups and picnic tables. Restrooms, showers, recreation room, swimming pool, hot tub, and coin laundry are available. Leashed pets are permitted.

Reservations, fees: Reservations are accepted; $35 per night. Major credit cards accepted. Open year-round.

Directions: In Palm Springs, drive one mile south on Palm Canyon Drive. Turn right on Mesquite Avenue and go to 211 West Mesquite on the left

Contact: Happy Traveler RV Park, tel. (760) 325-8518 or fax (760) 778-6708.

13 Palm Springs Oasis RV Resort

    2

This popular wintering spot is for RV cruisers looking to hole up in the Palm Springs area for awhile. Palm Springs is only six miles away.

Location: Near Palm Springs; map I7, grid h1.

Campsites, facilities: There are 140 RV sites with full hookups. Restrooms, showers, cable TV and modem hookups, two swimming pools, whirlpool, 18-hole golf course, tennis courts, coin laundry, and propane gas are available. Some facilities are wheelchair accessible. Leashed pets are permitted.

Reservations, fees: Reservations are accepted; $25 to $32 per night, $1 per person per night for more than two people. Major credit cards accepted. Open year-round.

Directions: In Cathedral City, drive to 36-100 Date Palm Drive. The camp is on the corner of Gerald Ford Drive and Date Palm Drive.

Contact: Palm Springs Oasis RV Resort, tel. (760) 328-4813, tel. (800) 680-0144, or fax (760) 328-8455.

14 Indian Wells RV Park

    1

Indio is a good-sized town midway between the Salton Sea to the south and Palm Springs to the north. In the summer, it is one of the hottest places in America. In the winter, it is a favorite for "snowbirds," that is, RV and trailer owners from the snow country who migrate south to the desert for the winter.

Location: In Indio; map I7, grid i3.

Campsites, facilities: There are 381 RV sites, most with full hookups. Picnic tables and fire grills are provided. Restrooms, showers, cable TV hookups, three swimming pools, two therapy pools, fitness room, horseshoes, shuffleboard courts, putting green, planned activities, ice, dog run, barbecue, and coin laundry are available. Some facilities are wheelchair accessible. Leashed pets are permitted.

Reservations, fees: Reservations are accepted; $18 to $33 per night. Major credit cards accepted. Open year-round.

Directions: In Indio on Interstate 10, take the Jefferson exit. As you exit, stay in the right lane and turn right at the light. Follow Jefferson Street south for three miles. The park is on the left at 47-340 Jefferson Street.

Contact: Indian Wells RV Park, tel. (760) 347-0895, tel. (800) 789-0895, or fax (760) 775-1147.

15 Outdoor Resorts Motorcoach Resort & Spa

    7

For owners of tour buses, motor coaches, and lavish RVs, it doesn't get any better than this in Southern California. This is the sole motorhome-only park in California and it is set close to golf, shopping, and restaurants. Jeep tours of the surrounding desert canyons and organized recreation events are available.

Location: In Indio; map I7, grid i4.

Campsites, facilities: There are 419 sites for RVs only with a minimum length of 25 feet. No trailers or pick-up truck campers are allowed.

Full hookups and cable television and modem hookups are provided. Restrooms, showers, swimming pool, tennis court, sauna, whirlpool, coin laundry, and an 18-hole golf course are available. Some facilities are wheelchair accessible. Leashed pets are permitted.

Reservations, fees: Reservations are accepted; $40 to $55 per night. Major credit cards accepted. Open year-round.

Directions: From Palm Springs, take Interstate 10 east to the Jefferson exit. Stay in the right lane as you exit and then turn right at the light on Jefferson. Drive through the intersection at Highway 111 and continue one block south to 48th Avenue. Turn left and drive one-fourth mile to the park on the left side of the road at 80-394 48th Avenue.

Contact: Outdoor Resorts Motorcoach, tel. (760) 775-7255, tel. (800) 371-9988 (California only), tel. (800) 892-2992 (outside California), or fax (760) 347-0875.

16 Corn Springs

   4

Just think: If you spend a night here, you can say to darn near anybody, "I've camped someplace you haven't." I don't know whether to offer my condolences or congratulations, but Corn Springs offers a primitive spot in the middle of nowhere in desert country. What the heck, if you are stuck for a spot while cruising Interstate 10, this will seem like paradise. The side trip to Joshua Tree National Park to the north is also well worth the adventure, as is the tramway ride available west of Palm Springs for an incredible view of the desert. On the other hand, if it's a summer afternoon, tell me, just how do you spend the day here when it's 115 degrees?

Location: Near Indio; map I7, grid i6.

Campsites, facilities: There are 14 sites for tents or RVs and one group site. Picnic tables and fire grills are provided. Vault toilets are available. No drinking water is available. Leashed pets are permitted.

Reservations, fees: No reservations; $6 per night. Open year-round.

Directions: From Indio on Interstate 10, drive 60 miles east to Corn Springs Road. Exit right on Corn Springs Road and drive eight miles to the campground at the end of the road.

Contact: Bureau of Land Management, Palm Springs Field Office, tel. (760) 251-4800 or fax (760) 251-4899.

17 Cottonwood

 4

If you enter Joshua Tree National Park at its southern access point, this is the first camp you come to. The park visitor center, where maps are available, is a mandatory stop. This park is vast, high desert country, highlighted by unique rock formations, occasional scraggly trees, and vegetation that manages to survive the bleak, roasting summers. This camp is set at 3,000 feet. A trailhead is available here for an easy one-mile nature trail, where small signs have been posted to identify different types of vegetation. You'll notice, however, that they all look like cacti (the plants, not the signs, heh, heh).

Location: In Joshua Tree National Park; map I7, grid i9.

Campsites, facilities: There are 62 sites for tents or RVs up to 40 feet long. There is a group campground adjacent to this one that has three sites for up to 25 people each. Group site number two is wheelchair accessible. Picnic tables and fire grills are provided. Drinking water and flush toilets are available. Leashed pets are permitted.

Reservations, fees: No reservations for individual sites; $10 per night. Reserve group sites at (800) 365-CAMP (800-365-2267); $25 group fee per night, plus $10 park entrance fee per vehicle. Open year-round.

Directions: From Indio, drive 35 miles east on Interstate 10. Take the Twentynine Palms exit (near Chiriaco Summit) and drive seven miles north on the park entrance road to the campground on the right.

Contact: Joshua Tree National Park, tel. (760) 367-5500 or fax (760) 367-6392.

18 Piñon Flat

 6

The Cahuilla Tewanet Vista Point is just two miles east of the camp and provides a good, easy side trip, along with a sweeping view to the east of the desert. A primitive trail is available two miles away to the southeast via Forest Road 7S01 off a short spur road (look for it on the left side of the road). This hike crosses a mix of sparse forest and high desert terrain for 10 miles, passing Cactus Spring five miles in. Desert bighorn sheep are sometimes spotted in this area. The elevation is 4,000 feet.

Location: Near Cahuilla Tewanet Vista Point in San Bernardino National Forest; map I7, grid j0.

Campsites, facilities: There are 18 sites for tents or RVs up to 22 feet long. Picnic tables and fire rings are provided. Drinking water and vault toilets are available. Some facilities are wheelchair accessible. Leashed pets are permitted.

Reservations, fees: No reservations; $8 per night. Open year-round.

Directions: From Palm Desert, drive 14 miles southwest on Highway 74 to the camp on the right.

Contact: San Bernardino National Forest, San Jacinto Ranger District, tel. (909) 659-2117 or fax (909) 659-2107.

19 Lake Cahuilla County Park

 7

Lake Cahuilla covers just 135 acres, but those are the most loved 135 acres for miles in all directions. After all, water out here is as scarce as polar bears. The park provides large palm trees and a 10-acre beach and waterplay area. In the winter it is stocked with trout, and in the summer, with catfish. No swimming is allowed. Only car-top boats are permitted, and a speed limit of 10 mph is enforced. An equestrian camp is also available, complete with corrals. A warning: The wind can really howl through here, and temperatures well over 100 degrees are typical in the summer. If it weren't for this lake, they might as well post a sign on Interstate 10 that says, "You are now entering Hell."

Location: Near Indio; map I7, grid j3.

Campsites, facilities: There are numbered, primitive sites and 60 RV sites (50 with electric and water hookups and 10 with no hookups). There is also a group area with collapsible horse corrals and equestrian trails. Fire grills and picnic tables are provided. Restrooms, showers, sanitary disposal station, playground, swimming pool, and an unpaved, beach boat launch are available. No gas motors are allowed. Leashed pets are permitted.

Reservations, fees: Reservations at (800) 234-PARK ($6.50 reservation fee); $12 to $16 per night, $4 per night for each extra vehicle, $2 pet fee. Weekly rates are available. Major credit cards accepted. Open year-round, closed Tuesday, Wednesday and Thursday in summer.

Directions: From Interstate 10 in Indio, take the Monroe Street exit and follow Monroe Street south for 10 miles to Avenue 58. Turn right and continue three miles to the lake at the end of the road.

Contact: Lake Cahuilla County Park, tel. (760) 564-4712 or fax (760) 564-2506.

20 Tool Box Spring

   5

This is a lightly used campground well off the beaten track. More like off the beaten universe. That makes it perfect for people who want to be by themselves when they go camping. The Ramona trail begins at the campground, heads out to the north, and provides an easy hike-in backpack option, 3.5-miles one way. In the winter, call for road conditions to determine accessibility. The elevation is 6,500 feet.

Location: In San Bernardino National Forest; map I7, grid j0.

Campsites, facilities: There are six tent sites. Picnic tables and fire grills are provided. Vault toilets are available. No drinking water is available. Garbage must be packed out. Leashed pets are permitted.

Reservations, fees: No reservations; no camping fee. An Adventure Pass ($30 annual fee) or $5 daily fee per parked vehicle is required. Open year-round.

Directions: Traveling southeast just past Lake Hemet on Highway 74, you'll see Forest Road 6S13 (paved, then dirt) on the right. Turn right and drive about four miles. Turn left on Forest Road 5S13 and drive 4.5 miles to the camp on the left.

Contact: San Bernardino National Forest, San Jacinto Ranger District, tel. (909) 659-2117 or fax (909) 659-2107.

CHAPTER 19

KIM WEIR

DESERT SAND DUNES

MAP 19

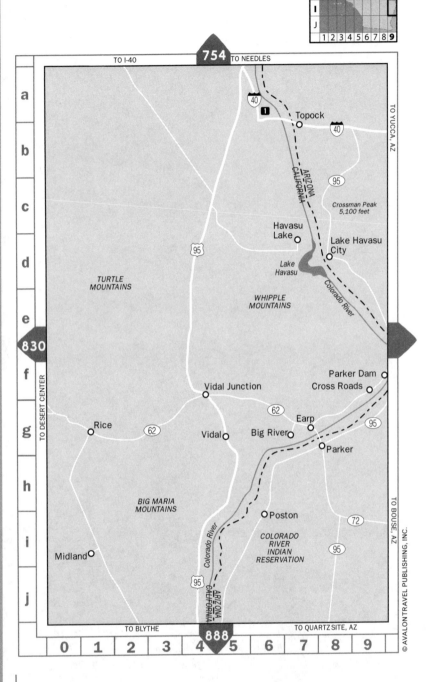

754 TO NEEDLES

TO I-40

TO YUCCA, AZ

40

1 Topock

ARIZONA
CALIFORNIA

40

95

Crossman Peak
5,100 feet

Havasu
Lake

Lake Havasu
City

95

*Lake
Havasu*

TURTLE
MOUNTAINS

WHIPPLE
MOUNTAINS

Colorado River

830

TO DESERT CENTER

Parker Dam

Cross Roads

Vidal Junction

95

Rice

62

62

Earp

Big River

Vidal

Parker

95

BIG MARIA
MOUNTAINS

72

Poston

Colorado River

COLORADO
RIVER
INDIAN
RESERVATION

95

Midland

95

ARIZONA
CALIFORNIA

TO BOUSE, AZ

TO BLYTHE

TO QUARTZSITE, AZ

888

© AVALONTRAVEL PUBLISHING, INC.

CHAPTER 19

1 Moabi Regional Park

  7

The adjacent Colorado River provides the main attraction, the only thing liquid around these parts that isn't contained in a can or bottle. The natural response when you see it is to jump in the water and everybody does so, with or without a boat. You'll see lots of wild and crazy types having the times of their lives on the water. The boating season is a long one here, courtesy of that desert climate.

Location: On the Colorado River; map 19, grid a6.

Campsites, facilities: There are more than 600 sites for tents or RVs, most with full hookups. Picnic tables and fire grills are provided at most sites. Restrooms, flush toilets, showers, laundry facilities, store, ice, playground, two sanitary disposal stations, and a boat ramp are available. Some facilities are wheelchair accessible. Leashed pets are permitted.

Reservations, fees: Reservations are accepted Monday through Friday, 8 a.m. to 4 p.m.; $12 to $20 per night per vehicle, $2 per person per night for more than six people, $1 pet fee. Major credit cards accepted. Open year-round.

Directions: From Needles, drive approximately 11 miles east on Interstate 40. Turn left on Park Moabi Road and continue a half mile to the park entrance at the end of the road

Contact: Moabi Regional Park, tel. (760) 326-3831 or fax (760) 326-3272; website: www.co.sanbernardino.ca.us/parks/moabi.

CHAPTER 15

A COMMON SIGHT
IN SOUTHERN CALIFORNIA

MAP J5

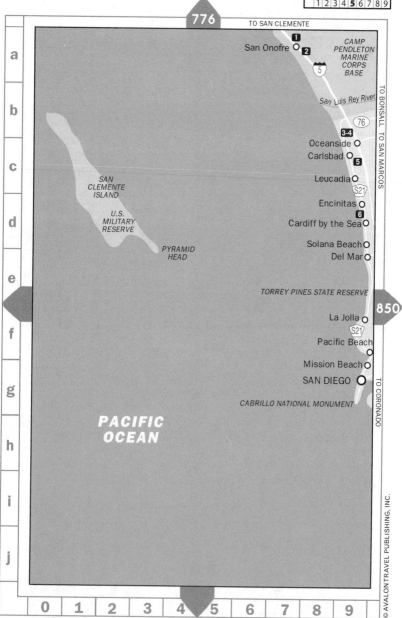

776

TO SAN CLEMENTE

a

1
San Onofre O **2**

*CAMP
PENDLETON
MARINE
CORPS
BASE*
5

b

San Luis Rey River

TO BONSALL   TO SAN MARCOS

76

3-4
Oceanside O
Carlsbad O **5**

c

*SAN
CLEMENTE
ISLAND*

Leucadia O
S21

*U.S.
MILITARY
RESERVE*

Encinitas O
6
Cardiff by the Sea O

d

*PYRAMID
HEAD*

Solana Beach O
Del Mar O

e

TORREY PINES STATE RESERVE

◆   **850** ◆

La Jolla O
S21

f

Pacific Beach
O

Mission Beach O

g

SAN DIEGO O

CABRILLO NATIONAL MONUMENT

TO CORONADO

h

*PACIFIC
OCEAN*

i

j

0 1 2 3 4 5 6 7 8 9

© AVALON TRAVEL PUBLISHING, INC.

CHAPTER J5

1 San Onofre State Beach: Bluff Area

 7

This camp may appear perfect at first glance, but nope, it is very noisy. Both the highway and train tracks are within very close range, you can practically feel the ground rumble, and that's not all. With Camp Pendleton just on the other side of the freeway, there is considerable noise from helicopters and other operations. Too bad. This is one of three parks set along the beach near San Clemente, just off the busy Coast Highway. The others are San Clemente State Beach and Doheny State Beach, both situated to the north. This area is one of the most popular in California for surfing. The shadow of the San Onofre Nuclear Power Plant is nearby.

Location: Near San Clemente; map J5, grid a7.

Campsites, facilities: There are 176 sites for tents or RVs up to 30 feet long, one group site for up to 50 people, and one hike-in/bike-in site. Picnic tables and fire rings are provided. Drinking water, flush toilets, and cold showers are available. A grocery store, coin laundry, and propane gas are available within about five miles. Leashed pets are permitted.

Reservations, fees: Reserve at tel. (800) 444-PARK (444-7275) or website: www.reserve america.com; $12 per night, $50 for the group site, $1 per person per night for the hike-in/bike-in site. Open year-round.

Directions: From San Clemente, drive three miles south on Interstate 5. Take the Basilone Road exit and drive south for two miles to the park.

Contact: San Onofre State Beach, tel. (949) 492-4872; Coast District Office, tel. (949) 492-0802.

2 San Onofre State Beach: San Mateo

 9

The camp is set inland with a nature trail available. It is a 1.1-mile walk to the beach, well known as the outstanding Trestles Surfing Area. Although this is a state beach, the camp is relatively far from the ocean. But it sure is a lot quieter than the option, the Bluffs.

Location: Near San Clemente; map J5, grid a7.

Campsites, facilities: There are 159 sites for tents or RVs, 47 with electric and water hookups. Fire grills are provided. A sanitary disposal station, hot showers, and flush toilets are available. A grocery store, propane gas, and coin laundry are nearby. Leashed pets are permitted. Some facilities are wheelchair accessible.

Reservations, fees: Reserve at tel. (800) 444-PARK (444-7275) or website: www.reserve america.com; $12 to $18 per night. Open year-round.

Directions: From Interstate 5 at the southern end of San Clemente, take the Cristianitos Road exit and drive inland 1.5 miles to the park entrance on the right.

Contact: San Onofre State Beach, tel. (949) 492-4872; Coast District Office, tel. (949) 492-0802.

3 Paradise by the Sea RV Resort

      7

This is a classic oceanfront RV park, but no tenters need apply. It's an easy walk to the beach. For boaters, Oceanside Marina to the immediate north is the place to go. Oceanside is an excellent headquarters for deepsea fishing, with charter trips available to Catalina Island, the kelp forests to the north offshore Camp Pendleton and San Onofre, as well as points south; contact Helgren's Sportfishing, tel. (760) 722-2133, to arrange charters. Camp Pendleton, a huge Marine Corps training complex, is to the north.

Location: In Oceanside; map J5, grid b9.

Campsites, facilities: There are 102 RV sites with full hookups; no pull-through sites. Restrooms, flush toilets, showers, cable TV hookups, swimming pool, whirlpool, clubhouse, banquet room, coin laundry, RV supplies, telephone, horseshoe pit, and a small grocery store are available. Boat rentals are nearby. Leashed pets are permitted with proof of vaccination.

Reservations, fees: Reservations are recommended; $30 to $39 per night, $2 per person per night for more than two people, $1 per night for each extra vehicle, $1 pet fee. Major credit cards accepted. Open year-round.

Directions: From Interstate 5 in Oceanside, take the Oceanside Boulevard exit. Drive west for a half mile to South Coast Highway. Turn left on South Coast Highway and go to 1537 South Coast Highway on the right.

Contact: Paradise by the Sea RV Resort, tel. (760) 439-1376 or fax (760) 439-1919; website: www.paradisebythesearvresort.com.

4 Casitas Poquitos

     7

There are three options for RV cruisers in the Oceanside area, and this is one of them. It's a short distance to the beach. For details on the area, see the entry for Paradise by the Sea RV Park.

Location: In Oceanside; map J5, grid b9.

Campsites, facilities: There are 140 RV sites with full hookups. Picnic tables and patios are provided. Flush toilets, showers, cable TV hookups, playground, coin laundry, recreation room, swimming pool, whirlpool, billiard room, propane gas, and a general store are available. Leashed pets are permitted.

Reservations, fees: Reservations are recommended; $27 to $38 per night, $2 per person per night for more than two people, $1 pet fee. Major credit cards accepted. Open year-round.

Directions: From Interstate 5 in Oceanside, take the Oceanside Boulevard exit. Drive west for a half mile. Turn left on South Coast Highway and drive 1.5 blocks to the park at 1510 South Coast Highway.

Contact: Casitas Poquitos, tel. (760) 722-4404.

5 South Carlsbad State Beach

     9

No reservation? Then likely you can forget about staying here. This is a beautiful state beach and, as big as it is, the sites go fast to the coastal cruisers who reserved in advance. The campground is set on a bluff, with half the sites overlooking the ocean. The nearby beach is accessible by a series of stairs. This is a phenomenal place for scuba diving and snorkeling, with a nearby reef available. This is also a popular spot for surfing and body surfing.

Location: Near Carlsbad; map J5, grid c9.

Campsites, facilities: There are 221 sites for tents or RVs up to 35 feet long. Picnic tables and fire rings are provided. Restrooms, drinking water, flush toilets, coin showers, and a sanitary disposal station are available. A lifeguard service is provided in summer. Some facilities are wheelchair accessible. Supplies and a coin laundry are available in Carlsbad. Leashed pets are permitted, but not on the beach.

Reservations, fees: Reserve at tel. (800) 444-PARK (444-7275) or website: www.reserve america.com; $12 per night. Open year-round.

Directions: From Carlsbad, drive four miles south on Pacific Coast Highway to the camp entrance on the right.

Contact: South Carlsbad State Beach, tel. (760) 438-3143; San Diego Coast District office, tel. (858) 642-4200.

6 San Elijo State Beach

 9

As with South Carlsbad State Beach, about half the sites overlook the ocean, that is, blufftop campgrounds. What more could you ask for? Well, er, for one thing, how about not so many trains? Yep, train tracks run nearby and the trains roll by several times a day. So much for tranquility. Regardless, it is a beautiful beach just north of the small town of Cardiff by the Sea. As at all state beaches, reservations are usually required to get a spot between Memorial Day weekend and Labor Day weekend. Nearby San Elijo Lagoon at Solana Beach is an ecological preserve. Though near a developed area, there are numerous white egrets, as well as occasional herons and other marine birds.

Location: In Cardiff by the Sea; map J5, grid d9.

Campsites, facilities: There are 171 sites for tents or RVs up to 35 feet long, and one hike-in/bike-in site. Picnic tables and fire grills are provided. Restrooms, drinking water, flush toilets, coin showers, sanitary disposal station, and a small store are available. A lifeguard service is available in the summer. Some facilities are wheelchair accessible. Leashed pets are permitted, but not on the beach.

Reservations, fees: Reserve at tel. (800) 444-PARK (444-7275) or website: www.reserve america.com; $12 to $18 per night, $1 per person per night for hike-in/bike-in site. Open year-round.

Directions: From Interstate 5 at Encinitas, take the Encinitas Boulevard exit and drive west for one mile to U.S. 101. Turn south on U.S. 101 and drive 3.5 miles to the campground on the right.

Contact: San Elijo State Beach, tel. (760) 753-5091; Coast District Office, tel. (858) 642-4200.

CHAPTER 16

THE PALOMAR OBSERVATORY

MAP J6

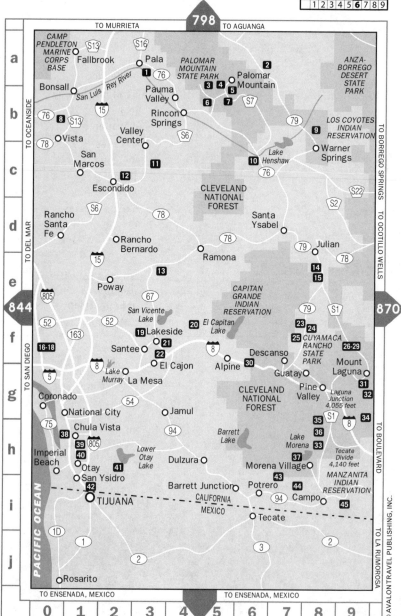

TO MURRIETA

798

TO AGUANGA

TO OCEANSIDE

CAMP
PENDLETON
MARINE
CORPS
BASE
Fallbrook

S13

S16

Pala

PALOMAR
MOUNTAIN
STATE PARK

2

ANZA-
BORREGO
DESERT
STATE
PARK

Bonsall

San Luis Rey River

1 76

PALOMAR
MOUNTAIN
STATE PARK

3 **4**

5 Palomar
Mountain

Pauma
Valley

6 **7**

S7

76 **8** S13

15

Rincon
Springs

S6

9

LOS COYOTES
INDIAN
RESERVATION

Vista

78

Valley
Center

Lake
Henshaw

Warner
Springs

TO DEL MAR

San
Marcos

11

10 76

TO BORREGO SPRINGS

Escondido

12

CLEVELAND
NATIONAL
FOREST

S22

S2

Rancho
Santa
Fe

S6

78

Santa
Ysabel

79

Julian

78

Rancho
Bernardo

78

Ramona

14

15

844

15

13

CAPITAN
GRANDE
INDIAN
RESERVATION

870

805

Poway

67

79

S1

52

San Vicente
Lake

23 **24**

52

19 Lakeside

20 El Capitan
Lake

25

CUYAMACA
RANCHO
STATE
PARK

26-29

163

16-18

Santee

21

8

22

El Cajon

Alpine

Descanso

30

Mount
Laguna

31

Lake
Murray

La Mesa

Guatay

32

5

Coronado

54

Jamul

CLEVELAND
NATIONAL
FOREST

Pine
Valley

Laguna
Junction
4,055 feet

National City

94

35 S1

34

75

Chula Vista

38

Barrett
Lake

36

8

39

805

Lake
Morena

33

Tecate
Divide
4,140 feet

Imperial
Beach

40

Lower
Otay
Lake

Dulzura

37

MANZANITA
INDIAN
RESERVATION

Otay

41

Morena Village

43

San Ysidro

42

Barrett Junction

Potrero

44

TIJUANA

CALIFORNIA
MEXICO

94

Campo

45

1D

Tecate

1

2

3

2

Rosarito

TO ENSENADA, MEXICO

TO ENSENADA, MEXICO

PACIFIC OCEAN

TO SAN DIEGO

© AVALON TRAVEL PUBLISHING, INC.

TO LA RUMOROSA

TO BOULEVARD

TO OCOTILLO WELLS

CHAPTER J6

(CONTINUED ON NEXT PAGE)

1 Rancho Corrído RV Park

      7

This RV layover is 10 miles east of Interstate 15, the main drag. A fishing pond is available for catch-and-release fishing only. It is a short drive to the Pala Indian Reservation and the Pala Mission to the east. The Palomar Observatory is 20 miles to the east, another possible side trip.

Location: Near the Pala Mission; map J6, grid a3.

Campsites, facilities: There are 210 sites for tents or RVs (110 with water, electric, and cable TV hookups) and 100 tent sites. Picnic tables and fire pits are provided. Restrooms, drinking water, flush toilets, showers, sanitary disposal station, modem hookups, clubhouses, gazebos, playground, small store, fishing pond, and coin laundry are available. Leashed pets are permitted.

Reservations, fees: Reservations are preferred; $19 to $24 per night, $7 per person (adult rate) per night for more than two people, $3 pet fee. Weekly rates available. Open year-round. Major credit cards accepted.

Directions: From Interstate 15, take the Highway 76 exit and drive east past the town of Pala. Continue east on Highway 76 for four miles to the camp at 14715 Highway 76 on the right.

Contact: Rancho Corrído, tel. (760) 742-3755 or fax (760) 742-3245; website: www.ranchocorrido.com.

2 Oak Grove

   4

Oak Grove camp is on the northeastern fringe of Cleveland National Forest at 2,800 feet. Easy access from Highway 79 makes this a popular camp. The Palomar Observatory is just five miles up the mountain to the west, but there is no direct way to reach it from the campground. Lake Henshaw is about a half-hour drive to the south. A boat ramp and boat rentals are available there.

Location: Near Temecula Creek in Cleveland National Forest; map J6, grid a6.

Campsites, facilities: There are 81 sites for tents or RVs up to 32 feet long. Picnic tables and grills are provided. Drinking water and flush toilets are available. Propane gas and groceries are nearby. Leashed pets are permitted.

Reservations, fees: No reservations; $15 to $20 per night. Open year-round.

Directions: From Aguanga, drive 6.5 miles southeast on Highway 79 to the camp entrance.

Contact: Cleveland National Forest, Palomar Ranger District, tel. (760) 788-0250 or fax (760) 788-6130.

3 Palomar Mountain State Park

      8

This developed state park is a short drive from the Palomar Observatory. There are four other campgrounds in the immediate area that are a short distance from the observatory. The elevation is 4,700 feet. This camp offers hiking trails and some fishing in Doane Pond (permit required, great for youngsters learning to fish). There are three excellent hikes, the Observatory Trail (4.5 miles), Boucher Trail (4 miles), and Lower Doane Valley Trail (3 miles). The view from Boucher Lookout is stunning, at 5,438 feet looking out over the valley below. At the Palomar Observatory you'll find the 200-inch Hale telescope, America's largest telescope. This is a private, working telescope, so there are no tours or public stargazing through it.

Location: Near the Palomar Observatory; map J6, grid a5.

Campsites, facilities: There are 31 sites for tents or RVs up to 21 feet long, three group sites for 15 to 25 people, and one hike-in/bike-in site. Picnic tables, grills, and food lockers are provided. Drinking water, flush toilets, and coin showers are available. Some facilities are wheelchair accessible. Leashed pets are permitted.

Reservations, fees: Reserve at tel. (800) 444-PARK (444-7275) or website: www.reserve america.com; $12 per night, $20 to $32 for group sites. Permit required for fishing pond. Open year-round.

Directions: From Interstate 15, turn east on Highway 76 and drive about 25 miles to County Road S6 (which brings you to the top of Palomar Mountain). At the top of the mountain turn left, go about 50 feet, turn left again on State Park Road/County Road S7, and drive about 3.5 miles to the park entrance.

Contact: Palomar Mountain State Park, tel. (760) 742-3462; Colorado Desert District, tel. (760) 767-5311.

◢ Fry Creek

   6

A small, seasonal stream, Fry Creek, runs near the camp. The elevation is 5,200 feet. On a clear night, you can see forever from Palomar Mountain. Literally. That's because the Palomar Observatory, just a short distance from this forested camp, houses America's largest telescope. With the 200-inch Hale telescope, it is possible for scientists to see 100 billion galaxies.

Location: Near the Palomar Observatory in Cleveland National Forest; map J6, grid a5.

Campsites, facilities: There are 12 tent sites and eight sites for tents or RVs up to 16 feet long. Picnic tables and fire rings are provided. Drinking water and vault toilets are available. A grocery store is nearby. Leashed pets are permitted.

Reservations, fees: No reservations; $12 per night. Open May through November.

Directions: From Interstate 15, head east on Highway 76 and drive about 25 miles to County Road S6 (the road that goes up to Palomar Mountain). At the top of the mountain, turn left and drive about nine miles to the campground entrance on the left. The road is not recommended for trailers.

Contact: Cleveland National Forest, Palomar Ranger District, tel. (760) 788-0250 or fax (760) 788-6130.

◢ Observatory

    4

This popular Forest Service camp is used primarily as a layover spot for campers visiting the nearby Palomar Observatory, housing the largest telescope in America. There are four other camps in the immediate area. The elevation is 4,800 feet. The trailhead for the Observatory Trail starts at this camp. This two-hour hike from the campground to the observatory includes one short, steep climb through woodlands, highlighted by a vista deck with a beautiful view of Mendenhall Valley, and then onward to the top and to the telescope viewing area.

Location: Near the Palomar Observatory in Cleveland National Forest; map J6, grid b5.

Campsites, facilities: There are 42 sites for tents or RVs up to 22 feet long (a few sites will accommodate RVs up to 28 feet long). Picnic tables and fire grills are provided. Drinking water and vault toilets are available. Leashed pets are permitted.

Reservations, fees: No reservations; $12 per night, double sites are $20 per night. Open May through November.

Directions: From Interstate 15, head east on Highway 76 and drive about 25 miles to County Road S6 (the road that goes up to Palomar Mountain). At the top of the mountain, turn left and drive about 8.5 miles to the campground entrance on the right.

Contact: Cleveland National Forest, Palomar Ranger District, tel. (760) 788-0250 or fax (760) 788-6130.

Crestline Group Camp

  4

This Forest Service camp is designed expressly for large groups planning to visit Palomar Observatory. For adventure information, see the entry for Palomar Mountain State Park. The elevation is 4,800 feet.

Location: Near the Palomar Observatory in Cleveland National Forest; map J6, grid b5.

Campsites, facilities: There is one group campsite for tents only. Picnic tables and fire grills are provided. Drinking water and vault toilets are available. A grocery store is nearby. Leashed pets are permitted.

Reservations, fees: Reservations are required; reserve at tel. (877) 444-6777 ($8.65 reservation fee) or website: www.reserveusa.com; $75 group fee per night. Major credit cards accepted. Open May through November.

Directions: From Interstate 15, head east on Highway 76 and drive about 20 miles to County Road S6 (the road that goes up to Palomar Mountain). Turn left and drive 6.5 miles. The campground is at the junction of County Roads S6 and S7.

Contact: Cleveland National Forest, Palomar Ranger District, tel. (760) 788-0250 or fax (760) 788-6130.

Oak Knoll

     5

The camp is set at 3,000 feet in San Diego County foothill country, among giant old California oaks. It is at the western base of Palomar Mountain, and to visit the Palomar Observatory and its awesome 200-inch telescope requires a remarkably twisty 10-mile drive up the mountain. A good side trip is driving to the Boucher Lookout in Palomar Mountain State Park. Trailheads for excellent hikes on Palomar Mountain include the Observatory Trail, (starting at Observatory) and the Doane Valley Loop (starting in Palomar Mountain State Park).

Location: Near the Palomar Observatory; map J6, grid b5.

Campsites, facilities: There are 46 sites for tents or RVs, many with full or partial hookups. Restrooms, drinking water, flush toilets, showers, playground, swimming pool, clubhouse, baseball diamond, coin laundry, propane gas, and groceries are available. Leashed pets are permitted.

Reservations, fees: Call ahead for available space; $20 to $24 per night, $3 per person per night for more than two people, $1 pet fee. Open year-round.

Directions: From Interstate 15, turn east on Highway 76 and drive about 20 miles to County Road S6 (the road that goes up to Palomar Mountain). Turn left and drive one block to the campground.

Contact: Oak Knoll, tel. (760) 742-3437; website: www.oakknoll.net.

Guajome County Park

    5

Guajome means "home of the frog" and, yep, so it is with little Guajome Lake and the adjacent marsh, both of which can be explored with a delightful two-mile hike. The lake provides a bit of fishing for warm-water species, mainly sunfish and catfish. Because of the wetlands, a huge variety of birds will stop here on their migratory journeys, making this a favorite area for bird-watching. There are also trails available for horseback riding. A historic adobe in the park is a must-see.

Location: In Oceanside; map J6, grid b0.

Campsites, facilities: There are 35 RV sites with water and electrical hookups. Picnic tables and fire grills are provided. Restrooms, drinking water, flush toilets, showers, sanitary disposal station, and a playground are available. A grocery store and propane gas are nearby. Leashed pets are permitted.

Reservations, fees: Reservations at tel. (858) 565-3600 ($3 reservation fee); $14 per night, eight person maximum per site, $1 pet fee. Major credit cards accepted. Open year-round.

Directions: From Oceanside, drive seven miles east on Highway 76/Mission Avenue.

Turn right on Guajome Lakes Road and drive to the entrance.

Contact: San Diego County Parks Department, tel. (858) 694-3049.

Indian Flats

   6

Indian Flats is a remote campground, set at 3,600 feet just north of Pine Mountain. A highlight here is that the Pacific Crest Trail passes only two miles down the road to the south. A two-mile hike south on the PCT will take you down into a canyon and the home of Agua Caliente Creek.

Location: Near the Pacific Crest Trail in Cleveland National Forest; map J6, grid b8.

Campsites, facilities: There are 17 sites for tents. Picnic tables and fire grills are provided. Drinking water and vault toilets are available. Leashed pets are permitted.

Reservations, fees: No reservations; $10 per night. Open May through March, closed April through June for protection of endangered species, the Arroyo Southwestern Toad.

Directions: From Warner Springs on Highway 79, drive two miles northwest on Highway 79. Turn right on Forest Road 9S05 and drive six miles to the campground.

Contact: Cleveland National Forest, Palomar Ranger District, tel. (760) 788-0250 or fax (760) 788-6130.

10 Lake Henshaw Resort RV

     7

Lake Henshaw is the biggest lake in San Diego County, yet it only has one camp. It's a good one, with the cabin rentals a big plus. The camp is on the southern corner of the lake, at 2,727 feet near Cleveland National Forest. Swimming is not permitted and a 10-mph speed limit is in effect. The fishing is best for catfish, especially in the summer, and at times decent for bass, with the lake-record bass weighing 14 pounds, four ounces.

Location: Near San Ysabel; map J6, grid c6.

Campsites, facilities: There are 164 sites for tents or RVs, many with full hookups. There are also 17 cabins with linens and kitchenettes. Flush toilets, showers, swimming pool, whirlpool, clubhouse, playground, sanitary disposal station, coin laundry, propane gas, boat and motor rentals, boat launch, bait and tackle shop, restaurant, and groceries are available. Some facilities are wheelchair accessible. A golf course is 10 miles away. Leashed pets are permitted.

Reservations, fees: Reservations for cabins only; family sites $14-16 per night, cabin fees are $45 to $60 per night, $1 pet fee. Major credit cards accepted. Open year-round.

Directions: From Santa Ysabel, drive seven miles north on Highway 79. Turn left on Highway 76 and drive four miles to the campground on the left.

Contact: Lake Henshaw Resort RV, tel. (760) 782-3487, tel. (760) 782-3501, or fax (760) 782-9224; website: www.lakehenshaw.com.

11 Woods Valley Kampground

     5

This privately operated park is set up primarily for RVs and is a short drive from Lake Wohlford to the south. Lake Wohlford has a 5-mph speed limit, which guarantees quiet water; canoes, inflatables, sailboats, and boats under 10 feet and over 18 feet are prohibited. It provides fair fishing for bass, bluegill, and catfish, best in late winter and spring.

Location: Near Lake Wohlford; map J6, grid c3.

Campsites, facilities: There are 59 RV sites, many with hookups, and 30 sites for tents or RVs. Picnic tables and fire barrels are provided. Restrooms, drinking water, flush toilets, showers, sanitary disposal station, swimming pool, kid's fishing pond, small farm, playground, supplies, and coin laundry are available. Leashed pets are permitted, except no pit bulls are welcome.

Reservations, fees: Reservations are accepted; $22 to $34 per night, $3 per person per night for more than four people; $3 per night for each extra vehicle, $3 pet fee. Open year-round.

Directions: From Escondido on Interstate 15, turn east on County Road S6 and drive northeast to Valley Center. Turn right on Woods Valley Road and drive two miles east to 15236 Woods Valley Road on the left.

Contact: Woods Valley Kampground, tel. (760) 749-2905; website: www.woodsvalley.com.

12 Dixon Lake Recreation Area

      7

Little Dixon Lake is the centerpiece of a regional park in the Escondido foothills. The camp is set at an elevation of 1,405 feet, about 400 feet above the lake's shoreline. No private boats are permitted, and a 5-mph speed limit for rental boats keeps things quiet. The water is clear, with fair bass fishing in the spring, and trout fishing in the winter and early spring. Catfish are stocked in the summer. A pretty and easy hike is available on the Jack Creek Nature Trail, a one-mile walk to a 20-foot waterfall.

Location: Near Escondido; map J6, grid c2.

Campsites, facilities: There are 45 sites for tents or RVs, some with full hookups. Picnic tables and fire grills are provided. Restrooms, drinking water, flush toilets, showers, boat rentals, bait, ice, snack bar, and a playground are available. Pets are not permitted.

Reservations, fees: Reservations are accepted; $12 to $16 per night, maximum of eight people per site, $2 per night for each extra vehicle. Group sites available. Major credit cards accepted. Open year-round.

Directions: In Escondido, drive four miles northeast on El Norte Parkway to La Honda Drive. Turn left and drive to 1700 North La Honda Drive at Dixon Lake.

Contact: Dixon Lake Recreation Area, tel. (760) 741-3328 or tel. (760) 839-4345; website: www.ci.escondido.ca.us.

13 Dos Picos County Park

      6

As a county park, this camp is often missed by folks relying on less complete guides. The park is quite picturesque, with plenty of shade trees and a small pond. Several nearby recreation options are in the area. San Vicente Lake is about 15 miles away, a prime bass lake open Thursday through Sunday from September through June. The elevation is 1,500 feet.

Location: Near Ramona; map J6, grid e3.

Campsites, facilities: There are 14 tent sites and 50 RV sites with electrical hookups. Picnic tables and fire grills are provided. Restrooms, drinking water, flush toilets, showers, and a playground are available. Supplies and a coin laundry are one mile away in Ramona. Leashed pets are permitted.

Reservations, fees: Reservations at tel. (858) 565-3600; $10 to $14 per night, maximum of eight people per site, $1 pet fee. Major credit cards accepted. Open year-round.

Directions: From Interstate 8 in El Cajon, drive 22 miles north on Highway 67. Make a sharp right on Mussey Grade Road and drive two miles to the park.

Contact: San Diego County Parks Department, tel. (858) 694-3094.

14 William Heise County Park

      6

This is a beautiful county park, set at 4,200 feet, that offers hiking trails and a playground, all amid pretty woodlands with a mix of oak and pine. A great hike starts right at camp (at the tent camping area) and is signed "Nature Trail." It joins with the Canyon Oak Trail and, after little more than a mile, links up with the Desert View Trail. Here you will reach an overlook with a beautiful view of Anza-Borrego Desert and the Salton Sea. The area surrounding the park is filled with recreation options. They include Cleveland National Forest to the immediate south, Lake Cuyamaca and Cuyamaca Rancho State Park to the southeast, the vast Anza-Borrego Desert State Park to the east, and the historic town of Julian.

Location: Near Julian; map J6, grid e8.

Campsites, facilities: There are 43 sites for tents only, 40 sites for tents or RVs, several group sites, and two cabins. Picnic tables and fire grills are provided. Restrooms, drinking water, flush toilets, showers, coin laundry, sanitary disposal station, and a playground are available. Supplies are available five miles away in Julian. Leashed pets are permitted.

Reservations, fees: Reservations at tel. (858) 565-3600; $12 to $14 per night, $35 per night for a cabin, eight person maximum per site, $1 pet fee. Major credit cards accepted. Open year-round.

Directions: From Highway 78 west of Julian, turn south on Pine Hills Road and drive two miles. Turn left on Frisius Drive and drive two miles to the park.

Contact: San Diego County Parks Department, tel. (858) 694-3049.

15 Pinezanita Trailer Ranch

    6

Set at an elevation of 4,680 feet in dense pine and oak, this camp has had the same owners, the Stanley family, for over 30 years. The fishing pond is a great attraction for kids (no license is required), but there's no swimming allowed. The pond is stocked with blue gill and catfish, some of which are 12 inches or longer. Two possible side trips include Lake Cuyamaca, five miles to the south, and William Heise County Park, about 10 miles to the north as the crow flies.

Location: Near Julian, map J6, grid e8.

Campsites, facilities: There are a total of 230 campsites, 40 for tents and 190 for RVs; 160 of the RV sites have partial hookups (electricity and sewer). There are also a few furnished cottages. Picnic tables and fire rings are provided. Restrooms, drinking water, flush toilets, showers, a general store, ice, propane, fishing pond, and a sanitary disposal station are available. Leashed pets are permitted.

Reservations, fees: Reservations accepted; campsites are $18 per night per vehicle (two people), cottages are $125 per night for two people (no children or pets in the cottages), $2 each additional camper, $2 per hookup and $2 pet fee. Major credit cards accepted. Open year-round.

Directions: From San Diego, drive east on Interstate 8 to the junction with Highway 79. Turn north on Highway 79 and drive 20 miles to the campground on the left.

Contact: Pinezanita Trailer Ranch, P.O. Box 2380, Julian, CA 92036-2380; tel. (760) 765-0429; website: www.pinezanita.com.

16 De Anza Harbor Resort

    5

Location means everything in real estate and campgrounds, and this private park passes the test. It is set on a small peninsula that is surrounded on three sides by Mission Bay, Sea World, and the San Diego Zoo. A beach and golf course are adjacent to the park. Mission Bay has 27 miles of shoreline, expansive beach frontage, great windsurfing, fantastic boating for water-skiing, and ocean access for deep-sea fishing. Note that a 5-mph speed limit is enforced on the northern bay, and on the entire bay after sunset.

Location: On Mission Bay; map J6, grid f0.

Campsites, facilities: There are 243 RV sites with full hookups and patios. Restrooms, drinking water, flush toilets, showers, playground, sanitary disposal station, coin laundry, modem hookups, recreation room, pool tables, bike rentals, boat ramp, propane gas, and a grocery store are available. Some facilities are wheelchair accessible. Leashed pets are permitted.

Reservations, fees: Reservations at (800) 924-7529; $18.50 to $72 per night (for Bay overlook sites), $3 per person per night for more than four people, $3 boats, $3 pet fee. Major credit cards accepted. Open year-round.

Directions: From southbound Interstate 5 in San Diego, take the Clairemont exit to Mission Bay Drive. Turn left and drive to North Mission Bay Drive. Turn right on De Anza Road and drive to 2727 De Anza Road on the right.

Contact: De Anza Harbor Resort, tel. (858) 273-3211 or fax (858) 274-0362.

Campland on the Bay

    5

No kidding, this is one of the biggest campgrounds on this side of the galaxy. With space for both tenters and RVers, you can usually find a spot to shoehorn your way into. It is set on Mission Bay, a beautiful spot and a boater's paradise. The park overlooks Kendall Frost Wildlife Preserve and Mission Bay, and includes a private beach. Water-skiing, windsurfing, and ocean access for deep-sea fishing are preeminent. Note that a 5-mph speed limit is enforced on the northern bay, and on the entire bay after sunset. Sea World, just north of San Diego, offers a premium side trip.

Location: On Mission Bay; map J6, grid f0.

Campsites, facilities: There are 750 tent and RV sites, most with full or partial hookups. Picnic tables and fire grills are provided. Restrooms, drinking water, flush toilets, showers, cable TV, phone, and modem hookups, swimming pools, hot tub, recreation hall, arcade, playground, sanitary disposal station, coin laundry, grocery store, RV supplies, propane gas, boat ramp, boat docks, water toy rentals, boat and bike rentals, and groceries are available. Leashed pets are permitted.

Reservations, fees: Reservations accepted up to two years in advance at (800) 422-9386 ($25 site guarantee fee); $29 to $52 per night, eight person per site maximum, $5 for boats and trailers, $30 for boat slip up to 20 feet, $3 pet fee. Major credit cards accepted. Open year-round.

Directions: From southbound Interstate 5 in San Diego, take the Balboa-Garnet exit. Drive straight on Mission Bay Drive to Grand Avenue. Turn right and drive one mile. Turn left on Olney Street and drive to Pacific Beach Drive. Turn left and drive a short distance to the campground entrance. From northbound Interstate 5 in San Diego, take the Grand-Garnet exit. Stay in the left lane and turn left on Grand Avenue. Turn left on Olney Street and continue as above.

Contact: Campland on the Bay, tel. (800) 422-9386, tel. (858) 581-4200 or fax (858) 581-4264; 20-minute waits can occur when making reservations; website: www.campland.com.

Santa Fe Travel Trailer Park

   1

This camp is a short drive from a variety of side trips, including the San Diego Zoo, Sea World, golf courses, beaches, sportfishing, and Tijuana.

Location: In San Diego; map J6, grid f0.

Campsites, facilities: There are 129 RV sites with full hookups. No tent camping is allowed. Restrooms, drinking water, flush toilets, showers, playground, swimming pool, hot tub, sanitary disposal station, cable TV, weight room, and coin laundry are available. Some facilities are wheelchair accessible. Leashed pets are permitted.

Reservations, fees: Reservations at (800) 959-3787; $31 to $47 per night, $2 person for more than four people, $2 pet fee. Major credit cards accepted. Open year-round.

Directions: In San Diego from Interstate 5, take the Balboa-Garnet exit (southbound). Make the first possible left to Damon Street. Turn left and drive to Santa Fe Street. Turn left and drive to the camp on the right at 5707 Santa Fe Street.

Contact: Santa Fe Travel Trailer Park, tel. (858) 272-4051 or fax (858) 272-2845.

19 Santee Lakes Regional Park

 6

This small regional park is 20 miles east of San Diego. Quiet, low-key boating is the name of the game here. Rowboats, pedal boats, and canoes are available for rent. The camp is set at 400 feet.

Location: Near Santee; map J6, grid f3.

Campsites, facilities: There are 172 sites for RVs with full hookups, including 57 sites for tents. Some barbecue grills are provided. Restrooms, drinking water, flush toilets, showers, sanitary disposal station, boat rentals, playground, swimming pool, grocery store, snack bar, recreation center, modem hookups, and coin laundry are available. Some facilities are wheelchair accessible. Leashed pets are permitted at campsites only.

Reservations, fees: Reservations are accepted; $18 to $32 per night, $1 per person per night for more than six people, $2 per night for each extra vehicle, $1 pet fee. Open year-round. Major credit cards accepted.

Directions: From Interstate 8 in El Cajon, drive two miles north on Highway 67 to the town of Santee. Turn left on Mission Gorge Road and drive 2.5 miles to Carlton Hills Drive. Turn right and drive to Carlton Oaks Drive. Turn left and drive a mile to the park on the right.

Contact: Santee Lakes Regional Park, tel. (619) 596-3143.

20 Lake Jennings County Park

 6

While this lake wasn't named after 'Ol Waylon (he's got a camp named after him in Littlefield, Texas), he wouldn't disown it if it were. It is a nice little backyard fishing hole and recreation area set at 850 feet, with easy access from Interstate 8. The highlights here are evening picnics, summer catfishing, and a boat ramp and rentals. Only one camp is available right at the lake, and this is it.

Location: On Lake Jennings; map J6, grid f4.

Campsites, facilities: There are 34 RV sites with full hookups, 34 RV sites with partial hookups, and 26 tent sites. Picnic tables and fire grills are provided. Restrooms, drinking water, flush toilets, showers, playground, and a sanitary disposal station are available. A grocery store is nearby. Leashed pets are permitted.

Reservations, fees: Reservations at (858) 565-3600; $12 to $16 per night, maximum of eight people per site, $1 pet fee. Open year-round.

Directions: From San Diego, drive 16 miles east on Interstate 8. Take Lake Jennings Park Road north to the park entrance.

Contact: San Diego County Parks Department, tel. (858) 694-3049.

21 Rancho Los Coches RV Park

 2

Nearby Lake Jennings provides an option for boaters and anglers and also has a less developed camp on its northeast shore. Vista Point on the southeastern side of the lake provides a side trip. For more information, see Lake Jennings County Park.

Location: Near Lake Jennings; map J6, grid f3.

Campsites, facilities: There are five tent areas and 137 RV sites with full hookups. Restrooms, drinking water, flush toilets, showers, sanitary disposal station, modem hookups, and coin laundry are available. A grocery store is one mile away. Leashed pets are permitted.

Reservations, fees: Reservations at (800) 630-0448; $29 per night, $3 per person per night for more than two people. Open year-round.

Directions: From El Cajon, drive east on Interstate 8 to the Los Coches Road exit. Go under the freeway, turn right on Highway 8 Business, and drive to the park entrance on the left at 13468 Highway 8 Business.

Contact: Rancho Los Coches RV Park, tel. (619) 443-2025 or fax (619) 443-8440; website: www.rancholoscochesrv.com.

22 Vacationer RV Park

    1

This camp is 25 minutes from San Diego, 40 minutes to Mexico. Discount tickets to area attractions such as the San Diego Zoo, Sea World, and the Wild Animal Park are available. It's not a real pretty place, and that is compounded with the very real chance of getting highway noise if you have a site at the back of the park. The RV sites are on asphalt and gravel. The elevation is 260 feet.

Location: Near El Cajon; map J6, grid f3.

Campsites, facilities: There are 158 sites with full hookups for RVs up to 40 feet long, including 20 pull-through sites. No tent camping is allowed. Restrooms, drinking water, flush toilets, showers, laundry, playground, recreation room, volleyball court, horseshoe pits, modem hookups, swimming pool, hot tub, sanitary disposal station, satellite TV, free video library, and a picnic area with barbecues are available. A grocery store is nearby. Some facilities are wheelchair accessible. Leashed pets are permitted.

Reservations, fees: Reservations at (619) 442-0904; $26.55 per night, $2 per person per night for more than two people. Major credit cards accepted. Open year-round.

Directions: On Interstate 8 in El Cajon, drive east for three miles to Greenfield Road exit. Take that exit, turn north and drive 100 feet to East Main Street. Turn left (west) and drive one-half mile to the park on the left.

Contact: Vacationer RV Park, tel. (619) 442-0904 or fax (619) 442-4378.

23 Green Valley

      8

Green Valley is the southernmost camp in Cuyamaca Rancho State Park. It is set at 3,900 feet, with Cuyamaca Mountain (6,512 feet) looming overhead to the northwest. A trailhead is available (look for the picnic area) at the camp for an easy five-minute walk to Green Valley Falls, and can be continued out to the Sweetwater River in a 1.5-mile round trip. Newcomers should visit the park headquarters, where exhibits detail the natural history of the area.

Location: In Cuyamaca Rancho State Park; map J6, grid f7.

Campsites, facilities: There are 81 sites for tents or RVs. Picnic tables and fire grills are provided. Restrooms, drinking water, flush toilets, and coin-operated showers are available. Some facilities are wheelchair accessible. A grocery store and propane gas are nearby. Leashed pets are permitted.

Reservations, fees: Reserve at tel. (800) 444-PARK (444-7275) or website: www.reserve america.com; $12 per night. Open year-round.

Directions: From San Diego, drive approximately 40 miles east on Interstate 8 to Highway 79. Turn north (left) and drive seven miles to the campground entrance on the left (at Mile Marker 4).

Contact: Cuyamaca Rancho State Park, tel. (760) 765-0755, or fax (760) 765-3021.

24 Los Caballos Equestrian & Los Vaqueros Group Equestrian

     8

These equestrian camps are among the most popular in Southern California, and plans and reservations must be secured far in advance of a trip. There are 110 miles of trails accessible out of the camp, amid a landscape of pine and oaks, at the edge of forest and meadows. The trails are shared with hikers, and the fire roads shared with mountain bikers as well.

Location: In Cuyamaca Rancho State Park; map J6, grid f8.

Campsites, facilities: There are 16 equestrian sites for tents or RVs, no hookups, one group camp that accommodates up to 80 people and 45 horses, and one cabin. Fire rings and picnic tables are provided. Restrooms, drinking water, flush toilets, and coin-operated showers are available. Two corrals are available at each site, two horses per site, and manure must removed, with shovels and trailers provided. Supplies are available nearby in Julian. Leashed pets are permitted at campsites and on paved roads only.

Reservations, fees: Reserve at tel. (800) 444-PARK (444-7275) or website: www.reserve america.com; $12 per night, $150 for group site, $15 for a cabin. Open April through November, weather permitting.

Directions: From Julian, drive south on Highway 79 for 10 miles to Stonewall Road. Turn left and drive one-quarter mile to Los Caballos Camp on the right, or continue one-half mile to Los Vaqueros Group Camp on the right.

Contact: Cuyamaca Rancho State Park, tel. (760) 765-0755, or fax (760) 765-3021.

25 Paso Picacho

     8

This camp is set at 4,900 feet in Cuyamaca Rancho State Park, best known for Cuyamaca Peak, 6,512 feet. The Stonewall Peak Trail is accessible from across the street. This is a 4.5-mile round-trip, featuring the climb to the summit at 5,730 feet. It's the most popular hike in the park, an easy to moderate grade, and completed by a lot of families. Another more ambitious hike is the trail up to Cuyamaca Peak, starting at the southern end of the campground, a 6.5-mile round-trip tromp (alas, on a paved road; at least it's closed to traffic) with a climb of 1,600 feet in the process. The view from the top is breathtaking, with the ocean, desert, and Salton Sea all within range. Park headquarters features exhibits about the area's Native Americans, gold mining, and natural history. That's where I learned that Cuyamaca means "The Rain Beyond."

Location: In Cuyamaca Rancho State Park; map J6, grid f7.

Campsites, facilities: There are 85 sites for tents or RVs, two group camps for up to 60 people, five cabins, and a nature den cabin. Fire grills and picnic tables are provided. Restrooms, drinking water, flush toilets, coin-operated showers, and a sanitary disposal station are available. Supplies are available nearby in Cuyamaca. Leashed pets are permitted.

Reservations, fees: Reserve at tel. (800) 444-PARK (444-7275) or website: www.reserve america.com; $12 per night, $75 for group site, $15 for a cabin. Open year-round.

Directions: From Julian, drive south on Highway 79 for 11 miles to the park entrance on the right.

Contact: Cuyamaca Rancho State Park, tel. (760) 765-0755, or fax (760) 765-3021.

26 Horse Heaven Group Camp

     3

Horse Heaven is set on the northeastern border of Cleveland National Forest at 5,500 feet, near Mount Laguna in the Laguna Recreation Area. The Pacific Crest Trail passes near the camp. Laguna and El Prado Group Camp provide nearby options. Side trip possibilities include visiting Little Laguna Lake to the immediate west, and Desert View Picnic Area to the south at Mount Laguna.

Location: Near the Pacific Crest Trail in Cleveland National Forest; map J6, grid f9.

Campsites, facilities: There are three group sites for tents or RVs. Picnic tables and fire grills are provided. Drinking water and vault toilets are available. You ca buy supplies in Mount Laguna. Leashed pets are permitted.

Reservations, fees: Reserve at tel. (877) 444-6777 ($8.65 reservation fee) or website: www.reserveusa.com; $60 to $150 per group per night. Open Memorial Day weekend through Labor Day weekend.

Directions: From San Diego, drive about 50 miles east on Interstate 8 to the Laguna Junction exit. Drive about 11 miles north on Sunrise Highway to the town of Mount Laguna. Continue north for two miles on Sunrise Highway/Laguna Mountain Road to the campground entrance road on the left.

Contact: Cleveland National Forest, Descanso Ranger District, tel. (619) 445-6235 or fax (619) 445-1753.

27 Laguna

    4

Laguna is set on Little Laguna Lake, one of the few lakes in America where "Little" is part of its official name. That's because for years everybody always referred to it as "Little Laguna Lake," and it became official. Yep, it's a "little" lake all right, a relative speck, with the camp on its eastern side at an elevation of 5,550 feet. A trailhead for the Pacific Crest Trail is a mile north on the Sunrise Highway/Laguna Mountain Road. Big Laguna Lake, which is actually a pretty small lake, is one mile to the west.

Location: Near Little Laguna Lake in Cleveland National Forest; map J6, grid f9.

Campsites, facilities: There are 30 sites for tents only, and 73 sites for tents or RVs up to 50 feet. Picnic tables and fire grills are provided. Restrooms, drinking water, flush toilets, and coin-operated showers are available. A grocery store and propane gas are available nearby. Some facilities are wheelchair accessible. Leashed pets are permitted.

Reservations, fees: Some sites are available by reservation only; reserve at tel. (877) 444-6777 ($8.65 reservation fee) or website: www.reserveusa.com; $14 per night. Open year-round.

Directions: From San Diego, drive about 50 miles east on Interstate 8 to the Laguna Junction exit. Drive about 11 miles north on Sunrise Highway to the town of Mount Laguna. Continue north for 2.5 miles on Sunrise Highway/Laguna Mountain Road to the campground entrance road on the left.

Contact: Cleveland National Forest, Descanso Ranger District, tel. (619) 445-6235 or fax (619) 445-1753.

28 El Prado Group Camp

   3

El Prado Group Camp is adjacent to Laguna and is a group camp option to Horse Heaven Group Camp. The elevation is 5,500 feet.

Location: In Cleveland National Forest; map J6, grid f9.

Campsites, facilities: There are five group sites for tents or RVs. Picnic tables and fire grills are provided. Drinking water and vault toilets are available. You can buy supplies in Mount Laguna. Leashed pets are permitted.

Reservations, fees: Reserve at tel. (877) 444-6777 ($8.65 reservation fee) or website: www.reserveusa.com; $45 to $150 per group per night. Open Memorial Day weekend through Labor Day weekend.

Directions: From San Diego, drive about 50 miles east on Interstate 8 to the Laguna Junction exit. Drive about 11 miles north on Sunrise Highway to the town of Mount Laguna. Continue north for 2.5 miles on Sunrise Highway/Laguna Mountain Road to the campground entrance road on the left.

Contact: Cleveland National Forest, Descanso Ranger District, tel. (619) 445-6235 or fax (619) 445-1753.

29 Agua Dulce Walk-In

 6

What you will find here are two walk-in group sites and five walk-in tent sites, south of the town of Mount Laguna. Little Agua Dulce Creek runs nearby, and the Desert View Picnic Area, two miles to the northwest, provides a side trip option. The Pacific Crest Trail passes nearby, skirting the Burnt Rancheria Camp. The elevation is 5,000 feet.

Location: Near the Pacific Crest Trail in Cleveland National Forest; map J6, grid f9.

Campsites, facilities: There are two walk-in group sites, and five individual walk-in sites for tents only. Picnic tables and fire grills are provided. Drinking water and vault toilets are available. Leashed pets are permitted.

Reservations, fees: Reserve at (877) 444-6777 ($8.65 reservation fee) or website: www.reserveusa.com; group sites $40 per night. Open Memorial Day weekend through Labor Day weekend.

Directions: From San Diego, drive approximately 50 miles east on Interstate 8 to the Laguna Junction exit. Drive about eight miles north on Sunrise Highway/Laguna Mountain Road to the campground entrance road on the left.

Contact: Cleveland National Forest, Descanso Ranger District, tel. (619) 445-6235 or fax (619) 445-1753.

30 Alpine Springs RV Resort

 3

This is one of the few RV parks in the area that welcomes tent campers. It is set in the foothill country in Alpine, eight miles from Lake Jennings to the west. See the entry for Lake Jennings County Park (about 10 minutes away) for more information. Other nearby lakes include larger El Capitan to the north and Loveland Reservoir to the south. Also nearby is the Viejas Casino.

Location: Near Lake Jennings; map J6, grid f6.

Campsites, facilities: There are 300 sites for tents or RVs, some with full or partial hookups. Picnic tables are provided. Restrooms, drinking water, flush toilets, showers, sanitary disposal station, coin laundry, and a swimming pool are available. No pets over 15 pounds are permitted.

Reservations, fees: Reservations are accepted; $18 to $20 per night, $3 per person per night for more than two people. Open year-round.

Directions: From Interstate 8 just east of Alpine, take the East Willows exit. Cross over the freeway and drive a third of a mile to 5635 Willows Drive on the left.

Contact: Alpine Springs RV Resort, tel. (619) 445-3162.

31 Wooded Hill Group

 4

This camp is set near Agua Dulce Camp, on the southern flank of Mount Laguna. The Pacific Crest Trail passes right by Burnt Rancheria, a mile up the road to the northwest. The elevation is 6,000 feet.

Location: Near the Pacific Crest Trail in Cleveland National Forest; map J6, grid g9.

Campsites, facilities: This group camp has 22 sites for tents or RVs. Picnic tables and fire grills are provided. Drinking water and vault toilets are available. A grocery store is nearby. Leashed pets are permitted.

Reservations, fees: Reserve at tel. (877) 444-6777 ($17.35 reservation fee); $165 group fee per night. Open Memorial Day weekend to Labor Day weekend.

Directions: From San Diego, drive approximately 50 miles east on Interstate 8 to the Laguna Junction exit. Drive about eight miles north on Sunrise Highway/Laguna Mountain Road to the campground entrance road on the left.

Contact: Cleveland National Forest, Descanso Ranger District, tel. (619) 445-6235 or fax (619) 445-1753.

32 Burnt Rancheria

 6

Burnt Rancheria is set high on the slopes of Mount Laguna in Cleveland National Forest, at an elevation of 6,000 feet. The Pacific Crest Trail runs right alongside this camp. It is quiet and private with large, roomy sites. Desert View Picnic Area, a mile to the north, provides a good side trip. Agua Dulce and Wooded Hill Group Camps are less than two miles away.

Location: Near the Pacific Crest Trail in Cleveland National Forest; map J6, grid g9.

Campsites, facilities: There are 51 sites for tents only and 58 sites for tents or RVs up to 50 feet. Picnic tables and fire grills are provided. Drinking water and vault toilets are available. Supplies are nearby in Mount Laguna. Leashed pets are permitted.

Reservations, fees: Some sites are available by reservation only; reserve at tel. (877) 444-6777 ($8.65 reservation fee) or website: www. reserveusa.com; $14 per night (two vehicle maximum). Open May through October.

Directions: From San Diego, drive approximately 50 miles east on Interstate 8 to the Laguna Junction exit. Drive about nine miles north on Sunrise Highway/Laguna Mountain Road to the campground entrance on the right.

Contact: Cleveland National Forest, Descanso Ranger District, tel. (619) 445-6235 or fax (619) 445-1753.

33 Boulder Oaks

 4

Boulder Oaks is easy to reach, just off Interstate 8, yet is a very small camp with an important trailhead for the Pacific Crest Trail running right by it. The elevation is 3,500 feet, set in the southern end of Cleveland National Forest and the Laguna Mountains. The camp is subject to closures in the spring to protect the Arroyo southwestern toad, an endangered species.

Location: Near Lake Morena in Cleveland National Forest; map J6, grid h8.

Campsites, facilities: There are six sites for tents only, 12 sites for tents or RVs, and 14 equestrian sites. Picnic tables and fire grills are provided. Drinking water and vault toilets are available. A grocery store is nearby. Leashed pets are permitted.

Reservations, fees: Equestrian sites reservations at tel. (877) 444-6777 ($8.65 reservation fee) or website: www.reserveusa.com; $12 per night for equestrian sites, $10 per night for individual sites. Open year-round.

Directions: From San Diego, drive east to Buckman Springs Road (five miles east of Pine Valley). Take the Buckman Springs off ramp. Turn right on Buckman Springs Road and drive a short distance to a four-way stop sign at Old Highway 80. Turn left and drive 2.5 miles to the campground.

Contact: Cleveland National Forest, Descanso Ranger District, tel. (619) 445-6235 or fax (619) 445-1753.

34 Cibbets Flat

 4

Cibbets Flat is at the southern flank of the Laguna Mountains, near Troy Canyon Creek. It is an obscure, fairly remote camp and staging area for the Pacific Crest Trail. A trailhead for the PCT is a mile southeast of camp, mostly used by hikers heading north across the Laguna Mountains. The elevation is 4,000 feet.

Location: On Troy Canyon Creek in Cleveland National Forest; map J6, grid g9.

Campsites, facilities: There are 23 sites for tents or small RVs. Picnic tables and fire grills are provided. Drinking water and vault toilets are available. Leashed pets are permitted.

Reservations, fees: No reservations; $10 per night (two vehicle maximum). Open year-round.

Directions: From San Diego, drive about 53 miles east on Interstate 8 to the Kitchen Creek/Cameron Station exit. Turn north on Kitchen Creek Road and drive 4.5 miles to the campground entrance on the right.

Contact: Cleveland National Forest, Descanso Ranger District, tel. (619) 445-6235 or fax (619) 445-1753.

35 Bobcat Meadows

 6

This camp, along with nearby Corral Canyon, caters primarily to OHV users. The camp is shaded with live oaks, and is a 10-minute drive to Corral Canyon camp. This camp is similar, but it has no water. The more spacious sites and privacy can make up for that. The elevation is 3,800 feet.

Location: In Cleveland National Forest; map J6, grid g8.

Campsites, facilities: There are 16 sites for tents and pickup truck campers. Picnic tables and fire pits are provided. Vault toilets are available. No drinking water is available. Garbage must be packed out. Leashed pets are permitted.

Reservations, fees: No reservations; no camping fee. Adventure Pass ($30 annual fee) or a $5 daily fee per parked vehicle is required. Open year-round.

Directions: From El Cajon, drive east on Interstate 8 for 34 miles to Buckman Springs Road. Turn south and drive 3.5 miles to Corral Canyon Road (Forest Road 17S04), marked by a sign "Camp Morena." Turn right (west) (still on 17S04) and drive two miles to Camp Morena. Continue 4.2 miles on a one-lane dirt road to Four Corners. Bear left at the Y instersection (still 17S04) and drive one mile to the campground on the left. These roads are not recommended for RVs or trailers.

Contact: Cleveland National Forest, Descanso Ranger District, tel. (619) 445-6235 or fax (619) 445-1753.

36 Corral Canyon

    6

This camp is a primitive campsite set adjacent to a network of OHV trails leading out 24 miles into the Corral Canyon area, hence the name. Most of the routes lead into a chaparral landscape. The camp is set at 3,500 feet, and is primarily used by the OHV crowd.

Location: In Cleveland National Forest; map J6, grid h8.

Campsites, facilities: There are 20 sites for tents and pickup truck campers. Picnic tables and fire rings are provided. Drinking water and vault toilets are available. Garbage must be packed out. Leashed pets are permitted.

Reservations, fees: No reservations; no camping fee. Adventure Pass ($30 annual fee) or a $5 daily fee per parked vehicle is required. Open year-round.

Directions: From El Cajon, drive east on Interstate 8 for 34 miles to Buckman Springs Road. Turn south and drive 3.5 miles to Corral Canyon Road (Forest Road 17S04), marked by a sign "Camp Morena." Turn right (west) (still on 17S04) and drive two miles to Camp Morena. Continue 4.2 miles on a one-lane dirt road to Four Corners. Bear right at the Y intersection (still 17S04) and drive one mile to the campground on the left. These roads are not recommended for RVs or trailers.

Contact: Cleveland National Forest, Descanso Ranger District, tel. (619) 445-6235 or fax (619) 445-1753.

37 Lake Morena County Park

      7

Yes, Lake Morena is out in the boondocks, but it's well worth the trip. If you like to fish for bass, don't miss it. The county park camp is set on the southern shore, at an elevation of 3,200 feet. The lake is just south of Cleveland National Forest and only seven or eight miles from the California/Mexico border. When full, it covers 1,500 acres, but water levels can fluctuate a great deal here. Catch rates for bass can be excellent, and some bass are big; the lake record weighed 19 pounds, two ounces. Boat rentals are available nearby.

Location: Near Campo; map J6, grid h7.

Campsites, facilities: There are 90 sites for tents or RVs, some with partial hookups, and two cabins. Picnic tables and fire grills are provided. Restrooms, drinking water, flush toilets, and showers are available. A grocery store, boat ramp, and rowboat rentals are nearby. Leashed pets are permitted.

Reservations, fees: Reservations at tel. (858) 565-3600; $10 to $16 per night, maximum of eight people per site, cabins $25 per night, $1 pet fee. Open year-round.

Directions: From San Diego, drive approximately 53 miles east on Interstate 8. Take the Buckman Springs Road/County Road S1 exit and drive 5.5 miles south. Turn right on Oak Drive and follow signs to the park. Turn left on Lake Morena Drive and drive to 2330 Lake Morena Drive.

Contact: San Diego County Parks Department, tel. (858) 694-3049.

38 International Motor Inn RV Park

    3

Easy access from Interstate 5 is a big plus here, but call ahead for available space. For nearby side trips, head west to Imperial Beach, south to Tijuana, or east to Otay Lake with its mega-sized bass and catfish.

Location: Near Imperial Beach; map J6, grid h0.

Campsites, facilities: There are 42 RV sites with full hookups. Picnic tables and patios are provided. Restrooms, drinking water, flush toilets, showers, swimming pool, whirlpool, and coin laundry are available. Leashed pets are permitted.

Reservations, fees: Reservations are accepted; $25.42 per night, $2 per person per night for more than two people. Major credit cards accepted. Open year-round.

Directions: From Interstate 5, take the Via de San Ysidro exit and drive south on Calle Primera to the park at 190 East Calle Primera, next to Motel 6.

Contact: International Motor Inn RV Park, tel. (619) 428-4486.

39 Chula Vista Marina and RV Park

        6

This RV park is close to San Diego Bay, a beautiful, calm piece of water where water-skiing is permitted in designated areas. An excellent swimming beach is available, and conditions in the afternoon for windsurfing are also excellent.

Location: In Chula Vista; map J6, grid h1.

Campsites, facilities: There are 237 RV sites with full hookups. Restrooms, drinking water, flush toilets, showers, modem hookups, TV hookups, playground, heated swimming pool and spa, game room, marina, fishing pier, free boat launch, coin laundry, propane gas, and groceries are available. Some facilities are wheelchair accessible. Leashed pets are permitted.

Reservations, fees: Reservations at (800) 770-2878; $28.50 to $53 per night, $3 per night for each extra vehicle, $1 pet fee. Major credit cards accepted. Open year-round.

Directions: From Interstate 5 in Chula Vista, take the J Street Marina Parkway exit and drive west a short distance to Sandpiper Way. Turn left and drive to 460 Sandpiper Way on the left.

Contact: Chula Vista Marina and RV Park, tel. (619) 422-0111 or fax (619) 422-8872; website: www.gocampingamerica.com/chulavista.

40 San Diego Metropolitan KOA

       1

This is one in a series of parks set up primarily for RVs cruising Interstate 5. Chula Vista is between Mexico and San Diego, allowing visitors to make side trips east to Lower Otay Lake, north to the San Diego attractions, south to Tijuana, or "around the corner" on Highway 75 to Silver Strand State Beach. Nearby San Diego Bay is beautiful with excellent water-skiing (in designated areas), windsurfing, and a great swimming beach.

Location: In Chula Vista; map J6, grid h1.

Campsites, facilities: There are 64 tent sites, 206 RV sites with full hookups, and a few cabins. Picnic tables and barbecue grills are provided. Restrooms, drinking water, flush toilets, showers, modem hookups, playground, sanitary disposal station, coin laundry, swimming pool, whirlpool, bike rentals, propane gas, and groceries are available. Some facilities are wheelchair accessible. Leashed pets are permitted.

Reservations, fees: Reservations at (800) 762-KAMP; $29 to $37.50 per night, $41 to $49 per night for cabins, $5 per night for each extra vehicle, $4 per person per night for more than two people. Major credit cards accepted. Open year-round.

Directions: From Interstate 5 in Chula Vista, take the E Street exit and drive three miles east. Turn north on Second Street and drive to the park on the right at 111 North Second Street.

Contact: San Diego Metropolitan KOA, tel. (619) 427-3601 or fax (619) 427-3622; www.sandiegokoa.com.

41 Sweetwater Summit Regional Park

 7

This regional park overlooks the Sweetwater Reservoir in Bonita. This camp has equestrian sites with corrals for the horses, and only a $1 fee per horse.

Location: Near Sweetwater Reservoir in Bonita; map J6, grid h2.

Campsites, facilities: There are 60 sites for tents or RVs with partial hookups. Twenty-two of the sites have horse corrals. Picnic tables and fire grills are provided. Restrooms, drinking water, flush toilets, showers, and a sanitary disposal station are available. Leashed pets are permitted.

Reservations, fees: Reservations at (858) 565-3600; $14 to $16 per night, maximum of eight people per site, $1 pet fee. Open year-round.

Directions: From San Diego, drive south about 10 miles on Interstate 805 to Bonita Road. Go east on Bonita Road to San Miguel Road. Proceed on San Miguel Road another two miles to the park entrance on the left.

Contact: San Diego County Parks Department, tel. (858) 694-3049.

42 La Pacifica RV Park

 1

This RV park is less than two miles from the Mexican border, with regular Mexicoach bus service from the park to downtown Tijuana and back. Do this trip just once and you will find out how two miles can be the equivalent of a million miles.

Location: In San Ysidro; map J6, grid i1.

Campsites, facilities: There are 177 RV sites with full hookups and individual lawns and patios. Flush toilets, showers, heated swimming pool, whirlpool, recreation room, sanitary disposal station, coin laundry, and propane gas are available. All facilities are wheelchair accessible. Leashed pets under 20 pounds are permitted.

Reservations, fees: Reservations at (888) 786-6997; $22 per night. Major credit cards accepted. Open year-round.

Directions: From Interstate 5 in San Ysidro, drive east on Dairymart Road to San Ysidro Boulevard. Turn left and drive to the park on the left at 1010 San Ysidro Boulevard.

Contact: La Pacifica RV Park, tel. (619) 428-4411, or fax (619) 428-4413.

43 Potrero County Park

 3

If you are looking for a spot to hole up for the night before getting through customs, this is the place. It is just a heartbeat away from the customs inspection station in Tecate. A good side trip is to the nearby Tecate Mission Chapel, where you can pray that the guards do not rip your car up in the search for contraband. But why waste energy worrying? It's a lot easier just to live clean, be clean.

Location: Near the Mexican border; map J6, grid i7.

Campsites, facilities: There are 32 sites for tents or RVs, with electrical hookups. Picnic tables and fire grills are provided. Restrooms, drinking water, flush toilets, showers, playground, and a sanitary disposal station are available. You can buy supplies in Potrero. Leashed pets are permitted.

Reservations, fees: Reservations at (858) 565-3600; $10 to $12 per night, maximum of eight people per site, $1 pet fee. Open year-round.

Directions: From San Diego, drive 42 miles east on Highway 94 to Potrero Valley Road. Drive north one mile on Potrero Valley Road to Potrero Park Road. Continue east on Potrero Park Road one mile to the park entrance.

Contact: San Diego County Parks Department, tel. (858) 694-3049.

44 Lake Morena RV Park

 6

This camp is near the southern side of Lake Morena, a great lake for fishing and off-season vacations. It is one of three camps near the lake and the best for RVs. Lake Morena, at 3,200 feet, is a large reservoir in the San Diego County foothills and is known for big bass. The lake record weighed 19 pounds, two ounces. The lake has a paved ramp and rowboat rentals.

Location: Near Campo; map J6, grid i7.

Campsites, facilities: There are 27 RV sites with full hookups and 17 with partial hookups. Picnic tables are provided. Flush toilets, showers, propane gas, and coin laundry are available. Leashed pets are permitted. Some facilities are wheelchair accessible.

Reservations, fees: Reservations are recommended; $22 per night, $2 per person per night for more than four people. A deposit is required on three-day weekends. Open year-round.

Directions: From San Diego, drive approximately 53 miles east on Interstate 8. Take the Buckman Springs Road/County Road S1 exit and drive 5.5 miles south. Turn right on Oak Drive and drive 1.5 miles. Turn left on Lake Morena Drive and drive to the park on right at 2330 Lake Morena Drive.

Contact: Lake Morena RV Park, tel. (619) 478-5677 or fax (619) 478-5031.

45 Outdoor World RV Park and Campground

 4

The town of Boulevard is centrally located for a wide variety of recreation possibilities. Some 10 miles to the north is Mount Laguna, with hiking trails available. Some 30 minutes to the south is the nearest point of entry to Mexico, at Tecate. Fishing at Lake Morena or Lake Cuyamaca is also a possibility, as is soaking in nearby hot springs.

Location: In Boulevard; map J6, grid i9.

Campsites, facilities: There are 138 sites for tents or RVs, 122 with full hookups and 16 with partial hookups. There are also some primitive tent camping sites. A clubhouse, pool table, restrooms, showers, horseshoes, fire rings, and a group camping area are available. Some facilities are wheelchair accessible. Leashed pets are permitted; Dobermans, Rottweilers and pit bulls are prohibited.

Reservations, fees: Reservations are recommended; $15 to $18 per night, $1 per person per night for more than two people. Weekly and monthly rates are also available. Open year-round.

Directions: From San Diego, take Interstate 8 east for 65 miles (past Alpine) to the Live Oak Springs exit. Take that exit and turn south and drive three miles to Tierra del Sol Road. Turn right and drive one-quarter mile to Highway 94. Turn right and drive three miles to Shasta Lane. Turn left and drive three-quarters mile to the campground on the left.

Contact: Outdoor World RV Park and Campground, 37133 Highway 94, Boulevard, CA 91905; tel. (619) 766-4480.

KIM WEIR

DESERT LANDSCAPE
WITH ROCK FORMATIONS

MAP J7

746 TO INDIO

TO CAHUILLA

a

ANZA-BORREGO
DESERT STATE PARK

195

86

111

1
2
3
4

CHOCOLATE
MOUNTAIN
IMPACT
AREA

Desert
Shores

b

SALTON SEA
STATE
RECREATION
AREA

5

TO NILAND

SALTON
SEA
BEACH

7

Borrego
Springs

Salton
Sea

6

8

S22

9

Salton
City

c

SALTON
SEA NAVAL
TEST
RANGE

S3

OCOTILLO WELLS
STATE VEHICLE
RECREATION AREA

10

78

11-12

13

Ocotillo
Wells

d

14

TO JULIAN

15

16

78

86

e

ANZA-BORREGO
DESERT STATE PARK

850

882

TO BRAWLEY

17

Agua Caliente
Springs

f

18

Westmorland

Superstition
Mountain
759 feet

19

20

S2

CARRIZO
IMPACT AREA
(CLOSED TO PUBLIC)

g

21

U.S. NAVAL AERIAL
GUNNERY RANGES
(CLOSED TO PUBLIC)

S30

MANZANITA
INDIAN
RESERVATION

22

Carrizo
Mountain
2,408 feet

Imperial

h

CAMPO
INDIAN
RESERVATION

8

Ocotillo

S80

Seely

23

Summit
4,350 feet

Mountain Springs Pass
3,241 feet

8

Plaster
City

EL CENTRO

Boulevard

i

Jacumba

98

S29

CALIFORNIA

MEXICO

Mount
Signal

TO CAMPO

TO TECATE, MEXICO

j

La Rumorosa

2

Colonia
Progreso

0 1 2 3 4 5 6 7 8 9

TO PINE VALLEY

© AVALONTRAVEL PUBLISHING, INC.

CHAPTER J7

1 Headquarters

 5

This is the northernmost camp on the shore of the giant Salton Sea, that vast, shallow, and unique lake. It is set at the recreation area headquarters, just south of the town of Desert Beach at an elevation of 227 feet below sea level. Corvina fishing can be quite good at this lake in the summer, though hot as the devil. If winds are hazardous, a red beacon on the northeast shore of the lake will flash. If you see it, get to the nearest shore.

Location: In the Salton Sea State Recreation Area; map J7, grid a7.

Campsites, facilities: There are 25 sites for tents or RVs up to 32 feet long, several with electrical hookups, 15 RV sites with full hookups, and several hike-in/bike-in sites. Picnic tables and fire grills are provided. Restrooms, drinking water, flush toilets, showers, sanitary disposal station, grocery store, and propane gas are available. Some facilities are wheelchair accessible. Boating, fishing, and an exhibit area is nearby. Leashed pets are permitted.

Reservations, fees: Reserve at tel. (800) 444-PARK (444-7275) or website: www.reserve america.com; $10 to $14 per night, and $1 per person per night for hike-in/bike-in site. Open year-round.

Directions: From Mecca, drive southeast on Highway 111 for 11 miles to the entrance on the right.

Contact: Salton Sea State Recreation Area, tel. (760) 393-3052 or (760) 393-3059.

2 Mecca Beach

This is one of the camps set in the Salton Sea State Recreation Area on the northeastern shore of the lake. For details, see the entry for Headquarters.

Location: In the Salton Sea State Recreation Area; map J7, grid a7.

Campsites, facilities: There are 110 sites for tents or RVs, six with partial hookups. Picnic tables and fire grills are provided. Drinking water and vault toilets are available. Restrooms, drinking water, flush toilets, showers, groceries, propane gas, gas station, and restaurant are available 1.5 miles north at Headquarters. Leashed pets are permitted.

Reservations, fees: No reservations; $10 per night. Open year-round.

Directions: From Mecca, drive southeast on Highway 111 for 12.5 miles to the entrance on the right.

Contact: Salton Sea State Recreation Area, tel. (760) 393-3052 or tel. (760) 393-3059.

3 Corvina Beach

This is by far the biggest of the campgrounds on the Salton Sea. For details about the Salton Sea, see the entry for Headquarters.

Location: In the Salton Sea State Recreation Area; map J7, grid b7.

Campsites, facilities: There are 500 primitive sites for tents or RVs. Drinking water and chemical toilets are available. Groceries and a gas station are available nearby. Leashed pets are permitted.

Reservations, fees: No reservations; $10 per night. Open year-round.

Directions: From Mecca, drive southeast on Highway 111 for 14 miles to the entrance on the right.

Contact: Salton Sea State Recreation Area, tel. (760) 393-3052 or tel. (760) 393-3059.

4 Salt Creek Primitive Area

Every camp has some claim to fame, however obscure. This one gets the award for the least likely place you want to visit on the Salton Sea. Why? No water. Even a water purifier won't work with the high-saline lake water, unless you're a corvina. For details on the Salton Sea State Recreation Area, see the entry for Headquarters.

Location: In the Salton Sea State Recreation Area; map J7, grid b8.

Campsites, facilities: There are 150 primitive sites for tents or RVs. Chemical toilets are available. No drinking water is available. Leashed pets are permitted.

Reservations, fees: No reservations; $10 per night. Open year-round.

Directions: From Mecca, drive southeast on Highway 111 for 17.5 miles to the entrance on the right.

Contact: Salton Sea State Recreation Area, tel. (760) 393-3052 or tel. (760) 393-3059.

5 Fountain of Youth Spa

Natural artesian steam rooms are the highlight here, but I didn't seem to get any younger. This is a vast private park, set near the Salton Sea. See the entry for nearby Red Hill Marina County Park for side trip options.

Location: Near the Salton Sea; map J7, grid b9.

Campsites, facilities: There are about 300 primitive sites and 546 RV sites with full hookups. Flush toilets, showers, natural artesian steam rooms, hydrojet pools, swimming pools, recreation center, sanitary disposal stations, modem hookups, coin laundry, barber shop, beauty parlor, masseur, church services, propane gas, and groceries are available. Some facilities are wheelchair accessible. Leashed pets are permitted.

Reservations, fees: No reservations; $16 to $25 per night, $1 per person per night for more than two people. Major credit cards accepted. Open year-round.

Directions: From Indio, drive 44 miles south on Highway 111 to Hot Mineral Spa Road. Or from Niland drive 15 miles north on Highway 111 to Hot Mineral Spa Road. Turn north on Hot Mineral Spa Road and drive about four miles to the park on the left.

Contact: Fountain of Youth Spa, tel. (888) 8000-SPA, or tel. (760) 354-1340 or fax (760) 354-1558; website: www.foyspa.com.

6 Bombay Beach

     5

All in all, this is a strange looking place, with the Salton Sea, a vast body of water, surrounded by stark, barren countryside. This camp is set in a bay along the southeastern shoreline, where a beach and nature trails are available. Nearby to the south is the Wister Waterfowl Management Area. The Salton Sea is California's unique saltwater lake set below sea level, where corvina can provide lively sportfishing.

Location: In the Salton Sea State Recreation Area; map J7, grid c9.

Campsites, facilities: There are 200 sites for tents or RVs. Drinking water and chemical toilets are available. A store, restaurant, marina, and boat launch are available nearby. Leashed pets are permitted.

Reservations, fees: No reservations; $10 per night. Open year-round.

Directions: From Niland, drive northwest on Highway 111 for 18 miles to the entrance on the left.

Contact: Salton Sea State Recreation Area, tel. (760) 393-3052, or (760) 393-3059.

7 Borrego Palm Canyon

   4

This is one of the best camps in Anza-Borrego Desert State Park with two excellent hikes available. The short hike into Borrego Palm Canyon is like being transported to another world, from the desert to the tropics, complete with a small waterfall, a rare sight in these parts. The Panorama Outlook Trail also starts here. An excellent visitor center is available, offering an array of exhibits and a slide show. The elevation is 760 feet.

Location: In Anza-Borrego Desert State Park; map J7, grid b1.

Campsites, facilities: There are 52 RV sites with full hookups, 65 sites for tents or RVs, and five group tent campsites for 10 to 24 people. Picnic tables and fire grills are provided. Restrooms, drinking water, flush toilets, and showers are available. Some facilities are wheelchair accessible. A grocery store, coin laundry, and propane gas are nearby. Leashed pets are permitted.

Reservations, fees: Reserve at tel. (800) 444-PARK (444-7275) or website: www.reserveamerica.com; $10 to $16 per night, $18 group fee. Open year-round.

Directions: From Borrego Springs, drive 2.5 miles west on County Road S22 and Palm Canyon Drive to the campground entrance.

Contact: Anza-Borrego Desert State Park, tel. (760) 767-5311 or fax (760) 767-3427.

8 Culp Valley Primitive Camp Area

    4

Culp Valley is set near Peña Springs and offers a trailhead for a hike routed to the northeast to the high desert. An enjoyable side trip is to the Panorama Outlook at Borrego Palm Canyon, about a 15-minute drive north on County Road S22. The elevation is 3,400 feet.

Location: Near Peña Springs in Anza-Borrego Desert State Park; map J7, grid c0.

Campsites, facilities: This is an open camping area in Anza-Borrego Desert State Park. It can be used for tents or RVs. Vault toilets are available. No drinking water is available. No open fires are permitted. Garbage must be packed out. Leashed pets are permitted.

Reservations, fees: No reservations; $5 per vehicle per night. Open year-round.

Directions: From Borrego Springs, drive southwest on County Road S22 for 8 miles to the camp entrance.

Contact: Anza-Borrego Desert State Park, tel. (760) 767-5311 or fax (760) 767-3427.

9 Arroyo Salado Primitive Camp Area

 5

This camp is a primitive spot set along (and named after) an ephemeral stream, the Arroyo Salado. A few miles to the west is the trailhead for the Thimble Trail, which is routed south into a wash in the Borrego Badlands. The elevation is 800 feet.

Location: In Anza-Borrego Desert State Park; map J7, grid c4.

Campsites, facilities: This is an open camping area in the Anza-Borrego Desert State Park. It can be used for tents or RVs. Vault toilets are available. No drinking water is available. Garbage must be packed out. Open fires are not allowed. Leashed pets are permitted.

Reservations, fees: No reservations; $5 per vehicle per night. Open year-round.

Directions: From Borrego Springs, drive about 16 miles east on County Road S22 to the camping area.

Contact: Anza-Borrego Desert State Park, tel. (760) 767-5311 or fax (760) 767-3427.

10 Tamarisk Grove

 5

They've got drinking water here, and that's the number one reason this is one of the most popular camps in this desert park. It is one of three camps in the immediate area, so if this camp is full, primitive Yaqui Well to the immediate west and Yaqui Pass to the north on Yaqui Pass Road provide alternatives. The Cactus Loop Trail, with the trailhead just north of camp, provides a hiking option. This is a 2.5-mile loop that passes seven varieties of cacti, some as tall as people. The elevation is 1,400 feet.

Location: In Anza-Borrego Desert State Park; map J7, grid d1.

Campsites, facilities: There are 27 sites for tents or RVs. Picnic tables and fire grills are provided. Restrooms, drinking water, flush toilets and coin showers are available. Some facilities are wheelchair accessible. Leashed pets are permitted.

Reservations, fees: Reserve at tel. (800) 444-PARK (444-7275) or website: www.reserve america.com; $10 per night. Open year-round.

Directions: From Borrego Springs, drive south on County Road S3 (which becomes Yaqui Pass Road) for 12 miles to the intersection with Highway 78 and the campground.

Contact: Anza-Borrego Desert State Park, tel. (760) 767-5311 or fax (760) 767-3427.

11 Yaqui Well Primitive Camp Area

 2

This camp is used primarily as an overflow area if the more developed Tamarisk Grove Camp is full. The Cactus Loop Trail, a 2.5-mile loop hike that passes seven varieties of cacti, starts at Tamarisk Grove. The elevation is 1,400 feet.

Location: In Anza-Borrego Desert State Park; map J7, grid d1.

Campsites, facilities: This is an open camping area in Anza-Borrego Desert State Park. It can be used for tents or RVs. Vault toilets are available. No drinking water is available. Garbage must be packed out. Open fires are not permitted. Leashed pets are permitted.

Reservations, fees: No reservations; $5 per vehicle per night. Open year-round.

Directions: From Borrego Springs, drive about five miles south on County Road S3. Turn right on Yaqui Pass Road/County Road S3 and drive about six miles to the camping area on the right.

Contact: Anza-Borrego Desert State Park, tel. (760) 767-5311 or fax (760) 767-3427.

12 Yaqui Pass Primitive Camp Area

 1

This extremely primitive area is set beside rough Yaqui Pass Road at an elevation of 1,730 feet. The camping area is a large, open, sloping area of asphalt, where it is darn near impossible to get an RV level. The trailhead for the Kenyan Loop Trail is to the immediate south. This spot is often overlooked because the Tamarisk Grove Camp nearby provides drinking water and a feature trail. Why campers are charged anything to camp here is astounding. Rangers should rather pay the campers.

Location: In Anza-Borrego Desert State Park; map J7, grid d1.

Campsites, facilities: This is an open camping area in Anza-Borrego Desert State Park. It can be used for tents or RVs. No drinking water or toilets are available. Garbage must be packed out. Leashed pets are permitted.

Reservations, fees: No reservations; $5 per vehicle per night. Open year-round.

Directions: From Borrego Springs, drive about five miles south on County Road S3. Turn right on Yaqui Pass Road/County Road S3 and drive about four miles to the camping area on the left.

Contact: Anza-Borrego Desert State Park, tel. (760) 767-5311 or fax (760) 767-3427.

13 Ocotillo Wells SVRA

 4

This can be a wild place, a giant OHV camp where the population of Ocotillo Wells can go from 100 to 5,000 overnight, no kidding. Some locals call the OHV crowd "escapees" and watch stunned as they arrive every February for two or three weeks. OHV events are held here occasionally as well. Mountain bikers also use these trails. One great side note is that the first Saturday of November is "Desert Cleanup Day," when OHV users will clean up the place. The non-OHV crowd can still use this camp, but most come in the winter on weekdays, when activity is lower. The landscape is barren desert, dry as an iguana's back. A few shade ramadas are provided on site.

Location: In Ocotillo Wells; map J7, grid d4.

Campsites, facilities: There are 125 dispersed primitive sites for RVs or tents. No hookups. Picnic tables and fire rings are provided. Vault and chemical toilets are available. No drinking water is available. A shower building is available near the ranger station, and another is 3.5 miles east at Holmes Camp. A store, restaurants, propane, and gas stations are available 3 miles away in Ocotillo Wells. Leashed pets are permitted.

Reservations, fees: No reservations; no fee, 30-day maximum stay per year. Open year-round.

Directions: From Borrego Springs, drive south on Borrego Springs Road for 17 miles to Highway 78. Turn east (left) and drive six miles to the park entrance on the left. Continue 1 mile to the ranger station.

Contact: Ocotillow Wells SVRA, tel. (760) 767-5391, or fax (760) 767-4951.

14 Stagecoach Trails RV, Equestrian & Wildlife Resort

 6

You want space? You got space. That includes 600,000 acres of public lands bordering this RV campground, making Stagecoach Trails Resort ideal for those who love horseback riding and hiking. Seventy-five corrals at the campground let you know right away that this camp is very horse friendly. In addition, Stagecoach Trails Resort provides the perfect jumping-off place for trips into neighboring Anza-Borrego Desert State Park. The resort's name comes from its proximity to the old Wells Fargo Butterfield Stageline Route.

Location: Near Julian; map J7, grid e0.

Campsites, facilities: There are 286 RV sites with full hookups, most of which are pull-through. There is also a primitive camping area for tents with 75 horse corrals and five trailers. Picnic tables and fire rings are provided. Restrooms, drinking water, flush toilets, showers, a heated pool, recreation room, banquet room, store, modem hookups, coin laundry, two sanitary disposal stations, and propane gas are available. The facilities are wheelchair accessible. Pets are permitted.

Reservations, fees: Reservations at (877) TWO-CAMP; $12 to $20 per night, $5 per night for each extra vehicle, $3 per person per night for more than two people, trailers $40 to $50 per night, $3 per night per horse. Major credit cards accepted. Open year-round.

Directions: From Escondido, drive east on Highway 78 to Ramona, and continue on Highway 78 for 15 miles to Santa Ysabel and Highway 79. Turn north (left) and drive 14 miles to County Road S2/San Felipe Road. Turn right and drive 17 miles to Highway 78. Turn right (west, towards Julian) and drive 0.4 mile to County Road S2 (Great Southern Overland Stage Route). Turn left and drive four miles to the resort on the right.

Contact: Stagecoach Trails Resort, 7878 Overland Stage Route, Julian, CA 92036; tel. (760) 765-2197; website: www.stagecoachtrails.com.

15 Butterfield Ranch

      3

Butterfield Ranch is an ideal layover spot for RV cruisers visiting nearby Anza-Borrego Desert State Park who want a developed park in which to stay overnight. Note that there is no gas available in Julian after 6 p.m. and that the nearest gas station is 36 miles to the east.

Location: Near Anza-Borrego Desert State Park; map J7, grid e0.

Campsites, facilities: There are 500 sites in all, with 300 full-hookup RV sites and 200 tent sites. Restrooms, hot showers, sanitary disposal station, playground, two swimming pools, whirlpool, coin laundry, recreation room, country store, fishpond free for kids, and a petting farm are available. Leashed pets are permitted.

Reservations, fees: Reservations at (800) 522-6502; $16 to $26 per night, $2 per night per pet. Open year-round.

Directions: From Escondido, drive east on Highway 78 to the town of Ramona, and continue east on Highway 78 for 14 miles to County Road S2/San Felipe Road. Turn right (south) and drive 12 miles to the campground entrance on the right.

Contact: Butterfield Ranch, tel. (760) 765-1463 or fax (760) 765-2083.

16 Fish Creek

    3

This primitive camp is set just inside the eastern border of Anza-Borrego Desert State Park, at the foot of the Vallecito Mountains to the west. A few miles north of camp is the Elephant Trees Discovery Trail, a 1.5-mile hike highlighted by weird trees that are a variety of colors and mostly 5-10 feet tall with crumpled bark. This is the closest camp to the Ocotillo Wells State Vehicular Recreation Area, which is 12 miles to the north.

Location: In Anza-Borrego Desert State Park; map J7, grid e3.

Campsites, facilities: There are eight sites for tents or RVs. Vault toilets are available. No drinking water is available. Garbage must be packed out. Leashed pets are permitted.

Reservations, fees: No reservations; $5 per vehicle per night.

Directions: From Highway 78 in Ocotillo Wells, drive 12 miles south on Split Mountain Road to the campground.

Contact: Anza-Borrego Desert State Park, tel. (760) 767-5311 or fax (760) 767-3427.

17 Vallecito County Park

    3

This nice county park in the desert gets little attention in the face of the other nearby attractions. These include the Agua Caliente Hot Springs, Anza-Borrego Desert State Park to the east, and Lake Cuyamaca and Cuyamaca Rancho State Park about 35 miles away. The elevation is 1,500 feet.

Location: Near Anza-Borrego Desert State Park; map J7, grid f0.

Campsites, facilities: There are 44 sites for tents or RVs. Picnic tables and fire grills are provided. Drinking water, flush toilets, and a playground are available. Leashed pets are permitted.

Reservations, fees: Reservations at (858) 565-3600; $10 to $14 per night, maximum of eight people per site, $1 pet fee. Major credit cards accepted. Open Labor Day weekend through Memorial Day weekend; closed June, July and August.

Directions: From Julian, drive 12 miles east on Highway 78. Turn right (south) on County Road S2/San Felipe Road and drive 18 miles to the park entrance on the right.

Contact: San Diego County Parks Department, tel. (858) 694-3049; website: www.co.san-diego.ca.us/parks.

18 Agua Caliente County Park

     3

Everything is hot here. The weather is hot, the coffee is hot, and the water is hot. And hey, that's what "Agua Caliente" means—hot water, named after the nearby hot springs. Anza-Borrego Desert State Park is also nearby. If you would like to see some cold water, Lake Cuyamaca and Cuyamaca Rancho State Park are about 35 miles away. The elevation is 1,350 feet.

Location: Near Anza-Borrego Desert State Park; map J7, grid f0.

Campsites, facilities: There are 104 RV sites with full or partial hookups and 36 sites for tents or RVs. Picnic tables and fire grills are provided. Restrooms, drinking water, flush toilets, showers, swimming pool, therapy pool, and a playground are available. Groceries and propane gas are nearby. No pets are allowed. Some facilities are wheelchair accessible.

Reservations, fees: Reservations at (858) 565-3600; $10 to $14 per night, maximum of eight people per site. Major credit cards accepted. Open Labor Day weekend through Memorial Day weekend; closed June, July and August.

Directions: From San Diego, take Interstate 8 east to the town of Ocotillo. From there, take County Road S2/San Felipe Road north for 25 miles to the park entrance on the right. From Julian, drive 12 miles east on Highway 78. Turn right on County Road S2/San Felipe Road and drive 21 miles south to the park entrance road on the right.

Contact: San Diego County Parks Department, tel. (858) 694-3049; website: www.co.san-diego.ca.us/parks.

19 Cottonwood

    4

This camp is set on the western edge of the McCain Valley Wildlife Management Area. Like most Bureau of Land Management camps, it is little known and little used. It is occasionally frequented by backcountry horsemen. The elevation is 4,000 feet.

Location: In the McCain Valley Wildlife Management Area; map J7, grid g0.

Campsites, facilities: There are 29 sites for tents or RVs. Picnic tables and fire grills are provided. Drinking water and vault toilets are available. Two group horse corrals are also available. Leashed pets are permitted.

Reservations, fees: No reservations; $6 per night. Open year-round.

Directions: From San Diego, drive approximately 70 miles east on Interstate 8 to the Campo/Boulevard exit. Turn right, then left on the southern frontage (county) road/Highway 98, and continue east for two miles to the intersection with McCain Valley Road. Turn left on McCain Valley Road and drive about 13 miles to the campground.

Contact: Bureau of Land Management, El Centro Field Office, tel. (760) 337-4400 or fax (760) 337-4490.

20 Bow Willow

    4

Bow Willow Canyon is a rugged setting that can be explored by hiking the trail that starts at this camp. A short distance east of the camp, the trail forks to the south to Rockhouse Canyon. For a good side trip, drive back to County Road S2 and head south over Sweeney Pass for the view at the Carrizo Badlands Overlook.

Location: Near Bow Willow Canyon in Anza-Borrego Desert State Park; map J7, grid g2.

Campsites, facilities: There are 14 sites for tents or RVs. Picnic tables and ramadas are provided. Vault toilets are available. Drinking water is limited. Leashed pets are permitted.

Reservations, fees: No reservations; $7 per night. Open year-round.

Directions: From Interstate 8 in Ocotillo, turn north on County Road S2 and drive 14 miles to the gravel campground entrance on the left.

Contact: Anza-Borrego Desert State Park, tel. (760) 767-5311 or fax (760) 767-3427.

21 Mountain Palm Springs Primitive Camp Area

    4

A plus for this camping area is easy access from County Road S2, but no water is a giant minus. Regardless of pros and cons, only hikers will get the full benefit of the area. A trail leads south to Bow Willow Creek (and Bow Willow) and onward into Bow Willow Canyon. The Carrizo Badlands Overlook is on the southeast side of Sweeney Pass, about a 10-minute drive south on County Road S2. The elevation is 950 feet.

Location: In Anza-Borrego Desert State Park; map J7, grid g2.

Campsites, facilities: This is an open camping area in Anza-Borrego Desert State Park. It can be used for tents or RVs. Chemical toilets are available. No drinking water is available. Open fires are not permitted. Garbage must be packed out. Leashed pets are permitted.

Reservations, fees: No reservations, $5 per vehicle per night. Open year-round.

Directions: From Interstate 8 in Ocotillo, turn north on County Road S2 and drive 15 miles to the camp entrance road on the left.

Contact: Anza-Borrego Desert State Park, tel. (760) 767-5311 or fax (760) 767-3427.

22 Lark Canyon OHV

    5

This is a small camp that few know of, set at 4,000 feet in the McCain Valley National Cooperative and Wildlife Management Area. It is near a popular off-highway-vehicle area. Many dirt bikers use it as their base camp.

Location: In the McCain Valley Wildlife Management Area; map J7, grid h2.

Campsites, facilities: There are 15 sites for tents or RVs. Picnic tables and fire grills are provided. Drinking water and vault toilets are available. Leashed pets are permitted.

Reservations, fees: No reservations; $6 per night. Open year-round.

Directions: From San Diego, drive approximately 70 miles east on Interstate 8 to the Campo/Boulevard exit to McCain Valley. Turn right, and then turn left on the frontage (county) road, and continue east for two miles to the intersection with McCain Valley Road. Turn left on McCain Valley Road and drive three miles to the campground.

Contact: Bureau of Land Management, El Centro Field Office, tel. (760) 337-4400 or fax (760) 337-4490.

23 Rio Bend RV Park

     5

This RV park is set at 50 feet below sea level near Mount Signal, about a 20-minute drive south of the Salton Sea. For some, this region is a godforsaken wasteland, but hey, that makes arriving at this park all the more like coming to a mirage in the desert. The park is usually well maintained, and management does what it can to offer visitors recreational options. It's hot out here, sizzling most of the year, but dry and cool in the winter, the best time to visit.

Location: Near El Centro; map J7, grid h7.

Campsites, facilities: There are 228 sites with full hookups for RVs, and a group area with 42 sites with partial hookups. Picnic tables are provided. A heated pool, spa, shuffleboard, volleyball, two small stocked lakes, golf course, coin laundry, and telephone, cable, and modem hookups are available. Some facilities are wheelchair accessible. A small store is nearby. Leashed pets are permitted.

Reservations, fees: Reservations are accepted; $13 to $26 per night, $2 for more than two people. Major credit cards accepted. Open year-round.

Directions: From El Centro, drive west on Interstate 8 for seven miles. Take the Drew Road exit and then drive south on Drew Road for one-quarter mile to the park on the right at 1589 Drew Road.

Contact: Rio Bend RV Park, tel. (760) 352-7061 or fax (760) 352-0055; website: www.riobendrv.com.

PRICKLY
PEAR

MAP J8

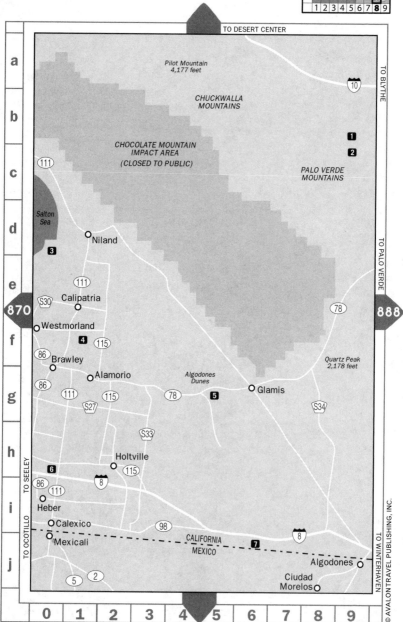

TO DESERT CENTER

TO BLYTHE

a

Pilot Mountain
4,177 feet

CHUCKWALLA
MOUNTAINS

b

CHOCOLATE MOUNTAIN
IMPACT AREA
(CLOSED TO PUBLIC)

1

2

PALO VERDE
MOUNTAINS

c

111

d

Salton
Sea

Niland

3

TO PALO VERDE

e

111

S30

Calipatria

870

888

78

f

Westmorland

86

4

115

Brawley

Quartz Peak
2,178 feet

g

86

Alamorio

111

115

S27

Algodones
Dunes

78

5

Glamis

S34

h

S33

Holtville

6

115

TO SEELEY

i

8

86

111

Heber

Calexico

TO OCOTILLO

j

Mexicali

98

CALIFORNIA
MEXICO

7

8

Algodones

TO WINTERHAVEN

5

2

Ciudad
Morelos

0 1 2 3 4 5 6 7 8 9

© AVALON TRAVEL PUBLISHING, INC.

882 Southern California

CHAPTER J8

1 Wiley's Well

 4

Like its neighbor to the south, Coon Hollow, this camp is attractive to snowbirds, rockhounds, and stargazers. Geodes and agates can be collected. The desert landscape is extremely stark.

Location: West of Blythe; map J8, grid b9.

Campsites, facilities: There are 13 sites for tents or RVs. No hookups. Picnic tables and fire grills are provided. Vault toilets are available. No drinking water is available. A sanitary disposal station is nearby. Leashed pets are permitted.

Reservations, fees: No reservations; $20 per week, $100 per season. Fees charged only during winter. Summer is free. Open year-round.

Directions: From Blythe, drive west on Interstate 10 for 15 miles to Wiley's Well Road. Turn left (south) and drive eight miles to the campground on the right.

Contact: Bureau of Land Management, Palm Springs Field Office, (760) 251-4800 or fax (760) 251-4899.

2 Coon Hollow

 4

Coon Hollow is out in the middle of nowhere, but rockhounds and stargazers have found it anyway; it's ideal for both sports. Rockhounding, in particular, can be outstanding with several geode and agate beds nearby. Hobby rock-collecting is permitted. Commercial rock poaching is not. The site, ideal for winter camping, attracts snowbirds and is set in a desert landscape at an elevation of 800 feet.

Location: West of Blythe; map J8, grid c9.

Campsites, facilities: There are 27 sites for tents or RVs. No hookups. Picnic tables and fire grills are provided. Vault toilets are available. No drinking water is available. A sanitary disposal station is nearby. Leashed pets are permitted.

Reservations, fees: No reservations; $20 per week, $100 per season. Fees charged only during winter. Summer is free. Open year-round.

Directions: From Blythe, drive west on Interstate 10 for 15 miles to Wiley's Well Road. Turn left (south) and drive 12 miles to the campground on the right.

Contact: Bureau of Land Management, Palm Springs Field Office, (760) 251-4800 or fax (760) 251-4899.

3 Red Hill Marina County Park

 3

This county park is near the south end of the Salton Sea, one of the weirdest places on Earth. Set 228 feet below sea level, it's a vast body of water covering 360 square miles, 35 miles long, but with an average depth of just 10 feet. It's an extremely odd place to swim, bobbing around effortlessly in the highly saline water. Fishing is often good for corvina in spring and early summer. Several wildlife refuges are in the immediate area, including two separate chunks of the Imperial

Wildfowl Management Area, to the west and south, and the huge Wister Waterfowl Management Area, northwest of Niland. For side trip options, see the entry for Bombay Beach.
Location: Near the Salton Sea; map J8, grid d0.

Campsites, facilities: There are 40 sites for tents or RVs, 12 with hookups. Picnic tables, cabanas, and barbecue pits are provided. Flush toilets, showers, and a boat launch are available. The water at this site is not certified for drinking. Leashed pets are permitted.

Reservations, fees: No reservations; $7 to $12 per night, $2 per night for each extra vehicle, with a 14-day limit. Open year-round.

Directions: From Niland, drive five miles south on Highway 111 to Sinclair Road. Turn right and drive to Garst Road. Go right and follow the road to the end (about 1.5 miles). Go left on Red Hill Road and follow it to the marina and campground at the end of the road.

Contact: Red Hill Marina County Park, tel. or fax (760) 348-2310.

Wiest Lake County Park

    4

This is a developed county park along the southern shore of Wiest Lake, which adjoins the Imperial Wildfowl Management Area to the north. Wiest Lake is just 50 acres, set 110 feet below sea level, and a prized area with such desolate country in the surrounding region. Water-skiing and windsurfing can be excellent, although few take advantage of the latter. The Salton Sea, about a 20-minute drive to the northwest, is a worthy side trip.

Location: On Wiest Lake; map J8, grid f1.

Campsites, facilities: There are 20 tent sites and 24 RV sites with full hookups. Picnic tables and fire grills are provided. Restrooms, flush toilets, showers, and a sanitary disposal station are available. A grocery store, coin laundry, and propane gas are nearby. Leashed pets are permitted.

Reservations, fees: No reservations; $7 to 12 per night, $2 per night for each extra vehicle. Open year-round.

Directions: From Brawley, drive approximately five miles north on Highway 111. Turn right on Rutherford Road and drive two miles to the park entrance on the right.

Contact: Wiest Lake County Park, tel. (760) 344-3712, tel. (760) 339-4384, or fax (760) 339-4372.

5 Imperial Sand Dunes Rec Area

   1

Gecko (for individual sites) and Roadrunner (group area) are two of the three camping options at Imperial Sand Dunes Recreation Area (Midway is the other). There isn't a tree within a million miles of this camp. People who wind up here all have the same thing in common: they're ready to ride across the dunes in their dune buggies or off-highway vehicles. Other recreation options include watching the sky and waiting for a cloud to show up. A gecko, by the way, is a harmless little lizard. I've had them crawl on the sides of my tent. Nice little fellows.

Location: East of Brawley; map J8, grid g5.

Campsites, facilities: There are numerous dispersed sites for tents or RVs. Vault toilets and a trash bin are available. No drinking water is available. Leashed pets are permitted.

Reservations, fees: No reservations; $10 per week, $30 per season. Open year-round.

Directions: From Brawley, drive east on Highway 78 for 27 miles to Gecko Road. Turn south on Gecko Road and drive three miles to the campground entrance on the left. To reach Roadrunner Group Camp, continue for two miles to the campground at the end of the road.

Contact: Bureau of Land Management, El Centro Resource Area, 1661 South Fourth Street, El Centro, CA 92243; tel. (760) 337-4400 or fax (760) 337-4490.

6 Country Life RV

     2

You'd best have air conditioning. This is an RV parking lot on the desert flats about a 10-minute drive north of the Mexican border. Nearby side trips include the Salton Sea to the north, little Sunbeam Lake County Park to the west and, if you need to sober up, the Mexican border customs to the south.

Location: Near El Centro; map J8, grid h0.

Campsites, facilities: There are six tent sites and 150 RV sites with full hookups. Restrooms, drinking water, flush toilets, showers, limited modem hookups, swimming pool, clubhouse, coin laundry, propane gas, and groceries are available. Some facilities are wheelchair accessible. Leashed pets are permitted.

Reservations, fees: Reservations are recommended; $15 to $18.50 per night, $1 per person per night for more than two people. Open year-round. Major credit cards accepted.

Directions: From Interstate 8 in El Centro, take the Highway 111 exit and drive a quarter mile north. Turn left on Ross Road and drive a short distance to the campground entrance on the left.

Contact: Country Life RV, tel. (760) 353-1040 or fax (760) 352-1948.

7 Midway

   6

This is off-highway headquarters, a place where people bring their three-wheelers, four-wheelers, and motorcycles and act like lunatics without anybody even raising an eyebrow. That's because a large area has been set aside just for this type of recreation. As you drive in you will enter the Buttercup Recreation Area, which is part of the Imperial Sand Dunes Recreation Area. You do what you please, camp wherever you like, and nobody beefs. See listing for Imperial San Dunes for more options.

Location: In the Imperial Sand Dunes Recreation Area; map J8, grid j6.

Campsites, facilities: There are several primitive sites for tents or RVs. Pit toilets are available. No drinking water is available.

Reservations, fees: No reservations; $10 per week, $30 per season. Open year-round, weather permitting.

Directions: From El Centro, drive east on Interstate 8 for about 40 miles to Sand Hills. Turn south on Gray's Wells Road and drive three miles. The road turns from pavement to dirt and then dead-ends; camping is permitted anywhere in this region.

Contact: Bureau of Land Management, El Centro Field Office; tel. (760) 337-4400 or fax (760) 337-4490.

KIM WEIR

CHAPTER 19

ROCKS AND SCRUB

MAP J9

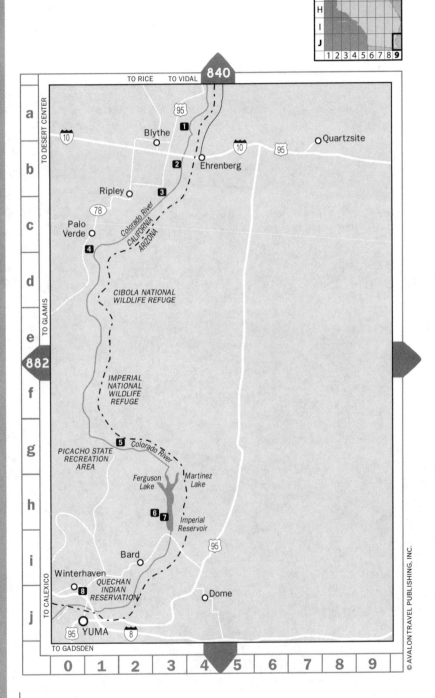

TO RICE   TO VIDAL   **840**

95

a   TO DESERT CENTER

10

Blythe   **1**

10   **95**   ○ Quartzsite

b   **2**   Ehrenberg

3

Ripley ○

78

c   Palo
Verde ○   *Colorado River*
    CALIFORNIA
    ARIZONA

4

d   *CIBOLA NATIONAL
WILDLIFE REFUGE*

e   TO GLAMIS

882

f   *IMPERIAL
NATIONAL
WILDLIFE
REFUGE*

g   **5**   *Colorado River*

*PICACHO STATE
RECREATION
AREA*

*Ferguson
Lake*   *Martinez
Lake*

h   **6** **7**

    *Imperial
Reservoir*

i   Bard ○   **95**

    Winterhaven

j   TO CALEXICO   **8**   *QUECHAN
INDIAN
RESERVATION*   ○ Dome

    95 ○ YUMA   **8**

TO GADSDEN

0   1   2   3   4   **5**   6   7   8   9

© AVALON TRAVEL PUBLISHING, INC.

CHAPTER J9

1 Mayflower County Park

       6

The Colorado River is the fountain of life around these parts and, for campers, is the main attraction to this county park. It is a popular spot for water-skiing. There is river access here in the Blythe area. This span of water is flanked by agricultural lands, although there are several developed recreation areas on the California side of the river south of Blythe near Palo Verde.

Location: On the Colorado River; map J9, grid a3.

Campsites, facilities: There are 28 tent sites and 152 RV sites with piped water and electrical hookups provided. Picnic tables and fire grills are provided. Restrooms, drinking water, flush toilets, showers, sanitary disposal station, and a boat ramp are available. Leashed pets are permitted.

Reservations, fees: Reservations are accepted; $15 to $16 per night, $2 boat launch fee, $2 pet fee. Major credit cards accepted. Open year-round.

Directions: From Blythe, drive 3.5 miles northeast on Intake Boulevard/U.S. 95 to Sixth Av-

enue. Turn right on Sixth Avenue and drive three miles to the park entrance directly ahead.

Contact: Mayflower County Park, tel. (760) 922-4665.

2 Destiny Riviera Resort

       6

This RV park is set up for camper-boaters who want to hunker down for awhile along the Colorado River and cool off. Access to the park is easy off Interstate 10, and a marina is available, both big pluses for those showing up with trailered boats.

Location: Near the Colorado River; map J9, grid b3.

Campsites, facilities: There are 285 RV sites, many with full or partial hookups. Picnic tables are provided. Restrooms, showers, swimming pool, spa, cable TV, modem hookups, coin laundry, store, card room, boat ramp, and propane gas are available. A golf course is within five miles. Leashed pets are permitted; no pit bulls, Dobermans or Rottweilers.

Reservations, fees: Reservations are accepted at (800) RV-DESTINY (783-3784); $18 to $29 per night, $20 per night for each extra vehicle. Major credit cards accepted. Open year-round.

Directions: From Blythe, drive two miles east on Interstate 10 to the Riviera Drive exit. Follow it to 14100 Riviera Drive on the right.

Contact: Riviera Blythe Marina, tel. (760) 922-5350 or fax (760) 922-0599; website: www.destinyrv.com.

3 Destiny McIntyre Park

      3

This RV park sits on the outskirts of Blythe on the Colorado River, with this stretch of river providing good conditions for boating, water-skiing, and other water sports. Fishing is an option, with a variety of fish providing fair results, including striped bass, largemouth bass, and catfish roaming the area.

Location: On the Colorado River; map J9, grid b3.

Campsites, facilities: There are 140 tent sites and 160 RV sites, including 11 pull-through sites, with full hookups. Picnic tables and fire rings are provided. Restrooms, drinking water, flush toilets, showers, sanitary disposal station, propane gas, snack bar, grocery store, bait, ice, and a boat ramp are available. Some facilities are wheelchair accessible. Pets are permitted from Nov. 1 to March 31.

Reservations, fees: Reservations at (800) RV-DESTINY; $20 to $37 per night per vehicle, $20 per night for each extra vehicle, $4 per person per night for more than two people. Major credit cards accepted. Open year-round.

Directions: From Blythe on Interstate 10, drive seven miles south on Intake Boulevard to the foot of 26th Avenue and the park entrance on the left.

Contact: Destiny McIntyre Resort, tel. (760) 922-8205; website: www.destinyrv.com.

4 Palo Verde County Park

    5

This is the only game in town, with no other camp around for many miles. It is set near a bend in the Colorado River, not far from the Cibola National Wildlife Refuge. To get to the boat ramp available at the Palo Verde Oxbow BLM site on the Colorado River, take the gravel road between mileposts 77 and 78 off Highway 78 and drive west for five miles to the river. This stretch of river is a good one for powerboating and water-skiing. The best facilities for visitors are available here and on the west side of the river between Palo Verde and Blythe, with nothing available on the east side of the river.

Location: Near the Colorado River; map J9, grid c1.

Campsites, facilities: There are an undesignated number of sites for tents or RVs. Flush toilets and a playground are available. No drinking water is available. A boat ramp is available at the Palo Verde Oxbow BLM site five miles west on the Colorado River. A grocery store, coin laundry, and propane gas are available in Palo Verde. Leashed pets are permitted.

Reservations, fees: No reservations; no fee. Open year-round.

Directions: From Palo Verde, drive three miles south on Highway 78 to the signed campground exit on the left.

Contact: Palo Verde County Park, tel. (760) 339-4384.

5 Picacho State Recreation Area

      6

To get here, you really have to want it. It's way out there, requiring a long drive north out of Winterhaven on a spindly little road. The camp is on the southern side of Taylor Lake on the Colorado River. The park is the best deal around for many miles, though, with a boat ramp, water-skiing, good bass fishing, and occasionally, crazy folks having the time of their lives. The sun and water make a good combination.

Location: Near Taylor Lake on the Colorado River; map J9, grid g2.

Campsites, facilities: There are 58 sites for tents or RVs up to 40 feet long, three group sites for 25 to 100 people, and several boat-in campsites. Picnic tables and fire grills are provided. Drinking water, pit toilets, sanitary disposal station, solar showers, camp store, and a boat launch are available. Some facilities are wheelchair accessible. Leashed pets are permitted.

Reservations, fees: Group site reservations only at tel. (760) 393-3059; individual sites $12, group sites $26. Open year-round.

Directions: From Highway 8 in Winterhaven, take the Winterhaven/Fourth Avenue exit. Turn left on Fourth Avenue and then turn right on County Road S24. Turn left on Picacho Road and drive under the railroad tracks. Continue on Picacho Road. When you cross the American Canal, the road becomes dirt. Continue north for 18 miles on the winding dirt road (not suitable for large RVs) to the campground. This takes about an hour.

Contact: Picacho State Recreation Area, tel. (760) 393-3059, or (760) 996-2963; Colorado Desert District, tel. (760) 767-5311.

6 Squaw Lake

     6

Take your pick. There are two camps near the Colorado River in this area (the other is Senator Wash). This one is near Squaw Lake, created by the nearby Imperial Dam on the Colorado River.

Location: Near the Colorado River; map J9, grid h3.

Campsites, facilities: There are 80 sites for tents or RVs. Picnic tables and fire grills are provided. Drinking water, flush toilets, cold showers, and a boat ramp are available. Some facilities are wheelchair accessible. Leashed pets are permitted.

Reservations, fees: No reservations; $5 per vehicle per day. There is a maximum 14-day limit. Open year-round.

Directions: From Yuma, Arizona, drive approximately 23 miles northeast on Imperial Highway/County Road S24 to Senator Wash Road. Turn left and drive about three miles to the campground on the right.

Contact: Bureau of Land Management, Yuma Field Office, tel. (520) 317-3200 or fax (520) 317-3250.

7 Senator Wash Recreation Area

     6

This campground is set in a large recreation area that borders the Colorado River. Specifically, it is nestled between Senator Wash Reservoir to the west and Squaw Lake (created by the Imperial Dam on the Colorado River) to the southeast. It is a vast, virtually unmonitored area, far less developed than the area

north from Palo Verde to Blythe. In other words, there's darn near nothing out here, except, that is, for this camping area and its nearby boat ramp.

Location: Near Senator Wash Reservoir; map J9, grid h3.

Campsites, facilities: There are an undesignated number of sites for tents or self-contained RVs. No drinking water is available. Vault toilets are available at the north shore. Drinking water, flush toilets, showers, and a boat ramp are available a quarter mile from the south shore. Some facilities are wheelchair accessible. Camping at the boat ramp is not permitted. Leashed pets are permitted.

Reservations, fees: No reservations; $5 per vehicle per day. There is a maximum 14-day stay. Open year-round.

Directions: From Yuma, Arizona, drive approximately 23 miles northeast on Imperial Highway/County Road S24 to Senator Wash Road. Turn left and drive about three miles to the campground on the left.

Contact: Bureau of Land Management, Yuma Field Office, tel. (520) 317-3200 or fax (520) 317-3250.

8 Sans End RV Park

  5

Sans End is only seven miles from Mexico, and lots of people who stay here like to cross the border for shopping and fun. The high season at this RV park is January to March, and no wonder, because it is blazing hot here in the summer. The Colorado River provides recreational opportunities near Imperial Dam. Boat ramps are available in Yuma and Winterhaven. Some areas of this stretch of water are marshy wetlands that provide an opportunity for duck hunting in the fall and early winter. For anglers, there are some big catfish roaming these waters. Whatever you choose to do, remember this: The magic is in each moment, so live in the moment and string them together: Life is no dress rehearsal!

Location: In Winterhaven; map J9, grid j0.

Campsites, facilities: There are 167 sites for RVs and a few sites for tents. Restrooms, showers, recreation hall with pool table, coin laundry, and shuffleboard are available. Leashed pets are permitted.

Reservations, fees: No reservations; $21 per night. Open year-round.

Directions: From Yuma, Arizona, take Interstate 8 west and then exit on Winterhaven Drive. Follow Winterhaven to the RV park at 2209 West Winterhaven Drive.

Contact: Sans End RV Park, 2209 West Winterhaven Drive, Winterhaven, CA 92283; tel. (760) 572-0797.

RESOURCE GUIDE

THE AUTHOR AT MUIR HUT,
11,965 FEET

JEFFREY PATTY

RESOURCE GUIDE

National Forests

The Forest Service provides many secluded camps and allows camping anywhere except where it is specifically prohibited. If you ever want to clear the cobwebs from your head and get away from it all, this is the way to go.

Many Forest Service campgrounds are quite remote and have no drinking water. You usually don't need to check in or make reservations, and sometimes, there is no fee. At many Forest Service campgrounds that provide drinking water, the camping fee is often only a few dollars, with payment made on the honor system. Because most of these camps are in mountain areas, they are subject to winter closure due to snow or mud.

Dogs are permitted in national forests with no extra charge and no hassle. Always carry documentation of current vaccinations.

National Forest Adventure Pass

Angeles, Cleveland, Los Padres and San Bernardino National Forests require an Adventure Pass for each parked vehicle. Daily passes cost $5; annual passes are available for $30. You can buy Adventure Passes at national forest offices in Southern California and dozens of retail outlets and on-line vendors. The new charges are use fees, not entrance fees. Holders of Golden Age and Golden Access (not Golden Eagle) cards can buy the Adventure Pass at a 50% discount at national forest offices only, or at retail outlets for the retail price. When you buy an annual Adventure Pass, you can also buy up to three additional annual Adventure Passes for $5 per family vehicle. Major credit cards are accepted at most retail and on-line outlets, but not at forest service offices.

You will not need an Adventure Pass while traveling through these forest, nor when you've paid other types of fees such as camping or ski pass fees. However, if you are camping in these forest and you leave the campground in your vehicle and park outside of the campground for recreation purposes, such as at a trailhead, day use area, near a fishing stream, etc., you will need an Adventure Pass for your vehicle. You also need an Adventure Pass if camping at a no-fee campground. More information about the Adventure Pass program, including a listing of retail and on-line vendors, can be obtained by website: www.fsadventurepass.org.

National Forest Reservations

Some of the more popular camps, and most of the group camps, are on a reservation system. Reservations can be made up to 240 days in advance, and up to 360 days in advance for groups. To reserve a site call (877) 444-6777 or visit the website: www.reserveusa.com. The reservation fee is usually $8.65 for a campsite in a national forest, and major credit cards are accepted. Holders of Golden

Age or Golden Access passports receive a 50 percent discount for campground fees, except for group sites.

National Forest Maps

National Forest maps are among the best you can get for the price. They detail all backcountry streams, lakes, hiking trails, and logging roads for access. They cost $6, sometimes more for wilderness maps, and can be obtained in person at forest service offices, or by contacting U.S. Forest Service, Attn: Maps Sales, P.O. Box 587, Camino, CA 95709, tel. (530) 647-5390, fax (530) 647-5389, or website: www.r5.fs.fed.us/visitorcenter. Major credit cards are accepted if ordering by telephone.

Forest Service Information

Forest Service personnel are most helpful for obtaining camping or hiking trail information. Unless you are buying a map or Adventure Pass, it is advisable to phone to get the best service. For specific information on a national forest, contact the following offices:

USDA Forest Service
Pacific Southwest Region
1323 Club Drive
Vallejo, CA 94592
tel. (707) 562-USFS (707-562-8737)
website: www.r5.fs.fed.us

or
Information Center
3070 Camino Heights Drive
Camino, CA 95709
tel. (530) 644-6048
fax (530) 295-5624

Angeles National Forest
701 N. Santa Anita Avenue
Arcadia, CA 91006
tel. (626) 574-1613
fax (626) 574-5233
website: www.r5 fs.fed.us/angeles

Humboldt-Toiyabe National Forest
1200 Franklin Way
Sparks, NV 89431
tel. (775) 355-5301
fax (775) 355-5399
website: www.fs.fed.us/htnf

Cleveland National Forest
10845 Rancho Bernardo Road, #200
San Diego, CA 92127-2107
tel. (858) 674-2901
fax (858) 673-6192
website: www.r5.fs.fed.us/cleveland

Inyo National Forest
873 N. Main Street
Bishop, CA 93514
tel. (760) 873-2400
fax (760) 873-2458
website: www.r5.fs.fed.us/inyo

Eldorado National Forest
100 Forni Road
Placerville, CA 95667
tel. (530) 622-5061
fax (530) 621-5297
website: www.r5.fs.fed.us/eldorado

Klamath National Forest
1312 Fairlane Road
Yreka, CA 96097-9549
tel. (530) 842-6131
fax (530) 841-4571
website: www.r5.fs.fed.us/klamath

Lake Tahoe Basin Management Unit
870 Emerald Bay Road, Suite 1
South Lake Tahoe, CA 96150
tel. (530) 573-2600
website: www.r5.fs.fed.us/ltbmu

Lassen National Forest
2550 Riverside Drive
Susanville, CA 96130
tel. (530) 257-2151
fax (530) 252-6428
website: www.r5.fs.fed.us/lassen

Los Padres National Forest
6755 Hollister Avenue, Suite 150
Goleta, CA 93117
tel. (805) 968-6640
fax (805) 961-5729
website: www.r5.fs.fed.us/lospadres

Mendocino National Forest
825 N. Humboldt Avenue
Willows, CA 95988
tel. (530) 934-3316
fax (530) 934-7384
website: www.r5.fs.fed.us/mendocino

Modoc National Forest
800 W. 12th Street
Alturas, CA 96101
tel. (530) 233-5811
fax (530) 233-8709
website: www.r5.fs.fed.us/modoc

Plumas National Forest
P.O. Box 11500
159 Lawrence Street
Quincy, CA 95971
tel. (530) 283-2050
fax (530) 283-7746
website: www.r5.fs.fed.us/plumas

San Bernardino National Forest
1824 Commercenter Circle
San Bernardino, CA 92408-3430

tel. (909) 383-5588
fax (909) 383-5770
website: www.r5.fs.fed.us/
sanbernardino

Sequoia National Forest
900 W. Grand Avenue
Porterville, CA 93257
tel. (559) 784-1500
fax (559) 781-4744
website: www.r5.fs.fed.us/sequoia

Shasta-Trinity National Forest
2400 Washington Avenue
Redding, CA 96001
tel. (530) 244-2978
fax (530) 242-2233
website: www.r5.fs.fed.us/shastatrinity

Sierra National Forest
1600 Tollhouse Road
Clovis, CA 93611
tel. (559) 297-0706
fax (559) 294-4809
website: www.r5.fs.fed.us/sierra

Six Rivers National Forest
1330 Bayshore Way
Eureka, CA 95501
tel. (707) 442-1721
fax (707) 442-9242
website: www.r5.fs.fed.us/sixrivers

Stanislaus National Forest
19777 Greenley Road
Sonora, CA 95370
tel. (209) 532-3671
fax (209) 533-1890
website: www.r5.fs.fed.us/stanislaus

Tahoe National Forest
631 Coyote Street
Nevada City, CA 95959
tel. (530) 265-4531
fax (530) 478-6109
website: www.r5.fs.fed.us.tahoe

State Parks

The California State Parks system provides many popular camping spots in spectacular settings. These campgrounds include drive-in numbered sites, tent spaces, and picnic tables, with showers and bathrooms provided nearby. Reservations are often necessary during the summer. Although some parks are well known, there are still some little-known gems in the state parks system where campers can enjoy seclusion, even in the summer.

Due to fee reductions for camping, day use, tours, and boating, the state parks now provide about the best deal in camping in the country. Add-on fees for premium sites, peak season visitation, reservations, pets, extra vehicles, and boat launching have been eliminated at state parks. In addition, fees have been reduced for day use, museum and other tours, parking, boat mooring, swimming pool use, and cabin rentals. You can now camp at a state park for as little as $1 per person per night at many walk-in or bike-in sites.

State Park Reservations

Most of the state park campgrounds are on a reservation system, and campsites can be booked up to seven months in advance at these parks. There are also hike-in/bike-in sites at many of the parks, and they are available on a first-come, first-served basis. Reservations can be made by telephone or on-line by phoning (800) 444-PARK (800-444-7275) or website: www.ReserveAmerica.com. Major credit cards are accepted for reservations, but are generally not accepted in person at the parks.

Discounts are available for persons age 62 and older. A reduced camping fee is also available to holders of the Disabled Discount Pass or the Disabled Veteran/Prisoner of War Pass.

For general information about California State Parks, contact:

California Department of Parks and Recreation
Office of Information
P.O. Box 942896
Sacramento, CA 94296
tel. (916) 653-6995
website: www.parks.ca.gov

National Parks

California's national parks are natural wonders, ranging from the spectacular yet crowded Yosemite Valley to the remote and rugged Lava Beds National Monument. Reservations for campsites are available five months in advance for many of the national parks in California. In addition to campground fees, expect to pay a park entrance fee ranging from $5 to $20 per vehicle (you can buy

Golden Eagle annual passes). This entrance fee is valid for seven days. Various discounts are available for holders of Golden Age and Golden Access passports, including a 50% reduction of camping fees (group camps not included) and a waiver of park entrance fees.

For Yosemite National Park reservations, call (800) 436-PARK (800-436-7275) or visit the website: reservations.nps.gov/. Major credit cards accepted.

For all other national parks, calle (800) 365-CAMP (800-365-2267) or visit the website: reservations.nps.gov/. Major credit cards are accepted.

National Park Service
Pacific West Region
600 Harrison Street, Suite 600
San Francisco, CA 94107-1372
tel. (415) 427-1304
fax (415) 427-1485
website: www.nps.gov

Cabrillo National Monument
1800 Cabrillo Memorial Drive
San Diego, CA 92106-3601
tel. (619) 557-5450
fax (619) 557-5469
website: www.nps.gov/cabr

Channel Islands National Park
1901 Spinnaker Drive
Ventura, CA 93001
tel. (805) 658-5730
fax (805) 658-5799
website: www.nps.gov/chis

Death Valley National Park
P.O. Box 579
Death Valley, CA 92328-0579
tel. (760) 786-2331
fax (760)786-3283
website: www.nps.gov/deva

Devils's Postpile National Monument
c/o Sequoia and Kings Canyon
National Parks
47050 Generals Highway
Three Rivers, CA 93271

tel. (559) 565-3341
website: www.nps.gov/depo

Golden Gate National Recreation Area
Fort Mason, Building 201
San Francisco, CA 94123
tel. (415) 556-0560
website: www.nps.gov/goga

Joshua Tree National Park
74485 National Park Drive
29 Palms, CA 92277-3597
tel. (760) 367-5500
fax (760) 367-6392
website: www.nps.gov/jotr

Lassen Volcanic National Park
P.O. Box 100
Mineral, CA 96063-0100
tel. (530) 595-4444
website: www.nps.gov/lavo

Lava Beds National Monument
P.O. Box 867
Tulelake, CA 96134
tel. (530) 667-2282
website: www.nps.gov/labe

Pinnacles National Monument
5000 Highway 146
Paicines, CA 95043
tel. (831) 389-4485
website: www.nps.gov/pinn

Point Reyes National Seashore
Point Reyes Station, CA 94956-9799
tel. (415) 663-1092
fax (415) 663-8132
website: www.nps.gov/pore

Redwood National and State Parks
1111 Second Street
Crescent City, CA 95531
tel. (707) 464-6101
website: www.nps.gov/redw

Santa Monica Mountains
National Recreation Area
401 W. Hillcrest Drive
Thousand Oaks, CA 91360
tel. (805) 370-2301
website: www.nps.gov/samo

Sequoia and Kings Canyon
National Parks
47050 Generals Highway
Three Rivers, CA 93271-9651
tel. (559) 565-3341
website: www.nps.gov/seki

Smith River
National Recreation Area
P.O. Box 228
Gasquet, CA 95543
tel. (707) 457-3131
fax (707) 457-3794

Whiskeytown-Shasta-Trinity
National Recreation Area
P.O. Box 188
Whiskeytown, CA 96095
tel. (530) 246-1225 or (530) 242-3400
website: www.nps.gov/whis

Yosemite National Park
P.O. Box 577
Yosemite National Park, CA 95389
tel. (209) 372-0265 or (209) 372-0200
for 24-hour recorded message
website: www.nps.gov/yose

U.S. Army Corps of Engineers & reservations

Some of the family camps and most of the group camps operated by the U.S. Army Corps of Engineers are on a reservation system. Reservations can be made up to 240 days in advance, and up to 360 days in advance for groups. To reserve a site, call (877) 444-6777 or visit the website: www.reserveusa.com. The reservation fee is usually $8.65, and major credit cards are accepted. Holders of Golden Age or Golden Access passports receive a 5 percent discount for campground fees, except for group sites.

U.S. Army Corps of Engineers
South Pacific Division/San Francisco District
333 Market Street
San Francisco, CA 94105
tel. (415) 977-8272
website: www.spn.usace.army.mil/

U.S. Army Corps of Engineers
Sacramento District
1325 "J" Street
Sacramento, CA 95814
tel. (916) 557-5100
website: www.spk.usace.army.mil/

U.S. Army Corps of Engineers
Los Angeles District
911 Wilshire Boulevard/P.O. Box 532711

Los Angeles, CA 90053
tel. (213) 452-3908
fax (213) 452-4191
website: www.spl.usace.army.mil/

Bureau of Land Management

Most of the BLM campgrounds are primitive and in remote areas. Often, there is no fee charged for camping. Holders of Golden Age or Golden Access passports receive a 50 percent discount, except for group camps, at BLM fee campgrounds.

Bureau of Land Management
California State Office
2800 Cottage Way, Room W-1834
Sacramento, CA 95825-1886
tel. (916) 978-4400
website: www.ca.blm.gov

California Desert District Office
6221 Box Springs Boulevard
Riverside, CA 92507
tel. (909) 697-5200
fax (909) 697-5299
website: www.ca.blm.gov/cdd

Alturas Field Office
708 W. 12th Street
Alturas, CA 96101
tel. (530) 233-4666
fax (530) 233-5696
website: www.ca.blm.gov/alturas

Arcata Field Office
1695 Heindon Road
Arcata, CA 95521-4573
tel. (707) 825-2300
fax (707) 825-2301
website: www.ca.blm.gov/arcata

Bakersfield Field Office
3801 Pegasus Drive
Bakersfield, CA 93308
tel. (661) 391-6000
fax (661) 391-6040
website: www.ca.blm.gov/bakersfield

Barstow Field Office
2601 Barstow Road
Barstow, CA 92311
tel. (760) 252-6000
fax (760) 252-6099
website: www.ca.blm.gov/barstow

Bishop Field Office
785 N. Main Street, Suite E
Bishop, CA 93514-2471
tel. (760) 872-4881
fax (760) 872-2894
website: www.ca.blm.gov/bishop

Eagle Lake Field Office
2950 Riverside Drive
Susanville, CA 96130
tel. (530) 257-0456
fax (530) 257-4831
website: www.ca.blm.gov/eaglelake

El Centro Field Office
1661 S. 4th Street
El Centro, CA 92243
tel. (760) 337-4400
fax (760) 337-4490
website: www.ca.blm.gov/elcentro

Folsom Field Office
63 Natoma Street
Folsom, CA 95630
tel. (916) 985-4474
fax (916) 985-3259
website: www.ca.blm.gov/folsom

Palm Springs/
South Coast Field Office
690 W. Garnet Avenue
N. Palm Springs, CA 92258
tel. (760) 251-4800
fax (760) 251-4899
website: ca.blm.gov/palmsprings

Redding Field Office
355 Hemsted Drive
Redding, CA 96002
tel. (530) 224-2100
fax (530) 224-2172
website: www.ca.blm.gov/redding

Ukiah Field Office
2550 N. State Street
Ukiah, CA 95482
tel. (707) 468-4000
fax (707) 468-4027
website: www.ca.blm.gov/ukiah

Other valuable resources

State Forests

California Department
of Forestry and Fire Protection
Resource Management
P.O. Box 944246
Sacramento, CA 94244-2460
tel. (916) 653-5121
fax (916) 653-4171
website: www.fire.ca.gov

Jackson Demonstration State Forest
802 N. Main Street
Fort Bragg, CA 95437
tel. (707) 964-5674
fax (707) 964-0941

County/Regional Park Departments

Del Norte County Parks
840 Ninth Street, Suite 11
Crescent City, CA 95531
tel. (707) 464-7230
fax (707) 464-5824

East Bay Regional Park District
2950 Peralta Oaks Court

P.O. Box 5381
Oakland, CA 94605-0381
tel. (510) 635-0135
fax (510) 635-3478
website: www.ebparks.org

Humboldt County Parks
1106 Second Street
Eureka, CA 95501
tel. (707) 445-7651
fax (707) 445-7409

Marin Municipal Water District
220 Nellen Avenue
Corte Madera, CA 94925
tel. (415) 945-1455
fax (415) 927-4953
website: www.marinwater.org

Midpeninsula Regiona
Open Space District
330 Distel Circle
Los Altos, CA 94022
tel. (650) 691-1200
fax (650) 691-0485
website: www.openspace.org

Pacific Gas and Electric Company
FERC/Land Projects
2730 Gateway Oaks, Suite 220
Sacramento, CA 95833
tel. (916) 386-5164
fax (916) 720-7044
website: www.pge.com/recreation

San Diego County
Parks and Recreation Department
5201 Ruffin Road, Suite P
San Diego, CA 92123
tel. (858) 694-3049
fax (858) 495-5841
website: www.co.san_diego.ca.us/
parks

San Mateo County
Parks and Recreation Department
455 County Center, Fourth floor
Redwood City, CA 94063-1646
tel. (650) 363-4020
fax (650) 599-1721
website: www.eparks.net

Santa Clara County
Parks and Recreation
298 Garden Hill Drive
Los Gatos, CA 95032
tel. (408) 358-3741
fax (408) 358-3245
website: www.parkhere.org

State and Federal Offices

U.S. Fish and Wildlife Service
1849 "C" Street NW
Washington, DC 20240
website: www.fws.gov

U.S. Geological Survey
Branch of Information Services
P.O. Box 25286, Federal Center
Denver, CO 80225

tel. (888) ASK-USGS (888-275-8747)
website: earthexplorer.usgs.gov

California Department
of Fish and Game
1416 Ninth Street, 12th floor
Sacramento, CA 95814
tel. (916) 653-6420
fax (916) 653-1856
website: www.dfg.ca.gov

Information Services

Lake County Visitor
Information Center
875 Lakeport Boulevard
Lakeport, CA 95453
tel. (800) 525-3743 or (707) 263-9544
fax (707) 263-9564
website: www.lakecounty.com

Mammoth Lakes Visitors Bureau
P.O. Box 48
Mammoth Lakes, CA 93546
tel. (800) 367-6572
fax (760) 934-7066
website: www.visitmammoth.com

The Nature Conservancy
201 Mission Street, Fourth floor
San Francisco, CA 94105
tel. (415) 777-0487
fax (415) 777-0244
website: www.tnccalifornia.org

Shasta-Cascade
Wonderland Association
1699 Highway 273
Anderson, CA 96007
tel. (800) 474-2782 or (530) 365-7500
fax (530) 365-1258
website: www.shastacascade.org

Map Companies

Earthwalk Press
5432 La Jolla Hermosa Avenue
La Jolla, CA 92037
tel. (800) 828-MAPS (800-828-6277)

Map Center
2440 Bancroft Way
Berkeley, CA 94704
tel. (510) 841-6277
fax (510) 841-0858

Map Link
30 South La Patera Lane, Unit 5
Santa Barbara, CA 93117
tel. (805) 692-6777
fax (800) 627-7768
website: www.maplink.com

Tom Harrison Maps
2 Falmouth Cove
San Rafael, CA 94901
tel./fax (800) 265-9090 or
(415) 456-7940
website: www.tomharrisonmaps.com

U.S. Forest Service
Attn: Map Sales
P.O. Box 587
Camino, CA 95709
tel. (530) 647-5390
fax (530) 647-5389
website: r5.fs.fed.us/visitorcenter

U.S. Geological Survey
Branch of Information Services
P.O. Box 25286, Federal Center
Denver, CO 80225
tel. (888) ASK-USGS (888-275-8747)
or (303) 202-4700
fax (303) 202-4693
website: earthexplorer.usgs.gov

INDEX

CAMPGROUND INDEX

Tom Stienstra

Tom Stienstra has made it his life's work to explore the West, traveling 200 days a year camping, hiking, fishing, and boating, always searching for the best of the outdoors and writing about it.

He is the nation's top-selling author of outdoor guidebooks. In 1999 and 2000, Amazon.com honored his book *California Camping* as the No. 1 outdoor book in the world. In the past 10 years, Stienstra was twice named national Outdoor Writer of the Year, newspaper division, by the Outdoor Writers Association of America.

He also has been awarded as California Outdoor Writer of the Year four times, most recently in 2000.

He is the outdoors writer for the *San Francisco Chronicle,* which distributes his column on the New York Times News Service. He can be reached directly on the Internet at www.TomStienstra.com/.

He lives with his family in Northern California.

His books include:

California Camping
California Hiking (with Ann Marie Brown)
California Fishing
California Recreational Lakes & Rivers
California Wildlife (with illustrator Paul Johnson)
Easy Camping in Northern California
Epic Trips of the West
Pacific Northwest Camping
Sunshine Jobs, Career Opportunities Working Outdoors
Tom Stienstra's Outdoor Getaway Guide: Northern California

> *"When you're 90 percent done with a book,*
> *it means you only have 50 percent to go."*

AVALON
TRAVEL
publishing

BECAUSE TRAVEL MATTERS.

AVALON TRAVEL PUBLISHING knows that travel is more than coming and going—travel is taking part in new experiences, new ideas, and a new outlook. Our goal is to bring you complete and up-to-date information to help you make informed travel decisions.

AVALON TRAVEL GUIDES feature a combination of practicality and spirit, offering a unique traveler-to-traveler perspective perfect for an afternoon hike, around-the-world journey, or anything in between.

WWW.TRAVELMATTERS.COM

Avalon Travel Publishing guides are available at your favorite book or travel store.

FOR TRAVELERS WITH SPECIAL INTERESTS

GUIDES

The 100 Best Small Art Towns in America • Asia in New York City
The Big Book of Adventure Travel • Cities to Go
Cross-Country Ski Vacations • Gene Kilgore's Ranch Vacations
Great American Motorcycle Tours • Healing Centers and Retreats
Indian America • Into the Heart of Jerusalem
The People's Guide to Mexico • The Practical Nomad
Saddle Up! • Staying Healthy in Asia, Africa, and Latin America
Steppin' Out • Travel Unlimited • Understanding Europeans
Watch It Made in the U.S.A. • The Way of the Traveler
Work Worldwide • The World Awaits
The Top Retirement Havens • Yoga Vacations

SERIES

Adventures in Nature
The Dog Lover's Companion
Kidding Around
Live Well

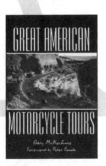

MOON HANDBOOKS

provide comprehensive coverage of a region's arts, history, land, people, and social issues in addition to detailed practical listings for accommodations, food, outdoor recreation, and entertainment. Moon Handbooks allow complete immersion in a region's culture—ideal for travelers who want to combine sightseeing with insight for an extraordinary travel experience.

USA

Alaska-Yukon • Arizona • Big Island of Hawaii • Boston
Coastal California • Colorado • Connecticut • Georgia
Grand Canyon • Hawaii • Honolulu-Waikiki • Idaho • Kauai
Los Angeles • Maine • Massachusetts • Maui • Michigan
Montana • Nevada • New Hampshire • New Mexico
New York City • New York State • North Carolina
Northern California • Ohio • Oregon • Pennsylvania
San Francisco • Santa Fe-Taos • Silicon Valley
South Carolina • Southern California • Tahoe • Tennessee
Texas • Utah • Virginia • Washington • Wisconsin
Wyoming • Yellowstone-Grand Teton

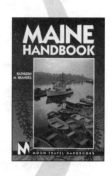

INTERNATIONAL

Alberta and the Northwest Territories • Archaeological Mexico
Atlantic Canada • Australia • Baja • Bangkok • Bali • Belize
British Columbia • Cabo • Canadian Rockies • Cancún
Caribbean Vacations • Colonial Mexico • Costa Rica • Cuba
Dominican Republic • Ecuador • Fiji • Havana • Honduras
Hong Kong • Indonesia • Jamaica • Mexico City • Mexico
Micronesia • The Moon • Nepal • New Zealand • Northern Mexico
Oaxaca • Pacific Mexico • Pakistan • Philippines • Puerto Vallarta
Singapore • South Korea • South Pacific • Southeast Asia • Tahiti
Thailand • Tonga-Samoa • Vancouver • Vietnam, Cambodia and Laos
Virgin Islands • Yucatán Peninsula

www.moon.com

www.travelmatters.com

User-friendly, informative, and fun:
Because travel *matters.*

Visit our newly launched web site and explore the variety of titles and travel information available online, featuring an interactive *Road Trip USA* exhibit.

also check out:

www.ricksteves.com

The Rick Steves web site is bursting with information to boost your travel I.Q. and liven up your European adventure.

www.foghorn.com

Visit the Foghorn Outdoors web site for more information on the premier source of U.S. outdoor recreation guides.

www.moon.com

The Moon Handbooks web site offers interesting information and practical advice that ensure an extraordinary travel experience.

U.S.~METRIC CONVERSION

1 inch = 2.54 centimeters (cm)
1 foot = .3048 meters (m)
1 yard = 0.914 meters
1 mile = 1.6093 kilometers (km)
1 km = .6214 miles
1 fathom = 1.8288 m
1 chain = 20.1168 m
1 furlong = 201.168 m
1 acre = .4047 hectares
1 sq km = 100 hectares
1 sq mile = 2.59 square km
1 ounce = 28.35 grams
1 pound = .4536 kilograms
1 short ton = .90718 metric ton
1 short ton = 2000 pounds
1 long ton = 1.016 metric tons
1 long ton = 2240 pounds
1 metric ton = 1000 kilograms
1 quart = .94635 liters
1 US gallon = 3.7854 liters
1 Imperial gallon = 4.5459 liters
1 nautical mile = 1.852 km

To compute celsius temperatures, subtract 32 from Fahrenheit and divide by 1.8. To go the other way, multiply celsius by 1.8 and add 32.

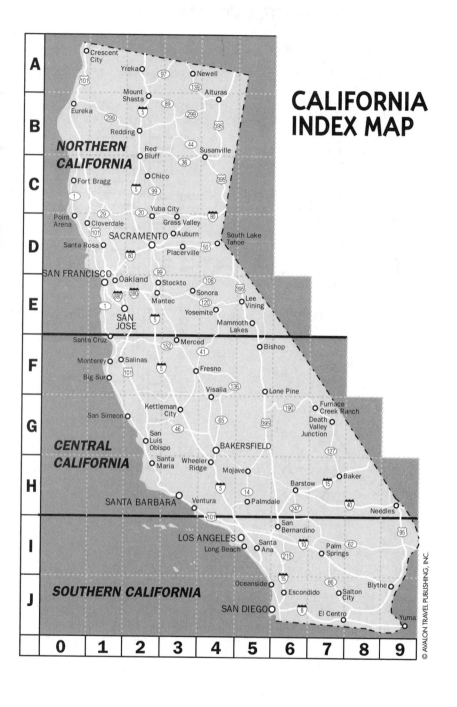

CALIFORNIA
INDEX MAP

NORTHERN CALIFORNIA

CENTRAL CALIFORNIA

SOUTHERN CALIFORNIA

Crescent City
Yreka
Newell
Mount Shasta
Alturas
Eureka
Redding
Red Bluff
Susanville
Fort Bragg
Chico
Point Arena
Cloverdale
Yuba City
Grass Valley
SACRAMENTO
Auburn
South Lake Tahoe
Santa Rosa
Placerville
SAN FRANCISCO
Oakland
Stockton
Sonora
Mantec
Lee Vining
SAN JOSE
Yosemite
Mammoth Lakes
Santa Cruz
Merced
Bishop
Monterey
Salinas
Big Sur
Fresno
Visalia
Lone Pine
Kettleman City
Furnace Creek Ranch
San Simeon
Death Valley Junction
San Luis Obispo
BAKERSFIELD
Santa Maria
Wheeler Ridge
Mojave
Baker
Barstow
SANTA BARBARA
Ventura
Palmdale
Needles
San Bernardino
LOS ANGELES
Santa Ana
Palm Springs
Long Beach
Oceanside
Escondido
Salton City
Blythe
SAN DIEGO
El Centro
Yuma

© AVALON TRAVEL PUBLISHING, INC.

A B C D E F G H I J

0 1 2 3 4 5 6 7 8 9

MAPS

NOTES

NOTES

NOTES

NOTES

NOTES

Will you have enough stories to tell your grandchildren?

Yahoo! Travel

DO YOU YAHOO!?

NOTES

NOTES

NOTES